STATUTORY INTERPRETATION

STATUTORY INTERPRETATION

Codified, with a critical Commentary

F. A. R. Bennion MA (Oxon), Barrister

*Former UK Parliamentary Counsel; sometime
Lecturer and Tutor in Jurisprudence
at St Edmund Hall Oxford*

London
Butterworths
1984

| England | Butterworth & Co (Publishers) Ltd |
| | 88 Kingsway, LONDON WC2B 6AB |

Australia Butterworths Pty Ltd
SYDNEY, MELBOURNE, BRISBANE, ADELAIDE, PERTH, CANBERRA and HOBART

Canada Butterworth & Co (Canada) Ltd
TORONTO and VANCOUVER

New Zealand Butterworths of New Zealand Ltd
WELLINGTON and AUCKLAND

Singapore Butterworth & Co (Asia) Pte Ltd
SINGAPORE

South Africa Butterworth Publishers (Pty) Ltd
DURBAN and PRETORIA

USA Butterworth Legal Publishers
ST PAUL, Minnesota; SEATTLE, Washington; BOSTON, Massachusetts
AUSTIN, Texas and D & S Publishers, CLEARWATER, Florida

©

Butterworths & Co. (Publishers) Ltd.
1984

Bennion, F.A.R.
  Statutory interpretation : codified with a critical commentary.
  1. Law—Great Britain—Interpretation and construction
  I. Title
  344.108′22   KD691.A

ISBN 0-406-25920-8

Printed and bound by The Whitefriars Press Ltd, Tonbridge, Kent

To *William Roscoe,* of Liverpool
1753–1831

Those who live only for the world, and in the world, may be cast down by the frowns of adversity; but a man like Roscoe is not to be overcome by the reverses of fortune. They do but drive him in upon the resources of his own mind; to the superior society of his own thoughts; which the best of men are apt sometimes to neglect, and to roam abroad in search of less worthy associates. He is independent of the world around him. He lives with antiquity and posterity, in the generous aspirings after future renown.

Washington Irving *The Sketch Book*

Contents

The Code: Summary of Parts

The Code: Arrangement of Sections

Part III – The Enactment and the Facts

Preliminary

The Enactment

The Facts of the Instant Case

The Opposing Constructions of the Enactment

Part IV – The Legal Meaning of an Enactment

Nature of the Legal Meaning

Grammatical Meaning of an Enactment

Part V – Legislative Intention

Nature of Legislative Intention

Filling in the Textual Detail

Part VI – Guides to Legislative Intention

Preliminary

Part IX – Extent and Application of Enactments

Territorial Extent of an Enactment

Part X – The Informed Interpretation Rule: Legislative History

Preliminary

Pre-enacting History

Enacting History

How to Use this Book

This book is designed to serve at all levels, from mere dip to thoroughgoing research. Because it examines the subject in depth, the book may appear difficult. Like most appearances, that is deceptive. The difficult books are the ones that treat their material superficially. This book is no more abstruse than its subject.

The book takes the form of a Code. (Man, said Lévi-Strauss, is a structure-making animal.) Drafted in a way similar to that used for Acts of Parliament, the Code is divided into numbered sections. These are arranged in Parts, each with a brief introductory note. The Parts are presented in two Divisions. Division One contains the gist, while Division Two consists of supplementary provisions.

Each section of the Code is followed by a critical commentary. The commentaries include numerous examples, many of which are relevant to more than one section. To facilitate cross-referencing, the examples are numbered in the order in which they appear in each commentary. When a cross-reference from another commentary is made, this takes the form of the section number followed by the number of the example. Thus Example 3 in the commentary on s 377 is cross-referenced as Example 377.3.

Suggestions to the user

* *To gain a thorough knowledge of the subject* Read the book from beginning to end: it forms a connected narrative, with pictures and stories.

* *To gain a competent grasp* Read Division One of the book: it refers to all the salient points.

* *To acquire an outline knowledge* Read the Code without the Commentary.

* *To acquire an outline with less trouble* Read Division One of the Code without the Commentary.

* *For a bird's-eye view* Glance through the Arrangement of Sections (pp xi to xxiii).

* *To ascertain the rules, principles, presumptions and canons of construction* Study Part VI.

* *To solve a particular problem* Consult Part VII.

* *To look up a particular point* Use the very full Index.

* *For court technique* See Appendix A.

* *For a checklist of interpretative criteria* See Appendix B.

* *For terms defined in the Code or Commentary* See Appendix C.

* *For updated text of Interpretation Act 1978* See Appendix D. {All but relatively minor details of the Interpretation Act 1978 are also reproduced in the appropriate place in the body of this work.} The explanatory white paper on the 1978 Act prepared by the Law Commission is reproduced in Appendix E.

Introduction

The search is for order. Parliament attempts to achieve this in its enactments, but not always with success. That is why, as Lord Hailsham of St Marylebone LC observed in *Johnson v Moreton* {[1980] AC 37, at p 53.}, nine-tenths of all cases reaching the House of Lords turn on statutory interpretation. In his 1983 Hamlyn lectures, Lord Hailsham broadened even this striking remark by saying that over nine out of ten cases heard on appeal before the Court of Appeal or the House of Lords either turn upon, or involve, the meaning of words contained in enactments of primary or secondary legislation. {*Hamlyn Revisited: the British Legal System Today* p 65.} A similar proportion no doubt applies in reported cases generally.

Yet statutory interpretation is still not regarded as a subject meriting thoroughgoing research, or serious academic exposition. Legal practitioners still are not grounded in it. People who think about these things sense that something is wrong. Our system stages *Hamlet*, but forgets the Prince of Denmark.

There is however one recent gain. Our courts have moved on from the old simplistic view. No longer is a problem of statutory interpretation settled by applying some talisman called the 'literal rule', or the 'golden rule', or the 'mischief rule'. Nowadays we have purposive construction, coupled with respect for the text and a recognition by judges that interpreting a modern Act is a matter sophisticated and complex. Rules of thumb are out. The only golden rule, as Shaw said, is that there are no golden rules.

This development has a valuable consequence. What struck many as being arbitrary and unconnected 'rules', each colliding with other such 'rules', are now perceived from a more rational aspect. It is rather like the appearance of familiar scattered islands when seen at last from the air. Each had seemed quite separate. Now from aloft we recognise that the seabed unites them.

Our system produces a written text (acknowledged to express the will of the legislature) which has the remarkable ambition of directing the conduct of citizens. This is not seen as remarkable, but that is what it is. To aspire to direct, for years into the future, the endlessly varied actions of millions of people by a brief verbal formula, necessarily bearing the cramping impress of its own day, is remarkably ambitious.

That the product must be an approximation does not detract from its validity, or lessen its social importance. Law consists of statements and elucidations of statements. Each legislative formula is imperfect, as all things human are. Elucidation, often but not always by the courts, has the function of alleviating this.

The natural and reasonable desire that statutes should be easily understood is doomed to disappointment. Thwarted, it shifts to an equally natural and reasonable desire for efficient tools of interpretation. If statutes must be obscure, let us at least have simple devices to elucidate them. A golden rule would be best, to unlock all mysteries.

Alas there is no golden rule. Nor is there a mischief rule, or a literal rule, or any other cure-all. Instead there are a thousand and one interpretative *criteria*. Fortunately, not all of these present themselves in any one case; but those that do yield factors that the interpreter must figuratively weigh and balance.

That is the nearest we can get to a golden rule, and it is not very near. If striving could do it, a true golden rule would in this work be presented to the reader. It can't.

Licking the wounds, while manfully concealing our disappointment, let us face the truth. Acts of Parliament are prepared unscientifically and in haste. They seek to regulate a future which is certain only of constant surprise. Some Acts embody a Civil Service response to the lessons of practical administration. Others are the product of partisan politics, and liable to swift reversal. Others again spring from shifting moralities, or embattled religions, or other fancied certainties in an always uncertain world. Furthermore society is a coalition; and compromise invests almost all of these well-intentioned measures. Here and there deals have been done. The draftsman has then striven to paper over the cracks.

When all that can be said has been said, and the human best has been done, we are forced to acknowledge that Acts use only words.

Acts so faultily engendered pass in rapid succession before busy judges, advised by busier advocates. Few of these actors have the time, or are equipped, for cool and deep analysis. Yet learned judges lean to the delivery of impromptu and pithy (and therefore doubly inaccurate) descriptions of the nature of statutes and the principles governing their interpretation.

Often quotable, these get quoted. Not being based, as a rule, either on profound research or blinding insight, they tend to agree neither with each other nor with the real nature of the subject-matter. Yet we are obliged respectfully to recognise, and humbly to accept, that principles of interpretation, when not laid down by Parliament itself, are devised or adopted by the courts and no one else. It is the self-imposed task of the commentator to reconcile them.

This Code accordingly sets out the current principles governing the construction of Acts and other legislative instruments, as laid down or adopted by the courts (with some slight help from Parliament). The intention is that the Code should be self-consistent. Contradictory utterances cannot both be right, and so cannot both be law.

The Code is accompanied by a Commentary, described as 'critical'. The epithet is chosen advisedly. It is the legal scholar's basic attribute to question, to challenge, to sift and weigh, and to take nothing he is told for granted. A book on statutory interpretation that sets out to be a mere pottage of dicta is, like any other law book so planned, of little use.

To be critical is not to be immodest, or lacking in respect for learned judges. A bold appraising legal writer can take comfort and courage from Lord Cockburn's long-ago assessment of Hume's *Criminal Commentaries*. When dealing with statutory interpretation, the jurist of today writes about a vital subject in disarray. Seeking to expound this in an enlightened and helpful fashion, he hears that scholarly voice from the old Edinburgh bench –

'. . . before any one can deserve the praise of being an enlightened expounder of a system of law not previously explained or methodised, the past actings of courts ought not to be merely stated, but criticised, so that future tribunals may be guided and the public instructed on defects and remedies.'

{Lord Cockburn *Memorials of His Time* (1856) p 102.}

The present writer has not felt such lack of respect for learned judges as to suppose they would wish to silence his findings of error, at whatever level. We all make mistakes, in the law as elsewhere; and we can all learn and improve. The only failing is to pretend it is not so. The operation of a book like this merely repeats what must be done every time any of the judicial dicta come up for consideration in the lawyer's chambers or the courtroom itself. The method of reconciliation was indicated by a Canadian voice echoing Cockburn's: we must look more closely at what judges do than at what they say. {J A Corry 'The Interpretation of Statutes' (reprinted in revised form in E A Driedger *The Construction of Statutes* App I) p 205.}

When Lord Goddard CJ remarked in *R v Wimbledon JJ, ex p Derwent* {[1953] 1 QB 380, at p 384.} that a court cannot add words to a statute or read words into it that are not there, he echoed what many judges have said. Yet the fact is that the express words of every Act have the shadowy accompaniment of a host of implicit statements. Either these statements are taken to be implied by law (because not expressly disapplied), or they arise from the words of the enactment or its context. In many cases of doubtful construction the real question, often not perceived, is whether the manifold implications include one that settles the doubt.

Furthermore Acts by implication delegate to the authoritative interpreter what must be recognised as a law-making function. Through the dynamic processing effected by their decisions, judges fill in gaps Parliament has unavoidably left. Later interpreters construe the larger text.

The whole idea of governing by fixed words inscribed on tablets is fascinating and strange. The words, which because of the inadequacy of language and the infinite variety of circumstance can from the beginning never be better than approximate, are frozen in their imperfect state until amended. Parliamentary amendment is difficult, and subject to the same constraints. Meanwhile the inadequate words grow less and less apt.

The temptation the court feels is to depart from the literal meaning in order to do justice or make sense. Yet this natural urge marks a failure in communication. Words are designed for no other purpose than to transmit a message. If what the words say is rejected in favour of a meaning reached by other means, the message has not got through. Those who trustingly read it, and in good faith acted accordingly, are confounded.

Between the grammatical meaning and the overall legal meaning, courts now draw a conceptual distinction. The two usually correspond, but sometimes there is doubt. Here concepts are useful. The question is always: does the grammatical meaning truly give effect to Parliament's imputed intention? If it does not, the legal meaning will be something else.

In searching for the legal meaning of a doubtful enactment, the court now proceeds by identifying, determining and weighing. It identifies the general interpretative criteria that are relevant in the instant case (of which there may be many). It determines by reference to these criteria the specific factors that, on the wording of the enactment and the facts of the instant case, are decisive. It weighs the factors that tell for or against each of the opposing constructions put forward by the parties. Then it gives its decision.

The aim of the Code is to describe this modern common-law system of statutory interpretation, presenting it in a coherent, self-consistent way. Attention is also paid to the learning of the past, without knowledge of which our present system cannot be understood. The old lawyers still have much to teach.

Summary of the Code

The Code consists of twenty-two Parts, arranged in two Divisions. Division One, containing seven Parts, deals with the gist of the matter, while Division Two contains supplementary material. All the fifteen Parts contained in Division Two are introduced by provisions in Division One, which is therefore comprehensive.

Each Part of the Code begins with a brief introduction. What now follows amounts to a précis of these.

Division One

Part I of the Code explains who the interpreter is, and why he occupies that role. Broadly, there are four types of interpreter: the legislator, the court or other enforcement agency, the jurist, and the subject (or his adviser). The interpreter's duty is to arrive at the *legal* meaning of the enactment. Either this is plain, or there is a real doubt.

The subject must obey, and is not excused by ignorance. If he disobeys there may be criminal or civil sanctions, or both. Acts are enforced by various functionaries, including government departments, local authorities, the police, prosecutors, courts and tribunals, sheriffs and bailiffs. All, in varying degree, need to interpret statutes.

The powers and functions of the courts are examined. Then Part I concludes with the vital matter of judicial legislation under the doctrine of precedent, otherwise known as *stare decisis* or dynamic processing.

Part II examines the nature and provenance of the three kinds of legislative text: the Act of Parliament, prerogative instruments, and delegated legislation. No one can properly interpret any of these without expert knowledge of their peculiar characteristics.

Part III sets out the anatomy of the elements wherein a doubt as to the legal meaning of an enactment resides, with a view to showing how such a doubt is resolved. The *enactment*, whether contained in an Act, prerogative instrument, or item of delegated legislation, is always the unit of enquiry. The doubt concerns the interaction between the facts of the instant case and the combined effect of the *factual outline* laid down by the enactment and the *legal thrust* the enactment imparts when the actual facts are within the outline. If there is doubt as to the factual outline or the legal thrust (or both), the interpreter needs to consider the *opposing constructions* of the enactment.

Part IV explores the concept of the legal meaning of the enactment, that is the meaning which truly reflects the imputed legislative intention. We see that very often the legal meaning corresponds to the grammatical meaning. Grammatical ambiguity is investigated. The other type of grammatical difficulty, concerning semantic obscurity, is explained.

Next we pass to the vital topic of *strained* construction. We see that, in the last analysis, an enactment is given either a literal or a strained interpretation. For sound constitutional reasons, judges dislike admitting this. Nevertheless it holds the key to the whole problem of statutory interpretation.

Part V shows us that the sole object in statutory interpretation is to arrive at the legislative intention. We see what is meant by this concept, and that it is not a mere myth or fiction. Parliament entrusts the courts with the task of spelling out its imputed intention, even where no actual intention existed.

Part VI of the Code is its heart. Having seen in Part V that legislative intention is the paramount criterion in statutory interpretation, we now examine the principal guides to arriving at that intention. We call these the interpretative criteria. They may be divided into (1) binding *rules*, (2) *principles* derived from general legal policy, (3) *presumptions* as to what Parliament had in mind, and (4) linguistic *canons* of construction.

Rules The basic rule is that where the interpretative guides or criteria conflict with one another, the problem is to be resolved by weighing and balancing the factors concerned.

Detailed rules are that the interpreter must have regard to the juridical nature of an enactment, and must bring to bear an *informed* approach. He must follow a meaning which is plain on an informed construction, and apply the basic rule in other cases. Common sense must be employed, and the court of construction must strive to implement rather than defeat the object of the Act. It must also bear in mind the precise function of each type of component within an Act. Rules laid down by statute must be observed.

Principles The principles of construction are derived from general legal policy. Law should serve the public interest, yet be just. Subjects should not be penalized under a doubtful law. Law should be predictable, and should not in general operate retrospectively. It should be coherent and self-consistent, and not subject to casual change. The municipal law should not conflict with public international law.

Presumptions The text of the Act is the primary indication of legislative intention, and it is presumed (though this presumption, like the others, may be displaced) that the literal meaning is to be applied. The court is to implement the remedy provided by Parliament for the 'mischief'; and it is presumed that a purposive construction should if possible be given.

Regard is to be had to the consequences of a particular construction, and it is presumed that an 'absurd' result was not intended. Nor were drafting errors meant by Parliament to go uncorrected, or evasion be permitted. The legislator is taken to intend that ancillary rules of general law should be applied, including legal maxims. Finally it is presumed that Parliament intended updating by the court to be effected where necessary to implement the legislative intention.

Canons The logic of language is discussed, and then the construction of an Act as a whole is described. We look at the interpretation of broad terms, and individual words and phrases. Finally we consider the familiar linguistic canons (such as the *ejusdem generis* principle) that in any verbal passage are used to elaborate the literal meaning of words and phrases.

Part VII completes Division One. It shows the practical way of arriving at the legal meaning of the enactment where there is real doubt as to which of the opposing constructions should be adopted.

The doubt is resolved by first assembling the relevant guides to legislative intention, or interpretative criteria, out of all those collected in Part VI of the Code or dealt with elsewhere. From them we extract, in the light of the facts of the instant case and the wording of the enactment, the relevant interpretative *factors*. The two 'bundles' of factors respectively favouring each of the opposing constructions are figuratively weighed one against the other. Whichever, all things considered, comes out heavier in the juristic scales is preferred.

Division Two

Part VIII of the Code deals with the temporal operation of an enactment, that is its commencement, amendment from time to time, and final repeal. The account includes such difficult and often misunderstood or neglected matters as extra-statutory concessions, the practice of 'double repeal', savings, expiry, desuetude, transitional provisions, and retrospective operation.

After temporal matters, we turn in Part IX to territorial and personal operation. We first consider the rules regarding the territory or territories in which an enactment is law, known as its 'extent'. We continue with an explanation of the principles which govern the application of an enactment to some persons and matters but not to others.

Next come two Parts that give further details of the informed interpretation rule mentioned above. Part X deals with the important aspect of that rule which is concerned with legislative history. The treatment divides this history into three compartments, respectively describing the use of pre-enacting, enacting and post-enacting history. Part XI contains amplifying material covering such matters as the 'context' of an enactment, the need to restrict admission of historical information so as to avoid unpredictability and unjustified lengthening of legal proceedings, and the need for adequate information *before* any judgment is made as to whether or not the enactment is doubtful.

Part XII describes the functions of the various components of an Act, with a view to the application of the functional construction rule mentioned above. All the components form part of what is put out by Parliament as its Act. Furthermore s 19 of the Interpretation Act 1978 has the effect of requiring them all to be taken into account (for what they are worth). The components fall into three groups, namely operative components (mainly sections and Schedules), amendable descriptive components such as the long title, preamble and short title, and unamendable descriptive components such as headings and punctuation. Part XII concludes with four sections dealing with ways in which external provisions may be incorporated into an Act.

Part XIII expounds more fully, in its application to statutory interpretation, the principle of legal policy that persons should not be penalized under a doubtful law. Although often referred to as though limited to criminal statutes, this principle in fact extends in varying degrees to any form of detriment. The detriments are gone through, with attention paid to the European Convention on Human Rights. The treatment covers constructions of an enactment which involve danger to human life or health, restriction of freedom of the person, prejudice to family rights, interference with freedom of religion, assembly, association or speech, or detriment to property or other economic interests, status or reputation, or legal rights.

We next have six Parts amplifying the treatment of *presumptions* sketched out above.

Part XIV explains the presumption that Parliament intends the courts to apply the remedy it provides for curing a mischief, based on the 400-year old resolution in *Heydon's Case*. Part XV follows on by presenting the modern version of what used to be called the mischief rule, namely purposive construction. This may require either a literal or a strained interpretation.

Part XVI gives details of the presumption that Parliament does not intend 'absurd' consequences to flow from the application of its Act, one aspect of the related presumption requiring a consequential construction. In this context 'absurd' means contrary to sense and reason. The presumption leads to avoidance by the interpreter of six types of undesirable consequence. These are: an unworkable or impracticable result, an inconvenient result, an anomalous or illogical result, a futile or pointless result, an artificial result, and a disproportionate counter-mischief.

Part XVII gives details of the presumption that Parliament does not intend its Act to be evaded. This is another aspect of the presumption that Parliament requires a consequential construction. It is necessary to distinguish legitimate ways of getting round an Act (avoidance) from illegitimate ways (evasion).

Part XVIII spells out the effect of the presumption that Parliament is taken to intend general rules of law to apply so far as relevant for the purposes of the enactment under enquiry. Part XIX does the same for those principles of law that are embodied in legal maxims.

The Code ends with three Parts dealing with linguistic canons of interpretation.

Part XX expands remarks made earlier on the use of deductive or syllogistic reasoning. The treatment is elementary, but makes the point that it is a universal canon of the construction of verbal expressions that language is to be treated as used in accordance with the rules of logic.

Part XXI deals with the linguistic canons which govern the straightforward interpretation of individual words and phrases, while Part XXII explains the linguistic canons which govern the elaboration of meaning of individual words and phrases by the drawing of certain inferences. Several of these are embedded in well-known Latin maxims, such as *noscitur a sociis*, *ejusdem generis*, *reddendo singula singulis*, and *expressio unius est exclusio alterius*.

Conclusion

As the ultimate concentrate, we can do no better than offer the opening words of Maxwell's great work–

> Statute law is the will of the legislature; and the object of all judicial interpretation of it is to determine what intention is either expressly or by implication conveyed by the language used, so far as necessary for the purpose of determining whether a particular case or state of facts which is presented to the interpreter falls within it.

True when written in 1875, this remains true today. One imagines the learned author, as he contemplated with proper humility his first edition, struggling to get right every word of this initial paragraph, and triumphantly succeeding.

Introduction

It is symptomatic of the confusion that has bedevilled this vexed subject that, when preparing the first edition to be published after Maxwell's death (the third in all), an officious editor saw fit to scrap Maxwell's opening passage. The present author, in a gesture of deserved respect, is humbly pleased to reclaim it.

Table of statutes

References in this Table to *Statutes* are to Halsbury's Statutes of England (Third Edition) showing the volume and page at which the annotated text of the Act will be found.

Page references printed in bold type indicate where the Act is set out in part or in full.

Table of cases

Page numbers set in bold type refer to pages on which cases are considered in Examples.

O

P

S

T

The Common-Law System of Statutory Interpretation

PART I

The Interpreter

Introduction to Part I We begin this survey of statutory interpretation at the beginning. Who is the interpreter, and why does he interpret? First, some preliminaries. There is no distinction between *construe* and *interpret* (s 1). The interpreter must arrive at the *legal* meaning (s 2). Either this is plain, or there is a *real* doubt (s 3).

Broadly, there are four types of interpreter. Although usually not a lawyer, the *legislator* needs to understand the law he is changing and the legal effect of what he does (s 4). The *court* both interprets and legislates (s 5). The *jurist* provides guidance, often unheeded (s 6). Last comes the *subject*, most closely concerned of all (s 7).

Sections 8 to 14 explain the position of the subject. He must obey (s 8), and is not excused by ignorance (s 9). Statutory requirements may be mandatory or merely directory (s 10). Contracting out or waiver may or may not be allowed (ss 11 and 12). If the subject disobeys there may be criminal (s 13) or civil (s 14) sanctions, or both.

Who is to impose these sanctions? Whoever he is, he must know how to interpret statutes. His overall function is to *enforce* what Parliament has enacted. If not enforced, it is futile.

So we look at government departments and other administrators (s 15), those empowered to issue licences (s 16), the police and other investigators (s 17), the prosecutors (s 18), and the adjudicators (ss 19 to 24). The last bring us to such topics as judicial notice (s 21), appellate jurisdiction (s 23), and judicial review (s 24). We briefly look at those ultimate indispensables who *physically* enforce judgments (s 25).

Finally we consider the vital matter of legislation by precedent, otherwise known as *stare decisis* or dynamic processing (s 26).

PRELIMINARY

1. To 'construe' or 'interpret'?

This Code proceeds on the basis that there is no material distinction between the 'construction' and the 'interpretation' of an enactment. The terms are interchangeable, though it is more natural to speak of 'interpreting' a word or phrase and 'construing' an extended passage.

COMMENTARY

We are now engaged in a discussion about words. These are the sole instruments by which a law can be framed, and then promulgated. It is altogether typical, and entirely symptomatic, that even before we start there must be an argument

3

over the terms we are to employ. What word must be used to describe what we are about?

Some pundits talk of statutory *interpretation*. Others prefer the term *construction*. A few seek to attach quite different meanings to each. So we must be plain.

This Code draws no significant distinction between 'construe' and 'interpret'. In the view of the Canadian expert Professor Driedger, statutes are in general to be 'construed'. Driedger believes that only where there is some ambiguity, obscurity or inconsistency is the term 'interpret' fitting. {E A Driedger *The Construction of Statutes* p ix.}

Dias regards 'interpretation' as relating to what the legislature meant to refer to and 'construction' as applying to the purpose it meant to accomplish. {R W M Dias *Jurisprudence* (4th edn, 1976) p 220.}

These are vain distinctions, as Bentham perceived-

> 'People in general when they speak of a *Law* and a *Statute* are apt to mean the same thing by the one as by the other. So are they when they speak of *construing* and *interpreting*.'

{*A Comment on the Commentaries* p 99.}

Sir Rupert Cross agreed. He declined to draw a distinction between 'interpret' and 'construe', feeling that it lacked an agreed basis. {*Statutory Interpretation* p 18.} The leading Act on the subject bears this out. It calls itself the Interpretation Act 1978 but refers throughout to 'construction'. {See also Administration of Justice Act 1969, s 12 (3) (a), set out at p 65 below}.

This Code follows Bentham and Cross. Such differences as exist in the use of the two terms in contemporary English are matters of nuance rather than distinct meaning. In some of the contexts with which we are concerned 'interpretation' suggests itself as the most fitting word, while in others one would speak more naturally of 'construction'. It is, as so often in the linguistic field, a question of 'feel'.

The reader may 'interpret' anything from a single word to an entire Act. He 'construes' a sentence or a longer passage, but not a word by itself. Interpretation perhaps connotes, more than construction does, the idea of determining the legal effect. Construction is more concerned with extracting a grammatical meaning. But there is no hard and fast line.

2. Interpreter's duty to arrive at legal meaning

The interpreter's duty is to arrive at the *legal* meaning of the enactment, which is not necessarily the same as its grammatical meaning. This must be done in accordance with the rules, principles, presumptions and canons which govern statutory interpretation (in this Code referred to as the interpretative criteria, or guides to legislative intention). The court is never entitled, on the principle *non liquet* (it is not clear), to decline the duty of determining the legal meaning of a relevant enactment.

COMMENTARY

This section of the Code states the principle that any person or body charged with the function of applying an enactment is under a duty to arrive at its *legal* meaning. {As to the types of interpreter see ss 4 to 7 of this Code.} This is to be done in accordance with the principles laid down by law for carrying out the function of statutory interpretation (in this Code referred to as the interpretative criteria, or guides to legislative intention). They are described in Part VI of this Code.

One reason why people have found the subject of statutory interpretation difficult is that they have thought it easy. They have not taken the trouble to investigate it with the care and deliberation required. Learned judges sum up the whole matter in a sentence. Learned academics relegate it to a small area of some preliminary course in jurisprudence, constitutional law or legal history. No one would suppose, from the way it is treated, that this area of expertise nowadays forms the subject of nine-tenths of all appeals on points of law. {See *Johnson v Moreton* [1980] AC 37 at p 53.}

To master the principles of statutory interpretation it is necessary to be clear about who is interpreting, what they are interpreting, and why. The duties and functions of the interpreter vary in every case. The one common factor is that he or she is always in search of the legal meaning of the enactment.

The legal meaning usually corresponds to the grammatical or literal meaning. If this were never so, the system would collapse. If it were always so, there would be no need for treatises on statutory interpretation. The cases when it is not so are the object of our enquiry. The key is this concept of the legal meaning. It is fully explained in Part IV of this Code.

3. Real doubt as to legal meaning

If, on an informed interpretation, there is no real doubt that a particular meaning of an enactment is to be applied, that is to be taken as its legal meaning. If there is real doubt, it is to be resolved by applying the interpretative criteria. For this purpose a doubt is 'real' only where it is substantial, and not merely conjectural or fanciful.

COMMENTARY

If, on an informed construction, the interpreter feels doubtful as to the meaning of the enactment his first step is to decide whether the doubt is real, that is whether it is one the law will recognise. Here the interpreter needs to bear in mind that, as Lord Cave LC put it, 'no form of words has ever yet been framed . . . with regard to which some ingenious counsel could not suggest a difficulty'. {*Pratt v South Eastern Rly* [1897] 1 QB 718, at p 721. See also Example 323.30.} Interpreters thus need to be on guard against plausible advocates.

In his *Apologia pro Vita Sua*, Cardinal Newman said that ten thousand difficulties do not make a doubt. Though he spoke of theological difficulties, the point is valid in relation to statute law. There may be numerous difficulties surrounding the legal meaning of an enactment. Once these are penetrated, it usually emerges as not truly uncertain.

The value of the concept of 'real doubt' is that it reminds us not to be put off by hairsplitting or unduly recondite argument. That is the less acceptable face of legal scholarship or advocacy; though those who feel confident need to beware of hubris. Coke said, when commenting on a *quaere* in Littleton-

'. . . grave and learned men may doubt, without any imputation to

them; for the most learned doubteth most, and the more ignorant for
the most part are the more bold and peremptory.'

{Co Litt 338a.}

The law recognises a doubt over the meaning of an enactment as 'real' only
where it is substantial, and not merely conjectural or fanciful. As Lord Diplock
said: 'Where the meaning of the statutory words is plain and unambiguous it is
not for the judges to invent fancied ambiguities . . .' {*Duport Steels v Sirs* [1980]
1 All ER 529, at p 541.}

To similar effect was the remark by Viscount Simonds that if a judge 'forms
his own clear judgment and does not think that the words are "fairly and equally
open to divers meanings" he is not entitled to say that there is an ambiguity'.
{*Kirkness v John Hudson & Co Ltd* [1955] AC 696, at p 712.} Lord Reid
pointed out that presumptions such as that in favour of construing penal Acts
strictly apply only where 'after full inquiry and consideration one is left in real
doubt'. {*DPP v Ottewell* [1970] AC 642, at p 649.} See Example 84.6.

Informed interpretation In determining whether there is real doubt, the
enquirer must bring to bear an informed interpretation. The rule laid down by
Oliver LJ in relation to taxing Acts is of general application-

> 'Accepting once more that the subject is not to be taxed except by
> clear words, the words must, nevertheless, be construed in the
> context of the provisions in which they appear and of the intention
> patently discernible on the face of those provisions from the words
> used.'

{*Wicks v Firth (Inspector of Taxes)* [1982] 2 All ER 9, at p 17.}

The informed interpretation rule is set out in s 119 and further described in
Parts X and XI of this Code.

TYPES OF INTERPRETER

4. Types of interpreter: the legislator

A legislator needs to be an interpreter in order to understand both the
law he is altering and the Bill by which he alters it. Most legislators are
not lawyers however, and need to rely on skilled advice.

COMMENTARY

By an unavoidable paradox, the person who lays down the law is usually
unfitted to understand it. Since statutory interpretation is based upon the
intention of the legislator as chiefly manifested in the words he has used, this
presents problems.

The legislator is concerned with the main lines of policy. He leaves it to the
experts to get the details right. Yet at any moment in the progress of a Bill some
minor point of detail may assume importance. This is a democratic safeguard.
The draftsman or other expert cannot count on any detail escaping attention. So
he ensures that it would pass scrutiny.

Nevertheless the legislator cannot escape responsibility. He is a law-maker, and
must see himself as such. When not a trained lawyer, he must try to come to

terms with the law. He must insist on proper explanations, and not be easily satisfied.

5. Types of interpreter: courts and other enforcement agencies

Legislation may (expressly or by implication) allow existing procedures to apply for the enforcement of its provisions, or may set up new enforcement procedures, or may do partly one and partly the other. The public agencies charged by law with the function of administering and otherwise enforcing legislation can be divided into various categories, according to whether their function is administrative, authorising, investigating, prosecuting, adjudicating or executive. An agency may fall into more than one category (for example it may be both an authorising agency and an investigating agency). Agencies of all kinds need to interpret legislation in carrying out their functions. For some, such as the courts, this is a central feature; while for others it is peripheral.

COMMENTARY

The duty of an enforcement agency is to arrive at the intention of Parliament, as expressed and implied in the Act (and any delegated legislation made under it) or spelt out by previous processing. Nevertheless modern legislation leaves a great deal of practical detail to be supplied on a day-to-day basis by executive officials. There is little new in this. The Twelve Tables of ancient Rome set the pattern. They did not contain the whole law, even for that primitive society. As Buckland tell us: 'They stated general rules: the countless details, especially of form, were left to be elucidated by officials'. {W W Buckland *A Textbook of Roman Law* (2nd edn, 1950) p 2.}

Existing enforcement procedures Legislation operates within the context of existing law. Where an Act does not disapply a legal doctrine relevant to its enforcement, the interpreter infers that Parliament intended the doctrine to have effect for that purpose. {In this Code 'enforcement' is used in a wide sense as including the administration of an Act generally.} This intention becomes explicit where the Act uses a free-standing legal term such as 'offence' or 'contract' without express amplification. {As to the use in Acts of free-standing legal terms see p 354 below.}

The way existing law applies in relation to each type of enforcement agency is outlined in the commentaries on ss 15 to 26 of this Code.

New enforcement procedures Sometimes Parliament considers existing procedures to be inadequate, and deems it necessary to include in an Act special provisions for its enforcement. These too are described in relation to each type of enforcement agency in the commentaries on ss 15 to 26 of this Code.

Mixed provisions It is unlikely that an Act would completely supersede existing enforcement provisions. Where these are not considered altogether suitable the usual course is to modify them, but only so far as necessary.

Enforcement agencies The interpreter needs to be aware, at least in broad outline, of the various state agencies used to administer and otherwise enforce the provisions of Acts of Parliament and other legislation. Accordingly the next seven sections of the Code attempt a brief description of these.

6. Types of interpreter: the jurist or text writer

The jurist or text writer differs from most other interpreters of legislation in taking an overall view of the law operating within his chosen field. The jurist's function is to rise above particular enactments and factual situations. He must enunciate general principle, and essay broad description.

A textbook, article or other learned text, the author of which is qualified by virtue of being a judge or barrister (whether practising or not), is treated by the courts as a work of persuasive authority. The *weight* of this imputed authority solely depends on the reputation of the author.

Legal writings, whether or not works of authority, may also be relevant in furnishing a source of facts or law of which the court is obliged to take judicial notice. They may include reasoning which the advocate can adopt as part of his argument, or the court as part of its judgment.

COMMENTARY

The British, a pragmatic race, distrust theory. Custom and common law, the bases of our legal system, depend on the accretion of one practical instance upon another. Relatively few members of the judiciary have seen it as their function, or recognised it as their ability, explicitly to lay down general principle. The tendency of the British judge is primarily directed to deciding the *lis*, the instant case before the court. In that everyday forum the parties appear as flesh and blood creatures, and abstract law takes second place. Their story, one of recent fact, is usually evidenced by living witnesses who can be cross-examined. This is what the pragmatist prefers.

Hence the respect for 'our lady the common law', whose earthy provenance is innumerable occasions of pragmatic justice. Thus is explained the judicial distrust of legislation, necessarily framed in the abstract and hopefully seeking to regulate by general language an always uncertain future.

So we have a threefold uneasy system. The elected politician, powerfully aided (indeed often led) by an expert civil service, lays down rules *in advance*. His commands, presented as those of Parliament, are deliberate prospective commands. The appointed judge, drawn from the ranks of practitioners who throughout their careers have ministered to individual clients, looks to the instant case and nurses his human desire to do justice. The academic jurist, placed very much at a distance, is oppressed by the expectations of those who provide his remuneration. He is required to teach and administer within the university. Few think he should serve as an unpaid oracle to the judiciary.

This is a state of affairs which in 1932 a Cambridge law professor, H C Gutteridge, told a law lord, Lord Atkin, he had always regarded as a great misfortune. Gutteridge lamented what he called the almost complete lack of contact between the practitioner and the academic lawyer in England. He went on-

> 'The gulf between the two is very wide - much wider than it is in America or on the Continent. The reason for this is no doubt the historical development of the teaching of English law and the fact that the Universities were late in the field, but it has led to the

development of an inferiority complex on the part of the teacher
which is bad for the teaching of law and also inimical to the future of
English law. There is so much that the Judge and the practitioner
cannot do because they have not got the time to spare, but which
ought to be done and can only be done by the academic lawyer.'

{Extract from a letter reproduced in G Lewis *Lord Atkin* (Butterworths, 1983) p
225.}

Gutteridge went on to suggest that each Inn of Court should appoint a
'teacher to the Bench'. In his reply {P 228.} Atkin ignored this presumptuous
suggestion, and delivered the tart rejoinder that it would help if law teachers
'showed up at times as discriminating champions of the profession'. The
position remains the same today.

The three elements in our law have stayed elaborately apart. It is one way to
run a legal system, but perhaps not the best way. The English take pride in their
common law, and their robust insular historic resistance to the reception of
Roman law doctrines.

No doubt by that resistance they gained much, but they also lost a little. On
the continent, where Roman law was received, the jurist and his opinions
(*responsa prudentium*) are honoured throughout the profession. *La doctrine* is in
Europe the central body of law furnished by the writings of its jurists (including
those on the bench). Here in England the judges look almost exclusively to the
opinions of their brethren.

The European practice derives from classical Rome. Buckland identifies the
jurists of the Augustan age as 'the real builders of the great fabric of Roman
law'. {W W Buckland *A Textbook of Roman Law* (2nd edn, 1950) p 20.} The
jurist's *interpretatio* is a source of law, along with rescripts and edicts. He
ponders the general principles of the law, taking an overview. Judges, busy with
day-to-day affairs, seek his advice: sometimes in a walk across the Forum.
{Cicero *De Oratore* 3 33 133, cited here despite Brett LJ's dismissive remark
that 'to quote Cicero for such a purpose is too ambitious' (*Ex p Chick* (1879) 11
Ch D 731, at p 738).} He instructs the advocate on points of law, as well as
instructing pupils. He acts as assessor to judges, and even dictates their
judgments. Buckland says-

> 'Much of the Praetor's edict was due only nominally to him, but was
> the work of his more learned councillors. Further, they were active in
> producing juristic literature; for the purposes of legal development it
> was their most important work.'

{W W Buckland *A Textbook of Roman Law* (2nd edn, 1950) p 22.}

English lawyers have tended to take a different view. With them, it is judicial
decision in an actual case before the court that gives the valid stamp. Blackstone
criticised the *Institutes* of Justinian as in themselves 'extremely voluminous and
diffuse'. In addition, he went on-

> ' . . . the idle comments, obscure glosses, and jarring interpretations
> grafted thereupon by the learned jurists, are literally without
> number. And these glosses, which are mere private opinions of
> scholastic doctors, and not, like our books of Reports, judicial
> determinations of the courts, are all of authority sufficient to be

vouched and relied on; which must needs breed great distraction and confusion in their tribunals.'

{Kerr Bl (4th edn, 1876) iii 335.}

Fathers of English law Our judges have nevertheless paid great respect to the opinions of jurists and commentators who may be described as the fathers of our law, such as Bracton, Glanvill, Littleton and Coke.

When counsel sought to dismiss Coke's view on the meaning of a phrase in a poor law statute of Elizabeth I {39 Eliz 1 c 3} as 'an opinion written in a closet, off-hand, without any discussion, and not confirmed by any decision in court' Lord Lyndhurst LC was unimpressed. He said: 'I do not think the House would feel justified in putting a construction on the Act inconsistent with the commentary of Lord Coke'. {*Mayor etc of Newcastle v A-G* (1845) 12 Cl & F 402, at p 419. See also *Strother v Hutchinson* (1837) 4 Bing NC 83, at p 89; *Gorham v Bishop of Exeter* (1850) 5 Ex 630; *Ecclesiastical Commrs v Parr* [1894] 2 QB 420, at p 428; *Wilmot v London Road Car Co* (1910) 27 TLR 4.}

Being called on to determine the meaning of the word 'forge' in s 20 of the Forgery Act 1861, Kelly CB relied on the writings of early jurists-

> 'When, however, we look at all these authorities and to the text-writers of the highest reputation such as Comyns (Dig tit Forgery A 1), Bacon (Abr tit Forgery A) and Coke (3 Inst 169) we find there is no conflict of authority. Sir M Foster (Foster's *Criminal Cases* 116), *Russell on Crime* (Vol 2 p 709, 10th edn) and other writers all agree there is no definition of the word 'forgery' in 24 & 25 Vict c 98, but the offence has been defined by very learned authors and we think the case falls within their definition.'

{*R v Ritson* (1869) LR 1 CCR 200, at p 203. Cf *Camden (Marquis) v IRC* [1914] 1 KB 641.}

Parliament itself recognised the authority of early jurists. Thus the statute 5 Eliz 1 c 1 (1562) provided that it should not be lawful to kill a person attainted in a *praemunire*, 'any law, statute, opinion, or exposition of law to the contrary notwithstanding'. It is scarcely imaginable that a modern Act would use such language.

Later writings More recent authors have often been cited. {See, e g, *Re Warner's Settled Estates, Warner to Steel* (1881) 17 Ch D 711, at p 713; *The Hansa Nord* [1976] QB 44, at pp 59, 72; *Winkworth v Christie, Manson & Woods Ltd* [1980] 1 All ER 1121, at p 1134; *R v Uxbridge JJ, ex p Commr of Police of the Metropolis* [1981] 3 All ER 129, at p 137; *Phonogram Ltd v Lane* [1981] 3 All ER 182, at p 187.} Sometimes indeed a judge will openly acknowledge his debt to an author, as Lloyd J did in relation to *Gough on Company Charges*. {*NV Slavenburg's Bank v Intercontinental Natural Resources Ltd* [1980] 1 All ER 955, at p 974 ('a book to which I am much indebted').}

However the tendency of judges has been to place relatively small reliance on the writings of modern jurists - though there have been many exceptions, particularly in the field of criminal law. {See, eg, *Re Castioni* [1891] 1 QB 149; *R v Stephenson* [1979] 2 All ER 1198, at pp 1201 and 1203; *R v Kelly* [1981] 2 All ER 1098, at pp 1101 and 1104.} The typical current attitude is illustrated by Lord Wilberforce's warning of 'the dangers, well perceived by our predecessors but tending to be neglected in modern times, of placing reliance on textbook authority for an analysis of judicial decisions'. {*Johnson v Agnew* [1979] 1 All ER 883, at p 892. The predecessors are not named, and it is difficult to guess who they are.} Lord Diplock is similarly dismissive-

> 'It may be that greater reliance than is usual in the English courts is placed on the writings of academic lawyers by courts of other European states where oral argument by counsel plays a relatively minor role in the decision-making process. The persuasive effect of learned commentaries, like the arguments of counsel in an English court, will depend on the cogency of their reasoning. Those to which your Lordships have been referred contain perhaps rather more assertion than ratiocination . . .'

{*Fothergill v Monarch Airlines Ltd* [1980] 2 All ER 696, at p 708. For an academic riposte attacking the tendency of judges themselves to engage in mere assertion, see Murphy and Rawlings 'After the Ancien Regime: The Writing of Judgments in the House of Lords 1979/1980 Part I' (1981) 44 MLR 617.}

The opening words of this dictum understate the true European view, which is illustrated by Article 167 of the Treaty of Rome. This places jurists on a level with judges themselves by saying that the qualification for appointment of judges to the Court of Justice of the European Communities {Called 'the European Court' by the European Communities Act 1972 (see s 1 and Sch 1 Pt II).} is that they-

> ' . . . shall be chosen from persons whose independence is beyond doubt and who possess the qualifications required for appointment to the highest judicial offices in their respective countries *or who are juarisconsults of recognised competence* . . .'

{Emphasis added.}

It is a feature of English law, says the biographer of Lord Atkin, 'that most of its best modern jurisprudence is to be found in the great opinions and judgments in the Law Reports and not in academic writings'. {G Lewis *Lord Atkin* (Butterworths, 1983) p 63.}

Nevertheless some textbooks, going into edition after edition, have acquired the status of legal monuments. Lord Goddard CJ once remarked that justices of the peace were accustomed to treat Stone's *Justices' Manual* 'with almost the respect paid to the Bible'. {*Bastin v Davies* [1950] 1 All ER 1095, at p 1096. See also *R v Adams* [1980] 1 All ER 473, at p 478; *NV Slavenburg's Bank v Intercontinental Natural Resources Ltd* [1980] 1 All ER 955, at p 962.}

Also treated as authoritative are the opinions of expert bodies such as the Law Commission, whose reports are frequently relied on by the courts. {See, e g, *Re J S (a minor)* [1980] 1 All ER 1061, at p 1065.} No author's text, from those of Coke downwards, is treated by the courts as of more than persuasive authority. Under our system, binding authority is reserved for judicial decisions.

Judges and barristers   The tradition of the courts has been to treat as works of authority only those written by members of the Bar or judges drawn from their ranks. {*Re Thompson* [1936] Ch 676, at p 680; *Tichborne v Weir* (1892) 67 LT 735, at p 736.}

Living and deceased authors   The ancient legal tradition is that no author can be cited as an authority in his own lifetime. {*Union Bank v Munster* (1887) 37 Ch D 51, at p 54; *Tichborne v Weir* (1892) 67 LT 735, at p 736; *Greenlands Ltd v Wilmshurst* (1913) 29 TLR 685, at p 687; *Re Ryder and Steadman's Contract* [1927] 2 Ch 62, at p 74; *Nicholls v Ely Beet Sugar Factory Ltd* [1936] Ch 343, at p 349 (where Lord Wright MR paid a neat compliment to the octogenarian Sir Frederick Pollock by saying his *Law of Torts* was 'fortunately not a work of authority').} Megarry V-C has given, extra-judicially, the following explanation for this doctrine-

> ' . . . quite apart from any possible *mala fides*, a living author might well insert in his book a passage dealing with a problem which he had himself encountered in practice and later falls to be litigated; and views expressed on a problem which has been presented to the author *ex parte*, as it were, may well prove unsound when the contentions of the other side come to be examined.
>
> True, any defect in the author's views in no wise depends upon whether or not he survives the trial; an *ex parte* opinion is an *ex parte* opinion, whether the author watches the trial from this world or the next. Yet the passage of years and the activities of those who edit the books of the departed tend to produce criticism and sometimes the elimination of frailties, and so give greater confidence in what remains.
>
> Further, many books by dead authors represent mature views after a lifetime of studying and, often, practising in the particular branch of law concerned, whereas all too many books by the living are written by those who, laudably enough, have merely hoped to learn the rudiments of a subject by writing a book about it.'

{*Miscellany-at-Law* pp 327-8.}

Perhaps the most cogent argument for the writings of the dead is that the authors can no longer change their minds. Lord Denning regarded the notion that books by living authors are not works of authority as 'exploded'. He said that 'the more recent the work, the more persuasive it is'. {(1947) 63 LQR 516.} This view is adopted in the formulation of this section of the Code.

Books by draftsmen of Acts   Judicial opinions have differed as to the value in interpretation of a commentary by the draftsman. In early times a judge might have an opportunity to lay down in court the meaning of an Act he had drafted himself. Hence Hengham CJ's famous rebuke to counsel: 'Do not gloss the statute; we understand it better than you do, for we made it'. {YB 33-35 Edw 1 (RS) 82, at p 83.}

Lord Ellesmere LC observed in the sixteenth century that 'those that were the penners and devisers of statutes have been the greatest light for exposition'. {Cited T R F Plucknett 'Ellesmere on Statutes' (1944) 60 LQR 242, at p 246.} Yet in *Hilder v Dexter* {[1902] AC 474.} Lord Halsbury LC abstained from delivering a speech because the case concerned an Act he had drafted himself. He said {P 477.}-

> 'I have more than once had occasion to say that in construing a statute I believe the worst person to construe it is the person who is responsible for its drafting'. He is very much disposed to confuse

what he intended to do with the effect of the language which in fact has been employed. At the time he drafted the statute, at all events, he may have been under the impression that he had given full effect to what was intended, but he may be mistaken in construing it afterwards just because what was in his mind was what was intended, though, perhaps, it was not done.'

{See also *Danford v McAnulty* (1883) 8 App Cas 456, at p 460; *Re Castioni* [1891] 1 QB 149, at p 167; *Vacher & Sons Ltd v London Society of Compositors* [1913] AC 107, at pp 113, 126.}

On the other hand a leading draftsman, Sir Courtenay Ilbert, pointed out that the draftsman 'often can, from his knowledge of the history and intention of an enactment, give a clue to its true construction'. {*Legislative Methods and Forms* (1901) p 93.}

Practice Acts are often drafted within the context of current legal practice, and the opinions of text writers may be relied on in later years as a form of *contemporanea expositio*: in other words as evidencing what Lord Cairns referred to as 'the constant practice of the profession'. {*Alexander v Kirkpatrick* (1874) LR 2 HL (Sc) 397, at p 400. See also *Basset v Basset* (1744) 3 Atk 203, at p 208; *Re Ford and Hill* (1879) 10 Ch D 365, at p 370; *Henty v Wray* (1882) 21 Ch D 332, at p 348; *Re Ryder and Steadman's Contract* [1927] 2 Ch 62, at p 84; *Bromley v Tryon* [1952] AC 265, at pp 274-5; *Marshall v Cottingham* [1981] 3 All ER 8, at p 11.} On the other hand the opinions of text writers may help to *form* practice. As Lord Goddard CJ said of a passage in Bell's *Sale of Food and Drugs*-

'If a statement has appeared in a well-known textbook for a number of years and has never been dissented from by a judicial decision, it would be most unfortunate to throw doubt on it, *after it had been acted upon by justices and their clerks for so long*.'

{*Bastin v Davies* [1950] 1 All ER 1095, at p 1096. Emphasis added.}

Judges will not however be deterred from rejecting a longstanding opinion if convinced it is wrong. In *Langdale v Danby* {[1982] 3 All ER 129.} the House of Lords dismissed a note which had appeared unaltered in the *Supreme Court Practice* for 70 years. Lord Bridge said that the note 'is unfortunately most misleading' and that the case cited as authority for the opinion it expressed 'is no authority at all'. {P 136. See also *New Zealand Government Property Corpn v H M & S Ltd* [1982] 1 All ER 624, at p 627.}

Adoption as part of counsel's argument If the court declines to accept a proferred text as authoritative, counsel is permitted to adopt it as part of his argument. {*Greenlands Ltd v Wilmshurst* (1913) 29 TLR 685, at p 687; *Suffolk County Council v Mason* [1979] 2 All ER 369, at p 379.} Its weight is then limited to what acceptance it may command purely as argument, without reliance on its author's reputation. The judge may choose to refer to the cited passage approvingly in his judgment, when it will gain a cachet thereafter adding weight to its status as an expression of the author's personal opinion. {See, e g, *Suffolk County Council v Mason* [1979] 2 All ER 369, at p 386.} This may be done even though the passage in question was not referred to in argument. {See, e g, *Faulkner v Talbot* [1981] 3 All ER 468, at p 473.}

Foreign jurists The courts will accept the writings of foreign jurists as indications of the law of their own country {See, e g, *Winkworth v Christie, Manson & Woods Ltd* [1980] 1 All ER 1121, at p 1133 (US law of chattels).}, or of the European Community {See, e g, *Phonogram Ltd v Lane* [1981] 3 All ER 182, at p 186.}, or as laid down by a treaty. {See, e g, *Fothergill v Monarch Airlines Ltd* [1980] 2 All ER 696, at p 701.}

7. Types of interpreter: the subject and his adviser

The subject who is bound by legislation must be classed as an interpreter of it. Nevertheless, unless himself an expert, the subject is unwise to trust to his own unaided understanding. His professional adviser must stand with him.

COMMENTARY

Sir Thomas More, the Lord Chancellor executed by Henry VIII, wrote in his *Utopia*: 'All laws are promulgated to this end, that every man may know his duty; and, therefore, the plainest and most obvious sense of the words is that which must be put upon them'. {*Utopia*, Book II.} This might well apply in Utopia, but sadly it does not hold good in real life.

The duty of obedience to an Act requires that the citizen shall construe the Act correctly. Since legal knowledge is needed to arrive at an informed interpretation of Acts, the fulfilment of this requirement presents obvious difficulties. {For the informed interpretation rule see s 119 of this Code. As to the rule that ignorance of the law (which includes mistaken understanding of it) provides no excuse for infringement see s 9.} The existence of these difficulties can only strengthen the importance of predictable construction by courts applying an Act. {As to predictable construction see s 130 of this Code. The general duty of courts and other enforcement agencies is discussed in ss 15 to 26.}

It is true our judges continue to insist that Acts should be drafted so as to be understood by the citizen. Lord Diplock, complaining of the drafting of the notorious s 17 of the Employment Act 1980, said-

> ' . . . what the law is, particularly in the field of industrial relations, ought to be plain. It should be expressed in terms that can be easily understood by those who have to apply it even at shop floor level . . . Absence of clarity is destructive of the rule of law.'

{*Merkur Island Shipping Corpn v Laughton* [1983] 2 WLR 778, at p 790.}

The idea that labour legislation in our complex society should be capable of being understood *as promulgated* by workers on the shop floor is indeed utopian. The only legislation a layman can safely rely on as promulgated is designed for the purpose, and there is little enough of that. One rare example is the notice regarding liability for a hotel guest's property. This was drafted for the purpose of being displayed in hotels. {The terms of the notice are set out in the Schedule to the Hotel Proprietors Act 1956. See Example 10.8.}

For the rest, a lay person must rely on processed versions of the enactment, such as official leaflets and advertisements. Or he must seek expert advice. {For a general discussion of the problem see Bennion *Statute Law* (2nd edn, 1983) chap 10.}

Where an enactment falls to be construed by a legal adviser, the adviser's function is to determine, in the light of the facts of the instant case, the legal meaning which the court is most likely to place upon the enactment if the matter should come to litigation.

There is a conceptual difference between the position of the court when called upon to rule on the meaning of an enactment and the position of anyone else. If a professional adviser is asked what the law is on some point he is in effect asked to say what he thinks a court would decide if the point came before it. Indeed Holmes J, unwitting founder of the American realist school of jurisprudence, went so far as to say that 'prophecies of what the courts are likely to do in fact and nothing more pretentious are what I mean by the law'. {'The Path of the Law' *Collected Legal Papers* p 173.}

The position is similar with a teacher instructing his students, or a textbook writer seeking to expound the law. Even a non-judicial functionary (such as an administrative official) is obliged to base his position on what the court would be likely to decide if the matter were litigated. While each of these may feel a temptation to set forth the decision a court *ought* to reach, in practice his need is to arrive at a forecast of the decision a court is *most likely* to reach.

We now go on to examine various aspects of the subject's position.

THE SUBJECT

8. The subject: duty to obey legislation

Every person to whom an Act applies is under a legal duty to comply with it. The same is true of a legislative instrument made under prerogative or delegated powers.

COMMENTARY

It is of the nature of legislation that the persons to whom it applies should have a legal duty to obey it. {As to who is subject to an Act see s 30 and Part IX of this Code.} These persons may be private citizens, private corporations, or public officials or bodies. Under the British system it makes no difference. All persons are equally obliged to obey the law, and there is no separate system for the enforcement of public administrative enactments. {The duty to enforce Acts is dealt with in ss 15 to 26 of this Code. As to the modern judge-made distinction between private law and public law see p 68 below.}

Often the sanctions for breach of a statutory duty are specified in the Act itself. Where this is not done, it is inferred that Parliament intended to rely instead on sanctions arising under principles of the general law. These are described in later provisions of the Code. {See ss 13 (criminal sanctions) and 14 (civil sanctions).}

Moral duty of obedience Questions concerning the moral, as opposed to the legal, content of the duty of obedience are mainly beyond the scope of this work. A distinction is sometimes drawn between *mala in se*, namely acts or omissions which are morally wrong regardless of what the law has to say, and *mala prohibita*, which are wrong only because the law forbids them. Except in so far as this distinction has any legal effect, it is unnecessary to pursue it here. {As to its legal significance see the discussion at p 741 below of how far mens rea is required in statutory offences.}

All that we need note is that even *mala prohibita* deserve to be regarded by citizens with the respect due to a law made on their own behalf by their elected representatives. That even local government councillors are representatives rather than delegates was recognised by the House of Lords in *Bromley LBC v Greater London Council* {[1982] 1 All ER 129, *per* Lord Diplock at p 165.} The principle applies *a fortiori* to Members of Parliament.

Blackstone, writing in the eighteenth century, adopted with his own variations the idea of the social contract put forward by Locke and Rousseau. He called it the 'original contract'-

> 'But though society had not its formal beginning from any convention of individuals, actuated by their wants and fears; yet it is the *sense* of their weakness and imperfection that *keeps* mankind together, that demonstrates the necessity of this union, and that, therefore, is the solid and natural foundation, as well as the cement, of civil society. And this is what we mean by the original contract of society ... namely, that the whole should protect all its parts, and that every part should pay obedience to the will of the whole; or, in other words, that the community should guard the rights of each individual member, and that, in return for this protection, each individual should submit to the laws of the community; without which permission of all, it was impossible that protection could certainly be extended to any.'

{Kerr Bl (4th edn, 1876) i 29.}

In a later passage Blackstone remarks that every man, when he enters society, thereby acquires an advantage. In return he 'gives up a part of his natural liberty as the price of so valuable a purchase; and in consideration of receiving the advantages of mutual commerce, obliges himself to conform to those laws which the community has thought proper to establish'. {Ibid, p 97.} The moral component of this duty of obedience increased in modern times with the final arrival of full adult suffrage. {Representation of the People (Equal Franchise) Act 1928.}

House of Lords   The role of the non-elected House of Lords in the enactment of legislation admittedly reduces the representative character of statute law. This drawback is mitigated by various factors.

The House of Lords, while providing a contribution based on the wisdom and experience of its members, plays only a small part in determining the policy content of Acts. It can however voice (and on rare occasions insist on implementing) the current opinions of the electorate. The House of Lords acts as a revising chamber for Bills (though nearly all amendments made in either House of Parliament to Bills which become law are in fact drafted by parliamentary counsel). Perhaps the most important constitutional function of the House of Lords is to serve as a brake on any desire of a particular House of Commons to prolong, or even perpetuate, its own existence.

Types of duty   The duty imposed by an Act may be absolute or *sub modo*. A duty is absolute where it arises irrespective of the will of the person under the duty. It is a duty *sub modo* where the subject activates the duty himself, as by seeking an advantage obtainable only by first discharging the duty. {See Example 12.1.}

How far compliance need be exact   The courts do not take an over-fussy view in determining whether a purported compliance satisfies the requirements of the Act. As Oliver LJ put it: 'In my judgment it is not necessary, in construing a statutory expression, to take leave of one's common sense . . .' {*Exxon Corpn v Exxon Insurance Consultants International Ltd* [1981] 3 All ER 241, at p 249. As to the commonsense construction rule see s 122 of this Code.}

Example 1   In *Banque de l'Indochine et de Suez SA v Euroseas Group Finance Co Ltd* {[1981] 3 All ER 198.} it was held that the requirement in s 108(1) of the Companies Act 1948 that a company should 'have its name mentioned in legible characters' in letters and notices did not require the registered name to be reproduced in full. It was sufficient if words like 'Company' and 'Limited' were abbreviated, so long as there was no possibility of confusion.

Example 2   On the other hand it was held in *Singer v Trustee of the property of Munro* {[1981] 3 All ER 215.} that the duty to send a notice to a person was not complied with by sending it to his solicitor. 'It is . . . a common fallacy to think that solicitors have an implied authority on behalf of their clients to receive notices'. {*Per* Walton J at p 218. But see s 356 of this Code.} Solicitors have a way of charging for anything they do.

On the other hand a mere literal compliance without the substance will not suffice. Here implication may need to be drawn on. {As to the use of implication in statutory interpretation see ss 107 to 110 of this Code.}

Example 3   Section 8 of the Bills of Sale Act 1878 requires a bill to set forth the consideration for which it was given. In *Ex p Johnson* {(1884) LT Vol L 214.} it was held that by implication this meant the consideration must be *truly* set forth.

Example 4   Similarly the requirement imposed on an employer by s 1 of the Employment Protection (Consolidation) Act 1978 to give the employee a written statement of the terms of his employment must import the requirement that the particulars given shall be *correct*. Otherwise the purpose of the enactment would clearly be frustrated. {The decision in *Brown v Stuart, Scott & Co* (1981) ICR 166 must be taken as wrongly decided on this point: see C Mogridge 'Giving Written Particulars of Employment - A Valueless Exercise?' (1981) 131 NLJ 1250.}

Over-performance   A duty is regarded as discharged where more is done than the duty requires. This is in accordance with the maxim *omne majus continet in se minus* (the greater includes the less). {5 Co Rep 115; Dig 50, 17, 110; Jenk Cent 208.} The maxim prevails generally in the law, an example of its operation being the rule that tender of a sum larger than the amount of a debt is a good tender. No counter-demand must however be made (for example a demand of change on tender of an excessive amount). The rule corresponds to the rule that where an act is permitted, anything less is included in the permisssion. {*R v Cousins* [1982] 2 All ER 115 (where actual force is permissible, a threat to use force is also permissible). See also Broom Leg Max 310 (power to lease for 21 years imports power to lease for a shorter period). See further s 122 of this Code.}

Hardship   In general hardship is not accepted as an excuse for lawbreaking. {*R v Botfield* (1982) *The Times* 22 March.} Absolute necessity may however be a defence. {As to necessity see s 352 of this Code.}

Ignorance of law   As to ignorance of law see ss 9 and 45 of this Code.

Directory and mandatory requirements   As to the distinction between directory and mandatory statutory requirements see s 10 of this Code.

Contracting out and waiver   As to when contracting out or waiver is allowed see s 11 of this Code. For cases where this is not permissible see s 12.

9. The subject: *ignorantia juris neminem excusat*

Ignorance or mistaken understanding of legislation is not accepted in law as an excuse for failure to comply with it.

COMMENTARY

Blackstone said that it is the subject's business to be thoroughly acquainted with the law 'for if ignorance of what he *might* know were admitted as a legitimate excuse, the laws would be of no effect, but might always be eluded with impunity'. {Kerr Bl (4th edn, 1876) i 28. See also Lord Ellenborough CJ in *Bilbie v Lumley* (1802) 2 East 469, at p 472, and the biting sarcasm of Knight Bruce LJ in *Walker v Armstrong* (1856) 8 De G M & G 531 at p 538.}

This knowledge of the law is required to be accurate. Blackstone said of mistakes as to the purport of a law: 'if a man thinks he has a right to kill a person excommunicated or outlawed, wherever he meets him, and does so, this is wilful murder'. {Kerr Bl (4th edn, 1876) iv 21.} He went on-

> 'For a mistake in point of law, which every person of discretion not only may, but is bound and presumed to know, is in criminal cases no sort of defence. *Ignorantia juris, quod quisque tenetur scire, neminem excusat*, is as well a maxim of our own law, as it was of the Roman.'

{Ibid.}

While this is true, it should be appreciated that enforcement of the criminal law in practice largely depends on popular ignorance of its provisions. For example if all criminals knew of, and insisted on, their right of silence there would be relatively few convictions. Sir Robert Mark, a former Commissioner of Police of the Metropolis, said in 1978-

> '. . . let me make it quite clear that I am one of those who believe that if the criminal law and the procedures relating to it were applied strictly according to the book, as a means of protecting society it would collapse in a few days.'

{*In the Office of Constable* pp 54-6. Elsewhere in this autobiographical work Mark notes that 'the two classes most immune from the criminal law are lawyers and police, if only because they know most about it' (p 102).}

The maxim Blackstone cites in the above passage is a narrower version of one relied on by Hale: *ignorantia eorum quae quis scire tenetur non excusat* (ignorance of those things which everyone is bound to know affords no excuse). {Pl Cr 42.} In Coke's version there is a prefatory phrase to show the rule does not extend to ignorance of fact: *Ignorantia facti excusat; ignorantia juris non excusat.* {1 Co Rep 177.}

Mistake as a defence If, through mistake of law, a person believes he is committing an offence when he is not, he is not guilty of the offence. If, through a combined mistake of law and fact in a case requiring mens rea, the defendant believes he is doing something the law forbids (when it does not forbid that thing) he is not guilty even though the actual facts constitute the actus reus of a different offence.

Example 1 In *R v Taafe* {[1984] 1 All ER 747.} the House of Lords considered the case of a man who thought he was smuggling money, and that to do so was in offence. In fact to smuggle money was not an offence; but the parcels in question contained cannabis. D was convicted under s 170(2) of the Customs and Excise Management Act 1979 of being 'knowingly concerned' in a fraudulent evasion of a prohibition on the importation of cannabis. *Held* The conviction was wrong. D's mistake of law could not convert the importation of currency into a criminal offence, and his mistake of fact prevented him from having the mens rea required for the offence charged. {As to mens rea see p 741 below.}

Ignorance by a foreigner It makes no difference to the application of the rule that the subject is a foreigner, and therefore less likely than a citizen to possess knowledge of the law. {*R v Esop* (1836) 7 C & P 456.} The rule is not based on fairness, but on expediency. One who enters a foreign land is necessarily under an obligation to acquaint himself with its relevant laws. See further s 222 of this Code.

No presumption of actual knowledge The better view is that the law does not truly import a presumption of legal knowledge. As Lord Atkin put it-

> 'For my part I am not prepared to accept the view that there is in law any presumption that any one, even a judge, knows all the rules and orders of the Supreme Court. The fact is that there is not and never has been a presumption that everyone knows the law. There is the rule that ignorance of the law does not excuse, a maxim of very different scope and application.'

{*Evans v Bartlam* [1937] AC 473, at p 479. Cf the remark by Scrutton LJ that 'It is impossible to know all the statutory law, and not very possible to know all the common law' (1921) 1 Camb L J 6, at p 19. See further pp 121–122, below.}

Effect on interpretation The rule is sometimes stated as a reason why a straightforward interpretation should be given. Professor Glanville Williams cites with approval the maxim from Book II of More's *Utopia* given in the commentary to s 7 above. {Glanville Williams 'Statute Interpretation, Prostitution and the Rule of Law' (comprised in *Crime, Proof and Punishment,*

Essays in memory of Sir Rupert Cross) p 71.} Unfortunately however it has to be accepted that modern statute law is not in general capable of accurate understanding by laymen. That is one reason why we have a legal profession. {See s 262 of this Code. As to the informed interpretation rule see s 119.}

As an element in 'reasonableness'   Many modern Acts use the concept of reasonableness in judging behaviour. The question arises whether a person can be heard to argue that his behaviour was not unreasonable because it was prompted by ignorance of the relevant legal rule.

Example 2   Under s 67(2) of the Employment Protection (Consolidation) Act 1978, the time limit for lodging a complaint of unfair dismissal may be extended if the industrial tribunal is satisfied that it was 'not reasonably practicable' for it to be lodged in time. This is a question of fact, and in *Palmer v Southend-on-Sea Borough Council* {[1984] 1 All ER 945, at p 955.} May LJ suggested that a valid reason for delay might be ignorance by the complainant of his legal right to complain, particularly where this was induced by misinformation from the employer.

Not applicable to executive instrument   Although the rule that ignorance forms no excuse is applicable to every type of law, it does not apply to an executive instrument made (under powers conferred by law) in relation to a named person only.

Example 3   In *Lim Chin Aik v R* {[1963] AC 160.} the accused was the subject of an *ad hoc* order prohibiting him by name from entering Singapore. Since the order had not been brought to his notice, the accused was held by the Privy Council not to be guilty of infringing it. Lord Evershed said that unless there was something the subject of the order could do as a practical matter there was no reason for penalising him: 'it cannot be inferred that the legislature imposed strict liability merely in order to find a luckless victim'. {P 174. As to strict liability in statutory offences see pp 362, 758–759 and 783–784 below.}

Parliamentary Bills   Although a Bill in progress through Parliament is not of course law, the courts will take judicial notice of it where relevant. {As to the doctrine of judicial notice see s 21 of this Code.}

A person cannot establish a claim for misrepresentation based on statements of what a Bill contains. He is taken to know that the Bill may be changed before finally passing, or may never be passed at all. {*Mandeville v Greater London Council* (1982) *The Times* 28 January.}

Where Act disapplies rule   As with every other principle of law, an Act may disapply the rule that ignorance is no excuse.

Example 4   Section 13(5) of the Companies Act 1976 provides as follows-

> 'No person shall act as auditor of a company at a time when *he knows* that he is disqualified for appointment to that office; and if an auditor of a company *to his knowledge* becomes so disqualified during his term of office he shall thereupon vacate his office and give notice in

writing to the company that he has vacated it by reason of such disqualification.'

{Emphasis added.}

It was held by the Divisional Court in *Secretary of State for Trade and Industry v Hart* {[1982] 1 All ER 817.} that this provision meant what it said. If a company auditor, because of his ignorance of the law, did not realise he was disqualified he committed no offence by continuing to serve (even though he was aware of the facts which caused the disqualification).

Section 13(5) runs counter to the reasons underlying the doctrine now under discussion, and is for that reason open to criticism. Woolf J commented {Pp 821–822.} that Parliament might need to amend it so as to reverse a perhaps inadvertent encouragement to wilful ignorance of what the law requires.

See further ss 45 and 130 of this code and Example 322.6.

10. The subject: mandatory and directory requirements

This section applies where-

(a) a person ('the subject') may be affected by a thing done under an enactment, and

(b) the effectiveness of that thing is subject to the performance by any person ('the person bound') of some duty ('the relevant duty'), and

(c) the relevant duty is not complied with, and

(d) the intended consequence of the failure to comply is not stated in the legislation.

In ascertaining, in a case where this section applies, the effect of the failure to comply with the relevant duty, it is necessary to determine whether the duty was intended by the legislature to be mandatory or merely directory. For this purpose it may be relevant to consider whether the person affected and the person bound are the same, and whether the thing done under the enactment is beneficial or adverse to the person affected.

Where the relevant duty is held to be mandatory, the failure to comply with it will invalidate the thing done under the enactment.

Where the relevant duty is held to be merely directory, the failure to comply with it will not invalidate the thing done under the enactment; and the law will be applied as nearly as may be as if the duty had been complied with.

COMMENTARY

Where a duty arises under a statute, the court, charged with the task of enforcing the statute, needs to decide what consequence Parliament intended should follow from breach of the duty.

This is an area where legislative drafting has been markedly deficient. Draftsmen find it easy to use the language of command. They say that a thing 'shall' be done. Too often they fail to consider the consequence when it is not done. What is not thought of by the draftsman is not expressed in the statute. Yet the courts are forced to reach a decision.

It would be draconian to hold that in every case failure to comply with the relevant duty invalidates the thing done. So the courts' answer has been to devise a distinction between mandatory and directory duties. Terms used instead of 'mandatory' include 'absolute', 'obligatory', 'imperative' and 'strict'. In place of 'directory', the term 'permissive' is sometimes used. Use of the term 'directory' in the sense of permissive has been justly criticised. {See Craies *Statute Law* (7th edn, 1971) p 61 n 74.} However it is now firmly rooted.

Where the relevant duty is mandatory, failure to comply with it invalidates the thing done. Where it is merely directory the thing done will be unaffected (though there may be some sanction for disobedience imposed on the person bound). {As to sanctions for breach of statutory duty see s 13 of this Code (criminal sanctions) and s 14 (civil sanctions).}

The exact meaning of 'invalidate' here depends on the circumstances. In some cases the thing done will be wholly void; in others merely voidable. The principle was thus stated by Lord Wilberforce in a case where the relevant duty was to observe natural justice-

> 'This argument led necessarily into the difficult area of what is void and what is voidable, as to which some confusion exists in the authorities. Their Lordships' opinion would be, if it became necessary to fix on one or other of these expressions, that a decision made contrary to natural justice is void, but that, until it is so declared by a competent body or court, it may have some effect, or existence, in law. This condition might be better expressed by saying that the decision is invalid or vitiated.'

{*Calvin v Carr* [1979] 2 WLR 755, at p 763.}

Consequential construction This is an area where consequential construction is applied. {For consequential construction see s 140 of this Code.} If the court were to hold that the most trivial breach of an apparently absolute duty is to be treated as vitiating the relevant transaction, the consequences would often be out of all proportion to the lapse.

Example 1 Section 34 of the Revenue (No 2) Act 1861 said that no copy of a bill of sale should be filed in any court unless the duly-stamped original was produced. In *Bellamy v Saull* {(1863) 32 LJQB 366.} a bill was filed without production of the stamped original. *Held* The duty was merely directory, and the default did not vitiate the registration. The court arrived at this conclusion by considering the mischief, which was loss of stamp duty. It would have produced unnecessarily extreme consequences to hold the registration void. {See also *Vita Food Products Inc v Unus Shipping Co Ltd* [1939] AC 277 (bills of lading 'shall' contain statement that Hague rules apply: directory only).}

The legislative intention There is no rule of thumb in this matter. As was said by Lord Campbell CJ-

> 'No universal rule can be laid down ... It is the duty of courts of justice to try to get at the real intention of the legislature by carefully attending to the whole scope of the statute to be construed.'

{*Liverpool Borough Bank v Turner* (1861) 30 LJ Ch 379, at p 380.}
   Lord Penzance supported this view in a dictum that still holds true-

> 'I believe, as far as any rule is concerned, you cannot safely go further
> than that in each case you must look to the subject-matter, consider
> the importance of the provision and the relation of that provision to
> the general object intended to be secured by the Act, and upon a
> review of the case in that aspect decide whether the enactment is what
> is called imperative or only directory . . .
> I have been very carefully through all the principal cases, but upon
> reading them all the conclusion at which I am constrained to arrive is
> this, that you cannot glean a great deal that is very decisive from a
> perusal of these cases. They are on all sorts of subjects. It is very
> difficult to group them together, and the tendency of my mind, after
> reading them, is to come to the conclusion which was expressed by
> Lord Campbell in the case of *Liverpool Bank v Turner*.'

{*Howard v Bodington* (1877) 2 PD 203, at p 211. Cf *Salford Union (Guardians) v
Dewhurst* [1926] AC 619, at p 633.}
   Sir Arthur Channell said-

> 'When the provisions of a statute relate to the performance of a
> public duty and the case is such that to hold null and void acts done
> in respect of this duty would work serious inconvenience or injustice
> to persons who have no control over those entrusted with the duty,
> and at the same time would not promote the main object of the
> legislature, it has been the practice to hold such provisions to be
> directory only, the neglect of them, though punishable, not affecting
> the validity of the acts done.'

{*Montreal Street Rly Co v Normandin* [1917] AC 170, at p 174.}
   The interpreter's task is always to scrutinize the Act and determine, in the
light of its particular provisions, the legal consequence most likely to have been
intended for breach of the duty. Nevertheless it is necessary for the law to
categorize.
   Without legal categories, the law has little chance of being orderly and
predictable. Yet these are desirable qualities, which the courts try to cultivate.
{As to the need for predictability see s 130 of this Code.} Accordingly the courts
have worked out the two categories mentioned in this section of the Code. A
statutory duty is said to be either mandatory or directory.

Implied duties   The distinction applies even though the duty is imposed merely
by implication.

Example 2   Rule 14(2) of the Magistrates' Courts Rules 1968 {SI 1968/1920.}
states that at the conclusion of the evidence for the complainant 'the defendant
may address the court'. By implication, this imposes on the court a duty to hear
the defendant. This duty is mandatory. Failure to comply with it will therefore
vitiate the conviction. {*Disher v Disher* [1963] 3 All ER 933.}
   A duty to do a thing in a certain way by implication imports a duty not to do it
in any other way.

Example 3   Section 12 of the Metropolitan Building Act 1855 required that

the walls of buildings should be constructed of brick, stone or other incombustible material. In *Stevens v Gourley* {(1859) 29 LJCP 1.} it was held that this by implication prohibited, and therefore rendered illegal, their construction with any other material.

In many cases the rules of natural justice impose implied mandatory duties. {See, eg, *Ridge v Baldwin* [1964] AC 40 (dismissal of chief constable void where rules of natural justice not complied with). See further s 335 of this Code.}

We now give examples of the areas of law where the distinction between mandatory and directory duties is applied.

Jurisdiction Where a court or tribunal whose jurisdiction is laid down by Act is under a statutory duty *not* to make a certain type of order, the duty is mandatory. A purported order made in contravention of the duty will be void as made in excess of jurisdiction. {See, eg, *B v B* [1961] 2 All ER 396; *Public Prosecutor v Koi* [1968] AC 829, at p 852; *R v Kettering JJ, ex p Patmore* [1968] 1 WLR 1436.}

A court can hardly confer jurisdiction on itself; and it certainly cannot do so in disregard of an injunction by Parliament. A court order made without jurisdiction is necessarily a nullity. {*Barker v Palmer* (1881) 8 QBD 9.} In *R v Ingram* {(1697) 2 Salk 593.} the statute 13 Hen 4 c 7 (1411), requiring justices to try rioters 'within a month', was held to confer jurisdiction to try them after the month had elapsed. This would be decided differently today. So too would *Foot v Truro* {(1725) 1 Stra 625.}, where aldermen were held able to act effectively notwithstanding that their term of office had expired.

Failure to comply with Rules of the Supreme Court does not nullify the proceedings, but is to be treated as an irregularity. {RSC Ord 2 r 1.} Irregular proceedings may by order be set aside. {RSC Ord 2 r 2.}

Statutory procedures Modern regulatory Acts often confer power on public authorities to take coercive action of one sort or another. The legislation lays down a procedure to be followed, and the question often arises of the effect of a failure by the authority to take one of the prescribed steps. If the step is mandatory, the failure vitiates the exercise of the statutory power. If the step is merely directory, the failure will not be fatal.

In deciding whether the step is mandatory or directory, the court considers the broad policy of the Act and the principle of fairness to the subject. The policy is not to be frustrated by a mere technicality. On the other hand the subject is not to be prejudiced by the neglect of a safeguard inserted by Parliament for his protection.

The need to strike this balance was expressed by Lord Denning MR in *Munnich v Godstone RDC.* {[1966] 1 WLR 427.} After citing the remark by Viscount Simonds in *East Riding County Council v Park Estate (Bridlington) Ltd* {[1957] AC 223, at p 233.} that there must be strict and rigid adherence to formalities, Lord Denning went on-

> 'We found that many people were taking an undue advantage of that statement. Formalities were being used to defeat the public good. So we no longer favour them ... We now reject technicalities and apply the simple test enunciated by Upjohn LJ in [*Miller-Mead v Minister of Housing and Local Government* {[1963] 2 QB 196, at p 232.}]: 'Does the

[enforcement notice] tell him fairly what he has done wrong and what he must do to remedy it?'

Lord Hailsham LC has said: 'Where Parliament prescribes that an authority with compulsory powers should inform the subject of his right to question those powers, prima facie the requirement must be treated as mandatory'. {*London & Clydeside Estates Ltd v Aberdeen District Council* [1979] 3 All ER 876, at p 881 See also Lord Keith of Kinkel at p 893.}

Interference with liberty   Where an Act confers a right to interfere with the freedom of any individual, the prescribed conditions are treated as mandatory and must be strictly complied with.

Example 4   An Act authorising the detention of lunatics prohibited the reception of a lunatic in an asylum without the furnishing of a medical certificate in a prescribed form. The form was required to include the street and number of the house where the alleged lunatic had been medically examined. *Held* This requirement was mandatory. Where it was not complied with, the Act did not justify the detention of the lunatic. {*R v Pinder* (1855) 24 LJQB 148. Cf *Re Shuttleworth* (1846) 9 QB 651; *Ex p Van Sandau* (1846) 1 De G 303, 15 LJBk 13.}

It follows that court procedures touching on the liberty of the subject, whether they are criminal or civil, must be substantially complied with. {See s 290 of this Code.}

Example 5   In *R v Phillips* {[1939] 1 KB 63.} the depositions of prosecution witnesses were taken by *reading over* depositions previously made by them in committal proceedings against another accused. *Held* This contravened the requirements of s 17 of the Indictable Offences Act 1848, and the resulting convictions would be quashed. Lord Hewart CJ said {P 68.}-

'The terms of s 17 of the Indictable Offences Act 1848 are imperative and if they are complied with the accused person hears the witness give his evidence so that he is able to object to any question that may be put to him improperly . . . '

{Cf *R v Pearce* [1981] Crim LR 639 (consent of Attorney-General not obtained to prosecution).}

Interference with property   Where an Act confers a right to claim money or otherwise interfere with the property of a person, the prescribed conditions will be treated as mandatory. {Cf s 295 of this Code.}

Example 6   Section 7 of the Coast Protection Act 1949 enables an authority to include in a works scheme a provision whereby, within a period stated in the scheme, costs can be recovered from landowners. In *Cullimore v Lyme Regis Corporation* {[1961] 3 All ER 1008.} the period stated was six months, but the authority did not serve demand notices until 23 months had elapsed. *Held* the time limit was mandatory, and the demands were therefore void.

Conferring of a right or benefit   Where legislation confers some right or benefit on a person which he would not have at common law, the conditions laid down as to the accrual of the right or benefit, unless purely formal, are mandatory. If they are not complied with the right or benefit will not accrue.

Example 7   The Engraving Copyright Act 1734 conferred on designers of prints the exclusive right of printing them during the period of 14 years after the day of publication. The Act added 'which [day] shall be truly engraved, with the name of the proprietor, on each plate'. *Held* This requirement was an essential element in the conferring of the copyright, and if it was not observed the right did not accrue. {*Newton v Cowie* (1827) 5 LJ (OS) CP 159; *Avanzo v Mudie* (1854) 10 Ex 203.}

Example 8   Section 2(3) of the Hotel Proprietors Act 1956 limits the liability of a hotel proprietor for loss of or damage to property brought to the hotel, provided a notice in the prescribed form is displayed. In a case under the predecessor of this enactment it was held that this relief did not apply if the displayed notice was inaccurate in a material particular. {*Spice v Bacon* (1877) 2 Ex D 463. Cf *Gregson v Potter* (1879) 4 Ex D 142.}

Voting   Where a right to cast any kind of vote is given by statute, the duty to comply with the conditions laid down is usually mandatory. Failure to comply, except in an immaterial respect, will cause the vote to be void. {As to what is an immaterial, and therefore merely directory, requirement see *Woodward v Sarsons* (1875) LR 10 CP 733; *Ackers v Howard* (1886) 16 QBD 739; *Phillips v Goff* (1886) 17 QBD 805. For a basic requirement held merely directory see Example 93.2. As to voting rights see further pp 723–724 below.}

Example 9   The Local Government Act 1972 states that, in the case of an equality of votes at a meeting of a local authority, the person presiding at the meeting shall have a second or casting vote. {S 99 and Sch 12 para 39(2).} The Act also states that at any meeting of the council the chairman, if present, shall preside. {S 99 and Sch 12 paras 5(1), 11(1), 17(1), 27(1).} In *Re Wolverhampton Borough Council's Aldermanic Election* {[1962] 2 QB 460.}, a case under corresponding provisions of the Local Government Act 1933 (expressed in terms of the mayor rather than the chairman), the mayor, though present, had allowed another council member to preside. *Held* The casting vote of the person presiding was void.

Form of notices etc   Where the wording of a notice or similar document is prescribed, while the duty to serve the notice may be mandatory the precise form of words is usually directory only. What matters is that the substance should be conveyed.

Example 10   Article 8 of Sch 1 to the Carriage by Air Act 1932 required consignment notes to 'contain the following particulars' (specifying them). In *Samuel Montagu & Co Ltd v Swiss Air Transport Co Ltd* {[1966] 2 QB 306.} Lord Denning MR said {P 314} that this should not be given 'so rigid an interpretation as to hamper the conduct of business'. He went on: 'I do not interpret the article as meaning that the waybill must contain the statement *verbatim*. It is sufficient if it contains a statement to the like effect'. {See also *Thomas v Kelly* (1888) 13 App Cas 506, *per* Lord Macnaghten at p 520 (a bill of sale need not be 'a verbal and literal transcript of the statutory form').}

Purely technical contraventions Even where the duty is mandatory, the court will not nowadays hold it to be contravened because of a purely formal or technical defect. This may be described as a defect that does not materially impair the remedy intended to be provided by the enactment for the mischief to which it is directed. {See *Munnich v Godstone RDC* [1966] 1 WLR 427, cited above. As to the doctrine of the mischief see s 138 and Part XIV of this Code.}

This development means that some decisions of the past would not be followed today. {See, eg, *Noseworthy v Overseers of Buckland-in-the-Moor* (1873) LR 9 CP 233 (notice required to be sent to a person's address as described in voters' list sent instead to a different address which was where he actually lived).}

Matters arising after duty performed Where the relevant duty is complied with at the time, the act done is not vitiated by later developments which, had they occurred earlier, would have meant that the duty should have been performed in a different way.

Example 11 Section 33(1) of the Caravan Sites and Control of Development Act 1960 conferred a right of appeal against an enforcement notice on any of seven specified grounds. Section 33(4) said: 'An appeal ... shall be made to the Minister by a written notice *which shall indicate the grounds on which the appeal is brought'*. In *Chelmsford RDC v Powell* {[1963] 1 WLR 123.} it was held that where, after the service of the notice, a further ground of appeal arose, the italicised words did not prevent the additional ground from being considered on the hearing of the appeal.

Mandatory injunctions The question of whether a duty is mandatory or merely directory is relevant in determining whether the court should exercise its discretion to order a mandatory injunction, or grant an order of mandamus, to compel obedience to it. The discretion is likely to be exercised where the duty is mandatory and the person bound refuses to carry it out. {*R v Epsom and Ewell Corpn, ex p R B Property Investment (Eastern) Ltd* [1964] 2 All ER 832 (where demolition order has become operative, the local authority 'shall serve' a notice to quit on the occupier: Housing Act 1957, s 22(1)).}

Where a court or tribunal is given in terms a *power* to exercise a certain jurisdiction, this may be construed as imposing a mandatory *duty* to act. This will arise where there is no justification for failing to exercise the power. In such cases, as it is often put, 'may' is held to mean 'shall'. {*Macdougall v Paterson* (1851) 11 CB 755, at p 773; *Morisse v Royal British Bank* (1856) 1 CB (NS) 67, at pp 84-5; *Re Eyre and Leicester Corpn* [1892] 1 QB 136; *Sheffield Corpn v Luxford* [1929] 2 KB 180; *Re Shuter (No 2)* [1960] 1 QB 142; *Annison v District Auditor for the Metropolitan Borough of St Pancras* [1962] 1 QB 489. See also Bennion *Statute Law* (2nd edn, 1983) p 199.} Where however a genuine discretion to act or not act is conferred there can be no compulsion to act. {*Julius v Bishop of Oxford* (1880) 5 App Cas 214.} See also Example 189.3.

11. The subject: where contracting out and waiver allowed

A person entitled to the performance of a statutory duty, where the case is within the principle *quilibet potest renuntiare juri pro se introducto* (a person may renounce a right introduced for his benefit), can effectively waive performance of the duty by the person bound; and that person can effectively contract out of performing the duty.

COMMENTARY

The question whether it is legally possible to contract out, or waive performance, of a statutory duty depends as always on the wording of the legislation. A well-drafted modern Act makes the matter clear. The opposing maxims respectively cited in this and the next section derive from a time when such clarity was rare, and Acts were the subject of disorganised composition. {See s 76 of this Code.} Nevertheless the maxims have their uses even today. The starting point must always be what the Act actually says.

The contrast is between cases where the policy of the Act allows contracting out and cases where it does not. Here changes in the outlook and *mores* of the community (which judges inevitably and rightly reflect) are particularly relevant.

In the Victorian age of laisser faire courts were ready, even anxious, to assume that Parliament intended persons of full capacity to be able to give up statutory benefits if they wished. Thus we find Lord Halsbury remarking sardonically in a colliery case: 'The statute discloses the view that the mine-owner and the persons employed in the mine were not, in the contemplation of the legislature, fit to be trusted to make their own bargains'. {*Netherseal Co v Bourne* (1889) 14 App Cas 228, at p 235).} In *Rumsey v North Eastern Railway* {(1863) 14 CB (NS) 641.} it was held that a railway company could freely contract out of its statutory duty to allow passengers to bring luggage on their journey.

The modern welfare state believes it to be for people's own good that they should not be exposed to any risk of being overreached. Thus in *Guardians of Salford Union v Dewhurst* {[1926] AC 619.} the House of Lords held that an employer could not contract out of a statutory duty to pay a pension. The reason was expressed by Pollock MR {P 664.} in somewhat quaint language-

> ' . . . the public should be safeguarded from the melancholy spectacle
> of seeing a man who had done work and been in a responsible
> position during years of his life, suffering from poverty and distress
> by reason of the fact that no adequate provision had been made to
> enable him to spend his latter years in reasonable comfort.'

The principles here discussed apply to statutory duties of every kind, provided they have some identifiable beneficiary. Included are duties which are not absolute, but arise only *sub modo*. {For an explanation of this distinction see p 16 above.}

An Act which imposes a duty, whether absolute or *sub modo*, should do two other things as well. It should make clear what are the consequences of disobedience, and it should say whether it is possible lawfully and effectively to get out of performing the duty. In this section we are concerned only with the latter question. {As to the consequences of disobediece when these are not stated in the Act see s 13 (criminal sanctions) and s 14 (civil sanctions). The distinction between directory and mandatory requirements is explained in s 10.}

Where the Act is not clear, careful scrutiny of the wording may be necessary to glean Parliament's implied intention. {See commentary on next section.}

Origin of maxim   The maxim *quilibet potest renuntiare juri pro se introducto* (a person may renounce a right introduced for his benefit) is mentioned by Coke. {2 Inst 183. See also 10 Rep 101.} Another version is *omnes licentiam habent his, quae pro se indulta sunt, renunciare* (everyone has liberty to renounce those things which are granted for his own benefit). {C 1, 3, 51.} Comparison may be made with the maxim *modus et conventio vincunt legem* (custom and agreement overrule law) {2 Co Inst 73.}, which however has a strictly limited application.

It is an element in the concept of property that the right to it can be given up if the owner thinks fit. Where the right is conferred by Act, this liberty to renounce is precluded only where Parliament so intends. Such an intention may exist on grounds of public policy, or where other persons have an equal right which might be adversely affected by the renunciation. The intention may be set out expressly, or may be left to be inferred.

Waiver of a defence   Many of the cases in which the principle has been applied concern the waiver of statutory defences. In general it is taken that when Parliament provides for such a defence it intends the party entitled to the defence to be able to waive it (whether by conduct or by an agreement not to rely on the defence).

This doctrine is in accordance with the usual rule whereby what is pleaded is within the control of the party pleading. In the High Court a party, in any pleading subsequent to a statement of claim, is required to plead specifically any matter which he alleges makes any claim or defence of the opposite party not maintainable, 'for example . . . any relevant statute of limitation'. {RSC Ord 18 r 8(1). As to waiver of a defence of limitation see *East India Co v Paul* (1849) 7 Moo PC 85; *Wright v John Bagnall & Sons* [1900] 2 QB 240; *Lubovsky v Snelling* [1944] KB 44. Ord 18 r 8(1) would also apply to, e g, the requirement of a written memorandum imposed by enactments such as the Statute of Frauds 1677, s 4 and the Law of Property Act 1925 ss 40(1), 43 and 44. See also *Graham v Ingleby* (1848) 1 Exch 651; *Park Gate Iron Co v Coates* (1870) LR 5 CP 634; *Wilson v McIntosh* [1894] AC 129. As to the implied importation of rules of pleading see p 750 below.}

Other steps in litigation   Where a procedural rule is laid down for the benefit of a party to litigation, that party can usually waive compliance with it. {This does not apply to a requirement for the court's consent - see pp 32–33 below.} Service of an originating summons is required by the Rules of the Supreme Court in the interests of defendants. Under the practice known as appearance *gratis* a defendant could waive service of such a summons, and enter an unconditional appearance. {*Oulton v Radcliffe* (1874) LR 9 CP 189; *Pike v Nairn & Co Ltd* [1960] Ch 553. The practice is now superseded: see Ord 10 r 1(3).}

Duty to give notice   Many Acts impose, either absolutely or *sub modo*, a duty to give notice of certain matters. If there is no express or implied indication that absence of notice is fatal, the person entitled to notice can waive the requirement. {*Toronto Corpn v Russell* [1908] AC 493; *Stylo Shoes Ltd v Prices Tailors Ltd* [1960] Ch 396.}

Act for benefit of limited class   A distinction is drawn between benefits for a particular class of persons and benefits for the community generally. In the former case the class can renounce the benefit; but a general benefit cannot be renounced. {*Great Eastern Rly v Goldsmid* (1884) 9 App Cas 927.}

Facts must be fully known Conduct by a person will not be taken to amount to the waiver of his statutory right unless it appears that he was aware of all the facts establishing the right. Waiver can arise only from presumed intention to give up a right.

Conduct does not raise this presumption if it occurred in ignorance of relevant facts. In *Chapman v Michaelson* {[1908] 2 Ch 612.} Eve J said the party renouncing must have been in a position 'to appreciate what his true legal rights were'. {P 622.}

Waiver must be by beneficiary Waiver of a statutory right is ineffective if not made by the beneficiary of the right. {Co Rep 23; Broom Leg Max 312 (waiver of notice by indorser of bill of exchange does not affect antecedent indorsers).} Where there are joint beneficiaries, waiver by one will bind them all. {*Nicholson v Revell* (1836) 4 A & E 675, at p 683. See also Broom Leg Max 313.}

Equally, a third person cannot *object* to the waiver of a right by the beneficiary.

Example 1 In *Hebblethwaite v Hebblethwaite* {(1869) LR 2 P & D 29.} this principle proved relevant. Section 3 of the Evidence Further Amendment Act 1869 provided that 'no witness shall be liable to be asked or bound to answer any question tending to show that he or she has been guilty of adultery'. The respondent, relying on this provision, objected when a witness was asked whether she had committed adultery with him. The witness however did not claim the benefit of the rule. It was held that the respondent could not invoke the rule, since 'it was not intended to narrow the sources of evidence, but to protect the witness'. {P 30. Cf *R v Kinglake* (1870) 22 LT (NS) 335 (evidence of witness who waives the privilege of non-incrimination cannot be impugned on that ground).}

12. The subject: where contracting out and waiver not allowed

Where a person is entitled by virtue of legislation to the performance of a duty by another person, and the case is within the principle *pacta privata juri publico derogare non possunt* (a public right is not overridden by the agreements of private persons), then the person under the duty cannot effectively contract out of performing it and the beneficiary cannot effectively waive its performance.

COMMENTARY

The question whether it is possible to contract out, or waive performance, of a statutory duty depends as always on the wording of the legislation. A well-drafted modern Act makes the matter clear. The two maxims respectively cited in this and the previous section derive from a time when such clarity was rare, and Acts were the subject of disorganized composition. {See s 76 of this Code.} Nevertheless the maxims have their uses even today. {For the general principles governing their use see the preliminary part of the commentary on s 11.}

Where wording precludes contracting out   The Act should make clear whether contracting out is or is not permitted. If the wording is doubtful, the court must reach its conclusion in the light of the interpretative criteria. {As to the interpretative criteria see Part VI of this Code.}

Example 1   Section 46(1) of the Rent Act 1977 states that where rates borne by the landlord are increased, the recoverable rent shall be correspondingly increased by the amount of the increase. Section 46(2) qualifies this statement-

> 'Where the amount of the recoverable rent is increased by virtue of this section, the increase shall not take effect except in pursuance of a notice of increase served by the landlord on the tenant and specifying the increase and the date from which it is to take effect.'

This imposes on the landlord a duty *sub modo*. He is not bound to serve a notice of increase. He must however serve one if he wants to obtain reimbursement of the added rates. Without such a notice the increase in rent 'shall not take effect'.

In *Aristocrat Property Investments Ltd v Harounoff* {(1982) *The Times* 1 March.} the Court of Appeal, reversing the county court, held that this wording was clear and did not permit of waiver or contracting out. Oliver LJ said-

> 'There were conditions precedent to the operation of recovery of rent. It was not open to the tenant to waive that and render himself liable to that which was not recoverable.'

{See also *Ryan v Oceanic Steam Navigation Co* [1914] 3 KB 731 (steamer ticket contract held void for non-compliance with statutory form).}

Example 2   In the earlier case of *Edwards v Edwards* {(1876) 2 Ch D 297.} Mellish LJ had dealt with a similarly uncompromising enactment. 'If', he said, 'the legislature says that a deed shall be "null and void to all intents and purposes whatsoever", how can a court of equity say that in certain circumstances it shall be valid?' {P 297. Note the greater economy of language by the Rent Act draftsman, which is in line with modern drafting technique. One cannot achieve more than that a notice 'shall not take effect', and it is now thought one should not say more.} Mellish LJ went on to add that courts of equity had given relief on equitable grounds in such cases arising under old Acts of Parliament but this was not done in the case of modern Acts 'which are framed with a view to equitable as well as legal doctrines'. {Ibid.}

Almost as certain is the enactment which is in affirmative terms, carrying the clear implication that what is not stated expressly is implicitly denied.

Example 3 Curtis v Perry   {(1802) 6 Ves 739.} concerned an Act which stated that a ship was to be treated as the property of the person in whose name it was registered. Nantes, in whose name a ship was registered, had for years allowed the ship to be regarded in the trade as the joint property of himself and his partners. The court held, on the petition of the creditors of Nantes (in opposition to the creditors of the partnership), that the long-continued acquiescence of Nantes could not operate as a waiver of his statutory right to be considered sole owner.

Clear as such cases may be, it is even better for the draftsman to put the matter beyond dispute by stating expressly whether or not contracting out is permitted. Section 77(3) of the Sex Discrimination Act 1975 says-

'A term in a contract which purports to exclude or limit any provision of this Act . . . is unenforceable by any person in whose favour the term would operate apart from this subsection.'

{For other examples see Merchant Shipping Act 1894 s 156; Landlord and Tenant Act 1927 s 9; Agricultural Holdings Act 1948 s 65; Licensing Act 1953 s 17(4) (as to which see *Wooler v North Eastern Breweries* [1910] 1 KB 247); Hire-Purchase Act 1965 ss 18(3), 29, 30; Consumer Credit Act 1974 s 173; Race Relations Act 1976 s 72.}

Severable agreements   Where a contract contains a void term purporting to relieve a person of the obligation to perform a statutory duty, the remaining terms will not be affected provided they can be severed. {*Netherseal Colliery Co Ltd v Bourne* (1889) 14 App Cas 228; *Stanton v Brown* [1900] 1 QB 671.} Severance is not possible where an illegal consideration is the basis, or one of the bases, for all the provisions of the contract. {*Carlton Hall Club v Laurence* [1929] 2 KB 153. Cf p 761 below.}

Origin of maxim   The maxim *pacta privata juri publico derogare non possunt* (a public right is not overridden by the agreements of private persons) is cited by Coke. {7 Rep 23.} In his discussion of it, Broom says-

' . . . the consent or private agreement of individuals cannot render valid any contravention of the law, nor can it render just, or sufficient, or effectual that which is unjust or deficient in respect to any matter which the law declares to be indispensable and not circumstantial merely.'

{Broom Leg Max 308. See also p 317 below.}

Public policy   Where it is clear that the Act, upon grounds of public policy, does not intend its provisions to be set aside by private bargain the courts will so hold. {As to principles of public policy (or legal policy) see s 126 of this Code.}

Example 4   This rule was applied, in relation to protective provisions concerning insurance policies, in *Equitable Life Assurance Society of USA v Reed*. {[1914] AC 587.} Lord Dunedin said {P 595.}-

'Their lordships have no doubt that this is a section intended to lay down a rule of public policy, and that it is impossible for either an assured or an assurer to contract himself out of it or to waive its effect.'

Criminal procedure   The law has taken the view that accused persons should not be able effectively to waive procedural requirements of the criminal law. These are imposed in the interests of justice, with a view to securing a fair trial and true verdict. It is not for the accused, even under legal advice, to attempt to forego that protection the law thinks right to give him. {*A-G for New South Wales v Bertrand* (1867) LR 1 PC 520; *Park Gate Iron Co Ltd v Coates* (1870) LR 5 CP 634; *Westmore v Paine* [1891] 1 QB 482.}

Where leave of court required   If Parliament has considered it necessary to require the leave of the court to some step in litigation, the parties cannot contract out of the duty to obtain leave. {*Soho Square Syndicate Ltd v E Pollard & Co Ltd* [1940] Ch 638; *Bowmaker Ltd v Tabor* [1941] 2 KB 1.}

Duty of court If the parties to litigtion have made a contract which is void because of the principle set out in this section then, as with any other illegal contract, it is the duty of the court to intervene so as to prevent an improper order being made. {Cf *Scott v Brown, Doering & Co* [1892] 2 QB 724; *North Western Salt Co v Electrolytic Alkali Co* [1914] AC 461. As to the effect of Acts in rendering contracts illegal see s 345 of this Code.}

13. The subject: criminal sanction for disobedience (the offence of contempt of statute)

Except where criminal sanctions are expressly laid down by the legislation in question, it is taken to be the legislator's intention, unless the contrary intention appears, that contravention of an enactment shall constitute the offence known as contempt of statute. For this at common law the offender, on conviction on indictment, is liable, subject to any other enactment, to imprisonment for such term as the court thinks fit, or a fine of any amount, or both.

COMMENTARY

Blackstone defined a criminal offence as 'an act committed, or omitted, in violation of a public law, either forbidding or commanding it'. {Kerr Bl (4th edn, 1876) iv 4.} A public general Act is the prime example of a public law.

It is the essence of a legal command that there shall be a sanction for disobedience to it; since otherwise the so-called command would be a mere entreaty or 'pious aspiration'. {*Cutler v Wandsworth Stadium Ltd* [1949] AC 398, *per* Viscount Simonds at p 407).} It would not be a command at all, but a *brutum fulmen* or harmless thunderbolt. {Pliny *Historia Naturalis* ii xliii.}

Sanctions for disobedience of a statute may be criminal or civil, or both. {As to civil sanctions see s 14 of this Code.} Where there is clearly no civil sanction, the inference is stronger that a penal sanction is intended.

Coke's name for this general offence was contempt of the king's law: 'whensoever an act of parliament doth generally prohibit any thing ... the party grieved shall not have his action only for his private reliefe, but the offender shall be punished at the kings suit for the contempt of his law'. {2 Inst 163.}

Later commentators have referred to disobedience to an Act's commands as 'contempt of the statute'. {See, e g, Broom and Hadley *Commentaries on the Laws of England* (1869) iv 45, following Hawkins *Pleas of the Crown* (1788) ii c 25 s 4.} Punishment for contempt of statute is a common law {*R v Robinson* (1759) 2 Burr 799.} rule under which the court may have a discretion as to whether to quash the indictment. {*R v Savage* (1698) 1 Ld Raym 347.}

It is accordingly to be presumed that disobedience to a command made by or under a public general Act is intended by Parliament to constitute an offence. Often, particularly with modern Acts, the enactment states this expressly, and lays down the punishment. Where it fails to do so, the common law rule is that the punishment shall be as stated in this section of the Code. {*Thomas Hollingworth's Case* (1620) Cro Jac 577; *R v Jones* (1735) 2 Stra 1146; *R v Davis* (1754) Say 163; *R v Wright* (1758) 1 Burr 543; *R v Robinson* (1759) 2 Burr 800;

R v Boyall (1759) 2 Burr 832; *R v Smith* (1780) 2 Doug KB 441; *R v Harris* (1791) 4 TR 202; *R v Gregory* (1833) 5 B & Ald 555; *R v Price* (1840) 11 A & E 727; *Fox v R* (1859) 29 LJMC 54; *R v Walker* [1875] LR 10 QB 355; *R v Hall* [1891] 1 QB 747; *R v Tyler* [1891] 2 QB 588, at p 592; *A-G v London and North Western Rly* [1900] 1 QB 78; *The Torni* [1932] P 78, at p 90; *Rathbone v Bundock* [1962] 2 QB 260; *R v Lennox-Wright* [1973] Crim LR 529; Hawkins *Pleas of the Crown* (1788) ii c 25 s 4; Archbold *Pleading, Evidence and Practice in Criminal Cases* (37th edn, 1969) para 6.}

Example 1   Section 1(4) of the Human Tissue Act 1961 states that where the removal and use for medical purposes of any part of a human corpse is authorised by the section-

> 'No such removal shall be effected except by a fully registered medical practitioner, who must have satisfied himself by personal examination of the body that life is extinct.'

In *R v Lennox-Wright* {[1973] Crim LR 529.} the accused, a layman, gained acceptance as a member of the medical staff of a hospital by forged credentials. One day he removed the eyes from a corpse. He was thereupon indicted for 'Doing an act in disobedience of a statute by removing parts of a dead body, contrary to s 1(4) of the Human Tissue Act 1961'.

The defence objected that the Act was merely regulatory and created no offence; and that it provided no punishment for contravening s 1(4). *Held* The law is well settled that if a statute *prohibits a matter of public grievance to the liberties and securities of the subject or commands a matter of public convenience (such as repairing of highways or the like)* all acts or omissions contrary to the prohibitions of the command of the statute are misdemeanours at common law punishable by indictment unless such method manifestly appears to be excluded by statute. {Emphasis added.}

Width of the rule   The italicised restrictive words in the above passage derive from a statement in *Hawkins' Pleas of the Crown.* {(1788) ii c 25 s 4.} They are however inappropriate in relation to a public general Act. Every such Act is taken to deal with a matter of public grievance, and to be for the public convenience. {See s 127 and Part XIV of this Code. As to the distinction between public and private Acts see s 28 of the Code.}

This appears to be recognised, at least to some extent, in Stephen's statement of the rule-

> 'Every one commits a misdemeanour who wilfully disobeys any statute of the realm by doing any act which it forbids, or by omitting to do any act which it requires to be done, *and which concerns the public or any part of the public*, unless it appears from the statute that it was the intention of the legislature to provide other penalty for such disobedience.'

{*Digest of the Criminal Law* art 152 (9th edn, 1950) p 120). Emphasis added.}

Here the italicised passage still purports to restrict the rule, but the restriction says no more than that a public Act concerns the public, which is self-evident. The only conceivable case where the restriction might apply is that of a public Act which began life as a hybrid Bill, that is one affecting both public and private rights. These are comparatively rare however. {See p 86 below.} In *R v Richards* {(1800) 8 TR 634.} disobedience was held not to be indictable where the statutory duty was for the benefit only of those entitled to use a particular private road. {See also *R v Pawlyn* (1664) 1 Sid 208.}

Blackstone stated the rule in unrestricted form as 'disobedience to any act of parliament, where no particular penalty is assigned'. {Kerr Bl (4th edn, 1876) iv 109. See also Yale *arguendo* in *Williams v Evans* (1876) 1 Ex D 277, at p 280.} Halsbury's *Laws* stated the rule in general terms: 'Every breach of a statutory command is, in the absence of specific provisions, indictable at common law as a misdemeanour'. {2nd edn, vol 36 para 675. The change made in the third edition (vol 44 para 952) was apparently occasioned only by the abolition of the distinction between felony and misdemeanour effected by s 1(1) of the Criminal Law Act 1967.}

Unless the contrary intention appears   Where the legislation specifically provides a penalty for disobedience, it is presumed that this displaces the penalty dealt with in this section of the Code. {*Anon* (1702) 2 Ld Raym 991; *R v Dixon* (1716) 10 Mod 335; *R v Robinson* (1759) 2 Burr 799; *R v Boyall* (1759) 2 Burr 832; *Couch v Steel* (1854) 3 E & B 402; *R v Hall* [1891] 1 QB 747; *Metropolitan Police Commr v Curran* [1976] 1 WLR 87, at p 99; cf *R v Buchanan* (1846) 8 QB 883.} Where an Act declares a certain activity to be 'unlawful' but goes on to provide penalties for some only of its manifestations, the implication may be that the remainder are *not* rendered criminal. {*Sales-Matic Ltd v Hinchcliffe* [1959] 1 WLR 1005 (relating to the statement in s 21 of the Betting and Lotteries Act 1934 that 'subject to the provisions of this Part of this Act, all lotteries are unlawful').} This is an aspect of the *expressio unius* principle, by which express mention of one thing by implication excludes another. {As to the principle see s 389 of this Code.}

Subject to any other enactment   The punishment stated in this section of the Code is subject to any general statutory modification of penalties such as is laid down by s 7 (absolute and conditional discharge) of the Powers of Criminal Courts Act 1973.

Law Commission recommendation   In 1976 the Law Commission recommended that the rule set out in this section of the Code be abrogated on the ground that whenever Parliament intends breach of a statute to be punished it says so expressly. {*Report on Conspiracy and Criminal Law Reform* (1975-6) Law Com No 76, para 6.5.} This overlooks the fact that Acts are drafted in knowledge of the rule. If the rule did not exist, draftsmen might feel it necessary to insert specific penal provisions more frequently.

So far this recommendation of the Law Commission has not been acted on. If it were to be implemented it seems that this should be done only for future Acts, so that allowance could be made in their drafting.

14. The subject: civil sanction for disobedience (the tort of breach of statutory duty)

Where legislation imposes a duty on any person, it is presumed to be the intention, unless the contrary intention appears, that if damage results to any other person by reason of his failure to comply with that duty, he shall be taken to commit the tort of breach of statutory duty, and be liable to the other person or his estate accordingly.

COMMENTARY

As stated above {P 33.}, it is the essence of a legal command that there shall be a sanction for disobedience to it. Sanctions for disobedience to a statute may be criminal or civil, or both. {As to criminal sanctions see s 13 of this Code.}

Here it has to be remembered that the objects of criminal and civil law are different. In very broad terms, the criminal law exists to punish wrongdoing, remove dangerous criminals from circulation, and deter potential wrongdoers from offending; while the object of civil law is to compensate the victim. Parliament may intend to visit breaches with both types of sanction, or one or other of them alone. {See *Wilson v Merry* (1868) LR 1 HL(Sc) 326, *per* Lord Chelmsford at p 341.}

Where there is clearly no criminal sanction, the inference is stronger that a civil sanction is intended. Where a particular sanction is specifically provided for, this suggests, under the *expressio unius* principle, that no other sanction (whether civil or criminal) was intended. {*Atkinson v Newcastle & Gateshead Waterworks Co* (1877) 2 Ex D 441; *Phillips v Britannia Hygienic Laundry Co* [1923] 2 KB 832, at p 841; *Witham Outfall Board v Boston Corpn* (1926) 136 LT 756; *Monk v Warbey* [1935] 1 KB 75, at p 84. As to the *expressio unius* principle see s 389 of this Code.}

It will be seen that the position is not free from difficulty. This prompted Lord du Parcq to utter the following courteous suggestion to draftsmen-

> 'To a person unversed in the science or art of legislation it may well seem strange that Parliament has not by now made it a rule to state explicitly what its intention is in a matter which is often of no little importance, instead of leaving it to the courts to discover, by a careful examination and analysis of what is expressly said, what that intention may be supposed probably to be . . .
>
> I trust, however, that it will not be thought impertinent, in any sense of that word, to suggest respectfully that those who are responsible for framing legislation might consider whether the traditional practice, which obscures, if it does not conceal, the intention which Parliament has, or must be presumed to have, might not safely be abandoned.'

{*Cutler v Wandsworth Stadium Ltd* [1949] AC 398, at p 410.}

This plea has fallen on deaf ears. Since it was uttered, relatively few Acts have contained provisions on the lines suggested by Lord du Parcq. {For examples of such provisions see Consumer Credit Act 1974, s 170; Sex Discrimination Act 1975, s 62; Race Relations Act 1976, s 53.}

Where sanction provided   As Lord Tenterden CJ said: 'Where an Act creates an obligation, and enforces the performance in a specified manner, we take it to be a general rule that performance cannot be enforced in any other manner'. *Doe d Bishop of Rochester v Bridges* {(1831) 1 B & Ad 847, at p 859. See also *Stevens v Evans* (1761) 2 Burr 1152, at p 1157; *Stevens v Jeacocke* (1848) 11 QB 731, at p

741; *Wake v Mayor of Sheffield* (1884) 12 QBD 145; *R v County Court Judge of Essex* (1887) 18 QBD 704, at p 707; *Clegg Parkinson & Co v Earby Gas Co* [1896] 1 QB 592, at p 595; *Wilkinson v Barking Corpn* [1948] 1 KB 721, at p 724; *Lonrho Ltd v Shell Petroleum Co Ltd* [1981] 2 All ER 456, at p 461.}

The 'general rule' is stronger in these days of precision drafting, where the draftsman may be expected to insert a remedy where one is truly intended. {For precision drafting see s 76 of this Code. As to when the 'general rule' does not apply see *Waghorn v Collison* (1922) 91 LJKB 735, at pp 736 and 738.}

Where in one provision a statute both lays down a new right or duty and links it with a tailor-made remedy, the implication is strong that no other remedy is intended to be available.

Example 1 An Act empowered harbour undertakers to remove any sunken ship from the harbour and recover the expenses of doing so from the ship's owner in a magistrates' court. In *Barraclough v Brown* {[1897] AC 615.} undertakers applied for a declaration of their right to recover damages in respect of such expenses.

Held The only remedy available was the one laid down by the Act, namely an order of a magistrates' court. Lord Herschell LC said {P 620.} that the appellant could not claim to recover by virtue of the statute and yet insist on doing so by means other than those prescribed by the statute. Lord Watson said {P 622.}-

> 'The right and remedy are given *uno flatu*, and the one cannot be dissociated from the other. By these words the legislature has, in my opinion, committed to the summary court exclusive jurisdiction, not merely to assess the amount of expenses to be repaid to the undertaker, but to determine by whom the amount is payable, and has therefore by plain implication enacted that no other court has any authority to entertain or decide these matters.'

{*Craies* treats this as an ouster of jurisdiction (*Statute Law* (7th edn, 1971) p 247); but in fact it was a novel judicial procedure as to which no High Court jurisdiction was ever conferred.}

Where no sanction provided If a duty is imposed for the benefit of the public, or a certain section of the public, and no means of enforcing the duty is laid down, the presumption is that a civil remedy was intended.

Example 2 Section 3(4) of the Housing (Homeless Persons) Act 1977 requires local authorities to ensure that accomodation is made available for the homeless. No sanction for breach of this duty is laid down by the Act. In *Thornton v Kirklees Metropolitan Borough Council* {[1979] 2 All ER 349.} the plaintiff brought an action for damages in respect of breach of this duty. *Held* The action was well-founded. Roskill LJ said {Pp 357-8.}-

> 'First, where an Act imposes a duty on a public authority and provides an administrative remedy by way of complaint to the Minister or to some other body, that almost invariably excludes the right of action in the courts; secondly, and conversely, where the

statute imposes a duty on a public authority or on anyone else for the benefit of a specified category of persons, but prescribes no special remedy for breach of duty, it can normally be assumed that a civil action for damages will lie.'

The tort of breach of statutory duty The common law treats breach of statutory duty as a tort. {*Thornton v Kirklees Metropolitan Borough Council* [1979] 2 All ER 349, at p 357. For the implied importation by statutes of the general rules of tort law see s 339 of this Code.} It follows that statutory references to 'tort' include breach of statutory duty. {*American Express Co v Brtish Airways Board* [1983] 1 All ER 557.}

If (1) Parliament forbids a thing to be done, and (2) in contravention of this it is done, and (3) the victim suffers damage, then prima facie the victim is entitled to recover from the wrongdoer. Coke said that 'whensoever an act of parliament doth generally prohibit any thing' the party grieved shall have his action 'for his private reliefe'. {2 Inst 163. See also *Monk v Warbey* [1935] 1 KB 75, *per* Greer LJ at p 81.}

Equally, where (1) Parliament requires a thing to be done, and (2) in contravention of this it is not done, and (3) some person suffers damage, then prima facie the victim is entitled to recover. {*Ashby v White* (1703) 2 Ld Raym 938 (returning officer wrongfully refused to accept plaintiff's vote at an election). Cf *Tozer v Child* (1857) 26 LJQB 151 (returning officers held to be quasi-judges, so that no action lay).} The presumption is particularly strong where the Act lays down a duty to pay money.

Example 3 Under the statute 11 & 12 Vict c 14 (1848) money had accrued due to a retired police constable. An application being made to attach this sum as a debt, it was objected that the sum was not truly a debt and so could not be attached. *Held* It must be treated as a debt, since otherwise the intention of Parliament would not be fulfilled. Lord Coleridge CJ said-

> 'It appears to me to be nonetheless a debt because no particular mode
> of enforcing the payment is given by the statute. When there is a
> statutory obligation to pay money, and no other remedy is expressly
> given, there would be a remedy by action.'

{*Booth v Traill* (1883) 12 QBD 8, at p 10.}
Either way, the prima facie presumption may be displaced by indications to the contrary.

Unless the contrary intention appears In this field the usual caveat 'unless the contrary intention appears' is particularly important. Quite often the contrary intention does appear. We have mentioned above one instance, namely the application of the *expressio unius* doctrine. Another is the not infrequent case where the Act expressly states that no civil remedy lies. {See, e g, Representation of the People Act 1949 ss 50(2) and 51(2); Radioactive Substances Act 1960 s 19(5)(a); Water Resources Act 1963 s 135(8); Medicines Act 1968 s 133(2).}

The essential point to bear in mind is that every enactment is passed to remedy a mischief. {As to the doctrine of the mischief see s 138 and Part XIV of this Code.} The first question to ask in determining whether a breach of statutory duty constitutes a tort is therefore this. Is the damage suffered by the plaintiff the type of mischief the enactment set out to remedy? Only if the answer is yes will the breach constitute a tort.

Example 4 An order made under s 75 of the Contagious Diseases (Animals) Act 1869 required ship owners carrying cattle on deck to fit pens. These were intended to separate cattle, so as to guard against murrain. In *Gorris v Scott* {(1874) LR 9 Ex 125.} the owner of sheep washed overboard in a storm sued for breach of this duty. If there had been pens fitted, the sheep would have been safe in the storm. *Held* The action failed. The mischief of animals being washed overboard was not the mischief to which the enactment was directed. Pollock CB said {P 131.}-

> 'The Act was passed *alio intuitu* . . . the precautions directed may be useful and advantageous for preventing animals from being washed overboard, but they were never intended for that purpose, and a loss of that kind caused by their neglect cannot give a cause of action.'

Example 5 *Cutler v Wandsworth Stadium* {[1949] AC 398.} concerned the requirement in s 11(2) of the Betting and Lotteries Act 1934 that occupiers of dog-racing tracks should make available for bookmakers 'space on the track where they can conveniently carry on bookmaking'. A bookmaker sued for damages on the ground that space had not been made available for him. *Held* The mischief to which the enactment was directed was lack of sufficient bookmaking services for members of the public attending races, not lack of facilities to enable a particular bookmaker to carry on his business. The action therefore failed. {See also *Newman v Francis* [1953] 1 WLR 402 (no cause of action where plaintiff injured by dog whose owner contravened park byelaws, since they were for the protection and regulation of the park only).}

Example 6 Sanctions orders made under the Southern Rhodesia Act 1965 were designed to remedy the mischief constituted by the Unilateral Declaration of Independence ('UDI') which had been made by the Smith regime in Southern Rhodesia. They were not intended to give a cause of action to individuals who suffered economic damage through breach of the orders. As Fox LJ said-

> 'I cannot think they were concerned with conferring rights either on individuals or the public at large. Their purpose was the destruction, by economic pressure, of the UDI regime in Southern Rhodesia; they were instruments of state policy in an international matter.'

{From an unreported judgment in the court below cited approvingly by Lord Diplock in *Lonrho Ltd v Shell Petroleum Co Ltd* [1981] 2 All ER 456, at p 462.}

If the damage is within the statutory mischief, the next question is whether the plaintiff is a member of the class Parliament intended to relieve. He may have suffered damage of the kind contemplated by the statute, yet still not be one of the intended beneficiaries. As Maugham LJ said, an action for breach of statutory duty must be brought 'by a person pointed out on a fair construction of the Act as being one whom the Legislature desired to protect'. {*Monk v Warbey* [1935] 1 KB 75, at p 85.}

Example 7 In *Buxton v North-Eastern Railway Co* {(1868) LR 3 QB 549.} a bullock got through a gap in a fence on to the railway line. This caused a train accident, in which the plaintiff was injured. He sued for breach of the duty imposed by s 68 of the Railways Clauses Consolidation Act 1845. The section begins with the following introductory words-

> 'The company shall make and at all times thereafter maintain the following works *for the accomodation of the owners and occupiers of lands adjoining the railway . . .*'

{Emphasis added.}

The relevant provision of s 68 refers to the erection of fences 'for separating the land taken for the use of the railway from the adjoining land not taken, and protecting ... the cattle of the owners or occupiers thereof from straying thereout'. *Held* The plaintiff could not recover, since s 68 was intended only for the protection of owners and occupiers. {See also *Square v Model Farm Dairies (Bournemouth) Ltd* [1939] 2 KB 365 (s 2 of the Food and Drugs (Adulteration) Act 1928 passed for benefit of purchasers only, and not those to whom they passed on food); *Ex p Island Records Ltd* [1978] Ch 122 (Performers' Protection Acts 1958 to 1972 passed for benefit of performers only, and not recording companies: see also *RCA Corpn v Pollard* [1982] 3 All ER 771).}

If the damage is within the statutory mischief, and the plaintiff is within the class of sufferers Parliament intended to relieve, the next question is this. Was the defendant in the required state of mind? Some statutory duties impose strict liability, while others are not broken unless there is negligence. What the latter impose is a duty to take reasonable care. This qualification may be express of implied.

Example 8   An example of an express provision is s 2 of the Occupiers' Liability Act 1957. This imposes on occupiers of land what it calls the 'common duty of care', defined as a duty to take such care as in all the circumstances is reasonable to see that the visitor will be reasonably safe. Here the plaintiff cannot recover unless he proves negligence (or of course recklessness or deliberate intention).

In *Caswell v Powell Duffryn Colliery Co* {[1940] AC 152, at p 168.} Lord Macmillan stated as a general proposition that 'if the plaintiff can show that there has been a breach of the statute he has established the existence of negligence. It remains for him to prove that the accident was due to that negligence'.

This dictum appears misconceived. The question is always for what (if for anything) did Parliament intend to give a civil remedy not spelt out in the Act? There is no certainty that Parliament intended to require the presence of negligence; and it is confusing to call breach of a strict liability in every case 'negligent'.

Example 9   Section 72 of the Metropolis Management Act 1855 imposed on the vestry a duty of properly cleaning the sewers vested in them by the Act. In *Hammond v Vestry of St Pancras* {(1874) LR 9 CP 316.} a civil action was brought for breach of this duty. *Held* No action would lie without proof of negligence. Brett LJ said {P 322.}-

> 'It would seem to me to be contrary to natural justice to say that Parliament intended to impose upon a public body a liability for a thing which no reasonable care or skill could obviate. The duty,

notwithstanding, may be absolute, but if so, it ought to be imposed in the clearest possible terms.'

Consequential construction Consideration of consequences plays a large part in this field. {As to consequential construction see s 140 of this Code.} Where Parliament is dealing with a new or increased social mischief involving high risk to individuals, the likelihood is that it intends adequate protection to be given to them. This particularly applies where personal injury is involved. {*Black v Fife Coal Co Ltd* [1912] AC 149, at p 165; *Cutler v Wandsworth Stadium Ltd* [1949] AC 398, at p 413.}

Example 10 In *Groves v Lord Wimborne* {[1898] 2 QB 402.} the defendant was in breach of a statutory duty to fence dangerous machinery, for which the Act laid down a penalty of £100. As a consequence the plaintiff workman suffered serious injury. *Held* The plaintiff was entitled to damages. The fine was not recoverable by the injured party and 'the legislature cannot have seriously intended that whether the workman suffered death or mutilation the liability of the master should never exceed £100'. {*Per* Rigby LJ at pp 414-5.}

Example 11 The Road Traffic Act 1930 was passed to deal with the growing danger to life and limb posed by motor cars on public roads. Section 35(1) required the owner of a car to be covered by third-party insurance, a penal sanction being laid down. In *Monk v Warbey* {[1935] 1 KB 75.} the plaintiff was injured by a negligent driver to whom the owner had lent his car, and who was not covered by his insurance policy. *Held* The plaintiff was entitled to recover damages from the owner. Maugham LJ said {Pp 85-6.}-

> 'There is sufficient ground for coming to the conclusion that s 35 was passed for the purpose of giving a remedy to third persons who might suffer injury by the negligence of the impecunious driver of a car . . . It was within the knowledge of the Legislature that negligence in the driving of cars was so common an occurrence with the likelihood of injury to third persons that it was necessary in the public interest to provide machinery whereby those third persons might recover damages . . .'

{See also *Couch v Steel* (1854) 3 E & B 402 (defendant bound under statutory penalty to keep medicines on shipboard for health of crew: seaman who suffered through breach held entitled to recover damages). Cf *Vallance v Falle* (1884) 3 QBD 109 (defendant bound under statutory penalty to hand over seaman's discharge certificate: no civil remedy for breach).}

Other remedy available The likelihood that Parliament intended breach of the statute to amount to a tort is lessened where some other civil remedy is available. This may be under another statute {*Square v Model Farm Dairies (Bournemouth) Ltd* [1939] 2 KB 365.} or at common law. {*Phillips v Britannia Hygienic Laundry Co* [1923] 2 KB 832, at p 842.} A statutory duty does not extinguish a corresponding common-law duty, unless the contrary intention appears. {*Glossop v Heston Local Board* (1879) 12 Ch D 102, at pp 110-111; *East Suffolk Catchment Board v Kent* [1941] AC 74, at p 89; *Read v Croydon Corpn* [1938] 4 All ER 654; *Barnes v Irwell Valley Water Board* [1939] 1 KB 21.} Sometimes the

Act expressly states that other causes of action are not affected. This was done for example by the Water Resources Act 1963, s 135(8) {See *Cargill v Gotts* [1981] 1 All ER 682.} and the Control of Pollution Act 1974 s 105(2). {See *Budden v British Petroleum Ltd* (1980) 130 NLJ 603. See also (1981) 131 NLJ 1026.}

Malice   If Parliament did not intend to give a civil remedy for breach of the statute, the fact that the person bound acted maliciously will not in itself create a remedy. {*Davis v Bromley Corpn* [1908] 1 KB 170.} Judicial review may however be available. {See s 24 of this Code.}

Remedies in tort   The remedies available for the tort of breach of statutory duty are the same as for tort generally. {*Building and Civil Engineering Holidays Scheme Management Ltd v Post Office* [1966] 1 QB 247.}

Relator actions   A person or body entitled to restrain apprehended breaches of statutory duty may apply to the Attorney-General for that official to bring a relator action against the person bound. Here the Attorney-General acts in pursuance of his constitutional function as guardian of the public interest.

Once the Attorney-General's consent to the action has been obtained, the actual conduct of the proceedings is in the hands of the relator, who is responsible for the costs. {Administration of Justice (Miscellaneous Provisions) Act 1933 s 7.} The question of giving consent is solely for the Attorney-General, and the court cannot intervene. {*London County Council v A-G* [1902] AC 165.}

An action may be brought by the Attorney-General at the relation of a local authority to enforce a byelaw of that authority. {*A-G v Ashbourne Recreation Ground Co* [1903] 1 Ch 101.} Where an enactment is persistently flouted by a person, regardless of frequent convictions, a relator action may be brought against him.

Example 12   In contravention of s 102 of the Manchester Police Regulation Act 1844, Mr and Mrs Harris each operated a flower stall which projected on to a footway near the entrance to a public cemetery. The penalty laid down by the Act was limited to a small fine, which was regarded by the defendants as a business expense. During a period of two years Mr Harris was convicted 74 times under s 102, and Mrs Harris 34 times. Finally, on the relation of the Town Clerk, a relator action was brought for an injunction, which was granted. {*A-G v Harris* [1961] 1 QB 74.} Sellers LJ said {P 86.}-

> 'It cannot, in my opinion, be anything other than a public detriment for the law to be defied, week by week, and the offender to find it profitable to pay the fine and continue to flout the law.'

Pearce LJ referred to 'the community's general right to have the laws obeyed'. {P 92. See also J Ll G Edwards *The Law Officers of the Crown* pp 286-295.}

Judicial review   As to remedies for breach of statutory duty by way of judicial review, in succession to the prerogative writs of mandamus, certiorari and prohibition, see s 24 of this Code.

Equitable remedies   Since the High Court and County Courts possess the old equity jurisdiction, the remedies this provided are available in relation to breach of statute. As Farwell J stated-

' ... there was nothing to prevent the Court of Chancery from granting an injunction to restrain the infringement of a newly created statutory right, unless the Act of Parliament creating the right provided a remedy which it enacted should be the only remedy, subject only to this, that the right was such a right as the [Court of Chancery] under its original jurisdiction would take cognisance of.'

{*Stevens v Chown* [1901] 1 Ch 894, at p 904. Cf *A-G v Sharp* [1931] 1 Ch 121. As to equitable remedies for breach of statutory duty see further pp 731–733 below.}

Law Commission recommendation In 1969 the Law Commissions recommended the enactment of a general provision to the effect that breach of a statutory provision is intended to be actionable as a tort unless the contrary is expressly stated. {*The Interpretation of Statutes* (1969) LAW COM No 21, SCOT LAW COM No 11, para 38 and App A.} This has not been acted on. {See Bennion 'Another Reverse for the Law Commissions' Interpretation Bill' (1981) 131 NLJ 840.}

See also Example 393.2.

ENFORCEMENT AGENCIES

15. Enforcement agencies: administrative agencies

Administrative or executive agencies with the function of enforcing legislation include government departments, public statutory bodies, bodies administering nationalised industries, and local authorities.

COMMENTARY

Government departments Every Act falls within the responsibility of one or more government departments. Except in so far as an Act contains express provision naming its administering agency, constitutional practice requires the Prime Minister to determine (either directly or by delegated authority) which Minister, and therefore which government department, is to have the responsibility of administering it. In making such allocations the Prime Minister acts (on behalf of the Crown) in exercise of a prerogative power.

Even where an Act does name its administering authority the Act can be amended by Order in Council. This must be made on government advice, so the choice of responsible Minister effectively rests with the Prime Minister even though Parliament has expressed its own intention. Power to make such Orders in Council is conferred by s 1 of the Ministers of the Crown Act 1975. {A consolidation Act replacing, inter alia, the Ministers of the Crown (Transfer of Functions) Act 1946.} Later Acts naming their administering authorities are presumed to be intended, by implication, to be made subject to s 1.

Subsection (1) of s 1 states that the Order in Council may-

'(a) provide for the transfer to any Minister of the Crown of any functions previously exercisable by another Minister of the Crown;

(b) provide for the dissolution of the government department in the charge of any Minister of the Crown and the transfer to or distribution among such other Minister or Ministers of the Crown as may be specified in the Order of any functions previously exercisable by the Minister in charge of that department;

(c) direct that functions of any Minister of the Crown shall be exercisable concurrentlly with another Minister of the Crown, or shall cease to be so exercisable.'

Subsection (2) of s 1 adds that an Order in Council may contain incidental, consequential and supplemental provisions, including provisions 'for such adaptations of the enactments relating to any functions transferred as may enable them to be exercised by the Minister to whom they are transferred and his officers'.

The power conferred by s 1 is needed only where the prerogative powers exercisable by the Prime Minister are restricted by some statutory provision. The 1975 Act contains an express saving for 'any power exercisable by virtue of the prerogative of the Crown in relation to the functions of Ministers of the Crown'. {S 5(5).}

Incoming governments usually remodel the ministry. This meant, in the light of the earlier practice of naming the Minister or department responsible in the Act, that transfer of functions orders became frequent and complicated. In recent years this difficulty has been lessened by the practice of referring in Acts to 'the appropriate Minister' or (more commonly) to 'the Secretary of State'. In the former case the Act goes on to define the appropriate Minister as, in effect, the one for the time being nominated by the Prime Minister. In the latter case the matter is dealt with by the Interpretation Act 1978, which defines 'Secretary of State' as meaning one of Her Majesty's principal Secretaries of State. {S 5 and Sch 1. See also Ministers of the Crown Act 1975 s 2. See further p 140 below.}

The question of which of the Secretaries of State (for example the Home Secretary or the Defence Secretary) is to be responsible for a function conferred on 'the Secretary of State' by a particular Act can thus be dealt with from time to time administratively. In such cases, and also where an Act is silent as to its administration, the question of which department is to be responsible for it is decided by or on behalf of the Prime Minister without statutory restriction.

The government department currently responsible for the administration of an Act is very often the one that dealt with its original enactment. Even where the ministry is later remodelled, the departmental unit responsible for the enactment of the Act usually goes on being responsible for adminstering it (even though the unit may be transferred to another department). This ensures continuity from the inception of an Act throughout its period of operation. Indeed there is continuity as respects a particular subject-matter, even though one Act dealing with it succeeds another. This is important from the point of view of interpretation.

The government department which plans an Act and steers it through Parliament usually has very definite ideas about what it is intended to mean. Sir Idwal Pugh, a senior civil servant, expressed the position in these words-

' . . . one thing the department, and a Minister in the department, above all want is that their intentions should be carried out, right or wrong. There is nothing worse for a department than to legislate and then find that the Bill that it conceived (now an Act) does not actually do what it thought it was going to do because its meaning has been overthrown or questioned in some case.'

{Broadcast on Radio 3, 14 November 1983.}

The Act is administered in accordance with this approach. In many cases, particularly with regulatory Acts, it will be the department's view of interpretation and not the courts' which will in practice prevail. This is because few questions of interpretation will reach the courts.

Other administrative agencies Sometimes Parliament sets up a special administrative agency for the purposes of an Act, or of a series of Acts in a particular field.

Example 1 For example the rise of the concept of consumer protection led to the passing of the Fair Trading Act 1973, which established the Office of Fair Trading. The Act proceeded, as is usual, not by establishing the Office of Fair Trading as such, but by providing for the appointment of 'an officer to be known as the Director General of Fair Trading [who] may appoint such staff as he may think fit . . .' {S 1.} The practical effect was the same.

The 1973 Act gave the Office of Fair Trading certain functions in relation to the supply of goods to consumers. {S 2.} When in the following year Parliament decided to make new provision to protect consumers in credit and hire transactions it used the administrative machinery ready to hand and enlarged the functions of the Office of Fair Trading to cover this too. {Consumer Credit Act 1974 Part I. The Office has also been given statutory functions in relation to monopolies, mergers and restrictive trade practices.} The remarks made above about government departments apply in a similar way to agencies of this kind, except that such agencies are more remote from the enactment process.

Local authorities Local authorities are frequently selected by Parliament for the administration of Acts in fields such as housing, planning and public health. They carry out these functions under the supervision of the relevant government department however. Uniformity of administration is secured by the issue by the department to the local authorities of advisory circulars.

Court supervision Where an enactment falls to be interpreted in the first instance by an executive or administrative authority it is presumed, unless the contrary intention appears in the relevant enactment, that the decisions of the authority are subject to review by the court.

Authoritative determinations under an enactment often fall to be made by executive or administrative bodies or persons, such as ministers of the Crown or their officials. Unless the contrary intention appears, these are subject to review by the court (though the court's powers are necessarily limited). Only in extreme cases can the decision of the administrator be overturned on appeal to the court. The guiding principle is that Parliament has thought fit to entrust the decision to the named administrator and no one else. Only if there is bad faith or basic error can a reviewing court intervene, though powers on appeal may be wider. {As to judicial review see s 24 of this Code. For the implied incorporation in statutes of common-law rules relating to decision-making see s 335.}

16. Enforcement agencies: authorising agencies

Regulatory Acts often set up or make use of authorising agencies, namely agencies (such as licensing authorities) having the statutory function of authorising persons to carry on activities regulated by the Act and of withholding authorisation from persons the agency considers unsuitable. Authorising agencies often have supervisory functions in addition.

COMMENTARY

The traditional sanction for infringement of an Act is the direct penal sanction, usually imposed by stating that the infringement shall constitute an offence and then going on to set out the penalties. This method requires the prohibited acts or omissions to be specified with particularity in the Act. {As to penal sanctions see s 13 of this Code.}

Sometimes it is not possible to specify this amount of detail. The object of the Act may be to raise standards in a particular trade for example. While it may work to treat extreme cases of unfair trading as criminal, the overall aim can best be achieved by a system of licensing and supervision. So the Act requires traders to seek a licence or other authorisation from an appointed authorising agency. Instead of labelling certain anti-social acts or omissions criminal, the Act proceeds by saying that socially *desirable* acts are criminal if not done under licence. Then provision is made for a licence to be refused or withdrawn if the licensee does not meet the standards required (in accordance with the Act) by the authorising agency.

The Office of Fair Trading has licensing functions of this kind under the Consumer Credit Act 1974. {See s 21 (persons carrying on a consumer credit business or consumer hire business) and s 147 (persons carrying on an ancillary credit business).} For estate agents on the other hand a licensing system has been rejected. Instead, the less elaborate method has been adopted of simply authorising the Office of Fair Trading to prohibit unfit persons from practising. Where such a restriction is not in force the agent is free from control under the Act. {Estate Agents Act 1979 s 3.}

Older Acts placed this kind of supervisory function on magistrates. {For example in relation to pawnbrokers (Pawnbrokers Act 1872 s 40), publicans (Licensing Act 1964 Pt I) and bookmakers (Betting, Gaming and Lotteries Act 1963 s 3).}

Local authorities frequently procure for themselves statutory licensing powers under local Acts (for example in relation to such establishments as coffee bars or massage parlours). Some professional bodies perform statutory supervisory functions (for example the Law Society in relation to the requirement that solicitors shall be in possession of practising certificates). {Solicitors Act 1974 ss 9-18.}

In relation to statutory procedures of the kind dealt with by this section of the Code, the courts are rarely troubled with questions of interpretation.

Example 1   In the ten years since the passing of the Consumer Credit Act 1974 there have been no reported court decisions on the interpretation of the licensing provisions, even though more than 100,000 licences have been issued.

It is in practice the authorising agency that sets the standard of conduct within the usually wide bounds of discretion fixed by the enabling Act.

17. Enforcement agencies: investigating agencies

The enforcement of legislation largely depends on investigating agencies, namely bodies (such as police forces and statutory inspectorates) with the function, whether generally or in relation to a particular Act or class of Acts, of receiving complaints of infringement, investigating possible infringements (whether on complaint or not) and gathering evidence with a view to the institution of criminal or civil proceedings.

COMMENTARY

The principal investigating agencies are the police forces. These are in modern times established and regulated by statute, though still based on the ancient office of constable.

Every person appointed to be a member of a police force is required to be attested as a constable and declare that he will-

' ... to the best of my power cause the peace to be kept and preserved, and prevent all offences against the persons and properties of Her Majesty's subjects ... and to the best of my skill and knowledge discharge all the duties [of the office of constable] faithfully according to law.'

{Police Act 1964 s 18 and Sch 2.}

The concept of the king's peace is fundamental to our criminal law. In early times prosecutions were known as 'suits of the peace'. Thus in an Act of 1503 (5 Hen 4 c 15) it was declared that the king had agreed to stop the suit of his peace for certain offences. As Blackstone said, 'all crimes are treated by the law as being *contra pacem domini regis*'. {Kerr Bl (4th edn, 1876) i 134.} When Chief Justice Thorpe was condemned to be hanged for bribery he was said *sacramentum domini regis fregisse*. {Rot Parl 25 Edw 3.}

The criminal law is now mainly in statutory form. A constable cannot 'prevent all offences' without knowing which acts and omissions constitute offences and which do not. He cannot carry out his duties 'faithfully according to law' without knowledge of what the law requires. Although legal advice and guidance is usually available to them, police officers must when necessary themselves construe enactments, and for that purpose must be aware of the principles of statutory interpretation.

The same applies to other public officials charged with the duty of investigating offences, such as trading standards officers, tax inspectors and customs officials.

See also Example 80.5.

18. Enforcement agencies: prosecuting agencies

The enforcement of legislation by courts and tribunals requires the existence of prosecuting agencies, namely bodies with the function of deciding whether or not to bring a prosecution (or where appropriate a civil action), and if so of assuming responsibility for its conduct. While these are mainly public bodies, the law has always relied to a greater or lesser extent on private persons to enforce the law.

COMMENTARY

As well as being the main investigating agencies, police forces are also the main prosecuting agencies, though in England and Wales they are supplemented by the Director of Public Prosecutions and his staff. The office of the DPP was set up by the Prosecution of Offences Act 1879, which was repealed and replaced by the Prosecution of Offences Act 1979. This requires the DPP, under the supervision of the Attorney-General, to undertake and advise on the institution of criminal proceedings. {S 2.}

This supervisory function is bestowed on the Attorney-General in recognition of the principle that all offences are against the peace of the Queen, whose officer he is. Blackstone describes why all prosecutions are in the name of the Crown, and why the Crown (in the shape of the executive) may pardon but must never sit in judgment, in a passage including these words-

> 'All offences are against either the peace of the sovereign or his Crown and dignity. For though in their consequences they generally seem, except in the case of treason, and a very few others, to be rather offences against the kingdom than the Crown; yet, as the public . . . has delegated all its power and rights, with regard to the execution of the laws, to one visible magistrate, all affronts to that power, and breaches of those rights, are immediately offences against him . . . He is therefore the proper person to prosecute for all public offences and breaches of the peace, being the person injured in the eye of the law.'

{Kerr Bl (4th edn, 1876) i 239.}

The reference to 'breaches of the peace' in this passage is not to be confused with references in such Acts as the Public Order Act 1936 s 5 to breaches of the peace in the narrow sense, as betokening actual violence.

Certain government departments also employ officials to handle the prosecution of offences against Acts for the administration of which the department is responsible.

Enforcement of an Act does not only concern the bringing of prosecutions in the criminal courts. Infringements of the Act may call for other forms of procedure, for example the revocation of a licence by an authorising agency or the institution of civil proceedings for an injunction. The taking of the decision to start enforcement proceedings of any kind marks the dividing line between the administrative and the judicial spheres of enforcement. Up to that point the decisive view on the meaning of the relevant enactment has been that of an administrative authority. Thereafter the court takes over.

The significant case here is where the administrative authority decides *not* to begin proceedings. If proceedings are brought, the court will ultimately determine the meaning and effect of the enactment. But if they are not brought (and the case we are concerned with is where they are not brought because of the view taken, no doubt by some official, on the interpretation of the enactment) then the matter never comes to court at all. The view of the official, whether right or wrong, has prevailed.

This is of profound significance to the carrying out of the legislative purpose of Parliament. In an extreme case the wishes of Parliament can be entirely frustrated if police or other officials responsible for enforcement adopt a negative policy.

Example 1 On 22 April 1966 the Commissioner of Police of the Metropolis issued an instruction to senior officers. Its purport was that no proceedings were to be taken against clubs for breach of the Gaming Acts unless there were complaints of cheating or a club had become the haunt of criminals. The Court of Appeal held that the adoption of such a policy was 'deplorable'. {*R v Commr of Police of the Metropolis, ex p Blackburn* [1968] 2 QB 118, *per* Lord Denning MR at p 138.} Lord Denning said-

'The law has not been enforced as it should. The lawyers themselves are at least partly responsible. The niceties of drafting and the refinements of interpretation have led to uncertainties in the law itself. This has discouraged the police from keeping observation and taking action ... No longer will we tolerate these devices. The law must be sensibly interpreted so as to give effect to the intentions of Parliament; and the police must see that it is enforced. The rule of law must prevail.'

{Ibid, p 138.}

Elsewhere in his judgment Lord Denning made it clear that it is the duty of every chief constable to enforce the law-

'He must take steps so to post his men that crimes may be detected; and that honest citizens may go about their affairs in peace. He must decide whether or no suspected persons are to be prosecuted; and, if need be, bring the prosecution or see that it is brought. But in all these things he is not the servant of anyone, save of the law itself.'

{Ibid, p 136.}

Prosecution policy Parliament has proved curiously reluctant to lay down prosecution policy. It enacts, often in great detail, the laws which determine when an act or omission constitutes an offence. Equally it enacts the laws which set up and regulate the enforcement agencies. What it has never done is specify the criteria which are to govern decisions to prosecute or not prosecute in cases where it is likely that a prosecution, if brought, would succeed.

It is impractical to investigate and prosecute more than a small proportion of the offences known or suspected to have been committed. Even where a suspected offence is investigated, and sufficient evidence collected, it may for various reasons be inexpedient to prosecute. The factors affecting the decision can be divided into those relevant to the offence and those relevant to the offender. First we consider those relevant to the offence.

It may be thought inexpedient to institute a prosecution if the offence is technical, or the Act creating it is obsolete. {But there is no doctrine of desuetude in relation to United Kingdom Acts: see 188 of this Code.} Another possible reason is staleness of the offence. Except where the enactment creating a summary offence otherwise provides, a prosecution for it must be brought within six months. {Magistrates' Courts Act 1980 s 127.} There is no such general restriction in relation to indictable offences, but it still may be thought oppressive to prosecute after a number of years have passed.

Again, there may be an international dimension to the offence (for example a need to bring witnesses from abroad, or a desire to exchange a willing prisoner for hostages). Another adverse factor may be the risk of harm to an essential witness (eg, a young child in a sex case). Or there may be risks of political disturbance or labour unrest if a prosecution is brought. A factor tending the other way is growth in the incidence of a particular offence, leading to an increased prosecution rate with the hope of stamping it out.

Factors related to the offender include advanced age and illness, either of which may render a trial a cruel imposition. High social status may bring disproportionate punishment for a minor offence. Relationship of the offender to the victim can be a compelling factor. A wife injured by her husband may have to go on living with him. Prospects for the rehabilitation of the marriage will not be improved by the vicissitudes of trial and sentence. Then again legal factors may enter the equation. Perhaps the suspect is already undergoing punishment for a more serious offence, or has agreed to turn Queen's evidence in the trial of an accomplice, or has to be persuaded to come voluntarily from overseas in order to testify in another trial.

It is clear that the interests of justice require prosecution policy to be sensible and consistent. The Royal Commission on Criminal Procedure, reporting in 1981, said that, subject to justifiable local variations, prosecution policy over the whole country should be uniform. Witnesses to the Commission expressed concern about the disparity of policy between different agencies, giving as an example 'the zeal with which social security frauds are prosecuted . . . contrasted with the relatively limited extent to which income tax defaulters are prosecuted'. {Cmnd 8092, para 7.43.} The Commission recorded that police forces had not found it easy to achieve consistency in the treatment of shoplifters, and said that such consistency was desirable. {Ibid, para 7.46.}

Another aspect is the question of which offence should be charged when the evidence covers more than one. Judges sometimes criticise prosecutors for selecting for charge an offence considered too minor in view of the facts. {See, e g, *R v Bodmin JJ, ex p McEwen* [1947] KB 321.} Prosecuting agencies 'have the duty to exercise great care in selecting the proper charges to prefer'. {*R v Canterbury and St Augustine's JJ, ex p Klisiak* [1981] 2 All ER 129, *per* Lord Lane CJ at p 139.}

Nevertheless, as with the question of whether to prosecute at all, Parliament has not so far seen fit to provide detailed guidance. {As to official prosecution policy see *The criteria for prosecution: Note by the Director of Public Prosecutions* (Appendix 25 to *The Investigation and Prosecution of Criminal Offences in England and Wales: The Law and Procedure*, issued by the Royal Commission on Criminal Procedure in January 1981, Cmnd 8092-1.}

See also Examples 14.12 and 82.1.

19. Enforcement agencies: courts and other adjudicating authorities

A court is an agency charged with the function of exercising the judicial power of the state. Only a court as thus defined has the power authoritatively to determine what the law is, and therefore what is the legal meaning of a relevant enactment. Some courts and other adjudicating agencies operate at first instance, while others (or sometimes the same ones in another capacity) operate as appellate or reviewing agencies.

COMMENTARY

Blackstone said that a court 'is defined to be a place wherein justice is judicially administered'. {Kerr Bl (4th edn, 1876) iii 22.} This definition is completed by the statutory requirement that justice shall be so administered only 'after the laws and usages of this realm, without fear or favour, affection or illwill'. {Promissory Oaths Act 1868 s 4.} The requirement follows the common law, as laid down in *Prohibitions del Roy* {(1607) 12 Co Rep 63.}: 'the King in his own person cannot adjudge any case . . . but this ought to be determined and adjudged in some Court of Justice, according to the law and custom of England'.

Parliament currently endorses this concept of the judicial power. Thus s 19 of the Contempt of Court Act 1981 defines the expression 'court' as meaning any tribunal or body exercising the judicial power of the state.

The 'court' may be a judge, stipendiary magistrate or other authority possessing expert legal knowledge. On the other hand the deciding agency may be a bench of lay magistrates, a jury, or some other lay body. In the latter case it is likely to be required to reach its decision under the guidance of a legal expert comprised in the 'court', though this is not invariable.

Another relevant distinction is between the court of first instance and the court of appeal or review. Inferior courts and tribunals are essentially controlled by the courts which exercise the Crown's judicial function. For example Burn, explaining how the latter controlled ecclesiastical courts, said they have-

'. . . the *exposition* of such statutes or acts of parliament as concern either the extent of the jurisdiction of [ecclesiastical courts] or the matters depending before them. And therefore if [ecclesiastical courts] either refuse to allow these acts of parliament, or expound them in any other sense than is truly and properly the exposition of them, the king's great courts of common law may prohibit and control them.'

{R Burn *The Ecclesiastical Law* (9th edn, 1842). Emphasis added.}

Powers of appeal or review are inevitably incomplete. For example, a jury acquittal cannot be challenged on the ground of mistake of law by the jury. A reviewing court (as opposed to an appellate court) is not free to substitute its own view of how a discretion should have been exercised for that of the body entrusted with the discretion in the first place. Even an appellate court refrains from disturbing the decision below without a weighty reason. {As to the implied incorporation in statutes of common-law rules relating to decision-making see s 335 of this Code.}

Some tribunals have mixed lawyer and non-lawyer membership. This may even be the case with an appellate tribunal. The Employment Appeal Tribunal, for example, consists of two lay members and a legally-qualified chairman. Not infrequently the lay members outvote the chairman *on questions of law*. {See A N Khan 'Who is Employed' (1983) 127 SJ 416. See further p 62 below.}

Court jurisdiction Parties cannot by their agreement confer upon a court any jurisdiction which under the Acts establishing the court it does not possess. {*Heyting v Dupont* [1963] 1 WLR 1192; *Re Aylmer, ex p Bischoffsheim* (1887) 20 QBD 258; *London Corpn v Cox* (1867) LR 2 HL 239.} If it were not so, private persons would have the power to compel a judge to act merely because they wished it: which is absurd.

Example 1   In *Re Hooker's Settlement* {[1955] Ch 55.} it was sought to persuade Danckwerts J to consent to the exercise of a power of revocation contained in a settlement. He held that he lacked jurisdiction to do this, and that the parties could not by their agreement supply the lack. He pointed out that-

> '. . . an ordinary person has not the power, which the legislature has
> . . . to impose upon a judge of the Chancery Division a jurisdiction
> which is not given him by the procedure of the courts or by any
> statute.'

{P 58. In fact the jurisdiction of the Chancery Division, as of the Supreme Court generally, is now wholly statutory.}

Danckwerts J went on to add that if this were not so the jurisdiction of the courts would be 'capable of extension in a very undesirable and improper manner . . . A judge could be compelled to act as arbitrator in commercial disputes or even in a question about a race'. {Ibid.}

This obvious restriction is often stated in clear terms by the relevant Act.

Example 2   Section 12(7) of the Increase of Rent and Mortgage Interest (Restrictions) Act 1920 stated that where the rent payable in respect of any tenancy was less than two-thirds of the rateable value of the premises 'this Act shall not apply to that rent or tenancy'.

In *J & F Stone Lighting & Radio Ltd v Levitt* {[1947] AC 209.} it was argued that by taking part in proceedings in the county court purporting to be brought under the Act the parties could, in defiance of s 12(7), enable the court to deal with the matter. Lord Thankerton responded: 'It is idle to suggest that either estoppel or *res judicata* can give the court a jurisdiction under the Rent Restriction Acts which the statute says it is not to have'. {P 216. As to estoppel in relation to statutes see pp 732 and 751 below.}

In some cases the Act conferring jurisdiction does so in affirmative terms, leaving it to be inferred that what is not expressly given by the Act is to be taken as withheld. An example is the legislation setting up the Lands Tribunal. In *Essex County Council v Essex Incorporated Church Union* {[1963] AC 808.} it was held by the House of Lords that the parties could not consent to give the Tribunal a jurisdiction not within the words of the Act.

The adjudicating function of courts and other authorities is considered in s 20 of this Code.

20. Enforcement agencies: function of adjudicating authorities

The function of a court or other adjudicating authority when trying a case is to ascertain the relevant facts and apply to them the relevant law. In so far as the relevant law is contained in a particular enactment, the authority's function is therefore to apply the enactment. This requires it to determine, on an informed interpretation, the legal meaning of the enactment as it applies to the facts of the instant case.

The nature of this task differs according to whether the enactment has been previously processed by judicial or administrative decision or is still unprocessed. Either way, the legal meaning of the enactment may be disputed by the parties or be undisputed. If it is undisputed, and the court itself feels no real doubt, the court applies the agreed meaning. If it is disputed, the court must decide between the opposing constructions advanced by the parties - always retaining the power of rejecting both the constructions advanced and applying its own view of Parliament's intention.

COMMENTARY

Under the British constitution, the function of determining authoritatively the meaning of a parliamentary enactment is entrusted to the judiciary. In the words of Richard Burn they have the exposition of Acts, which must not be expounded 'in any other sense than is truly and properly the exposition of them'. {See p 51 above.} This is but one aspect of the court's general function of applying the relevant law to the facts of the case before it. The starting point is therefore to consider this function.

The court is to find out the law by an informed approach, not one founded in ignorance. {As to the informed interpretation rule see s 119 of this Code.} A relevant enactment is to be given its *legal* meaning, which may differ from its grammatical meaning. {As to the legal meaning see s 2 of this Code.} If the legal meaning has been the subject of judicial decision, the court may not have a free hand. Under the doctrine of precedent it may be obliged to defer to the previous ruling, or at least treat it as of persuasive authority. {See s 26 of this Code.}

The meaning of most enactments is so clear that the parties do not dispute it. If there is a dispute the court must decide between the opposing constructions put forward, unless it rejects both and forms its own view. {As to opposing constructions see s 84 of this Code.}

The court's decision must be determined by what it considers to be the intention of Parliament, as expressed in the enactment. {See Part V of this Code.} Nevertheless the judiciary necessarily have a large hand in spelling out Parliament's imputed intention. 'The essence of the interpretation of statutes', said Donaldson MR, 'is an earnest seeking after the intention of Parliament or perhaps, more accurately, the deemed intention of Parliament'. {*Gubay v Kington (Inspector of Taxes)* [1983] 2 All ER 976, at p 983.}

The seeking must always be done with good faith, but there is wide scope for the judge's own view of what is just (and Parliament is taken never to intend what is unjust). The judiciary are inclined to believe, with Trollope, that-

> 'It is true that one must put up with wrong, with a great deal of wrong. But no one need put up with wrong that he can remedy.'

{*Framley Parsonage* p 7.}

The judges, by the nature of their office, are able to remedy much that is wrong. Nevertheless they are required, at least under modern doctrine, to stay close to the meaning of the legislators' words. {See ss 136 (primacy of text) and 137 (primacy of literal meaning) of this Code.} In arriving at the legal meaning the court, subject to relevant legal rules, is master of its own procedure. {*R v Wormwood Scrubs Prison Board of Visitors, ex p Anderson* [1984] 1 All ER 799.} It therefore has the power, indeed the duty, to consider such aspects of the legislative history of the enactment as may be necessary to arrive at the legal meaning. {As to legislative history see s 119 and Part X of this Code.}

21. Enforcement agencies: doctrine of judicial notice

Under the doctrine of judicial notice, a court or other adjudicating authority will in certain circumstances accept the existence of a law or fact relevant to the interpretation of an enactment without the necessity of proof.

COMMENTARY

The doctrine of judicial notice has several applications in statutory interpretation. These are dealt with at the appropriate places in the Code. Here we merely outline the general principle, which is expressed in the maxim *lex non requirit verificari quod apparet curiae* (the law does not require verification of what is apparent to the court). {9 Co Rep 54.}

This maxim may originally have related to the court record, for elsewhere Coke expresses it as: 'That which is apparent to the court by necessary collection out of the record need not be averred'. {Co Litt 303b.} The record here meant is the *roll* of what is called a court of record. It does not include the rolls of inferior courts, nor of any courts (such as those in other countries) which do not proceed *secundum legem et consuetudinem Angliae*. {Co Litt 260a.} However the doctrine of judicial notice is of much wider application than this.

Judicial notice of law   A judge is taken to know the *general* law prevailing within the area of his jurisdiction. The rule is an ancient one, going back to *The Prince's Case* {(1606) 8 Co Rep 1a, 13b.} Having been sworn to apply the laws and usages of the realm {Promissory Oaths Act 1868 s 4.}, a judge is assumed to have knowledge of what he has thus bound himself to administer.

As Lord Devlin put it, the judge has a mandate from the Crown to apply the law of the land. {*The Judge* p 87.} Reasonably enough, the law treats him as equipped to do this. No person is qualified for judicial office unless he possesses specified professional qualifications and experience. These are presumed to endow him with inherent legal knowledge: *judex est lex loquens*. {7 Co Rep 4.}

The judge is nevertheless entitled to refresh his memory of the law by whatever means appear suitable. Furthermore it has been judicially accepted that judges are liable to make mistakes in law. In a case turning on the meaning of s 19 (penalty points) of the Transport Act 1981 Lord Lane CJ said-

> ' . . . this court sympathises with courts which have to grapple with this sort of legislation. It may be said that it would be very surprising if judges did not make mistakes in this branch of their work.'

{*R v Kent* [1983] 3 All ER 1, at p 3.}

The general law of which judicial notice is taken comprises the common law (including principles of equity), established customs prevailing within the jurisdiction of the court in a particular geographical area (such as gavelkind and borough English) or among a particular class of people (such as the law merchant), and Acts of Parliament required by statute to be judicially noticed (that is all Acts passed before 1851 which so provide and all Acts passed after 1850 which do not otherwise provide). {Interpretation Act 1978 ss 3 and 22(1), Sch 2 para 2. In practice only personal Acts otherwise provide (see p 87 below).} Also required by statute to be judicially noticed is the law of the European Communities. {European Communities Act 1972 s 3(2).}

Delegated legislation The Interpretation Act 1978 pointedly avoids any pronouncement on whether judicial notice is to be taken of delegated legislation. Since s 23(1) of the Act, which applies most of its provisions to such legislation, excepts s 3 (judicial notice of Acts) it might be said that by implication, in accordance with the maxim *expressio unius est exclusio unius* {See s 389 of this Code.}, the Act intends that judicial notice shall *not* be taken of delegated legislation.

This would be too simple. The better view appears to be that at common law judicial notice is to be taken of delegated legislation made under a public general Act and published by authority. {See *Snell v Unity Finance Ltd* [1964] 2 QB 203; *Palastanga v Solman* (1962) 106 Sol Jo 176.} In a white paper on the Bill for the Interpretation Act 1978 {Law Com No 90, Cmnd 7235, para 9. The text is set out in Appendix E below.}, the Law Commissions, who were responsible for drafting the Act, criticised the Interpretation Act 1889 (which it replaced) as 'selective, not to say capricious' in its application to subordinate legislation. In view of this it is surprising and regrettable that the point was not dealt with by the 1978 Act, along with other improvements described in the white paper.

Judicial notice of fact The court will not require evidence of notorious facts, but will accept them as existing without need of proof. Such facts have been judicially defined for this purpose as 'matters generally known to well-informed people'. {*Escoigne Properties Ltd v IRC* [1958] AC 549, *per* Lord Denning at p 566.}

This includes the ordinary attributes of human nature. Lord Wilberforce remarked-

'As was said in *Transport Publishing Co Pty Ltd v Literature Board of Review* (1956) 99 CLR 111 at 118 there is such a thing as ordinary human nature which is not a subject for proof by evidence.'

{*Gold Star Publications Ltd v DPP* [1981] 2 All ER 257, at p 259.}
Or as Sir Carleton Allen put it: 'the judge frequently has to act, on his own knowledge of the world and of men, as a kind of super-juryman'. {*Legal Duties* p 71.} Knowledge of the world includes, for example, the fact that 'drugs are a great danger today' {*Yeandel v Fisher* [1966] 1 QB 440, at p 446.} or that at sea flags of convenience provide cheap labour. {*N W L Ltd v Woods* [1979] 3 All ER 614, at p 622.}

Judicial notice is also taken of the facts of nature. Thus Serjeant Shee once said in argument: 'the Court will take judicial notice that rain falls from time to time'. The Court (of Common Pleas) did not demur. {*Fay v Prentice* (1845) 14 LJCP 298, at p 299.}

Since they are by law taken to be advised of everything known to well-informed people, it follows that judges must keep themselves well informed. There used to be an affectation by the judiciary that they were unaware of vulgar phenomena. This aroused scorn. Scrutton LJ complained that 'It is difficult to know what judges are allowed to know, though they are ridiculed if they pretend not to know'. {*Tolley v J S Fry & Sons Ltd* [1930] 1 KB 473, 475 (see [1931] AC 333).} The supposed need to pretend ignorance of popular phenomena was finally exploded when Vinelott J said in a 1982 case-

'I think I am entitled to take judicial notice of the fact that the late

Elvis Presley was resident in and performed largely within [the United States].'

{*RCA Corpn v Pollard* [1982] 2 All ER 468, at p 479. See further s 82 of this Code.}

Expert knowledge   Judges will take notice of non-legal expertise if it bears on legal matters. Thus Lord Keith said of the contractor's principle that it was a 'notoriously unreliable' method of valuation. {*Western Heritable Investment Co Ltd v Husband* [1983] 3 All ER 65, at p 69.}

Meaning of words   As to judicial notice of the meaning of words see s 375 of this Code.

22. Enforcement agencies: adjudicating authorities with original jurisdiction

In its legislation, Parliament makes use of a variety of adjudicating authorities with original jurisdiction: that is courts and tribunals with the function of hearing and determining civil or criminal cases at first instance.

COMMENTARY

The *existence* of a statutory right or duty in a particular case depends both on law and fact. Where a right does exist the question of whether it has been *infringed* also depends on law and fact. The position is similar in relation to the breach of a duty. Under our system the determination of these questions is entrusted to some form of adjudicatory process.

The public agencies responsible for activating the adjudicatory process are briefly surveyed above. {See ss 15 to 18.} In this section we turn to the first level of the adjudicatory process, which is in the hands of authorities exercising original jurisdiction and operating at first instance.

We saw above {S 5.} that an Act may either make use of existing enforcement procedures or create new ones. Within that concept, we find that Acts either allow existing adjudicating authorities to exercise original jurisdiction in relation to alleged infringements of the Act or they set up a new adjudicating agency (usually a tribunal) for that purpose. We now give a brief account of the principal agencies operating at first instance in England and Wales. {Corresponding agencies exist in Northern Ireland. In Scotland, which has its own legal system, there are differences which are not from the point of view of statutory interpretation substantial.}

High Court of Justice   Under s 1 of the Supreme Court Act 1981, the High Court of Justice is constituted as a part of the Supreme Court of England and Wales. The section provides for the Court of Appeal and the Crown Court to be the other two constituent parts of the Supreme Court.

The Lord Chancellor is President of the Supreme Court, which does not in practice sit as a court. Nor is its name any more than an umbrella description of the constituent elements. The name is an inappropriate one, because neither collectively nor individually are the elements in any way 'supreme'. The discrepancy arose when s 20 of the Supreme Court of Judicature Act 1873, which provided for the abolition of the appellate jurisdiction of the House of Lords and the Privy Council, was repealed before it had come into force. There have been many subsequent Acts by which a more appropriate name could have been substituted, but the opportunity was never taken.

Having constituted the High Court by its full name, the Supreme Court Act 1981 thereafter refers to it simply as the High Court. The Act, a consolidation Act, thus effects a slight change in the name bestowed by the Act it replaced. This was the Supreme Court of Judicature (Consolidation) Act 1925, s 1 of which gave the name as 'His Majesty's High Court of Justice', to which it seems (because of the earlier wording of that section) that the words 'in England' were to be treated as added. By similar reasoning the full name should now be taken to be 'the High Court of Justice in England and Wales'.

The Interpretation Act 1978 says that 'High Court' means, in relation to England and Wales, 'Her Majesty's High Court of Justice in England'. {S 5 and Sch I.} The definition was not altered, as apparently it should have been, to correspond with the change in nomenclature effected by the 1981 Act. It seems that in relation to England and Wales references in Acts to 'the High Court' should now be taken to refer to the court as renamed by the 1981 Act.

The High Court is a superior court of record. {Supreme Court Act 1981 s 19(1).} A *superior court* is a court which is not subject to the control of any other court by prerogative writ or order. A *court of record* is a court whose proceedings historically were enrolled or recorded. Blackstone said this was 'for a perpetual memorial and testimony', adding that the records 'are of such high and super-eminent authority that their truth is not to be called in question'. {Kerr Bl (4th edn, 1876) ii 23. As to the juridical nature of the record see *Blay v Pollard* [1930] 1 KB 628 and *London Passenger Transport Board v Moscrop* [1942] AC 347. See also Earl Jowett *Dictionary of English Law*, tit 'Stet processus' (where it is stated that 'there is under the modern practice no record in an action').}

The concept of the 'record' is expanded by the requirement that a shorthand note be taken of evidence, summing up and judgment {RSC Ord 68.} In the High Court, recording equipment now makes the full text of counsel's speeches also available. {*Home Office v Harman* [1982] 1 All ER 532, *per* Lord Diplock at p 538.} As to the right under American law of inspecting the 'judicial record' see *Home Office v Harman*. {[1982] 1 All ER 532, *per* Lord Scarman at p 548.}

All courts of record are courts of the sovereign. At common law no other court has authority to fine or imprison for contempt not committed in the face of the court. {*R v Clement* (1821) 4 B & Ald 218.} The latter rule has been modified by statute. {See, e g, Magistrates' Courts Act 1980 s 63 and Contempt of Court Act 1981 s 17).}

The High Court consists of the Lord Chancellor, the Lord Chief Justice, the President of the Family Division, the Vice-Chancellor and not more than eighty puisne judges styled Justices of the High Court. {Supreme Court Act 1981 s 4.} Although pronounced 'puny', the word puisne does not refer to a status diminutive by comparison with senior judges. It comes from the French *puis ne* (later born). An equivalent term is *simplex justiciarius*, a judge not chief in any court.

The High Court sits in three divisions, the Queen's Bench Division (presided over by the Lord Chief Justice), the Chancery Division (in practice presided over by the Vice-Chancellor, though the Lord Chancellor is the nominal

President) and the Family Division. In addition, the Commercial Court and the Admiralty Court form part of the Queen's Bench Division and the Patents Court forms part of the Chancery Division. {Supreme Court Act 1981 s 5.} The High Court may also sit as a prize court. {Ibid, s 27.}

Owing to the method of archival drafting employed, it is not possible to state with reasonable brevity the original jurisdiction of the High Court. {Archival drafting is so called because it requires any person desiring to understand its full effect to consult legal and historical archives: see s 286 of this Code.} Section 19(2)(b) of the Supreme Court Act 1981 says that the High Court shall have such civil and criminal jurisdiction as was exercisable by it 'immediately before the commencement of this Act'. This sends the enquirer back to s 18 of the Supreme Court of Judicature (Consolidation) Act 1925 with its reference to 'the jurisdiction formerly vested in, or capable of being exercised by' various courts including the Courts of Common Pleas at Westminster, Lancaster and Durham respectively and the Court of Exchequer 'both as a court of revenue and as a common law court'. {As to the historical origins of the present jurisdiction see *Walker v Walker* [1919] AC 947 and *Board v Board* [1919] AC 956.}

At first instance the High Court has a very wide original jurisdiction in civil matters. This is cut down by statute only where it is considered appropriate to give a lesser court or tribunal initial jurisdiction. {See below. The provisions currently defining the jurisdiction and powers of the High Court are ss 19-44 of the Supreme Court Act 1981. As to the jurisdiction of the High Court to exercise judicial review see s 24 of this Code.}

Crown Court   The Crown Court is a superior court of record. {Supreme Court Act 1981 s 45(1). For the meaning of this see p 57 above.} Although constituted by the Supreme Court Act 1981 as a single court, it in fact sits in numerous localities in England and Wales. When sitting in the City of London it is known as the Central Criminal Court. {Supreme Court Act 1981 s 8(3).}

Crown court judges are normally circuit judges or recorders, though any High Court judge is empowered to sit. {Ibid, s 8(1).} The judges sit alone except when sitting with justices of the peace or (in the City of London) with the Lord Mayor or aldermen. {Ibid, s 8(1)(c) and (3).} The main function of the Crown Court is to try criminal cases on indictment, for which it has exclusive jurisdiction. {Ibid, s 46(1).} Here the Crown Court acts as the successor to the ancient courts of assize and quarter sessions, which were abolished by the Courts Act 1971. {See ss 1(2) and 3.}

The criminal jurisdiction of the Crown Court covers offences wherever committed, including 'offences within the jurisdiction of the Admiralty of England'. {Ibid, s 46(2).} The Crown Court also has a small original jurisdiction in civil matters. {The enactments conferring this civil jurisdiction are the following: National Parks and Access to the Countryside Act 1949 s 31; Firearms Act 1968 s 21(6) and (7) and Sch 3 Pt. I; Highways Act 1980 s 56(2).}

County courts   County courts are inferior civil courts set up throughout England and Wales and regulated by the County Courts Act 1959 as amended. Since the passing of the Courts Act 1971 they have been staffed (like the Crown Courts) by circuit judges. {Courts Act 1971 Pt III.} There are monetary limits on the various types of county court jurisdiction. These limits are from time to time adjusted to keep pace with inflation. Except where a particular enactment otherwise provides, the High Court has concurrent jurisdiction with the county court.

Magistrates' courts Justices of the peace, who before the expansion of the powers of local authorities in the nineteenth century also possessed widespread administrative functions, still retain much of their importance as adjudicating agencies. Some courts are staffed by legally-qualified stipendiary magistrates, while in others lay justices continue to sit. They are invariably advised by legally-qualified clerks.

The criminal jurisdiction of magistrates' courts relates to the trial of summary offences and the hearing of committal proceedings for indictable offences. In modern offence-creating Acts it is the invariable practice to specify whether a new offence is to be triable on indictment or summarily (or either way). Schedule 1 to the Magistrates' Courts Act 1980 specifies offences triable either way. Part I of the Act regulates the criminal jurisdiction and procedure of magistrates' courts. Proceedings (whether for a summary or an indictable offence) are initiated by the *laying of an information* before a justice of the peace and the issue of a summons or warrant. {Magistrates' Courts Act 1980 s 1.}

The civil jurisdiction and procedure of magistrates' courts is regulated by Part II of the Magistrates' Courts Act 1980. Proceedings are initiated by the *making of a complaint* to a justice of the peace and the issue of a summons. {Ibid, s 51. See Example 23.1.} Unlike the criminal jurisdiction, the civil jurisdiction of magistrates' courts is narrow. It is conferred by individual Acts, and is now mainly confined to domestic and family matters such as separation, maintenance and adoption.

Tribunals Various enactments confer adjudicating functions on tribunals, leaving the courts to play a supervisory role only. Since the passing of the Tribunals and Inquiries Act 1958, which set up the Council on Tribunals, this body has had the function of keeping under review the constitution and working of the numerous tribunals now listed in Sch I to the Tribunals and Inquiries Act 1971 (a consolidating Act) as amended.

Among the more important listed tribunals are the industrial tribunals, {These were first established under s 12 of the Industrial Training Act 1964.}, the Commissioners for the general and for the special purposes of the income tax {Respectively appointed under s 2 and s 4 of the Taxes Management Act 1970.}, the Lands Tribunal {Constituted under the Lands Tribunal Act 1949 s 1(1)(b).}, the Immigration Appeals Tribunal {Established by s 1 of the Immigration Appeals Act 1969.}, and the supplementary benefits appeal tribunals. {Constituted in accordance with Sch 4 to the Supplementary Benefits Act 1976.} See further pp 728–30 below.

23. Enforcement agencies: adjudicating authorities with appellate jurisdiction

Unless the contrary intention appears from the enactment conferring jurisdiction, the decisions of a court exercising original jurisdiction are subject to rights of appeal conferred by the general law. The decisions of any other type of enforcement agency may be subject to ad hoc rights of appeal.

COMMENTARY

From the point of view of statutory interpretation, the distinction between original and appellate jurisdiction is an important one. At first instance, the enforcement agency gives its decision on the meaning and effect of an enactment directly. The agency will usually have heard legal argument from each side as to the way its decision should go. Except in so far as interpretative processing of the enactment has previously occurred, the agency will not however be concerned with a view of the enactment's meaning and effect held by any other authority. {For the interpretative processing of enactments see s 26 of this Code.}

On appeal the position is different. Another authority has already given its decision; and the appellate body must now pay careful consideration to the reasons for it. If the decision involved an error of law, this must be corrected. If it involved an improper exercise of discretion, the appellate body must substitute its own view. The principle was summed up by Lord Atkin in a dictum described by May LJ in *Tsai v Woodworth* {(1983) *The Times* 30 November.} as the *locus classicus*-

> 'Appellate jurisdiction is always statutory ... and while the apppellate court in the exercise of its appellate power is no doubt entirely justified in saying that normally it will not interfere with the exercise of the judge's discretion except on grounds of law, yet if it sees that on other grounds the decision will result in injustice being done it has both the power and the duty to remedy it.'

{*Evans v Bartlam* [1937] AC 473, at p 480.}

We now give, in ascending order of importance, a description of the main types of appellate authority.

Magistrates' courts   Certain Acts confer appellate jurisdiction on magistrates' courts, for example in relation to licensing decisions by local authorities. Thus s 2(4) of the Nurses Agencies Act 1957 provides that a person who is refused a licence to carry on an agency for the supply of nurses may appeal to a magistrates' court, 'who may make such order as they think just'.

Appeals from other minor authorities operating locally also lie to magistrates' courts.

Example 1   Where a drainage authority serve a notice requiring an obstruction to a watercourse to be removed, the recipient of the notice may appeal to a magistrates' court. {Land Drainage Act 1976 (a consolidation Act) s 19(1).} The appeal is a civil proceeding, instituted by way of complaint under the Magistrates' Courts Act 1980. {Ibid, s 19(2).} The appellate court may make 'such order as it thinks fit', but guidelines are laid down to limit the width of this discretion. {Ibid, s 19(6) and (7).}

County courts   A small number of Acts confer on county courts appellate jurisdiction in civil matters similar to that entrusted to magistrates' courts. It is not possible to detect any principle governing Parliament's choice between the two kinds of court: the present distributon is largely a matter of historical accident. Thus the consolidation Act which, as noted above, confers jurisdiction on magistrates' courts in relation to watercourse obstruction appeals goes on to allocate appeals against demands for drainage charges to the county court. {Land Drainage Act 1976 s 57(1).} The county court is required to confirm, annul or modify a demand 'as it thinks just'. {Ibid, s 57(3).}

The unsatisfactory way in which these matters are dealt with is further illustrated by s 62 of the Local Government Act 1948. Section 62 says-

> 'So much of any statutory provision as authorises or requires any dispute arising in relation to water rates to be determined by a court of summary jurisdiction [i e a magistrates' court] shall have effect as if it authorised or required that dispute to be determined by the county court . . .'

This provision displays several of the defects of our system of legislative drafting, viz: (1) the same thing is called by different names ('court of summary jurisdiction' and 'magistrates' court'); (2) the wording is ambiguous (is the new jurisdiction of the county court in place of or additional to that of the magistrates?); (3) the amendment is not effected directly by textual amendment but indirectly by 'asifism'. {As to this much-used drafting technique see Bennion *Statute Law* (2nd edn, 1983) pp 124, 137-8, 181, 184-5, 200-3, 257.} On the last point it may be remarked that if the draftsman had been required to devise the words needed for textual amendment he would have been unlikely to perpetrate the ambiguity. It should also be said that this type of drafting is less likely today. Our drafting techniques have considerably improved in recent times.

Although s 62 of the Local Government Act 1948 remains on the statute book, it no longer means what it says. The Act setting up the Lands Tribunal provided that-

> 'There shall be referred to and determined by the Lands Tribunal . . . any question on which, but for this provision, an appeal . . . to the county court would or might be made by virtue of s 62 . . . of the Local Government Act 1948.'

{Lands Tribunal Act 1949, s 1(3)(e).}

Crown Court As successor to the courts of quarter sessions, the Crown Court possesses appellate jurisdiction in certain civil matters. {All the appellate and other jurisdiction of quarter sessions was transferred to the Crown Court by s 8 of and Sch 1 to the Courts Act 1971.}

Example 2 The Land Drainage Act 1976 provides for a further appeal to the Crown Court from decisions of magistrates' courts on appeals against decisions of drainage authorities given under s 18 of the Act. {Land Drainage Act 1976 s 19(8). See Example *1*.} The right of appeal is conferred on 'a person aggrieved'. {This is a *broad term* frequently used in such cases. As to the interpretation of such broad terms see s 150 of this Code.}

For a list of the enactments now conferring civil appellate jurisdiction on the Crown Court see Sch 1 to the Courts Act 1971 as amended.

The main appellate jurisdiction of the Crown Court is in criminal matters. Section 108 of the Magistrates' Courts Act 1980 gives any person who is convicted by a magistrates' court after a plea of *not guilty* a right of appeal to the

Crown Court against his conviction. The section affords an appeal against sentence whether the plea was *guilty* or *not guilty*.

Section 48 of the Supreme Court Act 1981 contains important provisions spelling out the powers which, subject to any particular enactment, the Crown Court has on an appeal. They apply whether the appeal is in a civil or criminal matter, and are to the following effect.

1. The Crown Court may correct 'any error or mistake' in the order or judgment incorporating the decision appealed from. {Supreme Court Act 1981 s 48(1). The tautology here is remarkable, since the English language does not admit any difference between 'error' and 'mistake'. We have the authority of a former Lord Chancellor for the statement that this kind of drafting is never either excusable or necessary. {Earl Jowitt *The Dictionary of English Law* (1st edn, 1959), tit: 'Tautology'.}

2. The Crown Court may (1) confirm, reverse or vary the decision, or (2) remit the matter (with its opinion) to the authority which made the decision, or (3) make such other order as it thinks just. {Supreme Court Act 1981 s 48(2). This adds that in the third case the order may exercise any power the authority appealed from might have exercised. This is clearly too narrow, and should be taken to apply also in the first case where the decision is varied.}

3. If the appeal is against conviction or sentence, the Crown Court can impose any punishment (whether more less severe) that the court appealed from could have awarded. {Supreme Court Act 1981 s 48(4).} This means that a person cannot effectively appeal against his conviction only (having perhaps no complaint against the sentence). The appellate court can always increase the sentence if it thinks fit.

Appellate tribunals   An Act which sets up a tribunal with original jurisdiction sometimes goes on to establish a second-tier body to hear appeals from it. Similarly, where a new tribunal has been constituted it may prove so successful that later Acts add to its jurisdiction and finally crown the structure with appellate machinery.

This occurred with industrial tribunals, which were originally set up under s 12 of the Industrial Training Act 1964 for the relatively unimportant purpose of determining appeals by employers assessed to a levy under the Act. Subsequent Acts expanded the jurisdiction of industrial tribunals to a much wider field, including unfair dismissal and contravention of the Equal Pay Act 1970. Eventually industrial tribunals were handling thousands of cases a year, and Parliament decided that a second-tier appellate body was needed.

For this purpose the Employment Appeal Tribunal was established by s 87 of the Employment Protection Act 1975. {Repealed and replaced by the Employment Protection (Consolidation) Act 1978: see s 135 of that Act.} It consists of judges of the High Court or Court of Appeal (and at least one judge of the Court of Session), together with lay members having special knowledge or experience of industrial relations. The Tribunal's jurisdiction (not confined to appeals from industrial tribunals) relates only to questions of law. {Employment Protection (Consolidation) Act 1978 s 136.}

High Court   From a decision of the Crown Court in its civil jurisdiction, an appeal lies to the Divisional Court by way of case stated. {Supreme Court Act 1981 s 28(1).} The decision of the Crown Court may be questioned by any party to the proceedings on the ground that it 'is wrong in law or is in excess of jurisdiction'. {Ibid.} The right of appeal does not apply to a decision under the Betting, Gaming and Lotteries Act 1963, the Licensing Act 1964 or the Gaming Act 1968 where, by any provision of those Acts, the decision is to be final. {Ibid, s 28(2).}

Various other enactments give rights of appeal to the Divisional Court from decisions of enforcement agencies. These are expressed either as a right of appeal simpliciter or as a right to have a case stated. Examples are: Tribunals and Inquiries Act 1971 s 13(1) as amended (appeal from various tribunals mentioned in Sch 1 to the Act) and s 13(5) (further appeal from decisions of the Secretary of State on appeals from traffic commissioners); Agriculture (Miscellaneous Provisions) Act 1954 s 6 (appeal from Agricultural Land Tribunals); Town and Country Planning Act 1971 s 246 (further appeal from decisions of the Secretary of State on appeals against planning notices).

In some Acts a formula has been adopted which has been found ambiguous. This states that the person in question 'may, according as rules of court may provide, either appeal to the High Court against the decision on a point of law or require the [authority making the decision] to state and sign a case for the opinion of the High Court'. {Tribunals and Inquiries Act 1971 s 13(1); Town and Country Planning Act 1971 s 246(1).} It is not clear whether this enables rules of court to lay down which of the two types of appeal is to operate in a particular case, or whether the appellant must be allowed to choose for himself.

A quasi-appellate jurisdiction is conferred on the High Court by enactments requiring the approval of the court before some scheme or arrangement can take legal effect. {See, e g, Leasehold Reform Act 1967 s 19 (scheme giving landlord rights of management).} As to the powers of the High Court on judicial review see s 24 of this Code.

Court of Appeal Under the Supreme Court Act 1981 the Court of Appeal consists of two divisions, the Civil Division and the Criminal Division. These are respectively presided over by the Master of the Rolls and the Lord Chief Justice. {Supreme Court Act 1981 s 3. The court is a superior court of record: s 15(1).}

With limited exceptions, the Court of Appeal has jurisdiction to hear and determine appeals from any decision of the High Court in a non-criminal matter where the decision is not by any enactment declared to be 'final'. {Supreme Court Act 1981 ss 16(1) and 18(1)(c).} The only right of appeal from the High Court to the Court of Apppeal in a criminal matter is in relation to contempt of court. {Administration of Justice Act 1960 s 13.}

The principal exception in civil cases concerns 'leapfrogging' appeals. These are appeals which, under Part II of the Administration of Justice Act 1969, lie direct from the High Court to the House of Lords. {See p 65 below.} Also excepted are appeals from the High Court when acting as a prize court, which lie to Her Majesty in Council in accordance with the Prize Acts 1864 to 1944. {Supreme Court Act 1981 s 16(2).}

Certain appeals require the leave either of the court below or the Court of Appeal. {See Supreme Court Act 1981 s 18.}

Subject to certain restrictions, an appeal on a question of law lies direct to the Court of Appeal (Civil Division) from a county court. The provision conferring this right says that a party may appeal if he is 'dissatisfied with the determination or direction of the judge in point of law or upon the admission or rejection of any evidence'. {County Courts Act 1959 s 108.}

The main appellate function of the Criminal Division of the Court of Appeal concerns appeals from the Crown Court in relation to cases tried on indictment. This is conferred by s 45 of the Criminal Appeal Act 1968. On an appeal against conviction, leave to appeal (or a certificate of the trial judge) is required unless the ground of appeal 'involves a question of law alone'. {Ibid, s 1(2).}

The wording of the 1968 Act is interesting in that it contemplates three other possible types of appeal: (1) on a ground which 'involves a question of fact alone'; (2) on a ground which 'involves a question of mixed law and fact'; and (3) on 'any other ground which appears to the Court of Appeal to be a sufficient ground of appeal'. {Ibid.}

The criteria specified by the 1968 Act for allowing an appeal against conviction are of great importance-

> '(a) that the verdict of the jury should be set aside on the ground that under all the circumstances of the case it is unsafe or unsatisfactory; or (b) that the judgment of the court of trial should be set aside on the ground of a wrong decision of any question of law; or (c) that there was a material irregularity in the course of the trial.'

{As to the desirable method of presenting and arguing appeals against conviction see Bennion 'Propositions of Law in Conviction Appeals' [1984] Crim LR 282.}

Then follows the famous proviso, under which thousands of convictions have been upheld nothwithstanding a breach of the foregoing formula or its predecessor-

> 'Provided that the Court may, notwithstanding that they are of opinion that the point raised in the appeal might be decided in favour of the appellant, dismiss the appeal if they consider that no miscarriage of justice has actually occurred.'

The proviso has been criticised as giving the judges too much discretionary power. {Kenny said that the proviso 'makes for no little uncertainty in the result of appeals': *Outlines of Criminal Law* (15th edn, 1946) p 589.} Justice normally means justice according to law, and *ex hypothesi* the law here has not been obeyed. By the usual British genius for logically indefensible compromise the proviso works in practice, however, and avoids the scandal attached to acquittals of undoubted rogues on a technicality. Nevertheless this has to be recognised as one more example of how an incorrect interpretation of an Act may in effect prevail.

The current grounds of appeal against conviction (given above) derive from s 9 of the Criminal Appeal Act 1907, which set up the old Court of Criminal Appeal. When that court was abolished by the Criminal Appeal Act 1966, the grounds were largely reproduced in defining the jurisdiction of the Court of Appeal (Criminal Division).

Some changes were, however, made. In the proviso the word 'substantial' was dropped before 'miscarriage of justice'. The first ground (paragraph (a)) was changed from the previous criterion that the jury's verdict was 'unreasonable or cannot be supported having regard to the evidence'. This involved a change of substance in fresh evidence cases. The Court of Appeal will not now order a retrial if, after assessing the fresh evidence, they do not regard it as rendering the verdict unsafe or unsatisfactory. {*Stafford v DPP* [1974] AC 878. The decision was criticised by Lord Devlin as undermining the right to trial by jury: *The Judge* pp 148-176.} The power to order a retrial where new evidence is admitted arises under s 7 of the Criminal Appeal Act 1968.

'Leapfrogging' appeals   In civil cases the stage of appeal to the Court of Appeal can be dispensed with in certain cases where the High Court is satisfied that a point of law of general public importance is involved. {Administration of Justice Act 1969 Pt II.} The appeal then goes direct to the House of Lords, provided that House concurs and all the parties in the case also agree. {Ibid, ss 12(1)(c) and 13(2).} Applications for the concurrence of the House of Lords 'shall be determined without a hearing'. {Ibid, s 13(3).}

Proceedings are excluded from the leapfrogging procedure if, by virtue of any enactment, no appeal lies to the Court of Appeal. The point of law must be one that-

> '(a) relates wholly or mainly to the construction of an enactment or of a statutory instrument, and has been fully argued in the proceedings, or
> (b) is one in respect of which the judge is bound by a decision of the Court of Appeal or of the House of Lords in previous proceedings, and was fully considered in the judgments given by the Court of Appeal or the House of Lords (as the case may be) in those previous proceedings.'
> {Ibid, s 12(3).}

Paragraph (a) marks a recognition by Parliament of the special importance attaching to questions of statutory interpretation.

House of Lords   An appeal lies to the House of Lords from any decision of the Court of Appeal. {Appellate Jurisdiction Act 1876 s 3; Criminal Appeal Act 1968 Pt II.} Section 3 of the Appellate Jurisdiction Act 1876 also provides, by a piece of archival drafting, for an appeal to lie to the House of Lords from an order or judgment of 'any Court in Scotland from which error or an appeal at or immediately before the commencement of this Act lay to the House of Lords by common law or by statute'. {As to archival drafting see s 286 of this Code.}

An appeal also lies to the House of Lords from a decision of the High Court where it is (1) a decision of a Divisional Court of the Queen's Bench Division in a criminal cause or matter {Administration of Justice Act 1960 s 1(1)(a).} or (2) a 'leapfrogging appeal'. {As to these see above.} The House also has certain other appellate powers, for example from courts in Northern Ireland.

The leave of the court below or the House of Lords is required for appeals to that House. {Administration of Justice (Appeals) Act 1934 s 1; Administration of Justice Act 1960 s 1(2); Criminal Appeal Act 1968 s 33(2).} In the case of criminal appeals, leave is given only where the court below certifies that a point of law of general public importance is involved and it appears to that court or to the House of Lords that the point is one that ought to be considered by that House. {Administration of Justice Act 1960 s 1(2); Criminal Appeal Act 1968 s 33(2).}

Section 4 of the Appellate Jurisdiction Act 1876 provides that-

'Every appeal shall be brought by way of petition to the House of
Lords, praying that the matter of the order or judgment appealed
against may be reviewed before Her Majesty the Queen in her Court
of Parliament, in order that the said Court may determine *what of
right, and according to the law and custom of this realm, ought to be done
in the subject-matter of such appeal.*'

{Emphasis added.}
This is a rare example of an attempt by Parliament to spell out the nature of the
function exercised in administering the judicial power of the state. Note that the
appeal is recognised to be in reality to *the High Court of Parliament*. This follows
the early common-law doctrine laid down in *Prohibitions del Roy* {(1607) 12 Co
Rep 63.} that, while the Monarch cannot sit at first instance-

'. . . the King hath his Court, viz in the Upper House of Parliament,
in which he with his Lords is the supreme Judge over all other
Judges; for if error be in the Common Pleas, that may be reversed in
the King's Bench; and if the Court of King's Bench err, that may be
reversed in the Upper House of Parliament, by the King, with the
assent of the Lords Spiritual and Temporal, without the Commons:
and in this respect the King is called the Chief Justice . . .'

Appeals to the House of Lords are nowadays heard only by law lords. Section
5 of the Appellate Jurisdiction Act 1876 describes these as comprising the Lord
Chancellor, the Lords of Appeal in Ordinary and such peers of Parliament as
hold or have held 'high judicial office'. {For the meaning of this expression see
Appellate Jurisdiction Act 1876 s 25 as amended by the Appellate Jurisdiction
Act 1887 s 5.} Other peers have not exercised their theoretical right to sit since
the case of *Bradlaugh v Clarke*. {(1883) 8 App Cas 354. See also *O'Connell's Case*
(1844) 11 Cl & Fin 155 and the House of Lords debate reported in 2 Macqueen's
Rep 577 (1856).}
It is accepted that the House of Lords has a wide-ranging function of
overseeing the working of the law. While a lower court might shrink from
declaring some long-standing construction or practice incorrect, the House of
Lords takes a larger view.

Example 3 Considering the power conferred on a constable by s 2(4) of the
Criminal Law Act 1967 to arrest without warrant anyone whom, with
reasonable cause, he suspects to have committed an arrestable offence, Latey J
said that by implication Parliament had left it to the courts to impose fetters on
this power if they thought right. He went on to say that where powers of arrest
had for a long period been exercised to obtain evidence it would not be right for
the courts 'at any rate below the level of the House of Lords' to impose a fetter
on them. {*Mohammed-Holgate v Duke* [1983] 3 All ER 526, at p 534.}
Until 1966 the House of Lords was bound by its own previous decisions, on
the ground that they established the law in such a way as to be binding on all
subjects including their Lordships. {*London Street Tramways Co Ltd v London
County Council* [1898] AC 375; *Radcliffe v Ribble Motor Services* [1939] AC
215.} On 26 July 1966 the Lord Chancellor announced that this rule would no
longer be followed. He said that while precedent is an indispensable foundation,
providing certainty and a basis for orderly legal development, it must not be

allowed to cause injustice or unduly restrict proper development of the law. {[1966] 1 WLR 1234; [1966] 3 All ER 77.}

Judicial Committee of the Privy Council The Judicial Committee of the Privy Council is constituted under the Judicial Committee Act 1833 as amended, and when sitting consists mostly of law lords. Its main jurisdiction is in relation to appeals from Commonwealth and colonial courts. It also hears appeals from decisions of professional disciplinary bodies. {See, e g, Medical Act 1956 s 36(3); Dentists Act 1957 ss 29(1) and 40(4); Opticians Act 1958 s 14(1); Professions Supplementary to Medicine Act 1960 s 9(3); Veterinary Surgeons Act 1966 s 17(1); Medical Act 1978 s 11(6).}

The Judicial Committee of the Privy Council has jurisdiction to hear appeals against pastoral schemes {Pastoral Measure 1968 s 96(3).} and from the Arches Court of Canterbury and the Chancery Court of York. {Ecclesiastical Jurisdiction Measure 1963 s 8.} Its jurisdiction to hear and determine a suit of *duplex querela* was in 1963 transferred to the Court of Ecclesiastical Causes reserved. {Ecclesiastical Jurisdiction Measure 1963 ss 10(1)(b) and 82(1).}

24. Enforcement agencies: judicial review

On judicial review of a matter concerned with public law, the High Court may make an order of mandamus, prohibition or certiorari. Or the High Court may, in lieu of such an order, make a declaration, or grant an injunction. In certain circumstances, damages may be awarded. The High Court may also on judicial review grant an injunction in the nature of quo warranto in respect of a public office.

COMMENTARY

This section of the Code outlines the effect of s 31(1) of the Supreme Court Act 1981. The remaining subsections of s 31, together with the provisions of RSC Ord 53, set out the detailed rules governing judicial review. This is carried out mainly through what are called prerogative orders.

We now give a brief summary of the mechanism underlying the public law remedy which operates by the use of these prerogative orders. The substance of the remedy, concerning the way decisions under statutory powers are arrived at, is dealt with later. {See s 335 of this Code. As to enactments purporting to oust or curtail judicial review see pp 747–750 below.}

The primary purpose of judicial review, and the recent increase in its importance, are indicated in a 1981 dictum of Lord Roskill {*IRC v National Federation of Self-Employed and Small Businesses Ltd* [1981] 2 WLR 722, at p 751.}-

> ' . . . in the last thirty years, no doubt because of the growth of central and local government intervention in the affairs of the ordinary citizen since the 1939–45 war, and the consequent increase in the number of administrative bodies charged by Parliament with the performance of public duties, the use of prerogative orders to check a usurpation of power by such bodies to the disadvantage of the

ordinary citizen, or to insist on due performance by such bodies of their statutory duties and to maintain due adherence to the laws enacted by Parliament, has greatly increased.'

On judicial review the High Court exercises 'a supervisory and not an appellate jurisdiction', and its approach is necessarily different from its approach when acting as a court of appeal. {*Pickwell v Camden LBC* {[1983] 1 All ER 602, *per* Forbes J at p 612.}

The making of a prerogative order is discretionary {*O'Reilly v Mackman* [1982] 3 All ER 1124, *per* Lord Diplock at p 1133.}; and it will not be made where the Act in question provides its own form of remedy. In such cases, the High Court requires a complainant to use the specific statutory remedy rather than applying for a prerogative order. {*R v Registrar of Joint Stock Companies* (1888) 21 QBD 131; *Cumings v Birkenhead Corpn* [1972] Ch 12; *R v Powys County Council, ex p Smith* (1982) *The Times* 16 June.} It seems that this rule does not apply to prohibition. {*Channel Coaling Co v Ross* [1907] 1 KB 145.} The fact that the time laid down by the Act for performance of the duty in question has elapsed will not preclude relief. {*Stepney BC v John Walker & Sons Ltd* [1934] AC 365.}

The general supervisory jurisdiction of the High Court on judicial review is based on what is called the *Wednesbury* principle. {*Norwich City Council v Secretary of State for the Environment* [1982] 1 All ER 737, at p 749; *Pickwell v Camden LBC* [1983] 1 All ER 602, at p 612. As to the *Wednesbury* principle see p 69ff below.} Under this name, the principle applies only in matters of administrative law or public law (as opposed to private law). {*O'Reilly v Mackman* [1982] 3 All ER 1124; *Davy v Spellthorne BC* [1983] 3 All ER 278; *Tsai v Woodworth* (1983) *The Times* 30 November.} However the principle appears in other areas of law; for example, a similar supervisory jurisdiction is exercised by the High Court in appeals from magistrates' courts by way of case stated. {*Bracegirdle v Oxley* [1947] 1 KB 349.}

The distinction between public and private law was explained by Lord Wilberforce in *Davy v Spellthorne BC* {[1983] 3 All ER 278, at p 285}, which concerned the problems that may arise when both public law and private law elements are present in a case-

> 'The expressions "private law" and "public law" have recently been imported into the law of England from countries which, unlike our own, have separate systems concerning public law and private law. No doubt they are convenient expressions for descriptive purposes. In this country they must be used with caution, for, typically, English law fastens not on principles but on remedies. The principle remains intact that public authorities and public servants are, unless clearly exempted, answerable in the ordinary courts for wrongs done to individuals. But by an extension of remedies and flexible procedure it can be said that something resembling a system of public law is being developed.'

Although judicial review is a public-law remedy, this does not preclude its being available for the enforcement of a duty imposed by a private Act. {*R v London & North-Western Rly* [1899] 1 QB 921.}

The sanction for disobedience to a prerogative order is attachment, or fining,

for contempt of court. A civil action for damages may also lie at the suit of any party injured. Lord Diplock has said that judicial statements on matters of public law, if the statements were made before 1950, are likely to be misleading in modern conditions. {*IRC v National Federation of Self-Employed and Small Businesses Ltd* [1981] 2 WLR 722, at p 736.}

The Wednesbury principle In *Associated Provincial Picture Houses Ltd v Wednesbury Corporation* {[1948] 1 KB 223.} a local authority had power under s 1(1) of the Sunday Entertainments Act 1932 to grant Sunday cinema licences under the Cinematograph Act 1909 'subject to such conditions as the authority think fit to impose'. The local authority decided to impose a condition that no child under fifteen should be admitted to a cinema on a Sunday. The condition was challenged as unreasonable and/or ultra vires. *Held* The authority had not acted unreasonably or ultra vires in imposing the condition.

What has become known as the *Wednesbury* principle is stated in the following passages from the judgment of Lord Greene MR (Pp 228-230.}-

> ' ... first, we are dealing with not a judicial act, but an executive act {In fact the principle is applied both to judicial and executive acts.}; secondly, the conditions which, under the exercise of that executive act, may be imposed are in terms, so far as language goes, put within the discretion of the local authority without limitation ... It is not to be assumed prima facie that responsible bodies like the local authority in this case will exceed their powers; but the court, whenever it is alleged that the local authority have contravened the law, *must not substitute itself for that authority* ... a person entrusted with a discretion must, so to speak, *direct himself properly in law*. He must call his own attention to the matters which he is bound to consider. He must exclude from his consideration matters which are irrelevant to what he has to consider ... if a decision on a competent matter is so unreasonable that *no reasonable authority could ever have come to it*, then the courts can interfere ... It is not what the court considers unreasonable, *a different thing altogether*.'

{Emphasis added.}

It should be added for completeness that this dictum applies not only to a positive decision which is 'unreasonable' in this special sense, but to a decision *not* to act which is similarly unreasonable. Either way, the feature is what amounts to a failure by the decision-making authority to carry out the function which Parliament has entrusted to it. The reviewing court is not to say that it would have decided differently: Parliament has not appointed it to take the decision. The function of the reviewing court is to pronounce whether, in a realistic sense, the enforcement agency has or has not carried out its statutory task.

The term 'judicial review' was formally applied to this type of procedure only when it was introduced by rules of court in 1977. Under the procedure, an applicant for relief is not (as hitherto) defeated because he has asked for the wrong remedy. {See *IRC v National Federation of Self-Employed and Small Businesses Ltd* [1982] AC 617, *per* Lord Scarman at pp 647-648.} By applying for 'judicial review' overall, he is treated as asking for whichever of the prerogative orders or other remedies may be found by the High Court to be appropriate on the facts of his case as proved.

This 1977 reform drastically ameliorated the position of applicants for prerogative orders. It removed the disadvantages, particularly in relation to discovery, which previously made this an inadequate remedy. {*O'Reilly v Mackman* [1982] 3 All ER 1124, *per* Lord Diplock at p 1134.}

The three leading remedies available on judicial review are mandamus, prohibition and certiorari, the latter two being available only against an inferior court, tribunal or other body which acts *judicially*. {As to the meaning of this concept see commentary on s 335 of the Code.} We now look at these remedies in turn.

Mandamus   The writ of mandamus (from the Latin, 'we command') was a prerogative writ which, as finally developed, became an original writ issuable out of the Crown side of the King's Bench wherever the applicant had a legal right arising out of the public status of the respondent, but no other specific remedy. {*Bagg's Case* (1615) 11 Co Rep 93b; *Benson v Paull* (1856) 6 E & B 273.} It commanded the respondent to satisfy the right.

Section 7(1) of the Administration of Justice (Miscellaneous Provisions) Act 1938 said that the prerogative writ of mandamus should no longer be issued by the High Court. Instead, s 7(2) of the Act provided that in any case where the High Court would have had jurisdiction to order the issue of a *writ* of mandamus requiring any act to be done it might make an *order* of mandamus requiring it to be done.

These provisions of the 1938 Act were repealed by the Supreme Court Act 1981. {S 152(4) and Sch 7.} In their place, the 1981 Act, by a piece of archival drafting {As to archival drafting see s 286 of this Code.}, gave the High Court power to make orders of mandamus 'in those classes of cases in which it had power to do so immediately before the commencement of this Act'. {S 29(1).}

The unsatisfactory nature of archival drafting is shown by the fact that the courts are steadily widening their power to make prerogative orders, so that the power does not in fact remain what it was at an earlier period. For example the former strict rules regarding such matters as locus standi and the nature of the court record have been greatly relaxed. {*IRC v National Federation of Self-Employed and Small Businesses Ltd* [1981] 2 WLR 722, *per* Lord Roskill at p 751.}

Prerogative orders of mandamus have frequently been issued to compel performance of public-law duties imposed by statute. For example: to compel tax commissioners to repay tax overpaid {*R v Commrs for the Special Purposes of the Income Tax Acts* (1888) 21 QBD 313.}; to order an education authority to pay teachers on a proper basis {*Board of Education v Rice* [1911] AC 179.}; to require a local authority to levy a rate and satisfy a precept {*R v Poplar Metropolitan BC (No 2)* [1922] 1 KB 95.}; to order a licensing committee to hear and determine an application under the Theatres Act 1843 {*R v Flint County Council Licensing Committee, ex p Barrett* [1957] 1 QB 350.}; to compel a housing authority to serve statutory notices to quit where a demolition order has become operative. {*R v Epsom and Ewell Corpn, ex p R B Property Investments (Eastern) Ltd* [1964] 1 WLR 1060.}

Obviously mandamus will not lie unless there is really a statutory duty as alleged. Thus in *R v Great Western Railway Company* {(1893) 69 LT 572.} an application to require the company to keep a track in repair failed when it was held that on the true construction of the enactment the company was empowered but not compelled to lay down and maintain the track.

Prohibition The old prerogative writ of prohibition issued out of the King's Bench, Chancery, Exchequer or Common Pleas. Its purpose was to prevent an inferior court from acting in excess of jurisdiction, or without any jurisdiction at all. Its ambit was much the same as that of certiorari, the practical difference being that prohibition lay up to the point when the inferior court made its order and certiorari thereafter.

The main targets of prohibition in earlier times were the ecclesiastical courts. {*R v Chancellor of St Edmundsbury and Ipswich Diocese* [1948] 1 KB 195.} In modern times prohibition was extended to 'judicial' functions of administrative bodies. {*R v Electricity Commrs, ex p London Electricity Joint Committee* [1924] 1 KB 171 (writ of prohibition issued to prevent holding of public inquiry to consider invalid scheme); see also *Estate & Trust Agencies (1927) Ltd v Singapore Improvement Trust* [1937] AC 898.} The fact that the enactment provides for a decision to be confirmed by Parliament or any other body does not preclude prohibition while the confirmation is pending. {*R v Electricity Commrs, ex p London Electricity Joint Committee* [1924] 1 KB 171, *per* Atkin LJ at p 198. The judgment of Atkin LJ contains a full historical treatment of prohibition and certiorari.}

Section 7(1) of the Administration of Justice (Miscellaneous Provisions) Act 1938 provided that the prerogative writ of prohibition should no longer be issued by the High Court. Instead, s 7(2) of the Act provided that in any case where the High Court would have had jurisdiction to order the issue of a *writ* of prohibition prohibiting any proceedings or matter it might make an *order* of prohibition prohibiting the proceedings or matter.

These provisions of the 1938 Act were repealed by the Supreme Court Act 1981. {S 152(4) and Sch 7.} In their place, the 1981 Act, by a piece of archival drafting {Archival drafting is explained in s 286 of the Code. As to its unsatisfactory nature in relation to prerogative orders see p 70 above.}, gave the High Court power to make orders of certiorari 'in those classes of cases in which it had power to do so immediately before the commencement of this Act'. {S 29(1).}

Certiorari The prerogative writ of certiorari (from the Latin 'to be more fully informed (or made certain) of') was the pre-eminent supervisory instrument. It issued only out of the Crown side of the King's Bench, though there was an analogous procedure, known as the bill of certiorari, in Chancery matters.

The writ of certiorari commanded judges or officers of inferior courts to certify or return, by what was known as a 'speaking order', the records of a cause in their courts, to the end that justice might be done. On inspection of this the superior court might quash the record, for example for error of law on its face {*R v Northumberland Compensation Appeal Tribunal* [1952] 1 KB 338; *R v Southampton JJ, ex p Green* [1976] QB 11; *R v Greater Birmingham Supplementary Benefit Appeal Tribunal, ex p Khan* [1979] 3 All ER 759; *R v Crown Court at Knightsbridge, ex p International Sporting Club (London) Ltd* [1981] 3 All ER 417.}, or excess of jurisdiction {*R v Licensing Authority for Goods Vehicles for the Metropolitan Traffic Area, ex p B E Barrett Ltd* [1949] 2

KB 17; *R v Blundeston Prison Board of Visitors, ex p Fox-Taylor* [1982] 1 All ER 646.}, or want of natural justice. {As to natural justice see pp 730–731 and 741–743 below.} It seems that even where an order has, in accordance with the empowering enactment, been approved by each House of Parliament it may still be subject to certiorari. {*R v Electricity Commrs, ex p London Electricity Joint Committee* [1924] 1 KB 171.} Except as provided by an enactment, such resolutions have no legislative effect. {See p 99 below.}

Section 7(1) of the Administration of Justice (Miscellaneous Provisions) Act 1938 provided that the prerogative writ of certiorari should no longer be issued by the High Court. Instead, s 7(2) of the Act provided that in any case where the High Court would have had jurisdiction to order the issue of a *writ* of certiorari removing any proceedings or matter into the High Court or any division thereof for any purpose it might make an *order* of certiorari removing the proceedings or matter.

These provisions of the 1938 Act were repealed by the Supreme Court Act 1981. {S 152(4) and Sch 7.} In their place, the 1981 Act, by a piece of archival drafting {Archival drafting is explained in s 286 of the Code. As to its unsatisfactory nature in relation to prerogative orders see p 70 above.}, gave the High Court power to make orders of prohibition 'in those classes of cases in which it had power to do so immediately before the commencement of this Act'. {S 29(1).}

Declaration or injunction   Section 31(2) of the Supreme Court Act 1981 provides that on an application for judicial review the High Court, where it appears 'just and convenient', may make a declaration, or grant an injunction, instead of making an order of mandamus, prohibition or certiorari. The meaning of this phrase was thus explained by Lord Scarman-

' . . . the application for judicial review, where a declaration, an injunction or damages {Damages can be awarded on judicial review where these could have been obtained if the matter had been raised by action: Supreme Court Act 1981 s 31(4).} are sought, is a summary way of obtaining a remedy which could be obtained at trial in an action begun by writ; and it is available only where in all the circumstances it is just and convenient. If issues of fact, or law and fact, are raised which it is neither just nor convenient to decide without the full trial process, the court may dismiss the application or order, in effect, a trial.'

{*IRC v Rossminster Ltd* [1980] AC 952, at p 1025.}

As to the last sentence of this dictum, it should be noticed that the High Court can in effect require the applicant to proceed (if at all) by writ if it refuses leave to make the application for judicial review. {Such leave is required by the Supreme Court Act 1981 s 31(3).} On the other hand, proceeding by writ may be held an abuse of the process of the court if the matter concerns public law and judicial review is the appropriate remedy because, for example, speed is required in the public interest. {*O'Reilly v Mackman* [1982] 3 All ER 1124, at p 1133.}

Nevertheless, the fact that a person could have challenged an act or omission by judicial review does not preclude him from relying on its nullity or illegality in other proceedings.

Example 1 In *R v Jenner* {[1983] 2 All ER 46.} the accused was convicted of failing to comply with a stop notice issued under s 90(1) of the Town and Country Planning Act 1971. This prohibited him from parking lorries, tipping rubbish, and carrying out other specified activities on certain land. At his trial the accused sought to show that the stop notice was invalid as contravening the requirement of s 90(2) of the Act that a stop notice should not prohibit activities begun more than twelve months earlier.

The trial judge ruled that the proper way of challenging a stop notice was by judicial review, and disallowed this defence. The accused appealed. *Held* The fact that no steps had been taken to quash the stop notice on judicial review did not mean that it could not be challenged in other proceedings in which the question of its validity or otherwise was material.

Where it deems it sufficient to declare the law in question, rather than making an order carrying the sanction of punishment for contempt of court, the High Court, on an application for judicial review, will content itself with making a declaration. If it does so, the declaration must be in terms which resolve the question of law at issue. However the court may state the grounds for the decision in the alternative, thus leaving the detail of the law to some extent uncertain. {See, e g, *R v Secretary of State for the Environment, ex p Greater London Council* (1983) *The Times* 2 December.} This is obviously unsatisfactory from the point of view of the use of the decision as a precedent. {As to processing of enactments by the court see s 26 of this Code.}

Quo warranto It is a noble, as well as an ancient, challenge to cry Quo warranto? By what right do you exercise this power? Power without right is tyranny. Yet right itself may be equivocal, as it was when Edward I established the old writ of *Quo warranto*. The Statute of Gloucester 1278 empowered the king to enquire by what right former royal estates, or exceptional franchises which infringed the royal prerogative of justice or taxation, were exercised by their present owners. To be legitimate, the right could only have been granted by royal charter or warrant. No such justification was possessed by the usurping barons who presumed on the weakness of John or Henry III.

It became accepted that the onus lay on the defendant to show that he had a right to exercise an office, franchise, liberty or privilege belonging to the Crown. The high prerogative writ of quo warranto also lay for neglect or misuse of a Crown office. Where the Crown succeeded, judgment of forfeiture or ousterlemain was given. The writ inquired by what right or authority the respondent supported his claim. {J Chitty jun *Prerogatives of the Crown* (1820) p 336.}

The writ was superseded by informations in the nature of quo warranto, which were in turn abolished by s 9 of the Administration of Justice (Miscellaneous Provisions) Act 1938. This substituted a new procedure whereby application could be made for an injunction. This was nevertheless applied with the old law in mind.

Example 2 In *Barnard v National Dock Labour Board* {[1953] 2 QB 18.} the Court of Appeal held that the delegation by the London Dock Labour Board, a statutory body, of its disciplinary functions to a port manager was unlawful. The manager's purported suspension of workers was therefore a nullity. Denning LJ said {P 42.}-

> ' . . . we are not asked to interfere with the decision of a statutory tribunal; we are asked to interfere with the position of a usurper . . . These courts have always had a jurisdiction to deal with such a case. The common law courts had a regular course of proceeding by which they commanded such a person to show by what warrant - quo warranto - he did these things. Discovery could be had against him, and if he had no valid warrant, they ousted him by judgment of ouster . . . Side by side with the common law jurisdiction of quo warranto the courts of equity have always had power to declare the orders of a usurper to be invalid and to set them aside. So at the present day we can do likewise.'

The matter is now dealt with by ss 30 and 31(1)(c) of the Supreme Court Act 1981. These provide that, on an application for judicial review in a case where a person not entitled to do so acts in a public office, the High Court may grant an injunction restraining him from doing so, and may declare the office vacant. The offices in question are 'any substantive office of a public nature and permanent character which is held under the Crown or which has ben created by any statutory provision or royal charter'. {S 30(2). For meaning of 'statutory provision' see s 151(1).}

See also Example 181.2.

25. Enforcement agencies: executive agencies ancillary to adjudicating authorities

Adjudicating authorities are assisted by officials employed by executive enforcement agencies, such as court bailiffs and sheriffs' officers. The duty of these officials is to implement, in accordance with the enactments governing their functions, the orders made by the adjudicating authorities.

COMMENTARY

The concept of the enforcement of laws depends finally on the physical carrying into effect of the orders of the court. No interference with this can be allowed. As was said of such interference in a seventeenth-century case: 'It is a contempt to the court, and an attachment shall be granted; for it should not be in any one's power to defeat the rules of this court, or render them ineffectual'. {*Butler's Case* (1696) 2 Salk 596. See also *Rantzen v Rothschild* (1865) 13 LT 399; *Davis v Barlow* (1911) 18 WWR 239; *Hubbard v Woodfield* (1913) 57 Sol J 729; *Z Ltd v A and others* [1982] 1 All ER 556.}

Under our constitution, it is the function of the sheriff, as the chief officer of the Crown in every county, to see to the execution of all process issuing from the superior courts. {Kerr Bl (4th edn, 1876) i 307.} For this purpose under-sheriffs and bailiffs are appointed to carry out the physical task of enforcing obedience.

Blackstone wrote this of the bailiffs of his own time-

> ' . . . as these are generally plain men, and not thoroughly skilful in this latter part of their office, that of serving writs, and making

executions, it is now usual to join special bailiffs with them, who are generally mean persons employed by the sheriffs on account only of their adroitness and dexterity in hunting and seizing their prey. The sheriff being answerable for the misdemeanors of these bailiffs, they are therefore usually bound in an obligation with sureties for the due execution of their office, and thence are called bound-bailiffs, which the common people have corrupted into a much more homely appellation.'

{Kerr Bl (4th edn, 1876) i 308. The homely appellation is of course 'bum-bailiff', which the Oxford English Dictionary innocently defines as the bailiff that catches the debtor in the rear.}

All public officers charged with the duty of executing court judgments and orders are required to observe, and so where necessary construe, the enactments governing that function. {See, e g, Judgments Act 1838; Execution Act 1844; Sheriffs Act 1887; Administration of Justice Act 1956 Pt IV; Attachment of Earnings Act 1971.} Unlike the agencies described in the preceding sections of this Code, they are not however concerned with the application, and therefore the construction or interpretation, of legislation generally. Their importance in statutory interpretation is accordingly small.

26. Enforcement agencies: dynamic processing of legislation by

In so far as Parliament does not convey its intention clearly, expressly, and completely, it is taken to require the enforcement agencies who are charged with the duty of applying legislation to spell out the detail of its meaning.

This may be done either-

(a) by finding and declaring implications in the words used by the legislator, or

(b) by regarding the breadth or other obscurity of the express language as conferring a delegated legislative power to elaborate its meaning in accordance with public policy (including legal policy) and the purpose of the legislation.

Either way, the operation, referred to in this Code as the dynamic processing of the enactment, influences the future legal meaning of the enactment by producing what this Code refers to as sub-rules. In the production of sub-rules, the courts have a predominant role by virtue of the fact that other processors are placed under their authority.

COMMENTARY

This section of the Code outlines the two ways by which the meaning of an enactment may be elaborated by dynamic processing. They are described in more detail in ss 107 to 114 of this Code.

Without the force of precedent, justice would be at the caprice of the individual mind. {G Lewis *Lord Atkin* (Butterworths, 1983) p 171.} The final arbiter is the court, by virtue of its appellate and supervisory jurisdiction. The court is guided, and sometimes bound, by precedent. Kerr LJ said-

'The interpretation of the intention of Parliament as expressed in our statutes is a matter for the courts. Once the meaning of an Act of Parliament has been authoritatively interpreted, at any rate by the House of Lords at a judicial sitting as our highest tribunal, that interpretation is the law, unless and until it is thereafter changed by Parliament . . . This does not involve any substitution of the views of the judges on questions of policy or discretion for those of the authority concerned, but merely the interpretation of the will of Parliament as expressed in its enactments. Thereafter any change in the law from its definition by the courts again devolves to Parliament alone.'

{*R v London Transport Executive, ex p Greater London Council* [1983] 2 All ER 262, at p 267.}

This is the conventional view, but it understates the judicial role. Moreover it overlooks the fact that, by a policy announcement of the Lord Chancellor in 1966, the House of Lords has ceased to be bound by its own previous decisions. {[1966] 1 WLR 1234; [1966] 3 All ER 77. See p 66 above.}

The truth is that courts are inescapably possessed of some degree of legislative power. Enacted legislation lays down rules *in advance*. The commands of Parliament are deliberate prospective commands. The very concept of enacted legislation postulates an authoritative interpreter who operates ex post facto. No such interpreter can avoid legislating in the course of exercising his function. Vinogradoff expressed this truth in his *Common Sense in the Law* {(2nd edn 1946) p 106.}-

' . . . legislation as a source of law is inseperable from a process of interpretation by the Courts, which in itself amounts to a subordinate source of law. It is impossible to curtail the freedom of judges in analysing cases and applying general rules in ways not premeditated by the legislators . . . another factor asserts itself by the side of that of deliberate prospective commands, namely, the force of public opinion and of professional opinion as manifested in the action of judges. They are undoubtedly persons in authority, but their voice has a decisive weight in such questions not merely on account of this external authority, but chiefly by reason of the necessities imposed by logic, by moral and by practical considerations.'

Except in relation to the particular purpose of the Act under interpretation, Vinogradoff is here referring to what is known as public policy or legal policy. {See s 126 of this Code. Purposive construction is described in s 139 and Part XV.}

Judicial confirmation of this view is found in many judgments. Lord Cottenham LC goes farther, and acknowledges that judges even change plain meanings and apply a strained construction-

'It cannot be denied that in some cases the plain meaning of an Act of Parliament has been changed by a course of judicial decisions, each going a little and a little further, so that at length the courts have adopted a construction widely different from that which would, but for such interpretations, have been put upon the plain intent of the words. In all such cases you are to take into consideration, not merely the words of the Act of Parliament, but the decisions on them, *which may be said to have been all but imported into the words of the Act.'*

{*Earl of Waterford's Claim* (1832) 6 Cl & F 133, at p 172 (emphasis added). See also Examples 110.3 and 253.2. As to strained construction generally see ss 92 to 97 of this Code.}

Admittedly this was said in the days of equitable construction. {As to equitable construction see s 94 of this Code.} Nevertheless the italicised words still have an application today.

Often Parliament intentionally leaves large gaps to be filled in by the courts.

Example 1 In the Acts governing the licensing of premises for the sale of intoxicating liquor, nothing is said about the rules that are to apply in the obvious case where the licensee is physically absent from the premises during the permitted hours. As a result the courts have been obliged to supply the deficiency in a long line of cases. When the House of Lords was asked to arrive at a ruling which would in effect annul these decisions as precedents, Lord Reid said-

> 'One might have expected to find in the Licensing Acts some provisions regulating the position in the common case of a licence holder being absent from the premises during the permitted hours, but there appears to be none. So, if the courts have in effect legislated to fill the gap, I think we should leave matters as they are.'

{*Vane v Yiannopoulos* [1965] AC 486, at p 498.}

Pejorative meaning of 'interpretation' Attempts have often been made by law-givers to prevent the glossing of their edicts. Thus Justinian forbade under severe penalties all commentaries on his legislation. {Const Deo Auctore, sec 12; Const Tanta, sec 21.}

Pufendorf mentions the law of Bologna which enacted that whoever drew blood in the streets should be severely punished. The law went on to add that its words 'should be taken precisely, *without any interpretation*'. {Pufendorf, ed Kennett, *Of the Law of Nature and Nations* (4th edn, 1729) p 540 (emphasis added).} This, says Pufendorf, bore hardly on a barber who was indicted for innocently and humanely opening the vein of a sick person in the street.

In England a sixteenth-century meaning of 'interpretation' imported the notion of what was later called equitable construction. {See s 94 of this Code.} By this, the 'interpretation' of the text was equated to its corruption. {This view has been endorsed on the Statute Roll itself: see p 348 below.} Medieval lawyers justified corruption of the text by the argument that, as an enactment acquires formal rigidity, its words must be saved from ossification by judicial departures from the literal meaning. {As to the modern doctrine of updating construction see s 146 of this Code.} These departures were described by contemporaries as 'interpretations'. {See T F T Plucknett 'Ellesmere on Statutes' (1944) 60 LQR 242, at p 247.}

In 1794 the Prussian legal code *Allgemeines Landrecht* forbade recourse to learned opinion and precedent in its interpretation. {See C K Allen *Law in the Making* (4th edn, 1946) p 113.} In modern times the first republican constitution of Ghana was described by its draftsman as a 'mechanism' based on the assumption that words have a fixed and definite meaning. {See Bennion

Constitutional Law of Ghana (Butterworths 1962) p 111.} Such attempts to fortify the intention of the original legislator are vain, and invariably ineffective.

If the forbidding of 'interpretation' fails, legislators sometimes try statutory direction of the method by which it is to be done. Many American states included in their constitutions instructions on this point. Arizona, for example, enjoined that words and phrases contained in legislation 'shall be construed according to the common and approved use of the language'. {Ariz Rev Stat Ann (1955) 1.213: see D Mellinkoff *The Language of the Law* p 10. As to similar attempts in the British Commonwealth see Bennion *Statute Law* (2nd edn, 1983) pp 89-90.} Such efforts are likely to be equally vain.

Tacit parliamentary approval of processing Where Parliament does not intervene to reverse or modify processing effected by courts or officials it can be taken tacitly to approve it. As Professor Pearce has said: 'if a legislature has chosen not to make any change in an Act following upon its interpretation by the judiciary, it is strong ground for thinking that the legislature is satisfied wth the court's ruling'. {D C Pearce *Statutory Interpretation in Australia* (2nd edn, 1981) p 6. Cf the treatment of custom in H L A Hart *The Concept of Law* pp 45-8.}

For this principle of 'tacit legislation' to apply, a reasonable period must have elapsed after the processing within which Parliament might, if it chose, have legislated the other way. The point strengthens the validity of processing as in effect a function exercised under power impliedly delegated by the legislature. {For the position where Parliament re-enacts the processed enactment, for example in a consolidation Act, see p 515-517 below.}

This concept of 'tacit legislation' has been disputed. Yet its broad truth is simply demonstrated. If for any reason Parliament *strongly disapproves* of the law as currently laid down by an enactment (with or without processing) it will hastily take steps to change it.

For example an incoming government will procure the rapid reversal of contentious changes made by its predecessor. {As to party-political enactments see s 304 of this Code.} Or a sudden emergency will lead to very quick enactment of necessary measures. {It is not at all unusual for an urgent Act to pass through all its stages in both Houses of Parliament in one day.} Or a wholly unacceptable decision of the courts will speedily be reversed by legislation. {See, e g, s 72 of the Supreme Court Act 1981, reversing the decision of the House of Lords in *Rank Film Distributors Ltd v Video Information Centre* [1981] 2 All ER 76.}

If we find that Parliament invariably alters what it disapproves we may arrive at the following syllogism-

> *Parliament always changes laws it dislikes.*
> *Parliament does not change this law.*
> *Therefore Parliament does not dislike this law.*

A similar concept of 'tacit legislation' applies where an old Act is suffered to remain in force. {As to updating construction in such cases see s 146 of this Code. See further Example 93.5.}

Sub-rules Processing of enactments by enforcement agencies produces an elaboration of the literal meaning of the enactment. Under the doctrine of precedent, this elaboration may be of binding or merely persuasive authority.

When an Act is included in a codification, such elaboration of its meaning will to a greater or lesser extent be rendered by the codifier expressly. {As to codification see s 233 of this Code.} Where the court makes use of interstitial articulation in its judgments this too will verbalise the elaboration of the statutory language which is effected by the decision. {As to interstitial articulation by the court see s 114 of this Code.}

Whether verbalised in these ways or not, dynamic processing by the interpreter develops the law as laid down by Parliament. {See s 78 of this Code. For an extended discussion of dynamic procesing see Bennion *Statute Law* (2nd edn, 1983) Pt III.} It is also developed by formal delegated legislation. {Delegated legislation is dealt with in ss 50 to 70 of this Code.}

Unjustified production of sub-rules Courts sometimes elaborate a statutory concept unnecessarily. When a draftsman uses a familiar word by itself, he usually intends it to be given its unadorned normal meaning. In *R v Lawrence* {[1981] 1 All ER 974, at p 978.} Lord Hailsham protested against the criminal courts giving 'recklessly' a refined and detailed meaning. It is a word, he pointed out, that has been in ordinary use for over a thousand years and possesses no separate legal meaning.

Similarly Lord Morris of Borth-y-Gest said of 'self-defence' in *Palmer v R* {[1971] 1 All ER 1077, at p 1088.}-

'The defence of self-defence is one which can and will be readily understood by any jury. It is a straightforward conception. It involves no abstruse legal thought. It requires no set words by way of explanation. No formula need be employed in reference to it. Only common sense is needed for its understanding.'

PART II

The Text

Introduction to Part II   Having dealt in Part I with the interpreter, we now look at what he is to interpret. In turn we examine three kinds of legislative text, the Act of Parliament, the prerogative instrument, and delegated legislation.

We define an Act of Parliament (s 27), and describe the various types of Act (s 28). The interpreter's obvious need to understand the nature of what he is interpreting is spelt out (s 29). An Act operates in time, in relation to particular persons and matters, and territorially (s 30).

The uniquely overriding nature of an Act is then described (ss 31 to 33). Crown immunity is discussed (s 34). We embark on the validating procedure (ss 35 and 36). Royal assent is important because paradoxically it shows the true nature of what binds us (ss 37 to 42). Though little used, the Parliament Acts 1911 and 1949 demonstrate how the non-elected House of Lords is reconciled with democracy (ss 43 and 44).

The way the text of an Act is finally settled reveals a little-known residual function of the Crown (s 45). Publication of Acts is briefly surveyed (s 46). Finally we look at the possibility of challenging an Act's validity (s 47).

We deal only briefly with prerogative instruments, because of their diminished importance (ss 48 and 49). Made on the advice of Ministers, they are to be construed in much the same way as Acts. This illustrates the close relation between the executive and the legislature under our system.

Lastly we deal with delegated legislation. Apart from the need to bear always in mind the enabling Act, this again is construed in much the same way as primary legislation.

After considering the nature of delegated legislation (s 50), and the control over it retained by Parliament (s 51), we look at the different types of delegate (ss 52 to 56). The delegate has a duty to act (s 57), but must not exceed his powers (s 58). The rule of primary intention directs our scrutiny to the *purpose* of the enabling Act (s 59). Other principles of interpreting delegated legislation are discussed (s 60).

Then follows a discussion of the various types of delegated instrument (ss 61 to 66). Sub-delegation is explained (s 67). The treatment of delegated legislation ends with commencement, amendment and revocation (ss 68 to 70).

ACTS OF PARLIAMENT

27. Act of Parliament: definition

An Act of the United Kingdom Parliament (in this Code referred to as an Act) is a *law* made by the Queen in Parliament, that is to say enacted by the Queen's most Excellent Majesty by and with the advice and consent of the Commons and (except where the Act is passed under the

Parliament Acts 1911 and 1949) the Lords Spiritual and Temporal, in Parliament assembled.

Subject to the provisions of any Act, the procedure by which this threefold consent is arrived at, signified and communicated is a matter for internal regulation by Parliament alone.

COMMENTARY

The text to be construed, so far as concerns the principles of statutory interpretation, is that either of an Act of Parliament or of a legislative instrument brought forth under the authority of an Act or by virtue of the prerogative. {See ss 50 to 70 of this Code (delegated legislation) and ss 48 and 49 (prerogative instruments). The interpretative criteria are the same for all these. {As to the interpretative criteria, or guides to legislative intention, see Part VI of this Code.}

We begin with the Act of Parliament, which furnishes the paradigm text. The definition of an Act is necessarily drawn from constitutional law. In a country such as Britain, lacking a written constitution, that means the law accepted by the courts as fundamental. For our courts, acceptance of the need for threefold consent is rooted in a judicial history continuous since the Norman Conquest. Coke said in his *Institutes*-

> 'There is no act of parliament but must have the consent of the lords, the commons, and the royal assent of the king, and as it appeareth by records and our books, whatsoever passeth in parliament by this threefold consent, hath the force of an act of parliament.'

{4 Co Inst 24.}

Coke also said that a purported Act 'penned *that the king with the assent of the Lords* . . . or *that the king with the assent of the commons* . . .' is no Act of Parliament. {*The Prince's Case* (1606) 8 Co Rep 1a, at p 13b.

The first statute of the Parliament of England was the Statute of Merton 1235. The doctrine of threefold consent requiring a Bill to be passed by both Houses and then given royal assent before it could be classed as an Act was not established at the time of the earliest statutes, some of which remain in force. One of the latter is Magna Carta, first signed by John in 1215 and confirmed some thirty-eight times before the close of the Middle Ages. {Halsbury's *Statutes of England* (3rd edn) vi 389.}

The doctrine of threefold consent was firmly established by the end of the thirteenth century, as evidenced by the statute Revocatio Novarum Ordinationum. {15 Edw 2 (1322).} The statute enacted that-

> ' . . . the matters which are to be established for the estate of our lord the King and of his heirs, and for the estate of the realm and of the people, shall be treated, accorded and established in Parliaments, by our lord the King, and by the assent of the prelates, earls, and barons, and the commonalty of the realm; *according as it hath been heretofore accustomed.*'

{Emphasis added.} See further ss 37 and 47 of this Code.

The assemblies giving consent to a Bill must be validly constituted, that is summoned by the Monarch. Doubts as to whether the assemblies of Lords and Commons meeting in 1688 without regal summons constituted valid Houses of Parliament were set at rest by subsequent legislation. {1 Will & Mar c 1, s 1 (1688); Crown and Parliament Recognition Act 1689.} This might seem a question-begging procedure, but illegality firmly enough prevailing falls to be treated as legality. What before passed as legality is then consigned to history.

It is an offence to take part in the proceedings of a body other than Parliament which (necessarily falsely) purports to assume any function of Parliament. {Convention (Ireland) Act Repeal Act 1879.}

Even in recent times courts have occasionally been asked to decide whether an ancient statute was validly enacted.

Example 1 In *Swaffer v Mulcahy* {[1934] 1 KB 608.} this task was placed upon MacKinnon J in relation to the *Estatuz del Eschekere*, of uncertain date. The learned judge found himself able to avoid resolving a difficult historical conundrum. He held that, even if the alleged statute was not valid as an Act of Parliament, it was nevertheless declaratory of the common law. {See also *Merttens v Hill* [1901] 1 Ch 842. Challenges to validity are dealt with in the following sections of this Code: s 47 (Acts of Parliament) and s 75 (enactments).}

Evidence of threefold consent In the absence of convincing evidence that what purports to have been done by either House of Parliament was in fact not done, the record of the Journals of the relevant House must be taken as conclusive. Where such opposing evidence is adduced, the court will consider it in the light of the rules of parliamentary procedure. {As to judicial notice of parliamentary procedure see *Garbutt v Durham Joint Committee* [1906] AC 291, at p 297, *per* Lord James.}

The Journals are published annually. By the Evidence Act 1845 s 3, copies of the Journals purporting to be printed by the printers to the Crown or either House are to be admitted as evidence in any court. {The Act does not extend to Scotland: s 5.} The Documentary Evidence Act 1882 s 2 extends this to printing by Her Majesty's Stationery Office, by whom the Journals are nowadays published. See further s 47 of this Code.

Control over procedure The authority for stating that parliamentary procedure is not open to challenge elsewhere is primarily the Bill of Rights 1688. This declares that 'proceedings in Parliament ought not to be impeached or questioned in any court or place out of Parliament'. {1 Will & Mar sess 2 c 2.} The rights of Parliament in this respect are not confined to those set out in the Bill of Rights, but go wider. {Erskine May *The Law, Privileges, Proceedings and Usage of Parliament* (20th edn, 1983), p 80.}

It is a long-recognised principle that each House has exclusive control over its own proceedings. {*Ibid*, p 77. See also *Bradlaugh v Gossett* (1884) 12 QBD 271; *Bilston Corpn v Wolverhampton Corpn* [1942] Ch 91; *Harper v Home Secretary* [1955] Ch 238. See also the Australian case of *Clayton v Heffron* (1960) 34 ALJR 378.} It follows from the principle of exclusive control, says Erskine May, that—

' . . . either House may vary its own peculiar forms, without question elsewhere, and without affecting the validity of any Act which has received, *in proper form*, the ultimate sanction of the three branches of the legislature.'

{P 606. Emphasis added.}

The words 'in proper form' appear to beg the question, but are presumed to refer to the form considered proper by Parliament itself rather than anyone else. The control of each House over its own procedure is of course subject to specific provisions in any Act of Parliament. {For an example of such provisions see Statutory Orders (Special Procedure) Act 1945 s 6.} Remarks outside Parliament slighting an order of either House may constitute a breach of privilege. {Erskine May *Loc cit* p 154.}

Types of Act   For the distinction between public general Acts and private (that is local or personal) Acts see s 28 of this Code.

Meaning of 'statute'   The term statute has no precise meaning in English law, but in current practice is used interchangeably with public general Act. It did not come into common use until towards the end of the thirteenth century. {H G Richardson and G Sayles 'The Early Statutes' (1934) 50 LQR 201.}

In early times, before the rise of regular parliaments, the term statute was applied to formal pronouncements of a legislative character by the king, usually in conjunction with his council. It derives from the Latin *statutum*, meaning a decree, decision or law, though the term was not used as a substantive in classical Latin. {H G Richardson and G Sayles 'The Early Statutes' (1934) 50 LQR 201 note 1.}

Sir Carleton Allen has given us the following description of early statutes-

'Sometimes they seem to have proceeded from the monarch himself and sometimes they were the solemn act of the King on the advice of his Council; they might be imperative, or declaratory, general or local, or even in the form of a grant, confirmation or resolution rather than of a sovereign command. They were, in short, simply decrees of the central government, undoubtedly of great force and authority, but of no uniform pattern and of no clearly defined scope; nor could they be otherwise, for, as we have seen, there was at this period no mature conception of a distribution of powers and a monarch had to keep order in his realm as best he could.'

{*Law and Orders* (1945) p 19.}

The fact was that in the first period after the Norman Conquest no distinction was drawn between executive or administrative pronouncements and those of a legislative character. This is characteristic of primitive and unsettled societies. Legislation supposes order, and some continuity of institutions.

So we find that in Norman England various central decrees were promulgated. These might be called statutes. Equally they might be given other names, such as *provisions, constitutions, graces, assizes, etablissements, ordinances, charters, writs,* or *dicta.*

Gradually the idea of legislation by Parliament developed, and the term *statute* was applied to this. In the seventeenth century we find Hobbes saying that the positive laws of all places are statutes. {T Hobbes *Dialogue of the Common Laws* (1681) p 30.} The word statute is used to denote fundamental law, whether of God or man. Thus Coverdale translates verse 12 of the 118th psalm as 'Praysed be thou O Lorde, O teach me thy statutes'. In the eighteenth century Blackstone refers to statutes as including all *leges scriptae,* or written laws of the kingdom. {Kerr Bl (4th edn 1876) i 60.}

The term *statute law* is used to denote either (a) the law contained in statutory form, whether in Acts or delegated legislation, or (b) the law governing the enactment, operation, interpretation and enforcement of statutes. The phrase 'by the statute' was anciently used to denote a measure, price or rate fixed by one of the statutes of the realm. An indictment for an offence created by Act formerly charged it as having been committed 'against the form of the statute in such case made and provided'. {C S Kenny *Outlines of Criminal Law* (15th edn, 1946) p 625.}

A parliamentary Bill is not a statute. {*Willow Wren Canal Carrying Co Ltd v British Transport Commission* [1956] 1 WLR 213.} Yet it may have some relevance in law. {See pp 99–100 below.}

28. Act of Parliament: types of

Acts can be classified in various ways, though the interpretative criteria are virtually the same for all. The main distinction is between public general Acts and private (that is local or personal) Acts. Another distinction is between permanent and temporary Acts.

The following categories of public general Act have special characteristics: law reform Acts (of which particular varieties are consolidation Acts, codification Acts, declaratory Acts and Statute Law Reform Acts), technical financial Acts (consisting of Appropriation Acts and Consolidated Fund Acts), adoptive Acts (including clauses Acts) and indemnity Acts.

COMMENTARY

Acts of the United Kingdom Parliament, whilst all equally possessing the overriding character arising from the doctrine of parliamentary supremacy {See s 31 of this Code.}, may be classified in various ways. Certain distinctions formerly employed (for example between 'remedial' Acts and others) are no longer useful.

Public general Acts Public general Acts are so called not because they necessarily extend to the whole country but because they are of importance to the community generally. {*R v London County Council* [1893] 2 QB 454, *per* Bowen LJ at p 462. As to the territorial extent of Acts see ss 195 to 220 of this Code.} Public general Acts are the main vehicle of legislation. They are far more important than private Acts, which are given chapter numbers in two separate series. {See s 278 of this Code.} Public general Acts are published by Her Majesty's Stationery Office both individually and in annual volumes. {See p 121 below.}

The decision to number and publish an Act in the series of public general Acts is taken by reference to its Parliamentary history, that is to its having been introduced and passed under the procedure applicable to public Bills. {As to this procedure see Erskine May *The Law, Privileges, Proceedings and Usage of*

Parliament (20th edn, 1983) chap XXII.} A public general Act results from a public Bill, that is one introduced by a member of the House of Commons or the House of Lords. A public Bill goes through various stages in each House of Parliament, always under the wing of a member of that House. {For the procedure see s 36 of this Code.} If at any stage no member can be found who is interested in taking it forward, the Bill drops.

A Bill introduced as a public Bill does not lose that character by reason of the fact that, because of its 'hybridity' the standing orders relating to private business are found also to apply to it. {Erskine May *The Law, Privileges, Proceedings and Usage of Parliament* (20th edn, 1983) p 588.} An Act of this kind may be said to be both public and private. {*Ingram v Foot* (1701) 12 Mod Rep 611.}

Private Acts   A private Act is one coming into existence on the giving of royal assent to a private Bill, that is one founded upon a petition deposited by the promoter (who may be anyone *except* a member of the House of Commons or the House of Lords).

A private Bill goes through a procedure different to that of a public Bill. It must be advertised, and its promoter must satisfy a parliamentary committee that it deserves to be enacted. It changes the law in a limited way purely for the benefit of its promoter; and Parliament has to make sure no one else will be unfairly prejudiced by it. Usually the promoter appears by counsel, a member of the Parliamentary Bar instructed by Parliamentary agents. This is a vestige of the ancient idea that a Bill is a petition presented to the king in Parliament by his subjects, craving some benefit. Except for these differences, the procedure relating to public Bills applies in the same way to private Bills.

Under modern practice private Acts are published, in the same way as public general Acts (though in a different series), by Her Majesty's Stationery Office. This enables personal Acts, which are not judicially noticed, to be proved simply by production of the HMSO print. {Evidence Act 1845 s 3; Documentary Evidence Act 1868 s 2.}

The components of private Acts are now the same as those of public general Acts, though the preamble (always present in a private Act) is rare in modern public Acts. The last invariable difference disappeared in 1960, when the standing order forbidding punctuation of private Bills was abrogated. Public Bills have been fully punctuated for centuries, as the careful research of David Mellinkoff has shown. {David Mellinkoff, *The Language of the Law* pp 157ff. See further s 284 of this Code.}

Local Acts and personal Acts   Private Bills are further subdivided into local Bills and personal Bills. On enactment these become local Acts and personal Acts respectively.

The royal assent formula for a local Bill is the same as for public Bills. {See ss 37 to 42 of this Code.} For a personal Bill (such as a marriage or estate Bill) the formula is '*Soit fait comme il est desiré*' ('Let it be done as it is desired)'. The same distinction is followed in relation to chapter numbers. {See s 278 of this Code.} Local Acts are numbered in a separate series using lower case roman figures. The series comprising personal Acts is numbered in italic arabic figures. There are thus three series of chapter numbers altogether.

Although from the parliamentary viewpoint both local Acts and personal Acts are private Acts, they are from the evidential viewpoint declared to be public Acts to be judicially noticed as such unless the contrary is *expressly* provided by the Act. {Interpretation Act 1978 s 3 (emphasis added). This replaced a similar provision in the Interpretation Act 1889 (s 9). That in turn reproduced s 7 of Lord Brougham's Act 1850 (13 & 14 Vict c 21). As to the use of 'expressly', in contradistinction to 'unless the contrary intention appears', the phrase normally employed in the Interpretation Act 1978, see Appendix D below.} In practice such contrary provision is invariably inserted in personal Acts, but never in local Acts.

There are a great many local Acts, usually promoted by local authorities. They regulate matters such as behaviour in public parks, the control of public processions, and the licensing of coffee bars or massage parlours. They are local and private Acts, but for the purpose of judicial notice they are by virtue of s 3 of the Interpretation Act 1978 public Acts - because they do not say otherwise. {As to the doctrine of judicial notice see s 21 of this Code.}

Personal Acts do say otherwise. They concern named individuals only, for example by regulating their family trusts or estates, or granting them naturalisation, or allowing them to marry within the prohibited degrees of affinity. Here the practice is for the personal Act to declare itself not to be a public Act. Judicial notice is not taken of it. It requires to be proved in court.

Permanent Acts and temporary Acts Most Acts are permanent. This does not mean that they cannot be repealed, but only that they remain in force until they *are* repealed. {For repeals see ss 178 to 186 of this Code.} Sometimes however Parliament deems it expedient to provide that an Act shall expire after a specified period. Often there is provision for extension of the period by resolution of each House of Parliament. Where this provision is not made, but it is nevertheless desired to continue the Act in force, it is included in the annual Expiring Laws Continuance Act.

Law reform Acts Law reform Acts include consolidation Acts, codification Acts, declaratory Acts and Statute Law Revision Acts. Of these, the most important under our present system are consolidation Acts. We briefly describe the other three varieties before returning to these.

Codifying Acts A codifying Act restates the whole law on a topic, whether common law or statutory. Unfortunately it has not been found possible to enact more than a handful of these Acts. They are not therefore important from the point of view of statutory interpretation. {As to codifying Acts see Bennion *Statute Law* (2nd edn, 1983) pp 81-84. For the interpretation of such Acts see s 233 of this Code.}

Declaratory Acts A declaratory Act or enactment declares what the law is on a particular point, often 'for the avoidance of doubt'. The subject-matter may be a rule either of common law or statute. Since a declaratory provision does not purport to change the law, it is presumed to have retrospective effect. {As to retrospectivity see ss 190 to 194 of this Code.} All this means is that the law as so declared is taken always to have been law (in the case of a common law rule) or to have been law since the commencement of the relevant enactment (in the case of statutory provisions). {As to the commencement of enactments see ss 164 to 169 of this Code.}

Statute Law Revision Acts   A Statute Law Revision Act is passed to tidy up the statute book by repealing with savings provisions that are obsolete, or otherwise effecting purely technical changes. {As to these Acts see Bennion *Statute Law* (2nd edn, 1983) pp 80-81.}

While saving space in editions of revised statutes, the repeal of spent provisions can be unfortunate. They may need to be referred to in order to construe other provisions that remain alive. {See p 579 below.} Furthermore savings may have the effect that repealed enactments are not altogether dead after all. {For an extraordinary instance of this see Example 182.1.} Savings also prevent common law rules from returning when enactments abrogating them are repealed. {See s 182 of this Code.}

Consolidation Acts   A consolidation Act is intended to confine within one Act provisions from various Acts that are *in pari materia*. {For the meaning of this term see pp 516–517 below. From the viewpoint of interpretation, there is only one distinction to be drawn in relation to consolidation Acts. That is between straight consolidation and consolidation with amendments. {As to this distinction, and the rules relating to the interpretation of consolidation Acts, see s 232 of this Code. For the various types of consolidation Act, and the methods by which they are passed see Bennion *Statute Law* (2nd edn, 1983) pp 73-80.}

Technical financial Acts   Technical financial Acts consist of Appropriation Acts and Consolidated Fund Acts. They are purely formal, and relate only to the House of Commons control over public expenditure and taxation. They lack legislative character, and so do not concern us. They are to be distinguished from taxing Acts, which usually take the form of the annual Finance Act. Although taxing Acts have special characteristics from the point of view of parliamentary procedure, this does not affect their interpretation. {As to the interpretation of taxing Acts see s 295 of this Code.}

Adoptive and Clauses Acts   An adoptive Act is law only in areas where it has been adopted (by whatever procedure is laid down by the Act). Clauses Acts set out common-form provisions which are made law in a particular context by being incorporated in what is known as the special Act. Some Clauses Acts are also adoptive, combining the features of both types.

The Town Police Clauses Act 1847 is an adoptive Act. At the same time it is, as its short title indicates, a Clauses Act. These were a nineteenth-century phenomenon. Parliament does not pass them nowadays, though many are still on the statute book. They saved the trouble of procuring the passage of a local or private Act, or when they did not altogether do that, they at least greatly shortened the language needed in such Acts. By providing common-form provisions, they produced a useful standardisation of certain areas of law.

For example in the days of the railway mania, when the so-called railway king George Hudson was promoting one new company after another, Parliament was asked to pass, by the private Bill procedure, a great many railway Acts. It was found after a while that they all followed similar lines. So Parliament passed the

Railway Clauses Consolidation Act 1845. This contained all the common form provisions, and could be incorporated in each special Act promoted by an individual company. The same can be said of the Lands Clauses Consolidation Act 1845 and the Companies Clauses Consolidation Acts, and of others - for example the Harbours, Docks and Piers Clauses Act 1847. All these are still in force.

The device had other applications. Local authorities could adopt an Act for their area or not, as they chose. There were the Baths and Washhouses Acts 1846 to 1899 - the days before almost every house had its own bathroom and kitchen. There were the Burial Acts 1852 to 1906 and the Public Libraries Acts 1892 to 1919. When the cinema came in, it was left to each locality to decide whether it wanted Sunday cinemas, nothwithstanding the Lord's Day Observance Acts. This 'local option' was provided for by the Sunday Entertainments Act 1932.

The adoptive system is still very much alive today. For example s 204 of the Highways Act 1980 provides for the adoption by a local authority of an advance payments code for the making up of private streets. Again, s 2 of the Local Government (Miscellaneous Provisions) Act 1982 empowers a local authority to resolve that provisions relating to the licensing of sex shops (contained in Sch 3 to the Act) shall apply in their area.

Indemnity or validation Acts Acts of indemnity, amnesty or oblivion relieve named individuals or groups from liability for breaches of law. Validation Acts remove actual or possible disability. {See further Bennion *Statute Law* (2nd edn, 1983) pp 18-19.}

29. Act of Parliament: interpreter's need to understand nature of

An Act cannot be truly interpreted unless its nature is understood by the interpreter. First it is necessary to grasp the nature of law itself. Then the interpreter requires knowledge of the constitutional significance of an Act, the way the Bill for an Act originates, the procedure by which it is passed into law, and the principles under which the subsequent Act operates. It is necessary to distinguish between the operative and descriptive components of an Act. In the case of the operative components, the interpreter further needs to distinguish between the substantive and the merely temporal provisions. The territorial operation of an Act, and its application to particular persons, must also be understood.

COMMENTARY

This section of the Code stresses the interpreter's need to understand the relevant aspects of the nature of an Act of Parliament. This need is further developed in s 118 of the Code.

While not attempting a comprehensive definition of law, we must now consider the essential attributes of an Act as a component of the operative law of its territory. We are concerned with the contrast between the text of the Act as a verbal formulation and the text as a *law* currently applied and enforced by the authorities of the state. The contrast may be likened to that between a *floodlight* which is out of use or switched on.

While unbought and unconnected the floodlight resembles the Parliamentary Bill in that, unless and until adopted and activated, each remains an inoperative product of human ingenuity. The Bill that has received royal assent but is not yet in force may be compared to the floodlight that has been bought and connected but is not yet switched on. Later, when operative, each has a pronounced effect (in accordance with its designed function) on the environment within which it is placed. This metaphor of the floodlight is further developed in the commentary on s 30 of this Code. Meanwhile we go on to examine the nature of an Act.

To grasp the special peculiarities of his science or art, the interpreter needs to understand the special peculiarities of the mode of verbal communication known as an Act of Parliament. Physically, it consists of words printed on paper, bound up as a booklet. Conceptually, it is a great deal more than that. What it is is something very complex indeed.

First, there are the obvious complications of its form and arrangement. An Act is not just a series of statements, such as one might find in a novel or a history. It is laid out in a special way. Its features reveal the long development of our legislative process. To interpret it properly one needs to be familiar with the machinery by which it is enacted. {See s 36 of this Code.} Again, some of an Act's features are given special meaning by statutory provisions.

Example 1   By virtue of the Acts of Parliament (Commencement) Act 1793, repealed and re-enacted by the Interpretation Act 1978 {See s 4.}, the printed date of assent appearing on the front of an Act is to be taken as the date of its *commencement* unless the contrary intention appears. {As to the commencement of Acts see ss 164 to 169 of this Code.}

Not all the laws that impinge on an Act are contained in other Acts. Many are judge-made. Here we must take into account *implications*. These include not only the inferences that arise from the words used, and the context. Also to be borne in mind by the interpreter are a host of implications imported by operation of law. Some of this incorporated law is statutory, the obvious example being the Interpretation Act 1978. Much of it is judge-made. {For the implied incorporation of general law see s 144 and Part XVIII of this Code. As to ancillary legal maxims see s 145 and Part XIX. For the incorporation of statutory rules see s 125.}

An Act takes its place as part of the corpus juris, or body of law. Unless it otherwise provides, it operates in accordance with general legal principles. Thus a penal enactment operates in accordance with principles of criminal law. Although it defines an offence in terms of *any person* there is an implication that this does not apply to children below the age of criminal responsibility, or adults lacking mental capacity. In the same way an Act about contracts has written into it by implication the relevant rules of contract law, and so on. On top of all this, there are imported the judge-made rules of statutory interpretation.

So an Act differs from ordinary prose in its special provenance, layout and features; and in the implications as to its meaning that arise by presumptions as to Parliament's intent, or by operation of law.

The differences go deeper than that. An Act is a *law*. We say it is 'in force'.

This is not just metaphor. The physical force of the state lies behind the Act. In the last resort, physical coercion will be used to compel obedience to it.

Why is this so? Why is it that these printed words on paper, accompanied by their implications, are backed up by the power of the state? We might attempt to explain it by saying that police officers, and tax collectors, and bailiffs, and trading standards inspectors, and all the rest, do as they do because that is what they are paid for.

We know this is not a sufficient explanation. They do it for that reason, but also because these words on paper are recognised by them as expressing the will of the sovereign legislature of our society. Most of their fellow-citizens (if not quite all) go along with this view. They would say as much in any opinion poll. That marks the basic difference between ordinary prose and legislative prose.

So we see that the real distinguishing feature of an Act of Parliament is that it is an expression of the will of the accepted legislator. It is worth some effort to find out just what that means in a free society. Anyone would prefer to live under a system that respects him and protects his interests rather than one that regards him as a pawn or cipher, to be dealt with at the will of a despotic master.

The peremptory knock on the house door in the middle of the night, followed by intrusion and arrest unsupported by legal warrant, has been the fear and fate of many. We remember the Roman soldier in Matthew: 'I say to this man, Go and he goeth; and to another, Come and he cometh; and to my servant, Do this, and he doeth it'. {Matthew vii 20.} That sort of arbitrary ukase is the opposite of what we understand and cherish as the rule of democratic law.

So to grasp the principles of statutory interpretation, one needs to understand the nature of what is being interpreted. We proceed therefore to an account of the legislative process as it operates in the Westminster Parliament.

Substantive and temporal provisions It is useful to distinguish substantive provisions, conveying the full operative effect of the Act, from temporal provisions, concerned only with aspects of its becoming or ceasing to be fully operative. The latter can be divided into commencement provisions, transitional provisions and repealing provisions. A full explanation of these is set out in Part VIII of this Code. Their outline characteristics are further discussed in the next section.

30. Act of Parliament: territorial, temporal and personal operation of

An Act has effect as law (a) in the territory to which it *extends* (its territorial operation), and (b) while it is *in force* in that territory (its temporal operation), and (c) in relation to the persons and matters to which it *applies* (its application).

COMMENTARY

An Act has a territorial, a temporal and a personal dimension. It has a territory or territories within which it forms part of the law. It operates for a finite period between its commencement and its repeal (or expiry). As part of its temporal operation, it may at its beginning and end be modified by transitional provisions. During its course it may be amended by or under the authority of

Parliament. At all times it is modified by judicial and other processing. It applies to some persons and matters within or outside its territory, but not others. All these things may be spelt out in the Act, or left wholly or in part to implication.

In a simple case an entire Act operates for a definite period as a component of the law of a single territory. More complex instances arise where portions of an Act are brought into force at different times, or in different territories, or both.

Example 1   An Act might be passed which came into force in the United Kingdom on royal assent but conferred power on Her Majesty, by Order in Council, to apply it with modifications to the Channel Islands. {See, e g, Trustee Savings Banks Act 1969 s 99.} If, as is very common nowadays, the United Kingdom commencement instead became operative piecemeal by Ministerial order, the result would be a complex pattern of various provisions coming into force in different territories at different times.

Here we may return to the analogy of the floodlight which was embarked upon in s 29 of this Code. The idea of an Act as operative law in the territory to which it extends is like the idea of the floodlight switched on at night and illuminating the area within its range. {For a different metaphor, of the Act as part of the legal *atmosphere*, see p 491 below.}

The comparison has obvious limitations. A floodlight operates in a purely physical way. The Act has a physical manifestation, as words on paper. It has physical consequences, as when the police make an arrest under the powers it bestows. But the essence of an Act is mental, rather than physical. It is not repealed by the destruction of all copies of it. It belongs to the world of the mind, and hence has more complications than the floodlight.

One type of complication concerns the idea of coming into force and ceasing to be in force. When a light is switched on or off the effect is straightforward. With an Act it is less simple. An Act is 'switched on' at commencement and 'switched off' by repeal. It, or some parts of it, may be switched on and off more than once.

Example 2   Section 41(1) of the Local Government, Planning and Land Act 1980 authorises the Secretary of State to direct that ss 17A and 17B of the General Rate Act 1967 shall cease to have effect. By s 41(2) of the 1980 Act he is authorised to make a subsequent order bringing those sections back again into force. This is indeed the light-switch analogue.

Time presents many difficulties in statute law. The problem of retrospectivity is continually troublesome. {See s 194 of this Code.} So too are transitional aspects concerned with commencement. Transitional problems also arise in relation to repeals. The text of an Act may be divided, conceptually speaking, between substantive and temporal provisions. Another distinction separates operative and descriptive components.

A further source of complication concerns amendments. One can alter a floodlight (for example by substituting a more powerful bulb). This may be likened to an amendment increasing the penalty for contravention of an Act. Usually however amendments to an Act have a more complex operation.

An Act may be either a principal Act or an amending Act. An amending Act also consists both of substantive and temporal provisions. One amending Act may follow another, until the original principal Act has been considerably altered. At each stage there are both substantive and temporal aspects. The position can be rendered schematically as follows (where the original Act is called Act A and two successive amending Acts are called Act B and Act C)-

1. Act A is passed, containing substantive provisions ('S1') and temporal provisions ('T1').

2. Act B is passed, containing substantive provisions ('S2') which amend S1, and also containing its own temporal provisions ('T2').

3. Act C is passed, containing substantive provisions ('S3') which repeal some of the provisions in S1 and further amend others. Act C also contains its own temporal provisions ('T3').

This is a simple scheme. The reality may be much more complicated. For example Act C might amend T1, or S2. Or there might be far more than two amending Acts. The point to note is that, however complex the position, under the British practice the successive temporal provisions are expressed independently of each other. They do not dovetail in the way succeeding amendments are likely, under the system of textual amendment now largely in use, to dovetail with the original substantive provisions. {For textual amendment see s 171 of this Code.}

This is despite the fact that conceptually there are only two texts, however many times the original Act is amended. These respectively embody the ongoing substantive and the ongoing temporal provisions. Using the above model, this can be illustrated as follows-

Text 1 (substantive provisions): S1 + S2 + S3.

Text 2 (temporal provisions): T1 + T2 + T3.

Obviously neither text remains the same throughout, though it could remain in each case a single text if the amendments were all made in textual form. For substantive provisions this is usually now done. It is never done for temporal provisions, which remain separate and independent (and thereby, it must be said, are rendered unnecessarily complicated). {For a way in which the temporal provisions might with advantage be presented in a form corresponding to their conceptual nature by employing the Jamaica Schedule technique see Bennion *Statute Law* (2nd edn, 1983) pp 277-9, as expanded in (1981) 131 NLJ 356 and 586.}

Further complications involve territorial extent. While a floodlight illuminates all objects within a given range equally (if at an intensity diminishing with distance), the operational effect of an Act it is not so simple. Although the idea that an Act forms part of the law of a specific territory is straightforward, it does not solve all problems of jurisdiction. Some Acts have extra-territorial effect, often to an indeterminate degree. On the other hand, foreigners within the area of jurisdiction may be differently affected by the Act than citizens are. Sometimes they may not be affected at all (as for example when they have diplomatic immunity).

An Act has no effect as part of the law of a territory unless it is in force in the territory. That is, the Act must be in the period between commencement and repeal. Since the law disregards fractions of a day, the period of operation starts at the first moment of one day and ends at the last moment of another. {This is not invariably so: see p 413 below.} If the Act extends to two territories in different time zones, it operates in each according to local time. Even though its period of operation for each territory is nominally identical it may thus be in force in one territory at a moment when it is not in force in the other. {*R v Logan* [1957] 2 QB 589.}

The courts are required to take judicial notice of an Act, even though it has not yet come into force. {Interpretation Act 1978, s 3. As to the doctrine of judicial notice see s 21 of this Code.} The same applies after its repeal. {Ibid.} Courts will also, as part of their duty to take judicial notice of matters generally known, have regard where relevant to the fact that a Bill is passing through Parliament (or even that the intention to introduce it has been made known). Nevertheless the Bill can have no operative effect until the commencement of the ensuing Act.

Example 3   In *R v Kynaston* {(1926) 19 Cr App R 181.} a man was 'convicted' of an offence under a section of an Act which had not yet been brought into force. Quashing the purported conviction on appeal, Lord Hewart CJ remarked that the prosecution of the appellant resembled nothing more than the pulling at a bell-handle without there being a bell at the other end. {P 181.}

The detailed application of the principles governing the temporal and territorial operation of Acts and their application is dealt with in Part VIII of this Code.

31. Act of Parliament: doctrine of parliamentary sovereignty

Under the doctrine of unlimited parliamentary sovereignty prevailing in the United Kingdom, an Act can lay down any proposition of law whatsoever (in the sense that that proposition will on the Act's commencement become law in the territory to which it extends).

COMMENTARY

The judges fully accept the supremacy of Parliament as a keystone of the British constitution. In itself this is enough to settle the matter. As Lord Devlin said: 'The law is what the judges say it is'. {*Samples of Lawmaking* p 2.} If the judges say unanimously, as they do, that the laws made by Parliament have sovereign overriding effect, that establishes the proposition. It remains established unless and until the judges start saying something different.

Example 1   In *R v Jordan* {[1967] Crim LR 483.} Colin Jordan, leader of the British Nazi Party, applied for habeas corpus on the ground that the Race Relations Act 1965, under which he was imprisoned, was invalid as being a curtailment of free speech. *Held* Parliament is supreme, and there is no power in the courts to quash the validity of an Act of Parliament. The ground of the application was therefore completely unarguable.

The question of invalidity is further dealt with in s 47 (Acts) and s 75 (enactments) of this Code. The overriding effect of an Act is described in s 32.

The fact that any proposition in an Act is good law does not mean it is necessarily *effective* law. This aspect is explored below. {See p 177.}

32. Act of Parliament: overriding effect of

An operative Act, as the expression of the will of the sovereign legislature, overrides inconsistent provisions of pre-existing law (whether statutory or not) and is itself overridden by any inconsistent subsequent Act.

COMMENTARY

When passed, an Act takes its place as a part of the *corpus juris*, or body of existing law. Modern Acts are usually tailored to fit neatly within this large and complex framework, so far as is possible. They spell out what their effect is on existing rules of law.

This spelling out is not necessary for legal operation however. With or without it, the overriding effect of a new Act follows as a consequence of the fact that the Act expresses the sovereign will of Parliament. By the same token, a present Act cannot curtail the ambit of any future Act.

The overriding effect applies to existing law of all kinds. Thus Richard Burn, after explaining that the ecclesiastical law of England consists of civil (i e Roman) law, canon law, common law and statute law, went on-

'When these laws do interfere and cross each other, the order of preference is this: the civil law submitteth to the canon law; both of these to the common law; and all three to the statute law.'

{R Burn *The Ecclesiastical Law* (9th edn, 1842). See also p 125 below and Example 386.1.}

Effect on existing law   To describe the way Acts operate on existing law one can use the image of a floor upon which rugs are spread. The floor consists of unwritten law or *lex non scripta* (in other words common law, rules of equity, and customary rules). The fusion of law and equity by the Supreme Court of Judicature Act 1873 was continued by ss 36-44 of the Supreme Court of Judicature (Consolidation) Act 1925, and is now provided for by s 49 of the Supreme Court Act 1981.

An Act is like a rug laid down on this floor. The Act conceals, for the area it covers, the texture underneath. That texture becomes visible again if the rug is removed (that is the Act is repealed). This is the position at common law. It is by statute considerably modified, so that repeal does not revive a common law rule. {See s 182 of this Code.}

An Act lying as it were on the floor of unwritten law may in time itself be overlaid. When later on another rug is put down (that is a further Act on the subject is passed), any portion of existing law it covers is *pro tanto* blocked out. In ordinary language, a later Act overrides inconsistent earlier Acts.

So far as it is not tailored to repeal or amend these expressly, the later Act does so by implication. Such implications in relation to earlier Acts are dealt with below, and are not further considered here. {See s 180 of this Code.} We return now to the effect of Acts on unwritten law. Acts may abolish unwritten rules, or may amend them. Or an Act may take over from the previous law and provide instead an enacted version of the old rule (with or without amendment).

Abolition of common law rules   There are many examples of the abolition of common law rules by statute. In tort for example, the defence of common employment was abolished by an Act of 1948. {Law Reform (Personal Injuries) Act 1948 s 1.} An Act of 1970 ended common law actions for enticement, seduction and the harbouring of a wife or child. {Law Reform (Miscellaneous Provisions) Act 1970 s 5.}

The cause of action strangely entitled *criminal conversation* was abolished in 1857. {Matrimonial Causes Act 1857 s 59.} The related right of a husband to obtain damages for adultery from a divorce co-respondent was ended by the Law Reform (Miscellaneous Proceedings) Act 1970 s 4. The tort of detinue was abolished by an Act of 1977. {Torts (Interference with Goods) Act 1977 s 2.}

In contract, the action for breach of promise of marriage was abolished in 1970. This was done by saying that for the future such a promise should 'not have effect as a contract giving rise to legal rights'. {Law Reform (Miscellaneous Provisions) Act 1970 s 1.} This wording prompts one to ask whether such a promise is to create a contract *not* giving rise to legal rights or no contract at all. The question is deliberately made unanswerable, which shows how statutes can obscure the outlines of common law doctrine.

Several common law crimes were abolished by s 13 of the Criminal Law Act 1967. The way they were described by the Act is of interest. It abolished-

> ' . . . any distinct offence under the common law in England and Wales of maintenance (including champerty, but not embracery), challenging to fight, eavesdropping or being a common barrator, a common scold or a common night walker . . . '

{S 13(1). In the case of maintenance and champerty, corresponding liability in tort was abolished by s 14 of the Act.}

A notable change in the field of criminal law was the abolition in 1967 of the concepts of felony and misdemeanour. {Criminal Law Act 1967 s 1.} It is interesting that the reforming Act said not that the concepts were abolished (as indeed they were) but that all *distinctions* between them were abolished. It then went on to apply to former felonies not only the *law* relating to misdemeanours but the *practice* too.

It is not unusual for statutes to recognise and apply practice as distinct from law. Thus the Finance Act 1894 s 8(1) applied to the newly-created tax called estate duty 'the existing law and practice' relating to death duties. To perpetuate existing practice in this way inevitably creates difficulty for statute users of the future. They are required to refer to procedures which by then may no longer be observed (or even remembered). In the case of estate duty this difficulty precluded consolidation of the Acts imposing it throughout the eighty years for which it was in operation. The technique is known as archival drafting. {See s 286 of this Code.}

In the law of real property, the rule in *Shelley's Case* {*Wolfe v Shelley* (1581) 1 Co Rep 93b.} was abolished by the Law of Property Act 1925 s 131. This referred to it as 'the rule of law known as the Rule in Shelley's case', which is the usual way to refer in legislation to common law doctrines.

The same Act also abolished what it referred to as 'The rule of law prohibiting the limitation, after a life interest to an unborn person, of an interest in land to the unborn child or other issue of an unborn person'. {S 161.} The rule was commonly known either as the double possibility rule or the rule in *Whitby v Mitchell*. Clearly the draftsman did not feel it safe to rely on either of these labels.

Modification of common law rules   More frequent are statutory provisions modifying common law rules rather than abolishing them altogether. It is not necessary to cite more than one or two examples.

The Law of Property Act 1925 s 162 modified a rule it described as 'the rule of law relating to perpetuities'. Forty years later the description was simplified to 'the rule against perpetuities'. {Perpetuities and Accumulations Act 1964, *passim.*}

Doctrines of contract {E g frustration (Law Reform (Frustrated Contracts) Act 1943) and implied terms (Supply of Goods (Implied Terms) Act 1973.} and tort {E g measure of damages (Law Reform (Personal Injuries) Act 1948 s 2) and contribution between tortfeasors (Law Reform (Married Women and Tortfeasors) Act 1935 s 6.} have been very frequently altered by statute. Even more numerous have been modifications of criminal law rules. {E g as to sexual offences (by the Sexual Offences Acts 1956 and 1967 in particular) and theft (by the Theft Acts 1968 and 1978).}

A common law rule may be modified *indirectly*. Instances of this arise where Acts authorise the carrying out of an activity which without the statutory cover would constitute an actionable tort.

Example 1　This is well illustrated by *R v Pease*. {(1832) 5 H & N 679; 4 B & Ad 30.} In the early days of railways the plaintiff suffered damage when his horse, on a road passing alongside the track of the Stockton and Darlington Railway, was frightened by the noise of the engines. The court held that in giving the railway company authority to build and operate its undertaking Parliament must have intended to authorise the likely consequences. {For this doctrine see pp 738–739 below. As to the presumption that common law rights are not taken away without compensation see s 295 of this Code.}

Enacting of common law rules　Sometimes an Act will replace a common law rule by a corresponding rule in statutory form. This may be done without modification of the rule, in which case it amounts to straight codification. {Codification is explained in s 233 of this Code.} Alternatively the newly-created statutory rule may, to a greater or less extent, differ from the common law rule it replaces.

Example 2　The treatment of the crime of conspiracy by the Criminal Law Act 1977 affords a typical example of such difference. Section 1 of the Act defines conspiracy in terms narrower than were used by the common law. Under that section, the crime of conspiracy is committed only where the agreement in question relates to the commission of an offence. At common law it is committed if the agreement was to do any unlawful act (or a lawful act by unlawful means), whether or not the unlawfulness involved criminality. The Act then says that 'the offence of conspiracy at common law is hereby abolished'. {S 5(1).}　This is followed by a saving: for some purposes common law conspiracy is to survive. The saving is in s 5(2), which reads-

> 'Subs (1) above shall not affect the offence of conspiracy at common law so far as relates to conspiracy to defraud, and s 1 above shall not apply in any case where the agreement in question amounts to to a conspiracy to defraud at common law.'

Even where a common law rule is entirely replaced by statute, it may be appropriate for the court, in applying the statutory provision, to seek guidance from the old rules.

Example 3　In *Handley v Handley* {[1891] P 124.} Lindley LJ held that the discretion as to custody of the children of divorced parents given to the court by s 35 of the Matrimonial Causes Act 1859 overruled 'both the common law rules and the Chancery rules'. He added: 'The judge is not bound to follow any of these rules, though he will have regard to them in exercising his discretion . . . ' {P 127. See also *R v Sodhi* (1978) 66 Cr App R 260 (common law power to vary sentences on convicted persons made statutory); *D v D* [1979] 3 All ER 337 (approbation of marriage as bar to nullity replaced by statutory bar).}

Custom   Within the area where it applies, custom corresponds to common law. If an unwritten rule is universal, it is common law; if confined to one area or class it is custom. {*Lockwood v Wood* (1844) 6 QB 50; Bract 1a, 2a; Brit 1a, 33b, 187b; Litt 170; Co Litt 110b; Finch 77; 1 Noy 17; Cowp 375; 1 Bl Comm 67. See further CK Allen *Law in the Making* (4th edn, 1946) chaps I and II.} What is said above as to the effect of statute on common law rules applies equally to its effect on customary rules.

In earlier times it was not unusual for customary rights such as the right to take tolls to be superseded by local Acts. Where an Act 'embraced and confirmed' a right which previously existed by custom or prescription the effect was that the right became thenceforward a statutory right, and that the lower title by custom or prescription was merged in and extinguished by the higher title. {*New Windsor Corpn v Taylor* [1899] AC 41, at p 49.}

The usage of a particular district cannot vary general law. {*R v Saltren* (1784) Cald 444.} A local custom in Southampton that a pound of butter should weigh eighteen ounces was ruled to be ineffective since it conflicted with the Act 14 Cha 2 c 26 (1662). {*Noble v Durell* (1789) 3 TR 271.} In the same way an Act overrides rules derived from a royal charter or franchise, or prescription. {*Mayor of Manchester v Lyons* (1882) 22 Ch D 287; *Abergavenny Improvement Commissioners v Straker* (1889) 42 Ch D 83, at p 89.}

A recent example of an Act overriding custom is the Costs of Leases Act 1958: see *Cairnplace Ltd v CBL (Property Investment) Co Ltd.* {[1984] 1 All ER 315.}

Royal prerogative   As to the overriding by an Act of prerogative rights see pp 129–130 below.

33. Act of Parliament: uniqueness of

Apart from Acts, and instruments made under the royal prerogative, no instrument made by Parliament, or by the Monarch or either House of Parliament separately, or by any other organ of the state, has the quality of law *proprio vigore* (by its own force). If an instrument so made does have legislative effect, it is as delegated legislation operating by virtue of an Act.

COMMENTARY

Prerogative instruments   See ss 48 and 49 of this Code.

Delegated legislation   See ss 50 to 70 of this Code.

This section of the Code states the rule, enunciated as early as 1323 but not fully established until the twentieth century, that Parliament can legislate only by Act. {The 1323 reference is contained in the third section of the statute *Revocatio Novarum Ordinationum* (15 Edw 2).} The same applies to the constituent elements of Parliament, with the sole exception of the Crown in relation to its prerogative powers. Other bodies are not recognised by the courts as having power to make law (though by agreement they may bind their own members).

The last power of the Monarch to legislate, otherwise than by prerogative instrument, disappeared with the repeal of the Statute of Proclamations. {31 Hen 8 c 8 (1539).} This repeal was effected by an Act of 1547. {1 Edw 6 c 12.} The Statute of Proclamations, passed at the instance of Henry VIII in 1539, gave the king power to make proclamations having the force of an Act of Parliament. Maitland called it the *Lex Regia* of England. {F W Maitland *The Constitutional History of England* p 253.}

Even so the Statute of Proclamations was limited. It did not purport to authorise any interference with common law or statute law, nor with 'any lawful and laudable customs of this realm'. Although a famous charter of monarchy, it was not so despotic as seems at first sight; nor was it used extensively. All the same, it must be recognised as a great surrender of principle by Parliament. No comparable surrender was ever thereafter made until the passing of the European Communities Act 1972.

Even into the early nineteenth century, the question of whether the House of Commons had power to legislate on its own remained undecided. The House still claimed to make law by its resolutions. With the passing of the Reform Bill of 1832 this claim acquired greater democratic persuasiveness. Yet powerful spirits, such as Stockdale and later Bowles, opposed it.

In 1839 Stockdale, considering himself defamed by criticisms reported as having been uttered in the Commons, sued Messrs Hansard (the printers of the House) for libel. The official reporter had truthfully repeated what was said on the floor of the House. The Commons required his employers to plead that in publishing his report they had acted under the orders of a court superior to any court of law. This was the High Court of Parliament, whose orders it was said could not be questioned in any other of the Queen's courts.

The Court of Queen's Bench rejected this inspired plea by Messrs Hansard. It held that only the Queen in Parliament could make and unmake laws. {*Stockdale v Hansard* (1839) 9 A & E 1.} In compliance with this judgment, the Parliamentary Papers Act 1840 was passed to give the force of law to the disputed Commons ruling.

Gibson Bowles challenged a later attempt by the Commons to give its resolutions the force of law. The practice had grown up of levying taxes merely on the strength of a resolution of the Committee of Ways and Means approving the Budget proposals. Bowles sued the Bank of England, seeking a declaration that the Bank was not empowered by such a resolution to deduct income tax at source from his dividends.

The court ruled in his favour. {*Bowles v The Bank of England* [1913] 1 Ch 57.} The practice successfully challenged by Bowles was then validated by the Provisional Collection of Taxes Act 1913. {See now the Provisional Collection of Taxes Act 1968, a consolidation Act.}

Statutory effect of a Bill Sometimes (but only by virtue of an Act of Parliament) a parliamentary Bill has statutory effect. The following are examples. Under the Acts of Parliament (Expiration) Act 1808 the introduction of a Bill to continue an expiring Act keeps the Act alive even though the date for expiry arrives before the Bill is passed. Under s 2 of the Parliament Act 1911 the date of second reading of a Bill may have statutory significance. {See s 44 of this Code.} Under s 1(4) of the Provisional Collection of Taxes Act 1968 a taxing resolution ceases to have the force of law unless a Bill relating to the tax is read a second time or amended within a certain period.

Except where given statutory effect in this way, a Bill in the course of its passage through Parliament has no legislative effect since it might not pass. {*A-G v Racecourse Betting Control Board* (1935) 152 LT 146; *British & Colonial Furniture Co Ltd v Mc Ilroy (No 1)* [1951] 1 All ER 404; *Willow Wren Canal Co v BTC* [1956] 1 WLR 213.} The position regarding such a Bill is however a matter of public knowledge of which the court, where relevant, takes judicial notice. {As to judicial notice see s 21of this Code.}

34. Act of Parliament: whether binding the Crown

Since an Act is made by the Queen in Parliament for the regulation of subjects, it follows that, unless the contrary intention appears, the Act does not bind the Crown itself. The Crown may however, again unless the contrary intention appears, take advantage of an Act if it chooses to do so. This principle, in both its aspects, is known as the doctrine of Crown immunity.

COMMENTARY

The doctrine of Crown immunity was thus expressed by Baron Alderson: 'it is inferred prima facie that the law made by the Crown . . . is made for subjects, and not for the Crown'. {*A-G v Donaldson* (1842) 10 M & W 117, at p 123. Cf *A-G for Ceylon v Silva* [1953] AC 461.} Or as Plowden put it-

'. . . it is not an Act without the King's assent, and it is to be intended that when the King gives his assent he does not mean to prejudice himself or to bar himself of his liberty and his privilege, but he assents that it shall be a law among his subjects.'

{Plowd 240.}
Diplock LJ expressed the principle as 'laws are made by rulers for subjects'. {*British Broadcasting Corpn v Johns (Inspector of Taxes)* [1965] Ch 32, at p 78.}

The contrary idea of a Monarch binding himself by his own statute, and thereafter being answerable for breach of it in his own court, nevertheless presented itself even in early times. Edward I guarded against it in the final chapter of the Statute of Westminster I. {3 Edw 1 (1275) c 50.} This chapter remains unrepealed, in token of the continuing operation of the doctrine of Crown immunity. It reads-

'And forasmuch as the King hath ordained [the preceding chapters] unto the honour of God and holy church, and for the commonwealth, and for the remedy of such as be grieved, he would not that at any other time it should turn in prejudice of himself, or of his crown; but that such right, as appertains to him, should be saved in all points.'

Traces appear in early sources of the idea that the Crown might generally be bound by its own statute. These are attributable to attempts by the barons and the church severally to limit the effective sovereignty of the king. A later factor is the effort of the judges to preserve the common law against royal or parliamentary encroachment. All these elements are found in the report of the *Case of Ecclesiastical Persons*. {(1601) 5 Co Rep 14b.} The following is an extract from what is now seen to be an erroneous statement of the common law-

> 'In divers cases the King is bound by Act of Parliament, although he be not named in it, nor bound by express words. And therefore all statutes which are made to suppress wrong, or take away fraud, or to prevent the decay of religion, shall bind the King although he be not named: for religion, justice, and truth are the sure supporters of the crown and diadems of Kings.'

{See also Bac Abr, Prerogative (E); *Willion v Berkley* (1561) 1 Plowd 223, at 226; *Case of a Fine Levied by the King, Tenant in Tail* (1604) 7 Co Rep 32a; *Magdalen College, Cambridge Case* (1615) 11 Co Rep 70b, at p 72a; *R v Archbp of Armagh* (1722) 1 Stra 516.}

This is a relic of the exploded idea that some Acts are 'remedial' while others are of a different character. The true doctrine is that all Acts are to be treated as beneficial in intent, there being no sound method of distinguishing between Acts in this regard. {See p 295 below.}

Ambit of 'the Crown' The doctrine of Crown immunity is not limited to the Monarch personally, but extends to all bodies and persons acting as servants or agents of the Crown, whether in its private or public capacity. In particular the doctrine embraces all elements of the executive government, from ministers of the Crown downwards. {*Town Investments Ltd v Department of the Environment* [1978] AC 359.} This brings in government departments and their civil servants, members of the armed forces, and other public bodies or persons. The question of where the line is to be drawn in relation to the last-named occasions frequent difficulty.

In *Gilbert v Corporation of Trinity House* {(1886) 17 QBD 795, at p 801.} Day J suggested the test of whether the person or body in question is an 'emanation of the Crown'. This was rejected by Denning LJ in the leading case of *Tamlin v Hannaford* {[1950] 1 KB 18, at p 22.} He preferred the test of 'whether it is properly to be regarded as the servant or agent of the Crown'. {See *International Rly Co v Niagara Parks Commission* [1941] AC 328, at p 342-3.}

The Denning test is borne out by modern Acts referring to the doing of acts 'on behalf of' or 'for the purposes of' the Crown. {See, e g, Sex Discrimination Act 1975 s 85(1), (2) and (10).} Under the best modern drafting practice an Act setting up a new public authority makes clear whether or not it is to be treated as acting on behalf of the Crown. {E g Town and Country Planning Act 1947 s 3(3) (Central Land Board).}

Many bodies are nowadays constituted by statute for public purposes. If largely autonomous, even though under some degree of public control, such bodies are not treated as acting on behalf of the Crown (i e Government). Thus in *Tamlin v Hannaford* {[1950] 1 KB 18.} Denning LJ rejected the finding that the British Transport Commission, set up by the Transport Act 1947 to run the nationalised railways, was within the doctrine. It was true, he said, that the Minister of Transport could appoint the members of the Commission and give them directions. He went on {[1950] 1 KB 18, at p 24.}-

'These are great powers but still we cannot regard the corporation as being [the Minister's] agent, any more than a company is the agent of the shareholders, or even of a sole shareholder. In the eye of the law, the corporation is its own master and is answerable as fully as any other person or corporation. It is not the Crown and has none of the immunities or privileges of the Crown. Its servants are not civil servants, and its property is not Crown property. It is as much bound by Acts of Parliament as any other subject of the King. It is, of course, a public authority and its purposes, no doubt, are public purposes, but it is not a government department nor do its powers fall within the province of government.'

{See also *Maritime Bank of Canada (Liquidators) v Receiver-General of New Brunswick* [1892] AC 437 (provincial government); *Cooper v Hawkins* [1904] 2 KB 164; *Chare v Hart* (1918) 88 LJKB 833; *Commrs of Public Works v Pontypridd Masonic Hall Co Ltd* [1920] 2 KB 233; *Bank voor Handel en Scheepvaart NV v Administrator of Hungarian Property* [1954] AC 584 (custodian of enemy property); *British Broadcasting Corpn v Johns (Inspector of Taxes)* [1965] Ch 32 (broadcasting authority).}

The doctrine of Crown immunity applies to the Crown in its overseas dependent territories in much the same way as in the United Kingdom. {See the Australian cases of *Roberts v Ahern* (1904) 1 CLR 406; *Pirrie v McFarlane* (1925) 36 CLR 170; *Essendon Corpn v Criterion Theatres Ltd* (1947) 74 CLR 1, at p 28. As to the composition of Her Majesty's overseas territories see s 211of this Code (independent dominions) and s 210 (others).} In the overseas territories of the Crown the matter is of course subject to any relevant provisions of the local law. Where an Act of the United Kingdom Parliament extends to an overseas territory the ambit of 'the Crown' in relation to the Act will include the Crown in right of the Government of that territory. {*R v Secretary of State for the Home Department, ex p Bhurosah* [1968] 1 QB 266 (Queen of Mauritius); *Mellenger v New Brunswick Development Corpn* [1971] 1 WLR 604 (Queen of New Brunswick); *R v Secretary of State for Foreign and Commonwealth Affairs, ex p Indian Assn of Alberta* [1982] 2 All ER 118.}

Scope of the doctrine The doctrine of Crown immunity means that the Crown can claim to be exempt from any onerous enactment, for example one imposing taxation. {*Coomber v Berkshire JJ* (1883) 9 App Cas 61, at pp 66, 76; *A-G v De Keyser's Royal Hotel Ltd* [1920] AC 508, at p 526. Tax exemption may also arise under the prerogative: *Coomber v Berkshire JJ* (1883) 9 App Cas 61, at p 71; *Madras Electricity Supply Corpn Ltd v Boarland (Inspector of Taxes)* [1955] AC 667.} Thus premises owned by the Crown were held not to be subject to the Rating Acts {*Jones v Mersey Docks and Harbour Board* (1865) 11 HLC 443, at p 508.}, the Rent Acts {*Rudler v Franks* [1947] KB 530; *Wirral Estates v Shaw* [1932] 2 KB 247.} or the Town and Country Planning Acts. {*Minister of Agriculture, Fisheries and Food v Jenkins* [1963] 2 QB 317.} Vehicles driven by Crown servants on Crown business were held not to be subject to the Locomotives Act 1865. {*Cooper v Hawkins* [1904] 2 KB 164.} The position was changed when s 16 of the Motor Car Act 1903 applied the 1865 Act to servants of the Crown. Later acts concerned with the regulation of road traffic have continued this subjection.

The Crown is not subject to the orders of the court in cases where an action against the Crown could not be brought. This is laid down by s 21(2) of the Crown Proceedings Act 1947, which states-

> 'The court shall not in any civil proceedings grant any injunction or make any order against an officer of the Crown if the effect . . . would be to give any relief against the Crown which could not have been obtained in proceedings against the Crown.'

This is an important element in the division between judicial and executive authority, and is strictly enforced.

Example 1 In *R v Secretary of State for the Home Department, ex p Kirkwood* {[1984] 2 All ER 390.} the applicant for judicial review, who was charged with offences in the United States carrying the death penalty, sought to uphold a stay on his extradition. *Held* There was no difference in substance between the stay and an injunction. The stay therefore contravened s 21(2) and was invalid.

The doctrine of Crown immunity has an indirect as well as a direct application. Thus in *Re Automatic Telephone and Electric Co Ltd's Application* {[1963] 1 WLR 463.} the Restrictive Trade Practices Act 1956 was held not to apply to an agreement to which the Crown was not a party but which was supplemental to an agreement to which the Crown was a party. On the other hand Crown lessees are generally bound by Acts, except in so far as the Crown's reversion may be adversely affected.

As to the application of the doctrine to private Acts see *Mersey Docks and Harbour Board v Lucas* {(1883) 8 App Cas 891, at p 902.} and *Stewart v River Thames Conservators.* {[1908] 1 KB 893, at p 901.}

Express contrary intention Where it is intended that the Crown shall be subject to the provisions of an Act, the usual practice is to insert a provision near the end of the Act saying 'this Act binds the Crown'. A corresponding procedure is followed where it is desired that a particular provision, rather than the whole Act, shall be binding on the Crown (e g 'this section binds the Crown').

Implied contrary intention An intention to bind the Crown may appear by implication. This is subject to the general rule that where such an implication would contradict any criterion laid down by law for inferring legislative intention (such as the doctrine now under discussion) the basis for the implication must be strong enough to outweigh that criterion. {*Thomas v Pritchard* [1903] 1 KB 209, at p 212; *A-G v Hancock* [1940] 1 KB 427, at pp 431, 439. As to the interpretative criteria see Part VI of this Code.}

The principle of implied contrary intention is sometimes described by saying that there needs to be a *necessary* implication against Crown immunity. Thus in *Bombay Province v Bombay Municipal Corporation* {[1947] AC 58, at pp 61-2.} it was held that an intention to bind the Crown is not to be inferred merely from the fact that the Act will not operate smoothly and efficiently if the Crown is not bound. {Cf *Premchand Nathu & Co Ltd v Land Officer* [1963] AC 177 (Act would have only limited operation if Crown not bound).} In *Gorton Local Board v Prison Commissioners* {(1887), reported in [1904] 2 KB 165n.}, Day J went so far as to say, in insisting on *necessary* implication before the Crown could be bound {P 167n.}-

'There are many cases in which such implication does not necessarily arise, because otherwise the legislation would be unmeaning. That is what I understand by "necessary implication".'

Insistance on necessary implication is typical of the unrealistic attitude displayed by many judges in resisting implied meaning in statutes. {See pp 245–247 below.} The question is always what did Parliament intend? It is answered by drawing any proper inference. Thus it is proper to infer that an enactment giving exemption from 'parliamentary rates, taxes, and payments whatsoever' binds the Crown since most taxes are levied by and on behalf of the Crown. {*Stewart v Thames Conservancy* [1908] 1 KB 893.}

It has been held not proper to infer, by applying the *expressio unius* principle, that because certain provisions of an Act are stated not to bind the Crown, therefore the remainder are intended to do so. {*Bombay Province v Bombay Municipal Corpn* [1947] AC 58, at p 65. See also *Smithett v Blythe* (1830) 1 B & Ad 509, at p 519; *Weymouth Corpn v Nugent* (1865) 6 B & S 22, at p 34; *Hornsey UDC v Hennell* [1902] 2 KB 73, at p 80; *A-G v Cornwall County Council* (1933) 97 JP 281. As to the *expressio unius* principle see ss 389 to 394 of this Code.} Where an Act contained a general saving for the Crown it was held that this did not prevent a particular enactment within the Act from binding the Crown where it was clearly intended to do so. {*Stewart v River Thames Conservators* [1908] 1 KB 893. See also *Yarmouth Corpn v Simmons* (1878) 10 Ch D 518, at pp 527-8.}

Taking of benefit by Crown   The Crown may take advantage of a statute, even though not bound by it. {*Willion v Berkley* (1561) 1 Plowd 223, at 243; *Case of a Fine Levied by the King, Tenant in Tail* (1604) 7 Co Rep 32a; *A-G v Tomline* (1880) 15 Ch D 150; *Cayzer, Irvine & Co v Board of Trade* [1927] 1 KB 269, at p 294; *Town Investments Ltd v Dept of the Environment* [1976] 1 WLR 1126 (reversed on other grounds [1978] AC 359).} This is a manifestation of the principle of legal policy that law should serve the public interest. {See s 127 of this Code.} Under modern conditions, the Crown is presumed to serve the public interest. Therefore for the Crown to take advantage of a statute is deemed to be for the public benefit.

Parliament itself has recognised this rule. Section 31(1) of the Crown Proceedings Act 1947 says-

'This Act shall not prejudice the right of the Crown to take advantage of the provisions of an Act of Parliament although not named therein; and it is hereby declared that in any civil proceedings against the Crown the provisions of any Act of Parliament which could, if the proceedings were between subjects, be relied upon by the defendant as a defence . . . may, subject to any *express* provision to the contrary, be so relied on by the Crown.'

{Emphasis added. As to the effect of the word 'express' see Example 108.14.}

The public is required to be fair, so the Crown must accept the disadvantages as well as the advantages: 'when the Crown elects to act under the authority of a statute, it, like any other person, must take the powers it thus uses *cum onere*'. {*A-G v De Keyser's Royal Hotel* [1920] AC 508, *per* Lord Moulton at p 549.}

The usual qualification also applies that the Crown cannot take the benefit of a statute if the contrary intention expressly or impliedly appears. {*R v Cruise* (1852) 2 I Ch R 65.}

If the enactment carefully spells out in detail the effect of the Act on the Crown there may be little room left for implication.

Example 2   Thus the Law Officers advised in 1983 that the Crown could not by implication take advantage of the Town and Country Planning Act 1971 so as to allow the sale of Crown land complete with planning permission for development. Without such permission the Crown land would sell for less, even though the buyer might confidently expect that his own application for planning permission would later succeed. This rigidity could only harm the public interest, yet the precise wording of s 266 (Crown land) of the 1971 Act was held to make this obviously desirable course impossible. {See in particular s 266(1)(b), where the word 'otherwise' was regarded as fatal.}

Nevertheless the whole policy of legislation, as being for the public good, indicates that the Crown should whenever possible be enabled to take advantage of an enactment. Where, as in Example 2, no one is injured by allowing the Crown to claim benefit and the public interest is served, it seems that the court ought, as the servant of the public interest, to allow a strained construction where this is necessary to achieve the desirable end.

35. Act of Parliament: need for validation

An instrument is accepted as an Act only where it has been validated as such in accordance with constitutional law. Under the constitutional doctrine of threefold consent, an Act is validated by being passed as a Bill by both Houses of Parliament (or by the House of Commons alone under the Parliament Acts 1911 and 1949), and then receiving royal assent.

COMMENTARY

This section states the rule that an instrument purporting to be made by Parliament does not rank as an Act of Parliament unless it has undergone the necessary validating procedure. In countries with written constitutions the procedure is spelt out by the constitution. In Britain the procedure is to be gathered informally from historical sources.

The criterion is whether the courts, guided by these sources, will recognise a Parliamentary instrument as an Act - or indeed as law at all. This is what Hart calls the 'rule of recognition', distinguishing valid legal injunctions from others. {H L A Hart *The Concept of Law* p 92.} See further s 27 of this Code.

Early statutes   The doctrine requiring a Bill to be passed by both Houses and then given royal assent before it could be classed as an Act of Parliament was not established at the time of the earliest statutes, some of which remain in force. The doctrine was first clearly enunciated in *The Prince's Case*. {(1606) 8 Co Rep 1a. See also *Pylkington's Case* YB 33 Hen VI, 17, pl 8; *College of Phistians v Cooper* (1675) 3 Keb 587.} It was not invariably applied even in later years.

Thus a Bill for a general pardon was *first* signed by the king, and then had *one* reading in each House. {Hatsell *Parliamentary Precedents* 3.69.}

Even in recent times the court has occasionally been asked to decide whether an ancient statute is valid. {See Example 27.1.}

Parliament Acts 1911 and 1949 As to the procedure by which the consent of the House of Lords is dispensed with under the Parliament Acts 1911 and 1949 see ss 43 and 44 of this Code.

We now proceed to look at the procedure by which threefold consent is given.

36. Act of Parliament: enactment procedure

A Bill is treated as passed by both Houses of Parliament only where it is passed (with or without amendment) by the House in which it is introduced and then-

(a) is passed by the second House in the form in which it is received by that House, or

(b) is passed by the second House with one or more amendments to which the first House agrees, or

(c) is passed by the second House with one or more amendments, and ultimately both Houses agree to such amendments by either House (if any) as are insisted on.

COMMENTARY

From the point of view of statutory interpretation, it is important to consider exactly what is the form of words to which the validating process is applied. In the case of a public Bill the starting point is the handing in of the intended text of the Bill to the Public Bill Office of the House in which the Bill is first introduced. The handing in is done by or on behalf of the Member presenting the Bill. In the case of Government Bills it is done by the draftsman. Rules of procedure of each House require that after the Bill is given a formal first reading by that House, its text is to be printed.

Thereafter the procedure differs slightly according to whether the Bill was first introduced in the Commons or the Lords. We start by describing the procedure for a Lords Bill.

Procedure for a Lords Bill Every peer entitled to sit in the House of Lords has the right to introduce a Bill. Most Bills which attain the statute book after first introduction in the Lords are introduced by a peer who acts on behalf of the Government. Nevertheless the Lords procedure is the same whatever the provenance of the Bill. A Government whip moves the first reading, which is almost invariably agreed to. {There have been rare occasions in modern times when first reading has been opposed, for example in the case of the Parliament (No 6) Bill 1969. The first reading of the Statute of Westminster 1931 (Amendment) Bill 1943 was negatived.}

The further progress of the Bill depends on the response of the House. If the second reading is moved, a debate on this question usually takes place. It is concerned only with the principles of the Bill. The alternative is to approve or negative second reading without debate. This is comparatively rare. If, with or without debate, the second reading is negatived the Bill proceeds no further.

If the Bill is given a second reading the next stage is clause-by-clause consideration in Committee. Here textual amendments to the Bill may be made. The term *amendment* is reserved for amendments in the strict sense, namely those alterations to the wording of the Bill which are made by order of the House. {As to the making of alterations informally by clerks in the Public Bill Office, see pp 108–109 below.}

After the Committee stage the Bill as amended is reported to the House. On the Report stage further amendments may be made. The next stage is third reading. Occasionally, even though it has proceeded so far, a Bill is negatived on third reading. Otherwise, after the motion for third reading has been agreed to, the motion is put 'that the Bill do now pass'. At none of the three 'readings' is the text of a Bill actually read out in the House.

Having been thus passed by the Lords, the Bill is taken to the Commons. The procedure for this is as follows. First, a document known as the House Bill is prepared in the Public Bill Office of the House of Lords. This is a print of the Bill (as finally agreed to by the Lords) interleaved with blank pages and bound in red tape. A manuscript endorsement in Norman French is made on the top of the front page and signed by the Clerk of the Parliaments. It reads *Soit baillé aux Communes* (let it be sent to the Commons).

The House Bill is then tied with red tape to a Message informing the Commons that 'the Lords have passed the [short title] Bill to which they desire the agreement of the Commons'. A Lords' clerk wearing wig and gown then carries the House Bill and Message to the bar of the House of Commons, bows to the Speaker, hands the Bill to the Serjeant-at-Arms, bows again and retires.

The standing orders of the House of Lords (though not those of the House of Commons) permit House Bills to be transmitted between the Houses informally if occasion requires. The effect is the same. Whether it is transmitted formally or informally, receipt of the Bill is entered in the minutes of the receiving House.

If by mistake a Bill is handed over without the required endorsement it must be returned to the original House, since the receiving House has then no authority to proceed. The Bill is returned informally unless the receiving House has entered upon consideration of it, when a motion by that House is required.

The Lords Bill is now in the possession of the Commons. If a member of the House of Commons informs the clerks at the table that he intends to take charge of the Bill it is thereupon deemed to be given a first reading. Otherwise it lapses.

Having been given a first reading, the Bill is subjected in the Commons to the same successive stages as described above in relation to the Lords. If the Bill is passed by the Commons with one or more amendments, the amendments are entered in the House Bill that was brought from the Lords.

On the passing of the Bill by the Commons (with or without amendment) the Clerk of the House of Commons or, in his absence, the Clerk Assistant endorses at the top of the first page of the House Bill brought from the Lords the appropriate formula. This is written immediately underneath the endorsement previously made by the Clerk of the Parliaments. If the Bill is unamended the formula is *A ceste Bille les Communes sont assentus* (To this Bill the Commons have assented). If a single amendment has been made the words *avecque une amendment* are inserted after *Bille*. In the case of two or more amendments the insertion is *avecque des amendemens*.

The House Bill is now tied with green tape to a Message informing the Lords that 'the Commons agree to the [short title] Bill without amendment' [or, as appropriate, 'with an amendment to which they desire the agreement of the Lords' or 'with amendments to which they desire the agreement of the Lords']. The Message and Bill are then carried to the Lords by a Commons' clerk in wig and gown. He is received by a Lords' clerk at the wicket gate of the Bar. The clerks exchange bows and the Message and Bill are handed over. The Bill is now once more in the possession of the Lords. If it was not amended by the Commons, it awaits royal assent. If however it was amended, at least one further stage is necessary.

There are three possible cases: (1) all the amendments made by the Commons are agreed to by the Lords; (2) they are all agreed to subject to one or more further amendments; (3) one or more of them is disagreed to. The House Bill is endorsed accordingly by the Clerk of the Parliaments. It is returned to the Commons (with any amendments entered) by the same procedure.

In the first of the three cases mentioned above, the endorsement on the House Bill is *A ces amendemens* (or *A cette amendement* if there is only one) *les Seigneurs sont assentus*. In the second case the words *avecque une amendement* or *avecque des amendemens* are inserted before *les Seigneurs*. In the third case the House Bill is returned accompanied by reasons for the disagreement. The formula is then *Ceste Bille est remise aux Communes avecque des Raisons* (or *une Raison*, where appropriate). Amendments disagreed to are underlined. If disagreements are persisted in, and the Bill continues its journeys between the Houses, different coloured ink is used for the successive endorsements.

In the first case, the Bill is now ready for royal assent. In the second and third cases, exchanges between the Houses continue for as long as may be necessary to secure agreement or, failing this, until it is clear that the Bill is lost for the session. The exchanges are conducted by means of Messages, and further endorsements as appropriate are made on the front of the House Bill. Where the exchanges end in agreement, it is the duty of the Clerk of the Parliaments to ensure that the final text of the House Bill corresponds exactly to what has been agreed by both Houses.

When a Bill has passed both Houses, the House Bill relating to it is kept until royal assent in the office of the Clerk of the Parliaments. This does not apply to a Bill for granting aids or supplies to the Crown, for example a Consolidated Fund Bill. Here the House Bill would be returned to the custody of the Clerk of the House of Commons if royal assent to the Bill were about to be signified by Commission. In practice this does not happen under modern conditions.

Procedure for a Commons Bill The above account describes the procedure applicable to a Bill that originates in the Lords. Where the Commons is the first House, the same procedure is followed with obvious adaptations. Such differences as do exist are insignificant. One difference is that with a Bill introduced in the Commons the House Bill is bound in green tape rather that red. These two colours have been used for many years to characterise each House respectively, for example in relation to the benches and decorative scheme of the debating chambers and the printing of insignia on Parliamentary papers.

Informal alterations to Bills In whichever House the Bill originates, the same strict rules apply to the making of alterations in the House Bill so as to bring its text into the condition necessary for royal assent. Here, as already indicated, we need to distinguish between amendments properly so called and other changes. Amendments are made by order of either House in the course of proceedings on the Bill. Most amendments are made at Committee stage or on Report. Other changes, known as printing corrections, are made informally by or under the direction of the Clerk of Public Bills of either House.

Printing corrections The principles governing the making of printing corrections may be expressed in the form of the following rules.

Rule 1 Except as mentioned in rules 2 to 7 below, no alterations may be made in the House Bill except such as are required to give effect to *amendments* (as defined above).

Rule 2 A clerk in the Public Bill Office, on the advice of the draftsman, decides on the place in the Bill at which each new clause or Schedule added by amendment is to be inserted. {This applies only to amendments made in the Commons. In the Lords, amendments to add new clauses or Schedules indicate the position they are to take in the Bill.}

Rule 3 Changes are made by a clerk in the Public Bill Office in the *numbers* of sections and other provisions, and in cross-references to such numbers, where the changes are made necessary by amendments adding or deleting material.

Rule 4 Where the text of the House Bill contains a misprint, and it is clear what the correct version should be, it is for the Public Bill Office to correct the error. If it is not clear what the correction should be the error must be allowed to remain (unless, there being further stages of the Bill's progress to come, the error can be put right by an amendment).

Rule 5 A clerk in the Public Bill Office, on the advice of the draftsman, may alter marginal notes or punctuation where this is made necessary or desirable by reason of amendments made to the Bill.

Rule 6 Rule 5 applies also to any cross-heading within the body of the Act or a Schedule.

Rule 7 A clerk in the Public Bill Office changes references to the year in cases where the Bill concludes its passage in the year subsequent to that in which it was introduced. {As to further changes made by the clerks following the signifying of royal assent, see p 120 below. As to changes made in the enacting formula where the Bill is passed under the Parliament Acts 1911 and 1949, see p 117 below.}

Final text It will be seen from the foregoing account that the text to which royal assent is given is that of the House Bill prepared by the first House as subsequently altered (1) to reproduce the effect of subsequent amendments agreed to by both Houses, and (2) to incorporate printing corrections.

As shown in the description given at p 113 below of the assent procedure, the Queen does not in practice see the corrected House Bill. All that is put before

Her Majesty at the time of assent is the short title. {As to the short title see s 275 of this Code.}

37. Act of Parliament: royal assent (two-stage procedure)

Royal assent to an Act requires two stages. Only on completion of the second stage is assent effectively given. First, the Queen's assent must be *signified* by letters patent under the Great Seal signed with Her Majesty's own hand, as described in section 38 of this Code. Second, that assent must be *communicated* to Parliament in one of the ways described in section 39.

COMMENTARY

The royal assent procedure is of interest and importance in throwing light on the true nature of legislation. Particular significance attaches to the fact that, while the Queen herself has practically no actual knowledge of the contents of the Bills to which she assents, the Clerk of the Parliaments is under a constitutional duty to act on Her Majesty's behalf in this respect.

Royal assent to an Act requires two stages. Only on completion of the second stage is assent effectively given. First, the Queen's assent must be *signified* by letters patent under the Great Seal signed with Her Majesty's own hand. Second, that assent must be *communicated to Parliament* in one of the ways set out in s 39 of this Code.

This two-stage requirement, is not always understood - even by the draftsmen of Acts. The Parliament Act 1911 in two places provides that a Bill shall become an Act of Parliament (when the requirements of the 1911 Act are satisfied) 'on the Royal Assent being signified'. {See ss 1(1) and 2(1).}

No doubt inadvertently, this appears to dispense with the need for assent to be communicated to Parliament where the Parliament Act procedure is followed. A similar error was made by the draftsman of the Act that gave effect to the abdication of Edward VIII. {His Majesty's Declaration of Abdication Act 1936 - see the opening words of s 1(1), which provide for the Act to take effect on royal assent being *signified*.} Royal assent procedure is now governed by the   Royal Assent Act 1967. This repealed the Royal Assent by Commission Act 1541, which had hitherto dealt with the matter. By a saving referring to 'the form and manner customary before the passing of this Act' the 1967 Act prevented the former practice from becoming obsolete. {See s 1(1)(a).} Until the passing of the Act of 1541 the monarch was required to communicate his assent to Parliament in person.

38. Act of Parliament: royal assent (signification of)

The Queen's assent to an Act is signified by letters patent under the Great Seal signed with Her Majesty's own hand.

COMMENTARY

Letters patent are formal communications by the sovereign, with the Great Seal affixed. They are otherwise described as letters overt or *literae patentes*. Letters patent are so called because they are *open* not secret, being at all times available for inspection to confirm the authority they bestow.

Royal assent is signified by letters patent signed with Her Majesty's own hand (the sign manual) and sealed on behalf of the Lord Chancellor by the Clerk of the Crown in Chancery (commonly known as the Clerk of the Crown).

This post, now held by the Permanent Secretary to the Lord Chancellor, places its holder in charge of the Crown Office. The Clerk of the Crown succeeded to the functions in relation to letters patent of the Clerk of the Petty Bag on the abolition of the latter office by the Great Seal (Offices) Act 1874. {See s 5 of that Act.} He is appointed by Her Majesty by warrant under the sign manual. {Great Seal (Offices) Act 1874 s 8).}

The seal used for the signifying of royal assent is the Wafer Great Seal. This is a wafer impressed with the same device as the Great Seal of the United Kingdom. It is placed on the document rather than being suspended from it. The use of the wafer instead of the pendant Great Seal is authorised by s 4 of the Crown Office Act 1877.

It is the duty of the Clerk of the Crown, in consultation with the Government, to procure the signifying of the royal assent at the earliest opportunity after a Bill becomes *ready for assent*. It becomes so ready at the moment when both Houses have passed the Bill, and have agreed together on all amendments made to it.

When a date has been fixed for royal assent, all Bills which are ready for assent must be presented for the Queen's assent by the Clerk of the Crown. There is no power to withhold a Bill from assent, whether on the instructions of the Government or anyone else. {See Erskine May *The Law, Privileges, Proceedings and Usage of Parliament* (20th edn, 1983) p 597: 'from that sanction they cannot be legally withheld'.} Nor, under the modern constitutional convention, may the Queen refuse assent. The last time assent was refused was by Queen Anne in 1707, in relation to a Scottish militia Bill. {*Lords' Journals* (1705-1709) p 506.}

The above rules are to some extent misleading. One of the strengths of Britain's unwritten constitution is the reserve power it contains. In a near-revolutionary situation the occasion might still arise for the withholding of royal assent, if only by way of delaying tactics. This might be done on the advice of Ministers, or by the Monarch of her own motion.

Wording of letters patent The precise wording of the letters patent is important for the light it throws on the true nature of the assent process. It is currently laid down by the Crown Office Rules Order 1967. {SI 1967/802. The order was made under s 3(1) of the Crown Office Act 1877.}

The wording varies slightly according to the method by which the assent is to be communicated to Parliament. The method most commonly used since the passing of the Royal Assent Act 1967 is *notification*. For royal assent by notification in the usual case where two or more Bills are included the wording of the letters patent is as follows {For ease of reading, the text is here broken up into its grammatical clauses. In practice the text is printed in unbroken form.}-

'ELIZABETH THE SECOND by the Grace of God of the United Kingdom of Great Britain and Northern Ireland and of Our other Realms and Territories Queen Head of the Commonwealth Defender of the Faith

To Our right trusty and right well beloved the Lords Spiritual and

Temporal and to Our trusty and well beloved the Knights Citizens and Burgesses of the House of Commons in this present Parliament assembled GREETING:

FORASMUCH as in Our said Parliament divers Acts have been agreed upon by you Our loving subjects the Lords Spiritual and Temporal and the Commons the short Titles of which are set forth in the Schedule hereto but the said Acts are not of force and effect in the Law without Our Royal Assent

AND forasmuch as We cannot at this time be present in the Higher House of Our said Parliament being the accustomed place for giving Our Royal Assent to such Acts as have been agreed upon by you Our said subjects the Lords and Commons

We have therefore caused these Our Letters Patent to be made and have signed them and by them do give Our Royal Assent to the said Acts

WILLING that the said Acts shall be of the same strength force and effect as if We had been personally present in the said Higher House and had publicly and in the presence of you all assented to the same

COMMANDING ALSO [name of Lord Chancellor] Chancellor of Great Britain to seal these Our Letters with the Great Seal of Our Realm

AND ALSO COMMANDING that this Our Royal Assent be notified to each House of Parliament separately pursuant to the Royal Assent Act 1967

AND after this Our Royal Assent shall have been notified to both Houses of Parliament the Clerk of Our Parliaments to endorse the said Acts in Our name as is requisite and to record these Our Letters Patent and the said Acts in manner accustomed

AND FINALLY We do declare that after this Our Royal Assent given and notified as aforesaid then and immediately the said Acts shall be taken and accepted as good and perfect Acts of Parliament and be put in due execution accordingly

IN WITNESS whereof We have caused these Our Letters to be made Patent

WITNESS Ourself at Westminster the .... day of ..... in the .... year of Our Reign

By The Queen Herself - signed with Her Own Hand'

The only other assent procedure now in use is assent by Commission at the time of prorogation of Parliament. Where this procedure is to be carried out the wording of the letters patent substantially differs from that given above only in one place. This is the passage immediately following 'AND ALSO COMMANDING'. Instead of 'that this Our Royal Assent be notified to each House of Parliament separately pursuant to the Royal Assent Act 1967' the wording directs the names of persons to be inserted as Commissioners, giving by way of example the names of the Duke of Gloucester and the Archbishop of Canterbury.

The names so inserted are to be followed by the names (as Commissioners) of the Lord Chancellor and at least two other Lords of the Privy Council. The Commissioners, or any three or more of them, are commmanded 'to declare this Our Royal Assent in the said Higher House in the presence of you the said Lords and Commons'.

Whether assent is to be by notification or commission, the Crown Office has the function of drawing up the letters patent for presentation to Her Majesty for signature. On the day fixed for signing of the letters patent the list of Bills ready for assent is sent to the Clerk of the Crown over the signature of the Clerk of the Parliaments, and is the authority for the issue of the letters patent.

The Acts are indicated in the schedule to the letters patent by specifying the short titles only. This is authorised by s 3 of the Crown Office Act 1877. The short title used is that conferred by the Bill, and not that by which the Bill was referred to in Parliament if different. An example of such a difference is the annual Appropriation Act, referred to during its passage through Parliament as the Consolidated Fund (Appropriation) Bill.

The short titles are listed in the order in which the Bills become ready, or are expected to become ready, for assent (except that Bills for granting aids or supplies to the Crown are placed first). It is a striking illustration of the extent to which royal assent has become a mere formality that Her Majesty does not have before her the texts, or even the long titles, of the Bills to which she signifies assent. Indeed these are not even communicated to officials of the Queen's Household (colloquially known as The Palace).

Another striking fact is that it is the practice, *after* the Queen has signed the letters patent, for the Clerk of the Crown to alter the schedule in manuscript when occasion demands. A listed Bill may be *struck out* if, having been inserted in anticipation of the Bill being passed by the second House in time for the assent ceremony, it proves not to be ready for assent on the date fixed for notification or prorogation. Similarly, though more rarely, a Bill which becomes ready unexpectedly may be *inserted* in the schedule after the Queen has signed the letters patent. Such alterations are made only with the informal approval of The Palace.

This practice in relation to alteration of the letters patent accords with the duty of the Clerk of the Crown to present for royal assent all Bills which are ready at the time it is given. The purely formal role played by the Queen herself also reflects the fact that officials of the House of Lords *act on behalf of the Crown*. Another manifestation of this constitutional principle is the responsibility of the Clerk of the Parliaments, on behalf of the Crown, to settle the text of the Act and procure its enrolment and publication. {See s 45 of this Code.}

39. Act of Parliament: royal assent (communication of)

The Queen's assent to an Act is communicated to Parliament in one of the following ways-

(a) by Her Majesty in person in Parliament; or
(b) by being pronounced by a Commission in the presence of both Houses of Parliament; or
(c) by being notified to each House of Parliament, sitting separately, by the Speaker of that House (or in the case of his absence by the person acting as such Speaker).

COMMENTARY

Assent in person Before the passing of the Royal Assent by Commission Act 1541 assent was required to be communicated to Parliament by the sovereign in person. Evidence of the practice before the reign of Henry VIII is scanty, but we know that from the accession of that king in 1509 until commissions were authorised by the Act of 1541 assent was pronounced in person only at the close of each session.

In the following two reigns (of Edward VI and Mary) commissions were not used. Indeed it was not until the reign of George III that commisssions outnumbered attendances by the sovereign in person. {J C Sainty *Parliamentary Functions of the Sovereign since 1509* (House of Lords Record Office Memorandum No 64).}

The last royal assent pronounced by the sovereign in person was that of Queen Victoria at a prorogation on 12 August 1854. {Erskine May *The Law, Privileges, Proceedings and Usage of Parliament* (20th edn, 1983) p 599.} This was also the last occasion on which Parliament was prorogued by the monarch in person. {Ibid, p 274.}

Section 1(2) of the Royal Assent Act 1967 states that nothing in the provisions introducing the new notification procedure affects the power of Her Majesty to declare her assent in person in Parliament. Since it seems unlikely that this ceremony will be revived, details of it are not given here.

Assent by commission   Section 1(1)(a) of the Royal Assent Act 1967 states that an Act of Parliament is duly enacted if assent, being signified by letters patent as explained above, 'is pronounced in the presence of both Houses in the House of Lords in the form and manner customary before the passing of this Act'. This piece of archival drafting refers to assent by commission under the Royal Assent by Commission Act 1541 (repealed by the Royal Assent Act 1967 s 2(2). {As to archival drafting see s 286 of this Code.}

As it required the Commons to be summoned to attend in the House of Lords, the ceremony of assent by commission (like the former assent in person) often constituted an unwelcome interference with Commons business. This MPs were inclined to resent. Ancient formalities, still observed, give the Commons an opportunity (never taken in modern times) to repel such interference.

The summons to attend in the Lords is delivered by the Sovereign's personal attendant in the Upper House, the Gentleman Usher of the Black Rod. When the Sovereign gave assent in person, Black Rod *commanded* the attendance of the Commons (as opposed to merely desiring it under the commission procedure). Either way, the Commons invariably barred his entrance. This action originated with the infamous attempt by Charles I in 1642 to arrest the five Members (Hampden, Pym, Holles, Hesilrige and Strode). Indignant at this breach of privilege, the House of Commons began, and has ever since continued, to assert its right of freedom of speech and uninterrupted debate by symbolically and momentarily barring entrance to the Monarch's representative.

Although kept alive by the 1967 Act, the ceremony of assent by commission is now used only once in a session at the time of prorogation. Since the Commons have by then finished their business, and are anyhow required to attend in the Lords for the prorogation ceremony, the former objection does not apply. The procedure is as follows.

Three or more of the Commissioners named in the letters patent sit on a form placed between the throne and the woolsack. They commmand the Gentleman Usher of the Black Rod to go to the Commons chamber and tell the members of that House that their attendance is desired. Mr Speaker, accompanied by some

MPs, walks to the Bar of the Lords. The letters patent are read out by the Reading Clerk. Then the short title of the first Bill is read out by the Clerk of the Crown. It is followed by the assent formula in Norman French recited by the Clerk of the Parliaments. The wording is *La Reyne le Veult* (the Queen wills it).

A different formula is used for a Supply Bill, that is a Bill granting aids or supplies to the Crown, such as a Consolidated Fund Bill or a Finance Bill. Here the wording is *La Reyne remercie ses bons sujets, accepte leur benevolence et ainsi le veult* (the Queen thanks her loyal subjects, accepts their bounty and wills it so). If assent were ever refused, the formula would be *La Reyne s'avisera* (the Queen will consider).

The House Bill is not produced at the assent ceremony, but lies on the table. An exception would arise in the case of a Bill for granting aids and supplies to the Crown, for example a Consolidated Fund Bill. Here, as explained above {P 108 above.} Errors have occurred over this on two occasions. Both were Commons after the Bill has been passed by the Lords (which in this case is always the second House).

When under the former practice assent to Bills granting aids and supplies was given by commission, the House Bill was brought up by the Speaker of the House of Commons. The Bill received assent before all other Bills. The House Bill was handed by Mr Speaker to the Clerk of the Parliaments for him to pronounce the assent formula. This procedure would still be followed if such a Bill received assent at the time of prorogation. This would be unusual however. The normal time for prorogation nowadays is October or November, when financial Bills for the session will have been safely passed some time previously.

Following the assent ceremony, Parliament is prorogued. The Lord Chancellor reads out the Royal Speech, and the commission for prorogation is then read out by the Reading Clerk. Finally, the Lord Chancellor announces prorogation. The Commissioners leave the Chamber and both Houses disperse.

Assent by notification Section 1(1)(b) of the Royal Assent Act 1967 provides that the fact that Her Majesty has signified assent may be 'notified to each House of Parliament, sitting separately, by the Speaker of that House or in the case of his absence by the person acting as such Speaker'. Such notification completes the assent process, and s 1(1) provides that thereupon the Act 'is duly enacted'.

The notification is accomplished by reading out a suitable formula, followed by the short titles of the Acts in question. The formula differs in the two Houses, being simpler in the Lords. Before the notification is read out in the Lords the letters patent, bearing the royal sign manual and with the Wafer Great Seal affixed, are taken to the table of the House of Lords as evidence that it is proper for the Lord Chancellor (as Speaker of that House) or his deputy to read out the notification. In the Commons a list of the short titles of the Acts signed by the Clerk of the Crown provides similar authority for Mr Speaker.

40. Act of Parliament: royal assent (absence or illness of Monarch)

In the event of the Monarch's absence from the United Kingdom, royal assent to Bills may be signified by Counsellors of State appointed under the Regency Acts 1937 to 1953. Similar provisions of these Acts apply where the monarch suffers from illness not amounting to such infirmity of mind or body as warrants a regency.

COMMENTARY

Provisions whereby, during the Monarch's absence from the United Kingdom, royal assent to Bills may be signified by Counsellors of State are contained in the Regency Act 1937 s 6 and the Regency Act 1953 s 3. The function is to be exercised jointly by the Counsellors of State, or by such number of them as may be specified in the letters patent appointing them. {Regency Act 1937 s 6(3).}

The letters patent may impose conditions on the exercise of any function of the Counsellors of State, but the legislation does not itself restrict the Bills to which they may signify assent.

Similar provisions apply where the monarch suffers from illness not amounting to such infirmity of mind or body as warrants a regency. {Regency Act 1937 s 6(1).}

41. Act of Parliament: royal assent (demise of the Crown)

Death or abdication of the Monarch does not alter the procedure for signifying and communicating royal assent, since on the demise of the Crown there is deemed in law to be no interval between the cessation of the reign of one Monarch and the accession of his successor.

COMMENTARY

In consequence of the disunion of the sovereign's natural body from his body politic, the kingdom is by operation of law transferred or demised to his successor, so that the royal dignity remains perpetual. {Plowd 177. See His Majesty's Declaration of Abdication Act 1936 s 1(1).} There is in law no interval between the death of a monarch and the accession of his successor: 'the king never dies'. {*Calvin's Case* (1609) 4 Co Rep 1a, 10b.}

In the event of the death or abdication of the Monarch during the interval between the passing of a Bill and the signifying of royal assent, the letters patent would be prepared for the signature of the successor to the Crown.

Acts done by one Monarch have the like effect as if done by his successor. Accordingly death or abdication of the Monarch during the interval between signature of the letters patent and communication of the assent to Parliament would not affect the validity of the letters patent; and the assent signified by them would be pronounced or otherwise communicated in the normal way.

42. Act of Parliament: royal assent (regency)

In the case of a regency, the regent would have the same functions and powers in relation to royal assent as the Monarch, except that the regent would not have power to assent to any Bill for changing the order of succession to the Crown.

COMMENTARY

The authority for this statement is the Regency Act 1937 s 4(2). A similar restriction is laid down by that provision in relation to any Bill altering the protestant church in Scotland.

43. Act of Parliament: validation under Parliament Acts 1911 and 1949 (money Bills)

A certified money Bill must, unless the House of Commons otherwise orders, be presented for royal assent although it has not been passed by the Lords if it is a Bill which -

(a) is passed by the Commons, and

(b) is sent up to the Lords at least one month before the end of the session, and

(c) is not passed by the Lords unamended within one month after it is sent up to them.

COMMENTARY

The Parliament Act 1911 (as amended by the Parliament Act 1949) provides an exception to the constitutional rule that an Act requires the agreement of *both* Houses of Parliament. In cases falling within either of the categories respectively described in this and the next following section, a Bill passed by the Commons becomes law notwithstanding that it lacks the approval of the Lords.

The House of Commons have power to prevent the operation of this statutory overriding of the Lords' veto should they think fit to do so. In practice this would enable the majority party in the Commons, up to the last minute, to arrange a compromise with the Lords. {So far the occasion for using this preventive power has not arisen.}

Only three Acts have been passed under the provisions of the Parliament Act 1911 as amended. None originated as money Bills, all three falling within the next following section. Separate Commissions were issued for royal assent. {That is the Commissions were separate from those issued for Bills passed by both Houses in the normal way, though a single Commission was issued covering the two Bills enacted under the Parliament Act 1911 in the year 1914.} In a future case no doubt a similar course would be followed in relation to notification under the Royal Assent Act 1967. {That is separate letters patent would be signed and sealed to cover a single Act enacted, or two or more Acts enacted at around the same time, under the Parliament Acts 1911 and 1949.}

Section 4(1) of the Parliament Act 1911 provides a special enacting formula for Bills receiving assent under the Act. Section 4(2) gives authority to alter the Bill by a printing correction so that this formula can be substituted without the need for an amendment.

Section 1(2) of the Parliament Act 1911 defines a 'money Bill' as a public Bill which in the opinion of Mr Speaker contains *only* provisions dealing with specified financial matters. The word 'only' prevents *tacking*, that is dispensing with Lords' consent for provisions which are not financial by including them in a money Bill. The matters specified include taxation, the expenditure of public funds, and the national debt. Local government expenditure is not included. Section 1(3) of the Act lays down the procedure for the certifying by Mr Speaker of Bills falling within the definition.

So far, no Bill falling within this category has yet been rejected by the House of Lords. The only practical effect of the statutory procedure has therefore been the operation of the requirement that whenever a money Bill is sent up to the Lords, the House Bill must bear Mr Speaker's certificate that it is a money Bill. This is laid down by s 1(3) of the Parliament Act 1911, which adds that the certificate must also appear on the Bill 'when it is presented to [Her] Majesty for assent'. It applies even though the Lords have *passed* the money Bill (which in practice they invariably do). Since, as explained above, Bills are not actually presented to Her Majesty this requirement is not in practice complied with. The certificate is conclusive, and cannot be questioned in any court. {Parliament Act 1911 s 3.}

44. Act of Parliament: validation under Parliament Acts 1911 and 1949 (other Bills)

Any public Bill (other than a certified money Bill, or a Bill to prolong the life of Parliament beyond five years, or a Bill to confirm a provisional order) must, unless the House of Commons otherwise orders, be presented for royal assent although it has not been passed by the Lords if it is a Bill which-

(a) is passed by the Commons in two succesive sessions, and
(b) is passed by the Commons in the second session not less than one year after the Commons gave it a second reading in the first session, and
(c) is sent up to the Lords at least one month before the end of each of the two sessions, and
(d) in the second session is neither passed by the Lords unamended nor passed by them only with amendments to which the Commons agree.

COMMENTARY

The Parliament Act 1911 (as amended by the Parliament Act 1949) provides an exception to the constitutional rule that an Act requires the agreement of *both* Houses of Parliament. In cases falling within either of the categories respectively described in this and the preceding section, a Bill passed by the Commons becomes law notwithstanding that it lacks the approval of the Lords.

The House of Commons have power to prevent the operation of this statutory overriding of the Lords' veto should they think fit to do so. In practice this would enable the majority party in the Commons, up to the last minute, to arrange a compromise with the Lords. {So far the occasion for using this preventive power has not arisen.}

Only three Acts have been passed under the provisions of the Parliament Act 1911 as amended. All fall within this section. They are the Welsh Church Act 1914, the Government of Ireland Act 1914 and the Parliament Act 1949.

Separate Commissions were issued for royal assent. {That is the Commissions were separate from those issued for Bills passed by both Houses in the normal way, though a single Commission was issued covering the two Bills enacted under the Parliament Act 1911 in the year 1914.} In a future case no doubt a similar course would be followed in relation to notification under the Royal Assent Act 1967. {That is separate letters patent would be signed and sealed to cover a single Act enacted, or two or more Acts enacted at around the same time, under the Parliament Acts 1911 and 1949.}

Section 4(1) of the Parliament Act 1911 provides a special enacting formula for Bills receiving assent under the Act. Section 4(2) gives authority to alter the Bill by a printing correction so that this formula can be substituted without the need for an amendment.

When a Bill falling within this section is presented for royal assent it is required to bear Mr Speaker's certificate that the statutory provisions have been complied with. {Parliament Act 1911 s 2(2).} Since, as mentioned above {P 113.}, Bills are not in practice presented for royal assent this is a dead letter. The certificate is deemed to be conclusive, and cannot be questioned in any court (Parliament Act 1911 s 3).

Bill to prolong the life of Parliament The time fixed for the maximum duration of Parliament was reduced to five years by s 7 of the Parliament Act 1911, which amended the period of seven years fixed by the Septennial Act 1715.

45. Act of Parliament: final settling of text and promulgation

Royal assent to an Act having been communicated, it becomes the constitutional duty of the Crown, acting through its officer the Clerk of the Parliaments, to-

(a) settle the final text of the Act, and
(b) procure entry of the text on the Parliament Roll and the Chancery Roll, and
(c) procure publication of the text by the Queen's Printer of Acts of Parliament.

The validity of an Act does not however depend in any way on the carrying out of this duty, nor on any other form of promulgation.

COMMENTARY

Although the reality is now very different, the enacting formula still speaks of an Act as made 'by' the Crown. That remains the theoretical position. In finalising the details of the text, the Crown still has a minor part to play. For this purpose it acts through its officer the Clerk of the Parliaments, who in turn acts through officials of the Public Bill Office of the House of Lords. {The Clerk of the Parliaments is appointed by the Crown under s 2 of the Clerk of the Parliaments Act 1824. The short title to this Act, incorrectly bestowed by the Short Titles Act 1896, was corrected by the Statute Law (Repeals) Act 1978 s 2 and Sch 3 para 2.}

Settling the text of the Act As soon as royal assent to an Act has been notified or pronounced, a copy of the Act is prepared for the printer. This is done in the Public Bill Office of the House of Lords, using the following method. A copy of the latest print of the Bill is obtained. When necessary, this is altered in manuscript or by the insertion of printed amendments (or in both ways) so that it exactly corresponds to the final version of the House Bill.

At this stage, there may be made further printing corrections of the kind authorised by rules 2 to 7 set out above. {See p 109.} In addition, the alterations needed to turn the form of a Bill into that of an Act are made. Apart from obvious adaptations, these include insertion of the chapter number and date of assent.

After examination in the Public Bill Office of the House of Lords to verify its accuracy, a proof of the printed Act is certified as correct by the Clerk of Public Bills and returned, with a request for its immediate publication, to the Queen's Printer of Acts of Parliament. {An office which, by virtue of letters patent of Queen Victoria dated 3 October 1888, is held by the official who is Controller of Her Majesty's Stationery Office.}

Entry on the Rolls Two copies of the Act are then printed on vellum. After a further examination in the Public Bill Office to ensure their correctness, these are endorsed with the appropriate royal assent formula and signed by the Clerk of the Parliaments. They then become the official copies of the Act.

One of the official copies is placed in the custody of the Public Record Office in Chancery Lane, London. By this action it is treated as becoming part of the Chancery Roll (see below). The other official copy is retained in the House of Lords. It is deposited among the records stored in the Victoria Tower. By this action it is treated as becoming part of the Parliament Roll (see below).

Rolls A roll was a parchment which could be rolled up by hand in the form of a pipe. Additions were stitched to the original to preserve continuity and prevent the insertion of false documents.

Chancery Roll The Chancery Roll consists of records of the Chancery of England. This was originally the office of the King's clerks under the Chancellor, or keeper of the king's seal. Since royal assent to Acts has always been signified by letters patent under the king's seal, it naturally followed that enrolment of the text of Acts should be in the Chancery.

The Chancery Roll was kept in the Tower of London until removed in the time of Edward II to the Rolls Office in Chancery Lane, London. This was renamed the Public Record Office by the Public Record Office Act 1838. {1 & 2 Vict c 94.} The Roll is still stored there, along with modern accretions, though the main Record Office has been transferred to Kew.

The matter is now regulated by the Public Records Act 1958, which transferred the direction of the Public Record Office from the Master of the Rolls to the Lord Chancellor. The Act provides however that the records of the Chancery of England (including those created after the commencement of the Act) are to remain in the custody of the Master of the Rolls.

For an example of inspection by the court of the text of an Act on the Chancery Roll see the report in the Law Journal of *R v Casement*. {(1917) 86 LJKB (n s) 467, at p 482.}

Parliament Roll The Parliament Roll (or Rolls of Parliament) is the record of the proceedings of Parliament kept in the Victoria Tower of the House of Lords. In the period following the Norman Conquest, all parliamentary Bills were drawn in the form of petitions to the king. These were entered, together with the king's reply, in the Rolls of Parliament. At the end of the session the judges converted them into the form of a single Statute divided into chapters. This was entered on that portion of the Rolls of Parliament known as the Statute Roll.

This concept of the Parliament Roll continues to the present time, though the vellum copies of each Act are now separate. The Parliament Rolls are still stored in the Record Office housed in the Victoria Tower of the Palace of Westminster. {See M F Bond *Guide to the Records of Parliament.*}

The practice of engrossing Acts on the Parliament Roll was discontinued in 1849. {*Claydon v Green* (1868) LR 3 CP 511, *per* Willes J at p 522. See also H Hardcastle *Statutory Law* (1st edn, 1879) p 241.} Section 7 of Lord Brougham's Act {(1850) 13 & 14 Vict c 21.} provided that each Act passed after 10 June 1850 should be a public Act, to be judicially noticed as such, unless the contrary was expressly provided by the Act. {See now Interpretation Act 1978 s 3.} Section 3 of the Evidence Act 1845 provides that other Acts may be proved by production of a copy purporting to be printed by the Queen's printer.

The Parliament Roll may be inspected to verify the accuracy of a print produced of an Act. {*R v Jefferies* (1721) 1 Stra 446; *Price v Hollis* (1813) 1 M & S 105; *Barrow v Wadkin* (1857) 24 Beav 327, at p 330; *R v Haslingfield* (1874) LR 9 QB 203, at p 209.}

Publication of Acts Prints for publication exactly correspond to the official copies on vellum. The texts of public general Acts are published separately by Her Majesty's Stationery Office. HMSO also publish annual volumes of the Acts. {See further s 46 of this Code.}

It sometimes happens that errors are discovered in the published print of an Act. The practice then is for the Clerk of the Parliaments to authorise HMSO to issue corrigendum slips. This is sometimes done even where the error is in the vellum copy.

The practice is thus at variance with the statement in *Craies* that 'The printers and officials clearly have no power to alter in any way the copy assented to, and it is for the judges or in the last resort for the legislature, to correct the error'. {Craies *Statute Law* (7th edn, 1971) p 522.} What *Craies* refers to as 'the copy assented to' is the *House Bill* in the form it is in at the time assent is pronounced or signified. Nevertheless this House Bill is not available to persons outside Parliament. Such persons cannot therefore look behind the Parliament Roll.

Effect of promulgation Acts of the Westminster Parliament have never depended upon promulgation for their validity. They are fully binding even upon persons who can have had no opportunity to read them or even to learn of their passing.   This doctrine goes back at least as far as the fourteenth century, when knowledge of what had been enacted by Parliament was not easily come by. Thorpe CJ said in *R v Bishop of Chichester* {YB 39 Ed 3 (1364) 7. Cited in abridged form 4 Co Inst 26.} that-

' . . . every one is bound to know what is done in Parliament, even although it has not been proclaimed in the country; as soon as

Parliament has concluded any matter, the law presumes that every person has cognizance of it, for Parliament expresses the body of the realm.'

Later Lord Ellenborough put it in this way: 'Public Acts of Parliament are binding upon every subject, because every subject is in judgment of law privy to the making of them, and therefore supposed to know them...' {*R v Sutton* (1816) 4 M & S 532, at p 542.} Blackstone said that the people are present 'by their representatives' at the passing of Acts {1 Comm 184.} Selden more realistically said that ignorance of the law excuses no man 'not that all men know the law, but because 'tis an excuse every man will plead, and no man can tell how to confute him'. {*Table Talk* (1689) p 99 of edition of 1892. As to ignorance of law see further s 9 of this Code.}

The practical need for promulgation depends on the fact that, if the authors of legislation are to secure their object, people must know of what they have done. In days long before the development of mass media of communication this spreading of knowledge was accomplished through the action of the king's officer, the sheriff. Statutes would be proclaimed in the county court, successor to the Saxon shire moot, of which in medieval times the sheriff was president. {*R v Sutton* (1816) 4 M & S 532, at p 542.}

For this purpose an official copy of the Act, under the Great Seal, would be sent to the counties. This was known as an *exemplification*. Another name for it was an *inspeximus*, that being the first word of the exemplification (meaning 'we have inspected').

An accompanying precept required the sheriff to proclaim the statute not only in the full county court but also in the townships. He was required to make copies and transmit them to knights of the shire, justices of the peace and other leading figures. {1 Stat Realm, Intr p lxxxvii. See also 4 Co Inst 26, 28; 1 Bl Comm 184.}

Later statutes were proclaimed at the cross or market place by the town crier or other official. Oral proclamations were made at churches until this was stopped by the Parish Notices Act 1837, which instead required them to be communicated by written notice fixed to the church door.

In 1796 the authorities ordered printed copies of the statutes to be distributed throughout the country as soon as possible after enactment. In 1801 the House of Commons passed a resolution requiring the King's Printer to supply copies of Acts to listed judicial and administrative officers. This practice continues. The list, which is revised from time to time, is known as the promulgation list.

Modern position   It is now accepted that the authorities have a moral and practical duty to promulgate statute law in an effficient manner. The arrangements for publicising public general Acts of Parliament are inevitably more effective than apply to private Acts, statutory instruments, byelaws and other lesser legislation. It follows that the more important rules should be in statutory form, but this is not always understood or acted upon.

Example 1   Schedule 1 to the Indictments Act 1915 contained important rules as to the form of indictments. The power to amend these conferred by ss 1 and 2 of the Act {Amended by s 56 of, and para 17 of Sch 8 to, the Courts Act 1971.} was used to remove the rules from the Act altogether. Instead they now appear, in amended form, in the Indictment Rules 1971. {SI 1971/1253.} Furthermore the forms of indictment formerly set out in the Act do not even appear in the statutory instrument. Instead, provision is made for such forms to be 'for the time being approved by the Lord Chief Justice'. {Indictment Rules 1971 r 5(2).} No provision is made for the forms so approved to be promulgated.

46. Act of Parliament: official published editions

Where an Act cites (by year, statute, session or chapter) another Act which is included in any revised edition of the statutes printed by authority, the reference is to be read, unless the contrary intention appears, as referring to that edition.

Where an Act cites (by number or letter) a section or other portion of another Act which is included in any revised edition of the statutes printed by authority, the reference is to be read, unless the contrary intention appears, as referring to that edition.

COMMENTARY

This section derives from the Interpretation Act 1978 s 19(1)(a).

Where an Act included in an official revised edition is referred to in another Act, the reference is to be taken (in the absence of indication to the contrary) as being to the text as printed in that edition. This requirement would be of significance only where there was a material discrepancy between different versions of the text; but in such a case it would raise more problems than it solved.

Revised editions The first official collection of statutes was published by the Record Commission in the early nineteenth century under the title *Statutes of the Realm*. Since these published statutes were not described as *revised*, and did not purport to be in revised form, they are presumably not within s 19(1)(a) of the Interpretation Act 1978. {See however s 19(1)(b), p 868 below.}

There have since been four official collected editions of the statutes, as follows.

1. The edition called *Statutes Revised*, consisting of 18 volumes, completed in 1885.
2. The edition called *Statutes Revised*, consisting of 24 volumes, published by instalments between 1888 and 1929.
3. The edition called *Statutes Revised*, consisting of 32 volumes, published in 1950.
4. The edition called *Statutes in Force*, arranged under 131 titles, begun in 1972 and completed in 1981 (though continuously updated since).

{For further details of the published editions of the statutes see Bennion *Statute Law* (2nd edn, 1983) chap 8. For cases where this section does not apply see Interpretation Act 1978 s 19(1)(b) and (c), p 868 below.}

There have thus been four successive editions of the statutes published by authority. Only the first three however are described as *revised*. Nevertheless it is thought the fourth (and current) edition also merits this epithet, and thus falls within s 19(1)(a) of the Interpretation Act 1978.

Often the same Acts appear in more than one edition. The versions might differ, yet s 19(1)(a) ignores this possibility.

It is arguable that a reference in an Act to another Act should be treated as referring to the text of it as contained in the official edition current immediately following the date of royal assent. If it were thereafter succeeded by a later edition giving a different version that would not alter the reference. Again, s 19(1)(a) ignores this possibility.

It is also arguable that if there were a discrepancy between a collected edition and the Queen's Printer copy the latter should prevail. Moreover if there should be a material inconsistency between the vellum copies {For these see p 120 above.} and the text as printed in any official published version, the vellum copies should on principle prevail. Yet s 19(1)(a) of the Interpretation Act 1978 ignores the existence of the vellum copies altogether.

Fortunately, material discrepancies between the vellum copies and later published editions are virtually unknown. This renders the problems posed by s 19(1)(a) of the Interpretation Act 1978 more theoretical than practical.

See further p 126 below.

47. Act of Parliament: challenges to Act's validity

The only ground on which a purported Act may be held invalid is that it has not received the necessary threefold consent. Parliament has power by a later Act to confirm or deny the validity of a doubtful Act, but subject to this it is for the court or tribunal before which a purported Act is propounded to rule on any challenge made to its validity.

COMMENTARY

Defects in enactment procedure The preceding sections of this Part of the Code set out the validating procedure by which an instrument becomes a public general Act. This may be briefly described in Coke's phrase as *threefold consent*. {The phrase must be taken to include twofold consent in cases where the consent of the House of Lords is dispensed with under the Parliament Acts 1911 and 1949: see ss 43 and 44 of this Code.} If a purported Act has received threefold consent the judges will not deny it validity. {See D V Cowen 15 MLR 282 and J Winterton 92 LQR 591. As to the question of whether a particular provision of an Act, as opposed to the Act as a whole, may be invalid see s 75 of this Code.}

Here it is necessary to draw a distinction between ancient and modern statutes. The question whether an early instrument is to be classed as an Act is a historical one, turning on the rise of Parliament in medieval times. Difficulty is caused here by the obvious fact that the requirement of threefold consent did not spring into being overnight, but was the outcome of developments spanning several centuries. The question whether a particular ancient instrument is or is not to be classed as a public general Act is not of practical importance today and will not be investigated here. {See s 27 of this Code. The matter is also dealt with in Bennion *Statute Law* (2nd edn, 1983) pp 15-17.} For an instance of where the question did arise in a modern case, and was sidestepped on the ground that the ancient instrument was merely declaratory of the common law, see Example 27.1.

Modern Acts A further sub-division is called for in the case of Acts passed (or alleged to have been passed) in modern times.

For this purpose modern times may be taken to begin around 1400, by which date, as stated at p 82 above, the doctrine of threefold consent had become fully established.

The six centuries to our own day must here be separated into two periods. Until the end of the seventeenth century, the view was tenable that the validity of an Act which had received threefold consent could be defeated on the ground that its provisions infringed natural law or were otherwise beyond the competence of Parliament. Since that time such a challenge has not been sustainable. Nor can it be argued that an Act is vitiated by fraud or other bad faith on the part of legislators {*Fletcher v Peck* (1810) 6 Cranch 87 (Act alleged to have been procured by bribing MPs).} or promoters {*British Railways Board v Pickin* [1974] AC 765 (promoters of private Act alleged to have misled Parliament by false recital).} Since the United Kingdom Parliament is not confined by a written constitution, no question of constitutional infringements can arise. {Cf *Bribery Commissioner v Ranasinghe* [1965] AC 172.} The only serious present-day question (it has given no trouble in practice) concerns the possible allegation that a purported Act has not in fact received threefold consent.

Challenge to threefold consent An instrument put forward as a post-1400 Act is met with the argument that it is not an Act at all because it did not receive threefold consent. Can such an allegation be sustained?

First we need to understand that the courts fully accept Parliamentary supremacy in our constitution. The Judicial Committee of the Privy Council has said that the judges are not at liberty to reject an Act: 'for that were to set the judicial power above that of the legislature, which would be subversive of all government'. {*Logan v Burslem* (1842) 4 Moore PC 284, at p 297.}

The judges, said Willes J, 'do not sit here as a court of appeal from Parliament'. {*Lee v Bude & Torrington Rly* (1871) LR 6 CP 576, at p 580.} On the contrary, he said, they sit only 'as servants of the Queen and the legislature'. {Ibid, p 582.} As Ungoed-Thomas J put it-

'What the statute itself enacts cannot be unlawful, because what the statute says and provides is itself the law. It is the law which prevails over every other form of law, and it is not for the court to say that a parliamentary enactment, the highest law in this country, is illegal.' {*Cheney v Conn* [1968] 1 All ER 779, at p 782. See also *Labrador Co v R* [1893] AC 104, at p 123.}

By such dicta the courts make clear that they fully accept the supremacy of Parliament. To affirm that one will obey an Act does not however dispense with the need to establish that it truly *is* an Act. Nor does the doctrine of judicial notice take the matter very much further. Section 3 of the Interpretation Act 1978 says that (unless the contrary is expressly provided by the Act in question) an Act is to be judicially noticed as such. If it is really an Act it therefore does not need to be proved: the judge is taken to know it. But suppose it is not really an Act at all?

If a doubt is raised, the obvious way to resolve it is to look at the Parliament Roll or the Chancery Roll. If the Act is enrolled its genuineness is surely conclusive. As Lord Campbell said in *Edinburgh and Dalkeith Railway Co v Wauchope* : 'All that a court of justice can do is to look to the Parliamentary roll ...' {(1842) 8 Cl & F 710, at p 725.}

Such inspections have from time to time been made. It was done at the trial of Sir Roger Casement, as appears from the report in the Law Journal. {*R v Casement* (1917) 86 LJKB (NS) 482, at p 486. See further p 782 below, dealing with the presumption of regularity expressed by the maxim *omnia praesumuntur rite et solemniter esse acta.*} An enrolled copy purporting to be not less than twenty years old is presumed genuine as an 'ancient writing'. {Evidence Act 1938 s 4.}

There are however two difficulties about total reliance on the Rolls. An Act may be relevant in judicial proceedings because it is referred to in another Act, but in such a case by statute the reference is not to the other Act as it appears on the Rolls, but as it is officially published. {Interpretation Act 1978, s 19(1)(a). See s 46 of this Code.} This appears to make inclusion of an Act in the relevant official publication conclusive; at least where there is no convincing evidence that it is not an 'Act' at all.

The second difficulty is that, while absence from the Rolls indicates that the alleged Act is not genuine and presence on the Rolls indicates the contrary, neither indication is conclusive. A mistake may have been made by the responsible authorities or (though it would be difficult to credit) there might even have been a deliberate falsification.

There are dicta to suggest that the courts would not entertain such speculations. Lord Campbell said in *Edinburgh & Dalkeith Rly v Wauchope* {(1842) 8 Cl & F 710, at p 725.} that if the Parliament Roll indicates that threefold consent has been given to a Bill-

> ' . . . no Court of Justice can inquire into the mode in which it was introduced into Parliament, nor into what was done previous to its introduction, nor what passed in Parliament during its progress in its various stages through both Houses.'

{See also *R v Countess of Arundel* (1616) Hob 109; *Lee v Bude & Torrington Rly* (1871) LR 6 CP 576, at p 582.}

To which Megarry V-C has appended a pertinent question: 'But does this cover a case where in one House there were no stages at all?' {*Miscellany-at-Law* p 346. Cf F W Maitland *Constitutional History of England* pp 381-2.} In now going on to examine whether it is permissible to go behind an entry (or lack of entry) of an alleged Act on the Rolls we look in turn at the various elements of threefold consent.

Evidence that Commons did not pass Bill Here the first question would be whether the Journals of the House of Commons indicated that the Bill had been passed. Copies of the Journals are admissible in evidence. {See p 83 above.} It seems that the court will not admit evidence contradicting an entry in a Journal, so if the Journal indicated that the Bill was passed that would be conclusive.

Notice of the passing of a Bill is also included in the Official Report (Hansard), but this does not constitute evidence. {Speaker's ruling, 461 HC Official Reports 1347.} Evidence may however be accepted from the reporter in person. {*Tranton v Astor* (1917) 33 TLR 383, at p 385). The leave of the House is not now required for this. {See pp 530–531 below.} If the matter is evidenced by an entry in the Journals of either House there is no difficulty, since s 3 of the Evidence Act 1845 authorises reference in court to such entries.

If the Journal indicated that an Act entered in the Rolls had *not* been passed,

and the matter were brought to the notice of the authorities of the House, there can be little doubt that appropriate corrective action would be taken. It is stated in *Erskine May* that-

> 'If an informality be discovered during the progress of a Bill through the House in which it originated, that House will either order the Bill to be withdrawn, or will annul the informal proceeding itself, and all subsequent proceedings . . .'

{Erskine May *The Law, Privileges, Proceedings and Usage of Parliament* (20th edn, 1983) p 606. For an example of an irregularity on third reading cured by the resolution that the Bill 'do now pass' see Megarry V-C *A Second Miscellany-at-Law* p 106.}

Once a Bill has left the House in which it originated, irregularities cannot be corrected in this way. A distinction is then drawn between fundamental irregularities and lesser errors. The latter are cured by royal assent. As *Erskine May* puts it, 'a departure from the usage of Parliament, during the progress of a Bill, will not vitiate a statute'. {Ibid.} A fundamental error, if discovered, would almost certainly be dealt with by validating legislation. There appears however to be no case on record where a Bill has received royal assent without having been passed by the Commons.

Evidence that Lords did not pass Bill The immediately preceding passage applies to evidence that the Lords did not pass a Bill, except that Hansard is not part of the official record of the House.

One Lords case is on record, relating to a private Bill. It had passed the Commons but not the Lords, and was given royal assent in mistake for another Bill dealing with the same subject. The irregularity was cured by the passage of a special Act thirteen days later. This treated the correct Bill as having received assent on the day in question, and deemed the other Bill not to have received assent then. {7 & 8 Vict c xix (1844).}

In the reign of Elizabeth I, the Commons sent up a Bill it had passed but did not insert on it the required endorsement. {The endorsement is *Soit baillé aux seigneurs*: see p 107 above.} The Bill was returned to the Commons as the Lords had no warrant to proceed with it. {*Erskine May* p 607.}

Evidence that amendments not agreed by both Houses Both Houses must not only pass a Bill, but must agree on any amendments that have been made to it. {See p 108 above.} Errors have occurred over this on two occasions. Both were corrected by subsequent Acts. {See as to the first case 10 Geo 4 cc 51 and 63 (1829) and as to the second 6 & 7 Vict c lxxxvi (1843).}

Errors in connection with royal assent Erskine May records only one case where a Bill which had passed both Houses did not receive royal assent. This was the Bill for the attainder of the Duke of Norfolk in 1546. An Act of Mary declared the attainder void. {1 Mary, No 27 (Stat of the Realm i, p lxxv).} The Act said that the Attainder Bill-

> ' . . . remayneth in verie dede as no Acte of Parlyament, but as a bill onelie exhibited in the saide Parlyament, and onelie assented to by the saide lordes and comons, and not by the saide late king.'

{Ibid, p 608.}

Erskine May also mentions two cases (in 1809 and 1821 respectively) where the titles of Bills were transposed on royal assent. Again the error was corrected by a subsequent Act. {1 & 2 Geo 4 c xcv (1821).}

Bill of Rights   Article 9 of the Bill of Rights (1688) states that debates and proceedings in Parliament must not be impeached or questioned in any court or place out of Parliament. {See p 83 above.} This inhibits the courts from calling into question the validity of the internal functioning of Parliament.

Summary as to defects in enactment procedure   It will be seen from the above that there have been very few cases recorded of defects in the enactment procedure, and that where they have come to light they have been speedily corrected by validating legislation. Although there is a theoretical possibility that the courts might be called upon to declare an Act invalid on proof of a fundamental defect in procedure, the likelihood of its happening remains remote. It seems that the proper course for the court to take if the point were raised would be to adjourn the proceedings to enable the authorities in Parliament to enquire into the matter and bring forward speedy validating legislation if found necessary.

Nevertheless the topic of procedural invalidity warrants notice, if only because an ultimate safeguard against abuse is needed. If a so-called Act were proved not to have received the necessary threefold consent, the courts would in the last resort have to acknowledge and declare the fact. Otherwise they would be enforcing, contrary to the judicial oath {Promissory Oaths Act 1868 s 4.}, provisions that were not law.

Invalidity on other grounds   It may be alleged that an Act which has undoubtedly received threefold consent is invalid on some other ground. Such an allegation is likely to be misconceived because it is difficult to imagine how any other ground of invalidity could exist, whether for an Act as a whole or for any provision of an Act. This is a consequence of the doctrine of parliamentary sovereignty, discussed above. {See s 31.}

One possible case concerns disqualification of members. A person may be disqualified from sitting and voting in either House on various grounds. {See Erskine May *The Law, Privileges, Proceedings and Usage of Parliament* (20th edn, 1983) chap 3.} In certain circumstances the seat of a disqualified person automatically becomes vacant. If a Bill were 'passed' by members some of whom were disqualified in this way, and the majority for the Bill was less than the number disqualified, it could be argued that the Bill had not truly passed that House. {See *Martin v O'Sullivan (Inspector of Taxes)* [1982] STC 416, affd (1984) *The Times* 7 March (allegation that MPs were disqualified as holders of offices of profit under the Crown rejected).}

For completeness, mention should also be made of art 18 of the Union with Scotland Act 1706. This restricts the power of the United Kingdom Parliament to alter pre-union Scottish law. The restriction only affects 'laws which concern private right' (as opposed to 'the laws concerning publick right policy and civil government'). No alteration must be made 'except for evident utility of the subjects within Scotland'.

There is no record of any Act being held invalid for contravention of this provision. Since Acts are presumed to be for the public benefit {See s 127 of this Code.}, it is unlikely that a court would hold its vague formula to be infringed.

An exception would be an Act which overtly discriminated against the inhabitants of Scotland, but the case is inconceivable. Such statutory discrimination as does occur is in favour of, rather than against, the Scots (for example in relation to industrial subsidies).

Even though not formally invalid, an enactment may be practically ineffective: for example because it conflicts with a provision of the Treaty of Rome. This aspect is dealt with in s 75 of the Code.

PREROGATIVE INSTRUMENT

48. Prerogative instrument: nature of

Vestiges of the royal prerogative not taken away by statute still give the Crown certain primary law-making powers. Orders in Council in exercise of these powers are made only on the advice of Ministers, and operate subject to provisions made by or under any Act.

COMMENTARY

The royal prerogative is regulated by law, that is by common law and above all by statute: 'the King hath no prerogative, but that which the law of the land allows him'. {*The Case of Proclamations* (1611) 12 Co Rep 74.} The law now allows the prerogative very little scope.

In the seventeenth century an attempt was made to get round this rule that the prerogative is regulated by law. The device used was that of *non obstante*. This worked through the issue of royal instruments announcing that they had effect *non obstante aliquo statuto in contrarium* (notwithstanding any statute to the contrary). Under Stuart domination, the judges then sitting in Westminster Hall accepted that the statutes were overridden.

This judicial surrender did not last for long. The device of *non obstante* was, as Blackstone put it, 'effectually demolished by the Bill of Rights at the revolution, and abdicated Westminster Hall when James II abdicated the kingdom'. {Kerr Bl (4th edn, 1876) i 305.}

In modern times the prerogative has been mainly of importance as a source of primary legislation in respect of war and emergency, and the government of Crown colonies and other dependent territories. In the former connection, it remains an important reserve power of government. This is illustrated by the Requisitioning of Ships Order 1982, made at the time of the Falklands War. That the prerogative legislative power is still capable of development is shown by the Criminal Injuries Compensation Scheme which was set up by proclamation on 1 August 1964. {*R v Criminal Injuries Compensation Board, ex p Thompstone* [1983] 1 All ER 936, at p 939. See also *R v Criminal Injuries Compensation Board, ex p Lain* [1967] 2 QB 864, *per* Diplock LJ at p 886.}

The legislative aspect of the prerogative power to declare war was thus described by Willes J in *Esposito v Bowden* {(1857) 7 E & B 763, at p 781.}-

> 'The force of a declaration of war is equal to that of an Act of Parliament prohibiting intercourse with the enemy except by the Queen's licence. As an Act of State, done by virtue of the Prerogative exclusively belonging to the Crown, such a declaration carries with it all the force of law.'

While carrying the force of law, an act of state is not generally within the cognizance of the courts. {*Sobhuza II v Miller* [1926] AC 518. See further pp 493–494 below.} However the modern doctrine is to distinguish acts of state (operating in relation to foreigners) from prerogative acts (relating to subjects). {*Re Ferdinand, ex-Tsar of Bulgaria* [1921] 1 Ch 107, at p 139.} In this sense, the courts retain jurisdiction over prerogative instruments. {*The Zamora* [1916] 2 AC 77.} For a recent example of the exercise of this jurisdiction see *Post Office v Estuary Radio Ltd* {[1968] 2 QB 740.}, which concerned the interpretation of the Territorial Waters Order in Council 1964.

Statutory curtailment of prerogative   Doubt sometimes arises as to whether, and if so to what extent, an Act is intended to curtail the prerogative power to legislate.

The historical tendency has been for prerogative powers to be enlarged, regulated, and finally superseded by Acts of Parliament. Thus a series of Acts to deal with the power to take land for the defence of the realm began in 1708. The successive Acts dealt piecemeal with various aspects of land requisition until replaced by the comprehensive Defence Act 1842. This has remained in force, though amended and supplemented by many subsequent Acts.

Where it legislates comprehensively in a field occupied by the prerogative, the presumption is that Parliament intends the Act, rather than the prerogative, thereafter to apply. This was laid down by the House of Lords in *A-G v De Keyser's Royal Hotel* {[1920] AC 508.}, where the question concerned the Crown's prerogative right to take land for the defence of the realm without the need to pay the compensation required by the Defence Act 1842. Lord Parmoor said {P 576.}-

> ' . . . where a matter has been directly regulated by statute there is a necessary implication that the statutory regulation must be obeyed, and that as far as such regulation is inconsistent with the claim of a Royal Prerogative right, such right can no longer be enforced.'

See further p 304 below.

Of course Parliament can always make clear that it intends the prerogative to remain untouched, as by saying expressly that the Act shall not bind the Crown. {As to the general doctrine of Crown immunity from legislation see s 34 of this Code.} Or the prerogative may be specifically mentioned. {See, e g, Emergency Powers (Defence) Act 1939 s 9.}

49. Prerogative instrument: interpretation of

Allowing for the difference in provenance, Orders in Council made under the prerogative are construed in the same way as Acts.

COMMENTARY

In effect, prerogative Orders in Council constitute legislation by the government or executive. This is taken to have the same general intention as Parliament, so that the same interpretative criteria apply as in the case of Acts. {As to the interpretative criteria see Part VI of this Code.} Thus the principles of judicial review apply to powers exercisable under a prerogative instrument in the same way as to statutory powers. {*R v Secretary of State for the Foreign and*

Commonwealth Office, ex p Council of Civil Service Unions (1984) The Times, 17 July 1984.}

An obvious exception operates in relation to construction by reference to the components of the instrument, called by this Code functional construction. {Functional construction is dealt with in s 124 and Part XII of the Code.} The components of an Act differ in nature and juristic significance from those of a prerogative Order in Council. The latter closely resemble those of an Order in Council made under delegated powers. {As to functional construction of such Orders in Council see s 62 of this Code.}

Difference in provenance Allowing for the difference in provenance of a prerogative Order in Council from that of an Act amounts to little more than recognising that, apart from Government statements on the Order made in Parliament and any debates arising from them, there will be lacking the parliamentary information usually made available as to the mischief to which an Act is directed, and the nature of the remedy provided to remedy it. {See Part XIV of this Code. As to legislative history see Part X.}

Since the intention of a particular goverment is a more straightforward concept than the intention of a complex legislature such as the Queen in Parliament, this difference is likely if anything marginally to simplify the task of interpretation. {As to legislative intention see Part V of this Code.}

DELEGATED LEGISLATION

50. Delegated legislation: nature of

An item of delegated legislation is an instrument made by a person or body (in this Code called the delegate) under legislative powers conferred by Act (in the Code called the enabling Act). The corpus of delegated legislation is divided into instruments which are statutory instruments (within the meaning of s 1 of the Statutory Instruments Act 1946) and other legislative instruments made under statutory powers.

COMMENTARY

The delegation of legislative power by means of an enabling Act is, by a paradox, an aspect of the grant of *executive* power. The position is thus summed up by *Erskine May-*

> 'It has been recognised that the greater number of details of an essentially subsidiary or procedural character which can be withdrawn from the floors of both Houses, the more time will be available for the discussion of major matters of public concern. Consequently, legislative power is often conferred upon the executive by statute, and various arrangements are made for parliamentary scrutiny of its exercise.'

{Erskine May *Parliamentary Practice* (20th edn, 1983) p 609.}

The delegate is usually a functionary of the executive, whether formally (as in the case of a Minister) or de facto (as in the case of the Queen in Council, who acts only on the advice of Ministers). An exception arises where the judiciary are given statutory power to make rules of court. {As to delegated legislation generally see: Report of the Committee on Ministers' Powers (Donoughmore Committee, 1932) Cmd 4060; C Carr *Delegated Legislation* (Cambridge, 1921); C Carr *Concerning English Administrative Law* (1941); C K Allen *Law in the Making* (7th edn, 1964); C K Allen *Law and Orders* (3rd edn, 1965); W Graham Harrison *Notes on the Delegation by Parliament of Legislative Powers* (1931); Report of the Select Committee on Delegated Legislation (1952-53) HC 301; Reports of the Joint Committee on Delegated Legislation (1971-72) HL 184, HC 475 (1972-73) HL 188 and 204, HC 407 and 468, and subsequently.}

In earlier times the executive power was wholly vested in the Crown. The change to the modern system was gradually effected by statute; and was thus described by Maitland in 1888-

> 'Open the statute book, on almost every page of it you will find "it shall be lawful for the Treasury to do this", "it shall be lawful for one of the Secretaries of State to do that". This is the result of a modern movement, a movement which began, we may say, about the time of the Reform Bill of 1832. The new wants of a new age have been met in a new manner - by giving statutory powers of all kinds, sometimes to the Queen in Council, sometimes to the Treasury, sometimes to a Secretary of State, sometimes to this Board, sometimes to the other.'

{F W Maitland *The Constitutional History of England* p 417.}

Reasons for delegation There are many reasons why Parliament finds it necessary to delegate legislative power. These may be summarised as follows.

(1) Modern legislation requires far more detail than Parliament itself has time or inclination for.

(2) To bring a complex legislative scheme into full working operation, consultation with affected interests is required. This can best be done *after* Parliament has passed the outline legislation, since it is then known that the new law is indeed to take effect and what its main points are. {For a useful discussion of this process of consultation, including a list of Acts which require such consultation to be carried out, see G C Thornton *Legislative Drafting* (2nd edn, 1979) pp 251-254.}

(3) Some details of the overall legislative scheme may need to be tentative or experimental. Delegated legislation affords an easy means of adjusting the scheme without further recourse to Parliament.

(4) Within the field of a regulatory Act new developments will from time to time arise. By the use of delegated legislation the scheme can be easily altered to allow for these. {This principle is even applied to taxation, as for example in the case of the Import Duties Act 1958, under which hundreds of taxing orders were made from time to time.}

(5) If a sudden emergency arises it may be essential to give the executive wide and flexible legislative powers to deal with it whether or not Parliament is sitting. {See Emergency Powers Act 1920.}

See further s 59 of this Code.

Unless the contrary intention appears from the enabling Act, the power to make delegated legislation may be exercised from time to time as occasion requires. {Interpretation Act 1978 s 12.}

For implementing Act The essential function of delegated legislation is to carry out the purpose of the enabling Act. Early forms of delegation were expressed in those terms, and gave the delegate a free hand.

Example 1 Thus the Recovery of Small Debts (Scotland) Act 1825 s 23 conferred on justices a general power to make rules and orders 'for carrying into effect the provisions and purpose of this Act'.

Example 2 The Poor Law Amendment Act 1834 gave very wide powers which were carried through into the Poor Law Act 1930. Section 136(1) of the 1930 Act said: 'for executing the powers given to him by this Act, the Minister shall make such rules, orders and regulations as he may think fit for ... *the management of the poor*. {Emphasis added.}

Wide powers of this kind were commonly inserted in colonial legislation throughout the period of the British Empire, but at home Parliament came to insist on tighter control. {For a modern provision giving very wide powers of this kind see Local Government Act 1972 s 254(1).}

Where a social problem requiring legislation exists, a common governmental response is to set up a departmental committee to enquire into the matter and report. An Act is then passed to implement the committee's recommendations (or such of them as are approved). Occasionally the Act, instead of itself effecting the necessary legal changes, entrusts this task to a delegate.

Example 3 In 1927 a committee was set up to enquire into the use of artificial humidity in factories making cotton cloth. The committee's report recommended the making of certain regulatory provisions. Parliament then passed the Factory and Workshop (Cotton Cloth Factories) Act 1929. Section 1(1) of this referred to the committee's recommendations and went on simply to empower the Secretary of State to make regulations 'for the purpose of giving effect to the recommendations contained in the report'.

During any interval between the passing and commencement of an enabling Act, delegated legislation may be made under it for the purpose of bringing any of its provisions into force, or giving full effect to a provision after it comes into force. {Interpretation Act 1978 s 13. This reproduced with minor amendments s 37 of the Interpretation Act 1889. As to the amendments see Law Com No 90 (Cmnd 7235) App, para 3 (set out at p 878 below). The amendments were made in the light of *R v Minister of Town and Country Planning* [1951] 1 KB 1 and *Usher v Barlow* [1952] Ch 255.}

Must not conflict with Act Unless the enabling Act so provides, delegated legislation cannot override any Act - and certainly not the enabling Act itself. {*Re Davis, ex p Davis* (1872) 7 Ch App 526, at p 529.} Indeed it is taken not to be authorised to override any rule of the general law. {5 Co Rep 63a; *Hall v Nixon* (1875) LR 10 QB 152, at p 159; *Rossi v Edinburgh Corpn* [1905] AC 21. See further s 58 of this Code.} This principle arises from the very nature of delegated legislation, and does not need to be stated in the enabling Act. {In earlier times less afraid of tautology, such statements were included: see, e g, Recovery of Small Debts (Scotland) Act 1825 s 23.}

Has effect as if made by Act Subject to the rule just mentioned that it must not conflict with general law, a provision of delegated legislation has statutory force.

That is its effect is the same as if it were contained in an Act. {*Dale's Case* (1881) 6 QBD 376, at p 398; *Re Langlois and Biden* [1891] 1 QB 349, at p 355; *Kruse v Johnson* [1898] 2 QB 91, at p 96; *Re Macartney, Brookhouse v Barman* (1920) 36 TLR 394.}

Formerly this would usually be spelt out in the enabling Act. {The practice has been traced back to the Statute of the Staple 1385: W Graham Harrison *Notes on Delegated Legislation* p 66.}

Example 4 Thus the great Reform Act of 1832, giving power to make legislative instruments laying down altered dates and times, said that these 'shall be deemed to be of the same force and effect as if they had in every instance been mentioned in this Act'. {Representation of the People Act 1832 s 80. Cf Civil Procedure Act 1833 s 1.} A few current Acts contain this provision. {See, e g, Emergency Powers Act 1920 s 2(4).} The effect is the same, whether or not the enabling Act spells it out. {*Institute of Patent Agents v Lockwood* [1894] AC 360, at p 361.}

While a *valid* item of delegated legislation has statutory effect, words saying that it is to 'have effect as if enacted in this Act' will not avail to achieve this effect if the instrument is ultra vires. {As to the doctrine of ultra vires see s 58 of this Code.}

May amend Act   The enabling Act may confer power on the delegate to amend the enabling Act itself, or any other Act. A provision conferring such power was formerly known as a Henry VIII clause, since it was supposed to reflect that monarch's autocratic tendencies. {C K Allen *Law and Orders* pp 100-102. See also *R v Minister of Health, ex p Wortley RC* [1927] 2 KB 229.}

Such provisions began to appear in the second half of the nineteenth century. {See, e g, Factory Acts Extension Act 1867 s 14; Anatomy Act (1832) Amendment Act 1871 s 2.} They are often used in relation to local Acts.

Example 5   Thus the Public Health Act 1875 s 303 confers power to 'repeal, alter or amend' by provisional order any local Act 'which relates to the same subject-matter as this Act'. {For a modern example see Mental Health Act 1983 s 144.}

It is not unknown even for moden Acts to give power to amend, or even repeal, public general enactments by delegated legislation.

Example 6   Thus the Local Government Act 1972 s 252(1) gives power to make modifications in any public general Act, or any instrument 'of a legislative character'.

{Another recent example is the House of Commons Disqualification Act 1975 s 5 (power to amend list of offices set out in Sch 1 to the Act). See also Town and Country Planning Act 1971 s 287(6).}

Delegated power is often given to amend monetary limits in Acts. {See, e g, Companies Act 1967 s 48(2); Gas Act 1972 s 19(1); Consumer Credit Act 1974 s 181.} Sweeping general powers to increase the amounts of fines imposed by Act are conferred by recent legislation. {See Magistrates' Courts Act 1980 s 143; Criminal Justice Act 1982 s 38.}

Apart from a power to amend the enabling Act, delegated power may be given to modify its effect from time to time.

Example 7 Thus s 50(1) of the Supreme Court of Judicature (Consolidation) Act 1925 said that *subject to rules of court* costs should be in the discretion of the court or judge. {Emphasis added. See now Supreme Court Act 1981 s 51(1).} This meant that, while the Act itself gave full discretion on costs to the court or judge, delegated legislation could curtail or even remove this. {As to the precise juridical nature of such provisions see *EMI Records Ltd v Ian Cameron Wallace Ltd* [1982] 2 All ER 980, *per* Megarry V-C at p 987.}

Sub-delegation By a three-tier system, an Act may authorise a Minister to make regulations controlling the making of byelaws by a subordinate authority. {See, e g, Sea Fisheries Regulation Act 1966 s 5 (byelaws by local fisheries committees).} Commentators have detected in some cases as many as *five* tiers in delegated legislation. {See J A G Griffith and H Street *Principles of Administrative Law* (5th edn, 1973) pp 59-66. See further pp 146 and 152 below.} Sub-delegation is dealt with below. {See s 67 of this Code.}

Terminology The Interpretation Act 1978 uses the term 'subordinate legislation' rather than delegated legislation. The former term is defined as 'Orders in Council, orders, rules, regulations, schemes, warrants, byelaws and other instruments made or to be made under any Act'. {Interpretation Act 1978 s 21(1).} This Code prefers the more descriptive term 'delegated legislation' because the central concept of the delegation of legislative power by Parliament is a crucial one, and needs constantly to be borne in mind when interpreting such instruments.

Judicial control The courts have long maintained a right to superintend delegated legislation, though their powers are necessarily limited by the terms of enabling Acts. In relation to byelaws, the courts have exercised a more stringent supervision than in the case of other forms of delegated legislation. {As to byelaws see p 144 below and s 65 of this Code.} The general position of the courts is thus explained by Lord Greene MR-

> 'All that the court can do is to see that the power which it is claimed to exercise is one which falls within the four corners of the powers given by the legislature and to see that the powers are exercised in good faith. Apart from that the courts have no power at all to enquire into the reasonableness, the policy, the sense or any other aspect of the transaction.'

{*Carltona Ltd v Commrs of Works* [1943] 1 All ER 560, at p 564. See also *Lewisham BC v Roberts* [1949] 2 KB 608; *Minister of Agriculture and Fisheries v Matthews* [1950] 1 KB 148. Various aspects of judicial control are dealt with in the following sections of this Code: 24 (judicial review); 57 (duty to exercise delegated powers); 58 (doctrine of ultra vires); 59 (rule of primary intention); 65 (byelaws); 67 (sub-delegation); 335 (natural justice etc).}

Parliamentary control As to parliamentary control over delegated legislation see s 51 of this Code.

51. Delegated legislation: parliamentary control of

In conferring a delegated legislative power, Parliament often retains some measure of control over the exercise of the power. For example it may require instruments to be laid before Parliament; and may make them subject to affirmative or negative procedure.

COMMENTARY

Although Parliament is often compelled to delegate legislative power, it prefers to retain some measure of control over the exercise of the power. This especially applies where the delegated legislation deals with matters of considerable importance. {See C Carr 'Parliamentary Control of Delegated Legislation' (1956) Public Law 200; J E Kersell *Parliamentary Supervision of Delegated Legislation*. Cf J R Mallory 'Parliamentary Scrutiny of Delegated Legislation in Canada' (1972) Public Law 30; Indian Law Institute *Delegated Legislation in India*.}

Normally such controls do not extend to the *amendment* of delegated legislation by Parliament, since this has the effect of converting it into primary legislation. An exception is provided by s 2 of the Emergency Powers Act 1920. Under this, regulations made following a proclamation of emergency require confirmation by resolutions of both Houses of Parliament, and 'may be added to, altered or revoked' by such resolutions. {Emergency Powers Act 1920 s 2(4). For another exception see s 2(1) of the Easter Act 1928. For a list of enactments conferring power on Parliament to amend delegated legislation see Report of the Joint Committee on Delegated Legislation (HL 184, HC 475 of 1971-2) p 181.}

Laying before Parliament   Some enabling Acts require delegated legislation to be laid before Parliament after being made. {See 36 MLR 64.} The meaning of this is explained in s 4 of the Statutory Instruments Act 1946, and in the Laying of Documents Before Parliament (Interpretation) Act 1948.

It appears that the duty to lay is mandatory. {As to the distinction between mandatory and directory statutory duties see s 10 of this Code.} For this reason it has been considered necessary to pass Indemnity Acts where the duty to lay was not carried out.

Example 1   This happened in respect of a series of wartime fire services regulations: see National Fire Service Regulations (Indemnity) Act 1944. In the debate on the Bill for this Act the Attorney-General stated that the duty to lay was mandatory. {HC Deb vol 42 col 1246.}

Example 2   It happened more recently in relation to certain town and country planning legislation: see Town and Country Planning Regulations (London) (Indemnity) Act 1970.

The Supreme Court of Barbados ruled that the duty to lay was mandatory in *Biggs v Commr of Police*. {(1982) 8 CLB 576. But see *Bailey v Williamson* (1873) LR 8 QB 118, at p 132; *Starey v Graham* [1899] 1 QB 406, at p 412; *Metcalfe v Cox* [1895] AC 328.}

Affirmative resolution procedure   Affirmative resolution procedure is said to have been first employed by the Military Manoeuvres Act 1897. {C K Allen

Law and Orders p 66.} It usually requires the passing of a resolution by *both* Houses of Parliament before the instrument becomes effective. The enabling Act may require a draft of the instrument to be approved before it can be made. {See, e g, Consumer Credit Act 1974 s 181(2). For a case where a time limit is imposed for the laying of the draft see Industry Act 1975 s 15(4).} Or the Act may say that an instrument, though made, shall not have effect, or shall cease to have effect, if affirmative resolutions are not passed. {See, e g, Sea Fish (Conservation) Act 1967; Legal Advice and Assistance Act 1972 s 11(2); Industry Act 1975 s 15(1).}

Negative resolution procedure Negative resolution procedure is a less rigorous form of parliamentary control than affirmative procedure. It enables either House of Parliament to defeat the instrument by passing a resolution annulling it or praying that it be annulled.

Example 3 An early example is furnished by the Lunacy Regulation (Ireland) Act 1871 s 118, which provided that either House of Parliament might by resolution annul an order made under the Act.

Sometimes, instead of providing for annulment of an order already made, the enabling Act requires the order to be laid in draft. If within a specified period a negative resolution is passed the matter can proceed no further. {See, e g, Census Act 1920 s 1(2).}

Mixed procedure Exceptionally, some parts of an instrument may be subject to affirmative procedure while others are subject to negative procedure. {See, e g, Census Act 1920 s 1(2).} Here the parts of the draft instrument subject to affirmative procedure are distinguiished for parliamentary purposes by being printed in italics.

Scrutiny Committee To replace the previous separate systems which had prevailed since 1944, the practice was adopted by the two Houses of Parliament in 1973 of appointing a sessional Joint Committee on Statutory Instruments. This is known as the Scrutiny Committee. Its duty is to draw to the special attention of Parliament any statutory instrument that calls for scrutiny. Among the specified grounds are that the instrument-

imposes a charge on the public revenues;

is made under an enactment excluding it from challenge in the courts;

purports to have retrospective effect where the enabling Act does not so provide;

has been unjustifiably delayed in publication;

gives rise to doubt as to whether it is *intra vires*;

appears to make an unusual or unexpected use of the powers conferred by the enabling Act;

requires elucidation as to its form or purport;

is defective in its drafting.

137

Some delegated instruments concerned with money are the responsibility of the House of Commons alone. {See p 139 below.} For these a separate sessional scrutiny committee is constituted, known as the House of Commons Select Committee on Statutory Instruments.

52. Delegated legislation: types of delegate (H M The Queen)

The only primary legislative power possessed by the Crown is either by virtue of the royal prerogative or as an element in the legislature known as the Queen in Parliament. Nevertheless an Act may authorise the Queen to make instruments having the force of law. Usually these are to take the form of Orders in Council, but other forms (such as proclamations or declarations) may be used instead.

COMMENTARY

Whenever in early times it was doubtful whether the royal prerogative extended to a matter with regard to which the King desired legislative power, or the exercise of the prerogative might be disputed, Parliament was asked to grant the necessary power. The outstanding example of this was the Proclamation by the Crown 1539. {See p 99 above.} Earlier still, the statute 11 Edw 3 c 1 (1337) prohibited the exporting of wool unless otherwise ordained by the King in council. Later, the Mutiny Act 1717 gave the King power to legislate for the army.

In modern times powers of delegated legislation bestowed on the Queen are most usually to be exercised by Order in Council. It is the modern constitutional convention that in exercising Her powers of delegated legislation the Queen acts only on the advice of Ministers.

Orders in Council   An Order in Council is an order made by the Queen by and with the advice of the Privy Council. The full name of the latter is 'the Lords and others of Her Majesty's Most Honourable Privy Council'. {Interpretation Act 1978 s 5 and Sch 1.} The jurisdiction of the Privy Council extends only to Great Britain. {Union with Scotland (Amendment) Act 1707 s 1.} The Privy Council of Northern Ireland was put in abeyance by s 32(3) of the Northern Ireland Constitution Act 1973.

An Order in Council is usually drafted in the Department concerned with administering the enabling Act, though an unusually important Order may be drafted by Parliamentary Counsel. Its ratification by the Queen and Privy Council is a formality.

Proclamations   The Emergency Powers Act 1920 s 1 empowers the Queen, where it appears to her that events threatening the nation's essentials of life have occurred, or are about to occur, to issue a proclamation of emergency. For another example of a royal power to legislate by proclamation see Coinage Act 1870 s 11. By implication, such powers are taken to be exercisable only on the advice of Ministers. {For the implied incorporation of such principles of constitutional law see s 334 of this Code.}

Declarations It is rare for an Act to provide for royal declarations. One example is the Coroners (Amendment) Act 1926. Section 4(4) of this provided for the abolition of the office of Admiralty Coroner 'if His Majesty is pleased to declare in Council that it is his will' to relinquish the right of making appointments to the office. Under this provision there was made the Admiralty Coronership (Abolition) Declaration 1927. {S R & O 1927 675.}

53. Delegated legislation: types of delegate (Privy Council)

Certain Acts confer delegated legislative power on the Privy Council alone.

COMMENTARY

The full name of the Privy Council is 'the Lords and others of Her Majesty's Most Honourable Privy Council'. {Interpretation Act 1978 s 5 and Sch 1.} The jurisdiction of the Privy Council extends only to Great Britain. {Union with Scotland (Amendment) Act 1707 s 1. The Privy Council of Northern Ireland was put in abeyance by s 32(3) of the Northern Ireland Constitution Act 1973.}

Delegated legislative powers conferred on the Privy Council alone usually concern its supervisory functions in relation to bodies incorporated by royal charter and regulated by Act. The instruments made under these powers are styled Orders of Council. {See, e g, Medical Act 1950 s 34(1); Opticians Act 1958 ss 7(5), 9(4), 10(4), 15(4), 17(3), 18(4), 20(4) and 25; Professions Supplementary to Medicine Act 1960 s 2(3); Veterinary Surgeons Act 1966 ss 3 and 25; Medical Act 1978 s 27.}

54. Delegated legislation: types of delegate (House of Commons)

In recognition of the exclusive power of the House of Commons over the raising and expenditure of public money, Parliament has by Act endowed certain orders of that House with legislative effect.

COMMENTARY

The Crown, as the executive power, is charged by the constitution with responsibility for the management of the public revenue of the state, and with the making of payments for the public service. Acting on the advice of Ministers, the Crown makes known to the House of Commons the financial requirements of the Government, and that House in return grants such aids or supplies as are needed. It provides by taxation, and by the appropriation of other sources of public income, the ways and means to meet the supplies it has granted. The Crown demands money, the Commons grant it, and the Lords assent to the grant. {Erskine May *Parliamentary Practice* (20th edn, 1983) p 750.}

An example of a delegated legislative power conferred on the House of Commons is provided by the Provisional Collection of Taxes Act 1968 s 1. This enables the House to pass resolutions which, for a limited period only, have statutory effect as if contained in an Act. {As to the legislative effect of certain financial resolutions and Bills see p 99 above. For the passing of money Bills under the Parliament Acts 1911 and 1949 see s 43 of the Code.}

55. Delegated legislation: types of delegate (Ministers)

In the case of most delegated legislation the appointed delegate is a Minister of the Crown.

COMMENTARY

The reasons why in the case of most delegated legislation the appointed delegate is a Minister are explained above. {See s 50 of this Code.}

Secretaries of State   In early times there was only one Secretary of State. Henry VIII appointed a second in 1539. {F W Maitland *The Constitutional History of England* p 392.} In 1601 the king's secretary became 'our principal Secretary of State' {Ibid.} The number grew to five in the nineteenth century, and remained at about that level until the Second World War.

Since around 1960 it has become usual to designate almost every senior Minister of the Crown as a Secretary of State rather than a Minister. His civil servants are then designated a Department rather than a Ministry. Acts conferring functions simply refer to 'the Secretary of State' rather than specifying a particular Minister. {Exceptions arise only where it is considered politically necessary to identify the Secretary of State concerned, or there is more than one involved. See, e g, 23 & 24 Vict c 34 (1860) s 2.}

By virtue of the Interpretation Act 1978, the expression 'Secretary of State' is taken to mean one of Her Majesty's Principal Secretaries of State. {S 5 and Sch 1.} It is for the Prime Minister to say which one. The system has the convenience that the reallocation by the Prime Minister of statutory functions between Ministers can be achieved without amending the relevant Acts. {See further pp 43–44 above.}

56. Delegated legislation: types of delegate (others)

There is no restriction on the types of person or body to whom Parliament may delegate legislative power. The delegate need not be one established by Act. Nor need the delegate be in the public domain, though this is usually the case.

COMMENTARY

Parliament has unfettered legislative power. {See s 31 of this Code.} It follows that, if it seems to Parliament expedient, a portion of this power may be delegated to anyone.

Example 1   Thus we find one delegate judicially described as a 'domestic executive body which the Legislature has thought fit in the public interest to entrust with important statutory powers'. {*Rowell v Pratt* [1938] AC 101, *per* Lord Maugham at p 103 (boards empowered under Agricultural Marketing Acts 1931 to 1933).}

57. Delegated legislation: duty to exercise delegated powers

Where an Act confers power on any person or body to make delegated legislation, the power may be either mandatory or discretionary. Where it is merely discretionary, the recipient is nevertheless under a duty to exercise the discretion properly.

COMMENTARY

The intention of Parliament in conferring a power to make delegated legislation may be that the power shall in any event be exercised, though the details of its exercise are necessarily left to the judgment of the delegate (subject to any reserved or confirming power in anyone else). On the other hand Parliament may intend to leave the question whether or not the power is to be exercised to the judgment of the delegate. Even here, the delegate must take the decision whether or not to exercise the power on a proper basis. {As to the principles governing the exercise of statutory decision-making powers see s 335 of this Code.}

Where the delegate fails to carry out a duty to make delegated legislation, or improperly exercises a discretion conferred on him in this regard, the remedy of judicial review is available. {As to judicial review see s 24 of this Code.}

Example 1 The Secretary of State for the Environment failed to make certain regulations under the Town and Country Planning Act 1971 with respect to the structure plan for Greater London. His reason was that the Government had embarked on a policy of abolishing the Greater London Council. The Council applied for judicial review. *Held* The Secretary of State ought to have made the regulations, and a declaration to that effect would be granted.

The court based its decision on three different views of the relevant enactments: (1) they placed a duty on the Secretary of State to make the regulations; (2) alternatively, they conferred a power which in all the circumstances was coupled with a duty to make them; (3) in the further alternative, they conferred a mere discretion which the Secretary of State, in refusing to make the regulations, had wrongfully exercised. {*R v Secretary of State for the Environment, ex p Greater London Council* (1983) *The Times* 2 December. As to failure to make a commencement order see pp 415–416 below.}

58. Delegated legislation: doctrine of ultra vires

Any provision of an item of delegated legislation is ineffective if it goes outside the powers which (expressly or by implication) are conferred on the delegate by the enabling Act. The provision is then said to be ultra vires (beyond the powers). This applies even where the instrument has been sanctioned by a confirming authority. Except where to do so would produce an instrument the effect of which the delegate would or might not have approved, the court has power to modify the instrument so as to remove its ultra vires quality.

COMMENTARY

It is self-evident that a power to do something extends only to that thing. A purported exercise of the power that extends to a different thing is to that extent not an exercise of the power at all. In so far as it purports to depend on that power, it is therefore void in that respect. As R F V Heuston has put it: 'the power exercised must be the power conferred'. {*Essays in Constitutional Law* (2nd edn, 1964) p 171. See Example 334.2.}

Here it is necessary to be clear just how far the power extends. An express power to do X may by implication also cover Y and Z. The power then extends to X, Y and Z.

Implications may *restrict* the delegated power. Like any other Act, an enabling Act imports implied ancillary legal rules {See s 144 and Part XVIII of this Code.} and implied ancillary legal maxims. {See s 145 and Part XIX.} Any of these may have a limiting effect.

Example 1   Section 47 of the Prisons Act 1952 empowers the Secretary of State to make rules for the regulation and management of penal establishments, and for the classification, treatment, employment, discipline and control of persons required to be detained in them. Under this power the Prison Rules 1964 were made. Rule 34(8) says that a prisoner shall not be entitled to communicate with any person in connection with any legal or other business except with the leave of the Secretary of State. Rule 37A purports to limit rights of communication between a prisoner and his legal adviser. The rules also confer on the Secretary of State power to make standing orders. Under this power a standing order was made which prohibits a prisoner's letter from including allegations against prison officers.

In *Raymond v Honey* {[1982] 1 All ER 756.} the respondent was a prisoner who was a party to certain legal proceedings. He wrote a letter to his solicitor which included an allegation of theft against a prison officer. The letter was stopped by the prison governor. The prisoner then prepared an application to the High Court for the committal of the governor for contempt of court in respect of the stopping of the letter. This application too was stopped. *Held* The governor was guilty of contempt of court. The power conferred by s 47 could not be taken to allow the making of rules which hindered the basic right of a citizen to unimpeded access to the courts. Lord Wilberforce said {Pp 760-1.}-

> 'In my opinion there is nothing in the Prison Act 1952 that confers a power to make regulations (*sic*) which would deny, or interfere with, the right of the respondent, as a prisoner, to have unimpeded access to a court. Section 47 . . . is quite insufficient to authorise hindrance or interference with so basic a right. The rules themselves must be interpreted accordingly, otherwise they would be ultra vires . . . The standing orders, if they have any legislative force at all, cannot confer any greater powers than the regulations which, as stated above, must be construed in accordance with the statutory power to make them.'

{See also *Chester v Bateson* [1920] 1 KB 829. Cf *R v Housing Appeal Tribunal* [1920] 3 KB 334 (delegated instrument authorising the condemnation of a person unheard). For the implied importing of general legal rules conferring rights under natural justice see pp 730–731 below.}

Purported confirmation of invalid provision   It follows that it does not add a scrap of validity to an excessive exercise of the power that it has been confirmed by the authority appointed for that purpose by the enabling Act. {*Ipswich Taylors' Case* (1614) 11 Co Rep 53; *Stationers' Company v Salisbury* (1693) Comb 221; *R v Wood* (1855) 5 E & B 49; *Slattery v Naylor* (1888) 13 App Cas 446; *Kennaird v*

Cory & Son [1898] 2 QB 578; *London and Westcliff Properties Ltd v Minister of Housing and Local Government* [1961] 1 WLR 519.} The only thing that can save the ultra vires provision is a fresh legislative initiative by an authority whose powers *are* wide enough to cover it, for example the passing of a confirmatory Act by Parliament. This applies even though the named confirming authority is one or both Houses of Parliament. By themselves, these have no legislative authority except as delegates. {See s 33 of this Code.}

Nor, for the same reason, can an ultra vires instrument be saved by words in the enabling Act which say that instruments made under the power 'shall have effect as if contained in this Act'. The position is summed up in the following dictum of Lord Sumner in *R v Ministry of Health, ex p Yaffé* {[1931] AC 494, at p 503.}, concerning a scheme made under the Housing Act 1925-

> 'The confirmation makes the scheme speak as if it was contained in an Act of Parliament, but the Act of Parliament in which it is contained is the Act which provides for the framing of the scheme, not a subsequent Act. If therefore the scheme, as made, conflicts with the Act, it will have to give way to the Act. The mere confirmation will not save it. It would be otherwise if the scheme had been per se embodied in a subsequent Act, for then the maxim to be applied would have been *posteriora derogant prioribus*. But as it is, if one can find that the scheme is inconsistent with the provisions of the Act which authorises the scheme, the scheme will be bad, and that can only be gone into by way of proceedings in certiorari.'

{See also *Hoffman la Roche (F) & Co AG v Secretary of State for Trade and Industry* [1975] AC 295.}

Ratification by Parliament   As the dictum of Lord Sumner just cited indicates, a later Act may ratify, and thereby validate, an ultra vires instrument. Here it must be clear that Parliament had the ultra vires point in mind, and did not merely continue the instrument assuming it to be valid. {See *Re Fletcher, ex p Fletcher v Official Receiver* [1955] 2 All ER 592.}

Disapplying the doctrine   Attempts have been made to disapply the ultra vires doctrine. Thus s 39(3) of the Small Holdings and Allotments Act 1908 said confirmation of an order 'shall be conclusive evidence that the requirements of this Act have been complied with, and that the order has been duly made and is within the powers of this Act'. {See also Housing, Town Planning &c Act 1909 Sch 1 para 2; Education Act 1918 s 34(1); Salmon and Freshwater Fisheries Act 1923 s 16(5); Housing Act 1925 Sch 3 para 2; Agricultural Marketing Act 1931 s 1(8).} Such a statement is a logical contradiction, yet since the intention of Parliament is the paramount consideration in statutory interpretation, some attempt must be made to clothe it with meaning.

The position can reduced to this form. The enabling Act says-

(a) The Minister may do X.
(b) If the Minister does Y, but certifies that Y is to be treated for this purpose as if it were X, the power conferred by (1) shall be taken to extend to Y.

This is not an illogical proposition in itself, but it poses the question of where the line is to be drawn. Plainly the Minister cannot put any proposition he likes into the Y category, or Parliament would have delegated all its powers to him. {See *Ex p Ringer* (1909) 25 TLR 718; cf *Damodhar Gordhan v Deoram Kanji* (1875) 1 App Cas 332.}

Byelaws compared to other instruments   The operation of the doctrine of ultra vires is wider in relation to byelaws than statutory instruments. {For the nature of byelaws see s 65 of this Code.} This is because in relation to byelaws the courts regard themselves as entitled to examine not only the scope of the power but the reasonableness of its exercise. The unreasonableness of a statutory instrument is not a ground for holding it ultra vires. {*Buckley v National Westminster Bank plc* (1983) *The Times* 24 October (prescribed forms not invalid even though 'calculated to puzzle, perplex or mislead' the user).}

The distinction is illogical, but is based on the historical fact that the courts have regarded it as their particular duty to safeguard the public against petty oppression at the hands of over-zealous authorities with byelaw-making powers. Originally such powers derived from royal charters, and the common-law rules were formed in that connection. {See *Slattery v Naylor* (1888) 13 App Cas 446, *per* Lord Hobhouse at p 452.}

A distinction is drawn by the courts in this regard between bodies established for the public good, such as local government authorities, and those established for private profit. {According to Channell J (*Williams v Weston-super-Mare UDC* (1907) 98 LT 537, at p 539), the distinction derives from the judgment of Lord Russell of Killowen CJ in *Kruse v Johnson* [1898] 2 QB 91.}

As to the byelaws of a local authority, Lord Russell of Killowen CJ said in *Kruse v Johnson* {[1898] 2 QB 91, at p 99.}-

> 'They ought to be supported if possible. They ought to be, as has been said, "benevolently interpreted" and credit ought to be given to those who have to administer them that they will be reasonably administered.'

Cozens-Hardy MR observed that the courts 'ought to assume, and assume strongly, that the local authority is [*sic*] exercising their duty honestly and doing their best for the benefit of the locality; they being entrusted by Parliament with powers for that express purpose'. {*Williams v Weston-super-Mare UDC (No. 2)* (1910) 103 LT 9, at p 11.}

Severance   Where possible, the court will sever the provision which is ultra vires from the rest of the instrument. {*Clark v Denton* (1830) 1 B & Ad 92, at p 95; *Dyson v London and North-Western Rly Co* (1881) 7 QBD 32; *Fielding v Thomas* [1896] AC 600; *Strickland v Hayes* [1896] 1 QB 290; *Potato Marketing Board v Merricks* [1958] 2 QB 316; *Dunkley v Evans* [1981] 3 All ER 285.} If the instrument consists of a collection of separate units, each of which is say a rule, a regulation or a byelaw, severance is likely to be easier.

The question of severance does not depend on a 'blue-pencil test'. The court will sever the invalid provision from the valid notwithstanding that this cannot be done neatly by textual amendment.

Example 2   The West Coast Herring (Protection of Fishing) Order 1978 {SI 1978/930.} prohibits herring fishing within a specified area. The area defined by the Order includes certain waters adjoining Northern Ireland. Under the enabling Act, the Sea Fish (Conservation) Act 1967 as amended by the Fishery Limits Act 1976, the Ministers who made the 1978 Order were not empowered to legislate for the Northern Ireland waters. It was not possible to rectify the Order by textual amendment. *Held* The Order was ultra vires the Ministers who made it only in so far as it affected the Northern Ireland waters. The remainder of the Order was good.

Ormrod LJ cited {P 287.} the following test given in Halsbury's Laws {4th edn vol 1 para 26.}: 'Unless the invalid part is inextricably interconnected with the valid, a court is entitled to set aside or disregard the invalid part, leaving the rest intact'. He also cited with approval {P 287.} a test propounded in the Australian case of *Olsen v City of Camberwell Corpn.* {[1926] VLR 58, at p 68.} This states that severence is only impossible where-

'... the enactment with the invalid portion omitted is so radically or substantially different a law ... as to warrant belief that if all could not be carried into effect, the legislative body would not have enacted the remainder independently.'

Both these statements suggest a need for some kind of spatial separation within the text of the offending instrument. However the court in *Dunkley v Evans* ruled that just as this was not necessary in the case of a declaration so it could be dispensed with where ultra vires was relied on in other ways. Ormrod LJ said {P 288.}-

'We can see no reason why the powers of the court to sever the invalid portion of a piece of subordinate legislation from the valid should be restricted to cases where the text of the legislation lends itself to judicial surgery or textual emendation by excision.'

This ruling means that the judicial process involved is not truly 'severance' but 'modification'. The court has power to modify the wording of an item of delegated legislation so as to leave it without any ultra vires effect. The only limit on the power is that it cannot be used to produce an instrument the overall effect of which the delegate, if made aware of the ultra vires point at the time of making the instrument, would or might not have approved.

Other examples of ultra vires provisions Here are some further examples of delegated legislation held to be ultra vires.

Example 3 Regulations made under a power enabling commissioners to make regulations as to 'any matter for which provision appears to them to be necessary for the purpose of giving effect to this Act' purported to exclude the subject from the courts and made the commissioners sole judge of the appropriate tax. *Held* These provisions were ultra vires. {*Customs and Excise Comrs v Cure & Deeley Ltd* [1962] 1 QB 340.}

Example 4 A byelaw made under s 109 of the Railways Clauses Consolidation Act 1845 purported to require *any* passenger not producing a ticket to pay the full fare, but the enabling Act restricted the power to passengers travelling with intent to avoid payment. *Held* The byelaw was ultra vires. {*Dearden v Townsend* (1865) LR 1 QB 10.}

Example 5   A rule of court purported to deal with Crown privilege (now known as public interest immunity) in a way which went beyond practice and procedure and encroached on substantive law. *Held* The rule was ultra vires. {*Re Grosvenor Hotel (London) Ltd (No 2)* [1965] Ch 1210.}

See further s 59 of this Code. As to the invalidity of byelaws see further s 65.

59. Delegated legislation: rule of primary intention

There are various types of delegated legislation, but all are subject to certain fundamental restraints. Some of these restraints are dealt with individually in sections 51, 57 and 58 of this Code. Underlying the whole concept of delegated legislation is the basic principle that the legislature delegates because it cannot directly exert its will in every detail. All it can in practice do is lay down the outline. This means that the intention of the legislature, as indicated in the outline (that is the enabling Act), must be the prime guide to the meaning of delegated legislation. In the Code this is referred to as the rule of primary intention.

COMMENTARY

The reason why the legislature delegates is that it cannot itself go into sufficient detail. There are various explanations for this. The legislature has not time to examine all the small print required. There may have to be an interval between adopting the principle of the legislation and settling its detail. Interested parties may need to be consulted on what the ultimate fine print should say. If they are not consulted, the legislative scheme will not work as well as it might, or even may not work at all.

Then again there is the concept of the continuing Act. Even when the whole structure, fine print and all, has been fully worked out, it will still be necessary to monitor how far it succeeds in practice. Practical experience is bound to suggest alterations to the scheme. Yet it is not possible to keep amending an Act in the light of day-to-day experience of its working. The government department responsible for administering the Act will not be allowed facilities to bring forward one amending Bill after another. {See also p 132 above.}

The answer is a two-tier Act, sometimes known as a skeleton Act. (In *Neill v Glacier Metal Co Ltd* {[1965] 1 QB 16, at p 27.}, Sachs J called it a 'streamlined' Act.) The top tier is laid down by Parliament in the Act itself. The second tier is laid down in delegated legislation, which can easily be adjusted in the light of experience of its working. {There may even be a third tier: see p 135 above.} But the intention of the legislature, as indicated in the Act conferring the delegated power, must always be the prime guide to the meaning of the delegated legislation. {*Rickards v A-G of Jamaica* (1848) 6 Moo PC 381, at p 398; *Macfisheries (Wholesale and Retail) Ltd v Coventry Corpn* [1957] 1 WLR 1066; *Hargreaves v Alderson* [1964] 2 QB 159; *Allford v Allford* [1965] P 117.}

The delegate is not intended to travel wider than the primary object of the legislature. {*Gorris v Scott* (1874) LR 9 Ex 125, atp 130; *Phillips v Britannia Hygienic Laundry Co* [1923] 2 KB 832, at p 842.} His function is to serve and promote that object, while at all times remaining true to it. That is the rule of primary intention. {See *Institute of Patent Agents v Lockwood* [1894] AC 347, *per* Lord Herschell at p 360.}

The following version of the rule, as stated in an Australian case {*Shanahan v Scott* (1957) 96 CLR 245, at p 250.}, was endorsed by the Judicial Committee of the Privy Council in *Utah Construction and Engineering Pty Ltd v Pataky* {[1965] 3 All ER 650, at p 653.}-

> '[Power delegated by an enactment] does not enable the authority by regulations to extend the scope or general operation of the enactment but is strictly ancillary. It will authorize the provision of subsidiary means of carrying into effect what is enacted in the statute itself and will cover what is incidental to the execution of its specific provision. But such a power will not support attempts to widen the purposes of the Act, to add new and different means of carrying them out or to depart from or vary its ends.'

The court will assume that the delegate intended to conform to the rule of primary intention, and will construe ambiguous provisions in the instrument accordingly. 'In other words, the courts will not be astute to ascribe to the person by whom the legislation was made an intention to make ultra vires provision.' {Halsbury's Laws (4th edn) vol 44 para 1002 n 3. As to the doctrine of ultra vires see s 58 of this Code.}

60. Delegated legislation: other principles of interpretation

Allowing for the difference in provenance, delegated legislation is construed in the same way as an Act.

COMMENTARY

Apart from the rule of primary intention described in s 59 of this Code, delegated legislation is construed on lines similar to those applicable in the case of Acts. The courts generally show no disposition to distinguish here, and many of the leading cases on statutory interpretation concern delegated legislation.

In effect, most delegated legislation constitutes legislation by the government or executive. This is taken to have the same general intention as Parliament, so that the like rules, principles, presumptions and linguistic canons apply as in the case of Acts. {For these see Part VI of this Code.} The matter was thus summed up by the Law Commissions in their 1969 report on statutory interpretation: 'it seems clear that the courts when dealing with [delegated] legislation apply the same general common law principles of interpretation which they apply to statutes'. The only exception noted was the obvious one related to the ultra vires doctrine (which applies to delegated legislation, but not to statutes of the Westminster Parliament). {Law Commissions *The Interpretation of Statutes* (1969) Law Com No 21; Scots Law Com No 11, para 77. As to the ultra vires doctrine see s 58 of this Code.}

Functional construction   An obvious exception operates in relation to construction by reference to the components of the instrument (called by this Code 'functional construction'). {Functional construction is dealt with in s 124 and Part XII of this Code.}

The components of an Act differ in nature and juristic significance from those of an item of delegated legislation. In turn the latter vary according to the nature of the instrument, whether an order, rules, regulations or whatever. The components are described in the sections of this Code dealing with the respective instruments. {See ss 62 (orders), 63 (regulations), 64 (rules), 65 (byelaws), 66 (other instruments).}

Difference in provenance Allowing for the difference in provenance of an item of delegated legislation from that of an Act amounts to little more than recognising that, apart from Government statements on the item in Parliament and any debates arising from them, there will be lacking the parliamentary information usually made available as to the mischief at which an Act is directed, and the nature of the remedy provided for it. {See Part XIV of this Code. As to legislative history see Part X.}

Since the intention of a particular goverment is a more straightforward concept than the intention of a complex legislature such as the Queen in Parliament, this difference is likely if anything marginally to simplify the task of interpretation. {As to legislative intention see Part V of this Code.}

Another difference to bear in mind is that the quality of drafting tends to be lower in the case of delegated legislation, little of which is drafted by parliamentary counsel. {See s 76 of this Code.} There are even degrees of accuracy and precision within the category of delegated legislation itself.

Example 1 Thus the Immigration Act 1971 s 3(2) contemplated that informal rules would be made for the administration of the Act, and required the Secretary of State to lay before Parliament *statements of the rules*. Lord Roskill said of the rules in question-

> 'These rules are not to be construed with all the strictness applicable to the construction of a statute or statutory instrument. They must be construed sensibly according to the natural meaning of the language which is employed. The rules give guidance to the various officers concerned and contain statements of general policy regarding the operation of the relevant immigration legislation.'

{*Alexander v Immigration Appeal Tribunal* [1982] 2 All ER 768, at p 770.}

Not only the drafting but the scrutiny given to it varies according to the type of instrument. As Viscount Maugham said in *Liversidge v Anderson* {[1942] AC 206, at p 223.}-

> ' . . . regulations pursuant to an Act of Parliament do not receive the same attention and scrutiny as statutes, and it is important to remember that, though they may be annulled, they cannot be amended in either House . . . so that errors in language, if detected, cannot be corrected. There are, of course, no three readings and no committee stage in either House.'

{As to annulment, which is not always available but depends on the terms of the enabling Act, see s 51 of this Code.}

Interpretation Act Section 11 of the Interpretation Act 1978 says that expressions used in any legislation made under a power conferred by an Act, have, unless the contrary intention appears, the same meaning as they bear in the Act. This applies to all delegated legislation made after 1889.

{Interpretation Act 1978 s 23(1) and Sch 2 para 1.} It gives statutory effect to the rule laid down in *Blashill v Chambers*. {(1884) 14 QBD 479, at p 485. See also *Potts (or Riddell) v Reid* [1943] AC 1.}

If the definition in the enabling Act of a term also used in delegated legislation is amended, this will have the effect of amending the delegated legislation too. {Interpretation Act 1978 s 11, as modified by ss 20(2) and 22(1). See *Re Simpkin Marshall Ltd* [1958] 3 All ER 611.}

Definitions set out in the Interpretation Act 1978 in relation to Acts also apply to delegated legislation made after 1 January 1979 (the date of commencement of the Interpretation Act 1978). {Interpretation Act 1978 s 23(1). As to delegated legislation made before that date see Interpretation Act 1978 s 23(1) and Sch 2 Pt II.}

Explanatory notes Most statutory instruments have at the end a note with a heading such as the following-

'EXPLANATORY NOTE
(This Note is not part of the Regulations)'

Departments are under instruction to include such notes wherever helpful. They are limited to simple explanation, and must not be argumentative. Nor should they attempt to construe the instrument in such a way as to encroach on the interpretative function of the courts.

The regular practice of including these notes began in 1943 with Defence Regulations, though such notes were occasionally included from a much earlier date. {See Report of the Committee on Ministers' Powers (Donoughmore Committee) (Cmd 4060, 1932) p 66.} The practice was accepted by the House of Commons in a ruling of June 1939 which stated that an explanatory note must represent the facts, must be essentially of an uncontroversial and explanatory nature, and must not prejudice readers in favour of the instrument.

For a case where the court relied on one of these explanatory notes see *Herbert v Pauley*. {(1964) Loc Govt Rep 647.}

61. Delegated legislation: types of instrument (statutory instruments)

The principal category of delegated legislation is that denoted by the term 'statutory instrument'. This category includes all statutory Orders in Council. It also includes all orders, rules, regulations or other legislation made by Ministers of the Crown under statutory powers which are expressed in the enabling Act to be exercisable by statutory instrument or (in the case of pre-1948 enabling Acts) are of a legislative character. Individual Acts make ad hoc provision for legislation made under them by other authorities to be included within the category of statutory instruments.

COMMENTARY

Until 1883 there was no general control over the form and publication of delegated legislation in the United Kingdom. In that year, following complaints of difficulties caused by the growing volume of such legislation and the failure to make it sufficiently known to the public, the Rules Publication Act 1893 was passed. This required all 'statutory rules' to be numbered in one series and published by the Queen's Printer. It applied to rules, regulations or byelaws which were made under an Act of Parliament and either related to procedure in courts of justice or were made by Her Majesty in Council or a Government department. Thereafter, until 1947, annual volumes of these instruments, under the name 'Statutory Rules and Orders' were published by HMSO.

The definition of 'statutory rules' in the 1893 Act was found to be too narrow, and the Act was replaced by the Statutory Instruments Act 1946. By this the new term 'statutory instrument' was applied to the instruments mentioned in this section of the Code. {Statutory Instruments Act 1946 s 1; Statutory Instruments Regulations 1947 (SI 1948/1) reg 2 and Sch.}

The operative components of a statutory instrument vary with its nature, depending on whether it is an order, regulations, rules or whatever. These components are described in the sections of this Code dealing with the respective instruments. {See ss 62 (orders), 63 (regulations), 64 (rules), 66 (other instruments).}

The descriptive components are common to every type of statutory instrument. Each has a heading which reads: STATUTORY INSTRUMENTS, with underneath the year and number of the instrument. Below that comes a heading denoting the subject-matter, followed by the title by which the instrument may be cited. Then comes some wording in italics giving relevant dates, such as the date of making, the date of laying before Parliament, and the date of coming into operation. Finally by way of preliminary matter comes a recital of the powers under which the instrument is made. Normally this ends, by way of precaution in case any relevant power is missed out, with the ancient sweeping-up formula 'and of all other powers enabling him in that behalf'.

Immediately after the making of any statutory instrument, it must be sent to the Queen's Printer (in effect HMSO). It is given a number in the SI series, of which the numbering starts again at the beginning of each calendar year. Except where otherwise provided by or under any Act, copies of the instrument must as soon as possible be printed and sold by the Queen's Printer. {Statutory Instruments Act 1946 s 2; Statutory Instruments Regulations 1947 (SI 1948/1) reg 3.}

Statutory Instruments Issue List   Her Majesty's Stationery Office is required to publish the Statutory Instruments Issue List, popularly known as the daily list. {Statutory Instruments Act 1946 ss 3(1), 8(1); Statutory Instruments Regulations 1947 (SI 1948/1) reg 9.} This gives the number, title and date of issue of statutory instruments first issued by HMSO during the period to which the list relates.

62. Delegated legislation: types of instrument (orders)

The term *order* is used for instruments which have an executive flavour and express an obvious command. Very often their effect is limited to a particular moment in time, rather than being continuing.

COMMENTARY

As its name indicates, a statutory order, though a form of legislation, has an executive character. Thus an order will bring an Act into force, or trigger a repeal or amendment.

Components of an order The operative components of an order, corresponding to the sections of an Act, are usually called *articles*. An article is divided into *paragraphs*. As with Acts, an appendix to the order is called a *Schedule*, and forms part of the order. The components of a Schedule are called paragraphs, with the subdivisions being called sub-paragraphs. While it has been doubted whether the headings within an Act form part of the Act {See s 281 of this Code.}, there can be no doubt that the headings within an order form part of the order.

Provisional orders The provisional order is a device for lessening the parliamentary burdens imposed by the need to secure the passing of private Bills. It is a relatively modern development. {For the origin and scope of provisional orders see A S Quekett 'Local Government and Devolution' (1918) 34 LQR 357.}

Special procedure orders Where by any Act passed after 20 December 1945 power to make or confirm orders is conferred on any authority, the Statutory Orders (Special Procedure) Acts 1945 and 1965 apply to the order. The Acts are also applied to certain Acts passed before that date, and can be applied to other such Acts. {Statutory Orders (Special Procedure) Act 1945 s 8.}

The effect is that the order is of no effect until it has been laid before Parliament and has been brought into operation in accordance with those Acts. {Statutory Orders (Special Procedure) Act 1945 s 1(2).} This requires advertising of the order, considering of petitions against it, and parliamentary approval or rejection of the order. {For examples of powers to make special procedure orders see Acquisition of Land (Authorisation Procedure) Act 1946 Sch 1 paras 9, 11(1), 12, 14; Atomic Energy Act 1946 s 7(3); Town and Country Planning Act 1971 ss 244 and 249(2); Local Government Act 1972 s 240; Land Drainage Act 1976 s 109(4); Civil Aviation Act 1982 ss 44(9), 46(4), 48(5), 51, Sch 10 Pt II para 9.}

63. Delegated legislation: types of instrument (regulations)

As their name indicates, regulations have a continuous regulating effect. Like Acts, they are 'always speaking'. They would be embodied in the enabling Act if conditions made this possible.

COMMENTARY

Regulations are genuinely legislative in character. Apart from the rule of primary intention {See s 57 of this Code.} and the question of ultra vires (See s 58 of this Code.}, regulations share the character of Acts and are construed in the same way.

Components of regulations Each operative component of a set of regulations, corresponding to a section of an Act, is called a *regulation*. A regulation is divided into *paragraphs*. As with Acts, an appendix to regulations is called a *Schedule*, and forms part of the regulations. The components of a Schedule are called paragraphs, with the subdivisions being called sub-paragraphs. While it has been doubted whether the headings within an Act form part of the Act {See s 281 of this Code.}, there can be no doubt that the headings within a set of regulations form part of the instrument.

64. Delegated legislation: types of instrument (rules)

The term 'rules' is mainly reserved for instruments, such as rules of court, which regulate judicial or other procedure.

COMMENTARY

Rules have the same nature as regulations, except that the term rule is usually reserved for an instrument dealing with the procedure of a court, tribunal, corporation or other statutory body.

Components of rules Each operative component of a set of rules, corresponding to a section of an Act, is called a *rule*. A rule is divided into *paragraphs*. As with Acts, an appendix to rules is called a *Schedule*, and forms part of the rules. The components of a Schedule are called paragraphs, with the subdivisions being called sub-paragraphs. While it has been doubted whether the headings within an Act form part of the Act {See s 281 of this Code.}, there can be no doubt that the headings within a set of rules form part of the instrument.

65. Delegated legislation: types of instrument (byelaws)

The term 'byelaw' is used for delegated legislation made by local authorities, public utilities and other public bodies. Usually the extent of byelaws is limited to a relatively small geographical area, or to the operations of a particular body only.

COMMENTARY

Byelaws are essentially used for local or other limited regulation. Thus s 235(1) of the Local Government Act 1972 gives local authorities power to make byelaws 'for the good rule and government' of their area, and for 'the prevention and suppression of nuisances therein'. {As to other public authorities see, e g, Water Act 1945 ss 17 and 18; Water Resources Act 1963 s 79; Sea Fisheries Regulation Act 1966 ss 5 to 12; Forestry Act 1967 s 46; Civil Aviation Act 1971 s 31; Airports Authority Act 1975 s 9.} Power to make byelaws is contained in most Clauses Acts. {As to Clauses Acts see pp 88–89 above.} The special authority of the courts in relation to byelaws is explained in the commentary to s 50 of this Code. {See p 144 above. See also Examples 108.12 and 351.3.}

By a three-tier system, an Act may authorise a Minister to make regulations controlling the making of byelaws by a subordinate authority. {See, e g, Sea Fisheries Regulation Act 1966 s 5 (byelaws by local fisheries committees).}

Components of byelaws Each operative component of a set of byelaws, corresponding to a section of an Act, is naturally called a *byelaw*. A byelaw is divided into *paragraphs*. As with Acts, an appendix to byelaws is called a *Schedule*, and forms part of the byelaws. The components of a Schedule are called paragraphs, with the subdivisions being called sub-paragraphs. While it has been doubted whether the headings within an Act form part of the Act {See s 281 of this Code.}, there can be no doubt that the headings within a set of byelaws form part of the instrument.

Confirmation A power to make byelaws usually states that they require confirmation. Thus ss 235 and 236 of the Local Government Act 1972 state that byelaws made by a local authority shall not have effect until confirmed by the Secretary of State. Before this can be given, an opportunity of objection must be afforded.

Unreasonableness A byelaw is void if it is unreasonable. The meaning of this concept was thus explained by Diplock LJ in *Mixnam's Properties Ltd v Chertsey UDC* {[1964] 1 QB 214, at p 237.}-

‘ . . . the kind of unreasonableness which invalidates a bye-law is not the antonym of “reasonableness” in the sense in which that expression is used in the common law, but such manifest arbitrariness, injustice or partiality that a court would say: “Parliament never intended to give authority to make such rules; they are unreasonable and ultra vires” . . .’

The concept is equivalent to the *Wednesbury* principle, as applied in judicial review. {*Pickwell v Camden LBC* [1983] 1 All ER 602, at p 613. As to the *Wednesbury* principle see pp 68–69 above.} It has been held to be ‘unreasonable’ in this sense for a byelaw to purport to exclude arbitration. {*Paul v Wheat Commission* [1937] AC 139. See also *Kruse v Johnson* [1898] 2 QB 91; *Friend v Brehout* (1914) 111 LT 832.}

Uncertainty As to when a byelaw is void for uncertainty see p 204 below.

Non-legislative byelaws The term byelaw is sometimes used for the regulations applying to members of corporations or other bodies. {See, e g, *Tobacco Pipe Makers' Company v Loder* (1851) 16 QB 780.} Byelaws of this kind do not constitute delegated legislation, since their character is contractual rather than legislative. Corporations established by royal charter are deemed to have power to make similar byelaws. {*Piper v Chappell* (1845) 14 M & W 624. As to where such byelaws are ultra vires or otherwise void see *R v Coopers' Company of Newcastle* (1798) 7 TR 543; *R v Cutbush* (1768) 4 Burr 2204; *Carter v Sanderson* (1828) 5 Bing 79.}

66. Delegated legislation: types of instrument (others)

There is no restriction on the name that an enabling Act may use to describe the delegated legislation to be made under it. Terms employed include the following, in addition to those dealt with in ss 62 to 65 of this Code: proclamation, warrant, declaration, scheme, general notice, direction, ordinance, legislative instrument.

COMMENTARY

In 1932 the Donoughmore Committee complained about the confused nomenclature in this field. They said it was 'not only due to the use of many different words for the same thing' but was 'aggravated by the use of the same word for different things'. {Report of the Committee on Ministers' Powers (1932) Cmd 4060 p 18.} Since then consistency has improved in British legislation, though oddities are still possible. {See, e g, the Crown Office Rules Order 1967 (SI 1967/802). Is this 'rules' or an 'order'? The last word of the title is what decides.}

Proclamation   The term proclamation is reserved for announcements made by or under the authority of the Crown. {See pp 99 and 138 above.}

Warrant   The term warrant is used for royal directions or those made by HM Treasury. Thus s 11 of the National Savings Bank Act 1971 empowers the Treasury by warrant to fix the amount of certain fees incurred under the Act. {See also s 26 of the Act.}

Declaration   As to declarations see p 139 above.

Scheme   The term scheme is used where, as the name suggests, power is given to make detailed arrangements for some matter considered to be in need of general statutory supervision or administration. {See, e g, Agricultural Marketing Act 1958 Pt I (agricultral marketing schemes); Job Release Act 1977 s 1 (job release schemes).} For an example of a case concerning a statutory scheme see *R v Ministry of Health, ex p Yaffé* [1931] AC 494 (scheme under Housing Act 1925 s 40).}

General notice   The term general notice is used for minor administrative announcements (which may have legislative effect) of which wide notice needs to be given. Usually they are issued under regulatory Acts. {See, e g, the definition of the term in Consumer Credit Act 1974 s 189(1) and its use in ss 2(4), 6(2), 22(8), 30(5), 31(3)(a) and 31(6) of the Act. See also Estate Agents Act 1979 s 33(1).}

Direction   Sometimes an enabling Act uses the term direction for what amounts to an order. {See, e g, the powers conferred on the Treasury by the Exchange Control Act 1947 ss 24(2), 25(3)-(5), 26, 27, 32 and 34(2).} As to the applicable considerations see the remarks concerning orders in s 62 of this Code.

The term direction is perhaps more properly reserved for purely executive instructions. Examples include the power conferred on the appropriate Minister by s 75(1)(a) of the Road Traffic Regulation Act 1967 to give 'general or other directions' regarding the erection of traffic signs, and the power conferred on the Secretary of State by s 12 of the Fair Trading Act 1973 to give directions to the Director General of Fair Trading.

Ordinance   The term ordinance is used for delegated legislation made by the governor or other administering authority in a colony or other dependent territory. The ordinance is the primary form of legislation in the territory, and often gives power to make regulations and other sub-delegated instruments.

Legislative instrument The term legislative instrument, a useful all-embracing term to describe delegated legislation and distinguish it from executive instruments, is little used in Britain. {For a detailed account of its use in Ghana see Bennion *Constitutional Law of Ghana* (Butterworths, 1962) pp 262-9.} As to the concept of the legislative, as opposed to executive, instrument, see s 61 of this Code and Example 50.6.

67. Delegated legislation: sub-delegation

Unless the contrary intention appears, an Act empowering a body or person to make delegated legislation does not authorise the delegate in turn to empower a sub-delegate to act in this respect on his behalf. This rule does not preclude a delegate from acting through appropriate agents under his control.

COMMENTARY

The principle of this section is expressed in the maxim *delegata potestas non potest delegari* (a delegated power cannot be delegated). {2 Co Inst 597.} This is a rule that applies in law wherever the authority conferred involves the reposing of trust and confidence in the chosen agent. That such is usually the case where the agent is authorised to make binding general law is self-evident. It was indicated in a description of delegated legislation given by the court in *R v Burah*. It described it as-

'Legislation, conditional on the use of particular powers, or on the exercise of a limited discretion, *entrusted by the legislature to persons in whom it places confidence . . .*'

{(1878) 3 App Cas 889, at p 906 (emphasis added). See also *Jackson, Stansfield & Sons v Buttterworth* [1948] 2 All ER 558, at pp 564-6, 575.}

Unless the contrary intention appears Parliament sometimes (though rarely) includes a specific power of sub-delegation. Thus s 1(3) of the Emergency Powers (Defence) Act 1939 provided that Defence Regulations made under powers delegated by the Act 'may provide for empowering such authorities, persons or classes of persons as may be specified in the Regulations to make orders, rules and byelaws for any of the purposes for which such Regulations are authorized by this Act to be made'. Such powers have been judicially criticised as evading necessary publicity. {*Blackpool Corpn v Locker* [1948] 1 KB 349, *per* Scott LJ at pp 362, 369.}

Other forms of sub-delegation The principle does not prevent the delegate from providing in the instrument for the reasonable delegation of powers conferred by it where these are not legislative. Nor can there be any objection to the conferring by the delegate of power *on himself* to legislate on a future occasion. {See Example 58.1 above.}

Acting through others In view of the multifarious duties assigned to Ministers and other functionaries, it is obviously necessary for them to make use of the services of their officials in discharging statutory functions. {*R v Skinner* [1968]

2 QB 700. As to the performance of statutory functions generally see *R v Race Relations Board, ex p Selvarajan* [1975] 1 WLR 1686. On when a civil servant acts as the alter ego of his Minister and when he carries out official duties in his own capacity see *Williams v Home Office (No 2)* [1981] 1 All ER 1211, at pp 1232-3.} This does not necessarily mean that Parliament is taken to intend a Minister to leave the making of delegated legislation to his staff. The question is one of the construction of the enabling Act, and for instruments of importance it may be inferred that the Minister himself, or at least his political deputy, was intended to exercise personal judgment.

Sometimes the matter is dealt with expressly in the enabling Act. Thus the Fair Trading Act 1973 provides that anything authorised or required by or under any enactment to be done by the Director General of Fair Trading *other than the making of a statutory instrument* may be done by any member of his staff who is authorised generally or specially in that behalf in writing by him. {Fair Trading Act 1973, s 1 and Sch 1 para 7.} This means that the making of delegated legislation other than statutory instruments (for example general notices {See p 154 above.}) may be delegated by the Director General.

68. Delegated legislation: commencement of

Notwithstanding that it contains a statement to the contrary, an item of delegated legislation does not come into operation until reasonable steps have been taken for the purpose of bringing its purport to the notice of persons likely to be affected by it. Where the item is a statutory instrument, the issuing of the instrument by Her Majesty's Stationery Office is taken to constitute the taking of such steps.

COMMENTARY

The first sentence of this section is based upon the rule laid down in *Johnson v Sargant & Sons* {[1918] 1 KB 101.} and given parliamentary recognition by s 3(3) of the Statutory Instruments Act 1946. The second sentence derives from s 3(1) and (2) of that Act.

Issue of SIs by HMSO   Her Majesty's Stationery Office is required to publish lists showing the date upon which every statutory instrument printed and sold by them was first issued. In legal proceedings a copy of such a list is conclusive evidence of the date of first issue. {Statutory Instruments Act 1946 s 3(1).}

Statement of commencement date   The modern practice is for an item of delegated legislation to contain a provision specifying the date or dates of commencement of its provisions. Such references are to the *beginning* of the day specified. {Interpretation Act 1978 ss 4 and 11.}

Criminal offences   Section 3(2) of the Statutory Instruments Act 1946 spells out the meaning inherent in this section of the Code by providing that it is a defence for a person charged with an offence consisting of a contravention of a statutory instrument *if printed and sold by the Queen's printer* to prove that the instrument had not been issued by Her Majesty's Stationery Office (HMSO) at the date of the alleged contravention.

The defence is defeated if the prosecution prove that reasonable steps had nevertheless been taken to bring the purport of the instrument to the notice of persons affected. {See *Jones v Robson* [1901] 1 KB 673; *Defiant Cycle Co v Newell* [1953] 2 All ER 38; *R v Sheer Metalcraft Ltd* [1954] 1 All ER 542.}

69. Delegated legislation: amendment of

Where an Act confers power to make-

(a) rules, regulations or byelaws; or
(b) Orders in Council, orders or other delegated legislation to
be made by statutory instrument,

it implies, unless the contrary intention appears, a power, exercisable in the same manner and subject to the same conditions or limitations, to amend any instrument made under the power.

COMMENTARY

This follows the wording of s 14 of the Interpretation Act 1978. {Reproducing in amended form s 32(3) of the Interpretation Act 1889. As to the amendments see Law Com No 90 (Cmnd 7235) App, para 4. (set out at p 878 below)} Note that, in the case of rules, regulations and byelaws only, the implied power to amend exists whether or not the instrument is a 'statutory instrument'. {As to statutory instruments see s 61 of this Code.}

Implied amendment As to the implied amendment of delegated legislation by amending the enabling Act see p 149 above.

Amendment by Parliament As to the power of either House of Parliament to amend delegated legislation see p 136 above.

70. Delegated legislation: revocation of

Where an Act confers power to make-

(a) rules, regulations or byelaws; or
(b) Orders in Council, orders or other delegated legislation to
be made by statutory instrument,

it implies, unless the contrary intention appears, a power, exercisable in the same manner and subject to the same conditions or limitations, to revoke (with or without re-enactment) any instrument made under the power.

COMMENTARY

This follows the wording of s 14 of the Interpretation Act 1978. {Reproducing in amended form s 32(3) of the Interpretation Act 1889. As to the amendments see Law Com No 90 (Cmnd 7235) App, para 4.} Note that, in the case of rules, regulations and byelaws only, the implied power to revoke exists whether or not the instrument is a 'statutory instrument'. {As to statutory instruments see s 61 of this Code.}

Revocation by confirming authority   An authority with power to confirm delegated legislation may also possess the power to revoke it. {See, e g, Sea Fisheries Regulation Act 1966 s 8.}

Revocation by repeal of enabling Act   In the absence of any saving, the repeal of an enabling enactment by implication revokes delegated legislation made under it. {*Watson v Winch* [1916] 1 KB 688; *R v Ellis* (1921) 125 LT 397. As to savings on repeal see s 182 of this Code.} The same applies on expiry of a temporary enabling Act. {*R v Wicks* [1946] 2 All ER 529, at p 531.}

As to the effect where an Act repeals and re-enacts an enabling enactment see s 185 of this Code.

Effect of revocation   The term 'revoke' is used in relation to delegated legislation with the same meaning as the term 'repeal' has in relation to Acts. As respects delegated legislation made after 1 January 1979 (the date of commencement of the Interpretation Act 1978), the provisions set out in ss 182 to 184 and s 186 of the Code in relation to the repeal of Acts also apply to the revocation of delegated legislation. {Interpretation Act 1978 ss 14 and 23(1). As to the revocation of delegated legislation made before that date see Interpretation Act 1978 s 23(1) and Sch 2 Pt II.}

PART III

The Enactment and the Facts

Introduction to Part III It is desired to arrive at the legal position on some matter. This involves a number of separate points, most of which are straightforward. One, concerning the meaning of a legislative provision, gives rise to doubt. This Part of the Code sets out the anatomy of the constituent elements, with a view to showing how such a doubt is resolved.

The doubt concerns the interaction between the facts of the instant case and the combined effect of the *factual outline* laid down by the legislative provision in question and the *legal thrust* that provision imparts when the facts are within the outline (s 71).

First we isolate the legislative words in which the doubt resides. This is the 'enactment', which forms the unit of our enquiry (s 72). We must understand the nature of an enactment (s 73). To arrive at the wording that is relevant to our own case, we may be helped by the technique of selective commination (s 74).

In rare instances we may wish to challenge the enactment's validity (s 75). In every case we need to know whether its composition is precise or disorganised (s 76). Either way we presume the drafting is in other respects competent (s 77).

In arriving at the relevant enactment, we needed to have in mind the facts of our own case. We now look at them more closely, and work out the relevant factual outline, or generalised factual situation that triggers the enactment (s 78). This may be wholly laid down by the enactment itself, or elaborated by judicial sub-rule. Does the doubt concern the ambit of this factual outline?

Next we look at the legal thrust of the enactment, in case the doubt concerns the nature or scope of that (s 79).

With the factual outline in mind, we distinguish the relevant facts of our case from those that are irrelevant (s 80). Is any material fact doubtful or disputed? If so, how is it to be proved (s 81)? Will judicial notice be taken of it (s 82)? Does it involve a question of law, or is it purely a matter of fact and degree (s 83)?

If we decide there is arguable doubt as to the factual outline or the legal thrust (or both), we then work out the opposing constructions of the enactment (s 84).

PRELIMINARY

71. The enactment and the facts

The court is not required to determine the meaning of an enactment in the abstract, but only when applied to the relevant facts of the case before it. The existence of a statutory right or duty in a particular case depends (a) on a question of law, namely whether an operative enactment which in certain circumstances confers that right or imposes that duty has effect as law, and (b) on a question of fact, namely whether those circumstances exist in that case.

COMMENTARY

Because the court exercises the judicial power of the state {See ss 19 to 24 of this Code.}, it has a twofold function. First it is required to decide the *lis*, that is the dispute between the parties who are before it in the instant case. Secondly it has the duty, so that justice according to law may be seen to be done and the law in question may be known, of indicating the legal principle held to be determinative of the *lis*.

Rules of law, as Sir Carleton Allen said {*Law and Orders*, p 160.}, are something more than abstract propositions of logic. They depend for their effect on relevance to certain states of fact. Where a legal proposition is laid down by statute, the court is not required to arrive at the meaning of the enactment *at large*. What it must do is identify the factual outline treated by the enactment as triggering its operation, and then determine how the facts of the instant case relate to this. If they fall within it, the court must finally identify, and by its order give effect to, the legal thrust of the enactment.

The importance of the facts in law is stated as follows by the Committee on Legal Education-

> 'The law cannot be properly applied until [the facts] are ascertained.
> If the facts are wrong, the advice of the most learned lawyer will be,
> at best, worthless - and may be dangerous.'

{*Report of the Committee on Legal Education* (1971) Cmnd 4595.}

That an enactment may have fundamentally different meanings in relation to different facts was recognised by Lord Brightman in a dictum on the Statutes of Limitation-

> 'A limitation Act may . . . be procedural in the context of one set of
> facts, but substantive in the context of a different set of facts.'

{*Yew Bon Tew v Kenderaan Bas Maria* [1982] 3 All ER 833, at p 839.}

So the practical question for the court is not what does this enactment mean in the abstract, but what does it mean *on these facts?* The point was concisely put by Lord Somervell of Harrow-

> 'A question of construction arises when one side submits that a
> particular provision of an Act covers the facts of the case and the
> other side submits that it does not. Or it may be agreed it applies, but
> the difference arises as to its application.'

{*A-G v Prince Ernest Augustus of Hanover* [1957] AC 436, at p 473.}

Lord Diplock put the point at greater length in *Roberts Petroleum Ltd v Bernard Kenny Ltd* {[1983] 1 All ER 564, at p 567.} Referring to the function of the Court of Appeal, he said-

> 'The primary duty of the Court of Appeal on an appeal in any case is
> to determine the matter actually in dispute between the parties. Such
> propositions of law as members of the court find necessary to state
> and previous authorities to which they find it convenient to refer in
> order to justify the disposition of the actual proceedings before them
> will be tailored to the facts of the particular case.'

However this covers only the first half of the judicial function described in the first paragraph of this commentary, and suggests that the court's duty does not go beyond the facts of the instant case. That is too narrow, particularly in relation to an appellate court.

Because most of its decisions are not taken further, the Court of Appeal is arguably our most important appellate court. Yet Lord Diplock here describes its role in terms more befitting the old courts of Nisi Prius. The primary function of the Court of Appeal, he says, is to determine the *lis*. For this it tailors the law to fit the facts of the case before it. The inference is that its pronouncements on law are of no general application.

This is to ignore an important constitutional function of the appellate courts, which is to lay down principles of law. In his book *Precedent in English Law*, Sir Rupert Cross quoted with approval the remark by Paton and Sawer {G W Paton and G Sawer 63 LQR (1947) p 461.} that the function of a court is not only to give judgment, but also to *lay down a principle consistent with that judgment*. {R Cross *Precedent in English Law* (3rd edn, 1977) p 99.} This applies a fortiori to the Court of Appeal. It is at the root of the doctrine we know as *stare decisis*, or dynamic processing. {As to this see s 26 of this Code.}

There is a twofold aspect to an enactment's operation. First there is its meaning in isolation from any one set of facts. Second there is the question of whether particular factual circumstances exist which trigger its operation. Statutory interpretation is concerned with both aspects. It can offer a general description of an enactment's effect, or an answer to the question of how it applies in a particuler case. To the practitioner and his client, the latter is likely to be of more significance.

This leads to an important point. In practice most disputes about statutory interpretation are likely to turn on which of two alleged meanings is correct. One is the meaning favoured by the plaintiff (or potential plaintiff), while the other is the meaning which suits his opponent. In criminal matters the terms prosecutor and accused would be substituted. Sometimes other terms, such as petitioner and respondent, are appropriate.

Where a point of law arises in litigation there are generally in contention two sides, and *therefore two meanings*. What matters to the litigants is which meaning the court will prefer. This practical point needs to be borne in mind by those who seek either to expound or to understand the principles of statutory interpretation.

Pleading   The distinction between fact and law is relevant in pleading. The general rule is that pleadings must state material facts but not law. {RSC Ord 18 r 7.} A pleading may however raise a point of law where it is considered doubtful and might have to be settled by the court. {RSC Ord 18 r 11. As to implied importation of rules of pleading see p 750 below.}

This rule does not entitle courts to decide abstract questions of law, even where the parties consent. The function of the court is 'to decide questions of law when arising between the parties *as the result of a certain state of facts*'. {*Stephenson, Blake & Co v Grant, Legros & Co Ltd* (1917) 86 LJ Ch 439 (emphasis added). See also *Glasgow Navigation Co v Iron Ore Co* [1910] AC 293; *Sumner v William Henderson & Sons* [1963] 2 All ER 712.}

Juries   The distinction between fact and law also divides the functions of judge and jury. Here the rule is expressed by Coke in the form *ad questiones facti non respondent judices; ad questiones juris non respondent juratores.* {Co Litt 295.}

This is subject to certain exceptions. For example the content of a rule comprised in the law of a foreign country is a question of fact but is to be decided by the judge. Holmes doubted the wisdom of this: '. . . courts recognize the statutes of the jurisdiction judicially, although the laws of other jurisdictions, with doubtful wisdom, are left to the jury'. {*The Common Law* 151. As to judicial notice of law and fact see s 21 of this Code. As to the difficulty of distinguishing law and fact see C K Allen *Law and Orders* pp 159-162.}

See also Example 333.4.

THE ENACTMENT

72. The enactment: the unit of enquiry in statutory interpretation

For the purposes of statutory interpretation, the unit of enquiry is an enactment whose legal meaning in relation to a particular factual situation falls to be determined. Where the combined effect of two or more enactments is in question each in turn is treated as a unit of enquiry, their combined effect then falling to be determined. To discover in the first place which are the relevant enactments, it is necessary to frame the question of law at issue.

COMMENTARY

The enactment is the unit of enquiry in statutory interpretation because what has to be ascertained is the legal meaning of a statutory proposition (alone or in combination with others) when related to given facts. Regard must be had not only to the *wording* of the enactment embodying the proposition but also to all other relevant interpretative factors (of which there may be many). {As to interpretative factors see Part VI of this Code.}

While a case sometimes requires the application of more than one such proposition, each still has to be examined separately. If, when the meanings of the several propositions as applied to the facts in question have been arrived at, they are found to conflict then further techniques may be required to resolve the problem. {See index references to *Repugnancy.*}

Identifying the relevant enactment   Although the enactment is the unit of enquiry in this sense, the problem usually starts farther back. Here we may begin with the very nature of law itself.

Laws are contrivances for bringing about public ends, the larger of which are identical in all systems. There is no practical difficulty in distinguishing a law from other things. The practical difficulties lie elsewhere.

This brings us to an essential, though neglected, aspect of the idea of law. It concerns the concept of *how law is embodied.* If one accepts, with the necessary qualifications, Austin's view that law is a command, what form does the full command take? Where are its various terms expressed, and how does one find them out?

Jurists devote much thought to the problem of how law is to be defined, and distinguished from other normative systems. Yet little attention has been paid to that existential problem which concerns the *nature* of a thing that is *unquestionably* law. Its substance might be ectoplasm, for all students of the jurists have been taught about it.

Take the injunction Thou shalt not kill. It may be said that this is a moral injunction, and not law at all. We can easily remove that objection, and at the same time show by the use of an extreme case the nature of our difficulty.

Suppose Parliament passed a Homicide Act of just two sections, as follows-

1. The existing law of homicide is hereby abolished.
2. From now on the law of homicide is: Thou shalt not kill.

It is unlikely that Parliament would pass such an Act, but it is not impossible. If it did do so, there is not the slightest doubt the Act would be law. The argument is not, as so many arguments about the concept of law turn out to be, whether the propositions are properly described as 'law'. The interesting question is what do these and other propositions of undoubted 'law' consist of?

We will return to this question, but let us first supply some facts. D, a man of sound mind, decides that tomorrow he will secretly shoot dead a female relative who D knows has included a substantial legacy for him in her will. Tomorrow comes round, and D carries out his plan.

There cannot be the slightest doubt that D has contravened s 2 of our Homicide Act. Though exiguous in its wording, the section does at least cover plain murder. On different facts, its legal meaning would be doubtful. If D were aged only nine, or suffered from delusions, or had acted in hot blood, doubts would arise. Even on the simple facts as given, there is still at least one doubt. What is to be D's punishment for contravening the Homicide Act?

Here we come to the nub of our problem of the nature of law. If this Homicide Act were indeed placed on the statute book, all doubts would have to be resolved one way or another by the courts. They would not do this arbitrarily or capriciously, but *in accordance with law*. Where, apart from the two brief sections of the Homicide Act, is this 'law' located? How is it embodied? What do we do to find and know it?

If this undoubted law is indeed embodied, it must be embodied in words. We cannot conceive of human positive law existing otherwise than in words. But which words? After some cases have been decided under the new Homicide Act, there will be some judgments to point to. But a judgment is not usually expressed in the form of a law (perhaps it ought to be). And what of the law before the judgments are given? Where is that 'embodied'?

It is no use the reader impatiently saying there would never be such an Act as our Homicide Act. The practical point is that *every* Act leaves some aspects of its operation unstated. Exceptions held to be essential are left to be inferred. Consquences of infringement are not fully spelt out. And so on. What we are talking about is a universal attribute of law (though present in extreme form in our Homicide Act).

We return to the central question. How is law embodied? We know it must be embodied in words, but where are these words? Some are assembled in command language within Acts and delegated legislation. Some are in diffuse judgments, often conflicting. Some are in the commentaries of jurists and text writers. Some are in official guidelines, circulars, handouts and advertisements. Some, although in a real sense part of the existing law, *are as yet unuttered*.

Such words as have been uttered vary in the degree of their precision, and in their authority. They do not fit comfortably together. They change with time, not always explicitly. The words that might have been uttered in 1950 if the right case had arisen in that year will be different by the time they do come to be uttered in 1980, when the case has at last come along but in a changed social setting.

All this presents difficulty for the subject who wants to know where he stands on some matter governed by law. At one end of the scale is the clearcut case. D, in the example above, gets a plain answer if he asks whether his projected killing of a relative would infringe our simple Homicide Act.

But as we pass down the scale, the giving of right answers becomes more and more difficult. We get deeper into that shadowy area of dependence on some person's discretion, or another's interpretation. As we seek for the answer law gives to our problem, we grope for implications, attempt to reconcile conflicting dicta, search for the ratio decidendi of some crucial decision. All too often there is no clear answer; but we do best if we start by framing a clear question.

As this section of the Code says, to discover which are the relevant enactments, it is necessary to frame the question of law at issue. It is not just a matter of what does the law say on these facts? Mostly, that is too general. In D's case, given above, the doubt is exposed only where a more precise question is framed. On the facts of D's case, to what punishment is he liable?

When we have worked out what we want to know, we can direct our attention to the enactment that may give us the answer. Having identified the enactment under enquiry, we enter the proper field of statutory interpretation. {As to the method of identifying the enactment see further Bennion *Statute Law* (2nd edn, 1983) chap 10. See also Example 88.1.}

73. The enactment: nature of an 'enactment'

An 'enactment' is a *proposition* expressed in an Act or other legislative text. The effect of the proposition is that, when facts fall within an indicated area (in this Code called the factual outline), specified legal consequences (in the Code called the legal thrust) shall ensue.

The proposition constituting an enactment may, as is most usual, be embodied in a single sentence of the Act or other instrument. Or it may fall to be collected from two or more sentences, whether consecutive or not.

In this Code the term 'enactment' is to be construed accordingly, and 'the legislator'-

(a) in relation to an enactment contained in an Act, means Parliament;
(b) in relation to an enactment contained in a prerogative instrument, means the maker of the instrument;
(c) in relation to an enactment contained in an item of delegated legislation, means (having regard to the terms of the enabling Act), the delegate.

COMMENTARY

This section of the Code defines an enactment as a single statutory proposition, whether contained in an Act, a prerogative instrument, or an item of delegated legislation. The enactment consists of the words that are *expressed*, though it is likely to have implied meanings as well.

The essence of the proposition is that, if facts fall within a certain outline, specified legal results follow. The nature of this twofold aspect is spelt out below. {See ss 78 (factual outline) and 79 (legal thrust).}

The concept of the enactment is central to statutory interpretation. This is because difficulties about meaning are usually centred on one proposition only. It may be enunciated in a single sentence, or fall to be gathered as the combined meaning of several statements (whether or not consecutive).

Bentham said that a law is either a proposition or an assemblage of propositions. {*A Comment on the Commentaries* p 76.} He added-

'A proposition (I use the word in the sense Logicians use it) consists of three things: The two terms, *subject* and *predicate*: and the *copula* that connects them'.

This recognises that a coercive legal formula may be based either on one legislative statement or on the combined effect of several legislative statements. Indeed there is a sense in which the *full* legal meaning of an enactment cannot be gained without penetrating to the extremities of the legal system as a whole.

This truth is brilliantly expounded in an unsigned article entitled 'Jurisprudence' in the famous eleventh edition of the *Encyclopedia Britannica*. {(1911) vol 15 pp 574-5.} The following extracts give some idea of the argument-

'A law, like any other command, must be expressed in words, and will require the use of the usual aids to expression. The gist of it may be expressed in a sentence which, standing by itself, is not intelligible; other sentences locally separate from the principal one may contain the exceptions and the modifications to which that is subject. In no one of these taken by itself, but in the substance of them all taken together, is the true law, in Austin's sense, to be found ... The bare prohibiton of murder without any penalty to enforce it would not be a law. To prohibit it under penalty of death implies a reference to the whole machinery of criminal justice by which the penalty is enforced. Taken by themselves, the rules of procedure are not, any more than canons of interpretation, complete laws in Austin's sense of the term. But they form part of the complete expression of true laws.'

{For the canon that an Act is to be read as a whole see s 149 of this Code. As to the implied importation of relevant legal rules and maxims see ss 144 and 145.}

Other meanings of the term 'enactment' Although the Code concentrates on the meaning of 'enactment' outlined above, it should be pointed out that as used in legislation this term is also capable of other meanings.

The term enactment can refer to a subsection, or sometimes a whole section. It may even denote an entire Act. {See *Wakefield and District Light Railways Co v*

Wakefield Corpn [1906] 2 KB 140, *per* Ridley J at p 146.} It may also be used with reference to the whole or a part of a statutory instrument. {See, e g, Ministers of the Crown (Parliamentary Secretaries) Act 1960 s 4(2), Sch 2; Charities Act 1960 s 48(2), Sch 7 Pt Ic.} This variation of meaning calls for care in construing a passage of an Act or other instrument in which the term is used.

While a single word may come under examination as the root of an ambiguity or obscurity, a word in itself can have little significance. Every written word needs a verbal context to raise any question of its meaning; and the enactment provides this context. The enactment consists of words which in most cases have been carefully chosen by the draftsman to provide the maximum possible of both connotation and denotation (though as denotation increases connotation tends to diminish, and vice versa).

The nature of an enactment was recognised by Parliament in a clause contained in s 35(1) of the Interpretation Act 1889. {The clause is not reproduced in the Interpretation Act 1978, which replaced the 1889 Act.} This said that 'any enactment may be cited by reference to the section or subsection of the Act in which the enactment is contained'. The clause (in itself an 'enactment') is an example of how even a part only of a sentence, when amounting to a complete proposition, may constitute a legislative unit of this kind.

Earlier s 2 of Lord Brougham's Act {(1850) 13 & 14 Vict c 21.} had said that-

' ... all Acts shall be divided into Sections, if there be more Enactments than One, which Sections shall be deemed to be substantive Enactments ...'

Usually an enactment consists either of the whole or a part of a single sentence. One sentence may thus contain two or more enactments. The practice in modern common-law drafting is to number the sentences of an Act separately. {As to the distinction between common-law and civil-law drafting see Bennion *Statute Law* (2nd edn, 1983) pp 25-28.} This means that a sentence is normally either a subsection (where, as is now usual, a section of an Act is divided into subsections) or a section by itself (where it is not). When contained in a Schedule the sentence will correspondingly be in most cases a subparagraph or paragraph.

Examples of an 'enactment' are to be found throughout the statute book. It often requires some skill to identify and isolate the relevant formula.

Example 1   Section 5 of the Public Order Act 1936 runs as follows-

'Any person who in any public place or at any public meeting-

(a) uses threatening, abusive or insulting words or behaviour, or
(b) distributes or displays any writing, sign or visible representation which is threatening, abusive or insulting,

with intent to provoke a breach of the peace or whereby a breach of the peace is likely to be occasioned, shall be guilty of an offence.'

{This reproduces the wording of s 5 as substituted by the Race Relations Act 1965 s 7. For a communition of this see Example 74.1.}

This section contains many different propositions (and therefore many 'enactments'). Each one defines a different unlawful act, and can be stated separately without departing from the language Parliament has used. For instance, one of the many offences created by the section can be expressed in this way-

> 'Any person who in any public place uses insulting behaviour, whereby a breach of the peace is likely to be occasioned, shall be guilty of an offence.'

As we shall see, although this may correspond to the offence charged, it cannot always safely be treated in a particular case as if it formed the entirety of the section. The other words in the section may colour its legal meaning, and an Act is always to be construed as a whole. {See s 149 of this Code.} Nevertheless the interpreter can be helped in carrying out his task if the relevant proposition in the section is reduced in this way to a simplified form {For the treatment of this by selective comminution see Example 74.2.}

Example 2 Another example of a part-sentence enactment was provided by May J when he said-

> 'The important part of the statute *which I think needs construction* are (*sic*) the words "if and only if [the judge] is satisfied that it would be unfair to that defendant to refuse to allow the evidence to be adduced or the question to be asked".'

{*R v Lawrence* [1977] Crim LR 492 at p 493, approved by the Court of Appeal in *R v Mills (Leroy)* (1978) 68 Cr App R 327. Emphasis added.}
This referred to s 2(2) of the Sexual Offences (Amendment) Act 1976, which placed a limitation on the power of the judge at a rape trial to give leave for the investigation of the sexual experience of the complainant. May J found the provisions clear, except for the proposition quoted by him in the above passage. This, he graphically said, *needed construction*.

A special type of part-sentence enactment is the *proviso*, which in itself may comprise more than one enactment. {As to the proviso see s 268 of this Code.}

Multi-sentence enactments A single proposition under scrutiny may sometimes represent the combined meaning of a number of separate sentences, not necessarily found in one place in the Act. Here the term 'enactment' is taken to relate to the entire proposition. This usage is fortified by the fact that, unless the contrary intention appears, statutory references in the singular are taken to include the plural. {Interpretation Act 1978 s 6(c).} A statutory reference to 'an enactment' therefore usually includes, where appropriate, two or more related enactments.

Plurality of enactments An Act may contain more than one enactment bearing on the point at issue. Or relevant enactments may be scattered between two or more Acts. In such cases the meaning and effect of each enactment falls to be examined separately (though not in isolation from the others). What has then to be applied is the resultant of the enactments combined.

Prerogative instrument See ss 48 and 49 of this Code.

Delegated legislation See ss 50 to 70 of this Code. As to the words in parenthesis in paragraph (c) of this section see s 59 (rule of primary intention) of this Code.

74. The enactment: selective comminution

The technique of comminution can assist the understanding of a highly-compressed product of modern precision drafting. The technique gets its name from the Latin word *comminuere*, to fragment or splinter an object, or otherwise divide it into its constituent parts. The statutory provision in question is set out in a way which spatially separates its constituent grammatical clauses. For ease of reference these can be allotted numbers.

Where the enactment under enquiry consists of a part only of a provision, a further advantage can be obtained by omitting from a comminution of the provision carried out as mentioned above the components that have no relevance to the point at issue in the instant case. This *selective* comminution simplifies the argument by removing irrelevant statutory material.

COMMENTARY

That compression of language can be an obstacle to the understanding of modern statutes is recognised by the judiciary. Ministers, said Donaldson MR, should modify policies which are too refined to be expressed in basic English. Though they might find it frustrating to do this, he added, 'it is part of the price which has to be paid if the rule of law is to be maintained'. {*Merkur Island Shipping Corpn v Laughton* [1983] 1 All ER 334, at p 351. As to the problem of compression generally see Bennion *Statute Law* (2nd edn, 1983) pp 119-126.}

Unfortunately there is little prospect that this advice of Donaldson MR will be heeded. Working out a comminution of a provision under scrutiny, and using the resulting numbering for reference in argument, can assist in mitigating the difficulty of ready comprehension.

It should always be possible to comminute a product of precision drafting in this complete and accurate way, admitting only trivial verbal adjustments of the kind referred to by draftsmen as 'carpentry'. {As to the contrast between precision drafting and disorganised composition see s 76 of this Code.}

Example 1   The following is a comminution of s 5 of the Public Order Act 1936 as substituted by s 7 of the Race Relations Act 1965 {For the official version of this see Example 73.1.}-

    (1) Any person who in any public place or at any public meeting
    (2) uses threatening, abusive or insulting words or behaviour
  OR
    (3) distributes or displays any writing, sign or visible representation
    which is threatening, abusive or insulting
    (4) with intent to provoke a breach of the peace
  OR
    (5) whereby a breach of the peace is likely to be occasioned
    (6) shall be guilty of an offence.

{For a book-length model of comminution see Bennion *Consumer Credit Control* (Oyez Longman, 1976 to date), where the provisions of the Consumer Credit Act 1974, in conjunction with statutory instruments made under it, are restated in this way.}

Selective comminution Selective comminution formally isolates those of the express words of the enactment that are relevant to the facts of the instant case. The technique of compression used by modern draftsmen leads to long sections, often divided up into complex and indigestible subsections. It can be of great help to get out of the way the irrelevant provisions.

Example 2 The following is a version of the comminution of s 5 of the Public Order Act 1936 set out in Example 1 which confines the wording to a particular offence-

(1) Any person who in any public place
(2) uses insulting behaviour
(3) with intent to provoke a breach of the peace
(4) shall be guilty of an offence.

{For a case on this provision see Example 84.3}

Here a word of caution is required. Although the brief formula given in this Example is extracted from the section without alteration, it cannot necessarily be treated as if it formed the entirety of the section. Other words located elsewhere in the section, or in other parts of the Act, may colour its meaning: an Act is to be construed as a whole. {See s 149 of this Code.} Subject to this caveat, the application of which is not likely to make much difference in the general run of cases, it is helpful to abbreviate a section in this way.

It should always be possible to produce an abbreviation of this kind. Even if not actually produced to the court, notionally it forms the subject of the enquiry into meaning. What needs to be grasped is that an enactment is less a specific portion of an Act than a *proposition* which, though always to be gathered from the words of the Act (and not usually significantly departing from them), fluctuates in its notional composition so as to address the particular point at issue.

The statute user has to develop a technique of skimming through a provision and mentally picking out the bits that matter in the case he has before him. If his mind can learn to blot out the irrelevant words, the remainder will read continuously and make sense. Carrying out a selective comminution merely gives effect to the mental act that in any case needs to be carried out. This need is accepted by judges.

Example 3 Lord Scarman cited an enactment in a form he described as 'trimmed of words inessential for present purposes' in *Riley v A-G of Jamaica*. {[1982] 3 All ER 469, at p 475.}

Example 4 In *R v Ludlow* {[1971] AC 29, at p 38.} Lord Pearson used the technique in relation to r 3 of Sch 1 to the Indictments Act 1915. {Revoked and replaced by the Indictment Rules 1971.} The rule allowed joinder of charges in an indictment 'if those charges are founded on the same facts, or form or are a part of a series of offences of the same or a similar character'. Lord Pearson said of the two offences charged in *Ludlow*-

> 'This question can be narrowed, because these two offences were not presented as being part of some larger series of offences and they were not of the same character. Thus the question comes to be whether these two offences formed a series of offences of a similar character.'

J R Spencer used selective comminution to telling effect when exposing weaknesses in s 22 of the Theft Act 1968. {'The Mishandling of Handling' [1981] Crim LR 682, at p 684.}

A refinement of the technique where *defined terms* are included in the relevant enactment was suggested by Donaldson MR in *Bland v Chief Supplementary Benefit Officer*. {[1983] 1 All ER 537, at p 539.} He called the process 'reconstructing' the relevant subsection 'to make it slightly more intelligible'. The refinement was to set out in the selective comminution the full meanings of the defined terms included in the enactment.

75. The enactment: challenges to validity of

A valid Act or instrument cannot contain an invalid enactment, though an enactment may for some reason be ineffective.

COMMENTARY

The question of the invalidity of an entire Act is dealt with in s 47 of this Code. This section considers challenges limited to the enactment under enquiry. In fact such a challenge would be misconceived. Either a purported Act is wholly invalid or it is wholly valid.

Ineffective enactments   There are various reasons why an enactment, though it cannot be said to be invalid, may nevertheless be ineffective. We now consider these.

Impossibility   The statement that Parliament can do anything except turn a man into a woman has been traced back at least to 1648. {R E Megarry *A Second Miscellany-at-Law* p 107.} Even that statement has been challenged as too narrow, since Parliament can very easily say that 'for the purposes of this Act' a man shall be deemed to be a woman. {Cf *Taff Vale Rly Co v Cardiff Rly Co* [1917] 1 Ch 299, *per* Scrutton LJ at p 317.}

It is true that, as Wilde J once observed, Parliament cannot alter the law of nature. {*Crow v Ramsey* (1671) T Jo 10, at p 12; 84 ER 1123} But it can, as it pleases, alter the law of the United Kingdom and its dependencies. Moreover it can say that for the purposes of the enactment the law of nature shall be something quite different from what it really is. If the result is impossible to carry out it will not be carried out. But the judges and other enforcement agencies are under a duty to ensure that it is carried out as nearly as may be. {As to statutory duties which are impossible to carry out see s 351 of this Code. For the construction of meaningless words in Acts see s 374.}

Example 1   Section 127 of the Highways Act 1959 made it an offence for a 'gipsy' to encamp on a highway without lawful authority or excuse. The term gipsy usually refers to one of Romany blood, but in *Mills v Cooper* {[1967] 2 QB 459, at p 467.} Lord Parker CJ said: 'That a man is of the Romany race is, as it seems to me, something which is really too vague of ascertainment, and impossible to prove . . .'

In view of this impossibility it became necessary to find some alternative meaning for the term. Diplock LJ, the other judge, said {P 468.} that the word must be given its popular meaning, adding 'which I would define as a person without fixed abode who leads a nomadic life . . .' It is highly doubtful if this really is the popular meaning of gipsy, but the court was plainly driven to it.

Example 2 Section 41 of the Housing Repairs and Rents Act 1954 (later consolidated as s 18 of the Rent Act 1968) dealt with the following subletting problem. Premises are let as a whole, in such a way as to be outside the Rent Acts. Then a part of them is sublet so that the subletting is within the Rent Acts. The superior letting comes to an end. How is Rent Act protection to be preserved for the subletting?

Section 41 dealt with this by erecting a hypothesis which in some circumstances was, if taken literally, factually impossible. It said that the operation of the Rent Acts should be the same 'as if in lieu of the superior letting there had been separate lettings of the sub-let part and the remainder of the premises, *for the like purposes as under the superior letting*'. {Emphasis added.}

Maunsell v Olins {[1975] 1 All ER 16.} concerned the application of this provision to a farm. The superior letting was of the farm as a whole, and was therefore outside the Rent Acts. The subletting related to a cottage on the farm, and was within the Rent Acts. Section 41 required the impossible hypothesis that a farm cottage, *let by itself*, was for use not as a dwelling but for agricultural operations. *Held* It was necessary to give a strained construction to the word 'premises' so as to exclude farms from its ambit. {The House of Lords divided three to two on this desperate remedy.}

Enactment purporting to curtail legislative power Sometimes an Act is passed which contains provisions purporting to be incapable of amendment or repeal. Such a provision is not void, but ineffective. The one thing a sovereign legislature cannot do is truncate its own sovereignty by restricting its successors. A parliament sovereign today must also be sovereign tomorrow. What is technically called a *clausula derogatoria* is therefore ineffective. *Non impedit clausula derogatoria quo minus ab eadem potestate res dissolvantur a qua constituuntur* (a derogatory clause does not prevent things from being dissolved by the same power which created them). {Bac Max Reg 19.}

Example 3 Section 7 of the Acquisition of Land (Assessment of Compensation) Act 1919 said that the provisions of any Act authorising land to be acquired-

> ' . . . shall, in relation to the matters dealt with in this Act, have effect subject to this Act, and in so far as inconsistent with this Act, those provisions shall cease to have effect *or shall not have any effect*'.

{Emphasis added.}

In *Ellen Street Estates Ltd v Minister of Health* {[1934] 1 KB 590.} it was argued that the italicised words overrode a later provision in the Housing Act 1925. Taken literally they did. They could have had no other meaning or intention but to control subsequent legislation. But the Court of Appeal rejected them. Maugham LJ said that the legislature-

> ' . . . cannot, according to our constitution, bind itself as to the form of subsequent legislation, and it is impossible for Parliament to enact

that in a subsequent statute dealing with the same subject-matter there can be no implied repeal'.

{Ibid, p 597. See also *Vauxhall Estates Ltd v Liverpool Corpn* [1932] 1 KB 733. As to implied repeal see s 180 of this Code.}

Surrender of territory   Even the rule precluding curtailment of future legislative power has an apparent exception, though on examination it will be found to be no more than an aspect of the nature of law. A surrender of territory necessarily involves a surrender of legislative power in relation to that territory. That a state can surrender portions of its territory is undoubted, but this is not in itself a legislative act. {*Blackburn v A-G* [1971] 1 WLR 1037.} The diminution in legislative power is merely a consequence. Although the legislature may recognise the surrender of territory, it cannot by its own act effect it.

The twentieth-century transformation of the British colonial empire into a Commonwealth largely consisting of independent self-governing states provides many examples of such surrender of sovereignty. Until this occurred, the Westminster Parliament possessed power to legislate for every one of the territories included in the Empire. This reflected the political fact of territorial sovereignty. As Lord Denning MR put it in the *Canadian Indians Case*: 'The colonies formed one realm with the United Kingdom, the whole being under the sovereignty of the Crown'. {*R v Secretary of State for Foreign and Commonwealth Affairs, ex p Indian Association of Alberta* [1982] 2 All ER 118, at p 123.}

What later occurred was described by Lord Denning in these words-

> ' . . . that law was changed in the first half of the present century, *not by statute, but by constitutional usage and practice*. The Crown became separate and divisible, according to the particular territory in which it was sovereign'.

{Pp 127-8. Emphasis added.} The 'constitutional usage and practice' by which this change was effected received the recognition of the United Kingdom legislature in s 4 of the Statute of Westminster 1931.

The famous remark by Lord Sankey in *British Coal Corpn v The King* {[1935] AC 500, at p 520.} that 'the Imperial Parliament could, as a matter of strict law, repeal s 4 of the Statute', if it was ever true, must be taken as no longer so. The worldwide process of Commonwealth maturity is virtually complete, and the Westminster Parliament can now legislate for the independent states of the Commonwealth only by their consent if at all.

What this means is that, by a vestigial arrangement, the power of the Westminster Parliament in relation to the independent countries of the Commonwealth is to be no more than that of a delegate. The delegation is not granted for all future occasions. It is to be engineered, as and when required, *ad hoc*. Since the Canada Act 1982 'patriated' the Canadian constitution, this residual power remains only in relation to Australia and New Zealand. {Canada Act 1982 s 2. See s 200 of this Code.}

Enactment said to be 'unconstitutional'   Parliamentáty sovereignty involves that no Act of Parliament can be held void as being unconstitutional. The same applies to a provision of an Act. De Tocqueville said-

> 'In England the Parliament has an acknowledged right to modify the constitution; as therefore the constitution may undergo perpetual

changes, it does not in reality exist; the Parliament is at once a legislative and a constituent assembly'.

{De Tocqueville *Oeuvres Complètes* (14th edn) Vol I pp 166-7.}

Dicey pointed out that being a 'legislative' assembly Parliament can make ordinary laws and being a 'constituent' assembly it can make laws which 'shift the basis of the constitution'. {A V Dicey *Law of the Constitution* (9th edn, 1939) p 88.} This all-embracing power is necessary to secure that no aspect of political sovereignty remains unallocated. {Cf Bennion *Constitutional Law of Ghana* (Butterworths, 1962) pp 111-8.}

Thus for example Parliament has power to extend its own life, notwithstanding the requirements of the Septennial Act 1715 as modified by s 7 of the Parliament 1911. In *Norman v Golder* {(1944) 171 LT 369.} the plaintiff, appearing in person, argued that the Finance Act 1942 was not competently passed because the annual prolongation of the life of Parliament by wartime Acts was invalid. {The Acts were the Prolongation of Parliament Act 1940, the Prolongation of Parliament Act 1941, the Prolongation of Parliament Act 1942, the Prolongation of Parliament Act 1943 and the Prolongation of Parliament Act 1944.} Lord Greene MR said of the plaintiff-

> 'He has obviously spent a great deal of time in interesting research into various constitutional matters in this country, but I do not think I should be justified in doing more, while paying a tribute to his industry, than to say that to argue before this court that Parliament is not entitled to prolong its own life is really an argument which does not call for any reasoned refutation. It is fundamental in this country that parliament can do what it pleases.'

{*Norman v Golder* (1944) 171 LT 369, at p 371; 26 TC 293, at p 299. Other reports of the case do not include this passage.}

The proposition that no enactment can be void as being unconstitutional was not fully established until the revolution of 1688. Earlier it was held for example that an Act could not truncate the royal prerogative. In 1637 Finch CJ said: 'No Act of Parliament can bar a King of his regality.' {*The Case of Ship Money* (1637) 3 St Tr 825, at p 1235.}

Alteration of requirement for threefold consent   The proposition that an Act may without restriction alter the constitution involves that it may interfere with the requirement for threefold consent itself. The Parliament Act 1911 did this by removing the need for Lords' consent in certain cases, and was widened in its operation by the Parliament Act 1949. {See ss 43 and 44 of this Code.} No judge has suggested that these Acts were invalid, though it is true the question has not come up for decision in any court.

There have from time to time been proposals to abolish the House of Lords altogether, and it seems there would be nothing to prevent this if current Bill procedure were used. Dicey said that an Act to abolish the House of Lords 'can be repealed as it has been passed by Parliament'. {A V Dicey *Law of the Constitution* (9th edn, 1939) p 89.} Repeal by itself would not resurrect the vanished House of Lords. To be effective the repealing Act would have to include provision for the setting up of a new second chamber. This would not be the old House of Lords, even though the Act should say that it 'shall be treated in all respects as if it were' the old House.

Current Bill procedure must accord with current law, and there are many precedents for Acts altering this procedure. {See, e g, Statutory Orders (Special Procedure) Act 1945 s 6.} If, as has been suggested, an Act were to be passed containing Bill of Rights provisions and entrenching them so that an amending Bill would require a two-thirds majority that would be binding. Such a Bill would indeed require a two-thirds majority, since those responsible would be acting illegally if they presented it for royal assent without. But the amending Bill, so passed, could itself abolish the requirement of a two-thirds majority for the future. {See E C S Wade *Constitutional Fundamentals* chap 3; R W M Dias *Jurisprudence* (4th edn, 1976) pp 112-132.}

Enactment said to be contrary to natural law   Another ground on which, until modern times, it might have been alleged that Acts could be held invalid was that their provisions were contrary to reason, or natural law, or the law of God. {*Dr Bonham's Case* (1610) 8 Co Rep 114a (when an Act 'is against common right and reason . . . the common law will control it and adjudge such Act to be void'); *Day v Savadge* (1614) Hob 85 (an Act 'made against natural equity, as to make a man a judge in his own case, is void in itself'); *R v Love* (1651) 5 St Tr 43, at p 172 (whatever is contrary to scripture, or to 'right reason which is maintained by scripture [cannot be] the law of England, but the error of the party which did pronounce it'); *Calladay v Pilkington* (1694) 12 Mod 513 ('Let an Act be ever so charitable, yet if it give away the property of a subject it ought not to be countenanced'); see also *R v Earl of Banbury* (1693) Skin 517, at p 527; *City of London v Wood* (1701) 12 Mod Rep 669 at p 687; *Mercer's Company v Bowker* (1725) 1 Stra 639, 3 Inst 111. For a detailed discussion see C K Allen *Law in the Making* (4th edn, 1946) pp 366-381.}

Once again, such a ground of invalidity would not be entertained today. Our judges follow Blackstone, who said-

'If Parliament would positively enact a thing to be done which is unreasonable, there is no power in the ordinary forms of the Constitution that is vested with authority to control it'. {1 Comm 91.}

Despite Blackstone's certainty however, the contrary argument was seriously maintained until the middle of the nineteenth century. In the first edition of his *Legal Maxims*, published in 1845, Broom cited as still operative the maxim *summa ratio est quae pro religione facit.* {Co Litt 341a.} For this he cited Blackstone's translation: 'If ever the laws of God and man are at variance, the former are to be obeyed in derogation of the latter'. {1 Bla Com (16th edn) 58 n (6).} Broom commented that if a statute were made directly contrary to the law of God, as for instance if it were enacted that no one should give alms to any object, in ever so necessitous a condition, such an Act would be void. {Broom *Legal Maxims* (1st edn, 1845) 18.}

The error here is to confuse law and morality. A legal system imports its own system of duty. By definition, whatever is contrary to the law is unlawful. It does not necessarily follow that whatever is unlawful is morally wrong. The width of the divide depends on how far (if at all) the legal system departs from morality. Broom came as near as is possible to bridging the gap when he said-

'In order to form a correct judgment on this subject, it is necessary to take into consideration, that the true principle both of moral and positive law is, in effect, the same - viz utility, or the general welfare; and that the disobedience of either sort of precept must be presumed to involve in it some kind of mischievous consequence, if for no other reason, yet for this, that such example of disobedience may encourage others to violate laws of a beneficial character, and tend to lessen that general reverence which ought to be entertained by the community for the institutions of the country.'

{Broom *Legal Maxims* (1st edn, 1845) 18.}
The modern position was stated in 1871 by Willes J in *Lee v Bude & Torrington Rly-*

'It was once said . . . that if an Act of Parliament were to create a man judge in his own cause, the Court might disregard it. That dictum, however, stands as a warning, rather than an authority to be followed. We sit here as servants of the Queen and the legislature. Are we to act as regents over what is done by parliament with the consent of the Queen, lords and commons? I deny that any such authority exists . . . The proceedings here are judicial, not autocratic, which they would be if we could make laws instead of administering them'.

{(1871) LR 6 CP 576, at p 582.}

European Communities Act 1972 The combined effect of ss 2 and 3 of the European Communities Act 1972 is to make Community law (as expounded by the European Court) part of British law. Furthermore Community law overrides inconsistent British law, whether the latter derives from a date before or after that of the Community law in question. {See Bennion *Statute Law* (2nd edn, 1983) chap 6.}

This does not however mean that inconsistent British law is *invalid*. In *Farrall v Department of Transport* {(1982) *The Times* 16 October, 133 NLJ 1040.} the applicant sought a declaration that s 85 of the Road Traffic Act 1972 was void as being inconsistent with a Community law relating to the general validity throughout the EEC area of driving licences granted in a member state. The application was rejected. Stephen Brown J said the applicant-

' . . . is seeking a declaration which it would be impossible to grant. It is a misunderstanding that any statute can be regarded as null and void because of the European Treaty. What is required is that the member state shall introduce regulations or legislation which shall give effect to decisions which are binding because of the Treaty.'

{Such regulations were shortly after made: see the Driving Licences (Community Driving Licence) Regulations 1982 (SI 1982/1555}
The last sentence of this dictum is inappropriate where Community law is directly applicable. Here the position was stated by Lord Denning MR in *Macarthys Ltd v Smith* {[1981] 1 All ER 111, at pp 120-1.} The case concerned the combined effect of the Equal Pay Act 1970 (as amended by the Sex Discrimination Act 1975) and Article 119 of the Treaty of Rome. Lord Denning said-

' . . . the provisions of art 119 of the EEC Treaty take priority over anything in our English statute on equal pay which is inconsistent with art 119. That priority is given by our own law. It is given by the European Communities Act 1972 itself. Community law is now part of our law; and whenever there is any inconsistency, Community law has priority. It is not supplanting English law. It is part of our law which overrides any other part which is inconsistent with it . . . it was said that, in [the 1970 Act as amended by the 1975 Act], our parliamentary draftsmen thought they were carrying out, and intended to carry out, the provisions of the EEC Treaty . . . The employers had no right to look at our English statute alone. They ought throughout to have looked at the EEC Treaty as well. Community law is part of our law by our own statute, the European Communities Act 1972. In applying it, we should regard it in the same way as if we found an inconsistency between two English Acts of Parliament; and the court had to decide which had to be given priority.'

The last sentence of this dictum is, with respect, inaccurate. The usual doctrine is that if two Acts are inconsistent the later prevails. {See s 180 of this Code.} The doctrine with regard to directly-applicable Community law is that it prevails whether later or earlier. {See John Parris (1984) 134 NLJ 165-6.}

Where, it may be asked, does this leave the doctrine of Parliamentary sovereignty described in s 31 of the Code? It is submitted that it leaves it unimpaired. In a later Act, Parliament is presumed to intend to comply with overriding Community law. To achieve this the court will where necessary give a strained construction to the enactment. If however the later enactment made clear, for example by express words to that effect, an intention by Parliament to override the relevant Community law the court would give effect to this. It would operate, to that extent, as an amendment of s 2 of the European Communities Act 1972.

Enactment said to contravene international law   It is said that international law is part of the law of the United Kingdom. {Blackstone *Commentaries* (17th edn) Book IV p 67; *Heathfield v Chilton* (1767) 4 Burr 2016; *R v Immigration Officer, ex p Thakrar* [1974] QB 684.} Whether this is so or not, it is quite clear that an Act can override any provision of international law, or of a treaty to which this country is a party. As Wade and Phillips put it-

> 'The supremacy of Parliament is not limited so far as British courts are concerned by the rules of international law. The courts have nothing to do with what foreign States consider a usurpation. Neither are they concerned whether an Act of Parliament is ultra vires on the ground that it contravenes generally accepted principles of international law.'

{E C S Wade and G G Phillips *Constitutional Law* (6th edn, 1960) p 46. See *Mortensen v Peters* (1906) 8 F (Ct of Sess) 93.}

The position with regard to treaties was stated by Diplock LJ in *Saloman v Commrs of Customs and Excise*-

> 'If the terms of the legislation are clear and unambiguous, they must be given effect to whether or not they carry out Her Majesty's treaty obligations, for the sovereign power of the Queen in Parliament

extends to breaking treaties (see *Ellerman Lines v Murray* {[1931] AC 126.}), and any remedy for such a breach of an international obligation lies in a forum other than Her Majesty's own courts.'

{[1966] 3 WLR 1223. As to the presumption that an enactment is intended to comply with relevant rules of public international law unless the contrary intention appears see s 134 of this Code. As to the duty to take into account that the consequence of a particular construction may be to infringe international law see pp 492ff below.}

Summary We see that, whatever may have been the position in the past, an Act that has received threefold consent cannot now be declared void on any ground. It follows that neither can any provision contained in the Act.

This is not the same thing as saying that no provision of an Act can be ineffective. In recent times the courts have come very near to refusing to implement attempts by Parliament to place administrative decisions beyond judicial challenge. {See p 747ff below.} An Act may be ineffective if as a matter of fact it is incapable of implementation. Drafting errors may render a provision ineffective. But provided it is contained in an Act to which threefold consent has been validly given, an enactment cannot be challenged as being in any sense a nullity.

76. The enactment: precise or disorganised?

In ascertaining the legal meaning of an enactment it is necessary first to determine whether the drafting is precise or imprecise. Modern British Acts are produced by *precision drafting*, where (although there are occasional lapses) the draftsman aims to use language accurately and consistently, and moreover is allowed himself to draft any amendments made to the Act during its parliamentary progress. Older Acts are frequently the subject of *disorganized composition*. Here the text may be the product of many hands; and the language is often confused and inconsistent. Then again delegated legislation may be drafted with less precision than Acts. The technique of interpretation applied to any enactment can only be as precise and exacting as the method of drafting permits.

COMMENTARY

If an enactment is sloppily drafted, so that the text is confused, contradictory or incomplete in its expression, the interpreter cannot insist on applying strict and exact standards of construction. It is therefore necessary at the outset, having regard to its date, to assess the style of drafting. If a form of words reproduced from an earlier enactment is under examination, the date of that may be the crucial one.

Precision drafting The need for precision in drafting was recognised by Stephen J in a famous passage noticed by Lord Thring {*Practical Legislation* p 9.}-

'I think that my late friend, Mr [John Stuart] Mill, made a mistake upon the subject, probably because he was not accustomed to use language with that degree of precision which is essential to anyone who has ever had, as I have on many occasions, to draft Acts of Parliament, which, although they may be easy to understand, people continually try to misunderstand, and in which, therefore, it is not enough to attain to a degree of precision which a person reading in good faith can understand; but it is necessary to attain, if possible, to a degree of precision which a person reading in bad faith cannot misunderstand. It is all the better if he cannot pretend to misunderstand it.'

{*Re Castioni* [1891] 1 QB 149, at p 167. See p 240 below.}

Legislative drafting in Britain has now reached a high degree of precision. This warrants the deployment of corresponding precision by judges and practitioners when legislation is dealt with in court. It is true that draftsmen occasionally fall short of this demanding standard. Such inevitable human failure should not prevent statute users from understanding how fully developed the current drafting technique is, and what benefits can be gained from it.

This high level of precision in modern drafting is recognised by the judiciary. Thus Lord Reid said in *Luke v Inland Revenue Comrs* {[1963] AC 557, at p 577.}: 'our standard of drafting is such that [the need to do violence to the words] rarely emerges'. In *Wills v Bowley* {[1982] 2 All ER 654, at p 682.} Lord Bridge referred to 'a modern statute, using language with the precision one expects'. In *Jennings v United States Government* {[1982] 3 All ER 104, at p 116.} Lord Roskill remarked that until comparatively recently 'statutes were not drafted with the same skill as today'. {See also Brandon LJ's comments in *London Borough of Hammersmith and Fulham v Harrison* [1981] 2 All ER 588, at p 598 on the contrast in drafting standards between the early Rent Acts and the Housing Act 1980.}

Disorganized composition   The unified control essential to clarity in legislation was lost at an early stage in the emergence of the Houses of Parliament. The turning point came in the last years of the fifteenth century. Until then, it was usually the judges who drafted Acts after the king had accepted a prayer by the Commons in general terms for the grant of a particular remedy. An exception was Magna Carta, which was mainly drafted by the papal legate Stephen Langton, whom Thring called the 'prince of draftsmen' (*Practical Legislation* p 2).}

Thereafter the petition *formam cuiusdam actus in se continens* was used. Parliament considered not merely the general policy of the proposed statute, but the exact wording. {T F T Plucknett 'Ellesmere on Statutes' (1944) 60 LQR 242, at pp 247-8.} The executive had little control over the wording of amendments Parliament chose to make.

Executive control was not fully regained until the present century. Within this gap of some five hundred years the distinguishing feature of the statute book was its disorganised composition. As Lord Loreburn LC said-

'. . . from early times courts of law have been continuously obliged, in endeavouring loyally to carry out the intentions of Parliament, to observe a series of familiar precautions for interpreting statutes, so imperfect and obscure they often are.'

{*Nairn v University of St Andrews* [1909] AC 147, at p 161. See F E Bradley 'Modern Legislation in the United Kingdom' (1894) 10 LQR 32.}

Sir Harold Kent, himself a draftsman, refers to the statutes of the mid-nineteenth century, 'with their appalling tracts of unparagraphed, unpunctuated matter, with the cc 'eyancer's predilection for repeating everything again and again'. (*In on the Act* (1979) p 24).}

Lord Brougham said of mid-ninteenth century statutes—

'No system whatever, nothing approaching to systematic is to be seen; all is random, all haphazard, all blind chance, all acting in the dark, without rule or guide, or compass or concert.'

{Cited J E Eardley Wilmot *Lord Brougham's Law Reports* (London, 1860) 117.}

The modern transformation started with the establishment of the Parliamentary Counsel Office under Thring in 1869. {For an account see Bennion *Statute Law* (2nd edn, 1983) chap 2.} By this a single government department came to be responsible for the drafting of all government Bills not solely relating to Scotland or Ireland. A uniform technique was adopted, which to the present day has steadily improved in exactness and precision.

It is important to grasp the essence of this transformation. The difference, as has been said, is between organised and disorganised composition. With disorganised composition there is in reality no coherent meaning. One statement contradicts another. Within a single statement there are glaring defects. As Grove J politely put it in *Ruther v Harris* {(1876) 1 Ex D 97, at p 100.}, the language 'is not strictly accurate and grammatical'.

Example 1 The enactment with which *Ruther v Harris* was concerned, s 21 of the Salmon Fishery Act 1861, furnishes a typical example of disorganised composition. It says that between certain hours no person 'shall fish for, catch, or kill, by any means other than a rod and line any salmon'. The mention of both fishing for and catching salmon clearly indicates that the unsuccessful as well as the successful angler contravenes the section. Yet it continues by saying that any person contravening the section 'shall forfeit all fish taken by him, and any net or moveable instrument used by him *in taking the same*'. {Emphasis added.} The court robustly held that the net of a person who had caught no fish was forfeit.

That particular error is likely to have been the fault of the original draftsman. An error probably caused by an ill-considered amendment in Parliament also fell to be dealt with by Grove J in the year 1876.

Example 2 Section 78 of the Highway Act 1835 was a very long section concerned with improper driving of horse-drawn vehicles. It was equipped with no less than three sidenotes, all of which referred only to *drivers*. In the middle of the section however there appears a prohibition of furious *riding* of any horse or beast. The machinery provisions of the section, imposing penalties and dealing with the refusal of an offender to disclose his name, are solely in terms of drivers. Again the court was robust. Grove J refused to hold that the legislature had made the 'absurd mistake' of creating riding offences without affixing any punishment for them. { *Williams v Evans* (1876) 1 Ex D 277, at p 282.}

Yet in truth the legislature had indeed made that absurd mistake. What the court did was come to the rescue of the legislature by correcting its error. That regularly had to be done with the sort of disorganised composition the courts were constantly required to grapple with before the advent of modern precision drafting. As to the contribution formerly made by ill-considered parliamentary amendments to disorganised composition see the remarks by Lord James in *Garbutt v Durham Joint Committee*. {[1906] AC 291, at p 297.} While such errors can still happen today, they are rare. See also Examples 90.3 and 107.1.

One aspect of disorganised composition is failure by the draftsman to comprehend the law he is engaged in altering. {As to errors of this sort see pp 318, 337, 344, 352–353 and 754–755 below.}

As to the technique of construing disorganised composition see s 90 of this Code. See also ss 137 and 142 and Example 147.1.

Delegated legislation   As to the lower standard of drafting in delegated legislation see p 148 above.

77. The enactment: drafting presumed competent

Whether the enactment is a product of precision drafting or disorganised composition it is to be presumed that it was in other respects competently drafted, so that the accepted principles of grammar, syntax and punctuation, and other accepted principles of language, are taken to have been observed and the draftsman is presumed to have executed his task with due knowledge of the relevant law.

COMMENTARY

Precision drafting and disorganized composition   See s 76 of the Code. This section of the Code relies on an aspect of the legal principle expressed in the maxim *omnia praesumuntur rite et solemniter esse acta* (all things are presumed to be correctly and solemnly done). {Co Litt 6.} While draftsmen undoubtedly err from time to time, they are presumed (where the point is in doubt) not to do so. Accordingly the court will prefer to follow a construction which flows from a reading based on correct drafting rather than one based on an assumption of error. As Lord Hewart CJ said-

> 'It ought to be the rule and we are glad to say that it is the rule that words are used in an Act of Parliament correctly and exactly and not loosely and inexactly. Upon those who assert that the rule has been broken, the burden of establishing their proposition lies heavily . . .'

{*Spillers Ltd v Cardiff Assessment Committee* [1931] 2 KB 21, at p 43. Approved by Lord Macmillan in *New Plymouth Borough Council v Taranak Electric Power Board* [1933] AC 680, at p 682.}

Example 1   Article 16(3)(a) of the Local Authorities (England) (Property, etc) Order 1973, made under s 254 of the Local Government Act 1972, provides for the transfer to successor authorities of 'liabilities' attaching to former local authorities. In *Walters v Babergh District Council* {(1983) *The Times* 21 June.} the court rejected the argument that 'liabilities' did not cover a breach of duty which at the date of transfer had not yet become actionable because resulting damage had not then occurred. Woolf J said-

> 'If the draftsman had not used words appropriate to cover potential liabilities, it would only be because he was so crassly incompetent as not to appreciate that for actions in tort it is not sufficient to have a breach of duty; there also has to have been damage ... the word "liabilities" is capable of some amplitude of meaning and, in the present context, is wide enough to apply to contingent or potential liabilities.'

While the draftsman is assumed to have ordinary competence in the law, his human limitations are recognised.

Example 2   Grifiths LJ said of the draftsman of the Agricultural Holdings Act 1948 for example-

> '... much as I admire and hold in awe the powers of parliamentary draftsmen, I am unwilling to assume that the author of this Act had at the forefront of his mind when drafting Sch 6 the case of *Tew v Harris* {(1847) 11 QB 7, 116 ER 376.} to be found in the English Reports and decided over a century earlier.'

{*University College, Oxford v Durdy* [1982] 1 All ER 1108, at p 1115.}

Disorganised composition   Clearly the presumption of correct drafting is less strong where the enactment is the subject of disorganized composition rather than precision drafting. {See s 76 of this Code.}

78. The enactment: the factual outline

An enactment lays down a legal rule in terms which show that the rule is triggered by the existence of certain facts. The enactment indicates these facts in outline form (in the Code referred to as the statutory factual outline). Any actual facts which fall within the statutory outline thus trigger the legal thrust of the enactment, unless the court narrows the literal meaning of the statutory factual outline in order to carry out the true intention of Parliament.

Where the court finds it necessary to narrow the statutory factual outline because its literal meaning goes wider than Parliament's intention, the court indicates what the narrower outline is. Alternatively, the statutory factual outline may be thought to need clarification by the court.

Either way, the court processes the enactment by laying down a sub-rule from which can be drawn a description (in the Code referred to as the judicial factual outline) of the narrower or more precise range of facts that will in future cases trigger the operation of the enactment.

COMMENTARY

The facts that trigger the operation of an enactment are indicated by it in outline form, that is discarding immaterial features. Very often this will show that both physical and mental facts have to be present. In criminal law the terms *actus reus* and *mens rea* are traditionally used, though they have recently been frowned on by the House of Lords. {*R v Miller* [1983] 2 AC 161, at p 174.}

Example 1   The Criminal Damage Act 1971 s 1(1) specifies several offences. A selective comminution of one of these reads-

'A person who without lawful excuse damages any property belonging to another, being reckless as to whether any such property would be damaged, shall be guilty of an offence.'

Here the statutory factual outline can be set out as follows.

(1) The subject is any person with criminal capacity.
{The last three words are *implied* (see s 340 of this Code).}
(2) The actus reus is without lawful excuse damaging any property belonging to another.
(3) The mens rea is being reckless as to whether any such property would be damaged. {See further as to this provision Example 5}

The factual outline of a legal rule may contain alternatives, in the sense that the same legal thrust applies in two or more possible factual situations. {Lord Diplock has given the example of buggery at common law 'which could be committed with a man *or* a woman *or* an animal' (*R v Courtie* [1984] 1 All ER 740, at p 744).} In criminal law this raises difficult questions as to whether the rule creates one offence only, or more than one. {See pp 744–746 below.}

The statutory factual outline is often too wide for juridical purposes. Grammatically it includes, or may be thought to include, some factual situations which are, and others which are not, intended to trigger the operation of the enactment. Alternatively, the statutory factual outline may be thought to need clarification, for example by the finding of implications as to mental states. {See Examples 108.3 and 108.5.}. In either case it is for the court to determine the sub-rules which lay down the boundary or clarify the provision. {As to judicial sub-rules see s 26 of this Code.} It does this by working out a *judicial* factual outline. {See Example 5.}

The *relevant* factual outline identifies the situations which, in relation to the legal rule or sub-rule in question, are material on the actual facts. For example, if a man charged with murder claims to be absolved because what he admittedly killed was *non compos mentis*, the limited enquiry is concerned only with whether the crime of murder extends to the killing with malice aforethought of persons who are *non compos mentis*.

It is the function of a court accurately to identify this area of relevance. The basis of the doctrine of precedent is that like cases must be decided alike. This requires a correct identification of the factual outline that triggers the rule on actual facts such as are before the court.

In his book *Precedent in English Law*, Sir Rupert Cross insisted that under the doctrine of precedent judgments must be read in the light of the facts of the cases in which they are delivered. {(3rd edn, 1977) p 42.} The principle is the same whether the case is decided under a rule of common law or statute law.

Example 2 In his famous judgment in *Donoghue v Stevenson* {[1932] AC 562, at p 599.}, Lord Atkin carefully marked out the area of relevance arising from the facts of the instant case (in our language the judicial factual outline). The liability of a bottler who launches upon the market a sealed bottle of ginger beer containing a decomposing snail was extended just so far as Lord Atkin's careful words indicate-

> ' . . . a manufacturer of products, which he sells in such a form as to show that he intends them to reach the ultimate consumer in the form in which they left him with no reasonable possibility of intermediate examination, and with the knowledge that the absence of reasonable care in the preparation or putting up of the products will result in an injury to the consumer's life or property, owes a duty to the consumer to take that reasonable care.'

Note that this dictum, while going into detail about the type of product and method of sale, gives no detail about what conduct actually constitutes negligence. This is left as a broad area not, as a matter of law, to be divided up by judicial sub-rules. Otherwise, as Professor Atiyah has said-

> ' . . . the generalising power of the negligence concept would very likely be lost, because multiplication of specific instances and subdivisions of the law would surely obscure what those instances and subdivisions have in common.'

{P S Atiyah 'The Legacy of Holmes Through English Eyes' (1983) 63 Boston Univ LR 341, at p 356. See also *Qualcast (Wolverhampton) Ltd v Haynes* [1959] AC 743, at p 758.}

It is open to a subsequent court, asked to follow such a precedent as *Donoghue v Stevenson* {[1932] AC 562.}, to assert that the judicial generalisation of facts (or factual outline) went wider than was justified. Equally, a subsequent court may declare that the generalisation should have gone wider still, as has happened with the developing tort of negligence. Subject to that, the decision stands as a guide to the rule or sub-rule in question. {See R Cross *Precedent in English Law* (3rd edn, 1977) pp 60-78.}

Without a carefully-delimited factual outline, any question of the meaning of an enactment is likely to be academic. To be more exact, it may demand the impossible by seeking in a compact expression the resultant of endless possibilities. The unlikelihood of achieving this no doubt explains that dislike frequently displayed by judges for hypothetical questions of law.

Example 3 This dislike was illustrated by the Lords' rejection of a clause, in what became the Rating and Valuation Act 1928, which would have empowered the relevant Minister to refer to the High Court questions of law unrelated to specific facts. {See 47 LQR 44.}

Judgments on points of interpretation should be read in the light of this need for a factual outline. Lord Halsbury LC described how the relevant outline is drawn by extending the facts of the instant case-

> 'Every judgment must be read as applicable to the particular facts proved or assumed to be proved, since the generality of the expressions which may be found there are not intended to be

expositions of the whole law but govern and are qualified by the particular facts of the case in which such expressions are to be found.'

{*Quinn v Leathem* [1901] AC 495, at p 506. See R Cross *Precedent in English Law* (3rd edn, 1977) pp 59-61.}

Judicial statements of principle must be related to the facts of the instant case, but the juristic function of the court is to *generalise* those facts as Lord Atkin did in the dictum cited above. He did not limit his famous statement of the 'good neighbour' principle to snails found in bottles of ginger beer. He widened 'a manufacturer of ginger beer' to 'a manufacturer of products'. Ginger beer in a bottle became any product in a container such that the manufacturer intended it to reach the ultimate consumer with no reasonable possibility of intermediate examination. And so on.

The ratio decidendi of a case involves postulating a general factual outline. This is part of the rule laid down or followed by the case, since a legal rule imports a factual situation to which it applies. If the facts of a later case fit within this outline but demand amendment of the legal thrust of the rule, the outline is too broadly stated. If on the other hand the facts of a later case do not fit into the outline, but do elicit the same legal response, the outline is too narrow.

When the court determines which of the opposing constructions of the enactment is the right one on the facts of the instant case it is often, under the doctrine of precedent, thereby laying down a sub-rule. In doing so it should make clear what is the factual outline relative to that sub-rule. This does not always seem to be appreciated, even in the highest judicial quarters.

Example 4   In *Roberts Petroleum Ltd v Bernard Kenny Ltd* {[1983] 1 All ER 564, at p 567.} Lord Diplock said-

> 'Even when making successive revisions of drafts of my own written speeches for delivery on appeals to this House, which usually involve principles of law of wider application than the particular case under appeal, I often find it necessary to continue to introduce subordinate clauses supplementing or qualifying the simpler, and stylistically preferable, wording in which statements of law have been expressed in earlier drafts.'

The clear but remarkable implication from this dictum is that the decisions of the House of Lords are relevant only to the particular facts of the instant case, and of scarcely more juridical value than is elsewhere in his speech attributed by Lord Diplock to those of the Court of Appeal. {See p 160 above.} This is disturbing because it seems to import a rejection by the Law Lords of the very constitutional function appellate judges are appointed to carry out.

Lord Diplock here complains at having to qualify broad statements of law. He is not necessarily obliged to do so.

Example 5   In *R v Caldwell* {[1981] 1 All ER 961.} Lord Diplock surprisingly laid down a largely objective test for recklessness. The provision in question was the Criminal Damage Act 1971 s 1(1), a selective comminution of which relative to *Caldwell* reads-

'A person who without lawful excuse damages any property belonging to another, being reckless as to whether any such property would be damaged, shall be guilty of an offence.'

Lord Diplock laid down a sub-rule as to the meaning of 'reckless' here. The following restates this limited version of s 1(1) to include the sub-rule.

(1) A person who without lawful excuse damages any property belonging to another

(2) by doing an act which in fact creates an obvious risk that the property will be damaged

(3) without giving any thought to the possibility of there being any such risk

OR

(4) recognising that there is some risk involved and nevertheless going on to do the act

(5) shall be guilty of an offence.

The reference to 'an obvious risk' in clause (2) introduces an objective test which brought from Professor J C Smith the anguished query: 'Can we really afford the House of Lords as an appellate criminal court?'. {[1981] Crim LR 393.} Robert Goff LJ expressed his 'unhappiness' at having to follow this ruling in *Elliott v C (a minor)*. {[1983] 2 All ER 1005, at p 1010. As to judicial embroidering of such simple statutory concepts as recklessness see Bennion 'Leave My Word Alone' (1981) NLJ 596).}

Lord Diplock in *Caldwell* was faced with a simple choice. He could have ruled that recklessness, like negligence, is a pure question of fact for the jury. He rejected this, and elected to lay down a sub-rule by way of modification of the statutory factual outline. He was not obliged to do so, but it was his right if he saw fit. It is well recognised that courts are entitled to elaborate statutory broad terms in this way.

Why then does Lord Diplock complain that facts constrain him to qualify broad statements of law almost out of existence? Law is about facts. Without facts, there would be, and would need to be, no law. A legal rule (whether common-law or statutory) applies not just to the facts of the instant case. It applies in relation to a defined band or segment of fact. The definition of this is part of the rule. It identifies the situations that are subject to the legal consequence laid down by the rule. It has to be defined, for it must almost inevitably go wider than the facts of the instant case.

Mistaken facts Unless the court makes clear what are the material facts upon which it bases its decision, that decision is unlikely to carry weight as a precedent. Where an appeal is brought on a question of law, the appellate court ought to decide the issue on the same facts as were found by the court below. This may appear obvious, but it is sometimes departed from.

Example 6 In the leading case of *Inland Revenue Comrs v Hinchy* {[1960] AC 748.} the House of Lords reached its decision on facts different from those considered in the courts below. Lord Keith of Avonholm said {P 785.} that if the true facts had been appreciated by the Court of Appeal, that Court might have decided the case the other way.

Formal logic   As to the treatment of the factual outline with the aid of principles of formal logic see s 148 and Part XX of this Code.

See further ss 80 to 83 of this Code and Example 84.3.

79. The enactment: the legal thrust

The legal thrust of an enactment is the effect in law produced by the enactment where the facts of the instant case fall within the statutory or judicial factual outline.

COMMENTARY

The sole purpose of an enactment is to achieve a particular legal effect. The thrust of this is triggered by the occurrence of facts falling within the enactment's factual outline. {As to the factual outline see s 78 of this Code.} Problems of statutory interpretation concern either the exact nature of the factual outline, or the exact nature of the legal thrust, or both. Respectively, these turn on *when* the enactment operates and *how* it operates.

In criminal law the legal thrust of an enactment is usually expressed by saying that where the factual outline is satisfied the person in question is 'guilty of an offence'. The legal consequences of this by way of punishment and so forth may be spelt out or left to the general law.

The legal thrust of other types of enactment may be more complex, and thus give rise to more difficult questions of statutory interpretation. For an illustration of problems concerning the legal thrust of enactments see Example 84.4.

Formal logic   As to the treatment of the legal thrust with the aid of principles of formal logic see s 148 and Part XX of this Code.

THE FACTS OF THE INSTANT CASE

80. The facts: relevant and irrelevant facts

In dealing with the actual facts of the instant case it is necessary (1) to identify the relevant enactment, (2) to ascertain the statutory or judicial factual outline, and (3) to separate the material facts of the case from those that, in accordance with the factual outline, are immaterial.

COMMENTARY

Factual outline   See s 78 of this Code.
While the question is always What does the enactment mean *in relation to these facts?* it is necessary to separate material from immaterial facts. A great many of the actual facts of a case are irrelevant. The name of a party is irrelevant (unless a question of identity is in issue). The particular moment when an incident happened is irrelevant (unless time is of the essence), and so on. It often requires skill to determine, in relation to the triggering of a particular enactment, which of the actual facts are relevant facts. On the other hand this operation is sometimes quite straightforward.

Example 1   A man named Brown is accused of murdering a woman named Mrs Green on Shrove Tuesday by running her down in the High Street with his Fiat car. Brown pleads that he cannot be guilty of murder because s 2 (diminished responsibility) of the Homicide Act 1957 applies. On the question of the interpretation of s 2 in Brown's case, the fact that his name is Brown, that the victim's name was Green, that the event took place on Shrove Tuesday, and so on, are all irrelevant (though any of them might be relevant on other aspects of the case).

Generalising the facts   While a fact may be relevant, it may still be necessary to strip it of its inessential features in order to arrive at its juristic significance. This is particularly true where the decision on that fact later comes to be treated as a precedent. In Example 1 the factual details surrounding the killing of Mrs Green might, for the purpose of applying s 2, have fallen to be reduced simply to the fact that (apart from s 2) Brown was guilty of murder.

Where the enactment is very simple, the facts which trigger it can be stated very simply. Caution is always necessary however.

Example 2   Section 1 of the Murder (Abolition of Death Penalty) Act 1965 says 'No person shall suffer death for murder'. The statutory factual outline to which this applies might be stated as 'a conviction of murder'. This would not be strictly accurate however, since s 1 does not apply to convictions anywhere in the world. After referring to the extent provision in the 1965 Act, namely s 3(3), we arrive at the following as the statutory factual outline: 'a conviction of murder by a court in Great Britain, or by a court-martial in Northern Ireland'.

Over-generalising the facts   Where a court articulates the meaning of an enactment but describes the generalised facts in terms that are too wide, its decision, to the extent that it is expressed too widely, will be of merely persuasive authority. A decision can be a binding precedent only in relation to similar facts, that is facts that do not *materially* differ from those of the instant case.

Example 3   In *Sclater v Horton* {[1954] 2 QB 1.} the Court of Appeal articulated the meaning of s 8 (rent arbitrations) of the Agricultural Holdings Act 1948 'by considering the section in isolation and not by reference to the facts of the case'. {*Per* Eveleigh LJ in *University College, Oxford v Durdy* [1982] 1 All ER 1108, at p 1112.} On facts materially different from those in *Sclater v Horton*, the decision, on usual principles of *stare decisis*, would not bind. {*University College, Oxford v Durdy* [1982] 1 All ER 1108, *per* Kerr LJ at pp 1117ff. Eveleigh LJ expressed disagreement (p 1112) but it is submitted the principle is clear.}

Need for clear thought   It is not always straightforward to determine precisely which facts need to be proved in order to trigger the enactment, in other words what the statutory factual outline is. {As to the factual outline see s 78 of this Code.}

Example 4   Section 9 (drink driving) of the Road Traffic Act 1972 says that in certain circumstances a person may be 'required' to provide a specimen for a laboratory test, and that if without reasonable excuse he refuses he commits an offence. In *Hier v Read* {[1977] Crim LR 483.} D, having been required to provide a specimen, was first asked to sign a consent form. He refused to sign the form unless he had read it, but the opportunity to do this was refused by the police. *Held* A requirement to provide a specimen after signing a consent form which one is not allowed to read is not a 'requirement' within the meaning of the Act. Accordingly no offence was committed.

Note that this case called for a careful assessment of just what the factual outline was. It was important to avoid confusion of thought. For example it might have been said that the behaviour of the police in refusing to allow D to read the consent form furnished him with a 'reasonable excuse' as contemplated by s 9. This would have been faulty reasoning, because that stage was never reached. On the facts, there had not been any valid 'requirement'.

The case also illustrates that the relevant factual outline need not always be comprehensively stated. A full statement, covering all possible cases, of what is a 'requirement' within s 9 of the Road Traffic Act 1972 might run to many pages. All that was needed here was a statement dealing only with cases where the defendant as asked to sign a consent form which he is not allowed to read. Once it is clear that, whatever the full factual outline may be, the instant case is outside it, the matter is concluded.

The enactment is triggered by a particular factual situation comprised in the factual outline. This statutory description must be 'transferred' to the material facts of the instant case, or as it were fitted over them to see if it corresponds. Here it is important to grasp exactly which facts are relevant.

Example 5   Green v Moore {[1982] 1 All ER 428.} concerned the interpretation of a multiple broad term, 'wilfully obstructs a constable in the execution of his duty', as used in the Police Act 1964 s 51(3). The duties of constables are multifarious. In a particular case under s 51(3) it is first necessary to identify the duty concerned.

In *Green v Moore* the duty in general terms was that of supervising licensed premises. The police are required to ensure that such premises are lawfully conducted. The licensee must go on being 'fit and proper' if he is to continue to hold a justices' licence. {Licensing Act 1964 s 3(1).} If they have evidence that these requirements are not made out, it is the duty of the police to oppose renewal of the licence. So the police must collect information about the various licensed premises in their area, and must ensure that the information is kept up to date.

In pursuance of this general duty, the police in *Green v Moore* organised a 'police support group' to make surprise visits to licensed premises. By tipping off the landlord of one of these, the appellant prevented the group from making a planned surprise visit on the night of 27 June 1980. Although it was normally open well after the official closing time, on that night the pub closed promptly. The appellant was convicted of an offence under s 51(3), and the conviction was upheld on appeal.

This decision was (mistakenly) critcised on the following grounds. It is the duty of the police to prevent crime. By the appellant's tip-off no crime (of after-hours drinking) was committed at those premises on the night of 27 June. He therefore helped the police in their duty rather than obstructing them. {M D Cohen 'Is it a Crime to Prevent a Crime?' (1982) 126 Sol Jo 603.}

It will be seen however that the tip-off did more than just prevent the commission of a crime on that night. It also interfered with the carrying out of the general police duty of checking that these particular licensed premises were lawfully conducted. That is the ground on which *Green v Moore* can be distinguished from *Bastable v Little* {[1907] 1 KB 59.}, where the police whose duties were obstructed by a tip-off were solely concerned with detecting speed limit infringements on a particular road by unknown persons.

The fallacy, as Donaldson LJ said in *Green v Moore* {P 433.}, is 'to think that the only lawful duty of a constable is to detect offences'. In construing a multiple broad term, it is necessary to pay close attention to the precise meaning of each element *in relation to the facts of the instant case*. In s 51(3) cases it is necessary first of all to identify the precise nature of the police duty which is alleged to have been obstructed.

European Court The European Court is not apparently inhibited by the difficulty of construing enactments without reference to fact. While it gives rulings on the Treaty of Rome and Community regulations it is 'careful not to rule on their application to the facts of the case, which is the function of the national court'. {*Per* Dillon J in *MacMahon v DHSS* (1982) *The Times* 21 July.} However it seems that the European Court could not refrain from ruling on the factual *outline*, since this is a pure question of law.

Law and fact As Blackstone put it, when the fact is found it is for the judge 'to determine the law arising upon that fact'. {Kerr Bl (4th edn, 1876) iii 24.} Blackstone gives an example based on demurrer, an 'issue upon matter of law'. {*Loc cit* p 324.} His example relates to a trespass alleged to have been committed while hunting-

> 'As, in an action of trespass, if the defendant in his plea confesses the fact, but justifies it *causa venationis*, for that he was hunting; and to this the plaintiff demurs, that is, he admits the truth of the plea, but denies the justification to be legal: now, on arguing this demurrer, if the court be of opinion that a man may not justify trespass in hunting, they will give judgment for the plaintiff; if they think that he may, then judgment is given for the defendant.'

{Ibid, p 332.}

Although Blackstone's example relates to an issue at common law, exactly the same principle applies where the question turns on the meaning of an enactment. The principle of interpretation arising from the adversarial nature of our legal proceedings is of considerable importance. It means that in practice there is not a wide range of possible meanings of an enactment, among which a choice is to be made. Where real doubt exists, the choice is usually between one of two meanings only. The task of the interpreter is first to find out and assess the criteria favouring or denying each of the two meanings, then to work out the factors arising from these, and finally to decide which set of factors outweighs the other. {See further as to law and fact s 83 of this Code.}

Presentation to court For the assistance of the court it is desirable for an advocate to prepare and present a summary of the relevant facts on which he relies. {As to briefs to the court see s 263 of this Code.}

Usually a case contains a mass of facts. Most of these are irrelevant to the legal issues involved. The art of the advocate is to analyse the facts and present them in a way which strips them of irrelevant detail. If any are in dispute the analysis can initially be presented in the alternative. When the court determines the disputed facts the advocate will, if the determination is made by a judge or other legally-qualified functionary, have an opportunity of crystallising his legal argument by reference to the facts as so found.

This is a crucial operation for counsel who is preparing an opinion or an address to the court. He or she has to fit the facts to the law and the law to the facts. It is a two-way running operation, where each of the two elements acts and reacts on the other as one goes along.

The essence of the operation is *selection*. There is a lot of law about; counsel must select the bits that are relevant. There is a constant interplay between the segment of law that is relevant and the facts that are relevant in applying that segment of law or in other words fall within the factual outline.

Finally the advocate or adviser is satisfied that he has weeded out the irrelevant facts and the irrelevant law. He may then find some *relevant* facts missing from what remains. At that point he must check whether these missing facts can be ascertained and proved. Other relevant facts may be contested or otherwise doubtful, and the decision of the case will then depend on whether they are proved or not. Even facts which do not appear doubtful may fail to get proved. An advocate must be resourceful, and prepared always for the witness who does not come up to his proof, or who fails under cross-examination. {See further ss 81 and 82 of this Code.}

81. The facts: proof of relevant facts

It is the duty of the parties (or usually in practice their advocates) to satisfy the court of the relevant facts. This may be done by oral or written evidence or by admissions. Or in certain circumstances the court may take judicial notice of a relevant fact.

In case of doubt or dispute it is the duty of the court to make findings as to the relevant facts. Except in the case of findings by a jury, the court may be required to state the facts upon which its interpretation of a relevant enactment was based so that this can be reviewed by an appellate court.

COMMENTARY

Under the adversarial system of British law the judge acts as arbiter not inquisitor. He reaches his decision only on the facts as placed before him by the parties. If the facts are disputed he must decide the dispute, and lay down the law accordingly. (This does not apply where a jury or other lay tribunal is charged with the fact-finding function.) His finding of fact may be subject to appeal.

Unless the court makes clear what are the material facts upon which it bases its decision, that decision is unlikely to carry weight as a precedent. Where an appeal is brought on a question of law, the appellate court ought to decide the issue on the same facts as were found by the court below. This may appear obvious, but it is sometimes departed from. {See Example 78.6}

Judicial notice of facts As to the doctrine of judicial notice see ss 21 and 82 of this Code.

82. The facts: judicial notice

The court will take judicial notice of notorious facts generally known to well-informed people.

COMMENTARY

Judicial notice For the general principles underlying the doctrine of judicial notice of law or fact see s 21 of this Code.

The usual result of applying the doctrine of judicial notice to a fact which is material because within the relevant factual outline {See s 78 of this Code.} is to avoid the need for evidence. Where however a jury is involved the matter may involve an important question of law.

As a rule it is for the jury to determine questions of fact. {See s 71 of this Code.} Where however a relevant fact is one of which the court takes judicial notice it is withdrawn from the jury and becomes effectively a question of law. The courts welcome this because it reduces the risk of varying decisions by different juries on what are substantially the same facts.

Example 1 Section 1 of the Prevention of Crime Act 1953 makes it an offence to have an 'offensive weapon' in a public place. This is defined as, inter alia, any article made or adapted for use for causing injury to the person. In *R v Simpson* [1983 3 All ER 789.} the Court of Appeal held that the court must take judicial notice of the fact that a flick knife is made for use for causing injury to the person. Lord Lane CJ {P 793.} said that there was great scope for unevenness in the administration of the law if it was to be left in each case to a jury to decide whether or not a flick knife was an offensive weapon *per se*, since the identical weapon might be the subject of different decisions by different juries. {See also *Gibson v Wales* [1983] Crim LR 114.}

Judge's private knowledge It is necessary to distinguish between judicial notice of notorious facts and judicial knowledge of non-notorious facts which is obtained otherwise than by evidence.

The principle is expressed in the maxim *non refert quid notum sit judici, si notum non sit in forma judicii* (it matters not what is known to the judge if be not known judicially). {3 Buls 115.} It is unfair to the parties for a judge to act on his private knowledge without providing an opportunity for its being tested by cross-examination or refuted by other evidence. It means that the judge is in effect passing upon the admissibility and weight of his own testimony.

83. The facts: matters of fact and degree

Where facts are ascertained, the question of whether they fit the factual outline and so trigger the enactment may not have an obvious answer. It is then what is called a matter of fact and degree. Such matters depend on the view taken by the fact-finding tribunal. If the fact-finding tribunal has directed itself properly in law and reached its decision in good faith, the decision is beyond challenge.

COMMENTARY

A matter of fact and degree marks the limit of statutory interpretation. After the relevant law has been ascertained correctly, it becomes a question for the judgment of the magistrate, jury, official, or other fact-finding tribunal to determine whether the matter is within or outside the factual outline laid down by the enactment. {As to the factual outline see s 78 of this Code.}

As Woolf J said on the question whether certain persons were members of a 'household' within the meaning of the Family Income Supplements Act 1970 s 1(1), there are always three possibilities:

(1) The only decision the tribunal of fact can, as a matter of law, come to is that the persons concerned *are* members of the household.

(2) The only decision the tribunal of fact can, as a matter of law, come to is that the persons concerned *are not* members of the household.

(3) It is proper to regard the persons concerned as being members or not being members of the household, depending on 'the view which the fact-finding tribunal takes of all the circumstances as a matter of fact and degree'.

{*England v Secretary of State for Social Services* [1982] 3 FLR 222, at p 224. See also *R v Birmingham Juvenile Court, ex p N (an infant)* [1984] 2 All ER 688.}

Difficulties over a matter of fact and degree usually arise in connection with *broad terms*, such as the word household in the above case.

Example 1   Section 3(1) of the Supplementary Benefits Act 1976 provides for payment of benefit 'to meet an exceptional need'. In *Supplementary Benefits Officer v Howell* {(1984) *The Times* 11 April.} the claimant had been given benefit to pay for new clothes to be worn at job interviews. *Held* This was wrong in law. The broad term in question did not confer a discretion, but stated a legal requirement. Fox LJ said that, since there was no defintion of the ordinary English words *exceptional need*, 'it would generally be a matter of fact and degreee whether the case came within them'. {See also *Edwards v Bairstow* [1956] AC 14, *per* Lord Radcliffe at p 33.}

The interpretation of broad terms is further discussed in s 150 of this Code.

THE OPPOSING CONSTRUCTIONS OF THE ENACTMENT

84. Opposing constructions on particular facts

The usual circumstance in which a doubtful enactment falls to be construed is where the respective parties each contend for a different meaning of the enactment in its application to the facts of the instant case (in this Code referred to as the opposing constructions). The opposing constructions may often (though not always) be suitably characterised as the *wider* and the *narrower* construction respectively.

A construction put forward may rely entirely on the literal meaning, or may elaborate (but still correspond to) the literal meaning, or may depart from the literal meaning in favour of a strained meaning. The court, where it considers (or prefers to say) that the literal meaning is unambiguous, will tend to decide in favour of what it regards as the unglossed literal meaning and reject other versions.

COMMENTARY

The usual circumstance in which a doubtful enactment falls to be construed by the court is where the respective parties each contend for a different meaning of the enactment in its application to the facts of the instant case. The Code refers to these as the *opposing constructions* of the enactment.

The position was explained by Lord Normand in *A-G v Prince Ernest Augustus of Hanover* {[1957] AC 436, at p 467.}-

> 'The courts are concerned with the practical business of determining a *lis*, and when the plaintiff puts forward one construction of an enactment and the defendant another, it is the court's business ... after informing itself of what I have called the legal and factual context ... to consider in the light of this knowledge whether the enacting words admit of both the rival constructions put forward.'

Lord Normand went on to explain that where the enacting words or, as they are more descriptively called, the operative words {See p 565 below.}, admit of both constructions, that is are grammatically ambiguous, the matter will be decided by reference to interpretative factors such as the preamble to the Act in question. Where they are unambiguous the choice is between a literal and a strained construction. {The matter is fully developed in Part IV of this Code.}

Wide and narrow meaning It is often said of the opposing constructions that one presents a wide and the other a narrow meaning of the enactment. This is a convenient usage, but it requires care. It is necessary to remember that one is speaking of a wider or narrower construction of the enactment forming the unit of enquiry, and not necessarily of the Act as a whole. An enactment which is the unit of enquiry may be a proviso cutting down the effect of a substantive provision. A wider construction of the proviso then amounts to a narrower construction of the substantive provision. {As to strict and liberal construction see s 154 of this Code.}

In a few cases, there may be no sense in which an opposing construction is 'wider' or 'narrower'. For example an enactment may determine whether a person who undoubtedly needs a licence for some activity needs one type of licence (say a category A licence) or another (category B). If the legal meaning of the enactment is uncertain, the opposing constructions will respectively require a category A and a category B licence.

Role of the court A construction put forward may elaborate, but still correspond to, the literal meaning, or it may depart from the literal meaning. The court, where it considers (or prefers to say) that the literal meaning is unambiguous, will tend to reject the opposing constructions put forward and decide in favour of the unvarnished literal meaning. However some enactments are on their face open to rival interpretations, regardless of particular facts.

Example 1 Lord Wilberforce said of s 18 of the Rent Act 1968: 'the section is certainly one which admits, almost invites, opposing constructions'. {*Maunsell v Olins* [1975] 1 All ER 16, at p 20.}

Where the enactment is grammatically ambiguous, the opposing constructions put forward are likely to be alternative meanings each of which is grammatically possible. Where on the other hand the enactment is grammatically capable of one meaning only, the opposing constructions are likely to contrast an emphasised version of the literal meaning with a strained construction. The court will tend to prefer the former, while wishing to reject the need for any emphasis in favour of the unvarnished words.

Example 2 In *IRC v Trustees of Sir John Aird's Settlement* [1983] 3 All ER 481.}, a tax avoidance case concerning capital transfer tax, the Court of Appeal were called on to construe para 6(7) of Sch 5 to the Finance Act 1975 as originally enacted. {Having been found defective, para 6(7) was repealed and replaced by s 105 of the Finance Act 1976.} Counsel for the Inland Revenue put forward several alternative arguments, but the court preferred the one based on the unglossed literal meaning. It may be conjectured however that the other arguments helped to convince the court that the Inland Revenue's case was to be preferred. {The case is further discussed below, p 552. For an extensive discussion published before the Court of Appeal hearing and urging reversal of the decision of the court below (which occurred) see Bennion 'Scientific Statutory Interpretation and the Franco Scheme' (1983) British Tax Rev 74.}

Professor Neil MacCormick expressed the position in this way-

> 'The parties move the court for a decision in their favour supported by a particular 'version' or 'reading' of the law, in turn backed up by consequentialist arguments and arguments of principle.'

{*Legal Reasoning and Legal Theory* p 214. See also pp 100 ff.}

Several points of doubt The particular versions or readings of an enactment may deal with more than one point of interpretation.

Example 3 *Parkin v Norman* {(1982) 126 Sol Jo 359.} raised two distinct points on the relevant factual outline. {As to the factual outline see s 78 of this Code.} The case concerned the meaning of provisions in s 5 of the Public Order Act 1936, as amended by s 7 of the Race Relations Act 1965. {For the official version of s 5 see Example 73.1.} A selective comminution of this reads-

(1) any person who in any public place
(2) uses insulting behaviour
(3) whereby a breach of the peace is likely to be occasioned
(4) shall be guilty of an offence.

The male defendant (D) was convicted of this offence and appealed. He was accused of indecent behaviour in a public lavatory, the only witness present being a policeman in plain clothes (P). D admitted that his behaviour was of an insulting nature. His testimony was accepted that he did not intend it to be insulting and that P was not in fact insulted. D argued that clause (2) of the above could be fully expressed as follows-

(2) uses behaviour which is of an insulting nature, and which he intends to be insulting, and which in fact insults another person

P argued for the following version-

(2) uses behaviour which is of an insulting nature (whether or not he intends it to be insulting, and whether or not another person is in fact insulted)

D's version requires three elements to be proved by the prosecution. In this case only the first was proved. P's version, which was preferred by the court, requires only the first to be proved.

This was not the end of the matter. There was dispute also about clause (3) of the above. D argued that its legal meaning was accurately indicated by the literal meaning as it stood, namely-

(3) whereby a breach of the peace is likely to be occasioned

P argued that its legal meaning was accurately expressed as follows-

(3) whereby a breach of the peace is *liable* to be occasioned

The facts showed that in the face of D's behaviour a breach of the peace was possible but unlikely. The court upheld the appeal on this ground, McCullough J saying that the word 'likely' was not to be treated as if it read 'liable'.

Defining the legal point   The legal point at issue in a case can usually be reduced to a small compass, though care and effort may be needed to define it accurately. This preliminary care and effort is worth while, for it avoids unnecessary argument and consequent lengthening of court proceedings. As Sir Edward Coke said in the seventeenth century of complaints that too many authorities were cited to the court-

'This were easily holpen, if the matter (which ever lieth in a narrow room) were first *discerned*, and then that everyone that argueth at the bar would either speak to the purpose or else be short.'

{Co Rep: Preface to Part X.}

Once counsel have (it is hoped) 'spoken to the purpose', the court gives its decision by reference to the opposing constructions put forward. Some advocates put them forward more clearly than others.

Example 4   Inland Revenue Commissioners v Hinchy {[1960] AC 748.} turned on the meaning of a phrase in s 25(3) of the Income Tax Act 1952 which concerned the legal thrust of that provision. {As to the legal thrust see s 79 of this Code.} Lord Reid said {P 766.}-

'I can now state what I understand to be the rival contentions as to the meaning of s 25(3). The appellants contend that "treble the tax which he ought to be charged under this Act" means treble his whole liability to income tax for the year in question . . . It is not so easy to state the contrary contention briefly and accurately.' {P 766.}

The art of determining precisely which is the most helpful yet plausible construction to advance to the court is an important forensic accomplishment. Reed Dickerson says that-

> 'A knack for detecting the two (or more) meanings which are being confused in a disputed verbal question is of more service in reasoning than the most thorough knowledge of the moods and figures of the syllogism.'

{*Materials on Legal Drafting* p 63.}

Alternative arguments   It is often wise for an advocate to put forward alternative legal arguments, rather than relying on one argument only to support his or her side of the case.

Example 5   Thus an advocate may put forward a construction of the enactment supported by arguments X, Y and Z, of which argument X is based on an unglossed literal construction of the enactment, argument Y on an implication alleged to have been intended by Parliament, and argument Z on a strained construction. All three lead to the same result in his favour, and in the view of the court each may reinforce the others. When finding for his side the court, while perhaps being impressed by arguments Y and Z (without necessarily saying so), is likely to base its judgment on argument X, the unglossed literal meaning. {See Example 2.}

The adversarial system   Under British law, it is for each party to frame for the court the view of the law on which he relies. 'In the system of trial which we have evolved in [England] the judge sits to hear and determine the issues raised by the parties . . . ' {*Per* Denning LJ in *Jones v National Coal Board* [1957] 2 QB 55, at p 63.}

Scottish law takes a similar view, and the system of pleading in that country requires each party to enunciate both the law and the facts on which he relies-

> 'Reduced to its essentials, the Scottish system of pleading involves stating conclusions, or general requests for the particular form of legal remedy desired by the pursuer, and supporting these by a condescendence or statement of those facts of the particular case which the pursuer believes to be and offers to prove true, and which, he thinks, justify him in asking for the remedy . . . the whole is completed by pleas in law for each party requesting the Court's action in the ways concluded for with special reference to the facts of the case . . . '

{D M Walker 'The Theory of Relevancy' (1951) 63 *Juridical Review* 1, at p 3.}

As the author of this passage later says, the pleader needs to 'construct a valid legal syllogism'. {Ibid, p 14. For a discussion of the kind of syllogism involved in arguing that particular facts give rise to an identified legal result through the operation of a relevant enactment see Part XX of this Code.}

Lord Eldon said that 'truth is best discovered by powerful arguments on both sides of the question'. {*Ex p Lloyd* (1822) Mont 70 at p 72 (n.).} The need for clear argument is particularly obvious when a new Act is under consideration. Lord Porter said of the interpretation of new Acts-

'However skilled [the draftsman] may be in his art, many doubtful cases must remain which can only be allocated to their proper position by the clash of intellects which argument in the Courts can alone provide.'

{'Case Law in the Interpretation of Statutes' (Presidential address to the Holdsworth Club of the University of Birmingham, 1940) p 2.}

The role of counsel Normally the court chooses between the arguments placed before it, rather than embarking on a line of its own. This puts a heavy responsibility on counsel. It is reinforced by professional rules of conduct requiring counsel to draw to the court's attention unfavourable authorities.

The significant role thus played by the arguments of counsel was recognised by Lord du Parcq when he said both sides before him had agreed on the meaning of a statutory phrase, adding 'If there had been any argument to the contrary effect the problem before your Lordships might have presented a different aspect . . .' {*Nugent-Head v Jacob (Inspector of Taxes)* [1948] AC 321, at p 331. Cf *R v Khan* [1982] 3 All ER 969, at p 971 ('it is conceded by the Crown . . .').}

If an advocate fails to put forward convincing arguments to support his side's construction of the enactment, he may find himself in the position of counsel for the plaintiff in *Marshall v Cottingham*. {[1981] 3 All ER 8.} Megarry V-C said of him {At p 13.}-

'Counsel for the plaintiff, if I may say so, was barking up the wrong tree; and when in his reply counsel for the receiver indicated the right tree, counsel for the plaintiff had no bark left.'

If neither advocate manages to find compelling reasons the responsibility passes to the court. It is submitted, despite the dictum of Lord du Parcq cited above, that the court ought not to feel itself inhibited by the fact that what seems to it the correct view of the law was advanced by neither side in argument. Counsel should however be given an opportunity to comment on the conclusion reached in such a judicial departure.

In *Roberts Petroleum Ltd v Bernard Kenny Ltd* {[1983] 1 All ER 564, at p 567.} Lord Diplock referred to-

' . . . agreement or concessions, tacit or explicit, as to the applicable law, made by counsel for the litigating parties in what they conceived to be the interests of their respective clients in obtaining a favourable outcome of the particular case.'

This serves as a warning of one ground on which a judicial decision may be suspect as a precedent laying down authoritative sub-rules.

No real doubt The court may hold that the case does not, after all, turn on a point of construction. This amounts to saying that there is no 'real doubt' as to the meaning. {For the concept of 'real doubt' see s 3 of this Code.}

Example 6 An enactment regulating taxis made it an offence for an unlicensed cab to display a notice which 'may suggest' that the vehicle is being used for hire. The opposing constructions for 'may suggest' put forward in the magistrates' court were (1) 'is reasonably likely to suggest' and (2) 'might

197

possibly suggest'. The Divisional Court rejected both constructions, holding that on the facts opposing constructions were not needed. There could be no doubt that the notice in question fell within the wording of the enactment as it stood. {*Green v Turkington* [1975] Crim LR 242.}

A particular version or reading   In the remark quoted above {P 194.}, Professor MacCormick says that the parties each support their argument by putting to the court a particular 'version' or 'reading' of the relevant enactment. These are what the Code calls the opposing constructions. We now need to look more closely at the *form* in which they are put forward.

In Example 3 the opposing constructions are shown as textual amendments to the wording of the enactment. This is at one extreme. The other extreme is where counsel does not attempt any verbal formulation at all. In Example 6, for instance, counsel for the defence might simply have argued that there was no way in which the notice displayed in his vehicle could plausibly be taken to suggest that the vehicle was used for hire.

In the middle range of argument counsel may attempt *some* degree of verbal formulation without seeking to cast it as a complete textual amendment of the enactment.

Similar variations are found in judgments, which tend to follow the way in which counsel have presented their arguments to the court.

Unless (as happened in Example 6) the court determines that the enactment is so clear as to rule out any room for opposing constructions, the decision in favour of one of the constructions on offer must mean that in law the enactment is taken to correspond to that one.

If the favoured construction was presented as a textual amendment of the enactment, then the court has in effect found that the enactment is to be treated (in relation to facts of that kind) as having been originally worded in that amended form. Even if, at the other extreme, the favoured construction was presented without any attempt at verbal formulation it must still be possible to construct a textual amendment which corresponds to the effect of the judgment. This involves a notional *reconstruction* of the wording of the enactment. Even where the court finds it unnecessary (as in Example 6) such a reconstruction is always possible. The product is in this Code referred to as a judicial 'sub-rule'.

These matters are further explored below. {See ss 107 to 114 of the Code.} The present discussion may be concluded by saying that, assuming the court's judgment is or can be presented in the form of a textual reconstruction of the enactment, or sub-rule, the law is in a sense treating the enactment as having been in that form all along. It might be said that Parliament *implied* that the enactment should be treated as being in that form, though in many cases that would stretch the concept of implication rather far. Alternatively, it may be accepted that the court has acted on a delegation of legislative power implied by the words Parliament has used.

Whichever view is taken, since legislative intention is always the ultimate criterion it can invariably be said that by its judgment the court has determined that Parliament did indeed intend the enactment to have the meaning conveyed by the putative reconstruction or sub-rule. Subject to any question as to how far the court's finding is to be taken as a precedent, the enactment formulated by Parliament has been authoritatively developed by the court.

See also Examples 89.1, 114.1, 161.1, 162.1, 284.3, 284.5 and 316.8.

PART IV

The Legal Meaning of an Enactment

Introduction to Part IV This Part explores the concept of the *legal* meaning, first mentioned in s 2 of the Code. Its nature as the meaning truly reflecting the legislative intention is described (s 85).

Very often the legal meaning corresponds to the grammatical meaning. The latter is examined (s 86). Grammatical ambiguity is investigated (ss 87 to 89). The other type of grammatical difficulty, concerning semantic obscurity, is explained (s 90). Where the enactment is obscure, the court is required to arrive at the 'corrected version'. A precise indication of what constitutes the 'literal meaning' is given (s 91).

Next we pass to the vital topic of strained construction. In the last analysis, an enactment is given either a literal or a strained interpretation. The nature of the latter is discussed (s 92). The need for it is explained (s 93). The relevance of the former doctrine of equitable construction is touched on (s 94). Repugnancy, which logically *demands* some form of strained construction, is described (ss 95 and 96). Finally we notice that the same verbal formula may have a different legal meaning in different contexts.

NATURE OF THE LEGAL MEANING

85. Nature of the legal meaning

As stated in s 2 of this Code, the interpreter is required to determine and apply the *legal* meaning of the enactment, that is the meaning that conveys the legislative intention. This usually corresponds to the grammatical meaning of the verbal formula that constitutes the enactment. If however the verbal formula, in its application to the facts of the instant case, is ambiguous the legal meaning will be in doubt. Even where the verbal formula is not ambiguous, there may be real doubt as to the legal meaning because the relevant factors drawn from the criteria laid down by law as guides to the legislative intention tend in different directions.

COMMENTARY

The distinction between literal and legal meaning lies at the heart of the problem of statutory interpretation. An enactment consists of a verbal formula. Unless defectively worded, this has a grammatical meaning in itself. The unwary reader of this formula (particularly if he is not a lawyer) may mistakenly conclude that the grammatical meaning is all that concerns him. If he were right, there would be little need for books on statutory interpretation. Indeed, so far as concerns law embodied in statute, there would scarcely be a need for law books of any kind.

Unhappily this state of being able to rely on grammatical meaning does not prevail in the realm of statute law; nor is it likely to. In some cases the grammatical meaning, when applied to the facts of the instant case, is ambiguous. Furthermore there needs to be brought to the grammatical meaning of an enactment due consideration of the relevant matters drawn from the context (using that term in its widest sense). This need for an 'informed' interpretation is explained in s 119 of the Code.

Consideration of the enactment in its context may raise factors that pull in different ways. For example the desirability of applying the clear literal meaning may conflict with the fact that this does not remedy the mischief that Parliament intended to deal with. {Causes of doubt are examined in detail in Bennion *Statute Law* (2nd edn, 1983) chaps 12 to 18.}

This Part of the Code now proceeds to refine in some detail the concept of grammatical meaning. It needs to do this because, before the interpreter can arrive at an informed interpretation of an enactment, he must be quite clear what its meaning is in itself (that is apart from any consideration of outside matters). Finally this Part deals with departures from the grammatical meaning, that is strained construction. This may be required where other factors outweigh the desirability of applying the literal meaning.

Legislative intention   The nature of legislative intention is dealt with in Part V of this Code, while the guides to it are described in Part VI. Finally Part VII explains how to arrive at the legal meaning of a doubtful enactment by use of these guides.

GRAMMATICAL MEANING OF AN ENACTMENT

86. Grammatical meaning: nature of

The grammatical meaning of an enactment is its linguistic meaning taken in isolation, that is the meaning it bears when, as a piece of English prose, it is construed according to the rules and usages of grammar, syntax and punctuation, and the accepted linguistic canons of construction.

COMMENTARY

The starting point in statutory interpretation must always be the ordinary linguistic meaning of the words used. This meaning may be clear, ambiguous or obscure. Even when clear, it may not correspond to the legal meaning of the enactment. The legal meaning, which is the meaning that counts, may depend on a strained construction. {For the legal meaning see s 85 of this Code. As to strained construction see ss 92 to 97.}

The reader needs to use care in determining the grammatical meaning. In English (unlike Latin), even the order of the words can be crucial.

Example 1   The draftsman of the Sunday Closing (Wales) Act 1881 deferred its coming into operation by an unintended twelve months when in the commencement provision (s 3) he tied this to 'the day next appointed' for the holding of the annual licensing meeting. It was held that he should instead have referred to 'the next day appointed'. {*Richards v MacBride* (1881) 51 LJMC 15.}

Linguistic canons of construction   As to these see ss 147 to 152 of this Code.

Doubt as to grammatical meaning   The reference above to a 'clear' grammatical meaning is not limited to the case where the linguistic meaning is clear from the start. There may be difficulties in arriving at the grammatical meaning, even before legal questions are considered. As Pollock CB said, 'grammatical and philological disputes (in fact all that belongs to the history of language) are as obscure and lead to as many doubts and contentions as any question of law'. {*Waugh v Middleton* (1853) 8 Ex 352, at p 356.}

Nevertheless, as this passage recognises, there is a clear conceptual difference between grammatical meaning apart from legal considerations and the overall meaning taking those considerations into account. While it may sometimes be difficult to draw in practice, this distinction is an essential one if statutory interpretation is to be not only an art but a science.

87. Grammatical meaning: ambiguity

Where, in relation to the facts of the instant case, the enactment is ambiguous, that is grammatically capable of more than one meaning, the legal meaning is the one to which on balance the factors arising from the relevant interpretative criteria accord the greater weight.

COMMENTARY

In aid of precision, this makes it clear that in the Code the term 'ambiguity' is reserved for cases where there is more than one meaning that is grammatically apt.

Whereas in the 'clear meaning' case examined in the previous section a real doubt is unlikely (and where it does exist will probably be overborne by the weight attached to the literal meaning), here we deal with a case which *ex hypothesi* must be doubtful. {As to the plain meaning rule see s 120 of this Code.} The draftsman has produced, whether deliberately or inadvertently, a text which from the grammatical point of view is capable, on the facts of the instant case, of bearing either of the opposing constructions put forward.

The way difficulty can be lessened by concentrating on the opposing constructions of an enactment in a particular factual situation is demonstrated by considering how ambiguity is usually treated by commentators. Pufendorf, for example, tells us that logicians distinguish between a single word and a sentence-

> 'Both of these Cases the *Rhetoricians* call *ambiguous*. But the *Logicians* are more nice, who, if the Variety of Significations lies in a Word, call it *equivocal*, if in a sentence, *ambiguous*.'

{*Of the Law of Nature and Nations* (4th edn, 1729) p 537.}

Pufendorf gives as a choice example of ambiguity the answer of Charles V to the French ambassador when, on behalf of his master, the ambassador

201

demanded that the dukedom of Milan be surrendered: 'That which pleases my brother the French king, pleases me also'. {Ibid.}

The 'equivocal' nature of a word when taken on its own is not usually significant in construing an enactment. As Lord Reid said-

> 'A provision is not ambiguous merely because it contains a word which in different contexts is capable of different meanings. It would be hard to find anywhere a sentence of any length which does not contain such a word. A provision is, in my judgment, ambiguous only if it contains a word or phrase which *in that particular context* is capable of having more than one meaning.'

{*Kirkness (Inspector of Taxes) v Hudson* [1955] AC 696 at p 735. Emphasis added.}

Lord Reid here points out by implication that the inherent uncertainty of meaning possessed by many words is normally cured in a particular case by the context, that is by the selection of other words in the sentence.

Judicial attitudes   Out of respect for Parliament, judges tend to avoid stigmatizing an enactment as 'ambiguous'. The court will always prefer to say that it is following the literal meaning, and to reject arguments based on the supposed existence of ambiguity, implication or the need for strained construction. For this purpose it will often place a refined or unexpected construction on the literal meaning, so as to bring it within the facts of the instant case. As Murphy and Rawlings say of House of Lords decisions: 'Characteristically, rather than acknowledge an ambiguity, the Law Lords assert the absence of any problem'. {'After the Ancien Regime: The Writing of Judgments in the House of Lords 1979/1980 Part I' (1981) 44 MLR 617 at p 628.}

Judges prefer to resolve what is in fact an ambiguity by simply asserting that the meaning is 'clear'. Advocates, learning by experience of this propensity, allow for it in the way their arguments are framed.

Types of ambiguity   Commentators distinguish between *semantic ambiguity* (caused by the fact that one word may in itself have several meanings), *syntactic ambiguity* (arising from the grammatical relationship of words as they are chosen and arranged by the draftsman), and *contextual ambiguity* (where there is conflict between the enactment and its internal or external context). {See, e g, Reed Dickerson *Materials on Legal Drafting* (West Publishing Co) pp 55-6.}

Reed Dickerson criticises lawyers who 'persist in using the word "ambiguous" to include vagueness'. {Ibid, p 57.} This Code however concentrates on the situation arising on the particular facts of the instant case. Here, if there are two possible grammatical meanings of the enactment it is *ambiguous*, whether this arises from vagueness, or what Dickerson calls a 'squinting modifier' (that is a modifying word or phrase possibly looking at two or more different substantives), or any other cause. {See Example 88.1.}

Resolving ambiguity   As this section states, where in relation to the facts of the instant case the enactment is ambiguous the legal meaning is the one to which on balance the factors arising from the relevant interpretative criteria accord the greater weight. The method of resolving such a doubt is set out in Part VII of this Code.

See also Examples 114.1, 157.1, 284.4 and 321.2.

88. Grammatical meaning: general and relative ambiguity

Grammatical ambiguity can be divided into *general ambiguity*, where the enactment is ambiguous quite apart from any particular set of facts, and *relative ambiguity*, where it is ambiguous only in relation to certain facts.

COMMENTARY

General ambiguity Here the ambiguity is universal. Whatever the factual situation, there will be doubt as to the legal meaning of the enactment.

Example 1 Section 92(1) of the County Courts Act 1959 empowers a judge to order proceedings to be referred to arbitration. Subs (3) of that section says-

'On any such reference the award of the arbitrator ... shall be entered as the judgment in the proceedings and shall be as binding and effectual to all intents as if given by the judge:

Provided that the judge may, if he thinks fit, on application made to him within such time as may be prescribed, set aside the award, or may, with the consent of the parties, revoke the reference or order another reference to be made in the manner aforesaid.'

A proposition (or 'enactment') located within the above subsection formed the unit of enquiry in *Leung v Garbett.* {[1980] 2 All ER 436.} The enactment in question can be selectively comminuted in this form-

'The judge may, with the consent of the parties, revoke the reference or order another reference to be made in the manner aforesaid.'

{As to selective comminution see s 74 of this Code.}

The general ambiguity here is this. Does the phrase 'with the consent of the parties' govern both limbs or only the first? In other words, can the judge order another reference even though the parties do not consent? It might be thought there is no ambiguity at all. The structure and punctuation of the sentence indicate that the qualifying phrase applies to both limbs. Yet the Court of Appeal in *Leung v Garbett* held otherwise. {See further Example 89.1.}

Relative ambiguity Here the enactment is ambiguous only in relation to certain facts. This type of ambiguity was thus described by Lord Dilhorne when considering a phrase in para 3(1) of Sch 5 to the Finance Act 1975-

'I do not think the words "interest in possession in settled property" are equally open to divers meanings. It is the determination of the application of those words to particular circumstances which gives rise to difficulty.'

{*Pearson v IRC* [1980] 2 All ER 479 at p 484.}

Relative ambiguity would arise in the arbitration enactment cited in Example 1 if say the facts raised a doubt as to whether the parties had or had not consented (within the meaning of the enactment) to the revocation of a reference. While it is clear that consent to revocation is needed, it may not be clear whether particular facts do or do not amount to consent for this purpose. There might for example be acquiescence rather than formal consent, or some question of estoppel.

Relative ambiguity might arise in relation to the enactment mentioned in Example 84.6 if the wording of the notice used on the vehicle in question were more equivocal than in that case.

Relative ambiguity typically arises where the draftsman uses a *broad term* with a penumbra of doubt at the periphery. {The interpretation of broad terms is dealt with in s 150 of this Code.}

Voidness for uncertainty   The interpreter is not permitted to declare an enactment containing a broad term or other ambiguous expression void for uncertainty. The uncertainty is intended to be resolved by the interpreter, whether an administrative official or the court. This can be looked on as a delegation by Parliament of legislative power. A corresponding rule applies to uncertainty in statutory instruments and most other delegated legislation. {As to the interpretation of delegated legislation generally see ss 59 and 60 of this Code.}

The position is different with byelaws however. {As to byelaws see s 65 of this Code.} A byelaw may be declared void if uncertain in its terms. {*Scott v Pilliner* [1904] 2 KB 855; *Leyton UDC v Chew* [1907] 2 KB 283.} The same applies to executive instruments made under statutory authority. Thus an enforcement notice requiring the occupant of premises to comply with a planning condition that he be employed 'locally' in agriculture or forestry was held void for uncertainty. {*Alderson v Secretary of State for the Environment* (1983) *The Times* 10 October.}

89. Grammatical meaning: ambiguity and 'opposing constructions'

A grammatical ambiguity in an enactment is best resolved by considering it in the light of opposing constructions of the enactment on the particular facts of the instant case.

COMMENTARY

The advantage of treating a problem of statutory interpretation from the viewpoint of opposing constructions in a given factual situation is stated above. {See s 84.} Even where the ambiguity is general rather than relative, discussion may be helped by considering the enactment in the context of various possible sets of facts. {As to general and relative ambiguity see s 88 of this Code.}

It is to be noted that the concept of opposing constructions does not *necessarily* depend on there being a particular set of facts. In a case of general ambiguity the law can be stated in terms of opposing constructions without reference to particular facts.

Example 1   Thus the general ambiguity in the arbitration enactment discussed in Example 88.1 can be expressed by framing the opposing constructions as follows-

Construction A The judge may, with the consent of the parties, order another reference to be made in the manner aforesaid.

Construction B The judge may, with or without the consent of the parties, order another reference to be made in the manner aforesaid.

In a case of relative ambiguity, the facts *must* be brought into the equation. They can however be generalised - though not so far as to lose the statement of the ambiguity. To avoid complicating the equation by consideration of unnecessary factual detail, the art is to refine the statement of the facts to the essential outline. Returning to the example of relative ambiguity given above in relation to the arbitration enactment, {P 204.} we may describe the correct approach as follows.

There is agreed to be no general ambiguity. Both sides accept that the appropriate comminution is: 'The judge may with the consent of the parties revoke the reference'.

Let us say that there is no dispute that the *plaintiff* has consented to revocation. The dispute is in relation to the *defendant*. Suppose he says that he never consented, or if he did his consent was effectively withdrawn after issue of the summons. Evidence is adduced to the court about this. Correspondence is argued over. Witnesses are orally examined about the conduct of the defendant. What the evidence boils down to is that the plaintiff told the defendant of his own consent and invited the defendant to consent too, but the defendant neither refused nor agreed. Then, after service of the summons, he told the plaintiff that he denied consenting - but that if he had consented the consent was now withdrawn.

There are thus two questions of construction for the court. The opposing constructions, using comminution and articulating the relevant detail to be added to what Parliament has said, might be framed as follows-

Plaintiff's construction

(1) The judge may, with the consent of the parties, revoke the reference.

(2) For the purposes of subsection (1) above, a party who does not before the commencement of proceedings refuse a request for his consent made by the other is taken to consent to revocation of the reference.

(3) A consent given before the commencement of proceedings cannot be withdrawn thereafter.

Defendant's construction

(1) The judge may, with the consent of the parties, revoke the reference.

(2) For the purposes of subsection (1) above, a party who does not expressly give his consent shall not be deemed to do so by implication.

(3) A consent given by a party may be withdrawn at any time before the judge revokes the reference.

We see that subsection (1) is the same in both constructions. The two questions for decision are posed in the two versions of subsections (2) and (3). For the plaintiff to win he must convince the court that his versions of these are both correct. The defendant wins if the court finds for him on either of his versions.

It is not suggested that litigation normally proceeds by framing alternative constructions in this way (though it might be more satisfactorily conducted if it did). {For a limited example of the use of the technique see *R v Schildkamp* [1971] AC 1, *per* Lord Guest at p 15.} The purpose here is rather to demonstrate the true nature of the interpretative process. Even though it is not always carried through to the stage of articulating the opposing versions of what the enactment means, these are what the argument is in fact about.

The above discussion illustrates another important truth. *Enactments contain a great many implications, and confer a great many delegated powers on the court.* Suppose the court upholds the plaintiff's construction. It does so for one of two reasons, or for a mixture of both.

The first reason is that the court considers the plaintiff's construction to correspond to the meaning intended by Parliament. It is not expressed in this detail, but what is not expressed must be taken as implied. The second reason is that the court considers that Parliament has delegated to it the power to work out the detail for itself. Under the doctrine of precedent this will have a legislative effect.

Another point illustrated by the foregoing is the immense complexity of statute law. The opposing constructions examined represent but a tiny fraction of the possible constructions inherent in just one proviso of one section of an Act. Other possible factual situations (of which the range may for some enactments be virtually infinite) will, if and when they arise, call forth other opposing constructions of the enactment. The potential is unlimited. We learn from this that it is not at all surprising that statutes can be difficult to interpret. We also learn that great care and thought are required to arrive at the correct meaning. {This technique of verbalising the opposing constrictions, called by the Code 'interstitial articulation', is further discussed below (ss 112 to 114).}

Weighing the opposing constructions Whether the ambiguity is general or relative, there are two possible situations. Either the opposing constructions are evenly balanced grammatically or they are not. If they are, then the particular weight conferred on a meaning because it is the literal meaning favours neither side, and other criteria will wholly decide the issue. If they are not, then one meaning will have more claim than the other to be the literal meaning and will carry more weight accordingly (quite apart from the weight of other interpretative factors). {The method of resolving such problems is explained in Part VII of this Code. As to the presumption favouring the literal meaning. See s 137.}

The case of the ambiguous enactment is the commonest in which the court is required to carry out an exercise in statutory interpretation. It mainly arises from the use of ellipsis by the draftsman. {The reasons for the widespread use of ellipsis are explained in Bennion *Statute Law* (2nd edn, 1983), chap 12.}

Broadly, ellipsis takes one of two forms: *implication* or *delegation*. The courts do not always make clear which form they believe was used. Indeed the courts dislike the idea of both concepts, and prefer whenever possible to say that the meaning is clear. This preference is shown even where the course of the argument indicates that two views are possible; and needs to be allowed for by the advocate.

90. Grammatical meaning: semantic obscurity and the 'corrected version'

Where, in relation to the facts of the instant case, the wording of the enactment is disorganised, garbled or otherwise semantically *obscure*, it is first necessary to determine what was the intended grammatical meaning. The version of the enactment thus arrived at is in this Code referred to as 'the corrected version'. The corrected version is then dealt with as if it had been the actual wording of the enactment.

COMMENTARY

This deals with the enactment that, either generally or only in relation to facts such as those of the instant case, has no proper 'grammatical' meaning (including the case where the grammatical version obviously intended is presented defectively). {For the grammatical meaning see s 86 of this Code.}

Such textual errors may arise because of the drafting vice of *compression*. Or the text may be garbled. Or there may be an incompleteness in the text or an underlying basic error of fact or law. We are not here concerned with ordinary verbal *ambiguity* however. {This is dealt with in ss 87 to 89 of the Code.} Nor does this section cover doubt caused by the repugnancy of the enactment with some other provision. {As to this see Index references to *Repugnancy*.} Again, we are not here concerned with arguable or debatable errors, but only those that are manifest and beyond denial.

When the text is thus semantically obscure, the interpreter's first task is to remedy the obscurity by notionally putting the words into the grammatical form most likely to have been intended (the 'corrected version'). This may be straightforward when the error is a simple one such as the mere transposition of words. Often the task may be very difficult, but it still has to be done. Then, having arrived at the corrected version, the interpreter goes on to apply the interpretative criteria to it in the usual way.

Example 1 Section 10(2) of the House of Commons Disqualification Act 1975 says that the enactments 'specified in Sch 4 to this Act' are repealed. The Act contains no Sch 4. It does however have Sch 3, which is headed 'Repeals'. Other internal evidence confirms that Sch 3 is the one intended. The court will not frustrate Parliament's intention by applying the literal meaning of s 10(2). Instead it will apply a corrected version referring to the enactments 'specified in Sch 3'.

Compression The modern draftsman's need for brevity leads to much use of compressed language. This may cause nothing more serious than difficulty in comprehension (which does not count as 'obscurity' for the purpose of this Code). Sometimes however it goes further.

Example 2 Section 22(1) of the Theft Act 1968 defines the offence of 'handling' stolen goods in terms which include the case where a person 'dishonestly undertakes or assists in their retention, removal, disposal or realisation by or for the benefit of another person, or if he arranges to do so'. As J R Spencer has demonstrated by using the technique of commination, these few words identify no fewer than 32 different prohibited acts. {'The Mishandling of Handling' [1981] Crim LR 682, at p 684.}

When the words are disentangled by comminution they yield some meaningless combinations. For example it becomes apparent that it is an offence in relation to stolen goods dishonestly to 'undertake their retention by another person'. Spencer describes this is as 'nonsense'. {Ibid. As to the drafting vice of compression see Bennion *Statute Law* (2nd edn, 1983) pp 119-126.}

Difficulty in comprehension   Judges sometimes experience difficulty in finding any meaning in enactments brought before them, particularly in the field of taxation. In *St Aubyn v A-G* {[1952] AC 15 at p 30.} Viscount Simonds said of a claim arisng under s 46 of the Finance Act 1940-

> 'It involves the consideration of provisions which are, I think, of unrivalled complexity and difficulty and couched in language so tortuous and obscure that I am tempted to reject them as meaningless'.

Other areas of law have proved difficult too. Of s 12 of the Agricultural Holdings Act 1923 Goddard LJ said: 'For myself, I am not ashamed to admit that I have not the least idea what subs (8) means'. {*Bebb v Frank* [1939] 1 KB 558, at p 568.} Of s 4 of the Trade Marks Act 1938, MacKinnon LJ said-

> 'In the course of three days hearing of this case I have, I suppose, heard s 4 . . . read, or have read it for myself, dozens if not hundreds of times. Despite this iteration I must confess that, reading it through once again, I have very little notion of what the section is intended to convey. . .'

{*Bismag Ltd v Amblins (Chemists) Ltd* [1940] Ch 667, at p 687.}

On s 8 of the Workmen's Compensation Act 1925 Scrutton LJ said: 'If I am asked whether I have arrived at the meaning of the words which Parliament intended I say frankly I have not the slightest idea'. {*Green v Premier Glynrhonwy Slate Co Ltd* [1928] 1 KB 561, at p 566. For further citations see the Renton Report and other sources cited on p 374 below. See also s 374 of this Code.}

In considering such judicial complaints it is necessary, as indicated above, to distinguish real from apparent obscurity. Many of the complaints relate to texts whose difficulty is due not to any grammatical or other defect but to the complexity of the subject-matter or the inelegance of the drafting. Such problems can usually be cleared up by textual treatments such as composite restatement, and are not within the scope of the present work. {For the problem of text-comprehension generally see Bennion *Statute Law* (2nd edn, 1983) chap 11. As to composite restatement see ibid, chap 27.}

Where the obscurity is real and not merely apparent, the judge is compelled to find a meaning (which in some cases amounts to saying that he must virtually invent one). Courts are not permitted to say *non liquet* (it is not clear). {See s 2 of the Code.}

With some garbled texts it is quite obvious what the intended version was. That is then the one to be taken. In other cases it may be less clear, and the court must do the best it can.

Two-stage treatment of obscurity The interpretative treatment of an obscure enactment is thus, on a true analysis, a two-stage one. Having arrived at the 'corrected version' by notionally restoring the enactment to a grammatical condition, the interpreter goes on to deal with it as if it had been in that condition to start with. It does not necessarily follow that the corrected version of the enactment is to be given a literal construction.

If, therefore, the interpreter is dealing with a garbled text where the words have got into the wrong order, he puts the words into the right order and then considers afresh how to construe the corrected text. The original semantic obscurity at that stage becomes irrelevant. Its existence must not be allowed to distract the interpreter from the main task of construction.

As well as the semantic obscurity, the enactment might for example suffer from general or relative ambiguity. This must be dealt with as if the semantic obscurity had not existed, once that has been got out of the way. {For an example see p 664 below.} Or the obscure enactment, when corrected, may call for a strained construction. The point is that having cleared up the obscurity which prevented the words from having a clear grammatical meaning, the court must still proceed to enquire whether the clear grammatical meaning really reflects Parliament's intention.

Example 3 Section 9 of the Lands Clauses Consolidation Act 1845 deals with compensation for compulsory acquisition of land payable to persons under a disability such as insanity. The section is sloppily drafted. It is dealing with two kinds of compensation, but it muddles them up. First there is compensation for *taking* land, amounting to the market value of the land taken. Then there is compensation for severance and injurious affection in relation to land which is *not* taken, but remains with the landowner. Section 9 says-

> 'The *purchase money or compensation* to be paid for any lands to be purchased or taken from any party under any disability . . . and the *compensation* to be paid for any permanent damage or injury *to any such lands* [shall be as specified].'

The trouble lies in those words 'any such lands'. The word 'such' is an adjective that often gives trouble. It modifies the noun to which it is attached by referring to a description which has been or is to be given. The trouble is that draftsmen often refer back or forward to the wrong description.

Here the reference back made by the phrase 'any such lands' is grammatically to the phrase 'any lands to be purchased or taken from any party under any disability'. But it is not the lands taken that suffer damage from severance or injurious affection: it is the lands that remain. What the draftsman wanted to do was refer back only to the part of that phrase which refers to 'any party under any disability'. He wanted to talk about the compensation to be paid to a party under disability for severance or injurious affection to the land he retained. But that is not the grammatical meaning of the words used. It is sloppy drafting, or what this Code calls 'disorganised composition'. {See s 76.}

Let us see what the court did about rectification in the case of s 9 of the Lands Clauses Consolidation Act 1845, which we have just been looking at. Brett J said-

> 'The word "such" . . . would seem at first to apply to lands purchased or taken; but if so read, it is insensible. It is a canon of construction that, if it be possible, effect must given to every word of

an Act of Parliament . . . but that if there be a word or phrase therein to which no sensible meaning can be given, it must be eliminated. It seems to me therefore that the word "such" must be eliminated from this part of the clause.'

{*Stone v Yeovil Corpn* (1876) 1 CPD 691, at p 701.}

However the true corrected version is not as stated by Brett J, which would leave the meaning of 'lands' at large instead of being limited to the lands of persons under disability. The true corrected version runs as follows-

'The purchase money or compensation to be paid for any lands to be purchased or taken from any party under any disability . . . and the compensation to be paid for any permanent damage or injury *to any lands retained by any such party* [shall be as specified].'

In this instance the defect of meaning was patent on the face of the enactment. In other cases the cause of obscurity is a defect of meaning due to some fact that does not appear from the face of the enactment. It is not so much that there is a grammatical flaw as that the enactment just does not make sense having regard to the obvious factual situation with which it is dealing.

Example 4   It is a well-known fact that in a trial on indictment the accused pleads either guilty or not guilty. If he pleads guilty there is no verdict because he is not put in charge of the jury. So an enactment worded as if there were *always* a verdict in a trial on indictment is bound to be obscure.

This was the case with s 4(3) of the Criminal Appeal Act 1907, which said-

'On an appeal against sentence the Court of Criminal Appeal shall, if they think that a different sentence should have been passed, quash the sentence passed at the trial, and pass such other sentence warranted in law *by the verdict* . . . as they think ought to have been passed'.

In *R v Ettridge* {[1909] 2 KB 24.} the court hearing an appeal against sentence by a prisoner who had pleaded guilty rectified s 4(3) by deleting the words 'by the verdict'. The court claimed the right to 'reject words, transpose them, or even imply words, if this be necessary to give effect to the intention and meaning of the Legislature'. {P 28.}

See further s 142 of this Code and Example 284.3.

91. Grammatical meaning: use of the phrase 'literal meaning'

In this Code the 'literal meaning' of an enactment in relation to the facts of the instant case (taking the enactment in isolation from any other enactment)-

(a) where the enactment is clear (that is with one grammatical meaning only), is the grammatical meaning;

(b) where the enactment is ambiguous (that is grammatically capable of two or more meanings), is any of the grammatical meanings;

(c) where the enactment is semantically obscure (that is without any straightforward grammatical meaning), is the grammatical meaning of the corrected version or, where the corrected version is grammatically capable of two or more meanings, is any of those meanings.

COMMENTARY

The nature of the grammatical meaning is explained in s 86 of this Code. The purpose of this section is to lay down, by reference to the grammatical meaning, a universal definition of the term *literal meaning*.

The practical consequence for the science or art of statutory interpretation is that it becomes possible to treat an enactment as being given either a literal construction (that is one corresponding to the 'literal meaning') or what this Code refers to as a strained construction. {As to strained construction see ss 92 to 97 of the Code.}

Admittedly there may (in the case of ambiguity) be more than one literal meaning. Nevertheless by this treatment the basic questions of statutory interpretation become essentially few in number. Where the enactment or (in the case of semantic obscurity) its corrected version is not ambiguous the question for the interpreter is: shall it be given a literal or strained construction in arriving at the *legal meaning* (which is always what matters)? {As to the concept of the legal meaning see s 85 of this Code.} Where it is ambiguous the questions are first, which of the ambiguous meanings is more appropriate, and second, should it in any case be given some other (strained) meaning?

STRAINED CONSTRUCTION

92. Strained construction: nature of

Where, on the facts of the instant case and taken by itself, an enactment has a clear grammatical meaning, it is a strained construction to give it a different meaning. Where it has two or more grammatical meanings (or in other words is ambiguous) it is a strained construction to give it a meaning other than one of the grammatical meanings. Where it is semantically obscure, it is a strained construction to give it a meaning other than the grammatical meaning, or one of the grammatical meanings, of the corrected version.

COMMENTARY

Using the term 'literal meaning' as comprehensively defined in s 91 of the Code, this section can be summed up by saying that a strained meaning of an enactment is any meaning other than its literal meaning.

Pufendorf, after pointing out 'that distinction of the *Rhetoricians* between the *Letter* and the *Design*', tells us of a law that makes it a capital offence for any foreigner to presume to mount the walls of the city. In a particular siege a foreigner mounts the wall, and beats down the enemy soldier who was about to scale it.

'Now the *Letter* is against the Foreigner, the *Design* for him; according to which no doubt Judgment ought to be given; for the *Design* of the Law was to prevent any Foreigner from mounting the Walls as a Spy; which Reason in the present Case ceases.'

{Pufendorf tr Kennett *Of the Law of Nature and Nations* (4th edn, 1729) pp 538-9). The last words refer to the maxim *cessante ratione legis, cessat ipsa lex* (Co Litt 70).}

It is of advantage in understanding the science or art of statutory interpretation if, at least in a treatise of this sort, a spade is called a spade. The judiciary, solely (one supposes) out of respect for Parliament, often prefer not to come down to earth in this way when obliged to give enactments a strained construction. Yet as MacKinnon LJ robustly said-

'When the purpose of an enactment is clear, it is often legitimate, because it is necessary, to put a strained interpretation upon some words which have been inadvertently used . . . '

{*Sutherland Publishing Co v Caxton Publishing Co* [1938] Ch 174, at p 201.}

This is a device not unknown to the law generally. Writing on constructive manslaughter, David Cowley said for example-

'It is common practice for lawyers to attach the label "constructive" to a term or concept which is being extended beyond its natural meaning or subjected to a strained interpretation.'

{'Constructive Manslaughter: New Limits' (1983) 133 NLJ 503.}

Usurping the legislative function?   Some judges have been reluctant to accept the legitimacy of strained construction in any circumstances. Thus, in a dictum cited by Sir Rupert Cross as being of crucial importance, Lord Reid said-

'It is a cardinal principle applicable to all kinds of statutes that you may not *for any reason* attach to a statutory provision a meaning which the words of that provision cannot reasonably bear.'

{*Jones v DPP* [1962] AC 635, at p 668 (emphasis added); cited R Cross *Statutory Interpretation* p 29.}

There are however very many cases cited in this book where courts have attached meanings to enactments which by no stretch of the imagination could be called meanings the words are grammatically capable of bearing if that qualification is to be allowed any genuine significance. {See also *Re Lockwood* [1957] 3 WLR 837 and the commentary at (1958) LQR 25-7.} The truth is that sometimes the arguments against a literal construction are so compelling that even though the words are not, within the rules of language, capable of another meaning they must be given one.

In *Magor & St Mellons RDC v Newport Corpn* {[1952] AC 189.} Viscount Simonds, referring to the suggestion by Denning LJ in the court below that judges should 'fill up the gaps and make sense of the enactment' {[1950] 2 All ER 1226 at p 1236.}, said: 'It appears to me to be a naked usurpation of the legislative function under a thin disguise of interpretation'. {P 190.} This dictum has been criticised as too extreme. {See R Cross *Interpretation of Statutes* p 167.} It is submitted however that it was justified in relation to Lord Denning's version of purposive construction. This followed the extreme

Continental model rather than the more carefully delineated British version. {The principle of purposive construction as followed in Britain is fully described in Part XV of this Code. For the contrast between the British and European versions. See s 320}

In general it must be pointed out that to assert, in the face of the innumerable cases where judges have applied a strained construction, that there is no power to do so is to infringe the *principium contradictionis* or logical principle of contradiction. {This is demonstrated in s 362 of the Code.}

93. Strained construction: need for

There are broadly four reasons which may justify (and in some cases positively require) the strained construction of an enactment: (1) a repugnance between the words of the enactment and those of some other enactment; (2) consequences of a literal construction so undesirable that Parliament cannot have intended them; (3) an error in the text which plainly falsifies Parliament's intention; (4) the passage of time since the enactment was originally drafted.

COMMENTARY

This section of the Code states in very broad outline the main reasons why sometimes a strained construction of an enactment is necessary. In many actual cases, the reasons overlap. Each reason is related to the intention of Parliament (the only ultimate criterion). {Legislative intention is dealt with in Part V of this Code.}

As Blackstone pointed out, it is not always enough for a lawyer to say *ita lex scripta est* (thus the law is written). {Kerr Bl (4th edn, 1876) i 17.} The reason Blackstone gave for saying this (which related to the education of a lawyer) also explains the legitimacy of allowing strained construction of statutes in proper cases-

'If practice be the whole [the law student] is taught, practice must also be the whole he will ever know; if he be misinstructed in the elements and first principles upon which the rule of practice is founded, the least variation from established precedents will totally distract and bewilder him; *ita lex scripta est* is the utmost his knowledge will arrive at: he must never aspire to form, and seldom expect to comprehend, any arguments drawn *a priori*, from the spirit of the laws, and the natural foundations of justice.'

The following dicta by literalist judges appear to rule out strained construction altogether. Such dicta are erroneous if taken literally.

In *R v City of London Court Judge*, Lord Esher MR said {[1892] 1 QB 273 at p 290.}-

'If the words of an Act are clear, you must follow them, even though they lead to a manifest absurdity. The court has nothing to do with the question whether the legislature has committed an absurdity.'

In the same case Lopes LJ said {P 301.}: 'I have always understood that, if the words of an Act are unambiguous and clear, you must obey those words, however absurd the result may appear ...' In *R v Skeen and Freeman* Lord Campbell CJ said {(1859) 28 LJMC 91 at p 94.}-

> 'Where by the use of clear and unequivocal language, capable of only one construction, any thing is enacted by the legislature we must enforce it, although in our own opinion, it may be absurd or mischievous.'

{As to the many instances of departure from the literal meaning in cases of 'absurdity' see Part XVI of this Code.}

In *R v Wimbledon JJ, ex p Derwent* {[1953] 1 QB 380 at p 384.} Lord Goddard CJ said: 'A court cannot add words to a statute or read words into it which are not there'. {As to the wide variety of cases where words are to be 'read into' a statute see ss 107 to 110 of this Code.}

In *Warburton v Loveland* {(1832) 2 D & Cl (HL) 480, at p 489.} Tindal CJ said: 'Where the language of an Act is clear and explicit, we must give effect to it, whatever may be the consequences ... ' {As to the many cases where consequential construction impels a departure from the literal meaning see s 140 of this Code.}

In *R v Oakes* {[1959] 2 QB 350 at p 354.} Lord Parker CJ said-

> 'It seems to this court that where the literal reading of a statute ... produces an intelligible result, clearly there is no ground for reading in words or changing words according to what may be the supposed intention of Parliament.'

{An enactment may be 'intelligible' and yet not produce the result Parliament intended; see below in this commentary.}

The so-called 'literal rule'   The dicta cited above reflect the so-called literal rule of statutory interpretation. This supposed rule would require the literal meaning of an enactment to be applied whatever the consequences and however unlikely they were to correspond with what Parliament intended.

The so-called literal rule is fallacious because words will not bear the weight it seeks to place upon them. This was neatly expressed by Pufendorf-

> 'The *Boeotians* made a League with the *Spartans,* and one of the Articles was, That they should deliver up *Panactum*; which they did indeed deliver up, but first demolish'd it.'

{Pufendorf, tr Kennett *Of the Law of Nature and Nations* (4th edn, 1729) p 535.}

For the court to apply the literal meaning regardless of consequences is contrary to the judicial oath requiring a judge to do right. {Promissory Oaths Act 1868 s 4.} Consequences of always applying the literal meaning can be so extreme that they could not conceivably have been intended. To give effect to them therefore would not be to 'do right'.

Example 1   A remarkable example of the truth of this assertion is found in a case decided in the United States. An Act empowering local authorities to cease to maintain highways in their area contained a section worded as follows-

> '8. All laws and parts of laws, and particularly Act 311 of the Acts of 1941, are hereby repealed.'

{Act 17 of 1945 of the State of Arkansas, cited R E Megarry *A Second Miscellany-at-Law* p 184.}

Clearly what has happened here is that some words have accidentally dropped out. The literal meaning of s 8 is that all laws of the state of Arkansas are abrogated. If the so-called literal rule were applied the state would be left without law. Faced with this dire consequence, the court is obliged to supply the missing words and hold that only laws inconsistent with the provisions of the Act are to be treated as repealed.

This bizarre enactment, which might be given the soubriquet of the 'universal repealer', is mentioned here because its extreme nature clinches the point. An error perpetrated in Arkansas ought not to be repeated in Britain; but it could be. And if it were, the court would be compelled to deal with it in the same way. By a reductio ad absurdum, the universal repealer disproves the literal rule of interpretation.

Example 2 A case almost as extreme as that of the universal repealer occurred in New Zealand. Parliament had been dissolved, but by mistake the Governor-General issued his warrant for the holding of the ensuing general election later than was prescribed by the relevant constitutional enactment. A case was brought to establish that the returns in the election were therefore a nullity. This would have meant that there would be a power vacuum in the state which no one could lawfully fill. *Held* The time requirement must be treated as directory rather than mandatory, so that the election was after all valid. {*Simpson v A-G of New Zealand* [1955] NZLR 271.}

Many less extreme examples of the neccessity for strained construction, and consequent disproof of the so-called 'literal rule' of statutory interpretation, could be given from our own law. Here are two.

Example 3 Section 8 of the Agricultural Holdings Act 1948 provides for the appointment by the relevant Minister of an arbitrator to determine rent adjustments. Various provisions of the Act turn on the moment of time when an arbitrator is 'appointed', and it is established by case law that this is when, with the arbitrator's assent, the instrument of appointment is signed and sealed. {*Sclater v Horton* [1954] 2 QB 1.}

One provision of the Act causes difficulty on this construction. Paragraph 6 of Sch 6 requires the parties to deliver statements of their respective cases to the arbitrator within 28 days from his appointment. Suppose notification of the appointment to one of the parties is accidentally delayed? The Court of Appeal had no hesitation in applying a strained construction to deal with this. Eveleigh LJ robustly said-

> 'It is true that para 6 of Sch 6 might cause injustice if literally construed, but that is a reason for the court to avoid a strict construction of the paragraph and not a reason for departing [elsewhere in the Act] from the natural meaning of the word 'appoint' ... A benevolent construction in accordance with natural justice is readily achieved by reading into para 6 the requirement that a party must have notice before time begins to run against him.'

{*University College, Oxford v Durdy* [1982] 1 All ER 1108, at p 1111.}

Example 4 Section 38(1) of the Children and Young Persons Act 1933 allows unsworn evidence of a child of tender years to be received in a criminal trial.

The provision goes on to say that where evidence admitted by virtue of it is given on behalf of the prosecution the accused shall not be liable to be convicted unless *that evidence* is corroborated by some other material evidence in support thereof implicating him. {Emphasis added.}

In *DPP v Hester* {[1973] AC 296.} a child called by the prosecution gave unsworn evidence which was not so corroborated. However other prosecution evidence, while not corroborating that of the child, was by itself fully sufficient to justify the conviction. The child's evidence was surplusage and could be ignored without risk of injustice.

On the literal meaning of the enactment the conviction was required to be quashed. Evidence had been admitted by virtue of s 38(1) but had not been corroborated. So the accused was not liable to conviction. Grammatically, the words are capable of no other meaning. The House of Lords upheld the conviction, Lord Diplock simply saying of the literal meaning: 'so preposterous an intention cannot reasonably be ascribed to Parliament'. {*DPP v Hester* [1973] AC 296, at p 323.}

More than one one literal meaning   It has been demonstrated above that there is no such thing as a literal rule of interpretation where the enactment has one grammatical meaning only. A fortiori the same applies where the enactment is grammatically ambiguous. If a single straightforward meaning is not necessarily to be followed, there can be even less justification for insistence on following one meaning or other of a grammatically ambiguous enactment.

Yet judges of the highest repute state the contrary. Cited above was the first sentence of a dictum by Lord Reid in *Jones v DPP* {[1962] AC 635 at p 688. The dictum is cited at p 212 above.} The second sentence of the dictum relates to the case where there is more than one literal meaning. The full passage reads-

'It is a cardinal principle applicable to all kinds of statutes that you may not for any reason attach to a statutory provision a meaning which the words of that provision cannot reasonably bear. If they are capable of more than one meaning, then you can choose between those meanings, but beyond that you must not go.'

This is the literal rule in another guise and, with great respect to Lord Reid, cannot be supported.

Law Commissions   In 1969 the Law Commissions criticised the courts for giving undue weight to the literal meaning-

'There is a tendency in our systems, less evident in some recent decisions of the courts but still perceptible, to over-emphasise the literal meaning of a provision (i e the meaning in the light of its immediate and obvious context) at the expense of the meaning to be derived from other possible contexts ... '

{*The Interpretation of Statutes* (Law Com No 21) para 80(c). This statement by an official body might itself be criticised as encroaching on the constitutional principle that in the absence of parliamentary intervention it is for the courts alone to determine the weight to be attached to the various factors involved in statutory interpretation.}

Leaving it to Parliament The literalist argument is that if enactments are construed literally and this produces injustice it is for Parliament to pass corrective legislation. As constitutional theory this is impeccable; but in practice it breaks down. Parliament is far too busy to respond quickly whenever the law needs rectifying, and with some emotive topics parliamentary agreement on what the remedy should be is not forthcoming.

Example 5 The Sunday Observance Act 1677 forbade Sunday trading, but s 3 of the Act provided an exception for 'meat'. In *Slater v Evans* {[1916] 2 KB 403.} it was argued that the word meat should be construed to include ice cream. Darling J said-

> 'This is not an effective way of getting rid of the statute. In my opinion the best way to attain that object is to construe it strictly, in the way the Puritans who procured it would have construed it; if that is done *it will very soon be repealed.*'

{P 405 (emphasis added). Cf *Pocock v Pickering* (1852) 18 QB 789, *per* Coleridge J at p 798. See also Example 128.4.}

The court decided the case accordingly, but the Act was not repealed until more than half a century had elapsed. {By the Statute Law (Repeals) Act 1969, an Act confined to repealing enactments that by that date had ceased to have any practical effect.}

The truth is that the parliamentary timetable is almost always congested; and it is impracticable to remedy statutory defects as they arise. Moreover on many topics (of which Sunday observance is one) agreement as to the best remedy is not easy to find. Legislators who cannot agree on a matter that is not pressing are unlikely to do anything about it. That is a political fact of life that literalist judges need to bear in mind.

When Parliament really meant it One limited ground on which the literalist dicta cited above can be justified is where the court is satisfied on an informed interpretation {As to informed interpretation see s 119 of this Code.} that the literal meaning reproduces *the actual intention* of the legislature.

If the result of a literal construction appears absurd or mischievous, the court must ask itself whether Parliament really meant it. There is a presumption that Parliament does not intend to do anything that will produce an absurd result. {See s 141 and Part XVI of this Code.} If the court thinks that what it considers to be absurd was really and truly contemplated by Parliament, and was deliberately intended, then the court must defer to that.

The true rule Instead of attempting to rule out altogether departures from the literal meaning, what interpreters need to do is recognise that the literal meaning carries great weight but may in rare cases be outweighed by other interpretative criteria. To this we can add a related proposition. The stronger the claim of a particular meaning to be the clear literal meaning, the weightier will the factors arising from opposing criteria need to be if it is to be displaced. {As to the primacy of the literal meaning see further s 137 of this Code. For the possibility that literalist dicta reflect, and are intended to defer to, the 'ideal' image of Parliament see p 231 below.}

94. Strained construction: former 'equitable construction'

In former times the practice of giving a strained meaning to statutes was known as equitable construction. This term had no more than an oblique reference to the technical doctrines of equity, but mainly indicated a free or liberal construction.

COMMENTARY

Equitable construction was felt to be required for two reasons. The first concerned the need to soften the harshness of some general rule laid down by Parliament. As Buckland and McNair said in their *Roman Law and Common Law-*

> 'In all systems of law, at all stages except the most primitive, there is a constant conflict between two methods of interpretation, the strict and the "equitable", sometimes expressed as being between *verba* and *voluntas*, which is not quite the same. There is both in Roman and in English law a steady tendency towards the triumph of the "equitable" doctrine.'

{(2nd edn, 1952, p xviii.}

The other reason for so-called equitable construction arose from an opposite consideration. Early statutes were drawn by the judges, and lacked precision of language. In a case in 1305 Hengham CJ told counsel that he must not gloss the statute, adding: 'we understand it better than you do, for we made it'. [YB 33-35 Edw I (RS) 82, at p 83.] Often the wording of statutes was not settled until after the close of the session in which they were passed. It seemed quite natural for the judges to continue the drafting process in court. As Coke put it-

> 'Equity is a construction made by the judges, that cases out of the letter of a statute, yet being within the same mischief, or cause of the making of the same, shall be within the same remedy, that the statute provideth; and the reason hereof is, for that the law-makers could not possibly set down all cases in express terms.'

{1 Co Inst 24(b).}

The principle of equitable construction was described in a sixteenth-century case as follows-

> 'For everything which is within the intent of the makers of the Act, although it be not within the letter, is as strongly within the Act as that which is within the letter and intent also.'

{*Eyston v Studd* (1574) 2 Plowd 459; 75 ER 692. See also *Stradling v Morgan* (1584) 1 Plowd 199; 75 ER 308 (quoted in *Cox v Hakes* (1890) 15 AC 506 at p 518); *Vernon's Case* (1572) 4 Co Rep 1a, at p 4a; *Turtle v Hartwell* (1795) 6 Term Rep 426, at p 429; *Johnes v Johnes* (1814) 3 Dow 1, at p 15; *Lyde v Barnard* (1836) 1 M & W 101, at p 113; *Hay v Perth Lord Provost and Magistrates* (1863) 4 Macq 535, at p 544; *Shuttleworth v Le Fleming* (1865) 19 CBNS 687, at p 703; *Re Bolton Estates, Russell v Meyrick* [1903] 2 Ch 461. See Example 146.28.}

Dwarris described equitable construction in this way-

'Sometimes the makers of a statute put the strongest cases, and, by construction, the lesser shall be included; here the cases are put by way of example, and not as excluding other things of a similar nature. Where, moreover, the words are general, and a statute is only declaratory of the common law, it shall extend to others besides the persons or things named. Sometimes, on the contrary, the expressions used are restrictive, and intended to exclude all things which are not enumerated. Thus, where certain specific things are taxed, or subjected to any charge, it seems probable, that it was intended to exclude everything else even of a similar nature, and, *a fortiori*, all things different in *genus* and description from those which are enumerated; for instance it is agreed that mines in general are not rated to the poor within the stat. 43 Eliz. c. 2, and that the mention in that statute of coal-mines is not by way of example, but in exclusion of all other mines.'
{2 Dwarr Stats 712.}

Towards the end of the eighteenth century a reaction set in favouring literal construction. {See *Brandling v Barrington* (1827) 6 B & C 467, at p 475; *A-G v Sillem* (1864) 2 H & C 431, at p 532.} Nevertheless in his selection of legal maxims first published in 1845, Broom could still write-

'In interpreting an act of Parliament ... it is not, in general, a true line of construction to decide according to the strict letter of the act; but the Courts will rather consider what is its fair meaning, and will expound it differently from the letter, in order to preserve the intent.'

{H Broom *Legal Maxims* (1st edn, 1845) p 299.}

As might be expected of an early-nineteenth century American lawyer, Sedgwick, author of a textbook on statutory interpretation, wrote disparagingly of equitable construction-

'Here we find cases ... where laws have been construed, not merely without regard to the language used by the legislator, but in defiance of his expressed will. Qualifications are inserted, exceptions are made, and omitted cases provided for, and the statute in truth remoulded, by the mere exercise of the judicial authority. It is vain to seek for any principle by which these decisions can be supported, unless it be one which would place all legislation in the power of the judiciary.'

{*Statutory Interpretation and Constitutional Law* (2nd edn, 1874) 261.}

Some of the grounds on which it is nowadays regarded as legitimate to depart from the literal meaning find their counterpart in the old doctrine of equitable construction. The difference is that present-day judges give unquestioned acceptance to the supremacy of Parliament, and strained constructions are applied in accordance with clearly-defined principle rather than judicial whim. At least this is the position in relation to legislation of the United Kingdom Parliament. Where legislation of the European Communities applies in Britain it is interpreted (at the behest of the European Court) on expansive lines more strongly reminiscent of the old English doctrine of equitable construction. {See Bennion *Statute Law* (2nd edn, 1983) chap 6.}

95. Strained construction: where enactment repugnant to another enactment within the Act

Where, on the facts of the instant case, the literal meaning of the enactment under enquiry is inconsistent with the literal meaning of one or more other enactments in the same Act, the combined meaning of the enactments is to be arrived at. To the extent that this combined meaning is inconsistent with the literal meaning of the enactment under enquiry, a strained meaning of that enactment is required. This is without prejudice to the possibility that the interpretative criteria may require some other meaning to be treated as the legal meaning of the enactment.

COMMENTARY

Where there are two or more conflicting provisions within an Act, the interpreter of any is logically impelled to reconcile them. An amalgamated text must notionally be produced before the interpreter can advance towards the legal meaning. Thereafter the relevant portion of the combined text needs to be construed (in the ordinary way) as indicated by the interpretative criteria. It may still be ambiguous, or require a strained construction. {As to ambiguity see ss 87 to 89 of this Code. For the nature of strained construction see s 92.}

Judges often complain of inconsistency within an Act. For example Lord Hewart CJ said of Schs 1 and 2 to the Shops (Sunday Trading Restrictions) Act 1936-

> 'Sir William Jowitt {Later Earl Jowitt LC.}, appearing on one side in this case, frankly admitted that the provisions of these two Schedules, taken together, and compared and contrasted with each other, were, to his mind, unintelligible.'

{*London County Council v Lees* [1939] 1 All ER 191, at p 196.}

An Act is to be read as a whole. If provisions within it conflict, a combined version has to be worked out. {See further s 149 of this Code.}

96. Strained construction: where enactment repugnant to a descriptive component of the Act

Where, on the facts of the instant case, there is a discrepancy between the enactment under enquiry and a descriptive component of the Act containing it, the discrepancy is to be dealt with in accordance with the functional construction rule. This may in rare cases require (or be thought to require) a strained construction to be given to the enactment.

COMMENTARY

This section of the Code is concerned with the problem of the enactment whose meaning is clear when the enactment is considered on its own, but conflicts with a descriptive component such as a sidenote or preamble. A more complicated case arises when the meaning of the enactment, taken alone, is doubtful and the doubt is compounded or apparently resolved by a descriptive component.

Functional construction rule The functional construction rule, which relates to the effect on the interpretation of an enactment of non-operative components such as headings and sidenotes, is explained in s 124 and Part XII of this Code.

97. Strained construction: same words may have different legal meanings

Since, in the light of the interpretative criteria which apply to a particular enactment, its legal meaning may be held to correspond either to the literal meaning or to a strained meaning, it follows that the legal meaning of a particular verbal formula may differ according to its statutory context.

COMMENTARY

This final section of Part IV of the Code states the important principle that an identical verbal formula may have different meanings in different Acts, or even within the same Act. If the grammatical meaning of the formula is clear, the applicable interpretative criteria may require the literal meaning to be given to it in one place but a strained meaning in another. If the formula is grammatically ambiguous, it may have one of its literal meanings in one place and the other literal meaning in the other. Further combinations are obviously possible.

This flexibility in the meaning of a verbal formula arises from the fact that automatic literalism is rejected in statutory interpretation. Legislative intention is always the ultimate guide to legal meaning, and this varies from Act to Act. {Legislative intention is dealt with in Part V of this Code.}

Example 1 In *Liversidge v Anderson* {[1942] AC 206.} the House of Lords considered the legal meaning of reg 18b of the Defence (General) Regulations 1939, under which the appellant had been detained in time of war. The crucial words were-

> 'If the Secretary of State *has reasonable cause to believe* any person to be of hostile origin or associations, or to have been recently concerned in acts prejudicial to the public safety or the defence of the realm, or in the preparation or instigation of such acts, and that by reason thereof it is necessary to exercise control over him, he may make an order against that person directing that he be detained.'

{Emphasis added.}

The appellant brought an action for false imprisonment against the Secretary of State, and claimed particulars of the grounds on which he had reasonable cause to believe the specified matters. *Held* (Lord Atkin dissenting): The appellant was not entitled to the particulars because, provided he acted in good faith, the question of fact was for the Secretary of State alone to determine.

The opposing constructions were as follows.

> (1) (for the Secretary of State): 'If the Secretary of State, acting in good faith, considers he has reasonable cause to believe . . . '
> (2) (for the appellant): 'If the Secretary of State in fact has reasonable cause to believe . . . '

As the dissenting Lord Atkin forcibly pointed out, construction (2) represented the literal meaning, while construction (1) was a strained construction. Lord Atkin said: 'I protest, even if I do it alone, against a strained construction put on words with the effect of giving an uncontrolled power of imprisonment to the Minister'. {P 244.}

Why did the majority of the House of Lords adopt a strained construction, even though the principle against doubtful penalization went against it?. {The principle is described in Part XIII of this Code. As to its application in cases involving imprisonment, see s 290.} The answer can be summed up by saying that in wartime another legal principle namely that favouring the safety of the state, was considered stronger. {As to this principle see p 289 below.}

Where there is no such strong criterion favouring a strained construction of this common formula, the literal meaning will be applied. This was done for example in *IRC v Rossminster Ltd* {[1980] 1 All ER 80.}, which concerned the formula as stated in s 20C of the Taxes Management Act 1970.

In that case Lord Scarman said that the ghost of *Liversidge v Anderson* cast no shadow on s 20C. He added: 'And I would think it need no longer haunt the law'. {P 104.} The latter comment seems, with respect, to indicate a basic misapprehension. *Liversidge v Anderson* remains good law on facts such as arose in that case. The controversy surrounding the decision solely concerned the question of whether the majority were right in their weighing of the relevant interpretative factors, and did not affect the principle concerning which the case is here used as an example. {For details of the controversy surrounding *Liversidge v Anderson* see G Lewis *Lord Atkin* (Butterworths, 1983) pp 132-157. For another example of the application of the principle dealt with in this section of the Code see *Customs and Excise Comrs v Cure & Deeley Ltd* [1962] 1 QB 340, at p 367. See also Example 93.3.}

PART V

Legislative Intention

Introduction to Part V The sole object in statutory interpretation is to arrive at the legislative intention. This Part examines what is meant by the concept. Its place as the paramount criterion is explained (s 98). It is shown not to be a mere myth or fiction (s 99). To understand it we need to know the nature of legislation (s 100). The duplex approach to it is explained (s 101).

Parliament delegates to the courts the function of spelling out its intention (s 102). We discuss the case where no actual intention existed (s 103). Sometimes the words accidentally fit facts that were never foreseen (s 104). Intention is distinguished from purpose or object (s 105) and from motive (s 106).

NATURE OF LEGISLATIVE INTENTION

98. Legislative intention: the paramount criterion in interpretation

An enactment has the legal meaning taken to be intended by the legislator. In other words the legal meaning corresponds to the legislative intention.

COMMENTARY

Definitions As to the meanings of the terms 'enactment' and 'legislator' see s 73 of this Code. As to the concept of the *legal* meaning see Part IV.

It is axiomatic that Parliament is to be taken to have an intention in everything it does; and that the function of the court is to find out and declare that intention. This is the paramount, indeed only ultimate, criterion. Lord Radcliffe expressed it thus-

> 'There are many so-called rules of construction that courts of law have resorted to in their interpretation of statutes but the paramount rule remains that every statute is to be expounded according to its manifest and expressed intention.'

{*A-G for Canada v Hallett & Carey Ltd* [1952] AC 427, at p 449.}
Pufendorf said-

> 'The true End and Design of *Interpretation* is, *to gather the Intent of the Man from most probable Signs*. These *Signs* are of two sorts, *Words*, and *other Conjectures*, which may be considered separately, or both together.'

{Pufendorf, tr Kennett *Of the Law of Nature and Nations* (4th edn, 1729) p 535.}

Part V Legislative Intention

As Halsbury's *Laws of England* puts it: 'The object of all interpretation of a written instrument is to discover the intention of the author as expressed in the instrument.' {4th edn, Vol 36, para 578.}

Sometimes *will* is used as a synonym for intention. Thus Maxwell started his famous treatise on the interpretation of statutes by saying 'Statute law is the will of the legislature . . .' {*Maxwell on the Interpretation of Statutes* (1st edn, 1875) p 1.} In our own day Donaldson MR has said that 'the duty of the courts is to ascertain and give effect to the will of Parliament as expressed in its enactments'. {*Corocraft v Pan-Am* [1969] 1 QB 616, at p 638.}

The will, be it noted, is that of the Parliament that passed the Act containing the enactment in question. Members of later Parliaments may have diffferent ideas, but if they suffer the enactment to remain law they are taken to endorse and continue it in its original intention. {As to such 'tacit legislation' see p 78 above.} This is subject always to the dynamic processing carried out from time to time by the courts. {As to dynamic processing, by which the wording of the enactment is filled out by judicial sub-rules having either binding or persuasive authority, see s 26 of this Code.}

An Act is the single product of a single constitutional entity. The Act and its producer Parliament (more fully the Queen in Parliament) each have a notional unity, though the reality and substance of the matter do not entirely correspond to this ideal. Nevertheless the constitutional theory of legislation cannot be ignored by the interpreter. An uneasy combination of theory and fact (with a sprinkling of fiction) is what this Part essays to capture. Legislative intention, as Lord Watson said, is a 'very slippery phrase'. {*Saloman v Saloman & Co Ltd* [1897] AC 22, at p 38.} That is far from meaning that it is unimportant or illusory.

Statutory interpretation is concerned with written texts, in which an intention is taken to be embodied, and by which that intention is communicated to those it affects. The idea that a society should govern itself by verbal formulas, frozen in the day of their originators yet continuing to rule, is a remarkable one. It is pregnant with unreality, yet can scarcely be improved upon. Those concerned with working out its effect have an important role, in which sincerity must be uppermost. An Act, it must be stressed, is a statement by the democratic Parliament. What the interpreter is required to do is give just effect to that statement.

The text of the statement is the indication of what was intended: *animus hominis est anima scripti* (the intention of a man is the soul of what he writes). {3 Bulstr 65.} At the same time there may be very many *implied* meanings, enlarging those expressed by the words used in the text. In addition the court has a certain degree of delegated legislative power.

Historical Down the centuries, a great number of judicial dicta support the view that legislative intention is the paramount criterion. In early times no general interpretative principles were followed by the courts. Even of a period as late as the first half of the fourteenth century it could be said that the science of statutory interpretation was so little developed in England that—

'. . . the courts themselves had no ordered ideas on the subject and were apt to regard each case on its merits without reference to any

224

other case - still less to any general canons of interpretation - and trust implicitly in the light of nature and the inspiration of the moment.'

{T F T Plucknett *Statutes & their Interpretation in the First Half of the Fourteenth Century* p 39.}

This is what is known as palm tree justice, universal (except for the accretions of custom) in primitive communities.

During the following two centuries, as certain types of case began to repeat themselves, the judges laid the foundations of the present system. Coke identified the court's duty as being to interpret an Act 'according to the intent of them that made it'. {4 Inst 330.} This dictum has been judicially approved many times, one of the latest endorsements being by Viscount Dilhorne in *Maunsell v Olins*. {[1975] 1 All ER 16, at p 19.}

The resolution in *Heydon's Case* {(1584) 3 Co Rep 7a. See s 301 of this Code.} laid down that the office of all the judges is 'to add force and life to the cure and remedy, according to the true intent of the makers of the Act, *pro bono publico*'. Blackstone remarked that the courts both profess and are bound 'to interpret statutes according to the true intent of the legislature'. {Kerr Bl (4th edn, 1876) iii 222.} Lord Halsbury LC summed up the position in *Eastman Photographic Materials Co Ltd v Comptroller-General of Patents, Designs and Trade-Marks* {[1898] AC 571 at p 575.}-

> 'Turner LJ in *Hawkins v Gathercole* {(1855) 6 DM & G 1, at p 21.}, and adding his own high authority to that of the judges in *Stradling v Morgan* {(1584) 1 Plowd 204.}, after enforcing the proposition that the intention of the Legislature must be regarded, quotes at length the judgment in that case: that the judges have collected the intention "sometimes by considering the cause and necessity of making the Act ... sometimes by foreign circumstances" (thereby meaning extraneous circumstances), "so that they have ever been guided by the intent of the Legislature, which they have always taken according to the necessity of the matter, and according to that which is consonant to reason and good discretion". And he adds: "We have therefore to consider not merely the words of this Act of Parliament, but the intent of the Legislature, to be collected from the cause and necessity of the Act being made, from a comparison of its several parts, and from foreign (meaning extraneous) circumstances so far as they can justly be considered to throw light upon the subject".'

Lord Blackburn said in *River Wear Commissioners v Adamson* {(1877) 2 App Cas 743, at p 763.}: 'In all cases the object is to see what is the intention expressed by the words used'. As it was succinctly put by Lord Lane CJ: when *interpreting* an Act the court must be careful not to *misinterpret* Parliament's intention. {*A-G's Reference (No 1 of 1981)* [1982] 2 All ER 417, at p 422.}

In the wording of its Acts, Parliament has frequently referred to, and by implication confirmed, the criterion of intention. A typical example is s 4 of the statute 2 Geo 3 c 19 (1762), where a penalty was imposed for things done 'contrary to the true intent and meaning of this Act'. In the present day we have the Interpretation Act 1978 throughout attributing meanings to Acts 'unless the contrary intention appears'. {See, e g, s 5.}

The idea that there is an actual intention behind every legislative enactment is akin to the idea that there is an actual rule behind every common-law judgment. As Dias says, the quest for the intention of the legislature can be no less elusive than the search for the *ratio decidendi* of a case. {*Jurisprudence* (4th edn, 1976) p 219.}

The search for a necessitated legislative intention (located perhaps, like the necessitated common-law rule, *in nubibus*) involves a sophisticated variant of inductive reasoning. Induction properly so-called is a process by which existent unobserved phenomena are inferred from observed phenomena. Here observed phenomena (written enactments or judgments) are often employed to construct some principle not previously existent by any usual criterion of being. Frequently it resides *in posse* rather than *in esse*. In other words, the process allows for development.

Both for common law and for statute law, this process of what may be uncharitably (and inaccurately) called make-believe is a necessary one. It is required if we are to make of the law a living system, reasonably certain yet responsive to unexpected needs of a society in flux. Without it the law would tend to petrify, and thus to some extent fail in its social purpose.

99. Legislative intention: is it a myth?

Legislative intention is not a myth or fiction, but a reality founded in the very nature of legislation.

COMMENTARY

Many commentators have mistakenly written off the concept of legislative intention as unreal. Dias says that reference to intention 'seems to be superfluous'. {R W M Dias *Jurisprudence* (4th edn, 1976) p 219.} Corry says intention is a myth. {J A Corry 'The Interpretation of Statutes' (1935), reprinted in E Driedger *The Construction of Statutes* (1976) p 203.} N J Jamieson says it is a fiction. {'Towards a Systematic Statute Law' (1976) Otago LR 568.}

The biographer of Lord Atkin, in a chapter devoted to statutory interpretation, goes so far as to say that the very Parliament whose intention must be discovered is 'an imaginary one'. {G Lewis *Lord Atkin* (Butterworths, 1983) p 118.} Even Cross regarded legislative intention as no more than a 'linguistic convention'. {R Cross *Statutory Interpretation* p 35. At p 36 he calls it a 'linguistic convenience'.} Driedger says-

> 'The "intention of Parliament" is, in a sense, a fiction. It is not an intention formulated by the mind of Parliament, for Parliament has no mind; and it is not the collective intention of the members of Parliament for no such collective intention exists. The only real intention is the intention of the sponsors and the draftsman of the bill that gave rise to the Act; but that is not the intention of Parliament. The "intention of Parliament" can only be an agreement by the majority that the words in the bill express what is to be known as the intention of Parliament.'

{E Driedger *The Construction of Statutes* (1976) p 82.}

The concluding sentence of this extract suggests that the parliamentary majority could with the like effect (that is none at all) agree that the words in the Bill express what is to be known as the intention of the deity. This is to miss the substance of the concept of intent entirely.

Max Radin is even more dismissive of legislative intention. It is 'a futile bit of fiction' and 'a transparent and absurd fiction'. The least reflection, he says, makes clear that the law maker, *der Gesetzgeber*, *le législateur*, 'does not exist'. {'Statutory Interpretation' (1930) 43 Harv LR 863 at pp 881 and 870.}

Reed Dickerson rightly objects that such statements as these deprive the word intention of a well-understood meaning. There really is something approaching an institutional state of mind, says Dickerson - and this should be recognised. He continues-

'Asserting that there is no such thing as legislative intent because a legislature, as an abstraction, cannot intend anything, is like asserting that there is no such thing as ptomaine poisoning because food ptomaines are not in themselves poisonous.'

{Reed Dickerson *Materials on Legislative Drafting* (1981) p 51.}

The objection goes deeper than that. If, as Lewis and Radin say, the law maker does not exist, what human mind first thinks and then validates the legislative text? It is not made into law otherwise than through the agency of the human mind.

A famous conjecture supposed that a million monkeys dancing for a million years on a million typewriters might at random reproduce the plays of Shakespeare. Acts of Parliament are not produced at random, or by monkeys. Neither are they yet produced (as in the future they conceivably may be) by computers. {As to this possibility see Bennion 'LEGOL and the Electronic Home Lawyer' (1981) *Law Society's Gazette* p 1334.} Under our present system Acts are produced, down to the last word and comma, by people. The law maker may be difficult to identify. It is absurd to say that he does not exist.

As Dickerson argues, 'legislative intent is ultimately rooted in individual intents'. {Reed Dickerson *Materials on Legislative Drafting* (1981) p 51.} These go right down to the democratic roots. Allen grasped this when he said that laws are not solely the creation of individuals who happen to compose the legislative body-

'Legislators, at least in democratic countries, are still representative enough to be unable to flout with impunity the main currents of contemporary opinion'.

{C K Allen *Law in the Making* (4th edn, 1946) p 388.}

Allen might have added that on the contrary legislators *reflect* such currents.

Clearly the idea that there is no true intention behind an Act of Parliament is anti-democratic. It denies the remarkable success of the British in developing a mechanism whereby enacted law can broadly reflect the national will. This it does in modern Britain in no merely fictitious sense. If it were not so revolution would be a constant threat.

One must recognise that legislation is an open activity. It is conducted in a glare of publicity. The protagonists, retained to represent the electorate, do so in various ways. Political parties strive to secure popular support. An individual MP feeds on the repute of his party, but also needs to gain the voters' approval on his own account. Even non-elected peers are listening posts. Civil servants depend ultimately on public acceptance of what they do. Legislating governments, formed or sustained by these elements, do not survive long if they fail to satisfy the populace.

An Act is usually the product of much debate and compromise, both public and private. The intention that emerges as the resultant of these forces is not to be dismissed as in any sense illusory. Such dismissal marks a failure to grasp the true nature of legislation. The judges know this well enough; and would not dream of treating a legislative text as having no genuine intendant. As was said by Lord Simon of Glaisdale-

> 'In essence drafting, enactment and interpretation are integral parts of the process of translating the volition of the electorate into rules which will bind themselves'.

{*Black-Clawson v Papierwerke* [1975] 1 All ER 810, at p 847. For a discussion of the elements within the concept of legislative intention that may justly be termed fictitious see s 101 of this Code. As to the argument that the fact that particular circumstances were never foreseen makes intention a fiction, see s 103 of the Code.}

100. Legislative intention: the nature of legislation

In arriving at the meaning taken to be intended by Parliament the court has regard to the nature of the enactment as part of an Act passed under a certain procedure by a sovereign representative legislature.

COMMENTARY

An enactment is not to be construed as if it were a piece of ordinary prose. This section of the Code spells out the nature of an enactment as a *legislative* pronouncement. {See also s 72 of this Code.} Ignorance of that nature leads to misunderstanding of the nature of legislative intention itself.

The nature of a legislative pronouncement is complex. The British Parliament, despite the non-elective basis of the House of Lords, is the democratic instrument whereby the people's voice is reflected in public action.

Legislation is either government-inspired or government-backed. From this it is sometimes deduced that Parliamentary validation is a mere rubber stamp. That conclusion overlooks a vital fact. It is accepted that no government can survive if it loses the support of the House of Commons (to identify the democratic heart of Parliament). The truth of which this is a consequence appears to be less easily grasped. It is that, in practical if not theoretical terms, government is an emanation of Parliament.

Modern government is the practical, working, administrative and executive arm of the democratic Parliament. To say that legislation is the work of government is therefore to say that, at one remove, it is the work of the people's representatives. To complain that Parliament is only in *form* a law-making body, as Parris for one has done {*Constitutional Bureaucracy* p 184; cited Miers and Page *Legislation* p 14.} is to stand the truth on its head. Moreover it overlooks the point that Parliament is quite capable of asserting its true control by amending of its own choice, or even rejecting altogether, Bills submitted by government for its approval.

The nature of an Act as the product of a complex democratic process must carry weight with the interpreter. It is too simple to say with Gray that the judge must guess what the legislature 'would have intended on a point not present to its mind, if the point had been present'. {*The Nature and Sources of Law* (2nd edn, 1921) p 173.} It is more that the judge must bear always in mind *whose words he is expounding.*

The draftsman It needs to be recognised that the draftsman, as composer of the text, has an intention as to its meaning. It should however be understood that, although the present British practice is to entrust responsibility for the drafting of an Act to a single expert draftsman, his work in carrying out broad government policy is at all stages modified and controlled by the views of the civil servants instructing him and (so far as it is thought necessary to consult them on the more minute details of the policy) by the views of Ministers.

If, as parliamentary counsel still like to believe, the draftsman is to be looked upon as equivalent to a barrister in chambers, then civil servants and their Ministers constitute his clients. Decisions and comments by the clients play a vital part in settling the wording of the Act. It is a team product that is submitted to the legislature. The same team is normally responsible for the wording of amendments made to the Bill in the course of its passage. These facts need to be borne in mind when references are made in this work to 'the draftsman'.

Obviously the intention of the draftsman should correspond to that of the legislators. Judges assume that this is so. Thus in referring to a provision of the Interpretation Act 1889 Lord Morris of Borth-y-Gest said: 'Prima facie it can be assumed that in the processes which lead to an enactment both draftsman and legislators have such a provision in mind'. {*Blue Metal Industries Ltd v R W Dilley* [1970] AC 827, at p 846. See now the Interpretation Act 1978.}

In fact the draftsman's intention is likely to be much more detailed than the legislators'. Judges now recognise this. On refined points of interpretation, analysis will usually be more straightforward and realistic if conducted in terms of the draftsman's intention rather than that of a mass of legislators. This truth was spelt out by Lord Simon of Glaisdale-

'The court sometimes asks itself what the draftsman must have intended. This is reasonable enough: the draftsman knows what is the intention of the legislative initiator (nowadays almost always an organ of the executive); he knows what canons of construction the courts will apply; and he will express himself in such a way as accordingly to give effect to the legislative intention. Parliament, of course, in enacting legislation assumes responsibility for the language of the draftsman. But the reality is that only a minority of legislators will attend debates on the legislation. Failing special interest in the subject-matter of the legislation, what will demand their attention will be something on the face of proposed legislation which alerts them to a questionable matter. Accordingly, such canons of construction as that words in a non-technical statute will primarily be interpreted according to their ordinary meaning or that a statute establishing a criminal offence will be expected to use plain and unequivocal language to delimit the ambit of the offence (ie that such a statute will be construed restrictively) are not only useful as part of that common code of juristic communication by which the draftsman signals legislative intention but are also constitutionally salutory in helping to ensure that legislators are not left in doubt as to what they are taking responsibility for.'

{*Ealing LBC v Race Relations Board* [1972] AC 342, at pp 360-1.}

In a later case Lord Simon went so far as to say that a court of construction must put itself into the place of the draftsman, and ascertain the meaning of the words used in the light of all the circumstances known by the draftsman. {*Maunsell v Olins* [1975] 1 All ER 16, at p 26. Lord Simon was dissenting, but not on this point.} Lord Simon has also referred to what he calls 'the irrebuttable ascription to Parliament of a draftsman's knowledge of the law in relation to which Parliament is legislating'. {*Black-Clawson v Papierwerke* [1975] 1 All ER 810, at p 845.}

Draftsmen themselves dislike being brought into the argument. The tradition of the Parliamentary Counsel Office is that the draftsman is anonymous. This is taken to remarkable lengths, the impression being given that the Act somehow drafted itself.

Thus Sir Henry Rowe, a former First Parliamentary Counsel, rebuked Cumming-Bruce LJ for several times referring in *Governors of the Peabody Donation Fund v Higgins* {[1983] 3 All ER 122.} to what the draftsman intended. The result should have been arrived at, said Rowe, 'by examining the section within the framework of the Act rather than by an attempt to look into the draftsman's mind'. {'What was in the Draftsman's Mind?: an Unnecessary Inquiry' (1984) 128 Sol Jo 3.}

This is the opposite of realism, and treats the law in a take-it-or-leave-it cavalier manner as being handed down from on high. Unfortunately the subject is not in a position to take it or leave it, and needs all the help he can get. {As to the position of the subject see ss 7 to 14 of this Code.}

101. Legislative intention: the duplex approach

In construing legislation it is necessary to bear in mind both the concept of the ideal legislature and the fact of the fallible draftsman, and produce a synthesis between them. This duplex approach to legislative intention requires an Act to be construed with due regard to the fact that its text is both-

(a) a text validated by a legislature which is treated by the constitution as sovereign and infallible, and whose members are all taken to share in the intention embodied in the text notwithstanding that certain of them may in fact have disagreed with, or been unaware of, some or all of the Act's provisions; and

(b) a text produced by a fallible draftsman who is not a legislator but possess an intention taken to be adopted by the legislature.

COMMENTARY

As has been shown, legislative intention is not a myth. {See s 99 of this Code.} Yet there are, it must be admitted, traces of fiction in the concept. Parliament is deemed to adopt the intention of the draftsman. Since the words of the Act must stand as the voice of Parliament as a whole, legislators who in fact opposed the measure are deemed to share in its intention. (Unlike an appellate court, Parliament does not formally register dissenting opinions in the text of its measures.) The Queen, who assents to Bills without even seeing them, is deemed to share in Parliament's intention. {As to royal assent procedure see ss 36 to 42 of this Code.} Daines Barrington, writing in the eighteenth century, went so far so far as to assert that successive Parliaments must together be regarded as a single author. {*Observations on the Statutes* (2nd edn, 1767) p iii.}

Also fictional is the concept nourished by the courts of Parliament as an 'ideal' body, incapable of error. Thus Grove J remarked in *Richards v McBride* {(1881) 8 QBD 119 at p 122.} that one cannot assume a mistake in an Act of Parliament. To like effect was Lord Halsbury's dictum that-

> '*Whatever the real fact may be* I think that a court of law is bound to proceed on the assumption that the legislature is an ideal person that does not make mistakes.'

{*Income Tax Special Purposes Commissioner v Pemsel* [1891] AC 531 at p 549 (emphasis added).}

Legislative intent tends to become more and more unreal as, while its Act remains law, the enacting Parliament recedes into the distant past. Blackstone said: 'The fairest and most rational method to interpret the will of the legislator, is, by exploring his intentions *at the time when the law was made*'. {Bl Comm (1813 edn) 128. Emphasis added.} Since an Act is 'always speaking' {See p 355 below.} it must be taken always to have an intention behind it. Apart from exceptional cases, this continuing intention must in practice, *pace* Blackstone, be related to current conditions, rather than those prevailing at the time the Act was passed. The matter is explored below. {See s 146.}

These incidental fictions serve a purpose, useful if it is not misunderstood. The ideal aspect of Parliament promotes social stability and public respect for the law. It also encourages the courts to respect the legislature and its commands, and strive to render them effective. On the other hand the interpreter must not lose sight of Lord Halsbury's 'real fact'. {See above.} If pushed too far, the concept of the 'ideal' legislature can produce unfortunate results. It may inhibit the court from recognising drafting errors and where permissible correcting them. It may colour the language of judgments, and for the unwary may make them misleading.

One aspect of reality that needs to be recognised is that there is both a political element and a civil service element in the production of an Act. The draftsman and other civil servants provide the actual text, based on a thorough working-out of the details of policy, a full assessment of the practical considerations, and a survey of likely consequences. The political element combines government policy and the views of the nation's representatives in the legislature. The Minister tells the civil servant what the public want (and also what the public will not stand for). The parliamentarian validates the result or not, as (subject to the whipping procedure) he thinks fit.

So we see that there is a dichotomy. On the one hand the ideal, august, infallible legislature. On the other the human, inadequate, legislative workshop. Between the two the answer lies. In construing legislation it is necessary to bear both in mind, producing a synthesis between them. This is the duplex approach to legislative intention.

The judges, respectful of the political realities, serve as the creative link between the ideal legislature and its human agents. With sensitive antennae, they usually manage to give an effect to an Act (however long ago it may have been originally passed) which accords with the ethos of their own day. Only comparatively rarely are modern judges forced by intractable words to admit defeat.

Example 1 An example of how our judges see their duty in this respect is furnished by Lord Templeman. Faced by the argument that the wording of an Act precluded sensible flexibility in relation to the amendment by a farmer of his statement of case in a tenancy arbitration, the learned judge robustly said-

> 'Although there may be some difficulty in knocking sense into the Agricultural Holdings Act 1948, we have not yet got to the stage where arbitrators and county court judges can foist on the Act the kind of machinery that is more appropriate to the ages of Lord Eldon and the Circumlocution Office than it is to the twentieth century.'

{*E D & A D Cooke Bourne (Farms) Ltd v Mellows* [1982] 2 All ER 208, at p 223.}

Judges of the present day feel no inhibition about referring to the 'real' side of the equation of parliamentary intention. If they are to achieve the fusion demanded by the duplex approach, this is necessary.

So we find Lord Simon of Glaisdale for example referring to the factual relationship between Parliament and the draftsman. He points out that the individual member of Parliament may very well not know the law about which he is legislating, then says-

> 'The draftsman knows the legal effect that the person for whom he is drafting wants to bring about; and he will draft accordingly, against his understanding of the prevailing law, and using as a code of communication to the courts of construction various canons of construction.'

{*Black-Clawson v Papierwerke* [1975] 1 All ER 810, at p 845.}

There is thus a recognition by the courts that the actual intention of the drafting team and the participating legislators has a part to play in arriving inductively at the 'ideal' intention. Treatment of the role of participating legislators is more difficult, because many of them may have attended debates and voted merely in accordance with the whips' directions and without true consideration of the provisions of the Bill. {See *British Railways Board v Pickin* [1974] AC 765, *per* Lord Wilberforce at p 796.}

An 'ideal' legislator never promulgates a meaningless enactment. Even if the court finds difficulty in attributing a meaning to the words actually used, it will strive to reach one. Moreover it will strive for a meaning that will achieve the purpose of the enactment.

This principle of interpretation means that the subject cannot just ignore an enactment binding on him because it seems meaningless. The language of command is different from other languages, which have to accept the status quo (whereas command alters it). So special rules apply to the meaning of a statute, because it exists to be obeyed. In other contexts an incoherent statement can be ignored. To ignore an incoherent command, simply because of its incoherence, is to risk incurring the sanctions visited upon disobedience.

102. Legislative intention: delegation to the court

Apart from any express delegation by the Act to named authorities, Parliament is taken to delegate to the court of construction the ultimate working out of the meaning intended by it (as expressed in the enactment under enquiry).

COMMENTARY

There is a limit to what Parliament can say by the words it uses, even allowing for the obvious implications present in those words. For this reason Parliament often expressly delegates power to spell out the detail, as for example by the making of statutory instruments or the laying down of guidelines. But in addition to any such express delegation, Parliament also delegates by implication the power to work out meaning. Since the court is charged with the function of enforcing enactments it is, as a necessary corollary, charged with the function of laying down what they mean. {The general function of the court is explained in ss 19 to 26 of this Code.} Government departments administering an Act necessarily need to work out the detail of its meaning. {As to the functions of administrative agencies generally see ss 15 to 18 of this Code.}

They do this under the direction of any rulings that may be given by the courts. In all cases Parliament is taken to delegate to the courts the ultimate function of spelling out the detail where dispute as to its intended meaning arises. This delegation is necessarily involved in the fact that Parliament has entrusted to the courts the function of applying, and therefore construing, its Acts.

The working out of detail by administering officials and courts is called by the Code 'dynamic processing', the product being called a 'sub-rule'. {See s 26 of this Code.} Once an enactment has been processed in this way it no longer suffices to interpret it solely by reference to its wording. The relevant sub-rules must be ascertained and applied.

103. Legislative intention: where no actual intention existed

Where, in relation to the facts of the instant case, it appears that neither the legislators nor the draftsman possessed an actual intention, Parliament is nevertheless taken to have had an intention; and the enactment is to be construed accordingly. This involves expounding the verbal formula of the enactment creatively, using its wording as a guide to the imputed intention.

COMMENTARY

The test is What did Parliament mean by these words? rather than What did Parliament mean in the abstract? {See p 325 below.} Thus the text is to apply to the facts of a particular case whether or not anyone concerned with its drafting and validation as law foresaw that facts of precisely that kind would arise.

Great difficulties in interpretation may occur where it seems that no one held an actual intention in relation to the application of the enactment to the kind of facts arising in the instant case. The operation of the words used is then 'blind', and only the court can modify the 'blind' literal meaning (unless Parliament elects to intervene with an amending Act). What principles should guide the court?

One reason why there is no clearcut answer is that the absence of true intention can never be surely known. It is mere conjecture, however likely in a particular case to be well-founded. All that can be said is that when it seems well-founded the courts are likely to be more willing than usual to adopt a strained construction. {As to strained construction see ss 92 to 97 of this Code.}

On the main objects of the Bill, everyone who was concerned in the parliamentary processes is likely to have possessed an actual intention. On the detailed provisions and minutiae, only the draftsman may have known what the Bill provided for. Even he cannot have had an actual intention in relation to unforeseeable events occurring since the date of its passing. Where significant errors occurred in the drafting, not even the draftsman will have had an actual intention that effect should be given to the literal meaning of the erroneous words.

Does lack of real intent make 'intention' fictional? The fact that an enactment may apply in circumstances never actually foreseen by Parliament is sometimes used to support the argument, discussed in s 99 of this Code, that legislative intention is a fiction or myth. Thus Glanville Williams says-

> 'When interpreting statutes the courts often announce that they are trying to discover "the intention of the legislature". In actual fact, if a court finds it hard to know whether a particular situation comes within the words of a statute or not, the probability is the situation was not foreseen by the legislature, so that the Lords and Members of Parliament would be just as puzzled by it as the judges are. Here "the intention of the legislature" is a fiction'.

{*Learning the Law* (11th edn, 1982) 99.}

Here it needs to be borne in mind that the true legislative intention may have been to delegate to the interpreter the task of working out the detailed application of a broad term. {As to the interpretation of broad terms see s 150 of this Code.}

Radin objects that intention cannot be imputed to a legislature because the chance that of several hundred men each will have exactly the same solutions in mind is 'infinitesimally small'. {'Statutory Interpretation' (1930) 43 Harv LR 863, at p 870.} An Act, he says, is not, like a literary text, the product of a single author. {Ibid, p 868.}

But even if the Act were the product of a single author (say some oriental despot), this would not ensure that the author's genuine intention would extend to all future possibilities. The despot, like our draftsman, would be likely to make mistakes and perpetrate ambiguities. But we would not say his intention is a fiction. To do so would amount to saying that there can be no genuine intention behind any normative text - not even such a text as one of Lord Chesterfield's letters to his son. This is indeed absurd.

Because an author cannot foresee everything or be all-wise, his prescription is not deprived of genuine intention. It is merely that the intention is necessarily incomplete.

With an enactment the position is similar to that prevailing in the case of contracts, about which Lord Denning said that often 'the intention of the parties is not clear, for the simple reason that they never formed an intention: so the court has to attribute an intention to them'. {*Fribance v Fribance* [1957] 1 WLR 384, at p 387.} The court when construing an enactment always has to 'attribute an intention' to Parliament. This may range from an intention actually held by many legislators to one actually held by nobody but found to be implicit in the words used.

Guess what the legislator would have said?   Cross cites the following statement from *The Nature and Sources of Law* by the American jurist Gray-

> 'The fact is that the difficulties of so called interpretation arise when the legislature had no meaning at all; when the question which was raised on the statute never occurred to it; when what the judges have to do is, not to determine what the legislature did mean on a point which was not present to its mind, but to *guess* what it would have intended on a point not present to its mind, if the point had been present.'

{(2nd edn, 1921) p 173 (emphasis added); cited R Cross *Statutory Interpretation* p 25.}

Gray's statement is erroneous. It overlooks the importance of the text, wherein the clue to imputed intention must always be sought. {See s 136 of this Code.} In so far as the court does make a 'guess', it must be one informed by the wording of the Act and arrived at in accordance with the recognised guides to legislative intention. {As to these guides see Part VI of this Code.} It must not be merely speculative. Nor must it attribute to the legislature a hindsight it could not possess.

104. Legislative intention: unforeseen facts and accidental fit

Where facts arise that were unforeseen by Parliament, but which the words of the enactment accidentally fit, it may be necessary to depart from the literal meaning in order to give effect to the imputed intention.

COMMENTARY

In relation to an unforeseen concatenation of events, the wording of an enactment, if construed literally, may be found to 'fit' in a way which was never designed and may be contrary to the presumed legislative intention. In such cases a strained rather than a literal construction may be applied. {Literal and strained constructions are dealt with in Part IV of this Code.}

Example 1   By s 61 of the Finance Act 1976 Parliament brought within the charge to income tax certain fringe benefits provided for company employees. They were defined as-

> '... accomodation (other than living accomodation), entertainment, domestic or other services, and other benefits and facilities of whatsoever nature (whether or not similar to any of those mentioned above in this subsection) ...'

This covered a very wide area, and no legislator could foresee all the specific benefits that in the years to come would fall within its literal meaning.

One company, ICI, decided to benefit its employees by setting up an educational trust to provide university scholarships for their children. These were clearly benefits within s 61, but there was an accidental fit with another tax enactment. Section 375 of the Income and Corporation Taxes Act 1970 provides a tax exemption for 'income arising from a scholarship'. The Court of Appeal held that this exemption did not apply. {*Wicks v Firth* [1982] 2 All ER 9.} As Watkins LJ said, s 375 was first enacted as s 28 of the Finance Act 1920 'when fringe benefits and taxation of them were unheard of'. {P 19.} On appeal, the House of Lords reversed this ruling and applied the literal meaning of s 375. {[1983] 1 All ER 151.} It is submitted that the reasoning of the Court of Appeal is to be preferred.

Example 2   Section 13 of the Sexual Offences Act 1956 makes it an offence 'to procure the commission by a man of an act of gross indecency with another man'. {By virtue of s 4 of the Sexual Offences Act 1967 s 13 is, with certain exceptions, disapplied where the indecent act is not done in a public place.} A private prosecution was brought under s 13 against a theatrical producer who had 'procured' the staging in a public theatre of a play in which two naked male actors performed a simulated homosexual rape. {*R v Bogdanov* (1982) (unreported). The magistrate issued a summons and the accused was committed for trial, but the proceedings were later terminated by a *nolle prosequi.*}

Section 13 re-enacted the notorious Labouchère amendment, which had been introduced without debate as s 11 of the Criminal Law Amendment Act 1885. All that Mr Labouchère said when introducing the clause was that it was directed against 'assaults'. {HC Deb 6 August 1885, col 1397.} Clearly Parliament never envisaged that its wording might be thought to cover simulated acts in the theatre. That it was possible to get the prosecution on its feet was due to the failure of s 2(4) of the Theatres Act 1968 to disapply s 13 in addition to disapplying, as it did, s 4 (indecent exhibitions) of the Vagrancy Act 1824. No doubt the draftsman understandably failed to foresee this type of accidental fit.

Accidental fit not contrary to intention   The fact that there is an accidental fit of the words of the enactment to the facts of the instant case does not always mean that a strained construction is necessary.

Example 3   Section 61(1) of the Factories Act 1961 required compliance with certain safety provisions 'as respects every chain, rope or lifting tackle used for the purpose of *raising* or lowering persons, goods or *materials*. {Emphasis added.} *Ball v Richard Thomas and Baldwins Ltd* {[1968] 1 All ER 389.}

concerned the application of s 61(1) to an operation whereby the 'scab' which formed when molten metal dripped on to the floor of a steel works was detached. This was done by attaching the 'scab' to a crane and using the crane's power to loosen and then lift it. This was not the normal use of a crane, but there was in a literal sense a 'raising' of 'materials'. *Held* The operation fell within s 61(1), although Parliament was unlikely to have had it in mind. Otherwise there would be no statutory safeguard in an admittedly dangerous operation.

Cases like these illustrate a dilemma inherent in statute law. Should the court, after investigating the legislative history, act on the obvious fact that neither Parliament nor the draftsman would have had in mind the possibility of a 'fit' such as has occurred? Or should the statute book be looked on as an interlocking whole, to be applied automatically without regard to the dates and circumstances when the relevant provision was originally enacted?

Our system arranges itself uneasily between these positions, showing a marked preference for the former. Thus, unlike that of many other countries, our statute book is not arranged under titles on a one Act-one subject basis. {As to the doctrine of the free-standing Act see pp 374–375 below. See also Examples 289.3 and 305.2.}

105. Legislative intention: intention distinguished from purpose or object

The distinction between the purpose or object of an enactment and the legislative intention governing it is that the former relates to the mischief to which the enactment is directed and its remedy, while the latter relates to the legal meaning of the enactment.

COMMENTARY

The distinction between purpose and intention in relation to statutory interpretation is that, while purpose has an overall reference to the mischief which the enactment is designed to remedy, intention is taken for practical purposes to relate to the imputed meaning and effect of the enactment in its application to particular factual situations. {See Example 106.3.}

A construction which furthers the purpose or object is described as a *purposive construction*. {See s 139 of this Code.} Provisions of an Act may deal with two or more distinct 'mischiefs', and the Act then has a corresponding number of 'purposes'. {As to the distinction between purpose and object see p 239 below.}

106. Legislative intention: intention distinguished from motive

The distinction between motive and intention is that, while the former relates to the political reasons for the historical decision to legislate in that way at that time for that purpose, the latter relates to the legal meaning of the enactment.

COMMENTARY

The court is concerned with motive only to the extent that it may throw light on intention. It is the legal meaning of the enactment that in the end matters to the court, not the reason why it was passed.

The reason why Parliament chose to legislate on the subject at the time and in the way it did is by definition a political rather than a legal matter (though not necessarily party-political). Virtually all Bills that get through are introduced (or at least supported) by the government. In introducing a Bill, the government may be carrying out its election manifesto, or responding to a sudden emergency or outbreak of public clamour, or merely going through the normal processes of administration. By its action it brings into play the political wisdom that Blackstone called 'the prudence of the legislature'. {Kerr Bl (4th edn, 1876) iv 247.}

This prudence gauges, for example, the weight of the sanction needed to deter infringements. Blackstone cites a quaint example from the old law of the Isle of Man. To steal a horse or an ox was not felony but mere trespass 'because of the difficulty in that little territory to conceal them or carry them off'. To steal a fowl, which was easily accomplished, was by contrast a capital offence. {Kerr Bl (4th edn, 1876) iv 12.}

Sometimes the motive for enacting a particular provision is odd. Occasionally it is bizarre.

Example 1 It seems that for over a century the Master of the Rolls has sat in the Court of Appeal, rather than in his traditional seat at first instance, simply because a Victorian Parliament considered it impossible to staff an appellate court which would be worthy to sit in judgment on the great Jessel MR. {Lord Evershed MR *The Court of Appeal in England* p 12. The provision effecting this elevation of Jessel MR (and willy nilly his successors too) was the Supreme Court of Judicature Act 1881 s 2.}

As part of its duty of informed interpretation {As to the informed interpretation rule see s 119 of this Code.}, the court takes note of the political reasons behind an enactment without canvassing their merits.

Example 2 In one trade union case Lord Denning MR began his judgment by pointing out that the subject-matter, the question of the union closed shop, was a matter of political controversy. He went on: 'So, like Agag (1 Samuel XV, 32) the court must tread delicately'. {*Taylor v Co-operative Retail Services Ltd* (1982) *The Times* 13 July. It will be remembered that King Agag's delicacy did not avail him, for he was at once despatched as a sacrificial offering.}

The correct judicial approach was thus described by Lord Diplock in a case dealing with a Transport Act passed thirteen years earlier-

> 'The extent to which public passenger transport ought to be treated as a social service to persons in the area in which it operated, rather than as a quasi-business enterprise which ought to do its best to pay its own way out of the fares it charged to passengers, was then, as it still is, a matter of political controversy. Into the merits of that controversy your Lordships, in your judicial capacity, must scrupulously refrain from entering; but recognition that it existed is, in my view, of considerable relevance to a proper understanding of the language of the Act.'

{*Bromley LBC v Greater London Council* [1982] 1 All ER 129, at p 164. Cf Salmon LJ's remarks in *Blackburn v A-G* [1971] 2 All ER 1380, at p 1383, where, after saying that he deprecated litigation the purpose of which was to influence political decisions, he added: 'Such decisions have nothing to do with these courts'.}

Example 3 In the mid-1970s there was a public outcry, led by the soi-disant 'women's movement', against certain aspects of the law of rape. One objection concerned the way 'mud-slinging' evidence about the complainant's morals could be adduced by the defence so as to damage her credit. The government commissioned an inquiry by the Advisory Group on the Law of Rape, which produced a report. {Cmnd 6352 (the Heilbron Report).} The Sexual Offences (Amendment) Act 1976 was based on this report. Section 2 of the Act requires the court to exclude certain evidence unless satisfied that the exclusion would be 'unfair' to the defendant. Parliament's intention, purpose or object, and motive may be briefly described as having been respectively as follows.

Intention That if an application to admit the evidence is made to the judge he shall ask himself whether to exclude it would be unfair to the defendant. Only if satisfied that exclusion would be unfair shall he admit it.

Purpose or object To ease the lot of rape victims by allowing questions affecting the issue of guilt while disallowing those which merely go to the credit of the complainant as a witness, allowance being made for the 'grey' area in between. {*R v Viola* [1982] 3 All ER 73. As to the distinction between intention and purpose see s 105 of this Code.} If it is desired to make a further distinction between the 'object' and the 'purpose' (which seems an unnecessary refinement), the former may be described as being to ease the victims' lot and the latter as being the remainder of the above statement.

Motive To still a public clamour, and add to the repute of the government, by remedying what was regarded by some as a mischief.

FILLING IN THE TEXTUAL DETAIL

107. Filling in the detail: implications (nature of)

Parliament is presumed to intend that the literal meaning of the express words of an enactment is to be treated as elaborated by taking into account all implications which, in accordance with the recognised guides to legislative intention, it is proper to treat the legislator as having intended. Accordingly, in determining which of the opposing constructions of an enactment to apply in the factual situation of the instant case, the court seeks to identify the one that embodies the elaborations intended by the legislator.

COMMENTARY

Implications arise either because they are directly suggested by the words expressed or because they are indirectly suggested by rules or principles of law not disapplied by the words expressed.

'General principle' approach   There is much current pressure for legislation to take the form of brief injunctions. The Renton Committee argued that-

> 'The adoption of the "general principle" approach in the drafting of our statutes would lead to greater simplicity and clarity. We would, therefore, like to see it adopted wherever possible.'

{*The Preparation of Legislation* 1975 Cmnd 6053, para 10.13.}

The drawback is that this leads to undue reliance on implications. Statutes need to allow for the sort of person Stephen J had in mind in the passage from his judgment in *In re Castioni* {[1891] 1 QB 149, at p 167 cited on pp 177–178 above.}-

The draftsman   In ordinary speech it is a recognised method to say *expressly* no more than is required to make the meaning clear (the obvious implications remaining unexpressed). The draftsman of legislation, striving to be as brief as possible and use ordinary language, needs to adopt the same method. On this the following remark by the distinguished American draftsman Reed Dickerson is apposite-

> 'It is sometimes said that a draftsman should leave nothing to implication. This is nonsense. No communication can operate without leaving part of the total communication to implication.'

{*Materials on Legal Drafting* p 133.}

The draftsman is nevertheless constrained by the need for precision described in the ductum by Stephen J mentioned above, and relies on implications as little as possible. Necessarily this still leaves large scope for their use however.

So the interpreter of legislation needs to accept that it is a fact of language, indeed a fact of life, that every statement consists not only of what is expressed but also of what is implied. Neither portion is more compelling than the other (though there will be more room for argument about the content of what is implied). The implications may arise from the language used, or from the context, or from the application of some external rule. They are of equal force, whatever their derivation.

This conveys an important truth about the role of a draftsman. He drafts express provisions, but one might also say that he drafts implications. At all events he needs to be well aware of the implications that arise from the express words he is using. *So do his readers.*

Ellipsis   The device of leaving unsaid some portion of what the writer means is known as ellipsis. It is necessarily used to a large extent in the drafting of Acts of Parliament, even where the draftsman does not employ the 'general principle' approach favoured by the Renton Committee.

Example 1   Sir Carleton Allen, discussing s 4 of the Statute of Frauds {(1677) 29 Car 2 c 3.}, said-

> ' . . . the statute refers to a contract "not to be performed within one year from the making thereof". To be performed by whom? By one party or by both? When the case arises in which the contract cannot be wholly performed by one party within the year, but *may* be so performed by the other party, the Court cannot simply refuse to

"read something into the statute": it is bound to decide how the general policy of the Act applies to this case, and in order to do so, it has to look for what is called "the implied will of the legislator".'

{*Law in the Making* (4th edn, 1946) 411.}

The example discussed by Allen is one where the language of the enactment is obviously elliptical. The court cannot avoid filling in the gaps when cases requiring this arise.

Example 2 Another instance is furnished by *Russian and English Bank v Baring Bros* {[1936] AC 405.}, where it was held that to make the enactment work it was necessary to find an implication that a dissolved foreign company could be required to go through a process of winding up in England as though it had not been dissolved.

In such cases the court may decide that there was a genuine intention on the point, and take the intended meaning as implied. Or it may decide that what Parliament intended to do was *delegate* the function of filling in the gap to the court. Where the express words give no clue to the unspoken meaning, it may be more realistic to draw the latter conclusion. {The reasons for the use of ellipsis are explained at greater length in Bennion *Statute Law* (2nd edn, 1983) chap 12.}

Are implications genuine or fictional? In s 99 of this Code the argument that legislative intention is a 'fiction' was examined. The concept of implied meaning is closely connected to the concept of intention. We speak of a person implying something when we wish to say that he intended to convey it by the words he chose to use, even though it was not expressed in those words.

Obviously draftsmen, and even legislators themselves, *sometimes* possess a real intention without feeling it necessary to put it into words. The implication is then undoubtedly 'genuine'. Equally obviously, implications often reside in express language even where the fact was not present to the user's mind. Rather than calling these 'fictitious', it is perhaps more accurate to refer them to the literary or other context from which they spring.

As respects express words, we can equate intention with the literal meaning. This aid is absent when it comes to implications. This means that the question of whether a suggested implication was genuinely intended becomes more difficult. The position is similar to that in contract law where it is not certain whether an 'implied term' is referable to the actual intention of the parties or is imposed by a rule of law.

Expressum facit cessare tacitum An implication cannot properly be found which goes against an express statement. This principle is stated in the maxim *expressum facit cessare tacitum* (statement ends implication). {See s 388 of this Code.} It is not permissible to find an implied meaning where this contradicts the grammatical meaning. Where therefore the court holds that the legal meaning of an enactment contradicts the literal meaning, it is not finding an implication but applying a *strained* construction. {See ss 92 to 97 of this Code.}

Treating implied words as incorporated It will be seen that there is a necessary consequence of the fact that the express words of an enactment fall to be treated as enlarged by all proper implications. So far as these are relevant in the case before it, the court *treats the enactment as if it were worded accordingly.* As Coleridge J said in *Gwynne v Burnell* {(1840) 7 Cl & F 572, at p 606.}-

'If . . . the proposed addition is already necessarily contained, although not expressed, in the statute, it is of course not the less cogent because not expressed.'

{As to whether the implication needs to be *necessary* see s 109 of this Code.}

This echoed Coke's maxim that *verba illata est inesse videntur* (words inferred are to be considered as incorporated). {Co Litt 359.}

Thus in Example 122.5 although the express words of the enactment under enquiry were 'A person may use such force as is reasonable ....' the court applied the enactment as if it read 'A person may use such force *or threat of force* as is reasonable . . .' Since indeed it was a threat and not actual force that was in question in the instant case, only the implied portion was needed. We therefore arrive at the operative words of the enactment for that case as being 'A person may use such threat of force as is reasonable . . .'

Here the implication is spelt out in words the draftsman might have used. To do this is to adopt the technique of interstitial articulation, coupled with selective comminution. {As to interstitial articulation see ss 112 to 114 of this Code. For selective comminution see s 74.} While it is helpful to proceed in this way, it is not essential. What is implied is a meaning, and not necessarily a particular verbal formula.

108. Filling in the detail: implications (are they legitimate?)

Despite some judicial dicta to the contrary, the finding of proper implications within the express words of an enactment is a legitimate, indeed necessary, function of the interpreter.

COMMENTARY

Judges are sometimes reluctant to recognise the widespread use of ellipsis by the legislative draftsman. Thus Lord Goddard CJ said that a court 'cannot add words to a statute or read words into it which are not there'. {*R v Wimbledon JJ, ex p Derwent* [1953] 1 QB 380.} In a famous dictum, Rowlatt J said of taxing Acts: 'Nothing is to be read in, nothing is to be implied'. {*Cape Brandy Syndicate v IRC* [1921] 1 KB 64, at p 71.} Such dicta are not to be relied on. The interpreter's task is always to arrive at the legislative intention. As shown in s 107 of this Code and below in this commentary, this intention is often manifested by implications.

Judges sometimes object, when an implied meaning is suggested by the advocate, that if Parliament had intended such a qualification of the express words it could easily have said so. This is not a reliable test. Pressed to be brief, the draftsman is forced to leave much of what he intends to implication. Judging when this can safely be done, and when on the other hand express provision is necessary, is one of the trickiest drafting decisions.

Example 1 Section 5(1) of the Misuse of Drugs Act 1971 says it is unlawful for a person to have a controlled drug in his possession. A Scottish judge said of this-

'The decision in *R v Carver* {[1978] QB 472.} seems to entail the importation into s 5(1) of a qualification to the term "controlled drug", namely "which is capable of being used". If that be the case, it would add an additional onus on the prosecution to prove that fact. If Parliament had intended that such a qualification should be added it would have been simple to give express effect to it.'

{*Per* the Lord Justice-Clerk (Wheatley) in *Keane v Gallacher* (1980) JC 77, at p 81 (approved by Lord Scarman in *R v Boyesen* [1982] 2 All ER 161, at p 165).}

While the decision not to infer an intention by Parliament that the drug should be of a usable amount was no doubt correct, the court ought not to have relied on the argument that, if it wished to produce this result, Parliament could easily have said so. It might indeed have been easy to say so. But it would have been impossible to say *everything* that was intended; and why should this particular statement have been singled out?

Judicial recognition of ellipsis To set against the dicta quoted above, there are very many cases where judges have recognised the existence of implied meanings. Blackstone typically said of a seventeenth-century statute {1 Cha 1 c 1 (1625).} that it 'does not prohibit, but rather impliedly allows' innocent Sunday amusements after the time of divine service. {Bl Comm 1765, iv 52.} Because it is important to dispel the false idea that implied meanings are not to be discovered and declared by the interpreter, we go on to give a number of examples of the true rule.

Example 2 In *Ex p Johnson* {(1884) *Law Times* Vol L 214.} the court considered the requirement in s 8 of the Bills of Sale Act 1878 that a bill of sale to which the Act applies 'shall set forth the consideration for which such bill of sale was given'. Bowen LJ said that s 8 'means - it does not say so in words, but it says so impliedly - that the consideration must be *truly* set forth'. {P 217; emphasis added.}

Example 3 In *Leicester v Pearson* {[1952] 2 QB 668.} the Divisional Court held that a regulation requiring precedence to be given to persons on a pedestrian crossing contained an implied requirement for negligence to be proved when establishing an infringement. Justifying a bold judicial gloss, Hilbery J said this was just such a regulation 'as requires one, in construing it, to introduce some qualifying words and to construe it as though those qualifying words were written into the regulation'. {P 672.}

Example 4 In *NWL Ltd v Woods* {[1979] 3 All ER 614, at p 630.} Lord Scarman said that s 29(1) of the Trade Union and Labour Relations Act 1974 'makes express what might well be thought to have been implicit' in the Trade Disputes Act 1906.

Example 5 In *Sweet v Parsley* {[1970] AC 132, at p 163.} Lord Diplock said that statutory words describing prohibited conduct are 'to be read as subject to the implication' that a certain mental element is necessary.

Example 6 In *University College, Oxford v Durdy* {[1982] 1 All ER 1108.} Griffiths LJ {At p 1115.} referred to an enactment as 'implicitly' requiring the receipt of notice, while Eveleigh LJ {At p 1111.} spoke of the need to 'read in' such a requirement.

Example 7 In *Robertson v Day* {(1879) 5 App Cas 63, at p 69.} the Judicial Committee of the Privy Council said of words in an Australian Land Act: 'It is doing no violence to the language to read the words as if slightly elliptical ...'

Example 8 In *Lord Advocate v AB* {(1898) 3 Tax Cases 617.} the court held that words in s 21(4) of the Taxes Management Act 1880 referred back to the preceding subsection 'though perhaps it may be said that the words are a little elliptical'.

Example 9 In *Commonwealth of Australia v Bank of New South Wales* {[1950] AC 235, at p 295 (emphasis added).} it was said by the court that-

> 'It is a somewhat elliptical but by no means an impossible use of language to speak of a decision *upon* a certain question when what is meant is a decision in a suit, which cannot be decided without the determination of that question, or, more shortly, a decision *involving* a certain question or involving the *determination* of a certain question.'

Example 10 In *IRC v Hinchy* {[1959] 1 QB 327, at p 335.} it was said that s 48 of the Income Tax Act 1952 expressed in clearer and lengthier language 'what is intended to be conveyed by the elliptical expression in s 25(3), "the tax which he ought to be charged"'.

Example 11 In *British Railways Board v Dover Harbour Board* {[1964] 1 Lloyd's Rep 428, at p 439.} the learned judge said that-

> ' ... the wording is, on any possible interpretation, elliptical and it seems to me to result from seeking to compress within a single sentence the limitations of the duration of existing and future liability on existing and future guarantees.'

Example 12 In *British Airports Authority v Ashton* {[1983] 3 All ER 6.} Mann J considered the legal meaning of a byelaw made under s 9(1) of the Airports Authority Act 1965. Paragraph (h) of s 9(1) authorised a byelaw to require any person, if so requested by a constable, to leave an aerodrome subject to the Act. The byelaw in question followed this language. Mann J said {P 12.}-

> ' ... there must be an implied limitation on the power of request in that a request to leave made capriciously would not support a prosecution for failure to leave. We agree that there must be an implied limitation.'

Legislative recognition of ellipsis Parliament itself acknowledges its reliance on implications by occasionally including in its Acts an express statement that a particular implication is *not* to be taken as intended.

Example 13 Section 12(4) of the Administration of Justice Act 1960 reads-

> 'Nothing in this section shall be construed as *implying* that any publication is punishable as contempt of court which would not be so punishable apart from this section.'

{Emphasis added. Cf s 6(b) of the Contempt of Court Act 1981.}

On the other hand Parliament sometimes incautiously assumes that the only way to convey a meaning is by express words.

Example 14 Lord Brougham's Act {13 & 14 Vict c 21 (1850).} was designed to shorten the language used in Acts by laying down certain meanings unless in a particular case these were displaced. Sections 4 and 7 use such statements as 'unless the contrary be expressly provided and declared' (by a particular Act). Willes J dealt with this unecessarily restrictive language in his usual robust way-

> 'It is not easy to conceive that the framer of [Lord Brougham's Act], when he used the word 'expressly', meant to suggest that what is necessarily or properly implied by language is not expressed by such language. It is quite clear that whatever the language used necessarily and naturally implies is expressed thereby.'

{*Chorlton v Lings* (1868) LR 4 CP 374, at p 387.}

While such a strained construction is no doubt salutary, it is necessary to preserve in discussion of statutory interpretation the important distinction between express and implied meaning. Nor are implied meanings always *necessary*. A passage may be open to more than one implied meaning, when the court will adopt the most appropriate. This point is further discussed in s 109 of this Code.

109. Filling in the detail: implications (when legitimate)

The question of whether an implication should be found within the express words of an enactment depends on whether it is proper, having regard to the accepted guides to legislative intention, to find the implication; and not on whether the implication is 'necessary' or 'obvious'.

COMMENTARY

Must implication be 'necessary'? It is sometimes suggested by judges that only necessary implications may legitimately be drawn from the wording of Acts. Thus Lord Watson said that-

> ' ... what the legislature intended to be done or not to be done can only be legitimately ascertained from what it has chosen to enact either in express words or by reasonable and necessary implication.'

{*Salomon v Salomon* [1897] AC 22, at p 38.}

This is too narrow. The necessity referred to could only be *logical* necessity, but requirements of logic are not the only criteria in determining the meaning of a literary text. While the implications intended are a matter of inference, it is often pyschological rather than logical inference that is involved.

The principle was accurately stated by Willes J when he said that the legal meaning of an enactment includes 'what is necessarily *or properly* implied' by the language used. {*Chorlton v Lings* (1868) LR 4 CP 374, at p 387 (emphasis added).}

Must implication be 'obvious'?   Another way the rule is sometimes put by judges is that the implication must be 'clear' or 'obvious'. Thus in *Temple v Mitchell* {(1956) SC 267, at p 272.} Lord Justice-Clerk Thomson said: 'There is no express provision, and I cannot discover any clear implication'.

This is also open to objection. Courts of construction are not usually troubled with a 'clear' provision. On the contrary they exist to give judgment where the law is not clear but doubtful. There is likely to be a fine balance to be struck where one side claims that a particular implication arises and their opponents deny it.

When an implication is 'proper'   The question of whether an implication should be found within the express words of an enactment depends on whether it is proper or legitimate to find the implication in arriving at the legal meaning of the enactment, having regard to the accepted guides to legislative intention. These guides are summarized in Part VI of this Code, but the crucial factor in a particular case may be found anywhere in the Code. {For the technique of arriving at the legal meaning see Part VII of this Code.}

It is for the court to decide whether a suggested implication is 'proper'. This may involve a consideration of the rules of language or the principles of law, or both together. Where the point is doubtful it will, as always in interpretation, call for a weighing and balancing of the relevant factors. {See ss 158 to 163 of this Code.}

For example it may be held improper to find an implication which imposes onerous burdens. Thus Blackstone said of an 'old opinion' to the effect that an enactment saying that an accused person 'be not admitted to challenge' more than twenty jurors meant that he could be subjected to the *peine forte et dure* if he challenged 21: 'so heavy a judgment, or that of conviction, which succeeds it, shall not be imposed by implication'. {Kerr Bl (4th edn, 1876) iv 366.}

This consideration as to the 'weight' to be attached to a suggested implication where it would impose burdens no doubt explains the reluctance of judges to find implications in taxing Acts. Warner J referred to-

' ... the well-established principle that in tax cases, the words to be interpreted and applied are those of the relevant statutory provision, not those of glosses put on them by judges.'

{*Page (Inspector of Taxes) v Lowther* (1982) *The Times* 24 November. See also the dictum of Rowlatt J cited above (p 242).}

Such a judicial remark betrays an unfortunate ignorance of the basis both of statutory interpretation and stare decisis. The fact is that such glosses are *not* to be ignored. On the contrary they form an important element in the law, from which neither taxation nor any other area is exempt. {See s 26 of this Code.}

The court should never proceed on the basis that the finding of implications is somehow an *improper* technique in interpretation. It is not really a device which, as Shaw LJ once appeared to suggest in a case involving musical and dramatic performers, resembles a forensic version of the illicit still-

'To distil from the language of the section a specific duty to performers would involve an illicit process of interpretation. That the product might be potable cannot justify *the method* or the result.'

{*Ex p Island Records Ltd* [1978] Ch 122, at p 139 (emphasis added).}

Here the point in question was whether s 1 of the Dramatic and Musical Performers' Protection Act 1958, in making it an offence to record performances without the consent of the performers, intended to give them by implication a civil remedy. While it was no doubt right to deny such a remedy, the judical condemnation of the *method* of finding an implied meaning is, with respect, unfortunate.

Implication versus presumption Where a presumption as to Parliament's intention favours one construction, an implication favouring the opposing construction can be drawn less easily, and needs to be more strongly based. This point is discussed in relation to the various presumptions. {See for example the commentary on s 34 (presumption that an Act does not bind the Crown) of this Code.}

110. Filling in the detail: implications affecting related law

The fact that Parliament has by an enactment declared its express intention in one area of law may carry an implication that it intends corresponding changes in related areas of law, or in relevant legal policy.

COMMENTARY

Sir Rupert Cross thought there were grounds for saying that in England a legislative innovation is received fully into the body of the law, to be reasoned from by analogy in the same way as any other rule of law. {*Precedent in English Law* (3rd edn, 1977) p 170.} He went on-

'Whether the courts regard legislation as the equal or superior of judge-made law when it is cited as an analogy upon which to found a decision must be regarded as an open question. There is no convincing reason why superiority in analogical force should always be attributed to legislation.'

In fact the position has been rather the reverse. The courts have treated legislation as being an analogical source inferior to judge-made law; and have commonly disregarded it altogether.

However the courts do accept that where a legislative innovation is based on a point of principle, the effect of receiving it into the body of the law is to treat the principle in question as thereafter embodied in legal policy. Thus Acts such as the Race Relations Act 1976, the Sex Discrimination Act 1975 and the Equal Pay Act 1970 are taken to indicate that it has become the general policy of the law to counter the relevant types of injurious personal discrimination whenever opportunity offers. This was recognised by Lord Morris of Borth-y-Gest in the following dictum relating to racial discrimination-

'My Lords, by enacting the Race Relations Acts 1965 and 1968 Parliament introduced into the law of England a new guiding principle of fundamental and far-reaching importance. It is one that affects and must influence action and behaviour in this country within a wide-ranging sweep of human activities and personal relationships.'

{*Charter v Race Relations Board* [1973] AC 868, at p 889. Cf the remarks by

Lord Denning MR on the effect of the European Communities Act 1972 in *Re Westinghouse Uranium Contract* [1978] AC 547, at p 564. See also Example 12.4.}

Presumably where an enactment of this kind is repealed the courts would take the opposite line and treat the relevant principle as expunged from the law.

Where courts follow statutory analogy Cross gives the following instances of where the courts have followed the analogy of some statutory rule.

Example 1 In pursuance of the maxim 'equity follows the law', it was held that in an equitable claim analogous to the common law action for money had and received the court would follow the spirit of the Limitation Act 1623 and hold the claim barred after a lapse of six years. {*Re Robinson* [1911] 1 Ch 502.}

Example 2 In *R v Bourne* {[1939] 1 KB 687.} the question of whether an abortion was 'unlawful' within the meaning of s 58 of the Offences against the Person Act 1861 was decided by analogy with a test laid down by Parliament in s 1(1) of the Infant Life (Preservation) Act 1929. This indicates that the law does not condemn an act against the foetus if done in good faith for the purpose only of preserving the life of the mother.

Example 3 Where a tax ruling had been reversed by statute, the House of Lords regarded its ratio decidendi as no longer authoritative in analogous cases. {*Thomson v Moyse* [1961] AC 967.}

Example 4 In *Broom v Morgan* {[1953] 1 QB 597, at p 609. Cf *Dutton v Bognor Regis UDC* [1972] 1 QB 373.} a similar view was taken by the Court of Appeal in relation to the abrogation by the Law Reform (Personal Injuries) Act 1948 of the rule of common employment laid down in *Priestley v Fowler*. {(1837) 3 M & W 1.}

Where courts reject statutory analogy Cross fails however to observe that there are many instances where the courts have declined to follow a statutory analogy. Here are two examples.

Example 5 At common law, suicide was a felony. The *felo de se* was required to be buried in the highway with a stake through his body, and his goods were forfeited. {C S Kenny *Outlines of Criminal Law* (15th edn, 1946) p 127.} Although these ignominies were later removed, the stigma remained. Because of it the common law raised a presumption (to be observed for example by coroners) that suicide was not to be lightly assumed.

Then, by s 1 of the Suicide Act 1961, the rule of law that made suicide a crime was abrogated. The Act said nothing about the above presumption. Did it remain, or was it by implication abolished too? An implied intention had to be found one way or the other. In *R v City of London Coroner, ex p Barber* {[1975] Crim LR 515.} it was held that the correct implication was that the stigma of suicide (and with it the presumption) remained in the law.

Example 6 To similar effect was the ruling in *Knuller v DPP* {[1973] AC 435.}, where it was held by the House of Lords that the decriminalisation of homosexual practices by consenting male adults in private did not imply that Parliament thereby intended to abolish the rule that the promotion of such practices was contrary to public policy. Lord Reid said: 'I find nothing in the Act to indicate that Parliament thought or intended to lay down that indulgence in these practices is not corrupting.' {At p 457.}

See also Example 133.5. As to the general relevance of legal policy in statutory interpretation see s 126 of this Code.

111. Filling in the detail: dynamic processing by the court (stare decisis)

As explained in s 26 of this Code, there are various ways in which the text of an enactment as promulgated by the legislature may later be authoritatively glossed by courts and other functionaries with the effect of developing and elaborating the detail of its legal meaning. By virtue of the doctrine of precedent or stare decisis, the sub-rules that are the result of judicial processing have either binding or persuasive authority. It follows that where an enactment has been the subject of judicial decision, the legal meaning of the enactment is thereafter to be ascertained in the light of that decision, according to the doctrine of precedent. The court has to that extent *processed* the enactment.

Nevertheless the court, in laying down a decision (whether of binding or merely persuasive authority), is empowered only to declare the legislative intention. If it appears to a later court, in the light of the guides laid down for arriving at that intention, that the decision did not truly reflect it, the later court will overrule or distinguish the decision (if and so far as it can legitimately do so).

COMMENTARY

As explained in the commentary on s 26 of this Code, for purposes of comment and explanation, it is convenient to employ the term 'sub-rules' to denote the infilling which is the product of the things that are authoritatively done to develop and expand the legal meaning of an Act *after* it is passed by Parliament.

Few Acts remain for very long in pristine condition. They are quickly subjected to a host of processes. Learned commentators dissect them. {As to such commentaries see s 6 of this Code.} Officials administer them. {For the functions of the various official enforcement agencies see ss 15 to 18 of this Code.} Courts pronounce on them. {The general function of the courts is explained in ss 19 to 24 of this Code.} When practitioners come to advise upon the legal meaning, they need to take account of all this. The Act is no longer as Parliament left it. It has been processed.

This Code is concerned only with *dynamic* processing, the kind which develops and elaborates the legal meaning and effect of the pristine Act. We are not here concerned with *static* processing, which merely furnishes aids to comprehension. {For static processing see Bennion *Statute Law* (2nd edn, 1983) Part IV.}

Judges tend to discourage the view that processing elaborates the legal effect of the words used by Parliament. Thus Lord Reid said of tax legislation generally-

> 'There is a wealth of authority on this matter and various glosses on
> or paraphrases of the words in the act appear in judicial opinions,
> including speeches in this House. No doubt they were helpful *in the
> circumstances of the cases in which they were used*, but in the end we
> must always return to the words in the statute ...'

{*Laidler v Perry* [1966] AC 16, at p 30. Emphasis added.}

The italicised words in this passage display the traditional restrictiveness of
judges, but they are with respect inaccurate. A judicial precedent applies not
only to the circumstances of the case in which it is laid down but also to
comparable circumstances in other cases. If it were not so there would be no
doctrine of precedent. This is the concept of the *factual outline*, described in s 78
of this Code.

Sub-rules   The gloss that results from processing an enactment is not usually
articulated in a form which combines the enactment and the gloss into a unified
text. {For this type of articulation, called by this Code *interstitial* articulation,
see ss 112 to 114 of the Code.} Whether it is expressed in this way or not, the
legal result is the same: the broad rules laid down by the enactment are
supplemented by more detailed rules. Where the processor is the court,
ultimately charged by Parliament with the authoritative interpretation of its
Acts, these detailed provisions operate as authoritative 'sub-rules'.

Earlier decision erroneous   The principle that the court will attempt to
distinguish an earlier decision where, in the light of the interpretative criteria, it
seems that it did not reflect Parliament's intention was thus expressed by Robert
Goff LJ-

> 'In my opinion, although of course the courts of this country are
> bound by the doctrine of precedent, sensibly interpreted,
> nevertheless it would be irresponsible for judges to act as automatons
> (*sic*), rigidly applying authorities without regard to consequences.
> Where therefore it appears at first sight that authority compels a
> judge to reach a conclusion which he senses to be unjust or
> inappropriate, he is, I consider, under a positive duty to examine the
> relevant authorities with scrupulous care to ascertain whether he can,
> within the limits imposed by the doctrine of precedent (always
> sensibly interpreted), legitimately interpret or qualify the principle
> expressed in the authorities to achieve the result which he perceives
> to be just or appropriate in the particular case.'

{*Elliott v C (a minor)* [1983] 2 All ER 1005, at p 1010. See further R Cross
Precedent in English Law (3rd edn, 1977) pp 165-176.}

112. Filling in the detail: interstitial articulation

Fully to enunciate the legal meaning of an enactment requires
articulation of the detailed propositions which, while not stated in the
express words of the enactment, are either taken to be implied or are held
to be there by the exercise of legislative power delegated to the court.

When the application of the enactment to particular facts is being determined, it thus becomes possible to restate the enactment in an expanded version which includes the expression (in relation to facts of that kind) of precisely what it was that the legislator, or in practical terms the draftsman, is determined to have left unsaid. This articulation puts into words what the Act is taken to be saying. The precision of modern drafting makes such restatement in most cases relatively straightforward. In this Code it is referred to as interstitial articulation.

COMMENTARY

This section of the Code explains the technique of interstitial articulation, by which the relevant unexpressed provisions of an enactment can be converted to express form by as it were filling out the interstices between the express words. The method is akin to that of codification, by which the effect of judicial decisions is reduced to legislative form. {See s 233 of this Code.}

  Full details of the technique of interstitial articulation are given in the commentaries on ss 113 and 114 below. {See also Example 387.4.} It is further extensively described by the present author in his book *Statute Law*. {2nd edn, 1983; see pp 235ff. For further examples of the use of the technique by the present author see 'Penalty points - a transitional problem' (1982) *LS Gaz* 1622 (pseudonymous); 'Scientific Statutory Interpretation and the Franco Scheme' (1983) British Tax Review 74; 'Propositions of Law in Conviction Appeals' [1984] Crim LR p 282. See also, as to an articulation relating to s 3 (making off) of the Theft Act 1978: [1980] Crim LR 670; [1982] Crim LR 612; [1983] Crim LR 205 and 573-4.}

113. Filling in the detail: interstitial articulation by the advocate

When in argument an advocate puts to the court his construction of the enactment in question, it is helpful for this to be expressed in the form of an interstitial articulation.

COMMENTARY

As explained in s 84 of this Code, the parties to a case involving a disputed point of statutory interpretation usually argue for opposing constructions of the enactment. If each advocate puts to the court a precise form of words embodying what he asserts to be the legal meaning, this crystallises his argument and tends to shorten the proceedings. {For a detailed example of how this technique of advocacy can be put into effect see Example 84.3. See also the sources listed above on this page.}

114. Filling in the detail: interstitial articulation by the court

The court, in its judgment, may usefully express its determination of the legal meaning of a relevant enactment in the form of an articulation of the unexpressed words of the enactment.

COMMENTARY

It would improve the clarity of legal reasoning if judges accepted that when they construe a statute what they are in substance doing is *declaring* or making explicit certain of its implied or unexpressed provisions. As Neil MacCormick puts it, the statute is *concretised* through the process of judicial interpretation. {*Legal Reasoning and Legal Theory* pp 188, 218.}

It is helpful in many ways when judges accept a responsibility to *articulate* what seems to them an appropriate version of those provisions which their judicial function requires them to concretize. The judiciary thus, to a limited but important extent, resume their ancient function of formulating the enacted law. {As to this function see Bennion *Statute Law* (2nd edn, 1983) p 244.} Within the verbal interstices provided by the express wording of an enactment there then grow, decision by decision, the concrete details needed to spell out its meaning in particular cases.

The technique may be compared to Bentham's suggestion that, whenever a statute is interpreted liberally, the judge should draw up a statement to be placed before the legislature indicating how the statute should be amended, the proposed amendment to have the force of law if not vetoed by Parliament within a specified time. {*Of Laws in General* (ed H L A Hart, 1970) p 241.} Bentham was no doubt aware that by his 'liberal' judgment, at least where it constitutes a precedent, the judge has already in effect laid down an 'amendment' which has the force of law. What Bentham's proposal would achieve in addition is the textual expression of the effect of this.

Interstitial articulation is sometimes essayed by judges, though usually this is informal.

Example 1   Mears v Safecar Security Ltd {[1982] 2 All ER 865.} concerned the interpretation of s 11(1) of the Employment Protection (Consolidation) Act 1978. In the course of his judgment Stephenson LJ said {P 872.}-

> 'Section 11(1) is, in my judgment, ambiguous and the ambiguity is not resolved by sub-s (5). Subsection (1) might mean "Where an employer does not give an employee any statement purporting to be a statement as required by s 1 or 4(1) or 8 ..." or "Where an employer has failed to give an employee any statement in accordance with s 1 or 4(1) or 8 ...".'

Example 2 Where a taxable person fails to make VAT returns, the Commissioners are empowered by s 31 of the Finance Act 1972 to assess the amount of tax due to the best of their ability, but an assessment 'of an amount of tax due for any prescribed accounting period' must not be made later than a specified date. Prescribed accounting periods are of three months duration.

In *S J Grange Ltd v Commissioners of Customs and Excise* {[1979] 2 All ER 91. The case is further discussed in Example 321.5.} it was argued that the quoted words meant that a separate assessment must be made for each accounting period, even though the Commissioners would find the provision impractical. The Court of Appeal rejected this construction. Lord Denning MR said {P 101.}-

> 'I can see the force of [the argument]. It is literally correct. But it leads to such impracticable results that it is necessary to do a little

adjustment so as to make the section workable. This can be done by reading in a few words, such as Bridge LJ suggested in the course of the argument. That is, after "for any prescribed accounting period" read in these words "which is included in the notice of assessment".'

Here it may be noted that what Lord Denning described as 'a little adjustment' could more accurately be called a declaration by the court of the unexpressed words that were to be taken as implied. By including such an articulation in its judgment, a court gives *precise* guidance as to what the law on the point is.

This helps in a number of ways.

Advantages of judicial articulation First it helps the parties to the case in considering whether to bring or resist an appeal. If an appeal is brought, the articulation helps the appellate court to decide whether or not the court below has erred in its construction of the enactment.

From the point of view of the law generally, the articulation by the court of the relevant provision makes the enactment clearer from then on. This assists future potential litigants, and indeed all who are concerned to administer, expound or alter the enacted law in question.

Perhaps the most powerful argument in favour of this technique of interstitial articulation by the court is that it can hardly fail to reduce the number of cases that are wrongly decided. This is because it requires the argument to be thought through with a stringency and thoroughness not necessitated by more conventional methods.

A further point is that, over a period, the judicial articulations of unexpressed provisions of an Act would collectively form materials for a *codification*. Their existence in reported judgments would greatly ease the well-known problems of carrying out a codification of processed enactments on conventional lines. These obstacles have so far effectively prevented any substantial codification of our law.

Finally it may be pointed out that the need for interstitial articulation by the courts, coupled usually with selective comminution {As to selective comminution see s 74 of this Code.}, arises from the immense complexity of modern statute law.

The opposing constructions put forward in actual cases usually represent but a tiny fraction of the possible meanings inherent in an enactment. Other possible factual situations (of which the range can be infinite) will, if and when they arise, call forth other pairs of opposing constructions of their own. The potential in the case of a particular enactment may be without limit. This makes it not at all surprising that statutes are difficult to construe, and that great care and thought are required to arrive at their correct legal meaning in any one case.

It will be seen that the most effective procedure, both for arriving at the correct decision in the instant case and for optimum use of that case as a precedent, is to treat the words of the enactment as supplemented by a number (in some cases infinitely great) of notional or implied formulas. These correspond to what this Code calls sub-rules. {See ss 26 and 111 of this Code.}

By the technique of interstitial articulation, such of these formulas as are needed to decide a particular case are picked out and declared by the court, acting with the assistance of the advocates appearing before it. The formulas thus articulated are not confined merely to the facts of the instant case, but are expressed in a general form so as to apply to any facts of a similar kind. {For the concept of the 'factual outline' see s 78 of this Code.} Thereafter the formulas are on record as dynamic processing of the enactment in question.

For another example of interstitial articulation by a judge see *East London Railway Co v Whitechurch*. {(1874) LR 7 HL 81, *per* Lord Cairns LC at p 88. See also Example 325.4.}

PART VI

Guides to Legislative Intention

Introduction to Part VI Having seen in Part V of the Code that legislative intention is the paramount criterion in statutory interpretation, we now examine the principal guides to arriving at that intention. These may be divided into binding rules, principles derived from general legal policy, presumptions as to what Parliament had in mind, and linguistic canons of construction. We begin by looking at the nature of these various guides or criteria (s 115).

Rules are dealt with in ss 116 to 125. The nature of a rule is described (s 116). The basic rule is stated (s 117). This is that where the guides conflict with one another the problem is to be resolved by weighing and balancing the factors concerned. Detailed rules follow. The interpreter must have regard to the juridical nature of an enactment (s 118). He must bring to bear an *informed* approach (s 119). If, on an informed interpretation, the meaning is plain (that is there is no real doubt), that plain meaning must be followed (s 120). In other cases the basic rule must be applied (s 121). Common sense must be used (s 122). The court must strive to implement rather than defeat the object (s 123). The precise function of each type of component must be borne in mind (s 124). Rules laid down by statute must be observed (s 125).

Sections 126 to 134 describe the various *principles* that are derived from legal policy. The nature of legal policy is explained (s 126). Then the principles are gone through. Law should serve the public interest (s 127). It should be just (s 128). Persons should not be penalized under a doubtful law (s 129). Law should be predictable (s 130), and should not operate retrospectively (s 131). It should be coherent and self-consistent (s 132), and not subject to casual change (s 133). The municipal law should not conflict with public international law (s 134).

We now pass to the *presumptions* as to legislative intention. Their nature is explained (s 135). The text of the Act is the primary indication (s 136), and it is presumed (though this presumption, like the others, may be displaced) that the literal meaning is to be applied (s 137). The court is to implement the remedy provided by Parliament for the 'mischief' (s 138); and it is presumed that a purposive construction should be given (s 139). Regard is to be had to the consequences of a particular construction (s 140), and it is presumed that an 'absurd' result was not intended (s 141). Nor were errors to go uncorrected (s 142), or evasion be permitted (s 143). Parliament is taken to intend that ancillary rules of general law should be applied (s 144), including legal maxims (s 145). Finally it is presumed that Parliament intended updating by the court to be effected where necessary to implement the legislative intention (s 146).

Part VI ends with the linguistic *canons* of construction. First their nature is explained (s 147). The logic of language is discussed (s 148). Construction of an Act as a whole is described (s 149). We look at the interpretation of broad terms (s 150), and individual words and phrases (s 151). Finally we consider the familiar canons, such as the *ejusdem generis* principle, that are used to elaborate the literal meaning of words and phrases.

PRELIMINARY

115. Nature of the guides: rules, principles, presumptions and canons

The guides to legislative intention consist of various rules, principles, presumptions and linguistic canons applied at common law or laid down by statute for assisting in statutory interpretation. In this Code they are collectively referred to as the guides to legislative intention or the interpretative criteria.

COMMENTARY

The paramount object in statutory interpretation is to discover what the legislator intended. {See s 98 of this Code.} This intention is primarily to be ascertained from the text of the enactment in question. That does not mean the text is to be construed merely as a piece of prose, without reference to its nature or purpose. On the contrary, in the light of its nature and purpose its detail is treated as filled in by implications and previous judicial processing. {See ss 107 to 114 of this Code.} For arriving at the implications, and determining (if one is the judge) or predicting (if one is not) how judicial processing on the facts of the instant case will be carried out, certain guides are provided by law.

These guides mainly consist of the rules, principles, presumptions and canons of construction which, over the centuries, the courts have laid down or adopted for that purpose in accordance with their constitutional function of declaring the intention of Parliament as embodied in its Acts. In addition, but to a relatively unimportant extent, Parliament has directly laid down certain rules of construction in the Interpretation Act 1978 and elsewhere.

As it is convenient to have collective terms by which to refer to these judicial and statutory injunctions, this Code calls them the guides to legislative intention, or the interpretative criteria. They are peculiar in that, while most general legal rules or principles directly govern the actions of the subject, these directly govern the actions of the court.

There is however an indirect effect on the subject. Since the court is obliged to apply an enactment in accordance with the interpretative criteria, persons governed by the enactment are well advised to read it in that light. The law in its practical application is not what an Act says but what a court says the Act means.

How the guides operate The way the interpretative criteria operate can be shown schematically as follows.

A question of the legal meaning of an enactment ('enactment E') arises. {As to legal meaning see s 2 and Part IV of this Code.} Opposing constructions of enactment E are put forward by the respective parties in relation to the facts of the instant case. {As to opposing constructions see s 84 of this Code.} Say the plaintiff puts forward construction P and the defendant construction D.

In the light of the facts of the instant case and the guides to legislative intention, constructions P and D are considered in turn by the court. On examining construction P the court finds that some of the interpretative criteria produce factors that tell in its favour. The plaintiff might call them 'positive factors'. Other criteria produce factors ('negative factors') that tell against construction P. The court repeats the process with construction D, and then assesses whether on balance P or D comes out as more likely to embody the legislator's intention.

A variety of interpretative criteria are likely to be relevant, but to simplify the example suppose there are only two: the primacy of the literal meaning and the desirability of purposive construction. In relation to construction P, a positive factor is that it corresponds to the literal meaning while a negative factor is that it does not carry out the purpose of the enactment. In relation to construction D, a positive factor is that it does carry out the purpose of the enactment while a negative factor is that it is a strained construction. The court weighs the factors, and gives its decision. {The forensic techniques involved are fully described in Part VII of this Code.}

Obviously this brief analysis does not necessarily correspond to the steps actually taken in court. In practice the intellectual processes and interchanges usually occur in a less formal way. The persons involved are, after all, experts engaging in a familiar routine. But formal analysis must be attempted if we are to believe that the law has progressed much beyond that medieval palm-tree justice described by Plucknett as entire reliance on the light of nature and the inspiration of the moment. {See p 225 above.}

Interpretative criteria as part of the common law   Using the term common law in a broad sense, the interpretative criteria laid down or adopted by the courts may (except where they are statutory) be regarded as part of the common law. Lord Wilberforce has described the courts' development and application of them as 'the common law in action'. {*Express Newspapers Ltd v McShane* [1980] 2 WLR 89, at p 94.} Blackstone said-

> ' . . . the rules of expounding wills, deeds and acts of parliament . . . are doctrines that are not set down in any written statute or ordinance, but depend upon immemorial usage, that is upon common law, for their support.'

{Kerr Bl (4th edn, 1876) i 46. See also ibid, p 60. Blackstone was of course writing before the passage of the first Interpretation Act in 1850.}

Parliament is slow to intervene here. As Lord Scarman said-

> 'It has been axiomatic among lawyers and, indeed, in our legal professional thinking for a very long time that the interpretation of statutes is a matter for the judges; it is not a matter for legislation.'

{HL Deb 13 February 1980 col 276.}

Two points need to be made about treating the guides to legislative intention as part of the common law. The first is that the application of a guide in relation to one Act cannot be *binding* in relation to a different Act. This is because the weight to be given to a particular interpretative factor is not capable of precise assessment, and varies from Act to Act. As Cross said-

'A decision on the interpretation of one statute generally cannot constitute a binding precedent with regard to the interpretation of another statute.'

{R Cross *Statutory Interpretation* p 30.}

This is confirmed by the following dictum of Lord Bridge in *Wills v Bowley* {[1982] 2 All ER 654, at p 672.}-

'Your Lordships' decision in the instant case will be binding authority for nothing but the extent of a constable's power of arrest under s 28 of the [Town Police Clauses Act 1847].'

{As to the details of this important decision see pp 401–404 below.}

Here it should be noted that while this dictum is correct as to the point Lord Bridge no doubt had in mind, namely the effect of *Wills v Bowley* as an authority on similar words in other Acts, the decision *is* binding authority for the proposition that courts may in suitable cases adopt a strained consruction of an enactment. {As to strained construction see ss 92 to 97 of this Code.}

The second point is that judges frequently employ language appropriate to laying down a comprehensive rule of interpretation when they are merely sketching its outline. The reports are full of dicta which seek to capture a rule or principle in a few words when for its full and exact statement many are needed.

Example 1   Parke B (later Lord Wensleydale) said in a famous dictum that the plain meaning of an enactment must be followed 'unless that would lead to some absurdity, or some repugnance or inconsistency with the rest of the instrument'. {*Grey v Pearson* (1857) 6 HL Cas 61, at p 106.} This purports to be a binding rule embodying a full description of the excepted cases, but the reality is otherwise. {For the plain meaning rule see s 120 of this Code.}

Criteria laid down by statute   Occasionally, Parliament steps in to lay down general interpretative criteria directly. This is primarily for the purpose of shortening the language of Acts. {See the long title of Lord Brougham's Act of 1850, the first Interpretation Act (13 & 14 Vict c 21).} Such aids to brevity are in the interest of governments, since they save parliamentary time. Governments therefore take an interest in them, which is not the case with most things that assist in statutory interpretation. {As to the requirement of brevity in the drafting of legislation see Bennion *Statute Law* (2nd edn, 1983) pp 38-9.}

Types of interpretative criteria   Although the boundaries between them are far from clearcut, the guides to legislative intention can for convenience of exposition be divided into rules of construction, principles of law or public policy, presumptions of legislative intention and linguistic canons of construction. The detailed nature of these is discussed in the remainder of this Part. Here we conclude by suggesting that they can be broadly distinguished as follows.

A rule of construction is of binding force, but in cases of real doubt rarely yields a conclusive answer. A principle embodies the policy of the law, and is mainly persuasive. A presumption affords a prima facie indication of the legislator's inferred or imputed intention as to the working of the Act. A linguistic canon of construction reflects the nature or use of language and reasoning generally, and is not specially referable to legislation.

Because many criteria can arguably be placed in more than one category, these terms and distinctions are not always observed by courts and commentators. As an aid to consistency of treatment however, they are so far as practicable adhered to in this Code.

RULES OF CONSTRUCTION

116. Rules: nature of rules of construction

A rule of construction must be followed, though this does not necessarily (or even usually) mean that it will be certain in its application where real doubt as to the legal meaning exists.

COMMENTARY

A criterion is not deserving of the name *rule* unless it is compelling. The basic rule of statutory interpretation set out in s 117 of this Code is compelling, but does not take one very far. This tends to be the case with rules of statutory interpretation. Where a real doubt as to meaning exists, the matter becomes one of judgment rather than predetermined response. {As to real doubt see s 3 of this Code.}

A difference between a rule and a principle is said to be that rules never conflict with each other, whereas principles do. When one rule *appears* to conflict with another, the reason is that one or both are framed incorrectly (for example with the omission of recognised exceptions). Even principles however can (and should) be framed so as not to conflict. They may lead in different directions, but each has its weight.

The difference between rules and principles is further explored in the commentary on s 115 of this Code.

117. Rules: the basic rule of statutory interpretation

The basic rule of statutory interpretation is that it is taken to be the legislator's intention that the enactment shall be construed in accordance with the general guides to legislative intention laid down by law; and that where these conflict the problem shall be resolved by weighing and balancing the factors concerned.

COMMENTARY

The biggest mistake made about statutory interpretation is that the court selects which 'rule' it prefers, and then applies it in order to reach a result. The error perhaps originated with Professor J Willis, in what Cross called a 'landmark' article. {R Cross *Statutory Interpretation* p v. The article, ominously entitled 'Statutory Interpretation in a Nutshell', appeared in (1938) 16 Can Bar Rev 1.} After warning his readers that it is a mistake to suppose that there is only one rule of statutory interpretation because 'there are three - the literal, golden and mischief rules', Willis went on to say that a court invokes 'whichever of the rules produces a result which satisfies its sense of justice in the case before it'. {Loc cit p 16.}

Commentators are still making statements like this. For example Professor Pearce says-

> 'The interpretation of each Act must be approached as a task in itself and the fact that *the use of a particular interpretation maxim produced a particular result* in relation to another Act is irrelevant.'

{D C Pearce *Statutory Interpretation in Australia* (2nd edn, 1981) p 7 (emphasis added).}

If there ever were, there are certainly not now, just three 'rules' of statutory interpretation. The so-called literal rule dissolves into a presumption that the text is the primary indication of intention {See s 136 of this Code.} and that the enactment is to be given a literal meaning where this is not outweighed by other factors. {See s 137 of this Code.} The so-called golden rule dissolves into one factor that may outweigh the literal meaning, namely the presumption that an 'absurd' result is not intended. {See s 141 and Part XVII of this Code.} The so-called mischief rule dissolves into the presumption that Parliament intended to provide a remedy for a particular mischief {See s 138 and Part XV of this Code.} and that a purposive construction is desired. {See s 139 and Part XVI of this Code.} There are many other considerations.

The court does not 'select' any one of these, and then apply it to the exclusion of the others. The court takes an overall view, weighs all the relevant factors, and arrives at a balanced conclusion. The basic rule set out in the present section of the Code endeavours to state this truth.

The proposition stated in this section is a *rule* because it is the duty of the court to obey it in every case. As Cotton LJ said in *Ralph v Carrick* {(1879) 11 Ch D 873, at p 878.}, judges 'are bound to have regard to any rules of construction which have been established by the Courts'. It is the basic rule because it embraces all the guides to legislative intention that exist to be employed as and when relevant. {As to the nature of these guides see s 115 of this Code.}

The courts in no way seek to dictate to the legislature. Parliament and its delegates are taken to know the surrounding law however, and that includes the interpretative criteria. Parliament is entirely free to indicate in an Act that it does not wish a particular guide to legislative intention to apply to the interpretation of the Act. Indeed this is built into the statement of each criterion, which is always to be taken as including the phrase 'unless the contrary intention appears'.

The combination of these statements amounts to a conditional rule. The enactment *must* be accorded the meaning the court considers they lead to unless there is some inbuilt indication to the contrary. The presumption that this is Parliament's intention is conclusive, or *juris et de jure* (of law and from law). The contrary indication need not assume any particular form however, and may be express or implied.

For the sake of uniformity this Code uses throughout the formula of the Interpretation Act 1978, namely 'unless the contrary intention appears'. The reference to 'the contrary intention' includes *any* divergence from the rule laid down, however minor. Where the interpretative criterion is not left to apply by itself 'the contrary intention' appears, even though (as sometimes happens) the criterion is only partially disapplied. In other words the phrase 'unless the contrary intention appears' really means 'except where, and to the extent that, a different intention appears'.

Balancing of conflicting factors   The balancing of conflicting interpretative factors is dealt with in Part VII of this Code.

118. Rules: duty to have regard to juridical nature of the enactment

In construing an enactment of any kind, the interpreter must treat it, in accordance with the rules governing his function as such, with due regard to its juridical nature as an enactment of that kind.

COMMENTARY

As explained in s 28 of this Code, there are various types of enactment. Some legal qualities are common to all types, while others relate only to a particular type or types. The interpreter needs to be aware of the nature of what he is interpreting, and construe it accordingly. He thus needs to follow the appropriate rules described in Part II (The Text), Part VIII (Commencement, Amendment and Repeal of Enactments) and Part IX (Extent and Application of Enactments) of this Code.

If the interpreter is an enforcement agency of any kind, he must comply with the rules governing his function as such. {As to these rules see ss 15 to 26 of this Code.} The rules relating to obedience by the subject, and sanctions for disobedience, must be followed. {See ss 8 to 14 of this Code.}

In considering the particular enactment in question, the interpreter needs to observe the requirements set out in Part III of this Code as to such matters as the style of drafting of the enactment, the relevant factual outline, and the ascertainment of material facts.

See further s 124 of this Code.

119. Rules: the informed interpretation rule

It is a rule of law (in this Code called the informed interpretation rule) that the interpreter is to infer that the legislator, when settling the wording of an enactment, intended it to be given a fully informed, rather than a purely literal, interpretation (though the two usually produce the same result).

Accordingly, the court does not decide whether or not any real doubt exists as to the meaning of an enactment (and if so how to resolve it) until the court has first discerned and considered, in the light of the guides to legislative intention, the *context* of the enactment, including all such matters as may illumine the text and make clear the meaning intended by the legislator in the factual situation of the instant case.

For this purpose Parliament intends the court to permit the citation of any publicly-available material which, in accordance with the interpretative criteria, the court considers it proper to admit (whether unconditionally or *de bene esse*).

COMMENTARY

The informed interpretation rule is a necessary one. If the draftsman had to frame the enactment in terms suitable for a reader ignorant of past and contemporary facts and of legal principles (and in particular the principles of statutory interpretation), he would need to use far more words than is practicable in order to convey the meaning intended.

This is recognised by Lord Blackburn in his famous judgment in *River Wear Commissioners v Adamson*. {(1877) 2 App Cas 743.} After pointing out that in all cases the object of interpretation is to discern the legislative intention indicated by the words used, Lord Blackburn adds {Pp 575-6.}-

'But from the imperfection of language, it is impossible to know what that intention is without inquiring further, and seeing what the circumstances were with reference to which the words were used, and what was the object, appearing from those circumstances, which the person using them had in view.'

Dangers of the 'first glance' approach The informed interpretation rule is to be applied no matter how plain the statutory words may seem at first glance. Indeed the plainer they seem, the more the reader needs to be on guard. A first glance at an enactment is not a fully-informed glance. Without exception, statutory words require careful assessment of themselves and their context if they are to be construed correctly.

One danger of the first glance approach lies in what is sometimes called *impression*. When the human mind comes into contact with a verbal proposition, an impression of meaning is immediately formed. It may be difficult to dislodge. Judges often say that the matter before them is 'one of impression'. {See, e g, *Maunsell v Olins* [1975] 1 All ER 16, *per* Lord Wilberforce at p 25.}

This first impression may of course be confirmed as correct by later investigation. In one case Lord Denning MR said-

'My first impression was that the words "provision in relation to death or retirement" meant "provision about [death or] retirement". Nothing has been said in the arguments which has made me change that first impression.'

{*Garland v British Rail Engineering Ltd* [1979] 2 All ER 1163, at p 1168. The present author, as draftsman of the words in question, can confirm that Lord Denning's impression was indeed what was intended.}

On the other hand, as Goulding J said-

'It is the commonest thing for a judge to express, and indeed express decidedly, his mind at a particular moment in the proceedings, before he has heard all the addresses that are to be put to him. Any person who has dealt with judicial business knows that after forming a strong view one way you may be completely turned round by an advocate who draws matters to your attention which you had overlooked or forgotten, or who shows the weakness of some reasoning that appealed to you before.'

{*Re Reed (a debtor)* [1979] 2 All ER 22, at p 26.}

The question for the interpreter is not simply what the grammatical meaning of the words is. Words may have a perfectly plain meaning in themselves and yet not convey the intention of the legislator (for example because they are contradicted by other words elsewhere). Judges describe the true meaning as the 'spirit' of the enactment, as opposed to the literal meaning or 'letter'. Occasionally the spirit and the letter point different ways. Sometimes the interpretative criteria on balance indicate that the spirit is to prevail, and sometimes the letter.

In a passage cited with approval by Sir Rupert Cross, the Canadian draftsman Professor Driedger suggests that while in the days of so-called equitable construction the spirit prevailed, and in later times the letter prevailed, we now have the best of both. 'First it was the spirit and not the letter, then the letter and not the spirit, and now the spirit and the letter'. {*The Construction of Statutes* p 2, cited in R Cross *Statutory Interpretation* p 16. As to equitable construction see s 94 of this Code.}

Unfortunately, with respect to Professor Driedger, this is simply not true. If the spirit goes with the letter it does not matter which you follow. If the letter goes with the spirit the same applies. It matters only when the spirit and the letter lead in different directions. Then the interpreter is forced to choose. He cannot have both. He cannot have 'the spirit and the letter'. He must adopt either a literal or a strained construction. {See Part IV of this Code.}

Need to consider the facts Another aspect of the need for an informed interpretation relates to the factual situation in the case before the court. In order to determine the meaning of an enactment in a particular case it is necessary to know the relevant facts. It is on these facts that the parties submit to the court their opposing constructions of the enactment. {See s 84 of this Code.}

Lord Simon of Glaisdale said that he saw no reason why a court of construction of a statute should limit itself in ascertaining the 'matrix of facts' more than a court of construction of any other written material. {*Black-Clawson v Papierwerke* [1975] 1 All ER 810, at p 843.} Lord Simon was here referring to the remark by Lord Wilberforce in *Prenn v Simmonds* {[1971] 1 WLR 1381, at p 1384.} that-

'The time [has] long passed when agreements, even those under seal, were isolated from the matrix of facts in which they were set and interpreted purely on internal linguistic considerations.'

Legislative history The informed interpretation rule requires that, in the construction of an enactment, attention should be paid to relevant aspects of the state of the law before the Act containing it was passed, of the history of the enacting of that Act, and of the legal events which occurred in relation to the Act subsequent to its passing. In this Code these are collectively described as the legislative history of the enactment, and severally described as the pre-enacting, the enacting, and the post-enacting history. They are fully explained in Part X of this Code.

Subject to relevant legal rules, a court or other tribunal considering any enactment is master of its own procedure. {See, e g, *R v Wormwood Scrubs Prison Board of Visitors, ex p Anderson* [1984] 1 All ER 799.} It therefore has the power, indeed the duty, to consider such aspects of the legislative history of the enactment as may be necessary to arrive at its legal meaning.

Further details of the rule Certain further aspects of the informed interpretation rule are dealt with in Part XI of this Code.

120. Rules: the plain meaning rule

It is a rule of law (in this Code called the plain meaning rule) that where, in relation to the facts of the instant case-

(a) the enactment under enquiry is grammatically capable of one meaning only, and
(b) on an informed interpretation of that enactment the interpretative criteria raise no real doubt as to whether that grammatical meaning is the one intended by the legislator,

the legal meaning of the enactment corresponds to that grammatical meaning, and is to be applied accordingly.

COMMENTARY

This sets out the plain meaning rule, namely that where the meaning is plain it must be followed. For this purpose a meaning is 'plain' only where no relevant interpretative criterion (whether relating to material within or outside the Act) points away from that meaning. {For the nature of the interpretative criteria see s 115 of this Code.} As it is put in Halsbury's *Laws of England-*

'If there is nothing to modify, nothing to alter, nothing to qualify the language which a statute contains, the words and sentences must be construed in their ordinary and natural meaning.'

{4th edn, Vol 36 para 585.}

The rule determines the operation of nearly every enactment, simply because nearly every enactment has a straightforward and clear meaning with no counter-indications. As Sir Rupert Cross put it-

'The essential rule is that words should generally be given the meaning which the normal speaker of the English language would understand them to bear in their context at the time when they were used. It would be difficult to over-estimate the importance of this rule because the vast majority of statutes never come before the courts for interpretation. If it were not a known fact that, in the ordinary case in which the normal user of the English language would have no doubt about the meaning of the statutory words, the courts will give those words their ordinary meaning, it would be impossible for lawyers and other experts to act and advise on the statute in question with confidence.'

{R Cross *Statutory Interpretation* p 1.}

It is salutary to bear this in mind. The science or art of statutory interpretation deals in the main with the pathology of law, when something has gone wrong. Usually nothing does go wrong.

264

Lawyers, like medical practitioners, need to be on guard against losing sight of the general prevalence of healthy conditions. Chalmers remarked that 'lawyers see only the pathology of commerce, and not its healthy physiological action, and their views are therefore apt to be warped and one-sided'. {*Sale of Goods* (12th edn, 1945) p 182.} Twining and Miers express similar views-

> 'Broken contracts and broken marriages represent only a small proportion of all contracts and marriages, and the law has at least as important a role to play in the creation of these relationships as in the clearing up of the mess after things have gone wrong.'

{*How To Do Things With Rules* (1st edn, 1976) pp 66-7.}
The plain meaning rule was expressed by Lord Reid as follows-

> 'In determining the meaning of any word or phrase in a statute the first question to ask always is what is the natural or ordinary meaning of that word or phrase in its context in the statute. It is only when that meaning leads to some result which cannot reasonably be suppposed to have been the intention of the legislature that it is proper to look for some other possible meaning of the word or phrase.'

{*Pinner v Everett* [1969] 3 All ER 257, at p 258.}
This may be compared to the following dicta by Lawton LJ: 'The only safe and correct way of construing statutes is to apply the plain meaning of the words'. {*McCormick v Horsepower Ltd* [1981] 2 All ER 746, at p 751.} 'As the meaning of the words . . . is clear, and no ambiguity, whether patent or latent, lurks within them, under our rules for the construction of Acts of Parliament the statutory intention must be found within those words.' {*Macarthys Ltd v Smith* [1979] 3 All ER 325, at p 332. See also *Sussex Peerage Case* (1844) 11 Cl & Fin 85, at p 143; *Fordyce v Bridges* (1847) 1 HL Cas 1, at p 4; *The Argos (Cargo ex), Gaudet v Brown* (1873) LR 5 PC 134, at p 153; *Philpott v President, etc of St George's Hospital* (1857) 6 HL Cas 338, at p 349; *River Wear Commissioners v Adamson* (1877) 2 App Cas 743, at p 755; *Hornsey Local Board v Monarch Investment Building Society* (1889) 24 QBD 1, at p 5; *London and North-Western Railway Co v Evans* [1893] 1 Ch 16, at p 27; *R v Titterton* [1895] 2 QB 61, at p 67; *Salomon v A Salomon & Co Ltd* [1897] AC 22, at p 3; *Vacher & Sons Ltd v London Society of Compositors* [1913] AC 107, at p 117; *Inland Revenue Commissioners v Smyth* [1914] 3 KB 406, at p 420; *Watney, Combe, Reid & Co Ltd v Berners* [1915] AC 885, at p 893; *Re Jenkins* [1931] 2 Ch 218, at p 231.}

Ambiguity Where on the facts of the instant case the enactment is grammatically ambiguous, {See ss 87 to 89 of this Code.} the meaning to be followed is determined by weighing the interpretative factors in the manner explained in Part VII of this Code.

Semantic obscurity Where the enactment is semantically obscure, the interpreter first arrives at the 'corrected version'. {See s 90 of this Code.} This is then treated as if it were the actual text, of which the meaning may be either 'plain' or not. In other words the plain meaning rule either will or will not apply to the corrected version.

Where meaning not 'plain'   For cases where the plain meaning rule does not apply see s 121 of this Code.

121. Rules: rule where meaning not 'plain'

Where, in relation to the facts of the instant case, the plain meaning rule does not apply (because paragraphs (a) and (b) of s 120 of this Code are not satisfied), the legal meaning of the enactment is to be ascertained in accordance with Part VII of this Code.

COMMENTARY

Where the plain meaning rule does not apply (either directly or to the 'corrected version' of a semantically obscure enactment {See s 90 of this Code.}), the legal meaning is arrived at by weighing the interpretative factors as explained in Part VII of this Code.

122. Rules: the commonsense construction rule

It is a rule of law (in this Code referred to as the commonsense construction rule) that when considering, in relation to the facts of the instant case, which of the opposing constructions of the enactment would give effect to the legislative intention, the court should presume that the legislator intended common sense to be used in construing the enactment.

COMMENTARY

Many judicial dicta say that common sense, or good sense, or native wit, or the reason of the case, are expected by Parliament to be applied in the interpretation of its laws. Indeed common sense is a quality frequently called for in law generally. {See, e g, *R v Rennie* [1982] 1 All ER 385, *per* Lord Lane CJ at p 389.} English law is at bottom a sensible thing. {G Lewis *Lord Atkin* (Butterworths, 1983) p 170.}

Here are some examples of the innumerable dicta of this kind which have been uttered in relation to statutory interpretation {See also Examples 80.4, 289.3, 305.2, 323.12, 363.3, 364.1 and 368.4.}

Lord Goddard CJ: 'A certain amount of common sense must be applied in construing a statute.' {*Barnes v Jarvis* [1953] 1 WLR 649, at p 652.}

May LJ (on s 1(1) of the Criminal Damage Act 1971)-

> 'We would only say that an unintentional act followed by an intentional omission to rectify it or its consequences, or a reckless omission to do so when recklessness is a sufficient mens rea for the particular case, should only be regarded in toto as an intentional or reckless act [for the purposes of the enactment] *when reality and common sense* so require . . .'

{*R v Miller* [1982] 2 All ER 386, at p 392 (emphasis added).}

Lord Denning MR (on the Housing (Homeless Persons) Act 1977: '. . . this court held, *as a matter of good sense,* that you have to look at the position when [the plaintiff] left Italy.' {*Lambert v Ealing London Borough Council* [1982] 2 All ER 394, at p 397 (emphasis added). Cf the remark by Lord Bridge (dissenting) in *Din v London Borough of Wandsworth* [1981] 3 All ER 881 that it 'offends commonsense' to say that a man is intentionally homeless for the purposes of the Act where he left his home in anticipation of eviction (p 897).}

McCullough J (on the meaning of 'cause' in various enactments): 'The word "cause" is to be given its ordinary commonsense meaning and any attempt to introduce refinements is to be deprecated'. {*F J H Wrothwell Ltd v Yorkshire Water Authority* (1983) *The Times* 31 October.}

Viscount Cave LC: '. . . this conclusion is in accordance, not only with the terms of the several Acts and Orders, but with *the reason of the case*'. {*A-G v Great Southern and Western Rly Co of Ireland* [1925] AC 754, at p 765.}

Robert Goff LJ: 'On a commonsense approach someone who has sniffed glue and taken toluene by inhalation is someone who has taken drugs . . .' {*Bradford v Wilson* [1983] Crim. LR 482.}

Bowen LJ: 'If a court is invested by Act of Parliament with a discretion, that discretion, like other judicial discretions, must be exercised according to common sense . . .' {*Gardner v Jay* (1885) 29 Ch D 50, at p 58.}

Example 1 A driver (D) stopped his car on the nearside of a street. He looked in his mirror, but saw no approaching traffic. He then opened his door a few inches. An overtaking vehicle which D had not seen collided with the door. D was charged with an offence under reg 117 of the Motor Vehicles (Construction and Use) Regulations 1973, namely opening the door of a motor vehicle on a road so as to cause danger to other road users.

W, the driver of the overtaking vehicle, was proved to have driven too close to D's car. D was not negligent. Yet if D had not opened his door there would have been no danger to W, and no collision. On a literal reading of reg 117, D was guilty.

Held D was not guilty. On a common-sense view the regulation must be read as subject to the implication that other road users said to be endangered must be behaving with ordinary prudence. It would not contravene the regulation to cause danger only to another road user who was not looking where he was going. {*Sever v Duffy* [1977] Crim LR 484. For another example see *Beck v Scholz* [1953] 1 QB 570.}

Draftsman's silence It follows that when a particular matter is not expressly dealt with in the enactment this may simply be because the draftsman thought it went without saying.

Example 2 Section 4(2) of the Courts Act 1971 provides that lay justices when sitting with a judge of the Crown Court are themselves to be treated as judges of that court. Lord Widgery CJ said that in arriving at decisions the full court must play its part. He went on-

> 'All one need add today is really a glimpse of the obvious, so obvious that no doubt the draftsman did not think it necessary to put it in the Act, namely, that in matters of law the lay justices must take a ruling from the presiding judge in precisely the same way as the jury is required to take his ruling when it considers its verdict.'

{*R v Orpin* [1974] 2 All ER 1121, at p 1123.}

Failure of common sense   Where the court fails to employ common sense it may be right to conclude that the decision is arrived at *per incuriam* and should, when opportunity offers, be overruled.

Example 3   In *R v Reynolds* {[1981] 3 All ER 849.} the Court of Appeal held that s 17(3) of the Juries Act 1974 required a verdict to be quashed if there had not been compliance with both limbs of the statutory requirement that a trial court-

> '. . . shall not accept a verdict of guilty [by a majority] unless the foreman of the jury has stated in open court the number of jurors who respectively agreed to and dissented from the verdict.'

The court held that for the foreman merely to state the number who agreed, leaving the number of dissenters to be inferred by simple arithmetical deduction would not suffice. Shaw LJ justified this by saying that otherwise the defendant could be prejudiced, since the minority might not have made up their minds.

The decision was severely criticised by the Court of Appeal in a later case. {*R v Pigg* [1982] 2 All ER 591.} There Lord Lane CJ said that 'applying common sense to the matter' it must follow that if ten of the jury were stated to have agreed in the verdict the other two dissented. He dismissed Shaw LJ's reason in Reynolds by using consequential construction. He pointed out that it involved the untenable proposition that a jury could never return a majority verdict if one of their number refused to make up his mind. Lord Lane regretted that 'this is apparently an area where common sense does not apply'. {Pp 594-5.} On appeal the House of Lords upheld this view and overruled the decision in *Reynolds*. {*R v Pigg* [1983] 1 All ER 56.}

Greater includes less   The requirement that common sense shall be used in interpretation brings in such obvious principles as that the greater includes the less. This is a principle the law recognises in many contexts: *Omne majus continet in se minus*. {5 Co 115.}

Example 4   The statute 22 & 23 Cha 2 c 1 (1670) was passed to deal with the prevalent practice of slitting the nose of a person one disliked. {It was called the Coventry Act after Sir John Coventry, a victim of the practice (Kerr Bl (4th edn, 1876) iv 206).} In *R v Coke and Woodburn* {(1722) 6 St Tr 212.} prisoners indicted under the Act for unlawfully slitting the nose of the brother-in-law of one of them 'with intent to maim or disfigure him' raised the defence that their true intent was to murder him. The court directed the jury that where as in this case a man attempted murder with an instrument (a hedge-bill) which was likely to disfigure the victim he could be found guilty under the statute. The two were condemned and executed.

Example 5   Section 3(1) of the Criminal Law Act 1967 states that a person may use such force as is reasonable in the prevention of crime. Milmo J said in *R v Cousins* {[1982] 2 All ER 115, at p 117.}-

> 'It is , of course, true that the charge against the defendant was not that he used force but that he threatened to use force. However if force is permissible, something less, for example a threat, must also be permissible . . .'

{Emphasis added.}

Example 6 Section 3(4) of the Unsolicited Goods and Services Act 1971 says that the Act is not to apply to contracts made before its commencement. In *Thomson Yellow Pages Ltd v Pugh* {[1975] Crim LR 118.} it was held that this must be taken to apply also to a dealing which did not amount to an effective contract.

Example 7 *Nationwide Building Society v Registry of Friendly Societies* {[1983] 3 All ER 296.} concerned the question whether a scheme providing for the granting of index-linked loans by a building society contravened the requirement in s 1(1) of the Building Societies Act 1962 that a society is limited to making 'advances'. These, it was argued, require repayment of the principal with interest. Under the scheme the borrower might have to pay as 'principal' a sum greater than the amount advanced, though the sum to be so paid by him could not be less than this amount. *Held* The scheme was valid. The requirement for repayment of the principal in full was satisfied by a requirement for payment of a greater amount. {See also *R v Vestry of St Pancras* (1890) 24 QBD 371 (power to pay a pension of a certain amount includes power to pay a smaller amount).}

Common sense may not provide an answer where the elements are incommensurable. Thus one cannot measure whether an actual minor assault is 'greater' or 'less' than a threat to carry out a major assault.

Example 8 In the Australian case of *Rosza v Samuels* {[1969] SASR 205.} a taxi driver repelled a minor assault from a passenger by producing a knife and threatening to cut the passenger to bits with it. *Held* The taxi driver was guilty of assault, and the plea of self defence failed. Only if the defendant would have been entitled actually to use the knife was he entitled to threaten to use it.

It is arguable that one should in law be entitled, for a good reason (such as self-defence), to threaten to do more than it would be lawful to carry out. Common sense may even suggest this, but since the elements are incommensurable there is no such guideline as that 'the greater includes the less'. {See *R v Cousins* as reported in [1982] Crim LR 444.}

The concept that the greater includes the less is akin to the reverse concept that it is common sense to assume that an Act remedying a lesser mischief is also intended to remedy a greater mischief of the same class.

Example 9 It was held that tenements were 'houses' and not 'other buildings' within the meaning of s 42(1) of the Housing Act 1957 since otherwise, while a group of eight unfit houses in which sixteen families lived could be declared a clearance area, a group of eight unfit houses in which ninety families lived could not. 'It would be strange indeed if the section had to be construed so that it was effective to abolish the smaller evil but not the greater'. {*Quiltotex Co Ltd v Minister of Housing and Local Government* [1966] 1 QB 704, per Salmon LJ at p 712.}

Separate ingredients Where the enactment uses a phrase mentioning two or more ingredients, it is common sense to conclude that if the ingredients are each present separately the description is met. Caution is needed however where the phrase has a special meaning amounting to more than the sum of its parts. {As to composite expressions see s 364 of this code.}

Example 10 Article 3 of the Industrial Training Levy (Hotel and Catering) Order 1981 {SI 1981/705.} imposes a levy on businesses providing 'board and lodging' for guests or lodgers. In *Leech Leisure Ltd v Hotel and Catering Industry Training Board* {(1984) *The Times* 18 January.} it was argued that a self-catering establishment which provided lodging, and also operated a cafe in which cooked meals and snacks could be consumed, was liable to the levy. *Held* The phrase 'board and lodging' is a composite one, and it is not satisfied where lodging is provided and, as an independent activity, food is also made available.

Formal ambiguity Formal or syntactical ambiguity can sometimes be resolved by the use of common sense. In *The Complete Plain Words*, a manual written to improve the use of language by civil servants, Sir Ernest Gowers cited as an example of formal ambiguity an instruction contained in a child care handbook: 'If the baby does not thrive on raw milk, boil it'. {(2nd edn, 1973) p 191.} The way the instruction is worded raises a theoretical doubt which common sense is enough to resolve. The same is true of a government regulation cited by Gowers- 'No child shall be employed on any weekday when the school is not open for a longer period than four hours.' {Ibid, p 163.}

Juries and lay magistrates Where the enactment is to be applied by persons who are not lawyers it is particularly important that room should be found for a commonsense approach. Referring to the test laid down by Lord Widgery CJ in *Bocking v Roberts* {[1974] QB 307, at p 309.} for construing s 5(1) of the Misuse of Drugs Act 1971, Lord Scarman said-

'Lord Widgery CJ was here emphasising the need for a practical approach; and he formulated a test which, whatever its limitation in logic, enables a jury or a bench of magistrates to make a commonsense judgment on the facts of a case without importing into the offence an element, i e 'usability', which is not mentioned in the statute creating it.'

{*R v Boyesen* [1982] 2 All ER 161, at p 164.}

123. Rules: *ut res magis valeat quam pereat*

It is a rule of law that the legislator intends the interpreter of an enactment to observe the maxim *ut res magis valeat quam pereat*; so that he must construe the enactment in such a way as to implement, rather than defeat, the legislative intention.

COMMENTARY

It is a rule of law that an Act is to be construed so that its provisions are given force and effect rather than being rendered nugatory. As Dr Lushington put it-

' . . . if very serious consequences to the beneficial and reasonable operation of the Act necessarily follow from one construction, I apprehend that, unless the words imperatively require it, it is the duty of the Court to prefer such a construction that *res majis (sic) valeat, quam pereat.*'

{*The Beta* (1865) 3 Moo PCC NS 23, at p 25 (for fuller details see Example

140.2). For an example of the application of this principle in a tax case see *Whitney v IRC* [1926] AC 37.}

Here it should be noted that, even where the words do 'imperatively require' a particular meaning, the court may in an extreme case find it necessary to arrive at a different one. {See s 93 of this Code.}

The *ut res magis* principle requires inconsistencies within an Act to be reconciled. Blackstone said: 'One part of the statute must be so construed by another, that the whole may, if possible, stand: *ut res magis valeat quam pereat*'. {Kerr Bl (4th edn, 1876) i 64. As to the reconciling of inconsistencies within an Act see s 149 of this Code. For purposive construction see s 139 and Part XV of the Code.} The principle also means that, if the obvious intention of the enactment gives rise to difficulties in implementation, the court must do its best to find ways of resolving these. {See Examples 107.2 and 313.3.}

124. Rules: the functional construction rule

It is a rule of law (in this Code called the functional construction rule) that in construing an enactment the significance to be attached to each type of component of the Act or other instrument containing the enactment must be assessed in conformity with its legislative function as a component of that type.

COMMENTARY

The enactment is the unit of enquiry in statutory interpretation. {See s 72 of this Code.} It is however to be construed by reference to the entirety of the Act or other instrument in which it is contained. {See s 149 of this Code.} So that this operation can be correctly performed, the interpreter needs to read the Act or other instrument with due regard to the juridical nature of its various components. {See s 118 of tis Code.} The remainder of this commentary is framed in terms of an Act, but similar principles apply to delegated legislation. {As to the components of various types of delegated legislation see ss 62 to 66 of this Code.}

Enactment procedure   The starting point is the enactment procedure. This tells us how the various components get into an Act, and what their true status is. It needs to be remembered that an Act consists of the entirety of the text to which royal assent is given. That is what Parliament puts out as its Act. {For enactment and Royal Assent procedures see ss 35 to 45 of this Code.}

Despite dicta to the contrary, the court, when interpreting an enactment, ought not to question the validity of anything within the Act comprising it. {As to challenges to validity see ss 47 (Acts) and 75 (enactments) of this Code.} Nor ought the court to feel in any way inhibited from taking due account of all components of the Act.

The incapacity of the courts to challenge the procedure by which a purported Act of Parliament has found its way on to the statute book is underlined by the ninth article of the Bill of Rights, with its statement that 'proceedings in

Parliament ought not to be impeached or questioned in any court or place out of Parliament'. The courts have held that it contravenes this provision to impugn the report of a Commons Select Committee. {*Dingle v Associated Newspapers Ltd* [1960] 1 All ER 294.} Yet they have not felt themselves precluded by it from impugning the validity of certain components of an Act, such as punctuation. Thus Lord Reid said in *IRC v Hinchy* {[1960] AC 748, at p 765}-

> 'Even if punctuation in more modern Acts can be looked at (which is very doubtful), I do not think one can have any regard to punctuation in older Acts.'

{For punctuation as a guide to interpretation see s 284 of this Code.}

The truth is that any suggestion that certain components of an Act are to be treated, for reasons connected with their parliamentary history, as not being part of the Act is unsound and contrary to principle. As Scrutton LJ said in relation to the short title-

> ' . . . I do not understand on what principle of construction I am not to look at the words of the Act itself to help me understand its scope in order to interpret the words Parliament has used in the circumstances in which they were legislating.'

{*Re the Vexatious Actions Act 1886 - in re Bernard Boaler* [1915] 1 KB 21, at p 40.}

Yet there are many instances of such suggestions in the reports. Avory J made the quite incorrect statement that headings and marginal notes 'are inserted after the Bill has become law'. {*R v Hare* [1934] 1 KB 354, at p 355.} Phillimore LJ referred to a 'general rule of law' to the effect that marginal notes must be disregarded 'upon the principle that those notes are inserted not by Parliament nor under the authority of Parliament, but by irresponsible persons'. {*Re Woking UDC* [1914] 1 Ch 300, at p 322.}

Printing corrections   The 'irresponsible persons' referred to by Phillimore LJ are the parliamentary clerks, who are empowered *by Parliament* to make what are known as printing corrections to Bills. {See pp 108–109 above.} In fact, the marginal notes in an Act are *not* inserted by parliamentary clerks, but are contained either in the Bill as introduced or in new clauses added by amendment. What the clerks very occasionally do is to alter, on the advice of the draftsman, a marginal note which because of amendments made to the Bill or for some other reason, is inaccurate.

Furthermore the clerks are not 'irresponsible persons'. They are subject to the authority of Parliament. Objection may be taken by a Member to anything done by a parliamentary official in relation to a Bill; and it would be open to either House, if it thought fit, to order rectification of a printing correction which it considered unsuitable.

To suppose that the components of a Bill which are subject to printing corrections cannot be looked at in interpretation of the ensuing Act is to treat them as in some way 'unreliable'. No other ground could possibly justify their being ignored. Yet this goes against another principle of law, expressed in the maxim *omnia praesumuntur rite et solemniter esse acta donec probetur in contrarium* - all things are presumed to be rightly and duly performed unless the contrary is proved. {See s 355 of this Code.} This is an important principle in many fields of law. There is no justification for excluding Acts of Parliament from its purview.

Law Commissions' Bill Uncertainty caused by conflicting judicial dicta led the Law Commissions in 1969 to suggest the enactment of a clarifying provision permitting reference to all components of an Act. {*The Interpretation of Statutes* Law Com No 21, Scot Law Com No 11. See clause 1(1)(a) of the appended Bill.} The Government did not take up the Bill, and attempts by Lord Scarman to procure its enactment in 1980 and 1981 were unsuccessful. {For an account of the Law Commissions' Bill and Lord Scarman's efforts to persuade Parliament to adopt it see Bennion 'Another Reverse for the Law Commissions' Interpretation Bill' (1981) 131 NLJ p 840.}

Comparison with statutory instruments The suggestion that any component of an Act in the form in which it receives royal assent is in some way not 'part' of the Act is open to objection on another ground. It introduces a distinction between the interpretation of Acts and that of statutory instruments. Such a distinction would be anomalous and unacceptable.

A statutory instrument, while sometimes subject to Parliamentary procedure, is hardly ever capable of amendment by Parliament. {See p 136 above.} It follows that the instrument is not subject to the making of printing corrections by parliamentary clerks. The headings, marginal notes and punctuation of a statutory instrument must necessarily therefore be treated as being as much part of the instrument as any other component. To avoid an unjustified distinction (never drawn in practice), the same must be taken to be true of an Act.

In their 1969 report on statutory interpretation, the Law Commissions said 'it seems clear that the courts when dealing with [delegated] legislation apply the same general common law principles of interpretation which they apply to statutes'. The only exception noted was the obvious one related to the *ultra vires* doctrine (which applies to delegated legislation, but not to statutes of the Westminster Parliament). {See *The Interpretation of Statutes* (LAW COM No 21) para 77. As to the ultra vires doctrine see s 58 of this Code.}

The correct approach Knowledge of the relevant parliamentary procedure (including royal assent procedure) will assist the interpreter to give correct weight to each component of an Act, judged as an aid to construction. Some components, although part of the Act, carry little if any weight for this purpose: they are intended as nothing more than quick guides to content. Other components (for example the long title) owe their presence in the Act wholly or mainly to the procedural rules applicable to parliamentary Bills, and are to be regarded in that light.

These matters are more fully explained in the sections of this Code dealing with the respective components. {See Part XII of the Code.} On the general aspect, it is submitted that the following dicta from the speeches of Lord Reid and Lord Upjohn in *R v Schildkamp* {[1971] AC 1.} correctly sum up the position, if allowance is made for the fact that they ignore two major factors. One is the point, made above, that the entire product is put out by Parliament as its Act. The other is the fact that by law a reference to an Act is a reference to it *as officially published*. {Interpretation Act 1978 s 19(1). See s 46 of this Code.}

'The question which has arisen in this case is whether and to what extent it is permissible to give weight to punctuation, cross-headings and side-notes to sections in the Act. Taking a strict view, one can say that these should be disregarded because they are not the product of anything done in Parliament. I have never heard of an attempt to move that any of them should be altered or amended, and between the introduction of a Bill and the Royal Assent they can be and often are altered by officials of Parliament acting in conjunction with the draftsman.

But it may be more realistic to accept the Act as printed as being the product of the whole legislative process, and to give due weight to everything found in the printed Act. I say more realistic because in very many cases the provision before the court was never even mentioned in debate in either House, and it may be that its wording was never closely scrutinised by any member of either House. In such a case it is not very meaningful to say that the words of the Act represent the intention of Parliament but that punctuation, cross-headings and side-notes do not.

So, if the authorities are equivocal and one is free to deal with the whole matter, I would not object to taking all these matters into account, provided that we realise that they cannot have equal weight with the words of the Act. Punctuation can be of some assistance in construction. A cross-heading ought to indicate the scope of the sections which follow it but there is always a possibility that the scope of one of these sections may have been widened by amendment. But a side-note is a poor guide to the scope of a section, for it can do no more than indicate the main subject with which the section deals.'

{*R v Schildkamp* [1971] AC 1, *per* Lord Reid at p 10.}

'It must always be remembered that cross-headings, punctuations [*sic*] and marginal notes are not part of the Bill passing through Parliament in this sense that they cannot be debated and amended as the Bill passes its various stages, in marked contrast to the preamble and long title. These cross-headings and marginal notes are put there in the first place by the Parliamentary draftsman but as the Bill proceeds may be altered (probably in consultation with the draftsman) by the officials of Parliament to accord with amendments made to the body of the Bill as it progresses.'

{*R v Schildkamp* [1971] AC 1, *per* Lord Upjohn at p 27.}

Other aspects of functional construction   Apart from the distinctions between components which have been mentioned so far, there is another type of distinction to be drawn. A component of one kind, for example a section of an Act, may be used in different ways and thus have different functions.

A section or similar item may be one of the substantive provisions of the Act, or it may be purely concerned with the machinery of bringing the Act into operation. Difficulty is caused by the fact that under our system provisions of the latter type (known as commencement and transitional provisions) are not clearly differentiated in the arrangement of the Act. {See s 30 of this Code. For

commencement provisions see s 164 to 169 of this Code. Transitional provisions
are dealt with in s 189.

That internal distinctions of this kind may be relevant in interpretation is
illustrated by the following dictum of Nourse J in relation to s 45(4) and (8) of
the Development Land Tax Act 1976-

> 'One thing which is clear about sub-ss (4) and (8) is that the former is
> a permanent provision and the latter is a transitional one. On a
> superficial level I can see the attractions of the argument which
> appealed to the Special Commissioners. But I think it would be very
> dangerous, in trying to get to the effect of the permanent provision,
> to attach too much weight to the particular wording of the
> transitional one.'

{*IRC v Metrolands (Property Finance) Ltd* [1981] 2 All ER 166, at p 183.}

125. Rules: rules laid down by statute

Parliament often finds it convenient to lay down limited rules of
interpretation by statute. Whether or not framed as such, these are in
essence *definitions* of some word or phrase, which must then be
understood in the stipulated sense. They may be general, or restricted to
the appearance of the defined term in the defining Act. Whether it is so
stated or not, they do not apply if the contrary intention appears from the
Act in which the defined term is used. The definition may be simple or
complex.

A term may be defined in an Act for one or more of the following
reasons-

(a) to clarify the meaning of a common word or phrase by
stating that it does or does not include specified matters (in
this Code referred to as a clarifying definition);

(b) to use the term as a *label* denoting a complex concept that
can then be referred to merely by use of the label (in the Code
referred to as a labelling definition);

(c) to attract a meaning already established in law, whether by
statute or otherwise (in the Code referred to as a referential
definition);

(d) to exclude a meaning that otherwise would or might be
included in the term (in the Code referred to as an
exclusionary definition);

(e) to add a meaning that otherwise would or might not be
included in the term (in the Code referred to as an enlarging
definition);

(f) to provide a full statement of the meaning of the term (in
the Code referred to as a comprehensive definition).

COMMENTARY

This section of the Code states the various reasons for which definitions may be
included in legislation, and describes the corresponding types of definition. The

word 'term' is used because a statutory definition may be of a single word or of a phrase of any length. The term must then be understood in the stipulated sense. {See, e g, *R v Britton* [1967] 2 QB 51.} Wherever the term appears, the text must be read as if the full definition were substituted for it. {*Thomas v Marshall* [1953] AC 543, *per* Lord Morton at p 556; *Suffolk County Council v Mason* [1979] 2 All ER 369, *per* Lord Diplock at p 374.} This may not be framed as a definition, but will have a defining effect.

There are many ways in which a term may be defined. The obvious form of a simple definition is 'T means D'. There are other possibilities, for example 'T includes D' or 'T does not include D'. A definition may be obliquely expressed.

Example 1   Section 19(1) of the Housing (Homeless Persons) Act 1977 says-

> 'Any reference in this Act to a person having a local connection with an area is a reference to his having a connection with that area [in specified ways].'

This is a form commonly used. It is not in terms a definition of the phrase 'a person having a local connection', but that is its purpose and effect. {See further Example 2.}

Potency of the term itself   Whatever meaning may be expressly attached to a term, the dictionary meaning of the term exercises some sway over the way the definition will be understood by the court. As Richard Robinson remarked, 'it is not possible to cancel the ingrained emotion of a word merely by an announcement'. {*Definition* (Oxford, 1952) p 77.}

Example 2   Thus in interpreting the definition set out in Example 1, which explains that a person is to be taken to have, or not to have, a 'local connection' with a place by reference to stated concepts (such as normal residence, employment, and family connections), the court will treat the stated concepts not in their ordinary sense but as *coloured* by the overall idea of 'local connection'. {*Eastleigh BC v Betts* [1983] 2 All ER 1111, *per* Lord Brightman at p 1120.}

The potency of the term defined may spring from its legal rather than its dictionary meaning.

Example 3   Gaming has a meaning at common law. It is also given an apparently comprehensive definition in s 55(1) of the Betting, Gaming and Lotteries Act 1963. In *McCollom v Wrightson* {[1968] AC 522.} the House of Lords considered whether this definition was coloured by the common law meaning. *Held* The common law meaning must be taken to apply so as to cut down the width of the statutory definition.

Simple and compound definitions   A definition is simple where it defines the term without bringing in other terms which have received, or need, definitions of their own. Where it does bring in such terms it is a compound definition. It is also a compound definition where it has more than one limb.

Unexpected meaning   The terms of a definition may produce a meaning that is unexpected or unlikely. This does not require the meaning to be rejected if the wording of the definition is clear. It does however suggest caution, and has attracted judicial censure. {See, e g, *Lindsay v Cundy* (1876) 1 QBD 348, at p 358; *Bradley v Baylis* (1881) 8 QBD 195, at pp 210, 230; *R v Commrs under the Boilers Explosion Act 1882* [1891] 1 QB 703, at p 716.}

Example 4 Section 175 of the Factories Act 1961 was held to require a film studio to be treated as a 'factory', since articles (namely films) were made there. {*Dunsby v British Broadcasting Corporation* (1983) *The Times* 25 July. Cf *Savoy Hotel Co v London County Council* [1900] 1 QB 665, at p 669 (Savoy Hotel a 'shop').}

Example 5 The verb *empty* has the clear and well-understood meaning of removing the contents so that there is nothing left. Yet if you 'empty' a bulk container by the tap provided there may be a residue. This led the draftsman of an official circular to define 'draining a bulk tank' as 'removing the liquid contents that remain after emptying'. {Cited E Gowers *The Complete Plain Words* (2nd edn rev 1977) p 234.}

Different definitions of same term A term may be defined differently in different Acts, according to the purpose of the Act. {See, e g, *Earl of Normanton v Giles* [1980] 1 All ER 106, *per* Lord Wilberforce at p 109 (varying definitions of 'livestock').} It is even possible for a term to have different meanings within the same Act.

Example 6 The definition of 'wild bird' in the Protection of Birds Act 1954 s 14(1) runs-

> '"wild bird" in sections 5, 10 and 12 of this Act means any wild bird, but in any other provision of this Act does not include pheasant, partridge, grouse (or moor game), black (or heath) game, or, in Scotland, ptarmigan.'

It may be noted that as well as exemplifying the use of a term in an Act with different meanings, this definition also illustrates the application of the *expressio unius* principle. {For this see s 389 of the Code.} It could scarcely be argued that the reference in say s 5 of the Act to a wild bird did not include a ptarmigan in Scotland. {But what of a ptarmigan that had strayed across the border?}

Definitions with substantive effect It is a drafting error (less frequent now than formerly) to incorporate a substantive enactment in a definition. A definition is not expected to have operative effect as an independent enactment. If it is worded in that way, the courts will tend to construe it restrictively and confine it to the proper function of a definition.

Example 7 In s 3 (the interpretation section) of the Railways Clauses Consolidation Act 1845, the following appears-

> 'The word "justice" shall mean justice of the peace acting for the county . . . or place where the matter requiring the cognizance of any such justice shall arise, *and who shall not be interested in the matter* . . .'
> {Emphasis added.}

In *Wakefield Board of Health v West Riding & Grimsby Rly Co* {(1865) LR 1 QB 84.} the question arose of whether the italicised words were merely descriptive or had the substantive effect of preventing an interested justice from acting even though the parties agreed. *Held* The former was the correct view. Cockburn CJ said {P 86.} that the words were inserted *ex abundanti cautela-*

' . . . in the apprehension that justices, if not warned of what the law is, might act although interested. Had it been intended to render an interested justice absolutely incompetent, notwithstanding that both parties might waive the objection, a positive enactment to this effect would have been inserted.'

{See also Example 342.4.}

Unless the contrary intention appears   Whether the defining enactment says so or not, a definition applies only where the contrary intention does not appear. This is because the legislator is always free to disapply a definition, whether expressly or by implication. {*Meux v Jacobs* (1875) LR 7 HL 481, at p 493; *Robinson v Barton Eccles Local Board* (1883) 8 App Cas 798, at p 801; *Law Society v United Service Bureau* [1934] 1 KB 343; *Jobbins v Middlesex County Council* [1949] 1 KB 142, at p 160; *Parkes v Secretary of State for the Environment* [1979] 1 All ER 211, at p 214; *Strathern v Padden* (1926) JC 9.}

Failure to keep to the definition   The interpreter needs to remember that draftsmen are fallible creatures. Richard Robinson said-

'In stipulating a meaning for a word, a writer demands that his reader shall understand the word in that sense whenever it occurs in that work. The writer thereby lays upon himself the duty of using the word only in that sense, and tacitly promises to do so, and tacitly prophesies that he will do so. But sometimes a writer does not use the word only in the sense he has stipulated. Then his stipulation implied a false promise and a false prediction.'

{*Definition* (Oxford, 1952) p 64.}
    Where it is clear that the draftsman has forgotten his definition, the court may need to give the term its ordinary meaning.

Failure to define a term   Sometimes the draftsman fails to define a term which the courts feel is too vague by itself. This usually betokens uncertainty by the draftsman as to the precise legislative intention. Or it may be desired to leave to the courts the development of the concept in question.

Example 8   Taxing Acts have been notoriously subject to this kind of vagueness. Except where a brand new tax is introduced, it is very difficult to make a fresh start with the drafting of tax legislation. Legislators are anxious to know what increase or decrease in liability would be involved, and this cannot be stated with any precision. Accordingly we are stuck with infelicities going back to the age of disorganised composition. {For the contrast between precision drafting and disorganised composition see s 76 of this Code.} Lord Macmillan expressed his displeasure at the result-

'The Income Tax Acts nowhere define "income" any more than they define "capital"; they describe sources of income and prescribe methods of computing income, but what constitutes income they discreetly refrain from saying. Nor do they define "profits or gains"; while as for "trade", the "intepretation" section of the [Income Tax 1918] only informs us, with a fine disregard of logic, that it "includes every trade, manufacture, adventure or concern in the nature of trade".'

{*Van Den Berghs Ltd v Clark* [1935] AC 431, at p 438. See now s 526(5) of the Income and Corporation Taxes Act 1970, where the definition of 'trade' castigated by Lord Macmillan is reproduced unchanged.}

Sometimes the draftsman misses an opportunity to label a complex concept so as to clarify the meaning of the enactment. {See, e g, the Employment Act 1980 s 17. If the draftsman had referred to 'blacking' in relation to sub-ss (3) and (4) and 'picketing' in relation to sub-ss (5) this much-criticised section would have been less dificult to understand.} This is an example of the vice of *anonymity*. {For an account of this and other drafting vices see Bennion *Statute Law* (2nd edn, 1983) chap 11.}

Failure to define term correctly Sometimes a draftsman causes confusion by defining an established term in a misleading way.

Example 9 Section 1(2) of the Parliament Act 1911 defines 'Money Bill' as used in the Act. {See s 43 of this Code.} Unfortunately the definition allots it a meaning slightly different from that borne by the term in parliamentary usage. Erskine May comments-

' . . . the number of bills which are money bills in both senses of the term is sufficiently large to create the mistaken belief that the term has only one meaning. As the framers of the Parliament Act did not realize the inconvenience of using an established term in a new and partly different sense, the resulting ambiguity must be frankly recognized.'

{Erskine May *The Law, Privileges, Proceedings and Usage of Parliament* (20th edn, 1983) p 857.}

Abandonment of a definition Sometimes a term is given a definition which is omitted in later legislation within the same field. Here it is assumed, unless the contrary intention appears, that the definition is intended to continue to apply.

Example 10 Class XI of the Town and Country Planning (Use Classes) Order 1948 {SI 1948/954.} referred to the use of premises as a 'wholesale warehouse' or as a 'repository', and went on to give definitions of these terms. The order was replaced by the Town and Country Planning (Use Classes) Order 1950 {SI 1950/1131.}, which contained a similar provision but omitted the definitions. In *Newbury District Council v Secretary of State for the Environment* {[1980] 1 All ER 731, at p 736.} Viscount Dilhorne said-

'The definitions of "repository" and "wholesale warehouse" were omitted from the 1950 and subsequent use classes orders but, if it had been the intention that these words should bear a different meaning from that they bore in 1948 to 1950, I would have expected that to have been made clear.'

We now go on to consider in turn the six types of definition described in this section. A particular definition may fall within more than one category.

Clarifying definitions   The purpose of a clarifying definition is to avoid doubt as to whether the term does or does not include specified matters. As Viscount Dilhorne said: 'It is a familiar device of a draftsman to state expressly that certain matters are to be treated as coming within a definition to avoid argument on whether they did (*sic*) or not.' {*IRC v Parker* [1966] AC 141, at p 161.}

A term may have a fairly certain meaning, yet give rise to uneasiness by the draftsman about leaving it to stand alone. His remedy is to specify the main ingredients, and rely for any others on the term itself. This greatly reduces the danger area. The form is 'T means A, B, C or D, or any other manifestation of T'.

Example 11   Section 72(5) of the Supreme Court Act 1981 includes the following definition-

' "intellectual property" means any patent, trade mark, copyright, registered design, technical or commercial information or other intellectual property;'

Labelling definitions   A labelling definition uses a term merely as a label to denote some more complex concept. Instead of the draftsman having to keep repeating the description of the concept, the label alone can be used. In its simplest form, a labelling definition may be very brief.

Example 12   Section 57(1) of the Courts Act 1971 stated that in the Act ' "the Judicature Act 1925" means the Supreme Court of Judicature Act 1925'. This gave the slight advantage of enabling three words to be dropped whenever the 1925 Act was mentioned. A common method for an amending Act is to use the label 'the principal Act'.

A labelling definition may be in indirect form.

Example 13   Section 58(5) of the Employment Protection (Consolidation) Act 1978 states-

'Any reason by virtue of which a dismissal is to be regarded as unfair in consequence of subs (1) or (3) is in this Part referred to as an inadmissible reason.'

{Donaldson MR criticised the draftsman's choice of label here by referring to 'what is quaintly called "an inadmissible reason"': *Carrington v Therm-A-Stor Ltd* [1983] 1 All ER 796, at p 797.}

Sometimes an unskilful draftsman does not expressly define what the label is to mean, but relies on implications arising from the term selected as a label. In such a case the court is expected to confirm and enforce the implications; though this expectation may not always be realised.

Example 14 Section 180 of the Licensing Act 1964 empowers magistrates to grant to the holder of a justices' on-licence covering any premises-

> ' . . . a licence (in this Act referred to as an "occasional licence") authorising the sale by him of any intoxicating liquor [at *other* premises].'

The Act contains no explanation of the term 'occasional', except that s 180(2) requires the applicant for an occasional licence to serve on the police a notice stating 'the place and occasion' for which it is required.

Clearly the implication is that there has to be some event, such as a wedding or other celebration, which could properly be called an 'occasion'. This is not the best way to draft, but nevertheless the intention is clear. However in *R v Bow Street Stipendiary Magistrate, ex p Commissioner of Police of the Metropolis* {[1983] 2 All ER 915.} Glidewell J succumbed to the argument, advanced by an on-licensee who had forgotten to renew his licence, that this act of forgetfulness itself constituted an 'occasion'. This ruling, which may be regarded as perverse, confirms that implications, however obvious the draftsman may think them, are not as safe as express words.

Referential definitions A referential definition attracts a meaning already established in law, whether by statute or otherwise. Thus s 45(1) of the Charities Act 1960 includes this definition: '"ecclesiastical charity" has the same meaning as in the Local Government Act 1894'. {See also Example 21.}

This method carries a danger. Suppose the Act referred to is amended or repealed? Here the principle is clear. Unless the amending or repealing Act contains an indication to the contrary, the amendment or repeal does not affect the meaning of the referential definition.

Exclusionary definitions An exclusionary definition deprives the term of a meaning it would or might otherwise be taken to have.

Example 15 One of the earliest exclusionary enactments was the Treason Act 1351, stated in its preamble to be enacted because 'divers opinions have been made before this time what case should be adjudged treason, and what not'. By not mentioning them, the Act excluded certain forms of violently anti-social conduct which had earlier been charged as treason, such as highway robbery and kidnapping for ransom. {See J G Bellamy *The Law of Treason in England in the later Middle Ages* pp 59ff.} Here a modern exclusionary technique is not to charge undoubted treasons (such as those perpetrated by the IRA) as such.

It tends to mislead if a wide term is artificially cut down by an exclusionary definition.

Example 16 The long title of the Animal Boarding Establishments Act 1963 says it is 'An Act to regulate the keeping of boarding establishments for animals'. All the way through, the Act refers to 'animals'. Only when the reader gets to the definition section at the end is he informed that in the Act '"animal" means any dog or cat'! {S 5(2).}

The title of an Act may warn the reader, and so justify a definition of this kind. The definition of 'suspected' as 'suspected of being diseased' could be criticised if it were not contained in the Diseases of Animals Act 1950. {See s 84(4).}

Enlarging definitions   An enlarging definition is designed to make clear that the term includes a matter that otherwise would or might be taken as outside it.

Example 17   Section 454(3) of the Income and Corporation Taxes Act 1970 begins: 'In this Chapter, "settlement" includes any disposition, trust, covenant, agreement or arrangement . . .' In *Thomas v Marshall* {[1953] AC 543, at p 556.}, Lord Morton, considering an earlier version of this in s 42 of the Income Tax Act 1952, said: 'the object of the subsection is, surely, to make it plain that . . . the word "settlement" is to be enlarged to include other transactions which would not be regarded as "settlements" within the meaning which that word ordinarily bears'. {See further Example 18.}

The typical form of an enlarging definition is 'T includes X'. This is taken to signify 'T means a combination of the ordinary meaning of T plus the ordinary meaning of X'. In other words the mention of X does not affect the application of the enactment to T in its ordinary meaning. {*Nutter v Accrington Local Board* (1878) 4 QBD 375, at p 384; *Deeble v Robinson* [1954] 1 QB 77, at pp 81-2; *Ex p Ferguson* (1871) LR 6 QB 280, at p 291.}

An enlarging definition may not fall to be applied to its full literal extent.

Example 18   Thus the House of Lords have held the definition considered in Example 17 to be restricted by implication to 'settlements' (in the enlarged sense) which contain an element of bounty. {*IRC v Plummer* [1979] 3 All ER 775.}
   An enlarging definition may make the term include a division of the matter in question.

Example 19   Section 58(6) of the Employment Protection (Consolidation) Act 1978 states-

> 'In this section, unless the context otherwise requires, references to a trade union include references to a branch or section of a trade union.'

{For another example see *Bradley v Baylis* (1881) 8 QBD 210, at p 230 (part of a dwelling house).}
   Where an enactment contains an enlarging definition of a term, words used in connection with the term in its normal meaning are by implication required to be modified as necessary.

Example 20   One speaks of the *grant* of a lease but of the *making* of an agreement for a lease. By s 32(5) of the Housing Act 1961 'lease' includes an agreement for a lease. Section 33(5) of the Act says that in the application of s 33 to a lease 'granted for a term part of which falls before the grant' that part is to be left out of account. *Held* In the case of an agreement for a lease the words 'granted' and 'grant' are to be treated as adapted accordingly. {*Brikom Investments Ltd v Seaford* [1981] 2 All ER 783.}

Comprehensive definitions   A comprehensive definition sets out to provide a full statement of everything that is to be taken as included in the term.

Example 21   Section 46 of the Charities Act 1960 includes the following: ' "charitable purposes" means purposes which are exclusively charitable according to the law of England and Wales'. This comprehensively describes the concept in question. It is also an example of a referential definition, since it draws on the legal meaning of 'charity'.

Interpretation Act 1978   The general interpretation Act currently in force is the Interpretation Act 1978. This replaced the Interpretation Act 1889, which in turn replaced the first interpretation Act, known as Lord Brougham's Act 1850. {13 & 14 Vict c 21.}

The basic idea of an interpretation Act is indicated by the long title to Lord Brougham's Act: 'An Act for shortening the Language used in Acts of Parliament'. Indeed the Act was given the popular short title of 'the Acts of Parliament Abbreviation Act'. {J E Eardley-Wilmot *Lord Brougham's Law Reforms* (London, 1860) 117.} An interpretation Act is thus essentially a collection of *labelling definitions*. {As to the function of a labelling definition see above p 280.} It does not operate in such a way as to change the essential effect of an enactment.

Example 22   In *Blue Metal Industries Ltd v R W Dilley* {[1970] AC 827.} the Judicial Committee of the Privy Council considered the effect of a provision of the Interpretation Act 1897 of New South Wales corresponding to s 6(c) (singular words include the plural, and vice versa) of the Interpretation Act 1978. Section 185 of the Companies Act 1961 (NSW) provided for the compulsory transfer of shares on a takeover involving the transfer of shares in a company 'to another company'. The question was whether the 1897 Act made s 185 apply where there were two or more transferee companies. *Held* It did not. Lord Morris of Borth-y-Gest said {P 848 (emphasis added).}-

'The Interpretation Act is a drafting convenience. It is not to be expected that it would be used so as to change the character of legislation. Acquisition of shares by two or more companies is not merely the plural of acquisition by one. It is quite a different kind of acquisition with different consequences. It would presuppose *a different legislative policy*.'

The currently updated text of the Interpretation Act 1978 is set out in Appendix D. {See pp 865ff below. The text of the explanatory white paper on the Act is set out in Appendix E, pp 877ff.} Its main provisions are dealt with in the appropriate sections of this Code. We now explain certain of its definitions for which there is no other convenient place in the Code. {As to the dates from which these provisions operate see Interpretation Act 1978 s 22. For their application to delegated legislation see Interpretation Act 1978 s 23.}

The term 'person'   The term 'person' includes a body of persons, whether corporate or unincorporate. {Interpretation Act 1978 s 5 and Sch 1. See *Law Society v United Services Bureau Ltd* [1934] 1 KB 343 ('person' in Solicitors Act 1932 s 46 confined to person who could become a solicitor, excluding corporations); *Davey v Shawcroft* [1948] 1 All ER 827 (committee a 'person'); *Boarland v Madras Electrical Supply Corpn Ltd* [1954] 1 All ER 52, at p 57 (the Crown, as a corporation sole, is a 'person').}

Gender   Unless the contrary intention appears, words importing the masculine gender include the feminine and vice versa. {Interpretation Act 1978 s 6.}

Number   Unless the contrary intention appears, words in the singular include the plural and vice versa. {Interpretation Act 1978 s 6.} This may require selective pluralising or singularising in complex cases. {See *Number 20 Cannon Street Ltd v Singer and Friedlander Ltd* [1974] Ch 229. See also Bennion *Statute Law* (2nd edn, 1983) pp 194-5.}

Time   Subject to s 3 of the Summer Time Act 1972 (references to points of time during summer time period), whenever an expression of time occurs in an enactment this is taken to refer to Greenwich mean time, unless it is otherwise specifically stated. {Interpretation Act 1978 s 9.} References to a 'month' mean a calendar month. {Interpretation Act 1978 s 5 and Sch 1.}

Distance   In the measurement of any distance for the purposes of an Act, that distance, unless the contrary intention appears, is to be measured in a straight line on a horizontal plane. {Interpretation Act 1978 s 8.}

Land   A reference to 'land' includes buildings and other structures, land covered by water, and any estate, interest, easement, servitude or right in or over land. {Interpretation Act 1978 s 5 and Sch 1.} This is an extremely important definition, which is often overlooked. {See, e g, *Westminster City Council v Haymarket Publishing* [1981] 2 All ER 555.} Failing to take it into account can lead to difficulty because it is an enlarging definition of unexpected extent. An unsuspecting reader might be surprised, for example, that a reference to 'land' includes a mere right of way.

Powers and duties   Where an enactment confers a power or imposes a duty it is implied, unless the contrary intention appears, that the power may be exercised, or the duty is to be performed, from time to time as occasion requires. {Interpretation Act 1978 s 12(1).} This is an important provision, often overlooked in practice. {See, e g, *R v Adams* [1980] 1 All ER 473.}

Duplicated offences   Where an act or omission constitutes an offence under two or more enactments, or both under an enactment and at common law, an alleged offender, unless the contrary intention appears, is liable to be prosecuted and punished under either or any of those enactments or at common law, but must not be punished more than once for the same offence. {Interpretation Act 1978 s 18.} This follows the common law rule. {*Wemyss v Hopkins* (1875) LR 10 QB 378. For the meaning of 'the same offence' see *R v Thomas* [1950] 1 KB 26. As to the effect of agreeing that two charges shall be heard together see *Williams v Hallam* [1943] 112 LJKB 353.}

Statutory definitions generally   For a list of terms defined generally by Act see the title ACT OF PARLIAMENT in the official *Index to the Statutes.*

Free-standing terms Some terms have a meaning in law which exists for all purposes, and not just for the purposes of a named enactment. These are discussed below. {See s 366 of this Code.}

PRINCIPLES DERIVED FROM LEGAL POLICY

126. Principles: nature of legal policy

A principle of statutory interpretation embodies the policy of the law, which is in turn based on public policy. The court presumes, unless the contrary intention appears, that the legislator intended to conform to this legal policy. A principle of statutory interpretation can be described as a principle of legal policy formulated as a guide to legislative intention.

COMMENTARY

No Act can convey expressly the fullness of its legal effect. Indeed only a small proportion of this intended effect can be conveyed by the words of the Act. For the rest, Parliament assumes that interpreters will draw necessary inferences. One inference is that, unless the contrary intention appears, Parliament expects relevant aspects of legal policy to be applied. An Act does not operate in a vacuum, but as a part of the whole *corpus juris* or body of legal rules and principles.

Nature of a principle Here it is necessary to remember the juridical distinction between principles and rules. {See s 115 of this Code.} A rule binds, but a principle guides: *principiorum non est ratio*. {2 Buls 239.} If an enactment incorporates a rule, it makes that rule binding in relation to the purposes of the Act. But if it attracts a principle it leaves scope for flexible application. The clue is given by this. General *principles* of law and public policy underlie and support the *rules* laid down by the whole body of legislation. If it were not so the rules would be merely arbitrary.

Even where a rule does appear arbitrary (for example that one must drive on the left), there is likely to be a non-arbitrary principle underlying it (road safety is socially desirable). Legal rules, as MacCormick says-

'... singly, or much more commonly, in related groups may be conceived of as tending to secure, or being aimed at securing, some end conceived as valuable, or some general mode of conduct conceived to be desirable: to express the policy of achieving that end, or the desirability of that general mode of conduct, in a general normative statement, is, then, to state "the principle of the law" underlying the rule or rules in question.'

{*Legal Reasoning and Legal Theory* p 156.}

In his seminal article entitled 'The Model of Rules', Dworkin discussed a principle of law relied on by the court in the famous American case on statutory interpretation *Riggs v Palmer*. {(1899) 115 NY 506, 22 NE 188. The article appeared in (1967) 35 U Chi LR 14. It is reprinted, under the title 'Is law a system of rules?' in R Dworkin (ed) *The Philosophy of Law* p 38. It is also included in R Dworkin *Taking Rights Seriousy* pp 22ff.} The court had to construe a wills statute the wording of which, if taken literally, gave certain property to the grandson of the man whose will was before the court. The intended beneficiary had however murdered his grandfather.

The New York court said that all laws-

' ... may be controlled in their operation and effect by general, fundamental maxims of the common law. No one shall be permitted to profit by his own fraud, or to take advantage of his own wrong, or to found any claim upon his own iniquity, or to acquire property by his own crime.'

{115 NY 509; 22 NE 189. This 'maxim of the common law' is called a rule of public policy in the curiously-named Forfeiture Act 1982, which codifies the *Riggs v Palmer* principle for British law: see s 1(1). As to this particular 'rule' (properly called a principle) see further s 354 of this Code.}

Dworkin commented that the standards mentioned by the New York court were not the sort we think of as legal rules-

'They seem very different from propositions like "The maximum legal speed on the turnpike is sixty miles an hour" or "A will is invalid unless signed by three witnesses". They are different because they are legal principles rather than legal rules.'

{Ibid, p 45.} It may be noted that of the two examples of rules cited by Dworkin the first directly bears on the citizen (by telling him that he must not drive above the specified speed) while the other is more in the nature of a direction to the court (ordering it to disallow a will not signed by three witnesses). This is an incomplete analysis, since both court and citizen are to some extent affected by both rules. Its relevance will appear in the course of the following discussion.

Before considering how Dworkin elaborates this distinction between principles and rules we need to make two criticisms of the way the New York court in *Riggs v Palmer* expressed the principles cited. These criticisms go to the heart of an understanding of statutory interpretation.

First, it is not correct (at least in relation to a sovereign legislature such as the British Parliament) to speak of an enactment as being 'controlled' by the common law. The true analysis is that the legislature is presumed to intend, where it does not disapply it, that any relevant principle of common law shall apply to fill out the Act's meaning and effect. {See s 144 of this Code.}

Second, it is a mistake to express a principle in the form 'No one shall be permitted to take advantage of his own wrong'. In that form the principle is plainly incorrect. The law often permits, indeed helps, people to take advantage of their own wrong (for example the squatter whose ultimate title is gained under a statute of limitation). To misstate a principle in this way is to encourage the mistaken idea that statutory interpretation is a trackless jungle of conflicting rules. Instead, the principle should be stated in a form such as 'It is desirable that a person should not be permitted to take advantage of his own wrong'.

Dworkin distinguishes a principle from a rule in this way. Rules are applicable in an all-or-nothing fashion. A principle 'states a reason that argues in one direction, but does not necessitate a particular decision'. {*Loc cit* p 47.} In a passage encapsulating the essence of the matter, Dworkin goes on-

'If a man has or is about to receive something, as a direct result of something illegal he did to get it, then that is a reason which the law will take into account in deciding whether he should keep it. *There may be other principles or policies arguing in the other direction - a policy of securing title, for example, or a principle limiting punishment to what the legislature has stipulated.* If so our principle may not prevail, but that does not mean that it is not a principle of our legal system, because in the next case, *when these countervailing considerations are absent or less weighty,* the principle may be decisive.

All that is meant, when we say that a particular principle is a principle of our law, is that the principle is one which officials must take into account, if it is relevant, as a consideration inclining in one direction or another . . . Principles have a dimension that rules do not - the dimension of weight or importance. When principles intersect . . . one who must resolve the conflict has to take into account the relative weight of each. This cannot, of course, be an exact measurement, and the judgment that a particular principle or policy is more important than another will often be a controversial one. *Nevertheless it is an integral part of the concept of a principle that it has this dimension, that it makes sense to ask how important or how weighty it is.*

{*Loc cit* pp 47-8 (emphasis added). The reference to 'officials' clearly includes judges. For what amounts to an endorsement of this analysis by the House of Lords see *Maunsell v Olins* [1975] AC 373, *per* Lord Reid at p 382. As to the weighing operation see ss 158 to 163 of this Code.}

Principles and policy We next need to relate principles to the general policy of the law. Dworkin distinguishes between a principle and a policy. A legal principle confers a *right*, in the sense that the litigant has a right that the court shall take into account any relevant principle. It is 'a standard that is to be observed'. {R Dworkin *Taking Rights Seriously* p 22. Dworkin's 'rights thesis' goes a step further and claims that the litigant has a right to the *decision* pointed out by the relevant principles.}

By contrast Dworkin defines a policy as a standard 'that sets out a goal to be reached, generally an improvement in some economic, political, or social situation deemed desirable'. {Ibid.} This sounds more like a social policy than a legal policy. It is the policy of an Act not dealing with 'lawyer's law', where Parliament sets out to remedy a *social mischief*. {As to the social mischief see s 302 of this Code.}

The principle that underlies traffic regulations (road safety is desirable) is an element of social policy. It may point to the mischief and remedy of a particular enactment, and assist in purposive construction. {As to purposive construction see s 139 and Part XV of this Code.} It is not the sort of principle this section of the Code is concerned with.

What we are now concerned with is the body of general principles which has been built up by the judiciary over the centuries, and is referred to as legal policy. (It is also referred to as public policy; but it is the judges' view of public policy, and confined to justiciable issues.) Public policy in this sense has been judicially described as 'a very unruly horse'. {*Richardson v Mellish* (1824) 2 Bing 252.} It is not a concept that admits of precise definition. {*Egerton v Brownlow* (1853) 4 HLC 1; *Besant v Wood* (1879) 12 Ch D 620; *Davies v Davies* (1887) 36

Ch D 364.} Nevertheless it is clear that it exists, and has a powerful influence on the interpretation of statutes.

The nature of legal policy   Legal policy consists of the collection of principles the judges consider it their duty to uphold. The principles cannot be numbered, and are constantly being developed. {See pp 293–294 below.} Legal policy is equivalent to what the Germans call *rechtspolitik*. It is directed always to the well being of the community. Thus it was said by the court in *R v Higgins* {(1801) 2 East 5.} that 'All such acts and attempts as tend to the prejudice of the community are indictable'.

The framing of legal policy goes to the root of the judicial function as understood in Britain. {It might be more seemly to say England and Wales, since the present author disclaims any learning in Scots law. However legal policy seems common throughout the United Kingdom, as should be so since this is a unitary state with one legislature.} The judges do not exactly invent legal policy: it evolves through the cases. Yet the function is an important creative one, even in relation to statutes. Friedmann remarked that in his auxiliary function as interpreter of statutes, 'the task of the judge is to leave policy to the elected organs of democracy and to interpret such policy intelligently'. {W Friedmann *Legal Theory* (2nd edn, 1949) p 315.} Yet it is inescapable that judge-made legal policy shall be a seamless web thrown over both common law and statute law.

The constituent elements of legal policy are drawn from many sources. These include parliamentary enactments, past judgments, ideas of natural law, and the writings of jurists. The sources are not all legal however. Religious, philosophical and economic doctrine enters in. Political reality flavours the mixture. International obligations are not forgotten. Common sense and savoir faire bind the whole together. {As to the effect of parliamentary enactments see further s 110 of this Code.}

Example 1   In *R v Lemon* {[1979] 1 All ER 898.} the House of Lords were called on to decide a question which Lord Scarman described as 'one of legal policy in the society of today'. {P 927.} This was whether the common law offence of blasphemous libel requires proof only of an intention to publish the offending matter, or whether what Lord Diplock called 'the mental element or mens rea' {P 900.} in the offence requires proof that the accused actually intended to cause offence. Their Lordships agreed that, as Lord Scarman said {P 925.}, the point was open for their decision as a matter of principle. Lord Scarman went on: 'And in deciding the point your Lordships are not saying what the law was in the past or ought to be in the future but what is required of it in the conditions of today's society'.

In reaching its decision the House took many considerations into account, including developments in the law of evidence and penal policy, the tendency of recent Acts in comparable fields, the decline in the public importance of the Church of England, the absence of convictions for blasphemy during the preceding half century, the need for consistency in various departments of the law of libel, the need for social tranquillity in a multiracial society, and our international obligations under the European Convention on Human Rights. The House divided by 3 to 2 in favour of the stricter view.

Elements of legal policy The underlying basis of legal policy is the welfare of the inhabitants: *salus populi est suprema lex.* {13 Co Inst 139. The principle is found in Cicero (*De Legibus* III iii 8).} Locke said laws 'ought to be designed for no other end ultimately but the good of the people'. {*Of Civil Government* (Dent 1924) p 189.} Blackstone said that the only true and natural foundations of society are the wants and fears of individuals. {Kerr Bl (4th edn, 1876) iv 28.} It follows that in the formation of legal policy public opinion plays its part, and is never far from the judge's mind. {See, e g, *Foley v Foley* [1981] 2 All ER 857, *per* Eveleigh LJ at p 861 (on a claim for maintenance by a divorced wife, 'public opinion would readily recognise a stronger claim founded on years of marriage than on years of cohabitation').}

The principle that law should serve the public interest is explained in s 127 of this Code. We now briefly mention the other main elements of legal policy.

Justice A primary aim of legal policy is to do justice, and the courts assume that Parliament does not intend injustice. {See s 128 of this Code.}

State security Legal policy is concerned to keep the community secure from political dangers both external and internal. In essence these are directed against the freedom of the inhabitants to run their society as they think fit, and maintain control over it and themselves. Such dangers involve the use or threat of armed force. {See further pp 665 and 777 below.}

Preserving the peace The concept of the Queen's peace is central to legal policy. Civilised living demands tranquil social conditions; and that disputes should be settled peaceably. {See pp 297–298, 490–491 and 742–743 below.} The prerequisite is a democratic system with full adult suffrage.

Health A society cannot function if human life is not safeguarded, and the agencies of disease controlled. The law seeks to further this end so far as it can. {See s 289 of this Code.}

Morality Lord Mansfield said that the court is the *custos morum* of the people. {*R v Delaval* (1763) 3 Burr 1434, at p 1438.} Two centuries later, Lord Simonds confirmed this-

> 'There remains in the courts of law a residual power to enforce the supreme and fundamental purpose of the law, to conserve not only the safety and order but also the moral welfare of the State.'

{*Shaw v Director of Public Prosecutions* [1962] AC 220, at p 267. For criticism of this view see J Andrews 'Conspiracy and Criminal Law Reform' [1976] Crim LR 483, at pp 491-2. See also *Knuller (Publishing, Printing and Promotions) Ltd v Director of Public Prosecutions* [1973] AC 435. For a more cautious view by Scrutton LJ see *Re Wigzell, ex p Hart* [1921] 2 KB 835, at p 859.}

Example 2 A remarkable illustration of the effect of this doctrine on statutory interpretation is furnished by *R v Chapman*. {[1959] 1 QB 100.} Section 19(1) of the Sexual Offences Act 1956 makes it an offence to take an unmarried girl under 18 out of the possession of her parent or guardian with the intention that she shall have *unlawful* sexual intercourse. {Emphasis added.} In *Chapman* the defendant was found guilty even though the girl was over marriageable age and freely consented to intercourse. Willing fornication is not a crime, yet the law treats it as 'unlawful'.

Example 3   The effect of the *custos morum* doctrine on statutory interpretation is further illustrated by *R v Drury*. {[1975] Crim LR 655.} The relevant enactment was s 28 of the Sexual Offences Act 1956, a selective comminution of which reads-

> 'It is an offence for a person to encourage the commission of an indecent assault on a girl under the age of sixteen for which he is responsible, that is of whom he has the custody, charge or care.'

Few would say that an adult had the 'custody, charge or care' of a 14-year old girl merely because she came baby-sitting to his home one evening. Yet it was so held in *Drury*, where the defendant had encouraged a 17-year old youth to behave indecently with the girl.

The *content* of the moral system imported by the *custos morum* doctrine is a question of growing difficulty in modern conditions. It includes religious doctrine, but is this still exclusively Christian? It used to be said that Christianity is part of the law of England, which must mean that Christian tenets are part of legal policy. {See *R v Taylor* (1676) 1 Vent 293.} Yet Lord Sumner branded this statement as 'mere rhetoric' in *Bowman v Secular Society Ltd.* {[1917] AC 406, at p 457.} Rightly or wrongly, Lord Devlin said extra-judicially in 1959-

> 'But the law has never yet had occasion to inquire into the differences between Christian morals and those which every right-minded member of society is expected to hold. The inquiry would, I believe, be academic. Moralists would find differences; indeed they would find them between different branches of the Christian faith on subjects such as divorce and birth-control. But for the purpose of the limited entry which the law makes into the field of morals, there is no practical difference.'

{*The Enforcement of Morals* p 23.}

When the law enforces morality with penal sanctions, it may be doubted whether this is truly a 'limited entry'.

Lord Devlin also said in 1959 that a moral principle is part of the law if any twelve jurors would unanimously hold it to be so. {*The Enforcement of Morals* p 15.} On many moral issues such unanimity is unlikely today. Yet judges show themselves slow to abandon entrenched principles of the past. Where the sanction is a trial on indictment however, the jury has the last word. Lord Morris said in *Shaw v Director of Public Prosecutions* {[1962] 220, at p 292.}-

> 'Even if accepted public standards may to some extent vary from generation to generation, current standards are in the keeping of juries, who can be trusted to maintain the corporate good sense of the community and to discern attacks upon values that must be preserved.'

It is a triumph of English law that, where penalties are most severe, the final arbiter of legal policy should be not the Law Lord but the humble juror.

Obedience to Parliament   It is basic to judge-made legal policy in Britain that it subserves the will of Parliament. {See s 31 of this Code.} If Parliament indicates by legislation that it desires the policy of the law to take a novel turn, the judges will respond. This has happened recently with Acts against race and sex discrimination. {See s 110 of this Code.}

Consistency and integrity of the law   As interpreters of statute and enunciators of the common law, the judiciary have the responsibility to maintain the consistency and coherence of the law as a whole. This includes both legal doctrines and their practical application. {See s 132 of this Code.} It involves assuming that Parliament does not intend to make casual changes in the law. {See s 133 of this Code.} Another aspect is that the law should be *predictable*. {See s 130 of this Code.} Again, use should not be made of legal institutions (such as the marriage ceremony) for indirect ends. {*Brodie v Brodie* [1917] P 271; *Vervaeke v Smith (Messina and A-G intervening)* [1982] 2 All ER 144. Cf *Re Shusella* (1982) *The Times* 23 June (treating court as debt-collecting agency).}

Equality before the law   It is a basic principle of British legal policy that the law should afford equal treatment for all, or what Dworkin calls 'equal concern and respect'. {R Dworkin *Taking Rights Seriously* pp 180-3, 272-8.}

Liberty removed not granted   A legal system may treat its citizens as having no rights except those specifically granted by law. Or it may on the contrary treat them as possessing the freedom to do anything they wish, except where the law otherwise decrees. English law takes the latter course, and lends its aid to the working out of this presumptive freedom. Thus Jessel MR said that 'contracts when entered into freely and voluntarily shall be held sacred and shall be enforced by Courts of Justice'. {*Printing and Numerical Registering Co v Sampson* (1875) LR 19 Eq 462, at p 465.}

Under the doctrine of equality before the law, mentioned above, the principle that libery is removed not granted is of general application. It is thus available to those in positions of authority as well as to citizens.

Example 4   The principle was relied on by the police in *Malone v Commr of Police of the Metropolis (No 2)* {[1979] 2 All ER 620.} The plaintiff was a private citizen whose telephone had been tapped by the police under authority of a Crown warrant. Megarry V-C said {P 638.}-

> 'Finally there is the contention that as no power to tap telephones has been given by either statute or common law, the tapping is necessarily unlawful. The underlying assumption of this contention, of course, is that nothing is lawful that is not positively authorised by law. As I have indicated, England is not a country where everything is forbidden except what is expressly permitted . . .
> The notion that some express authorisation of law is required for acts which meet with 'general disfavour', and 'offend against proper standards of behaviour', and so on, would make the state of the law dependent on subjective views on indefinite concepts, and would be likely to produce some remarkable and contentious results. Neither in principle nor in authority can I see any justification for this view, and I reject it.'

It is a consequence of this aspect of legal policy that penal enactments should be construed strictly. Where the law curtails some liberty of action, it places a penal sanction on disobedience. Since that liberty exists unless taken away, no sanction can properly be imposed until it is clear that it *has* been taken away. {For the detailed working out of the principle against doubtful penalization see s 129 and Part XIII of this Code.}

Prohibition of restraints Legal policy as worked out by the judiciary has tended to frown on restraints placed on freedom by private persons. This particularly applies in the field of trade and employment. Thus Lord Macnaghten said : 'All interferences with individual liberty of action in trading, and all restraints of trade themselves, if there is nothing more, are contrary to public policy and therefore void'. {*Nordenfelt v Maxim Nordenfelt Guns and Ammunition Co* [1894] AC 535, at p 565.} James V-C said: 'Public policy requires that every man shall be at liberty to work for himself, and shall not be at liberty to deprive himself or the State of his labour, skill or talent, by any contract he enters into'. {*Leather Cloth Co v Lorsont* (1869) LR 9 Eq 345, at p 353.} Those governing a profession or trade may not unjustly exclude members-

> 'The common law of England has for centuries recognised that a man has a right to work at his trade or profession without being unjustly excluded from it. He is not to be shut out from it at the whim of those having the governance of it. If they make a rule which enables them to reject his application arbitrarily or capriciously, not reasonably, that rule is bad. It is against public policy.'

{*Nagle v Fielden* [1966] 2 QB 633, *per* Lord Denning MR at p 644.}

The law also objects to the withdrawal of property from commerce. Thus Jekyll MR said in 1732-

> ' ... great mischief would arise to the public from estates remaining for ever or for a long time inalienable or untransferable from one hand to another, being a damp to industry and a prejudice to trade, to which may be added the inconvenience and distress that would be brought on families whose estates are so fettered.'

{*Stanley v Leigh* (1732) 2 P Wms 686.}

From this sentiment arose such doctrines as the rule in *Whitby v Mitchell* {(1890) 44 Ch D 85. The rule was abolished by the Law of Property Act 1925 s 161.}, and the rules against perpetuities and accumulations. {See Perpetuities and Accumulations Act 1964.}

International relations It is the policy of the law to respect treaty obligations and the comity of nations. The law presumes that Parliament feels likewise. Thus Donaldson LJ said in *Cheall v Association of Professional, Executive, Clerical and Computer Staff* {[1982] 3 All ER 855, at p 886. See also *Schering Chemicals Ltd v Falkman Ltd* [1981] 2 WLR 848.} that 'in matters of legal policy regard should be had to this country's international obligation to observe the [European Convention on Human Rights] as interpreted by the European Court of Human Rights'. {As to the European Convention see s 134 and Part XIII of this Code. The general principle that Parliament intends to comply with public international law is dealt with in s 134. For the implied incorporation of rules of private international law see s 342.}

Residual categories The courts retain a residual power to declare matters contrary to public policy on the ground that they imperil the welfare of the state and its inhabitants. This must be so, for of its nature the general policy of the law cannot admit of areas of national life that it must not penetrate. It operates always subject to the provisions of any relevant Act, but admits no other restriction.

Example 5 Desiring that Lord Alford should strive to attain for himself elevation as Duke (or at least Marquis) of Bridgewater, a testator devised lands to him for 99 years and then to the heirs male of his body. A proviso added that if Lord Alford should not in his lifetime acquire the dignity of the Marquis or Duke of Bridgewater, the estates should pass from his heirs male immediately on his decease. *Held* The proviso was void as contrary to public policy. {*Egerton v Brownlow* (1853) 4 H L Cas 1. Cf *Re Wallace* [1920] 2 Ch 274, where this decision was distinguished in the case of a baronetcy ('a barren title . . . the possession of [which] is a matter of indifference, so far as the welfare of the State or of the public at large is concerned').}

It is true that judges prefer to play down their role in relation to legal policy. This is in line with their constitutional reluctance to admit to being legislators. Thus Lord Thankerton said that the proper function of the courts is to 'expound, and not to expand' such policy. {*Fender v Mildmay* [1938] AC 1, at p 23.}

However Lord Thankerton immediately went on to qualify this by saying it did not mean that the courts could not apply an existing principle of public policy to a new set of circumstances, 'where such circumstances are clearly within the scope of the policy'. It seems that the position was more accurately indicated by Lord Hailsham of St Marylebone in relation to public interest immunity: 'The categories of public interest are not closed, and must alter from time to time whether by restriction or extension as social conditions and social legislation develop'. {*D v NSPCC* [1978] AC 171, at p 230. Cf *McLoughlin v O'Brian* [1982] 2 All ER 298, *per* Lord Edmund-Davies at p 307 (there is always the possibility 'of a wholly new type of policy being raised'; *Cheall v Association of Professional, Executive, Clerical and Computer Staff* [1982] 3 All ER 855, *per* Donaldson LJ at p 887.}

Changes in legal policy The fact is that neither principles of law nor those of wider public policy are static. In their judgments, the courts reflect developments in these principles. In their Acts, legislators do likewise. There is an interaction between the two. As Lord Sumner said-

> 'The fact that opinion grounded on experience has moved one way does not in law preclude the possibility of its moving on fresh experience in the other; nor does it bind succeeding generations, when conditions have again changed.'

{*Bowman v Secular Society Ltd* [1917] AC 406, at p 467.}

On some points, legal policy may change drastically over a century. Lord Devlin referred to certain aspects of mid-nineteenth century legal policy as-

' . . . a Victorian Bill of Rights, favouring (subject to the observance of the accepted standards of morality) the liberty of the individual, the freedom of contract, and the sacredness of property, and which was highly suspicious of taxation.'

{*The Judge* p 15.}
Such a description would scarcely be apposite to the legal policy of today.

Legal policy changes in response to signals from all quarters, some subtle. The prevailing wind that is legal policy in a particular area backs or veers accordingly. Of its nature, said Lord Devlin, the law cannot be immediately responsive to new developments. It needs as a corrective 'the observation of the man up aloft who gauges the strength and direction of the winds of change'. {*The Enforcement of Morals* p 126.}

The more perceptive judges pick up the signals first. An aware judge tries to move in the direction he thinks the law ought to advance. 'If he has moved in the right direction, along the way his society would wish to go, there will come a time when the tethering-point is uprooted and moved nearer to the position he has taken'. {Lord Devlin *The Enforcement of Morals* pp 94-95.}

Legal policy and statutory interpretation Because it takes Parliament as intending that general principles of law should apply unless the contrary intention appears, the common law has developed specific principles of statutory interpretation by reference to those general principles. For example, from the general principle that it is undesirable that a person should be allowed to profit from his own wrong we have the principle of construction that if the literal meaning of an Act would permit a man so to profit it may be correct to infer an intention by the legislator that a strained construction should be given in such cases. {For this principle against wrongful self-benefit see s 354 of the Code. See also Examples 12.4 and 110.6.}

As indicated above, the interpretative criteria do not stand apart from legal principles generally. On the contrary, in the context of an enactment a principle can usually be expressed either in general form or as a principle of statutory interpretation. One can say to the citizen 'It is desirable that you should not be permitted to take advantage of your own wrong'. Or one can say to the court 'If the literal meaning of the Act enables a man to take advantage of his own wrong, it is likely that Parliament intended words of exception to be taken as implied'.

Even an interpretative criterion which appears to be limited to the construction of Acts will be found on analysis to have a wider base. For example the principle that a penal statute should be strictly construed is only an aspect of the principle of justice and fairness that a person should not suffer under a doubtful law (whether written or unwritten).

In a difficult case the number of relevant interpretative criteria may be high, and the task of the court in assessing their relative weight correspondingly difficult. In a statement of importance to any treatise on statutory interpretation, Dworkin says of legal principles generally that 'if we tried to list all the principles in force we would fail'. He adds-

'They are controversial, their weight is all important, they are numberless, and they shift and change so fast that the start of our list would be obsolete before we reached the middle.'

{R Dworkin (ed) *The Philosophy of Law* p 64. Although Dworkin is writing of

American law, his remarks are clearly applicable to common law countries generally.}

This crucial problem of weighing the factors produced by the interpretative criteria in a particular case is examined in detail in Part VII of this Code. The main criteria, and the considerations affecting their assessment, are set out in the various provisions of the present Part. But the categories are never closed, and the area of enquiry is very wide. What is important in a particular case is that no relevant consideration should escape notice. {For a checklist designed to assist in reducing the risk of this see Appendix B, p 857 below.}

For the concept of public policy in the European Communities see *R v Bouchereau*. {[1981] 2 All ER 924.}

127. Principles: that law should serve the public interest

It is the basic principle of legal policy that law should serve the public interest. The court, when considering, in relation to the facts of the instant case, which of the opposing constructions of the enactment would give effect to the legislative intention, should presume that the legislator intended to observe this principle. It should therefore strive to avoid adopting a construction which is in any way adverse to the public interest.

COMMENTARY

Legal policy The principle that law should serve the public interest is the basis of legal policy. For the general nature of legal policy see s 126 of this Code. As to the opposing constructions see s 84.

Lord Wright said that-

> 'In one sense every rule of law, either common law or equity, which has been laid down by the Courts, in that course of judicial legislation which has evolved the law of this country, has been based on considerations of public interest or policy.'

{*Fender v St John-Mildmay* [1938] AC 1, at p 38.}

Equally, all enactments are presumed to be for the public benefit, there being no sound method of distinguishing between them in this regard. {*The Swift* (1813) 1 Dods 320, at p 329; *Richards v MacBride* (1881) 51 LJMC 15, at p 16; *A-G v Hancock* [1940] 1 KB 427, at p 435; *London and North Eastern Rly Co v Berriman* [1946] AC 278, at p 313; *Bombay Province v Bombay Municipal Corpn* [1947] AC 58, at p 62-3; *London County Auxiliary and Territorial Forces Assn v Nichols* [1949] 1 KB 35, at p 45.} This means that the court must always assume that it is in the public interest to give effect to the true intention of the legislator. {As to legislative intention see Part V of this Code.}

Every legal system must concern itself primarily with the public interest. Hence the numerous Latin maxims beginning with the phrase *interest reipublicae* (it concerns the state). Continuations of this include: *ne maleficia remaneant impunita* (that wrongdoers are not left unpunished) {Jenk Cent 31; Wing Max 140.}; *ne sua re quis male utatur* (that no one should make a wrongful use of his property) {6 Co Rep 37.}; *quod homines conserventur* (that human life be preserved) {12 Co Rep 62.}; *res judicatas non rescindi* (that judgments be not rescinded) {2 Co Inst 360.}; *suprema hominum testamanta rata haberi* (that men's last wills be deemed valid) {Co Litt 236.}; *ut sit finis litium* (that lawsuits be not protracted) {Co Litt 303. See *Brown v Dean* [1910] AC 373, at p 374.}

One of the most troublesome conflicts in statutory interpretation is that between individual and group rights. Modern liberal ideas lay great stress on individual rights, but little on the converse. There is much talk of human rights, but no mention of human duties. {As to human rights see s 134 and Part XIII of this Code.}

Yet a proper balance has to be struck. Nor is this an even balance: *jura publica anteferenda privati* (public rights are to be preferred to private). {Co Litt 130a.} Lord Denning quoted the statement by Lord Reid in *A-G v Times Newspapers Ltd* {[1974] AC 273, at p 296.} that 'there must be a balancing of relevant considerations', and then added his own rider: 'The most weighty consideration is the public interest'. {*Wallersteiner v Moir* [1974] 1 WLR 991, at p 1005.}

Too great an emphasis on the principle against doubtful penalization {See s 129 and Part XIII of this Code.} can harm the public interest. The public suffers if dangerous criminals escape on a technicality, or taxes are improperly evaded. In time of war or other national emergency the need to curtail some human rights is greater, as the case of *Liversidge v Anderson* {[1942] AC 206.} illustrated. {See Example 97.1.} Other types of conflict are indicated in the following dictum of Lord Salmon-

> 'Cruelty to children is a most serious and fairly common social evil. The society for its prevention has done much successful work, a large proportion of which was made possible by the information received by the society. Your Lordships held that it was in the public interest that the identity of the society's informers should not be revealed for much the same reason as the identity of police informers is not revealed. If it were, informers would cease to inform. The result would be strongly against [the] public interest for in the one case little children would suffer and in the other case crime would increase.'

{*Science Research Council v Nasse* [1979] 3 All ER 673, at p 685.}

Example 1   Concern for the welfare of infants has led the courts to give a wide meaning to the term 'single woman' in the bastardy legislation. This reached a culmination in *Kruhlak v Kruhlak* {[1958] 2 QB 32.}, where a wife separated from her husband was treated as a 'single woman' for the purpose of obtaining a maintenance order against him under s 3 of the Bastardy Laws Amendment Act 1872. Devlin J said-

> 'The artificiality of the construction which the courts have given to the expression 'single woman' is brought into high relief when a wife asserts against her own husband that she is a single woman. Nevertheless once the point is reached when the fact of singleness is determined by looking at the actual state to which the woman has been reduced and not at her status in the eyes of the law, it seems to me that a woman whose husband has deserted her or cast her off can say to him, with as much force as she can say it to anyone else, that he has reduced her to living as a single woman.'

Different aspects of the public interest may conflict. In the case of public interest immunity, for instance, 'the balance . . . has to be struck between the public interest in the proper functioning of the public service (i e the executive arm of government) and the public interest in the administration of justice'. {*Burmah Oil Co Ltd v Bank of England (A-G intervening)* [1979] 3 All ER 700, *per* Lord Scarman at p 734.}

Where a literal construction would seriously damage the public interest, and no deserving person would be prejudiced by a strained construction to avoid this, the court will apply such a construction.

Example 2 Section 1 of the Mortmain and Charitable Uses Act 1888 provided that where real property or chattels real were transferred to a corporation not licensed to hold lands in mortmain the property 'shall be forfeited to Her Majesty'. In *A-G v Parsons* {[1956] AC 421.} the House of Lords was asked to apply the literal meaning where the effect would have been to vest in the Crown a worthless lease under which onerous repairing obligations were outstanding. *Held* The term 'forfeited' would be construed as *liable* to be forfeited, since otherwise-

' . . . any person holding a short unexpired residue of a leasehold interest would merely have to transfer that interest to a company without licence to hold lands in mortmain to make Her Majesty liable under the covenants contained in the lease.'

{*Per* Earl Jowitt at p 435. Lord Morton dissented on the ground that the words were unambiguous; as indeed they were.}

Example 3 In *Insurance Officer v Hemmant* {[1984] 2 All ER 533.} the Court of Appeal were called on to decide whether a mobility allowance under s 37A of the Social Security Act 1975 could be withdrawn when the beneficiary went to live permanently outside the United Kingdom. Section 37A(7) says that entitlement to a mobility allowance 'shall be determined as at the date when claim for the allowance is received'. *Held* This did not prevent the withdrawal. Oliver LJ said such a reading accorded with common sense-

' . . . for it is difficult to see why the legislature should have thought it either necessary or desirable to provide lifelong benefits at the expense of the British taxpayer for a person who might immediately leave the country and go to live elsewhere.'

In pursuance of well-established principles of legal policy regarding the public interest, the courts will apply a strict or, as the case may require, a liberal interpretation of expressions in an enactment. {As to strict and liberal construction see s 154 of this Code.}

Example 4 Section 1(1) of the Prevention of Crime Act 1953 says that a person is guilty of an offence 'who without lawful authority *or reasonable excuse* . . . has with him in any public place *an offensive weapon*. {Emphasis added.} In pursuance of the policy of upholding the Queen's peace, the courts have construed 'reasonable excuse' narrowly and 'offensive weapon' widely. It has not been left to juries to decide whether an excuse is reasonable: the scope of the expression has been curtailed by judicial sub-rules. {As to sub-rules see s 26 of this Code.} The adjective 'offensive' has been extended to cover defensive use. {See T M S Tosswill 'Defensive Weapons' (1981) 131 NLJ 1024.}

Construction in bonam partem   In pursuance of the principle that law should serve the public interest, the courts have evolved the technique of construction *in bonam partem*. If a statutory benefit is given on a specified condition being satisfied, it is presumed that Parliament intended the benefit to operate only where the required act is performed in a *lawful* manner. Thus where an Act gave efficacy to a fine levied on land, it was held to refer only to a fine lawfully levied. {Co Litt s 728. *Maxwell* states the principle more widely as 'Words are prima facie to be taken in their lawful and rightful sense': see *The Interpretation of Statutes* (12th edn, 1969) p 274. This goes beyond the principle underlying the construction, and forces *Maxwell* to say later (p 277) that a major exception to *in bonam partem* is the ability to tax unlawful profits. In fact this case is not within the principle to begin with.}

    Construction *in bonam partem* is related to three specific legal principles. The first is that a person should not benefit from his own wrong, expressed in the maxim *nullus commodum capere potest de injuria sua propria*. This is discussed in s 354 of the Code. Next is the principle *allegans suam turpitudinem non est audiendus*, which is discussed in s 345. If a person had to prove an unlawful act in order to claim the statutory benefit, this maxim would preclude him from succeeding. The third related principle is stated by Coke in the words *ubi quid generaliter conceditur inest haec exceptio si non aliquid sit contra jus fasque* (where a grant is in general terms there is always an implied provision that it shall not include anything which is unlawful or immoral). {Co Rep 78b.}

Example 5   Where goods are seized in execution under process of a county court, the power to distrain for rent conferred by s 102(3) of the County Courts Act 1984 does not apply if the goods do not belong to the debtor, since the seizure is then unlawful. {*Hughes v Smallwood* (1890) 25 QBD 306, *per* Wills J at p 309 (decided under the County Courts Act 1888 s 160). See also *Beard v Knight* (1858) 8 E & B 865; *Foulger v Taylor* (1860) 5 H & N 202. Cf *Gaskell v King* (1809) 11 East 165.}

Example 6   In *R v Hulme* {(1870) LR 5 QB 377.} the court was concerned with an enactment which entitled a witness to the grant of an immunity certificate where he 'shall answer every question' on certain matters. *Held* This was limited to answers given by the witness truthfully, to the best of his knowledge and belief.

Example 7   Section 12(5) of the Town and Country Planning Act 1947 said that, in respect of land which on the appointed day was unoccupied, planning permission was not required 'in respect of the use of the land for the purpose for which it was last used'. In *Glamorgan County Council v Carter* {[1963] 1 WLR 1.} the last use of the land had contravened a local Act. *Held* Section 12(5) did not apply. Salmon J said {P 5.}-

    'It seems to me plain on principle that [the occupier] could not acquire any legal right by the illegal uses to which she was putting the land. In my view it is plain that the use referred to in s 12(5)(c) . . . must mean lawful use, at any rate in this sense, that it cannot include use which constitutes the commission of a criminal or quasi-criminal offence.'

Equally a person does not forfeit a statutory right because he has abstained from acting illegally.

Example 8 In *R v Portsmouth City Council, ex p Knight* {(1983) *The Times* 18 July.} it was argued that the applicant was intentionally homeless within the meaning of s 17 of the Housing (Homeless Persons) Act 1977, and therefore not entitled to be rehoused. He had been a service licensee whose employment had come to an end, and with it his right to remain in the dwelling. Instead of waiting until his employers obtained a court order for possession, he quit the premises. *Held* If the applicant had remained in possession he would have been a trespasser. He was not to be treated as intentionally homeless because he had refrained from acting unlawfully. {Cf *R v Hillingdon London Borough Council, ex p Wilson* (1983) *The Times* 14 July (applicant, who had given up housing accomodation in Australia, would have contravened immigration laws if she had not done so).}

Construction *in bonam partem* applies where a disability is removed conditionally, since the removal of a disability ranks as a benefit.

Example 9 By virtue of s 41(1) of the Solicitors Act 1957, no solicitor 'who has not at some time been *in continuous practice* as a solicitor for a period of five years could take an articled clerk without special leave. {Emphasis added.} It was held in *Adlam v The Law Society* {[1968] 1 WLR 6.} that the italicised phrase should by implication be read as 'in continuous *lawful* practice', so that a continuously-practising solicitor who had in several years been late in renewing his annual practising certificate required special leave.

It is necessary to analyse the situation correctly in order to see whether there is scope for applying the *in bonam partem* principle.

Example 10 Section 16 of the Highway Act 1862 required a highway surveyor to conform in all respects to the orders of the board in the execution of his duties. This may not seem to give scope for the application of the principle, until one puts the matter another way. What s 16 also meant was that the board were entitled to require a surveyor to obey their orders. In *Mill v Hawker* {(1875) LR 10 Ex 92.} it was held that this did not extend to *unlawful* orders.

The court may refuse to apply the *in bonam partem* principle because it considers that the contrary intention appears. This may be because it is the practice in legislation of the kind in question to state expressly that the matter is limited to *lawful* transactions. Or some other way be provided for raising the question of illegality.

Example 11 Both these grounds were held to be present in *Governors of the Peabody Donation Fund v Higgins.* {[1983] 3 All ER 122.} The appellant claimed the benefit of s 37(1) of the Housing Act 1980, which refers to the case where 'a secure tenancy is assigned'. The purported assignment had been in contravention of the terms of the tenancy, and the respondent landlords claimed that it was therefore not within s 37(1). *Held* The appellant succeeded. The landlord's remedy was to seek possession under Ground 1 of Sch 4 to the

Housing Act 1980 on the ground of breach of an obligation of the tenancy. Furthermore if the draftsman of s 37(1) had intended to exclude such cases he would have followed the example of the Rent Act 1977 and said 'if a secure tenancy is *lawfully* assigned'.

The second reason for this decision is open to criticism. The *in bonam partem* principle is not referred to in the judgments, which are worded as though the court was unaware of it. The Housing Act 1980 has been held by the Court of Appeal not to be in pari materia with the Rent Acts {*London Borough of Hammersmith and Fulham v Harrison* [1981] 2 All ER 588, at p 597.}, which are in any case notoriously ill-drafted and chaotic. {See Example 333.1.} The courts need to bear in mind that parliamentary draftsmen are not specialists in a particular field of law, and cannot be expected to preserve consistency in unrelated provisions of this kind. On the other hand draftsmen ought to be able to rely on the courts' applying well-known principles of construction.

128. Principles: that law should be just

It is a principle of legal policy that law should be just, and that court decisions should further the ends of justice. The court, when considering, in relation to the facts of the instant case, which of the opposing constructions of the enactment would give effect to the legislative intention, should presume that the legislator intended to observe this principle. The court should therefore strive to avoid adopting a construction which leads to injustice.

COMMENTARY

Legal policy The principle that law should be just is an aspect of legal policy. For the general nature of legal policy see s 126 of this Code. As to the opposing constructions see s 84 of this Code.

Parliament is presumed to intend to act justly and reasonably. {*IRC v Hinchy* [1960] AC 748, *per* Lord Reid at p 768. See also *Mangin v IRC* [1971] AC 739, at p 746; *Nothman v London Borough of Barnet* [1979] 1 All ER 142, at p 148.} Justice here includes social justice {*Williams & Glyn's Bank Ltd v Boland* [1980] 2 All ER 408, *per* Lord Scarman at p 416.} or what is sometimes called distributive justice. {See R W M Dias *Jurisprudence* (4th edn, 1976) pp 276-285.} Yet injustice has been judicially described as not 'a practical test' {*Prudential Assurance Co Ltd v Newman Industries Ltd (No 2)* [1982] 1 All ER 354, at p 366.} and as meaning 'different things to different men'. {*Estmanco (Kilner House) Ltd v Greater London Council* [1982] 1 All ER 437, at p 444.}

Nevertheless the courts are always concerned to see that there is not a failure of justice {*R v Ward* (1848) 2 Car & Kir 759.} and that the well of justice remains clear. {*A-G v English* [1982] 2 All ER 903, at p 909.} Here courts rely on 'impression and instinctive judgment as to what is fair and just'. {*Home Office v Dorset Yacht Co Ltd* [1970] AC 1004, *per* Lord Pearson at p 1054. See also *Warden v Warden* [1981] 3 All ER 193, at p 196}

Example 1 In *Customs and Excise Commrs v Mechancial Services (Trailer Engineers) Ltd* {[1979] 1 ALL ER 501.} the Court of Apeal considered a value added tax provision which imposed tax at the higher rate on pleasure boats and related goods. If read literally, it extended this to couplings and winches sold separately - even though more than nine-tenths of them would be used in the assembly of lower-rated goods. *Held* The injustice of this consequence must be taken into account, and required a different construction. Browne LJ said-

> 'This decision will not prevent the Commissioners from recovering tax at the higher rate on all couplings and winches which are in fact used on [higher-rated goods] . . . What it will prevent is what I think the grossly unjust result that the Commissioners are authorised to levy the higher rate on the great majority of these goods which are used for purposes which have nothing to do with [such goods].'

Example 2 In *De Vesci (Evelyn Viscountess) v O'Connell* {[1908] AC 298.} the House of Lords allowed an appeal from a decision of the Irish Court of Appeal. This construed s 33(4) of the Land Law (Ireland) Act 1896 as requiring the court, on a statutory conveyance of a part of an area subject to a fee farm rent, to make an order which had the effect of prejudicing the interests of the proprietor of the rent, notwithstanding that he was a stranger to the transaction. Lord Macnaghten {P 310.} absolved the draftsman in these words-

> 'I do not think the framers of the Act are to blame for not deeming it possible that a land judge administering equity as between A and B would go out of his way to derogate from the rights of a third person who had nothing whatever to do with the matter in hand. The process vulgarly described as robbing Peter to pay Paul is not a principle of equity, not is it, I think, lightly to be attributed to the Legislature even in an Irish Land Act.'

Example 3 In *Coutts & Co v IRC* {[1953] AC 267.} the Crown demanded estate duty of £60,000 where by reason of the death of a trust beneficiary the income of another beneficiary was increased by a mere £1,976 per annum. Lord Reid said {P 281.}-

> 'In general if it is alleged that a statutory provision brings about a result which is so startling, one looks for some other possible meaning of the statute which will avoid such a result, because there is some presumption that Parliament does not intend its legislation to produce highly inequitable results.'

{See Example 322.10.}
It sometimes happens that injustice to someone will arise whichever way the decision goes. Here the court, as usual, carries out a balancing exercise.

Example 4 In a case concerning damages recoverable by a deceased's estate under the Law Reform (Miscellaneous Provisions) Act 1934, Lord Wilberforce said that there might in some cases be duplication of recovery. He went on-

> 'To that extent injustice may be caused to the wrongdoer. But if there is a choice between taking a view of the law which mitigates a clear and recognised injustice in cases of normal occurrence, at the cost of the possibility in fewer cases of excess payments being made, or

leaving the law as it is, I think that our duty is clear. We should carry the judicial process of seeking a just principle as far as we can, confident that a wise legislator will correct resultant anomalies.'

{*Pickett v British Rail Engineering Ltd* [1980] AC 136, at p 151. See s 347 of this Code.}

The courts nowadays frequently use the concept of *fairness* as the standard of just treatment.

Example 5   In *Cardshops Ltd v John Lewis Properties Ltd* {[1982] 3 All ER 746.} the Court of Appeal had to decide the amount of compensation for disturbance where a landlord served a notice of termination of a business tenancy under s 25 of the Landlord and Tenant Act 1954. The notice was served before the compensation provisions in s 37(2) of the 1954 Act were on 25 March 1981 amended by the Local Government, Planning and Land Act 1980 s 193 and Sch 33 para 4. The question was whether compensation should be on the old or new basis. *Held* The new basis applied. Waller LJ said-

> 'In my judgment the law to be applied in cases such as the present is the law at the date on which the tenant is obliged to quit, in this case 29 June 1981. I might add that I do not see any injustice to the landlords in such a conclusion. The policy of the Landlord and Tenant Acts is to hold the balance between landlord and tenant with an obligation on the landlord to pay compensation (and I assume fair compensation) when the tenant is dispossessed. If the unamended law was not achieving fairness I do not see that the landlord suffers injustice by having to pay what Parliament views as proper compensation.'

This concept of *fairness* is sometimes referred to as 'the aequum et bonum', after the maxim *aequum et bonum est lex legum* (that which is equitable and good is the law of laws). {Hob 224.} Speaking of the attempt by lawyers to give proper weight to the aequum et bonum, Lord Devlin has said-

> 'The sort of aequum et bonum which they are trying to handle is something which has unfortunately been squeezed out in the processing of a principle into a rule. The squeezing may happen in several ways. There may be an omission in the wording of the rule unnoticed at the time when the rule was framed, and then many English lawyers would like to use the aequum et bonum, as in other systems lawyers are allowed to do, to repair the omission. Or the particular case which the judge is considering may belong to a category for which the rule makes no provision at all . . .'

{*The Judge* p 87.}

129. Principles: that persons should not be penalized under a doubtful law

It is a principle of legal policy that a person should not be penalized except under clear law (in this Code called the principle against doubtful penalization). The court, when considering, in relation to the facts of the instant case, which of the opposing constructions of the enactment would give effect to the legislative intention, should presume that the legislator intended to observe this principle. It should therefore strive to avoid adopting a construction which penalizes a person where the legislator's intention to do so is doubtful, or penalizes him in a way which was not made clear.

COMMENTARY

Legal policy The principle against doubtful penalization is an aspect of legal policy. For the general nature of legal policy see s 126 of this Code. {The principle against doubtful penalization is dealt with at p 292 of the commentary on that section.} As to the opposing constructions see s 84 of this Code.

This section of the Code explores the application to statutory interpretation of the just principle that a person is not to be put in peril upon an ambiguity. {See also Examples 126.4, 191.1 and 191.2.}

Meaning of 'penal' and 'penalty' The term 'penal' has been treated as a term of art, and given various meanings depending on the context. {*Craies* says that the term is ambiguous, and discusses some of its possible meanings: *Statute Law* (7th edn, 1971) pp 525ff.} This is misconceived, because a law that inflicts hardship or deprivation of any kind is in essence penal. There are degrees of penalization, but the concept of detriment inflicted through the state's coercive power pervades them all. Accordingly this Code is not concerned with any technical rules as to what is or is not a penal enactment. The substance is what matters.

Nature of the principle Whenever it can be argued that an enactment has a meaning requiring infliction of a detriment of any kind, the principle against doubtful penalization comes into play. If the detriment is minor, the principle will carry little weight. If the detriment is severe, the principle will be correspondingly powerful. However it operates, the principle states that persons should not be subjected by law to any sort of detriment unless this is imposed by clear words. As Brett J said-

> 'Those who contend that a penalty may be inflicted must show that the words of the Act distinctly enact that it shall be incurred under the present circumstances. They must fail if the words are merely equally capable of a construction that would, and one that would not, inflict the penalty.'

{*Dickenson v Fletcher* (1873) LR 9 CP 1, at p 7.}
Maxwell says that-

> 'The strict construction of penal statutes seems to manifest itself in four ways: in the requirement of express language for the creation of an offence; in interpreting strictly words setting out the elements of an offence; in requiring the fulfilment to the letter of statutory conditions precedent to the infliction of punishment; and in insisting on the strict observance of technical provisions concerning criminal procedure and jurisdiction.'

{*The Interpretation of Statutes* (12th edn, 1969) pp 239-240. As to strict and liberal construction see s 154 of this Code.}

For reasons given above, this passage is too restrictive. Although criminal penalties are usually the most severe, the principle applies to any form of detriment. References in this work to 'penal' and 'penalty' are to be understood accordingly.

Deprivation without compensation   An obvious detriment is to take away rights without commensurate compensation. The common law has always frowned on this. Brett MR said-

'It is a proper rule of construction not to construe an Act of Parliament as interfering with or injuring persons' rights without compensation unless one is obliged so to construe it.'

{*A-G v Horner* (1884) 14 QBD 245, at p 257 (approved *Consett Iron Co v Clavering* [1935] 2 KB 42, at p 58; *Bond v Nottingham Corpn* [1940] Ch 429, at p 435). See also *Wells v London, Tilbury and Southend Rly* (1877) 5 Ch D 126, at p 130.}

The same applies where it is arguable that rights, though not taken away, are restricted. {*London and North-Western Rly Co v Evans* [1893] 1 Ch 16, at p 27; *Mayor etc of Yarmouth v Simmons* (1879) 10 Ch D 518, at p 527.}

The principle applies both to the rights of an individual and those possessed by the public at large. {*Forbes v Ecclesiastical Commrs* (1872) LR 15 Eq 51, at p 53; *R v Strachan* (1872) LR 7 QB 463, at p 465.}

It follows that although the intention to interfere with property or other rights is plain, there may still be a doubt as to whether adequate compensation is intended. A denial of this must be clearly stated. Lord Atkinson said it was a well-recognised 'canon of construction' that-

' . . . an intention to take away the property of a subject without giving him a legal right to compensation for the loss of it is not to be imputed to the legislature unless the intention is expressed in unequivocal terms.'

{*Central Control Board v Cannon Brewery Co* [1919] AC 744, at p 752 (cited *Marshall v Blackpool Corpn* [1933] 1 KB 688, at p 693; *Bournemouth-Swanage Motor Road and Ferry Co v Harvey & Sons* [1929] 1 Ch 686, at p 697; *Langham v City of London Corpn* [1949] 1 KB 208, at p 212. See also *Minister of Health v Stafford Corpn* [1952] Ch 730, at p 743.}

Where a statutory procedure exists for taking away rights with compensation, the court will resist the argument that some other procedure is available for doing the same thing without compensation. {*Hartnell v Minister of Housing* [1965] AC 1134; *Hall v Shoreham-by-Sea UDC* [1964] 1 WLR 240. See p 130 above.}

Common-law rights   The principle against doubtful penalization applies to the taking away of what is given at common law: 'Plain words are necessary to establish an intention to interfere with . . . common law rights'. {*Deeble v Robinson* [1954] 1 QB 77. The dictum is expressed to apply equally to contractual rights. See also *Gray v R* (1844) 11 Cl & F 427; *Levinger v R* (1870) LR 3 PC 282, at p 289.}

Detailed statutory codes   Where Parliament finds it necessary to lay down a detailed system of regulation in some area of the national life, the courts recognise that it may then be impossible to avoid inflicting detriments which, taken in isolation, are unjustified. The presumption against doubtful penalization is therefore applied less rigorously in such cases. As Lord Fraser of Tullybelton said-

'It must in my view be accepted that, in the application of a detailed statutory code such as that in [the Town and Country Planning Act 1971], or those which are commonly found in fiscal legislation, a measure of hardship may in some cases be unavoidable.'

{*Young v Secretary of State for the Environment* [1983] 2 All ER 1105, at p 1110.}

Doubt as to relieving provision It sometimes happens that a penal enactment contains provisions giving relief from the imposed penalty in specified cases. It may be clear that a particular detriment is imposed, unless the case can be brought within a problematical exception. Here the presumption against doubtful penalization requires that the exception be construed liberally (that is in favour of the subject). {For strict and liberal construction see s 154 of this Code.} If it is doubtful whether an exception to a penalty applies, it is doubtful whether the penalty itself applies.

Chancing one's arm Judges sometimes rule that criteria favouring the public good outweigh the principle against doubtful penalization, particularly where the conduct in question is regarded as *malum in se*. Professor Glanville Williams has commented that-

' . . . paradoxically, the courts seem frequently to feel a greater urge to extend the criminal law than the civil, apparently on the ground that a comprehensive criminal law is the greater public need. In defence of the judges, it may be said not only that we have an inadequate legislature but that people who chance their arms must take the consequences.'

{Glanville Williams 'Statute Interpretation, Prostitution and the Rule of Law' (comprised in *Crime, Proof and Punishment*, Essays in memory of Sir Rupert Cross) p 80.}

Professor Williams cites in support the famous statement by Holmes J about the problem of drawing a line-

'Wherever the law draws a line there will be cases very near each other on opposite sides. The precise course of the line may be uncertain, but *no one can come near it without knowing that he does so, if he thinks*, and if he does so it is familiar to the criminal law to make him take the risk.'

{*United States v Wurzbach* (1930) 280 US 396, at p 399. Emphasis added.}

Standard of proof Where an enactment would inflict a serious detriment on a person if certain facts were established then, even though the case is not a criminal cause or matter, the criminal standard of proof will be required to establish those facts. That is their existence will not be taken to be proved merely on a balance of probabilities. Proof must be beyond reasonable doubt, so that anyone testing it would feel sure.

Example 1   Under s 35 of the Agricultural Marketing Act 1958 a registered milk producer is precluded from selling milk except to the Milk Marketing Board. In *R v Milk Marketing Board, ex p Austin* {(1983) *The Times* 21 March.} the Board refused to purchase milk from the appellant following tests on the quality of his produce. *Held* The criminal standard of proof applied, and this had not been satisfied. Forbes J said: 'When a man's livelihood is at stake the standard of proof should not be lower than in criminal proceedings'.

Retrospectivity   The question of the retrospective operation of enactments goes wider than the principle against doubtful penalization. Accordingly it is discussed separately. {See s 131 of this Code.}

Detailed applications   The way the principle against doubtful penalization is applied in various areas of law is explained in Part XIII of this Code. More than one kind of penalization may arise in the same case, the most obvious example being the criminal offence. To hold that a doubtful provision gives rise to criminal liability may subject a person to the risk of detriments falling within one or more of the following sections of Part XIII: 289 (capital and corporal punishments), 290 (imprisonment), 291 (interference with marital and other family rights), 295 (fine or other economic loss), 296 (harm to reputation), 297 (infringement of privacy).

Sanctions for breach of statutory duty   As to the cases where the legislator is taken to intend that sanctions shall be imposed for breach of statutory duty see s 13 of this Code (criminal sanctions) and s 14 (civil sanctions).
   See further as to the principle against doubtful penalization s 154 of this Code.

130. Principles: that law should be predictable

It is a principle of legal policy that law should be certain, and therefore predictable. The court, when considering, in relation to the facts of the instant case, which of the opposing constructions of the enactment would give effect to the legislative intention, should presume that the legislator intended to observe this principle. It should therefore strive to reach a construction which was reasonably foreseeable by the parties concerned.

COMMENTARY

Legal policy   The principle that law should be certain and predictable is an aspect of legal policy. For the general nature of legal policy see s 126 of this Code.

Legal certainty   It is universally assumed that the law should be certain. As Locke wrote-

> 'To this end it is that men give up all their natural power to the
> society they enter into, and the community put the legislative power

into such hands as they think fit, with this trust, that they shall be governed by *declared laws*, or else their peace, quiet, and property will still be at the same uncertainty as it was in the state of Nature.'

{*Of Civil Government* p 186 (emphasis added).}

Shael Herman remarked that (as Montesquieu has taught us) 'certainty can positively affect the citizenry'. {'Quot judices tot sententiae: A study of the English reaction to continental interpretive (*sic*) techniques'. 1 *Legal Studies* 165, at p 180. Cf p 309 below.} Herman went on to say that 'if private actors know in advance the incidence of state intervention, they can adjust their activities to account for it, thereby avoiding the effect of sporadic legal catastrophes'.

In like vein Lord Denning quotes the attack by 'Junius' on Lord Mansfield's introduction into the eighteenth-century common law of equitable principles-

'Instead of those certain positive rules by which the judgments of a court of law should invariably be determined, you have fondly introduced your own unsettled notions of equity and substantial justice.'

{*What Next in the Law* p 23, citing *Letters of Junius* 14 November 1770.}

Here Lord Denning likens Lord Mansfield's role in legal development to his own. His point is that, just as eighteenth-century opponents of the introduction of equity were proved wrong by time, so will those be who insist on legal certainty in the twentieth century. The cases however are not parallel.

Lord Diplock illustrated the practical aspects of the need for legal certainty when describing the position of traders as regards the arbitration of their disputes-

'. . . it is in the interests of legal certainty that there should be some uniformity in the decision of arbitrators as to the effect, frustrating or otherwise, of [a certain type of event] on similar transactions in order that other traders can be sufficiently certain where they stand as to be able to close their own transactions without recourse to arbitration . . .'

{*Pioneer Shipping Ltd v BTP Tioxide Ltd, The Nema* [1981] 3 WLR 292, at p 305.}

Another illustration was given by Lord Brightman as respects the need to be able to rely on the certain operation of Limitation Acts-

'When a period of limitation has expired, a potential defendant should be able to assume that he is no longer at risk from a stale claim. He should be able to part with his papers if they exist and discard any proofs of witnesses which have been taken, discharge his solicitor if he has been retained, and order his affairs on the basis that his potential liability has gone.'

{*Yew Bon Tew v Kenderaan Bas Maria* [1982] 3 All ER 833, at p 839.}

These are but two illustrations of what it means to have certainty in the law. The essence is the good citizen's peace of mind. Being law-abiding, he can trust in remaining untroubled by vexatious manifestations of legality.

This element is regarded by most jurists as of the very essence of law. If law is not certain it is to that extent not known. Lord Diplock said-

'Unless men know what the rule of conduct is they cannot regulate their actions to conform to it. It fails in its primary function as a rule.'

{'The Courts as Legislators' (address to the Holdsworth Club of the University of Birmingham, 1965) p 16.1. Cf Bracton i 207 (tallage at will a badge of servitude).}

For the law not to be known is the ultimate injustice. Until the common law courts intervened, the Council of the North, an institution of government established in exercise of the royal prerogative by Henry VIII, operated under and enforced secret instructions from the king. Condemning this, Coke cited the maxim *misera est servitus, ubi jus est vagum aut incertum* (obedience is a hardship where the law is vague or uncertain). {4 Co Inst 246. The Council of the North was abolished by the statute 16 Cha 1 c 10 (1640). This also abolished the Court of Star Chamber, which was subject to similar objections.}

Being unjust, an uncertain law tends to arouse civil discord. Serjeant Carus said *arguendo* in *Stowel v Lord Zouch* {(1569) 1 Plowd 353.} that 'certainty [in law] is the mother of repose, and incertainty is the mother of contention'. Such contention is justified, because where the legislature does not provide certain law it fails in its elementary purpose and duty. The legislature is an organ of the state, which requires its members to conform to its will. Blackstone said-

'For since the respective members [of the state] are bound to conform themselves to the will of the state, it is expedient that they receive directions from the state declaratory of that its will. But as it is impossible, in so great a multitude, to give injunctions to every particular man, relative to each particular action, it is therefore incumbent on the state to establish general rules for the perpetual information and direction of all persons in all points, whether of positive or negative duty. And this, in order that every man may know what to look upon as his own, what as another's; what absolute and what relative duties are required at his hands; what is to be esteemed honest, dishonest, or indifferent; what degree every man retains of his natural liberty; what he has given up as the price of the benefits of society; and after what manner each person is to moderate the use and exercise of those rights which the state assigns him, in order to promote and secure the public tranquillity.'

{Kerr Bl (4th edn, 1876) i 33-4.}

Knowability   One guarantee of certainty is that the law should be known. Only if the state of the law on any point is obvious and manifest can any person be sure it will not be manipulated to his disadvantage. What is publicly known cannot be altered without publicity. Locke said that the legislature must govern 'by promulgated established laws, not to be varied in particular cases, but to have one rule for rich and poor, for the fovourite at Court, and the countryman at plough'. {*Of Civil Government* (Dent, 1924) p 189.}

Predictability   If the law is both known and certain it is predictable. Those affected by it can foresee how the court will apply it, and arrange their affairs accordingly. Holmes J, unwitting founder of the American realist school of jurisprudence, went so far as to suggest that this predictability was indeed the very essence of law: 'The prophecies of what the courts are likely to do in fact and nothing more pretentious are what I mean by the law'. {'The Path of the Law' *Collected Legal Papers* 173.}

The French legal system employs language which romantically suggests that the law itself foresees how it will be applied. The European Convention on Human Rights frequently uses a phrase which in the English version is rendered 'prescribed by law'. {See, e g, art 5.} The French version however says 'prévue par la loi'.

If the law is indeed to 'prévue' the decisions that will be arrived at in its name this imposes a self-denying ordinance on courts of construction. Without it judges may freely interpret statutes according to their own view of what is just. The danger of such latitude, in the words of Megaw LJ-

'. . . is not, indeed, that the judges become legislators, but that they may become legislators with widely differing, and perhaps unduly legalistic, views of the policy which is, or ought to be, behind the legislation. Hence the law, whatever it may gain in other respects, may in some cases suffer a loss in what has always been regarded as one of the essential features of law - uniformity; or at least predictability. Sometimes, in relation to the judicial view of "the presumed purpose of the legislation", it may be a case of *quot judices, tot sententiae*: whereas in relation to what the legislation has actually said, it is unlikely that judicial opinion would vary so widely.'

{*Ulster-Swift Ltd v Taunton Meat Haulage Ltd* [1977] 3 All ER 641, at pp 646–647. The Latin words are an adaptation of a phrase in Terence's *Phormio*. Translated this reads: so many men, so many opinions; his own a law to each (*quot homines tot sententiae; suus cuique mos*). Cf p 307 above.}

The truth was as so often expressed by Blackstone-

'. . . the liberty of all cases in an equitable light must not be indulged too far, lest thereby we destroy all law, and leave the decision of every question entirely in the breast of the judge. And law, without equity, though hard and disagreeable, is much more desirable for the public good, than equity without law: which would make every judge a legislator, and introduce most infinite confusion; as there would then be almost as many rules of action laid down in our courts, as there are differences of capacity and sentiment in the human mind.'

{Kerr Bl (4th edn, 1876) i 41.}

The classic modern statement of the need for predictability is that of Lord Diplock in *Black-Clawson International Ltd v Papierwerke Waldhof-Aschaffenberg AG* {[1975] 1 All ER 810, at p 836.}-

'The acceptance of the rule of law as a constitutional principle requires that a citizen, before committing himself to any course of action, should be able to know in advance what are the legal consequences that will flow from it. Where those consequences are regulated by a statute the source of that knowledge is what the statute says. In construing it the court must give effect to what the words of the statute would be reasonably understood to mean by those whose conduct it regulates. That any or all of the individual members of the two Houses of Parliament that passed it may have thought the words bore a different meaning cannot affect the matter. Parliament, under our constitution, is sovereign only in respect of what it expresses by the words used in the legislation it has passed.'

Predictability and literalism   It will be seen from this important dictum of Lord Diplock that there is a close connection between predictability and literal construction. If the literal meaning is clear, *and it is known that it will be enforced*, the citizen has all the information he needs. He may not agree with the law, but at least he knows what it is. The more courts are inclined to depart from the literal meaning in search of the legislative purpose, or merely of abstract justice, the less certain the law becomes.

Unfortunately there tends to be some inconsistency of judicial approach here. Now and then a judge such as Lord Denning arrives on the scene. By deliberately adopting a less literal interpretative technique than most of his colleagues, he introduces confusion into the law. Advisers may feel obliged to tender different advice according to whether or not a literalist judge is to try the case. Zander says : 'The result of the inevitable inconsistency as to the application of the literal approach is that it loses much of its claim to be the basis of greater certainty'. {*The Law-Making Process* p 51. The pages following this remark contain an interesting discussion of the problem.} The questionable thing about Zander's remark is whether the inconsistency is indeed *inevitable*. Are not the judiciary obliged to follow a common approach ?

Such is certainly the view of the House of Lords. In a comprehensive denunciation of the Denning ethos Lord Hailsham LC said-

> '. . . litigants would not have known where they stood. None could have reached finality short of the House of Lords, and, in the meantime, the task of their professional advisers of advising them as to their rights, or as to the probable cost of obtaining or defending them, would have been, quite literally, impossible. Whatever the merits, chaos would have reigned until the dispute was settled, and, in legal matters, some degree of certainty is at least as valuable a part of justice as perfection.'

{*Cassell & Co Ltd (No 2) v Broome* [1972] AC 1027, at p 1054 Lord Denning comments sardonically on this passage in his book *The Discipline of Law* (pp 312-3).}

Consistency in interpreting broad terms   Where by the use of a broad term Parliament has delegated to the court the working out of the detailed meaning of an enactment, the requirements of legal certainty and predictability mean that a consistent interpretation must be followed. {As to broad terms see s 150 of this Code.}

One example of this need for consistency lies in sentencing policy in criminal law. When establishing a criminal offence Parliament often lays down the minimum and maximum penalty. Sometimes however provision is made for a fine or imprisonment at the entire discretion of the court. Either way, the courts take great care to apply a 'tariff' of penalties with a view to consistency of treatment.

In every sphere, even-handed justice requires uniformity as between one citizen and another. Thus in valuation for rating great stress is placed on 'the tone of the list'. {*Re Hurren (a bankrupt)* [1982] 3 All ER 982, at p 986.}

Who should be able to predict? Inevitably in a discussion of certainty and predictability in statutory interpretation there comes the question of *who* should be able to know what the enactment requires. The obvious answer is: everyone affected by it. Lawyers are very well aware that this, though desirable, is not practicable in an advanced society. The Law Commissions, who should know better, have pandered to the impossible dream. In their 1969 paper on statutory interpretation they say-

> 'It is important . . . to bear in mind that a statute is directed not merely to the courts but also to the community at large, who will tend to read the statute without giving any very refined attention to the exact legal status of its different parts.'

{*The Interpretation of Statutes* (Law Com No 21) para 45.}
Even Blackstone was tempted to subscribe to this facile view when he wrote-

> 'It were endless to enumerate all the affirmative acts of parliament wherein justice is directed to be done according to the law of the land: and what that law is, every subject knows, or may know if he pleases; for it depends not upon the arbitrary will of any judge, but is permanent, fixed, and unchangeable, unless by authority of parliament.'

{Kerr Bl (4th edn, 1876) i 111-2.}
Judges and politicians too have succumbed to the temptation of acting as though in this regard the desirable were always the possible. It is notorious that the government which procured the passing of the Workmen's Compensation Act 1897 fondly thought that if the Act simply said that compensation was to be granted to a workman for an accident 'arising out of and in the course of his employment' workmen would know where they stood.

Even so acute a lawyer as Lord Macnaghten subscribed to this naive view when he said of the 1897 Act: 'Parliament is making a new departure in the interest of labour, and legislating for working men presumably in language that they can understand'. {*Fenton v Thorley* [1903] AC 443, at p 447. Seldom can the word 'presumably' have been asked to bear such weight.} The truth was that literally thousands of cases were brought before the courts in order to work out the legal meaning of these few simple words.

In fact, as explained above, statutes are to be given an *informed* interpretation. {See s 119 of this Code.} This is not possible for those without expert knowledge. If they attempt it they may fail to understand what the law is. Worse, they may believe it to be what it is not. {As to the dangers of this see s 9 of this Code.}

Lawyers should not glory in this need for an expertise they exist to provide. While inescapable, it is nevertheless unfortunate. Nor should lawyers distance themselves from the plain man's idea of what is just. In a shoplifting case Lord Lane CJ said that-

> '. . . the court should not be astute to find that a theft has taken place where it would be straining the language so to hold, or where the

ordinary person would not regard the defendant's acts, though possibly morally reprehensible, as theft.'

{*Kaur v Chief Constable for Hampshire* [1981] 1 WLR 578, at p 583.} The sentiment is echoed by H E Markson, who after discussing this and similar cases writes-

'. . . where possible, [legislative] language should be given its most obvious meaning, to accord with how the man in the street might answer problems posed by the words. Although this may not always be feasible, it is suggested that the courts could do much worse than to have that as a primary objective . . .'

{'Statutory Interpretation' (1982) 126 Sol Jo 215, at pp 216-7.}
Bentham grasped that laymen necessarily depend on experts to tell them what the law is-

'Is it not to be wished that a man could know for certain, the legal consequences of his doing an act before he does it? . . . I want somebody to do it [sc interpret the law] for me. But the somebody to answer my purpose fully, must be somebody who can make the conduct of the Law . . . *answerable to his prediction.*'

{*A Comment on the Commentaries* p 102. Emphasis added.}
This makes two important points. The layman needs an expert adviser, and the advice needs to be dependable.

Lord Diplock recognised the layman's need for an expert adviser when he said that legal certainty 'demands that the rules by which the citizen is to be bound should be ascertainable by him (or, more realistically, by a competent lawyer advising him)'. {*Fothergill v Monarch Airlines Ltd* [1980] 2 All ER 696, at p 705.}

The adviser also needs to be able to make the client understand the law, even if only in outline. The criminal law, which everyone must obey under penalty, particularly needs to be in a form where it can be grasped by the citizen. Thus Glanville Williams said-

'Penal statutes . . . should give the citizen reasonably clear guidance as to what is punishable, and where in its plain or primary meaning a penal statute does not reach conduct of a particular kind, the courts should not be astute to find some secondary meaning that will cover it. This principle is traditionally stated in the proposition that penal statutes should be construed strictly. It must be said that although the rule is still maintained in theory, it is nowadays rarely given practical effect. When the judges are morally outraged they tend to give the prohibitory law its widest rather than its narrowest extension . . .'

{Glanville Williams 'The Meaning of Literal Interpretation' (1981) 131 NLJ 1128, at p 1150. For examples of this wide construction in relation to soliciting for prostitution see Glanville Williams in *Crime, Proof and Punishment* (ed. Colin Tapper) 71. As to strict construction of penal enactments see s 129 and Part XIII of this Code.}

Over-subtlety One principle to be observed in rendering the law comprehensible is avoidance of over-subtle interpretation. As Coke said, *nimia subtilitas in jure reprobatur* (too great subtlety in law is condemned). {4 Co Rep 5. Another version mentioned by Coke in the same place is: *simplicitas est legibus amica* (simplicity is the friend of the laws).}

In a modern criminal case Lord Diplock rejected any complex meaning of the power of forfeiture contained in s 27 of the Misuse of Drugs Act 1971 with these words-

> 'That it should be necessary to have recourse to such erudite and intricate arguments in order to ascertain the meaning of a provision in a criminal statute which needs to be administered with reasonable consistency by hundreds of criminal courts throughout the land if justice is to be done would be discreditable to the English legal system.'

{*R v Cuthbertson* [1980] 2 All ER 401, at p 403.}

This reminds us that the administration of the law is not confined to those with expert legal knowledge. Lay magistrates, jurors, tribunal members, arbitrators, police officers, local and central government officials, tax inspectors and many more depend on understanding the law in order to carry out their function. {See ss 15 to 18 of this Code.} So the law is bound to avoid over-subtlety. {See also the remarks on 'hairsplitting' at p 5 above.}

On the other hand one cannot expect all the laws of a modern complex society to be simple. 'People' said Blackstone 'are apt to be angry at the want of simplicity in our laws: they mistake variety for confusion, and complicated cases for contradictory'. {Kerr Bl (4th edn, 1876) iii 333.}

Promoting settlement of disputes One advantage of predictability is that it encourages the settlement of disputes without recourse to litigation. Where litigation has been embarked upon, predictability helps to promote settlements without pursuing the litigation to the bitter end.

It is the policy of the law to promote settlement of disputes. Thus Lord Diplock, in referring to a judicial guideline as to the rate of interest to be adopted in relation to damages awards, said its purpose lay 'in promoting predictability and so facilitating settlements'. {*Wright v British Railways Board* [1983] 2 All ER 698, at p 706.}

131. Principles: that law should not operate retrospectively

It is a principle of legal policy that, except in relation to procedural matters, changes in the law should not take effect retrospectively. The court, when considering, in relation to the facts of the instant case, which of the opposing constructions of the enactment would give effect to the legislative intention, should presume that the legislator intended to observe this principle. The detailed spelling-out of this presumption is an aspect of the commencement, amendment and repeal of enactments, and is therefore dealt with in Part VIII of this Code (see ss 190 to 194).

COMMENTARY

Legal policy The principle against retrospective operation is an aspect of legal policy. For the general nature of legal policy see s 126 of this Code. As to the opposing constructions see s 84.

A person is presumed to know the law {See s 9 of this Code.}; and is required to obey the law. {See s 8 of this Code.} It follows that he should be able to trust the law. Having fulfilled his duty to know the law, he should then be able to act on his knowledge with confidence. The rule of law means nothing else. It follows that to alter the law retrospectively, where that is to the disadvantage of the subject, is a betrayal of what law stands for. Parliament is presumed not to intend such betrayal.

From the general principle governing retrospectivity it follows that the penalties imposed for any transgression of the law should not be altered to the detriment of the transgressor *after he has transgressed*. Any such alteration amounts to switching the rules while the event is still in progress, and is obviously unfair. Parliament is presumed not to intend to do this.

Rules of legal procedure are taken to be intended to facilitate the proper settlement of civil or, as the case may be, criminal disputes. Changes in such rules are assumed to be for the better. They are also assumed to be neutral as between the parties, merely holding the ring. Accordingly the presumption against retrospective penalization does not apply to them, since they are supposed not to possess any penal character. Indeed if they have any substantial penal effect they cannot be merely procedural.

For further details see ss 190 to 194 of this Code.

132. Principles: that law should be coherent and self-consistent

It is a principle of legal policy that law should be coherent and self-consistent. The court, when considering, in relation to the facts of the instant case, which of the opposing constructions of the enactment would give effect to the legislative intention, should presume that the legislator intended to observe this principle. The court should therefore strive to avoid adopting a construction which involves accepting that on the point in question the law is not coherent and self-consistent.

COMMENTARY

Legal policy The principle that law should be coherent and self-consistent is an aspect of legal policy. For the general nature of legal policy see s 126 of this Code. As to the opposing constructions see s 84 of this Code.

Consistency within the system of laws is an obvious benefit. It is acknowledged in the maxim *lex beneficialis rei consimili remedium praestat* (a beneficial law affords a remedy for cases which are on the same footing). {2 Co Inst 689.} This is also expressed as *in consimili casu, consimile debet esse remedium* (in similar cases there should be like remedies). {Hard 65.} The law should be as simple and straightforward as possible. It should avoid inconsistency and overlapping. {As to the need for predictability see s 130 of this Code. For the avoidance of anomalies and other unsatisfactory features see s 141 and Part XVI. As to the avoidance of overlapping remedies for breach of statutory duty see s 13 (criminal remedies) and s 14 (civil remedies). See also Example 311.1.}

One of the grounds on which Blackstone praised the old system of travelling assize judges was the resulting consistency in the law-

'These justices, though . . . varied and shifted at every assizes, are all sworn to the same laws, have had the same education, have pursued the same studies, converse and consult together, communicate their decisions and resolutions . . . And hence their administration of justice and conduct of trials are consonant and uniform; whereby . . . confusion and contrariety are avoided . . .'

{Kerr Bl (4th edn, 1876) iii 354.}

In reaching its decision, the court must bear in mind the effect the decision will have as a precedent. The court's duty, as Neil MacCormick has said, is 'to treat like cases alike, and therefore to treat this case in a way in which it will be justifiable to treat future cases'. {*Legal Reasoning and Legal Theory* p 150. As to the doctrine of precedent see s 26 of this Code.}

Thus the court will try to reach a decision that will avoid unnecessary or pointless litigation in future cases. The law seeks always to avoid what Hale CJ called 'endless suits and vexations'. {Cited in *Hargrave's Law Tracts* (1787) p 226 (see *A-G of New Zealand v Ortiz* [1982] 3 All ER 432, at p 442).}

Again the court will try to avoid cutting across established legal categories and procedures.

Example 1 In *Imperial Tobacco Ltd v A-G* {[1980] 1 All ER 866.} the House of Lords was asked to say that pronouncing on whether certain facts constituted a criminal offence was within the court's statutory power to grant a declaration. *Held* It was not within the statutory power, since it would usurp the function of the criminal court. Details of how the existence of such a jurisdiction would cut across clear legal divisions were given by Viscount Dilhorne {P 875.}-

'Such a declaration is no bar to a criminal prosecution, no matter the authority of the court which grants it. Such a declaration in a case such as the present one, made after the commencement of the prosecution, and in effect a finding of guilt or innocence of the offence charged, cannot found a plea of autrefois acquit or autrefois convict, though it may well prejudice the criminal proceedings, the result of which will depend on the facts proved and may not depend solely on admissions made by the accused. If a civil court of great authority declares on admissions made by the accused that that no crime has been committed, one can foresee the use that might be made of that at the criminal trial.'

Example 2 In *Vestey v IRC* {[1979] 3 All ER 976. See Example 1} the House of Lords justified its departure from the previous decision of the House in *Congreve v IRC* {[1948] 1 All ER 948.} on the ground that it could now see what Lord Edmund-Davies called {P 1003.} the 'startling and unacceptable' consequences of that decision when applied to circumstances never contemplated by the House when reaching it.

Duplication of offences The courts strive to avoid multiplying the number of offences that relate to the same factual situations.

Example 3 In *Low v Blease* {[1975] Crim LR 513.} the appellant was convicted of burglary contrary to s 9(1)(b) of the Theft Act 1968 on the ground that he had entered a house as a trespasser and used the telephone. *Held* The conviction would be quashed. Although the facts might be brought within the wording of s 9(1)(b), it was clear that s 13 (abstracting of electricity) of the Act was designed for such cases.

Duplication of remedies   Where a recognised civil remedy exists for a certain kind of wrong, the court will be reluctant to find that a different remedy also exists. {See, e g, *R v Lands Tribunal, ex p City of London Corpn* [1982] 1 All ER 892, *per* Lord Denning MR at p 894 (no case can be stated under Lands Tribunal Act 1949 s 3(4) on an interlocutory matter because 'there is ample other machinery available for interlocutory matters').} In a matrimonial case Ormrod LJ said 'if we have two courts with jurisdiction in a matter like this, there is bound to be confusion and waste of money'. {*Horner v Horner* [1982] 2 All ER 495, at p 497.} On the registration of company charges, Lloyd J held that a charge was not registrable both under the Bills of Sale Acts and the Companies Acts. {*NV Slavenburg's Bank v Intercontinental Natural Resources Ltd* [1980] 1 All ER 955, at p 975.}

Example 4   Where it was argued that copyright under the Copyright Act 1956 s 2(1) existed in the trade name 'Exxon', the court rejected this on the ground that 'it cannot really have been intended to give further rights of property in words or names which would naturally and properly qualify for excellent protection as registered trade marks or as the subject of passing-off actions'. {*Exxon Corpn v Exxon Insurance Consultants International Ltd* [1981] 2 All ER 495, *per* Graham J at p 503.}

   It is correlative to this principle that, where two systems do not occupy all the required space, the court should be ready to fill the gap.

Example 5   In *West Mercia Constabulary v Wagener* {[1981] 3 All ER 378.} Forbes J held that since magistrates were not empowered to issue a search warrant to deal with the proceeds of an alleged crime held in a bank account, the High court should fill the gap by using the power to preserve the subject matter of a cause of action which is conferred by RSC Ord 29 r 2. Forbes J said {P 382.}-

> 'If of course it were open to the justices to issue search warrants to deal with bank accounts in that way, it would seem to me these proceedings would be misconceived, because the appropriate remedy would be to go to the justices for such a warrant. But while counsel accepts that a warrant could not be issued in those circumstances it seems to me ... that this court should be ready to fill that particular gap.'

Where contrary intention appears   As always, the principle against duplication of remedies is displaced if it appears that such duplication was intended. {See, e g, *Tandon v Trustees of Spurgeon's Homes* [1982] 1 All ER 1086, *per* Lord Roskill at p 1094 (Leasehold Reform Act 1967 Sch 3 shows there is an overlap between that Act and Part II of the Landlord and Tenant Act 1954).}

133. Principles: that law should not be subject to casual change

It is a principle of legal policy that law should be altered deliberately rather than casually, and that Parliament should not change either common law or statute law by a sidewind, but only by measured and considered provisions. In the case of common law, or Acts embodying common law, the principle is somewhat stronger than in other cases. It is also stronger the more fundamental the change is.

The court, when considering, in relation to the facts of the instant case, which of the opposing constructions of the enactment would give effect to the legislative intention, should presume that the legislator intended to observe this principle. The court should therefore strive to avoid adopting a construction which involves accepting that Parliament contravened the principle.

COMMENTARY

Legal policy The principle that law should not be subject to casual change is an aspect of legal policy. For the general nature of legal policy see s 126 of this Code. As to the opposing constructions see s 84 of this Code.

The presumption that Parliament does not intend to make a radical change in existing law by a sidewind arises from the nature of the legislative process. It is, or should be, a serious business. Changes in the basic law, since they seriously affect everybody, are to be carefully worked out. The more fundamental the change, the more thoroughgoing and considered should be the provisions by which it is implemented. Such is the proper way to conduct the legislative processes of a civilised state.

One aspect of this is that the settlement of private rights should not be held to determine public rights. As we have mentioned, private rights give way to public. {See pp 30–33 above.} The principle is also expressed in the maxim *jura publica ex privato promiscue decidi non debent* (public rights ought not to be indiscriminately decided out of a private transaction).

Where these requirements are not met, the suspicion is raised that perhaps, although the words of the enactment seem to point that way, Parliament did not really intend a radical change in existing law. Since it has not produced a text of appropriate design, any uncertainty in the wording should be resolved in favour of the less extreme meaning. As Lord Devlin said-

> 'It is a well-established principle of construction that a statute is not to be taken as effecting a fundamental alteration in the general law unless it uses words that point unmistakably to that conclusion.'

{*National Assistance Board v Wilkinson* [1952] 2 QB 648.}

Thus the House of Lords has refused to place on s 56 of the Law of Property Act 1925 a construction which would overturn the doctrine of privity of contract. {*Beswick v Beswick* [1968] AC 58.} Similarly the Court of Appeal preserved the equity doctrine of mortgages in construing s 86(2) of that Act. {*Grangeside Properties Ltd v Collingwoods Securities Ltd* [1964] 1 WLR 139. Cf *London Permanent Benefit Building Society Ltd v De Baer* [1968] 2 WLR 465.}

Example 1   The wording of s 4(1) of the Criminal Evidence Act 1898 is somewhat curious. It runs-

> 'The wife or husband of a person charged with an offence under any enactment mentioned in the Schedule to this Act may be called as a witness either for the prosecution or defence and without the consent of that person.'

It is odd to contemplate calling the wife of an accused person as a witness for the defence without his consent, but that was not the point which concerned the House of Lords in *Leach v R.* {[1912] AC 305.} The question for decision was whether s 4(1), while clearly making the wife a *competent* witness for the prosecution, also made her a *compellable* one. The House ruled that it did not. Lord Atkinson said {P 311.}-

> 'The principle that a wife is not to be compelled to give evidence against her husband is deep seated in the common law of this country, and I think if it is to be overturned it must be overturned by a clear, definite and positive enactment, not by an ambiguous one such as the section relied upon in this case.'

Example 2   Widgery J held in a case on the Foreign Judgments (Reciprocal Enforcement) Act 1933 that-

> ' . . . one ought not to assume that this Act has made a substantial alteration in the common law approach to the enforcement of foreign judgments unless that intention can be found in express terms or by necessary implication.'

{*Société Co-operative Sidmetal v Titan International Ltd* [1966] 1 QB 828, at p 847. Judges often speak as if an implication cannot be admitted unless it is *necessary*. It is submitted that *proper* is a more appropriate term. The point is discussed in s 109 of this Code.} He added: 'In my judgment the intention cannot be found, and ought not lightly to be assumed'.

Example 3   In *Re Seaford* {[1968] P 53.} the Court of Appeal refused to hold that the doctrine of relation back of a judicial decision to the beginning of the day on which it was pronounced 'was, as a result of the Supreme Court of Judicature Act 1873 made applicable, as it were by a side-wind, in matrimonial proceedings before the newly constituted High Court'. {P 68.}

Example 4   In *R v Owens* {(1859) 28 LJQB 316.} the court held that an Act allowing a mayor to stand as a councillor did not enable him to act as returning officer at an election for which he was a candidate since it would not be legitimate to infer from the language used that the legislature had intended to repeal by a side-wind the principle that a man shall not be a judge in his own cause. As to this principle see s 353 of the Code. See also *R v Wimbledon LB.* {(1882) 8 QBD 459 at p 464 (the right to demand a poll is a common law incident of all popular elections).}

Restriction of wide words   Analogous rulings have been given in cases where wide terms have been held to be impliedly narrowed by reference to established doctrine. {See, e g, *Phipps v Pears* [1965] 1 QB 76 (a reference to 'advantages' in a property Act must be regarded as limited to an advantage known to the law).}

Presumption against taking away functions An aspect of the presumption now under discussion is that the court will be reluctant, in the absence of clear words, to construe an Act as taking away or cutting down an existing function conferred by law. Thus the function of the Chancery Division in representing the Crown as *parens patriae* will not easily be treated as set aside. {*Re S (an infant)* [1965] 1 WLR 483; see also *A v Liverpool City Council* [1982] AC 363. As to the general treatment by the courts of enactments purporting to oust their jurisdiction see pp 747–750 below.} An enactment which empowered the Commissioners for the special purposes of the Income Tax Acts to collect tax at source in a particular way was held not to take away the existing function of the General Commissioners to collect it in a different way. {*Grosvenor Place Estates Ltd v Roberts (Inspector of Taxes)* [1961] Ch 148, at p 148.}

Special protection for the common law The early struggles of the common law to establish itself against the claims of the king led judges to attempt to shield it from statutory encroachment. These efforts produced the theory that an Act was presumed not to be intended to change the common law. Thus Coke said that 'it is a maxim in the common law that a statute made in the affirmative without any negative expressed or implied doth not take away the common law'. {2 Inst 200.} Similarly it was said by the court in *Arthur v Bokenham* {(1708) 11 Mod 148, at p 150.} that statutes 'are not presumed to make any alteration in the common law further or otherwise than the Act doth expressly declare'.

Example 5 Section 107 of the Public Health Act 1875 gave a local authority power to take proceedings for nuisance. In *Tottenham UDC v Williamson & Sons Ltd* [1896] 2 QB 353 the Court of Appeal held that this did not cover proceedings which a private person could not take and which were unknown to the law. Kay LJ said {p 355.} 'Had that been the intention of the Act, I should have expected to find the new remedy, hitherto uknown to the law, stated in explicit terms'. Parliament reversed this decision when replacing s 107 with s 100 of the Public Health Act 1936. {See *Stoke-on-Trent City Council v B & Q (Retail) Ltd* [1984] 2 All ER 332, per Lord Templeman at pp 338–340.}

The presumption is weaker in the case of modern Acts. The common law is regarded by present-day draftsmen as not significantly different to the body of surrounding statute law. Under the conditions of today, *lex scripta* and *lex non scripta* are equally law. Neither is perhaps deserving of greater respect than the other, though *lex scripta* has overriding effect. {See s 32 of this Code.}

The truth of this can be tested quite simply. Suppose a question arose as to whether an Act impliedly overruled some aspect of the law of criminal conspiracy. The question would be decided in exactly the same way whether the Act was passed before or after the partial codification of that offence by the Criminal Law Act 1977. The enormous output of legislation in the past two hundred years has meant that whole areas previously regulated by the common law are now the province of statute law, whether enacted by way of codification, development or replacement of common law rules.

There is thus little difference in *quality* between common law and enacted law. To suggest otherwise brings one within the range of Lord Radcliffe's condemnation of 'mystical' methods of discovering the law. {*Galloway v Galloway* [1956] AC 299, at p 320.}

All that can legitimately be said is that *some* common law rules have deeper roots in our law than *some* statutory rules. Judges still pay respect to 'our lady the common law'. Thus we continue to find dicta like that of Lord Reid in *Black-Clawson International Ltd v Papierwerke Waldhof-Aschaffenburg AG* {[1975] 1 All ER 810, at p 815.} when he said that Parliament 'can be presumed not to have altered the common law farther than was necessary'. It is submitted that the better view is that earlier expressed by Lord Wright when he said that the principle that an Act of Parliament should be construed so as not to change the common law more than seemed unavoidable is now discredited. {(1945-7) 9 CLJ 2, at p 3.}

Effect of statute on common law rules   Where Parliament takes a particular view of a common law rule, this may influence the court in determining the (purely common-law) content of the rule. Thus in *R v D* {[1984] 1 All ER 574.} the Court of Appeal, in holding that the kidnapping of a child of tender years had never been an offence at common law, was influenced by the fact that Parliament had taken that view when passing an Act relating to child stealing in 1814. {54 Geo 3 c 101. The decision was reversed by the House of Lords: [1984] 2 All ER 449.}

This does not mean that the common law can be 'developed' to fill gaps in a statute which cannot be filled by legitimate implication or delegated legislative power.

Example 6   In *Malone v Commissioner of Police of the Metropolis* {[1979] 1 All ER 256, at p 270.} Roskill LJ described the proposition that the common law should be developed and extended by the court to permit retention of property seized by police under an enactment which did not justify such retention as 'an impossible argument'. Stephenson LJ said {P 266.}: 'Until I listened to this argument, I had never heard that the statute book was a source of the common law. The argument has nothing to commend it but its audacity'. {As to the effect of legislation in developing legal policy see however s 110 of this Code. See also Examples 180.2 and 334.1.}

134. Principles: that municipal law should conform to public international law

It is a principle of legal policy that the municipal law should conform to public international law. The court, when considering, in relation to the facts of the instant case, which of the opposing constructions of the enactment would give effect to the legislative intention, should presume that the legislator intended to observe this principle.

COMMENTARY

Legal policy   The principle that municipal or national law should conform to the principles of public international law is an aspect of legal policy. For the general nature of legal policy see s 126 of this Code. As to the opposing constructions see s 84 of this Code.

Public international law is what used to be called the law of nations, or *jus gentium*. {See Brownlie *Principles of Public International Law* (3rd edn, 1979).}

134. Principles: municipal law to conform to public international law

More strictly the *jus gentium*, originally distinguished from the *jus civile* or ancient law of Rome, was the body of legal rules found in all civilised states. {*Vocaturque jus gentium, quasi quo jure omnes gentes utuntur* (Just. Inst.).} As Maine put it, basing himself on Justinian-

> 'All nations, who are ruled by laws and customs, are governed partly by their own particular laws, and partly by those laws which are common to all mankind. The law which a people enacts is called the Civil Law of that people, but that which natural reason appoints for all mankind is called the Law of Nations, because all nations use it.'

{H S Maine *Ancient Law* pp 37-8.}

This overlooks what should be a central feature, namely that, when their thinking is not distorted by religious or other dogma, human beings, because of their common humanity, tend to arrive at similar social or municipal laws. Neverthless our courts do not assume that nations agree on the content of any particular rule. {*Re Queensland Mercantile and Agency Ltd* [1892] 1 Ch 219, *per* Lindley LJ at p 226.}

Public international law is not generally part of the municipal legal system, and so is not subject to the implied importation of legal rules dealt with in s 144 and Part XXI of this Code. It is for this reason that a United Kingdom court will not make a declaration as to the content of a rule of public international law or the effect of a treaty. {*Republic of Italy v Hambros Bank Ltd* [1950] Ch 314, at p 329; *Malone v Commr of Police of the Metropolis (No 2)* [1979] 2 All ER 620, at pp 627-8.}

Nor, where Parliament has refrained from legislating so as to give effect to a treaty, will the court find it easy 'to lay down new rules of common law or equity that will carry out the Crown's treaty obligations, or . . . discover for the first time that such rules have always existed'. {*Malone v Commr of Police of the Metropolis (No 2)* [1979] 2 All ER 620, *per* Megarry V-C at p 648.}

Again, where the words of an enactment have a wider application than the provisions of a relevant treaty, the treaty will not be held to cut down their ordinary meaning. {*The Norwhale* [1975] QB 589.}

However, a rule of public international law which is incorporated by a decision of a competent court then becomes part of the municipal law. {*Thai-Europe Tapioca Service Ltd v Govt of Pakistan* [1975] 1 WLR 1485, *per* Scarman LJ at p 1495.} Again, under the principle known as *adoption*, a rule of international law may be incorporated into municipal law by custom or statute. In all such cases the implied importation dealt with in s 144 of this Code would apply.

It is an important principle of public policy to respect the comity of nations, and obey treaties which are binding under public international law. Thus Diplock LJ said-

> ' . . . there is a prima facie presumption that Parliament does not intend to act in breach of [public] international law, including therein specific treaty obligations; and if one of the meanings that can reasonably be attributed to the legislation is consonant with the treaty obligations and another or others are not, the meaning which is so consonant is to be preferred.'

{*Salomon v Commrs of Customs and Excise* [1967] 2 QB 116, at p 143 (cf *Garland v British Rail Engineering Ltd* [1982] 2 All ER 1163, *per* Lord Diplock at p 415).}

Like so many judicial dicta on statutory interpretation, this overlooks the likelihood that there will be more than one factor bearing on a disputed interpretation. {As to the weighing of two or more conflicting interpretative factors by the court see Part VII of this Code.}

In *Post Office v Estuary Radio Ltd* {[1968] 2 QB 740, at p 757.}, which concerned an order made under the prerogative, Diplock LJ attributed to the Crown also this intention to respect treaty obligations. The courts in fact treat the need to observe treaties as a general matter of legal policy. {*A-G v British Broadcasting Corporation* [1980] 3 WLR 109, *per* Lord Scarman at p 130. As to legal policy see s 126 of this Code.}

In *Corocraft Ltd v Pan American Airways Inc* {[1968] 3 WLR 1273, at p 1281.}, a case on the Warsaw convention, Lord Denning MR put the point even more strongly-

> 'The Warsaw Convention is an international convention which is binding in international law on all the countries who have ratified it: and it is the duty of these courts to construe our legislation so as to be in conformity with international law and not in conflict with it.'

See also Example 324.1.

However it is clear that the correct principle is as stated by Diplock LJ. The prime duty of the courts is to carry out the intention of Parliament. Where Parliament makes it plain that it intends to infringe an international obligation, the court must comply.

Example 1 In *Collco Dealings Ltd v IRC* {[1962] AC 1.} the House of Lords was called on to construe s 4(2) of the Finance (No 2) Act 1955, which dealt with the tax-avoidance device known as dividend stripping. Section 4(2) was inconsistent with double taxation agreements made between the British and Irish governments, but the House of Lords held that s 4(2) must prevail. Viscount Simonds said {P 19.}-

> 'It is said that the plain words of the statute are to be disregarded . . . in order to observe the comity of nations and the established rules of international law. I am not sure on which of these high-sounding phrases the appellant company chiefly relies. But I would answer that neither comity nor rule of international law can be invoked to prevent a sovereign state from taking what steps it thinks fit to protect its own revenue laws from gross abuse, or to save its own citizens from unjust discrimination in favour of foreigners. To demand that the plain words of the statute should be disregarded in order to do that very thing is an extravagance to which this House will not, I hope, give ear.'

{See also *Niboyet v Noboyet* (1878) 4 PD 1; *Mortensen v Peters* (1906) 8 F (J) 93.}

This again is over-stated. The concepts of comity and public international law scarcely deserve the dismissive epithet 'high-sounding'; while all that need be said about what a 'sovereign state' such as Britain can do is that its legislature has unlimited and overriding power to lay down the municipal law. {See s 32 of this Code.}

European Convention on Human Rights The European Convention on Human Rights entered into force on 3 September 1953. {Its full name is the European

Convention for the Protection of Human Rights and Fundamental Freedoms. It is set out in Cmnd 8969.} To date it has been ratified by 21 nations, including the United Kingdom. For these it constitutes a treaty imposing the usual obligations and rights under a treaty in public international law. The machinery for enforcement of these consists of the European Commission of Human Rights and the European Court of Human Rights, both of which operate at Strasbourg. The United Kingdom has accepted the right of individual petition to the Commission, but has not made the Convention part of its municipal law.

It follows that the Convention does not directly govern the exercise of powers conferred by or under an Act. {*R v Secretary of State for the Home Department, ex p Fernandes* (1980) *The Times* 21 November; *R v Secretary of State for the Home Department, ex p Kirkwood* [1984] 2 All ER 390.} However it is presumed that Parliament, when it passes an Act, intends it to be construed in conformity with the Convention, unless the contrary intention appears. In *Taylor v Co-operative Retail Services Ltd* {(1982) *The Times* 13 July.} Fox LJ said in relation to closed shop legislation that the Convention is not a reliable guide to the intention of Parliament. Nevertheless the Convention is a treaty by which the United Kingdom is bound. It is, by virtue of the principle now under discussion, as reliable a guide to legislative intention as any other treaty.

Furthermore many of the principles embedded in the Convention correspond to, and may indeed be derived from, those of our own legal policy. {As to principles of legal policy see s 126 of this Code.} This appears from the passage in the preamble recording that the states parties agreed upon the Convention-

> 'Reaffirming their profound belief in those Fundamental Freedoms which are the foundation of justice and peace and are best maintained on the one hand by an effective political democracy and on the other by a common understanding and observance of the Human Rights upon which they depend; [and]
>   Being resolved, as the Governments of European countries which are like-minded and have a common heritage of political traditions, ideals, freedom and the rule of law . . .'

{Professor Fawcett, a former President of the European Commission of Human Rights, points out that the Constitution adopted by the USSR in 1977, while containing a Bill of Rights, gives equal prominence to what might be called Human Duties: 'Human Rights: Our Country in Europe' (Child & Co lecture 1983) p 3.}

The individual human rights specified in the European Convention are mentioned in their appropriate places in Part XIII of this Code.

Judicial notice Judicial notice is taken of rules and principles of public international law, even when not embodied in municipal law. {*Re Queensland Mercantile and Agency Ltd* [1892] 1 Ch 219, *per* Lindley LJ at p 226.} This also applies to treaties made by the British Crown. As Scarman LJ said in *Pan-American World Airways Inc v Department of Trade* {[1976] 1 Lloyd's Rep 257, at p 261 (emphasis added).}-

> 'If statutory words have to be construed or a legal principle formulated in an area of the law where Her Majesty has accepted

international obligations, our courts - *who, of course, take notice of the acts of Her Majesty done in the exercise of her sovereign power* - will have regard to the convention as part of the full content or background of the law. Such a convention, especially a multilateral one, should then be considered by the Courts even though no statute expressly or impliedly incorporates it into our law.'

{As to the doctrine of judicial notice generally see s 21 of this Code. The Courts will accept a Minister's certificate as to acts of sovereign power.}

Citation of treaties   The existence of the presumption dealt with in this section of the Code means that the court is obliged to consider any relevant rule of public international law, and permit the citation of any relevant treaty. For this reason it seems that Lord Parker CJ was mistaken when in *Urey v Lummis* {[1962] 1 WLR 826, at p 832.} he said it was not for the court to consider whether the United Kingdom had implemented the international Agreement regarding the Status of Forces of Parties to the North Atlantic Treaty.

Uniform statutes   An Act passed to give effect to an international agreement will be construed in the light of meanings attached to the agreement in other contracting states, so as to promote uniformity. {*Stag Line Ltd v Foscolo Mango & Co Ltd* [1932] AC 328, at p 350; *Riverstone Meat Co v Lancashire Shipping Co* [1961] AC 807, at p 869; *Compania Colombiana de Seguros v Pacific Steam Navigation Co Ltd* [1965] 1 QB 101; *Salomon v Commrs of Customs and Excise* [1967] 2 QB 116; *Leesh River Tea Co Ltd v British India Steam Navigation Co Ltd* [1967] 2 QB 250; *Post Office v Estuary Radio Ltd* [1967] 1 WLR 1396.} As Scott LJ said of an agreement designed to put an end to differing practices: 'the *maintenance* of uniformity in the interpretation of a rule after its international adoption is just as important as the initial removal of divergence'. {*The Eurymedon* [1938] P 41, at p 46 (emphasis added). See further F A Mann 'The Interpretation of Uniform Statutes' (1946) 62 LQR 278; 'Uniform Statutes in English Law' (1983) 99 LQR 376.} The treaty need not be referred to in the Act for the court to have regard to it. {*Salomon v Commrs of Customs and Excise* [1967] 2 QB 116.}

Interpretation of enactment by reference to terms of treaty   As to the interpretation of an enactment by reference to the terms of a relevant treaty see s 242 of this Code.

Vienna Convention   For the provisions relating to interpretation of treaties set out in the Vienna Convention on the Law of Treaties {Treaty Series No 58 (1980); Cmnd 7964.} see pp 539–541 below.}

Diplomatic privilege   As to diplomatic privilege see pp 494–495 below.

Extra-territorial extent and application of Acts   For presumptions based on rules of public international law regarding the territorial extent of Acts, and their application to foreigners, see Part IX of this Code.

PRESUMPTIONS AS TO LEGISLATIVE INTENTION

135. Presumptions: nature of presumptions as to legislative intention

A presumption affords guidance as to the legislator's prima facie intention regarding the working of the enactment.

COMMENTARY

As explained in s 98 of this code, legislative intention is the paramount criterion in statutory interpretation.

The common law has laid down various presumptions about what Parliament is likely to intend regarding the operation of an Act, for example that it is not to be evaded. The presumptions are not distinct from rules and principles of law, but are to a large extent drawn from them. At the same time they recognise the essential nature of legislation, and look in particular to its effective working.

Sections 136 to 146 of the Code set out the most important of these presumptions.

136. Presumptions: that text to be primary indication of intention

In construing an enactment, the text of the enactment, in its setting within the Act or instrument containing it, is to be regarded as the pre-eminent indication of the legislator's intention.

COMMENTARY

British courts, towards the end of the twentieth century, regard the text of Acts of the United Kingdom Parliament with great respect. When called upon to construe an Act, the court regards its primary duty as being to look at the text and say what, in itself, it means.

> 'The safer and more correct course of dealing with a question of construction is to take the words themselves and arrive if possible at their meaning without, in the first instance, reference to cases.'

{*Per* Lord Warrington of Clyffe in *Barrell v Fordree* [1932] AC 676, at p 682.}

The text is the starting point, and the centre of the interpreter's attention from then on. It is the text, after all, that is being interpreted.

The full working out of the principle of the pre-eminence of the text is explained in the provisions of this Code dealing with linguistic canons of construction. {See ss 147 to 152 and Parts XX to XXII.} One consequence of the principle is the respect paid to the literal meaning. {See s 137 of the Code.}

137. Presumptions: that enactment is to be given literal meaning

Prima facie, the meaning of an enactment which was intended by the legislator (in other words its legal meaning) is taken to be that which corresponds to the literal meaning (as defined in s 91 of this Code).

COMMENTARY

As explained in s 91 of this Code, the term 'literal meaning' corresponds to the grammatical meaning where this is straightforward. If however the grammatical meaning, when applied to the facts of the instant case, is ambiguous then any of the possible grammatical meanings may be described as the literal meaning. If the grammatical meaning is semantically obscure, then the grammatical meaning likely to have been intended (or any one of them in the case of ambiguity) is taken as the literal meaning.

The point here is that the literal meaning is one arrived at from the wording of the enactment alone, without consideration of other interpretative criteria. When account is taken of such other criteria (for the purpose of arriving at the *legal meaning* of the enactment), it may be found necessary to depart from the literal meaning and adopt a strained construction. {As to strained construction see ss 92 to 97 of this Code.} The initial presumption is however in favour of the literal meaning.

In other words, as this section of the Code says, the literal meaning of an enactment is prima facie to be treated as the legal meaning. There is a presumption in its favour, since Parliament is taken to mean what it says. The presumption is of very long standing, and is embodied in early maxims of the law.

Broom cites the maxim *Quoties in verbis nulla est ambiguitas, ibi nulla expositio contra verba non fienda est* (where nothing in the words is ambiguous, no exposition of them shall be made which is opposed to the words). {*Legal Maxims* (1st edn, 1845) Pp 266ff.} After discussing the application of this to contracts and other written instruments, Broom continues-

> 'It may scarcely be necessary to observe, that the maxim under consideration applies equally to the interpretation of an act of Parliament, the general rule being, that *a verbis legis non est recedendum.* {One must not depart from the words of a statute. See 5 Co Rep 119.} A court of law will not make any interpretation contrary to the express letter of a statute; for nothing can so well explain the meaning of the makers of the act as their own direct words, since *index animi sermo* {Language conveys the intention of the mind. See 5 Co Rep 118b.}, and *maledicta expositio quae corrumpit textum* {An exposition which corrupts the text is bad. See 4 Co Rep 35; *Sussex Peerage Case* (1844) 11 Cl & F 143.}, it would be dangerous to give scope for making a construction in any case against the express words, *where the meaning of the makers is not opposed to them, and when no inconvenience will follow from a literal interpretation.*'

{Ibid, p 268 (emphasis added). The final italicised words give the game away, and let in strained construction.}

This presumption in favour of literal interpretation was thus stated by a nineteenth-century Lord Chancellor, Lord Selborne -

> '. . . there is always some presumption in favour of the more simple and literal interpretation of the words of the statute . . .'

{*Caledonian Rly Co v North British Rly Co* (1881) 6 App Cas 114, at p 121.}

Judges of the present day show no inclination to abandon the presumption, despite the growing popularity of 'purposive' construction. {As to purposive construction see s 139 and Part XV of this Code.} As Lord Parker CJ said: 'the intention of Parliament must be deduced from the language used'. {*Capper v Baldwin* [1965] 2 QB 53, at p 61. As to this deductive process see s 148 and Part XX of the Code.}

Precision drafting One cause of the adherence of modern judges to the principle of literal construction is the increasing precision with which Acts are drafted. {See s 76 of this Code.}

When called upon to construe a written statement of a kind known to be expressed (as a rule) loosely and imprecisely, the interpreter approaches the task in a suitable frame of mind. Contradictions meet with no surprise. Incomplete statements, leaving something to the imagination of the reader, are expected. Interpreters of such imprecise compositions are of necessity very ready to do what Lord Denning once said the courts should always do with Acts, namely 'fill up the gaps'. {Cf the remarks of the same judge in *Seaford Court Estates Ltd v Asher* [1949] 2 KB 481, at p 499.}

Modern Acts are not drafted in this loose way however. While the draftsman deliberately leaves much to be implied, and procures the delegation by Parliament of much legislative power to the courts, he aims to achieve consistency of language and conceptual completeness. The product, as the courts recognise, must be interpreted accordingly.

One consequence is the need for close and careful scrutiny of the *minutiae* of the draftsman's language. Sir Carleton Allen pointed out that it is not to be supposed that literal interpretation, however pedantic it may seem at times, is a mere disputation of Schoolmen. {*Law in the Making* (4th edn, 1946) p 421. Cf the reference by Willis J to giving the words of an enactment 'the analytical attention of a medieval schoolman' (cited by Forbes J in *R v Rochdale Metropolitan Borough Council* [1982] 3 All ER 761 at p 767.} Allen went on to say-

> 'There is, no doubt, something slightly comic in the spectacle of a Bench of Judges anxiously dissecting a word or expression which the Plain Man thinks - though he is frequently mistaken - has a meaning too obvious for argument . . . But if rules of law are so framed that rights, liberties, and even lives may depend on vocables, then it is no mere intellectual exercise, but a positive duty - and one from which he would greatly prefer to be relieved - for the Judge to give the most precise value to *minutiae* . . . {Cf the remark by Lord Evershed MR: 'The judicial task of interpreting Acts is uncreative and barren, if intellectually exacting' (42 *Proceedings of the British Academy* (1956) 247.} It is even possible, in some circumstances, that the most ingenious literal interpretation of the law may be the most effective way of fulfilling its spirit. It was in such manner that Portia thwarted Shylock!'

Hairsplitting It should be noticed in relation to the *minutiae* that it is no use an interpreter trying to be more refined in his literal interpretation than the draftsman was in his drafting. Where, as happens particularly (though not exclusively) with older Acts, the draftsman has been generally careless or imprecise in his use of words, the courts recognise that nice distinctions cannot be based on differences or refinements of terminology. {See, e g, *Kammins Ballroom Co Ltd v Zenith Investments (Torquay) Ltd* [1971] AC 850, *per* Lord Diplock at p 882.} Attempts by counsel to go farther in this respect than the language justifies are apt to be condemned by the court as 'splitting hairs'. {See *R v Gleaves* (1977) (unreported), cited in *R v Reilly* [1982] 3 All ER 27, at pp 33 and 34.}

Example 1   Section 4(3) of the Criminal Law Act 1977 applied s 281(4) of the Customs and Excise Act 1952 to conspiracies to commit certain offences. Section 281(4) made provision for the case 'where any person has been detained for any offence for which he *is* liable to be detained under [certain Acts]'. {Emphasis added.} In *R v Whitehead* {[1982] 3 All ER 96, at p 103.} Donaldson LJ said that s 281(4) 'cannot be applied literally'. Parliament, he said, must have intended that the word 'is' should be read as 'would be'.

Weight to be attached to literal meaning   The literal meaning, at least of a modern Act, is to be treated as pre-eminent when construing the enactments contained in the Act. In general, the weight to be attached to the literal meaning is far greater than applies to any other interpretative criterion. The literal meaning may occasionally be overborne by other factors, but they must be powerful indeed to achieve this.

With older Acts, the weight attached to the literal meaning tends to be less. As Lord Bridge said of an Act of 1847, it is 'legitimate to take account, when construing old statutes, of the prevailing style and standards of draftsmanship'. {*Wills v Bowley* [1982] 2 All ER 654, at p 680.}

Even with older Acts, the judge is usually happier when sticking to what Parliament has said. Jessel MR expressed this feeling-

> 'Now in construing instruments, I have always followed the rule laid down by the House of Lords in *Grey v Pearson* {(1857) 6 HL Cas 61.} which is to construe the instrument according to the literal import, unless there is something in the subject or context which shows that that cannot be the meaning of the words.'

{*Lowther v Bentinck* (1874) LR 19 Eq 166, at p 169.}

Example 2   Section 4 of the Customs and Inland Revenue Act 1888 imposed an excise duty of two guineas on mechanically-propelled carriages with four wheels. In *Hollands v Williamson* {[1920] 1 KB 716.} the respondent owned a tricycle to which he had fitted a detachable 'auto-wheel' equipped with a small petrol engine. The road wheel of the device could be raised or lowered by hand. When lowered it touched the road surface and propelled the vehicle. The court held that the excise duty of two guineas was payable. The Earl of Reading CJ said-

> 'It is impossible to say that the tricycle did not become a carriage within the definition . . . when it had a fourth wheel attached to it and was propelled by mechanical power. The result of our decision is that under s 86 of the Finance (1909-10) Act 1910, if this tricycle is

propelled by mechanical power it also becomes a motor car. It seems perfectly absurd to call it a motor car, but we are bound by the terms of the Act . . . This decision may create difficulties, because there are statutory requirements with regard to motor cars which were never intended to apply to carriages of this description.' {P 717.}

Here we see that although to apply the literal meaning produced an 'absurd' result, this was not so extreme as to outweigh the pre-eminence of that meaning. Sometimes however so-called 'absurdity' may be so great as to induce the court to depart from the literal meaning. {See s 141 and Part XVI of this Code.}

Speculative departures   It is clear that mere speculation will not justify departure from the literal meaning. There must be real doubt before the question will even be entertained by the court. {As to 'real doubt' see s 3 of this Code.} Lord Haldane LC expressed the principle in *Lumsden v IRC* {[1914] AC 877, at p 892.}-

'But a mere conjecture that Parliament entertained a purpose which, however natural, has not been embodied in the words it has used, if they be literally interpreted, is no sufficient reason for departing from the literal construction.'

The so-called 'literal rule'   It will be seen from the above that there is no literal *rule* of interpretation in the sense that the literal meaning must invariably be followed. {See pp 214–216 above.} Determining when it is to be departed from is perhaps the interpreter's most difficult task.

Primacy of text   While this section of the Code states the primacy of literal construction, it is explained elsewhere that the prime *text* is that of the enactment in its immediate setting. It is this that is the unit of enquiry. {See s 72 of this Code. As to the pre-eminence of the text see s 136.}

Predictable construction   As to the relation of the need for predictability to literal construction see s 130 of this Code.

138. Presumptions: that court to apply remedy provided for the 'mischief'

Parliament intends that an enactment shall remedy a particular mischief. It is presumed therefore that Parliament intends the court, in construing the enactment, to endeavour to apply the remedy provided by it in such a way as to suppress that mischief.

COMMENTARY

Except in the case of purely declaratory provisions, the only reason for passing an Act is to change the existing law. So the reason for an Act's passing must lie in some defect in the existing law. If the existing law were not defective, Parliament would not need or want to change it. That defect is the 'mischief' to which the Act is directed. {See Example 10.1.}

This matter is one of some complexity. It is therefore dealt with in a separate Part of this Code, namely Part XIV.

Related to the concept of the mischief is the technique now known as purposive construction. This is dealt with in s 139 and Part XV.

139. Presumptions: that enactment to be given a purposive construction

A construction which promotes the remedy Parliament has provided to cure a particular mischief is now known as a purposive construction.

COMMENTARY

As explained in s 138 of this Code, the purpose or object of Parliament in passing an Act is to provide an appropriate remedy to serve as a cure for the mischief with which the Act deals. The legislative purpose of a particular enactment contained in the Act is to be arrived at accordingly.

This matter is one of some complexity. It is therefore dealt with in a separate Part of this Code, namely Part XV.

140. Presumptions: that regard to be had to consequences of a construction

It is presumed to be the legislator's intention that the court, when considering, in relation to the facts of the instant case, which of the opposing constructions of the enactment corresponds to its legal meaning, should assess the likely consequences of adopting each construction, both to the parties in the case and (where similar facts arise in future cases) for the law generally. If on balance the consequences of a particular construction are more likely to be *adverse* than *beneficent* this is a factor telling against that construction.

COMMENTARY

Consequential construction often calls for a strained interpretation. As a prelude to the following, reference may be made to the commentary on s 93 of the Code, which explains the need for strained interpretation in certain cases. This gives many examples of consequential construction, including the extreme case of the 'universal repealer'. {See pp 213ff. The universal repealer is described in Example 93.1. See also Examples 10.1, 127.2, 128.3 and 132.2.}

Consequential construction is of modern adoption. The earlier attitude of the judges was expressed by Lord Abinger CB in *A-G v Lockwood* {(1842) 9 M & W 378, at p 395.}-

> '... I cannot enter into a speculation of what might have been in the contemplation of the legislature, because they have not stated what they contemplated ... The Act of Parliament [in question] practically has had, I believe, a very pernicious effect - an effect not at all contemplated - but we cannot construe the Act by that result.'

The modern attitude is indicated by a dictum of Mustill J in *R v Committee of Lloyd's, ex p Moran* {(1983) *The Times* 24 June.}-

'. . . a statute or contract cannot be interpreted according to its literal meaning without testing that meaning against the practical outcome of giving effect to it . . .'

Some judges have gone so far as to suggest that the correct course is to *start* by considering which result would be desirable, and then see if the law permits it. Thus Lord Radcliffe said in *ICI Ltd v Shatwell* {[1965] AC 656, at p 675.}-

'My Lords, it sometimes helps to assess the merits of a decision, if one *starts by noticing its results* and only after doing that allots to it the legal principles upon which it is said to depend.' {Emphasis added.}

Lord Radcliffe went on say that in the instant case he had begun by considering the consequences of the apparent meaning of the enactment, and found these disquieting. He went on: 'I start then with the assumption that something must have gone wrong in the application of legal principles that produce such a result'. {[1965] AC 656, at p 676.}

Prima facie, as we have seen {S 120.}, the ordinary meaning of the words is to be followed. If the consequences are adverse, this presumption may be displaced. As Donaldson MR put it-

'Our task, as I see it, is to construe [the Act], and in so doing the prima facie rule is that words have their ordinary meaning. But that is subject to the qualification that if, giving words their ordinary meaning, we are faced with extraordinary results which cannot have been intended by Parliament, we then have to move on to a second stage in which we re-examine the words . . .'

{*Re British Concrete Pipe Association* [1983] 1 All ER 203, at p 205.}

The so-called 'golden rule'   The 'prima facie rule' referred to in the above dictum of Donaldson MR was called by Viscount Simon the 'golden rule'. {*Nokes v Doncaster Amalgamated Collieries* [1940] AC 1014, at p 1022.} Viscount Simon said: 'The golden rule is that the words of a statute must prima facie be given their ordinary meaning'. However the term golden rule is more usually applied to the precept Lord Blackburn, in *River Wear Commissioners v Adamson* {(1877) 2 App Cas 743, at p 764.}, described as 'what Lord Wensleydale used to call the golden rule'. Lord Blackburn went on to express this so-called rule as follows-

'. . . that we are to take the whole statute together, and construe it all together giving the words their ordinary signification, unless when so applied *they produce an inconsistency, or an absurdity or inconvenience* so great as to convince the Court that the intention could not have been to use them in their ordinary signification . . .'

{Emphasis added. For other possible meanings of the term 'golden rule' see Bennion *Statute Law* (2nd edn, 1983) pp 90-1. See also p 000 above.}

This was an attempt by Lord Blackburn to provide in a few words an all-embracing single prescription for the task of statutory interpretation. As such it was, like all such judicial attempts, over-ambitious and doomed to failure. The subject is not capable of being thus condensed. To try to do it is to invite confusion, as has indeed followed. {See R Cross *Statutory Interpretation* p v.}

The reference to 'an absurdity or inconvenience' in Lord Blackburn's dictum describes, if inadequately, consequential construction and the presumption dealt with in the next section of this Code. In particular it points to what the present section calls 'adverse' consequences of a particular construction. {The reference to 'inconsistency' points to repugnance between texts. As to this see p 220 above.}

Similar words were used in another formulation of the so-called 'golden rule', this time by Bramwell B-

> 'The golden rule of construction is that words are to be construed according to their natural meaning, unless such a construction would either render them senseless or would be opposed to the general scope and intent of the instrument, or unless there be some very cogent reason of convenience in favour of a different interpretation.'

{*Fowell v Tranter* (1864) 3 H & C 458, at p 461.}

Opposing constructions As explained above {S 84.}, the court is usually concerned to decide between opposing constructions of the enactment which are advanced by the parties in relation to the facts of the instant case. Consequential construction requires the consequences of adopting each of the constructions to be assessed. The position was thus described by Romer LJ in *Fry v IRC* {[1959] Ch 86, at p 105.}-

> 'It seems to us that on the language of [the section] neither the view of [the defendant] nor that of the plaintiff can be said to be obviously wrong. The court, then, when faced with two possible constructions of legislative language, is entitled to look at the *results* of adopting each of the alternatives respectively in its quest for the true intention of Parliament.'

{Emphasis added.}

Adverse and beneficent consequences The consequences of a particular construction may be regarded as 'adverse' if they are such that in the light of the interpretative criteria the court views them with disquiet. Any other consequences (whether merely neutral or positively advantageous) may be called 'beneficent'. For this purpose a consequence clearly intended by Parliament is to be treated as beneficent even though the judge personally dislikes it. The court is not permitted to canvass the merits of what Parliament has undoubtedly willed. {See p 217 above.}

It is only where there is 'real doubt' as to Parliament's true intention regarding the meaning of the enactment in relation to the facts of the instant case that the adverse-beneficent test comes into play, though the likelihood of a strongly adverse consequence may in itself raise doubt. {As to real doubt see s 3 of this Code.} The test covers a very wide field. For example a result is 'adverse' if it frustrates the purpose of the Act, or works injustice, or is contrary to public policy, or is productive of inconvenience or hardship, and so on. Parliament is presumed not to intend such consequences.

Consequences for the parties and the law In judging consequences it is important to distinguish consequences to the parties in the instant case and consequences for the law generally. It will generally be a straightforward matter to determine the effect on the court's final order of a finding in favour of one possible construction rather than the other. But the court must also bear in mind that under the doctrine of precedent its decision may be of binding, or at least persuasive, authority for the future. {See Example 122.3. As to the doctrine of precedent in relation to statutes see s 26 of this Code.}

Here the constraints on the court are similar to those arising in a common law case. Before reaching any decision on a new point of principle, whether in common law or statute, the court must carefully weigh its future effect on the law. Sometimes counsel opposing a particular finding paints in grim contours the likely consequence. This is known as the 'floodgates' argument. Counsel says, in effect, that if the court adopts his opponent's view of the legal rule in question this will open the floodgates to a spate of unmeritorious future claims. Lord Edmund-Davies once dealt with this type of argument in robust terms-

'My Lords, the experiences of a long life in the law have made me very familiar with this 'floodgates' argument. I do not, of course, suggest that it can invariably be dismissed as lacking cogency; on the contrary, it has to be weighed carefully, but I have often seen it disproved by later events.'

{*McLoughlin v O'Brian* [1982] 2 All ER 298, at p 307.}

The court may be less unwilling to adopt an 'adverse' construction where some functionary is interposed whose discretion may be so exercised as to reduce the practical ill-effects.

Example 1 Section 107(1)(a) of the Income Tax Act 1918 provided for a defaulting taxpayer to be subject to a penalty fixed by the General Commissioners. This was to be 'not exceeding £20 and treble the tax which he ought to be charged under this Act'. In *IRC v Hinchy* {[1960] AC 748.}, a case on the Income Tax Act 1952 (a consolidation Act re-enacting the 1918 Act as amended) Lord Reid said {P 769.}-

'I find it impossible to hold that the words "not exceeding £20 and treble the tax which he ought to be charged under this Act" in s 107(1)(a) of the Act of 1918 meant anything other than treble the whole tax which he ought to be charged for the relevant year. The argument for the more limited meaning adopted by the Court of Appeal is based almost entirely on the extravagant consequences which flow from giving the words in the present Act [which omitted the phrase 'not exceeding'] their natural meaning. But that argument loses almost all its force when applied to the Act of 1918. Under that Act the General Commissioners, an independent body, had full discretion to modify the penalty, and all that could then be said was that, owing to the increase in the rates of tax, the maximum penalty had become so high as to be extravagant in the great majority of cases.'

IRC v Hinchy {[1960] AC 748.} also illustrates the fact that consequential construction can rarely change the interpretation of an enactment if the literal meaning is incontrovertibly clear. Lord Reid found it 'difficult to believe that Parliament ever really intended' the consequences of the literal meaning (namely that the full penalty was exigible without remission in all cases). Nevertheless the wording of the enactment was crystal clear. Lord Reid said {P 767.}-

'But we can only take the intention of Parliament from the words which they have used in the Act, and therefore the question is whether these words are capable of a more limited construction. If not, then we must apply them as they stand, however unreasonable or unjust the consequences, and however strongly we may suspect that this was not the real intention of Parliament.'

{Cf the view of Cardozo J, a justice of the US Supreme Court: 'We do not pause to consider whether a statute differently conceived and worded would yield results more consonant with fairness and reason. We take the statute as we find it'. (*Anderson v Wilson* (1933) 289 US 20, at p 27.).}

Lord Reid's dictum goes wider than was necessary for the decision however, and must be read subject to a caveat. As the case of the 'universal repealer' {See Example 93.1.} shows, the consequences of a literal construction may in rare cases be so dire as virtually to compel the court to depart from it.

Consequences tending both ways   Since the consequences to be borne in mind are often of a wide variety it is not surprising that they may tend in both directions. Each of the opposing constructions may involve some adverse and some beneficent consequences. Lord Morris of Borth-y-Gest pointed this out in relation to anti-discrimination legislation-

'In one sense there results for some people a limitation on what could be called their freedom: they may no longer treat certain people, because of their colour or race, or ethnic or national origins, less favourably than they would treat others. But in the same cause of freedom, although differently viewed, Parliament has, in statutory terms now calling for consideration, proscribed discrimination (on the stated grounds) as being unlawful.'

{*Charter v Race Relations Board* [1973] AC 868, at p 889.}

This aspect calls for a nice balancing by the court of the relevant factors. Moreover they are to be weighed not in any narrow juristic sense, but from the viewpoint of the community at large. Our judges indeed need to be men and women of the world. {As to the weighing of interpretative factors see s 158 of this Code.}

Ambiguity and strained construction   As always when considering the interpretative criteria we find that the ultimate questions, in consequential construction as elsewhere, are related to the settling of ambiguity and the problem of strained construction.

Cardozo J said: 'Consequences cannot alter statutes, but may help to fix their meaning'. {*Re Rouss* (1917) 221 NY 81, at p 91.} Where the enactment is grammatically ambiguous {See ss 87 to 89 of this Code.} assessment of the consequences of each of the opposing constructions may certainly help to fix the meaning one way or the other. As Lord Reid said: 'It is always proper to construe ambiguous words in the light of the reasonableness of the consequences'. {*Gartside v IRC* [1968] AC 553, at p 612. See also *Fry v IRC* [1959] Ch 86, at p 105; *The R L Alston* (1882) 8 PD 5, at p 9; *Coutts & Co v IRC* [1953] AC 267, at p 281; *Brunton v New South Wales Commrs of Stamp Duties* [1913] AC 747, at p 759.}

Where the result of a literal construction is sufficiently 'adverse', the consequential construction principle may indicate a decision in favour of a strained construction. {As to strained construction see ss 92 to 97 of this Code.} To that extent the above dictum by Cardozo J may be considered wrong.

Example 2   Section 374 of the Merchant Shipping Act 1854 provided that a pilot's licence issued on any day should not continue in force beyond the following 31 January, but could be renewed on 31 January 'or any subsequent day'. If taken literally this required renewals of pilots' licences all to take place on one day of the year (31 January), since otherwise some pilots would necessarily be unlicensed for a period. In the High Court of Admiralty Dr Lushington applied a strained construction, whereby licensed pilots were enabled to obtain the renewal of their licences in good time before 31 January in each year. Dr Lushington said-

> 'Now, I am fain to confess, with regard to this 374th section, that any construction I put upon it, is subject to some difficulty and attended with inconvenience; and this being so, I look to the consequences of the different constructions upon that section proposed, and if very serious consequences to the beneficial and reasonable operation of the act necessarily follow from one construction, I apprehend that, unless the words imperatively require it, it is the duty of the Court to prefer such a construction that *res majis valeat, quam pereat*. It is stated in the argument, that unless the construction urged on the one hand of the Statute be adopted it will be next to impossible to have any licensed Pilot at all at certain periods of the year . . .'

{*Mann v Malcolmson (The Beta)* (1865) 3 Moo PCC NS 23.}

The reason for a strained construction in this case was that without it great commercial inconvenience would have been suffered by large numbers of seafarers, merchants and others. When faced with a substantial public evil of this sort, the court, as an organ of the state, is likely to feel itself obliged to surrender to the dictates of common sense and practical utility.

Beneficent consequence   There is a tendency to concentrate attention on adverse consequences, but it needs to be remembered that a court may be strongly influenced the other way. If a consequence is clearly desirable, the court will wish to give effect to it.

Example 3   Nationwide Building Society v Registry of Friendly Societies {[1983] 3 All ER 296.} concerned the question whether a scheme providing for the granting of index-linked loans by a building society contravened the requirement in s 1(1) of the Building Societies Act 1962 that a society is limited to making 'advances'. Holding that it did not, Peter Gibson J remarked that he would be loath to find that 'the very sensible proposals' made by the scheme were outside the section. {See Example 122.7.}

Strict and liberal construction   Where the application of an enactment yields an adverse result, the interpretative factors may on balance indicate that the court should curtail its application. {As to the interpretative factors see Part VII of this Code.} This is known as strict construction. Equally, where the application of an enactment yields a beneficent result the interpretative factors may on balance indicate that the court should widen its application. This is known as liberal construction. Strict and liberal construction are explained in s 154 of this Code.

Further discussion   A great many of the guides to legislative intention employ the idea of consequential construction. Nearest perhaps to Lord Blackburn's idea of 'absurdity or inconvenience' in his formulation of the so-called golden rule are those dealt with in s 141 and Part XVI of this Code. But there are many others. {See the following sections of this Part: 122, 123, 127–131, 138, 139, 146.}

141. Presumptions: that 'absurd' result not intended

The court seeks to avoid a construction that produces an absurd result, since this is unlikely to have been intended by Parliament. Here the courts give a very wide meaning to the concept of 'absurdity', using it to include virtually anything which appears inappropriate, unfitting or unreasonable.

In rare cases there are overriding reasons for applying a construction that produces an absurd result, for example where it appears that Parliament really intended it or the literal meaning is too strong.

COMMENTARY

In their dicta on statutory interpretation, the courts by tradition give 'absurd' a far wider import than it has in modern English (where it simply means foolish, ridiculous or silly). Judges keep to the older meaning. The Oxford English Dictionary puts this as: 'out of harmony with reason or propriety; incongruous, unreasonable, illogical'. It was in such a sense that Claudius told Hamlet his excessive mourning for a dead father was 'To reason most absurd'. {*Hamlet* I ii 103.} The derivation is from the Latin *surdus*, deaf. We commonly speak even today of a person being deaf to reason.

So it is not surprising to find the judge even in a 1982 case (on the sober question of the date from which interest should run on a judgment debt) saying that he is preferring one of the opposing constructions above the other 'in order to avoid absurd results'. {*Erven Warnink BV v J Townend & Sons (Hull) Ltd (No 2)* [1982] 3 All ER 312, at p 320.}

Example 1   The general approach of the courts is illustrated by *Williams v Evans*. {(1876) 1 Ex D 277.} The Highway Act 1835, a choice example of disorganized composition {As to this see s 76 of the Code.}, created an offence of furious horse riding but omitted to include this in the penalty provision. {See Example 76.2.} Grove J said that unless a strained construction were applied the court would in effect hold that the legislature had made an 'absurd mistake'. {P 282.} Field J agreed, adding-

> 'No doubt it is a maxim to be followed in the interpretation of statutes, that the ordinary grammatical construction is to be adopted; but when this leads to a manifest absurdity, a construction not strictly grammatical is allowed, if this will lead to a *reasonable* conclusion as to the intention of the legislature.'

{P 284. Emphasis added}

Cross, noting the wide use by the courts of the concept of absurdity, goes so far as to suggest that such words as 'repugnancy', 'inconsistency', 'anomaly' and 'contradiction' can all be 'properly subsumed under the word "absurdity" for the purposes of a brief exposition of the rules of statutory interpretation'. {*Statutory Interpretation* p 81.}

Certainly there are dicta supporting this view. However, repugnancy, inconsistency and contradiction (all as between different enactments) raise conceptual problems different to those where the 'absurdity' lies within a single provision. They are accordingly dealt with separately in this Code. {See s 149 (construction as a whole, s 173 (implied amendment) and s 180 (implied repeal)}

Even dealing with the other varieties of 'absurdity' is a matter of some complexity. It is therefore consigned to a separate Part of this Code, namely Part XVI.

142. Presumptions: that errors to be rectified

It is presumed that the legislator intends the court to apply a construction which rectifies any error in the drafting of the enactment, where this is required to give effect to the legislator's intention.

COMMENTARY

There are occasions when, as Parke B said, the language of the legislature must be modified, in order to avoid inconsistency with its manifest intentions. {*Miller v Salomons* (1852) 7 Ex 475, at p 553.} It has to be accepted that drafting errors frequently occur. {For an account of the various types of drafting error see Bennion *Statute Law* (2nd edn, 1983) chaps 16 to 18.} This has always been so; there is nothing new in it.

Blackstone remarked that 'in one statute only, 5 Anne, c 14, there is false grammar in no fewer than six places, besides other mistakes'. {(Kerr Bl 4th edn, iv 177-8).} In our own day we find Nourse J saying of s 3(3) of the Law of Property Act 1925 that it is possible, 'and no criticism of him at all', that the draftsman either overlooked or misunderstood the fact that the opening words were inappropriate because of the changes made by the 1925 property legislation. {*Re Rowhook Mission Hall, Horsham; Channing-Pearce v Morris* (1984) *The Times* 12 March.} During the two centuries intervening between these statements, we find many in similar terms.

It would not be right to allow such human mistakes to frustrate the will of Parliament. In 1977 an attempt was made by the Government to persuade Parliament to enact the Acts of Parliament (Correction of Mistakes) Bill. This would have provided a simple procedure for certain kinds of rectification, but was rejected. {For details of the Bill see K Smith and DJ Keenan *English Law* (6th edn, 1979) p 9. Cf Acts of Parliament (Mistaken References) Act 1830 (11 Geo 4 & 1 Will 4 c 71).} Parliament preferred to leave matters in the hands of the judiciary.

A flawed text has been promulgated as expressing the legislative intention. {As to legislative intention see Part V of this Code.} This needs judicial correction. Yet those who have relied on it are entitled to protection.

This raises a difficult conflict between literal and purposive construction. The courts tread a wary middle way between the extremes. The court must do the best it can to implement the legislative intention without being unfair to those who reasonably expect a predictable construction. {For the principle that the construction adopted should be predictable see s 130 of this Code.}

The cases where rectifying construction may be required can be divided into six categories. These are: the garbled or corrupt text; the incomplete text; errors of meaning; the *casus omissus*; the *casus male inclusus*; and the textual conflict. Before discussing these in turn, we mention a Scottish doctrine which in various forms appears of general application.

Nobile officium   In Scotland recourse may be had to the *nobile officium* (or noble office) of the court, a power derived from Roman law and corresponding to that of the Court of Equity in England. The reasoning underlying it suggests that courts elsewhere in the United Kingdom should be regarded as possessing equivalent powers within their general jurisdiction. The seventeenth-century Scottish jurist Stair said-

> 'Every court must have this power, unless there be a distinct court for equity, from that for law, as it is in England ... Other nations do not divide the jurisdiction of their courts, but supply the cases of equity and conscience, by the noble office of their supreme ordinary courts, as we do.'

{*Institutes of the Law of Scotland* iv 3. 1.}

In *The Practice of the Court of Session*, David Maxwell says {P 127.} that the following principles are settled in the case of statutes-

> 'Where a matter depends entirely on the construction of the words of a statute, there cannot be any appeal to the *nobile officium*; and it cannot be used to extend or derogate from the provisions of a statute. It is however available to parties to meet a *casus improvisus* in a statute; and where the intention of a statute is clear, but the machinery required for carrying out that intention is lacking, the *nobile officium* can under special circumstances be invoked to provide the necessary machinery.'

{Maxwell's footnote references are omitted here.}

Example 1   In *Lloyds and Scottish Finance Ltd v H M Advocate* {(1974) SLT Rep 3; [1975] Crim LR 108.} the *nobile officium* was apparently used to rectify a defect in s 23 of the Criminal Justice Act 1972. This section enabled a convict to be deprived by court order of his rights in any property used for the commission of an offence. In relation to England and Wales, the section clearly safeguarded the rights of any innocent person in the property. In relation to Scotland however, s 23(5) simply said that the property 'shall be disposed of as the court may direct'.

The sheriff ordered forfeiture of a car owned by an innocent finance company. *Held* The order was invalid. The High Court accordingly quashed the order. They directed that the car be sold, and the value of the finance company's interest paid to them out of the proceeds. The court said it would be manifestly inequitable that in Scotland there should be no protection for innocent owners when such protection was given in England and Wales. Reading s 23 as a whole, it was clear that Parliament intended that there should not be this anomaly 'but by a remarkable omission has failed to provide, in Scotland, any machinery by which that intention can be achieved'.

Garbled or corrupt text   An Act was once passed which imposed a duty to garble. {6 Anne c 68 (1707) s 3, empowering the Corporation of London to appoint a 'garbler' who, at the request of owners of spices or drugs 'shall garble the same'.} This used the word in a different sense to the one now intended, which is that of corrupting or spoiling.

A text may be garbled by the omission of words, the inclusion of unwanted words, the inclusion of wrong words, typographical errors or punctuation mistakes. The duty of the court is to rectify the text so as to give it the intended meaning. This produces what is in this Code called the corrected version. {See s 90.}

If a text is garbled, the fact is obvious. Obvious that is to those who are equipped with the learning a lawyer is presumed to possess, and read with care. Little of either was needed however with the statutory instrument authorising a defendant to apply to have the action transferred to 'the County Court in which he resides or carries on business'. {Salford Hundred Court of Record (Extension of Jurisdiction) Rules 1955 (SI 1955/1295) r 2.} It was obvious that some words had dropped out, and also obvious what the sense of them was. {Cf Example 93.1.} In other cases the error may not be quite so easy to rectify.

Example 2   One of the best-known examples of an incomplete text is s 6 of the Statute of Frauds Amendment Act 1828 (Lord Tenterden's Act). This runs as follows-

> ' . . . no action shall be brought whereby to charge any person upon or by reason of any representation or assurance made or given concerning or relating to the character, conduct, credit, ability, trade or dealings of any other person, *to the intent or purpose that such other person may obtain credit, money, or goods upon,* unless such representation or assurance is made in writing, signed by the party to be charged therewith.'

{Emphasis added.}

It seems clear that some words are missing at the end of the italicised passage. However in *Lyde v Barnard* {(1836) 1 M & W 101.} the three judges each took different views.

Gurney B said {P 104.} that he had no doubt that 'credit' should follow the word 'upon'. Parke B said {P 115.}-

> 'The words of the clause in question are, it is to be observed, clearly inaccurate, probably from a mistake by the transcriber into the

Parliamentary Roll. We must make an alteration in order to complete the sense . . .'

Parke B went on to suggest two alternative rectifications, giving different results.

Lord Abinger CB took a third course, namely to reject the word 'upon' as nonsensical. He regarded it as a remanet, the word having originally been 'thereupon' and having been partially struck through by the draftsman. He added {P 124.}-

'The printers of bills for the two houses seldom commit an error on the side of omission. Every thing which is not beyond doubt erased in MS is sure to be served up in print, and, if it should afterwards escape detection in committe, finds its way upon the rolls of Parliament, and into the Statute Book.'

{For other examples of omitted words see *Re Wainwright* (1843) 1 Ph 258; *A-G v Beauchamp* [1920] 1 KB 650.

Instead of intended words being omitted, unintended words may be included. {See Example 90.4.}

A further possibility is that the words are confused. {See Example 90.3.}

The Queen's printer sometimes corrects merely typographical errors.

Example 3   As originally promulgated, s 11(5) of the Landlord and Tenant (Rent Control) Act 1949 referred to s 6 (instead of s 7) of the Furnished Houses (Rent Control) Act 1946. This was corrected in subsequent published copies of the 1949 Act.

In other cases Parliament itself finds it necessary to step in.

Example 4   In 1879 an Act was passed with the clumsy short title of the Artizans and Labourers Dwellings Act (1868) Amendment Act 1879. The clumsiness did not stop there. Section 22(3) of the Act required loans under the Act to be secured by a mortgage 'in the form set forth in the Third Schedule hereto'. There was no Third Schedule; and nowhere in the Act was a mortgage form to be found. The mistake was put right in the following year, by an Act which apparently had the same draftsman. Its short title was the Artizans and Labourers Dwellings Act (1868) Amendment Act (1879) Amendment Act 1880.

Sometimes the error is made in transcribing an enactment for inclusion in a consolidation Act. Here there is an irrestistible inference that the original wording should be followed.

Example 5   Section 125(2) of the Law of Property Act 1922 empowered trustees to appoint agents for 'executing and perfecting assurances of property'. In s 23(2) of the Trustee Act 1925 this appears as a reference to *insurances* of property. {For a judicial comment on this see *Green v Whitehead* [1930] 1 Ch 38, *per* Eve J at p 45. For another consolidation Act case see *The Arabert* [1963] P 102.}

Two errors appear in the Repeal Schedule to the Interpretation Act 1978 (a consolidation Act). {Sch 3.} The short title of the National Health Service Reorganisation Act 1973 is given as 'The National Health Service Reorganisation Act 1973', while a reference is made to Sch 5 of the Medical Act

1978 instead of Sch 6. In neither case is there any doubt as to what was intended, and the court would read the references in their intended form.

Sometimes however there is doubt as to whether an apparent defect is a typographical error or was intended to be significant.

Example 7   Section 45(3) of the Finance Act 1965 originally said that references in Part III (capital gains tax) of the Act to a married woman living with her husband 'should be construed in accordance with section 361(1)(2) of the Income Tax Act 1952'. By the Income and Corporation Taxes Act 1970 s 537(2) and Sch 15, this was altered to refer to 'section 42(1)(2) of the Income and Corporation Taxes Act 1970' (a re-enactment of s 361 of the 1952 Act).

The wording of s 45(3) is odd in two repects. First, why is 'should' used instead of the invariable 'shall'? Is it a misprint, or is it intended to carry significance? Second, why does it refer to 'section 361(1)(2)'? Section 361 of the 1952 Act, like the replacing s 42 of the 1970 Act, consists of two subsections only (of which the second has a proviso). It is not the practice, when referring to the entirety of a section, to mention the subsections in this way. Was it an error, or was it intended to be significant? Was it perhaps intended to exclude the proviso to subs (2) ?

The puzzle was compounded by the fact that the draftsman of the consolidating 1970 Act reproduced the reference in the same form. This seemed to indicate that there was no error, but what could the meaning be? In *Gubay v Kington (Inspector of Taxes)* [1984] 1 All ER 513.} a divided House of Lords had great difficulty in reaching a conclusion. In the end the majority decided that these curiosities bore no significance. Section 45(3) meant what it would clearly have meant if it had said that references to a married woman living with her husband '*shall* be construed in accordance with *section 361* of the Income Tax Act 1952'. When there was an opportunity to correct this obviously obscure wording on consolidation one wonders why it was not taken, as it certainly should have been.

For other examples of typographical or verbal errors in Acts see Ecclesiastical Leases Act 1571 ('or' for 'of') {*Eton College v Minister of Agriculture, Fisheries and Food* [1964] Ch 274.}; Warrants of Attorney Act 1822 s 2 ('or execution issued' for 'and execution levied') {*Green v Wood* (1845) 7 QB 178, at p 185.}; County Courts Act 1850 s 13 ('may' for 'shall') {*Macdougall v Paterson* (1851) 11 CB 755, at p 773.}; Customs Consolidation Act 1876 s 186 ('offender' for 'apparent offender') {*Bernard v Gorman* [1941] AC 378.}; Arbitration Act 1889 s 5 ('may' for 'shall') {*Re Eyre and Leicester Corpn* [1892] 1 QB 136.}; Weights and Measures Act 1889 s 13 ('may' for 'shall') {*R v Roberts* [1901] 2 KB 17.}; Intestates' Estates Act 1890 s 6 ('testamentary' expenses of intestacy) {*Re Twigg's Estate* [1892] 1 Ch 579.}; Prevention of Corruption Act 1916 s 4(2) ('and' for 'or') {*R v Newbould* [1962] 2 QB 102.}; Official Secrets Act 1920 s 7 ('and' for 'or') {*R v Oakes* [1959] 2 QB 350.}; National Assistance Act 1948 s 44(3) ('on' for 'arising out of') {*Clapham v National Assistance Board* [1961] 2 QB 77.}; Sexual Offences Act 1956 s 19(1) ('unlawful' for 'immoral') {*R v Chapman* [1959] 1 QB 100.}; Road Traffic Act 1960 s 6(4) ('committing' for 'apparently committing') {*Wiltshire v Barrett* [1966] 1 QB 312.}; Hallmarking Act 1973 Sch 2 ('complies with' for 'is capable of complying with') {*Barge v Graham Brown (Oasis Trading) Ltd* [1981] 3 All ER 360, at p 362.}; Matrimonial Causes Act 1973 s 35(2) ('thereafter' for 'then') {*Warden v Warden*

[1981] 3 All ER 193, at p 196.}; Inheritance (Provision for Family and Dependants) Act 1975 s 1(3) ('shall be treated . . . if' for 'shall not be treated . . . unless') {*Re Beaumont decd, Martin v Midland Bank Trust Co Ltd* [1980] 1 All ER 266, at p 271.}; Limitation Act 1975 s 2A(1) ('damage' for 'damages').

As to words appearing in the wrong place in an Act see *R v Vasey and Lally* {[1905] 2 KB 748.} and *Local Government Board v South Stoneham Union.* {[1909] AC 57, at p 63.}

Errors of meaning   Rectification of a more substantial kind may be required where the meaning is vitiated by some error on the part of the draftsman which is not apparent on the face of the text. He may have misconceived the legislative project, or based the text on a mistake of fact. Alternatively he may have made an error in the applicable law, or mishandled a legal concept.

If the draftsman misconceives the factual nature of the legislative project his wording is likely to be ineffective. The court may be able to remedy this by applying a strained construction which accomodates the true facts without causing injustice or other disadvantage.

Example 7   Section 8(1) of the Food and Drugs Act 1955 says that a person who sells 'any *food* intended for, but unfit for, human consumption' commits an offence. {Emphasis added.} This misconceives the legislative project, which is to safeguard the public from being supplied (as food) with any *deleterious substance*. It should be immaterial whether the substance supplied is truly food or not. What matters is that it is supplied as being food.

In *Meah v Roberts* {[1977] Crim LR 678.} children asked for lemonade and were given corrosive caustic soda, some of which they drank. {Section 135(1) of the 1955 Act defines 'food' as including drink.} The defence argued that caustic soda is not food. *Held* To rectify the misconceived project, a strained construction was necessary. The expression 'sells any food' must be taken to mean 'sells anything (whether a food or not) *as* a food'.

Example 8   Section 110(1) of the Representation of the People Act 1983, requiring the name and address of the printer and publisher to appear on the 'face' of election material, misconceives the factual situation regarding election posters and leaflets. It assumes there are two quite different things, namely (1) the poster which is displayed and consists of one lettered surface only and (2) the leaflet which is held in the hand to be read and may consist of several pages. It overlooks the common fact that a single document may be in a form which enables it to serve both as a poster and a leaflet.

A selective comminution of s 110(1) runs-

> 'A person shall not print or publish any bill, placard or poster having reference to an election or any printed [promotional] document unless the bill, placard, poster or document bears upon its face the name and address of the printer and publisher.'

Cook v Trist {(1983) *The Times* 15 July.} concerned one of these double-purpose documents. Treated as a leaflet it complied with s 110(1), the required name and address being printed on its 'face'. The reverse side was printed as a poster, with the words 'please display'. It did not bear the name and address.

Held On a commonsense construction, the requirements of s 110(1) must be taken to apply twice over, taking the document first as a leaflet and then as a poster. The required name and address therefore had to appear both on the front and the back. {For the commonsense construction rule see s 122 of this Code.}

Example 9 Another illustration of the common drafting fault of misconceiving the project concerns the publication of notices inside and outside licensed betting offices. This might seem to be a simple matter, but in fact it is fraught with difficulty and requires the draftsman to keep a clear head.

Briefly, the difficulties arise because Parliament considers that certain information *must* be given to punters who have found their way *inside* a betting office, while certain information *must not* be given to persons who are *outside* a betting office and should not be encouraged to enter it. The simple-minded draftsman will deal with these situations by talking about the display of notices inside and outside the office respectively. Bookmakers, who tend to be less simple-minded, quickly discover that a notice may be placed inside an office so as to be visible through the window to those who are outside, and vice versa. In dealing with the resulting interpretative problems, the courts have tended to take a robust line where literal meanings give way to common sense and a desire to remedy the true mischief. {See, e g, *Roy William Robinson Ltd v Cox* (1968) 67 LGR 188; *Dunsford v Pearson* [1970] 1 WLR 222; *R v Newcastle upon Tyne Gaming Licensing Committee* [1977] 1 WLR 1135; *Windsors (Sporting Investments) Ltd v Oldfield* [1981] 2 All ER 718. As to the commonsense construction rule see s 122 of this Code.}

The wording of an enactment is sometimes based on an error as to a specific fact. Such errors can be of a most elementary nature, though few touch the depths of the Canadian regulation providing that, unless the context otehwise required, 'words of one gender include all other genders'. {Atomic Energy Regulations, reg 101(1)(m) (made under the Atomic Energy Act 1946).} Even Blackstone nodded in this respect, with his definition of felonious homicide as 'the killing of a human creature, of any age or sex, without justification or excuse'. {Kerr Bl (4th edn, 1874) iv 190.}

Factual errors may be difficult to rectify. An enactment is intended to provide a remedy for a mischief. {See s 138 and Part XIV of this Code.} If those who design the remedy are mistaken in the underlying fact, they are likely to get the remedy wrong. {See, e g, *Labrador Company v The Queen* [1893] AC 104 (mistake over ownership of land). See also *R v Haughton (Inhabitants)* (1853) 22 LJMC 89, at pp 92 and 94; *Hoani Te Heuheu Tukino v Aotea DMLB* [1941] AC 308; *IRC v Dowdall, O'Mahoney & Co* [1952] AC 401, at p 426. For an amusing example see the story 'Tods' Amendment' in Kipling's *Plain Tales from the Hills.*}

Factual errors become apparent with experience of the enactment's operation. Officials administering the Act will then try to 'tailor' it to accomodate the true facts. If the matter comes before a court, the modern judge will do likewise. He will be more than usually willing to apply a liberal construction. {As to strict and liberal construction see s 154 of this Code.}

Where the mischief concerns the operation of some legal rule, the remedy is likely to take the form of a modification of the rule. If the draftsman fails to understand the legal rule he is to modify, the modification is likely to be misconceived. The court, in construing the enactment, is then forced to take account of the draftsman's error. The court must do the best it can, being ready to apply a strained construction in order to tailor the enactment to the true legal rule.

Example 10 The Leasehold Property (Repairs) Act 1938 (which is still in force) was passed to assist tenants by interposing the supervision of the court where a landlord sought to enforce repairing covenants. As with so much legislation of this inter-war period (notably the Rent Acts), the 1938 Act was drafted in popular language and rode roughshod over the principles of conveyancing. It was not properly thought out. Section 1 provided that where a lessor served a notice relating to breach of a repairing covenant the tenant could serve a counter-notice claiming the benefit of the Act. This was stated to mean that the landlord could not proceed further without leave of the court.

Section 1(5) of the Act states that leave shall not be given unless the lessor 'proves' at least one out of five specified conditions. Unfortunately these are all drafted as though there could be no doubt that a breach had indeed occurred. The possibility that the very existence of the alleged breach might be in dispute did not to occur to the draftsman. {For an illustration of the difficulties thereby caused to the court see *Land Securities plc v Receiver for the Metropolitan Police District* [1983] 2 All ER 254.}

Example 11 Where a person is charged before a magistrates' court with an offence, and on conviction the court would have power to make a hospital order against him on grounds of insanity, s 60(2) of the Mental Health Act 1959 {Re-enacted as s 37(3) of the Mental Health Act 1983.} empowers the court, if satisfied that the accused did the act charged, to make a hospital order without convicting him. This overlooks the obvious possibility that the accused may be unfit to plead, so that no trial can take place in which evidence to 'satisfy' the court can be adduced. The point arose in *R v Lincoln (Kesteven) JJ, ex p O'Connor*. {[1983] Crim LR 621.}

Held Parliament must have intended that the power could be exercised in such cases, so it must be taken to intend that informal means of acquainting the court with the facts must be allowed, at least where those acting for the accused consent.

When a modern draftsman has to handle ancient law he is likely, not being trained in it, to make mistakes.

Example 12 The draftsman of the Commons Registration Act 1965 referred to land which, at the time of registration under the Act, is 'waste land of a manor'. {S 22(1) (definition of 'common land').} However the changes in the legal status of a manor, culminating in the abolition of copyhold tenure by the Law of Property Act 1922, have robbed this phrase of any precise legal meaning. To render the use of it legally precise, far more words are needed than this draftsman thought fit to employ. In the result the courts were forced to struggle for a meaning. Inevitably, they disagreed. The finally prevailing view of the Court of Appeal was given in *Box Parish Council v Lacey* {[1979] 1 All ER 113.}

Meaning narrower than the object (casus omissus) Where the literal meaning of the enactment goes narrower than the object of the legislator, the court may be required to apply a rectifying construction. Nowadays it is regarded as not in accordance with public policy to allow a draftsman's ineptitude to prevent justice being done. This was not always the case.

Example 13 Section 21 of the Matrimonial Causes Act 1857 empowered a magistrate to make an order protecting the property of a deserted wife. However it allowed the husband to apply for the discharge of such an order to 'the magistrate . . . by whom the order was made'. In a lecture given in 1933, Sir M S Amos told of what happened when in 1864 a Mr Sharpe sought to exercise this right-

> 'He discovered that the magistrate who had made the order was dead; and the question what was now his proper course of action came before a bench composed of Cockburn CJ, Blackburn and Shee JJ, who decided unanimously that this was a *casus omissus*, and that it was not competent for the husband to apply to some other metropolitan magistrate who might present the advantage of being alive.'

{'The Interpretation of Statutes' (1934) 5 CLJ 163. Although Amos did not give the case reference, it was presumably *Ex p Sharpe* (1864) 5 B & S 322.}

Here we have the classic conflict, between an unimaginative draftsman and an unyielding court. Sandwiched between them, incapable of helping himself, the innocent litigant is crushed. It is safe to say it would not happen today.

Meaning wider than the object (casus male inclusus) The intention of Parliament is to remedy a mischief. Since an Act is a coercive instrument, backed by the physical forces of the state, it is presumed that Parliament does not intend the enactment to go wider in its operation than is necessary to remedy the mischief in question.

Just as a case which is within the object of an enactment but outside its wording is described as a *casus omissus*, so it is appropriate to describe the reverse case as a *casus male inclusus*. {The name was suggested by Glanville Williams: see *Learning the Law* (11th edn, 1982), p 103.} It is unfortunate that the literal meaning of many enactments takes their coercive force wider than is necessary to remedy the mischief. Harman LJ remarked of the Leasehold Property (Repairs) Act 1938: 'Like most remedial Acts of that sort, it catches the virtuous in the net which is laid for the sinner'. {*Sidnell v Wilson* [1966] 2 QB 67, at p 79.}

Example 14 Section 32 of the Sexual Offences Act 1956 makes it an offence for a man 'persistently to solicit or importune in a public place for immoral purposes'. Heterosexual fornication is treated by the law as immoral or even 'unlawful'. {*R v Chapman* [1959] 1 QB 100.} It is therefore within the literal meaning of s 32, but the Divisional Court held in *Crook v Edmondson* {[1966] 2 QB 81.} that the literal meaning must be cut down so as to confine the application of s 32 to homosexual acts. {See also *R v Ford* [1977] Crim LR 688.}

Cessante ratione legis cessat ipsa lex This maxim, cited by Coke {Co Litt 70b.}, may be literally translated as 'the reason for a law having ceased, the law itself ceases'. This principle plainly does not apply to statutes, as to which there is no doctrine of desuetude. {See s 188 of this Code.}

The maxim has not however been applied with this temporal connotation. In the law generally, it has been used in a spatial rather than a temporal sense. The meaning is rather: in areas where the reason underlying the law is not applicable, the law does not apply.

Thus Broom cites as an example of the principle a qualification of the rule that a person contracting with an undisclosed principal can exercise a right of set-off which he has against the agent-

> 'Where, however, the party contracting either knew, had the means of knowing, or must, from the circumstances of the case, be presumed to have known, that he was dealing, not with a principal, but with an agent, the reason of the above rule ceases, and here the right of set-off cannot be maintained.'

{*Legal Maxims* (1st edn, 1845) p 69.}

It will be seen that this really amounts to a way of stating the undisclosed principal rule *with appropriate restrictions*. The same applies to the other examples cited by Broom of the maxim's application. So it is with Blackstone, who cites the maxim in connection with the exceptions to the defence of *autrefois attaint*. {Kerr Bl 4th edn, 1876) iv 350.}

At common law, where the rules are 'unwritten', the principle has an obvious place. It does not appear to have been applied to statutes, for obvious reasons. Nevertheless it may be thought to add some justification to the giving of a purposive-and-strained construction where the literal meaning goes wider than the object. {As to this type of construction see s 315 below.}

Textual conflicts Some form of rectification is essential where the court is faced with conflicting texts. If the texts are within the same Act, the conflict is generally to be resolved by construing the Act as a whole. {As to this see s 149 of this Code.} If the texts are in different Acts, the later usually prevails. {See ss 173 and 180 of this Code.}

Where the conflicting texts are in different Acts another possibility is that the Acts are not *in pari materia*, and that each text must be confined to its own sphere. {As to when Acts are *in pari materia* see pp 516–517 below.}

Example 15 Section 10 of the Contempt of Court Act 1981 states that no court may require a person to disclose the source of information contained in a publication for which he is responsible. In *Secretary of State for Defence v Guardian Newspapers Ltd* [1984] 1 All ER 453.} the Crown sought the return of a photocopy of a secret document supplied to the *Guardian* by a 'mole' in the Ministry of Defence, and published in that newspaper.

The photocopy was the property of the Crown, and bore markings which might have revealed the identity of the 'mole'. It had no intrinsic value. The Crown asked the court to exercise the discretion conferred on it by s 3 of the Torts (Interference with Goods) Act 1977 to order the handing over of the photocopy. The *Guardian* argued that this would be contrary to the literal meaning of s 10 of the 1981 Act. *Held* The literal meaning must be treated as subject to an implied exclusion of cases where there existed a proprietary right, and the Crown was entitled to its order.
{See also Examples 76.1, 76.2, 77.1, 77.2, 90.1, 90.3, 90.4, 93.1, 93.2, 93.4 and 342.3.}

143. Presumptions: that evasion not to be allowed

It is the duty of a court to further the legislator's aim of providing a remedy for the mischief against which the enactment is directed. Accordingly the court will prefer a construction which advances this object rather than one which attempts to find some way of circumventing it.

COMMENTARY

Consequential construction This is one of the numerous varieties of consequential construction {See s 140 of this Code.}.

Heydon's Case The duty of the court to further Parliament's aim of providing a remedy for the mischief against which the enactment is directed was laid down by the judges themselves in *Heydon's Case* {(1584) 3 Co Rep 7a at p 7b. See s 301 of this Code.}. They enunciated the principle expounded in this section and Part XVII of the Code by stating that-

> '... the office of all the Judges is always to make such construction as shall ... suppress subtle inventions and evasions for continuance of the mischief ... *pro privato commodo* (for private advantage).'

{See also *Magdalen College Case* (1615) 11 Co Rep 66b and Example 224.4.}

This basic principle embodies the necessary legal policy of any democratic state. As Blackstone said: the law will not suffer itself to be trifled with by evasions {Kerr Bl (4th edn, 1876) iv 232.}. In the words of Abbott CJ, it is a well-known principle of law that the provisions of an Act of Parliament shall not be evaded by shift or contrivance. {*Fox v Bishop of Chester* (1824) 2 B & C 635, at p 655.}. Or as was expressed in a maxim favoured by Coke: *quando aliquid prohibetur fieri, prohibitur ex directo et per obliquum* (whenever a thing is prohibited, it is prohibited whether done directly or indirectly). {Co Litt 223.}.

Fraud on the Act The courts have frequently held that a construction is to be preferred that prevents evasion of the intention evinced by Parliament to provide an effective remedy for the mischief against which the enactment is directed. When deliberately embarked on, such evasion is judicially described as a fraud on the Act.

Attempts to evade statutory requirements go back to the earliest times. Indeed the first statutes were themselves often enacted to remedy evasions of the common law. These evasions were frequent once the machinery of common law procedure had become fixed.

The Year Books are full of cases where legal process was abused for purposes of fraud or unconscionable delay. T F T Plucknett suggests that these abuses 'gave a strong impetus to the movement for a written statutory law'. {*Statutes & their Interpretation in the First Half of the Fourteenth Century* p 166.} He goes on-

> 'At first, perhaps, it was thought that precise, written, legislation would remove the evil, but the event proved the contrary. No sooner was a statute made, than we find reported in the Year Books numerous ingenious attempts to evade or circumvent the Act. Originally, perhaps, the result of legal chicanery, the new written and

published statutes themselves rapidly became the cause of further artifice, and the battle of wits between the legislature and the smart litigant has continued until our own day.' {Ibid.}

So prevalent was the evasion of statute law that we find a general injunction against it entered on the medieval Statute Roll-

'And every man . . . shall keep and observe the aforesaid ordinances and statutes . . . without addition, or fraud, by covin, evasion, art or contrivance, *or by interpretation of the words.*'

{10 Edw 3 st 3 (1336). Emphasis added.}

Judges always set their faces against allowing any person to drive a coach and horses through an Act - even though lawyers have been found in every age who were ready to help their clients do just that. Thus Craies complacently remarks: 'It has always been the pride of a competent conveyancer to be able, when required, to drive a coach and four, or six, through any Act of Parliament' {*Statute Law* (7th edn, 1971) p 77.}. This money-spinning posture has helped bring the legal profession into disrepute among the majority of citizens not able to afford the services of such proud and skilful practitioners.

To prevent evasion, the court turns away from a construction that would allow the subject (a) to do what Parliament has indicated by the Act it considers mischievous or (b) to refrain from doing what Parliament has indicated it considers desirable.

Either of these constructions may qualify as what is termed a fraud on a statute. In various forms, this expression has long been used by judges to describe attempts at the deliberate evasion of statutory requirements. Thus Lord Coleridge spoke of 'a fraud upon an Act of Parliament'. {*Ramsden v Lupton* (1873) LR 9 QB 17, at p 24.} Cockburn CJ said that-

' . . . the courts, from the time of Lord Mansfield, held that if a trader, in contemplation of bankruptcy, with a view to evade the bankruptcy law, preferred a particular creditor to the detriment of the rest, such a preference was a fraud upon the law.'

{*Bills v Smith* (1865) 6 B & S 314, at p 319. See also *Ex p Mackay* (1878) LR 8 Ch 643.}

Lord Eldon referred to 'a fraud on the law or an insult to an Act of Parliament' in *Fox v Bishop of Chester* {(1829) 1 Dow & Cl 416, at p 429.}.

The judicial attitude remains the same today, as is illustrated by two decisions on the Housing (Homeless Persons) Act 1977. These go opposite ways. In the first case the housing authority sought to evade its statutory duty, while in the second a homeless person tried to evade a limitation on that duty. Either way, the courts were alert to prevent evasion.

Example 1 Rejecting the argument that a woman who was accomodated in a refuge for battered wives was not 'homeless', and that therefore the local authority were under no duty to find accomodation for her, Hodgson J said that to accept the argument would involve 'watering down' the Act. {*R v Ealing London Borough Council, ex p Sidhu* (1982) *The Times* 16 January.}

Example 2 Concurring in a finding by the Court of Appeal that 'intentional' homelessness could arise where an earlier home, and not merely the previous home, had been intentionally abandoned, Kerr LJ said that this would be a sensible interpretation since a contrary construction of the Act 'would make it possible to drive a coach and horses through it'. {*Lambert v Ealing London Borough Council* [1982] 2 All ER 394, at p 400.}

The desire of the courts to prevent evasion of statutes is manifest in many fields.

Example 3 A regulation designed to restrict the number of juggernaut lorries allowed to encumber the roads imposed a length limit of 15 metres. A letout was provided for vehicles 'constructed and normally used for the conveyance of indivisible loads of exceptional length'. The term 'indivisible load' was defined as a load which could not without undue expense or risk of damage be divided into two or more loads.

A vehicle exceeding 15 metres in length was used to carry an exceptionally long container which could not be so divided. The container was constructed and used to transport livestock. *Held* The letout was intended for large unitary objects such as cranes and boilers. The 'load' referred to must be taken to be the goods themselves (in this case the livestock) and not their container. Lord Widgery CJ justified this strained construction by saying 'it cannot have been the intention of the legislature to allow the provisions of the regulations to be circumvented merely by packing goods into a larger receptacle'. {*Patterson v Redpath Brothers Ltd* [1979] 2 All ER 108, at p 111.}

Example 4 Where a house occupied by more than one 'household' is in defective condition, s 19(1) of the Housing Act 1961 empowers the local authority to direct that not more than a specified number of households shall occupy the house. A direction specifying a limit of three households was made in relation to a house mainly occupied by students in single rooms. Each student shared one of the three kitchens. *Held* It was open to magistrates to find that each student constituted a 'household'. Griffiths LJ, justifying this strained interpretation, said-

> 'During the course of the argument I had considerable doubt whether the word 'household' could be construed so as to include a student lodging in a single room. It certainly is not the meaning that is normally attached to the word 'household' which generally envisages a number of people living together rather than a single occupant in a single room. However, on reflection, I have been persuaded that it must be so construed in the context in which it is used in the Housing Act 1961, for unless it includes a person lodging in a single room, it means that lodging houses would be taken out of the code which is applied by the Act for houses in multiple occupation. This, I am satisfied, cannot have been the intention of Parliament.'

{*London Borough of Hackney v Ezedinma* [1981] 3 All ER 438, at p 442.}

Example 5 The Vaccination Act 1867 authorised a magistrate to summon a parent to appear with his child and, upon the appearance, to order the child to be vaccinated. *Held* A vaccination order could be made where the parent failed to produce the child, since otherwise the parent could evade the intention of Parliament that children should be vaccinated. {*Dutton v Atkins* (1871) LR 6

QB 373. See also *London School Board v Wood* (1885) 15 QBD 415 (parent did not satisfy the requirement to 'cause the child to attend school' where he sent him to school *without the school fees*) and *Ditton's Case* (1701) 2 Salk 490 (justices who were authorised to discharge an apprentice from his indenture *on the master's appearance before them* could do so even though the master failed to appear). Cf *R v A Justice for the Cinque Ports* (1886) 17 QBD 191; *London School Board v Wright* (1884) 12 QBD 578.}

Wider aspects of principle The principle requiring a construction against evasion is not limited to cases where a person has deliberately set out to get round the Act, perhaps with a motive connoting moral blame. It extends to other ways in which the integrity of an Act may be undermined, even unwittingly. This wider aspect is a matter of some complexity. It is therefore dealt with in a separate Part of this Code, namely Part XVII.

Evasion distinguished from avoidance See s 327 of this Code.

144. Presumptions: that ancillary rules of law apply

Unless the contrary intention appears, an enactment by implication imports any principle or rule of law (whether statutory or non-statutory) which prevails in the territory to which the enactment extends and is relevant to its operation in that territory (in this Code referred to as an 'implied ancillary rule').

COMMENTARY

An Act of Parliament is not a statement in a vacuum. Parliament intends its Act to be read and applied within the context of the existing corpus juris, or body of law. The Act relies for its effectiveness on this implied importation of surrounding legal principles and rules.

It is impossible for the draftsman to restate in express terms all those ancillary legal considerations which are, or may become, necessary for the Act's working. In this respect an Act is treated in the same way as a contract. With a contract, by importing established legal principles in accordance with the maxim *quando abest provisio partis, adest provisio legis* (when provision of party is wanting, provision of law is present), the law supplies what the parties have failed to say. {*Flack v Downing College, Cambridge* (1853) 13 CB 945, at p 960.} An Act requires treatment no less considerate.

The Barons of the Court of Exchequer in *Heydon's Case* {(1584) 3 Co Rep 7a, at p 7b. See s 301 of this Code.} stated as the first of the four things to be discerned and considered for the sure and true interpretation of all statutes: 'What was the common law before the making of the Act'. With the growth of parliamentary enactments in the ensuing four centuries, this reference now needs to be read as including statute law. {See p 635 below.}

An Act, unless merely declaratory, *changes* the existing body of law. That indeed is all it does. To understand the changes the Act is intended to make one therefore needs to begin, as the Barons of the Exchequer pointed out, by considering what was the relevant law beforehand. That was what Parliament desired to amend; and we infer that (save as so amended) Parliament intended it to go on applying.

Furthermore it is to be inferred that existing law is intended to continue not only generally, but *in relation to the operation of the Act itself*. As Lord Denning MR said of a royal proclamation relevant to the operation of the British North America Act 1867 but not mentioned in it-

> 'It was an unwritten provision which *went without saying*. It was binding on the legislatures of the Dominion and the provinces just as if there had been included in the statute a sentence: "The aboriginal peoples of Canada shall continue to have all their rights and freedoms as recognised by the royal proclamation of 1763".'

{*R v Secretary of State for Foreign and Commonwealth Affairs, ex p Indian Association of Alberta* [1982] 2 All ER 118, at p 125. Emphasis added.}

This is a principle of very great importance in statutory interpretation. Each relevant item of the existing law, so far as not altered by the Act in question (whether expressly or by implication) operates for the purposes of that Act just as if written into it. It goes without saying, in Lord Denning's homely phrase.

These imported principles and rules are in the Code and Commentary referred to as 'implied ancillary rules'. Rules which have been incorporated into the law as *maxims* are dealt with separately. {See s 145 and Part XX of this Code.} They are referred to as 'implied ancillary maxims'.

Implied ancillary rules range from the widest principles of legal policy to narrow technical rules. They include both statutory and non-statutory principles and rules. They may be substantive or procedural. Equally they may be domestic or international, civil or criminal. All that matters is that they should have a place in the law of the territory to which the Act extends.

This means that virtually the whole body of law is imported, by one enactment or another, as implied ancillary rules. The Code clearly cannot attempt to give full effect to this by reproducing all the implied rules. By doing so it would turn itself into a comprehensive legal digest, which is not the object. On the other hand it would not be satisfactory, having merely stated the principle, to leave it at that. Too many judicial dicta have insisted that nothing can be implied in Acts. There has been too much neglect of the vastly important role played by implications of one sort or another, and particularly these implications. {See, as to implications generally, ss 107 to 110 of this Code.}

Accordingly it seems best to present, albeit in outline, a full range of the more important implied ancillary rules. That is the purpose of Part XVIII of this Code. More elaborate detail in any area of law must be sought in the relevant specialist textbooks, or in a compendium such as Halsbury's *Laws of England*.

Unless the contrary intention appears As usual in the Code, this phrase, used throughout the Interpretation Act 1978, is adopted to signify that the rule stated in the Code applies except where the intention that it should not apply is indicated in the Act in question.

It is axiomatic that in its Act Parliament can always, if it chooses, disapply any existing principle or rule. It is equally axiomatic that, unless Parliament does so, the principle or rule, being relevant, applies. Thus Lord Pearce said of tribunals set up by Act-

' . . . it is assumed, unless special provisions provide otherwise, that the tribunal will make its enquiry and decision according to the law of the land.'

{*Anisminic Ltd v Foreign Compensation Commission* [1969] 2 AC 147, at p 195.}

Equally Byles J said that 'it is a sound rule to construe a statute in conformity with the common law, except where or in so far as the statute is plainly intended to alter the course of the common law'. {*R v Morris* (1867) LR 1 CCR 90 at p 95. See also *Lord Eldon v Hedley Bros* [1935] 2 KB 1, *per* Slesser LJ at p 24, and *R v Thomas* [1950] 1 KB 26, *per* Humphreys J at p 31).}

Disapplication or modification? Sometimes it is difficult to be sure whether or not Parliament does intend to disapply an ancillary rule. Or the problem may be whether the intention is to disapply a rule altogether or merely modify it. This can be particularly troublesome where the rule is peripheral to the subject-matter of the Act. Rules relating to surrounding areas of criminal law (such as inchoate offences or the position of accessories) present problems with many Acts, usually because the draftsman has overlooked them.

Draftsmen framing a new criminal offence tend to have a blind spot about such matters. There is no difficulty if the new offence is worded so as not to trespass on the peripheral area: the latter's rules then come in by implication as they stand. But suppose the draftsman forgets the peripheral area, and words the new offence so as inadvertently to trespass on some part of it?

Example 1 Section 1 of the Suicide Act 1961 abolishes the crime of suicide. However s 2(1) goes on to state that a person who 'aids, abets, counsels or procures' the actual or attempted suicide of another commits an offence. It is unclear whether or not this brings in the usual ancillary rules governing aiding, abetting etc (for example as to the need for and nature of *mens rea*). K J M Smith has discussed at length whether or not, as he puts it, the usual features of complicity were intended to be 'read into' the s 2(1) offence. {'Assisting in Suicide - The Attorney-General and the Voluntary Euthanasia Society' [1983] Crim LR 579.} The phrase 'read into' neatly describes that process of elaboration of the express words which is set out in this Part of the Code. {Cf the report of *R v Woolven* [1983] Crim LR 623, where the same phrase is used.}

Example 2 Section 4(2)(b) of the Misuse of Drugs Act 1971 makes it an offence 'to be concerned in the production of [a controlled drug] in contravention of [s 4(1) of the Act] by another'. This looks very like a description of aiding and abetting. Is it intended to replace the whole law on that aspect, or leave it standing so far as not inconsistent?' This is a difficult question to answer because the truth probably is that the draftsman did not think about the law of aiding and abetting, and so had no true intention in the matter. In a note on a case where the point rose for decision {*R v Farr* [[1982] Crim LR 745.}, Professor J C Smith comments-

'Being "concerned in" clearly covers much that would amount to ordinary aiding and abetting under the general law and might therefore be held to be intended to take the place of the general law. If this . . . is correct, the effect is that s 4(2) has a narrowing effect on liability, an effect which was most unlikely to have been intended by the draftsman or Parliament.'

After discussing other similar cases, Professor Smith ends with a warning to hasty draftsmen-

> 'Thus the use of the apparently wider words with the intention of *extending* liability may be a snare and a delusion to the draftsman and result in an unintended *narrowing* of liability.' {Emphasis added.}

Another example of this difficulty of determining how far Parliament intended to displace existing ancillary rules concerns the common law of markets. Where a market exists by charter or prescription, Parliament may pass an Act affecting it. This Act may in its case supplement the common law rules relating to markets, or abrogate them and substitute a statutory code. The Act may on the other hand do something in between. {See the extracts from *Pease and Chitty's Law of Markets and Fairs* (2nd edn, 1958), and accompanying comment by Judge FitzHugh QC, given in *Wakefield City Council v Box* [1982] 3 All ER 506, at pp 510-11.}

Geographical extent This section of the Code refers to the geographical extent of the Act because the implied ancillary rules will of course be those of the relevant territory. If for example an Act extends both to England and Scotland then, so far as the Act applies in England the implied ancillary rules will be those prevailing under English law while so far as the Act applies in Scotland they will be those of Scots law.

Thus in the Scottish case of *Temple v Mitchell* {(1956) SC 267.} the Second Division treated a difference in implied ancillary rules between England and Scotland as precluding the court from following English precedents in a Rent Act case. The English precedents were held to turn on 'a special doctrine of the English law of husband and wife not received in Scotland'. {Neil MacCormick *Legal Reasoning and Legal Theory* p 202. See also p 223.}

Legal policy Unless the contrary intention appears, Parliament is taken to intend its Act to conform to the broad principles of legal policy prevailing in the area to which the Act extends. As usual, the same principle applies to delegated legislation. {For the implied application of principles derived from legal policy see generally ss 126 to 134 of this Code.}

Example 3 Thus, on the question whether a local valuation court was an 'inferior court' within the meaning of provisions dealing with contempt of court in RSC Ord 52 r 1(2), Lord Scarman said-

> 'If the issue should ultimately be, as in this case I think it is, a question of legal policy, we must have regard to the country's international obligation to observe the European Convention [on Human Rights] as interpreted by the European Court of Human Rights.'

{*A-G v British Broadcasting Corpn* [1980] 3 All ER 161, at p 178.}

Example 4 Similarly Viscount Simon construed a statutory transfer of 'property' as not including employers' rights under contracts of service because it is the policy of the common law not to permit assignment of such rights without the employee's consent. Treating 'property' as a broad term which on the facts was ambiguous, Viscount Simon concluded that Parliament intended this term to bear a meaning which did not 'disregard fundamental principles'. {*Nokes v Doncaster Amalgamated Collieries* [1940] AC 1014, at p 1022.}

Rules of law   An Act may abrogate, modify or merely work in conjunction with an existing rule. Although within our terminology the rule is an 'implied ancillary rule', in fact it may be the enactment itself which is on the periphery.

Example 5   In *River Wear Commissioners v Adamson* {(1877) 2 App Cas 743.} the question was whether s 74 of the Harbours, Docks, and Piers Clauses Act 1847 imposed a new substantive liability on persons whose ships caused damage, or merely gave directions as to who should bear an existent common-law liability. In finding for the latter, the House of Lords treated the enactment as ancillary to the existing common-law right. Lord Cairns LC said that he could not look upon s 74 'as intending to create a right to recover damages in cases where, before the Act, there was not a right to recover damages *from someone*'. {P 750. Emphasis added.}

Free-standing terms   One of the most obvious ways in which Parliament indicates its intention to attract ancillary rules is by the use of a free-standing term. This is a word or phrase which is not defined in the Act but has a well-understood meaning at common law or otherwise.

Example 6   Section 14(1) of the Sexual Offences Act 1956 states that it is an offence 'for a person to make an indecent assault on a woman'. The Act contains no definition either of 'indecent' or 'assault'. Parliament is therefore taken to intend to apply the common-law meaning of these terms when taken together. {*R v Kimber* [1983] Crim LR 630.}

Implied ancillary rules relating to specific areas of law   The implied ancillary rules relating to the main areas of law are dealt with separately in Part XVIII of this Code. {See also s 145 and Part XIX, dealing with legal maxims that are by implication applied.}

145. Presumptions: that ancillary legal maxims apply

Unless the contrary intention appears, an enactment by implication imports the principle of any legal maxim which prevails in the territory to which the enactment extends and is relevant to the operation of the enactment in that territory (in this Code referred to as an 'implied ancillary maxim').

COMMENTARY

Parliament legislates within the general context of law and established legal principle. Therefore, as stated in s 144 of this Code, ancillary legal rules apply in the interpretation of enactments. However some principles of law are embodied in maxims. It follows that they too are imported (unless the contrary intention appears from the Act). The effect is to qualify the literal meaning of the enactment.

It is convenient to deal with some of these maxims separately from any legal rule relating to a particular area of law. This is because they cross the borders of established legal categories.

The term maxim is derived from the Latin *maxima*. Coke said that a maxim is so called 'Quia maxima est ejus dignitas et certissima auctoritas, atque quod maxime omnibus probetur'. {Co Litt 11a.}

Early English lawyers venerated maxims. Fortescue treated *maxima* and *regula* as identical. {*De Laudibus Legum Angliae* (1616) c 8.} In *Doctor and Student* {P 26.} maxims are described as 'of the same strength and effect in the law as statutes be'. Bacon said-

> 'Not only will the use of maxims be in deciding doubt and helping soundness of judgment, but, further, in gracing argument, in correcting unprofitable subtlety, and reducing the same to a more sound and substantial sense of law, in reclaiming vulgar errors, and, generally, in the amendment in some measure of the very nature and complexion of the whole law.'

{*Collection of Maxims*, preface.}

Some modern lawyers get irritated by maxims, and dislike the retaining of their Latin formulation. Lord Esher MR said: 'I detest the attempt to fetter the law with maxims'. {*Yarmouth v France* (1887) 19 QBD 647, at p 653. See also *Ballard v North British Rly Co* (1923) SC (HL) 43, *per* Lord Shaw of Dunfermline at p 56; *Ingram v United Automobile Services Ltd* [1943] 2 All ER 71, *per* du Parcq LJ at p 73 (his remark is not included in the report of the case set out in [1943] KB 612).}

The proper use of maxims is to treat them not as fetters, but as repositories of that wisdom the best lawyers contribute to human welfare. While a broadly-stated maxim is likely to have exceptions and require qualification, the law still finds a use for this way of expressing some basic principle. Coke said-

> 'It is holden for an inconvenience that any of the maxims of the law should be broken ... for that by infringing of a maxim, not only a general prejudice to many, but in the end a public uncertainty and confusion to all would follow.'

{Co Litt 152b.}

We have space to deal only with some of the more important maxims applicable in the construction of statutes. Even so their bulk is too great to be dealt with in this section. Accordingly they are described in Part XIX of the Code. Certain other maxims are dealt with in their appropriate places in the Code. {See Index.}

146. Presumptions: that updating construction to be applied

While it remains law, an Act is to be treated as always speaking. In its application on any date, the language of the Act, though necessarily embedded in its own time, is nevertheless to be construed in accordance with the need to treat it as current law.

With regard to updating, Acts can be divided into two categories, namely the Act that is intended to develop in meaning with developing circumstances (in this Code called an ongoing Act) and the Act that is intended to be of unchanging effect (in the Code called a fixed-time Act).

It is presumed that Parliament intends the court to apply to an ongoing Act a construction that continuously updates its wording to allow for changes since the Act was initially framed.

In particular where, owing to developments occurring since the original passing of an enactment, a counter-mischief comes into existence or increases, it is presumed that Parliament intends the court so to construe the enactment as to minimise the adverse effects of the counter-mischief.

COMMENTARY

This section states the principle, enunciated by the great Victorian draftsman Lord Thring, that an Act is taken to be always speaking. {*Practical Legislation* (1902) p 83.} While it remains in force, the Act is necessarily to be treated as current law. {As to the doctrine of 'tacit legislation' see p 358 below.} It speaks from day to day, though always (unless textually amended) in the words of its original draftsman.

With this principle in mind, the competent draftsman frames his language in terms suitable for continuing operation into the unforeseeable future. He does not conspicuously compose the Act as at the date of his draft. Rather, he aims to employ a continuous present tense. For example he uses, as Thring enjoined, the word *shall* as 'an imperative only, and not as a future'. {Ibid.}

Yet, since language (like human society) is continually in flux, the formula expressed in the words of one age may not feel comfortable as current law to its subjects in another. It might even fill them with the consciousness of governance from the grave: an always absurd, and sometimes intolerable, infliction. Where the words have changed their meaning, an interpreter may find it impossible to apply the original sense. Imagination and historical awareness are here required.

Each generation lives under the law it inherits. Constant formal updating is not practicable, so an Act takes on a life of its own. What the original framers intended sinks gradually into history. While their language may endure as law, its current subjects are likely to find that law more and more ill-fitting.

The intention of the originators, collected from an Act's legislative history, necessarily becomes less relevant as time rolls by. Yet their words remain law. Viewed like this, the ongoing Act resembles a vessel launched on some one-way voyage from the old world to the new. The vessel is not going to return; nor are its passengers. Having only what they set out with, they cope as best they can. On arrival in the present, they deploy their native endowments under conditions originally unguessed at.

The ongoing Act   In construing an ongoing Act, the interpreter is to presume that Parliament intended the Act to be applied at any future time in such a way as to give effect to the true original intention. Accordingly the interpreter is to make allowances for any relevant changes that have occurred, since the Act's passing, in law, social conditions, technology, the meaning of words, and other matters.

Just as the US Constitution is regarded as a 'living Constitution', so an ongoing British Act is regarded as a 'living Act'. {Thomas Grey called 'the living Constitution' Americans' characteristic contemporary metaphor, describing an instrument which permits the judiciary to elucidate the development and change in constitutional rights over time ('Do We Have an Unwritten Constitution?' (1975) 27 Stan L Rev 703, at p 711). Louis Lusky holds that the founding fathers conferred an 'implied right' of judicial revision (*By What Right?* (Charlottesville, Michie Co, 1975) p 21). Cf *M'Culloch v Maryland* (1819) 17 US 316.}

That today's construction involves the supposition that Parliament was catering long ago for a state of affairs that did not then exist is no argument against that construction. Parliament, in the wording of an enactment, is expected to anticipate temporal developments. Indeed the draftsman will try to foresee the future, and allow for it in his wording.

Example 1 On one view of the definition of 'superior court' in s 19 of the Contempt of Court Act 1981, it applied to a type of court that did not exist in 1981. In *Peart v Stewart* {[1983] 1 All ER 859, at p 861.} Lord Diplock said-

'I should . . . have reached the same conclusion on the construction of the definition of "superior court" in s 19, even if it were impossible to point to any existing court which complied with the description and one were driven to the conclusion that the draftsman was making anticipatory provision for possible new courts that might be subsequently created with the status of superior courts of record.'

An enactment of former days is thus to be read today, in the light of dynamic processing received over the years, with such modification of the current meaning of its language as will now give effect to the original legislative intention. The reality and effect of dynamic processing provides the gradual adjustment. It is constituted by judicial interpretation, year in and year out. It also comprises processing by executive officials. {As to dynamic processing by courts and officials see s 26 of this Code.}

Commentators often fail to take into account this processing factor. H L A Hart asserts that the Witchcraft Act 1735 was at all times applied in the same way, even though it remained in force for more than two centuries. {*The Concept of Law* pp 60-4.} This is obviously not so, as a study of the cases shows. {The Act was repealed by the Fraudulent Mediums Act 1951 s 2(a). A successful prosecution was brought under it as late as 1944 (*R v Duncan* [1944] KB 713).} 713).}

Rightly dismissing the argument that old Acts remain law *solely* because the current legislature tacitly endorses them, Hart mistakenly goes to the other extreme. He claims that old Acts remaining in force and those passed today have precisely the same juridical nature. There is, he says, 'nothing to distinguish the legal status of a statute of the present sovereign and an unrepealed statute of an earlier one'. {*The Concept of Law* p 64.} This is clearly not the case with most surviving statutes, if one examines the substance of the matter.

On an elementary level, it is true that there is no juristic difference between an ancient and a modern Act when both are unrepealed. Each is law, and each is 'speaking'. Yet from a realistic viewpoint they do not both speak in the same tones, or carry the same conviction. Any court of construction will accept and act upon these facts, yet Hart dismisses such realism as 'humdrum'. {*The Concept of Law* p 64.}

Tacit legislation Hart goes on to deride as 'absurd' the notion that the acquiescence of the current legislature in the survival of an old Act confers upon it added legitimacy. Yet the notion has some force. Where Parliament allows an ancient statute to continue in operation, this does convey a message to the court. In law, the concept of an act includes the omission to act.

Perhaps, as with the Justices of the Peace Act 1361 (which provides for binding over), the ancient statute remains in current use and is regarded as doing an effective job. Or perhaps, as with the remaining Lord's Day Observance Acts, the topic is too politically contentious for agreed reform to be practicable. Or, as with ancient constitutional statutes, Parliament may fear disproportionate opposition from conservationists if it attempts reform. There are various possible attitudes to ancient Acts that still have life in them, but one thing is clear. Parliament is not truly antagonistic to the old Act, or it would at once repeal it.

Indeed the same applies to Parliament's suffering a *common law* rule to continue. Maine even went so far as to assert that the common law is in reality a command of Parliament 'because they can repeal or alter or restate it at pleasure'. {H Maine *The Early History of Institutions* p 314.}

Similar considerations apply to legislative acceptance of the judicial processing of an enactment. When Parliament dislikes a court decision it takes steps to reverse it. {See p 78 above.} Failure to take such steps indicates acceptance if not downright approval. In law, acquiescence gives consent. As *Maxwell* says: 'the long acquiescence of the legislature in the interpretation put upon its enactment by notorious practice may, perhaps, be regarded as some sanction and approval of it'. {P B Maxwell *The Interpretation of Statutes* (12th edn, 1969) p 264.}

The inference of tacit approval of a legal rule grows stronger when Parliament does not take the opportunity to amend it which is afforded by the introduction of a Bill on the subject.

Whenever any of these factors apply, the courts will take judicial notice of the position, and construe the Act accordingly. {For the doctrine of judicial notice see s 21 of this Code.} They will certainly not regard a surviving ancient statute in precisely the same light as some new-minted mandated product of a government just returned to power.

Changes in the mischief The mischief at which an enactment was originally directed needs to be 'discerned and considered' in order to construe the enactment correctly. {See s 301 of this Code.} Difficulty can be caused by the obvious fact that while the enactment may continue in force the mischief on the ground is likely to change, or even (if Parliament's remedy works) disappear altogether.

Example 2 The statute 1 Ja 1 c 8 (1603) took away benefit of clergy where, even without malice aforethought-

> ' . . . one thrust or stabbed another, not then having a weapon drawn,
> or who had not then first stricken the party stabbing, so that he died
> thereof within six months after.'

Blackstone tells us that the mischief at which the Act was aimed was 'the frequent quarrels and stabbings with short daggers between the Scotch and the

English at the accession of James the First'. {Kerr Bl (4th edn, 1876) iv 193 n 1.} Blackstone added that being therefore temporary the statute 'ought to have expired with the mischief which it meant to remedy'. {Ibid.} It did not however do so, but remained on the statute book till long after Blackstone's own death. {It was repealed by 9 Geo 4 c 31 (1828).}

If the enactment is successful it will remove, or at least alleviate, the social mischief. {As to the social mischief see s 302 of this Code.} In the early days however the court will need to help the enactment achieve its object. At best, the enactment may have only partial success. Persons concerned to continue the mischief may attempt to do so. As time goes on, various factors may cause changes in the mischief or may lead to its disappearance. We can illustrate the position in schematic form.

Suppose that SM is a social mischief for which the best legal remedy (so far as law can provide a remedy) is the enactment E. E is accordingly passed into law. E will remain law until amended or repealed, which may be any period from a few months to several centuries. It is by no means certain that E will be amended or repealed at the moment the need for this arises. It follows that E may continue to have effect well after the conditions which caused it to be added to the statute book have significantly changed or even disappeared.

Example 3 It is the year 1772. Naval ships are built of seasoned oak. Burning tar for caulking is everywhere present in His Majesty's dockyards. There are also many malcontents. Arson of the ships is easy, and poses a grave danger to the state. This social mischief calls for a change in the law, effected by the passing of a statute we may call E. {In fact 12 Geo 3 c 24, named by the Short Titles Act 1896 the Dockyards, etc, Protection Act 1772.} This carries the death penalty, and is effective.

In time naval ships cease to be wooden. Instead they are constructed of iron, which is much less easily made the subject of arson. E nevertheless remains in force. This might be accounted for by the fact that at the same time sail gives way to steam. The new iron ships carry coal, which is burnt in their furnaces. Arson is still a risk.

The coal-burning iron ships are succeeded by diesel-powered steel ships. Arson becomes almost a practical impossibility. Still E remains in force. Still it imposes the death penalty, even after capital punishment for most crimes (including murder) has been abolished. Finally, long after it has ceased to be needed, E is repealed. {In the case of the Dockyards, etc, Protection Act 1772, this was effected by the Criminal Damage Act 1971 s 11.}

We see that in this instance E cured the legal mischief, which meant that (so far as law could do it) SM, the social mischief, was checked. Then, for reasons not altogether connected with law, SM changed in character. By reason of the severe penalty, it ceased to be an actual mischief and became potential only. Furthermore the potential harm was greatly reduced by changes in the ships. Yet the words of the Act remained exactly the same.

All we are here concerned with is how changes in SM affect the interpretation of E. E remains verbally the same, but as the years pass SM changes. Since an Act is always speaking, E (so far as concerns the mischief) must be construed from time to time with regard to the current state of SM.

Towards the end of E's life on the statute book, SM has dwindled to little or nothing. It is then not something that needs to be remedied. There is virtually no mischief to which E is now directed. E declines into the category of a technical or nominal law. If it is activated by a prosecution the court will react accordingly. It will criticise the bringing of the case. It will sum up against the prosecution. If the legal meaning of E is doubtful, it will give little weight to the factor of public safety and much weight to the principle against doubtful penalization.

We see that Hart is wrong, and there *is* a juridical difference between yesterday's Act and today's.

Changes in relevant law   After an Act is passed, later amendments of the corpus juris (perhaps carried out for a quite different purpose) may mean that the legal remedy provided by the Act to deal with the original mischief has become inadequate or inappropriate. In accordance with principles of legal policy, judges develop common law doctrines to deal with legal developments. {See, e g, *R v David Timmis* [1976] Crim LR 129 (common law crime of escape developed to accomodate modern arrest procedures where an offence has not necessarily been committed, eg, arrest for breathalyser test). For legal policy see s 126 of this Code.} Similar development is needed in statute law.

In theory this should not be so, because the keepers of the statute book should guard against it by promoting amending Acts as necesssary. Frequently this is not done however. The court must then, in interpreting an affected Act, make allowances for the fact that the surrounding legal conditions prevailing on the date of its passing have changed.

It also follows that legal references in an enactment must be updated to allow for change. {See 2 Co Inst 35 ('lords' in Magna Carta taken to include new ranks of nobility).} If for example an ongoing enactment refers to territories falling within the term 'colony', it applies at a particular time only to territories with the legal status of colonies *at that time*. Their status at the date of enactment is immaterial. {Cf *Pole-Carew v Craddock* [1920] 3 KB 109 and *Gissing v Liverpool Corpn* [1935] Ch 1 ('tax' in pre-income tax enactment held to include income tax).}

Draftsmen of amending Acts sometimes fail to realise that changes in surrounding law call for corresponding changes in the language they choose. Courts need to be aware of the difficulty this can cause. {As to differences in drafting technique at various periods see s 76 of this Code and *R v Manners* [1976] Crim LR 255.}

Example 4   The legal term *felony* originally meant 'liable to forfeiture'. {Kerr Bl (4th edn, 1876) iv 82.} When forfeiture was abolished by the Forfeiture Act 1870 it became irrelevant to retain the legal concept of felony. Yet it remained in common use until the passing of the Criminal Law Act 1967. {See s 1.}

A similar story can be told of the term *murder*, which originally meant a *secret* homicide. {Kerr Bl (4th edn, 1876) iv 195.} Blackstone remarks: 'But, this difference being totally abolished by statute 14 Edw 3 c 4 (1340), we must now . . . define murder in quite another manner'. {Ibid.}

Example 5   In *Nugent-Head v Jacob (Inspector of Taxes)* {[1948] AC 321, at p 322.}, Viscount Simon commented on a difficulty of this kind in the enactments relating to income tax-

'It is much to be regretted that the present statute law defining in what cases a married woman is herself liable to income tax . . . is not stated in plain and unambiguous language . . . As it is, the words now in operation are largely borrowed from Acts of 1803, 1805 and 1806, at which dates the effect of marriage on the property of a wife was very different from what it is today.'

When the question arises of whether an ongoing enactment covers a legal entity not known at the date it was passed, the key is whether it is of the same type or genus as things originally covered by the enactment.

Example 6 In *R v Manners* {[1976] Crim LR 255.} the question was whether the North Thames Gas Board, set up under the Gas Act 1948, was a 'public body' within the meaning of the Prevention of Corruption Acts 1889 to 1916. *Held* The question was what type of body was regarded in 1916 as a 'public body'. Applying that test, the North Thames Gas Board qualified. (This was reinforced by the fact that s 41(1) of the Gas Act 1948 excluded the Public Authorities Protection Act 1893, which would not have been necessary if Gas Boards were not public bodies.)

Where there has been a significant change in law since the enactment was framed, it is applied to the *substance* of the new law. If the original terminology referred to has been allotted a different meaning, the court will look at the substance behind the wording. The fact that the term referred to by the enactment is still in use does not mean the enactment will apply if the current use gives the term an essentially different meaning.

Example 7 Section 10 of the Extradition Act 1870 draws a significant distinction between persons *convicted* of an extradition crime and those merely *accused* of such a crime. Section 26 of the Act makes it clear that a person convicted under a foreign law *in contumacia* falls into the latter rather than the former category. This is because such a conviction is normally provisional, and may be reversed. {The section was designed to give statutory effect to the decision in *Re Coppin* (1866) LR 2 Ch App 47: see *Zezza v Government of Italy* [1982] 2 All ER 513, at p 517.}

In *Zezza v Government of Italy* {[1982] 2 All ER 513.} the House of Lords considered the application of these provisions in relation to Italian law. The appellant had been convicted in Italy in his absence, by a procedure described in the relevant Italian law (introduced in 1931) as *in contumacia*. The extradition treaty, made in 1873, said that a person should not be treated as a convict if the conviction was *in contumacia*. At that time under Italian law a conviction *in contumacia* was merely provisional, but under the 1931 law it was final (subject to a right of appeal which had been exercised in this case).

Held While the current Italian law used the expression *in contumacia*, it did so in a materially different sense from that used in the 1870 Act and the 1873 treaty. Although the conviction was in the absence of the accused it was in no sense provisional, and there was no further appeal. Accordingly it was right to treat the appellant as a person convicted, rather than merely as a person accused. Lord Roskill said {P 518.} that 'notwithstanding the name given to, or one might say the label attaching to, the Italian procedure . . . your Lordships should look at the true nature and effect of the procedure as it has operated in Italy since 1931'.

Also relevant are changes in judicial approach over the years. An Act might be differently construed before and after such a change.

Example 8   In *River Wear Cmrs v Adamson* {(1877) 2 App Cas 743.} the House of Lords, in refusing to hold a shipowner liable for damage caused to a pier by his ship without any fault, appeared to depart from the literal meaning of s 74 of the Harbours, Docks, and Piers Clauses Act 1847. Commenting on a suggestion by E A Driedger {*The Construction of Statutes* p 36.} regarding this decision, Sir Rupert Cross said-

> 'There is much force in Mr Driedger's suggestion that Lord Blackburn refused to believe that Parliament meant what it said, and, over the years, the courts have undoubtedly become less squeamish over the question of statutory impositions of civil liability without fault.'

{R Cross *Statutory Interpretation* p 83. Cross cites as an example of the 'less squeamish' approach *Kensington Borough Council v Walters* [1960] 1 QB 361.}

As to *criminal* liability without fault there has been a recent movement in the opposite direction. Lord Diplock said in 1980 {*R v Sheppard* [1981] AC 394, at pp 407-8.}-

> 'The climate of both parliamentary and judicial opinion has been growing less favourable to the recognition of absolute offences over the last few decades, a trend to which s 1 of the Homicide Act 1957 and s 8 of the Criminal Justice Act 1967 bear witness in the case of Parliament, and in the case of the judiciary is illustrated by the speeches in this House in *Sweet v Parsley* {[1970] AC 132.}.'

Change in another field was noted by Lord Diplock when he said in 1981 that 'Any judicial statements on matters of public law if made before 1950 are likely to be a misleading guide to what the law is today'. {*IRC v National Federation of Self-Employed and Small Businesses Ltd* [1981] 2 WLR 722, at p 736.} On the exercise of a discretion conferred by statute, Lord Diplock said in 1982-

> ' . . . an expression of opinion by [the House of Lords] as to the way in which a judicial discretion ought to have been exercised in circumstances as they existed many years ago, ought not to be regarded as immutable when circumstances have altered radically from those current when the judgment containing that expression of opinion was delivered.'

{*M V Yorke Motors (a firm) v Edwards* [1982] 1 All ER 1024, at p 1028. One of the changed circumstances relevant was the greater profit nowadays accruing to a debtor who delays payment.}

Changes in social conditions   Where relevant social conditions have changed since the date of enactment, what was then classed as a social mischief may not be so regarded today. {As to the doctrine of the social mischief see s 302 of this Code.} It is very difficult for the court to apply an enactment so as to 'remedy' what is no longer regarded as a mischief. {For the concept that the purpose of an enactment is to remedy a mischief see s 138 of this Code.} The consequence is an interpretation that minimises the coercive effect of the enactment and gives great weight to criteria such as the principle against doubtful penalization. {See s 129 and Part XIII of this Code.}

Example 9 Section 17 of the London Hackney Carriage Act 1853 makes it an offence for a cab driver to 'demand *or take* more than the proper fare'. {Emphasis added.} The literal meaning clearly includes taking a tip, whether demanded or not. A century later, the tipping of cab drivers had become an accepted social custom. In *Bassam v Green* {[1981] Crim LR 626.} both members of the Divisional Court stated obiter, without giving reasons, that tipping did *not* contravene s 17.

Example 10 Section 5(1) of the Housing Act 1957 (a consolidation Act) makes it unlawful 'to erect any back-to-back-houses intended to be used as dwellings for the working classes'. By 1957 the phrase 'working classes' had already been judicially declared obsolete. {*Green & Sons v Minister of Health (No 2)* [1948] 1 KB 34, at p 38.} Nor were back-to-back houses of the old slum variety any longer built (for one thing they would not have got planning permission). So the social mischief at which the original enactment was directed had vanished. In *Chorley Borough Council v Barratt Developments (North West) Ltd* {[1979] 3 All ER 634.} Blackett-Ord V-C performed the obsequies of s 5(1). It was not a case for applying the doctrine of developing the ongoing enactment; the enactment was obsolete.

If, as often happens, Parliament identifies a matter as a social mischief before a conservative judiciary is ready to do so the Act will receive a restricted construction until the judiciary catches up. This notoriously occurred with Acts dealing with the emancipation of women, from the Married Women's Property Act 1882 to the Sex Discrimination Act 1975. {See C E Odgers *The Construction of Deeds and Statutes* (5th edn, 1967) p 444, citing *Edwards v Porter* [1925] AC 1. See also *Viscountess Rhondda's Claim* [1922] 2 AC 339; *Peake v Automotive Products Ltd* [1978] QB 233; *Grieg v Community Industry* [1979] ICR 356; *The Times* (letters) 1 June 1978.}

Enactments dealing with property rights need to be construed in the light of social change.

Example 11 In *Williams & Glyn's Bank v Boland* {[1980] 2 All ER 408.} the House of Lords considered the position of a wife whose husband was the legal owner of the matrimonial home in which she had an equitable interest. They both lived in the house, but the husband mortgaged it to the bank without disclosing her interest. Did she have an overriding interest protected by s 70(1)(g) of the Land Registration Act 1925? This depended on whether she was 'in actual occupation'.
Held Earlier cases suggesting that in such circumstances the husband alone was in actual occupation were no longer applicable in view of changes in the respective social and legal status of husband and wife. Accordingly the wife was entitled to the protection of the Act. Lord Wilberforce said {P 411.}: 'The solution must be derived from a consideration in the light of current social conditions of the Land Registration Act 1925 and other property statutes'. {Cf *R v D* [1984] 2 All ER 449 (father no longer has absolute control over his child).}

Changes in the practices of mankind may necessitate a strained construction if the legislator's object is to be achieved.

Example 12   The Carriage by Air Act 1961 gives legislative force to the Warsaw Convention as amended at The Hague in 1955, which is set out in Sch 1. The Convention limits liability for loss of or damage to 'registered baggage', but does not explain what 'registered' means or what 'registration' entails. In *Collins v British Airways Board* {[1982] 1 All ER 302, at pp 305-6.} Lord Denning MR explained that originally airlines kept register books in which all baggage was entered, but that this had been discontinued. He added-

> 'What then are we to do? The only solution that I can see is to strike out the words "registered" and "registration" wherever they occur in the articles. By doing this, you will find that all the articles work perfectly, except that you have to find out what a "baggage check" is.'

{Cf *Marina Shipping Ltd v Laughton* [1982] 1 All ER 481, at p 487 (changes in shipping practices led to the change that a master was no longer to be treated as necessarily contracting on behalf of the owner).}

Similarly the earlier *processing* of an enactment may be disregarded if it is no longer appropriate in the light of changed conditions.

Example 13   This occurred with *R v Blane* {(1849) 13 QB 769.}, a decision on the meaning of the word 'bastard' in the Poor Law Amendment Act 1844. The court held that English bastardy statutes did not apply to a bastard born out of the jurisdiction, but this was reversed in *R v Bow Road JJ, ex p Adedigba*. {[1968] 2 QB 572.} Edmund Davies LJ said of *R v Blane* that 'the application of that decision to social conditions in the mid-twentieth century can lead to irrational and indeed unjust results'. {P 586. Cf *Dyson Holdings Ltd v Fox* [1975] 3 All ER 1030 (declining to follow the decision in *Gammans v Ekins* [1950] 2 KB 328 that a 'common law wife' is not a member of a tenant's family for purposes of the Rent Acts).}

Example 14   Section 3(2) of the Matrimonial Causes Act 1973 allowed a judge to authorise presentation of a divorce petition within three years of marriage on the ground of 'exceptional depravity'. In *C v C* {[1979] 1 All ER 556.} it was held by the Court of Appeal that this phrase must be construed in the light of current social conditions. Ormrod LJ said-

> 'The word "depravity" has fallen out of general use (it is not included in Fowler's *Modern English Usage*) so that it now conveys only a vague idea of very unpleasant conduct. In 1937 [when the phrase was first introduced into the divorce law by s 1 of the Matrimonial Causes Act 1937] it may have carried to contemporary minds a much more specific meaning, but norms of behaviour, particularly in the sexual sense, have changed greatly in the last 40 years. It is unlikely that the meaning . . . suggested by Denning LJ in *Bowman v Bowman* {[1949] P 353, at pp 356-7.} would find much support today.'

The Law Commissions have summed up this aspect with the remark that 'Particular presumptions of intention will ... be modified or even abandoned with the passage of time, and with the modification of the social values which they embody'. {*The Interpretation of Statutes* (1969) LAW COM No 21, para 34.}

Developments in technology   The nature of an ongoing Act requires the court to take account of changes in technology, and treat the statutory language as modified accordingly when this is needed to implement the legislative intention.

Example 15   Section 4 of the Foreign Enlistment Act 1870 makes it an offence for a British subject to accept any engagement in 'the military or naval service' of a foreign state which is at war with a friendly state. The mischief at which s 4 is aimed requires this phrase to be taken as now including air force service. {Cf *The International* (1871) LR 3 A & E 321 (laying of submarine cable).}

Textual updating of the 1870 Act was recommended in the Report of the Committee of Privy Councillors appointed to inquire into the recruitment of mercenaries {(1976) Cmnd 6569.}, but has not been done. Even so it seems that a modern court should treat 'military or naval service' in s 4 as including any service in the armed forces of the state in question.

If however changed technology produces something which is altogether beyond the scope of the original enactment, the court will not treat it as covered.

Example 16   In *Kingston Wharves Ltd v Reynolds Jamaica Mines Ltd* {[1959] AC 187.} the Judicial Committee of the Privy Council had to decide whether 18,000 lb powered tractors were 'carriages' within the meaning of an 1895 law. *Held* The legislator could not have intended articles of the weight and complexity of these tractors to be included.

Example 17   Section 3(1) of the Coroners Act 1887 (a consolidation Act) says that where a coroner is informed that the dead body of a person is lying within his jurisdiction, and certain conditions are satisfied, the coroner, whether or not the cause of death arose within his jurisdiction, shall hold an inquest.

The development of refrigeration and air freight services means that bodies can now easily be brought to England from foreign parts. In 1887 this was impossible, so there was no need for the Act to state that the death must have occurred in Britain. Now that new technology makes real the possibility that a decedent whose body is in Britain died abroad, the courts have had to decide whether a territorial limitation is to be treated as implied. The point arose in *R v West Yorkshire Coroner, ex p Smith* {[1982] 2 All ER 801 and 3 All ER 1098.}, where judicial opinion was divided. *Held* There was on balance no justification for applying a restriction on the width of s 3(1).

Again, if the social mischief against which the enactment is directed has disappeared or lessened the court may decline to develop the meaning of the language.

Example 18   Section 47 of the Shops Act 1950 required a launderette to be 'closed for the serving of customers' on a Sunday. It was open and in use, but no staff were present. The washing machines were all coin-operated. *Held* The reference in s 47 was confined to *personal* service, and there was no contravention.

The courts may develop the language for one purpose but not another. This will usually be because the weighting of the relevant interpretative factors is different. {As to the weighing of factors see Part VII of this Code.}

Example 19   In *Taylor v Goodwin* {(1879) 4 QBD 228.} a bicycle was held to be a 'carriage' within the meaning of a provision of the Highway Act 1835 prohibiting furious driving, whereas in *Williams v Ellis* {(1880) 49 LJMC 47.} a bicycle was held *not* to be a 'carriage' for the purpose of an enactment imposing taxation. {Cf *Simpson v Teignmouth Bridge Co* (1903) 72 LJKB 204 (bicycle not a 'carriage' etc under an Act imposing tolls).}

For other examples of allowance by the courts for developments in technology see *Gambart v Ball* {(1863) 32 LJCP 166.} (photography held within Engraving Copyright Act 1734); *A-G v Edison Telephone Co of London Ltd* {(1880) 6 QBD 244.} (telephone held to be a 'telegraph') {See also *Malone v Commr of Police of the Metropolis (No 2)* [1979] 2 All ER 620, at pp 630, 642; and cf *In re Regulation and Control of Radio Communications in Canada* [1932] AC 304 (does 'telegraph' include broadcasting?).}; *Parkyns v Preist* {(1881) 7 QBD 313.} (steam tricycle held to be a 'locomotive'); *Chappell & Co Ltd v Associated Radio Co of Australia Ltd* [1925] VLR 350.} (radio broadcast a 'performance in public' under pre-broadcasting Copyright Act); *Chapman v Kirke* {[1948] 2 KB 450, at p 452.} (electric tramcar held to be a 'stage carriage' within Stage Carriages Act 1832); *Lake Macquarie Shire Council v Aberdare County Council* {(1970) 123 CLR 327.} ('gas' in Act passed when there was only coal gas included liquified petroleum gas); *Imperial Chemical Industries of Australia and New Zealand Ltd v FCT* {(1972) 46 ALJR 35.} (salt-panning held to be 'mining'); *Barker v Wilson* {[1980] 2 All ER 81.} ('bankers' books' in s 9 of Bankers' Books Evidence Act 1879 held to include microfilm); *R v South London Coroner, ex p Thompson* {(1982) *The Times* 9 July.} (requirement in r 30 of Coroners Rules 1953 {SI 1953/205.} that coroner should 'take a note' satisfied by use of tape recorder); *Hawkins v Harold A Russett Ltd* {[1983] 1 All ER 215.} (clip-on container held part of lorry for purpose of overhang restrictions in reg 58 of Motor Vehicles (Construction and Use) Regulations 1978 {SI 1978/1017.})

Changes in meaning of words   Where an expression used in an Act has changed its original meaning, the Act may have to be construed as if there were substituted for that expression a term with a modern meaning corresponding to that original meaning. {*The Longford* (1889) 14 PD 34.} This may be described as the 'box' principle; and can be demonstrated schematically as follows. {The box principle does not take account of new things produced by technology or otherwise; it is solely concerned with changed meanings of words.}

An Act uses a term T1. The meaning of T1 at the date when the Act is passed indicates that it comprises A, B, C and D. (In other words T1 is like a box containing those four elements and no others.) By the time the instant case is heard, the meaning of T1 has changed. Now the box contains A, B, E and F, and nothing else. However, another term T2 is now in use. The box which is T2 contains, at the date of the instant case, the elements A, B, C and D (and no others). For the purposes of that case, the Act is to be read as if instead of T1 it used the term T2. (If there were in fact no new term T2, it would be necessary to use instead a form of words which embraced A, B, C and D, and nothing else.)

The box principle can be briefly described by asking whether it is necessary to treat the Act as textually amended in order that it shall mean today what it meant when passed. It is undoubtedly the correct approach to changes in the meaning of words, yet courts sometimes depart from it.

Example 20 The old meaning of the word *engine* was very wide. It derives from the Latin *ingenium,* and formerly meant any product of human ingenuity. Its modern meaning is much narrower, and denotes a mechanical contrivance with moving parts. Section 31 of the Offences against the Person Act 1861 makes it an offence to set or place 'any spring gun, mantrap, or other engine' calculated to endanger life. In *R v Munks* {[1964] 1 QB 304.} the accused rigged up an electrical trap designed to inflict a shock when his wife opened a french window. He was convicted of placing an engine, contrary to s 31.

Held The conviction would be quashed. Lord Parker CJ said {P 307.}-

' . . . as a matter of common sense, it is difficult to see how *today at any rate* one could aptly refer to these two electric wires as amounting to a spring gun, mantrap or other engine. The court has come to the conclusion that, particularly as this is a penal statute, the meaning to be given to it is the more limited meaning of "engine" as meaning a mechanical contrivance. It also accords with common sense, it seems to this court, as to the natural meaning *today* of "engine".'

{Emphasis added.}

The decision may well be correct as an example of the application of the *ejusdem generis* doctrine. {As to this doctrine see ss 378to 385 of this Code.} However the italicised passages run contrary to the box principle and are therefore, it is submitted, erroneous.

If it seems that the meaning of an expression used in an Act may have changed materially since the Act was passed, evidence may be adduced to establish the original meaning. {*London and North Eastern Rly Co v Berriman* [1946] AC 278, at p 312. See also *Hardwick Game Farm v Suffolk Agricultural and Poultry Producers Assn Ltd* [1966] 1 All ER 309, at p 323.}

Examples of expressions whose meanings have changed in ways significant to the application of legislation also include *blackmail* (a term once confined to the extorting of protection money for avoidance of rapine in the northern counties: 43 Eliz 1 c 13 (1601)); *discover* (this used to mean uncover rather than find; thus the statute 13 Eliz 1 c 2 (1571) made it a crime not to discover an offender); *fraudulent* (this formerly had a wide meaning equivalent to wrongful) {*A-G's Reference (No 1 of 1981)* [1982] 2 All ER 417.}; *indecent* (this once meant unbecoming or indecorous) {Kerr Bl (4th edn, 1876) iv 51. See *Abrahams v Cavey* [1967] 3 All ER 179 (disturbance in church).}; *lottery* (this formerly included any distribution of prizes by lot or chance; now it is confined to distributions for payment) {*Imperial Tobacco Ltd v A-G* [1979] 2 All ER 592, at p 606.}; *pillors and robbers* (as used in the Justices of the Peace Act 1361, this covers any disturber of the peace) {*Lansbury v Riley* [1914] 3 KB 229.}; *police* (this formerly meant the peace or good order of a place) {Kerr Bl (4th edn, 1876) iv 176-7.}; *sad* (once meaning sober and discreet; thus the statute 3 Hen 7 c 14

(1487) required a jury consisting of 'twelve sad men'); *seduce* (this once simply meant persuade: the statute 5 Geo 1 c 27 (1718) made it an offence to seduce artificers to settle abroad); *tory* (the statute 7 Wm 3 c 21 (1695) 'for better suppresssing tories, robbers, and rapparees' was repealed by the Statute Law Revision Act 1878); *trespasser* (this formerly meant any wrongdoer; later it was narrowed by reference to the tort of trespass) { *Wilson v Knubley* (1806) 7 East 128, at p 136.}.

The fixed-time Act A fixed-time Act is one which, contrary to the usual rule, was intended to be applied in the same way whatever changes might occur after its passing. It has as it were a once for all operation. It is to such an Act that the oft-quoted words of Lord Esher chiefly apply: 'the Act must be construed as if one were interpreting it the day after it was passed'. { *The Longford* (1889) 14 PD 34, at p 36. The dictum is also relevant to the box principle discussed above (pp 366–377).} An obvious example is the indemnity Act. {See s 28 of this Code.} There are various other possibilities.

Example 21 It was held in *Lord Colchester v Kewney* {(1866) LR 1 Ex 368, at p 380.} that s 25 of the Land Tax Act 1797, which exempted 'any hospital' from the land tax, was intended by Parliament to apply only to hospitals which were in existence at the time the Act was passed.

The presumption however is that an Act is intended to be an ongoing Act, since this is the nature of statute law: an Act is always speaking. So there must be some reason adduced on account of which Parliament is taken to depart in a particular case from this principle. One such reason is where the Act is of the nature of a *contract*. If an Act can be said to form or ratify a contract its meaning cannot properly be 'developed' in the usual way. An obvious example is an Act implementing an international convention. {See s 242 of this Code.} The convention itself may be subject to 'development', but that is another matter.

Similar principles apply to constitutional Acts relating to dependent territories.

Example 22 In a Canadian constitutional appeal Lord Sankey LC said-

'The process of interpretation as the years go on ought not to be allowed to dim or whittle down the provisions of the original contract upon which the federation was founded, nor is it legitimate that any judicial construction of the provisions of ss 91 and 92 should impose a new and different contract upon the federating bodies.'

{ *Re the Regulation and Control of Aeronautics in Canada* [1932] AC 54, at p 70.}

Example 23 It was held in *A-G for Alberta v Huggard Assets Ltd* {[1953] AC 420.} that the Tenures Abolition Act 1660 was of the nature of a compact between the king and his people in England and Wales, and thus did not extend to after-acquired territories of the Crown, such as those in Canada. Lord Asquith of Bishopstone said {P 442.}-

'It seems to their Lordships strained to suppose that such an Act, recording a compromise between the King of England and his people, the main object of which was the abolition of certain peculiarities of our insular mediaeval land tenure, was intended to apply to a vast tract of country thousands of miles away which was only inhabited at the time by a few Indians and half castes: people who had never smarted under wardships, marriage and primer seisin, and had almost certainly never heard of them.'

On the other hand an Act which actually lays down a constitution must be expected to develop. As Viscount Jowitt LC said of the British North America Act 1867: 'To such an organic statute the flexible interpretation must be given that changing circumstances require'. {*A-G for Ontario v A-G for Canada* [1947] AC 127, at p 154.}

An obvious instance of the Act which partakes of the nature of a compact is the private Act. The courts treat this as a contract between its promoters (or that portion of the public directly interested in it) and Parliament. {*Milnes v Mayor etc of Huddersfield* (1886) 11 App Cas 511; *Perchard v Heywood* (1800) 8 TR 468.} This brings into operation the principle *verba cartarum fortius accipiuntur contra proferentem* (the words of an instrument are to be taken most strongly against the party putting them forward). {Co Litt 36a.}

Example 24 It was held in *Perchard v Heywood* {(1800) 8 TR 468.} and *Sion College v Lord Mayor of London* {[1901] 1 KB 617.} that a private Act conferring exemption from 'all taxes whatsoever' applied only to taxes in force at the time of passing of the Act.

Increase in counter-mischief Where, owing to developments occurring since the original passing of an enactment, a counter-mischief comes into existence or increases, it is presumed that Parliament intends the court so to construe the enactment as to minimise the adverse effects of the counter-mischief.

As explained in s 326 of this Code, the courts assume that Parliament did not intend an enactment to give rise to a counter-mischief which is as great as or greater than the mischief the enactment was intended to remedy. The problem may be exacerbated where the counter-mischief has come into existence, or increased in gravity, since the date of the enactment. The difficulty is the same with a rule of common law, and the courts take a similar view in either case.

Example 25 The provision of fee scales for legal aid cases protects the public purse, speeds taxation of costs and obviates uncertainty. If however the scales are not updated to meet inflation, a counter-mischief of growing severity will develop. This was so in *R v Wilkinson* {[1980] 1 All ER 597.}, which concerned the scales set out in the Schedule to the Legal Aid in Criminal Proceedings (Fees and Expenses) Regulations 1968. {SI 1968/1230.} Robert Goff J said {P 609.}-

'I was astonished to learn that the figures specified in this Schedule have remained unaltered since 1960, and so have remained unaltered throughout one of the worst periods of inflation in the history of this country. In the result, by today's standards the figures can only be regarded as derisory.'

The only amelioration attempted was an amendment adding a new para 7(6) to the regulations. {Effected by the Legal Aid in Criminal Proceedings (Fees and Expenses) (Amendment) Regulations 1977 (SI 1977/875).} This allowed the taxing officer to exceed the scale where, taking into account specified matters, it did not provide fair remuneration. Robert Goff J commented on para 6(7) {P 610.}-

'. . . in practice, taxing officers treat it as a means of escape from the straitjacket of the Schedule, all interpreting the new para 6(7) very liberally, and some in consequence now disregarding the Schedule altogether. This attitude is most understandable in the circumstances . . . the result of preserving fixed scales unchanged over the past 19 years has not only been to provoke justified resentment on the part of the legal profession and measured criticism by the Royal Commission [on Criminal Procedure] {(1981) Cmnd 8092.}, but to drive those responsible for the taxation of costs to shut their eyes to what has become oppressive legislation.'

The learned judge did not criticise this strained construction of the regulations. On the contrary, he accepted it as being the correct way to remedy the counter-mischief that had grown up.

Example 26   The principle that court hearings should be conducted in public, enshrined in what is known as the rule in *Scott v Scott* {[1913] AC 417; see *Home Office v Harman* [1982] 1 All ER 532, *per* Lord Diplock at p 537.} is intended to remedy the mischief that judges might otherwise misbehave. There are however counter-mischiefs. One of these is the disturbance caused when multitudes of people throng the courts. The nuisance caused by this in the eighteenth century was thus described by Daines Barrington-

'An open court at present is generally so crowded by idle spectators, that no one who hath any real business to do can have access; or, if he procures access, he is not so much at his ease, as those whose interests are depending have a reasonable right to insist upon.'

{*Observations upon the Statutes* (2nd edn, 1767) p 101.}

In still earlier times these disturbances were regarded as a greater mischief than that remedied by the principle of free access to the courts. Accordingly, free access was cut down by statute. {13 Edw 1 cc 42 and 44 (1285), by which spectators were charged for admission to the courts.} In our own day, there has been the growth of different counter-mischiefs. In *Home Office v Harman* {[1982] 1 All ER 532, at p 537.} Lord Diplock called them 'side-effects'-

'My Lords, although the reason for the rule [in *Scott v Scott*] is to discipline the judiciary, to keep the judges themselves up to the mark, the form it takes, that justice is to be administered in open court where anyone present may listen to and report what was said, has inevitable side-effects that may not be conducive to the attainment of justice in the particular case, but which have to be accepted because of the general importance of maintaining the general rule. One of those side-effects is that any document or portion of a document that is read out orally in open court can be taken down in shorthand . . . and can be published as part of a report of the proceedings in the court, even though after it has been read aloud it turns out that it ought not to have been, because it is later ruled to be inadmissible in evidence.'

Lord Diplock went on to say that the adverse effect of the 'side-effects' or counter-mischiefs had increased considerably in recent years through the development of mechanical and electronic means of recording and reproduction of court proceedings. This fact clearly influenced the decision of the House of Lords in *Home Office v Harman* to restrict the freedom of using material obtained on an order of discovery.

Contemporanea expositio Whether an Act is an ongoing or a fixed-time Act, it may be necessary to determine how its meaning was understood at the time it was originally passed. For this purpose reference is made to sources of that time. This is known as *contemporanea expositio*, from the maxim given by Coke in the form *contemporanea expositio est optima et fortissima in lege* (contemporaneous exposition is the best and most powerful in law). {2 Co Inst 11. See also archival drafting, which is described in s 286 of this Code.}

Fixed-time Acts are construed as they were when passed. It was in relation to these that Coke enunciated his maxim. Speaking of Magna Carta, he said: 'This and the like were the forms of ancient Acts and graunts, and the ancient Acts and graunts must be construed and taken as the law was holden at the time when they were made'. {See Craies *Statute Law* (7th edn, 1971) p 80.}

Contemporaneous exposition is not confined to what courts decide. It extends to the *practice* of the legal profession. Furthermore it may embrace the way those who were bound by the Act in question behaved.

Example 27 In *Trustees of the Clyde Navigation v Laird* {(1883) 8 App Cas 658.} the question was whether the Clyde Navigation Consolidation Act 1858 required navigation dues to be paid on logs which were chained together and floated down the River Clyde. It was proved that from the passing of the Act until the present time (a period of a quarter of a century) these dues had been levied and paid without protest. Lord Blackburn said {P 670.} that this raised 'a strong prima facie ground' for thinking that there must exist 'some legal ground' for exacting the dues. Lord Watson however said {P 673.} that such usage was of no value.

While it is true that the actions of laymen are in themselves of little value on a question of statutory interpretation, it might be expected that traders would not for a lengthy period pay charges unless legal opinion supported the grounds for this. Traders often have legal advisers; and legal opinion on a matter affecting the pocket tends to become known.

Maxwell says-

> ' . . . the language of a statute must be understood in the sense in which it was understood when it was passed, and those who lived at or near the time when it was passed may reasonably be supposed to be better acquainted than their descendants with the circumstances to which it had relation, as well as with the sense then attached to legislative expressions.'

{P B Maxwell *The Interpretation of Statutes* (12th edn, 1969) p 264. See also *R v Casement* [1917] 1 KB 98, at p 138.}

In some judgments the doctrine of contemporaneous exposition is confused with something quite different, namely the undesirability of disturbing a settled construction. {See, e g, *Martin v Mackonochie* (1868) LR 2 PC 365, at p 391;

Bourne v Keane [1919] AC 815, at p 874; *Thompson v Nixon* [1966] 1 QB 103, at pp 109-110; *Re Holt's Settlement* [1969] 1 Ch 100, at p 115; Craies *Statute Law* (7th edn, 1971) p 81.} The only connection is that, under the principle of presumed continuity, the practice of today is presumed, unless the contrary is shown, to be the practice of yesterday too. {Jowitt *Dictionary of English Law* tit 'Life'.}

For understandable reasons, the courts dislike disturbing a long-continuing practice. This even applies where the practice seems wrong in law, for *communis error facit jus* (common error makes law). {4 Co Inst 240.}

Example 28   The statute 15 Ric 2 c 3 (1391) expressly provided that the Admiralty should have no jurisdiction over contracts made in the bodies of counties. Yet over a long period seamen entering into such contracts had been allowed to sue on them in the Admiralty court, where the remedy was better than in the common law courts. Holt CJ said that this was 'against the statute expressly, though now *communis error facit jus*'. {*Clay v Sudgrave* (1700) 1 Salk 33. See aslo *Alleson v Marsh* (1690) 2 Vent 181.}

Example 29   Section 1 of the Central Criminal Court Act 1834 empowered judges at the Old Bailey 'or any two of them' to try offences which might be tried under a commission of oyer and terminer for London or Middlesex. However from the passing of the Act it had been the practice, as with other courts acting under commissions of oyer and terminer, for Old Bailey courts to sit with a single judge. In *Leverson v R* {(1869) LR 4 QB 394.} this practice was upheld as lawful. It would clearly not have been in the public interest to rule that hundreds of convictions over a period of some 35 years were invalid. {As to the effect of settled practice see also *Gorham v Bishop of Exeter* (1850) 15 QB 52; *R v Cutbush* (1867) LR 2 QB 379, at p 382; *Hebbert v Purchas* (1871) LR 3 PC 605; *Re Holt's Settlement* [1969] 1 Ch 100, at p 115.}

In *Campbell College, Belfast (Governors) v Comr of Valuation for Northern Ireland* {[1964] 1 WLR 912.} the House of Lords rejected the argument that *contemporanea expositio* required the clear meaning of a century-old rating Act to be set aside. Viscount Radcliffe said {Pp 930-1.}-

> 'If I thought that a decision in favour of the appellants would be likely to have a far-reaching and disturbing effect upon the rating system and the distribution of the rating burden in Northern Ireland, I would be disposed to leave ill alone, whatever my personal views as to the law of the matter. But ... our inquiries suggest that no such large-scale disturbance is to be anticipated. If that is so, I think the balance of convenience inclines towards declaring now what we believe the law to be and always to have been.'

{As to the duty of courts to serve the public interest see s 127 of this Code.}

LINGUISTIC CANONS OF CONSTRUCTION

147. Canons: nature of linguistic canons of construction

A linguistic canon of construction reflects the nature or use of language generally. It does not depend on the legislative character of the enactment in question, nor indeed on its quality as a legal pronouncement. It applies in much the same way to all forms of language.

COMMENTARY

Linguistic canons of construction are not confined to statutes, or even to the field of law. They are based on the rules of logic, grammar, syntax and punctuation; and the use of language as a medium of communication generally.

When judges say, as they sometimes do, that the principles of statutory interpretation do not materially differ from the principles applicable to the interpretation of documents generally, it is these linguistic canons they have in mind. {See *Butler and Baker's Case* (1591) 3 Co Rep 25a, at p 27b; *Grey v Pearson* (1857) 6 HL Cas 61, at p 106; *Caledonian Railway Co v North British Rly Co* (1881) 6 App Cas 114, at p 131; *Lamplugh v Norton* (1889) 22 QBD 452, at p 459; *Curtis v Stovin* (1889) 22 QBD 513, at p 517; *Hawke v Dunn* [1897] 1 QB 579, at p 586.}

The linguistic canons of construction are used to arrive at the literal meaning of an enactment. {As to literal meaning see s 91 of this Code.}

148. Canons: use of deductive reasoning

The literal meaning of an enactment in its application to a particular factual situation is ascertainable by the process of reasoning known as deductive or syllogistic reasoning. In deciding between opposing constructions of an enactment, deductive reasoning is applied to each construction in turn.

COMMENTARY

Linguistic canons of construction For the general nature of linguistic canons of construction see s 147 of this Code.

Literal meaning For the literal meaning of an enactment see s 91 of this Code.

Inference is the mental operation which proceeds by so combining two propositions, called premisses, as to cause a consequent conclusion. Deductive or syllogistic inference proceeds from a universal premiss to a particular premiss. Since it is the nature of law to be universal, law is applied to facts syllogistically.

Because the logical methods available apply equally to all forms of verbal expression, it seems right to class them with general linguistic canons of construction.

Although it is beyond the scope of this work to examine in detail how deductive reasoning could be used in statutory interpretation, certain important aspects of this matter cannot be ignored. They are accordingly dealt with in Part XX of this Code.

149. Canons: construction of Act or other instrument as a whole

An Act or other legislative instrument is to be read as a whole, so that an enactment within it is not treated as standing alone but is interpreted in its context.

COMMENTARY

Linguistic canons of construction   For the general nature of linguistic canons of construction see s 147 of this Code.

The essence of construction of an instrument as a whole was caught by Holmes J in his remark that 'you let whatever galvanic current may come from the rest of the instrument run through the particular sentence'. {O W Holmes Jr 'The Theory of Legal Interpretation' (1898-99) 12 Harv LR 417.}

Doctrine of the free-standing Act   Under the British system, each Act (being drafted as such) is regarded formally as a separate legal entity, standing alone. Though a later Act may state that its text is to be taken as incorporating provisions of an earlier Act, this does not affect the independent status of the earlier Act.

The British system of free-standing Acts contrasts with the system found in most other Commonwealth countries where the whole statute book is a unit divided up into 'chapters'. Although British Acts are given a number known as a 'chapter number', this description is of no modern significance. {As to the chapter number see s 278 of this Code.}

The main relevance of the doctrine of the free-standing Act to statutory interpretation is that, while the enactment is the unit of enquiry {See s 72 of this Code.}, the Act containing the enactment is the main guide to its meaning. The doctrine favours indirect amendment of Acts rather than textual amendment, though in recent years textual amendment has been on the increase. {See s 171 of this Code.}

The doctrine of the free-standing Act no doubt originated in the nature of an early parliamentary Bill as a self-contained petition. An official report stated in 1835 that 'the statutes have been framed extemporaneously, not as parts of a system, but to answer particular exigencies as they occurred'. {*First Report of the Statute Law Commisioners*}

Maitland said that eighteenth-century statutes possessed 'a wonderfully empirical, partial and minutely particularising character', adding that in the so-called age of reason 'the British parliament seems rarely to rise to the dignity of a general proposition'. {Ency Brit (11th edn, 1910) ix 605.}

Continuance of the doctrine into the present day marks the British system as still unscientific and unorganised. There have been many complaints about this, but they have fallen upon deaf ears. {See the Renton Report ('The Preparation of Legislation', report of a Committee appointed by the Lord President of the Council, 1975, Cmnd 6053), republished by Sweet & Maxwell Ltd on behalf of the Statute Law Society. See also the following publications of the Statute Law Society (published on behalf of the Society by Sweet & Maxwell Ltd): *Statute Law Deficiencies* (1970), *Statute Law: the Key to Clarity* (1972), *Statute Law: A Radical Simplification* (1974), *Renton and the Need for Reform* (1979). And see Bennion *Statute Law* (2nd edn, 1983), pp 10-11.}

Uniform construction An Act should be capable of being given a uniform construction, so that it is construed in the same way throughout. The ability to do this depends on whether the Act is a product of precision drafting or disorganised composition. {As to this distinction see s 76 of the Code.} As Professor Pearce says-

> 'The issue will ultimately turn on the view the court forms of the care exercised by the draftsman in his choice of words. If it should be shown that a word has been used with different meanings in an Act, then the argument for consistent interpretation cannot stand. If, on the other hand, it is clear that a word is used throughout an Act to convey one meaning, then the burden of showing that there was an inconsistent use should be regarded as difficult to discharge.'

{D C Pearce *Statutory Interpretation in Australia* (2nd edn, 1981) p 33. For an example of the former case see *R v Huntingdon District Council, ex p Cowan* [1984] 1 All ER 58.}

We now look at this matter in more detail.

Construction ex visceribus actus Coke referred to construction *ex visceribus actus* (from the guts of the Act). He said that it is the most natural and genuine exposition of a statute to construe one part of it by another: 'for that best expresseth the meaning of the makers ... and this exposition is *ex visceribus actus*'. {1 Co Inst 381 1b. See Example 199.5.}

An Act is or should be a literary composition penned by one author at one time. A single spirit infuses it; and it moves together as a whole.

All words to be given meaning On the presumption that Parliament does nothing in vain, the court must endeavour to give significance to every word of an enactment. It is presumed that if a word or phrase appears in an enactment, it was put there for a purpose and must not be disregarded. {See Examples 75.3, 291.2 and 323.26.} This applies a fortiori to a longer passage, such as a section or subsection.

Thus where in *Albert v Lavin* {[1981] 1 All ER 628, at p 639.} Hodgson J said that in defining a criminal offence 'the word "unlawful" is surely tautologous' he was rebuked by Lawton LJ in a later case. {*R v Kimber* [1983] 3 All ER 316, at p 320.}

It may happen however that no sensible meaning can be given to some word or phrase. It must then be disregarded. As Brett J said in *Stone v Corpn of Yeovil* {(1876) 1 CPD 691, at p 701.}: 'It is a canon of construction that, if it be possible, effect must be given to every word of an Act of Parliament or other document; but that, if there be a word or phrase therein to which no sensible meaning can be given, it must be eliminated'.

Every word cannot be accorded a meaning if there is deliberate tautology.

Example 1 Brett MR said of the Bankruptcy Act 1883-

> 'The more ... I have considered this case the more difficult it appears to me to be, but I have come to the conclusion, though with great doubt, that the legislature intended this Act of Parliament to be verbose and tautologous, and intended to express itself twice over.'

{*Hough v Windus* (1884) 12 QBD 224, at p 232. The 1883 Act is an example of disorganised composition (as to this see s 76 of this Code).}

For recent examples of statutory tautology see *Hadmor Productions Ltd v Hamilton* {[1982] 1 All ER 1042, *per* Lord Diplock at p 1054.} and *R v Ashfors, ex p Bouzagon*. {(1983) *The Times* 4 July ('*unlawfully* entering . . . in breach of immigration laws').}

Words may be robbed of meaning by subsequent changes in the law.

Example 2   Section 6(3) of the Criminal Law Act 1967 states that where a person tried on indictment is found not guilty as charged, but the allegations include 'an allegation of another offence falling within the jurisdiction of the court of trial', the jury may find him guilty of that other offence. In 1971 the Crown Court was established, with exclusive jurisdiction in trial on indictment. {Courts Act 1971, ss 4 and 6. See now the Supreme Court Act 1981, ss 45 and 46.} In *R v Wilson (Clarence)* {[1983] 3 All ER 448, at p 451.} Lord Roskill remarked of s 6(3): 'The words "falling within the jurisdiction of the court of trial" can now be ignored since the creation of the Crown Court'.

Same words to be given same meaning   It is presumed that a word or phrase is not to be taken as having different meanings within the same instrument, unless this fact is made clear. Where threfore the context makes it clear that the term has a particular meaning in one place, it will be taken to have that meaning elsewhere. The matter is fully discussed in s 373 of this Code. {See Example 93.3.}

Different words to be given different meaning   Similarly it is presumed that the draftsman did not indulge in elegant variation, but kept to a particular term when he wished to convey a particular meaning. {The useful term *elegant variation* seems to have been invented by H W Fowler: see *Modern English Usage* pp 130-131.} Accordingly a variation in the term used is taken to denote a different meaning. Blackburn J said-

> 'It has been a general rule for drawing legal documents from the earliest times, one which one is taught when one first becomes a pupil to a conveyancer, never to change the form of words unless you are going to change the meaning . . . '

{*Hadley v Perks* (1866) LR 1 QB 444, at p 457. See also *R v Inhabitants of Great Bolton* (1828) 8 B & C 71, at p 74; *Re Stock & Share Auction & Banking Co* [1894] 1 Ch 736.}}

At the same place however Blackburn J recognised the possibility of elegant variation when he said that the legislature 'to improve the graces of the style and to avoid using the same words over and over again' may employ different words without any intention to change the meaning. It can only be said that this is bad drafting. Making use of pronouns when safe, the draftsman should otherwise stick to the same word. Graces of style are all very well, but in Acts of Parliament they take a far second place to certainty of meaning.

The exigencies of parliamentary amendment may lead to use of different words for the same meaning. {See *Lines v Hersom* [1951] 2 KB 682, at p 687.} In modern Acts this is rarely likely to happen, since the practice is for the Bill's draftsman also to draft any amendments made to it.

Where a difference of wording is inexplicable unless different meanings were intended, the court does its best to find those different meanings.

Example 3 Regulation 19 of the Docks Regulations 1934 required equipment to be 'tested and examined' before it was used in hoisting or lowering, and to be 'inspected' every three months. In *Gibson v Skibs A/S Marina and Orkla Grobe A/B and Smith Coggins Ltd* {[1966] 2 All ER 476.} Cantley J said-

> 'One would expect that when two different words, although practically synonymous in ordinary use, are employed in different parts of the same regulation dealing with the same kind of topic, they are intended to have some different meaning. It seems to me . . . that "examination" . . . is a more thorough and scientific process than "inspection" under these regulations. Indeed, "examination" . . . may require technical qualifications.'

Example 4 Section 1(1) of the Inheritance (Provision for Family and Dependants) Act 1975 sets out various categories of persons who may apply to the court for payment out of a deceased's estate. Paragraph (e) of s 1(1) specifies a person 'who immediately before the death of the deceased was being maintained, either wholly or partly, by the deceased'. In *Re Beaumont (deceased), Martin v Midland Bank Trust Co Ltd* {[1980] 1 All ER 266.} the question was whether a para (e) applicant had to show that the deceased had *assumed responsibility* for his maintenance. *Held* He did have to show this.

The decision was based on the fact that s 3(4) of the Act, in stating what had to be shown by a para (e) applicant, used words suggesting that responsibility would have been assumed. This contrasted with the wording of s 3(3) which, in relation to another type of applicant, envisaged that the deceased might or might not have assumed responsibility.

Consolidation Acts The presumption is weaker with Consolidation Acts, since these combine the work of different draftsmen executed at different times. It is notorious that tax consolidations suffer from this defect. Lord Reid said-

> 'It is no doubt true that every Act should be read as a whole, but that is, I think, because one assumes that in drafting one clause of a Bill the draftsman had in mind the language and substance of the other clauses, and attributes to Parliament a comprehension of the whole Act. But where, as [in the Income Tax Act 1952], quite incongruous provisions are lumped together and it is impossible to suppose that anyone, draftsman or Parliament, ever considered one of these sections in light of another, I think it would be just as misleading to base conclusions on the different language of different sections as it is to base conclusions on the different language of different sections in different Acts.'

{*IRC v Hinchy* [1960] AC 748, at p 766. See also *R v Riley* [1896] 1 QB 309, at p 323; *R v Burt, ex p Presbury* [1960] 1 QB 625, at p 632; *Gartside v IRC* [1968] AC 553. As to the construction of consolidation Acts see s 232 of this Code.}

Conflicting statements within one instrument Where two enactments within an Act or other instrument appear to conflict, it may be necessary to treat one as modifying the other. This depends on whether the appearance is true, or a product of the reader's carelessness. Much care, not always given, is needed in reading legislation.

If it is true, and no charity can construe the enactments as consistent with each other, then logic demands action. Such adjustment of the words must be effected as will make them maintainable by one and the same proponent in one and the same discourse.

If no other method of reconciliation seems possible, the court may adopt the principle that the enactment nearest the end of the instrument prevails. {*Wood v Riley* (1867) LR 3 CP 26, *per* Keating J at p 27 ('the known rule is that the last must prevail'). See also *A-G v Chelsea Waterworks Co* (1731) Fitzg 195 and the Australian cases of *Mt Isa Mines Ltd v FCT* (1976) 10 ALR 629, at p 639; *Ross v R* (1979) 25 ALR 137, at p 145.} However there are certain maxims, now to be discussed, which may afford assistance.

Generalibus specialia derogant   Where the literal meaning of a general enactment covers a situation for which specific provision is made by some other enactment within the Act or instrument, it is presumed that the situation was intended to be dealt with by the specific provision.

The maxim *generalibus specialia derogant* (special provisions override general ones) is found in Halkerston's Latin Maxims. {P 51. For the application of the principle in a case where the special provision is contained in a *later Act* see s 181 of this Code.} Acts very often contain general provisions which, when read literally, cover a situation for which specific provision is made elsewhere in the Act. This maxim gives a rule of thumb for dealing with such a situation: it is presumed that the general words are intended to give way to the particular. This is because the more detailed a provision is, the more likely is it to have been tailored to fit the precise circumstances of a case falling within it. {Lofft's King's Bench Rep. (1772-74) 351 (98 ER).} For a case where the principle was relied on see *Kidston v The Empire Marine Insurance Co Ltd.* {[1866] LR 1 CP 535, at p 546.}

Professor Pearce says-

> 'It is commonsense that the draftsman will have intended the general provisions to give way should they be applicable to the same subject matter as is dealt with specifically ... The draftsman often indicates his intention that this should be so by the inclusion of such words as "subject to this Act" in a general provision. But these words are included more by way of abundant caution as the overriding idea that an Act should be read as a whole has the effect of making all provisions subject to one another.'

{D C Pearce *Statutory Interpretation in Australia* (2nd edn, 1981) p 47.}

Other versions of the same concept are the following.

Generalia specialibus non derogant   {Jenk Cent 120.} The converse principle: general provisions do not override special ones. {For the application of this principle in a case where the general provision is contained in a *later* Act see s 181 of this Code.}

Clausula generalis non referta ad expressa   General words are taken not to be intended to disturb express stipulations. {8 Co Rep 154.}

Generalia verba sunt generaliter intelligenda   General words are to be understood generally. {3 Co Inst 76.} It is not to be supposed that the draftsman could have had in mind every possible combination of circumstances which may chance to fall within the literal meaning of general words.

Generalis clausula non porrigitur ad ea quae antea specialiter sunt comprehensa. A general clause does not extend to things previously dealt with by special provision. {8 Co Rep 154.}

Effect of specific on general provision   A specific provision within an Act is not usually of much relevance in construing one of the Act's general provisions *on other aspects*. This is because specific provisions may be inserted *ex abundanti cautela,* or otherwise without regard for the wider application of the general provision. Thus Lord Cairns LC said that a saving in a private Act is in the nature of a private bargain between promoter and objector. Such savings are not part of the general scheme of the Act 'and ought not to have any effect upon the construction of a general clause'. {*East London Rly Co v Whitechurch* (1874) LR 7 HL 81, at p 89.}

Disorganised composition   As with so many maxims, the need to apply this principle to provisions within the same Act arises only in the case of disorganised composition. In a precisely-drafted Act it is made clear which of any inconsistent provisions is intended to prevail. {As to the contrast between precision drafting and disorganised composition see s 76 of this Code.}

Judicial inadvertence   Sometimes judges fail to advert to the principle that an Act must be read as a whole.

Example 5   In *British Broadcasting Corporation v Ioannou* {[1975] QB 781.} the Court of Appeal took a point that had been missed in the court below and decided the case by reference to a particular paragraph in Sch 1 to the Trade Union and Labour Relations Act 1974. In a later case a differently constituted Court of Appeal acknowledged that this had been an error, since the earlier Court had overlooked the effect on the paragraph in question of other provisions in the Act. {*Dixon v British Broadcasting Corporation* [1979] 2 All ER 112.} Colin Ross has described how criminal courts go astray by not reading Acts as a whole. {[1981] Crim LR 808.}

Acts in pari materia   The concept that an Act is to be read as a whole is also applied to a group of Acts which are *in pari materia*. {As to these see pp 000ff below PART X}.
  See further s 259 of this Code.

150. Canons: interpretation of broad terms

A broad term is a word or phrase in an enactment which in its application to certain factual situations is vague and therefore necessarily ambiguous. A broad term may be either *static*, that is of constant meaning, or *mobile*, that is shifting in its meaning according either to the time when, or the place in which, it is applied (or both). As with any form of statutory ambiguity, the meaning of the term which is to be applied in relation to particular facts is determined by reference to the interpretative criteria.

COMMENTARY

Linguistic canons of construction For the general nature of linguistic canons of construction see s 147 of this Code.

For the sake of brevity, or because the enactment has to deal with a multiplicity of circumstances, the draftsman often uses a broad term. This has the effect of delegating legislative power to the courts and officials who are called upon to apply the enactment. The governing legal maxim is *generalia verba sunt generaliter intelligenda* (general words are to be understood generally). {3 Co Inst 76. See Examples 78.5, 80.5 and 83.1.} It is not to be supposed that the draftsman could have had in mind every possible combination of circumstances which may chance to fall within the literal meaning of general words. {For a detailed discussion of the concept of the broad term see Bennion *Statute Law* (2nd edn, 1983) chap 13.}

The broad term which is a substantive has been called a *nomen generale*. {*Hunter v Bowyer* (1850) 15 LTOS 281.} Other judicial descriptions of the broad term include 'open-ended expression' {*Express Newspapers Ltd v McShane* [1980] 2 WLR 89, at p 94.}, 'word of the most loose and flexible description' {*Green v Marsden* (1853) 1 Drew 646.} and 'somewhat comprehensive and somewhat indeterminate term'. {*Campbell v Adair* [1945] JC 29.}

The broadest terms, such as 'reasonable' or 'just', virtually give the court or official an unlimited delegated authority, subject to the remedies available on judicial review or appeal. {As to these see s 24 of this Code (judicial review) and s 23 (appeal).}

Narrowing of term by implication The width of a broad term when read literally is often intended by Parliament to be cut down by an implication arising from the words of the Act. Although the literal meaning of a broad term may on particular facts be found ambiguous, the court is often able to find an implication that reduces its width.

Example 1 Regulation 6 of the Imported Food Regulations 1968 {SI 1968/97} enabled a destruction order to be made where food was 'unwholesome'. A cargo of dates heavily infested with insects was unwholesome from the point of view of most uses, but not for the intended use, namely the manufacture of brown sauce. *Held* There was an implication that the broad term 'unwholesome' was intended to be limited so as to mean 'unwholesome when used as intended'. {*R v Archer, ex p Barrow Lane & Ballard Ltd* (1983) *The Times* 13 August. For another example, based on *Crook v Edmondson* [1966] 1 All ER 833, see Bennion *Statute Law* (2nd edn, 1983), p 148.}

Statutory guidelines The practice is growing of including in an Act which uses a broad term some indication of how Parliament intends the term to be construed. This is an important category of cases where rules of construction are laid down by statute. {See s 125 of this Code.}

Processed terms   The draftsman selects a broad term which is either a processed term or an unprocessed term. In the former case one of the interpretative factors will be the meaning given to the term in the cases which have processed it. {See s 26 of this Code.}

Again, a broad term may be either static or mobile (whether in time or place or both).

Static broad terms   A broad term is said to be static where the circumstances that fall within it are basically the same wherever they happen, and at whatever time. The term identifies the type of broad term which does not change its meaning according to time or place. {For examples see Bennion *Statute Law* (2nd edn, 1983), pp 149-150, where the terms discussed are 'accident', 'repairing', 'consent' and 'supply'.} With terms of this kind, precedents on the meaning of the term as used in other legislation are of direct relevance.

Broad terms mobile in time   A broad term is said to be mobile in time where the circumstances that fall within it are liable to differ according to the historic date of the facts in question. This identifies the type of broad term which changes its meaning according to time. {For examples see Bennion *Statute Law* (2nd edn, 1983), pp 150-4, where the terms discussed are 'objects of general concern', 'book', 'fancy bread', 'single woman', 'family', 'cruelty', 'dangerous', 'immoral purposes', 'fit for human habitation', 'working classes', and 'back-to-back houses'.}

With such terms it is necessary to be on guard when applying previous judicial decisions as to the meaning of the term. A meaning that was applicable in the circumstances prevailing at some past time may no longer be relevant if the circumstances have materially altered.

Broad terms mobile in space   A broad term is said to be mobile in space where the circumstances that fall within it are liable to differ according to the location of the circumstances in question. This identifies the type of broad term which changes its meaning according to the place or area in question. {For examples see Bennion *Statute Law* (2nd edn, 1983), pp 153-4, where the terms discussed are 'fit for human habitation', 'working classes', 'back-to-back houses', 'extraordinary traffic', 'neighbourhood' and 'special occasion'.} With such terms it is necessary to be on guard when applying previous judicial decisions as to the meaning of the term. A decision as to its meaning in one type of place may not be applicable to its meaning elsewhere.

Broad terms mobile in both time and space   A broad term is said to be mobile in both time and space where the circumstances that fall within it are liable to differ both according to the historic date of the facts in question and according to the location of the circumstances. This identifies the type of broad term which changes its meaning according both to time and place. For example the requirement contained in s 6 of the Housing Act 1957 to keep certain dwellings 'fit for human habitation' imports standards which vary in both time and place. {See Bennion *Statute Law* (2nd edn, 1983), pp 153-4.}

With such terms it is necessary to be especially careful when applying previous judicial decisions as to the meaning of the term. {See s 83 of this Code.}

151. Canons: interpretation of individual words and phrases

Particular canons of construction apply in relation to departures from the ordinary meaning, the interpretation of technical or foreign terms, and other matters concerned with the meaning of individual words and phrases. These are set out in Part XXI of this Code.

COMMENTARY

Linguistic canons of construction   For the general nature of linguistic canons of construction see s 147 of this Code.

Explaining how individual words and phrases are applied for purposes of statutory interpretation is a matter of some complexity. It is therefore dealt with in a separate Part of this Code, namely Part XXI.

152. Canons: elaboration of meaning of words and phrases

The courts use as aids to interpretation the linguistic canons of construction developed over the centuries to throw light on meaning generally, and not just in a legal context. These canons have the effect of elaborating the literal meaning of a word or phrase, usually by taking the elaborated meaning as having been implied by the author.

COMMENTARY

Linguistic canons of construction   For the general nature of linguistic canons of construction see s 147 of this Code.

Canons of construction such as the *ejusdem generis* principle and the maxim *expressum facit cessare tacitum* are in common use for purposes of statutory interpretation. The way they are used is a matter of some complexity. It is therefore dealt with in a separate Part of this Code, namely Part XXII.

PART VII

Arriving at Legislative Intention where Legal Meaning not 'Plain'

Introduction to Part VII   The plain meaning rule stated in s 120 of this Code indicates that where *on an informed construction* there is no real doubt, the plain meaning is to be applied. This Part shows the practical way of arriving at the legal meaning of the enactment where there *is* real doubt.

First the cause of the doubt must be ascertained (s 153). This may lead to either a strict or liberal construction being applied (s 154).

The doubt is resolved by first assembling the relevant guides to legislative intention, or interpretative criteria. These were discussed in Part VI. From them we extract, in the light of the facts of the instant case and the wording of the enactment, the interpretative *factors*. The nature of a factor is explained (s 155). In relation to either of the opposing constructions, a factor may be positive or negative (s 156). The problem is solved if we find all the factors pointing one way (s 157).

Where the relevant factors point in different ways, the interpreter embarks on the operation of *weighing* them. The rest of Part VII is concerned with this. We examine the nature of the operation (s 158). If the legislator has indicated how a particular factor should be assessed, this must be acted on (s 159). We consider the weighing operation in the key cases of grammatical ambiguity (s 160), semantic obscurity (s 161), and the possible need for a strained construction (s 162). Finally we note, in the closing section of Division One of the Code, that there may from time to time be changes in the way judges assess a particular factor (s 163).

PRELIMINARY

153. Ascertaining cause of the doubt

Where, in relation to the facts of the instant case, the plain meaning rule does not apply (because paragraphs (a) and (b) of s 120 of this Code are not satisfied), it is necessary to ascertain the cause of the doubt and then identify the relevant interpretative factors. A particular factor may both cause the doubt and provide, or help to provide, the means to resolve it.

COMMENTARY

As explained at p 211 above, the categories where there is real doubt about the legal meaning of an enactment in relation to particular facts can be reduced to two: *grammatical ambiguity* and the possible need for a *strained* construction.

Both types of doubt are to be resolved by weighing the relevant interpretative factors. {For the nature of the 'interpretative factors' see ss 155 to 157 of this Code.}

Semantic obscurity may also cause doubt, but this is a defect of a different nature. It is a corruption of the text which, when resolved by the working out of the 'corrected version', still leaves the possibility of ambiguity or the possible need for a strained construction. {As to the working out of the corrected version in cases of semantic obscurity see s 90 of this Code.}

It will be seen that in essence *there are only two kinds of doubt*, namely the doubt caused by grammatical ambiguity and the doubt over whether a straining of the literal meaning is called for. {As to use of the phrase 'literal meaning' see s 91 of this Code.}

Where a doubt is raised as to the legal meaning of an enactment, it is first necessary to determine whether the doubt is *real*. {See s 3 of this Code.} If it is a real doubt, the interpreter must then ascertain the cause of the doubt. Broadly, the cause will either be grammatical ambiguity or the circumstance that the relevant interpretative factors tend in different directions. {For an extended discussion of the causes of doubt see Bennion *Statute Law* (2nd edn, 1983) chaps 12 to 18.} In either case it will be necessary to identify the relevant factors and examine their nature.

In the latter case it may be that, as this section of the Code states, a particular factor both causes the doubt and gives the means to resolve it. If a literal construction would produce gravely adverse consequences, for example the endangering of national security, this will raise doubt as to whether it could really have been Parliament's intention that the court should apply the literal meaning. At the same time the presumption that Parliament does not intend to endanger national security will assist in the working out of the appropriate strained construction. {See also Example 157.1.}

154. Strict and liberal construction

Where the application of an enactment yields an *adverse* result (that is one detrimental to the subject or the state), the interpretative factors may on balance indicate that the court should curtail its application. This is known as strict construction.

Equally, where the application of an enactment yields a *beneficent* result (that is one beneficial to the subject or the state), the interpretative factors may on balance indicate that the court should widen its application. This is known as liberal construction.

COMMENTARY

A strict construction narrows the operation and effect of the enactment, whereas a liberal construction broadens it. If the enactment is coercive, a strict construction reduces its coerciveness. If the enactment is relieving, a liberal construction widens its relieving effect.

Principles of legal policy such as the principle against doubtful penalization {See s 129 and Part XIII of this Code.} and that in favour of the public good {See s 127 of this Code.} tend to indicate that the court should be ready to narrow the effect of a coercive enactment, and widen that of a relieving enactment.

However the true view is not that strict and liberal construction are in themselves interpretative criteria. They are simply methods or techniques by which the court *applies* the interpretative criteria. This may have been in Pollock CB's mind when he said: 'The distinction between a strict construction and a more free one has, no doubt, in modern times almost disappeared, and the question now is, *what is the true construction of the statute?*'. {*A-G v Sillem* (1864) 2 H & C 431, at p 509 (emphasis added).} However this would have been more accurately expressed as: All enactments are to be construed by the same method, but the result may in some cases yield a strict construction and in others a liberal one. {See Examples 60.1 and 127.4.}

Professor Glanville Williams put the matter in this way-

> 'The ancient rule was that penal statutes are to be construed strictly - that is, in favour of the defendant and against the prosecution - on the theory that the legislature must make its intention clear if it proposes to have people punished. The rule was important at a time when many crimes were punishable by death, but it has not necessarily lost all its value in these more lenient days.'

{Glanville Williams 'Statute Interpretation, Prostitution and the Rule of Law' (comprised in *Crime, Proof and Punishment,* Essays in memory of Sir Rupert Cross) p 71.}

This, like many judicial dicta, confuses the *technique* of strict or liberal construction with the *weight* to be given to relevant interpretative factors. Where the punishment is death, very great weight will be given to the principle against doubtful penalization; and in pursuance of that principle the court may feel obliged to give a very strict construction. Whenever the consequence of a particular construction is very severe, the court will wish to avoid it unless the merits favour such a result. {As to the 'merits' of a case see p 814 below.}

Example 1 Blackstone tells us of the lengths the judges would go to in strict construction so as to avoid capital punishment in doubtful cases-

> 'Thus the statute 1 Edw 6 c 12 (1547), having enacted that those who were convicted of stealing *horses* should not have the benefit of clergy, the judges conceived that this did not extend to him that should steal but one *horse*, and therefore procured a new Act for that purpose in the following year. To come nearer our own times, however, by the statute 14 Geo 2 c 6 (1740), stealing sheep, *or other cattle*, was made felony without benefit of clergy. But these general words "or other cattle", being looked upon as much too loose to create a capital offence, the Act was held to extend to nothing but mere sheep. And therefore, in the next session, it was found necessary to make another statute, 15 Geo 2 c 34 (1741), extending the former to bulls, cows, oxen, steers, bullocks, heifers, calves, and lambs, by name.'

{Kerr Bl (4th edn, 1876) i 63. See Example 380.5.}

Mixed consequences Very often however the consequences, and other relevant factors, will be mixed. {As to consequential construction see s 140 of this

385

Code.} Some will point one way, and some another. The decision whether to give a strict or liberal construction, or one which is neither strict nor liberal, will depend on the weighing of the factors. {As to this see ss 158 to 163 of the Code.}

For this reason over-simplistic judicial dicta on the point must be regarded with due reserve. A typical such dictum was that of Plowman J when he said: 'If the language of the statute is equivocal and there are two reasonable meanings of that language, the interpretation which will avoid the penalty is to be adopted'. {*Re HPC Productions Ltd* [1962] 2 WLR 51.} Here those essential words 'other things being equal' must be written in.

Professor J C Smith said in a comment on *R v Sibartie* {1983] Crim LR 470, at p 472.}: 'Though lip-service is from time to time paid to the principle that a penal statute must be construed strictly in favour of the accused, in practice that approach is out of fashion'. This is one more indication of how necessary it is to state the principles of statutory interpretation correctly. The *true* principle has never been that 'a penal statute must be construed strictly' (though it is often stated in such terms).

The correct formulation is that a penal statute must be construed with due regard to the principle against doubtful penalization, *along with all other relevant criteria*. Furthermor *penal* needs to be given a meaning which includes any form of detriment. {See p 303 above.} Judges today often find it necessary to give great weight to counter-principles such as the need to protect the public against vicious criminals. {On the other hand, additional factors may *reinforce* the principle against doubtful penalization: see, e g, *R v Bloxham* [1982] 1 All ER 582, *per* Lord Bridge at p 585.}

Terminology It should be mentioned that, as is usual in statutory interpretation, the judiciary here observe no uniformity in the use of terms. While the meaning of strict and liberal construction given above is the most common, judges may depart from it.

Example 2 Thus Scrutton LJ said of the Agricultural Holdings Act 1923: 'As by the Act he (the landlord) is being deprived of his common law rights, I think we must construe the Act with some liberality in his favour or scrutinise the tenant's claim with some strictness'. {*Turton v Turnbull* [1934] 2 KB 197, at p 201.} Here strict and liberal construction are seen as opposite sides of the same coin. In other words the same construction is regarded as both strict and liberal, which can only devalue the terms.

Again, instead of 'strict' judges may use terms like *limited* or *narrow*. Instead of 'liberal' they may say *wide* or *beneficial*.

INTERPRETATIVE FACTORS

155. Interpretative factors: nature of a factor

The term 'interpretative factor', in relation to an enactment, is used in this Code to denote a specific legal consideration which-

> (a) derives from the way a general interpretative criterion applies to the text of the enactment and the facts of the instant

case (and to other factual situations within the relevant factual outline), and

(b) serves as a guide to the construction of the enactment in its application to those facts.

COMMENTARY

In the terminology of this Code, an interpretative *criterion* is a general guide to legislative intention {See s 115.}, while an interpretative *factor* is a particular legal consideration which is derived from a general interpretative criterion but is tailored to the wording of the particular enactment and the nature of the particular facts of the instant case. It would apply in a similar way to other cases falling within the same factual outline. {As to the relevant factual outline see s 78 of this Code.}

There are many different criteria which may be relevant in deciding which of the opposing constructions of a doubtful enactment the court should adopt. {As to opposing constructions see s 84 of this Code.} The principle to be followed was stated by Lord Reid in *Maunsell v Olins* {[1975] 1 All ER 16, at p 18.} as follows-

'When doubt arises, rules of construction are relied on. They are not rules in the ordinary sense of having some binding force. They are our servants not our masters. They are aids to construction, presumptions or pointers. Not infrequently one "rule" points in one direction, another in a different direction. In each case we must look at all relevant circumstances, and decide as a matter of judgment what weight to attach to any particular "rule".'

No doubt when Lord Reid put the word rule in quotation marks here he meant to acknowledge that many of the interpretative criteria are not true rules. Some can however be formulated as such. The point is dealt with in s 115 of this Code.

The task in a particular case is to determine (by reference to general criteria) the specific factors which, in the light of the facts of the instant case, are relevant in construing the enactment for purposes of that case. Where, as frequently happens, factors tend in different directions the interpreter then has to weigh or evaluate them. This process is explained in ss 158 to 163 of the Code.

156. Interpretative factors: positive and negative factors

As respects a particular construction of the enactment, an interpretative factor may be either positive (tending in favour of that construction) or negative (tending away from it).

COMMENTARY

A particular factor may tend in favour or against one of the opposing constructions of the enactment. {As to opposing constructions see s 84 of this Code.} It is convenient to describe the factor as positive or negative in relation to that construction.

Usually a factor which is positive in relation to one of the opposing constructions will be reflected in a corresponding factor which is negative in relation to the other. Take for example the common case where the question is whether a literal construction ('Construction L') or a strained construction ('Construction S') shall be applied to the enactment. The positive factor in favour of Construction L that it gives effect to the literal meaning is reflected in the negative factor against Construction S that it does not give effect to the literal meaning.

This correspondence need not necessarily be present. In some cases a given factor may be positive (or negative) in relation to *both* the opposing constructions. This might happen for instance in the case of the 'universal repealer' given in Example 93.1. Here the literal meaning produces such dire consequences that they cannot have been intended. A strained construction becomes inevitable, but perhaps there is doubt as to which of two possible strained constructions should be applied.

In such a case we may call the opposing strained constructions Construction S1 and Construction S2. The negative factor that Construction S1 does not give effect to the literal meaning is not reflected in a corresponding positive factor that favours Construction S2. On the contrary, Construction S2 is subject to the same negative factor. The crucial difference may be that the 'literalist' negative factor is not as weighty for S1 as it is for S2. This would be the case if S1 departed less than S2 from the literal meaning.

The adverse weight of a negative factor may be less if some person's discretion is interposed by the exercise of which the adverse effect may be obviated or lessened. {See further p 400 below.}

Example 1   In *Forrest v Brighton JJ* {[1981] 2 All ER 711.} the House of Lords considered the meaning of s 108(1) of the Magistrates' Courts Act 1952. {Now s 133 of the Magistrates' Courts Act 1980.} This states that where a magistrates' court imposes two or more terms of imprisonment to run consecutively the aggregate shall not exceed six months. *Held* This did not prevent an aggregate exceeding six months where the sentences were imposed on separate occasions.

Lord Fraser of Tullybelton said {P 717.}-

'I recognise that the result of construing the subs-s in the way I consider to be correct is to leave room for what may seem to be an anomaly; provided the sentences are imposed on different days there is, in theory, no limit to the aggregate . . . But that is only theoretical, because in practice if the aggregate were going to be greatly in excess of 6 months . . . the magistrates' court would remit the case to a higher court for sentence.'

157. Interpretative factors: factors all pointing one way

Where upon investigating a grammatically ambiguous enactment it appears that the interpretative factors all point in favour of one of the opposing constructions and against the other, the doubt is to be resolved in favour of the first construction.

COMMENTARY

The rule stated in this section of the Code is self-evident, but is included for completeness. It is also worth considering the detailed application of the rule, since it is desirable to be sure that the result is arrived at correctly. To achieve this the court must ask itself the right questions.

The enactment is grammatically ambiguous. {For grammatical ambiguity see ss 87 to 91 of this Code.} There are two opposing constructions of the enactment as it applies to the facts of the instant case. {As to opposing constructions see s 84 of this Code.} The interpretative factors have been worked out. {As to this see ss 155 and 156 of the Code.} The interpreter either concludes that there is only one operative factor, or that there are two or more pointing in the same direction. Either way, the matter is concluded. There is no need for the process of assessing the respective weights of factors. {As to this weighing process where factors conflict see s 158 of the Code.}

Example 1 *Hobson v Gledhill* {[1978] Crim LR 45.} concerned the legal meaning of s 1(1) of the Guard Dogs Act 1975, a comminution of which reads-

(1) A person shall not use or permit the use of a guard dog at any premises
(2) unless a person ('the handler') who is capable of controlling the dog is present on the premises
(3) and the dog is under the control of the handler at all times while it is being so used
(4) except while it is secured so that it is not at liberty to go freely about the premises.

{This exactly reproduces the entire wording of s 1(1), the only change being the breaking up of the text into numbered clauses. As to the comminution of enactments in this way see s 74 of this Code.}

The question for the court was whether clause (2) applies when clause (4) is satisfied. In other words, does there need to be a handler on the premises when the dog is secured?

The court held that the enactment was 'ambiguous', though there is no grammatical ambiguity. As a matter of grammar, clause (2) applies whether or not the dog is secured. There is a real doubt, but on a true analysis it should be formulated differently.

The true doubt is whether a strained construction should be given, so that clause (4) is read as modifying clause (2) as well as clause (3). {As to strained construction see ss 92 to 97 of this Code.} The arguments for such a strained construction would be (1) that it is absurd to require a handler to be on the premises while the dog is secured, and (2) that s 1(2) of the Act (not included in the above comminution) suggests that this was not the intention.

We see that, as often happens, the court here used the word 'ambiguous' not in its grammatical sense but with a wide meaning equivalent to 'doubtful'. They held that the doubt was evenly balanced, and decided the case by applying a single factor drawn from the principle that a person should not be penalized under a doubtful enactment. {For this principle see s 129 of the Code.}

If the court chooses, as it often does, to proceed on the basis that the enactment is grammatically ambiguous when it is not, then this section of the

Code applies. In *Hobson v Gledhill* {[1978] Crim LR 45.} there were really three factors. On one hand was the desirability of applying the literal meaning of s 1(1). On the other were the absurdity of requiring the handler to be on the premises while the dog was secured, and the contextual effect of s 1(2). The court had to choose between these.

In fact what the court did was to hold that the opposing factors made the enactment 'ambiguous'. Whereupon a fourth factor, the undesirability of convicting the accused on an 'ambiguous' enactment was brought into play and treated as the sole factor.

The case illustrates the skill needed by an advocate when piloting a case of doubtful construction through the court. The case may need to be conducted on two levels: one the level of true analysis, and the other the adaptation of the true analysis to the way the matter is viewed by the court.

Strained construction   This section of the Code does not apply where there is only one grammatical meaning, but a strained construction may be needed. Here the factors inevitably point in different directions, and need to be weighed.

WEIGHING THE FACTORS

158. Weighing the factors: nature of the operation

Where s 157 of this Code does not apply to the construction of a doubtful enactment, it is necessary for the interpreter to assess the respective weights of the relevant interpretative factors and determine which of the opposing constructions they favour on balance. Unless, in the light of the factors, the court favours a third construction, it will adopt this favoured construction.

COMMENTARY

By the process described in s 156 of this Code, the relevant interpretative factors have been assembled. Section 157 of the Code does not apply. Some interpretative factors tend one way and some another.

We may speak of the factors tending in a certain direction as a *bundle* of factors. This is figurative, but then so is the idea of factors being 'weighed'. The court is unlikely even to consider the factors one by one, and certainly will not proceed in any mechanistic way. For the purpose of analysis however we must treat mingled processes as separated out.

We find that one bundle of factors favours one of the opposing constructions of the enactment, while the other bundle favours the other construction. {As to opposing constructions see s 84 of this Code.} There may be factors drawn from a single interpretative criterion in both bundles. *R v Horsham JJ, ex p Farquharson* {[1982] 2 All ER 269. See Example 159.1} illustrates this. It concerned the criterion of 'public interest'. This is very wide, and often (as here) comprises two or more competing interests. {For other examples see *Rogers v Secretary of State for the Home Department* [1973] AC 388, *per* Lord Simon of Glaisdale at p 407; *D v NSPCC* [1978] AC 171, at p 192; *Gaskin v Liverpool City Council* [1980] 1 WLR 1549, at p 1552; *Burmah Oil Co v Bank of England* [1980] AC 1090, at p 1129; *A-G v English* [1982] 2 All ER 903, at p 911.}

Once an advocate has assembled the bundles of factors which tell for and against the opposing constructions, he is in a position to devise the arguments he will present to the court. He aims to assemble as many factors that tend in his favour as possible. He wishes to convince the court that on balance it should decide in favour of his bundle of factors and reject his opponent's bundle. He frames his arguments accordingly, elevating his own factors and trying to demolish his opponent's.

The court will then be invited to assess or 'weigh' the factors. It is the task of the court to evaluate the two bundles and decide which on balance weighs heavier in the juristic scales. {*Maunsell v Olins* {[1975] 1 All ER 16, at p 18.} As Lord Denning MR put it in a different context-

'Let the advocates one after the other put the weights into the scales - the "nicely calculated less or more" - but the judge at the end decides which way the balance tilts, be it ever so slightly.'

{*The Due Process of Law* p 60.}

The process of weighing or balancing legal factors in order to arrive at a disputed rule or determine a *lis* is common throughout law, and not limited to statutory interpretation. Accordingly the general principles applicable to it operate in the field of statutory interpretation as elsewhere.

Wherever the law is doubtful, the court weighs or balances the factors telling in favour of or against a particular formulation of the rule, and arrives at its determination accordingly. This is an essential part of the forensic process, to which the judge is expected to bring certain qualities. Hart numbered among these-

'... impartiality and neutrality in surveying the alternatives; consideration for the interest of all who will be affected; and a concern to deploy some acceptable general principle as a reasoned basis for decision.'

{H L A Hart *The Concept of Law* p 200.}

Example 1 On the question of the admissibility in evidence of purloined documents, Warner J said-

' ... I must balance the public interest that the truth should be ascertained, which is the reason for the rule in *Calcraft v Guest* {[1898] 1 QB 759.}, against the public interest that litigants should be able to bring their documents into court without fear that they may be filched by their opponents, whether by stealth or by a trick, and then used by them in evidence.'

{*ITC Video Distributors v Video Exchange Ltd* [1982] 2 All ER 241, at p 246; see T R S Allan 'Filching Your Opponent's Papers in Court: When Privilege Cannot be Defeated by a Trick' (1983) 133 NLJ 665.}

Example 2 In relation to discovery of documents where public interest immunity is claimed Lord Edmund-Davies said the court may be obliged-

' ... to conduct a balancing exercise, consisting in weighing (a) the public interest in the due administration of justice against (b) the public interest established by the claim for immunity.'

{*Air Canada v Secretary of State for Trade* [1983] 1 All ER 910, at p 922.}

Example 3   In *Re W (a Minor)* {(1982) *The Times* 27 October.} Cumming-Bruce LJ gave a list of factors that are relevant in deciding a case of child custody. He went on to say that where the mother and child have been separated for a lengthy period it becomes in each case 'a very delicate weighing exercise' to determine whether the child should be uprooted and returned to its mother.

Example 4   A remarkable example of balancing legal factors occurred in *R v Allen.* {(1849) 1 Den 364.} The accused was indicted for allowing a boy of twelve to bugger him. He demurred on the undoubtedly true ground that at common law there is a conclusive presumption that a boy under fourteen is incapable of effecting penetration. {*R v Tatam* (1921) Cr App R 132.} *Held* It was contrary to public policy to allow the accused to escape, and notwithstanding the legal anomaly involved the indictment was good.

In terms of the interpretative criteria, this last decision may be shown as an example of where the requirements of common sense {See s 122 of this Code.} were regarded by the court as outweighing the objections to an anomaly. {As to the presumption against anomaly see s 323 of this Code.} The consideration of promoting the public good {See s 127 of this Code.} would also be relevant.

There are no fixed priorities as between various factors, since so much depends on the wording of the enactment and the particular facts. For example, in some cases the adverse consequences of a particular decision may be very likely to arise whereas in others they may be unlikely. {As to consequential construction see s 140 of this Code.}

Nevertheless there are some absolutes. Mere inconvenience will get a low rating, while injustice will weigh heavily. The literal meaning weighs heavily too. In one case Lord Wilberforce remarked that 'It would require a high degree of inconvenience to deter me from what seemed to me, on the language, the true meaning'. {*Tuck v National Freight Corpn* [1979] 1 All ER 215, at p 226.}

The judge may feel confident in his decision or agonise over it. In a borderline case he may find it very difficult to make up his mind.

Example 5   In *Westminster City Council v Ray Alan (Manshops) Ltd* {[1982] 1 All ER 771.} the Divisional Court was called on to construe s 14(1)(b) of the Trade Descriptions Act 1968. The defendants advertised a 'closing down sale' when the shop was not in fact closing down. Was this to make a false statement as to 'facilities' provided in the course of the trade? The court decided in the negative, but Woolf J said {P 775.}-

> 'I have come to that conclusion because this is a section which creates a penal offence. I have also come to it with some reluctance because, in my view, it would be desirable for there to be some protection for the public which prevented persons advertising something as a closing down sale if it is not such a sale.'

Subjective nature of the judicial assessment   The exact nature of judicial assessment has defied analysis. It was described by Professor Wisdom as 'a matter of weighing the cumulative effects of one group of severally inconclusive items against the cumulative effects of another group of severally inconclusive items'. {*Philosophy and Psycho-analysis* p 157.} Sir Rupert Cross showed that there is a point beyond which analysis cannot get-

'. . . even when judicial reasoning is based on the cumulative effect of several independent premisses, a time inevitably comes when all that the judge can say is "I have weighed the pros and cons which I have stated and I now give judgment for so and so in accordance with the principle I have formulated after weighing the stated pros and cons". The important thing is that it is of the essence of the judicial process that the pros and cons should first be weighed.'

{*Precedent in English Law* (3rd edn, 1977) pp 196-7.}

This state of affairs, though difficult, is manageable when only one judicial mind is involved. Often however there are several minds, particularly where a case is taken to appeal.

It is notorious that different judicial minds may, and frequently do, conscientiously arrive at differential readings. {The problem is examined in Bennion *Statute Law* (2nd edn, 1983) chap 23.} Nothing can be done about this. It is what in the following passage Neil MacCormick calls the bedrock-

'Judges evaluating consequences of rival possible rulings may give different weight to different criteria of evaluation, differ as to the degree of perceived injustice, or of predicted inconvenience which will arise from adoption or rejection of a given ruling. Not surprisingly, they differ, sometimes sharply and even passionately, in relation to their final judgement of the acceptability or unacceptability all things considered of a ruling under scrutiny. At this point we reach the bedrock of the value preferences which inform our reasoning but are not demonstrable by it. At this level there can simply be irresoluble differences of opinion between people of goodwill and reason.'

{*Legal Reasoning and Legal Theory* pp 105-6.}

Great difficulty may arise where different values are truly incommensurable, for example those respectively attached to property and human life. How do you equate personal freedom and public inconvenience? In one Irish case the court declined to allow duty-evaders to rely on the privilege against self-incrimination because 'so much public inconvenience would result from a contrary decision'. {*A-G v Conroy* (1838) 2 Jo Ex Ir 791, at p 792.}

In the end judges can find no better words to use than 'instinct' or 'feel'. {See, e g, the reference by Watkins LJ to 'an instinctive feeling that the event or act being weighed in the balance is too remote' (*Lamb v London Borough of Camden* [1981] 2 All ER 408, at p 421). As to the order of priority given by judges to different values see R W M Dias 'The Value of a Value-study of Law' (1965) 28 MLR 397. Cf Bentham *An Introduction to the Principles of Morals and Legislation* chap 4.} Some factors may have 'the nature of a makeweight'. {*Turner v Fenton* [1982] 1 All ER 8, *per* Warner J at p 18.}

We should not end this discussion without pointing out that the idea of judicial subjectivism, and its separation from objectivity can be taken too far. {As it has been by E A Driedger: see *The Construction of Statutes* pp 17-43.} It is true that the weight to be attached to a particular factor is not a precise resultant of the combination of the general criterion and the facts of the instant case. Our law is not so mechanistic and predetermined as that. Yet it is not accurate to say that the weight to be attached to a factor is a purely subjective matter, entirely dependent on the idiosyncrasies of particular judges.

393

It is expected that any judge in the system would arrive at much the same (even though not identical) weighting. A judge who consistently arrived at weightings markedly different from those of his brethren would be regarded by them as a maverick. The reason is that weights are not assessed in a vacuum.

Each judge comes to his task equipped with both experience and ability. The experience (compounded of learning and practice) shows him in a particular case how other judges have weighed similar factors. The ability equips him for the difficult intellectual task of assembliing and then assessing the factors bearing on his decision.

Number of factors   A large number of interpretative factors may be relevant in any one case, though in practice relatively few of them are likely to be referred to in the arguments or judgment.

Example 6   In a comparatively brief examination of the case of *Smith v Hughes* {[1960] 1 WLR 830.}, decided under s 1 of the Street Offences Act 1959, Professor Glanville Williams identified factors drawn from no fewer than eight relevant criteria. These were: (1) the principle that persons should not be penalized under a doubtful enactment; (2) the rules of formal logic; (3) the unlikelihood of a draftsman employing zeugma; (4) the principle *expressum facit cessare tacitum*; (5) the principle *noscitur a sociis*; (6) the presumption that Parliament intended to remedy a 'mischief'; (7) the legislative history of the enactment; (8) the principle that the construction should promote the public good. {Glanville Williams 'Statute Interpretation, Prostitution and the Rule of Law' (comprised in *Crime, Proof and Punishment*, Essays in memory of Sir Rupert Cross).}

Attitude of the court   While the above commentary represents the reality of the situation, the way a case is typically argued and decided is likely to obscure this. Judges prefer to say that the meaning they are adopting is the 'clear' meaning of the enactment. For various reasons, our courts like to show the result of a case as being free from doubt. If there is really an ambiguity they prefer not to acknowledge the fact. If they are really adopting a strained construction they prefer not to acknowledge that either. Having privately weighed the factors and decided which comes out heavier, the court will typically deliver a judgment which in terms is one-sided. That is it will tend to suggest that the law is clear and contrary arguments are of no account.

Example 7   In an evenly-balanced case Lord Diplock expressed his conclusion as follows-

> 'If there are two possible constructions of the definition of "superior court" in s 19 [of the Contempt of Court Act 1981], one of which would include and the other exclude a county court, the ambiguity ought to be resolved in favour of exclusion for three reasons.'

Lord Diplock went on to state the three reasons. Although he had indicated that there were two possible constructions, he made no mention of the interpretative factors which told in the opposite direction. {*Peart v Stewart* [1983] 1 All ER 859, at p 863.}

There are sound policy reasons for these attitudes, and it is not the purpose of this work to criticise them. Nor should we criticise advocates for framing their arguments in accordance with judicial preference. Indeed they are well advised to do so.

What in a work of this kind we must do is present a true analysis, even though its practical application may be indirect. Accordingly the argument in this, the key part of the book, is in terms of weighing the factors for and against a particular resolution of an ambiguity, or for and against a strained construction. {For a detailed guide to the operations involved from beginning to end in a case requiring statutory interpretation see Appendix A, p 855 below.}

159. Weighing the factors: where legislator has indicated a view

The wording of an enactment may indicate that the legislator has determined the relative weights which are to be given to certain factors, or at least wishes to give guidance on the matter. In such a case the court must conform to the legislative intention thus signified.

COMMENTARY

It sometimes happens that Parliament itself indicates the relative weights which it wishes to assign to competing factors. Since the interpreter must always strive to implement the legislative intention, such an indication must be followed.

Example 1 Section 3 of the Criminal Justice Act 1967 places a restriction on what may be reported about committal proceedings, but enables the restriction to be lifted in a particular case on the application of the defendant. In *R v Horsham JJ, ex p Farquharson* {[1982] 2 All ER 269.} Forbes J pointed out {P 274.} that s 3 involved the weighing and balancing of competing criteria concerning the public right to be informed of court proceedings and the need to ensure a fair trial. He rejected the suggestion that magistrates to whom an application under s 3 is made need to weigh these factors themselves-

> 'It would be wholly wrong to suggest, and I think there was a suggestion of it during the course of the argument, that the justices had any duty to weigh the interests of public reporting against the interests of the defence or the interests of justice. Any such balancing of interests had already been done by Parliament in enacting [s 3].'

It is not uncommon for Parliament to give some indication, by the way an Act is worded, of the weight it wishes the interpreter to give to relevant factors. Clearly such indications are to be looked for and respected.

160. Weighing the factors: grammatical ambiguity

Where, on the facts of the instant case, the enactment is grammatically ambiguous, the court weighs the interpretative factors to determine which of the grammatical meanings corresponds to the legislative intention. In certain cases the interpretative factors may indicate that all the grammatical meanings are to be rejected in favour of a strained construction.

COMMENTARY

Where the possible meanings of an ambiguous enactment are equally open grammatically, the choice of which to adopt will be determined by factors other than the primacy of the literal meaning. {As to grammatical ambiguity see ss 87 to 91 of this Code.} In other cases there will be a bias in favour of the meaning which is the more obvious grammatically. The fact that the enactment is ambiguous does not however rule out the possible need for a strained construction.

In case of grammatical ambiguity the court shows no reluctance to consider the interpretative factors other than the primacy of the literal meaning. Where on the other hand there is no grammatical ambiguity, the court is usually reluctant to consider these. A typical dictum is the following by Jessel MR-

' . . . where you have plain terms used in the enacting part of an Act of Parliament nothing less than manifest absurdity will enable a court to say that the ordinary and natural meaning of the terms is not the true meaning. Where there are two or more readings possible - that is, where there is ambiguity - there, of course, you let in arguments of inconvenience; arguments of the more useful or more likely interpretation may be fairly considered.'

{*Brown and Sons v The Russion Ship Alina* (1880) 42 LT 517, at p 518. For the reasons stated in s 141 of the Code, a very wide meaning must be given to the word 'absurdity' if this is to be considered an accurate statement of the present law.}

We now give an extended example of how the interpretative factors are used in cases of grammatical ambiguity.

Example 1   In *Pascoe v Nicholson* {[1981] 2 All ER 769.} the House of Lords was called upon to consider an ambiguity in the drink-driving provisions of the Road Traffic Act 1972. The question was whether these permitted a suspect who failed a breath test at one police station to be transferred to another police station in order to be given a blood test. A selective comminution of the relevant enactments reads as follows {With some 'carpentry' changes, this exactly reproduces the statutory language so far as it bears on the point in dispute. As to selective comminution see s 74 of this Code.}-

1. A person arrested for failing a breath test shall, while at a police station, be given an opportunity to provide a specimen of breath for a breath test there. {Based on Road Traffic Act 1972 s 8(7).}

2. A person who has been arrested for failing a breath test may, while at a police station, be required by a constable to provide a specimen for a blood test, if he has previously been given an opportunity to provide a specimen of breath for a breath test at that station under para 1 above and has failed that breath test. {Based on Road Traffic Act 1972 s 9(1).}

3. A person who, without reasonable excuse, fails to provide a specimen for a blood test in pursuance of a requirement imposed under para 2 above shall be guilty of an offence. {Based on Road Traffic Act 1972 s 9(3).}

4. Any person required to provide a specimen for a blood test under para 2 above may thereafter be detained at the police station until he passes a breath test. {Based on Road Traffic Act 1972 s 11.}

So far as it bears on whether the suspect can lawfully be transferred to another police station to take the blood test (perhaps because a police surgeon lives nearby), this says that 'while at a police station' the suspect must be given an opportunity to take a second breath test *there*. If he fails it he may, *while at that station* be required to provide a specimen of blood. Note that the *requirement* must be made at that station, but the Act is silent on where the specimen of blood must actually be given. Finally the Act says that a person required to provide a specimen for a blood test may *thereafter* be detained at 'the police station' until he sobers up. Clearly this means the police station where he then is.

It will be seen that the problem lies in para 2 of the above restatement. So far as concerns the place where the specimen is to be given, the words 'provide a specimen' are ambiguous. Some statement about place must be taken to be implied. What is it? This involves a piece of interstitial articulation. {As to the technique of interstitial articulation see ss 112 to 114 of this Code.} The prosecution might say that para 2 should be treated as in effect being worded as follows-

> (2) A person who has been arrested for failing a breath test may, while at a police station, be required by a constable to provide, *whether at that or some other police station*, a specimen for a blood test, if he has previously been given an opportunity to provide a specimen of breath for a breath test at that station under para 1 above and has failed that breath test.

The defence on the other hand might argue for the following version-

> (2) A person who has been arrested for failing a breath test may, while at a police station, be required by a constable to provide *at that station*, a specimen for a blood test, if he has previously been given an opportunity to provide a specimen of breath for a breath test at that station under para 1 above and has failed that breath test.

It will be seen that the only difference in the two versions lies in the italicised phrases. In both cases these are inserts into the official text. One or other of these inserted phrases must be treated as implied. The question for the court is which?

The positive factors in aid of the prosecution version are-

> (1) it promotes the convenience of the police and police surgeons and assists the administration of justice, and
> (2) it does not contradict the express wording.

The negative factors against the prosecution version are-

> (1) without clear authority it interferes with the liberty of the suspect by allowing him to moved about the countryside and possibly delaying his release, and
> (2) there is nothing in the wording to suggest it and indeed the wording of para 4 suggests the opposite, namely that Parliament

contemplated that the same police station would be the location throughout.

{This argument impressed the Divisional Court in *Butler v Easton* [1970] RTR 109, a decision overruled by *Pascoe v Nicholson*.}

The House of Lords found in favour of the prosecution. They decided the case on the basis that the statutory language was clear, since there were no words restricting the physical power of the police to move arrested persons from one place to another. On a true analysis it is submitted the statutory language was however grammatically ambiguous as to the point raised in the case.

161. Weighing the factors: semantic obscurity

Where, on the facts of the instant case, the enactment is semantically obscure, the court arrives at the 'corrected version', as stated in s 90 of this Code. For this purpose, where necessary it weighs the interpretative factors to determine the meaning that corresponds to the legislative intention. In certain cases the interpretative factors may indicate that the intended grammatical meaning is to be rejected in favour of a strained construction (that is the intended grammatical meaning is not the intended legal meaning).

COMMENTARY

In many cases of semantic obscurity, the intended version of the text is obvious. This particularly applies to obscurity caused by typographical errors. As explained in the commentary on s 90 of this Code, the interpreter's task is to arrive (actually or notionally) at the 'corrected version' of the text and then treat that as if it had been the original version. Thus it may ultimately be necessary to give it a strained construction. {As to strained construction see s 162 of this Code.}

In some cases of semantic obscurity, the intended grammatical meaning is not obvious. Here it may be necessary to apply the interpretative factors in the same way as in the case of ambiguity or the possible need for a strained construction. A frequent cause of such difficulty is the draftsman's use of compression.

Example 1   In *R v Wilson (Clarence)* {[1983] 3 All ER 448.} the House of Lords for the first time considered the legal meaning of s 6(3) of the Criminal Law Act 1967. This important subsection provides a general rule continuing and combining the rules of common law and the provisions of most of the statutes which enabled alternative verdicts to be returned in specific cases or types of cases. {*Per* Edmund Davies LJ in *R v Lillis* [1972] 2 QB 236, at p 240.} Its wording is as follows-

> 'Where, on a person's trial on indictment for any offence except treason or murder, the jury find him not guilty of the offence specifically charged in the indictment, but the allegations in the indictment amount to or include (expressly or by implication) an allegation of another offence falling within the jurisdiction of the court of trial, the jury may find him guilty of that other offence or of

an offence of which he could be found guilty on an indictment specifically charging that other offence.'

R v Wilson (Clarence) concerned an indictment for inflicting grievous bodily harm. Lord Roskill delivered the only full speech. In it he accepted {P 455.} that there could be an infliction of grievous bodily harm without an assault being committed. On an indictment charging this offence (and not stating that it was committed by an assault) the accused had been convicted, by virtue of s 6(3), of the offence of assault occasioning actual bodily harm. The question was whether s 6(3) allowed this.

Lord Roskill {P 453} essayed a comminution of s 6(3). {As to comminution see s 74 of this Code.} He did not go so far as to spell out the wording of this, but he indicated the basis for it. A *selective* comminution referable to the instant case would have run as follows {Emphasis added.}-

> 'Where the jury find him not guilty of the offence specifically charged in the indictment, *but the allegations in the indictment by implication include an allegation of another offence*, the jury may find him guilty of that other offence.'

The italicised words show the point of construction which was at issue. The indictment charged the infliction of grievous bodily harm, which can be committed with or without an assault. The 'offence specifically charged in the indictment' could in essence have been framed as: the infliction of grievous bodily harm with or without assault. Does this 'by implication include' an allegation of the offence of assault occasioning actual bodily harm?

In trying to answer this, we realise that we are faced with an example of semantic obscurity. The phrase 'the allegations in the indictment by implication include an allegation of another offence' is not good English. It is compressed legislative English.

What is the corrected version of this phrase? {For the 'corrected version' in cases of semantic obscurity see s 90 of this Code.} As is usual, the House of Lords declined to produce one in so many words. The analyst needs to produce one, but finds himself in difficulty. There are two possibilities, which we may call Version A and Version B.

> *Version A* '... the allegations in the indictment indicate an offence the ingredients of which in all cases constitute another offence'.
> *Version B* '... the allegations in the indictment indicate an offence the ingredients of which sometimes but not always constitute another offence'.

These, although not worked out as such by the House of Lords, are the opposing constructions. {For the concept of opposing constructions see s 84 of this Code.} To determine which one is to be adopted one needs to assemble the respective interpretative factors. The House of Lords, overruling *R v Springfield* {(1969) 53 Cr App R 608.} (in which Version A had been followed) adopted Version B. In doing so, as is usual, they concentrated on the positive factors.

The interpretative factors in favour of Version B were found to be as follows.

> (1) It reproduced the practice and opinion in the profession which had prevailed before the enactment of s 6(3). {P 452.} Since s 6(3) was intended to codify this, Version B is what one would expect.

(2) Using the text of s 6(3) as the primary indication of legislative intention {See s 136 of this Code.}, it could be said on linguistic grounds that the words 'amount to or include' point in favour of Version B. {P 453.}

(3) The following of Version A during the fourteen years since the decision in *R v Springfield* {(1969) 53 Cr App R 608.} had led to practical difficulties in the prosecution of offences. {See Lord Roskill at p 455, citing *R v Hodgson* [1973] 1 QB 565, at p 570. As to the presumption against a construction that causes practical difficulty see s 321 of this Code.}

The only factor against Version B mentioned by Lord Roskill was that it might cause injustice. {As to the presumption against a construction that causes injustice see s 128 of this Code.} Lord Roskill countered this by saying {P 456.}-

'If it be said that this conclusion exposes the defendant to the risk of conviction on a charge which would not have been fully investigated at the trial on the count in the indictment, the answer is that a trial judge must always ensure, before deciding to leave the possibility of conviction of another offence to the jury under s 6(3), that the course will involve no risk of injustice to the defendant and that he has had the opportunity of fully meeting that alternative in the course of his defence.'

This illustrates an important general point. An objection to a particular construction can often be met by showing that there is within the application of the enactment an element of *discretion*, by the wise exercise of which the adverse effect of that construction may be avoided. {See p 388 above and Example 156.1.}

162. Weighing the factors: need for strained construction

Where, on the facts of the instant case, the interpretative factors on balance indicate that the literal meaning of the enactment does not correspond to the legislative intention, it is necessary, as stated in ss 92 to 97 of this Code, to give the enactment a strained construction.

COMMENTARY

'Literal meaning'   As appears from s 91, this Code uses the term 'literal meaning' to include, in a case where the enactment is grammatically ambiguous, any one of the possible grammatical meanings.

Need for strained construction   As explained in the commentary on s 160 of this Code, all relevant interpretative factors are regularly brought into play when the enactment is grammatically ambiguous. Where however there is only one literal meaning, the position is different. The presumption, as stated in s 137 of this Code, is that the enactment is to be given its literal meaning. If this is to be departed from, the factors tending in the other direction must be compelling.

162. *Weighing the factors: need for strained construction*

As mentioned above {P 216.}, the tendency of judges is to say that a particular construction can be arrived at only where the words are reasonably capable of bearing it. This is the ordinary line taken by the courts. Wherever possible they mask departures from it by suggesting that the language *is* capable of bearing the desired meaning even though this is not so. The usual judicial policy was thus outlined by Lord Scarman in *Williams & Glyn's Bank Ltd v Boland* {[1980] 2 All ER 408, at p 417.}-

'... the judicial responsibility remains, to interpret the statute truly according to its tenor. The social background is, therefore, to be kept in mind but can be decisive only if the particular statutory provision under review is reasonably capable of the meaning conducive to the social purpose to which I have referred. If it is not, the remedy is to be found not by judicial distortion of the language used by Parliament but in amending legislation.'

This may apply even though the court is sure that the literal meaning does not correspond to the true intention. Thus in *Richards v MacBride* {(1881) 51 LJMC 15, at p 17.} Lopes J said that he could not doubt that it was the intention that the Sunday Closing (Wales) Act 1881 should come into operation throughout Wales in 1881, but that he was bound to read the words of the commencement provision (s 3) in their ordinary sense. By this, 'it is plain that the Act cannot come into operation till next year'.

Nevertheless, as explained in s 93 of this Code, the courts do sometimes find a compelling need to 'distort the language used by Parliament' in Lord Scarman's words. The weight of the factors adverse to the literal meaning is too great to ignore.

Many cases are cited in this work where a strained construction has been found necessary (even though the court has usually preferred to avoid admitting the fact). We now give a more extended example of how this was done by the House of Lords.

Example 1 This example is based on *Wills v Bowley*. {[1982] 2 All ER 654.} While illustrating how the House of Lords found it necessary to adopt a strained construction in that case, the example also illustrates the techniques of selective comminution {See s 74 of this Code.} and interstitial articulation. {See s 112 of this Code.} Although indicating some of the things counsel might do when using these techniques, the example does not purport to say what counsel involved in that case actually did.

Mr P is briefed to prosecute D (a female) at Cardiff magistrates' court. She is charged with two offences. One is an offence under s 28 of the Town Police Clauses Act 1847 ('the s 28 offence'). The other is the offence of assaulting three police officers in the execution of the duty imposed on them by that section of arresting her without a warrant ('the assault offence'). The facts are that the constables saw and heard D using obscene language in a street. When they tried to arrest her she became violent.

Mr P looks up s 28. He finds it is a long section, running to some three pages. He makes a selective comminution, limiting it to the provisions relevant in the instant case. This, while retaining the actual wording of s 28, reduces it to a mere 48 words. Mr P's version runs as follows-

Part I

(1) Every person who in any street,
(2) to the annoyance of the residents or passengers,
(3) uses any obscene language
(4) shall be [guilty of an offence].

Part II

(5) Any constable shall take into custody, without warrant,
(6) and forthwith convey before a justice,
(7) any person who within his view commits any such offence.

(This selective comminution is presented in two parts because the relevant portions of s 28 constitute two independent propositions and it is convenient to be able to refer to them separately.)

Mr P perceives that, in order to succeed on the assault charge, he needs to show that the power of arrest conferred by Part II of his selective comminution had really arisen. If the arrest was not lawful, then D was justified in resisting it.

Mr P finds there is some doubt about whether the evidence will establish what is required by clause (2) of his comminution. He realises that if the case goes to appeal he may have to uphold a conviction for the assault offence without his argument being supported by D's conviction for the s 28 offence. Indeed D may by that time have been acquitted of the s 28 offence.

Mr P then sees that, to obtain (and retain) a conviction for the assault offence, it may be necessary to convince the court that clause (7) of the comminution is wide enough to include a case where the constable reasonably believes the accused to be committing a s 28 offence even though this is not actually the case.

Mr P therefore prepares the following articulated version of clause (7)-

(7) any person who within his view-
(a) commits any such offence, or
(b) does any act which he reasonably believes constitutes such an offence.

The inclusion of para (b) in clause (7) amounts to a strained construction. The literal meaning of s 28 clearly confines the duty of arrest to cases where a s 28 offence is actually committed. Mr P prepares arguments justifying the strained construction.

Miss Q is briefed for the defence. She prepares a similar selective comminution to that of her opponent Mr P. She appreciates the point that has troubled him, and prepares an articulation of clause (7) that strengthens the wording in her client's favour. It runs as follows-

(7) any person who within his view does an act which actually constitutes any such offence.

The Cardiff magistrates acquit D of the s 28 offence. In relation to the assault offence, Mr P and Miss Q argue for their respective versions of clause (7). The bench prefer Mr P's version. They convict D of the assault offence on the ground that her behaviour fell within Mr P's clause (7)(b), and so rendered her arrest lawful.

D appeals by case stated to the Divisional Court, who dismiss her appeal. She then appeals to the House of Lords, who by three to two also dismiss the appeal. The majority agree that a slightly different version of Mr P's clause (7) is appropriate. It runs as follows-

(7) any person-
(a) who within his view commits any such offence,
or
(b) whom he honestly believes, on reasonable grounds derived wholly from his own observation, to have committed such an offence within his view.

The interpretative factors which were considered by Lord Bridge (who delivered the only full speech on behalf of the majority) to favour a strained construction importing the addition of the last-mentioned version of clause 7(b) were as follows.

(1) The drafting of s 28 is an instance of what this Code calls disorganised composition. {See s 76 of the Code.} There are a number of instances of older statutes, mainly of the nineteenth century, which confer power to arrest offenders without expressly including *apparent* offenders. Such inaccurate drafting cannot be construed as if it were precise. {Pp 672-3, 680, 682.}

(2) It is important to construe an enactment of this kind so as to maintain law and order. {Pp 673 and 677. For this presumption see pp 297–298 above.}

(3) It is desirable to arrive at a legal meaning of the enactment that is workable. {P 675. Lord Bridge cited a dictum by Swinfen Eady LJ in *Trebeck v Croudace* [1918] 1 KB 158, at pp 164-5. That case concerned the power conferred by s 12 of the Licensing Act 1872 to arrest a person 'who is drunk when in possession of any loaded firearms'. Swinfen-Eady LJ asked: 'Is it to be said that if [the constable] sees a drunken man in a street in possession of a gun and brandishing it about he must abstain from intervening unless he is sure that the gun is loaded, or otherwise risk an action being brought against him? Is he to wait until the drunken man shows that the gun was loaded by discharging it? And then perhaps it may no longer be a loaded firearm.' As to the presumption that Parliament did not intend an unworkable meaning see s 321 of this Code.}

(4) There is a need to avoid the artificial and 'nonsensical' result that a constable could only be sure his arrest was justified long after it occurred, when the court gave its decision. {Pp 680-1. For the presumption that an artificial result is not intended see s 325 of this Code.}

(5) It would be unfair to impale a constable (who under s 28 as originally enacted was liable to imprisonment for breach of the duty to arrest) 'on the horns of an impossible dilemma'. {P 681. As to the presumption that Parliament intends to act fairly see s 128 of this Code.}

The factors mentioned by Lord Bridge as militating against the strained construction were the following.

(1) It is desirable to respect the liberty of the subject. {Pp 673-4. Lord Bridge cited the 'much-quoted' observation by Pollock CB in *Bowditch v Balchin* (1850) 5 Exch 378, at p 381: 'In a case in which the liberty of the subject is concerned, we cannot go beyond the natural construction of the statute'. As to this principle see s 290 of the Code.}

(2) Judicial pronouncements of great weight have been made against a strained construction of similar enactments. {P 681. For the principles as to following binding or persuasive precedents see s 26 of this Code.}

(3) The inclusion of clause 7(b) goes against the presumption that the literal meaning is to be applied. {Lord Bridge did not apply this factor in so many words, but it is implicit in his speech. As to this presumption see s 137 of the Code.}

We might say of our imaginary Mr P and Miss Q that, through the effort of thinking out their respective articulations, they formed a more exact appreciation of what the enactment provides. This helped them to prepare a full and clear formulation of what, in the contention of each, the relevant law really was. The process of preparing his or her articulation, and the resulting ability to refer to these formulations in argument before the court, clarifies counsels' minds and assists the cogency and certainty of their arguments.

The court too is enabled by this means to concentrate on the exact point at issue. The final version of clause (7) given above is based on Lord Bridge's answer to the certified question in *Wills v Bowley*. {[1982] 2 All ER 654, at p 682.} It is submitted however that Mr P's version is preferable to that of Lord Bridge. The former slots properly into the structure of s 28, and correctly identifies the nature of the offence. Lord Bridge's version refers to 'an offence' in general terms. In stating that the grounds of belief must derive wholly from the constable's observation, Lord Bridge is more restrictive than the wording of s 28 appears to justify.

These defects (if such they be) are no doubt due to the fact that under the usual system argument is not directed to the precise wording of the key passage in the judgment, namely that which articulates the unexpressed portion of the relevant enactment. Indeed counsel before the House of Lords in *Wills v Bowley* are unlikely to have had an opportunity to comment on Lord Bridge's formulation of the answer to the certified question. In most cases before the courts there is not even the concentration of argument provided by a stated case.

163. Weighing the factors: changes in legal policy

The weight given by the courts to a particular interpretative criterion may change from time to time. This is to be borne in mind when considering, in the light of the binding or persuasive authority of relevant precedents, the weight to be attached in the instant case to a factor derived from that criterion.

COMMENTARY

The interpretative criteria, or guides to legislative intention, are set out in Part VI of this Code. From them, as explained in s 155 of the Code, interpretative factors are drawn by reference to the wording of the relevant enactment and the facts of the instant case. This section states the principle that, through changes in social policy or prevailing attitudes, the weight to be attached to a particular criterion may vary from time to time. The position was stated by R W M Dias as follows-

> 'Every social twist alters the balance and settles the values in a new pattern; the position today is different from what it was five years ago, and vastly different from what it was thirty years ago.'

{*Jurisprudence* (4th edn, 1976) p 260.}

Such shifts are common to the law generally, and not confined to statutory interpretation. Thus Lord Reid commented on 'a steady trend' towards regarding the law of negligence as depending on principle rather than precedent. {*Home Office v Dorset Yacht Co Ltd* [1970] AC 1004, at p 1026.} The development of the doctrine of natural justice is another example. {See s 335 of this Code.} So too is public interest, in relation to such matters as public interest immmunity. Lord Hailsham said-

> 'The categories of public interest are not closed, and must alter from time to time whether by restricton or extension as social conditions and social legislation develop.'

{*D v NSPCC* [1978] AC 171, at p 230. As to such developments see Neil MacCormick *Legal Reasoning and Legal Theory* pp 158-161. See also s 126 of this Code.}

The presumption, stated in s 137 of this Code, that an enactment is to be given its literal meaning varies in weight from time to time. At its height in the middle of the nineteenth century, it has declined somewhat in recent years.

All legal doctrines are subject to this kind of temporal variation.

Example 1 The lack of merit in tailor-made tax avoidance schemes led the House of Lords in *W T Ramsay Ltd v IRC* {[1981] 1 All ER 865.} to modify the well-known *Westminster* principle {*IRC v Duke of Westminster* [1936] AC 1.} by holding that even though each transaction in the scheme is 'genuine' and not a sham, if the sole object is tax avoidance this will not save it.

In a later case, Lord Diplock said that it would be disingenuous to suggest, and dangerous on the part of those who advised on elaborate tax-avoidance schemes to assume, that *W T Ramsey Ltd v IRC* {[1981] 1 All ER 865.} did not mark a significant change in the approach adopted by the courts. {*IRC v Burmah Oil Co Ltd* (1981) *The Times* 9 December.} In the same case Lord Scarman observed that it was of the 'utmost importance' that the business community and their advisers should appreciate that *Ramsay* marked a significant change.

DIVISION TWO

Supplementary Provisions

PART VIII

Commencement, Amendment and Repeal of Enactments

Introduction to Part VIII This Part amplifies, so far as concerns temporal operation, the account of the temporal, territorial and personal application of an Act set out in s 30 of the Code. Territorial extent and personal application are amplified in Part IX.

The first six sections of Part VIII deal with the commencement or coming into operation of an enactment. The meaning of the term 'commencement' is explained (s 164). Different types of commencement date are discussed (ss 165 to 168). The making of preparatory orders etc is dealt with (s 169).

Then follow eight sections about the amendment of enactments. The meaning of the term 'amendment' is explained (s 170). Different kinds of amendment are examined in turn (ss 171 to 175). We look at the difficult question of what a reference to an enactment is intended to mean after the enactment has been amended (s 176). Lastly we deal with extra-statutory concessions, which produce the effect of an amendment without there having been one in fact (s 177).

The next next eight sections consider repeal. The meaning of the term 'repeal' is explained (s 178). We pass to the practice of 'double repeal' (s 179), and the difficult concept of implied repeal (s 180). The effect of repeals, and of statutory savings etc, is considered (ss 181 to 186). We conclude with expiry (s 187) and desuetude (s 188).

Then follows a section on the important and often overlooked topic of the transitional provisions which pave the way for commencement, amendment or repeal (s 189).

The final group of sections in Part VIII is concerned with the vexed question of retrospective operation, or *ex post facto* law (briefly outlined at pp 313–314 above). We examine in more detail the general presumption against retrospectivity (s 190), and then go on to some detailed matters (ss 191 to 193). Finally we explain the common drafting failure that causes doubts over whether or not an enactment is intended to be retrospective (s 194).

COMMENCEMENT OF AN ENACTMENT

164. Commencement: meaning of 'commencement'

The 'commencement' of an Act or enactment is the time when it comes into force.

COMMENTARY

This definition of 'commencement' is laid down by the Interpretation Act 1978. {S 5 and Sch 1. As to what is meant by being in force see 30 of this Code. For

409

the meaning of 'enactment' see 71. See also Example 30.3.} Whatever the day of commencement may be, the Act, as Grove J put it, 'speaks from that day'. {*Richards v MacBride* (1881) 51 LJMC 15, at p 17.}

The commencement date may be the date of passing of the Act {See s 165 of this Code.}, or a date specified or indicated in the Act {See s 166 of this Code.}, or a date specified in a commencement order made by a Minister or other functionary. {See s 167 of this Code.} Different provisions of an Act may be brought into force on different dates. {See s 168 of this Code.}

In a typical modern session of Parliament the public general Acts passed, totalling perhaps seventy or eighty in number, will display a wide variety of commencement provisions. In an investigation carried out in 1979, a Statute Law Society working party found that, in relation to the 105 public general Acts passed between 1 January 1978 and the dissolution of Parliament in April 1979, the commencement situation was as follows-

> 41 Acts came into force on the date of passing;
> 12 Acts came into force on a date specified in the Act;
> 14 Acts came into force on the expiry of a period of one, two or three months after passing, being a period specified in the Act;
> 38 Acts were subject to the making of commencement orders by Ministers.

{[1980] Stat LR 40.}

Draftsmen are required to group all commencement provisions at the end of the Act, unless this is impracticable. Where a section includes a commencement provision applying to other parts of the Act, the sidenote must include the word 'commencement'. If commencement provisions are complex they must be put in a separate section or Schedule. Where possible, commencement dates for particular provisions should be specified in the Act itself. {These instructions were issued by the Management and Personnel Office in 1982: see *The Law Society's Gazette* 28 July 1982.}

165. Commencement: on passing of Act

Where no provision is made for the coming into force of an Act or provision of an Act, it comes into force at the beginning of the day on which the Act receives royal assent.

COMMENTARY

This reproduces s 4(b) of the Interpretation Act 1978. An Act is 'passed' at the moment when it receives royal assent {*Coleridge-Taylor v Novello & Co Ltd* [1938] Ch 608.}. The reference to 'no provision' being made relates (without practical exception) to different provision contained in the Act itself.

Section 4(b) of the Interpretation Act 1978 reproduces the effect of a provision previously contained in the Acts of Parliament (Commencement) Act 1793. This provision (repealed by the 1978 Act) stated that the date of royal assent to an Act, which the 1793 Act required to be endorsed on the Act, {As to this endorsement see s 279 of the Code.} should be the date of the Act's commencement 'where no other commencement shall be therein provided'.

The 1978 Act dropped the limitation suggested by the word 'therein' on the (unlikely) supposition that a commencement provision might be contained elsewhere than in the Act itself. In doing so it committed the solecism of denying its own statement. It cannot be the case that 'no provision is made' for commencement since the 1978 Act itself, in this very section, makes such provision.

Until the enactment of the Acts of Parliament (Commencement) Act 1793, all Acts passed in a Parliamentary session were deemed to come into effect (except where a particular Act otherwise provided) on the first day of the session. {4 Co Inst 25; *R v Wilde* (1671) 1 Lev 296; *A-G v Panter* (1772) 6 Brown 486; *Latless v Holmes* (1792) 4 TR 660; *Bryant v Withers* (1813) 2 M & S 123, at p 131.} This rule originated when a parliament had only one meeting and its enactments (passed in response to petitions) were not drawn up in the form of statutes until after those summoned to attend had dispersed.

The rule produced great injustice and inconvenience. The injustice is recited in the preamble to the Act of 1793, and evidenced by cases cited in the previous footnote. One inconvenience was that where two inconsistent Acts were passed in the same session it was not possible to say which overrode the other. {*R v Middlesex JJ* (1831) 2 B & Ad 818, at p 821.} Nowadays where it is desired that an Act shall modify, or otherwise operate in relation to, all other Acts passed in the same session, the old rule is revived by express words. {See, e g, Parliament Act 1949 s 1.}

At the beginning of the day   This gives statutory effect to the rule laid down in *Tomlinson v Bullock* {(1879) 4 QBD 230.} As to fractions of a day see p 93 above.

166. Commencement: on date specified in Act

An Act may state that it is to come into force at a time after its passing, which may be a specified calendar date, or the end of a specified period, or the date of a specified happening, or a time otherwise described. An Act may, by any similar description, state that it is to be treated as having come into force at a time *before* its passing.

COMMENTARY

This section of the Code deals with the case where an Act provides that it is not to come into operation on the date of its passing, but is to be treated as coming into effect on some other specified date. This may be after or before the date of passing.

The commencement of an Act which is not to come into force at its passing is sometimes postponed to a date specified in the Act (rather than one fixed by a later exercise of Ministerial discretion). The practice is an ancient one.

Example 1   Chapter 50 (the final chapter) of the Statute of Westminster the Second {13 Edw 1 (1285).}, which had a sidenote reading 'No Man shall depart from the King's court without Remedy', ran as follows-

> 'All the said Statutes [sc chapters 1 to 49 of the Statute] shall take effect at the Feast of St Michael next coming, so that by occasion of

any Offence done on this side the said Feast, contrary to any of these Statutes, no Punishment (Mention whereof is made within these Statutes) shall be executed upon the Offenders.

(2) Moreover, concerning the Statutes provided where the Law faileth, and for remedies, lest Suitors coming to the King's Court should depart from thence without Remedy, they shall have Writs provided in their Cases, but they shall not be pleaded until the Feast of St Michael aforesaid.'

{Statutes at Large (1761) i 229.}

The usual reason for a postponement of this kind is to allow persons affected to obtain copies or summaries of the Act, familiarise themselves with its provisions and adjust their affairs to comply with it. It may also be necessary for officials to prepare for the work entailed in administering the Act.

Departments are instructed that the postponement in such cases should be for a period of not less than two months (or three months in the case of consolidation Acts). {These instructions were issued by the Management and Personnel Office in 1982: see *The Law Society's Gazette* 28 July 1982.}

Specified calendar date   It is becoming comparatively rare for a calendar date to be specified in the Act. The reason is that it is always possible for there to be an unexpected hold-up in the progress of a Bill through Parliament. A commencement date which initially seems appropriate may then be rendered unsuitable, necessitating an amendment to the Bill. Successive hold-ups may make more than one such amendment necessary. The managers of government business in Parliament strive to avoid all unnecessary amendments, since they tend to use up precious government time.

A specified date may be used where it is desired that the Act shall not come into force until a considerable period has elapsed.

Example 2   The Equal Pay Act 1970, which introduced the principle of parity between the pay of men and women doing similar work, involved such a fundamental change in industrial and commercial practice that it was thought to require a period of more than five years between passing and commencement. The Act received royal assent on 29 May 1970. By s 9(1) its commencement date was fixed at 29 December 1975.

Commencement at end of a specified period   Where the reason for postponement is simply to give people time to prepare themselves for the operation of the Act, a fixed period is often the most convenient method. It is much used. By specifying a fixed period after assent (nowadays usually either two or three months), it is possible to avoid the problems mentioned above caused by uncertainty as to the date of assent.

The formula used is on the following lines: 'This Act shall come into force at the end of the period of ... months beginning with the day on which it is passed'. As Winn J said in *Hare v Gocher* {[1962] 2 QB 641, at p 646.}, these are 'words expressly chosen to avoid equivocation and to exclude the application of the general rule that the first day of a period should be excluded from a computation'.

412

Date of specified happening An Act may be linked to some public event, for example the ratification by the United Kingdom of a treaty to which the Act gives effect. It is then appropriate to tie the commencement of the Act to the event in question. So as to avoid argument about whether the event has indeed occurred (and if so on what date), the modern practice is to deal with this type of situation by the machinery of Ministerial order. {See s 167 of this Code.}

If it is desired to avoid the few hours' retrospectivity involved in the rule that, unless the contrary intention appears, an Act comes into force at the *beginning* of the day on which royal assent is given, the Act may include suitable words.

Example 3 On the abdication of Edward VIII, this was done to avoid the awkwardness of treating the king as abdicating some hours before he gave assent to the necessary Act (in which case he could not lawfully have assented to it): see the opening words of s 1(1) of His Majesty's Declaration of Abdication Act 1936.

Where the Act's commencement is expressly tied to the linked event, difficulty may arise if the connection is inadequately described.

Example 4 Richards v MacBride {(1881) 8 QBD 119.} concerned the commencement of the Sunday Closing (Wales) Act 1881. Section 3 of the Act provided that it should commence 'with respect to each division or place in Wales on *the day next appointed* for holding the general annual licensing meeting for that division or place'. {Emphasis added.} The italicised phrase caused great difficulty in relation to areas where a day *later* than royal assent had been appointed *before* royal assent. Did the words look to an *appointment* after assent, or merely to a *date* after assent (the appointment having been made before)?

The court had the impression that the Government had desired the Act to come into effect as soon as possible. *Held* The literal meaning was plain. Although, in the case before the court, the Act could without inconvenience to anyone have come into force on the forthcoming date appointed before assent had been given to the Act, it was decreed that commencement must be postponed to the date fixed by the *next* appointment in a year's time.

Date otherwise described There is no limit to the ways in which Parliament may choose to fix the time of commencement, although in modern practice the tendency is not to employ unusual methods. A date may be indicated by implication. {*Forbes v Fanshawe* Tr 1784 (cited in *Latless v Holmes* (1792) 4 TR 660, at p 661).}

Repeal before commencement Where a future date is specified by the Act for its commencement, it is open to Parliament to change its mind and repeal the Act or some part of it before the date of commencement arrives. Such repeal need not indeed betoken a change of mind. It is common practice to precede a consolidation Act by an amending Act 'tidying up' the area of law to be consolidated. When the consolidating Act finally comes into force it repeals the amending Act without its ever having become operative.

Example 5 The Agricultural Holdings Act 1906 was specified to come into force on 1 January 1909. Before that date it was repealed as to England and consolidated as part of the Agricultural Holdings Act 1908.

There may be other reasons for repeal before commencement. One is where an error is discovered.

Example 6   Schedule 6 to the Housing Act 1980 contained provisions amending Sch 11 to the Rent Act 1977. Before Sch 6 was brought into force, it was found that these were defective. Equivalent provision was therefore made by reg 2 of and Sch 1 to the Regulated Tenancies (Procedure) Regulations 1980. {SI 1980/1696. The regulations were made under s 74 of the Rent Act 1977.} In the explanatory note to these regulations it was stated that Sch 6 would not now be brought into force.

Retrospective commencement   Occasionally it may be considered necessary to give an Act retrospective effect. The position relating to retrospective operation is explained in ss 189 to 193 of this Code.

167. Commencement: on date specified by government order

An Act may state that it is to come into force on such date as Her Majesty may by Order in Council appoint, or as a specified Minister may by order made by statutory instrument appoint, or as may be otherwise appointed.

COMMENTARY

This describes the position where the whole Act is to be brought into force on one date by government order. Piecemeal commencement orders are dealt with in s 168 of this Code.

An Order in Council made under an Act is a statutory instrument. Under constitutional convention it is as much under government control as any other type of delegated legislation. {See s 50 of this Code.} Accordingly all commencement orders are effectively made by Ministers.

Advantages   This method of commencement gives the advantages of extreme flexibility. Before a new Act is brought into operation, any necessary statutory instruments which need to be made under it can be drafted. Full consultations can be held with the industry concerned. Explanatory material for the guidance of officials and the public can be prepared and absorbed. Further consideration can be given to the wisdom of any doubtful provisions and, if necessary, amendments to the Act can be sought from Parliament. The matter is under government control, and the Government, paying regard to political factors, can choose the most advantageous moment. These are the reasons which cause the commencement order method to be chosen for a large proportion of modern Acts.

Choice of date   Use of the word 'may' rather than 'shall' in the commencement provision indicates that, although Parliament has thought fit to pass the Act, it has chosen to leave the question of when it shall be brought into operation to Ministers. This recognises that unexpected factors may arise which make it in the Government's view inexpedient to allow the Act to come into force without some delay.

Although this is sometimes criticised as in effect allowing the civil service a suspending power, the remedy lies with Parliament. If it wishes to insist on an Act's coming into force within a certain period it can always use appropriate wording. {As to the denial of a suspending power see s 177 of this Code.}

Leaving the date to be appointed carries the risk that the need for a commencement order will be overlooked by the civil servants charged with the duty of administering the Act. This has occasionally happened, particlarly in colonial territories. {For examples see Bennion *Constitutional Law of Ghana* (Butterworths, 1962) p 380.}

Rarely, Parliament may insist on being given an opportunity to consider and, if thought fit, reject a proposed commencement order. Thus s 2(2) of the Easter Act 1928, which would cause the date of Easter to be fixed instead of variable, prevents a commencement order being made unless a draft of it has first been approved by both Houses of Parliament. No such draft has yet been approved.

Alternatively, Parliament may *specify* the date which, if Ministers decide to make a commencement order, is to be the one appointed.

Example 1 Section 9(2) of the Equal Pay Act 1970 gave the Secretary of State discretion to bring certain provisions of the Act into force earlier than the commencement date of 29 December 1975 specified by s 9(1), but stated that the day appointed by such an order must be 31 December 1973.

Enforced commencement Occasionally Parliament inserts a provision by which, if a commencement order has not been made by a certain date, the Act will come into force anyway.

Example 2 Section 5(2) of the Domestic Violence and Matrimonial Proceedings Act 1976 provided that if any provisions of the Act had not been brought into force by 1 April 1977 'the Lord Chancellor shall then make an order by statutory instrument bringing such provisions into force'.

Decision never to make commencement order Can a government lawfully decide, as a matter of policy, never to bring an Act (or part of an Act) into force at all? Certainly governments do as a matter of fact take such decisions. {For examples see N Tutt and H Giller 'Police Cautioning of Juveniles: the Practice of Diversity' [1983] Crim LR 587 (Children and Young Persons Act 1969 s 5); J R Spencer 'When is a Law not a Law' (1981) 131 NLJ 644 (Health and Safety at Work etc Act 1974 s 71). See also Example 166.6.} They can only apply until reversed, and this might always be done by a successor government. So the word 'never' is perhaps inapt; though on some matters there may be all-party agreement that an enactment should in effect be repealed by this form of inaction.

The official doctrine on the point was set out by Lord Elwyn-Jones LC in answer to a parliamentary question relating to the failure to bring into force s 7 of the Road Traffic Act 1974-

> ' . . . if the Act states that it shall come into force on a date to be fixed
> by order made by the Minister, and provides no more than that, it is
> within the discretion of the Minister as to when he brings the Act
> into force. Parliament may of course bring pressure to bear on him

and require him to justify any inactivity. But short of another Act, there is no way in which the Minister can be compelled *by Parliament* to bring that Act into operation.'

{HL Deb, 29 June 1977 (col 1110) Emphasis added.}
This statement must be literally true, but it overlooks the possibility that there might be another remedy, namely an application to the High Court for judicial review. {As to judicial review see s 24 of this Code.} A commencement order is a statutory instrument, and in *R v Secretary of State for the Environment, ex p Greater London Council* {(1983) *The Times* 2 December.} judicial review was allowed in the case of a failure by a Minister to make a statutory instrument, admittedly of a different kind. {See p 642 below.}

Two cases can be distinguished. The first, which is comparatively rare, is where the Act says the the Minister *shall* bring the provision into force. An example was given above in relation to the Domestic Violence and Matrimonial Proceedings Act 1976. Here a date was specified by which the Lord Chancellor was required to make a commencement order, and it seems that the High Court should have been willing to make a declaration on judicial review if the Lord Chancellor had failed to carry out this duty.

An example of a mandatory requirement where no date was specified is furnished by s 192(4) of the Consumer Credit Act 1974. This says that the Secretary of State 'shall' make orders bringing into operation the amendments and repeals set out in Schs 4 and 5 to the Act.

It is submitted that such mandatory provisions are to be taken to imply that the duty must be performed *within a reasonable time*. A contrary reading would enable a Minister to frustrate the clear intention of Parliament, which is contrary to the whole essence of statutory interpretation. {In fact the bulk of the last-mentioned amendments and repeals were not brought into force until 19 May 1985: Consumer Credit Act 1974 (Commencement No 8) Order 1983 (SI 1983/1551), arts 4 and 5. Is an interval of nearly eleven years a 'reasonable period'?}

The second type of case is the more usual one where the permissive 'may' is used. Here again it is submitted that the matter is within the scope of judicial review. A declaration was granted in *R v Secretary of State for the Environment, ex p Greater London Council* {(1983) *The Times* 2 December.} notwithstanding that some of the regulation-making powers there in question were couched in permissive terms. It is submitted that whenever parliament passes an Act it intends, unless the contrary intention appears, that all its provisions shall be brought into force within a reasonable time. There is no reason in principle why this matter of public law should be treated as withheld from the supervisory jurisdiction of the High Court.

Statutory defence   It does not seem that the defence under s 3(2) of the Statutory Instruments Act 1946 of non-issue of the instrument {See pp 156–157 above.} is available to a person charged with an offence under an Act brought into force by a statutory instrument. It can scarcely be said in such a case that the offence 'consists' of a contravention of the statutory instrument within the meaning of s 3(2) - even though but for the making of the instrument the charge could not have been brought.

168. Commencement: of different provisions on different days

An Act may state that its various provisions are to come into force (either wholly or for certain purposes only) on such dates as Her Majesty may by Order in Council appoint, or as a specified Minister may by order made by statutory instrument appoint, or as may be otherwise appointed.

COMMENTARY

Where power is given to bring the Act into force by order, it is now more usual to provide flexibility by enabling different provisions to be brought into force at different times. {See *R v Weston* [1910] 1 KB 17.} Furthermore any one provision may be brought into force at different times for different purposes. The commentary on s 167 of this Code applies to these cases also.

Departments are under instructions to minimise the number of commencement orders made for any one Act, and to rationalise their issue and the dates of commencement. The explanatory note to a commencement order should include commencement dates appointed by previous orders made under the Act in question. {These instructions were issued by the Management and Personnel Office in 1982: see *The Law Society's Gazette* 28 July 1982.}

169. Commencement: preparatory orders etc

Where an Act which (or any provision of which) does not come into force immediately on its passing confers power to make delegated legislation, or to make appointments, give notices, prescribe forms or do any other thing for the purposes of the Act, then, unless the contrary intention appears, the power may be exercised, and any instrument made thereunder may be made so as to come into force, at any time after the passing of the Act so far as may be necessary or expedient for the purpose-

(a) of bringing the Act or any provision of the Act into force; or

(b) of giving full effect to the Act or any such provision at or after the time when it comes into force.

COMMENTARY

This is derived from s 13 of the Interpretation Act 1978, and enables preparatory steps to be taken. Section 13 reproduces with minor improvements s 37 of the Interpretation Act 1889. {As to the effect of s 37 see *R v Minister of Town and Country Planning, ex p Montague Burton Ltd* [1950] 2 All ER 282; *Usher v Barlow* [1952] Ch 255.}

One of the purposes of s 13 is to avoid the difficulty that would otherwise arise if an Act contained a provision enabling the whole Act to be brought into force by commencement order. Since that provision would not itself be in force, the commencement order (on a literal construction) could never be made!

AMENDMENT OF AN ENACTMENT

170. Amendment: meaning of 'amendment'

To 'amend' an Act or enactment is to alter its legal meaning.

The *repeal* of an enactment constitutes the *amendment* of the Act containing it. Accordingly the rules applicable to repeals set out in ss 178 to 185 of this Code may also apply to an amendment.

An Act or provision of an Act may be amended in the same Session of Parliament in which the Act is passed.

COMMENTARY

Where an enactment is contained in an Act, the only provision having power to override it is a later Act, or an intra vires item of delegated legislation made under the same or a later Act. Where the enactment is contained in an item of delegated legislation, it may be altered by a later instrument made under the same power, or by or under a later Act. Where the enactment is affected by later Community law it may be treated as amended by that. {European Communities Act 1972 ss 2 and 3. See Bennion *Statute Law* (2nd edn, 1983) chap 6.

Amendment may be by alteration of the words (textual amendment) {See s 171 of this Code.}, or by indirect express amendment {See s 172 of this Code.}, or by implication. {See s 173 of this Code.} There is no rule to prevent an amendment being made that alters the whole basis of an Act.

Example 1   The Bill which became the Rules Publication Act 1893 was introduced at the instance of the Law Society solely to ensure notice and publication of rules of court, though it was greatly widened during its passage. Section 15(3) of the Administration of Justice Act 1925 amended the 1893 Act to *exclude* rules of court from its ambit, thus reversing its original effect. {See C K Allen *Law and Orders* p 58.}

Amendment may take the form of, or include, a repeal. If for example a section of an Act is deleted, it can be said that the section is repealed but the Act is amended. In so far as an amendment also constitutes a repeal, the rules relating to repeals will apply. These are set out in ss 178 to 185 of the Code.

Amendment in same Session   The last sentence in this section of the Code derives from s 2 of the Interpretation Act 1978. {Earlier s 1 of 13 & 14 Vict c 21 (Lord Brougham's Act 1850), and then s 10 of the Interpretation Act 1889. The words 'or provision of an Act' do not appear in s 2, but must be taken as implied.} It is not needed, being a statement of the obvious, but relates to the time when all statutes passed in a Session were treated as receiving royal assent at the beginning of the session. This doctrine was abolished by the Acts of Parliament (Commencement) Act 1793.

171. Amendment: textual amendment

Textual amendment is a form of amendment whereby the text of the Act or other instrument to be amended is expressly altered by the deletion, substitution or addition of words. The effect then is that the instrument can be reprinted as amended, and remains a single text.

Where the passage to be altered is described as running 'from' a specified word, phrase or other part of the instrument being amended, it includes that word, phrase or other part. Similarly, where the passage to be altered is described as running 'to' a specified word, phrase or other part, it includes that word, phrase or other part.

COMMENTARY

Textual amendment has the great advantage for the statute user that it enables the matter to be retained in one text. Although little used in Britain until recently, this method is now accepted as being the usual one. {See further Bennion *Statute Law* (2nd edn, 1983) pp 131-2.}

The second part of this section of the Code is drawn from s 20(1) of the Interpretation Act 1978. The following, in showing how it operates, gives a typical example of the modern technique of textual amendment.

Example 1   As originally enacted, s 13(1) of the Dentists Act 1957 ran as follows-

'Where the General Dental Council, with a view to permitting any person holding a Commonwealth or foreign diploma temporarily to practise dentistry in a hospital or other institution, give a direction that he be registered as respects practice in that hospital or institution for such a period as may be specified in the direction, that person shall, without showing that any requirements under the last foregoing section are fulfilled in his case, be entitled to be registered in the dentists register in accordance with the provisions of this Act subject to the entry against his name of the restrictions specified in the direction.'

The Dentists Act 1983 s 33(1) and Sch 2 para 6, provided for the following amendments to s 13 of the 1957 Act-

'(a) in subsection (1)-
(i) for the words from "Commonwealth" to "practice" substitute "recognised overseas diploma temporarily to practise dentistry in a particular post in a hospital or other institution, give a direction that he be registered as respects practice in that post";
(ii) omit the words from "without" to "case".'

The result of the amendments is to make s 13(1) read as follows-

'Where the General Dental Council, with a view to permitting any person holding a recognised overseas diploma temporarily to practise dentistry in a particular post in a hospital or other institution, give a direction that he be registered as respects practice in that post in that hospital or institution for such a period as may be specified in the direction, that person shall be entitled to be registered in the dentists register in accordance with the provisions of this Act subject to the entry against his name of the restrictions specified in the direction.'

419

The following points arise on the latter of the two amendments. First, it is accompanied by what is expressed to be a 'repeal' of the words omitted. This is located in Sch 3 to the 1983 Act. {As to the reason for what amounts to a double repeal see s 179 of this Code.} Second, although as a matter of common sense it follows that the pair of commas surrounding the phrase deleted by the second amendment must disappear along with the phrase, this is not stated. Except where to do so is impracticable, textual amendments ignore transitional punctuation and leave the user to make the obvious adjustments in it for himself.

Significance of wording used   No significance should usually be attached to variations in the way different draftsmen word directory provisions in textual amendments. Their object is almost always the same, i e to cause the enactment to be treated as having the new wording rather than the old. This is always subject to any commencement and transitional provisions that are included. {As to commencement provisions see ss 164 to 169 of this Code. For transitional provisions see s 189.}

For this reason Glidewell J was, it is submitted, mistaken when, in an unreported judgment in *R v Houghton, R v Donachie* {Cited with approval in *R v Clarke (Linda)* [1982] 3 All ER 232, at p 235.} he based his decision on the meaning of s 47(8) of the Criminal Law Act 1977 on the presence of the italicised words {Emphasis added.}-

> '(8) This section and paras 1 to 6 of Sch 9 to this Act and the Powers of Criminal Courts Act 1973 shall be construed *and have effect* as if this section and those paragraphs of the Schedule were contained in that Act.'

Admittedly the wording of this is unfortunate, and does not follow the usual pattern for textual amendment. It furnishes one more instance of the perils of the drafting device which, since it makes undue use of the phrase 'as if' and similar hypotheses, is known as *asifism*. {See Bennion *Statute Law* (2nd edn, 1983) pp 184-5, 200-2.} As to tautology generally see pp 375–376 above.

Rule in A-G v Lamplough   Textual amendment necessarily involves a certain degree of artificiality. At a date which may be long after its enactment, the Act is given a different wording. Clearly there will be transitional problems regarding events spanning the change, but these should be taken care of by the transitional provisions of the amending Act. A more subtle problem concerns the effect on the words that remain.

An Act is to be construed as a whole. {As to this principle see s 149 of the Code.} Are the unaltered words of the Act to be construed as meaning what they did before the others were amended? It was held in *A-G v Lamplough* {(1878) 3 Ex D 214.} that, unless the contrary intention appears from the amending Act, the answer is yes. {See further Bennion *Statute Law* (2nd edn, 1983) pp 281-2.}

However it is submitted that under modern practice the intention of Parliament when effecting textual amendment of an Act is to produce a revised text of the Act *which is thereafter to be construed as a whole*. Any repealed provisions are to be treated as never having been there, so far as concerns the application of the amended Act for the future.

Effect of amending Act It follows that the usual rule is that the function of the amending Act is to serve as an instrument for altering the text of the earlier Act, subject only to the need for commencement and transitional provisions. Unless the contrary intention appears, the other provisions of the amending Act should not affect the construction of words inserted by it into the earlier Act.

Example 2 Paragraph 1 of Sch 1 to the Immigration Act 1971 begins-

'The law with respect to registration as a citizen of the United Kingdom and Colonies shall be modified as follows:-
(a) in the British Nationality Act 1948, immediately before s 6, there shall be inserted as s 5A the provisions set out in Appendix A to this Schedule, and no person shall be entitled to be registered under or by virtue of s 6(1) of that Act except in the transitional cases allowed for by para 2 below.'

Section 33(2) of the Immigration Act 1971 says-

'It is hereby declared that, except as otherwise provided in this Act, a person is not to be treated *for the purposes of any provision of this Act* as ordinarily resident in the United Kingdom . . . at a time when he is there in breach of the immigration laws.'

{Emphasis addded.}

In *R v Secretary of State for the Home Department, ex p Margueritte* {[1982] 3 All ER 909.} the question was whether the italicised words in s 33(2) governed the new s 5A inserted by para 1 into the 1948 Act. If they did, para 1 was ineptly drawn. An inserting Act should modify the provisions it is inserting only from the point of view of their commencement and the transition. If there are substantive modifications they should be included in what is being inserted. *Held* The wording of para 1 of Sch 1 to the 1971 Act indicated that the new s 5A was intended to be a provision of the 1971 Act within the meaning of s 33(2).

See also Example 104.3.

172. Amendment: indirect express amendment

Where an Act or other instrument expressly amends an enactment, but does not do so by textual amendment, it is said to do it by indirect amendment (sometimes known as referential amendment).

COMMENTARY

An indirect amendment may or may not identify the enactment amended. Either way it produces the need to *conflate* the two texts and arrive at the combined legal meaning. {For the problems posed by conflation see Bennion *Statute Law* (2nd edn, 1983) pp 113-5.} Until recently this was the normal method of amendment in the United Kingdom. It has now been largely replaced by textual amendment. {As to this see s 171 of this Code.}

Example 1 An example of an indirect amendment which does not name the amended enactments is furnished by the opening words of s 1 of the Sex Disqualification (Removal) Act 1919, which is still in force-

'A person shall not be disqualified by sex or marriage from the exercise of any public function, or from being appointed to or holding any civil or judicial office or post, or from entering or assuming or carrying on any civil profession or vocation . . .'

The Act did not go on to include the consequential textual amendments required by this sweeping provision. {As to consequential amendments see s 175 of this Code.} This undoubtedly accounts for the failure of the Act to achieve its main purpose. {See Bennion 'The Sex Disqualification (Removal) Act - 60 Inglorious Years' (1979) 129 NLJ 1088.}

One striking aspect of this failure relates to the ordination of women. The Act undoubtedly removed the legal bar to the creation of women priests by the words 'A person shall not be disqualified by sex . . . from entering or assuming or carrying on any civil profession or vocation.' Yet everyone concerned has all along assumed that the contrary is the case.

173. Amendment: implied amendment

Where a later enactment does not expressly amend (whether textually or indirectly) an earlier enactment which it has power to override, but the provisions of the later enactment are inconsistent with those of the earlier, the later by implication amends the earlier so far as is necessary to remove the inconsistency between them.

COMMENTARY

If a later Act cannot stand with an earlier, Parliament (though it has not said so) is taken to intend an amendment of the earlier. This is a logical necessity, since two inconsistent texts cannot both be valid without contravening the principle of contradiction. {As to this principle see s 362 of the Code.} If the entirety of the earlier Act is inconsistent, the effect amounts to a repeal of it. The rules relative to repeals will then apply. {See ss 178 to 185 of this Code.} Similarly, a part of the earlier Act may be regarded as repealed where it cannot stand with the later.

Implied amendment often presents the statute user with difficult problems of *conflation*. {See Bennion *Statute Law* (2nd edn, 1983) pp 113-5.} For that reason it is objectionable, and to be avoided by draftsmen.

Statutory exposition   Where the legal meaning of an enactment is doubtful, and a later enactment having power to override it is so worded as to show that the legislator treated it as having a particular meaning, this is said to be a statutory exposition of it. {Jowitt *Dictionary of English Law* tit 'Statutory exposition'.}

Whether statutory exposition is equivalent to implied amendment depends on whether the later enactment indicates an intention to clarify the meaning of the earlier one (thus serving as a *declaratory* enactment), or merely refers to it. In the latter case it is of persuasive authority only. See further s 255 of this Code.

174. Amendment: amendment by delegated legislation

An Act may confer power for the amendment of itself or another Act by delegated legislation. An amendment made by the use of such a power is as effective as if made directly by an Act.

COMMENTARY

Provided it is not ultra vires, an amendment made by delegated legislation has the same effect as one made directly by Act. {For the doctrine of ultra vires see s 58 of this Code.} The practice of including such amending powers in Acts began in the second half of the nineteenth century, and has been applied in many Acts since. {See, e g, Factory Act Extension Act 1867 s 14; Anatomy Act (1832) Amendment Act 1871 s 2; Local Government Act 1888 s 108; Local Government Act 1894 s 80(1); Roads Act 1920 s 10; Rating and Valuation Act 1925 s 66; Mental Treatment Act 1930 s 15; Public Health Act 1936 ss 313-4; Highways Act 1959 s 288; Local Government Act 1972 s 252.}

Despite, the frequency of the use of this method by Parliament, there is still some judicial dislike of it.

Example 1 Barge v Graham Brown (Oasis Trading) Ltd {[1981] 3 All ER 360.} concerned the Hallmarking Act 1973, which confers power to amend its own provisions by statutory instrument. {See ss 4(7) and 17(2).} In agreeing with the finding of Forbes J as to the legal meaning of a provision of the Act as so amended, Donaldson LJ said {P 363.}-

'I have a suspicion that this is not what the draftsman of the Act intended. But since he has taken this quite remarkable power to alter the Act by statutory instrument, the remedy is in his own hands.'

This displays a strange ignorance of how statutes are drafted and administered. Parliamentary counsel does not choose to take such a power. He acts on instructions from the sponsoring department, and the result is approved (or not) by Parliament. The amending instruments are drafted not by parliamentary counsel, but by departmental officials. The remedy for any error is within the hands of the department, not those of parliamentary counsel. Moreover the power is not 'remarkable', but very commonly used.

Here the following remarks made by Lord Diplock 1n 1980 are in point-

'In purely domestic legislation . . . the choice of the actual words that are most apt to express with clarity and precision the intention of the promoters of the Bill (generally the executive government) will have been that of parliamentary counsel . . . The audience to whom the language that he chooses is addressed is the judiciary, whose constitutional function is to resolve any doubts as to what written laws mean; and the resulting Act of Parliament will be couched in language that accords with the traditional, and widely criticised, style of legislative draftsmanship which has become familiar to English judges during the present century and for which their own narrowly semantic approach to statutory construction, until the last decade or so, may have been largely to blame. That approach for which parliamentary draftsmen had to cater can hardly be better illustrated than by the words of Lord Simonds LC in *IRC v Ayrshire Employers Mutual Insurance Assn Ltd* {[1946] 1 All ER 637, at p 641.}:

"The section . . . s 31 of the Finance Act 1933, is clearly a remedial section . . . It is at least clear what is the gap that is intended to be filled and hardly less clear how it is intended to fill that gap. Yet I can come to no other conclusion than that the language of the section fails to achieve its apparent purpose and I must decline to insert words or phrases which might succeed where the draftsman failed."

The unhappy legacy of this judicial attitude, although it is now being replaced by an increasing willingness to give a purposive construction to the Act, is the current English style of legislative draftsmanship.'
{As to purposive construction see s 139 and Part XV of this Code.}

Power to amend an Act by delegated legislation is usually restricted to less important provisions. Such is not invariably the case however.

Example 2   Schedule 1 to the Indictments Act 1915 contained important rules as to the form of indictments. Sections 1 and 2 of the Act, as amended by s 56 of and para 17 of Sch 8 to the Courts Act 1971, empower the Crown Court rule committee to make rules 'varying or annulling' these statutory rules, and to make further rules with respect to the same matters. Unfortunately this has been construed as allowing Sch 1 to be altogether displaced by a mere statutory instrument. {Indictment Rules 1971, SI 1971/1253. For the objections to this course see pp 122–123 above.}

Official table   At the end of the official annual volume of public general Acts published by Her Majesty's Stationery Office, a table is given of textual amendments to Acts effected by statutory instruments made during the year.

175. Amendment: consequential amendment

An enactment may be amended in consequence of substantive provisions contained in a later Act or instrument. Such an amendment is known as a consequential amendment.

COMMENTARY

Apart from the occasional declaratory Act, the sole purpose of every new Act of Parliament is to change the law. If the existing law did what was required a new Act would not be needed. The main provisions of a new Act usually involve consequential minor changes to existing Acts, commonly known as consequentials.   Often these changes are widespread and numerous.

There are three ways of effecting consequential changes.

(1) No express consequentials are included in the new Act. Under the usual doctrine, the inconsistent provisions in the new Act simply override earlier law. The consequential amendments are thus effected purely by implication. {As to implied amendment see s 173 of this Code.}

(2) *General* consequentials are included in the new Act. These do not textually amend the inconsistent provisions of the existing law, but merely apply a general formula to them. {As to indirect express amendment see s 172 of this Code.}

(3) *Specific* consequentials are included in the new Act. These textually amend the affected provisions, which can thereafter be reprinted in their amended form. {As to textual amendment see s 171 of this Code.}

Method 3 is by far the most efficient for the statute user. He has the amended provision as a single text, and does not need to puzzle out how the new Act has altered the law. Often such puzzles are too difficult for the ordinary practitioner.

Modern practice is to use method 3 for the more obvious consequentials and method 2 for the rest. It would be desirable for the practice to be changed so that method 3 is always used except in the rare case where the confused state of the existing law makes method 2 the only one that is practical.

It will be objected, as it is to many suggestions for reform, that this will increase the work of the draftsman. The following answers to this objection may be given. Most of them apply to other reform proposals as well.

(a) While such a reform will increase the draftsman's work on the Bill in question, the overall long-term effect will be to make the law simpler. This will reduce the drafting workload on Bills generally.

(b) The advent of computer retrieval for statutes makes it easier than before for the draftsman to track down enactments that require consequential amendment.

(c) The draftsman of a Bill is uniquely qualified to know precisely what consequentials are needed.

(d) The draftsman can do the consequentials once and for all. For each user to struggle with them separately is inefficient.

(e) Since the ordinary user inevitably makes mistakes, the efficient working of the legal system suffers unnecessarily under the present method.

(f) The time thus unnecessarily spent by individual users adds to costs.

Sometimes an enactment is subjected to consequentials using both method 2 and method 3.

Example 1 The British Nationality Act 1981 is described in its long title as an Act 'to make fresh provision about citizenship and nationality'. It repeals the previous principal Act, the British Nationality Act 1948, except for a few minor provisions. One of these is s 3, a complex section which limits the criminal liability of certain classes of persons.

Section 52(6) of the 1981 Act is in the form commonly used for enacting consequentials by method 3. It reads: 'The enactments specified in Sch 7 shall have effect subject to the amendments there specified, being amendments consequential on the provisions of this Act'. The only amendment to the 1948 Act included in Sch 7 is one that adds a new subsection to s 3.

However, to glean the full updated effect of s 3 it is also necessary to apply some method 2 (that is indirect or non-textual) consequentials contained in s 51 of the 1981 Act. Section 3 is a criminal provision. It appears in *Archbold*. But it would be very difficult indeed for a practitioner, perhaps under pressure in court, to work out the updated effect of s 3 without undue expenditure of time and effort. Even then the ordinary practitioner might well get it wrong. Statutory drafting is difficult enough to understand when only the one text has to be considered.

The draftsman of a measure like the 1981 Act has everything at his fingertips. It is child's play for him to complete the task of updating enactments requiring consequential amendment. He can do it there and then, once and for all. It is very much more difficult for the busy practitioner, inexpert in statute law, to accomplish this task. Moreover it has to be done many times over by numerous practitioners, instead of just once by the draftsman.

The official answer to a complaint made about this was that the updating would be 'swept up in any future legislation'. But it may be years before Parliament gets round to doing this. Meanwhile the statute user is left to struggle, quite unnecessarily.

If this were just one isolated case it would matter little. Unfortunately this kind of thing goes on all the time. Cumulatively, it adds greatly to the complexity and obscurity of the statute book and the expenditure of needless time and effort by practitioners.

Missed consequentials When Parliament abolishes or alters a rule of law it is taken to intend that corresponding alterations shall be treated as made elsewhere in the law where these are consequential on the change in question. An alteration in one area of law often has repercussions in others. The draftsman aims to spell out what these are, but may fail to do so comprehensively. This may be because he is not aware of all the possible ramifications. In such cases an implication arises that the necessary changes were effected, even though not expressly. The courts construe existing legislation accordingly.

Example 2 Section 22 of the Firearms Act 1937 made it an offence for a person to have in his possession any firearm 'with intent by means thereof to endanger life'. When enacted, this covered a person who had possession of a firearm with intent to kill himself, suicide being a crime. On the passing of the Suicide Act 1961 suicide ceased to be a crime. Since there was thereafter no criminality in taking one's own life, there could be no criminality in endangering one's own life. Although the Suicide Act 1961 did not say so, it was treated as effecting a consequential amendment to this effect in s 22. {*R v Rex Norton* [1977] Crim LR 478. The case was decided on s 16 of the Firearms Act 1968 (a consolidation Act), which reproduced s 22. Cf *Bryan v Mott* (1976) 62 Cr App R 71; [1976] Crim LR 64. See also Example 351.8.}

176. Amendment: references to an amended enactment

Where an Act or other instrument refers to a particular enactment, the reference, unless the contrary intention appears, is a reference to that enactment as amended, and includes a reference thereto as extended or applied, by or under any other enactment, including any other provision of that Act or instrument.

COMMENTARY

This section of the Code follows s 20(2) of the Interpretation Act 1978. The reason for inserting it was officially given in para 8 of the white paper published by the Law Commissions on the Bill for the Act. {Cmnd 7235.} This is in the following terms-

'The great majority of Acts of Parliament contain references of some kind to other existing enactments which, or some of which, have been amended by intervening legislation. This raises the theoretical question whether the reference is intended to denote the enactment in the form in which it was originally passed or in the form in which it stands at the time of the reference. The intention is almost invariably the latter. Where it is not, words are added to make that clear - see for example para 7(1) of Sch 2 to the Acquisition of Land (Authorisation Procedure) Act 1946, which refers to ss 78 to 85 of the Railways Clauses Consolidation Act 1845 "as originally enacted and not as amended . . . by s 15 of the Mines (Working Facilities and Support) Act 1923".

Nevertheless the practice has grown up, no doubt to be on the safe side, of including in Acts which contain such references a clause to the effect that they are to be construed as referring to the enactments in question as amended by subsequent Acts. On an approximate estimate such a clause now appears in two out of every three Acts. Although the general purpose is the same, these clauses differ from each other in detail, ranging from the simplest form - "Any reference in this Act to any other enactment is a reference to that enactment as amended by any subsequent enactment" to the full treatment - "Unless the context otherwise requires, any reference in this Act to any other enactment is a reference thereto as amended, and includes a reference thereto as extended or applied, by or under any other enactment, including this Act".

Apart from the expenditure of paper and ink upon clauses *the need for which is at best doubtful,* these provisions are disturbing because it is seldom self-evident why the clause appears in different forms in different Acts, and does not appear at all in others.

We recommend accordingly that the consolidation should include a clause designed to eliminate these *ad hoc* clauses. Effect to this recommendation is given in clause 20(2) of the draft Bill.'

{Emphasis added.}

Unfortunately the change made by s 20(2) of the 1978 Act is far from clearing up the difficulties (hinted at in the italicised passage above). A formula of this type is a 'blind', or hit-and-miss, formula. It is aimed at something it cannot see. There are a wide variety of possible cases. The formula will be right for some, and wrong for others. It is up to the draftsman of each Act to judge whether the formula is right for the references he makes to other enactments, but that is often very difficult to do.

Subsequent amendments The biggest difficulty concerns subsequent amendments. We may illustrate this in schematic form.

> *1984* Act A is passed.
> *1985* Act B amends Act A.
> *1986* Act C, which contains a reference to Act A, is passed.
> *1988* Act D further amends Act A.

By virtue of s 20(2), restated in this section of the Code, the reference in Act C to Act A is in say 1987 to be read as a reference to Act A as amended by Act B.

But how is that reference to be read in say 1989? Is it to be read as referring to Act A as amended by Act B alone, or to Act A as amended by Acts B and D?

It will be seen that s 20(2) is ambiguous on this very difficult point. It might be thought that since the Law Commissions were inserting a new provision into the Interpretation Act they would have made sure that it was not ambiguous. As the passage reproduced above shows, the provision had been used many times previously. There was no excuse for getting it wrong.

Example 1   In *Willows v Lewis (Inspector of Taxes)* {(1981) *Times* 2 November.} Nourse J was faced with resolving this problem. Following the schematic treatment used above, we may show the position as follows-

> *1970* The Income Tax and Corporation Taxes Act 1970 ('the 1970 Act') is passed. It includes as s 540(3) a provision on similar lines to s 20(2) of the Interpretation Act 1978.
> *March 1975* The 1970 Act is amended so as to charge to tax 'payments of benefit under Chapters I to III of the Social Security Act 1975' ('the 1975 Act').
> *August 1975* An amendment, made by another Act, inserts into Part III of the 1975 Act a new type of benefit (called a mobility allowance).
> *1978-79* The appellant receives a mobility allowance.

The question was whether the mobility allowance was caught by the charging provision in the 1970 Act. *Held* It was not. Nourse J said that to treat s 540(3) of the 1970 Act as applying to future amendments was to give it 'a width of application which the wording, at best equivocal, could not bear, especially in a taxing statute'. {The decision was reversed for the future by the Finance (No 2) Act 1979 s 12 and Sch 2 para 3.}

177. Amendment: extra-statutory concessions

Where the legal meaning of a taxing enactment produces a charge which the tax authorities consider should not be imposed, or should be imposed in a way less onerous to the taxpayer, the practice is to grant an extra-statutory concession by which the charge is waived or alleviated accordingly. This has the de facto effect of an amendment to the enactment.

COMMENTARY

The extra-statutory concessions currently available are set out in a booklet published by the Board of Inland Revenue. This has the reference IR 1 (1970), and is supplemented by updating releases. {The concessions are also published in Halsbury's *Statutes of England* (3rd edn), Vol 34 App II.}

Constitutionality   It is sometimes alleged that, since Parliament has enacted the provisions in question, it is improper for the revenue authorities to alter their effect - even to the advantage of the subject.

Example 1   In *Commrs of Customs and Excise v Mechanical Services (Trailer Engineers) Ltd* {[1979] 1 All ER 501.} the Court of Appeal considered a VAT enactment which, if literally construed, would have taxed at the higher rate attributable to pleasure boats all components which were suitable for fitting to boat trailers, even though more than nine-tenths of such components were in point of fact fitted to lower-rated goods.

The Crown undertook that, if this literal construction were adopted by the court, hardship would be avoided by the granting of extra-statutory concessions. *Held* This was not a factor which could be considered when weighing the relevant considerations. Browne LJ said {P 507.}-

> 'I understand counsel for the Crown to be saying that the commissioners could and would deal with anomalies by not enforcing the law when they thought this inexpedient. This argument seems to raise echoes of the seventeenth century, when one of the great issues between King and Parliament was the general dispensing power, and I have no hesitation in rejecting it as an answer to counsel for the taxpayer company.'

{See also *R v Commrs of Customs and Excise, ex p Cook* [1970] 1 WLR 450, at pp 454-5. For a decision the other way see Example 252.1.}

The opposite argument On the other side it can be said that taxation is a special case. There is no general suspending or dispensing power; and the Bill of Rights (1688) declares any pretended exercise of such a power illegal. But taxes are given by Parliament as aids and supplies to the Crown.

After condemning the suspending and dispensing powers, the Bill of Rights goes on to refer to the 'levying of money for or to the use of the Crowne'. It does this in order to forbid taxation by pretence of prerogative, or 'for longer time or in other manner than the same is or shall be granted'; but does not deny the Crown's right to stay its grasp.

If the Crown, acting through its agents the revenue authorities, chooses to decline some part of granted aids and supplies out of mercy or fairness, it is scarcely for the Queen's justices to utter censure.

REPEAL OR EXPIRY OF AN ENACTMENT

178. Repeal: meaning of 'repeal'

To 'repeal' an Act is to cause it to cease to be a part of the corpus juris or body of law. To 'repeal' an enactment is to cause it to cease to be in law a part of the Act containing it.

A repeal may be either express or implied.

The *repeal* of an enactment constitutes the *amendment* of the Act containing it. Accordingly the rules applicable to amendments set out in ss 170 to 177 of this Code may also apply to a repeal.

An Act or provision of an Act may be repealed in the same Session of Parliament in which the Act was passed.

COMMENTARY

A repeal revokes or abrogates an Act or part of an Act. For delegated legislation the term 'revoke' is used instead, to like effect. Except where inapplicable, the provisions of this Code relating to repeals apply also to the revocation of delegated legislation.

A provision can effect a repeal only where contained in an instrument having power to override the Act in question. {See s 32 of this Code.} This may be another Act, or an item of delegated legislation made under an Act conferring power to repeal. An Act may repeal itself, or any provision contained in it. {See, eg the Government Trading Funds Act 1973, s 7 (5).}

The law has made use of many synonyms for the operation known as repeal, often in the same sentence. Thus the statute 19 Hen 7 c 28 s 1 {1503.} spoke of the 'reversall repelle adnullacion and advoydance' of a specified Act.

The desire to emphasise that an Act is consigned to limbo perhaps reached its extreme when a statute of Richard III was ordered to be 'annulled and utterly destroyed, [to be] taken out of the Roll of Parliament, and be cancelled and burnt, and be put in perpetual oblivion'. {R E Megarry *A Second Miscellany-at-Law* p 110.} There is no special wording required however, and the one word 'repeal' will delete the provision as effectively as any verbal jumping on its bones or scattering of its ashes.

Types of repeal   A repeal may be made textually, naming the repealed enactment. {This corresponds to textual amendment, and s 171 of this Code is relevant accordingly.} Or the repeal may be made by indirect express provision. {This corresponds to indirect express amendment, and s 172 of this Code is relevant accordingly.} Thus s 33 of the Supreme Court of Judicature Act 1875 repealed 'Any other enactments inconsistent with this Act'. Finally the repeal may be *implied*. {Implied repeal is explained in s 179 of this Code.}

Effect of repeal   At common law the repeal of an Act makes it as if it had never been, except as to matters past and closed. {See, e g, *Eton College v Minister of Agriculture* [1964] Ch 274.} It was laid down in *Tattle v Grimwood* {(1826) 3 Bing 493. See also *Mount v Taylor* (1868) LR 3 CP 645 (Act modifying earlier Act repealed, leaving the earlier Act standing).} that this even has the effect of reviving enactments repealed by the Act which has now gone. {Statutory modifications of the common law rule are described in s 181 of this Code.}

Thus anything done after the repeal in purported exercise of a repealed provision is a nullity. This applies even though the repealed provision has been re-enacted.

Example 1   In *Stowers v Darnell* {[1973] Crim LR 528.} the appellant had been convicted of using on a road *on 11 July 1972* a motor vehicle with defective tyres, contrary to s 64(2) of the Road Traffic Act 1960. However on 1 July 1972, s 64(2) had been repealed by the Road Traffic Act 1972 s 205(1) and Sch 9. Section 40(5) of the 1972 Act (which was a consolidation Act) reproduced the effect of s 64(2). *Held* The convictions related to alleged offences under what was at the time in question a non-existent Act, and would therefore be quashed. It was no answer that the repealing Act included provision in similar terms.

A repeal cannot go wider than the repealing Act. Thus an apparently comprehensive repeal may be limited if the Act is expressed not to apply to certain matters. {See D F Murray 'When is a repeal not a repeal?' (1953) 16 MLR 50.}

Too-wide repeal The court sometimes finds that the literal meaning of a repeal goes wider than seems right if Parliament's underlying intention is to be fulfilled. In accordance with its duty to give a rectifying construction where other factors do not rule this out, the court will then construe the repeal narrowly. {As to rectifying construction see s 142 of this Code.}

Example 2 In *Wigram v Fryer* {(1887) 36 Ch D 87, at p 99.} North J held that, in order to give working effect to an enactment providing for the erection of housing for the working classes, it was necessary to treat the powers conferred by a repealed enactment as being still available. {Cf Example 182.1.}

Repeal in same Session The last sentence in this section of the Code derives from s 2 of the Interpretatiion Act 1978. {Earlier s 1 of 13 & 14 Vict c 21 (Lord Brougham's Act 1850), and then s 10 of the Interpretation Act 1889. The words 'or provision of an Act' do not appear in s 2, but must be taken as implied.} It is not needed, being a statement of the obvious, but relates to the time when all statutes passed in a Session were treated as receiving royal assent at the beginning of the session. This doctrine was abolished by the Acts of Parliament (Commencement) Act 1793.

Repeal twice over It sometimes happens that the same provision is inadvertently repealed more than once.

Example 3 Section 5 of the Statute Law Revision (Substituted Enactments) Act 1876 was repealed by the Licensing Act 1961 {S 38 (3) and (4) and Sch 9 Part I.} and the SLR Act (Northern Ireland) 1954. It was then repealed all over again by the Statute Law (Repeals) Act 1971 s 1 and Sch Part IX.

To repeal what is already repealed has the same effect as killing a corpse, namely none at all. Since however Parliament is expected to do nothing in vain, it is as well to make sure that an apparent error of this kind has not got something behind it.

As to the practice of 'double repeal' see s 179 of this Code.

179. Repeal: the practice of 'double repeal'

It is a common practice in the drafting of repealing provisions to state in the body of the Act that the enactment shall 'cease to have effect' and also include it in the Repeal Schedule. The object is to draw the repeal to the attention of legislators considering the Bill for the Act (by including it in the body of the Bill) while at the same time enabling the Repeal Schedule to include all repeals made by the Act.

COMMENTARY

It is considered desirable that the columnar Repeal Schedule to an Act should be comprehensive. At the same time it is necessary to draw important repeals to the attention of MPs considering a Bill. The answer to the difficulty of satisfying both requirements is the practice of 'double repeal'.

Some judges and practitioners are unaware of the practice. This ignorance can have serious consequences.

Example 1 The House of Lords decision in *Commissioner of Police of the Metropolis v Simeon* {[1982] 2 All ER 813.} concerned the 'sus' offence laid down by s 4 of the Vagrancy Act 1824. This made it an offence for a 'suspected person' to be found loitering with intent to commit an arrestable offence.

The 'sus' provision was repealed by the Criminal Attempts Act 1981. On this Act's commencement date of 27 August 1981, more than 100 cases were awaiting trial for 'sus' offences. One of these concerned Simeon, whose alleged 'sus' offence was committed on 30 June 1981. The Divisional Court had granted him an order of prohibition preventing his trial being held.

Three sections of the 1981 Act are relevant. Section 8 said that the 'sus' provision 'shall cease to have effect'. Section 9 partially replaced the 'sus' provision by an alternative offence of interfering with vehicles. Section 10 said that the enactments mentioned in the Schedule to the 1981 Act 'are hereby repealed'. Included in the Schedule was the 'sus' provision.

Here it is necessary to consider the general savings made by s 16(1) of the Interpretation Act 1978 {These are explained in s 182 of this Code.}. A selective comminution of s 16(1) reads as follows-

'Where an Act repeals an enactment, the repeal does not, *unless the contrary intention appears*, affect any penalty or punishment incurred in respect of any offence committed against that enactment, or any legal proceeding in respect of any such penalty or punishment; and any such legal proceeding may be instituted or continued, and any such penalty or punishment may be imposed, as if the repealing Act had not been passed.'

{Emphasis added.}

In the Divisional Court the question was whether the italicised words prevented the general saving from authorising the trial of the applicant and (if he was considered guilty) his conviction and sentencing. The opposing constructions were {As to opposing constructions see s 84 of this Code.}-

(1) No 'contrary intention' appeared from the 1981 Act to prevent s 16(1) of the Interpretation Act 1978 from applying.

(2) A 'contrary intention' did appear. This was manifested by s 8 of the 1981 Act (which said that the 'sus' provision should 'cease to have effect'). Pending prosecutions could not therefore lawfully be completed. Since the new offence of interference with vehicles did not apply to acts done before the commencement date (27 August 1981) those on pending charges escaped.

The Divisional Court found for construction (2), and granted orders of prohibition and mandamus. They accepted the applicant's erroneous argument that there could be no reason for the double repeal except to manifest a 'contrary intention' and disapply s 16(1).

The prosecution appealed to the House of Lords, and on 16 July 1982 (five months after it had been given) the decision was unanimously reversed. Lord Roskill, who delivered the only judgment, said {P 816.}: 'with profound respect to the Divisional Court, I think they fell into error'. The Commissioner of Police of the Metropolis announced that he did not think it proper, after the time that had elapsed, to revive the 100 or more pending prosecutions. These therefore lapsed.

180. Repeal: implied repeal

Where a later enactment does not expressly repeal an earlier enactment which it has power to override, but the provisions of the later enactment are contrary to those of the earlier, the later by implication repeals the earlier in accordance with the maxim *leges posteriores priores contrarias abrogant* (later laws abrogate earlier contrary laws). This is subject to the exception embodied in the maxim *generalia specialibus non derogant*.

A like principle applies to the abrogation of a common law rule.

COMMENTARY

If a later Act makes contrary provision to an earlier, Parliament (though it has not said so) is taken to intend the earlier to be repealed. The same applies where a statutory provision is contrary to a common law rule.

This is a logical necessity, since two inconsistent laws cannot both be valid without contravening the principle of contradiction. {As to this principle see s 362 of the Code. For implied *amendment* see s 173.} The matter was thus described by A L Smith J-

> 'The test of whether there has been a repeal by implication by subsequent legislation is this: are the provisions of a later Act so inconsistent with, or repugnant to, the provisions of an earlier act that the two cannot stand together.'

{*West Ham Church Wardens and Overseers v Fourth City Mutual Building Society* [1892] 1 QB 654, at p 658.}

The possibility of implied repeal goes wider however than is indicated by the principle of contradiction. Other interpretative criteria may indicate implied repeal, for example the commonsense construction rule {See s 122 of this Code.} or the presumption that Parliament wishes to avoid an anomalous result. {See s 323 of this Code.}

Example 1 In *R v Davis* {(1783) 1 Leach 271.} it was held that a statute creating a capital offence was impliedly repealed by a later Act carrying a penalty of only £20.

Leges posteriores priores contrarias abrogant The maxim *leges posteriores priores contrarias abrogant* (later laws abrogate earlier contrary laws) is found in Coke. {1 Inst 25b.} It is a necessary consequence of the overriding nature of statutes. {See s 32 of this Code.} The principle is however subject to the countervailing principle expressed in the maxim *generalia specialibus non derogant*. {See s 181 of this Code.}

Presumption against implied repeal The courts presume that Parliament does not intend an implied repeal. {*The India* (1864) Brown & Lush 221 at p 224; *West Ham v Fourth City Mutual Building Society* [1892] 1 QB 654.} The presumption is stronger where modern precision drafting is used. {See s 76 of this Code.} In view of the difficulty of determining whether an alleged implication is really intended, the courts assume that, where it desires a repeal, Parliament will make itself plain by express words.

Example 2 In *Jennings v United States Government* {[1982] 3 All ER 104.} it was alleged by the defence that s 1 of the Road Traffic Act 1972 (as substituted by s 50 of the Criminal Law Act 1977) by implication abrogated the common law offence known as motor manslaughter. Section 1 is short and simple: 'A person who causes the death of another person by driving a motor vehicle on a road recklessly shall be guilty of an offence'.

Held There was still room for the operation of the common law offence, and it had not been abrogated. Lord Roskill said {P 114.} that earlier cases on implied repeal must be approached and applied with caution, since until comparatively late in the nineteenth century 'statutes were not drafted with the same skill as today'.

{See further s 181 of this Code, and Example 75.3.}

181. Repeal: *generalia specialibus non derogant*

Where the literal meaning of a general enactment covers a situation for which specific provision is made by another enactment contained in an earlier Act, it is presumed that the situation was intended to continue to be dealt with by the specific provision rather than the later general one. Accordingly the earlier specific provision is not treated as impliedly repealed.

COMMENTARY

The maxim *generalia specialibus non derogant* (a general provision does not derogate from a special one) is found in Jenkins' Exchequer Reports {Jenk Cent 120 (see 145 ER 84).}. For the application of the principle in a case where both provisions are contained in the same Act see p 378 above.

It may be found that, while a state of facts falls within the literal meaning of a wide provision, there is in an earlier Act a specific provision obviously intended to cover that state of facts in greater detail. Where the effect of the two enactments is not precisely the same, and the earlier one is not expressly repealed, it is presumed that Parliament intended it to continue to apply. {Lofft's KB Rep (1772-74) 351 (98 ER); *Kidston v The Empire Marine Insurance Co Ltd* [1866] LR 1 CP 535, at p 546; *Earl of Derby v Bury Improvement Commrs* (1869) 4 Ex 226. See also 6 Co Rep 65; 8 Co Rep 154; 11 Co Rep 59b; 3 Co Inst 76; Halk 51; Lofft 351.}

Thus in *Seward v The Vera Cruz* {(1884) 10 App Cas 59, at p 68.} the Earl of Selborne LC said-

' . . . where there are general words in a later Act capable of reasonable and sensible application without extending them to subjects specially dealt with by earlier legislation, you are not to hold that earlier and special legislation indirectly repealed, altered or derogated from merely by force of such general words, without any indication of a particular intention to do so.'

{See also *Garnett v Bradley* (1878) 3 App Cas 944; *Barker v Edger* [1898] AC 748, at p 754; *Blackpool Corpn v Starr Estate Co Ltd* [1922] 1 AC 27, at p 34; *Aberdeen Suburban Tramways Co v Magistrates of Aberdeen* (1927) SC 683, at p 689; *Walker v Hemmant* [1943] 1 KB 604; *Harlow v Minister of Transport* [1951] 2 KB 98; *R v Ramasamy* [1965] AC 1.}

Example 4 In *R v Horsham JJ, ex p Farquharson* {[1982] 2 All ER 269.} it was argued that the maxim *generalia specialibus non derogant* applied in the case of the following provisions-

> *The special provision*: s 8 of the Magistrates' Courts Act 1980, as amended by s 1 of the Criminal Justice (Amendment) Act 1981, makes special provision as to what can be reported in relation to committal proceedings.
> *The general provision*: s 4(2) of the Contempt of Court Act 1981 empowers the court in *any* legal proceedings to order that the publication of a report of the proceedings be *postponed* for a specified period.

The argument was that s 8 contained a complete code as to the reporting of committal proceedings, and that s 4(2) as not intended to alter this.

Held The argument failed, since on a true construction s 8 was not intended to be comprehensive and was not primarily concerned with the matters regulated by s 4(2). Lord Denning MR rejected the application of the maxim *generalia specialibus non derogant* because, as he said: 'There is still a place for s 4(2) . . .' {P 283.}

The principle may apply where two Acts (or groups of Acts), each operating independently of each other, are in question, and the facts of the instant case fall literally within the two different legislative schemes.

Example 5 Under s 108 of the Magistrates' Courts Act 1980 and s 9(2) and (4) of the Courts Act 1971 a precise statutory framework exists for the hearing of appeals against sentence from the magistrates' courts to the Crown Court. In *R v Battle JJ, ex p Shepherd* {(1983) *The Times* 26 April.} it was held by the Divisional Court that this precluded use of the general power of judicial review. Robert Goff LJ said that had the appeal proceeded in the Crown Court there would have been power to review the whole matter in the light of all the material in the case. It was difficult to conceive of circumstances where it would be proper for the Divisional Court to entertain an application where these full powers were not available.

182. Repeal: general savings

Where an Act passed after 1889 repeals an enactment, the repeal does not do any of the following (unless the contrary intention appears).

(1) Revive anything not in force or existing at the time at which the repeal takes effect.

(2) Affect the previous operation of the enactment repealed, or anything duly done or suffered under it.

(3) Affect any right, privilege, obligation or liability acquired, accrued or incurred under the enactment repealed.

(4) Affect any investigation, legal proceeding or remedy in respect of a right, privilege, obligation or liability acquired, accrued or incurred under the enactment repealed (and any such investigation, legal proceeding or remedy may be instituted, continued or enforced as if the repealing Act had not been passed).

(5) Affect any penalty, forfeiture or punishment incurred in respect of any offence committed against the enactment repealed.

(6) Affect any investigation, legal proceeding or remedy in respect of any penalty, forfeiture or punishment incurred in respect of any offence committed against the enactment repealed (and any such investigation, legal proceeding or remedy may be instituted, continued or enforced, and any such penalty, forfeiture or punishment may be imposed, as if the repealing Act had not been passed).

COMMENTARY

This section of the Code is derived from s 16(1) of the Interpretation Act 1978. Without significantly changing the wording, it attempts to present s 16(1) in a less complicated form. {S 16(1) reproduces s 38(2) of the Interpretation Act 1889, making no effort to improve the notoriously opaque drafting. The restriction to post-1889 Acts derives from the Interpretation Act 1978 s 22 and Sch 2 para 3.} By virtue of s 23 of the Interpretation Act 1978, the provision applies also to delegated legislation which is made after 1978 and effects the repeal or revocation of an enactment. {As to delegated legislation made before 1979 see *DPP v Lamb* [1941] 2 KB 89.}

The main effect of this provision is to modify the common law doctrine that at repeal the 'floodlight' is switched off, plunging everything illuminated by it into immediate darkness. {See pp 90–93 above.} The general savings reproduced here enable matters which are in progress at the time of repeal to be concluded.

Special savings   The general savings given here are often supplemented by special provisions in the repealing Act itself. Occasionally such special provisions may entirely displace these general savings. {See, e g, House of Commons Disqualification Act 1957, s 14(2).} Through inept drafting, the effect of a special saving may be to nullify the repeal and keep the supposedly repealed provision alive.

Example 1 The Chancery Amendment Act 1858 (known as Lord Cairns's Act) was repealed by the Statute Law Revision and Civil Procedure Act 1881 {S 3 and Sch.} and the Statute Law Revision and Civil Procedure Act 1883. {S 3 and Sch.} However, by the combined affect of s 4 of the 1881 Act and s 5 of the 1883 Act, the jurisdiction conferred by the principal section of Lord Cairns's Act, namely s 2 (which gave the Court of Chancery power to award damages), was not affected. Accordingly s 2, and the other sections of Lord Cairns's Act which contain provisions ancillary to s 2, maintain an uneasy existence as repealed provisions which are somehow still in force. {See *Leeds Industrial Co-operative Society Ltd v Slack* [1924] AC 851, at pp 861-863; *Johnson v Agnew* [1979] 1 All ER 883, at p 895. Cf Example 178.2.}

We now comment on the individual paragraphs of this section of the Code.

Paragraph 1 This operates to prevent the repeal of a repealing enactment from reviving enactments that enactment had repealed. {See p 430 above. This is also spelt out by s 15 of the Interpretation Act 1978, which applies to Acts passed after 1850.} In the same way the repeal of an enactment does not revive anything else (such as a contract or other obligation) which that enactment had rendered illegal or otherwise put an end to. {*Coates v Diment* [1951] 1 All ER 890.}

Furthermore it seems that para 1 also applies to rules of common law which had been abrogated by the repealed Act and were therefore 'not in force or existing' at the time the repeal took effect.

Example 2 Section 3(1) of the Nullity of Marriage Act 1971 was stated by s 3(4) of that Act to 'replace' the common law rule whereby a decree of nullity might be refused by reason of approbation, ratification or lack of sincerity. The Matrimonial Causes Act 1973 repealed the whole of the 1971 Act. {See s 54 and Sch 3.} Although the 1973 Act did not refer to the common law rule, it was held in *D v D* {[1979] 3 All ER 337.} not to have been revived by the repeal.

This application of para 1 to common law rules is unsatisfactory, and can be said to be contrary to principle. {See Aubrey L. Diamond *'Repeal and Desuetude of Statutes' Current Legal Problems* 1975 107 at pp 110–112.} The principle is that the common law exists as a seamless web of judge-made and customary rules and principles. It gives way to a statute while the statute is in force, but ought not to give way to it after the statute has gone. While it makes sense to say that a repealed statute does not revive when the repealing Act goes, this does not apply to the common law. The statute book, as currently in force, can be looked on as a whole. The common law ought in the same way to be a complete system, subject only to current Acts. It makes little sense to say that a rule of common law is occluded by statute when the statute in question has been repealed. {See *R v Secretary of State for the Foreign and*

Commonwealth Office, ex p Council of Civil Service Unions (1984) *The Times* 17 July 1984 (prerogative power held to revive on repeal of occluding enactment).}

Paragraph 2   The reference to 'anything duly done' avoids the need for procedural matters, such as the giving of notices, to be done over again {*R v West Riding of Yorkshire JJ* (1876) 1 QBD 220; *Heston and Isleworth UDC v Grout* [1897] 2 Ch 306, at p 311; *Hutchinson v Jauncey* [1950] 1 KB 574, at p 582.}.

Paragraphs 3 and 4   The right etc must have become vested by the date of repeal, i e it must not have been a mere right to take advantage of the enactment now repealed. {*Abbott v Minister of Lands* [1895] AC 425; *Hamilton Gell v White* [1922] 2 KB 422, at p 431. As to when a right 'accrues' for this purpose see *Lewis v Hughes* [1916] 1 KB 831; *Costello v Brown* (1924) 94 LJKB 220. Cf *Director of Public Works v Ho Po Sang* [1961] AC 901} If a right to damages has accrued, it is immaterial that the amount has not been quantified. {*Free Lanka Insurance Co v Ranasinghe* [1964] AC 541.}.

Being able to avail oneself of a statutory defence is not a 'right' for this purpose. {*Sifam Electrical Instrument Co Ltd v Sangamo Weston Ltd* [1971] 2 All ER 1074.}

A liability was held to be 'incurred' when the debtor had committed an act of bankruptcy. {*Re a Debtor (No 490 of 1935)* [1936] Ch 237.}

Paragraphs 5 and 6   At common law there could not be a conviction of an offence against a repealed enactment once the repeal had taken effect. This applied even though proceedings had been commenced previously. {*Bennett v Tatton* (1918) 88 LJKB 313.} Para 6 enables a prosecution which was begun before the repeal took effect to be completed. {*Postlethwaite v Katz* (1943) 59 TLR 248.}

Note that paras 5 and 6 do not apply where a penalty-creating provision is repealed, but the offence-creating provision is not. They only save a penalty etc for an offence *against the enactment repealed*. {See *Porter v Manning* (1984) *The Times* 23 March (repeal of Road Traffic Act 1972 s 93(3), which created no offence but merely provided for penalties).}

The working of paras 5 and 6 is illustrated by Example 179.1.

183. Repeal: substituted provisions (commencement)

Where an Act passed after 1850 repeals an enactment, and substitutes provisions for the enactment repealed, the latter remains in force until the commencement of the substituted provisions.

COMMENTARY

This derives from s 17(1) of the Interpretation Act 1978. It applies also to a revocation by delegated legislation made after 1978. {Interpretation Act 1978 s 23.} The restriction to post-1850 Acts derives from the Interpretation Act 1978 s 22 and Sch 2 para 2.

184. Repeal: re-enactment (adaptation of references)

Where an Act passed after 1889 repeals and re-enacts an enactment (with or without modification) then, unless the contrary intention appears, any reference in any other enactment to the enactment so repealed is to be construed as a reference to the provision re-enacted.

COMMENTARY

This derives from s 17(2)(a) of the Interpretation Act 1978. It applies also to a revocation by delegated legislation made after 1978. {Interpretation Act 1978 s 23.} The restriction to post-1889 Acts derives from the Interpretation Act 1978 s 22 and Sch 2 para 3.

This provision is intended for consolidation Acts, which may include minor modifications of existing law. If applied to anything else, it should be construed with great caution. This is because of the vagueness of the word 'modification' in the parenthesis. If it is held to cover anything more than minor modification it may alter rights and liabilities in unintended ways. {See *Brown v McLachlan* (1872) LR 4 PC 543; *Stevens v General Steam Navigation Co* [1903] 1 KB 890.}

The provision is subject to difficulties and objections similar to those discussed in the commentary on s 176 of this Code.

185. Repeal: re-enactment (preservation of delegated legislation)

Where an Act passed after 1978 repeals and re-enacts an enactment (with or without modification) then, unless the contrary intention appears, delegated legislation made, or having effect as if made, under the enactment repealed, in so far as it could be made under the provision re-enacted, has effect as if made under that provision.

COMMENTARY

This derives from s 17(2)(b) of the Interpretation Act 1978. The restriction to post-1978 Acts derives from the Interpretation Act 1978 s 22(1). As to the type of Acts for which this is intended see commentary on s 184 of this Code.

186. Repeal: re-enactment (preservation of other things done)

Where an Act passed after 1978 repeals and re-enacts an enactment (with or without modification) then, unless the contrary intention appears, anything done, or having effect as if done,under the enactment repealed, in so far as it could have been done under the provision re-enacted, has effect as if done under that provision.

COMMENTARY

This derives from s 17(2)(b) of the Interpretation Act 1978. The restriction to post-1978 Acts derives from the Interpretation Act 1978, s 22(1). As to the type of Acts for which this is intended see commentary on s 184 of this Code.

187. Expiry of an enactment

Unless the contrary intention appears, where a temporary enactment expires the effect is the same as if it had been repealed by an Act. However the general savings set out in s 182 of this Code apply to the expiry of a temporary enactment only where it is contained in an Act passed after 1978.

COMMENTARY

Apart from differences created by statute, the juridical effects of repeal and expiry are identical. {See *Moakes v Blackwell Colliery Co* [1925] 2 KB 64, at p 70.} In each case the legal floodlight is switched off. {As to this metaphor see pp 90ff above.} The only difference between a permanent and a temporary enactment is that with the latter the floodlight is on a time switch. Even so, a temporary enactment may be renewed (as by the annual Expiring Laws Continuance Act).

All this does not mean that a reference in an enactment to 'repeal' will apply without more to expiry. For this reason s 16(2) was added to the Interpretation Act 1978, so that the general savings which by statute applied to a repeal would also extend to an expired Act. {For these savings see s 182 of this Code.}

It has long been the practice to enact certain provisions, for example those relating to the armed forces and taxation, on a temporary basis only. {See pp 640–641 below.} In former times the practice of passing temporary Acts was more widespread than it is today.

Example 1   In the seventeenth century press censorship, based originally on the Royal Prerogative, was continued under the Licensing of the Press (1662). {14 Cha 2 c 33.} This was limited to two years, but was successively renewed up to 1679. After a gap of six years it was again renewed for seven years. {1 Ja 2 c 8 (1685) s 15.} It was further renewed until in 1695 the Commons refused to continue it, thus laying authors open to attacks of literary piracy. This resulted in the passing of the first Copyright Act in 1709. {8 Anne c 21.}

In modern times Acts are made temporary if experimental or controversial, or passed to deal with conditions which it is expected or hoped will be of limited duration. {See, e g, Prevention of Terrorism (Temporary Provisions) Act 1974 and Prevention of Terrorism (Temporary Provisions) Act 1976.} If not renewed, a temporary Act comes to an end in accordance with its own provisions. {*Willcock v Muckle* [1951] 2 KB 844.} If a Bill to continue it is not passed in time, it may be saved by the Acts of Parliament (Expiration) Act 1808. If it seems that it should be made permanent after all, this may be done. {See, eg, Expiring Laws Act 1969 s 1. This made permanent the Accommodation Agencies Act 1953 and the Children and Young Persons (Harmful Publications) Act 1955, effecting the necessary alterations to their wording. An earlier example is s 1 of the Treason Act 1817, which made 'perpetual' the Treason Act 1795.}

188. Desuetude

An enactment contained in an Act does not become inoperative through lack of use or the passage of time. This applies even though the enactment is disobeyed over a long period, and not enforced. Once in force, it remains in force until repealed.

COMMENTARY

Desuetude is a legal process by which, through disobedience and lack of enforcement over a long period, a statute may lose its force without express or implied repeal by Parliament. The doctrine of desuetude does not apply to United Kingdom Acts. {Under Scots law the doctrine does apply to Acts of the Parliament of Scotland: *Johnstone v Stott* (1802) 4 Paton (Sc App) 274 at p 285; *M'Ara v Magistrates of Edinburgh* (1913) SC 1059; *Brown v Magistrates of Edinburgh* (1931) SLT 456, at p 458. Desuetude may apply to part only of an Act of the Scottish Parliament: *Bute v More* (1870) 9 Macph 180; *M'Ara v Magistrates of Edinburgh* (1913) SC 1059.} This is salutory, since otherwise an enquiry would be needed before the subject could know whether or not an apparent Act bound him. The idea that an Act need not be applied if it had never been enforced was put forward in the fourteenth century. {See *R v Bishop of Lincoln* (1345) YB 19 Edw 3 (RS) 170.}, but was later rejected {*Stewart v Lawton* (1823) 1 Bing 374, at p 375.}

Example 1 A private Act of 1799 gave the inhabitants of a village the right to hold a fair or wake on certain land at Whitsuntide. In *Wyld v Silver* {[1963] 1 QB 169.} it was alleged that the right had fallen into abeyance through disuse over a long period. A purchaser of the land had been given planning permission to build houses on it, and claimed to be entitled to do so. *Held* The statutory right still subsisted, and the law would prevent any action being taken which rendered its exercise impracticable.

In *A-G v Prince Ernest Augustus of Hanover* {[1957] AC 436. See p 579 below.} the Attorney-General, *arguendo* in the court below {[1956] Ch 188, at p 208.}, expressly disclaimed reliance on any argument that the statute in question {(1705) 4 Anne c 16.} was a 'dead letter'.

Practical obsolescence Although there is no doctrine of desuetude in English law, an Act may in practice be a 'dead letter'. This may even apply to a relatively modern Act if it falls into disuse, or is not applied as intended. An example is the Sex Disqualification (Removal) Act 1919. {See pp 723–724 below.}

Where the court has a discretion as to the application of an Act, for example in relation to the sentence to be imposed for a statutory offence, it is likely to take account of practical obsolescence where it exists. So recently as 1979 Ormrod J cited approvingly Bacon's dictum: 'Therefore let penal laws, if they have been sleepers of long or if they be grown unfit for the present time, be by wise judges confined in the execution'. {*Imperial Tobacco Ltd v A-G* [1979] 2 All ER 592, at p 609.}

The courts are quite willing to apply the term 'obsolete' to an Act. {See, e g, Lindley LJ in *Dobbs v Grand Junction Waterworks* (1882) 10 QBD 337, at p 355.} Moreover where judges dislike an Act, their decisions tend to reflect the fact.

Example 2 This happened with the Limitation Act 1623. The judicial emasculation of this statute caused Lord Sumner to lament the difficulty of extracting-

> ' . . . anything that deserves to be called a principle from the decisions of three centuries, which have been directed to what is after all the task of decorously disregarding an Act of Parliament.'

{*Spencer v Hemmerde* [1922] 2 AC 507, at p 519. See also Examples 146.9 and 146.10 and Aubrey L. Diamond 'Repeal and Desuetude of Statutes' *Current Legal Problems* 1975 p 107 at pp 115–124.}

Unexpected revival An Act considered for centuries to be a dead letter may suddenly acquire a new lease of practical existence. It is there to be applied, if anyone is bold enough to do it. Thus Gladstone appointed suffragan bishops under the statute 26 Hen 8 c 14 (1534) after a lapse of nearly three centuries. {Craies *Statute Law* (7th edn, 1971) p 406n.}

TRANSITIONAL PROVISIONS

189. Transitional provisions

Where an Act contains substantive, amending or repealing enactments, it commonly also includes transitional provisions which regulate the coming into operation of those enactments and modify their effect during the period of transition. Where the Act fails to include such provisions expressly, the court is required to draw such inferences as to the intended transitional arrangements as, in the light of the interpretative criteria, it considers Parliament to have intended.

COMMENTARY

Transitional provisions are provisions which spell out precisely when and how the operative parts of an Act are to take effect. They serve a very useful purpose. Merely to say that an enactment comes into force on a specified date is often insufficient to produce a clear meaning. Failure by the draftsman to include adequate transitional provisions is frequently the cause of avoidable difficulty to statute users. {See Examples 122.6, 128.5 and 337.2.}

Example 1 In *Cardshops Ltd v John Lewis Properties Ltd* {[1982] 3 All ER 746.} the Court of Appeal (who were divided) were faced with the task of working out the intended transitional operation of s 47(5) of the Local Government,

Planning and Land Act 1980. Waller LJ said {P 749.}: 'The absence of any transitional provisions has made the construction of this section difficult because it is possible to argue in favour of more than one date.'

Where difficulty of this kind is experienced, the usual guides to interpretation must be applied. {For these see Part VI of the Code.} It was in that way that the Court of Appeal dealt with their problem in *Cardshops Ltd v John Lewis Properties Ltd.*

Need to look for transitional provisions It is important for the interpreter to realise, and bear constantly in mind, that what appears to be the plain meaning of a substantive enactment is often modified by transitional provisions located elsewhere in the Act. Often these are tucked away in an obscure place, where they are easily overlooked. The consequences of overlooking them can be serious.

Example 2 The transitional provisions in the Magistrates' Courts Act 1980 (a consolidation Act) were overlooked by numerous prosecutors and others concerned with the working of magistrates' courts. In several cases this required the discharging of juries and the obtaining of bills of indictment in the High Court. One commentator said-

> 'The confusion has arisen because many magistrates' courts have been committing all cases for trial under provisions of the Magistrates' Courts Act 1980, which came into force on July 6 [1981]. Yet tucked away in a schedule to the Act {Sch 8 para 2(1).} is a transitional provision unnoticed by many courts, to the effect that where proceedings began before July 6, committals should be made under the old enactments.'

{Terence Shaw (Legal Correspondent) *The Daily Telegraph* 30 September 1981.}

Example 3 In *R v Folkestone and Hythe Juvenile Court, ex p R (a juvenile)* {[1981] 3 All ER 840.} the Divisional Court dealt with another misunderstanding over the transitional provisions of the Magistrates' Courts Act 1980. The applicant for judicial review had been convicted by magistrates in proceedings which, by virtue of these transitional provisions, fell to be dealt with under the old procedure. He was committed for sentence to the Crown Court. In error the minute recording the conviction referred to it as having been made under the new Act. *Held* Since it was not strictly necessary to record the statute under which the conviction was effected, the error related to something that was mere surplusage. Accordingly it did not invalidate the committal. {As to the distinction between mandatory and merely directory enactments see s 10 of this Code.}

RETROSPECTIVE OPERATION OF ENACTMENTS

190. Retrospective operation: general presumption against

Unless the contrary intention appears, an enactment is presumed not to be intended to have a retrospective operation.

COMMENTARY

The essential idea of a legal system is that current law should govern current activities. Elsewhere in this work a particular Act is likened to a floodlight switched on or off {See pp 90–93 above.}, and the general body of law to the circumambient air. {See p 491 below.} Clumsy though these images are, they show the inappropriateness of retrospective laws.

If we do something today, we feel that the law applying to it should be the law in force today, not tomorrow's backward adjustment of it. Such, we believe, is the nature of law. Dislike of ex post facto law is enshrined in the United States Constitution {Art I s 9(3).} and in the constitutions of many American states, which forbid it.

The true principle is that *lex prospicit non respicit* (law looks forward not back). {Jenk Cent 284. See also 2 Co Inst 292.} As Willes J said, retrospective legislation is-

> '. . . contrary to the general principle that legislation by which the conduct of mankind is to be regulated ought, when introduced for the first time, to deal with future acts, and ought not to change the character of past transactions carried on upon the faith of the then existing law.'

{*Phillips v Eyre* (1870) LR 6 QB 1, at p 23. See also *Re Athlumney, ex p Wilson* [1898] 2 QB 547.}

Retrospectivity is artificial, deeming a thing to be what it was not. Artificiality and make-believe are generally repugnant to law as the servant of human welfare. {For the desire of courts to avoid an artificial result see s 325 of this Code.}

So it follows that the courts apply the general presumption that an enactment is not intended to have retrospective effect. As always, the power of Parliament to produce such an effect where it wishes to do so is nevertheless undoubted. {For the doctrine of parliamentary sovereignty see s 31 of this Code.} The general presumption therefore applies only unless the contrary intention appears.

The general presumption is stated in *Maxwell on the Interpretation of Statutes* in the following emphatic terms-

> 'It is a fundamental rule of English law that no statute shall be construed to have a retrospective operation unless such a construction appears very clearly in the terms of the Act, or arises by necessary and distinct implication.'

{(12th edn, 1969) p 215.}

This statement has received frequent judicial approval. {See, e g, *Carson v Carson* [1964] 1 WLR 511, at p 516.} It is however too dogmatically framed, and describes as a rule what (for reasons stated in s 115 of this Code) is really no more than a presumption which, in the instant case, may be outweighed by other factors. {As to the weighing of interpretative factors to arrive at the true legal meaning see Part VII of this Code.}

Where, on a weighing of the factors, it seems that *some* retrospective effect was intended, the general presumption against retrospectivity indicates that this should be kept to as narrow a compass as will accord with the legislative intention. {*Lauri v Renad* [1892] 3 Ch 402, at p 421; *Skinner v Cooper* [1979] 2 All ER 836.}

Apart from the general presumption itself, the question of retrospectivity is relevant to the application of various other guides to legislative intention. We have just mentioned one of them, namely the presumption against an artificial result. Now we go on to deal with others.

Principle against doubtful penalization   It is a general principle of legal policy that no one should suffer detriment by the application of a doubtful law. {See s 129 and Part XIII of this Code.} The general presumption against retrospectivity means that where one of the opposing constructions of an enactment would, without clear words justifying it, impose an ex post facto law, that construction is necessarily doubtful. {As to the opposing constructions see s 84 of this Code.} If the construction also inflicts a detriment, that is a second factor against it.

Lord Brightman said in *Yew Bon Tew v Kenderaan Bas Maria* {[1982] 3 All ER 833, at p 836.} that a retrospective enactment inflicts a detriment for this purpose-

'... if it takes away or impairs a vested right acquired under existing laws, or creates a new obligation, or imposes a new duty, or attaches a new disability, in regard to events already past.'

{This follows almost exactly the words of Craies (*Statute Law* (7th edn) p 387). See also *Re Athlumney, ex p Wilson* [1898] 2 QB 547, at p 551; *Smith v Callender* [1901] AC 297, at p 303; *West v Gwynne* [1911] 2 Ch 1, at p 15.}

The strongest case against retrospective penalization relates to the act of making something an offence which was not so when committed: *nullum crimen sine lege*. {As to the retrospective increase of penalties see p 448 below.}

European Convention on Human Rights   Article 7 of the European Convention on Human Rights states that no one shall be held guilty of any criminal offence on account of any act or ommission which did not constitute a criminal offence under national or international law at the time when it was committed. Where the act or omission did constitute an offence when committed, no penalty is to be imposed which is heavier than the one applicable at that time.

Article 7 is expressed not to prejudice the trial and punishment of any person for any act or omission which, at the time it was committed, was criminal according to 'the general principles of law recognised by civilised nations'. {As to the position of the European Convention on Human Rights in United Kingdom law see pp 322–323 above.}

Public good construction   One of the principles governing statutory interpretation is that the construction adopted should promote the public good. {See s 127 of this Code.} This criterion, like many others, can affect the question of whether an enactment should be given a retrospective construction.

Example 4   In *London Borough of Hammersmith and Fulham v Harrison* {[1981] 2 All ER 588.} the Court of Appeal was faced with the question of whether the provisions of the Housing Act 1980 giving a right of purchase to tenants of council houses should, by a strained construction, have retrospective effect. It was argued by tenants that the court should follow the precedent set by *Remon v City of London Real Property Co Ltd* {[1921] 1 KB 49.}, when this treatment was given to the security of tenure provisions of the Rent and Mortgage Interest (Restrictions) Act 1920. *Held* This would not be appropriate. While strong public welfare considerations had required the 1920 Act to be applied retrospectively, such was not the case here. Brandon LJ said {P 597.}-

> 'The 1920 Act, in relation to which *Remon*'s case was decided, was passed to deal with the critical housing shortage which followed the demobilisation of immense numbers of the armed forces after the end of the 1914-18 war. It was necessary that legislation to meet that situation should be passed, and that its remedial qualities should take effect, as quickly as possible . . . By contrast . . . the 1980 Act was not enacted in order to meet any immediate or urgent crisis in housing accomodation.'

The public good requires that evasion of statutes be prevented. {See s 143 and Part XVII of this Code.} This may account for the following dictum of Lord Greene MR about the tax avoidance provisions of s 18 of the Finance Act 1936-

> 'The fact that the section has to some extent a retroactive effect appears to us of no importance when it is realised that the legislation is a move in a long and fiercely contested battle with individuals who well understand the vigour of the contest.'

{*Lord Howard de Walden v IRC* [1942] 1KB 389, at p 398.}

Retrospective benefit   If the retrospective construction would confer a benefit on some person without inflicting a corresponding detriment on some other person, or on the public generally, the principle against doubtful penalization obviously does not apply. Furthermore the fact that such a benefit is conferred may even outweigh the general presumption against retrospectivity. If to confer such benefits appears to heve been the legislator's object, then the presumption that an enactment should be given a purposive construction will carry great weight. {As to purposive construction see s 139 and Part XV of this Code.} This is the justification for treating procedural provisions as retrospective. {See s 191 of this Code.}

191. Retrospective operation: procedural provisions

Because a change made by the legislator in procedural provisions is expected to be for the general benefit of litigants and others, it is presumed that it applies to pending as well as future proceedings. This presumption does not operate where, on the facts of the instant case, to apply it would contravene the principle that persons should not be penalized under a doubtful enactment.

COMMENTARY

A procedural change is expected to improve matters for everyone concerned (or at least to improve matters for some, without inflicting detriment on anyone else who uses ordinary care, vigilance and promptness). {As to the need for the latter see Example 1.}

Unless an enactment is clearly stated to be retrospective, there must, under the general presumption against retrospective operation, be doubt about whether Parliament really intended it to be so. Accordingly, where a person may suffer detriment under the enactment, there is brought into play the principle that persons should not be penalized under a doubtful enactment. {See s 190 of this Code.}

The question therefore is whether, *on the facts of the instant case*, the enactment is substantive or merely procedural. The italicised words are important, because an enactment may be substantive in the light of some facts but merely procedural on others. {See Example 1.}

Procedural provisons expected to be beneficial   Procedure and practice is the mere machinery of law enforcement. As Ormrod LJ said: 'The object of all procedural rules is to enable justice to be done between the parties consistently with the public interest'. {*Imperial Tobacco Ltd v A-G* [1979] 2 All ER 592, at p 605.}

If the procedural rules are defective, the legal apparatus works less efficiently and the public interest suffers. The appropriate authorities then seek to remedy the defect by changing, or persuading Parliament to change, the inadequate rule. If no one suffers thereby, it is sensible to apply this improvement to pending proceedings.

Limitaton Acts   Provisions laying down limitation periods fall into a special category. Although prima facie procedural, they are capable of effectively depriving persons of accrued rights. From the point of view of retrospectivity, they therefore need to be approached with care.

Example 1   In *The Ydun* {[1899] P 236.} the owners of the barque *Ydun* had a cause of action against a port authority, the Preston Corporation, in respect of the grounding of the barque on 13 September 1893. They had a limitation period of six years from that date within which to issue their writ. However on 1 January 1894 the Public Authorities Protection Act 1893 came into force (having been passed on 5 December 1893). This reduced the limitation period in such cases to six months. If it applied to their claim, the owners of the *Ydun* had only until 12 March 1894 to issue their writ. In fact they did not issue it until the original six-year period had nearly expired. *Held* The 1893 Act did apply, and the action was statute-barred.

In this case the relevant enactment was regarded as merely procedural. However, as Lord Brightman pointed out in a later case, on slightly different facts the same enactment would have been treated as substantive. {*Yew Bon Tew v Kenderaan Bas Maria* [1982] 3 All ER 833, at p 839.}

This would have been so if the barque had grounded say in May 1893. Then the new six-month limitation period referred to in the 1893 Act would have expired before the Act was passed, and so could not be complied with. That would have effectively deprived the plaintiffs of their cause of action. In *Yew Bon Tew v Kenderaan Bas Mara* {[1982] 3 All ER 833.} the Judicial Committee of the Privy Council held that in such cases the court would rule against a retrospective operation. {Cf *R v Chandra Dharma* [1905] 2 KB 335, *per*

Channell J at p 339 (prosecution could not be brought within extended period if old period had already expired when amending Act passed).}

Penalties for offences   It has been held that an enactment fixing the penalty, or maximum penalty, for an offence is merely procedural for the purpose of determining retrospectivity. {*DPP v Lamb* [1941] 2 KB 89; *Buckman v Button* [1943] KB 405; *R v Oliver* [1944] KB 68.}

This seems wrong in principle, as well as conflicting with our international obligations under the European Convention on Human Rights. Article 7 of this says: 'Nor shall a heavier penalty be imposed than the one that was applicable at the time the criminal offence was committed'. {To like effect is the United Nations Convention on Civil and Political Rights, art 15. As to the presumption that Parliament intends to comply with international obligations see s 134 of this Code.}

Example 2   In *R v Deery* {[1977] Crim LR 550.} the Northern Ireland Court of Criminal Appeal considered a case where the appellant had been sentenced to a greater term of imprisonment than was permitted by the enactment in question, s 19A of the Firearms Act (Northern Ireland) 1969, at the time the offence was committed. It was however within the increased maximum allowed by an amending order, the Firearms (Amendment) (Northern Ireland) Order 1976, which had been made before the trial. *Held* The sentence was contrary to law and would be reduced to within the maximum prevailing at the time the offence was committed.

Here the court declined to follow the English authorities, namely *DPP v Lamb* {[1941] 2 KB 89.}; *Buckman v Button* {[1943] KB 405.} and *R v Oliver* {[1944] KB 68.}. These do appear to be wrongly decided, unless justifiable on the ground that wartime conditions rendered the factor of public safety stronger than in peacetime (if conditions in Northern Ireland in 1976 can accurately be described as 'peacetime'). {Cf Example 97.1.}

In *R v Penwith JJ, ex p Hay* {(1979) 1 Cr App R (S) 265.} it was said by the Divisional Court that, where the maximum penalty for an offence is increased, this should not be applied to offences committed before the increase unless there is a clear legislative intention to this effect. {See also commentary on *R v Craig* [1982] Crim LR 132 at [1982] Crim LR 191-2.}

192. Retrospective operation: events occurring over a period

This section applies where an enactment is concerned with events occurring over a period and, on the facts of the instant case, a part but not the whole of the period had elapsed at the commencement of the enactment.

Where this section applies to a case, the court decides whether the enactment is subject to the principles governing retrospectivity by determining whether in substance the enactment, in relation to the facts of that case, is a current or future enactment. Only where it is a future enactment will it be retrospective if applied to the case.

COMMENTARY

Some of the most difficult problems concerning retrospectivity concern enactments that turn on events occurring over a period. If the enactment comes into force during the period is it retrospective or not?

Little guidance can be given beyond saying that it is necessary to look at the substance of the matter as indicated in this section. The problem ought never to arise, because the draftsman should have included transitional provisions that make clear the intention. {See s 194 of this Code.} Draftsmen however are fallible; and when they fail the court must do its best to sort out the result.

Example 1   Section 2 of the Poor Removal Act 1846 provided that-

' . . . no woman residing in any parish with her husband at the time of his death shall be removed . . . from such parish, for twelve calendar months after his death, if she so long continue a widow.'

Until the Act was passed, the appropriate authority had the right to remove the widow immediately after the death. The effect of s 2 thus operated over a period ('the relevant period') consisting of twelve months from the death, unless shortened by the remarriage, death or departure from the parish of the widow.

In *R v St Mary, Whitechapel* {(1848) 12 QB 120.} the relevant period had begun but not ended when s 2 came into force. The authority argued that at commencement they had a vested right to remove the widow. *Held* The removal itself was the substance of the matter. Since it had not been carried out before commencement, s 2 applied and was not to be treated as retrospective.

Example 2   Section 1(1) of the Defective Premises Act 1972 says that a person '*taking on work* for or in connection with the provision of a dwelling' owes a duty to see that the work is done properly 'so that as regards that work the dwelling will be fit for habitation when completed'. {Emphasis added.}

In *Alexander v Mercouris* {[1979] 3 All ER 305.} the Court of Appeal was asked to say whether this duty applied where the work was taken on before the commencement of the 1972 Act but completed after. *Held* The substance of the matter was the initial act of 'taking on' the work. The duty did not therefore arise unless the 'taking on' occurred after the commencement of the Act.

Example 3   Part I of the Finance Act 1972, under which VAT is charged, came into force on 1 April 1973. Part IV of the Value Added Tax (General) Regulations 1972 {SI 1972/1147.} provides that where goods are supplied under a hire agreement-

' . . . they shall be treated as being successively supplied on hire for successive parts of the period of the agreement and each of the successive supplies shall be treated as taking place when a payment under the agreement is received.'

In *Comrs of Customs and Excise v Thorn Electrical Industries Ltd* {[1975] 3 All ER 881.} the House of Lords considered a hire agreement made on 20 July 1972 and continuing in force after 1 April 1973. The appellants contended that it would be to apply the VAT legislation retrospectively if payments received under the agreement were taxed. *Held* The regulations made it clear that each hire payment was to be treated separately; and VAT was due on those made after 1 April 1973. Lord Morris of Borth-y-Gest said {P 890.}-

> 'The fact that as from a future date tax is charged on a source of income which has been arranged or provided for before the date of the imposition of the tax does not mean that a tax is retrospectively imposed.'

193. Retrospective operation: delegated powers

The same principles apply to a question as to the restrospective operation of delegated legislation as apply to Acts. However in the case of delegated legislation not only must the wording of the instrument itself be considered, but that of the Act under which it was made. Furthermore the doctrine of ultra vires needs to be taken into account. Similar considerations apply to the exercise of non-legislative delegated powers.

COMMENTARY

Since the principles regarding retrospectivity are based on public policy, it follows that they apply equally to delegated legislation. However the legislative intention needs to be gathered by considering both the enabling Act and the delegated instrument. If retrospectivity is beyond the power conferred by the Act, the doctrine of ultra vires comes into play. {As to this doctrine see s 58 of the Code.}

Delegated powers may relate to executive as well as legislative functions. Here similar principles apply, and it is necessary to determine the intention underlying the conferring of the power.

Example 1   Section 4 of the Mobile Homes Act 1975 empowers the occupier of a mobile home, on the default of the owner, to apply to the court for the grant of an occupation agreement complying with the Act. In *Grant v Allen* {[1980] 1 All ER 720.} the question arose of whether this empowered the court to grant a retrospective agreement relating back to the start of the occupation. *Held* The parties themselves could have entered into a retrospective agreement, and there was no reason why the court could not make one for them in suitable cases. Brandon LJ said {P 726.}-

> 'So far as the argument that a retrospective date of commencement would deprive an occupier of his rights to assign the agreement and to sell his mobile home on site *throughout* a minimum period of five years is concerned, we accept that there is some force in the argument. We do not, however regard it as sufficiently strong to lead to the conclusion that a retrospective date of commencement is so inconsistent with the Act as to be impliedly prohibited by it.'

{Emphasis addded.}

194. Retrospective operation: cause of doubt

Doubt as to whether an enactment is intended to be retroactive is usually caused by bad drafting. It is the duty of the draftsman to supply appropriate transitional provisions so as to make clear whether, and if so to what extent, the enactment has a retrospective effect.

COMMENTARY

Doubt as to whether or not an enactment is intended to be given retrospective effect is almost invariably due to failure by the draftsman to provide adequate commencement and transitional provisions. {For commencement provisions see ss 164 to 169 of this Code. For transitional provisions see s 189.} Too often there is undue reliance on the simple concept of an Act's coming into force at a particular moment in time, like the switching on of a floodlight. {As to this metaphor see pp 90–93 below.} In many cases the precise effect of this needs to be spelt out if uncertainty is to be avoided. {See Example 189.1.}

Example 1   Section 7(4) of the Matrimonial Proceedings and Property Act 1970 came into force on 1 January 1971. {S 43(2).} It began-

> 'If after the grant of a decree dissolving or annulling a marriage either party to that marriage *remarries*, that party shall not be entitled to apply for an order under s 2 or 4 of this Act against the person to whom he or she was married immediately before the grant of that decree . . .'

{Emphasis added.}

Sections 2 and 4 of the Act provided for orders making financial provision or adjusting property rights. Under the previous law, replaced by the 1970 Act, remarriage did not prevent the making of such orders. In *Bonning v Dodsley* {[1982] 1 All ER 612.} the question for the Court of Appeal was whether s 7(4) applied to a remarriage before 1 January 1971, so as to prevent a s 2 or 4 order being made in favour of the remarried spouse.

Held Section 7(4) must be taken as intended to apply only where the remarriage occurred on or after 1 January 1971, since otherwise divorced spouses would be deprived of their right to choose not to remarry (so as to retain their rights against the former spouse). The court arrived at this conclusion only with great difficulty, taking into account decisions reached with equal difficulty on other transitional problems under the Act. {See *Williams v Williams* [1971] P 271; *Powys v Powys* [1971] P 340.}

PART IX

Extent and Application of Enactments

Introduction to Part IX This Part amplifies, so far as concerns territorial extent and personal application, the account of the temporal, territorial and personal application of an Act set out in s 30 of the Code. Temporal operation is amplified in Part VIII.

Part IX consists of two groups of sections. The first deals with territorial extent, while the second describes the application of an enactment.

We first consider the basic rule regarding the territory or territories in which an enactment is law (s 195). The meaning of an Act's 'extent' is explained (s 196). An enactment should have a uniform meaning throughout its area, even where (as with England and Scotland) its operates within more than one legal system (s 197).

We examine what elements compose an Act's territory, embracing land masses, territorial waters, airspace etc (s 198). It is presumed, unless the contrary intention appears, that an Act extends to the United Kingdom but not beyond (s 199). The vestigial power of the Westminster Parliament to legislate for certain of Her Majesty's independent dominions is explained (s 200). This group of sections ends with definitions of twenty terms used in relation to the territorial extent of Acts (ss 201 to 220).

The second group of sections in Part IX begins with an explanation of the general principles governing the application of an enactment to some persons and matters but not to others (s 221). Then follow sections dealing respectively with the four main categories. These are application of the enactment to foreigners and foreign matters within the Act's territory (s 222), application to foreigners and foreign matters outside the Act's territory (s 223), application to British people and matters outside the territory (s 224), and application to persons and matters on the high seas and in other unappropriated territories (s 225).

Part IX ends with three sections showing how the law as to application of enactments deals with complex or artificial situations. These are the deemed location of an omission to act (s 226), the deemed location of a composite act or omission which takes place in several territories (s 227), and the deemed location of a company or other artificial person (s 228).

TERRITORIAL EXTENT OF AN ENACTMENT

195. Territorial extent: the basic rule

Although an enactment may be expressed in general terms, the area over which it is law excludes territories where Parliament lacks jurisdiction. It also excludes territories for which the legislator did not intend to legislate. That intent may be gathered from the operation of certain presumptions.

Parliament has ordinary jurisdiction to legislate for any of Her Majesty's dominions, excepting Her Majesty's independent dominions. In addition, Parliament has extraordinary jurisdiction to legislate for Australia and New Zealand. Parliament has no jurisdiction to legislate for any other territory.

COMMENTARY

Her Majesty's dominions For the meaning of the expression 'Her Majesty's dominions' see s 210 of this Code.

Australia and New Zealand For the nature of Parliament's power to legislate for Australia and New Zealand see s 200 of this Code.

The sections of the Code dealing with territorial extent are expressed in terms of enactments rather than Acts because it is possible for different provisions of an Act to extend to different territories.

Sometimes an Act states expressly what its extent is (or what the different extents of its various provisions are). Other Acts leave the matter to implication, and there may then be difficulty in arriving at what is to be taken as the true implication. Nevertheless certain presumptions apply, notably that unless the contrary intention appears an Act is taken to extend to the whole of the United Kingdom but not beyond. {See s 199 of this Code.}

It is necessary to distinguish between *extent* and *application*. Extent defines the area within which the enactment is law. Application is concerned with the persons and matters in relation to which the enactment operates. These may be within or outside the area of its extent. An enactment does not necessarily apply to all persons and matters even *within* the area of its extent. The question of application is dealt with separately. {See ss 221 to 228 of this Code.}

It is self-evident that an enactment cannot be law in an area outside Parliament's jurisdiction. For reasons of comity, Parliament avoids any impression that it is purporting to intrude into the area of jurisdiction of some other sovereign power. {As to the reasons of comity underlying limitations on extent and application of enactments see pp 496–497 below.}

An Act may operate in a foreign country by virtue of a provision of the law of that country which applies the Act. International conventions sometimes provide for this to be done.

Example 1 In pursuance of the Single Convention on Narcotic Drugs signed at New York on 30 March 1961, s 20 of the Misuse of Drugs Act 1971 says that a person commits an offence if in the United Kingdom he assists in or induces the commission in a foreign country of an offence against a 'corresponding law' of that country. {As to the meaning of 'corresponding law' see Misuse of Drugs Act 1971 s 36(1).}

In *R v Faulkner and Thomas* {[1977] Crim LR 679.} the defendants, on conviction under s 20, were sentenced according to the penalty scale for British drug offences rather than the much lower scale prevailing in the country in question. Commenting on the decision, Professor J C Smith said {Ibid.}: 'This is a very unusual offence in that its existence depends entirely on the law of some place outside the United Kingdom'. In fact it does not depend *entirely* on the foreign law, since s 20 provides the cutting edge. It is perhaps as near as one can get to the position where the law of one country prevails (as law) in another.

196. Territorial extent: meaning of 'extent'

The 'extent' of an Act is the geographical area throughout which it is law.

COMMENTARY

The 'extent' of an Act consists of the territory or territories throughout which, so long as it is operative, the Act forms part of the current body of law or *corpus juris*. {As to the geographical composition of this area see s 198 of the Code.}

An Act may specify its extent, or leave it to be inferred. Such inferences arise from the factors governing implied meaning, namely the words of the Act, the context of the Act and the operation of general legal rules. One such rule provides that, in the absence of any contrary indication, an Act is taken to extend throughout the United Kingdom but not beyond. {See s 199 of this Code. See also Example 80.2.}

Differential extent An Act need not have a uniform extent. Some of its provisions may have a wider extent than others, or may have a quite different extent. In the United Kingdom such cases are common, the principal reasons being the existence of different legal systems in England, Wales and Northern Ireland on one hand and Scotland on the other, and the existence at various periods of transferred legislative powers in Northern Ireland.

In modern Acts the details of differential extent are clearly spelt out.

Example 1 Thus s 120(3) of the Town and Country Planning Act 1947 says: 'This Act (except section 2 and subsection (2) of section 58 thereof) shall not extend to Scotland.' {For an example of a very detailed differential extent provision see the Administration of Justice Act 1982 s 77.}

Older Acts are often less clearly worded.

Example 2 A notorious example of obscurity is the Fires Prevention (Metropolis) Act 1774. Although the long title appears to limit the Act to London, it was held after much uncertainty that the wording of the important s 83 (which is still in force) indicated that that section at least extended throughout England and Wales. {*Sinnott v Bowden* [1912] 2 Ch 414 (See further Example 199.3). This is an example of disorganised composition: see s 76 of this Code.} The effect of differential extent is sometimes achieved by allowing the whole Act to extend throughout the United Kingdom, but including provisions *modifying* its operation in specified territories. For example the Army Act 1955 is of general extent, but s 214 specifies modifications which are to apply so far as the Act extends to Scotland. Section 215 lays down similar modifications for Northern Ireland.

Another common device is to enact separate but almost identical Acts for different territories. For example the Rent Act 1968 had much the same effect in England and Wales as the Rent (Scotland) Act 1971 did in Scotland.

Northern Ireland extent Statute users are sometimes puzzled by provisions such as s 18(6) of the National Heritage Act 1980, which says: 'This Act extends to Northern Ireland'. In view of the presumption that Acts extend to the whole of the United Kingdom except in so far as the contrary intention appears, there is clearly no need to state that an Act extends to Northern Ireland (or indeed to any other part of the United Kingdom).

In view of the principle that all words of an Act are if possible to be given a meaning {See pp 375–376 above.}, the reader might reasonably expect the words stating that an Act extends to Northern Ireland to add a significance not otherwise there. This is not the case however. The reason for this unnecessary provision (unnecessary that is from a purely legal aspect) is to save the government lawyers in Northern Ireland from having to comb through each Act to see whether or not their province is included.

197. Territorial extent: uniform meaning throughout area of extent

Unless the contrary intention appears, an Act extending to an area consisting of two or more territories is presumed to be intended to have a uniform meaning throughout that area.

COMMENTARY

Where an Act extends to more than one territory the presumption, in the absence of a contrary indication, is that Parliament intended the Act to operate in the same way throughout the area of its extent.

This presumption derives from the principle of equality before the law. {As to this principle see p 291 above.} A person affected by an Act is not to suffer an increased penalty, or enjoy an increased advantage, solely because of the place within the area of the Act's extent where he (or his property) happens to be located. As Craies puts it in relation to taxation-

'If a statute imposes a tax upon the whole United Kingdom, it is construed so far as its terms allow in such a way that like interests in property may be subject to like charges, wheresoever in the United Kingdom the property is situate, so that all the subjects of the kingdom may be taxed equally under the same circumstances.'

{*Statute Law* (7th edn, 1971) p 115.}

The principle does not however mean that powers under a *delegatory* enactment must necessarily be exercised in the same way in all places within the area of its extent. {As to delegated legislation see ss 50 to 70 of this Code.} Circumstances differ in different areas, and it is assumed that Parliament intended this to be taken into account as justifying differential treatment where appropriate.

The principle of uniform application may cause difficulty where an Act uses the technical terms of English law in circumstances where other legal systems are also involved. Scots law particularly has been the victim here. Lord Macnaughten said of an Income Tax Act-

' . . . in some cases certainly, and especially in the legislation of former days, the statute proclaims its origin and speaks the language

of an English lawyer, with some Scottish legal phrases thrown in
rather casually.'

{*Income Tax Commissioners v Pemsel* [1891] AC 531, at p 579).}

The correct approach is to penetrate to the substance of the English term and
apply it on the basis that it is intended to cover the corresponding Scots or
foreign term also. {This is a variant of the 'box principle' discussed above in
relation to updating construction: see pp 366–367.} Or as Lord Hardwicke said:
'You must, as in other sciences, reason by analogy'.

Lord Hardwicke's dictum was cited by Lord Macnaghten in *Income Tax
Commissioners v Pemsel*. {[1891] AC 531, at p 580.} Lord Macnaghten went on
to say that what Lord Hardwicke meant was-

'... you must take the meaning of legal expressions from the law of
the country to which they properly belong, and in any case arising in
the sister country you must apply the statute in an analogous or
corresponding sense, so as to make the operation and effect of the
statute the same in both countries.'

This accords with the principle of equality stated above. A thing is to be
regulated in the same way even though it has different legal names in different
countries. As Coke said, *nomina sunt mutabilia, res autem immobiles* (names are
changeable, but the things they denote are not). {6 Co Inst 66.} Unfortunately
there are some judicial dicta, quoted by Craies, which obscure this
straightforward principle.

Example 1 In *Braybrooke v A-G* {(1861) 9 HLC 150.}, where technical terms
of real property law were in question, Lord Campbell said that construction in
such cases must be 'not according to the technicalities of the law of real property
in England or in Scotland, but according to the popular use of the language
employed'. {P 165. As to the distinction between technical and ordinary
meaning see ss 363 to 368 of this Code.} It is submitted that this dictum can be
true only in the case where Parliament is to be taken to have used the technical
term in a popular sense. Yet Craies cites Lord Campbell's remark as being of
universal application. {*Statute Law* (7th edn, 1971) p 115.}

Example 2 In another questionable citation, this time from the case of *New
York Breweries Co v AG* {[1899] AC 62.}, Craies says that in the case Lord
Halsbury 'pointed out' that when used in an English taxing Act the terms
executor and administrator do not include persons who fill that character in
some other country. {Ibid, p 116.}

No such generalisation is in fact possible. The meaning of any term depends
on the language of the Act using it. If it appeared that Parliament's intention in
using the term 'executor' was to include persons who act in the capacity of an
executor in another country it would be necessary to interpret the term executor
in the Act as including such persons, whatever the term used to describe them
might be under the law of the other country.

Example 3 Another doubtful dictum, also cited by Craies, is the suggestion
made in *R v Slator* {(1881) 8 QBD 267, at p 272.} that where terms of art are
used which have a different meaning in England and Scotland they are to be

read in each country in the sense which they ordinarily bear there. Since that dictum inevitably means the Act will have a different effect in each country to which it extends, the dictum contravenes the principle of equality described in this section. The better view is that the court should endeavour to arrive at a compromise meaning which will produce territorial equality. {The dictum is cited on p 471 of Craies' *Statute Law*, where it is said that it 'must not be too implicitly followed'. See also Examples 142.1 and 366.4.}

We consider now some particular applications of the principle of uniform application. It should be stressed that these do not involve any variation of the principle, but are merely examples of its use.

Criminal statutes   It is particularly important that criminal enactments, which involve the liberty of the subject, should be construed in the same way throughout the area of the Act's operation. As Lord Goddard CJ said, 'it would be very unfortunate to have, on a similar set of facts, a conviction in England and no conviction in Scotland, or vice versa'. {*Cording v Halse* [1955] 1 QB 63, at p 70. The dictum does not of course apply where the criminal law of the two countries is intentionally different, as it is for example in relation to certain sexual offences.}

Taxing Acts   The principle of uniform application has often been stressed in relation to taxation. Thus Viscount Simon LC said in *Income Tax Commissioners v Gibbs* {[1942] AC 402.}-

> 'In construing a taxing statute which applies to England and Scotland alike, it is desirable to adopt a construction of the statutory words which avoids differences of interpretation of a technical character such as are calculated to produce inequalities of taxation between citizens of the two countries.'

{P 414. The Act was the Income Tax Act 1918, and the technical term in question was 'partnership'. See also *Lord Saltoun v Advocate-General* (1860) 3 Macq HL (Sc) 659; *Newman v Lipman* [1950] 2 All ER 832, *per* Lord Goddard at p 834; *Regional Properties Ltd v Frankenschwerth* [1951] 1 KB 631.}

Where for United Kingdom tax purposes an English legal term is employed, the Scottish courts must take judicial notice of the term and not treat it as a term of foreign law to be dealt with as a question of fact. {*IRC v Glasgow Police Athletic Association* [1953] AC 380. Here the term involved was 'charity'.}

Company law   Where a commercial Act applies throughout an area where trade is conducted on a common basis it is obviously important that the Act should have the same meaning everywhere in the area. {See *Re Wanzer Ltd* [1891] 1 Ch 305, which concerned the meaning of 'sequestration' in what is now s 228(1) of the Companies Act 1948. As to harmonisation within the EEC area see pp 175–176 above. See also pp 534–541 below.}

Comity between British courts   Where an Act extends to two or more countries of the United Kingdom, decisions on the Act of courts in one of those countries, though not binding on courts in the other country or countries, are treated by them as of persuasive authority. {*Blake v Midland Rly* (1852) 18 QB 93, *per* Coleridge J at p 109; *Ford v Wiley* (1889) 23 QBD 93, *per* Coleridge CJ at p 216.

See also *Cantiare San Rocco v Clyde Shipbuilding Co* [1924] AC 226, at pp 247-8 and *Chandler v Webster* [1904] 1 KB 493 (overruled in the Fibrosa [1943] AC 32).} In s 17(5) of the Railway and Canal Traffic Act 1888 Parliament recognised that courts in England, Scotland and Ireland might differ in their interpretation of the Act.

As between England and Scotland the position is affected by the Union with Scotland Act 1706. Article XVIII of this provides that laws which concern public right, policy and civil government may be made the same throughout the United Kingdom. These are contrasted with laws which concern private right, which may be altered only 'for evident utility of the subjects within Scotland'. {As to the effect of this on the legislative power of Parliament see pp 128–129 above.} The argument that it was illegitimate to apply in Scotland English decisions on a common Act which conflicted with those of Scottish courts failed in *Duncan v Findlater* (1839) 6 Cl & F 894 (see pp 902, 909).}

Lord Watson described the House of Lords as the *commune forum* for the reconciliation of the laws of England, Scotland and Ireland. {*Cooper v Cooper* (1888) 13 App Cas 88, at p 104.} Craies expresses the function of the House of Lords thus-

> 'In dealing with the statutes common to the whole of the United Kingdom, the House of Lords has to lay down rules applicable to all those countries alike, and to consider and reconcile, or select from, conflicting decisions of English, Scottish and Northern Irish courts upon such enactments.'

{*Statute Law* (7th edn, 1971) p 20.}

Commonwealth countries Where a British enactment has been adopted in a Commonwealth country, the courts in the United Kingdom will strive to preserve a uniform interpretation. This particularly applies where the subject-matter to some extent forms a common system, as with patents or copyright. In relation to Australian and New Zealand decisions on patent legislation, Lord Parker CJ said-

> 'One cannot shut from one's mind the desirability of having a homogeneous development of the law in all countries which have adopted our system of patent legislation. That desirability must result in a tendency of our courts to follow these decisions if it is possible to do so.'

{*R v Patents Appeal Tribunal, ex p Swift & Co* [1962] 2 QB 647. Cf *Consolidated Agencies Ltd v Bertram Ltd* [1965] AC 670 (Indian decisions on Tanganyika Act).}

In relation to Commonwealth territories from which a right of appeal lies to the Judicial Committee of the Privy Council, that Committee serves as a *commune forum* in the same way as the House of Lords does for the countries of the United Kingdom. {See p 688 below.}

See further s 199 of this Code.

198. Territorial extent: composition of an enactment's territory

Unless the contrary intention appears, where an enactment extends, or does not extend, to a particular territory this refers to-

(a) the land mass of that territory, including internal waters and islands within them, and

(b) the territorial waters, including the seabed under them (the 'territorial seabed'), and

(c) the airspace over the area comprised in paragraphs (a) and (b) above, and

(d) any part of the seabed adjoining the territorial seabed which has been reduced into possession by entry from the territorial seabed.

COMMENTARY

This spells out exactly what is meant by saying that an Act extends to a certain territory. Where the territory named constitutes the entirety of an independent state, such as the United Kingdom, the reference is taken to be to that area recognised to be the area of the state under international law, including its airspace and territorial waters. Under British law the power to declare what is the territory of the state is regarded as lying with the Crown in exercise of the prerogative. {*R v Kent JJ, ex p Lye* [1967] 2 QB 153.} Dependencies are not included unless specified or implied.

Difficulty may arise where the named territory forms a part only of a state, as is the case with Scotland in relation to the United Kingdom. While the land boundaries may be clear, the area of the territorial waters attributable to the territory is likely to be uncertain. This is because the concept of territorial waters belongs to a state, not to parts of a state. {See s 218 of this Code.}

Contrary intention   An Act may of course specify or imply that its reference to a particular territory is to be construed in a narrower or wider way than usual.

Example 1   In *Mortensen v Peters* {(1906) 43 Sc LR 872; 8 F (Just) 93.} it was held that the wording of the Herring Fishery (Scotland) Act 1889 implied an intention that the extent of the Act should go beyond the three-mile limit. The Law Commission have commented that in some recent Acts it is not clear upon what basis territorial limits are to be measured. {See pp 485–486 below.}

Paragraph (a)   As to internal waters see s 213 of this Code.

Paragraph (b)   As to territorial waters see s 218 of this Code. The ownership of the seabed lying under the territorial waters is somewhat doubtful. It was decided in *R v Keyn* {(1876) 2 Ex D 63.} that at common law the realm ended at the low-water mark. The Territorial Waters Jurisdiction Act 1878 was passed to reverse that decision for certain purposes, but did not refer to the seabed. {The question is discussed at length in Gibson 'The ownership of the seabed under British territorial waters' *International Relations* 6 (1978) 474.}

Where the territorial waters and seabed are relevant for the purposes of a particular Act, and the terms of the Act do not exclude them, it seems that the Act should be taken as intended to extend to them. This paragraph accordingly so provides. {See further commentary on para (c) below.}

Paragraph (c)   This accords with the principle *cujus est solum ejus est usque ad coelum et ad inferos* (he who possesses land has an interest in, and exclusive right to, that which is above it to an indefinite height and below it to the centre of the earth). {Co Litt 4a.}

Under this principle an invasion of airspace constitutes trespass at common law. {*Kelsen v Imperial Tobacco Co (of Great Britain and Ireland) Ltd* [1957] 2 All ER 343. But see *Saunders v Smith* (1838) as reported in 2 Jur 491, where Shadwell V-C said that sailing over another's land in a balloon would be 'too contemptible' for the law to notice. Cf *Kenyon v Hart* (1865) 6 B & S 249, *per* Lord Blackburn at p 252.} Section 40 of the Civil Aviation Act 1949, in providing that no action of trespass shall lie where an aircraft overflies property at a reasonable height, recognises the existence of the landowner's right over airspace.

Clearly there can be no private right more extensive than rights of sovereignty, and national territory therefore includes airspace. This was recognised in the preamble to the Air Navigation Act 1920 (repealed) which declared that

'the full and absolute sovereignty and rightful jurisdiction of His Majesty extends, and has always extended, over the air superincumbent on all parts of His Majesty's dominions and the territorial waters adjacent thereto'.

Paragraph (d)   There is clearly sovereignty over any part of the adjacent extra-territorial seabed which has been reduced into possession. This is recognised by art 7 of the Geneva Convention on the Continental Shelf. {See Law Commission *Report on the Territorial and Extraterritorial Extent of the Criminal Law* (1978) Law Com No 91 p 21 (footnote 84).} The Law Commission report that-

'For many years there have existed mines tunnelled from the land but lying underneath the seabed and extending beyond the accepted limits of territorial waters. Various powers in relation to the designated areas under which the mines were situated were given by the National Coal Board (Additional Powers) Act 1966, and they are regarded as mines to which the Mines and Quarries Act 1954 applies. This legislation would appear already to accord with international law since, quite apart from claims in respect of the continental shelf, the principle of the freedom of the high seas has no relevance in the context of occupation of the subsoil taking place by means of tunnelling from the shore through the subsoil lying underneath territorial waters; there can therefore be no objection to the assertion of sovereign rights over such workings.'

{*Loc cit* para 52. See also the Continental Shelf Act 1964.}

199. Territorial extent: presumption of United Kingdom extent

Unless the contrary intention appears, Parliament is taken to intend an Act to extend to each territory of the United Kingdom but not to any territory outside the United Kingdom.

COMMENTARY

The presumption that an Act extends throughout the area of the United Kingdom derives from the fact that Parliament is the only sovereign legislature for that area.

The presumption that an Act does not extend *beyond* the United Kingdom arises from the fact that other British territories, while not excluded from the jurisdiction of the Westminster Parliament, are not represented in it and mostly possess legislatures of their own. At least where the subject-matter of an Act is within the competence of the local legislature, it is presumed that Parliament did not, without saying so, intend to intrude on its preserve. Blackstone puts it in this way-

> 'The general run of laws, enacted by the superior state, are supposed to be calculated for its own internal government, and do not extend to its distant dependent countries, which, bearing no part in the legislature, are not therefore in its ordinary and daily contemplation. But when the sovereign legislative power sees it necessary to extend its care to any of its subordinate dominions, and mentions them expressly by name, or includes them under general words, there can be no doubt but then they are bound by its laws.'

{Kerr Bl (4th edn, 1876) i 75. See also C Ilbert *Legislative Methods and Forms* p 251.}

Express modification of the presumption Acts often rely on this presumption *sub silentio,* but modify it by stating that they do not extend to one or more of the territories of the United Kingdom.

Example 1 Thus s 87(6) of the Highways Act 1971 (repealed) said: 'This Act does not extend to Scotland or Northern Ireland'. It implied that the Act *did* extend to the rest of the United Kingdom, namely England and Wales.

Example 2 Exactly the same effect is produced by s 17(10) of the Housing Rents and Subsidies Act 1975. This does not rely on the presumption of United Kingdom extent but instead spells out the extent of the Act. It says: 'This Act extends to England and Wales only'.

Implied modification of the presumption Modern Acts state expressly when, and how far, they are departing from the presumption of United Kingdom extent. Older Acts are often less precise. For these it may be necessary to determine whether there is an implication modifying or disapplying the presumption.

Such a contrary implication may arise if the express wording is clearly inappropriate for the entire United Kingdom.

Example 3 The Act 14 Geo 3 c 78 (1774) was enacted, according to its long title, 'for the more effectually preventing Mischiefs by Fire' in various localities. The localities mentioned in the long title were all in or around London, but the wording of two of the sections, namely ss 83 and 86 (which are still in force), is quite general.

It was held in *Richards v Easto* {(1846) 3 Dow & L 515.} and *Filliter v*

Phipperd {(1847) 11 QB 347.} that s 86 is of general application. A similar ruling was later laid down as respects s 83. {*Ex p Gorely* (1865) 34 LJ Bk 1 (*per* Lord Westbury); *Sinnott v Bowden* [1912] 2 Ch 414.} Section 83 has been held not to extend to Scotland {*Westminster Fire Office v Glasgow Provident Investment Society* (1883) 13 App Cas 699: see Example 4.} or to Ireland. {*Andrews v Patriotic Assurance Co (No 2)* (1886) 18 LR Ir 355).} Despite these decisions the Act was given by the Short Titles Act 1896 the misleading short title of the Fires Prevention (Metropolis) Act 1774.

Problems are caused where the draftsman of an Act which is intended to extend throughout the United Kingdom uses language appropriate only for the legal system of England and Wales. {See s 197 of this Code.}

Example 4 In *Westminster Fire Office v Glasgow Provident Investment Society* {(1883) 13 App Cas 699.} Lord Watson said of s 83 of the Fires Prevention (Metropolis) Act 1774 that its tenor, and the remedies provided by it, indicated that it was not intended by the legislature to apply in Scotland or be administered by Scottish courts. {P 716.}

Example 5 In *R v Mallow Guardians* {(1860) 12 Ir CLR 35.} the question was whether the Common Lodging House Acts 1851 and 1853 applied to Ireland. Lefroy CJ said {P 40.}-

> 'Prima facie since the Union every Act applies to Ireland, but according to Lord Coke the construction of a statute is best made *ex visceribus actus*, and on looking carefully through the details of these Acts, I think abundant proof will be found of their inapplicability to Ireland'.

{As to construction *ex visceribus actus* see p 375 above.}

Such an indication of limited extent may be contradicted where an *express* extent provision does not exclude the territory.

Example 6 This happened in *Perth Water Commissioners v McDonald* {(1879) 6 R (Sc) 1050.} The question was whether the Act 35 & 36 Vict c 91 (1872), which related to borough funds, extended to Scotland. The language was unsuitable but on the other hand there was an exclusion clause which mentioned Ireland only, thus bringing in the principle *expressio unius est exclusio alterius*. {See s 389 of this Code.} Lord Moncrieff said

> 'Now, there are not words excluding Scotland from its provisions. Ireland is specially excluded, and the statute deals with interests which are the same on either side of the Border. The only reason for supposing that it was not meant to extend to Scotland is that it is drawn with such exclusive reference to English legislation and English institutions and procedure that though it would be easy enough to find equivalents in our usages for these requisites, it would be difficult, if not impossible, to follow out in Scotland the precise injunctions of the Act ... I incline to the opinion that the statute applies to Scotland because its object is general, and there are no words to exclude and no reason for excluding Scotland from its

operation, although I see great difficulties in the way of its practical application.'

{Pp 1055–1056. As to the question of uniform construction in different territories to which an Act extends see s 197 of this Code.}

200. Territorial extent: extent to Her Majesty's independent dominions

Canada   No Act of the Parliament of the United Kingdom passed after the coming into force of the Constitution Act 1982 set out in Schedule B to the Canada Act 1982 extends to Canada or its dependencies as part of their law.

Australia   No Act of the Parliament of the United Kingdom passed after the adoption of the Statute of Westminster 1931 extends to the Commonwealth of Australia or its dependencies unless it is expressly declared in the Act that the Parliament and Government of that Commonwealth have requested, and assented to, the enactment thereof:

Provided that this does not require the concurrence of the Parliament or Government of that Commonwealth in any law made by the Parliament of the United Kingdom with respect to any matter within the authority of the States of Australia, not being a matter within the authority of the Parliament or Government of the Commonwealth of Australia, in any case where it would have been in accordance with the constitutional practice existing before the commencement of the Statute of Westminster 1931 that the Parliament of the United Kingdom should make that law without such concurrence.

New Zealand   No Act of the Parliament of the United Kingdom passed after the adoption of the Statute of Westminster 1931 extends to to New Zealand, or to any of its dependencies, unless it is expressly declared in the Act that that country has requested, and assented to, the enactment thereof.

Other independent dominions   An Act of the Parliament of the United Kingdom does not extend to a country mentioned below, or to a dependency of that country, where the Act is passed on or after the country's independence day (the date specified after the name of that country).

The said countries are the following (being countries, in addition to Canada, Australia, and New Zealand, of which Her Majesty is Queen, but not in right of Her Government in the United Kingdom)-

Antigua and Barbuda (1 November 1981) {West Indies Act 1967; Antigua Termination of Association Order 1981 (SI 1981/1104); Antigua and Barbuda Constitution Order 1981

(SI 1981/1106).},

The Bahamas (10 July 1973) {Bahamas Independence Act 1973 s 1.},

Barbados (30 November 1966) {Barbados Independence Act 1966 s 1.},

Belize (21 September 1981) {Belize Act 1981 s 1(1); Belize Independence Order 1981 (SI 1981/1107).},

Fiji (10 October 1970) {Fiji Independence Act 1970 s 1.},

Grenada (7 February 1974) {West Indies Act 1967; Grenada Termination of Association Order 1973 (SI 1973/2157).},

Jamaica (6 August 1962) {Jamaica Independence Act 1962 s 1.},

Mauritius (12 March 1968) {Mauritius Independence Act 1968 s 1.},

Papua New Guinea (16 September 1975) {Papua New Guinea, Western Samoa and Nauru (Miscellaneous Provisions) Act 1980 s 2.},

Saint Christopher and Nevis (19 September 1983) {West Indies Act 1967; Saint Christopher and Nevis Termination of Association Order 1983 (SI 1983/800).},

Saint Lucia (22 February 1979) {West Indies Act 1967; Saint Lucia Termination of Association Order 1978 (SI 1978/1900).},

Saint Vincent (27 October 1979) {West Indies Act 1967; Saint Vincent Termination of Association Order 1979 (SI 1979/918).},

Solomon Islands (7 July 1978) {Solomon Islands Act 1978 s 1.},

Tuvalu (1 October 1978). {Tuvalu Act 1978 s 1. Tuvalu was formerly the Ellice Islands.}

COMMENTARY

Canada The first clause of this section derives from s 2 of the Canada Act 1982, which was brought into force on 17 April 1982 by a proclamation of that date issued by the Queen under s 58 of that Act. Section 2 of the Canada Act 1982 does not refer to dependencies, but these must be taken as included by necessary implication.

Australia The second clause derives from s 4 of the Statute of Westminster 1931. By virtue of s 10 of that Act, s 4 was not to extend to Australia unless adopted by the Commonwealth Parliament. This was done as from 3 September 1939 by the Statute of Westminster Adoption Act 1942 (No 56 of 1942). The adoption is revocable. {Statute of Westminster 1931 s 10(2).}

Section 1 of the Statute of Westminster 1931, which defines the term 'Dominion' as used in the Act, does not refer to dependencies. They must be taken as included by necessary implication.

For an example of the inclusion in an Act of the form of declaration

465

contemplated here see the preamble to His Majesty's Declaration of Abdication Act 1936. For a reference, falling short of such a declaration, to the agreement of Commonwealth governments to the passing of an Act see the preamble to the Royal Titles Act 1953.

New Zealand   The third clause derives from s 4 of the Statute of Westminster 1931. By virtue of s 10 of that Act, s 4 was not to extend to New Zealand unless adopted by the New Zealand Parliament. This was done on 25 November 1947 by the Statute of Westminster Adoption Act 1947 (No 38 of 1947). The adoption is revocable. {Statute of Westminster 1931 s 10(2).}

Section 1 of the Statute of Westminster 1931, which defines the term 'Dominion' as used in the Act, does not refer to dependencies. They must be taken as included by necessary implication.

For an example of the inclusion in an Act of the form of declaration contemplated here see the preamble to His Majesty's Declaration of Abdication Act 1936. For a reference, falling short of such a declaration, to the agreement of Commonwealth governments to the passing of an Act see the preamble to the Royal Titles Act 1953.

Other independent dominions   The fourth clause reproduces the common-form provision contained in Acts effecting or recognising the independence of former British territories in the Commonwealth. {Because of the different constitutional history of Papua New Guinea, this clause is not found in the Papua New Guinea, Western Samoa and Nauru (Miscellaneous Provisions) Act 1980. It appears however that, in recognising the independence of the territories, the Act must be taken to have similar effect.} The Acts do not refer to dependencies of these countries, but these must be taken as included by necessary implication.

The countries listed consist of the thirteen independent countries (other than Canada, Australia, and New Zealand) of which Her Majesty is Queen, but not in right of the United Kingdom government.

Independent Commonwealth countries which are republics, or are monarchies with monarchs other than Her Majesty, are not listed since there can be no doubt that, so far as the legislative powers of the United Kingdom Parliament are concerned, they are in the position of foreign countries. They do however recognise Her Majesty as Head of the Commonwealth.

When acting in that capacity, it seems that Her Majesty is not subject to the constitutional doctrine that she speaks and acts only on the advice of Her Ministers. This is in accordance with the political reality, since it would not be proper for any one Government to presume to 'advise' (in the technical sense understood in constitutional law) the Head of the Commonwealth. No doctrine has yet developed whereby the Governments of Her Majesty's independent dominions collectively tender advice to the Head of the Commonwealth.

See further s 210 of this Code.

201. Territorial extent: meaning of 'associated state'

Unless the contrary intention appears, in any Act passed on or after 16 February 1967 'associated state' means a territory maintaining a status of association with the United Kingdom in accordance with the West Indies Act 1967.

COMMENTARY

This section derives from the Interpretation Act 1978 s 5 and Sch 1.

The West Indies Act 1967 conferred on certain British possessions in the West Indies a status of 'association' with the United Kingdom. Under this the United Kingdom government ceased to have responsibility for the associated state except in relation to defence, external affairs and citizenship. {West Indies Act 1967 s 2.} Acts of the United Kingdom Parliament passed after the status came into existence and while it subsisted do not extend to the state unless its request and consent were signified or the Act relates to reserved matters. {West Indies Act 1967 s 3.}

The following were the original associated states: Antigua, Dominica, Grenada, Saint Christopher, Nevis and Anguilla, Saint Lucia and Saint Vincent. Either the United Kingdom or the state in question had power to terminate the status. {West Indies Act 1967 s 10.} This has now been done in all cases, so that the states have achieved full independence. {For details see s 200 of this Code.}

202. Territorial extent: meaning of 'baseline'

Under international law, the baseline is the line marking the limit of territorial waters on the landward side. The baseline of the United Kingdom is fixed by Orders in Council made in exercise of the royal prerogative.

COMMENTARY

A lack of unanimity prevails among the nations over those factors which in international law determine the baseline. It is generally agreed as a starting point that the baseline should (so far as possible) follow the low water line. Difficulty then arises in relation to bays and other indentations. For these it is agreed to be necessary to depart from the low water line and take a straight line from headland to headland (known as a bay-closing line).

The exact positioning of the sectors of baseline consisting of bay-closing lines has caused dispute. The common law drew the baseline (equivalent to the boundary of the realm) so as to leave on the landward side the enclosed waters of bays, gulfs, and the estuaries or mouths of great rivers. These internal waters were described as being *intra fauces terrae* (within the jaws of the land).

Apart from such enclosing lines, the baseline at common law followed the low water line. {See *R v Keyn* (1876) 2 Ex D 63; *The Fagernes* [1927] P 311.} It was disputed whether at common law the baseline advanced and retreated with the tide. {See *R v Keyn* (1876) 2 Ex D 63; *Constable's Case* (1601) 5 Co Rep 106a; *A-G v Chambers* 4 De Gex, Mac & Gor 206; *Embleton v Brown* (1860) 3 E & E 234.}

The latest international convention on the baseline of nations is the Geneva Convention on the Territorial Sea and the Contiguous Zone. {(1958) Cmnd 584.} As to this, and the Orders in Council made to implement it, see below.

Waters on the landward side of the baseline are known as internal waters. {See s 213 of this Code.}

United Kingdom baseline As to the existence and extent of the royal prerogative in relation to territorial waters see s 218 of this Code. The current order under the prerogative is the Territorial Waters Order in Council 1964. {SI 1965 III, p

6452A.} This was made so as to give effect in British law to the Geneva Convention mentioned above. The findings of hydrographic surveys on the west coast of Scotland later made necessary an adjustment of the baseline fixed by the 1964 order. {See Territorial Waters (Amendment) Order in Council 1979.}

The combined effect of the two orders is to fix the present United Kingdom baseline at the low water line (including low tide elevations) except where special provision is made for 'bays' (as defined by the 1964 order) and for certain parts of the Scottish coastline. Article 5 of the order defines a bay for this purpose as-

> 'An indentation of the coast such that its area (measured at low water) is not less than that of a semicircle whose diameter is a line drawn across the mouth of the indentation . . . joining the low water lines of its natural entrance points.'

The United Kingdom baseline is shown on large-scale charts drawn up under the authority of the Hydrographic Department of the Ministry of Defence. Changes in physical features caused by coastal erosion or accretion, or peculiarities of natural configuration, may however cause dispute as to whether a chart truly shows the location of the baseline at a time and place material in legal proceedings.

In such cases the usual standards of proof in civil or, as the case may be, criminal cases apply. In a civil case the plaintiff is thus required to prove the position of a point relative to the baseline only on a balance of probabilities. {*Post Office v Estuary Radio Ltd* [1968] 2 QB 740.}

In a criminal case the onus on the prosecution is the usual one of satisfying the court or jury of the position of the relevant baseline so that they feel sure. Either way, expert evidence is likely to be required.

203. Territorial extent: meaning of 'Berwick upon Tweed'

Berwick upon Tweed, though referred to in various Acts, is not the subject of a statutory definition. Berwick is a town at the mouth of the River Tweed, on the north bank. Under section 1 of, and Schedule 1 to, the Local Government Act 1972 it is a district within the non-metropolitan county of Northumberland. It therefore forms part of England.

COMMENTARY

Under the Local Government Act 1933 {Repealed by the Local Government Act 1972 s 272 and Sch 30.} Berwick was a non-county borough in the administrative county of Northumberland. {S 1 and Sch 1 Pt III.} Earlier it was a municipal borough and a county in itself.

Since the twelfth century the Tweed has constituted for most of its length the boundary between England and Scotland. Being on the Scottish side of the river, Berwick was included in that country until captured by Edward I in 1302. Until then it was one of the four royal burghs of Scotland.

Berwick was retaken by the Scots for a period in the fifteenth century, but from 1482 onwards was represented in the English Parliament. {Its liberties, franchises and customs were confirmed by the statutes 22 Edw 4 c 8 (1482) and

1 Ja 1 c 28 (1603). See also *R v Cowle* (1759) 2 Burr 834.} Certain writs of the courts at Westminster did not run into Berwick, though prerogative writs so ran and indictments concerning matters in Berwick were triable by a jury of the county of Northumberland. {Kerr Bl (4th edn, 1876) i 74; Cro Jac 543; 2 Rol Abr 292; stat 11 Geo 1 c 4 (1724). See also *Mayor of Berwick v Shanks* (1826) 3 Bing 459 and stat 5 & 6 Will 4 c 76 (1835) s 109.}

This checkered history led to the practice of mentioning Berwick specifically in statutory provisions dealing with the extent of Acts. {See, e g, Habeas Corpus Act 1679 s 11. Cf Parish Notices Act 1837 s 6.}

Any need for specific mention disappeared on the enactment of s 3 of the statute 20 Geo 2 c 42 (1746), which provided that references in Acts to England should be taken to include the town of Berwick upon Tweed. This Act, which had the long title *An Act to enforce the Execution of an Act of this session of Parliament, for granting to his Majesty several Rates and Duties upon Houses, Windows, or Lights*, was repealed except for s 3 by the House Tax Act 1803 s 84. Because s 3 was then the only surviving section, the Act was given the short title the Wales and Berwick Act 1746 by the Short Titles Act 1896. Section 3 was repealed by the Interpretation Act 1978. {S 25 and Sch 3.}

204. Territorial extent: meaning of 'British Islands'

Unless the contrary intention appears, in any Act passed after 1889 'British Islands' means the United Kingdom, the Channel Islands and the Isle of Man. The definition of 'British Islands', in its application to Acts passed after the establishment of the Irish Free State but before 1979, includes the Republic of Ireland.

COMMENTARY

This section derives from the Interpretation Act 1978 ss 5 and 22(1), Sch 1 and Sch 2 para 4(2). {It originated in the Interpretation Act 1889 s 18(1).} Since the partition of Ireland the expression has ceased to be appropriate and is seldom used. {It is used elsewhere in the Interpretation Act 1978 however: see the definition of 'colony' reproduced in s 207 of this Code.}

The second sentence of this section derives from the Interpretation Act 1978. {S 22 and Sch 2 para 4(2).} It originated in the Irish Free State (Consequential Adaptation of Enactments) Order 1923 (S R & O 1923/405) art 2 and Sch. The effect of this was continued by the Ireland Act 1949 s 3(1)(a)(iii).}

205. Territorial extent: meaning of 'British possession'

Unless the contrary intention appears, in any Act passed after 1889 'British possession' means any part of Her Majesty's dominions outside the United Kingdom. Where parts of Her Majesty's dominions outside the United Kingdom are under both a central and a local legislature, all parts under the central legislature are deemed, for the purposes of this definition, to be one British possession.

COMMENTARY

This derives from the Interpretation Act 1978. {S 5 and Sch 1. It originated in the Interpretation Act 1889 s 18(2). See also, in relation to British India, s 18A(1)(i) of the latter Act.}

206. Territorial extent: meaning of 'Channel Islands'

The Channel Islands, though referred to in various Acts, are not the subject of a statutory definition. They consist of the Bailiwick of Jersey and the Bailiwick of Guernsey, Alderney and Sark. They are not part of the United Kingdom, though included in the expression 'British Islands'. They are not colonies.

COMMENTARY

History   The islands of Jersey, Guernsey, Sark and Alderney, together with their appendages, were until the Norman conquest parcel of the duchy of Normandy. At the conquest they became united with the Crown of England. {Kerr Bl (4th edn, 1876) i 80.} Blackstone said that the Islands 'are governed by their own laws, which are for the most part the ducal customs of Normandy, being collected in an ancient book of very great authority entitled *Le Grand Coustumier*'. {Kerr Bl (4th edn, 1876) i 81.}

The islands have never been regarded as part of the kingdom of England however. {*Navigators and General Insurance Co Ltd v Ringrose* [1962] 1 All ER 97.} The ordinary writ or process of the English courts does not run there, though prerogative writs and orders do. {*Carus Wilson's Case* (1845) 7 QB 984; *IRC v Stype Investments (Jersey) Ltd* [1982] 3 All ER 419; *IRC v Stannard* (1984) *The Times* 14 February; Kerr Bl (4th edn, 1876) i 81.} The Habeas Corpus Act 1679 s 10 unnecessarily provides that habeas corpus shall run into 'the islands of Jersey or Guernsey'. It is unnecessary because as Blackstone says 'this and all other prerogative writs were issuable at common law to all the dominions of the Crown'. {Kerr Bl (4th edn, 1876) i 80. See also *R v Cowle* (1759) 2 Burr 856.}

Extent of Acts to Islands   It has long been established that an Act of the United Kingdom Parliament does not extend to the Channel Islands in the absence of an indication to this effect. {4 Co Inst 286; Kerr Bl (4th edn, 1876) i 81.} Such an indication may be given by words stating that the Act or a particular provision of it extends to the Channel Islands. {For an example see the Societies (Miscellaneous Provisions) Act 1940, s 12(2). A repealing or amending Act must similarly extend: see, as to the last-mentioned Act, s 6 of the Statute Law (Repeals) Act 1969.}

The modern practice is for an extent provision to refer to 'the Channel Islands', but earlier Acts specified the individual islands. {See, e g, the Parish Notices Act 1837 s 6.} Alternatively the Act may confer power to effect the extension, with or without modifications, by Order in Council. {For an example see Prevention of Terrorism (Temporary Provisions) Act 1974 s 11.} Another variant is for the Act to state that it extends to the Channel Islands but go on to give power to modify the Act, so far as it so extends, by Order in Council. {For an example see Trustee Savings Banks Act 1969 s 99.}

Registration of Acts Sometimes an Act, when providing for its extent to the Channel Islands, requires the Royal Courts of the Islands to register the Act, but the practice is by no means invariable. {For an example see National Debt Act 1972 s 19.} It has been suggested that an Act may not be binding in the Islands without registration of the Act in the rolls of the Royal Courts, and that such registration cannot be effected without the concurrence of the States (the local legislature). {Craies *Statute Law* (7th edn, 1971) pp 34, 477; *Ency Brit* (11th edn) v 842. Cf *Re States of Jersey* (1853) 9 Moore PC 185; *Re Jersey Prison Board* (year?) 8 St Tr (NS) 286, 1147; *Renouf v A-G for Jersey* [1936] AC 445.}

However this would effectively give the States a veto, and is contrary to principle. As the sovereign legislature of that part of Her Majesty's dominions, the United Kingdom Parliament has the same undoubted power to legislate for the Channel Islands as it has for any other part of those dominions. Registration by the Royal Courts is thus of mere historical interest, and cannot affect the validity or operation of the Act. {Cf *Du Boulay v Du Boulay* (1869) LR 2 PC 430.} Blackstone, after saying that the authority of the sovereign in council over the Channel Islands was said to be absolute, added 'but in modern times the legislation for these islands has generally been by act of parliament'. {Kerr Bl (4th edn, 1876) i 205. See also *Re States of Jersey* (1853) 9 Moore PC 185, at p 262.}

The Crown has power to direct the registration of any Act extending to the Channel Islands. This is done by Order in Council under the prerogative, and does not depend on any provision in the Act itself. One such Order in Council, dated 1 July 1731, went on to make this general pronouncement-

' ... for the future whenever any Act shall be passed in the Parliament of Great Britain relating to the said Islands of Jersey and Guernsey, printed copies of such Acts [*sic*] shall be transmitted by the Clerk of His Majesty's Privy council as soon as conveniently may be to the Royal Courts of the said Islands, signifying to them at the same time His Majesty's Pleasure, to Register and Publish the said Acts, and to cause the same to be carried into due execution.'

The practice is to signify the royal pleasure in every case by Order in Council, whether or not the Act contains a registration provision. It follows that such statutory registration provisions are otiose, and should not be included. {For the doctrine that effect is if possible to be given to every word of an Act see pp 375–376 above. The doctrine implies that draftsmen should not include otiose provisions, even where they are traditional.}

For a list of Acts which extend to the Channel Islands see the official *Index to the Statutes*, title CHANNEL ISLANDS See also E Lenfestey 'The Bailiwick of Guernsey in the Channel Islands'. {(1984) 10 CLB 417.}

Colony See s 207 of this Code, from which it will be seen that at all times the expression 'colony' has been confined to territories outside the British Islands.

207. Territorial extent: meaning of 'colony'

Post-1978 Acts Unless the contrary intention appears, in any Act passed after 1978 'colony' means any part of Her Majesty's dominions outside the British Islands except-

(a) countries having fully responsible status within the Commonwealth;
(b) territories for whose external relations a country other than the United Kingdom is responsible;
(c) associated states.

Pre-1979 Acts Unless the contrary intention appears, in any Act passed at any time after 1889 but before 1979 'colony' means any part of Her Majesty's dominions outside the British Islands except countries having fully responsible status within the Commonwealth and associated states, and includes-

(a) any colony within the meaning of section 18(3) of the Interpretation Act 1889 which was excluded, but in relation only to Acts passed at a later time, by any enactment repealed by the Interpretation Act 1978;
(b) any country or territory which ceased after that time to be part of Her Majesty's dominions but subject to a provision for the continuation of existing law as if it had not so ceased.

Federations Where parts of Her Majesty's dominions are under both a central and a local legislature, all parts under the central legislature are deemed for the purposes of this definition to be one colony.

COMMENTARY

Post-1978 Acts The first clause of this definition derives from the Interpretation Act 1978. {S 5 and Sch 1.} Paragraph (a) refers to countries, other than the United Kingdom, which are part of Her Majesty's independent dominions. {For these see s 211 of this Code.} Paragraph (b) refers to dependencies of countries falling within para (a). As to associated states see s 201 of this Code.

Pre-1979 Acts The second clause derives from the Interpretation Act 1978. {S 22(1) and Sch 2 para 4(3).} The repealed enactments referred to in para (a) are mainly common-form provisions of independence Acts which provided that the definition of 'colony' in s 18(3) of the Interpretation Act 1889 was no longer to apply to the newly-independent state. These followed the precedent set by s 11 of the Statute of Westminster 1931, which was also repealed by the Interpretation Act 1978. {S 25 and Sch 3.}

Paragraph (b) ensures that countries or territories which either left the Commonwealth on or after attaining independence or became republics within the Commonwealth continue to be within the definition of 'colony' for the purposes of pre-1979 Acts so far as this is appropriate. Provision for the continuation of existing law is commonly made for countries ceasing to be part of Her Majesty's dominions. {For an example see Ghana (Consequential Provision) Act 1960 s 1(1).}

Federations The final clause of this section derives from the Interpretation Act 1978. {S 5 and Sch 1.} It was formerly contained in the Interpretation Act 1889 s 18(3).

For a list of Acts which extend to the colonies see Index to the Statutes, title
COLONIES, PROTECTORATES, PROTECTED STATES AND TRUST TERRITORIES.

208. Territorial extent: meaning of 'England'

Unless the contrary intention appears, in an Act passed on or after 1
April 1974 'England' means, subject to any alteration of boundaries
under Part IV of the Local Government Act 1972, the area consisting of
the counties established by section 1 of that Act, together with Greater
London and the Isles of Scilly.

Unless the contrary intention appears, in an Act passed before 1 April
1974 'England' includes Berwick upon Tweed and Monmouthshire.

Unless the contrary intention appears, in an Act passed before the
Welsh Language Act 1967 'England' includes Wales.

COMMENTARY

The first clause of this section derives from the Interpretation Act 1978. {S 5
and Sch 1.} It originated in s 269 of the Local Government Act 1972, before the
enactment of which there was no full definition. It is remarkable that 'England'
is not a free-standing term but is thought to require definition. Until 1972 its
name was simply a matter of repute. It was 'that part of Britain called England'.
{See Statute Law Revision Act 1948 s 4(b).}

Greater London Unlike 'England', this is a free-standing term. It means the
area comprising the areas of the London boroughs, the City of London, the
Inner Temple and the Middle Temple. {London Government Act 1963 ss 2(1),
89(1).}

Islands As Blackstone put it, the smaller adjacent islands such as the Isle of
Wight, Portland, Thanet etc, 'are comprised within some neighbouring county,
and are therefore to be looked upon as annexed to the mother island, and part of
the kingdom of England'. {Kerr Bl (4th edn, 1876) i 79.}

Isles of Scilly Although part of England, the Isles of Scilly are a special case.
There is no statutory definition of the name, which is a free-standing term of
purely descriptive character.

The Isles of Scilly are situated off the coast of Cornwall. There are about forty
of them, of which only about half a dozen are inhabited. The Isles are
administered by a Council. {See Local Government Act 1972 s 265.}
Sometimes an Act otherwise extending to England and Wales is expressed not to
extend to the Isles of Scilly, or to extend to them subject to exceptions,
adaptations and modifications. {See, e g, Rent Act 1977 s 153.}

The second clause of this section derives from the Interpretation Act 1978. {S
22(1) and Sch 2 para 5(a).} It is explained in the commentaries on ss 203
(Berwick upon Tweed) and 215 (Monmouthshire) of this Code.

The final clause of this section derives from the Interpretation Act 1978. {S
22(1) and Sch 2 para 5(a).} The Welsh Language Act 1967 was passed on 27

473

July 1967. Section 4 of the Act repealed the provision of the Wales and Berwick Act 1746 by virtue of which references in Acts to England were taken to include Wales. See further the commentary on s 220 (definition of 'Wales') of this Code.

209. Territorial extent: meaning of 'Great Britain'

Great Britain consists of England, Scotland and Wales.

COMMENTARY

This definition is derived from art 1 of the Union with Scotland Act 1706, which states that the two kingdoms of England and Scotland shall from the year 1707 for ever be united into one kingdom by the name of Great Britain. {In fact the union took effect on 1 May 1707.} The reference to England in art 1 is deemed to include Wales. {Interpretation Act 1978 ss 22(1) and Sch 2 para 5(a).} The result is that the whole island is known as Great Britain. This includes its subsidiary islands (such as the Isle of Wight, the Isles of Scilly, the Orkneys and the Shetlands) but not the Isle of Man {See s 214 of this Code.} or the Channel Islands. {See s 206 of this Code.}

The idea of the island of Britain forming a political unit, in accordance with its geography, is an ancient one. The statute 1 Ja 1 c 1 (1603) declares, more figuratively than historically, that the island was formerly one kingdom. Henry VIII tried without success to unite the two kingdoms. A dynastic accident led to the union of the Crowns in 1603, but more than a century was to pass before full political union became possible on an enduring basis. {Cromwell brought about a temporary union during the interregnum.}

Coke found great similarity between the common law of England and Scotland, tracing it to the adoption by the Scots of the early treatise on English common law attributed to Glanvil. {4 Co Inst 345.} Blackstone said that the differences between the two legal systems arose-

' . . . from a diversity of practice in two large and uncommunicating jurisdictions, and from the acts of two distinct and independent parliaments, which have in many points altered and abrogated the old common law of both kingdoms.'

{Kerr Bl (4th edn, 1876) i 70.}
A potent cause of difference was the reception of Roman law in Scotland, largely through the close historical connection with France.

Article 18 of the Union with Scotland Act 1706 provides that the law of Scotland shall remain the same as before-

' . . . but alterable by the Parliament of Great Britain with this difference betwixt the laws concerning publick right policy and civil government and those which concern private right that the laws which concern public right policy and civil government may be made the same throughout the whole United Kingdom. But that no alteration be made in laws which concern private right except for evident utility of the subjects within Scotland.'
{As to the effect of this see pp 128–129 above.}

210. Territorial extent: meaning of 'Her Majesty's dominions'

The expression 'Her Majesty's dominions', though used in various Acts, is not the subject of a statutory definition. Unless the contrary intention appears, in any Act of the United Kingdom Parliament 'Her Majesty's dominions' means the territories to which for the time being Her Majesty's sovereignty and jurisdiction extend in right of Her Government in the United Kingdom.

COMMENTARY

The meaning of this expression was straightforward until the emergence in the British Empire of countries possessing what is referred to by the Interpretation Act 1978 as 'responsible status within the Commonwealth'. {This now somewhat inadequate phrase is contained in the definition of 'colony' in Sch 1 to the 1978 Act, reproduced in s 207 of this Code.}

Before that emergence, the dominions of the Crown consisted of all the territories over which full British sovereignty was exercised. Areas which were not British territory, such as protectorates, protected states and trust territories, were excluded from the ambit of the term. There was no need to consider in right of which of its governments the Crown ruled. Rule was plainly in right of the Imperial Government throughout.

Now that the long process of emergence is virtually complete, we can distinguish within the Commonwealth a number of countries which are independent of the United Kingdom Parliament in every sense. In the case of two others, namely Australia and New Zealand, independence is virtually complete but the United Kingdom Parliament possesses residual powers. As respects certain of these independent countries within the Commonwealth, Her Majesty remains Queen. This is however in right of Her Government in the country in question, and not that of the United Kingdom. {See the definition of the phrase 'Her Majesty's independent dominions' in s 211 of this Code.}

In the Acts regulating the emergence of independent members of the Commonwealth, little distinction is made between those independent countries which have retained the Queen as monarch and those which, while remaining within the Commonwealth, have become republics. Yet it is necessary to draw this distinction in relation to statutory references to 'Her Majesty's dominions'. An independent republic is clearly not part of Her Majesty's dominions, even though no Act has explicitly said this. The position is not altered by the fact that the republic recognises Her Majesty as Head of the Commonwealth.

In fact most independence Acts have *not* stated expressly that the country granted independence is to cease to be a part of Her Majesty's dominions, even though it is to become a republic. {For a list of these Acts see Index to the Statutes, title INDEPENDENCE ACTS.} The reason for this is sometimes a technical one, the constitution of the new state being laid down by Order in Council and not in the Act itself. {For an exception see the Lesotho Independence Act 1966 s 1, which states that the territories in question 'shall cease to form part of Her Majesty's dominions and shall become an independent kingdom under the name of Lesotho'.}

Another common reason is that, while retaining the Queen as head of state for a short period after independence, the country subsequently turns itself into a republic in exercise of its independent powers.

Example 1   This happened in the case of Ghana, which became independent under the Queen in 1957 and turned itself into a republic in 1960. As to the implied effect of the Ghana (Consequential Provision) Act 1960 in recognising that Ghana then ceased to be part of Her Majesty's dominions see Bennion *Constitutional Law of Ghana* (Butterworth, 1962) p 105.}

The grant of independence sometimes produces the result that a territory becomes a part of Her Majesty's dominions in right of the government of the new state even though it had not been part of Her dominions before.

Example 2   Again Ghana provides an example. Section 1 of the Ghana Independence Act 1957 provided that the territories of the former Gold Coast should 'together form part of Her Majesty's dominions under the name of Ghana'. This had the effect of *annexing* the Northern Territories protectorate and the Togoland trust territory. {See Bennion *Constitutional Law of Ghana* (Butterworth, 1962) p 61. Other examples are furnished by: Sierra Leone Independence Act 1961 s 1; Tanganyika Independence Act 1961 s 1; Malawi Independence Act 1964 s 1.}

Unless the contrary intention appears   Where a United Kingdom Act passed after the independence of a country refers to 'Her Majesty's dominions' with legislative effect in those dominions the reference must be taken not to include that independent country. This arises from the fact that the United Kingdom Parliament has given up its right to legislate for the independent countries of the Commonwealth other than Australia and New Zealand. {See s 200 of this Code.} Where however the term is used merely descriptively the context will indicate whether the narrower meaning given in this section is meant to be displaced.

The contrary intention may appear in an Act granting independence.

Example 3   Section 1(1) of the Gambia Independence Act 1964 states that certain territories 'shall together form part of Her Majesty's dominions under the name of The Gambia'. This is a wider use of the phrase 'Her Majesty's dominions', bringing in also Her Majesty's independent dominions. {As to these see s 211of this Code.}

A common-form clause in Independence Acts provides that, until contrary provision is made by some future Act, existing United Kingdom law shall continue to operate in relation to the newly independent country as if there had been no change in its status, that is as if it continued to form part of Her Majesty's dominions in the narrower sense. {See, e g, Botswana Independence Act 1966 s 2(1).}

It may in other cases be clear that the object of an enactment (as part of United Kingdom law) requires the expression 'Her Majesty's dominions' to include all territories of which Her Majesty is Queen.

Example 4   The object of s 25 of the Finance Act 1925 is to make Commonwealth governments liable to tax in relation to their trading in the United Kingdom. The section expressly refers to 'the Government of any part of [Her] Majesty's Dominions which is outside Great Britain and Northern Ireland'. {For another example see the Regency Act 1937 s 2(2).}

In right of Her Government in the United Kingdom   The concept that the Crown rules a territory 'in right of the government' of that territory was first given statutory recognition by the Crown Proceedings Act 1947. {See s 40(2)(c).} It has been used frequently since. {For a modern example see Protection of Aircraft Act 1973 s 27(2).} In the case of a dependent British territory outside the United Kingdom, the Crown rules in right of the government of that territory, even though the United Kingdom Parliament retains legislative power. {*R v Secretary of State for Foreign and Commonwealth Affairs, ex p Indian Assn of Alberta* [1982] 2 All ER 118.}

211. Territorial extent: meaning of 'Her Majesty's independent dominions'

Her Majesty's independent dominions consist of the following independent countries of which Her Majesty is Queen, together with their dependencies-

Antigua and Barbuda
Australia
Bahamas
Barbados
Belize
Canada
Fiji
Grenada
Jamaica
Mauritius
New Zealand
Papua New Guinea
Saint Christopher and Nevis
Saint Lucia
Saint Vincent
Solomon Islands
Tuvalu
United Kingdom.

COMMENTARY

For details of the status of these countries as independent dominions of the Queen see ss 200 and 210 of this Code.

212. Territorial extent: meaning of 'high seas'

The high seas are those parts of the sea that are not internal waters or territorial waters.

COMMENTARY

Internal waters   See s 213 of this Code.

Territorial waters   See s 218 of this Code.

This definition is taken from art 1 of the Geneva Convention on the High

Seas. {(29 April 1958) See the Continental Shelf Act 1964.} Its wording means in practice that any uncertainty as to whether particular waters are 'high seas' is to be resolved by reference to the meaning of 'territorial waters'. {But see *The Tolten* [1946] P 135, at 156.}

The term 'high seas' is unlikely to be used without definition in a modern Act. In older Acts this was often done.

Example 1   For an example of the use of 'high seas' undefined see the Slave Trade Act 1824 s 9. The wording of this implies that the term refers to seas beyond the Admiral's jurisdiction. {As to this see p 484 below.}

213. Territorial extent: meaning of 'internal waters'

Except for the purposes of an Act which otherwise provides, the internal waters of a territory are those waters lying within the baseline.

COMMENTARY

Baseline   See s 202 of this Code.

Provided the baseline is known, there can be no difficulty in determining which are the internal waters. Art 5 of the Geneva Convention on the Territorial Sea and Contiguous Zone {(1958) Cmnd 584.} expressly defines waters to landward of the baseline as 'internal waters'.

Equally, uncertainty as to the position of the baseline imports a corresponding uncertainty about whether relevant waters are internal or territorial.

While the internal waters clearly form part of the national territory, it does not follow that their area will be included in some local government district. That depends on whether the boundary of the district was drawn with internal waters in mind. At common law, internal waters are treated as being within the body of the adjacent county or counties. {*R v Keyn* (1876) 2 Ex D 63.}

214. Territorial extent: meaning of 'Isle of Man'

The Isle of Man, though referred to in various Acts, is not the subject of a statutory definition. The expression 'Isle of Man' refers to the Island of Man in the Irish Sea, together with the smaller islands appertaining to it. The Isle of Man is not part of the United Kingdom, though included in the expression 'British Islands'. It is not a colony.

COMMENTARY

The Isle of Man is the 'centrum' of the British Islands, being roughly equidistant from all the constituent countries. The description of it given in the Isle of Man Purchase Act 1765 was the 'island, castle, pele, and lordship of Man, and all the islands and lordships to the said Island of Man appertaining'. {S 1.} The Act vested the island in the Crown inalienably, and by virtue of this the Queen is Lord of Man. {Ibid. See also 43 Geo 3 c 123 (1803) and 6 Geo 4 c 34 (1825). The Isle of Man Purchase Act 1765 was repealed by the Statute Law (Repeals) Act 1976.} The island has its own Government. {See, e g, the

Colonial Stock Act 1892 s 3, and the Isle of Man Act 1979, long title, for statutory recognition of the Government.} The Queen's representative has the title of Lieutenant Governor of the Isle of Man.

Earlier history The island became Viking territory in the tenth century, and this has modelled its institutions till the present day. The last Scandinavian king was Magnus (1252-1265). The island was then ceded to the kings of Scotland. Edward I of England claimed it, and there followed a confused period until the Crown purchase of 1765 mentioned above. During most of this time the Earls of Derby were Lords of Man by virtue of Crown grant.

The island has never been regarded as part of the kingdom of England, even after its purchase by the Crown in 1765. Blackstone says it 'is a distinct territory from England, and is not governed by our laws'. {Kerr Bl (4th edn, 1876) i 79).} The ordinary writ or process of the English courts does not run there, though prerogative writs and orders do.

Common purse Since 1866 the Isle of Man Government has been paid by the United Kingdom Government its share of customs and similar duties. {29 & 30 Vict c 23 (1866).} These so-called common purse arrangements are currently regulated by the Isle of Man Act 1979. This requires the Commissioners of Customs and Excise to pay to the Treasurer of the Isle of Man 'the net Isle of Man share of common duties'. This is a free-standing term coined by s 2(2) of the Act. The duties in question are customs, excise and pool betting duties, value added tax and car tax. {Isle of Man Act 1979 s 1(1).}

Extent of Acts to Isle of Man Acts do not extend to the island unless they contain an indication to this effect. {4 Co Inst 284; 2 And 116; Kerr Bl (4th edn, 1876) i 79; stat 16 & 17 Vict c 107 s 346 (1853).} The island has its own legislature, the Tynwald. This has a Scandinavian form, and has been in continuous existence since the Viking invasion. It consists of the Lieutenant Governor, the House of Keys or lower house and the Legislative Council or upper house. The Tynwald has on occasion been granted power to amend Acts of Parliament. {For example s 1(3) of the Isle of Man Act 1958 (repealed) said that provision 'may be made by or under an Act of Tynwald' for amending Acts relating to customs.}

An indication of extent to the Isle of Man may be given in various ways. Sometimes the word 'extend' is used by itself (which is normal practice in Acts, and sufficient for the purpose). In other Acts the nature of extent is spelt out. Thus s 14(8) of the Isle of Man Act 1979 says that except for specified provisions 'this Act does not extend to the Isle of Man *as part of the law of the Island*'. {Emphasis added.} An Act which is to extend to the Isle of Man will very often extend to the Channel Islands also.

For a list of Acts extending to the Isle of Man see Index to the Statutes, title ISLE OF MAN. See also W Cain 'A note on the Isle of Man'. {(1984) 10 CLB 413.}

215. Territorial extent: meaning of 'Monmouthshire'

Monmouthshire was constituted as a county by section 2 of the Laws in Wales Act 1535, and later came to be considered part of England. By virtue of section 20 of the Local Government Act 1972 the former

Monmouthshire is now part of Wales, for the most part as a county under the ancient name of Gwent.

COMMENTARY

The Romans were the first recorded settlers in what became Monmouthshire. Moving through Glevum (Gloucester), the legions penetrated the territory west of the River Severn. Gloucester became one of the four *coloniae* of Roman Britain. On the Roman withdrawal the Welsh marches were subject to successive invasions.

At the time of the Heptarchy the area of Monmouthshire formed the Welsh kingdom of Gwent, whose inhabitants fiercely resisted attempted incursions by the West Saxons. The term Heptarchy, derived from Greek words meaning *seven rule*, designates the period of English history between the arrival of the Anglo-Saxons in 449 and the union of the English kingships under Egbert in 828. The term was first used in the sixteenth century, being adopted because of the belief of Camden and other historians that during this period there were seven identifiable kingdoms, namely Mercia, Wessex, Northumbria, East Anglia, Kent, Essex and Sussex. In fact this was an over-simplification, the power bases of the English kings having been during the period in question constantly in flux. The attempts at the invasion of Monmouthshire began in the seventh century. Later the kings of Gwent acknowledged Alfred as lord, and some Saxon settlement occurred.

In the ninth and tenth centuries the area was harried and partly settled by the Danes. The Welsh Chronicle records that in 1047 the whole of south Wales lay waste. In this year Irish invaders plundered and partly settled Gwent. By 1085 the Normans had subjugated almost the whole area. Although Gwent still ranked as Welsh territory at the time of the Doomsday survey, the town of Monmouth and other areas in it were assessed under Herefordshire. At the end of the fifteenth century there were no less than 24 separate Norman baronies in Gwent. The lords held their lands *per baroniam*, so that the writ of the king of England did not run in them.

The legal position was changed by the statute 27 Hen 8 c 26. This was given the short title The Laws in Wales Act 1535 by the Statute Law Revision Act 1948. This short title is inadequate to cover the full scope of the Act, and therefore misleading. The Act abolished the marches and united the 24 lordships to form Monmouthshire. {S 2.} Although the Act did not formally constitute the new county part of England, it provided for the English legal system to apply. {S 3.} Sheriffs were appointed in 1541, and Monmouthshire gradually came to be looked on as part of England. It was included in the Oxford circuit in the reign of Charles II.

Later the Welsh character of Monmouthshire reasserted itself. Acts passed in the late nineteenth century applied provisions designed for Wales to 'Wales and Monmouthshire'. {See the Sunday Closing (Wales) Act 1881 and the Welsh Intermediate Education Act 1889.} When the establishment of the Church of England in Wales was terminated by the Welsh Church Act 1914, Monmouthshire was included in the operation. The practice of linking Wales and Monmouthshire in legislation became invariable. {For a modern example see the Marriage (Wales and Monmouthshire) Act 1962.} Finally the wheel turned full circle when the Local Government Act 1972 restored

Monmouthshire to Wales, for the most part as a county under the ancient name of Gwent. {S 20 and Sch 4.}

216. Territorial extent: meaning of 'Northern Ireland'

Northern Ireland consists of the parliamentary counties of Antrim, Armagh, Down, Fermanagh, Londonderry and Tyrone, and the parliamentary boroughs of Belfast and Londonderry.

COMMENTARY

This derives from the Government of Ireland Act 1920. {S 1(2).} Although the definition is stated to apply only for the purposes of that Act, it now has general effect: Ireland (Confirmation of Agreement) Act 1925 Sch para 1.}

History The territory now constituting Northern Ireland became part of the United Kingdom under the Union with Ireland Act 1800, which took effect on 1 January 1801. On this date 'and for ever after' the kingdom of Great Britain and the kingdom of Ireland were united into one kingdom by the name of the United Kingdom of Great Britain and Ireland. {Article First.}

The Act provided for the United Kingdom to 'be represented in one and the same Parliament, to be stiled the Parliament of the United Kingdom of Great Britain and Ireland'. {Article Third.} Existing laws were to continue to apply in the respective territories, until altered by Parliament. {Article Eighth. See *Lane v Bennett* (1836) 1 M & W 70 at p 75; *Swifte v A-G for Ireland* [1912] AC 276.}

Separate legislatures and governments for Northern Ireland and Southern Ireland were established by the Government of Ireland Act 1920. These were subordinate to the United Kingdom government and parliament. In 1922 the south was given dominion status under the name of the Irish Free State. {Irish Free State (Agreement) Act 1922; Irish Free State Constitution Act 1922 (Session 2).}

The style of the Westminster Parliament was altered in 1927 to the Parliament of the United Kingdom of Great Britain and Northern Ireland. {Royal and Parliamentary Titles Act 1927 s 2(1).} In 1937 the name of the Irish Free State was changed to Eire. {Eire (Confirmation of Agreements) Act 1938 s 1. See *Murray v Parkes* [1942] 2 KB 123.} In 1948 it was changed again to the Republic of Ireland. Section 1 of the Ireland Act 1949 provided as follows-

'(1) It is hereby recognized and declared that the part of Ireland heretofore known as Eire ceased, as from 18 April 1949, to be part of His Majesty's dominions.

(2) It is hereby declared that Northern Ireland remains part of His Majesty's dominions and of the United Kingdom and it is hereby affirmed that in no event will Northern Ireland or any part thereof cease to be part of His Majesty's dominions and of the United Kingdom without the consent of the Parliament of Northern Ireland.'

On the abolition of the Parliament of Northern Ireland on 1 January 1974, sub-s (2) was re-enacted as s 1 of the Northern Ireland Constitution Act 1973 in terms which are identical except that for the words following 'without the consent of' there are substituted the words 'the majority of the people of Northern Ireland voting in a poll held for the purposes of this section in accordance with Sch 1 to this Act'.

Section 1 of the Ireland Act 1949 continues-

> '(3) The part of Ireland referred to in subsection (1) of this section is hereafter in this Act referred to, and may in any Act, enactment or instrument passed or made after the passing of this Act be referred to, by the name attributed thereto by the law thereof, that is to say, as the Republic of Ireland.'

Despite these changes the south of Ireland continues to be treated by the Westminster Parliament as to some extent a 'home' country.

Example 1   Without a licence for that purpose, the parent or guardian of a minor is prohibited from allowing him to 'go abroad' for the purpose of singing, playing, performing or being exhibited. {Children and Young Persons Act 1933 s 25(1).} The definition of 'abroad', which remains unaltered, is 'outside Great Britain and Ireland'. {Ibid s 30.}

Example 2   Section 2(1) of the Ireland Act 1949 declares that the Republic of Ireland 'is not a foreign country for the purposes of any law in force in any part of the United Kingdom'. {S 31 of the British Nationality Act 1981 continues the preferential treatment of Irish citizens.}

Further constitutional provision was made by the Northern Ireland Constitution Act 1973 and the Northern Ireland Assembly Act 1973. In place of the Stormont Parliament, the latter Act provided for the setting up of an elected assembly. Temporary provision for direct rule was however made by the Northern Ireland Act 1974. This put the assembly into suspense and authorized its legislative powers to be exercised instead by Order in Council.

Extent of Acts to Northern Ireland   As part of the United Kingdom, the province comes within the presumption that, unless the contrary intenton appears, an Act extends to it. {See s 199 of this Code.}

217. Territorial extent: meaning of 'Scotland'

Scotland is not the subject of a statutory definition. Its only land boundary, largely formed by the River Tweed, is coterminous with, and fixed by, the northern boundary of England. Its seaward boundaries are those of the former kingdom of Scotland and its islands, including the Hebrides and the Orkneys and Shetlands.

COMMENTARY

The name 'Scotland' is simply a matter of repute. It is 'that part of Britain called Scotland'. {See Statute Law Revision Act 1948 s 4(b).}

The name of the country originated in the 11th century from *Scotia*, derived from a portion of its population known as the tribe of Scots. Previously the name Scotia was applied to Ireland, from whence the original Scots are said to have come.

So far as it is bordered by the sea, there can be no doubt as to the boundaries of Scotland. The land boundary is coterminous with that of England. This is explained in s 208 of the Code. As to the union with England see s 209.

Hebrides The Hebrides became part of Scotland in 1266, when all claim to them was renounced by Magnus, king of Norway.

Orkneys and Shetlands The Orkneys and Shetlands became part of Scotland in 1468, when they were pledged by Christian I of Denmark to secure the dowry of his daughter Margaret on her betrothal to James III of Scotland. The dowry remains unpaid.

Berwick upon Tweed For the position of Berwick upon Tweed see s 203 of this Code.

218. Territorial extent: meaning of 'territorial waters'

Except for the purposes of an Act which otherwise provides, the territorial waters of the United Kingdom or a British possession are those waters which lie between the baseline and a line three nautical miles seaward of the baseline.

COMMENTARY

Baseline See s 202 of this Code.

History At common law the territorial waters did not form part of the realm. This was finally decided by the majority of the judges in the *Franconia* case. {*R v Keyn* (1876) 2 Ex D 63.} The decision contradicted Blackstone's remark that 'the main or high seas are part of the realm of England' {Kerr Bl (4th edn, 1876) i 84.} and also the view taken by Parliament in s 2 of the Foreign Enlistment Act 1870. {See also the Customs Consolidation Act 1876 s 179). Coke said that the main or high seas were not subject to the common law. {Co Litt 260.}

The decision in the *Franconia* case was reversed by the Territorial Waters Jurisdiction Act 1878. Expressing Parliament's concurrence with the minority opinion of the judges in that case, the preamble to the Act stated that the jurisdiction of the Crown 'extends and has always extended' over the open sea 'to such a distance as is necessary for the defence and security' of the country. In the eighteenth century this distance had become fixed at one marine league (three nautical miles). It then represented the range of cannon fire. The width of the territorial sea thus accorded with the maxim *terrae dominium finitur ubi finitur armorum vis* (the dominion of the land ends where the power of arms ends), sometimes known as the cannon shot rule.

The decision as to what constitutes territorial waters is now regarded as a matter within the royal prerogative. Lord Parker CJ said that-

' . . . [it] is a matter of sovereignty; it is a matter of the extension of sovereignty over the high seas, and, as such is particularly a matter for the Crown from time to time under the prerogative to determine.'

{*R v Kent JJ, ex p Lye* [1967] 2 QB 153, at p 174. Cf *Direct United States Cable Co v Anglo-American Telegraph Co* (1877) 2 App Cas 394. See also Examples 198.1 and 395.2.}

It is noteworthy however that the saving in s 5 of the Territorial Waters Jurisdiction Act 1878 refers to jurisdiction under the law of nations or by statute but not to the prerogative. {It is said that in this respect the existence of prerogative powers has been asserted only recently: see Edeson 'The Prerogative of the Crown to delimit Britain's maritime boundary' (1973) 89 LQR 364.}

Territorial Waters Jurisdiction Act The 1878 Act (which is still in force) is limited to criminal jurisdiction. This is in accordance with the way such matters have been traditionally dealt with by Parliament. Instead of declaring that the law of the territory extended to its waters, Parliament confined statutory interference to the matter of most important practical concern. Other aspects (such as the question of the tortious liability which on the mainland often accompanies a criminal act or omission) were left in doubt.

Section 2 of the Territorial Waters Jurisdiction Act 1878 states-

> 'An offence committed by a person, whether he is or is not a subject of Her Majesty, on the open seas within the territorial waters of Her Majesty's dominions, is an offence within the jurisdiction of the Admiral, although it may have been committed on board or by means of a foreign ship, and the person who committed such offence may be arrested, tried and punished accordingly.'

{In this passage 'ship' includes a hovercraft (Hovercraft (Application of Enactments) Order 1972, SI 1972/971) but not a foreign public vessel (*Chung Chi-Cheung v The King* [1939] AC 160).}

The office of Admiral probably dated from the thirteenth century and later carried the title Lord High Admiral. At common law the Admiralty jurisdiction extended only to treason, felony and conspiracy. {See Offences at Sea Act 1536, repealed by the Criminal Law Act 1967 s 10 Sch 3 Pt I.} Even as subsequently extended by statute, the jurisdiction apparently never extended to summary offences. By virtue of s 6 of the Courts Act 1971 the jurisdiction is now vested, so far as concerns England and Wales, in the Crown Court. {See further Law Commisson 'Report on the Territorial and Extraterritorial Extent of the Criminal Law' (1978) Law Com No 91; [1979] Crim LR 355, 778, 781.}

Section 7 of the 1878 Act contains a definition of the phrase 'the territorial waters of Her Majesty's dominions' as used in s 2 (the only place in the Act where it appears). In relation to the United Kingdom it means 'such part of the sea adjacent to the coast . . . as is deemed by international law to be within the territorial sovereignty of Her Majesty'. This would include sea areas, known as 'historical bays' or 'historical waters', which by long usage are internationally accepted as falling within the territory. {See p 467 above.} It principally refers however to the area for the time being accepted generally as constituting territorial waters. For the United Kingdom at the present day this means the area delimited by the Territorial Waters Order in Council 1964 as amended. {See below.}

Section 7 continues with a provision that has caused difficulty in interpretation-

' . . . and for the purpose of any offence declared by this Act to be within the jurisdiction of the Admiral, any part of the open sea within one marine league of the coast measured from low-water mark shall be deemed to be open sea within the territorial waters of Her Majesty's dominions.'

The drafting is clumsy, but the combined effect of the provisions appears to be this. An offence committed on the open sea is within the Admiral's jurisdiction if committed on what at the relevant time are regarded in international law as the territorial waters. Furthermore, even if committed *outside* those waters, it is still within the Admiral's jurisdiction if committed within three nautical miles of the low water line.

The purpose of the second limb of the definition was no doubt to avoid argument about what is or is not internationally agreed (notoriously a difficult matter) in cases where the offence is anyway within the three mile limit. {The Law Commission appear to take the contrary view, namely that only the second limb is applicable: Law Com No 91, para 20. This reading deprives the first limb of any meaning or purpose, and is contrary to the principle of statutory interpretation described at pp 375–376 above (all words of Act to be given meaning).}

Difficulty also arises from the fact that s 2 speaks only of offences committed 'on' the open seas. Under modern conditions it is of course possible for offences also to be committed under or above the sea. {As to the effect on interpretation of developments occurring after the passing of an Act see the treatment of updating construction in s 146 of this Code.}

Territorial Waters Order in Council 1964 The Territorial Waters Order in Council 1964 as amended {For details see above.} defines the United Kingdom territorial waters as being bounded by a line three nautical miles seaward of the baseline fixed by the order. {As to this baseline see s 202 of the Code.} Unless the contrary intention appears, it is assumed that a reference in an Act passed after the making of this order to the territorial waters or territorial sea is to be construed accordingly. {The Finance Act 1972 s 46(4) refers to 'the territorial sea'. It is not thought there is any difference in meaning between the two expressions.}

Home Secretary's certificate Since the question is one of the prerogative, the court will accept as conclusive (at least in civil cases) a certificate by the Home Secretary that a certain point is or is not within territorial waters. Thus in *The Fagernes* {[1927] P 311.} a certificate was given which stated that 'the spot where this collision is alleged to have occurred is not within the limits to which the territorial sovereignty of His Majesty extends'.

Where Act otherwise provides It is of course open to Parliament to provide in any particular Act for a different definition of territorial waters to apply for the purposes of the Act. In this connection the following comment by the Law Commission is of interest-

'In some recent Acts, it is not clear upon what basis the territorial limits are to be measured. Under the Protection of Wrecks Act 1973, indictable offences created by the Act may be committed in "the sea within the seaward limits" of territorial waters, "the sea" including "any estuary or arm of the sea". In others, it seems clear that measurement is to be made by reference to the 1964 order: see e g Marine etc Broadcasting (Offences) Act 1967, Wireless Telegraphy Act 1967 s 9(1) and Sea Fisheries Act 1968.'

{Law Com No 91, footnote 34.}

Fishery limits   Parliament may assert jurisdiction for certain purposes over the high seas. Thus fishery limits are not necessarily coterminous with territorial waters. {See the Fishery Limits Act 1976, which lays down limits extending over a strip two hundred miles from the relevant baselines.}

219. Territorial extent: meaning of 'United Kingdom'

Unless the contrary intention appears, in an Act passed before 12 April 1927 the term 'United Kingdom' means Great Britain and Ireland, while in an Act passed on or after 12 April 1927 it means Great Britain and Northern Ireland.

COMMENTARY

This section derives from the Interpretation Act 1978 ss 5 and 22(1), Sch 1 and Sch 2 para 4(1).

The expression 'the United Kingdom' originated on the union of England and Scotland in 1707. {See, e g, the reference in art 24 of the Union with Scotland Act 1706 to 'that part of the United Kingdom now called Scotland'.} The territory now constituting Northern Ireland became part of the United Kingdom under the Union with Ireland Act 1800, which took effect on 1 January 1801. On this date 'and for ever after' the kingdom of Great Britain and the kingdom of Ireland were united into one kingdom by the name of the United Kingdom of Great Britain and Ireland. {Article First.}

The style was altered in 1927 to the United Kingdom of Great Britain and Northern Ireland. {Royal and Parliamentary Titles Act 1927 s 2(2).} In general, references to the United Kingdom in Acts passed before the establishment of the Irish Free State do not include the Republic of Ireland. {Irish Free State (Consequential Adaptation of Enactments) Order 1923 (SR & O 1923/405).}

220. Territorial extent: meaning of 'Wales'

Unless the contrary intention appears, in an Act passed before 1 April 1974 the term 'Wales' means the dominion or principality of Wales, while in an Act passed on or after 1 April 1974 it means, subject to any alteration of boundaries made under Part IV of the Local Government Act 1972, the area consisting of the counties established by section 20 of that Act.

COMMENTARY

This section derives from the Interpretation Act 1978 ss 5 and 22(1) and Sch 1. It originated in s 269 of the Local Government Act 1972, before the enactment of which there was no full definition. As to the inclusion of the former county of Monmouth in Wales see s 215 of this Code. References to England in Acts passed between the passing of the Wales and Berwick Act 1746 and the Welsh Language Act 1967 were taken, by virtue of the former Act, to include Wales. {See p 469 above.}

The absorption of Wales, 'retreat of the ancient Britons', into England is thus described by Blackstone-

> 'Wales continued independent of England, unconquered and uncultivated, in the primitive pastoral state which Caesar and Tacitus ascribe to Britain in general, for many centuries; even from the time of hostile invasions of the Saxons, when the ancient and Christian inhabitants of the island retired to those natural intrenchments, for protection from their pagan visitants. But when these invaders themselves were converted to Christianity, and settled into regular and potent governments, this retreat of the ancient Britons grew every day narrower; they were overrun by little and little, gradually driven from one fastness to another, and by repeated losses abridged of their wild independence, till at length in the reign of Edward the First, who may justly be styled the conqueror of Wales, the line of their ancient princes was abolished, and the king of England's eldest son became their titular prince; the territory of Wales being then entirely annexed to the dominion of the Crown of England.'

{Kerr Bl (4th edn, 1876) i 68.}

The statute, or rather ordinance, effecting this annexation was the Statutum Walliae or Statute of Rhuddlan, promulgated in 1284. {12 Edw 1, repealed with savings by the Statute Law Revision Act 1887 s 1.} The term annexation should not here be understood in its modern sense: what the ordinance did was to render the area feudally subject to the English kings. It did not in general abrogate the local law.

The union was completed by the statute 27 Hen 8 c 26, which in 1948 was given the somewhat inadequate short title of the Laws in Wales Act 1535. {See Statute Law Revision Act 1948 s 5 and Sch 2. See also the Laws in Wales Act 1542.} By this, Wales was united with England and made subject to English law.

APPLICATION OF AN ENACTMENT

221. Application: general principles

Unless the contrary intention appears, and subject to any privilege, immunity or disability arising under the law of the territory to which an enactment extends (that is within which it is law), and to any relevant rule of private international law, an enactment applies to all persons and matters within the territory to which it extends, but not to any other persons and matters.

COMMENTARY

An Act is taken to be for the governance of the territory to which it extends, that is the territory throughout which it is law. {As to the territorial extent of Acts see s 195 of this Code.} Other territories are governed by their own laws. The principle of comity between nations requires that each nation should be left to govern its own territory.

An Act does not usually apply to acts or omissions taking place outside its territory, whether they involve foreigners or Britons. The basic principle is that words of written or unwritten law expressed in general terms are taken to be subject to an implied limitation which confines their effect to the territorial jurisdiction. Thus Viscount Simonds said that one obvious reason for restricting the apparent width of the literal meaning of an Act is 'a principle of comity which confines its operation within the territorial jurisdiction of the enacting State'. {*A-G v Prince Ernest Augustus of Hanover* [1957] AC 436, at p 462.}

Maxwell puts it this way-

> 'Under the general presumption that the legislature does not intend to exceed its jurisdiction, every statute is interpreted, so far as its language permits, so as not to be inconsistent with the comity of nations or the established rules of international law, and the court will avoid a construction which would give rise to such inconsistency unless compelled to adopt it by plain and unambiguous language.'

{P B Maxwell *The Interpretation of Statutes* (12th edn, 1969) p 183. The passage is based on a dictum of Sir James Hannen P in *Bloxam v Favre* (1883) 8 PD 101, at p 104. Cf *R v Anderson* (1868) LR 1 CCR 161, *per* Blackburn J at p 170.}

This is one of many instances where the express words of an Act are taken to be subject to implications altering their literal meaning. {As to implications in statutory interpretation see ss 107 to 110 of this Code.}

The rules of comity and international law reflect the obvious fact that it is for each territorial government to regulate the inhabitants and affairs of its own territory. In British colonial legislation the traditional phrase used to describe this function was the making of provision for *the peace, order and good government* of the territory. {See British Settlements Act 1887 s 2.}

In *Macleod v A-G of New South Wales* {[1891] AC 455, at p 458.} the Judicial Committee of the Privy Council adopted the opinion of Parke B expressed in his advice to the House of Lords in *Jeffreys v Boosey* {(1854) 4 HLC 815, at p 926.}-

> 'The legislature has no power over any persons except its own subjects - that is, persons natural-born subjects, or resident, or whilst they are within the limits of the kingdom. The legislature can impose no duties except on them, and when legislating for the benefit of persons must prima facie be considered to mean the benefit of those who owe obedience to our laws and whose interests the legislature is under a correlative obligation to protect.'

In relation to citizens of the territory who are within it, and matters within it having no foreign connection, the position is clear. They are subject to the laws of their territory, and no other laws compete with those.

Foreign element   Difficulties arise as to the operation of the enactment where there is a foreign element. A person within its territory is a foreigner. Property within the territory is owned by a foreigner. A citizen of the territory, for which its law retains some concern, does a significant act in a foreign country. And so on.

In explaining the general principles laid down by the courts in this field, we may speak in terms of what is and is not 'foreign'. A broad brush is needed, even though the actual position may not be clearcut for reasons such as the following. The extent of the enactment may not cover the whole area of Parliament's jurisdiction. There are three different categories of British citizenship. Independent Commonwealth countries are not regarded by British law as altogether 'foreign'. Special rules apply in the criminal field.

These and other complications mean that our analysis must be somewhat crude. In applying it, the interpreter needs to look for individual statutory rules modifying its generalised approach in the case of particular enactments. For the purpose of general propositions within the remainder of this Part, we divide people into 'Britons' and 'foreigners'. The terms 'British' and 'foreign' are to be understood accordingly.

To a limited extent cases with a 'foreign' element are dealt with by rules of private international law. Sometimes these are applied directly, by express enactment. {See, e g, the Civil Jurisdiction and Judgments Act 1982.} Others are imported by implication. {As to the implied importation of rules of private international law in the operation of enactments see s 342 of this Code.} Principles of public international law may also be relevant, though these are not by implication imported directly unless also part of the municipal law. {As to the relevance of public international law in statutory interpretation see s 134 of this Code.}

Apart from such rules, the matter is mainly dealt with by presumptions as to the intention of the legislator. These are described in the following sections of this Part. First we look at the nature of extra-territorial legislation.

Extra-territorial legislation In the British Commonwealth a mark of the attainment of full nationhood following colonial status has been taken to be the gaining of the power to legislate extra-territorially. Thus s 3 of the Statute of Westminster 1931 'declared and enacted that the Parliament of a Dominion has full power to make laws having extra-territorial operation'. {The Dominions referred to were Canada, Australia, New Zealand, South Africa, the Irish Free State and Newfoundland: s 1.} The United Kingdom Parliament, like that of any independent state, of course possesses this full power.

It is important to be clear what the power involves. A legislature does not have the capacity to *make law* for a territory outside its jurisdiction, so that what it enacts becomes part of the *corpus juris* of that external territory. The true position was put by Wheare-

> 'It is a mark of a sovereign, independent state that its legislature has power to make laws with extra-territorial effect. The nature and extent of this power should not be misunderstood. Extra-territorial legislation simply means legislation which attaches significance for courts within the jurisdiction to facts and events occurring outside the jurisdiction. This does not imply that one state can pass laws for another state, or that several systems of law will be in operation regulating a particular sphere within any given state.'

{K C Wheare *The Constitutional Structure of the Commonwealth* p 43.}

The latter part of this passage applies only as between independent sovereign states. Several systems of law may regulate the same matter in a dependent territory, or in one forming part of a federal or quasi-federal system. {As to the position of EEC legislation in the United Kingdom see pp 175–176 above.}

Similarly, the territory of a soveregn state may be divided into areas each having a different system of law. This is the position as between England and Wales on the one hand and Scotland on the other. In relation to such divided areas the same implied limitation on the operation of enactments is applied as prevails between different sovereign states.

Example 1   In *Forsyth v Forsyth* {[1948] P 125.} the Court of Appeal refused to make a maintenance order under an English Act against a deserting husband who at all material times had been domiciled and resident in Scotland.

Example 2   In *McCullie v Butler* {[1962] 2 QB 309.} it was held that 'solicitor' in the Legal Aid and Advice Act 1949 did not include a Scottish solicitor, who 'must be treated, for the purposes of taxation [of costs], simply as a foreign agent'. {P 313, *per* Diplock J.}

222. Application: foreigners and foreign matters within the territory

Unless the contrary intention appears, and subject to any privilege, immunity or disability arising under the law of the territory to which an enactment extends, and to any relevant rule of private international law, the enactment applies to foreigners and foreign matters within its territory as it applies to persons and matters within that territory belonging to it.

COMMENTARY

In identifying the persons and matters to which an Act applies, it is necessary to distinguish the territory where the Act is law from all other territories. {As to the general principles governing an Act's operation as part of the law of a territory see s 30 of this Code. The rules defining the territorial extent of an Act are set out in s 195.}

In considering the application of an Act to persons or matters belonging outside its territory (though at the time in question situated within that territory), the Act is not to be considered as standing by itself. A particular Act forms a part of the entire *corpus juris* (both written and unwritten) of its territory. Subject to any special provision made by the Act itself, its intended application is therefore taken to accord with the principles governing that body of law generally.

Where however a particular code of law has its own rules of territorial effect an Act within its ambit will, in the absence of a contrary indication, be taken as intended to conform to those rules. For an example see the rules as to the application of criminal law described in s 225 of this Code.

The law proceeds on the general assumption that by entering a territory a person who belongs outside submits to its laws, and also claims the benefit of them. Blackstone said that 'to kill an alien or an outlaw, who are all under the king's peace and protection, is as much murder as to kill the most regular born

Englishman; except he be an alien enemy in time of war'. {Kerr Bl (4th edn, 1876) iv 197-8.}

When discussing earlier how an Act operates as the law of a territory we used the image of a floodlight switched on and illuminating that territory. {See pp 90–93 above.} Now we vary the metaphor and think of the Act, together with the rest of the territory's laws, as providing the legal *atmosphere* the inhabitants breathe.

This concept derives from a remark by Lord Mansfield in *Somerset v Stewart.* {(1772) Lofft 1-19; 20 St Tr 1-82.} Towards the end of the eighteenth century, the owner of a slave named James Somerset brought him on a visit from Jamaica to England. While the owner went about his business, he claimed the right to imprison his human property in irons until the ship which had brought that property to England set sail again for Jamaica. Lord Mansfield gave his judgment-

'Every man who comes into England is entitled to the protection of English law, whatever oppression he may heretofore have suffered and whatever may be the colour of his skin. The air of England is too pure for any slave to breathe. Let the black go free.'

There are many decisions to the effect that, in the absence of contrary indication, an Act, as part of the general law, applies equally to all who are within its territory.

Example 1 *R v Inhabitants of Eastbourne* {(1803) 4 East 103.} concerned the position of alien paupers under the old poor law. The concept of 'settlement' of paupers, introduced by the Poor Relief Act 1601, meant that a pauper was taken to be attached to a particular parish which was then under a duty to support him. For this purpose he was deemed to be 'settled' in the place of his birth unless shown to have acquired a settlement elsewhere. The Court of Queen's Bench held that aliens could benefit from these provisions in the same way as citizens. Lord Ellenborough CJ said {P 107.}-

'As to there being no obligation for maintaining poor foreigners before the statutes ascertaining the different methods of acquiring settlements, the law of humanity, which is anterior to all positive laws, obliges us to afford them relief, to save them from starving; and those laws were only passed to fix the obligation more certainly, and point out distinctly in what manner it should be borne.'

Since that time there have been many welfare Acts providing facilities available to anyone who is in the country.

Example 2 The National Health Service Act 1946 required the appropriate Minister to establish a comprehensive health service designed to promote the physical and mental health of 'the people of England and Wales'. {S 1. Similar provision was made for Scotland by the National Health Service (Scotland) Act 1947.} This provision has been regarded as applying in the same way to all who find themselves within the territory to which the Act extends. This is shown by the fact that in 1949 Parliament gave power to impose charges under the Act for health facilities provided to persons not ordinarily resident in that territory. {National Health Service (Amendment) Act 1949 s 17.} The power has not been used.

In the housing field the welfare legislation has again been taken to apply to anyone in the country.

Example 3 The Housing (Homeless Persons) Act 1977 places a duty on local authorities in relation to 'a homeless person'. This is taken to include anyone who finds himself homeless within the Act's territory, whatever his nationality or origin. The House of Lords has accepted this notwithstanding that it presents serious problems for authorities whose area comprises an international airport.

Lord Wilberforce commented on the difficulties these 'airport cases' cause the London Borough of Hillingdon. Its area includes London Heathrow airport 'through which a number of persons arrive in this country who have no accomodation'. {*Islam v London Borough of Hillingdon* [1981] 3 All ER 901, at p 903.} Lord Wilberforce went on to remark {P 905.}-

> 'While . . . I entirely accept that immigrants as such are not intended to be excluded from the Act, I share Ackner LJ's misgiving whether, in relation to persons coming from overseas (whether the EEC or otherwise) . . . the Act is as well considered as it is undoubtedly well intentioned.'

This failure to deal adequately with the foreign dimension where an Act has no obvious international nexus is a common feature of our legislation. The attention of those concerned with preparing the Act is concentrated on the problems of the British public. Peripheral aspects escape notice until too late. This gives the courts difficulty in arriving at 'the intention of Parliament'. In any meaningful sense, this intention simply does not exist. {As to the task of the interpreter when dealing with this type of defect see s 103 of the Code.}

As well as enjoying the benefits of laws from which they are not expressly excluded, foreigners in the country must also accept the burdens the laws impose. As James LJ said in *Ex parte Blain* {(1879) 12 Ch D 522, at p 526.}, there is no doubt that an English Act applies 'to foreigners who, by coming into this country, whether for a long or a short time, have made themselves during that time subject to English jurisdiction'.

Foreigners and their property situated within the country 'are totally subject to our laws'. {*Gold Star Publications Ltd v DPP* [1981] 2 All ER 257, *per* Lord Wilberforce at p 259.} There can be no objection to their property, rights or interests within the country being subjected to legislative control by Parliament. {Ibid, at p 265, *per* Lord Roskill. See also (as to variation of trusts) *Re Seale's Marriage Settlement* [1961] Ch 574; *Re Paget's Settlement* [1965] 1 WLR 1046; *Re Ker's Settlement* [1963] Ch 553. As to foreigners' property, rights or interests *outside* the Act's territory see s 223 of this Code.} Thus land in England, although owned by an alien, is governed by English municipal law. {*Birtwhistle v Vardill* (1840) 7 Cl & F 895; *Freke v Lord Carbery* (1873) LR 16 Eq 461.}

Overseas property of resident foreigner The mere presence of a foreigner within the jurisdiction does not however bring his overseas property and affairs within the scope of its laws. The greatly increased mobility produced by modern air travel make this a vitally necessary rule. The overseas matters must have some nexus with the territory for its laws to apply.

Example 4 In *Colquhoun v Brooks* {(1888) 21 QBD 52. Affd by HL (1889) 14 App Cas 493.} the respondent, an Australian citizen resident in England, was a sleeping partner in a business wholly conducted in Australia. Part of his share of the profits was remitted to him in England. The remainder was retained in Australia. The Inland Revenue sought to charge tax on the unremitted profits by virtue of s 1 of the Income Tax Act 1853. A selective comminution of s 1 reads-

> 'Income tax is charged for and in respect of the annual profits accruing to any person resident in the United Kingdom from any trade, whether the same shall be exercised in the United Kingdom or elsewhere.'

Held Tax was not chargeable on the unremitted profits, even though the literal meaning of s 1 clearly covered them. Lord Esher MR said {Pp 56–59.} that, while it was impossible to have words larger than the words used, their literal application would produce a result absolutely contrary to the comity of nations. It would subject this country to remonstrances from foreign governments which it could not answer. He went on-

> ' . . . the English parliament cannot be supposed merely by reason of its having used general words to be intending to do that which is against the comity of nations. It is true that if we came to the conclusion that this had been intentionally done we must carry out the law and leave to the government of the country the task of answering objections, but unless that is perfectly clear we ought to limit the words so as to make them reasonable and proper . . .
>
> I come to the conclusion that the statute was only dealing with that with which it has a right to deal, and not with land or business carried on in other countries with which we have no right to interfere, and that the words must be limited, and do not apply to an absolutely foreign trade, no part of which is connected with this country.'

In addition English courts apply the rules of private international law, under which for example dispositions of personal property are governed by the law of the domicile. {As to the effect of private international law on the interpretation of statutes see s 342 of this Code.}

Privileges and immunities Certain doctrines based on the comity of nations provide an exception to the rule that resident aliens are intended to be treated by the law in the same way as citizens.

The doctrine of sovereign immunity excludes from the jurisdiction of the court property in the ownership, possession or control of a foreign sovereign state, or in which such a state claims an interest. {*Compania Naviera Vascongada v Steamship Cristina* [1938] AC 485; *United States of America v Dollfus Mieg et Cie SA* [1952] AC 582.} Equally the court cannot inquire into a sovereign act of state (including an act of war), whether by its own government or another. {*Duke of Brunswick v King of Hanover* (1844) 6 Beav 1 (affd (1848) 2 HL Cas 1); *D F Marais v G O C Lines of Communication, ex p D F Marais* [1902] AC 109; *Buttes Gas & Oil Co v Hammer* [1981] 3 All ER 616.}

Example 5 In *Mighell v Sultan of Johore* {[1894] 1 QB 149.} an Indian prince, while visiting England, entered into a contract to marry the plaintiff. He broke the contract, and she sued him for breach of promise. *Held* As the ruler of what for the purposes of the action was to be taken as an independent foreign state, the Sultan was immune from process. The Sultan had abandoned all right to contract with foreign states, and had placed his territory under British protection. The court held that he was, nevertheless, a foreign sovereign so far as immunity from British jurisdiction was concerned. Wills J said {P 153.}-

> 'The ground upon which the immunity of sovereign rulers from process in our courts is recognized by our law, is that it would be absolutely inconsistent with the status of an independent sovereign that he should be subject to the process of a foreign tribunal.'

Example 6 In *The Parlement Belge* {(1880) 5 PD 197.} an attempt was made in the Admiralty Division of the High Court to enforce the seizure of a ship to secure redress for collision damage. It was proved that the ship was the property of the King of the Belgians, being used to carry mails for the Belgian government as well as passengers and freight. The court held that sovereign immunity protected the ship from seizure. {Later judicial development withdrew this protection where the property was used for purely commercial operations: see *Campania Naviera Vascongado v Steamship Cristina* [1938] AC 485; *The Porto Alexandre* [1920] P 30. See now State Immunity Act 1978.}

Example 7 In the course of armed conflict between Malaysia and Indonesia, Indonesian troops were engaged in warlike operations on Malaysian territory. In *Public Prosecutor v Oie Hee Koi* {[1968] AC 829.} it was argued that an Indonesian soldier found in possession of firearms on Malaysian territory was in contravention of the Malayan Internal Security Act 1960 s 57(1), which made possession of firearms without lawful excuse an offence. *Held* The Act did not apply in such circumstances. Lord Hodson said {P 860.}-

> 'True that the language of s 57 covers "any person", but upon its proper construction s 57 cannot be read so widely as to cover members of the regular Indonesian armed forces fighting as such in Malaysia in the course of what, it has been assumed, was an armed conflict between Malaysia and Indonesia. The Act is an Internal Security measure, part of the domestic law, and not directed at the military forces of a hostile power attacking Malaysia.'

The decision depends on the concept of acts of state (including acts of war). It does not apply to persons who are engaged in unlawful insurrection, and do not act on behalf of a sovereign state. They are subject to the ordinary criminal law.

The immunities and privileges enjoyed by diplomatic agents of foreign and Commonwealth countries are regulated by the Vienna Convention on Diplomatic Relations, which came into force on 24 April 1964. Its main provisions were given the force of law in the United Kingdom by s 2 of the Diplomatic Privileges Act 1964. Parallel provision in relation to consular officers is made by the Vienna Convention on Consular Relations (implemented by the Consular Relations Act 1968).

Exterritoriality These various immunities and privileges are ascribed in international law to the principle of exterritoriality. Nowadays this is perhaps more usually called extra-territoriality. To avoid confusion, the latter term is however reserved in this work for the opposite concept of the application of an Act outside its territory.

The doctrine of exterritoriality applies both to persons and their property, and relates to all cases in which a state refrains from enforcing its laws within the territory of its jurisdiction. The doctrine thus extends to ships in territorial waters (in cases where the ship belongs to a foreign state and is used wholly or mainly for that state's public purposes). It is described by an eighteenth-century commentator in these terms-

> 'That as by one fiction of positive law an ambassador is considered as the representative of the nation which sends him, so by another like fiction of the same law he is considered as if he was out of the territory, though he is in it.'

{Rutherforth *Institutes* II (1756), ii, ix, para 20.603.}

Exterritoriality is also on some occasions granted by treaty in terms which extend to private citizens of a high contracting party. Examples include the treaties by which China formerly admitted English traders to certain enclaves, and the privileges of Christians under arrangements made with the Ottoman Porte.

Exterritoriality may apply to members of the armed forces of foreign states who are in authorised transit or temporary residence. The Visiting Forces Act 1952 allows certain matters concerning visiting forces in the United Kingdom to be dealt with by service courts applying their own law, instead of in accordance with local law. {See ss 2 and 3. The Act is applied to British colonies and dependencies by s 15.} Similar provision is made in relation to certain international organisations. {International Headquarters and Defence Organizations Act 1964 s 1.} A statutory limitation period does not begin to run against a claimant while the immunity operates. {*Musurus Bey v Gadban* [1894] 2 QB 352.}

Waiver The privileges and immunities mentioned above relate to legal process, and do not negative the existence of legal liability. They can be waived by those entitled to them, and the effect of such waiver is to restore the full operation of the original liability.

The right to waive a defence is in accordance with the principle expressed in the maxim *quilibet potest renunciare juri pro se introducto*: every man is entitled to give up a right introduced in his favour. {2 Co Inst 183; Co Litt 99a.} An insurer thus called upon to pay cannot resist on the ground that the waiver was a voluntary act. {*Dickinson v Del Solar* [1930] 1 KB 376. As to the plea of volenti non fit injuria see s 358 of this Code. See further as to waiver ss 11 and 12 of this Code.}

Disabilities There are certain statutory disabilities on aliens. These are taken to modify the express words of an Act unless the Act indicates that they are not to apply. Thus s 3 of the Act of Settlement (1700) precludes foreign-born persons whose parents are not British subjects from holding certain offices and positions. {As to express disapplication of this disability see the Aliens' Employment Act 1955 s 1. See also the Status of Aliens Act 1914 and the Aliens Restriction (Amendment) Act 1919.}

223. Application: foreigners and foreign matters outside the territory

Unless the contrary intention appears, and subject to any relevant rules of private international law, an enactment is taken not to apply to foreigners and foreign matters outside the territory to which it extends.

COMMENTARY

In this section, 'foreigner' is used in contradistinction to 'Briton'. {For the reasons for this crude nomenclature see p 489 above.} The wording of this section is similar to that of s 224 of this Code. Foreigners and Britons are treated separately in this way because the contrary intention more frequently appears in the case of Britons.

In identifying the persons and matters to which an enactment applies, it is necessary to distinguish the territory over which the Act is law from all other territories. {As to the territorial extent of enactments see s 195 of this Code. For the general principles as to application of enactments see s 221.} In considering what application an Act may have outside its territory, the Act is not to be considered as standing by itself. The individual Act forms merely a part of the entire *corpus juris* (both written and unwritten) of its territory.

Subject to any special provision made by the Act itself, the intended application (if any) of the Act outside its territory is therefore taken to accord with the general principles governing the external application of the body of territorial law. Where special principles are applicable to law of the kind dealt with by the Act (for example criminal law) these will of course apply to the Act as well.

If a legislature seeks to go beyond the basic function of government and legislate for foreigners outside its territory it is likely to displease other nations whose function it is usurping. This fact of international relations was recognised by Lindley MR in *Re A B & Co* {[1900] 1 QB 541.}, when replying to the argument that the court had power to make bankrupt a foreigner resident abroad-

> 'Unless Parliament has conferred on the court that power in language which is unmistakeable, the court is not to assume that Parliament intended to do that which might seriously affect foreigners who are not resident here and might give offence to foreign governments.'

{P 544. For a case where such unmistakeable language was used in relation to bankruptcy see *Theophile v S-G* [1950] AC 186 (foreigner who has ceased trading in England and left the country leaving debts unpaid is 'carrying on business in England' within the meaning of Bankruptcy Act 1914 s 1(2)(c)).}

In another case Lord Simon of Glaisdale (dissenting, but not on this point) referred to 'the undoubted principle that it is only exceptionally (and then by clear words) that United Kingdom legislation operates extra-territorially'. He went on to say that two concepts lie behind this rule, namely international comity and the concept 'that Parliament does not legislate where it has no effective power of enforcement'. He added-

> 'Other than quite exceptionally, sovereigns do not meddle with the subjects of foreign sovereigns within the jurisdiction of those foreign

sovereigns, a consideration inherently potent where international standards vary greatly.'

{*Gold Star Publications Ltd v DPP* [1981] 2 All ER 257, at p 261.}

Dr Lushington earlier stressed the same point when he said that 'the British Parliament has no proper authority to legislate for foreigners out of its jurisdiction', adding that 'no statute ought therefore to be held to apply to foreigners with respect to transactions out of British jurisdiction unless the words of the statute are perfectly clear'. {*The Amalia* (1863) 1 Moo PCC NS 471, at p 474.}

Subjection to law involves protection by the law in return, which foreigners out of the jurisdiction are not in a position to receive. As Blackstone put it, 'protection and subjection are reciprocal'. {Kerr Bl (4th edn, 1876) i 207.} Coke expressed the principle in the maxim *extra territorium jus dicenti impune non paretur* (the pronouncement of one who adjudicates beyond his jurisdiction can be disobeyed with impunity). {10 Co Rep 77. The maxim was cited by Lord Halsbury in *Cooke v Charles A Vogeler & Co* [1901] AC 102, at p 108.}

Example 1   In *Madrazo v Willes* {(1820) 3 B & Ald 353.} a foreign national recovered damages for the seizure by a British warship of a cargo of slaves in purported exercise of authority conferred by an Act held not to apply to foreigners when acting outside British territory.

Example 2   *Air-India v Wiggins* {[1980] 2 All ER 593.} concerned the ill-treatment of a consignment of parakeets flown from India to London, where all the relevant birds died before the aircraft entered United Kingdom airspace. The airline were convicted of contravening an order which read-

> 'No person shall carry any animal [defined to include birds] by sea, air, road or rail, or cause or permit any animal to be so carried, in a way which is likely to cause injury or unnecessary suffering . . .'

The House of Lords quashed the conviction. Lord Diplock {P 596.} cited with approval the following dictum of Lord Russell CJ-

> 'One other general canon of construction is this - that if any construction otherwise be possible, an Act will not be construed as applying to foreigners in respect to acts done by them outside the dominions of the sovereign power enacting.'

{*R v Jameson* [1896] 2 QB 425, at p 430.}

Lord Diplock said that if the Minister indeed had power to make the order in question 'such power must have been conferred on him by words in the statute so clear and specific as to be incapable of any other meaning'. He added that furthermore 'the words of the order must themselves be explicable only as a clear and unambiguous exercise of that power'. {P 596.}

The principle excluding foreigners abroad from the ambit of Acts does not apply only to onerous Acts. Even where an Act confers a benefit, its width will be taken to be impliedly restricted so as to exclude foreigners who are out of the jurisdiction.

Example 3   The Copyright Act 1709 gave a copyright to 'the author of any book'. The House of Lords held that this general phrase 'author' must be taken to include only authors who were either British subjects or were aliens resident in the territory covered by the Act at the time of publication of the work. {*Jeffreys v Boosey* (1854) 4 HLC 815.}

Lord Cranworth pointed out that copyright restricted the liberty of people to enjoy works. He said: 'the object of giving the privilege must be taken to have been a national object, and the privileged class to be confined to a portion of that community for the general advantage of which the enactment is made'. {P 955.} Lord Brougham added a reference to the fact that the legislature normally confined an Act 'to its own subjects over whom it has authority and to whom it owes a duty in return for their obedience'. {P 970.}

A modern Copyright Act will carefully spell out the position of foreigners under it, as indeed all modern Acts should do. {See Copyright Act 1956 Pt V. Cf *Princess of Reuss v Bos* (1871) LR 5 HL 176 (foreigners entitled to register a company in England where it was to do some business there).}

In the same way, a general reference in an enactment relating to the legal, administrative or other official arrangements of the territory will be treated as by implication confined to those arrangements.

Example 4 Section 67(1) of the Criminal Justice Act 1967 says that the length of a sentence of imprisonment imposed on an offender shall be treated as reduced 'by any period during which he was in custody . . . by an *order* of a *court* made in connection with any *proceedings* relating to that sentence or the offence for which it was passed'. {Emphasis added.} In *R v Bennett* {[1975] Crim LR 654.} the Court of Appeal treated the italicised words as relating only to matters within the jurisdiction. Imprisonment served in Canada prior to extradition for the offence was not therefore counted. {For criticism of this see Nigel Shepherd 'When is a Court not a Court' [1975] Crim LR 629. The criticism omits the reasoning given here.}

By analogy of reasoning, doctrines such as that of *autrefois acquit* do not take account of foreign proceedings. This does not however mean that the principle of fairness underlying such a doctrine will not be invoked in suitable cases to produce a similar result. {See *Treacy v Director of Public Prosecutions* [1971] AC 537, at p 561. See also *R v Roche* (1775) 1 Leach 134; *R v King* [1897] 1 QB 214; *R v Aughet* (1918) 13 Cr App R 101; *R v Thomas (Keith William)* (1984) *The Times* 12 April.}

Submission to the jurisdiction Since the principle of territoriality is implemented by placing a limitation on the jurisdiction of the court, it follows that a foreigner may bring himself effectively within the provisions of an Act by voluntarily submitting to the jurisdiction. {*Re Dulles' Settlement* [1951] Ch 265.} This is in accordance with the usual legal rule that a defence to an action may be waived. It is expressed in the maxim *quilibet potest renunciare juri pro se introducto* (every man is entitled to give up a right introduced in his favour). {2 Co Inst 183; Co Litt 99a. See further s 11of this Code.}

Extension where Act so provides We have described the normal presumption that an Act does not apply in relation to non-resident subjects and territories of other sovereign states. Now we turn to the cases where an Act specifically provides for transactions or persons in the territory, or deemed territory, of another state. {As to the rules relating to an Act's application to its own state's ships, aircraft and artificial installations when located outside the jurisdiction of any state see s 225 of this Code.}

It is not necessary to say very much about this aspect. No one seriously doubts that, if it wishes to do so, Parliament can legislate in any way it thinks fit. {See s 31 of this Code.} We therefore merely give here some examples of cases where Parliament has thought fit to legislate in a way exceeding normal principles of comity.

The most common instances arise in the field of criminal law. National policy not infrequently makes it necessary to punish offences laid down by an Act even though they are committed outside the Act's territory. Very rarely, it may even be necessary to punish foreigners for acts committed outside that area.

Example 5 The Criminal Jurisdiction Act 1975 s 1 provides that an act or omission by a person *of any nationality* which takes place in the Republic of Ireland shall constitute an offence where it would constitute an offence within a specified category if taking place in Northern Ireland. {For another example see Merchant Shipping Act 1894 s 687 (punishing offences committed abroad by foreigners employed on British ships). See also *R v Anderson* (1868) LR 1 CCR 161.}

Some crimes, such as terrorism or hijacking, tend to be international in character. Acts to combat them therefore need to have extra-territorial operation. {See, e g, the Suppression of Terrorism Act 1978 and the Hijacking Act 1971.} Piracy *jure gentium*, as part of the law of nations, is punishable in any country where the pirate is found. {*In the matter of Piracy jure gentium* [1934] AC 586. See Tokyo Convention Act 1967 s 4 and Sch; *Cameron v HM Advocate* (1971) SLT 333.} A grave breach of the Geneva Conventions on prisoners of war etc is made punishable in the United Kingdom even though committed by a foreigner out of the United Kingdom. {Geneva Conventions Act 1957 s 1.}

Extra-territoriality by necessary intendment If the purpose of an Act cannot be fully accomplished without giving the Act extra-territorial effect this may be implied. The doctrine as to such overriding implication may be referred to as the doctrine of extra-territoriality by necessary intendment, a phrase derived from British colonial legislation. {See, e g, the Colonial Laws Validity Act 1865 s 1.}

In *Jefferys v Boosey* {(1854) 4 HLC 815 at p 970.} Lord Brougham said-

> 'Nothing is more clear than that [the legislature] may ... extend its provisions to foreigners in certain cases and may, without express words, make it appear that such was the intendment of those provisions ... But the presumption is rather against the extension and the proof of it rather on those who maintain such to be the meaning of the enactment.'

In earlier times the intendment necessary for implied extra-territoriality was seldom to be found. Travel was difficult and communications poor. Parliament had small occasion to concern itself with the regulation of acts and omissions in foreign parts, even those of British subjects. Under modern conditions, the intendment is more often found to be present. It can exist in relation to any persons, but is most likely to apply to British citizens. We now examine the principles involved.

Extension to foreigners where objects of Act so require Although an Act may contain no express provisions rendering it operative in relation to foreigners outside the Act's territory, such operation may be implied. The implication must be strong enough to overcome the reverse implication that an Act is intended to apply only to persons and acts within its territory. Thus there must be an obvious United Kingdom interest.

Example 6 As an example of such an interest, where movements into or out of British ports were concerned it was held reasonable to expect an Act to operate even in relation to acts by foreigners out of the jurisdiction if those acts would have territorial repercussions. {*Air-India v Wiggins* [1980] 2 All ER 593, *per* Lord Scarman at pp 597-9.}

Example 7 On the other hand in *Clark (Inspector of Taxes) v Oceanic Contractors Inc* {(1981) *The Times* 11 November.} the British interest in tax collection was held not to raise an implication that a non-resident foreign company was bound to operate the PAYE system and deduct income tax when paying employees assessed to Schedule E tax. It made no difference that the company had a 'presence' in England in the shape of an office in respect of which it complied with the requirements of s 407 (delivery of documents etc to Registrar of Companies) of the Companies Act 1948.

In taxing Acts the question of extra-territorial operation is not infrequently left obscure.

Example 8 In *Astor v Perry* {[1935] AC 398, at p 416.} Lord Macmillan said of s 20 of the Finance Act 1922-

> 'The possible extra-territorial effects of the section were obviously not thought out and the task of reconciling the resulting conflict which the legislature has omitted to perform is imposed upon your Lordships.'

Where the draftsman has thought of the point, extra-territoriality may be indicated by express words.

Example 9 Section 1(2) of the Bankruptcy Act 1914 defines 'debtor' as including 'any person, *whether a British subject or not*, who at the time when any act of bankruptcy was done or suffered by him . . . was carrying on business in England'. {Emphasis added.} This was held by the House of Lords to cover an act of bankruptcy committed by a foreigner abroad. He had ceased trading in England and left the country, though leaving behind unpaid trade debts. {*Theophile v S-G* [1950] AC 186.}

In the case of the Fatal Accidents Acts 1846 and 1864 it has been held reasonable to infer that Parliament intended foreigners abroad to obtain compensation for what 'the law of every civilised country treats as an actionable wrong'. {*Davidson v Hill* [1901] 2 KB 606, *per* Kennedy J at p 612. See also Examples 127.3, 216.2 and 323.3.}

224. Application: Britons and British matters outside the territory

Unless the contrary intention appears, and subject to any relevant rules of private international law, an enactment is taken not to apply to Britons (using the term in contradistinction to 'foreigners') and British matters outside the territory to which it extends.

COMMENTARY

In this generalised account, 'Briton' is used in contradistinction to 'foreigner'. {For the reasons for this crude nomenclature see p 489 above.} The wording of this section is similar to that of s 223 of this Code. Foreigners and Britons are treated separately in this way because the contrary intention more frequently appears in the case of Britons, and different considerations operate.

In identifying the persons and matters to which an enactment applies, it is necessary to distinguish the territory over which the Act is law from all other territories. {As to the territorial extent of enactments see s 195 of this Code. For the general principles as to application of enactments see s 221.} In considering what application an Act may have outside its territory, the Act is not to be considered as standing by itself. The individual Act forms merely a part of the entire *corpus juris* (both written and unwritten) of its territory.

Subject to any special provision made by the Act itself, the intended application (if any) of the Act outside its territory is therefore taken to accord with the general principles governing the external application of the body of territorial law. Where special principles are applicable to law of the kind dealt with by the Act (for example criminal law) these will of course apply to the Act as well.

It is in relation to criminal law that Parliament has most often found it necessary to legislate in respect of acts done by Britons out of the jurisdiction. Except by virtue of an enactment, a citizen is not liable under English law for an offence committed out of the jurisdiction. {*R v Lewis* (1857) Dears & B 182.}

It is true that Lord Devlin went so far as to suggest that common law crimes contrary to the moral law do not have territorial limits. {*R v Martin* [1956] 2 QB 272, at p 285.} Presumably this would apply where, as frequently happens, a common law crime is reduced to statutory form (with or without modifications). More realistically, Viscount Simonds said that-

> ' . . . apart from those exceptional cases in which specific provision is made in regard to acts committed abroad, the whole body of the criminal law of England deals only with acts committed in England.'

{*Cox v Army Council* [1963] AC 48, at p 67.}
This echoes the remark by Lord Halsbury LC that 'All crime is local'. {*Macleod v A-G of New South Wales* [1891] AC 455, at p 458.}

Such exceptional provision is most likely to be made in relation to matters affecting the safety of the state. Here the concept of what is a 'Briton' is also likely to be framed in wide terms.

Example 1 The Treason Act 1351 provides, in words declaratory of the common law, that treason is committed (among other instances) 'if a man do . . .

be adherent to the King's enemies in his realm, giving them aid or comfort in the realm, *or elsewhere*. {Emphasis added.} In relation to external operation, this is an example of implication mixed with express provision. The implication, arising on the basis discussed above, is that the Act does not apply to foreigners acting in places outside British jurisdiction.

It is for the court to draw the dividing line between those who are 'foreigners' for this purpose and those who are not. In *Joyce v Director of Public Prosecutions* {[1946] AC 347.} the House of Lords held that an alien who held a British passport was claiming British protection. Therefore he owed allegiance in return, and so was within the 1351 Act. {Cf *R v Lynch* [1903] 1 KB 444 (British subject who acquired enemy nationality guilty of treason).}

The 1351 Act is ambiguous so far as activities out of the realm are concerned. Do the words 'or elsewhere' qualify 'be adherent to' as well as 'giving them aid and comfort'? In *R v Casement* {[1917] 1 KB 98.} the defence argued that they did not. To constitute treason, they said, the 'adherence' had to be in the realm, even though the aid or comfort might be administered elsewhere. The Court of Criminal Appeal rejected this argument on the ground that the allegiance follows the person of the subject. They cited the statute 35 Hen 8 c 2 (1543), relying on the reference in its long title to 'treasons commytted out of the Kinges Majesties domynions'.

Other criminal statutes dealing with offences overseas include: Criminal Jurisdiction Act 1802; Treason Felony Act 1848 s 3; Offences against the Person Act 1861 ss 9 and 10 (murder and manslaughter) and 57 (bigamy); Criminal Justice Act 1948 s 31 (offences by servants of the Crown); Foreign Enlistment Act 1870 ss 16 and 17; Perjury Act 1911 s 8; Explosive Substances Act 1883 (as amended) and Official Secrets Act 1911 s 10.

British enactments are applied to persons out of the jurisdiction because the policy of the Act, or legal policy generally, requires it. {As to legal policy see s 126 of this Code.} In the nature of things, this is more likely to happen with Britons than foreigners. They belong to the legislating territory, and are likely to return to it. Nowadays, their absence abroad may be very brief indeed. It would plainly be against legal policy for persons to be able to go abroad to commit their crime and then return without punishment. {As to the presumption against evasion of an Act see s 143 and Part XVII of this Code.}

Example 2 In *R v Russell (Earl)* {[1901] AC 446.} the House of Lords was concerned with s 57 (bigamy) of the Offences against the Person Act 1861. This states that a British subject commits bigamy if, being married, he 'shall marry any other person during the life of the former husband or wife, whether the second marriage shall have taken place in England or Ireland *or elsewhere*'. {Emphasis added.} The defence argued that the italicised words were intended to relate only to British territory. *Held* The words were not so limited. It would evade the purpose of the Act if an English couple could travel to a foreign country for a bigamous ceremony and then return. {Cf *Pugh v Pugh* [1951] P 482.}

Any person subject to military law who commits a civil offence anywhere in the world is guilty of an offence against the Army Act 1955. {See s 70 of the Act.} Corresponding provision applies to persons subject to naval law {Naval Discipline Act 1957 s 42.} or air-force law. {Air Force Act 1955 s 70.}

Under section 686 of the Merchant Shipping Act 1894, a British subject who, on a foreign ship to which he does not belong, commits an act which would be an offence if committed in England, may, if found within the jurisdiction of a court in England and Wales, be tried for it by that court. The section makes corresponding provision where the act would be an offence if committed in any other territory to which the Merchant Shipping Act 1894 extends and the offending British subject is found within that territory.

Where the offender does belong to the ship the theory 'presumably is that . . . he is more appropriately dealt with by the courts of the jurisdiction to which the ship belongs'. {[1981] Crim LR 45.} In *R v Kelly* {[1981] 2 All ER 1098, *per* Lord Roskill at p 1102.} the House of Lords held that the purpose of s 686 is to provide 'disciplinary control . . . over miscreant British subjects on board foreign ships'. There is no corresponding control over such subjects when travelling on foreign aircraft.

Taxing Acts frequently legislate in respect of property outside the jurisdiction. This even applies to land, which under rules of private international law is governed by the *lex situs*. {*Companhia de Mocambique v British South Africa Company* [1893] AC 602.}

Example 3 Section 28 of the Finance Act 1962 extended estate duty to land overseas. This did not however mean that British tax authorities were thereby given any direct right of recourse against foreign land. In accordance with principle, the provision was enforceable only indirectly, against property and persons within the jurisdiction.

Extension to Britons where objects of Act so require As mentioned in Example 2, if Britons were allowed with impunity to take brief trips overseas solely for the purpose of committing an illegal act, the law could be easily evaded. Again, the good name of Britain is thought to be tarnished when its citizens commit antisocial acts such as vandalism or hooliganism in foreign countries. {*R v Kelly* [1981] 2 All ER 1098.}

Parliament's concern for the reputation of Britain overseas was recognised by Lord Roskill when he said in *Gold Star Publications Ltd v Director of Public Prosecutions* {[1981] 2 All ER 257, at p 266.} that 'Parliament may well have intended that England and Wales should not become a source from which unrestricted supplies of obscene articles should flow unchecked . . . to other countries throughout the world'.

Nevertheless the most likely ground for the extra-territorial application of an Act to British subjects is that otherwise the Act will fail in its purpose.

Example 4 In the *Sussex Peerage Case* {(1844) 11 Cl & F 85.} the question was whether the provision of the Royal Marriages Act 1772 which requires the monarch's consent to certain marriages had extra-territorial effect. The judges advised that it had, since otherwise the objects of the Act would be frustrated. Tindal CJ said {P 1058.} that 'the mischief is remediless, and the power of the Sovereign nugatory, if the marriage, which in England would have been confessedly void, is to be held good and valid when celebrated out of the country'.

Example 5 The Slave Trade Act 1824, which rendered slave trading unlawful, did not specify what the territorial extent of the Act was. Since however it was a notorious fact that the trade against which the Act was directed was mainly conducted on the west coast of Africa it was held that the necessary intendment of Parliament must have been that the Act should apply to British subjects there. {*R v Zulueta* (1843) 1 Car & K 215.}

In *Santos v Illidge* {(1860) 8 CBNS 861, at p 870.} Bramwell B said: 'I cannot doubt that [the Slave Trade Act 1824] was intended to apply to the coast of Africa, where the slave trade was carried on. But was it intended to apply to the territories, or rather the interior of the territories, of the King of Portugal? Was it intended to apply to the state of Kentucky in North America? I think not'. {See also the Slave Trade Act 1843 s 1, which states that the 1824 Act applies to British subjects everywhere.}

The doctrine of extra-territoriality by necessary intendment was held not to apply to the warranty imported by the Fertilisers and Feeding Stuffs Act 1926 where the property in goods purchased passed before the ship carrying the goods reached England. {*Draper v Turner* [1965] 1 QB 424.} There was a similar ruling in relation to a provision requiring certain weights and measures to be used. It was held that it did not apply where the weighing was to be done in China, since otherwise 'a contract made in China would have to have English weights and measures sent out there'. {*Rosseter v Cahlmann* (1853) 8 Ex 361, *per* Parke B at p 363. As to the argument of inconvenience see s 322 of this Code.}

As explained above in relation to foreigners, the doctrine of extra-territoriality by necessary intendment may operate to the advantage, as well as to the detriment, of British citizens.

Example 6 This is illustrated by the Personal Injuries (Emergency Provisions) Act 1939 s 3. The reference here to 'war injuries' has been held to include injuries suffered outside the Act's territory. {*Howgate v Bagnall* [1951] 1 KB 265.}

Example 7 On the other hand in *Tomalin v S Pearson & Son Ltd* {[1909] 2 KB 61.} an English workman employed by an English company was sent by his employers to do work in Malta. In the course of this work an accident occurred in which the workman was killed. The Workmen's Compensation Act 1906 s 1(1) provided for compensation to be paid 'if in any employment personal injury by accident arising out of and in the course of the employment is caused to any workman'. *Held* These words were by implication limited to accidents occurring within the territory over which the Act was law.

British Nationality Act 1948 s 3(1) The British Nationality Act 1948 s 3(1), as amended, equates the criminal law applying to certain Commonwealth and Irish citizens in respect of acts done outside the United Kingdom to that applying to aliens. {S 3(1) was amended by the Criminal Jurisdiction Act 1975 s 1(4) and the British Nationality Act 1981 s 52 and Sch 7. In addition, certain expressions used in s 3(1) are modified by virtue of the new nationality provisions in the 1981 Act.}

Section 3(1) does not apply to any extra-territorial offence within the meaning of s 1(3) of the Criminal Jurisdiction Act 1975 or to the contravention of any provisions of the Merchant Shipping Acts 1894 to 1948. {The current collective title is 'the Merchant Shipping Acts 1894 to 1983' (see Merchant Shipping Act

1983 s 11(2)). As to whether the post-1948 Acts should be treated as within this reference, see s 288 of the Code.}

The effect of s 3(1) as amended is highly complex, and virtually impossible to summmarise accurately. The following gives an outline. The terms in italics are defined at the end.

1. Where an enactment creating an offence extends to any *British territory*, a *Commonwealth etc citizen* is not guilty of that offence by reason of an act or omission in a *Commonwealth etc country* unless he would be guilty of that offence if he were an *alien* and the act or omission occurred in a *foreign country*.

This assimilates the position of Commonwealth etc citizens to that of aliens so far as relates to crimes by them committed in Commonwealth etc countries.

Example 8   A Commonwealth etc citizen committing a treasonable act in his own country would not be guilty of an offence against the Treason Act 1351 so far as it has effect as part of the law of the United Kingdom. This is because an alien doing the same act in his country would not be so liable. If however the Treason Act 1351 also had effect in the law of the Commonwealth etc citizen's country his act would constitute an offence under that law. This result accords with the present independent status of former colonial territories.

2. Where an enactment creating an offence extends to any *British territory*, a *Commonwealth etc citizen* is not guilty of that offence by reason of an act or omission in a *foreign country* unless he would be guilty of that offence if he were an *alien*.

This has the same effect as para 1 above except that it relates to acts or omissions in foreign countries.

Definitions   The following are the meanings of the italicised terms in paras 1 and 2 above.

The term 'alien' means a person who is not any of the following, namely a British citizen, a British Dependent Territories citizen, a British Overseas citizen, a British subject under the British Nationality Act 1981 or a Commonwealth etc citizen. {The definition of 'alien' contained in s 32(1) of the British Nationality Act 1948 was repealed by the British Nationality Act 1981 s 52(8) and Sch 9. The definition given here derives from s 51(4) of the British Nationality Act 1981. The terms 'British citizen', 'British Dependent Territories citizen' and 'British Overseas citizen' are free-standing terms deriving respectively from Parts I, II and III of the British Nationality Act 1981. Part IV of the Act lays down who are British subjects under the Act.}

The term 'British territory' means the United Kingdom, the Channel Islands, the Isle of Man, a colony, a British protectorate or a United Kingdom trust territory. {See note at end of this Commentary.}

The term 'Commonwealth etc citizen' means a person who is a citizen of a country mentioned in Sch 3 to the British Nationality Act 1981, or a British subject under that Act, or a citizen of the Republic of Ireland. {Schedule 3 to the British Nationality Act 1981 lists the independent countries of the Commonwealth. Part IV of that Act defines who are British subjects under the Act.}

The term 'Commonwealth etc country' means a country mentioned in Sch 3 to the British Nationality Act 1981, a dependency of a country so mentioned, or the Republic of Ireland. {Schedule 3 to the British Nationality Act 1981 lists the independent countries of the Commonwealth. Dependencies of those countries are included by virtue of s 50(12) of that Act.}

The term 'foreign country' means a country which is neither a British territory nor a Commonwealth etc country. {This derives from the definition in s 32(1) of the British Nationality Act 1948, which was repealed by the British Nationality Act 1981 s 52(8) and Sch 9. See now s 50(1) of the 1981 Act.}

'British territory'   The position regarding the definition of this expression is somewhat obscure. Section 3(1) of the British Nationality Act 1948 refers to 'the laws of any part of the United Kingdom and Colonies or of any protectorate or United Kingdom trust territory'. That Act did not however define the phrase 'United Kingdom and Colonies' for this purpose. The meaning of 'protectorate' was regulated by s 30 of the Act, which is now repealed. {By the British Nationality Act 1981 s 52(8) and Sch 9. Section 38 of the 1981 Act provides for protectorates in a different way.} 'United Kingdom trust territory' was defined by s 32(1) of the British Nationality Act 1948, repealed by the British Nationality Act 1981 s 52(8) and Sch 9 and not replaced. The definition was 'a territory administered under the trusteeship system of the United Nations by [Her] Majesty's government in the United Kingdom'.
{See also Example 395.3.}

225. Application: high seas and other unappropriated territories

Unless the contrary intention appears, the application of an enactment to persons and matters on a ship, aircraft, or other craft or installation on or over the high seas or in any other unappropriated territory is regulated as follows. If the craft or installation is generally subject to the law of the United Kingdom, the enactment applies as it does to persons and matters within its territory. Otherwise it applies as it does to like persons and matters in foreign territory.

COMMENTARY

Some places on the earth's surface or above it are unappropriated territories outside the jurisdiction of any state, though nevertheless subject to public international law. {As to the effect of public international law in relation to statutory interpretation see s 134 of this Code.} The high seas are an obvious example. {For the meaning of 'the high seas' see s 212 of this Code.} The practice is for individual states to pass laws providing that when within such areas its ships, aircraft and other means of transportation, and its artificial installations, are to be treated as being in effect extensions of its own territory.

The nationality of a ship 'depends upon her ownership and upon that alone'. {*Chartered Mercantile Bank of India v Netherlands India Steam Navigation Co* (1883) 10 QBD 521, *per* Brett LJ at p 535.} This applies 'unless a ship be employed under letters of marque of Government, which make her become a ship of the Government'. {Ibid.} Furthermore 'the jurisdiction of a country is preserved over its vessels, though they may be in ports or rivers belonging to another nation'. {*R v Anderson* (1868) LR 1 CCR 161, *per* Bovill CJ at p 166. See also Offences at Sea Act 1799.}

This may be thought to justify the statement that a British ship on the high seas 'is in point of law a part of the United Kingdom'. {Earl Jowitt *Dictionary of English Law* tit Abroad, Offences committed.} In *R v Anderson* {(1868) LR 1 CCR 161.} the court referred to British ships as 'floating islands' and as such notionally to be regarded as extensions of the territory of England. {See pp 163 and 168.}

However this eminently sensible concept, which avoids much legal obscurity, has been stigmatised by the Law Commission as a 'picturesque metaphor . . . not well founded in legal principle'. {*Report on the Territorial and Extraterritorial Extent of the Criminal Law* (Law Com No 91, 1978) para 54, citing *Chung Chi-Cheung v The King* [1939] AC 160; *R v Gordon Finlayson* [1941] 1 KB 171; *Oteri v The Queen* [1976] 1 WLR 1272, at p 1276.}

This criticism may unfortunately be supported by the authorities, and particularly by the way Parliament has habitually dealt with the matter. Here however 'legal principle' in the true sense is conspicuously absent. The aim has almost invariably been to lay down a formula that works in practice whatever its theoretical defects may be. That after all is the British way.

A British ship other than a naval vessel is subject (wherever she may be) to the provisions of the Merchant Shipping Acts. Rather than speaking of 'the law in force' in a British ship on the high seas, these Acts operate by conferring jurisdiction on British courts in relation to events occurring on any such ship when outside the area of the court's normal jurisdiction.

Example 1 Thus s 684 of the Merchant Shipping Act 1894 provides that for the purpose of giving jurisdiction 'every offence shall be deemed to have been committed and every cause of complaint to have arisen either in the place in which the same actually was committed or arose, or in any place in which the offender or person complained against may be'. {See also ss 685-7 of the Act and ss 43, 84 and 86 of the Merchant Shipping Act 1906.}

By implication such provisions must be taken to apply the municipal law to persons on board the ship. This is because the references to concepts of the law, such as offences, would otherwise have no meaning. An act or omission is an 'offence' only in the context of some applicable system of law, since the concept of an offence, as employed in legislation, is a purely legal one. The same point arose in relation to aircraft under s 62(1) of the Civil Aviation Act 1949 before the repeal of that provision (see below). As to offences by British subjects aboard foreign ships see below.

In modern Acts, more carefully thought out provisions are found.

Example 2 Thus s 3(1) of the Continental Shelf Act 1964 provides, in relation to oil rigs and other installations in an area designated under the Act, as follows-

> 'Any act or omission which-
>> (a) takes place on, under or above an installation in a designated area or any waters within five hundred metres of such an installation; and
>> (b) would, if taking place in any part of the United Kingdom, constitute an offence under the law in force in that part,
> shall be treated for the purposes of that law as taking place in that part.'

Corresponding provision in relation to civil law is made by s 3(2) of the Act.

While it is an improvement on the Merchant Shipping Act provisions, s 3(1) still does not directly say that a specified system of law is in force on a North Sea oil rig or other installation within the Act. A straight answer is not therefore possible to a worker's enquiry 'What law governs us on this rig?'Our statute law commonly avoids dealing with such matters in a straightforward way. Instead it prefers to employ what has been called 'asifism'. {See Bennion *Statute Law* (2nd edn, 1983) pp 124, 184-5, 200-202, 257.}

The inadequacy of this indirect method is illustrated by the fact that the Continental Shelf Act 1964 finds it necessary to include an express provision giving a constable on an installation the same powers, protection and privileges he would have on the mainland. {S 11(3). As to prosecution of offences committed on an installation see s 11(1) and (2).} This provision, which would not be necessary if English or Scottish law were applied as a whole, invites speculation about what other rules of the general law might be needed but have not been thought of and expressly applied.

As regards aircraft there has been further improvement in the way the matter is dealt with. In place of the defective s 62(1) of the Civil Aviation Act 1949 we now have s 1(1) of the Tokyo Convention Act 1967. Section 62(1) was defective because it simply said that for the purpose of giving jurisdiction 'Any offence whatever committed on a British aircraft shall . . . be deemed to have been committed in any place where the offender may for the time being be'. For the reason given above in relation to the Merchant Shipping Acts, this begs the question of what system of law applies for the purpose of determining whether or not a particular act or omission *is* an offence, and if so what the punishment for it is. {See *R v Martin* [1956] 2 QB 272; *R v Naylor* [1962] 2 QB 527; *Cox v Army Council* [1963] AC 48.}

Section 1(1) of the Tokyo Convention Act 1967 runs as follows-

> 'Any act or omission taking place on board a British-controlled aircraft while in flight elewhere than in or over the United Kingdom which, if taking place in, or in a part of, the United Kingdom, would constitute an offence under the law in force in, or in that part of, the United Kingdom shall constitute that offence:
>
> Provided that this subsection shall not apply to any act or omission which is expressly or impliedly authorised by or under that law when taking place outside the United kingdom.'

This has less artificiality than the Continental Shelf Act provision given above. It makes clear that an actual offence is committed on the aircraft. Both provisions are however unsatisfactory in applying more than one system of criminal law. If the passenger or crew member is not guilty under English law he might still be caught under Scottish law , and vice versa. This is contrary to the principle of certainty regarded as necessary in law, and particularly criminal law. {See s 130 of this Code.}

The 1967 Act gives no definition of 'aircraft' as such. Presumably it would not apply to a spacecraft outside the earth's atmosphere, since that would not be flying in air and is not designed primarily for air flight. The Act is applied to hovercraft by the Hovercraft (Application of Enactments) Order 1972. {SI 1972/971.}

226. Application: deemed location of an omission

For the purpose of considering the application of an enactment, an omission to act is, unless the contrary intention appears, to be treated as taking place in the territory where the act ought to have been performed. Applying this test, an omission may fall to be treated as occurring in each of two or more territories.

COMMENTARY

The principle that an omission is to be treated as taking place where the act in question should have been performed is a matter of common sense. {As to the commonsense construction rule see s 122 of this Code.} Where it would have sufficed to perform the act in any of two or more territories, it follows that the omission must be treated as having taken place in all of them.

Example 1 In *Brinkibon Ltd v Stahag Stahl* {[1982] 1 All ER 293, at p 296.}, Lord Wilberforce said: 'Each of these acts should have been performed outside the jurisdiction and failure to do them must be similarly located'.

227. Application: deemed location of a composite act or omission

Where different elements of an act or omission occur in different territories, the act or omission is treated, for purposes of the application of the law of any territory, as occurring within the territory where the significant proportion of it took place. Applying this test, an act or omission may fall to be treated as occurring in each of two or more territories.

COMMENTARY

Lord Wilberforce described as 'composite acts' those acts 'of which some elements may occur within and some outside the jurisdiction'. {*Gold Star Publications Ltd v Director of Public Prosecutions* [1981] 2 All ER 257, at p 259. Cf Examples 192.1 to 192.3.}

In criminal law what usually matters is where the composite act or omission takes effect. That is where the significant proportion of it occurs. {See *R v Oliphant* [1905] 2 KB 67; *R v De Marny* [1907] 1 KB 388; *R v Stoddart* (1909) 2 Cr App R 217.} Apart from this it is difficult to frame any general rule, and the matter is usually dealt with by *ad hoc* provisions laid down either by Parliament or the courts.

Example 1 An example of a statutory rule for this purpose is s 10 of the Offences against the Person Act 1861, relating to murder and manslaughter. If a person who has been criminally 'stricken, poisoned, or otherwise hurt' out of England then dies of that treatment in England, a prosecution may be brought in England. Despite the general wording of this provision there has been held to be an implication that it is not to apply where the homicidal act was done by an *alien* outside the jurisdiction. {*R v Lewis* (1857) 26 LJMC 104; Dears & B 182.}

Example 2 An example of a judicial rule to deal with a composite act is furnished by the treatment of bastardy where impregnation occurs in one territory and the resulting child is born in another. In *R v Blane* {(1849) 13 QB 769.} a single woman born and domiciled in France gave birth in France to an illegitimate child. She had lived in England for the preceding thirteen years however, and had become pregnant there. Held: She could not obtain an affiliation order under English law.

Lord Denman CJ considered the place of birth of the child to be decisive: 'I am clearly of opinion that children born out of this country are not the subject of our bastardy laws'. {P 772.} Coleridge J agreed, giving as a reason that the relevant Acts were clearly framed in terms of births within some parish in England. {P 773.} He also applied a consequential construction related to his view that to find for the mother would establish an unworkable precedent-

> 'If the word "bastard" is . . . to comprehend any bastard born in any part of the world, an immense field of inquiry must be traversed respecting the status of children according to the different laws of different countries.'

{*Ibid.*} As to consequential construction by reference to the impractical or unworkable results of a particular reading see s 321 of this Code.

After a century had passed, improvements in communications rendered the difficulty less acute. This factor, together with changed social attitudes, led to the reversal of *R v Blane* by the Court of Appeal in *R v Bow Road JJ, ex p Adedigba*. {[1968] 2 QB 572. As to the effect on the construction of an Act of changes in social conditions after it was passed see s 146 of this Code.}

228. Application: deemed location of an artificial person

Artificial persons are treated as located in the country under whose law they were created. Where however they operate within any other territory, they may, by the law of that territory, be treated as present within it.

COMMENTARY

Bodies corporate and other artificial persons are equipped by law with a fictitious personality distinct from those of their human members. {*Sutton's Hospital Case* (1612) 15 Co Rep 32b; *Salomon v Salomon* [1897] AC 22.} Such bodies are deemed to be located in the territory under whose law they were created. If however they carry on any activities in another territory they are, in respect of those activities, subject to the law of that other territory. {As to whether a company registered in England can be liable under an English criminal statute for acts committed in a foreign country where they are lawful see *Macnee v Persian Investment Co* (1890) 44 Ch D 306; *Re International Securities Corpn Ltd* (1908) 24 TLR 837.}

This rule is inevitable. A corporation can act only through natural persons, who must themselves be present in the territory where they act. The law of a territory usually makes special provision for such cases.

Example 1 Thus we find the Companies Act 1948 laying down regulations governing companies incorporated outside Great Britain which have a place of business within it. {See Part X of the Act.}

As to the treatment of artificial persons in statutory interpretation see further Bennion *Statute Law* (2nd edn, 1983) pp 183-5.

PART X

The Informed Interpretation Rule: Legislative History

Introduction to Part X This Part and Part XI spell out the detail of the informed interpretation rule described in s 119 of the Code. This Part deals with the important aspect of that rule which is concerned with legislative history. It is dealt with in three compartments, respectively describing pre-enacting, enacting and post-enacting history. Before these are embarked on, a general explanation of the use of legislative history in statutory interpretation is given (s 229).

The basic rule as to use of pre-enacting history is then explained (s 230). The concept mainly relates to the state of the earlier law (s 231). Two special aspects of this are then considered. These respectively arise where the Act under enquiry is a consolidation Act (s 232) or a codifying Act (s 233).

We pass to the main area, enacting history. Its meaning is explained (s 234). The basic rule governing its use is set out (s 235). We then deal with the *sources* of enacting history, namely those referred to in the Act (s 236), committee reports leading up to the Bill for the Act (s 237), Hansard reports (s 238), amendments proposed to the Bill in Parliament (s 239), and explanatory memoranda accompanying the Bill (s 240). The special exclusionary rule relating to parliamentary proceedings is set out (s 241). The final source dealt with is the international treaty (s 242).

Next we look at the various ways in which enacting history materials are handled. Judicial notice may be taken of them (s 243). The court always has the right to inspect them (s 244). Counsel may read out extracts from them as of right or *de bene esse* (s 245). Counsel may use them as part of his argument (s 246).

Finally we consider the use made of these materials. They may indicate the view taken by Parliament as to the pre-Act law (s 247). They may help to ascertain the mischief with which Parliament was dealing (s 248). They may serve generally as a guide to Parliament's intention (s 249). They are of persuasive authority only (ss 250 and 251).

Part X concludes by describing post-enacting history. This shows the effect on the construction of an Act of events occurring after it was passed. We begin with the basic rule (s 252). Then we consider the effect of official statements on the meaning and operation of the Act (s 253). Delegated legislation made under the Act may throw light on its meaning (s 254). Later Acts, while not actually amending the Act, may indicate the view a later Parliament takes of it (s 255). Judicial decisions on the Act frequently affect, or at least explain, its meaning (s 256). Expert commentaries by a committee examining the working of the Act may be relevant to its construction (s 257). So too may commentaries by jurists (s 258).

PRELIMINARY

229. Legislative history as a guide to construction

The informed interpretation rule requires that, in the construction of an enactment, due attention should be paid to relevant aspects of the state of the law before the Act was passed, the history of its passing, and the events subsequent to its passing. In the Code this material is described collectively as the legislative history of the enactment, and severally as the pre-enacting, the enacting, and the post-enacting history.

COMMENTARY

Informed interpretation rule   As to the informed interpretation rule see s 119 of this Code. Reference to legislative history is an important component in informed interpretation.

This section states the principle explored in the following sections of this Part. An enactment does not stand alone. {As to the enactment see Part III af this Code.} It is part of the Act containing it. The Act in its turn is part of the corpus juris. The enactment must be construed in the light of its overall context. If it is not, the court may err. {For a case where knowledge of the pre-enacting and enacting history would probably have led the Court of Appeal to reach the opposite conclusion to the one it in fact reached see W A West 'The Intention of the Legislature' (1971) 87 LQR 471.}

Subject to relevant legal rules, a court considering an enactment is master of its own procedure. {*R v Board of Visitors of Wormwood Scrubs Prison, ex p Anderson* (1983) *The Times* 9 November.} The court therefore has the power, indeed the duty, to consider such aspects of the legislative history of the enactment as may be necessary to arrive at its legal meaning. In doing so it must give them their proper *weight*. {See s 259 of this Code. As to the weighing of interpretative factors see Part VII of the Code.}

Delegated legislation For a proper understanding of an item of delegated legislation, it is necessary not only to consider the wording of the enabling Act, but also the legislative history of that Act. {*Crompton v General Medical Council* [1982] 1 All ER 35, *per* Lord Diplock at p 37. As to delegated legislation see ss 50 to 70 of this Code.}

PRE-ENACTING HISTORY

230. Pre-enacting history: the basic rule

The interpreter cannot judge soundly what mischief an enactment is intended to remedy unless he knows the previous state of the law, the defects found to exist in that law, and the facts that caused the legislator to pass the Act in question.

COMMENTARY

Of those who argue that there is no need to know what the law was before the passing of the Act 'since it is certain what the law is now by statute', the first known book on statutory interpretation in England, written in the sixteenth century, said-

' . . . yet are they much deceived . . . for they shall neither know the statute nor expound it well, but shall as it were follow their noses and grope at it in the dark.'

{Cited by T F T Plucknett, who surmises that the author was Lord Ellesmere LC ('Ellesmere on Statutes' (1944) 60 LQR 242 at p 245).}

As to the mischief at which an enactment is directed see s 138 and Part XIV of this Code.

231. Pre-enacting history: the earlier law

Under the doctrine of judicial notice, the court is taken to know the relevant law prevailing within its jurisdiction. This applies both to past and present law. Accordingly there can be no restriction on the sources available to the court for reminding itself as to the content of any rule of law which prevails, or has prevailed, within its jurisdiction.

Where an Act uses a form of words with a previous legal history, this may be relevant in interpretation. The question is always whether or not Parliament intended to use the term in the sense given by this earlier history.

COMMENTARY

Judicial notice As to the general principles relating to judicial notice see s 21 of this Code.

Except in the case of declaratory, codifying or consolidating Acts, the sole purpose of an Act is to change the law. It is obviously relevant in the construction of an Act to take account of what the previous law on the topic was.

The position is described by Lord Diplock in a passage from his opinion in *Black-Clawson International Ltd v Papierwerke Waldhof-Aschaffenberg AG.* {[1975] 1 All ER 810, at p 835.} The case dealt with the legal meaning of s 8 of the Foreign Judgments (Reciprocal Enforcement) Act 1933, an Act passed more than 40 years before. Lord Diplock was considering the use that might legitimately be made of the so-called Greer Report {Report of the Foreign Judgments (Reciprocal Enforcement) Committee (1932) Cmd 4213.}, upon which s 8 was based. He said-

'As regards the first of these purposes [ascertainment of the pre-Act law] for which recourse may be had to the report, the Act deals with a technical subject-matter - the treatment to be accorded by courts in the United Kingdom to judgments of foreign courts. The expressions used in it are terms of legal art which were in current use in English and Scots law at the time the Act was passed. In order to understand their meaning the court must inform itself as to what the existing law was on this technical subject-matter. In order to do this it may have recourse to decided cases, to legal text-books or other writings of recognised authorities, amomg whom would rank the members of the committee. Their report contains a summary of the existing law, as they understood it. As such it is part of the material to which the court may have recourse for the purpose of ascertaining what was the existing law on the subject- matter of the Act.'

{See also *Vacher & Sons Ltd v London Society of Compositors* [1913] AC 107, at p 113; *Assam Rly and Trading Co Ltd v IRC* [1935] AC 445, at p 457-9; *Boy Andrew (Owners) v St Rognvald (Owners)* [1948] AC 140, at p 149.}

Where a subject has been dealt with by a developing series of Acts, the courts often find it necessary, in construing the latest Act, to trace the course of this development. By seeing what changes have been made in the relevant provision, and why, the court can better assess the current meaning.

Example 1   The treatment of road traffic offences is a good example of this. In *Jennings v United States Government* {[1982] 3 All ER 104, at p 115. See Example 180.2} Lord Roskill said that the defence argument could not be evaluated without a review of the legislative history beginning as far back as the Motor Car Act 1903.

Again, the court will often find it necessary to trace the course of judicial interpretation of earlier versions of the provision in order to apply the doctrine of *stare decisis* correctly. {As to this doctrine see s 26 of the Code.}

Use of term with previous history   Where an Act uses a form of words with a previous legal history, this may be relevant in interpretation. An obvious example is the free-standing legal term.

If the term was borrowed from different legislation, and had received judicial interpretation in its other context, that processing may be relevant to understanding its meaning in the present Act.

Example 2 In *Welham v Director of Public Prosecutions* {[1961] AC 103, at p 123.} Viscount Radcliffe, dealing with the phrase 'intent to defraud' in the Forgery Act 1913 s 4, remarked that since the Act had not included a definition of the phrase he could not doubt that it 'must be understood in the light of any established legal interpretation that prevailed at the date of the passing of the Act'.

The sole question is whether, in borrowing the word, Parliament also intended to borrow its previous processing. This can be a very difficult matter to determine.

If the two Acts are *in pari materia*, it is assumed that uniformity of language and meaning was intended. This attracts the considerations arising from the linguistic canon of construction that an Act is to be construed as a whole. {As to this see s 149 of the Code.} The following are *in pari materia*-

(1) Acts which have been given a collective title. {As to collective titles see s 288 of this Code.} This is a recognition by Parliament that the Acts have a single subject-matter.

(2) Acts which are required to be construed as one. {As to these see s 287 of this code.} Again there is parliamentary recognition of a single subject-matter.

(3) Acts having short titles that are identical (apart from the calendar year).

(4) Other Acts which deal with the same subject-matter on the same lines. Here it must be remembered that the Latin word *par* or *paris* means equal, and not merely similar. Such Acts are sometimes described as 'forming a code'. This

does not mean that the Acts are codifying Acts however. {As to codifying Acts see pp 97–98 above.}

The principle regarding Acts *in pari materia* was thus expressed by twelve judges in *Palmer's Case* {(1785) 1 Burr 445, at p 447.}: such Acts 'are to be taken together as forming one system, and as interpreting and enforcing each other'.

This has even been applied to repealed Acts within a group. In *Ex p Copeland* {(1852) 22 LJ Bank 17, at p 21.}, Knight Bruce LJ said-

> '[On a question of construction arising] upon a subsequent statute on the same branch of the law, it is perfectly legitimate to use the former Act, though repealed. For this I have the authority of Lord Mansfield, who in *R v Loxdale* {(1758) 1 Burr 445, at p 447.}, thus lays down the rule, "Where there are different statutes *in pari materia*, though made at different times, or even expired and not referring to each other, they shall be taken and construed together as one system and as explanatory of each other".'

{See also, to the like effect, *Barras v Aberdeen Steam Trawling and Fishing Co* [1933] AC 402, at p 411; *Powell v Cleland* [1948] 1 KB 262, at p 273; *Beaman v ARTS Ltd* [1949] 1 KB 550, at p 567; *Ealing Corpn v Ryan* [1965] 2 QB 486; *Caravans and Automobiles Ltd v Southall Borough Council* [1963] 1 WLR 690.}

It is however necessary to remain realistic. A draftsman who produces an amending Bill does not always have the time or industry to read through the whole of a mass of preceding legislation to make sure he drafts in full accordance with it. Harman LJ said: 'The broad principle laid down by Lord Mansfield in *R v Loxdale* as to the exposition of one statute by the language of another must be taken with a pinch of salt when a long series of Acts is being dealt with'. {*Littlewoods Mail Order Stores v IRC* [1961] Ch 597, at p 633.}

Mistake Sometimes it may be argued that Parliament's understanding of the earlier law was mistaken. This possibility is dealt with in s 244 of the Code. {See also Examples 125.10 and 323.14.}

232. Pre-enacting history: consolidation Acts

In the first instance, a consolidation Act is to be construed in the same way as any other Act. If however any real doubt as to its meaning arises, the following rules apply.

(1) Unless the contrary intention appears, an Act stated in its long title to be a consolidation Act is presumed not to be intended to change the law.

(2) In so far as the Act constitutes straight consolidation, its words are to be construed exactly as if they remained in the earlier Act.

(3) In so far as the Act constitutes consolidation with amendments, its words are to be construed as if they were contained in an ordinary amending Act.

(4) Straight consolidation consists of reproduction of the original wording without significant change. Consolidation with amendments is any other consolidation.

COMMENTARY

Real doubt   As to real doubt see s 3 of this Code.

A consolidation Act is intended to confine within one Act provisions from various Acts that are *in pari materia*. {For the meaning of this term see pp 516–517 above.} The object is to improve the form of the law without altering its substance. Obviously the court construing a consolidation Act should bear in mind that that is what it is. Unfortunately this does not always happen. {For an example see *R v Schildkamp* [1971] AC 1, at p 26.}

From the viewpoint of interpretation, there is only one distinction to be drawn in relation to consolidation Acts. That is between straight consolidation and consolidation with amendments. {For the various types of consolidation Act, and the methods by which they are passed see Bennion *Statute Law* (2nd edn, 1983) pp 73–80.} Here we need to look at the consolidation Act section by section.

Example 1   Suppose a consolidation Act consists of 100 sections. Of these, 90 are reproduced verbatim from the earlier Acts. A further seven are reproduced with insignificant changes due to 'carpentry', that is is the need to tailor the provisions to the new format. The remaining three embody amendments of substance, none of which affects the meaning of the other 97 sections. Here the 97 sections are to be construed as being straight consolidation, while the remaining three are consolidation with amendments.

Lord Herschell's rule   The rule laid down by Lord Herschell LC in relation to codifying Acts applies equally to consolidation Acts. {As to the rule see pp 519–520 below.} This is to the effect that, unless there is real doubt, such Acts should be given their ordinary meaning. This is but an aspect of the plain meaning rule. {See s 120 of this Code. For confirmation of this view see *Administrator-General of Bengal v Prem Lal Mullick* (1895) LR 22 IA 107, *per* Lord Watson at p 116.}

Straight consolidation   Under our system, the provisions in a straight consolidation are reproduced verbatim, apart from necessary 'carpentry'. The opportunity is not taken to improve the drafting, or give expression to the sub-rules produced by dynamic processing. {See Example 142.6. As to dynamic processing and sub-rules see s 26 of this Code.}

The result from the point of view of interpretation is that re-enactment in the form of straight consolidation makes no difference. It does not import parliamentary approval of judicial decisions on the earlier Acts, because Parliament has not had those decisions in mind. Not even the draftsman will have had them in mind. He will not have taken time to look them up, because his concern is simply to reproduce accurately the statutory wording. Each enactment is therefore to be construed as if it had remained in the original Act.

To those who understand the procedure for consolidation of enactments in Britain, it is self-evident that straight consolidation gives no added authority to earlier judicial decisions on a consolidated enactment. Yet counsel sometimes argue the contrary. When this happened in *Galloway v Galloway* {[1956] AC 299.}, Viscount Radcliffe said {P 320.}-

> 'I must confess that I do not lend a sympathetic ear to this . . . almost mystical method of discovering the law, least of all when it depends

upon a consolidating Act the function of which is to repeat, but not to amend, existing statute law.'

Even learned judges are not immune from the temptation to argue in this obviously incorrect way. {See, e g, *Mitchell v Westin* [1965] 1 WLR 297, at pp 306-7.}

It follows that it is important for the court to know, when construing a provision in a consolidation Act, whether that provision constitutes straight consolidation or consolidation with amendments. If practicable, recourse may for this purpose be had to materials relating to the enacting history.

Notwithstanding the general exclusionary rule, these may include parliamentary materials. {See *Beswick v Beswick* [1968] AC 58, at p 105. As to the exclusionary rule see s 241 of this Code.} Failing such recourse, the court is confined to a textual comparison of the consolidation Act with the enactment consolidated. {*MacConnell v Prill (E) & Co Ltd* [1916] 2 Ch 57, at p 63; *H v H* [1966] 3 All ER 560, at p 566.}

The presumption is that a consolidation Act is not intended to change the law. {*Gilbert v Gilbert and Boucher* [1928] P 1, *per* Scrutton LJ at p 8; *R v Governor of Brixton Prison, ex p De Demko* [1959] 1 QB 268, *per* Lord Evershed MR at pp 280-1.}

For examples of cases where there is real doubt, and the earlier law is looked at, see *Mitchell v Simpson* {(1890) 25 QBD 183, at p 188.}; *Smith v Baker* {[1891] AC 325, at p 349.}; *IRC v Hinchy* {[1960] AC 748, at p 768.}; *Barentz v Whiting.* {[1965] 1 WLR 433}.

233. Pre-enacting history: codifying Acts

In the first instance, a codifying Act is to be construed in the same way as any other Act. If however any real doubt as to its meaning arises, the following rules apply.

(1) Unless the contrary intention appears, an Act stated in its long title to be a codifying Act is presumed not to be intended to change the law.

(2) In so far as the Act constitutes consolidation of previous enactments (with or without amendment), the rules stated in s 232 of this Code apply.

(3) In so far as the Act constitutes codification (with or without amendment) of common-law rules or judicial sub-rules, reports of the relevant decisions may be referred to.

COMMENTARY

Real doubt   As to real doubt see s 3 of this Code.

Codification is relatively rare in Britain. {For a general treatment of the topic see Bennion *Statute Law* (2nd edn, 1983) pp 81-4.}

Lord Herschell's rule   Lord Herscell LC, to whose reforming zeal the few English codes are mainly due, laid down the following rule as to their interpretation-

'I think the proper course is, in the first instance, to examine the language of the statute, and to ask what is its natural meaning, uninfluenced by any considerations derived from the previous state of the law, and not to start with enquiring how the law previously stood, and then, assuming that it was intended to leave it unaltered, to see if the words of the enactment will bear an interpretation in conformity with this view. If . . . treated in this fashion it appears to me that its utility will be almost entirely destroyed and the very object with which it was enacted will be frustrated. The purpose of such a statute surely was that on any point specifically dealt with by it, the law should be ascertained by interpreting the language used, instead of, as before, by roaming over a vast number of authorities . . .'

{*Bank of England v Vagliano* [1891] AC 107, at p 144. See also, to the like effect, *Bristol Tramways v Fiat Motors* [1910] 2 KB 831, at p 836.}

Lord Herschell's rule that, unless there is real doubt, codifying Acts should be given their ordinary meaning is but an aspect of the plain meaning rule. {See s 120 of this Code. For a case where there was real doubt, and the previous law was looked at, see *Yorkshire Insurance Co Ltd v Nisbet Shipping Co* [1962] 2 QB 330.}

ENACTING HISTORY

234. Enacting history: meaning

The enacting history of an Act is the surrounding corpus of public knowledge relative to its introduction into Parliament as a Bill, and subsequent progress through, and ultimate passing by, Parliament. In particular it is the extrinsic material assumed to be within the contemplation of Parliament when it passed the Act. A text constituting an item of its enacting history may or may not be expressly mentioned in the Act. If inspected, it is unlikely to be self-explanatory. On the contrary it will probably require skilled evaluation.

COMMENTARY

This section describes the information comprised in what is known as the enacting history of any piece of legislation. It is described as the *surrounding* corpus of knowledge because the central source of information as to Parliament's intention must always be the text of the Act itself. That is the Act's sole function and purpose.

Irrespective of whether or not it is admissible in court, enacting history comprises reports and other material on which the Act is based, the text of the Bill and amendments proposed to it, reports of parliamentary debates and proceedings on the Bill, explanatory memoranda officially issued in connection with the Bill, and other contemporaneous material upon which Parliament may be presumed to have acted.

Much of this material emanates from the executive, rather than from the legislature itself. For example in former colonial territories there have been treated as included in enacting history such matters issuing from the executive as Colonial Office records, despatches of governors and opinions of Law

Officers. {See, e g, the Australian cases of *Ward v R* (1980) 142 CLR 308, at pp 322 and 332, and *Wacando v Commonwealth* (1981) 37 ALR 317, at p 328.}

Judicial notice It has been authoritatively said that judicial notice is to be taken of such facts 'as must be assumed to have been within the contemplation of the legislature when the Acts in question were passed'. {*Govindan Sellappah Nayar Kodakan Pillai v Punchi Banda Mundanayake* [1953] AC 514, at p 528. As to the doctrine of judicial notice see s 21 of this Code.}

Mention in the Act An item is not in any way precluded from being regarded as part of the enacting history because it is not expressly mentioned in the Act. This applies even where the item might have been expected to be mentioned because it is the purpose of the Act to give effect to what the item expresses. {*Salomon v Commrs of Customs and Excise* [1967] 2 QB 116.}

Evaluation of material In considering whether to admit an item of enacting history, the court needs to bear in mind that it is unlikely to be proper to take the item at face value. Material should not be used in the interpretation of the enactment without correct evaluation of its nature and significance. This may in some cases greatly prolong the court proceedings if the item is admitted. {As to the undesirability of this see s 260 of the Code.}

An official policy discussion paper produced in 1982 by the Australian Government commented that legislative history materials 'are not self-explanatory and require an often difficult exercise of evaluation'. {Cited in *Report of a Symposium on Statutory Interpretation held at Canberra on 5 February 1983* (Attorney-General's Department, Australian Government 1983) p 114.}

235. Enacting history: the basic rule

In fulfilment of the informed interpretation rule, but subject to the exclusionary rule stated in section 241 of this Code, the court may under proper safeguards have regard to any item of the enacting history of an Act as an aid to its construction.

In doing so the court is expected to bear in mind that law (even statute law) is, from the time of its creation, subject to a continuous process of development. This means that the intentions of the historical legislator may not indefinitely continue to carry interpretative weight (or at least the same weight). A fortiori this applies to the underlying intentions of bodies other than Parliament (such as committees of inquiry), upon whose proposals the Act is based.

COMMENTARY

This section of the Code continues what was said in s 119 as to the need for an informed interpretation. That section expressed the principle that in general, and subject to practical limitations, the interpreter can never be too well-informed. We here continue the argument in terms limited to information as to the circumstances in which the Act in question was passed by Parliament.

We now face the dilemma challenging all legislative texts. The central idea of legislation is to provide the citizen or his adviser with a structure which *in itself* constitutes a basis upon which he can safely stand. Once a building is erected the scaffolding can be taken down, and should thereafter be irrelevant. This may be defeated in the field of legislation by the inadequacy of language, the fallibility of legislators and the fact that the future they seek to regulate is unknown, and unguessable.

The precise function of enacting history in interpretation is determined by where the line is currently drawn by the courts. No systematic doctrine emerges from the cases. In what follows we endeavour to extract the inherent principles.

It is worth repeating that on a strict view the enacting history should be irrelevant, since the object of Parliament is to express its will entirely within the definitive text of the Act itself. This eminently convenient doctrine has unfortunately proved too idealistic and theoretical in practice. The essence of statutory interpretation lies in resolving the dichotomy between the 'pure' doctrine that the law is to be found in the Act and nowhere else, and the 'realist' doctrine that legislation is an imperfect technique requiring, for the social good, an importation of surrounding information.

In the upshot, this information is generally regarded as admissible (according to the weight it deserves to carry) unless there is some substantial reason requiring it to be kept out. In expounding the relevant rules it is necessary to distinguish-

(a) the main *sources* of enacting history (described in ss 236 to 242 of this Code),

(b) the *ways* in which enacting history is used in interpretation (described in ss 243 to 246), and

(c) the *purposes* for which it is used (described in ss 247 to 250).

Proper safeguards   The precautions the court needs to take before relying on enacting history are described in the course of the following discussion. The American Justice Frankfurter accurately summed up the constraining factors in these words-

'Spurious use of legislative history must not swallow the legislation so as to give point to the quip that only when legislative history is doubtful do you go to the statute. While courts are no longer confined to the language, they are still confined by it. Violence must not be done to the words chosen by the legislature. Unless indeed no doubt can be left that the legislature has in fact used a private code, so that what appears to be violence to language is merely respect to special usage. In the end, language and external aids, each accorded the authority deserved in the circumstances, must be weighed in the balance of judicial judgment.'

{'Some Reflections on the Reading of Statutes' (1947) 2 *The Record of the Association of the Bar of the City of New York* 213, at p 234. Though helpful, this passage is defective in failing to take note of drafting error (see s 142 of this Code). See also *Greenwood v United States* (1956) 350 US 366, at p 374.}

Courts ought not to make unexpected use of an item of enacting history. They certainly ought not to do so where this produces an opposite interpretation to what the user may legitimately have relied on. {See s 260 of this Code. For the predictable construction principle see s 130.} Professor J Richardson, Ombudsman of the Commonwealth of Australia, said-

'The important thing, I think, from the consumer's point of view is that if the High Court and the other courts are going to use extrinsic materials in interpreting Acts of Parliament then it's not sufficient for the High Court alone to have the message as to which materials they will use. Officials are called upon to administer Acts in departments, solicitors to advise clients on the same question. They ought to know too what classes or what particular types of extrinsic material the court would rely on in the particular cases they are called upon to advise. It's not sufficient to say the court has a discretion as to the extrinsic materials to be invoked. The court needs to go further, so that in future persons outside the courts required to apply legislation are confident as to extrinsic materials which may be used in the instances before them.'

{*Report of a Symposium on Statutory Interpretation held at Canberra on 5 February 1983* (A-G's Department, Australian Government 1983) p 27.}

The court 'goes further' in this sense by working out and adhering to a uniform practice, to which exceptions (if necessarily admitted on occasion) are kept strictly within bounds.

A further inhibiting factor is that the court, after admitting an item of legislative history, often finds that it carries the matter no further. The question of marginal utility arises here, since admitting the item inevitably adds to trial costs. In an Australian case the judge commented-

'I have necessarily ventured far into the use of legislative history only, in the outcome, to discover that it leads to no conclusion different from that which would have followed from a disregard of anything extrinsic to the words of the legislation itself.'

{*Dugan v Mirror Newspapers Ltd* (1979) 142 CLR 583, *per* Stephen J at p 599.}

Updating The second part of this section recognises that, as law develops, original source materials often become out of date. A remark of the Law Commissions in relation to Continental codes applies equally to Acts of Parliament-

'In Continental countries it is recognised that the interpretative weight of extraneous material contemporary with or preceding a code diminishes as the code develops its own momentum which tends to reduce reference to the intentions of the historical legislator.'

{'The Interpretation of Statutes' (1969) Law Com No 21, Scot Law Com No 11 p 43. As to the importance of this consideration in relation to the use of contemporaneous explanatory memoranda see s 240 of this Code. For updating construction see s 146.}

236. Enacting history: sources referred to in Act

Where the Act expressly refers to a document comprised in its enacting history, Parliament is presumed, unless the contrary intention appears, to intend that document to be used in the construction of the Act.

COMMENTARY

If the Act states that named sources may be referred to for the purpose of interpretation, the matter is free from doubt. Such express provision is rarely included however.

Example 1   One example is s 3 of the Civil Jurisdiction and Judgments Act 1982, which runs as follows-

> '(1) Any question as to the meaning or effect of any provision of the Conventions shall, if not referred to the European Court in accordance with the 1971 Protocol, be determined in accordance with the principles laid down by and any relevant decision of the European Court.
> (2) Judicial notice shall be taken of any decision of, or expression of opinion by, the European Court on any such question.
> (3) Without prejudice to the generality of subsection (1), the following reports (which are reproduced in the Official Journal of the Communities), namely-
>> (a) the reports by Mr P Jenard on the 1968 Convention and the 1971 Protocol; and
>> (b) the report by Professor Dr Peter Schlosser on the Accession Convention,
> may be considered in ascertaining the meaning or effect of any provision of the Conventions and shall be given such weight as is appropriate in the circumstances.'

It will be noticed that while sub- (3) of this contains a saving for sub- (1), it contains no saving for the right of the court to consult other items of legislative history if it thinks fit. The provision thus creates doubt, which tends to be a feature of provisions such as this intended to clarify the law.

In their 1969 report on statutory interpretation, the Law Commissions suggested the enactment of a provision contemplating that each future Act would include a statement of what legislative history materials could legitimately be used in interpreting that particular Act. {'The Interpretation of Statutes' (1969) Law Cp, No 21, Scot Law Com No 11 p 51. For the history of the attempts to secure the enactment of this and similar provisions see Bennion 'Another Reverse for the Law Commissions' Interpretation Bill' (1981) 131 NLJ 840. For similar suggestions in Australia see *Report of a Symposium on Statutory Interpretation held at Canberra on 5 February 1983* (Attorney-General's Department, Australian Government 1983) pp 20 and 24.}

This suggestion was not adopted because, although theoretically attractive, it presents insuperable problems. There may be a wide range of legislative history materials relative to a particular Act. These are bound to be of varying usefulness; and it is not helpful (and may be misleading) to give some of them the imprimatur of mention in the Act. Moreover when the Act is drafted it cannot always be foreseen which points of interpretation will give trouble in the future.

In the proceedings on clause 33 of the Theft Bill 1968 Lord Wilberforce moved, but after debate withdrew, an amendment stating that-

'Reference may be made, for the interpretation of this Act, to the Notes on Draft Theft Bill contained in Annexe 2 of Command 2977 {Eighth Report of the Criminal Law Revision Committee.} but this commentary shall be for guidance only and shall have no binding force.'

{(1968) 290 HL Deb, cols 897-913; see 'The Interpretation of Statutes' (1969) Law Com No 21, Scot Law Com No 11 p 38. The following year Lord Wilberforce put down a similar amendment to the abortive Animals Bill. For a similar (unsuccessful) attempt in Australia see *Report of a Symposium on Statutory Interpretation held at Canberra on 5 February 1983* (Attorney-General's Department, Australian Government 1983) p 56.}

Express authority not given Where a provision of the Act mentions a document but does not give express authority for it to be referred to in construing the Act, the meaning of the provision is as always a matter for interpretation. It is presumed however that if Parliament has thought fit to mention the document, and has not forbidden reference to it in interpretation, the inference is that it may be referred to. {See, e g, the Australian case of *Deputy Federal Commissioner of Taxation v W R Moran Pty Ltd* (1939) 61 CLR 735 (preamble of Act referring to report of prime ministers' conference).}

237. Enacting history: committee reports leading up to Bill

Before Parliament legislates on a topic, a committee of inquiry may be set up to investigate the alleged mischief and propose a remedy. This may be a Royal Commission, a parliamentary select committee, a departmental committee, or some other body. Its report may or may not be published; and may or may not be formally presented to Parliament. In any event the report constitutes part of the enacting history.

COMMENTARY

Committee reports are among the most useful sources of enacting history. Lord Simon of Glaisdale said-

'As to the statutory objective of [particular provisions of an Act], a report leading to the Act is likely to be the most potent aid; and, in my judgment, it would be mere obscurantism not to avail oneself of it. There is, indeed, clear and high authority that it is available for this purpose.'

{*Black-Clawson International Ltd v Papierwerke Waldhof-Aschaffenberg AG* [1975] 1 All ER 810, at p 844. See also Example 50.3.}

Lord Simon went on to mention, as part of this 'clear and high authority', the following: *River Wear Comrs v Adamson* {(1877) 2 App Cas 743, *per* Lord Blackburn at p 763.}, *Eastman Photographic Materials Co Ltd v Comptroller-General of Patents* {[1898] AC 571, *per* the Earl of Halsbury LC at p 573.} and *Hawkins v Gathercole* {(1855) 6 De GM & G 1, *per* Turner LJ at p 21.}

In another case Lord Diplock said-

'Where the Act has been preceded by a report of some official commission or committee that has been laid before Parliament and the legislation is introduced in consequence of that report, the report itself may be looked at by the court for the limited purpose of identifying the 'mischief' that the Act was intended to remedy, and for such assistance as is derivable from this knowledge in giving the right purposive construction to the Act.'

{*Fothergill v Monarch Airlines Ltd* [1980] 2 All ER 696, at p 706. As to purposive construction see s 139 and Part XVI of this Code.}

The weight to be given to a committee report depends on the standing and authority of the committee members, and the degree to which it appears Parliament followed their proposals.

The extent to which such reports may be referred to is discussed below as part of the general treatment of enacting history.

238. Enacting history: reports of parliamentary proceedings on Bill

Hansard reports, and other reports of parliamentary proceedings on the Bill which became the Act in question, are of obvious relevance to its meaning. They are often of doubtful reliability however. Special restrictions, set out in s 241 below, apply to their citation.

COMMENTARY

This section deals with the nature and utility of parliamentary reports as guides to meaning. The so-called exclusionary rule is described separately. {See s 241 of this Code.}

It is obvious that on many points of interpretation a reference to *Hansard* would clear the matter up. This arises where the point was specifically dealt with in debate either on the Bill or on a proposed amendment (whether added to the Bill or not). {For examples see 'The Interpretation of Statutes' (1969) Law Com No 21, Scot Law Com No 11 n 148.} There are however difficulties in applying this 'obvious' remedy.

Practicability To carry out satisfactory research in *Hansard* on a particular point of interpretation requires time and skilled effort. Even though the point appears to be dealt with satisfactorily in one place (perhaps on the occasion when the relevant provision was added to the Bill by an amendment), this cannot be relied on. There may well have been other occasions when the point was referred to in the parliamentary debates on the Bill. Furthermore the point may have been referred to in Parliament *outside* the debates on the Bill itself.

A Bill which becomes an Act goes through the stages of second reading, committee, report and third reading. It does this not once but twice, in each House of Parliament. At every stage there may be debate and amendment. All of these are reported. Statements made at one stage may be contradicted at another stage (or even on the same stage). Clause numbers change as amendments are carried, so that what ends up as say s 100 of the Act may have borne other numbers at various earlier stages of enactment.

To discover, conflate and accurately evaluate the various statements that may have been made in Parliament relative to the point at issue is a formidable task. The conclusions reached by the researcher will almost certainly be open to challenge. The court of construction can quickly find itself in an embarrassing morass.

A *selective* recourse to parliamentary materials is obviously undesirable. On one occasion when Lord Denning MR was guilty of trying this short cut he received a stern rebuke from the House of Lords. {*Hadmor Productions Ltd v Hamilton* [1982] 1 All ER 1042, *per* Lord Diplock at pp 1055-6.} Yet without being selective it is difficult to keep the operation within manageable bounds. As the Law Commission remarked-

' . . . our existing legislative procedures are not especially well adapted for the use of parliamentay material as an aid to interpretation; in particular, we do not have committee reports of the kind which, as an authoritative summary of the purpose and scope of a legislative proposal, are available to the courts in countries which make use of legislative history.'

{'The Interpretation of Statutes' (1969) Law Com No 21, Scot Law Com No 11 para 59.}

Availability Few legal practitioners have ready access to reports of parliamentary proceedings. The reports are published in different series, and are inadequately indexed. It requires considerable political expertise to evaluate them correctly. Lawyers, even including judges, do not in general possess this knowledge. {See 'The Interpretation of Statutes' (1969) Law Com No 21, Scot Law Com No 11 paras 60-2; Bennion 'The Need for Training in Statute Law' [1982] *The Law Society's Gazette* 219.}

Reliability What is said in Parliament is manifestly unreliable as a guide to the legal meaning of an enactment. {As to the legal meaning see s 2 of this Code.} Most politicians are not lawyers, and even when briefed by lawyers are likely to express legal propositions in an inaccurate, if not downright misleading, way.

Moreover the object of debate is persuasion. This may tend in the direction of enacting a particular provision, or it may tend against it. Even when competent, politicians acting as advocates are not always scrupulous. They tend to exaggerate, when they do not consciously deceive. No codes of ethics or disciplinary tribunals restrain them, as they do the barrister or solicitor arguing a point of statutory interpretation in court. The only restraint is parliamentary privilege, very rarely invoked in this connection.

The difficulty was well put by the Canadian jurist J A Corry, who said that the process of enacting legislation is not 'an intellectual exercise in the pursuit of truth but an essay in persuasion or perhaps almost seduction'. Corry suggested that 'to appeal from the carefully-pondered terms of the statute to the hurly-burly of Parliamentary debate is to appeal from Philip sober to Philip drunk'. {'The Use of Legislative History in the Interpretation of Statutes' (1954) 32 Can Bar Rev 624, at p 621-2.}

The American realist Charles P Curtis described the court which unrestrainedly pursues enacting history as 'fumbling about in the ashcans of the legislative process for the shoddiest unenacted expressions of intention'. {'A

Better Theory of Legal Interpretation' (1949) 4 *The Record of the Association of the Bar of the City of New York* 321).}

A further point may be added in conclusion. Once legislators realised that their statements might influence judicial interpretation, they would inevitably insert in them passages designed only for this purpose. Thus would be perverted, not only the judicial technique of interpretation, but the very legislative process itself.

239. Enacting history: amendments to Bill

Where the Bill which became the Act in question was amended during its passage through Parliament this may throw light on its meaning. So too may an amendment moved but not made. Special restrictions, set out in s 241 below, apply to these items of enacting history.

COMMENTARY

Under the current British system, amendments added to a Bill are almost invariably drafted by the draftsman of the Bill. In *Fothergill v Monarch Airlines Ltd* {[1980] 2 All ER 696, at p 705.} Lord Diplock described the position as being that the draftsman's advice will have been available on the wording of amendments. This is an understatement. In 99 cases out of 100 the draftsman will himself have drafted the amendment.

The Bill's draftsman drafts amendments so that they fit in, and leave the Bill as a coherent whole. The resulting Act is a seamless web, with no help to be gained from ascertaining which provisions were in the original Bill and which were added. The position may be different as regards an unsuccessful amendment moved by someone other than the promoters. If the history of this were admitted for purposes of interpretation it might prove significant.

Example 1   A case where reference to an amendment which was moved during the passage of the Bill would have settled the point at issue is *Viscountess Rhondda's Claim*. {[1922] 2 AC 339.} Lady Rhondda asserted the right to be allowed to take her seat in the House of Lords by reason of the statement in s 1 of the Sex Disqualification (Removal) Act 1919 that a person 'shall not be disqualified by sex or marriage from the exercise of any public function'.

During the passage of the Bill, a Commons amendment stating that the exercise of a 'public function' included sitting and voting in the House of Lords had been rejected as unnecessary. {CJ (1919) 330; LJ (1919) 431.} The Committee of Privileges refused to consider this amendment, and denied Lady Rhondda's claim. Lord Birkenhead LC however said that since the case was not being considered by the House of Lords in its judicial capacity the parliamentary history of the Act might have been admissible.

In an Australian case, Barwick CJ said-

' . . . I would wish to say that whilst I am quite clear that no relevant assistance can be obtained from speeches in the legislature, even from the second reading speech of the Minister introducing the Bill, I can see the possibility of relevant profit in knowing the changes which take place in the Bill between its introduction and its passage. These, unlike the speeches, result from action of the legislature itself. The changes may well be classified as *travaux préparatoires* to which heed is paid in other systems of law. However, authorities of long standing would not allow of this possible advantage being taken.'

{*South Australian Commr for Prices and Consumer Affairs v Charles Moore (Australia) Ltd* (1977) 139 CLR 449, at p 457. In Australia such materials may be admitted on constitutional points: *Tasmania v Commonwealth* (1904) 1 CLR 329, at p 333; *Seamens Union of Australia v Utah Development Co* (1978) 144 CLR 120, at pp 142-4. For a recent change in Australian law on this point see p 559 below.}

Whatever the difficulties about basing a judgment on material of this kind, there is nothing to stop the judge familiarising himself with it in private. This need not be done in connection with a particular case. It is part of what is contemplated by the informed interpretation rule. {See s 119 of this Code.}

240. Enacting history: explanatory memoranda

When a Bill is before Parliament, various kinds of explanatory material may be provided by the promoter of the Bill (usually the Government) for the use either of members of Parliament or of ministers seeking to explain the Bill's provisions. Since these are designed to throw light on the meaning of the Bill, they are of obvious relevance when the Bill has become an Act. Special restrictions however apply to these sources.

COMMENTARY

Explanatory and financial memoranda The promoter of a public Bill may preface it with what is called an Explanatory Memorandum. This explains the contents and objects of the Bill. It must be framed in non-technical language, and must not be argumentative. If passed by the Public Bill Office as satisfying these requirements, it appears on the front of the Bill when first printed by either House. When, following the making of amendments, the Bill is later reprinted the Explanatory Memorandum is dropped. This means that these memoranda are usually not accurate guides to the final Act.

Where the Bill is promoted by the Government, and involves expenditure, it must also be prefaced by a Financial Memorandum. {The doctrine of the exclusive financial initiative of the Crown means that a non-Government Bill cannot effectively require expenditure. As to this see pp 724–725 below.} A Financial Memorandum outlines the financial effect of the Bill, and gives estimates of the amount of money involved. The same principles apply to it as to an Explanatory Memorandum.

In practice, a Government Bill always includes an Explanatory Memorandum. Since 1968 this has included forecasts of changes in manpower requirements in the public sector expected to result from the Bill. {HC Deb (1968-69) 773 col 1546.} In the case of financial Bills, the two types of memoranda are combined in the form of what is called an Explanatory and Financial Memorandum.

Textual memoranda Where a Bill contains textual amendments to an Act, the effect of these may be indicated for the benefit of MPs in a separate textual memorandum. This reprints the affected provisions in full, incorporating the amendments. {See, e g, *Textual Memorandum on the Furnished Lettings (Rent Allowances) Bill 1972* Cmnd 5242. See further as to textual memoranda *The Preparation of Legislation* (Renton Report, 1975) Cmnd 6053 para 13.12; *Renton and the Need for Reform* (Sweet & Maxwell, 1979) pp 43-4 and 74-9.} An inferior alternative is the Keeling Schedule, which instead incorporates the written-out amendments in the Act itself. {For objections to the Keeling Schedule see Bennion *Statute Law* (2nd edn, 1983) pp 56-7.}

Statutory instruments   In 1943 the regular practice was adopted of adding an explanatory memorandum at the end of every statutory instrument. Like memoranda attached to Bills, these must be non-argumentative and factual. {For the use of such memoranda in interpretation see *Herbert v Pauley* (1964) 62 Loc Goct Rep 647.}

241. Enacting history: special restriction on parliamentary materials

Although, as stated in sections 238 to 240 above, parliamentary materials are of obvious relevance in statutory interpretation, the courts are inhibited in referring to them by considerations of comity, that is the courtesy and respect that ought to prevail between two prime organs of state: the legislature and the judiciary. Furthermore such materials are essentially unreliable; and pursuit of them involves an expenditure of time and effort that can only add to costs.

Accordingly such materials are not in general admissible for purposes of statutory interpretation. Nevertheless the court, as master of its own procedure, retains a residuary right to admit them where, in rare cases, the need to carry out the legislator's intention appears to the court so to require.

COMMENTARY

Parliament has always been jealous of interference in its proceedings by outsiders. Thus art 9 of the Bill of Rights (1688) {The short title was given by the Short Titles Act 1896 s 1 and Sch 1.} states that debates and other proceedings in Parliament ought not to be questioned in any court or place out of Parliament. Article 9 is declaratory of the law of Parliament, which may in fact go wider. {Erskine May *The Law, Privileges, Proceedings and Usage of Parliament* (20th edn, 1983) p 89.} It is also of course part of the general statute law binding on the courts.

The insistence, where so desired by either House, on privacy of debate, and consequent secrecy of reports of parliamentary proceedings, is also relevant. From it arose the asserted, and finally acknowledged, right of Parliament to control publication of such reports, and to punish infringements as a breach of privilege or contempt of Parliament.

In the view of the House of Commons, expressed in a resolution of 1818 {Erskine May *The Law, Privileges, Proceedings and Usage of Parliament* (20th edn, 1983) p 94.}, this meant that special leave of the House was required for reference to be made to Hansard or other parliamentary reports in court proceedings. On 31 October 1980 the Commons passed a resolution giving general leave for such references to be made, thus dispensing with the need for special leave in every case.

The resolution of 31 October 1980 does not affect the exclusionary rule laid down by the courts, except that it indicates the willingness of the House of Commons that its proceedings should be referred to in construing Acts. To this extent it weakens the argument for the exclusionary rule so far as it is based on comity.

In the House of Lords there has never been a requirement that the leave of the House be obtained for citation of Hansard reports in court. Indeed, although compiled since 1909 by officers of the House of Lords, Hansard is not formally a record of the House. The Clerk of the Records has nothing in his custody which he could produce to a court as the 'original' report of a debate.

The exclusionary rule The most recent authoritative statement of what is known as the exclusionary rule was given in the House of Lords in 1982 by Lord Diplock-

> 'There are a series of rulings by this House, unbroken for a hundred years, and most recently affirmed emphatically and unanimously in *Davis v Johnson* {[1979] AC 264.}, that recourse to reports of proceedings in either House of Parliament during the passage of the Bill that on a signification of royal assent became the Act of Parliament which falls to be construed is not permissible as an aid to its construction.'

{*Hadmor Productions Ltd v Hamilton* [1982] 1 All ER 1042, at p 1055. For rulings to similar effect see *Miller v Taylor* (1769) 4 Burr 2303, at p 2332; *R v Hertford College* (1878) 3 QBD 693, at p 707; *Escoigne Properties Ltd v IRC* [1958] AC 549, at p 566; *Shell-Mex & BP Ltd v Holyoak* [1959] 1 WLR 188, at p 202.}

In a case dealing with an international convention, Lord Diplock said: 'Hansard can never form part of the travaux préparatoires of any Act of Parliament whether it deals with purely domestic legislation or not'. {*Fothergill v Monarch Airlines Ltd* [1980] 2 All ER 696, at p 706.}

Speeches by Ministers The speech in Parliament by a minister or other promoter of a Bill explaining its purpose and effect might be thought of persuasive value. Yet as Lord Wright said in *Assam Railways and Trading Co Ltd v CIR* {[1935] AC 445, at p 458.}: 'It is clear that the language of a Minister of the Crown in proposing in Parliament a measure which eventually becomes law is inadmissible . . . '

Comity The prime reason for the exclusionary rule lies in the concept of comity. The constitutional desirability of mutual respect is the factor unique to this species of legislative history. While parliamentary materials partake of the other reasons inhibiting recourse to legislative history, this kind alone are in addition subject to the factor of comity. It is reasonable therefore to assume that it is comity and nothing else that produces the rule putting this particular type of legislative history virtually beyond the reach of courts of construction.

The rationale of this concept of comity was cogently put by Lord Hailsham LC in his 1983 Hamlyn lectures-

'From the constitutional viewpoint, I do not think it appropriate with a view to the comity between the different branches of Government, and their independence of each from the other, that the actual proceedings in Parliament should be the subject of discussion (and thereby inevitably criticism) in the courts both from the Bench and by counsel ... criticism of [what is said in Parliament] by judges, which would not only be legitimate but necessary were it to be admissible, would be constitutionally most undesirable.'

{See also (1980) 405 HL Deb cols 303-4.}

This truth was earlier perceived when the Ghana (Consequential Provisions) Act 1960 was drafted, at the time when the former Gold Coast colony first became a republic. This Act empowers the court to turn for help-

' ... to any text-book or other work of reference, to the report of any commission of inquiry into the state of the law, to any memorandum published by authority in reference to the enactment or to the Bill for the enactment and to any papers laid before [Parliament] in reference to it, but not to the debates in [Parliament].'

On this provision the present author (who was concerned in its drafting) made some comments that may be thought relevant to the British system of legislation-

'This marks a considerable increase in the [interpretative] sources made available to the court. It includes such things as Government White Papers and the [explanatory memorandum] published on the front of every Bill. In relation to textbooks it removes the argument that the author must be an established authority (or must even be dead) before the court can consider what he has to say. It does not of course interfere with the rule that where the words of an enactment are clear effect must be given to them. Nor does it prevent the court from attaching what weight it thinks fit to the sources named. The exclusion of references to debates in [Parliament] was explained in the memorandum to the Interpretation Bill as follows:

"There are two cogent reasons for their exclusion: first, it would not be conducive to the respect which one organ of State owes to another that its deliberations should be open to discussion in Court; and secondly it would greatly interfere with the freedom of debate if members had to speak in the knowledge that every remark might be subject to judicial analysis."

A third reason might be added, namely that the extempore answer of a Minister pressed to explain a provision in a Bill is not always a reliable guide to its meaning.'

{Bennion *Constitutional Law of Ghana* (Butterworth, 1962) pp 278-9. The reasoning here set out was approved by Sir Garfield Barwick, Chief Justice of Australia: 'Divining Legislative Intent' (1961) 35 ALJ 197. The Ghana provision was also referred to approvingly in 'Extrinsic Aids to Statutory Interpretation' (Australian Government, Canberra, 1982) paras 3.17-19 and 5.5, and in 'Symposium on Statutory Interpretation' (Australian Government, Canberra, 1983) paras 4.4-5.}

Australian law In Australia a recent Act has abolished the exclusionary rule. {Acts Interpretation Amendment Act 1984 s 7. See p 559 below.}

Disregard of exclusionary rule Despite the exclusionary rule, the court retains an overall control of its procedure, and if it thinks fit will disregard the rule.

Example 1 Thus in *R v Warner* {[1968] 2 WLR 1303, at p 1316.} Lord Reid said-

' . . . this case seems to show there is room for an exception where examining the proceedings in Parliament would almost certainly settle the matter immediately one way or the other.'

{For other examples of the citation of parliamentary history in court see YB 33 Edw 1 (1305) M. Term (Rolls edn) 82; *Ash v Abdy* (1678) 3 Swanst 664; *R v Wallis* (1793) 5 TR 375; *Re Mew* (1862) 31 LJBk 87; *Mounsey v Ismay* (1865) 3 H & C 486; *Hebbert v Purchas* (1871) LR 3 PC 605; *Ridsdale v Clifton* (1877) 2 PD 276; *R v Bishop of Oxford* (1879) 4 QBD 525, at pp 549, 550, 576; *South Eastern Rly v Railway Commrs* (1880) 5 QBD 217, at p 236; *Viscountess Rhondda's Claim* [1922] 2 AC 339, atp p 349-50; *Edwards v A-G for Canada* [1930] AC 124, at p 143; *Re C* [1937] 3 All ER 783, at p 787 (omitted from the report in [1938] Ch 121); *Beswick v Beswick* [1968] AC 58, at p 105; *Sagnata Investments Ltd v Norwich Corpn* [1971] 2 QB 614, at p 624; *Knuller (Publishing, Printing and Promotions) Ltd v Director of Public Prosecutions* [1972] 3 WLR 143, *per* Lord Reid at p 148; *R v Greater London Council, ex p Blackburn* [1976] 1 WLR 550, at p 556. See also (1937) 1 MLR 166; (1956) CLP 96.}

Despite Lord Diplock's vigorous dictum in *Hadmor* {P 531 above.}, it is not possible for a superior court to remove all discretion on such matters from courts below. They are questions of practice rather than strict law. As Salmon LJ said about whether the Court of Appeal is bound to follow its own previous decisions-

'The point about the authority of this court has never been decided by the House of Lords. In the nature of things it is not a point that could ever come before the House for decision.'

{*Gallie v Lee* [1969] 2 Ch 17, at p 49. See R W M Dias *Jurisprudence* (4th edn, 1976) pp 180-2.}

Courts must be in charge of their own procedure, and it is ultimately for the court with the duty of interpreting a particular enactment to decide what items of enacting history it will permit counsel to cite, having regard to the various relevant considerations (including the need not to protract the proceedings without commensurate benefit). {See s 260 of this Code.} The numerous precedents for citation of parliamentary material cancel out dicta saying it can *never* be done. Here, as elsewhere, the logical principle of contradiction applies. {This principle is explained in s 362 of the Code.}

Parliamentary proceedings which are legal rather than political are less likely to be excluded from citation. Thus the House of Lords, when construing a consolidation Act, has permitted reference to a report on the relevant Bill by the

Joint Committee on Consolidation Bills. {*Beswick v Beswick* [1968] AC 58, *per* Lord Upjohn at p 105.} The purpose of the reference was to ascertain whether anything in the proceedings before the Joint Committee weakened the usual presumption that, unless the contrary intention appears, a consolidation Act does not change the law. {See s 232 of this Code.}

An exception is also likely where the judicial proceedings themselves possess a quasi-legislative character. {Eg, proceedings on a peerage claim before the Committee of Privileges of the House of Lords: see *Viscountess Rhondda's Claim* [1922] AC 339, *per* Lord Birkenhead LC at pp 349-50).}

Citation by jurists   The artificiality of the so-called exclusionary rule is shown by the fact that if a text writer chooses to include an extract from *Hansard* in a discussion of the meaning of an enactment it may be allowed to be cited under the rule which permits recourse to such sources. Lord Denning MR said in 1979 {*R v Local Commissioner for Administration* [1979] 2 All ER 881, at p 898.}-

> 'According to the recent pronouncement of the House of Lords in *Davis v Johnson* {[1979] AC 264.}, we ought to regard Hansard as a closed book to which we as judges must not refer at all, not even as an aid to the construction of statutes.
>
> By good fortune, however, we have been given a way of overcoming that obstacle. For the Ombudsman himself in a public address to the Society of Public Teachers of Law quoted the relevant passages of Hansard as part of his address: and Professor Wade has quoted the very words in his latest book on Administrative Law. And we have not yet been told that we may not look at the writings of the teachers of law. Lord Simonds was as strict on these matters as any judge ever has been but he confessed his indebtedness to their writings, even very recent ones: see *Jacobs v London County Council* {[1950] AC 361, at p 374.}.

Lord Denning's argument may be thought disingenuous, since extracts from *Hansard* cannot accurately be described as 'writings of the teachers of law'. {As to reference to such writings in argument or judgments see s 6 of this Code.}

242. Enacting history: international treaties

A treaty may have three different kinds of status, considered as a source of law.

(1) An Act may embody, whether or not in the same words, provisions having the effect of the treaty (in this Code referred to as direct enactment of the treaty).

(2) An Act may say that the treaty is itself to have effect as law, leaving the treaty's provisions to apply with or without modification (in this Code referred to as indirect enactment of the treaty).

(3) The treaty may be left simply as an international obligation, being referred to in the interpretation of a relevant enactment only so far as called for by the presumption that Parliament intends to comply with public international law.

Whichever status a treaty has, its provisions may be referred to as an aid in the interpretation of a relevant enactment. So too may its preparatory work (travaux préparatoires), the decisions on it of foreign courts (*la jurisprudence*) and the views on it of foreign jurists (*la doctrine*).

COMMENTARY

A treaty {In this work the term 'treaty' is used to cover any type of international agreement.} is not self-executing in law. {*Fothergill v Monarch Airlines Ltd* [1980] 2 All ER 696, *per* Lord Wilberforce at p 699.} It may have any of the three different kinds of status described in this section of the Code. Only the first two are considered in this commentary. For the third, namely the case where the treaty is left simply as an international obligation (being referred to in the interpretation of a relevant enactment only so far as permitted by the presumption that Parliament intends to comply with public international law) see s 134 of this Code.

Direct enactment of treaty Except from one point of view, the most satisfactory way of giving legal effect to a treaty is by direct enactment. The internationally-agreed words cannot be suited to the legal systems of every participating state, and difficulties of interpretation must follow from indirect enactment. From this point of view it is best to produce a version tailored to the municipal system of the country concerned. This, if a United Kingdom Act, will be 'couched in the conventional English legislative idiom . . . designed to be construed exclusively by English judges'. {*Per* Lord Diplock in *Fothergill v Monarch Airlines Ltd* [1980] 2 All ER 696, at p 706. Presumably Lord Diplock intended his reference to embrace Scottish judges also.}

Example 1 A recent example of direct enactment of a treaty is furnished by the Arbitration Act 1975, the long title of which describes it as 'An Act to give effect to the New York Convention on the Recognition and Enforcement of Foreign Arbitral Awards'.

However direct enactment does not serve the need for uniformity in the application of a treaty. This need is particularly felt in relation to the operations of such bodies as intergovernmental agencies and multinational corporations, but it is of general import. Accordingly the tendency for indirect enactment is growing.

Indirect enactment of treaty Where the treaty is to be indirectly enacted, all that is needed is a short Act stating that the treaty shall have the force of law in the territory to which the Act extends. Perhaps the Act may go on to add one or two relatively minor modifications or clarifying provisions. The text of the treaty may or may not be scheduled to the Act. {The first English Act to have a treaty scheduled appears to have been the Carriage of Goods by Sea Act 1924, where the scheduled text was in fact a *draft* of the treaty: see *Fothergill v Monarch Airlines Ltd* [1980] 2 All ER 696, *per* Lord Roskill at p 717.}

With indirect enactment, instead of the substantive legislation taking the well-known form of an Act of Parliament, it has the form of a treaty. In other words the form and language found suitable for embodying an international agreement become, at the stroke of a pen, also the form and language of a municipal legislative instrument. It is rather like saying that, by Act of Parliament, a woman shall be a man. Inconveniences ensue.

One inconvenience is that the interpreter is required to cope with disorganised composition instead of precision drafting. {For the differences between these see s 76 of this Code.} The drafting of treaties is notoriously sloppy - usually for very good reason. To get agreement, politic uncertainty is called for. {As to politic uncertainty see Bennion *Statute Law* (2nd edn, 1983) chap 14.}

Example 2   In *Collins v British Airways Board* {[1982] 1 All ER 302, at p 305.} Lord Denning MR described as 'an amazing omission' the failure of the draftsman of the Warsaw Convention on International Carriage by Air to define what he meant by registration of baggage. This failure is thought to have arisen because of the difficulty of getting international agreement on registration procedures.

Another inconvenience of indirect enactment, mercifully rare, is that a text in some foreign tongue may become parcel of the law of England.

Example 3   Section 1(1) of the Carriage by Air Act 1961 states-

> 'Subject to the provisions of this section, the provisions of the Convention known as "the Warsaw Convention as amended at The Hague, 1955" as set out in the First Schedule to this Act shall . . . have the force of law in the United Kingdom in relation to any carriage by air to which the Convention applies . . .'

The First Schedule sets out both the English and French versions of the Convention. Section 1(2) of the Act goes on to provide that if there is any inconsistency between English and French versions *the text in French shall prevail.*

The consequences flowing from this were graphically described by Lord Wilberforce in *Fothergill v Monarch Airlines Ltd* {[1980] 2 All ER 696, at p 699.}-

> ' . . . it cannot be judged whether there is an inconsistency between two texts unless one looks at both. So, in the present case the process of interpretation seems to involve (1) interpretation of the English text, according to the principles on which international conventions are to be interpreted (see *Buchanan (James) & Co Ltd v Babco Forwarding and Shipping (UK) Ltd* {[1978] AC 141.} and *Stag Line Ltd v Foscolo Mango & Co Ltd* {[1932] AC 328, at p 350.}, (2) interpretation of the French text according to the same principles but with additional linguistic problems, (3) comparison of these meanings.'
> {See further pp 537-538 below.}

The interpretation of a treaty imported into municipal law by indirect enactment was described by Lord Wilberforce as being 'unconstrained by technical rules of English law, or by English legal precedent, but [conducted] on broad principles of general acceptation'. {*Buchanan (James) & Co Ltd v Babco Forwarding and Shipping (UK) Ltd* {[1978] AC 141, at p 152.} This echoes the dictum of Lord Widgery CJ that the words 'are to be given their general meaning, general to lawyer and layman alike . . . the meaning of the diplomat rather than the lawyer'. {*R v Governor of Pentonville Prison, ex p Ecke* [1974]

Crim LR 102. See also *Hobhouse v Wall* [1963] 2 QB 124.}

Court's right to consider text of treaty Dicta suggesting that the court is entitled to consult a relevant treaty only where the enactment is ambiguous can no longer be relied on. {See, e g, *Ellerman Lines Ltd v Murray* [1931] AC 126; *IRC v Collco Dealings Ltd* [1962] AC 1; *Warwick Film Productions Ltd v Eisinger* [1969] 1 Ch 508.} The true rule is that in this area, as in others, the court is to arrive at an *informed* interpretation. {For the informed interpretation rule see s 119 of this Code. As to recourse to treaties see also *Pyrene Co Ltd v Scindia Steam Navigation Co Ltd* [1954] 2 QB 402, at p 421; *Riverstone Meat Co Pty Ltd v Lancashire Shipping Co Ltd* [1961] AC 807; *Corocroft Ltd v Pan American Airways Inc* [1969] 1 QB 616; *Quazi v Quazi* [1979] 3 All ER 897, at pp 903, 908, 915.}

Lord Denning MR said in *Salomon v Comrs of Customs and Excise* {[1967] 2 QB 116, at p 141.} that his view that the relevant Act (passed to give effect to an international convention) should be construed in conformity with the convention had been confirmed by looking at the convention. He added-

> 'I think we are entitled to look at it, because it is an instrument which is binding in international law; and we ought to interpret our statutes so as to be in conformity with international law'.

{As to this principle see s 134 of the Code.}

This presumption of national policy applies also to the Crown. Thus the relevant treaty was admitted in construing the Territorial Waters Order in Council 1964, an instrument made under the royal prerogative. {*Post Office v Estuary Radio Ltd* [1968] 2 QB 740. As to prerogative instruments see ss 48 and 49 of this Code.}

The view taken by the courts as to recourse to the treaty has developed in recent years. {For the course of this development see *Fothergill v Monarch Airlines Ltd* [1980] 2 All ER 696, *per* Lord Roskill at pp 717-9.} It is now clear that a relevant treaty can be looked at even though not referred to in the Act. {*Salomon v Commrs of Customs and Excise* [1967] 2 QB 116.}

Treaty in foreign language Whether or not the foreign-language text of a treaty is part of our law, the court may be called upon to construe it. The principles applicable were stated by Lord Wilberforce in *Fothergill v Monarch Airlines Ltd* {[1980] 2 All ER 696, at p 700.}-

> 'My Lords, as in [*Buchanan (James) & Co Ltd v Babco Forwarding and Shipping (UK) Ltd* {[1978] AC 141.}], I am not willing to lay down any precise rule on this subject. The process of ascertaining the meaning must vary according to the subject matter. If a judge has some knowledge of the relevant language, there is no reason why he should not use it; this is particularly true of the French or Latin language, so long languages of our courts. There is no reason why he should not consult a dictionary, if the word is such that a dictionary can reveal its significance; often of course it may substitute one doubt for another ... In all cases he will have in mind that ours is an

537

adversary system: it is for the parties to make good their contentions. So he will inform them of the process he is using, and, if they think fit, they can supplement his resources with other material, other dictionaries, other books of reference, textbooks and decided cases. They may call evidence of an interpreter, if the language is one unknown to the court, or an expert if the word or expression is such as to require expert interpretation. Between a technical expression in Japanese and a plain word in French there must be a whole spectrum which calls for suitable and individual treatment.'

Meaning of 'preparatory work'   Travaux préparatoires, or preparatory work, is a phrase covering materials which record such matters as the proceedings of an international conference which produced the treaty in question. Thus in *Porter v Freudenberg* {[1915] 1 KB 857, at p 876.} Lord Reading CJ referred to 'statements made in a committee of the conference which prepared the Hague Convention of 1907 upon the Laws and Customs of war on land'. In relation to the Warsaw Convention on International Carriage by Air Lord Scarman said-

> 'Working papers of delegates to the conference, or memoranda submitted by delegates for consideration by the conference, though relevant, will seldom be helpful; but an agreed conference minute of the understanding on the basis of which the draft of an article of the convention was accepted may well be of great value.'

{*Fothergill v Monarch Airlines Ltd* [1980] 2 All ER 696, at p 716.}

Court's right to consider preparatory work   The court is entitled, in construing a treaty and any enactment based on it, to make cautious reference to the preparatory work of the treaty. {*Porter v Freudenberg* [1915] 1 KB 857, at p 876; *Post Office v Estuary Radio Ltd* [1968] 2 QB 740, at p 761; *Fothergill v Monarch Airlines Ltd* [1980] 2 All ER 696.} Lord Wilberforce suggested that this should be done only where the material involved is both public and accessible; and indisputably points to a definite legislative intention. {*Fothergill v Monarch Airlines Ltd* [1980] 2 All ER 696, at p 703.}

Court's right to consider la jurisprudence   For the purpose of securing uniformity of application internationally, as well as the correct interpretation of the treaty, the court is entitled to refer to decisions of foreign courts. {*Fothergill v Monarch Airlines Ltd* [1980] 2 All ER 696.}

Court's right to consider la doctrine   For the purpose of securing uniformity of application internationally, as well as the correct interpretation of the treaty, the court is entitled to refer to the writings of foreign jurists. {*Fothergill v Monarch Airlines Ltd* [1980] 2 All ER 696. As to admission of the writings of jurists generally see s 6 of this Code.}

Vienna Convention   The Vienna Convention on the Law of Treaties {Treaty Series No 58 (1980); Cmnd 7964.} contains provisions governing the interpretation of any treaty which was concluded after the date when the Vienna Convention entered into force, namely 27 January 1980. However these provisions, set out in s 3 of the Convention, codify existing public international law, and may be taken to apply to the interpretation of all treaties. {*Fothergill v Monarch Airlines Ltd* [1980] 2 All ER 696, *per* Lord Diplock at p 707.} They are also of interest in relation to statutory interpretation generally. Accordingly they are set out below.

'Section 3. Interpretation of Treaties

ARTICLE 31

General rule of interpretation

1. A treaty shall be interpreted in good faith in accordance with the ordinary meaning to be given to the terms of the treaty in their context and in the light of its object and purpose.
2. The context for the purpose of the interpretation of a treaty shall comprise, in addition to the text, including its preamble and annexes:

   (a) any agreement relating to the treaty which was made between all the parties in connexion with the conclusion of the treaty;

   (b) any instrument which was made by one or more parties in connexion with the conclusion of the treaty and accepted by the other parties as an instrument related to the treaty.
3. There shall be taken into account, together with the context:

   (a) any subsequent agreement between the parties regarding the interpretation of the treaty or the application of its provisions;

   (b) any subsequent practice in the application of the treaty which establishes the agreement of the parties regarding its interpretation;

   (c) any relevant rules of international law aplicable in the relations between the parties.
4. A special meaning shall be given to a term if it is established that the parties so intended.

ARTICLE 32

Supplementary means of interpretation

Recourse may be had to supplementary means of interpretation, including the preparatory work of the treaty and the circumstances of its conclusion, in order to confirm the meaning resulting from the application of article 31, or to determine the meaning when the interpretation according to article 31:

   (a) leaves the meaning ambiguous or obscure; or

   (b) leads to a result which is manifestly absurd or unreasonable.

ARTICLE 33
Interpretation of treaties authenticated in two or more languages

1. When a treaty has been authenticated in two or more languages, the text is equally authoritative in each language, unless the treaty provides or the parties agree that, in case of divergence, a particular text shall prevail.

2. A version of the treaty in a language other than one of those in which the text was authenticated shall be considered an authentic text only if the treaty so provides or the parties so agree.

3. The terms of a treaty are presumed to have the same meaning in each authentic text.

4. Except where a particular text prevails in accordance with paragraph 1, when a comparison of the authentic texts discloses a difference of meaning which the application of articles 31 and 32 does not remove, the meaning which best reconciles the texts, having regard to the object and purpose of the treaty, shall be adopted.'

Purposive construction of treaty   Paragraph 1 of art 31 of the Vienna Convention requires a combination of literal and purposive construction. {Whether this imports the British or European version of purposive construction is not clear. For the distinction between them see s 320 of this Code.} This must be taken as permitting a purposive-and-strained construction in appropriate cases. {For purposive-and-strained construction, the kind usually intended when 'purposive construction' is referred to, see s 315 of this Code.}

Example 4   In *Fothergill v Monarch Airlines Ltd* {[1980] 2 All ER 696.} the House of Lords considered the meaning of provisions of the Warsaw Convention as set out in Sch 1 to the Carriage by Air Act 1961. Article 26(2) of the scheduled Convention states that, in case of 'damage' to baggage, complaint must be made within seven days. The plaintiff complained within seven days that a seam of his suitcase had been torn away, but did not complain within seven days that some of the contents were missing. He argued that this loss was not within the term 'damage', and so did not need to be reported.

Held Although this might be true on a literal construction, it was necessary to depart from the literal meaning in order to give effect to the purpose, which was to enable the airline to take suitable steps when an incident was notified. Referring to the language of art 26(2), Lord Wilberforce remarked {P 702.} that 'some strain, if not distortion, seems inevitable'.

The matter was put right for the future by the addition of a new s 4A to the 1961 Act. {Carriage by Air and Road Act 1979 s 2.} The House of

Lords held in *Monarch Airlines* that this did not affect the interpretation of the provisions as they previously stood. {For a criticism of the decision in *Monarch Airlines* see F A Mann 'Uniform Statutes in English Law' (1983) 99 LQR 376. For another example of purposive construction of a treaty see *Quazi v Quazi* [1979] 3 All ER 897, at p 915.}

The *Monarch Airlines* decision marks a departure by the House of Lords from the view taken by it in *Ellerman Lines v Murray*. {[1931] AC 126.} Here a literal meaning was given to s 1(1) of the Merchant Shipping (International Labour Conventions) Act 1925, notwithstanding that this was arguably absurd, and contrary to the purpose of the labour convention the Act stated by its preamble that it intended to implement (at which the House of Lords declined to look). Lord Wilberforce had earlier said of the House's refusal to consider the labour convention in this case that it was 'atypical and in my opinion should no longer be followed'. {*Buchanan (James) & Co Ltd v Babco Forwarding and Shipping (UK) Ltd* [1978] AC 141, at p 153; but see F A Mann 'Uniform Statutes in English Law' (1983) 99 LQR 376.} As the examination of the case at pp 549–550 below shows, it is unlikely that 'looking' at the labour convention would in any case have affected the result.
{For other cases where the relevant treaty was consulted see *Pyrene Co Ltd v Scindia Steam Navigation Co Ltd* [1954] 2 QB 402, at p 421; *Riverstone Meat Co Pty Ltd v Lancashire Shipping Co Ltd* [1961] AC 807; *The Norwhale. Owners of the Vessel Norwhale v Ministry of Defence* [1975] QB 589.}

243. Enacting history: judicial notice of

No rule prevents the court from inspecting in private whatever materials it thinks fit to ensure that it is well informed, whether in relation to the case before it or generally. Where these materials constitute publicly-available enacting history, the court takes judicial notice of them.

COMMENTARY

As stated in s 119 of this Code, the court of construction, like the legislative draftsman, needs to be as well-informed as possible. No legal limitation is placed on the court's freedom to read in private any materials it thinks fit relating to the legislative history of any Act of Parliament, whether for the purposes of a particular case before it or in order to acquire information about current affairs generally. Lord Hailsham LC said-

> 'I always look at *Hansard*, I always look at the Blue Books, I always look at everything I can in order to see what is meant . . . The idea that [the Law Lords] do not read these things is quite rubbish . . . '

{(1981) HL Rep (5th series) col 1346.}
Lord Denning confirmed this view: 'Having sat there for five years, I would

only say: "I entirely agree and have nothing to add".' {*Hadmor Productions Ltd v Hamilton* [1981] 2 All ER 724, at p 731.}

Judicial notice   The general doctrine of judicial notice is described in s 21 of this Code. The Judicial Committee of the Privy Council held that-

' . . . judicial notice ought to be taken of such matters as the reports of Parliamentary Commissions and of such other facts as must be assumed to have been within the contemplation of the legislature when the Acts in question were passed.'

{*Govindan Sellappah Nayar Kodakan Pillai v Punchi Banda Mundanyake* [1953] AC 514, at p 528.}

244. Enacting history: inspection by court of

The court has an inherent power to inspect any material brought before it. This is to enable the court to determine whether the material is relevant to the point of construction in question, and if so whether it should be admitted.

COMMENTARY

It is never possible to say to the court 'you must not look at this'. The court is always entitled to inspect any document or other material which is or may be relevant in the proceedings. Even if the material turns out to be inadmissible, the court must be able to inspect it in order to ascertain that fact.

Where an enactment is to be applied, then, as the Law Commissions put it in their 1969 survey, 'a judge might wish to inform himself about the general legal and factual situation forming the background to the enactment'. {'The Interpretation of Statutes' (1969) Law Com No 21, Scot Law Com No 11 p 28.} The Law Commissions added-

'Provided the court thought that the information was relevant and reliable, there do not seem to be any specific limitations on the information to which the court might refer under [this] heading.' {Ibid.}

The word 'refer' in this passage is ambiguous, but it is taken to be equivalent to 'rely'. The court must be able to refer to material in the sense of inspecting it in order to determine whether or not it is 'relevant and reliable'.

Similarly judges often say 'look at' when what they mean is 'rely on'. Thus Lord Denning MR said in *Letang v Cooper* {[1965] 1 QB 232, at p 240}: 'But you cannot look at what the committee recommended, or at least, if you do look at it, you should not be unduly influenced by it'. {Cf *Katikiro of Buganda v A-G* [1961] 1 WLR 119, where the Judicial Committee refused to 'look at' a White Paper, but added that in any case it failed to establish the contention for which it was sought to be cited!}

245. Enacting history: recitals by counsel of

The court may, if it thinks fit, allow an advocate to read out, *de bene esse*, any material forming part of the enacting history of a relevant enactment for the purpose of implementing the informed interpretation rule or determining whether the material is admissible.

COMMENTARY

The court is master of its own procedure. If it thinks fit to allow an advocate to recite any material, in case it might be relevant, the court has power to do so.

De bene esse   As to the *de bene esse* principle see s 264 of this Code.

Excluded matters   Counsel are said to be under a duty not to cite to the court any excluded matter (such as *Hansard* reports). {For the exclusionary rule see s 241 of this Code.} Nevertheless the court can authorise this if it thinks fit. Lord Denning MR said-

> 'In most of the cases in the courts, it is undesirable for the Bar to cite Hansard or for the judges to read it. But in cases of extreme difficulty, I have often dared to do my own research. I have read *Hansard* just as if I had been present in the House during a debate on the Bill. And I am not the only one to do so.'

{*Hadmor Productions Ltd v Hamilton* [1981] 2 All ER 724, at p 731.}

Here Lord Denning referred to the fact that normally any citizen is entitled to be present in the public gallery and hear parliamentary debates. Judges are citizens. If they are entitled to witness debates, they must be entitled to read or hear reports of them.

Lord Diplock stresses that, while the judge may admit such reports, counsel may not introduce them without his permission-

> 'The rule that recourse to *Hansard* is not permitted as an aid to the construction of an Act of Parliament is one which it is the duty of counsel to observe in the conduct of their clients' cases before any English court of justice.'

{*Hadmor Productions Ltd v Hamilton* [1982] 1 All ER 1042, at p 1055.}

246. Enacting history: adoption as part of counsel's argument

It is a recognised technique for the court to permit counsel to lay before it, as part of his argument, any relevant material relating to the enacting history which the court thinks fit to allow.

COMMENTARY

The device of making questionable material part of one's argument is an old advocate's trick. Lord Hailsham LC, speaking of his time at the Bar, said of material such as *Hansard*-

> ' . . . I never let on for an instant that I had read the stuff. I produced it as an argument of my own, as if I had thought of it myself. I only took the trouble because I could not do the work in any other way.'

{(1981) 418 HL Rep (5th series) col 1346.}

To prove a negative   The court may permit counsel to cite an item of enacting history in support of his construction of the enactment where the purpose is to show that his construction is not contrary to that item. {*Cozens v North Devon Hospital Management Committee*; *Hunter v Turners (Soham) Ltd* [1966] 2 QB 318 (see *per* Thompson J at p 321). Cf *Beswick v Beswick* [1968] AC 58, *per* Lord Upjohn at p 105.}

247. Enacting history: to ascertain Parliament's view of the pre-Act law

Where a question arises as to the view the legislator took (whether correctly or not) regarding the law with which the enactment dealt, this is a matter of enacting history, and the usual rules apply.

COMMENTARY

This Code distinguishes between a pure question of what the pre-Act law was (when no question of admissibility of enacting history applies), and a question as to the peculiar view the legislator took of that law (which is to be treated in the same way as any other question of surrounding fact). This section deals with the latter aspect. {As to the former aspect see s 231 of this Code.}

Mistake by legislator as to pre-Act law   If Parliament legislates upon an erroneous view of the law, this is bound to affect construction. Lord Simon of Glaisdale said-

> 'Once it is accepted that the purpose of ascertainment of the antecedent defect in the law is to interpret Parliament's intention, it must follow that it is Parliament's understanding of that law as evincing such a defect which is relevant, *not what the law is subsequently declared to be.*'

{*Black-Clawson International Ltd v Papierwerke Waldhof-Aschaffenberg AG* [1975] 1 All ER 810, at p 845 (emphasis added). Lord Simon went on to say that on reflection he thought his hesitation on the point in *Povey v Povey* [1970] 3 All ER 612 was unjustified, and added a reference to *Barras v Aberdeen Steam Trawling and Fishing Co* [1933] AC 402.}

To this it should be added that the law as it really was may nevertheless be also relevant. {See s 231 of this Code.} Later in his speech Lord Simon refers to 'the irrebuttable ascription to Parliament of a draftsman's knowledge of the law in relation to which Parliament is legislating'. {P 845.} This perhaps puts the point rather too strongly, since the draftsman's intention is not the only one to be considered. {As to the duplex approach to legislative intention see s 101 of this Code.}

If it can be demonstrated that one of the opposing constructions put forward involves accepting that Parliament was mistaken as to the law, this may favour acceptance of the alternative construction. {*Black-Clawson International Ltd v Papierwerke Waldhof-Aschaffenberg AG* [1975] 1 All ER 810, *per* Lord Reid at p 815.} This is because of the comity or respect between judiciary and legislature. {As to this see pp 530–533 of this Code.}

Committee reports The report of a committee set up to examine the pre-Act law and make recommendations for its improvement may be treated as a guide to what Parliament thought that law was. As Lord Reid said in relation to the provision of the so-called Greer Report {Report of the Foreign Judgments (Reciprocal Enforcement) Committee (1932) Cmd 4213.} upon which s 8 of the Foreign Judgments (Reciprocal Enforcement) Act 1933 was based-

> 'I think we can take this report as accurately stating . . . the law as it was then understood to be, and therefore we are fully entitled to look at those parts of the report which deal with those matters.'

{*Black-Clawson International Ltd v Papierwerke Waldhof-Aschaffenberg AG* [1975] 1 All ER 810 at, p 814.}

Anticipation of change Parliament may word an enactment with a view to dealing with an expected future judicial development of the law. {See, e g, *Rookes v Barnard* [1964] AC 1129 (where the expected development did not in fact take place).}

248. Enacting history: to ascertain the mischief

Enacting history may be used to ascertain the mischief Parliament intended to remedy by the enactment, subject to the restrictions set out in section 241 of this Code.

COMMENTARY

The proposition that an enactment is intended to remedy a particular mischief is explained in s 138 and Part XIV of this Code. The need to use legislative history in order to ascertain the mischief was described by Lord Simon of Glaisdale in *Black-Clawson International Ltd v Papierwerke Waldhof-Aschaffenberg AG.* {[1975] 1 All ER 810, at p 843.} The case concerned the interpretation of s 8 of the Foreign Judgments (Reciprocal Enforcement) Act 1933. The item of legislative history in question was the so-called Greer Report {Report of the Foreign Judgments (Reciprocal Enforcement) Committee (1932) Cmd 4213.}, upon which s 8 was based. Lord Simon said-

> 'The first question is . . . whether the Greer report can be looked at in order to ascertain what was the 'mischief' which Parliament was seeking to remedy. 'Mischief' is an old, technical expression; but it reflects a firmly established and salutary rule of statutory construction. *It is rare indeed that a statute can be properly interpreted without knowing what was the legislative objective.*'

{Emphasis added. Cf *Maunsell v Olins* [1974] 3 WLR 835, at pp 847-9; *Holme v Guy* (1877) 5 Ch D 901.}

Committee reports The report of a committee set up to examine the mischief and make recommendations for its remedying may be treated as a guide to what Parliament thought the mischief was. As Lord Reid said in relation to the provision of the so-called Greer Report {Report of the Foreign Judgments (Reciprocal Enforcement) Committee (1932) Cmd 4213.} upon which s 8 of the Foreign Judgments (Reciprocal Enforcement) Act 1933 was based-

'I think we can take this report as accurately stating "the mischief"
... and therefore we are fully entitled to look at those parts of the
report which deal with [it].'

{*Black-Clawson International Ltd v Papierwerke Waldhof-Aschaffenberg AG*
[1975] 1 All ER 810 at, p 814. For details given by Lord Reid of the mischief so
found see p 815 of the report.}

In *Eastman Photographic Materials Co Ltd v Comptroller-General of Patents*
{[1898] AC 571.}, the House of Lords considered the meaning of a provision of
the Patents, Designs and Trade Marks Act 1888 based on the report of a
departmental commission. Lord Halsbury LC said {P 573.}-

' ... I think no more accurate source of information as to what was
the evil or defect which the Act of Parliament now under
construction was intended to remedy could be imagined than the
report of that commission.'

{Approved by Viscount Dilhorne in *Black-Clawson International Ltd v
Papierwerke Waldhof-Aschaffenberg AG* [1975] 1 All ER 810 at, p 821.}

Similarly the Court of Appeal in *Letang v Cooper* {[1965] 1 QB 201.} allowed
reference to a committee report for this purpose. {For other such references to
committee reports see *Rookes v Barnard* [1964] AC 1129; *Heatons Transport (St
Helens) Ltd v Transport and General Workers Union* [1973] AC 15; *National
Provincial Bank Ltd v Ainsworth* [1965] AC 1175; *Shenton v Tyler* [1939] Ch
620.}

In *Assam Railways and Trading Co Ltd v IRC* {[1935] AC 445, at p 458.},
Lord Wright stressed that the above-cited dictum of Lord Halsbury approved
the citation of the commission's report 'not directly to ascertain the intention of
the words used in the Act' but merely 'to show what were the surrounding
circumstances'.

249. Enacting history: as an indication of Parliament's intention

Parliament's overall intention is to be gathered from the words of the
Act. These are to be given an informed interpretation however, and
enacting history is an important element here.

The nature of the remedy provided by the enactment to counter the
mischief is of the essence of its meaning. Here above all the Act should
speak for itself, and be interpreted directly by the court. The court will
look with caution and reserve at any outside statement which purports to
lay down the legal meaning of a remedial provision in an Act.

Care must always be taken to guard against the possibility that an
intention suggested by the legislative history was in the end departed
from by Parliament.

COMMENTARY

Sections 247 and 248 of the Code and this section deal respectively with
Parliament's understanding of the pre-Act law, the mischief and the remedy. As
Lindley MR said-

'In order to interpret any statute it is as necesary now as it was when Lord Coke reported *Heydon's Case* to consider how the law stood when the statute to be construed was passed, what the mischief was for which the old law did not provide, and the remedy provided by the statute to cure that mischief.'

{*Re Mayfair Property Co* [1898] 2 Ch 28, at p 35. For a full description of *Heydon's Case* see s 301 of this Code.}

The remedy is bound up with the overall intention, always the key factor. The finding of the legislative intention is quintessentially the function of the court. On this the court must ultimately make up its own mind. {As to legislative intention see Part V of this Code.}

The courts have been inclined to reject outright any outside material which purports to state what an enactment really means. However it appears that the better view is that the court should not altogether deprive itself of recourse to any form of enacting history, but should regard it as of greater or less persuasive value. It certainly has no binding authority.

Non-adherence to preparatory material   Perhaps the most crucial consideration when dealing with enacting history materials is the possibility that Parliament changed its mind, or for some other reason departed from them.

In *Assam Railways and Trading Co Ltd v Comrs of Inland Revenue* {[1935] AC 445 at, p 458.}, where the House of Lords refused to permit counsel to refer to a recommendation in the Report of the Royal Commission on Income Tax {(1920) Cmd 615.} to explain a provision of the Finance Act 1920 as amended by the Finance Act 1927, Lord Wright said that committee reports are of little value 'because it does not follow that their recommendations were accepted'. {To the like effect see Lord Denning MR in *Letang v Cooper* [1965] 1 QB 232, at p 240.}

Lord Wright's dictum carries the implication that if there is some indication that a recommendation *was* accepted (eg, because its wording was copied into the Act) the objection to relying on it is removed. In any case, all enacting history must be inspected with great care and caution. As an indication of legislative intention, it is very far behind the actual words of the Act. {For the presumption that the text is the primary indication of intent see s 136 of this Code.}

250. Enacting history: as persuasive authority

Where an item of enacting history (other than a matter of pure fact) is admitted in interpretation, it is of persuasive authority only. The weight to be attached to it depends on its nature and the surrounding circumstances. On a strict view, its origin carries no weight in itself, and only the argumentative cogency of the material possesses validity. Where the literal meaning of the enactment is clear, the court is unlikely to allow it to be displaced by a contrary indication in the enacting history.

COMMENTARY

Except in so far as it is purely factual, that an item of legislative history comes from an impressive source, for example a high-powered committee which drew up the Bill for the Act, strictly should not add to its weight. The material should stand on its own feet, and not gain (or lose) cogency from its provenance. In other words cogency should here depend solely on the quality of argument displayed in the source.

Fact is here excluded because it is a matter of evidence (or judicial notice) rather than argument. For this purpose 'fact' must be taken to include expert opinion, whether of law or otherwise.

Preservation of the judicial function   It is the function of the court alone to declare the legal meaning of an enactment. If anyone else (such as the draftsman of the provision) purports to lay down what the legal meaning is the court will tend to react adversely, regarding this as an encroachment upon its constitutional sphere.

This aspect was clearly stated by Lord Wilberforce in *Black-Clawson International Ltd v Papierwerke Waldhof-Aschaffenberg AG* {[1975] 1 All ER 810 at, p 828.}, when considering whether a committee report could be relied on in construing s 8 of the Foreign Judgments (Reciprocal Enforcement) Act 1933-

> 'In my opinion it is not proper or desirable to make use of such a document as a committee or commission report, or for that matter of anything reported as said in Parliament, or any official notes on clauses, for *a direct statement of what a proposed enactment is to mean* . . . To be concrete, in a case where a committee prepared a draft Bill and accompanies that by a clause by clause commentary, it ought not to be permissible, even if the proposed Bill is enacted without variation, *to take the meaning of the Bill from the commentary* . . .
>
> Legislation in England is passed by Parliament, and put in the form of written words. This legislation is given legal effect on subjects by virtue of judicial decision, and it is the function of the courts to say what the application of words to particular cases or particular individuals is to be. This power which has been devolved on the judges from the earliest times is an essential part of the constitutional process by which subjects are brought under the rule of law - as distinct from the rule of the King or the rule of Parliament; and it would be a degradation of that process if the courts were to be merely a *reflecting mirror* of what some other interpretation agency might say . . .
>
> It is sound enough to ascertain, if that can be done, the objectives of any particular measure, and the background of the enactment; but to take the opinion, whether of a Minister or an official or a committee, as to the intended meaning in particular applications of a clause or a phrase, would be a stunting of the law and not a healthy development.'

{Emphasis added. See also Lord Reid at pp 814-5 and Lord Diplock at p 835.}

In the same case, Viscount Dilhorne made it clear that this approach does not preclude the court from 'looking at' any material it likes. {Pp 822-3. See s 244 of this Code.} What it means is that the court will not take orders from anyone but the legislature itself. As Lord Langdale put it in a nineteenth-century case: 'we must endeavour to attain for ourselves the true meaning of the language employed'. {*Gorham v Bishop of Exeter* (1850) 14 Jur 443; cited approvingly by Farwell LJ in *R v West Riding of Yorkshire County Council* [1906] 2 KB 676. But see s 257 of this Code.}

Drafting error The essential validity of the doctrine that the court must make up its own mind on the legal meaning of an enactment is demonstrated by the fact that outside commentators may be mistaken. Alternatively the draftsman may have made an error. It can be unfair if words which mean one thing are held to mean another merely because Parliament got them wrong.

As Viscount Dilhorne put it: 'Of course it may be that the language used in the draft Bill and in the Act is defective and does not carry out the committee's and Parliament's intention'. {*Black-Clawson International Ltd v Papierwerke Waldhof-Aschaffenberg AG* [1975] 1 All ER 810, at p 823. See also Lord Simon of Glaisdale at p 847.} Such errors may need to be corrected by strained construction, but this is entirely a matter for the court's free decision. {As to rectifying construction see s 142 of this Code.}

Clear literal meaning As always, the court arrives at the legal meaning of the enactment by weighing the interpretative factors respectively favouring the rival constructions. {See Part VII of this Code.} An item of enacting history may carry considerable persuasive force, but this is unlikely to avail if the literal meaning is thought to be clear in an opposite sense.

Example 1 In *Ellerman Lines v Murray* {[1931] AC 126.} the House of Lords had to construe s 1(1) and (2) of the Merchant Shipping (International Labour Conventions) Act 1925. The sub-ss were in the following terms-

'(1) Where by reason of the wreck or loss of a ship on which a seaman is employed his service terminates before the date contemplated in the agreement, he shall, notwithstanding anything in s 158 of the Merchant Shipping Act 1894, {This provided for the payment of wages up to the date of the wreck.} but subject to the provisions of this section, be entitled, in respect of each day on which he is in fact unemployed during a period of two months from the date of the termination of the service, to receive wages at the rate to which he was entitled at that date.

(2) A seaman shall not be entitled to receive wages under this section if the owner shows that the unemployment was not due to the wreck or loss of the ship and shall not be entitled to receive wages under this section in respect of any day if the owner shows that the seaman was able to obtain suitable employment on that day.'

The date contemplated by Murray's agreement for the termination of his service was 11 March. The ship was wrecked 13 days earlier, on 27 February. Murray remained unemployed for the following two months, and the owner was not able to show that this was not due to the wreck. Subsection (2) did not therefore apply.

The question was whether Murray was entitled to two months' wages under sub-s (1) notwithstanding that if the ship had not been wrecked he would have been entitled only to 13 days' further wages. Did the Act enable Murray to make a profit out of the wreck?

The long title to the Act stated that it was 'to give effect to certain Draft Conventions'. These were described in the preamble and included (in part) in Sch 1. The relevant provision (set out as art 2 of Part I of Sch 1) was inconclusive on the point at issue.

A selective comminution of the relevant parts of s 1 runs as follows-

> 'Where by reason of the wreck of a ship on which a seaman is employed his service terminates before the date contemplated in the agreement, he shall be entitled, in respect of each day on which he is in fact unemployed during a period of two months from the date of the termination of the service, to receive wages at the rate to which he was entitled at that date.'

If we insert the actual dates this reads (in abbreviated form)-

> 'Where, by reason of the wreck, his service terminates before 11 March he shall be entitled, in respect of each day on which he is in fact unemployed during the period beginning on 27 February and ending on 26 April, to receive wages at the rate to which he was entitled at 27 February.'

This is a perfectly clear unambiguous proposition. Although the shipowner argued that it was unfair, and not what the labour convention intended, the House held that it was far too plain to be contradicted by materials from the legislative history. As Lord Diplock said in *Hadmor Productions Ltd v Hamilton* {[1982] 1 All ER 1042, at p 1053}: 'I think that the meaning of the words in their application to the facts in the instant case is too plain and unambiguous to justify resort to legislative history'.

A more cogent argument than anything in the legislative history would have been that it was illogical to pay wages for a period after the service would anyway have terminated (see s 323 of this Code). Even this argument might have failed. The literal meaning is very plain, and there could be a humanitarian case for giving a shipwrecked seaman two months' wages regardless of when his service would have ended if the ship had got safely to port.

251. Enacting history: as binding authority

Enacting history is never of binding or compelling authority, the court's ultimate task being always to interpret the text of the enactment.

COMMENTARY

This section of the Code registers the fact that no background material can ever be of more than persuasive authority. It is always for the court to make up its mind as to its weight, when set against the literal meaning of the enactment. {As to the literal meaning see s 91 of this Code.} If the literal meaning is grammatically ambiguous, or obscure, enacting history may have a part to play in determining the legal meaning. Even here, it can never be of more than persuasive authority. {See s 250 of this Code.}

POST-ENACTING HISTORY

252. Post-enacting history: the basic rule

In the period immediately following its enactment, the history of how an enactment is understood forms part of the *contemporanea expositio*, and may be held to throw light on the legislative intention. The later history may, under the doctrine that an Act is always speaking, indicate how the enactment is regarded in the light of developments from time to time.

COMMENTARY

On a superficial view, it may be thought that nothing that happens after an Act is passed can affect the legislative intention at the time it was passed. This overlooks the two factors stated in this section.

Contemporanea expositio The concept of legislative intention is a difficult one. {It is explained in Part V of this Code.} Contemporary exposition helps to show what people thought the Act meant in the period immediately after it was passed. Official statements on its meaning are particularly important here, since every Act is supervised, and most were originally promoted, by a government department which may be assumed to know what the legislative intention was. {See s 253 of this Code.} The concept of *contemporanea expositio* is explained above. {Pp 371–372.}

Updating construction The doctrine that an Act is always speaking, and the consequences in the way of updating construction, are explained in s 146 of this Code.

253. Post-enacting history: official statements on meaning of Act

Official statements by the government department administering an Act, or by any other authority concerned with the Act, may be taken into account as persuasive authority on the meaning of its provisions.

COMMENTARY

The administration of every Act of Parliament is within the purview of some government department. This applies even where other public bodies (such as local authorities) are charged with the day-to-day operation of the Act. It follows that the relevant government department is frequently obliged to form a view as to the meaning of a doubtful enactment. This may happen before the point has come before any court, and arises simply as a matter of administration.

For example tax law cannot be administered without the taking of a view by the Inland Revenue or the Commissioners of Customs and Excise on doubtful points of statutory interpretation. These rulings are communicated to officials of the department and to taxpayers and their advisers. Often they are published, either individually or as part of a regular series. They stand until the court modifies or reverses them, or the department has second thoughts. The informed interpretation rule {See s 199 of this Code.} requires that an Act is to be interpreted in the light of such official rulings.

Example 1   In *Wicks v Firth (Inspector of Taxes)* {[1983] 1 All ER 151, at pp 154, 159.} the House of Lords had regard to a press release issued by the Inland Revenue on 14 June 1978 in relation to the tax treatment of scholarships awarded by employers to children of employees. Lord Bridge said {P 155.} that the release indicated that the Inland Revenue were prepared to treat as relieved from tax certain cases which, on the construction they now contended for, would be caught. He went on-

> 'This is not a decisive consideration, but in choosing between competing constructions of a taxing provision it is legitimate, I think, to incline against a construction which the Revenue are unwilling to apply in its full rigour but feel they must mitigate by way of extra-statutory concession, recognising, presumably, that in some cases their construction would operate to produce a result which Parliament can hardly have intended.'

Lord Templeman said {P 159.} 'the press release is not relevant to statutory construction'. This overlooks the importance of an informed interpretation, and the fact that the press release was undoubtedly part of the post-enacting history, or what in another case Walton J called the 'revenue context'. {*Oram (Inspector of Taxes) v Johnson* [1980] 2 All ER 1, at p 6.}. Its significance went to weight rather than relevance or admissibility.

Official statements of expenditure under an Act may be admitted as an indication of its legal meaning.

Example 2   In *Hanning v Maitland (No 2)* {[1970] 1 All ER 812.} the Court of Appeal admitted statistics showing that, whereas £40,000 a year was being appropriated by Parliament towards the expenses under a legal aid enactment, only about £300 a year was actually being expended. This followed a restrictive ruling on the operation of the enactment arrived at in an earlier decision of the Court of Appeal. It suggested that the ruling did not conform to Parliament's intention.

Altering a departmental ruling   If the department concerned at any time reaches the conclusion that their ruling is wrong in law it is their duty to alter it. They cannot be treated as in any way bound by it in future cases.

Example 3   In *IRC v Trustees of Sir John Aird's Settlement* {[1982] 2 All ER 929.} Nourse J referred to the fact that counsel for the Inland Revenue had informed him in the course of the hearing that they had accepted the general validity of a scheme of tax avoidance known as the simple General Franco scheme. {P 937. As to this scheme see p 194 above.} There was perhaps an implication from the judge's remarks that the Inland Revenue were in some way bound by this acceptance. However there can be no doubt that an administrative ruling of this kind does not bind the department in future cases. A government department has no power to legislate, and cannot of its own accord alter the true meaning of a statute. {*Vestey v IRC* [1979] 3 All ER 976, *per* Lord Wilberforce at pp 984-6; *Customs and Excise Commissioners v Mechanical Services (Trailer Engineers) Ltd* [1979] 1 All ER 501.}

Admissibility As always with legislative history, admissibility of official statements is at the discretion of the court. Formerly courts were less ready than now to allow such material to be cited. {See, e g, *Katikiro of Buganda v A-G* [1960] 3 All ER 849 (Government white paper).}

Often it is important for the court of construction to be aware of what statute users have been told by official pronouncements. It is clearly unjust for the subject to be penalized because a court reverses an official statement he has trusted in. {As to the principle that law should be just see s 128 of this Code.}

The position in relation to official processing of enactments is examined at length in Bennion *Statute Law* (2nd edn, 1983) chap 20. See also s 15 of this Code.

254. Post-enacting history: delegated legislation made under Act

Delegated legislation made under an Act may be taken into account as persuasive authority on the meaning of its provisions.

COMMENTARY

The position regarding delegated legislation as a guide to the meaning of an Act is similar to that in relation to official processing. {See s 253 of this Code.} Indeed delegated legislation closely resembles official processing, the difference being that the former is a type of formal legislation. {As to delegated legislation generally see ss 50 to 70 of this Code.}

An Act may be construed in the light of delegated legislation made under it. {See, e g, *Britt v Buckinghamshire County Council* [1963] 2 All ER 175; *Leung v Garbett* [1980] 2 All ER 436; *R v Uxbridge JJ, ex p Commissioner of Police of the Metropolis* [1981] 3 All ER 129).} On principle such legislation cannot amend an Act, except where power is given for it to do so. It follows that (apart from such excepted cases) a provision of delegated legislation which is inconsistent with an Act is likely to be held ultra vires and void. {See s 58 of this Code.}

255. Post-enacting history: later Acts

Where a later Act is *in pari materia* with an earlier Act, provisions of the later Act may be used to aid the construction of the earlier Act. In determining whether the later provision *alters* the legal meaning of the earlier, the test is whether or not Parliament intended to effect such an alteration.

COMMENTARY

The effect of later Acts really belongs to a consideration of the technique of amendment of Acts, which is described in ss 170 to 177 of this Code. Here we confine ourselves to Acts which are *in pari materia*. {For the meaning of this see pp 516–517 above.}

553

The principle underlying the treatment of Acts which are *in pari materia* is based on the idea that there is continuity of legislative approach to such Acts, and common terminology. {See Example 323.14.} A later Act may thus throw light on some aspect of an earlier. The principle is clear however. No change of meaning is to be taken as effected by the later Act unless this was intended. {*Casanova v R* (1866) LR 1 QB 444, at p 457.}

Such an intention is more readily gathered where the Acts are expressly required to be construed as one. This is a positive indication that Parliament has given its mind to the question. However because of the difficulties which have been caused by this concept of requiring Acts to be construed as one, the phrase has fallen out of use among draftsmen. It is a sloppy device, almost certain to lead to trouble. If an alteration of the earlier Act is intended, it should be made textually. {As to construction as one see s 287 of this Code.} This is one more aspect of ¨the distinction between precision drafting and disorganised composition. {As to this distinction see s 76 of the Code.}

Mistake by Parliament   Where it is clear that an enactment proceeds upon a mistaken view of earlier law, the question may arise of whether this effects a change in that law (apart from any amendment directly made by the enactment).

Here it is necessary to remember that, except when legislating, Parliament has no power to interpret the law. That function belongs to the judiciary. {See p 53 above.} When legislating, Parliament may, with binding effect, *declare* what the law is to be considered to be or have been. But a declaratory enactment must be intended as such. A mere inference that Parliament has mistaken the nature or effect of some legal rule does not in itself amount to a declaration that the rule is other than what it is. {*Dore v Gray* (1788) 2 TR 358, at p 365; *IRC v Dowdall, O'Mahoney & Co Ltd* [1952] AC 401, at pp 417, 421; *IRC v Butterley & Co Ltd* [1955] 2 WLR 785, at pp 807-8.}

However the view taken by Parliament as to the legal meaning of a doubtful enactment may be treated as of persuasive, though not binding, authority. {*Cape Brandy Syndicate v IRC* [1921] 2 KB 403, at p 414; *Camille & Henry Dreyfus Foundation Inc v IRC* [1954] Ch 672, at p 690.}

256. Post-enacting history: judicial decisions on Act

Under the doctrine of precedent or *stare decisis,* dynamic processing of an enactment by the court produces sub-rules which are of either binding or persuasive authority in relation to the future construction of the enactment. Where Parliament subsequently indicates that it adopts any such sub-rule, the status of the sub-rule becomes equivalent to that of legislation.

COMMENTARY

Sub-rules   As to sub-rules produced by dynamic processing see s 26 of this Code.

Subsequent adoption by Parliament   Parliament is normally presumed to legislate in the knowledge of, and having regard to, relevant judicial decisions. If therefore Parliament has a subsequent opportunity to alter the effect of a decision on the legal meaning of an enactment, but refrains from doing so, the implication may be that Parliament approves of that decision and adopts it. This is as aspect of what may be called *tacit legislation*. {See pp 357–358 above.}

Example 1 Section 2(1) of the Law Reform (Personal Injuries) Act 1948 says that, in assessing damages for loss of earnings or profits as a result of personal injury, there shall be deducted one half of certain national insurance or social security benefits receivable *during the five years following the accrual of the cause of action*. It says nothing about such benefits receivable after the five-year period has elapsed, even though at common law the whole of these might fall to be deducted.

In *Hultquist v Universal Pattern and Precision Engineering Co Ltd* {[1960] 2 QB 467.} the Court of Appeal held, where a disablement gratuity had been assessed at 14 per cent for life, that s 2(1) meant that only the first five years' payments could be deducted from damages for the injury. In the Social Security Act 1973, Parliament amended s 2 in ways which showed that they had the whole of its operation under review. The 1973 Act could easily have reversed or modified the effect of *Hultquist v Universal Pattern and Precision Engineering Co Ltd* {[1960] 2 QB 467.} had Parliament been minded to do so.

In *Denman v Essex Area Health Authority* {[1984] 2 All ER 621.} it was submitted that certain payments should be deducted in full after the five-year period elapsed. *Held* The submission would be rejected, since Parliament must be taken by implication to have adopted the decision in *Hultquist v Universal Pattern and Precision Engineering Co Ltd* {[1960] 2 QB 467.} Peter Pain J {P 625.} said 'Parliament thus gave its blessing to the decision'.

Consolidation and codification Straight consolidation or codification does not import any ratification by Parliament of judicial decisions. It does not have them under consideration, and so the case is outside the principle stated in this section. {See ss 232 (consolidation) and 233 (codification) of this Code.}

257. Post-enacting history: committee reports on Act

The court may treat as of persuasive authority in the construction of an enactment the view of an official committee reporting on the meaning of the enactment.

COMMENTARY

Where a Royal Commission, departmental committee or other official body makes a study of a sector of legislation and reports on its meaning, the court may treat this as providing authoritative guidance.

Example 1 The report of the Royal Commission on Criminal Procedure {1981 (Cmnd 8092).} contained an account of how the power of arrest conferred by s 2(4) of the Criminal Law Act 1967 and similar enactments should be exercised. {Para 3.66.} In *Mohammed-Holgate v Duke* {[1983] 3 All ER 526.} the Court of Appeal held that this account reflected the proper basis for the exercise of the power of arrest, and could be relied on as authoritative.

258. Post-enacting history: commentaries on Act

The writings of jurists and other learned commentators may be considered by the court in construing an enactment. There is now no requirement that the commentator be deceased before his writings can be regarded as authoritative. A commentary by the draftsman of the Act may be regarded as particularly helpful on points related to its intended meaning.

COMMENTARY

Learned commentaries undoubtedly form part of the post-enacting history, and are often taken into account by courts of construction. The matter is dealt with in s 6 of this Code.

PART XI

The Informed Interpretation Rule: Further Provisions

Introduction to Part XI This Part contains half a dozen general sections supplementary to the informed interpretation rule set out in s 119 of this Code, and particularly relevant to the consideration of legislative history (Part X).

The informed interpretation rule requires an enactment to be construed in its 'context'. The meaning of this is explained (s 259). A restriction is placed on the rule by the need to avoid unpredictability, and unjustified lengthening of legal proceedings (s 260). The need for full information *before* any judgment is made as to whether or not the enactment is doubtful calls for a two-stage approach (s 261). The information required by the interpreter includes legal expertise (s 262). The court is assisted by the preparation of briefs by counsel (s 263). Admission of information *de bene esse* is described (s 264).

259. Meaning of the 'context' of an enactment

For the purpose of applying the informed interpretation rule, the context of an enactment comprises, in addition to the other provisions of the Act containing it, the legislative history of that Act, the provisions of other Acts *in pari materia,* and all facts constituting or concerning the subject-matter of the Act.

COMMENTARY

Viscount Simonds stressed the interpreter's need to read and absorb the whole Act before deciding whether real doubt exists as to the legal meaning of an enactment-

> '... it must often be difficult to say that any terms are clear and unambiguous until they have been read in their context ... the elementary rule must be observed that no one should profess to understand any part of a statute ... before he has read the whole of it. Until he has done so he is not entitled to say that it or any part of it is clear and unambiguous.'

{*A-G v Prince Ernest Augustus of Hanover* [1957] AC 436, at p 463.}
  Or as Learned Hand J put it-

> ' ... the meaning of a sentence may be more than that of the separate words, as a melody is more than the notes, and no degree of particularity can ever obviate recourse to the setting in which all appear, and which all collectively create.'

{*Helvering v Gregory* (1934) 69 F (2d) 809, at p 810.}

Other judges have pointed out that it may not be enough even to read the whole Act. 'At first blush, I should have said that "member" [of a company] means what it says' said Roxburgh J, pointing to the importance of the legislative history of the enactment before him, 'but it is never safe to construe an Act of Parliament by paying undue attention to the meaning of words . . . the matter has a long history'. {*Re Consolidated Goldfields of New Zealand Ltd* [1953] Ch 689, at p 694.}

Speaking of the Acts relating to industrial disputes, Lord Scarman said-

'It is wrong to attempt to construe any section or subsection of these Acts without reference to their legislative purpose. And it is also necessary to have regard to the history of the statute law and the case law since 1906 for a full understanding of them. This history I would summarize as a shifting pattern of Parliamentary assertions and judicial responses, a legal point counterpoint which has been more productive of excitement than of harmony. The judges have been, understandably, reluctant to abandon common law and equitable principles, unless unambiguously told to do so by statute. Parliament has created ambiguity not through any lack of drafting skill but by its own changes of mind.'

{*NWL Ltd v Woods* [1979] 3 All ER 614, at p 630.}

The surrounding facts are also important to the understanding, and therefore correct interpretation, of an Act.

Example 1 Why does s 1(3)(a) of the Factories Act 1961 (a consolidation Act) require the inside walls of factories to be washed every *fourteen months*? An annual spring cleaning one could understand, but why this odd period? Sir Harold Kent, who drafted the original provision in the Factories Act 1937, gives the answer: factory spring cleaning takes place at Easter, and Easter is a movable feast. {H S Kent *In on the Act* (1979) p 88.}

One aspect of the informed interpretation rule is therefore that the interpreter should treat the express words of the enactment as illumined by consideration of its context or setting. The words are not deployed in a vacuum. Courts accordingly may have regard to the legislative history, the statutory context furnished by legislation *in pari materia,* and the common law context. The overall context of the Act provides the colour and background to the words used, and thus helps the interpreter to arrive at the meaning intended by Parliament.

Judges have not observed a uniform terminology in discussing statutory interpretation. Sometimes they use the word 'context' in a narrow sense. At other times they use it with a meaning so wide that it embraces virtually all the interpretative criteria. Thus Viscount Simonds said in *A-G v Prince Ernest Augustus of Hanover* {[1957] AC 436, at p 461.}-

' . . . words, and particularly general words, cannot be read in isolation: their colour and content are derived from their context. So it is that I conceive it to be my right and duty to examine every word of a statute in its context, and I use "context" in its widest sense . . . its preamble, the existing state of the law, other statutes in pari materia, and the mischief which I can, by those and other legitimate means, discern the statute was intended to remedy . . . I must admit to a consciousness of inadequacy if I am invited to interpret any part of any statute without a knowledge of its context in the fullest sense of that word.'

In the same case Lord Normand said: 'It is the merest commonplace to say that words abstracted from context may be meaningless or misleading'. {P 465.} Lord Somervell of Harrow added: 'It is unreal to proceed as if the court looked first at the provision in dispute without knowing whether it was contained in a Finance Act or a Public Health Act'. {P 473.}

260. Need to avoid unpredictability, and lengthening of proceedings

In determining whether consideration should be given to any item of legislative history or other informative material, and if so what weight should be given to it, regard is to be had to-

(a) the desirability of persons being able to rely on the ordinary meaning conveyed by the text of the enactment, taking into account its context in the Act or other instrument and the legislative intention; and

(b) the need to avoid prolonging legal or other proceedings without compensating advantage.

COMMENTARY

This section is taken from s 15AB(3) of an Australian statute, the Acts Interpretation Act 1901 as amended by the Acts Interpretation Amendment Act 1984 s 7. In turn s 15AB was derived from clause 5(3) of the draft Bill proposed in the present author's book *Statute Law* {(2nd edn, 1983) pp 269-70, 305-6.} Paragraph (a) reflects the predictability principle described in s 130 of this Code. Paragraph (b) is an aspect of the law's general concern that legal proceedings shall not be unduly protracted.

The informed interpretation rule does not go so far as to permit the court to take into account material which is not generally available. As Lord Reid said in *Black-Clawson v Papierwerke* {[1975] 1 All ER 810, at p 814.}: 'An Act is addressed to all the lieges and it would seem wrong to take into account anything that was not public knowledge at the time'.

A wide variety of materials are nevertheless publicly available, and this may cause problems for the practitioner who is called on to advise a client. The practitioner may have less learning than the judge; and also lack the time and the facilities needed for research. The situation of the ordinary citizen, who is not excused by saying he does not know the law, is even worse. As the Law Commissions have put it-

'A statute may ultimately have to be interpreted by the courts but it is directed to a wider audience. The citizen, or the practitioner whom he consults, may have a heavy burden placed upon him if the context in which a statute is to be understood requires reference to materials which are not readily available without unreasonable inconvenience or expense.'

{*The Interpretation of Statutes* (1969) Law Com No 21 para 60.}

What materials are admissible Outside the courtroom, while there are practical restrictions on what can be looked at there are no legal ones. Inside the courtroom, the position is different. Limitations have been placed by law on materials to which reference may be made. Reports of parliamentary proceedings on the Bill containing the enactment are generally excluded, for example. {See s 241 of this Code.}

Nevertheless the *mind* of the interpreter can never be too well-stocked. A conscientious judge, like a conscientious legislator or a conscientious draftsman, keeps himself fully informed about what is going on in the world. In his private room the judge is free to consult any materials he likes relative to a case before him. He will not rely on a specific source without affording counsel an opportunity to make submissions about it, but he will bring to bear an informed mind. His ultimate task is usually to determine the precise ambit of a statutory duty, and realistically this can only be what the moral philosopher Sir David Ross called 'duty *all things considered*'. {*Foundations of Ethics* p 84.}

Moreover, subject to relevant legal rules, a court or other tribunal considering an enactment is master of its own procedure. {See, e g, *R v Board of Visitors of Wormwood Scrubs Prison, ex p Anderson* (1983) *The Times* 9 November.} It therefore has the power, indeed the duty, to consider such aspects of the legislative history of the enactment as may be necessary to arrive at its legal meaning. In any proceedings, the court will draw the line between on the one hand unduly prolonging the proceedings by allowing excessive citation of source material, and on the other hand concluding the proceedings with an *ill-informed* judgment.

261. The two-stage approach to statutory interpretation

In interpreting an enactment, a two-stage approach is necessary. It is not simply a matter of deciding what doubtful words mean. It must first be decided, on an informed basis, whether or not there *is* a real doubt about the legal meaning of the enactment. If there is, the interpreter moves on to the second stage of resolving the doubt. (The experienced interpreter combines the stages, but notionally they are separate.)

COMMENTARY

It is important to notice that *two* decisions about meaning are contemplated and not, as is often supposed, one only. As Lord Upjohn said, 'you must look at all the admissible surrounding circumstances before starting to construe the Act'. {*R v Schildkamp* [1971] AC 1, at p 23.} Or as Professor Neil MacCormick put it: ' . . . we can't tell whether the case we are faced with is easy or hard until we have reflected on the principles as well as on the prima facie applicable rule or rules'. {*Legal Reasoning and Legal Theory* p 231.}

Sir Rupert Cross perceived that there are two stages of the judge's deliberations-

> ' . . . that at which he enquires whether the words are "in themselves precise and unambiguous", and that at which, having answered this question in the negative, he is seeking to resolve doubts arising from the terms employed by the legislature . . . no one is entitled to assert

that statutory words are unambiguous until he has read them in their
full context . . .'

{R Cross *Statutory Interpretation* pp 51, 110. The words 'having answered this
question in the negative' should not be read as indicating that a sentence which
is plain on its own requires no further consideration.}

The Law Commissions have also stressed the necessity of examining any
statutory expression in its full context before deciding whether it is clear and
unambiguous. {*The Interpretation of Statutes* (1969) Law Com No 21, para 74.
Cf, as to the 'two-stage' approach, *Maunsell v Olins* [1975] 1 All ER 16, *per* Lord
Simon of Glaisdale at p 29.}

Lord Simon of Glaisdale has said that where a report containing a draft Bill
and commentary is cited to the court-

> 'To refuse to consider such a commentary, when Parliament has
> legislated on the basis and faith of it, is for the interpreter to fail to
> put himself in the real position of the promulgator of the instrument
> *before* essaying its interpretation. It is refusing to follow what is
> perhaps the most important clue to meaning. It is perversely
> neglecting the reality, while chasing shadows. As Aneurin Bevan
> said: 'Why gaze in the crystal ball when you can read the book?''

{*Black-Clawson International Ltd v Papierwerke Waldhof-Aschaffenberg AG*
[1975] 1 All ER 810, at p 847. Emphasis added.}

262. Interpreter's need for legal knowledge

The interpreter of an enactment needs to be someone who is, or is
advised by, a person with legal knowledge. This is because an Act is a
legal instrument. It forms part of the body of law, and necessarily
partakes of the character of law. It cannot therefore be reliably
understood by a lay person. Moreover the meaning of the enactment
needed by the interpreter is its *legal* meaning.

COMMENTARY

An Act requires for its understanding a knowledge of the principles laid down
by law for the interpretation of statutes (in this Code referred to as the
interpretative criteria). {For these see Part VI of the Code.} Those principles in
turn demand particular knowledge as to the enactment which is the unit of
enquiry (for example concerning the relevant factual outline). {For the position
of the subject and his adviser see s 7 of this Code. For the enactment as the unit
of enquiry see s 72. For the factual outline see s 78.} At the end of it all,
asexplained in s 3 of the Code, it is the *legal* meaning that the interpreter seeks.

A basic aspect of the informed interpretation rule is therefore that the
interpreter needs to be informed in law. {For the informed interpretation rule
see s 119 of this Code.}

263. Briefs to the court

In appellate courts it is permissible for counsel to submit in advance to
the court a written outline of his argument. The outline (in this Code

referred to as a brief to the court) may include contextual information relative to the enactment which is the unit of enquiry.

COMMENTARY

The knowledge required for application of the informed interpretation rule comes into the possession of the court in one of two ways. {For the informed interpretation rule see s 119 of this Code.} Either the court takes judicial notice of it or it is proved by evidence. These are dealt with in detail elsewhere in this Code. {See ss 21, 82 and 243 (judicial notice) and s 81 (evidence).}

Counsel appearing in a case may furnish the court in advance with written details of either sort of information. Some courts provide guidance as to the form this should take. {See, e g, Practice Note [1983] 2 All ER 34 (Court of Appeal Civil Division); A Guide to Proceedings in the Court of Appeal Criminal Division [1983] Crim LR 415.}

It is always helpful to a court to receive advance notice of counsel's argument, including evidence proposed to be adduced. As respects judicial notice, a brief to the court may include material which refreshes the judicial memory on matters which are of common knowledge, and of which it may be asked to take judicial notice.

Brandeis briefs The brief to the court has been taken to extreme lengths in the United States. In the 1908 case of *Muller v Oregon* {208 US 412.} the constitutionality of a statute which limited the hours for which women could work was challenged. Louis Brandeis (later a distinguished justice of the US Supreme Court) was retained as counsel to uphold the statute. He submitted to the court a brief which contained two pages of legal argument followed by more than one hundred pages of contextual fact largely gleaned from published official reports. Briefs of this kind have since become common in the United States, and are known as Brandeis briefs.

There is no reason in principle why the Brandeis brief cannot be used in British courts. Judges discourage what they consider excessively long and complex briefs, but welcome the assistance given by compact summaries of the matters to be laid before them. {For a case where elaborate information was presented to the Court of Appeal as to the factual working of the supplementary benefits system (not however referred to in the judgments) see *R v Preston Supplementary Benefits Appeal Tribunal, ex p Moore* [1975] 1 WLR 624.}

264. Admission of information *de bene esse*

Where the court is doubtful of the admissibility of any contextual material, it may allow it to be cited *de bene esse* pending a decision on admissibility.

COMMENTARY

As master of his court, the judge may permit citation of doubtful material *de bene esse*. Use of this phrase in law goes back at least to 1272, it having been originally borrowed from the church. {T F T Plucknett (1946) 62 LQR 130.}

The rule stated in this section of the Code was recognised by Lord Simon of

Glaisdale in *Black-Clawson v Papierwerke* {[1975] 1 All ER 810, at p 841.} when he said-

> 'The matter was, in my judgment, put beyond doubt when your Lordships looked, de bene esse, at the report of the Greer Committee on Reciprocal Enforcement of Foreign Judgments.'

The principle of admission *de bene esse* is mainly referable to the doctrine of conditional relevancy in the law of evidence. {See the US legal dictionary *Words and Phrases*, DE BENE ESSE.}

> 'To take or do any thing *de bene esse*, is to accept or allow it as *well done for the present;* but when it comes to be more fully examined or tried, to stand or fall according to the merit of the thing in its own nature'.

{Tomlin's *Law Dictionary* (4th edn, 1835) tit. DE BENE ESSE (derived from Jacob's Law Dictionary).}

The consequence of such a reference on a point of statutory interpretation 'falling' rather than 'standing' would be that the court based no part of its judgment on the material so admitted. It would however have added to the judge's stock of factual knowledge in the same way as material looked at in the privacy of his chambers.

PART XII

The Functional Construction Rule

Introduction to Part XII This Part describes the functions of the various components of an Act, with a view to the application of the functional construction rule set out in s 124 of this Code. All the components form part of what is put out by Parliament as its Act. Furthermore s 19 of the Interpretation Act 1978 has the effect of requiring them all to be taken into account (for what they are worth). The components fall into three groups.

The first group consists of the operative components. Their nature is explained (s 265). They comprise sections (s 266), Schedules (s 267), provisos (s 268) and savings (s 269).

Next come the amendable descriptive components, whose nature is explained in s 270. They comprise the long title (s 271), the preamble if any (s 272), purpose clauses (s 273), recitals (s 274), the short title (s 275), and examples (s 276).

The third group consists of unamendable descriptive components, whose nature is dscribed in s 277. They comprise the chapter number (s 278), the date of passing (s 279), the enacting formula (s 280), headings (s 281), sidenotes (s 282), format (s 283), and punctuation (s 284).

Part XII concludes with four sections dealing with ways in which other provisions may be incorporated into an Act. The nature of this process is described (s 285). Archival drafting, requiring recourse by the interpreter to historical sources, is explained (s 286). Construction of Acts as one is dealt with (s 287). Lastly, collective titles are described (s 288).

OPERATIVE COMPONENTS OF ACT

265. Operative components of Act: nature of

The operative components of an Act are those that constitute Parliament's pronouncements of law. Operative components normally consist of *sections* and *Schedules*, either of which may incorporate a *proviso* or a *saving*.

COMMENTARY

Functional construction rule Under the functional construction rule set out in s 124 of this Code, the significance to be attached by the interpreter to any component of an Act must be assessed in conformity with its legislative function as a component of that type. This section explains the function of the operative components.

An operative component is often called an 'enactment'. {For the meaning of this term see s 73 of the Code.} The eminent Victorian draftsman Lord Thring used the word *declaration*. He said that an Act may be considered 'as a series of declarations of the Legislature . . .' {*Practical Legislation* p 26.}

Various terms are used by judges to refer to what the Code calls an operative component. Expressions such as 'enacting part', 'enacting provision', 'enacting words' or 'enacting portion' are employed. All four of these will be found in the speeches of the House of Lords in *A-G v Prince Ernest Augustus of Hanover*. {[1957] AC 436.} Nicholl MR referred to 'the purview or enacting part of the statute' in *Brett v Brett*. {(1826) 3 Addams 210, at p 216). This was doubly wrong, as appears below (p 570).}

The adjective *enacting* in this context is an obvious solecism. The enacting words are, if anything, the words at the beginning of an Act usually known as the enacting formula or purview. {See s 280 of this Code.} The mistake apparently derives from the fact that it was formerly the custom to preface *each section* of an Act by a formula such as 'Be it enacted' or 'Be it further enacted'. This practice was however rendered obsolete by s 2 of Lord Brougham's Act of 1850. {13 & 14 Vict c 21. See now the Interpretation Act 1978 s 1.} It is obviously wrong to continue a terminology which was justifiably used (if at all) only up to the middle of the nineteenth century. {The adjective *enacting* was also used in contrast to *declaratory*: see, e g, M D Chalmers *Sale of Goods Act 1893* (12th edn, 1945) p 197.}

The epithet *operative* is appropriate, since we are seeking to identify the parts of the Act that carry the direct message of the legislator, its 'cutting edge'. The term has also been used by judges and is accordingly adopted by this Code. {For examples of this judicial usage see *Glegg v Bromley* [1912] 3 KB 474, *per* Parker J at p 492 ('operative part'); *Commr of Stamp Duties v Atwill* [1973] AC 558, *per* Viscount Dilhorne at p 562 ('operative portion').}

The operative components are obviously by far the most important, for they carry the legislative message directly. All other components serve as commentaries on the operative components, of greater or less utility depending on their precise function.

266. Operative components of Act: sections

Where (as is usually the case) an Act contains more enactments than one, it is divided into sections. Each section is deemed to be a substantive enactment, without the need for enacting words other than the Act's initial enacting formula.

COMMENTARY

This derives from s 2 of Lord Brougham's Act of 1850 {13 & 14 Vict c 21.}, which was partly reproduced as s 8 of the Interpretation Act 1889. {See now Interpretation Act 1978 s 1.} In terms of 1850 conditions, the first sentence of this section represented the existing practice but the second was new.

The earliest statutes were not divided into sections. They had no formal structure, and delivered their message in whatever way seemed best to the author (usually one of the king's justices).

Later, different propositions, often quite unconnected, came to be bundled together in a single statute. A statute became the total legislative output of a Parliament, meeting at some town convenient to the king on one of his progresses. There might be only one day's sitting. Each item in the statute was called a chapter. Thus the Statute of Westminster the First (1275) had 51 chapters, of which one (c 50) remains.

When in the fourteenth century the Commons became established as a necessary party to legislation, it also became established that Parliament met in Westminster Hall. This was because the provincial towns had no hall big enough to accomodate the growing size of the House of Commons. Sessions of Parliament became longer, and statutes became individual Acts.

However the idea lingered that the output of an entire session could be looked on as one statute. Individual Acts were numbered as chapters of that supposed statute. Unless the contrary intention appeared, the chapters all came into force at the same moment of time, namely the beginning of the parliamentary session. {See p 411 above.} This was the literal consequence of the idea that all the Acts of the session formed one statute.

Another inconvenient rule was that each proposition included in a chapter had to be introduced by separate words of enactment. The idea that the enacting formula could be set out once for all at the beginning had not yet occurred to anyone. {As to the present enacting formula see s 280 of this Code.} Sometimes these enacting words would be prefaced by a statement of the purpose. The conjunction 'And' would join them all together.

Example 1   We may take an example from the last Act to be passed before Lord Brougham persuaded Parliament to reform the system. Section 8 of the Act 13 & 14 Vict c 20 (1850) starts off: 'And for the Purposes [*sic*] of exempting the Metropolitan Police District as herein-before provided, be it enacted, That . . .'

Lord Brougham's Act said that all Acts were to be divided into sections 'if there be more enactments than one', and that each section should be a substantive enactment without need for introductory words. Though useful, this had an unfortunate side-effect. By losing the introductory words, we also lost the statement of purpose. {See further s 273 of this Code.}

In debates on a Bill, the provision that on enactment becomes a section is referred to as a *clause* (though in the Bill itself the word 'section' is used). Sometimes judges and others loosely refer to sections of an Act as clauses. {See, e g, *R v Dibdin* [1910] P 57, *per* Moulton LJ at p 125.}

Example 2   The famous s 20 of the Representation of the People Act 1832, which extended the county franchise, was long known as the Chandos Clause because its insertion was moved in the House of Commons by the Marquis of Chandos, eldest son of the Duke of Buckingham.

In modern Acts, sections bear arabic numerals unbracketed. Until the second half of the nineteenth century roman numerals were employed.

Modern sections tend to be lengthy and complex.

Example 3   In a computer-assisted statistical analysis published in 1982, Dr Arbab-Dehkordi reported that the current Acts dealing with income tax, corporation tax and capital gains tax consisted of 1,198 sections and 129 Schedules. The average length of a section was 257 words, while the average Schedule contained 928 words. The longest section was s 60 of the Capital

Allowances Act 1968, which contained 1,925 words. {B Arbab-Dehkordi 'Statistical Analysis of Statutory Texts' *Computers and Law* May 1982 p 4.}

Unless the section is subdivided, the practice is to draft it as one sentence. {As to the reason for this see Bennion *Statute Law* (2nd edn, 1983) p 48. For exceptions see, e g, Coinage Act 1870 s 7 (three sentences); Supreme Court of Judicature Act 1881 s 9 (four sentences).}

Subsections   As sections grew longer, draftsmen began to sub-divide them. The sub-divisions are known as subsections. Each bears an arabic numeral in brackets. The subsections are related to the theme of the section, but each is drafted independently. Like the undivided section, the subsection usually consists of a single sentence. In debates on a Bill, subsections are referred to as such, and not as 'sub-clauses'.

Paragraphing   To aid the reader, the modern draftsman makes use of paragraphing in his undivided section, or in his subsection. The provision remains a single sentence, but is printed with indentations and paragraph numbers so as to bring out the sense and aid cross-referencing. The numbering of paragraphs is by bracketed small letters. Smaller divisions are referred to as sub-paragraphs, and then heads.

Judges take notice of the paragraphing as a guide to what are intended to be the units of sense. {See, e g, *The Eastman Photographic Materials Co Ltd v The Comptroller-General of Patents, Designs and Trade-Marks* [1898] AC 571, at pp 579, 584; *Nugent-Head v Jacob (Inspector of Taxes)* [1948] AC 321, at p 329. See further s 283 of this Code.}

Provisos   As to the proviso see s 268 of this Code.

Interpretation of a section   The section is the primary indication of Parliament's meaning and intention. {*Spencer v Metropolitan Board of Works* (1882) 22 Ch D 142, *per* Jessel MR at p 162.} The other main operative component, the Schedule, is to be read in the light of the inducing section. {As to Schedules see s 267 of this Code.} Collectively, the sections are known as the *body* of the Act.

It has been said by judges that the division of an Act into sections is arbitrary, and ought not to be treated as furnishing a guide to its construction. {See *R v Newark-upon-Trent (Inhabitants)* (1824) 3 B & C 59, at pp 63 and 71.} This sweeping generalisation might have contained some truth when it was uttered, in the days of disorganised composition. {As to this see s 76 of the Code.} With the precision drafting of today, the position is otherwise. Draftsmen take great care to design a section so that it deals with a single point; and the way the sections are organised and arranged is to be taken as a guide to legislative intention.

267. Operative components of Act: Schedules

The Schedule is an extension of the section which induces it. Material is put into a Schedule because it is too lengthy or detailed to be conveniently accomodated in a section, or because it forms a separate document (such as a treaty).

COMMENTARY

It is often found convenient to incorporate part of the operative provisions of an Act in the form of a Schedule. {For an early example see the Privilege of Parliament Act 1512.} The Schedule is always given a capital S. We speak of a Schedule 'to' an Act, but a section 'of' an Act.

A Schedule must be attached to the body of the Act by words in one of the sections (known as inducing words). It was formerly the practice for the inducing words to say that the Schedule was to be construed and have effect as part of the Act. {See, e g, Ballot Act 1872 s 28.} This is no longer done, being regarded as unnecessary. If by mischance the inducing words were omitted, the Schedule would still form part of the Act if that was the apparent intention.

The Schedule is often used to hive off provisions which are too long or detailed to be put in the body of the Act. This does not mean they are unimportant. Lord Wilberforce said of the capital gains tax introduced by the Finance Act 1965: 'Using a modern technique, Parliament has placed most of the working and detailed provisions in lengthy schedules'. {*Floor v Davis (Inspector of Taxes)* [1979] 2 All ER 677, at p 679.}

Another use of the Schedule is to set out in it some document, such as a treaty or convention, which is referred to in the body of the Act.

Example 1 The Carriage of Goods by Sea Act 1971 s 1(2) states: 'The provisions of [the Hague-Visby Rules], as set out in the Schedule to this Act, shall have the force of law'. In *The Hollandia* {[1982] 1 All ER 1076.} it was argued that this merely meant that the rules were enforceable at law as a contract. *Held* Section 1(2) meant that the rules had the full force of law. Sir Sebag Shaw said {P 1081.} that the effect was 'to imbue them with the character of a statutory enactment'.

Where the Schedule is in a form resembling sections, the units corresponding to sections are known as paragraphs. They do not have sidenotes. Sub-divisions of these are called sub-paragraphs. Further sub-divisions are known as heads or (illegitimately) paragraphs. If the Schedule is in tabular form the items are called entries.

Interpretation of Schedules Whether material is put in a section or a Schedule is usually a mere matter of convenience. Little significance should therefore be attached to it. As Brett LJ said in *A-G v Lamplough* {(1878) 3 Ex D 214, at p 229.}: 'A schedule in an Act is a mere question of drafting, a mere question of words. The schedule is as much a part of the statute, and is as much an enactment, as any other part'. {See also, to the like effect, *Flower Freight Co Ltd v Hammond* [1963] 1 QB 275; *R v Legal Aid Committee No 1 (London) Legal Aid Area, ex p Rondel* [1967] 2 QB 482; *Metropolitan Police Commr v Curran* [1976] 1 WLR 87.}

In *IRC v Gittus* {[1920] 1 KB 563, at p 576.}, Lord Sterndale MR gave the following guidance on conflicts between a Schedule and the inducing section-

> 'If the Act says that the Schedule is to be used for a certain purpose
> and the heading of the part of the Schedule in question shows that it
> is prima facie at any rate devoted to that purpose, then you must read
> the Act and the Schedule as though the Schedule were operating for
> that purpose, and if you can satisfy the language of the section
> without extending it beyond that purpose you ought to do it.'

But if in spite of that you find in the language of the Schedule words and terms that go clearly outside that purpose, then you must give effect to them and you must not consider them as limited by the heading of that part of the Schedule or by the purpose mentioned in the Act for which the Schedule is prima facie to be used. You cannot refuse to give effect to clear words simply because prima facie they seem to be limited by the heading of the Schedule and the definition of the purpose of the Schedule contained in the Act.'

{See also *IRC v Littlewoods Mail Order Stores Ltd* [1963] AC 135.}

This is to be preferred to the earlier dictum by Lord Cottenham that 'If the enacting part of the statute cannot be made to correspond with the schedule, the latter must yield to the former'. {*Re Baines* (1840) 12 A & E 227.} Also too mechanical is Lord Penzance's dictum that 'It would be contrary to the principles on which courts of law construe Acts of Parliament to enlarge the conditions of an enactment by reference to words given in a schedule'. {*Dean v Green* (1882) 8 PD 79.}

The question of conflicts between Schedule and inducing section is an aspect of the principle that an Act is to be construed as a whole. This is dealt with in s 149 of this Code.

Occasionally an Act may provide that a Schedule is to be interpreted in accordance with notes contained in it. {See, e g, Finance Act 1972 s 46(2).}

Headings   Since the Schedule as a whole is annexed to the Act, it is not possible to argue that headings in the Schedule are somehow not really 'part' of it, in the way some judges have done in the case of headings in the body of the Act. As explained above {P 271.}, this is a spurious distinction since the whole Act is the product of Parliament. {For the treatment of headings generally see s 281 of this Code. For a case where ambiguous words in a Schedule were construed by reference to a heading see *Qualter, Hall & Co Ltd v Board of Trade* [1962] Ch 273.}

268. Operative components of Act: the proviso

A proviso is a formula beginning 'Provided that . . .', which is placed at the end of a section or subsection of an Act, or of a paragraph or sub-paragraph of a Schedule, and the intention of which is to narrow the effect of the preceding words.

COMMENTARY

The proviso is an ancient verbal formula. {For early references to provisos in statutes see Hatsell *Parliamentary Precedents* 3.46 (1575); 3.114 (1660).} It enables a general statement to be made as a clear proposition, any necessary qualifications being kept out of it and relegated to the proviso. This aids understanding. The general statement is sometimes called the 'purview'. {See, e g, *A-G v Chelsea Waterworks* (1731) Fitzg 195.} This is based on a misconception however, for the purview is truly the enacting formula. {See s 280 of this Code.}

Example 1 Section 3(3) of the Obscene Publications Act 1959 states the circumstances in which forfeiture orders can be made by magistrates after a summons to show cause has been issued. It ends: 'Provided that if the person summoned does not appear, the court shall not make an order unless service of the summons is proved'.

Other drafting techniques can be used to achieve the same result. Thus s 3(3) could have employed the 'so however' formula. Instead of with the proviso, it would then have ended 'so however that if the person summoned does not appear . . .' Or the two propositions could have been presented as separate subsections (say subs-ss (3) and (4)). Here sub-s (3) might have begun 'Subject to subsection (4) . . .' Or sub-s (4) might have begun 'Notwithstanding anything in subsection (3) . . .'

The modern drafting practice is to use these latter methods rather than the proviso. Indeed many modern draftsmen would dispense even with the introductory words, and assume that in this example it was obvious that sub-s (4) was intended to cut down sub-s (3).

Whichever drafting method is used, it is clear that the interpretation should be the same.

Burden of proof The only operative significance of identifying a statement as a proviso lies in the burden of proof. Kenny said inaccurately of criminal statutes-

> 'The prosecution need not negative a proviso in a statute, and a distinction must be drawn between the enacting part of a law which the prosecution must normally negative and exceptions in a proviso within which the accused must bring himself.'

{C S Kenny *Outlines of Criminal Law* (15th edn, 1946) p 409.}

Example 2 Kenny cited as authority for this statement the case of *R v Audley*. {[1907] 1 KB 383.} The defendant was charged with bigamy elsewhere than in England and Ireland, contrary to s 57 of the Offences against the Person Act 1861. This section has a proviso beginning-

> 'Provided, that nothing in this section contained shall extend to any second marriage contracted elsewhere than in England and Ireland by any other than a subject of Her Majesty . . .'

Held the onus of proving that he was other than a subject of Her Majesty rested upon the defendant.

However Kenny failed to notice that the Indictments Act 1915 Sch 1 r 5(2) had changed the position. {This change was made earlier for magistrates' courts by s 39 of the Summary Jurisdiction Act 1879. See now Magistrates' Courts Act 1980 s 101.} Rule 5(2) is now embodied as rule 6(c) of the Indictment Rules 1971. {SI 1971/1253.} This says that is not necessary for the prosecution 'to specify or negative an exception, exemption, proviso, excuse or qualification'.

As Archbold remarked: 'This rule extends to exceptions generally the previous practice with regard to provisos in the case of statutory offences'. {J F Archbold *Pleading, Evidence & Practice in Criminal Cases* (37th edn, 1969) para 104.} It is thus for the defendant to raise and prove what is in substance an exception, *regardless of the form in which it is expressed*. {*R v Oliver* [1944] KB 68.} The civil standard of proof applies. {*Islington London Borough v Panico* [1973] 3 All ER 485.}

A similar change has occurred in civil proceedings. {See RSC Ord 18 r 8.}

Interpretation of a proviso   Judges have been in the habit of speaking as though a proviso did not form part of the 'enacting part' of the section in which it appears.

Example 3   In *Mullins v Treasurer of Surrey* {(1880) 5 QBD 170, at p 173.} Lush J said: 'When one finds a proviso to a section, the natural presumption is that, but for the proviso, the enacting part of the section would have included the subject-matter of the proviso'. {See also, to like effect, *West Derby Union v Metropolitan Life Assurance Co* [1897] AC 647, *per* Lord Watson at p 652. See also Example 356.3.}

While the substance of this dictum is undoubtedly correct, the treatment of the proviso as qualitatively different from the rest of the section is not. The entire section, including the proviso, is an operative component of the Act. {*Gubay v Kington (Inspector of Taxes)* [1984] 1 All ER 513, *per* Lord Scarman (dissenting, but not on this point) at p 519.}

Judges used to cast doubt on the value of a proviso in throwing light on the meaning of the words qualified by it. {See, e g, *West Derby Union v Metropolitan Life Assurance Co* [1897] AC 647, *per* Lord Watson at p 652 and Lord Herschell at p 655.} This is because provisos, like savings, were often put down as amendments to Bills by their opponents, and accepted to allay usually groundless fears. This still happens in the case of private Bills; but since the establishment of the Parliamentary Counsel Office in 1869 it has not been true of public general Acts.

In the case of precision drafting, the proviso is to be taken as limited in its operation to the section or other provision it qualifies. {*Leah v Two Worlds Publishing Co* [1951] Ch 393, at p 398; *Lloyds and Scottish Finance Ltd v Modern Cars & Caravans (Kingston) Ltd* [1966] 1 QB 764, at pp 780-781. As to the distinction between precision drafting and disorganised composition see s 76 of this Code.} Where the Act is the subject of disorganised composition, what is in form a proviso may in fact be an independent substantive provision. {*Rhondda UDC v Taff Vale Rly* [1909] AC 253, at p 258; *Eastbourne Corpn v Fortes Ltd* [1959] 2 QB 92, at p 107; *Commr of Stamp Duties v Atwill* [1973] AC 558. Cf *R v Dibdin* [1910] P 57, affd [1912] AC 533.} The proviso is then said not to be a 'true' proviso. {*Commr of Stamp Duties v Atwill* [1973] AC 558, at p 561. See Example 356.3.}

In the case of a proviso, the usual rule applies that an Act is to be construed as a whole. {See s 149 of this Code.} A section containing a proviso is also to be construed as a whole, within the Act. {*Jennings v Kelly* [1940] AC 206, at p 229.}

References   A reference to a section includes any proviso to the section, since the proviso forms part of the section. Thus the repeal of the section also repeals the proviso. {*Horsnail v Bruce* (1873) LR 8 CP 378, at p 385. But see *Piper v Harvey* [1958] 1 QB 439, where the proviso extended beyond the repealed enactment.} In accordance with principle, the repeal may be effected by implication. {*Whitehead v Smithers* (1877) 2 CPD 553.}

The proviso may be compared to a saving. {As to savings see s 269 of this Code.}

269. Operative components of Act: savings

A saving is a provision the intention of which is to narrow the effect of the enactment to which it refers so as to preserve some existing legal rule or right from its operation.

COMMENTARY

A saving resembles a proviso, except that it has no particular form. Furthermore it relates to an existing legal rule or right, whereas a proviso is usually concerned with limiting the new provision made by the section to which it is attached. {As to the proviso see s 268 of this Code.} A saving often begins with the words 'Nothing in this [Act] [section] [etc] . . .'

Very often a saving is unnecessary, but is put in *ex abundanti cautela* to quieten doubts.

Example 1 The Welsh Language Act 1967 deals with the use of Welsh in legal proceedings and matters. Its final provision is s 5(3), which reads: 'Nothing in this Act shall prejudice the use of Welsh in any case in which it is lawful apart from this Act'.

Example 2 The Statute Law (Repeals) Act 1977 is an instance of what is known as a Statute Law Revision Act. {See p 88 above.} Its long title says that it is-

'An Act to promote the reform of the statute law by the repeal, in accordance with recommendations of the Law Commission and the Scottish Law Commission, of certain enactments which (except in so far as their effect is preserved) are no longer of practical utility; and to facilitate the citation of statutes.'

Part XII of Sch 1 to the 1977 Act repeals certain obsolete provisions relating to the validation of marriages. Section 2 of the Act consists of a saving, as follows-

'The repeal by this Act of the enactments specified in Part XII of Schedule 1 to this Act does not affect the admissibility of any register of marriage, or copy, as evidence of marriage.'

Some savings are general, and of standing effect. An important example is s 16 of the Interpretation Act 1978, relating to the effect of repeals. {For a description of s 16 see s 182 of this Code.}

A saving may be qualified or conditional. {See, e g, *Royal Borough of Windsor and Maidenhead v Brandrose Investments Ltd* [1981] 3 All ER 38, at p 43 (referring to Town and Country Planning Act 1971 s 52(3)(a).}

Interpretation of savings The principles of interpretation applied to savings are similar to those applying to provisos. {See p 572 above.} Savings are regarded as unreliable guides to the provisions to which they are attached, for reasons sketched by Lord Simon of Glaisdale in the following dictum-

' . . . considerable caution is needed in construing a general statutory provision by reference to its statutory exceptions. "Saving clauses" are often included by way of reassurance, for avoidance of doubt or from abundance of caution. Section 27(9)(a) [of the Race Relations Act 1968] itself provides a striking example: it provides that nothing in the Act shall invalidate certain rules restricting certain classes of employment to "persons of particular birth, citizenship, nationality, descent or residence," and "residence," at least, is not conceivably within the ambit of s 1(1).'

{*Ealing London Borough Council v Race Relations Board* [1972] AC 342, at p 363.}

A saving is taken not to be intended to confer any right which did not exist already. {*Alton Woods' Case* (1600) 1 Co Rep 40b; *Arnold v Gravesend Corpn* (1856) 2 K & J 574, at p 591; *Butcher v Henderson* (1868) LR 3 QB 335; *R v Pirehill North JJ* (1884) 14 QBD 13, at p 19.}

An unsatisfactory feature of savings, and a reason why good draftsmen resist the addition of unnecessary savings, is that they may throw doubt on matters it is intended to preserve, but which are not mentioned in the saving. {See, e g, *Re Williams, Jones v Williams* (1887) 36 Ch D 573.} This is an aspect of the application of the *expressio unius* principle. {As to this see ss 389 to 394 of this Code.}

As an aspect of the principle against doubtful penalization, {See s 129 and Part XIII of this Code.} a saving is liberally construed. {*Foster v Pritchard and Whitroe* (1875) 2 H & N 151; *R v West Riding of Yorkshire JJ* (1876) 1 QBD 220; *Barnes v Eddleston* (1876) 1 Ex D 102.}

AMENDABLE DESCRIPTIVE COMPONENTS OF ACT

270. Amendable descriptive components of Act: nature of

An amendable descriptive component is a component which describes the whole or some part of the Act, and was subject to amendment (as opposed to a mere printing correction) when the Bill for the Act was going through Parliament. The following are amendable descriptive components: long title, preamble, purpose clause, recital, short title, example.

COMMENTARY

Functional construction rule   Under the functional construction rule set out in s 124 of this Code, the significance to be attached by the interpreter to any component of an Act must be assessed in conformity with its legislative function as a component of that type. This section explains the function of the amendable descriptive components.

Printing correction   As to printing corrections see pp 108–109 above.

Judges have often said that amendable descriptive components are not part of the Act. Thus Willes J, after asserting that the long title and other 'appendages' are not part of an Act, said of any Act passed after the practice of engrossing Acts on the Parliament Roll ceased in 1849-

'The Act, when passed, must be looked at just as if it were still entered upon a roll, which it may be again if Parliament should be pleased so to order; in which case it would be without these appendages . . .'

{*Claydon v Green* (1868) LR 3 CP 511, at p 522.}

After the lapse of more than a century without renewed use of the roll, it may confidently be asserted that this dictum is no longer good law, if indeed it ever was. As stated in the commentary on s 124 of this Code, the entire Act is put out by Parliament as its Act, and must be accepted as such. {See p 271 above.}

This might seem to make irrelevant the question of whether a descriptive component is or is not amendable in Parliament. That is no doubt strictly true. Out of deference to the numerous judicial dicta that draw the distinction, it is nevertheless adhered to in this Code. It should however be regarded as little more than a convenient demarcation line.

271. Amendable descriptive components of Act: long title

The long title of an Act (formerly and more correctly called the title) appears at the beginning of the Act. It is a remanet from the Bill which on royal assent became the Act. Its true function pertains to the Bill rather than the Act. It sets out in general terms the purposes of the Bill, and under the rules of parliamentary procedure should cover everything in the Bill. If the Bill is amended so as to go wider than the long title, the long title is required to be amended to correspond.

Although thus being of a procedural nature, the long title is nevertheless regarded by the courts as a guide to legislative intention.

COMMENTARY

The long title begins with the words 'An Act to . . .' It is not, as might appear to the uninstructed reader, a helpful summary of the Act's contents inserted for his convenience. It owes its presence to the procedural rules governing Parliamentary Bills.

The long title is thus drafted to comply with these procedural rules. It is not designed as a guide to the contents of the Act. It is a parliamentary device, whose purpose is in relation to the Bill and its parliamentary progress. Under parliamentary rules, a Bill of which notice of presentation has been given is deemed to exist as a Bill even though it consists of nothing else but the long title. Once the Bill has received royal assent, the long title is therefore vestigial.

One important way in which the long title may be influenced by parliamentary considerations concerns the doctrine of 'scope' in the House of Commons. This doctrine renders an amendment out of order if it is beyond the scope of the Bill. Where a Government Bill is contentious, the draftsman may seek to cut down the number of amendments that have to be debated by drawing the long title tightly. The officials of the House will treat this as narrowing the scope, though the scope does not entirely depend on the long title. {It should perhaps be mentioned that the doctrine of scope does not always succeed in keeping out extraneous material: see, e g, Theft Act 1968 s 30, which makes provision in relation to spouses going much wider than theft and related offences.}

In other cases the draftsman will be content with a broad and vague long title. From his point of view, this has the advantage of accomodating possible amendments to the Bill without requiring the long title to be amended.

Example 1 One of the broadest and vaguest long titles on record was attached to the statute 22 Hen 8 c 9 (1530). This was: 'An Act for poysonyng'. The Act was prompted by the crime of the Bishop of Rochester's cook, who murdered members of the Bishop's household by preparing a poisoned stew. In accordance with the *ex post facto* Act, he was sentenced to be boiled to death in the very pot used by him for the crime. {Radzinowicz *History of English Criminal Law* (1948) i 239.}

It will be seen that the function of the long title is complex. Its nature is often misunderstood. Learned judges have even been known to confuse the long title with other descriptive components of an Act.

Example 2 Some judges have confused the long title with a preamble. {As in *Ward v Holman* [1964] 2 QB 585, at pp 586-7; *Thornton v Kirklees* [1979] 2 All ER 349, at p 352; *Re Coventry decd* [1979] 3 All ER 815, at p 821 and *Kassam v Immigration Appeal Tribunal* [1980] 2 All ER 330, at p 332. For the preamble see s 272 of this Code.}

Example 3 Other judges, perhaps more surprisingly, have mistaken the long title for a heading. {See *Re Diplock's Estate* [1948] Ch 465; *Hodgson v Marks* [1970] 3 All ER 513. For headings see s 281 of this Code.}

Example 4 In other cases the long title has been judicialy referred to as the short title. {*The Ydun* [1899] P 236, at p 236; *R v East Powder Magistrates' Court* [1979] 2 All ER 329, at p 332; *R v Duncalf* [1979] 2 All ER 1116, at p 1120; *R v West Yorkshire Coroner* [1982] 2 All ER 801, at p 803. For the short title see s 275 of this Code.}

Example 5 Lord Porter called the long title of an Act its 'caption'. {'Case Law in the Interpretation of Statutes' (1940), Presidential address to the Holdsworth Club of Birmimgham University p 7.}

In the case of early statutes, the long title was known as the *rubric*, from the fact that it was sometimes printed in red. Hence the reference to interpretation *a rubro ad nigrum*, from the red to the black (letter).

Use of long title in interpretation There are many dicta to the effect that the long title is not part of the Act and should be disregarded. {See, e g, *Powlter's Case* (1610) 11 Co Rep 29a; *A-G v Weymouth* (1743) Ambl 20; *R v Wilcock* (1845) 7 QB 317; *Salkeld v Johnson* (1848) 2 Ex 256; *Claydon v Green* (1868) LR 3 CP 511.} Certainly since the emergence of parliamentary legislation in its modern form, these dicta are unsound in principle. The long title is undoubtedly part of the Act, though its value in interpretation has often been exaggerated by judges. {See, e g, *Fielding v Morley Corpn* [1899] 1 Ch 1, at pp 3,4; *Suffolk County Council v Mason* [1979] 2 All ER 369, at p 379; *Gold Star Publications Ltd v Director of Public Prosecutions* [1981] 2 All ER 257, at pp 260-261.}

The courts have been inconsistent on the question of whether the effect of operative provisions should be treated as cut down by the long title. This is to be expected, since the weight of other relevant factors is bound to vary. {As to the weighing of interpretative factors see s 158 of this Code.}

Example 6   In *Watkinson v Hollington* {[1943] 2 All ER 573} the Court of Appeal resorted to the long title to cut down the plain literal meaning of the phrase 'the levying of distress' in s 1(2) of the Courts (Emergency Powers) Act 1943 and exclude from it the impounding of trespassing cattle by the ancient remedy of levying distress *damage feasant*. This was because the consequence of applying the literal meaning of s 1(2) would have been unfortunate. {See p 676 below.}

Example 7   The long title of the Wills Act 1861 (Lord Kingsdown's Act) was 'An Act to amend the law with respect to wills of personal estate made by British subjects'. Section 3 of the Act ran: 'No will or other testamentary instrument shall be held to be revoked or to have become invalid, nor shall the construction thereof be altered, by reason of any subsequent change of domicile of the person making the same'. In *In the Estate of Groos* {[1904] P 269.} the court declined to limit the application of s 3 to British subjects merely because of the reference to them in the long title. {See also, to like effect, *Ward v Holman* [1964] 2 QB 580.}

In his book *Statutory Interpretation*, the late Sir Rupert Cross said 'it is by no means uncommon for the enacting words to go beyond the matters mentioned in the long title.' {P 158.} In fact a rule of Parliamentary procedure requires the long title to cover everything in a Bill, and to be amended if amendments to the operative provisions render this necessary. The rule is strictly enforced by Parliamentary officials.

Because of their mainly procedural character, mistakes are not infrequent in long titles.

Example 8   The long title to the Rating and Valuation Act 1928 included the words 'to provide for obtaining decisions on points of law with a view to securing uniformity in valuation'. These words relate to nothing in the body of the Act because the clause allowing such decisions to be obtained was dropped after protests made by the law lords.

Conclusion   We may summarise by saying that the long title is an unreliable guide in interpretation, but should not be ignored. It may arouse doubt where it appears to conflict with the operative parts of the Act; and this doubt should then be resolved in the usual way. {See Part VII of this Code.} It is not right to say with Slade LJ {*Manuel v A-G* [1982] 3 All ER 822, at p 831.} that the court is not entitled to look at the long title unless the operative provisions are ambiguous, because this strikes at the basis of the informed interpretation rule. {See s 119 of this Code.} As Lord Simon of Glaisdale said-

> 'In these days, when the long title can be amended in both Houses, I can see no reason for having recourse to it only in case of an ambiguity - it is the plainest of all guides to the general objectives of a statute. But it will not always help as to particular provisions.'

{*Black-Clawson International Ltd v Papierwerke Waldhof-Aschaffenberg AG*
[1975] 1 All ER 810, at p 844.}

To this it may be added that while the long title may be the plainest guide to
the objectives this is only because it is usually the only guide within the Act
itself. {As to other guidance see the following provisions of this Code: s
272 (preamble), s 273 (purpose clauses); s 274 (recitals), and s 119 and Part X
(legislative history etc).

{See also Examples 316.5 and 316.7.}

272. Amendable descriptive components of Act: preamble

The preamble is an optional feature in public general Acts, though
compulsory in private Acts. It appears immediately after the long title, and
states the reason for passing the Act. It may include a recital of the
mischief to which the Act is directed. When present, it is thus a useful
guide to the legislative intention.

COMMENTARY

Few modern public Acts contain a preamble. Where present it begins with the
word 'Whereas' or 'Albeit'.

Example 1   The Laws in Wales Act 1535 begins with words about the Welsh
language that might be controversial with some people today-

> 'Albeit the dominion, principality and country of Wales justly and
> righteously is, and ever hath been incorporated, annexed, united and
> subject to and under the imperial Crown of this Realm, as a very
> member and joint of the same [but] the people of the same dominion
> have and do daily use a speech nothing like nor consonant to the
> natural mother tongue used within this realm . . .'

It is interesting to compare this with the preamble to the Welsh Language Act
1967: 'Whereas it is proper that the Welsh language should be freely used by
those who so desire in the hearing of legal proceedings in Wales and
Monmouthshire . . .'

The preamble may be used as a guide to legislative intention. {1 Co Inst 79a;
Sussex Peerage Claim (1844) 11 Cl & F 85, at p 143; *Turquand v Board of Trade*
(1886) 11 App Cas 286; *Hollinrake v Truswell* [1894] 3 Ch 420, at pp 427-428;
Powell v Kempton Park Racecourse Co Ltd [1899] AC 143.} A sixteenth-century
judge remarked that the preamble is 'a key to open the minds of the makers of
the Act, and the mischiefs which they intended to redress'. {*Stowel v Lord Zouch*
(1569) 1 Plowd 353, *per* Dyer CJ at p 369.} Four centuries later we find Lord
Denning MR using almost the same language. {*Imperial Tobacco Ltd v A-G*
[1979] 2 All ER 592, at p 600.}

In *London County Council v Bermondsey Bioscope Co Ltd* {[1911] 1 KB 445, at
p 451.} Lord Alverstone CJ said: 'I . . . regret that the practice of inserting
preambles in Acts of Parliament has been discontinued as they were often of
great assistance to the courts in construing the Acts'. The reason for the
discontinuance in public Acts may be gathered from the view of Lord Thring
that-

' . . . it is not as a general rule advisable to enunciate the principle of an Act in a preamble, as the opponents of the Act are sure to select it as a battle-ground instead of dividing on the actual provisions of the Act.'

{*Practical Legislation* (1902) p 93.}

This remark by Lord Thring casts light on the general problem of obscurity in statutes. Draftsmen quickly learn that there are advantages in it. {The question is discussed in Bennion *Statute Law* (2nd edn, 1983) chap 14.}

The courts are reluctant to allow a preamble to override inconsistent operative provisions.

Example 2 It was laid down by the House of Lords in *A-G v Prince Ernest Augustus of Hanover* {[1957] AC 436.} that the preamble should not be allowed to contradict plain words in the body of the Act. These words naturalised as British subjects the descendants of the Electress Sophia of Hanover whenever they might be born. The preamble however said it was desirable that they should be naturalised 'in your Majesty's lifetime' (referring to Queen Anne). *Held* The preamble did not override the plain words. The applicant was entitled to naturalisation even though Queen Anne was dead. The decision made virtually all the crowned heads of Europe British subjects. {See also *Manuel v A-G* [1982] 3 All ER 822, *per* Slade LJ at p 831.}

The recital of facts in the preamble to an Act does not amount to conclusive proof that the facts are true; but constitutes prima facie evidence of them. {*R v Sutton* (1816) 4 M & S 532; *A-G v Foundling Hospital* [1914] 2 Ch 154; *Dawson v Commonwealth of Australia* (1946) 73 CLR 157, at p 175.} Further evidence is then admissible. {*DFC of T (NSW) v W R Moran Pty Ltd* (1939) 61 CLR 735 (court could refer to record of conference referred to in preamble).}

As to cases where judges have confused the preamble with the long title see Example 271.2. There is indeed a similarity between them as guides to legislative intent, though judges have never doubted that a preamble is part of the Act. {*West Ham v Iles* (1883) 8 App Cas 388. See also Example 300.4.}

Statute Law Revision Acts Through a misguided policy, many Statute Law Revision Acts have repealed preambles of Acts as being spent. Consequently revised editions of the statutes omit them. This is particularly unfortunate in view of the fact that, by virtue of s 19(1)(a) of the Interpretation Act 1978, the revised edition is taken to be the one referred to. {See pp 123–124 above.}

Since the preamble may be a guide to the legal meaning of an enactment, it is unsafe to construe the enactment without reference to the preamble; indeed to do so contravenes the informed interpretation rule set out in s 119 of this Code. Clearly the repeal of a proviso by a Statute Law Revision Act does not affect the meaning of the Act. {*Powell v Kempton Park Racecourse Co Ltd* [1899] AC 143.}

Private Acts In a private Bill the preamble is required to set forth the expediency of enacting the Bill. When a private Bill is referred to a select committee, and is opposed on the question of its general expediency, the promoters are called on to establish by argument and evidence that the Bill is expedient. This is known as proving the preamble. Failure to prove it usually means rejection of the Bill.

273. Amendable descriptive components of Act: purpose clauses

A purpose clause is an overt statement of the legislative intention. Such a clause is optional. When present, it is included in the body of the Act. It may apply to the whole or a part of the Act.

COMMENTARY

Instead of a preamble, {See s 272 of this Code.} an Act may contain one or more purpose clauses in the body of it. These are rare in British Acts, no doubt for the reason advanced by Lord Thring in relation to preambles. {See pp 578–579 above.}

Example 1   Section 488(1) of the Income and Corporation Taxes Act 1970 reads-

'This section is enacted to prevent the avoidance of tax by persons concerned with land or the development of land.'

In *Page (Inspector of Taxes) v Lowther* {(1983) *The Times* 27 October.}, the Court of Appeal held that a transaction which did not, and was not intended to, avoid tax nevertheless fell within s 488(2). Its clear words were not taken as being reduced in scope by the purpose clause. {For other examples see Income Tax Act 1952 s 412 (now Income and Corporation Taxes Act 1970 s 478), referred to by Viscount Dilhorne in *Vestey v IRC (Nos 1 and 2)* [1979] 3 All ER 976, at p 991; Finance Act 1936 s 18, referred to in *Latilla v IRC* [1942] 1 KB 299, at p 303; Public Health Acts Amendment Act 1890 s 51.}

In an Australian case Barwick CJ said that, without being definitive, a statement of intention included by Parliament in an Act 'may assist in the determination of the operative effect of the Act'. {*Re Credit Tribunal, ex p General Motors Acceptance Corpn, Australia* (1977) 14 ALR 257, at p 260.} Nevertheless it is clear from Example 1 that, like a preamble, a purpose clause is unlikely to be held to override the clear words of a detailed provision. {Cf the application of the maxim *generalia specialibus non derogant* in relation to the principle that an Act is to be construed as a whole, discussed in s 149 of this Code.}

Draftsmen dislike the purpose clause. They take the view that often the aims of legislation cannot usefully or safely be summarised or condensed by such means. A political purpose clause is no more than a manifesto, which may obscure what is otherwise precise and exact. Moreover detailed amendments made to a Bill after introduction may not merely falsify the purpose clause but even render it impracticable to retain any broad description of the purpose. The draftsman's view is that his Act should be allowed to speak for itself. {See *The Preparation of Legislation* (Renton Report) 1975, Cmnd 6053, para 11.7.}

The wider aspects of statements of the purpose of an Act or a particular enactment are discussed in s 316 of this Code. As to purpose clauses see further Bennion *Statute Law* (2nd edn, 1983) pp 98-100.

274. Amendable descriptive components of Act: recitals

A recital has the same function as a preamble, but is confined to a single section or other textual unit.

COMMENTARY

A recital is so called because it recites some relevant matter, often the state of facts that constitutes the mischief the provision is designed to remedy. There may be recitals in this sense within a preamble. {As to the preamble see s 272 of this Code.} Or indeed they may occur anywhere else in an Act. The specialised use of the term however confines it to a statement beginning 'Whereas . . .' which forms the prefix to a section or other textual unit.

Example 1 Section 1(3) of the Statute Law (Repeals) Act 1975 begins: 'Whereas this Act repeals so much of section 16(4) of the Marriage Act 1949 as requires a surrogate [ie deputy ecclesiastical judge] to have given security by his bond . . .' and then goes on to release surrogates from their bonds.
   An earlier form used the construction 'Forasmuch as . . .'

Example 2 Section 2 of the Laws in Wales Act 1535 begins with the words 'And forasmoche as there be many and dyvers lordshippes marchers within the said countrey or dominion of Wales . . .'
   {See also Examples 295.1, 295.5, 316.3 and 316.4.}
   A recital may be combined with a statement of intention, when it is called a purpose clause. {See s 273 of this Code.}

275. Amendable descriptive components of Act: short title

(1) The short title is a brief description by which the Act may be cited or referred to. In a modern Act the short title is usually given by the Act itself. For earlier Acts short titles were given by Statute Law Reform Acts such as the Short Titles Act 1896, or by popular attribution.
(2) An Act may continue to be cited by the short title authorised by any enactment notwithstanding the repeal of that enactment.
(3) Where any Act cites or refers to another Act otherwise than by its short title, the short title may, in any revised edition of the Statutes published by authority, be printed in substitution for that citation or reference.

COMMENTARY

The practice is now always to include in an Act a short title clause in common form. This may be the whole or part of a section.

Example 1 Section 43 of 1983 c 47 reads: 'This Act may be cited as the National Heritage Act 1983'.
   The draftsman strives to keep the short title brief, but does not always suceed. {See Example 142.4.}
   We now examine the elements of this common form clause.

'May be cited' The grant of permission is scarcely necessary. Where a reference is made in any text, whether legislative or not, the question is always what the intention was, as appearing from the text as a whole. There is no law against

referring to an Act in any way the writer fancies. Provided the intention is clear, effect will be given to it in the usual way.

It follows that if an error were made in referring to an Act (for example by getting the year wrong) this would not matter provided the Act intended could be identified from the context. {For an example see pp 340–341 above.} Acts have been known to have more than one short title. For example 9 & 10 Vict c 95 (1846) was known both as the Small Debts Act 1846 and the County Courts Act 1846. {See *Whitter v Peters* [1982] 2 All ER 369, at p 373.}

The final word 'Act'   Since it became the practice to insert short title clauses in Acts, the short title given has almost invariably ended with the word 'Act', followed by the calendar year. In the Act 22 & 23 Geo 5 c 4 however the short title given, presumably because this was a weighty constitutional Act with a direct application throughout the Commonwealth, was 'the Statute of Westminster, 1931'. {See s 12. As to the comma in this short title see below.}

Calendar year   Since it became the practice to insert short title clauses in Acts, the short title given has almost invariably ended with the calendar year in which the Act was passed. However the Short Titles Act 1896 created confusion by naming the statute 1 Will & Mar Sess 2 c 2 (1688) as simply 'the Bill of Rights'.

Comma in short title   Until the beginning of the session 11 & 12 Eliz 2 (1962), the short title included a comma before the calendar year, eg 'the Judicial Committee Act, 1833'. {Conferred by the Short Titles Act 1896 s 1 and Sch 1.} By direction of the Statute Law Committee the comma was then dropped. {(1966) 82 LQR 25.} Acts beginning with the Tanganyika Republic Act 1962 are thus given short titles which lack this comma.

Moreover earlier Acts originally equipped with a comma in their short title are now said to be correctly cited without one. {See, eg, the citation 'the Judicial Committee Act 1833' in s 2(5) of the Tanganyika Republic Act 1962.} The authority for this statement is a note, apparently based on the proposition that commas in Acts are to be disregarded, by the then First Parliamentary Counsel, Sir Noël Hutton. {(1966) 82 LQR 25).} It is of doubtful validity however, since the short title to an Act is conferred either by the Act itself or by a Short Titles Act or other Statute Law Revision Act. Neither the Statute Law Committee nor the First Parliamentary Counsel is empowered to override an Act of Parliament, though it has to be admitted that the point is scarcely worthy of the sort of special enactment required to meet it.

In earlier times short titles were given informally, eg Lord Brougham's Act, Fox's Libel Act, Michaelangelo Taylor's Act, Lord Cairns's Act, the Thellusson Act.

Short title as guide to meaning   When using the short title as a guide to legislative intention, it must be remembered that its function is simply to provide a brief label by which the Act may be referred to. This does not mean that such limited help as it can give must be rejected. As Scrutton LJ said-

' . . . the short title being a label, accuracy may be sacrificed to brevity; but I do not understand on what principle of construction I am not to look at the words of the Act itself to help me understand its scope in order to interpret the words Parliament has used in the circumstances in which they were legislating.'

{*Re the Vexatious Actions Act 1886 - re Bernard Boaler* [1915] 1 KB 21, at p 40.}

Judges not infrequently mention the short title as being at least confirmatory of one of the opposing constructions. {See, e g, *Lonrho Ltd v Shell Petroleum Co Ltd* [1981] 2 All ER 456, *per* Lord Diplock at p 462. As to the opposing constructions see s 84 of this Code.}

The fact that, apart from the year, two Acts have identical short titles will be taken as an indication that they are *in pari materia*. {*R v Wheatley* [1979] 1 All ER 954, *per* Bridge LJ at p 957. As to Acts *in pari materia* see pp 516–517 above.}

For cases where judges have confused the long title of an Act with the short title see Example 271.4.

Repeal of naming Act Subsection 2 of this section derives from s 19(2) of the Interpretation Act 1978. It anyway goes without saying. For reasons given above, all that matters is whether a reference sufficiently identifies the Act.

Revised editions Subsection 3 of this section derives from the Statute Law Revision Act 1893 s 3.

276. Amendable descriptive components of Act: examples

Where an Act includes examples of its operation, these are to be treated as detailed indications of how Parliament intended the enactment to operate in practice. If however an example contradicts the clear meaning of the enactment the latter is accorded preference, it being assumed in the absence of indication to the contrary that the framer of the example was in error.

COMMENTARY

If Parliament thinks fit to include in an Act examples of how the Act is intended to operate, these are clearly of strong persuasive authority. They show how Parliament itself contemplated the Act would work.

Judges have welcomed the assistance given by statutory examples. Lord Denning MR said-

'. . . one of the best ways, I find, of understanding a statute is to take some specfic instances which, by common consent, are intended to be covered by it. This is especially the case with a Finance Act. I cannot understand it by simply reading it through. But when an instance is given, it becomes plain. I can say at once: "Yes, that is the sort of thing Parliament intended to cover".'

{*Escoigne Properties Ltd v IRC* [1958] AC 549, at pp 565-6. See also *London Transport Executive v Betts* [1959] AC 213, at p 240.}

Jurists have asked for greater use of statutory examples. {See, e g, R W M Dias *Jurisprudence* (4th edn, 1976) p 244.} The Renton Committee suggested that more use be made of examples 'showing how a Bill is intended to work in particular situations'. {*The Preparation of Legislation* (1975, Cmnd 6053) para

20.2(9).} The Committee preferred that examples should be placed in Schedules. {Ibid.}

Where statutory examples are given it is the duty of the court to accept their guidance. Unless this is unavoidable, they should not be rejected on the ground that they are repugnant to the operative provisions of the Act. As the Judicial Committee of the Privy Council said in *Mahomed Syedal Ariffin v Yeoh Ooi Gark* {[1916] 2 AC 575, at p 581.}-

> 'The great usefulness of the illustrations, which have, though not part of the sections, been expressly furnished by the legislature as helpful in the working and application of the statute, should not be thus impaired.'

Form of examples   Statutory examples vary in their form. The most usual type is the parenthetical example, where the legislator for a moment turns aside from setting forth the rule by means of the usual generalised formula.

Example 1   In setting out the common duty of care owed by an occupier of premises to any visitor to the premises, s 2(3) of the Occupiers' Liability Act 1957 says that the occupier should expect a visitor to display the ordinary amount of care, 'so that (for example) in proper cases-

> (a) an occupier must be prepared for children to be less careful than adults; and
> (b) an occupier may expect that a person, in the exercise of his calling, will appreciate and guard against any special risks . . .'

{Similar examples are given in s 2(4) of the Occupiers' Liability Act 1957.}

Direct examples were given by s 2(2) of the Race Relations Act 1968. Section 2(1) of the Act made it unlawful to discriminate in the provision of 'any goods, facilities or services'. Section 2(2) began: 'The following are examples of the facilities and services mentioned in subsection (1) above . . .'

The Race Relations Act 1968 was repealed by the Race Relations Act 1976. {S 79 and Sch 5.} Section 20(2) of the Race Relations Act 1976 is on similar lines to s 2(2) of the Race Relations Act 1968, and also closely follows s 29(2) of the Sex Discrimination Act 1975. On the effect of the examples set out in s 29(2) of the Sex Discrimination Act 1975, Lord Fraser of Tullybelton, speaking for the majority of the House of Lords in *Amin v Entry Clearance Officer, Bombay* {[1983] 2 All ER 864, at p 872.} said-

> 'My Lords, I accept that the examples in s 29(2) are not exhaustive, but they are, in my opinion, useful pointers to aid in the construction of sub-s (1). Section 29 as a whole seems to me to apply to the direct provision of facilities or services, and not to the mere grant of the permission to use facilities. That is in accordance with the words of sub-s (1), and is reinforced by some of the examples in sub-s (2).'

{Lord Fraser then went on to spell out how the statutory examples given in s 29(2) operated. These examples were also relied on by Ackner LJ in *Kassam v Immigration Appeal Tribunal* [1980] 2 All ER 330 at p 335.}

The most elaborate examples in modern British legislation are contained in Sch 2 to the Consumer Credit Act 1974. The Act introduced many new terms, and the purpose of Sch 2 is to show how they are to be used. It is introduced by s 188 of the Act, which runs-

'(1) Schedule 2 shall have effect for illustrating the use of terminology employed in this Act.
(2) The examples given in Sch 2 are not exhaustive.
(3) In the case of conflict between Sch 2 and any other provision of this Act, that other provision shall prevail.
(4) The Secretary of State may by order amend Sch 2 by adding further examples or in any other way.'

Schedule 2 is in two Parts. Part I gives a list of the 31 new terms dealt with in the Schedule. Part II sets out 24 detailed examples. Each example is in two parts, respectively labelled *Facts* and *Analysis*.

On this Schedule, the Australian Attorney-General, Mr Peter Durack QC, commented: 'The advantages of using such techniques in appropriate cases have perhaps been ignored or undervalued, or both'. {*Symposium on Statutory Interpretation* (Canberra 1983) para 5.10.}

For an instance of examples in regulations see the University Elections (Single Transferable Vote) Regulations 1918 (S R & O 1918 No 1348) Sch 1.

Repugnant example   Where an example contradicts the clear meaning of an enactment the latter is accorded preference, it being assumed that the framer of the example was in error. This does not mean that the 'clear' meaning will always be followed however. There are cases when the court will apply a strained construction, and an example may *support* the reasons for doing so. A repugnant example cannot in itself justify departure from the literal meaning of an operative provision however. {*Mahomed Syedal Ariffin v Yeoh Ooi Gark* {[1916] 2 AC 575, at p 581. See also Consumer Credit Act 1974 s 188(3) (cited above), which is thought to express the general rule.}

UNAMENDABLE DESCRIPTIVE COMPONENTS OF ACT

277. Unamendable descriptive components of Act: nature of

An unamendable descriptive component is a component which describes the whole or some part of the Act, and is not subject to amendment (as opposed to a mere printing correction) when the Bill for the Act is going through Parliament. The following are unamendable descriptive components: chapter number, date of passing, enacting formula, heading, sidenote or marginal note, punctuation, format.

COMMENTARY

Functional construction rule   Under the functional construction rule set out in s 124 of this Code, the significance to be attached by the interpreter to any component of an Act must be assessed in conformity with its legislative function as a component of that type. This section and ss 278 to 284 explain the function of the unamendable descriptive components.

Printing corrections   As to the making of printing corrections by parliamentary clerks see pp 108–109 above.

An unamendable descriptive component is part of an Act, and may be used in interpretation so far as, having regard to its function, it provides a reliable guide. {For a refutation of dicta to the contrary, see commentary on s 124 of this Code.}

278. Unamendable descriptive components of Act: chapter number

Every Act bears a chapter number. Pre-1963 Acts are numbered serially from the beginning of the parliamentary session in which they were passed. Acts passed after 1962 are numbered serially from the beginning of the calendar year.

COMMENTARY

On the Queen's Printer copies of Acts, the calendar year and chapter number appear at the head.

Use in interpretation   The only significance of the chapter number for statutory interpretation is in determining which of two Acts receiving royal assent on the same date are to be treated as first in time. Thus where two Acts passed on the same day are inconsistent, the chapter numbers indicate which of them, being deemed the later, is to prevail.

Where two or more Acts receive assent by the same letters patent, chapter numbers are allocated according to the order in which the short titles are set out in the schedule to the letters patent. {As to enactment procedure see s 36 of this Code.} Accordingly where Acts are shown as receiving royal assent on the same day, the chapter number shows the deemed order of passing.

Chapters of sessions   An Act passed before the year 1963 was numbered as a chapter of the 'statute book of the session', that is the portion of the entire statute book that was enacted in the *parliamentary session* within which the Act was passed. {See p 411 above.}

Example 1   Thus the first Act to receive royal assent in the session 10 & 11 Eliz 2 (the Tanganyika Independence Act 1961) was numbered chapter 1 even though it received assent as late as 22 November in the calendar year 1961.

Under this system, each Act bore in abbreviated form the regnal year or years identifying the session in which it was passed, eg, '10 & 11 Eliz 2'. This was followed by the chapter number, eg, 'c 1'.

Regnal years   The regnal year runs from the anniversary of the date of accession of the Monarch.

Example 2   Queen Elizabeth II acceded to the throne on 6 February 1952. Accordingly each regnal year of Her reign begins on 6 February and ends on the following 5 February.

If, at the time the Act was printed, the parliamentary session had not progressed beyond the first of what were usually the two regnal years within which it was held, only that first year could be shown on copies of the Act. No assumption could be made that the session would pass into the next regnal year because, on an early end to the session (as with a dissolution of Parliament) or on the demise of the Crown, this would not in fact occur. So we find Acts printed with what turns out to be an incorrect regnal year.

Example 3 The Tanganyika Independence Act 1961 bears the regnal year 10 Eliz 2, though with hindsight we can see that the correct description would have been 10 & 11 Eliz 2.

Even when the Acts were gathered into the official annual volume these enforced errors were not corrected.

Example 4 Thus we find that the volume of public general Acts of 15 & 16 Geo 5 inaccurately shows the first 25 chapters of the session as having been passed in the (non-existent) session '15 Geo 5'.

Where, as used to happen frequently and can still happen today, there are two parliamentary sessions within one regnal year, the practice was to characterise the Acts of the first session as 'Stat 1' and those of the second as 'Stat 2'. This is because under early practice the entire legislative output of a session was regarded as one statute. {See p 411 above.}

Example 5 The Bill of Rights (1688) is cited as '1 W & M st 2 c 2'. {Kerr Bl (4th edn, 1876) i 61.}

Later practice has in such cases adopted an alternative formula using 'sess 1' and 'sess 2'. Thus the Bill of Rights is cited in the official Chronological Table of the Statutes as '1 Will & Mar sess 2 c 2'.

Until 1940, the official volumes of Acts were organised on a sessional, rather than an annual, basis. This meant that the 'statute book of a session', beginning at chapter 1 and ending with the concluding chapter of the session, was published as a whole in one or more volumes. Though logically impeccable, this arrangement was inconvenient once the short title, rather than the session and chapter, had become the accepted mode of citation of Acts. The short title indicates the calendar year of passing, not the session. A calendar year usually comprises the whole or part of two or more sessions, so the user did not know which sessional volume to consult. Starting with the year 1940, the official volumes of Acts contain only those passed in the calendar year in question.

Chapters of calendar years Section 1 of the Acts of Parliament Numbering and Citation Act 1962 brought to an end the ancient system of numbering Acts as chapters of the 'statute book of a session'. It states that-

> 'The chapter numbers assigned to Acts of Parliament passed in the year 1963 and every subsequent year shall be assigned by reference to the calendar year, and not the Session, in which they are passed; and any such Act may, in any Act, instrument or document, be cited accordingly.'

This does not spell out the precise method of citation intended as helpfully it might have done. In official printed copies of an Act the short title appears at the head, with underneath the chapter number in the form-

1963 CHAPTER 1

Where however a marginal citation is given in an Act of Parliament to a post-1962 Act referred to therein the form used is-

1963 c. 1.

It may be assumed that either form complies with s 1 of the Acts of Parliament Numbering and Citation Act 1962.

Surprise may be felt at the fact that it was thought necessary to pass an Act of Parliament in order to authorise the change from chapters of sessions to chapters of calendar years. The draftsman concerned justified it in these words-

'The change . . . had to be authorised by Act of Parliament, or so it was thought, because the previous system formed part of the law and custom of Parliament. Indeed it was arguable that it formed part of the law of nature, immune even from the reach of an Act, inasmuch as (whatever you choose to call it) an Act is a slice of the statute or statutes of a particular Session.'

{Sir Noël Hutton (1966) 82 LQR 24.}

Type face The type face used for a chapter number has a surprising importance.

The chapter number for a public general Act is in large arabic figures. It is in small roman for local Acts (including Provisional Order Confirmation Acts), and small *italicised* arabic for personal Acts (if printed).

The importance lies in the fact that the type face of the chapter number is the only thing that tells the reader which sort of Act he is looking at, or is being referred to in another Act. {Where another Act is referred to in an Act, the calendar year and chapter number are given in the margin.} This guide is not always reliable in the case of earlier Acts. Thus many private Acts of the reign of Queen Anne are shown in the Chronological Table of the Statutes as bearing large arabic numerals.

279. Unamendable descriptive components of Act: date of passing

The date of passing of an Act appears in square brackets after the long title.

COMMENTARY

The date of passing or assent is inserted in accordance with a duty imposed by the Acts of Parliament (Commencement) Act 1793. {33 Geo 3 c 13. The short title was conferrred on the Act by the Short Titles Act 1896.} This requires the Clerk of the Parliaments, in the case of every Act, to-

' . . . endorse (in English) . . . immediately after the title {I e the long title (see s 271 of this Code).} of such Act, the day, month and year when the same shall have passed and shall have received the Royal Assent; and such endorsement shall be taken to be a part of such Act.'

The wording of this calls for comment. It suggests that the passing of the Act and the receiving of royal assent are two different things, but in fact they are the same thing. {*R v Smith* [1910] 1 KB 17.} It speaks of 'receiving' royal assent. Does this mean, where the dates are different, the signification or communication of assent? {See s 37 of this Code.} It probably means the latter.

Commencement The significance of the date of passing is that, unless the contrary intention appears, it is also the date of commencement. {See s 165 of this Code.} As to the priority between two Acts passed on the same day, see s 278 of this Code.

280. Unamendable descriptive components of Act: enacting formula

The enacting formula or purview of an Act is the verbal formula expressing the Act's nature as a command of the sovereign legislature, namely the Queen in Parliament. It immediately follows the long title and date of passing unless there is a preamble, when it follows that.

In any revised edition of the statutes published by authority the enacting formula may be omitted.

COMMENTARY

The wording of the enacting formula or purview has varied, and is still not uniform. It is now purely formal, with no direct significance in interpretation.

The enacting words of early statutes were *Purveu est* or *Provisum est*, respectively law French and Latin versions of the formula *It is provided*. As might be expected, there was no uniformity however. When the House of Commons became established as an element in the making of statutes, the formula settled down on lines of which the Laws in Wales Act 1535 furnishes a typical example: ' . . . His Highness . . . hath by the deliberate advice consent and agreement of the Lords Spiritual and Temporal, and the Commons, in the present Parliament assembled, and by the authority of the same, ordained enacted and established . . . that . . .'

For most public general Acts the formula is now-

> Be it enacted by the Queen's most Excellent Majesty, by and with the advice and consent of the Lords Spiritual and Temporal, and Commons, in this present Parliament assembled, and by the authority of the same, as follows:-

Although the reality is now very different, the enacting formula thus still speaks of an Act as made *by* the Crown. In finalising the details of the text, the Crown still has a minor part to play. For this purpose, as we have seen, it acts through its officer, the Clerk of the Parliaments, who in turn acts through officials of the Public Bill Office. {See s 45 of this Code.}

Omission in revised editions The final sentence in this section is authorised by the Statute Law Revision Act 1894 s 4. No doubt through oversight, the authority is duplicated in the Statute Law Revision Act 1948 s 3(1)(a).

281. Unamendable descriptive components of Act: headings

A heading within an Act, whether contained in the body of the Act or a Schedule, is part of the Act. It may be considered in construing any provision of the Act, provided due account is taken of the fact that its function is merely to serve as a brief, and therefore necessarily inaccurate, guide to the material to which it is attached.

COMMENTARY

Headings are unamendable descriptive components. {See 277 of this Code.} Like anything else in what Parliament puts out as its Act, a heading is part of the Act, despite dicta to the contrary. {See s 124 of this Code.} However it is of very limited use in interpretation because of its necessarily brief and inaccurate nature.

Any heading can only be an approximation, and may not cover all the detailed matters falling within the provision to which it isattached. Furthermore it may fail to get altered when some amendment made in Parliament to those provisions would justify this. As Lord Reid said-

> 'A cross-heading ought to indicate the scope of the sections which follow it but there is always a possibility that the scope of one of these sections may have been widened by amendment.'

{*R v Schildkamp* [1971] AC 1, at p 10.}

However it is clear that, in accordance with the informed interpretation rule, {See s 119 of this Code.} modern judges consider it not only their right but their duty to take account of headings. {See, e g, *Dixon v British Broadcasting Corpn* [1979] 2 All ER 112, *per* Shaw LJ at p 116 ('it is requisite to look at the heading'; *Customs and Excise Commrs v Mechanical Services (Trailer Engineers) Ltd* [1979] 1 All ER 501, at p 509; *Lloyds Bank Ltd v Secretary of State for Employment* [1979] 2 All ER 573, at p 580; *Re Phelps (deceased)* [1979] 3 All ER 373, at p 377.}

Certain older dicta must now therefore be regarded as erroneous. Avory J said: 'Headings of sections . . . form no part of a statute. They are not voted on or passed by Parliament, but are inserted after the Bill has become law'. {*R v Hare* [1934] 1 KB 354, at p 355.} This is not correct. The entire Act is passed by Parliament, and is entered, or deemed to be entered, in the Parliament Roll with all non-amendable components included. These components mostly remain unchanged throughout the passage of the Bill. They are certainly not inserted after the Bill has become law.

Where a heading differs from the material it describes, this puts the court on enquiry. However it is most unlikely to be right to allow the plain literal meaning of the words to be overridden purely by reason of a heading. {See, e g, *Fitzgerald v Hall Russell & Co Ltd* [1970] AC 984, *per* Lord Upjohn at p 1000; *Pilkington Bros Ltd v IRC* [1982] 1 All ER 715, *per* Lord Bridge at p 723.} The House of Lords did this, it is submitted illegitimately, in *Infabrics Ltd v Jaytex Ltd* [1981] 1 All ER 1057. {For a detailed criticism of this decision see Bennion 'Can There Be an Infringing Copy Without a Copyright Infringement?' (1981) 131 NLJ 749.}

Judges have been known to refer to the long title of an Act as a 'heading', but this is an obvious inaccuracy. {See, e g, *Hodgson v Marks* [1970] 3 All ER 513, at p 525.}

282. Unamendable descriptive components of Act: sidenotes

A sidenote or marginal note to a section is part of the Act. It may be considered in construing the section or any other provision of the Act, provided due account is taken of the fact that its function is merely to serve as a brief, and therefore necessarily inaccurate, guide to the content of the section.

COMMENTARY

Sidenotes are unamendable descriptive components. {See 277 of this Code.} Like anything else in what Parliament puts out as its Act, a sidenote or marginal note (the terms are interchangeable) is part of the Act, despite dicta to the contrary. {See s 124 of this Code.} It may therefore be used by the interpreter. As Sir Rupert Cross said of this component: 'No judge can be expected to treat something which is before his eyes as though it was not there'. {*Statutory Interpretation* 113.} However the sidenote is of very limited use in interpretation because of its necessarily brief and inaccurate nature.

The function of a sidenote is as a brief indication of the content of the section. In early Acts a marginal note was in the nature of a precis of the section, often quite lengthy. {See, e g, the notes affixed to the statute 2 Geo 3 c 19 (1761).} A sidenote can only be an approximation, and may not cover all the detailed matters falling within the section to which it is attached. Furthermore it may fail to get altered when some amendment made in Parliament would call for this.

Sometimes a draftsman will use a sidenote to name some concept dealt with in the section. This may throw light on the intention.

Example 1 Section 6 of the Bail Act 1976 makes it an offence if a person who has been released on bail in criminal proceedings fails without reasonable cause to surrender to custody. The sidenote reads: 'Offence of *absconding* by person released on bail'. {Emphasis added.} Absconding is not the only possible reason for failing to surrender to bail. Does the sidenote restrict the width of the section? The answer is no. Such labels are given merely for convenience, and have no substantive effect. {See *R v Harbax Singh* [1979] 1 All ER 524, at p 525.}

Thring wisely said that the sidenotes, when read together in the arrangement of sections at the beginning of the Act, 'should have such a consecutive meaning as will give a tolerably accurate idea of the contents of the Act'. {*Practical Legislation* p 60.} This is an aim draftsmen pursue, and is illustrated by the arrangement of sections of the present Code.

If the sidenote contradicts the text this puts the interpreter on enquiry; but the answer may be that the draftsman chose an inadequate signpost, or neglected to alter it to match an amendment made to the clause during the passage of the Bill. Such facts are outside the knowledge of the interpreter, who must therefore adopt a rule not depending on them.

In *R v Schildkamp* {[1971] AC 1, at p 10.} Lord Reid said that 'a side-note is a poor guide to the scope of a section, for it can do no more than indicate the main subject with which the section deals.'

Example 2 In *Page (Inspector of Taxes) v Lowther* {(1983) *The Times* 27 October.}, while the Court of Appeal had 'full regard' to the sidenote of s 488 of the Income and Corporation Taxes Act 1970 ('Artificial transactions in land'), they nevertheless held that a non-artificial transaction fell within the section. Slade LJ said that the sidenote was 'somewhat misleading'. He added that it was a brief précis of the section and was therefore 'a most unsure guide to its construction'.

Upjohn LJ gave a precisely accurate indication of the role of the sidenote when he said: 'While the marginal note to a section cannot control the language used in the section, it is at least permissible to approach a consideration of its general purpose and the mischief at which it is aimed *with the note in mind.* {*Stephens v Cuckfield RDC* [1960] 2 QB 373, at p 383 (emphasis added).} The italicised words accurately show the relationship of this component to the informed interpretation rule set out in s 119 of this Code. Earlier inconsistent dicta must be treated as erroneous.

Thus Phillimore LJ referred to a 'general rule of law' to the effect that marginal notes must be disregarded 'upon the principle that those notes are inserted not by Parliament nor under the authority of Parliament, but by irresponsible persons.' {*Re Woking UDC* [1914] 1 Ch 300, at p 322.}

In fact, with occasional trifling exceptions, the marginal notes in an Act are *not* inserted by parliamentary clerks - or even draftsmen - but are contained either in the Bill as introduced or in new clauses added by amendment. Furthermore the clerks are not 'irresponsible persons'. They are subject to the authority of Parliament. Objection may be taken by a Member to anything they do in relation to a Bill; and it would be open to either House, if it thought fit, to order rectification of a printing alteration which it considered unsuitable.

Avory J said that 'marginal notes form no part of a statute'. He added: 'They are not voted on or passed by Parliament, but are inserted after the Bill has become law' {*R v Hare* [1934] 1 KB 354, at p 355.} This is not the case however. The entire Act is passed by Parliament, and is entered, or deemed to be entered, in the Parliament Roll with all non-amendable components included. These components mostly remain unchanged throughout the passage of the Bill. They are certainly not inserted after the Bill has become law.

Willes J, after asserting that the marginal notes and other 'appendages' are not part of an Act, said of any Act passed after the practice of actually engrossing Acts on the Parliament Roll ceased in 1849-

'The Act, when passed, must be looked at just as if it were still entered upon a roll, which it may be again if Parliament should be pleased so to order; in which case it would be without these appendages . . .'

{*Claydon v Green* (1868) LR 3 CP 511, at p 522.}

After the lapse of more than a century, during which Parliament has not returned to using the old Parliament Roll, it may confidently be asserted that this dictum is no longer good law, if indeed it ever was. Modern judges consider it proper to consider sidenotes, and gather what guidance they can from them. Thus Vinelott J said that the sidenote to s 488 of the Income and Corporation Taxes Act 1970 was a permissible and useful guide that threw a light on the mischief at which the section was aimed. {*Chilcott v IRC* [1982] STC 1, at p 23. See also *Re Phelps (deceased)* [1979] 3 All ER 373, at p 377.}

283. Unamendable descriptive components of Act: format

The layout or format is part of the Act. It may be considered in construing any provision of the Act, provided due account is taken of the fact that it is designed merely for ease of reference.

COMMENTARY

The format is an unamendable descriptive component. {See 277 of this Code.} It forms part of the Act as promulgated by Parliament, and is not to be disregarded by the interpreter. *Alcom Ltd v Republic of Colombia* [1984] 1 All ER 1. While meaning should certainly not depend on format, this may have a part to play in cases of doubt.

Megarry V-C said extrajudicially that 'both punctuation and arrangement may be of the highest importance in suggesting one interpretation and concealing another'. {(1959) 75 LQR 31.} This is the modern view. Earlier dicta to the contrary belong to the age of disorganised composition and erratic printing. {See, e g, *R v Newark-upon-Trent* (1824) 3 B & C 59, *per* Holroyd J at p 71. As to disorganised composition see s 76 of this Code.}

Paragraphing It is the modern practice to break a long section or subsection into paragraphs. {See p 568 above.} Where a provision consists of several numbered paragraphs with the word 'or' before the last paragraph only, that word is taken to be implied before the previous paragraphs after the first. {R E Megarry (1959) 75 LQR 29. Cf *Bricker v Whatley* (1684) 1 Vern 233; *Phillips v Price* [1958] 3 WLR 616.}

Parts A large Act may be divided into Parts. A smaller sub-division (whether there are Parts or not) is the *fasciculus*, which is a group of sections or paragraphs marked by a cross-heading.

It was the former practice for the opening section of a large Act to say that the Act was divided into Parts. {See, e g, Merchant Shipping Act 1854; Companies Act 1862. For the effect see *Inglis v Robertson* [1898] AC 616, *per* Lord Herschell at p 630.} Thring commended this by saying: 'It will thus be out of the power of courts of law to refuse to recognise the division into parts, as being a substantive portion of the Act'. {*Practical Legislation* p 60.} This was an aspect of the often-remarked 'war' waged by Victorian judges on parliamentary legislation. It has no place today.

The following statement of the reasons for dividing an Act into parts was given by Holroyd J in the Australian case of *Re The Commercial Bank of Australia Ltd* {(1893) 19 VLR 333, at p 375.}-

> 'When an Act is divided and cut into parts or heads, prima facie it is, we think, to be presumed that those heads were intended to indicate a certain group of clauses as relating to a particular object ... The object is prima facie to enable everybody who reads to discriminate as to what clauses relate to such and such a subject matter. It must be perfectly clear that a clause introduced into a part of an Act relating to one subject matter is meant to relate to other subject matters in another part of the Act before we can hold that it does so.'

Example 1 As an example of a case falling within the last part of this dictum, Professor Pearce cites *Chalmers v Thompson.* {(1913) 30 WN (NSW) 162. See D

C Pearce *Statutory Interpretation in Australia* (2nd edn, 1981) p 53.} A section of the Children's Protection Act (a consolidation Act) relating to ill-treatment of children appeared in a Part headed 'Adoption of Children'. The question was whether a child's *natural father* could be convicted of contravening the section. The court held that he could. They reached this result by consulting the pre-consolidation version, which was not divided into parts.

Footnotes   If material is put into the form of a footnote it is still fully a part of the Act, and must be construed accordingly. {*Erven Warnink BV v Townend & Sons (Hull) Ltd* [1982] 3 All ER 312, at p 316.}

For other cases where the court was guided in its construction of an enactment by its typography and layout see *Piper v Harvey*, {[1958] 1 QB 439 (see on this 101 Sol Jo 856-857).} *Re Allsop* {[1914] 1 Ch 1.} and *Dormer v Newcastle-on-Tyne Corpn.* {[1940] 2 KB 204.}

284. Unamendable descriptive components of Act: punctuation

Its punctuation forms part of an Act, and may be used as a guide to interpretation. Punctuation is generally of little weight however, since the sense of an Act should be the same with or without its punctuation.

COMMENTARY

Punctuation is a device not for making meaning, but for making meaning plain. Its purpose, as Bouvier said, is to denote the stops that ought to be made in oral reading, and to point out the sense. {*A Law Dictionary* (1839) vol 2, tit. PUNCTUATION.} Draftsmen are instructed that they should on no account allow the meaning to turn on the presence or absence of a punctuation mark. The good draftsman consciously drafts every clause with an eye to what its sense would be if all such marks were removed.

The courts have consistently said that in the original version Acts are not punctuated, and that punctuation forms no part of an Act. Research has shown this to be misconceived.

Parliament Roll   Acts were formerly engrossed on the Parliament Roll. This ceased at the end of 1849. {*Claydon v Green* (1868) LR 3 CP 511, at p 522.} It was replaced by the present practice whereby separate vellum copies of each Act are prepared. {See p 120 above.}

Judges have frequently stated, quite mistakenly, that punctuation marks were never entered on the Parliament Roll. Thus Cockburn CJ said: 'On the Parliament Roll there is no punctuation, and we therefore are not bound by the printed copies'. {*Stephenson v Taylor* (1861) 1 B & S 101, at p 106. See also, to the like effect, *Doe d Willis v Martin* (1790) 100 ER 882, at p 897: *R v Oldham* (1852) 169 ER 587, at p 588; *Barrow v Wadkin* (1857) 24 Beav 327, at p 330; *Duke of Devonshire v O'Connor* (1890) 24 QBD 468, at p 478; *IRC v Hinchy* [1960] AC 748, at p 765; *Hanlon v The Law Society* [1980] 2 All ER 199, *per* Lord Lowry at p 221. See also Example 5.}

Willes J took this to absurd lengths by saying that an Act passed after the practice of engrossment on the Roll had ceased must be looked at as if it contained no punctuation marks. This, he said, was because Parliament might at any time order such an Act to be entered on the Roll: 'in which case it would be without these appendages'. {*Claydon v Green* (1868) LR 3 CP 511, at p 522.}

The fact is that, while some Acts were engrossed on the Roll without punctuation, many did include punctuation marks. As that thorough American researcher Mellinkoff reports: 'English statutes were punctuated from the earliest days'. {D Mellinkoff *The Language of the Law* (1963) p 159.}

Example 1 When the enrolment of the Treason Act 1351 was examined by the judges in *R v Lynch* {[1903] 1 KB 444.} and *R v Casement* {(1917) 86 LJKB (NS) 484, at pp 484-486.} it was found that the enrolled Act was punctuated.

Nevertheless there was ample justification for the mistrust of punctuation in the printed versions of early statutes. The position is well put by Mellinkoff-

> 'The printers of statutes could not slough off questions of punctuation. The penman might hedge with an ambiguous squiggle, but the cutting of type involved decision and art, and the setting of type was not a casual act. Individual notions of punctuation varied. The raw materials the printers worked with were neither uniformly organized [nor uniformly] punctuated; and some printers themselves copied copies rather than originals.
>
> Each printer according to his own lights attempted to bring order to the disorder of the handwritten statutes, numbering sections, making marginal notes, and improving on the punctuation. These were all labours of typographical composition and not legislation, yet the statutes as fancied up by the printers were the only statutes ordinarily available to the profession. It is in this context - and in the context of the tradition that punctuation was for oral effect anyhow, not for grammatical sense - that it became understood that punctuation was no part of the statute, i e that what the printer did could not change the law.'

{D Mellinkoff *The Language of the Law* (1963) p 163.}

Because a comma, stop or apostrophe was small in the printer's fount it was easily dropped or misplaced. In manuscripts it could be mistaken by a copyist, or counterfeited by a blot or fold. All this led to distrust in the legal profession. The attorney's stock answer to a client who complained of an unpunctuated deed was: 'How would you like the title to your estate to depend upon a comma?' {R L Hine *Confessions of an Uncommon Attorney* (1946) p 20.}

Modern position As an aspect of precision drafting, {For this see s 76 of the Code.} modern Acts are carefully punctuated by or under the supervision of the draftsman. The printer has no part to play, and must faithfully reproduce the punctuation found in the vellum copies. {As to these see s 45 of the Code.}

Moreover the interpreter is by statute required to treat the published version of the Act, complete with punctuation, as authoritative. {See p 271 above.} Accordingly, in the absence of any indication that a mistake has occurred, the interpreter must take the printed punctuation as part of the Act, for what it is worth. Reliance cannot be placed on dicta such as this by Lord Reid: 'Even if punctuation in more modern Acts can be looked at (which is very doubtful), I do not think one can have any regard to punctuation in older Acts'. {*IRC v Hinchy* [1960] AC 748, at p 765.}

In a later case, Lord Reid said-

> 'Taking a strict view, one can say that [punctuation] should be
> disregarded because [it] is not the product of anything done in
> Parliament. I have never heard of an attempt to move that
> [punctuation marks] should be altered or amended, and between the
> introduction of a Bill and the Royal Assent they can be and often are
> altered by officials of Parliament acting in conjunction with the
> draftsman.'

{*R v Schildkamp* [1971] AC 1, at p 10.}

It is true that a punctuation change in a Bill may be made by what is known as
a printing correction. {As to these see pp 108–109 above.} Nevertheless the
whole Act as printed is put out by Parliament as its Act, and it is not for the
courts to treat any component of it as suspect. {As to this basic but often
disregarded principle see p 271 above.}

Most current judicial opinion accepts the view expressed extrajudicially by
Megarry V-C that 'both punctuation and arrangement may be of the highest
importance in suggesting one interpretation and concealing another'. {(1959) 75
LQR 31.} He went on-

> 'Nobody in his senses who was trying to interpret an obscure passage
> of prose would disregard all punctuation, from commas and
> quotation marks to brackets and full stops . . .'

{See also *Slaney v Kean* [1970] Ch 243, *per* Megarry J at p 252.}

Sir Noël Hutton, then First Parliamentary Counsel, appears to have
overlooked this wise judicial remark when writing a few years later in the same
journal that 'The only law about commas is that you pay no attention to them'.
{(1966) 82 LQR 24.}

Lord Shaw of Dunfermline said in a will case-

> 'Punctuation is a rational part of English composition and is
> sometimes quite significantly employed. I see no reason for depriving
> legal documents of such significance as attaches to punctuation in
> other writings.'

{*Houston v Burns* [1918] AC 337, at p 348. See also *Gauntlett v Carter* (1853) 17
Beav 586, at p 591, where commas were held 'a circumstance of importance'.}

Lord Shaw's words were later echoed by Lord Lowry-

> 'I consider that not to take account of punctuation disregards the
> reality that literate people, such as parliamentary draftsmen,
> punctuate what they write, if not identically, at least in accordance
> with grammatical principles. Why should not other literate people,
> such as judges, look at the punctuation in order to interpret the
> meaning of the legislation as accepted by Parliament?'

{*Hanlon v The Law Society* [1980] 2 All ER 199, at p 221.}

To ignore punctuation is indeed foreign to the ancient traditions of the law. In
early pleadings a punctuation mistake could be fatal, as Ruggle remarked in his
celebrated Latin comedy *Ignoramus*: *in nostra lege unum comma evertit totum
placitum.*

284. Unamendable descriptive components of Act: punctuation

In Scotland the Court of Justiciary has refused to ignore commas in a statute-

> 'Bills when introduced in Parliament have punctuation, and without such would be unintelligible to the legislators, *who pass them into law as punctuated*.'

{*Alexander v Mackenzie* (1947) SC(J) 155, at p 166. Emphasis added. Approved *Hanlon v The Law Society* [1980] 2 All ER 199, *per* Lord Lowry at p 221.}

Drafting error Where mistakes in punctuation occur, judges show little hesitation in rectifying them.

Example 2 In *Allnatt London Properties Ltd v Newton* {[1981] 2 All ER 290, at p 292.} Megarry V-C said of s 38(4)(b) of the Landlord and Tenant Act 1954 (as added by the Law of Property Act 1969 s 5) that 'for the errant semi-colon after the words "so specified" I have substituted the comma that lucidity demands'. {Cf the same judge's remarks in *Marshall v Cottingham* [1981] 3 All ER 8, at pp 10-12.}

Because punctuation ought not to make any difference to the grammatical meaning, it may assist in cases of doubt to read the words of the enactment *without* the punctuation provided. This will also help to avoid the mistake often made by judges and commentators of locating the cause of doubt in the punctuation when it truly arises from the choice or order of the words. {See, e g, R Cross *Statutory Interpretation* pp 114-115 and P B Maxwell *The Interpretation of Statutes* (12th edn, 1969) p 14, when compared to Examples 3 and 4.}

Example 3 Section 113 of the Housing Act 1957 deals with the conditions to be observed in the management of council houses. Subsection (4) reads-

> 'The local authority shall from time to time review rents and *make such changes, either of rents generally or of particular rents, and rebates* (if any) as circumstances may require.'

{Emphasis added.}

The italicised passage is obviously defective. In *Luby v Newcastle-under-Lyme Corpn* {[1965] 1 QB 214.} the Court of Appeal was asked to deal with the defect. The question was whether in relation to rebates the italicised words meant *make such rebates* or *make such changes [of] rebates*. *Held* The latter was the intended meaning. Harman LJ based his judgment on what he regarded as a mistaken comma after 'particular rents', which he held should be treated as omitted. 'The obligation', he said, 'is not to make rebates, *as grammatically it should have been if the comma were there*, but to make changes of rebates (if any)'. {P 229. Emphasis added.}

However the fact is that Harman LJ's removal of the comma does not give the passage the meaning held to be correct, as we see if all punctuation is removed from within the sentence-

> The local authority shall from time to time review rents and make such changes either of rents generally or of particular rents and rebates (if any) as circumstances may require.

Without changing the words or their order, we may gain assistance by presenting the opposing constructions using the device of comminution. The meaning found by the court ('the approved version') can be presented as-

(1) The local authority shall from time to time
(2) review rents
AND
(3) make such changes
(4) either of rents generally or of particular rents
AND
(5) rebates (if any)
(6) as circumstances may require.

The other version ('the rejected version') can be presented, again without altering any of the words or their order, in this way-

(1) The local authority shall from time to time
(2) review rents
AND
(3) make such
(3) changes either of rents generally or of particular rents
AND
(5) rebates (if any)
(6) as circumstances may require.

Comparing the two versions, we see that the rejected version is the grammatically correct one. The approved version, in order to make grammatical sense, requires the insertion of the preposition *of* at the beginning of our clause (5). The two commas do not assist comprehension of either version, and can be disregarded.

Was the court then wrong in choosing the approved version? The answer is that the court was right, but not for the reason given. The question is determined by applying the linguistic canon of construction requiring an Act to be construed as a whole. {See s 149 of this Code.} Another provision of the Housing Act 1957 (s 113(3)) gives a discretionary power to local authorities to grant rebates. The rejected version of s 113(4) (making the grant of rebates compulsory) would contradict this, and was clearly not intended by Parliament.

We see the true analysis to be that s 113(4) is subject to semantic obscurity through the omission of the preposition 'of' and the misuse of commas. The court was therefore required to produce the corrected version. {As to semantic obscurity and the 'corrected version' see s 90 of this Code.}

The same technique may be useful where the problem is not semantic obscurity but grammatical ambiguity. {As to this see ss 87 to 89 of this Code.}

Example 4   Section 10 of the Fugitive Offenders Act 1881 gave the court power to refuse to return an alleged offender if to do so 'would, having regard to the distance, to the facilities of communication, and to all the circumstances of the case, be unjust or oppressive or too severe'. However the power applied only where the words just quoted applied 'by reason of the trivial nature of the case, or by reason of the application for the return of the fugitive not being made in good faith in the interests of justice *or otherwise*'. {Emphasis added.}

The argument in *R v Governor of Brixton Prison, ex p Naranjan Singh* {[1962]

1 QB 211.} turned on whether a comma should be treated as inserted before the italicised words at the end of the passage last cited. The version preferred by the court ('the approved version') was that produced by inserting the comma. It can be rendered as follows, without altering the words or their order-

(1) by reason of the trivial nature of the case
OR
(2) by reason of the application for the return of the fugitive not being made in good faith in the interests of justice
OR
(3) otherwise.

The alternative version (the rejected version) can be rendered, again without alteration, as follows-

(1) by reason of the trivial nature of the case
OR
(2) by reason of the application for the return of the fugitive not being made in good faith in the interests of justice or otherwise.

Since the two versions have different meanings, but use the same words in the same order, it is obvious that there is grammatical ambiguity. How should this be resolved?

Here the absence of the comma before 'or otherwise' is a true interpretative factor. {As to interpretative factors see Part VII of this Code.} If the approved version were correct, one would expect to find a comma in position here.

Such considerations are always slight however, and there is a weighty factor the other way. The rejected version mentions only two considerations, triviality and bad faith. Neither has much to do with the two specified factors to which the court is required to have regard in the passage quoted above, namely the distance and the facilities of communication. This led the court to prefer the wider meaning, which admitted a variety of possible reasons for refusing the return of an alleged offender. It is one more example of the need to construe an Act as a whole. {As to this see s 149 of the Code.}

The importance of punctuation is increased when the alternative versions differ widely in meaning.

Example 5 In *Barrow v Wadkin* {(1857) 24 Beav 327.} Romilly MR was faced with a choice of punctuation between 'aliens, duties' and 'aliens' duties' in the statute 13 Geo 3 c 21 (1773). Both versions appeared in printed versions of the Act. Romilly MR inspected the Roll and found the phrase in question unpunctuated. He decided in favour of the former version, adding on the basis of his inspection: 'It seems that in the Rolls of Parliament the words are never punctuated'. {*Barrow v Wadkin* (1857) 24 Beav 327, at p 330. Since the inspection was made in his capacity of Master of the Rolls, it seems more likely that what Romilly MR inspected was actually the Chancery Roll.} This conclusion was strange because, as Mellinkoff reports, the enrolment of the Act in question contains two full stops, twelve hyphens and three apostrophes! {D Mellinkoff *The Language of the Law* (1963) p 158.}

A choice example of how grammatical ambiguity can be resolved one way or the other through the use of punctuation was given by the law reporter James Burrow in his *Essay on Punctuation* {(1772) p 11. Burrow also includes the rhyme in his *Settlement Cases* (1768) 629, at pp 636-637.}-

> Every lady in this land,
> Hath twenty nails upon each hand;
> Five and twenty on hands and feet,
> And this is true without deceit.

A rearrangement shows the truth-

> Every lady in this land hath twenty nails;
> Upon each hand five,
> And twenty on hands and feet;
> And this is true without deceit.

{The old rhyme is quoted by Megarry V-C in *Marshall v Cottingham* [1981] 3 All ER 8, at p 12.}

INCORPORATION OF PROVISIONS BY REFERENCE

285. Incorporation by reference: nature of

It is a common device of draftsmen to incorporate earlier statutory provisions by reference, rather than setting out similar provisions in full. This device saves space, and also attracts the case law and other learning attached to the earlier provisions. Its main advantage is a parliamentary one however, since it shortens Bills and cuts down the area for debate.

COMMENTARY

Sometimes the draftsman will keep the length of his Bill down by incorporating relevant provisions of some other Act. This is in accordance with the maxim *verba relata hoc maxime operantur per referentiam ut in eis inesse videntur* (words to which reference is made in an instrument have the same operation as if they were inserted in the instrument referring to them). {Co Litt 359.} The practice has been widely criticised by the courts. {See, e g, *Knill v Towse* (1889) 24 QBD 186, at pp 195-196; *Willingale v Norris* [1909] 1 KB 57, at p 61; *Chislett v Macbeth & Co* [1909] 2 KB 811, at p 815; *Woolley v Moore* [1953] 1 QB 43, at p 46.}

In the nineteenth century so-called Clauses Acts were passed. They contained common-form provisions which could be incorporated in local or private Acts. This technique of incorporation by reference is described above. {Pp 88-89.}

Such incorporation does not affect the separate identity of the several Acts. By implication it requires any necessary verbal adjustments to be made in the incorporated provisions, even though these are not spelled out. {*R v Whitehead* [1982] 3 All ER 96, *per* Donaldson LJ at p 103.}

Grouping of Acts   While each Act remains a separate entity, Acts dealing with the same subject-matter may be recognised as forming a group. They are said to be *in pari materia*. {As to this concept see pp 516-517 above.} They may be given a collective title. {See s 288 of this Code.} Formerly it was common to provide that a series of Acts *in pari materia* should be construed as one. {See s 287 of this Code.} This latter technique is liable to give rise to difficulty, and has fallen into disfavour.

There are a great many instances of the recycling by draftsmen of earlier statutory provisions of a similar kind to those they are required to produce.

Example 1 The draftsman of the Public Health Act 1875 was required to confer a power on local authorities to lay water mains. If set out afresh, this would have needed lengthy and complicated provisions. The draftsman had what seemed to him a better idea. He reflected that local authorities already had power to lay *sewers,* and that much the same process was involved in laying water mains. Accordingly what he said was this-

'Where a local authority supply water within their district, they shall have the same powers . . . for carrying water mains . . . as they have . . . for carrying sewers.'

{Public Health Act 1875 s 54. For the difficulties of interpretation thereby involved see *Jones v Conway and Colwyn Bay Joint Water Supply Board* [1893] 2 Ch 603. For a discussion of this case see p 702 below.}

The modern practice when applying provisions in another Act is to leave the reader to work out for himself what is involved. It was not always so. Some earlier Acts set out in full, with any modifications incorporated, the provisions that were applied in this way.

Example 2 The Transvaal Loan (Guarantee) Act 1907 provided for the raising and guarantee of a public loan for the Transvaal. Section 1(2) referred to s 1(2) to (6) of the South African Loan and War Contribution Act 1903. It said that these provisions-

' . . . which are set out in the Second Schedule to this Act, with the modifications shown in that schedule, shall apply, with respect to the guarantee, and the raising of the loan under this Act, as if they were herein re-enacted.'

The Second Schedule to the 1907 Act set out these provisions in full, with modifications indicated by italics.

The technique of incorporation has received so much judicial and other criticism that it is seldom used today. There are however occasional exceptions.

Example 3 Section 30(2) of the Transport Act 1981 says that ss 19 to 21 of the Act shall be construed as if they were contained in Part III of the Road Traffic Act 1972. In *Porter v Manning* {(1984) *The Times* 23 March.} Watkins LJ said that the reason for this was that Part III constituted a complete code regarding the licensing of drivers and, as parts of it were repealed by the 1981 Act, it could only remain complete if the new provisions of ss 19 to 21 were made part of it. {The usual modern method in such cases is to use the technique of textual amendment: see s 171 of this Code.}

286. Incorporation by reference: archival drafting

An enactment sometimes incorporates into the Act a whole body of law as it existed at a given time ('the relevant date'). This may include the practice prevailing on the relevant date, as well as the substantive law in force at that time. Often the provisions thus incorporated do not otherwise continue in force. The technique may be called archival drafting because it requires persons applying the Act after a considerable period has elapsed since the relevant date to engage in historical research in order to find out what the law thus imported amounts to.

The effect of archival drafting is to 'freeze' the body of law, so far as thus imported, in the form it was in on the relevant date. Subject to any amendments subsequently made for the purposes of the applying Act, the body of law is to be interpreted for those purposes at any subsequent time, unless the contrary intention appears, as if it had remained unaltered since that date.

COMMENTARY

Archival drafting may import previous legislation, or common law rules, or practice.

Example 1   Section 19(2) of the Supreme Court Act 1981, following earlier precedents, states that there shall be exercisable by the High Court 'all such . . . jurisdiction (whether civil or criminal) as was exercisable by it immediately before the commencement of this Act'. This relates back, by way of s 18 of the Supreme Court of Judicature (Consolidation) Act 1925, to the setting up of the High Court by the Supreme Court of Judicature Act 1873. Section 16 of the 1873 Act in similar language transferred to the new court the statutory jurisdiction of courts such as the Court of Queen's Bench and the Court of Chancery. It even brought in their *inherent* jurisdiction. {*Andrews v Barnes* (1888) 39 Ch D 133; *EMI Records Ltd v Ian Cameron Wallace Ltd* [1982] 2 All ER 980, at p 988; *The Despina GK* [1983] 1 All ER 1, at p 3.}

Many other examples could be cited. {See, e g, Crown Proceedings Act 1947 s 1, which makes it necessary to refer to all the enactments repealed by the Act together with the law and practice in relation to petitions of right; Solicitors Act 1974 s 50(2) (bringing in the practice relating to the long-vanished proctors); Post Office Act 1969 s 80 (bringing in former Civil Service practice). See also Examples 349.2. As to the disadvantages of archival drafting in relation to estate duty see Bennion *Statute Law* (2nd edn, 1983) pp 222-223.}

This form of drafting, which may be called archival drafting since it requires the reader to delve in the archives of the law, has the advantage of preserving continuity in the legal system. It suffers however from the grave defect that as time passes it becomes more and more difficult to discover precisely what the current law is.

Blackstone described the difficulty when he said, in relation to the 'court hand' formerly used to record legal records, that a record that was more than a century old at the time he wrote 'is now become the subject of science, and calls for the help of an antiquarian'. {Kerr Bl (4th edn, 1876) iii 331.} The very records disparagingly referred to by Blackstone may need to be consulted even today, to elucidate some point on the present jurisdiction of the High Court.

Despite the difficulties involved in giving effect to archival drafting, particularly after the passage of lengthy periods of time, it seems that it is the duty of the court to apply the imported law *as it existed on the relevant date*.

Lord Denning MR suggested the contrary in *Federal Commerce v Molena Alpha Inc* {[1978] 3 WLR 309, at p 338.} when he said of the grounds for equitable set-off as applying after the 'fusion' of law and equity effected by the Judicature Act 1873-

> 'These grounds were never precisely formulated before the Judicature Act 1873. It is far too late to search through the old books and dig them out . . . we have no longer to ask ourselves: what would the courts of common law or the courts of equity have done before the Judicature Act?'

This dictum, which is clearly contrary to the literal meaning of the incorporating provisions, also conflicts with the ruling by the House of Lords in *The Aries*. {[1977] 1 All ER 398. See 132 NLJ 815.} It is however supported by the principle described in s 321 of this Code.

287. Incorporation by reference: Acts construed as one

Where two Acts are required by a provision in the later Act to be construed as one, every enactment in the two Acts is to be construed as if contained in a single Act, except in so far as the context indicates that the later Act was intended to modify the earlier Act. The like principle applies where more than two Acts are to be construed as one, or where a part only of an Act is to be construed as one with other enactments.

COMMENTARY

This section is derived from a dictum of Lord Selborne LC concerning two Acts-

> 'It is to be observed that those two Acts are to be read together by the express provision of the seventh and concluding section of the amending Act; and therefore we must construe every part of each of them as if it had been contained in one Act, unless there is some manifest discrepancy making it necessary to hold that the later Act has to some extent modified something found in the earlier Act.'

{*Canada Southern Rly Co v International Bridge Co* (1883) 8 App Cas 723, at p 727. Followed *Hart v Hudson Bros Ltd* [1928] 2 KB 629; *Phillips v Parnaby* [1934] 2 KB 299. See also *Mather v Brown* (1876) 1 CPD 596.}
   Construction as one has the convenience of attracting for purposes of an amending Act the machinery provisions of the principal Act.

Example 1 The Highways Act 1971 was required to be construed as one with the principal Act, the Highways Act 1959. {Highways Act 1971 s 84(1).} Section 31(1) of the 1971 Act said that a builder's skip 'shall not be deposited on a highway without the permission of the highway authority'. In *York City Council v Poller* {[1976] Crim LR 313.} it was held that construction as one attracted s 280 of the 1959 Act, which required 'consents' under that Act to be in writing. Permission to deposit a skip had therefore to be in writing.
   While this method may be convenient for the draftsman, it is not so for the reader. Moreover it has dangers. Draftsmen seldom know what they are attracting when they require their Act to be construed as one with earlier Acts. There are telltale signs of this for those who know how to read them. In the

Example 1 case it may be surmised that the draftsman of s 31(1) did not know about s 280. If he had, he would have referred to 'consent' rather than 'permission', since 'consent' is the word invariably used in the 1959 Act.

Draftsmen are uneasily aware of this problem, and sometimes try to meet it by express provision.

Example 2   The draftsman of s 9 of the Supreme Court of Judicature Act 1881 wished that section to be construed as one with certain Acts. He ended the section with this sentence: 'This section, *so far as is consistent with the tenor thereof,* shall be construed as one with the said Acts'. {Emphasis added.} In fact the italicised words do no more than spell out what is meant by construction as one.

Construction as one often causes great difficulty to the interpreter. This is because it is a 'blind' form of drafting, far inferior to textual amendment. {As to textual amendment see s 171 of this Code.} Applied by the draftsman more or less automatically, it is bound to give rise to puzzling conjunctions.

Example 3   Section 15(1) of the Sale of Food (Weights and Measures) Act 1926 said that the Act was to be construed as one with the Weights and Measures Acts 1878 to 1926. Among these was the Weights and Measures Act 1889, s 21(2) of which made it an offence to deliver less coal than the amount mentioned in the delivery ticket or note. Section 12(6) of the 1926 placed certain conditions on the bringing of a prosecution 'in respect of an offence ... under *this Act*'. {Emphasis added.} The 1926 Act dealt only with food.

In *Phillips v Parnaby* {[1934] 2 KB 299.} the question was whether the s 12(6) conditions applied to a prosecution under s 21(1). Did the requirement that the Acts were to be construed as one convert the reference to 'this Act' in s 12(6) into a reference to the Weights and Measures Acts 1878 to 1926? *Held* The requirement did have this effect. Lord Hewart CJ expressed himself in great difficulty in arriving at a decision either way.

The case shows the sort of problems produced by this technique of incorporation. Although the draftsman of s 12(6) had written 'this Act', he had included elsewhere in the 1926 Act a provision which had the effect of changing these words into something else. This may be called the Chinese puzzle method of drafting, teasing and mocking the bemused reader. Lord Hewart CJ made his expostulations accordingly. {P 304.}

Judicial and other criticism has reduced the use of this pernicious drafting technique. Mackinnon LJ threw light on the reasons why it is employed.

Example 4   Mackinnon LJ was a member of the departmental committee whose proposals led to the Arbitration Act 1934. These called for major amendments to the principal Act, the Arbitration Act 1889. The committee strongly recommended that their proposals should be implemented by a comprehensive new Act, replacing the 1889 Act. Their advice was rejected, as s 21(4) of the 1934 Act shows-

> 'This Act shall be construed as one with the principal Act, and the
> principal Act, the Arbitration Clauses (Protocol) Act 1924, and the
> Arbitration (Foreign Awards) Act 1930, and this Act may be cited
> together as the Arbitration Acts 1889 to 1934.'

The latter part of this confers what is known as a collective title. {See s 288 of this Code.} Where Acts are to be included in a collective title and also construed as one, it is usual to say this in a combined provision. The reader cannot rely on this practice however, since it is sometimes departed from. {See, e g, Highways Act 1971 ss 84(1) and 87(2).}

Mackinnon LJ has recorded how the draftsman of the 1934 Act came to see him about this rejection of the committee's recommendation-

> 'I declined to take any interest in it: I reminded him of our request, but "Here", I said, "is the detestable thing - legislation by reference of the worst sort". By way of defence he said what we had proposed was impossible. A Bill so drafted would be intelligible to any MP of the meanest parts; he could debate every section of it, and move endless amendments.'

{'The Statute Book' (presidential address to the Holdsworth Club of the University of Birmingham, 1942) p 14.}

288. Incorporation by reference: collective titles

Where there are two or more Acts *in pari materia* the latest of them may include a provision to the effect that that Act and the earlier Acts in the series may be cited together by a title consisting of descriptive words usually ending with the calendar years of the first and last Act. This is known as a collective title. Such a provision has the like effect from the point of view of interpretation as a provision equipping an Act with a short title. As in the case of short titles, the collective title may alternatively be given by a Statute Law Revision Act.

COMMENTARY

A provision conferring a collective title usually takes the form followed for example by s 11(2) of the Merchant Shipping Act 1983. This runs as follows-

> '(2) This Act and the Merchant Shipping Acts 1894 to 1981 may be cited together as the Merchant Shipping Acts 1894 to 1983.'

Sometimes however the calendar years are omitted. Examples are the Lands Clauses Acts and the Income Tax Acts. {These collective titles are respectively conferred by the Interpretation Act 1978 Sch 1 and the Income and Corporation Taxes Act 1970 s 526(1)(b).}

Where there are only two Acts, the form is that which would have been employed in the Merchant Shipping Act 1897 if that Act had included a collective title provision (which it did not), namely-

> 'This Act and the Merchant Shipping Act 1894 may be cited together as the Merchant Shipping Acts 1894 and 1897.'

In this case a collective title was not bestowed until the number of Acts had grown to four. {See Merchant Shipping (Mercantile Marine Fund) Act 1898 s 9(2).}

Where two or more relevant Acts are passed in the same year, the later collective title provision takes the form followed for example by s 70(1) of the

Pilotage Act 1983: 'This Act . . . shall be included among the Acts that may be cited as the Merchant Shipping Acts 1894 to 1983'. The Pilotage Act 1983 is also an illustration of the fact that the descriptive words in the short title of an Act need not be the same as those in the collective title.

A collective title may include a part only of an Act. This may consist of named provisions (for example 'sections 4 to 13') or may be identified less precisely.

Example 1   The Fees (Increase) Act 1923 increased a wide range of fees, including some relating to merchant shipping. Section 11(2) provides that 'the Merchant Shipping Acts 1894 to 1921 . . . and this Act *so far as it amends those Acts* may be cited together as the Merchant Shipping Acts 1894 to 1923'. {Emphasis added.}

Updating of references   Where an enactment refers to a collective title, difficulty may arise when the collective title is later modified by the inclusion of further Acts. In most cases the reference requires updating to match, but this is seldom done expressly. Is it to be treated as done by implication, or is the reference to be treated as continuing to refer only to the Acts comprised in the original collective title?

Example 2   Section 3(1) of the British Nationality Act 1948 ends with the following proviso-

> 'Provided that nothing in this subsection shall apply to the contravention of any provision of the Merchant Shipping Acts 1894 to 1948.'

Since 1948 another fifteen Acts have been added to this collective title, which has now become the Merchant Shipping Acts 1894 to 1983. {Merchant Shipping Act 1983 s 11(2).} The policy of s 3(1) appears to require that the reference in the proviso should be treated as updated accordingly. Is the interpreter therefore to treat this as done?

There appears to be no authority on the point, which is a difficult one. It is hard to see how the successive Merchant Shipping Acts that altered the collective title after 1948 had any intention to amend s 3(1) of the British Nationality Act 1948. On the other hand the policy of s 3(1) requires that all current Acts which, at the time when it falls to be applied, are *in pari materia* with the Merchant Shipping Acts 1894 to 1948 should be treated as within the proviso.

It is submitted that the answer in such cases is to determine the policy of the provision containing the reference in question and be guided by that. Usually it will require a reference to a collective title to be treated as referring to the collective title as it stands at a time when the provision falls to be applied.

The formula used for the collective title may need to be changed where later Acts are different in scope.

Example 3   The collective title 'the Assurance Companies Acts' became too narrow when later Acts dealt with insurance companies also. When all the Acts were consolidated in 1958, the opportunity was taken to give a wider short title to the principal Act, which was called the Insurance Companies Act 1958. This consolidated the Assurance Companies Acts 1909 to 1946. By the time of the next consolidation in 1974, the current collective title was 'the Insurance Companies Acts 1958 to 1973'.

Short title The principles governing the use of a collective title in interpretation are similar to those applying in the case of the short title. {See s 275 of this Code.}

Statute Law Revision Acts For an example of the conferring of collective titles by a Statute Law Revision Act see the Short Titles Act 1896 s 2.

Construction as one The provision conferring a collective title often incorporates a statement that the Acts in question shall be construed as one, though this is less common than formerly. {See, e g, Fees (Increase) Act 1923 s 11(2).} As to the effect of a provision requiring Acts to be construed as one see s 287 of this Code.

The Principle against Doubtful Penalization

Introduction to Part XIII This Part expounds more fully the principle of legal policy set out in s 129 of this Code, namely that a person should not be penalized under a doubtful law. Although often referred to as though limited to criminal statutes, this principle in fact extends to any form of detriment.

The various detriments are gone through, with attention being paid to the provisions of the European Convention on Human Rights. First comes danger to human life or health (s 289). Then follow various kinds of interference: with freedom of the person (s 290), family rights (s 291), religion (s 292), free assembly and association (s 293), and free speech (s 294).

Next follows detriment to property and other economic interests (s 295), detriment to status or reputation (s 296), and infringement of privacy (s 297). Part XIII concludes by dealing with impairment of rights in relation to law and legal proceedings (s 298), and with other infringement of a person's rights as a citizen (s 299).

289. Danger to human life or health

One aspect of the principle against doubtful penalization is that by the exercise of state power the life or health of a person should not be endangered, except under clear authority of law.

COMMENTARY

Principle against doubtful penalization The presumption against imposition of a statutory detriment to health or safety without clear words is an aspect of the general principle against doubtful penalization. This general principle is explained in s 129 of the Code.

Whenever a particular construction of an enactment may endanger human life, or lead to detriment to a person's health or personal safety, the principle against doubtful penalization comes into play. In criminal law the death penalty is the most obvious example, though corporal punishment also comes into this category. {Penalties imposed by criminal law fall into several sections of this Part of the Code. Apart from the present section, imprisonment falls within s 290, and fines within s 295. All convictions impose a stigma, and are therefore within s 296. Other sections can be relevant; for example imprisonment may be regarded as interfering with family rights (s 291).}

An implied exception as to preservation of human life is imported whenever necessary into an enactment. Thus it was said in *Reniger v Fogossa* {(1550) 1 Plowd 1, at p 13 (*per* Robert Brook *arguendo*).}-

'When laws or statutes are made, yet there are certain things which are exempted and excepted out of the provision of the same by the law of reason, although they are not expressly excepted. As the breaking of prison is felony in the prisoner himself by the Statute de Frangentibus Prisonam {1 Ed 2 st 2 (1307).}: yet if the prison be on fire, and they who are in break the prison to save their lives, this shall be excused by the law of reason, and yet the words of the statute are against it.'

{In fact prison-breaking is a common law offence (2 Hawk c 18 s 21) and the statute of 1307 was an ameliorating one said to have been enacted for the benefit of the King's favourite Piers Gaveston: see Daines Barrington *Observations upon the Statutes* (2nd edn, 1767) p 144. Coke qualifies this passage in Brook's argument by inserting after 'fire' the words 'unlesse it be by the privity of the prisoner': 2 Co Inst 590. Cf *R v Rose* (1847) 2 Cox CC 329 ('revolt in a ship' justified to prevent master from unlawful killing of persons on board).}

When in a poor law case it was objected that the law gave an alien no claim to subsistence, Lord Ellenborough CJ said-

' . . . the law of humanity, which is anterior to all positive laws, obliges us to afford them relief, to save them from starving; and [the poor laws] were only passed to fix the obligation more certainly, and point out distinctly in what manner it should be borne.'

{*R v Inhabitants of Eastbourne* (1803) 4 East 103.}

The law requires convincing justification before it permits any physical interference, under alleged statutory powers, with a person's body. {See Examples 14.10 and 14.11.}

Example 1   RSC Ord 50 r 3 authorises the court or a judge to make, in connection with civil proceedings, any order for the 'inspection of any property or thing . . . as to which any question may arise therein [and] to authorise any samples to be taken, or any observation to be made or experiment to be tried' for obtaining full information or evidence.

In *W v W (1963)* {[1964] P 67.} the petitioner claimed a decree of nullity on the ground that the respondent was pregnant by another man at the time of the marriage. He asked the court to order, under Ord 50 r 3, the making of blood tests on himself, the respondent, and the child. *Held* Such an order, though within the literal wording, was precluded by the principle now under discussion. Cairns J said {Pp 70-71.} that if the petitioner's argument were right-

' . . . it would mean that in the case of a plaintiff alleging that he had suffered some internal injury by the defendant's negligence, it would be open to the court to direct that an extensive exploratory operation should be made by a surgeon on the plaintiff's body against his will . . . I do not consider that the word "thing" in the context of that rule includes the body or blood of a living person, nor that the taking of a sample includes the taking of a sample of blood from the veins of an unwilling human being. In my opinion, far more precise wording would be needed to enable the court to authorise any such interference with a person's body.'

{Cf *Aspinall v Sterling Mansell Ltd* [1981] 3 All ER 866 (medical examination by 'patch testing' refused where the method involved slight risk of causing dermatitis).}

Example 2 In *Prescott v Bulldog Tools Ltd* {[1981] 3 All ER 869.} the plaintiff brought an action for negligence against his employers in respect of noise-induced industrial deafness. The defendants wished the plaintiff to undergo medical tests which would require him to spend several days in hospital and would involve discomfort and some risk of minor injury. They offered in return to reimburse him for loss of wages during that time and make a token payment in addition. The plaintiff refused.

In determining whether the relevant statutory powers authorised the overriding of this refusal, Webster J drew the following distinctions between various types of medical examination-

' ... first, an examination which does not involve any serious technical assault, but involving only an invasion of privacy; second, an examination involving some technical assault, such as a palpation; third, an examination involving a substantial assault but without involving discomfort and risk; fourth, the same, that is to say a substantial assault, but involving discomfort and risk; and fifth, an examination involving risk of injury or to health.'

Webster J went on to say that the weight of reasonableness of a party's objections to medical examination must bear a very close correlation to the order in which he had listed the above distinctions. He then cited Scarman LJ's statement in *Starr v National Coal Board* {[1977] 1 WLR 63, at p 71.} that in relation to medical examination in personal injury cases one or other of the parties might have to accept an infringement of a fundamental human right cherished by the common law.

Webster J examined each type of test desired by the defence and decided that on balance some were reasonable while others were not. On the loss of liberty involved by an enforced stay in hospital to undergo tests, he said {P 876.}-

' ... the reasonableness of the defendants' request just outweighs the reasonableness of the plaintiff's objection, taking into account the fact that ... the whole process of litigation necessarily involves the parties and their witnesses in invasion or loss of liberty in various ways.'

Again, the court will be reluctant to arrive at a meaning which would hinder self-help by a person whose health is endangered.

Example 3 Section 5(1) of the Misuse of Drugs Act 1971 says that, subject to regulations under s 7 of the Act, it is unlawful for a person to have a controlled drug in his possession. Regulation 10(1) of the Misuse of Drugs Regulations 1973 {SI 1973/797.} authorises a doctor to have a controlled drug in his possession 'for the purpose of acting in his capacity as such'.

In *R v Dunbar* {[1982] 1 All ER 190.} the appellant was a doctor convicted of infringing s 5(1). He had no patients, and had obtained the controlled drug for self-administration. The trial judge ruled that a doctor treating himself was not acting in his capacity as such. *Held* The ruling was wrong, and the conviction would be quashed. Lord Lane CJ said {P 191.}-

> 'If the Crown were correct it would produce the extraordinary result that no doctor, who had quite properly in his drug cupboard a [controlled drug], and who quite properly decided that he required such a drug, for instance codeine, to alleviate either pain or sickness in himself, could administer to himself such a drug without committing a criminal offence. Similarly the sort of situation propounded by counsel for the appellant, where a doctor, again perfectly properly carrying morphine in his bag in a car, suffers an accident as a result of which he is in acute pain. If he were in those circumstances to remove an ampoule of morphine from his bag and inject himself to relieve the pain with morphine, he once again would be committing a criminal offence.'

European Convention on Human Rights   Article 2 of the European Convention on Human Rights requires everyone's right to life to be protected by law, and states that no one shall be deprived of his life intentionally save in the execution of a court sentence following conviction for a crime for which the law imposes the death penalty. Exceptions cover self-defence, lawful arrest, and action taken to quell riot or insurrection.

Article 3 of the Convention follows the Bill of Rights (1688) in prohibiting torture, and 'inhuman or degrading treatment or punishment'. {As to the status of the European Convention on Human Rights in United Kingdom law see pp 322–323 above.}

290. Physical restraint of the person

One aspect of the principle against doubtful penalization is that by the exercise of state power the physical liberty of a person should not be interfered with except under clear authority of law.

COMMENTARY

Principle against doubtful penalization   The presumption against imposition of a statutory impairment of liberty of the person without clear words is an aspect of the general principle against doubtful penalization. This general principle is explained in s 129 of the Code.

Freedom from unwarranted restraint of the person has always been a keystone of English law. It follows that an enactment is not held to impair this without clear words. {See Examples 10.4, 325.5 and 348.5.} As Goff LJ said in *Collins v Wilcock*: the fundamental principle, plain and incontestable, is that every person's body is inviolate'. {(1984) *The Times* 17 April. The dictum is not given in the law report, but in the news report on p 3. For the facts of the case see Example 1.}

This means that even the slightest touching of the body, if not justified, is unlawful.

Example 1 Section 2 of the Street Offences Act 1959 provides a procedure in relation to police cautioning of prostitutes. This does not confer any express powers on a constable. It says that, where a woman is cautioned by a constable, she may apply for a court order directing that the caution shall not be entered in her police records. In *Collins v Wilcock* {(1984) *The Times* 17 April.} the defendant appealed against her conviction of assaulting a police officer contrary to s 51(1) of the Police Act 1964. The incident happened when she refused to stop in the street for questioning. The officer took hold of her arm to restrain her, whereupon the defendant forcibly resisted. *Held* The conviction would be quashed. Section 2 contained no implied provision which overrode the principle against unjustified physical restraint of the person.

Goff LJ said that since the police officer took hold of the appellant's arm to restrain her, and was not proceeding to arrest her, that action went beyond the acceptable conduct of touching a person to engage his or her attention. It was therefore an unlawful battery. {See also *Rawlings v Till* (1837) 3 M & W 28.}

The main infringement of personal liberty that concerns the law is imprisonment under sentence of the court. The principle dealt with in this section of the Code therefore comes into play on the construction of any enactment under which a sentence of imprisonment might be imposed. {Penalties imposed by criminal law fall into several sections of this Part of the Code. Apart from the present section, capital and corporal punishments fall within s 289, and fines within s 295. All convictions impose a stigma, and are therefore within s 296. Other sections can be relevant; for example imprisonment may be regarded as interfering with family rights (s 291).}

The primary remedy for false imprisonment is what Blackstone called the great and efficacious writ of *habeas corpus ad subjiciendum*, directed to the person detaining, and commanding him to produce the body of the prisoner, with the day and cause of his caption and detention, *ad faciendum, subjiciendum, et recipiendum* (to do, submit to and receive whatever the court shall consider). {Kerr Bl (4th edn, 1876) iii 123; St Tr viii 142.}

This is a high prerogative writ, running into all parts of the Queen's dominions: 'for the sovereign is at all times entitled to have an account, why the liberty of any of her subjects is restrained, wherever that restraint may be inflicted'. {Kerr Bl (4th edn, 1876) iii 124; Cro Jac 543. As to the extent of Her Majesty's dominions see s 210 of this Code.} As Blackstone said, 'the glory of English law consists in clearly defining the times, the causes, and the extent, when, wherefore, and to what degree, the imprisonment of the subject may be lawful'. {Kerr Bl (4th edn, 1876) iii 126.}

That Parliament's concern for freedom from unjustified physical restraint remains unimpaired is illustrated by s 18(1)(h)(i) of the Supreme Court Act 1981. This provides an exception from the need for leave to appeal to the Court of Appeal 'where the liberty of the subject is concerned'.

Here the broad term 'concerned' has a narrower legal meaning, equivalent to 'where a person is in danger of losing his liberty'.

Example 2 In *Bowden v Yoxall* {[1901] 1 Ch 1.}, a case on the predecessor of s 18(1)(h)(i), the applicant sought to appeal from the refusal of an application by him for the committal to prison of the defendants. *Held* Although in a literal sense the appeal 'concerned' (that is was about) the liberty of the subject, in fact the liberty of the defendants was in no danger as things stood. The application for their committal having been refused, their liberty was not now at risk. Leave to appeal was therefore required.

This is an example of how the context by implication cuts down the literal meaning of an enactment. The intended or legal meaning of the phrase 'where the liberty of the subject is concerned' was here 'where the liberty of the subject is at risk'. It would have been better if those words had been used by the draftsman.

Freedom from physical restraint is respected by constitutional principles laid down at common law. {As to the implied importation of general rules of constitutional law see s 334 of this Code.

European Convention on Human Rights   Article 4 of the European Convention on Human Rights states that no one shall be held in slavery or servitude, or be required to perform forced or compulsory labour. Exceptions cover lawful imprisonment, military service, work to meet an emergency threatening the life or well-being of the community, and 'normal civic obligations'.

Article 5 of the Convention states that everyone has the right to liberty and security of person, and that no one shall be deprived of his liberty except in one of a number of specified cases. These cover lawful imprisonment, care of minors, and detention of lunatics, alcoholics, drug addicts, vagrants, and persons with infectious diseases.

Protocol 4 to the Convention forbids imprisonment merely on the ground of inability to fulfil a contractual obligation. It also states that, subject to obvious exceptions, everyone lawfully within the territory of the state shall have the right to liberty of movement (including freedom to choose his residence), and freedom to leave the state. {As to the status of the European Convention on Human Rights in United Kingdom law see pp 322–323 above.}

291. Interference with family rights

One aspect of the principle against doubtful penalization is that by the exercise of state power the family arrangements of a person should not be interfered with, nor his relationships with family members impaired, except under clear authority of law.

COMMENTARY

Principle against doubtful penalization   The presumption against imposition of a statutory detriment to family rights without clear words is an aspect of the general principle against doubtful penalization. This general principle is explained in s 129 of the Code.

The law has always concerned itself with the protection of the home. {As to the principle that a man's home is his castle see s 349 of this Code.} An interpretation that would make a person homeless is adopted with reluctance.

Example 1   In *Annicola Investments Ltd v Minister of Housing and Local Government* {[1968] 1 QB 631, at p 644.} Lawrence J said that one of the opposing constructions of the Housing Act 1957 s 42 put forward 'would result in the displacement of 36 families with no obligation on the local authority to provide any of them with alternative accomodation [while] the tenement itself could remain a deserted hulk'.

In considering the enactments relating to child care, Lord Scarman said-

> 'The policy of the legislation emerges clearly from a study of its provisions. The encouragement and support of family life are basic. The local authority are given duties and powers primarily to help, not to supplant, parents. A child is not to be removed from his home or family against the will of his parent save by the order of a court, where the parent will have an opportunity to be heard before the order is made. Respect for parental rights and duties is, however, balanced against the need to protect children from neglect, ill-treatment, abandonment and danger, for the welfare of the child is paramount.'

{*London Borough of Lewisham v Lewisham Juvenile Court JJ* [1979] 2 All ER 297, at p 319. Although uttered in relation to particular statutory provisions, it seems that this dictum reflects legal policy generally. As to the relevance of legal policy in statutory interpretation see s 126 of this Code.}

The courts lean in favour of the transmission of an intestate's estate to members of his family, rather than that it should pass to the state as *bona vacantia*.

Example 2 Section 47(5) of the Administration of Estates Act 1925 provided that where on intestacy the statutory trusts in favour of a class of relatives failed because no member of the class attained a vested interest, the estate should devolve as if the intestate had died without leaving any member of that class, *or issue of any member of that class*, living at his death. {Emphasis added. S 47(5) was inserted by the Intestates' Estates Act 1952 s 1(3)(c).}

In *Re Lockwood, Atherton v Brooke* {[1958] Ch 231.} the deceased died intestate. His only relatives were issue of his deceased aunts and uncles, who were excluded by the italicised words. If these words were applied it would mean that the estate would pass to the Crown as *bona vacantia*.

Held The italicised words produced an absurd and capricious result and would be disregarded. Apart from the *bona vacantia* point, s 47(5) would, if there had been relatives of the half-blood, have favoured them over the issue of those of the whole blood. Harman J said {P 238.}-

> 'I take this course because I am convinced that Parliament, in laying down rules for ascertaining next of kin, cannot have intended to promote those more remote over those nearer in blood.'

Yet that was the only meaning the italicised words could bear. Section 47(5) was repealed by the Family Provision Act 1966 ss 9, 10 and Sch 2.

{See also Examples 194.1 and 305.1.}

European Convention on Human Rights Article 8 of the European Convention on Human Rights states that everyone has the right to respect for his family life and his home, with exceptions for national security, public safety, economic wellbeing of the state, prevention of crime or disorder, protection of health or morals, and the freedom of others.

Article 12 of the Convention says that men and women of marriageable age have the right to marry and to found a family. Protocol 1 states that no person shall be denied the right to education, and adds that the state shall respect the right of parents to ensure that education is in conformity with their own 'religious and philosophical convictions'. {As to the status of the European Convention on Human Rights in United Kingdom law see pp 322–323 above.}

292. Interference with religious freedom

One aspect of the principle against doubtful penalization is that by the exercise of state power the religious freedom of a person should not be interfered with, except under clear authority of law.

COMMENTARY

Principle against doubtful penalization   The presumption against imposition of a statutory interference with religious freedom without clear words is an aspect of the general principle against doubtful penalization. This general principle is explained in s 129 of the Code.

The law of the United Kingdom is still predisposed to the Christian religion, particularly that form of it which is by law established (or in other words Anglicanism). However Parliament has discarded most of the former laws, such as the Corporation and Test Acts, which caused positive discrimination against persons of other faiths or none. {The Corporation Act 1661 (repealed by the Promissory Oaths Act 1871) confined elections to office in corporate towns to persons who within the past year had taken Holy Communion according to the rites of the Church of England. The so-called Test Act of 1672 (25 Cha 2 c 2) required persons holding civil or military office to be communicating members of the Church of England. It was repealed by 9 Geo 4 c 17 (1828).}

The House of Lords dismissed as 'mere rhetoric' Hale's statement that Christianity is 'parcel of the laws of England'. {*Bowman v Secular Society Ltd* [1917] AC 406, *per* Lord Sumner at p 458. The statement was made by Hale CJ in *R v Taylor* (1676) 1 Vent 293.} Yet the House of Lords has recently enforced, after an interval of more than half a century, the ancient offence of blasphemous libel as a safeguard solely of Christian believers. {*R v Lemon* [1979] 1 All ER 898. The previous recorded conviction for this offence was *R v Gott* (1922) 16 Cr App R 87.} Parliament, in passing legislation against unjustified discrimination, has markedly refused to extend the relief to victims of discrimination based on religious grounds.

In *R v Lemon* {[1979] 1 All ER 898.} Lord Scarman, remarking that the United Kingdom is now a plural society, expressed regret that the offence of blasphemous libel was not sufficiently comprehensive to protect the religious susceptibilities of adherents of other religions. {[1979] 1 All ER 898, at p 922.} As he said, such issues are questions of legal policy in the society of today. {P 927. See p 288 above.} It may be said that, apart from the one-sided nature of positive legal rules such as those relating to blasphemy, our legal policy is now in line with what is required by the *European Convention on Human Rights*.

Article 9 of this Convention states that, within obvious limitations, everyone has the right to freedom of thought, conscience and religion. This is stated to include freedom to change one's religion or belief, and freedom (either alone or in community with others, and either in public or private) to manifest one's religion or belief in worship, teaching, practice and observance. {As to the status of the European Convention on Human Rights in United Kingdom law see pp 322–323 above.}

Lord Scarman has said that by necessary implication art 9 'imposes a duty on all of us to refrain from insulting or outraging the religious feelings of others'. {*R v Lemon* [1979] 1 All ER 898, at p 927.}

293. Interference with free assembly and association

One aspect of the principle against doubtful penalization is that by the exercise of state power the freedom of a person to assemble and associate freely with others should not be interfered with, except under clear authority of law.

COMMENTARY

Principle against doubtful penalization The presumption against imposition of a statutory interference with freedom of association without clear words is an aspect of the general principle against doubtful penalization. This general principle is explained in s 129 of the Code.

Freedom of assembly and association is respected by constitutional principles laid down at common law. {As to the implied importation of general rules of constitutional law see s 334 of this Code.} As Dicey put it, the right of assembly is nothing more (and he might have added nothing less) than a view taken by the courts of the individual liberty of the subject. {A V Dicey *Law of the Constitution* (8th edn, 1915) p 499.}

Example 1 In *Beatty v Gillbanks* {(1882) 9 QBD 308.} local Salvation Army leaders were convicted of unlawful assembly for organising revival meetings and marches which would have been entirely peaceful if a hostile group had not sought to break them up by force. *Held* The conviction was wrong. Field J said {P 313.}-

> 'As far as these appellants are concerned there was nothing in their conduct when they were assembled together which was either tumultuous or against the peace. But it is said, that the conduct pursued by them on this occasion was such, as on several previous occasions, had produced riots and disturbances of the peace and terror to the inhabitants . . .
> Now I entirely concede that everyone must be taken to intend the natural consequences of his own acts . . . the finding of the justices amounts to this, that a man may be convicted for doing a lawful act if he knows that his doing it may cause another to do an unlawful act. There is no authority for such a proposition . . .'

European Convention on Human Rights Article 11 of the European Convention on Human Rights states that everyone has the right to freedom of peaceful assembly and to freedom of association with others, including the right to form and to join trade unions for the protection of his interests. There are exceptions for members of the armed forces, police and state administration, and the other usual qualifications. {As to the status of the European Convention on Human Rights in United Kingdom law see pp 322–323 above.}

294. Interference with free speech

One aspect of the principle against doubtful penalization is that by the exercise of state power a person's freedom of speech should not be interfered with, except under clear authority of law.

COMMENTARY

Principle against doubtful penalization   The presumption against imposition of a statutory restraint of free speech without clear words is an aspect of the general principle against doubtful penalization. This general principle is explained in s 129 of the Code.

Lord Mansfield said: 'The liberty of the press consists in printing without any previous licence, subject to the consequences of law'. {*R v Dean of St Asaph* (1784) 3 TR 428 (note). See also *R v Cobbett* (1804) 29 St Tr 1.}

Scarman LJ, in remarks concerning s 12(4) of the Administration of Justice Act 1960, referred to 'the law's basic concern to protect freedom of speech and individual liberty'. {*Re F (a minor) (publication of information)* [1977] Fam 58, at p 99. The dictum was approved by Lord Edmund-Davies on appeal ([1979] AC 440, at p 465).}

Example 1   In *Re X (A Minor)* {[1975] Fam 47.} it was sought to prohibit the publication of discreditable details about a deceased person on the ground that this might harm his infant child if the child became aware of them. *Held* The public interest in free speech outweighed the possible harm to the child, and the injunction would be refused.

Freedom of speech is respected by constitutional principles laid down at common law. {As to the implied importation of general rules of constitutional law see s 334 of this Code.}

European Convention on Human Rights   Article 10 of the European Convention on Human Rights says that everyone has the right to freedom of expression. This includes freedom to hold opinions and receive and impart information and ideas without interference by public authority, and regardless of frontiers. Licensing of broadcasting and cinemas is allowed, but not licensing of the press. Other restrictions such as 'are necessary in a democratic society' are allowed.

In a case concerning citizens' band radios, Lord Lane CJ said that under the Convention 'freedom of expression does not mean freedom to express yourself on 27 MHz'. {*R v Goldstein* [1982] 3 All ER 53, at p 61.}

Article 6 of the European Convention on Human Rights permits restrictions on the reporting of criminal trials. {As to the status of the Convention in United Kingdom law see pp 322–323 above.}

295. Detriment to property and other economic interests

One aspect of the principle against doubtful penalization is that by the exercise of state power the property or other economic interests of a person should not be taken away, impaired or endangered, except under clear authority of law.

COMMENTARY

Principle against doubtful penalization   The presumption against imposition of a statutory detriment to a person's property or other economic interests without clear words is an aspect of the general principle against doubtful penalization. This general principle is explained in s 129 of the Code.

It was said by Pratt CJ in the great case against general warrants, *Entick v Carrington* {(1765) 19 St Tr 1030, at p 1060.}, that-

> 'The great end for which men entered into society was to secure their property. That right is preserved sacred and incommunicable in all instances where it has not been abridged by some public law for the good of the whole.'

Blackstone said that the right of property is an absolute right, inherent in every Englishman: 'which consists in the free use, enjoyment, and disposal of all his acquisitions, without any control or diminution, save only by the laws of the land'. {Kerr Bl (4th edn, 1876) i 109.} He added: 'The laws of England are therefore, in point of honour and justice, extremely watchful in ascertaining and protecting this right'.

It follows that whenever an enactment is alleged to authorise interference with property the court will apply the principle against doubtful penalization. The interference may take many forms. All kinds of taxation involve detriment to property rights. So do many criminal penalties, such as fines, compensation orders and costs orders. {Penalties imposed by criminal law fall into several sections of this Part of the Code. Apart from those which fall within the present section, capital and corporal punishments fall within s 289, and imprisonment within s 290. All convictions impose a stigma, and are therefore within s 296. Other sections can be relevant; for example imprisonment may be regarded as interfering with family rights (s 291).}

Compulsory purchase, trade regulations and restrictions, import controls, forced redistribution on divorce or death, and maintenance orders are further categories. As so often in statutory interpretation, there are other criteria operating in favour of all these and the result is a balancing exercise. {As to the weighing of interpretative factors see Part VII of this Code.}

There are a great many decisions illustrating the reluctance of courts to countenance statutory interference with property rights unless the wording is clear. See for example *Harrod v Worship* {(1861) 30 LJMC 165.} (provision that a lender could not 'recover' any part of his principal when trader declared bankrupt did not abridge lender's rights as *mortgagee*); *Hammond v Hocking* (1884) 12 QBD 291, at p 292.} (Bills of Sale Act (1878) Amendment Act 1882 s 7 not to be so construed as to interfere with honest transactions or impair securities); *More v More* {[1962] Ch 424, at p 430.} (protection of rights of creditors on annulment of bankruptcy petition); *R v Evans* {[1963] 1 QB 979, at p 989.} (compensation order did not lapse with cessation of probation order); *Minister of Housing and Local Government v Hartnell* {[1965] AC 1134, at pp 1172-3.} (interference with planning rights of caravan site owner); *Allen v Thorn Electrical Industries Ltd* {[1968] 1 QB 487, at p 503.} (contractual rights not to be taken away on an ambiguity); *Director of Public Prosecutions v Ottewell*

{[1970] AC 642, at p 649.} (civil penalty only to be imposed on clear words).
{See also Examples 10.1, 10.6, 10.8, 12.3, 14.1, 58.4, 128.2, 142.15, 154.2, 357.1 and 367.6.}

Perhaps the most severe interference with property rights is expropriation. Buckley LJ said that-

' ... in an Act such as the Leasehold Reform Act 1967, which, although it is not a confiscatory Act is certainly a disproprietory Act, if there is any doubt as to the way in which language should be construed, it should be construed in favour of the party who is to be dispropriated rather than otherwise.'

{*Methuen-Campbell v Walters* [1979] 1 All ER 606, at p 620.}

Property rights include the right of a person who is sui juris to manage and control his own property. Nourse J referred to 'the general principle in our law that the rights of a person whom it regards as having the status to deal with them on his own behalf will not ... be overridden'. {*Re Savoy Hotel Ltd* [1981] 3 All ER 646, at p 657.} Nourse J excepted cases such as those where, on a construction summons under RSC Ord 15 r 13, a representative order may be made. (A construction summons under Ord 15 r 13 may relate to 'the construction of a written instrument, *including a statute*.) {Emphasis added.}

The rights of a trader are jealously watched by the courts, because of their consciousness of the importance of trade to national prosperity.

Example 1   Sections 10 and 11 of the Bankrupts Act 1623 {13 Eliz 1 c 5.} began with the recital: 'And for that bankrupts frequently convey over *their goods* and yet continue in possession and dispose of them ...' {Emphasis added.} The operative provision however empowered commissioners to sell for the benefit of creditors '*any* goods *or chattels*' entrusted to the bankrupt. {Emphasis added. This is a typical case of disorganised composition: see s 76 of this Code.}

It was held in *L'Apostre v Le Plaistrier* {(1708); cited in *Copeman v Gallant* (1716) 1 P Wms 314.} that the general words were to be explained and limited by the words of the recital. The decision was approved by Parker CB in *Ryall v Rolle* {(1749) 1 Atk 164, at p 174.}, who said 'for otherwise merchants could not correspond or carry on their business without great danger and great difficulty'.

Common law rights   The tendency is for the conferring of property rights to be by common law, and for their abridgement to be by statute. The courts, having created the common law, are jealous of attempts to deprive the citizen of its benefits.

Example 2   In *Newtons of Wembley Ltd v Williams* {[1965] 1 QB 560, at p 574.} Sellers LJ said of s 9 of the Factors Act 1889 'one must remember that it is taking away a right which would have existed at common law, and for myself I should not be prepared to enlarge it more than the words clearly permitted and required'.

Example 3   In *Turton v Turnbull* {[1934] 2 KB 197, at p 199.} Scrutton LJ said of a point on s 12 of the Agricultural Holdings Act 1923-

'As by the Act [the landlord] is being deprived of his common-law rights, I think we must construe the Act with some liberality in his favour and scrutinise the tenant's claim with some strictness.'

The social changes which have occurred since this case was decided in 1934 would now weigh the scales more heavily in favour of the tenant. {As to altered interpretation because of social change see s 146 of this Code.}

Where property rights given at common law are curtailed by statute, the statutory conditions must be strictly complied with. Thus Davies LJ said of the Landlord and Tenant Act 1954: 'The statute, as we all know, is an invasion of the landlord's right, for perfectly proper and sound reasons; but it must be construed strictly in accordance with its terms'. {*Stile Hall Properties Ltd v Gooch* [1979] 3 All ER 848, at p 851. See also *Methuen-Campbell v Walters* [1979] 1 All ER 606, at p 619.}

Example 4 Section 1 of the Law of Distress Amendment Act 1908 abridges a landlord's common law right of distress. For this reason it was said by Horridge J that the section had to be strictly construed to ensure that a person claiming immunity from distress under it complied with its provisions. {*Druce & Co Ltd v Beaumont Property Trust Ltd* [1935] 2 KB 257, at p 264; see also *Lawrence Chemical Co Ltd v Rubenstein* [1982] 1 All ER 653, at p 656. Cf *East Riding County Council v Park Estate (Bridlington) Ltd* [1957] AC 223, *per* Viscount Simonds at p 233 (Town and Country Planning Act 1947 highly technical and 'as it encroached on private rights, the court must insist on strict and rigid adherence to formalities'. As to strict construction see s 154 of this Code.}

Taxation A frequently-cited, though now questionable, dictum of Rowlatt J runs-

'. . . in a taxing Act one has to look at what is clearly said. There is no equity about a tax. There is no presumption as to a tax. Nothing is to be read in, nothing is to be implied. One can only look fairly at the language used.'

{*Cape Brandy Syndicate v IRC* [1921] 1 KB 64, at p 71. Approved, e g, by Viscount Simon LC in *Canadian Eagle Oil Co v R* [1946] AC 119, at p 140. For criticism of this dictum see p 242 above.}

There are many cases where the court has refused to adopt a construction of a taxing Act which would impose liability where doubt exists. See, for example, *Tomkins v Ashby* {(1827) 6 B & C 541, at p 542.} (stamp duty not to be charged unless intention plain); *Re Micklethwait* {(1855) 11 Ex 452, at p 456.} (subject not to be taxed without clear words); *Partington v A-G* {(1869) LR 4 HL 100, at p 122.} (equitable construction not admissible in a taxing statute); *Oriental Bank v Wright* {(1880) 5 App Cas 842, at p 856.} (clear and unambiguous language necessary); *IRC v R Woolf (Rubber) Ltd* {[1962] Ch 35, at pp 44-5.} (literal reading of definition of 'member' of a company in s 255(2) of Income Tax Act 1952 departed from where it would have made lending banker liable for surtax); *South West Water Authority v Rumble's* {[1984] 2 All ER 240.} (water rate not chargeable under s 30 of Water Act 1973 for 'facilities provided' where facilities not used by occupier).

However the modern attitude of the courts is that the revenue from taxation is essential to the running of the state, and that the duty of the judiciary is to aid its collection while remaining fair to the subject. {See, e g, *IRC v Berrill* [1982] 1 All ER 867, at p 880 (construction rejected which would have made it impossible for Inland Revenue to raise an assessment).} Here one must bear in mind the rule requiring the courts to observe the principle *ut res magis valeat quam pereat*. {As to this see s 123 of the Code.}

On taxing Acts, a dictum of Cardozo J in an American case is relevant: 'The construction that is liberal to one taxpayer may be illiberal to others'. {*Burnet v Guggenheim* (1933) 288 US 280, at p 286.} A common way by which traders avoid paying as much tax as they ought is by inflating the 'expenses' of the trade. On this Lord Wilberforce said in a case dealing with allowable expenditure on plant-

> 'I do not think that the courts should shrink, as a backstop, from asking whether it can really be supposed that Parliament desired to encourage a particular expenditure out of, in effect, taxpayers' money, and perhaps ultimately, in extreme cases, to say that this is too much to stomach.'

{*IRC v Scottish and Newcastle Breweries Ltd* [1982] 2 All ER 230, at p 233.}

Lord Thankerton said in 1948-

> 'Counsel are apt to use the adjective 'penal' in describing the harsh consequences of a taxing provision, but if the meaning of the provision is reasonably clear, the courts have no jurisdiction to mitigate such harshness.'

{*IRC v Ross & Coulter* [1948] 1 All ER 616, at p 625. See also *A-G v Carlton Bank* [1899] 2 QB 158, *per* Lord Russell of Killowen CJ at p 164 (taxing Act not to be construed differently from any other Act); *Cenlon Finance Co Ltd v Ellwood (Inspector of Taxes* [1962] AC 782, at p 794 ('discovering' an under-assessment to tax by the inspector does not require new facts).}

It is regarded as penal for a person to be taxed *twice over* in respect of the same matter. This is known as double taxation, and the courts seek to avoid it. {*IRC v Clifforia Investments Ltd* [1963] 1 WLR 396; *IRC v FS Securities Ltd* [1964] 1 WLR 742.} However the courts do not regard it as double taxation for a shareholder in a company to be taxed in respect of a gain upon which the company itself has previously borne tax. In *Furniss (Inspector of Taxes) v Dawson* {[1984] 1 All ER 530. See p 715 below.} Lord Brightman said-

> 'The element of double taxation exists whenever a shareholder sells at a profit his shares in a company that has itself realised a capital asset at a profit. I do not see any undesirable element of double taxation [in such cases].'

{See further s 347 of this Code.}

The courts are reluctant to adopt a construction permitting a person's tax liability to be fixed by administrative discretion.

Example 5   Section 412 of the Income Tax Act 1952 {Re-enacted as s 478 of the Income and Corporation Taxes Act 1970.} began with a recital stating that the section was intended for the purpose of preventing the avoidance of tax by arranging for income to be paid to non-residents. The Inland Revenue claimed to apply s 412 so as to tax beneficiaries under discretionary trusts regardless of whether they received any payment. For this purpose the Inland Revenue apportioned by administrative discretion the total income of the trustees in each year.

The House of Lords considered this practice in *Vestey v IRC (Nos 1 and 2)* {[1979] 3 All ER 976.} *Held* Notwithstanding previous House of Lords authority to the contrary, the practice was beyond what s 412 authorised and therefore illegal. Lord Wilberforce said {Pp 984-6.}-

'Taxes are imposed on subjects by Parliament. A citizen cannot be taxed unless he is designated in clear terms by a taxing Act as a taxpayer, and the amount of his liability is clearly defined. A proposition that whether a subject is to be taxed or not, or that, if he is, the amount of his liability is to be decided (even though within a limit) by an administrative body, represents a radical departure from constitutional principle . . .

This would be taxation by self-asserted administrative discretion and not by law. As the judge well said {[1979] Ch 177, at p 197.}, "One should be taxed by law, and not be untaxed by concession". The fact in the present case is that Parliament has laid down no basis on which tax can be apportioned where there are numerous discretionary beneficiaries . . .

I must regard this case therefore as one in which Parliament has attempted to impose a tax, but in which it has failed, in the case of discretionary beneficiaries, to lay down any basis on which it can be assessed or levied.'

As to the constitutional principle reserving the right of taxation to Parliament see p 724 below. As to extra-statutory concessions see s 177 of this Code. As to tax evasion and avoidance see s 327.

The courts will presume that Parliament did not mean to tax subjects in order to benefit foreigners, except where the intention to do this is clear (as in an Act for granting overseas aid). {*R v Barnet London Borough Council, ex p Shah* [1982] 1 All ER 698, *per* Templeman LJ at p 710.}

European Convention on Human Rights Protocol 1 to the European Convention on Human Rights says that every natural or legal person is entitled to the peaceful enjoyment of his possessions. No one is to be deprived of his possessions except in the public interest and by due process of law. {As to the status of the European Convention on Human Rights in United Kingdom law see pp 322–323 above.}

296. Detriment to status or reputation

One aspect of the principle against doubtful penalization is that by the exercise of state power the status or reputation of a person should not be impaired or endangered, except under clear authority of law.

COMMENTARY

Principle against doubtful penalization The presumption against imposition of a statutory detriment to status or reputation without clear words is an aspect of the general principle against doubtful penalization. This general principle is explained in s 129 of the Code.

The more a particular construction is likely to damage a person's reputation, the stricter the interpretation a court is likely to give. Any conviction for a criminal offence imparts a stigma, even though an absolute discharge is given. {*Director of Public Prosecutions for Northern Ireland v Lynch* [1975] AC 653, *per* Lord Edmund-Davies at p 707 ('the obloquy involved in the mere fact of conviction'). See also Example 110.5. Penalties imposed by criminal law fall into several sections of this Part of the Code. Apart from injury to reputation within this section, capital and corporal punishments fall within s 289, imprisonment within s 290, and fines etc within s 295. Other sections can be relevant; for example imprisonment may be regarded as interfering with family rights (s 291).}

If an offence carries a heavy penalty, the stigma will be correspondingly greater. {*Sweet v Parsley* [1970] AC 132, *per* Lord Reid at p 149 ('the more serious or more disgraceful the offence the greater the stigma').} This is an important consideration in determining whether Parliament intended to require mens rea. {See also *R v Phekoo* [1981] 3 All ER 84. For a general discussion see E Goffman *Stigma* (1968).}

European Convention on Human Rights   The European Convention on Human Rights does not reproduce the provision in the Universal Declaration of Human Rights 1948 stating that no one shall be subjected to 'attacks upon his honour and reputation'. {Art 12.} However art 10 of the European Convention on Human Rights, in conferring the right of free speech, does include an exception 'for the protection of the reputation or rights of others'. {As to the status of the European Convention on Human Rights in United Kingdom law see pp 322–323 above.}

297. Infringement of privacy

One aspect of the principle against doubtful penalization is that by the exercise of state power the privacy of a person should not be infringed, except under clear authority of law.

COMMENTARY

Principle against doubtful penalization   The presumption against imposition of a statutory infringement of privacy without clear words is an aspect of the general principle against doubtful penalization. This general principle is explained in s 129 of the Code.

An important element in the law's protection of privacy springs from the principle that a man's home is his castle. This is discussed in s 349 of the Code. Even outside the home, the courts tend to require clear words to authorise an invasion of privacy. {See Examples 126.4 and 294.1.}

Example 1   Section 186 of the Licensing Act 1964 says that a constable 'may at any time enter licensed premises . . . for the purpose of preventing or detecting the commission of any offence . . .' In *Duncan v Dowding* {[1897] 1 QB 575.} it was held that a predecessor of this section did not authorise a constable to enter unless he had some reasonable ground for suspecting a breach of the law.

There is no principle in English law by which documents are protected from discovery by reason of confidentiality alone. This does not mean that, in deciding whether to order discovery under statutory powers, an authority is intended to ignore the question of confidentiality. It is to be taken into account along with other factors. {See *Science Research Council v Nasse* [1979] 3 All ER 673, *per* Lord Wilberforce at p 679.}

For a case where breach of privacy had to be balanced against other human rights considerations see Example 289.2.

European Convention on Human Rights   Article 8 of the European Convention on Human Rights states that everyone has the right to respect for his private life and his correspondence, with exceptions for national security, public safety, economic wellbeing of the state, prevention of crime or disorder, protection of health or morals, and the freedom of others. {As to the status of the European Convention on Human Rights in United Kingdom law see pp 322–323 above.}

298. Impairment of rights in relation to law and legal proceedings

One aspect of the principle against doubtful penalization is that by the exercise of state power the rights of a person in relation to law and legal proceedings should not be removed or impaired, except under clear authority of law.

COMMENTARY

Principle against doubtful penalization   The presumption against imposition of a statutory detriment to legal rights without clear words is an aspect of the general principle against doubtful penalization. This general principle is explained in s 129 of the Code.

The rule of law requires that the law should apply equally, and that all should be equal before it. {*Richards v McBride* (1881) 51 LJMC 15, at p 16.} It also requires that all penalties be inflicted by due process of law, which in turn demands that there should be no uncovenanted interference with that process. In general, no citizen should without clear authority be 'shut out from the seat of justice'. {The phrase was used by Hodgson J in *Aspinall v Sterling Mansell Ltd* [1981] 3 All ER 866, at p 867. See Example 58.3.} This applies even to a prisoner. {*Raymond v Honey* [1982] 1 All ER 756, *per* Lord Wilberforce at p 760. See Example 58.1.}

These principles are embedded in various ancient constitutional enactments. Thus a chapter of Magna Carta enshrines the Crown's promise that a man shall not be condemned 'but by lawful judgment of his peers, or by the law of the land'. It goes on: 'We will sell to no man, we will not deny or defer to any man either justice or right'. {25 Edw 1 (1297) c 29.}

The statute 28 Edw 3 c 3 (1354) enacts that 'no man of what estate or condition that he be, shall be put out of land or tenement, nor taken, nor imprisoned, nor disinherited, nor put to death, without being brought to answer *by due process of law*'. {Emphasis added.} The Bill of Rights (1688) forbids excessive bail, excessive fines, and cruel and unusual punishments; and requires jurors to be duly empannelled and returned.

Trial by jury Alleged deprivation of the common law right to trial by jury will be strictly construed. Best CJ said-

> 'An Act of Parliament which takes away the right of trial by jury . . . ought to receive the strictest construction; nothing should be holden to come within its operation that is not expressly within the letter and spirit of the Act.'

{*Looker v Halcomb* (1827) 4 Bing 183, at p 188. See also *R v St Albans Juvenile Court, ex p Godman* [1981] 2 All ER 311, at p 314; *R v Amersham Juvenile Court, ex p Wilson* [1981] 2 All ER 315, at p 320. Cf *Gray v R* (1844) 11 Cl & F 427 (right of peremptory challenge).}

Conduct of proceedings The right to bring, defend and conduct legal proceedings without unwarranted interference is a basic right of citizenship. {See *Re the Vexatious Actions Act 1896 - in re Bernard Boaler* [1915 1 KB 21, at pp 34-5.} While the court has control, subject to legal rules, of its own procedure, this does not authorise any ruling which abridges the basic right.

The right covers the putting of legal argument before the court in such manner as the party or his advocate thinks fit, subject to the court's power to rule against tedious, repetitious, irrelevant or otherwise improper argument. Subject to this restriction, such authorities as the party or his advocate thinks fit to cite may be laid before the court. The attempt of the House of Lords in *Roberts Petroleum Ltd v Bernard Kenny Ltd* {[1983] 1 All ER 564.} to place severe restrictions on the citation of unreported cases runs contrary to this principle. Unreported cases have no less authority than reported cases. {See *The Law Society's Gazette* (1983) 1635; (1984) 257.}

Rights in relation to witnesses are jealously protected. If witnesses are deterred from coming forward, said Lord Langdale MR, it is impossible to administer justice: 'It would be better that the doors of the courts of justice were at once closed'. {*Littler v Thomson* (1839) 2 Beav 129, at p 131. See also *A-G v Butterworth* [1963] 1 QB 696.} The principle that a wife is not to be compelled to give evidence against her husband 'is deep seated in the common law of this country', and if it is to be overturned 'it must be overturned by a clear, definite and positive enactment, not by an ambiguous one such as [s 4(1) of the Criminal Evidence Act 1898]'. {*Leach v R* [1912] AC 305, *per* Lord Atkinson at p 311.}

In the case of a defendant, the right to conduct legal proceedings covers 'the right to defend himself in the litigation as he and his advisers think fit [and] choose the witnesses that he will call'. {*Starr v National Coal Board* [1977] 1 WLR 63, *per* Scarman LJ at p 71.} A defendant faced with a hopeless claim is deserving of the court's protection. Such a claim has a nuisance value, and should be dismissed as soon as possible. {See *Re Beaumont (deceased), Martin v Midland Bank Trust Co Ltd* [1980] 1 All ER 266, *per* Megarry V-C at p 276.}

A person's right to conduct legal proceedings as he thinks fit is highly regarded, and may even outweigh the right to personal liberty. {See Example 289.2.}

The removal of legal remedies is strictly construed.

Example 1 Section 4 of the Trade Disputes Act 1906 prohibited the bringing of an action 'in respect of any tortious act alleged *to have been committed* by or on behalf of a trade union'. {Emphasis added.} In *Boulting v Association of*

Cinematograph, Television and Allied Technicians {[1963] 2 QB 606.} Upjohn LJ said that this did not prevent the court from granting an injunction to prevent an *apprehended* injury. He went on {Pp 643-4.}-

'If a tort has been committed, the injured party is without remedy against the union ... a strict construction should be given to the section which, after all, is substantially interfering with the common law rights of the subject ... I think that unless prevented by clear words ... the court should be especially astute to prevent the commission of an unlawful act where the tortfeasor can by statute escape the usual consequences of his aggression once committed.'

A strict construction is applied to provisions allowing technical defences. {*Sanders v Scott* [1961] 2 QB 326.} It is presumed that a party is not to be deprived of his right of appeal. {*Mackey v Monks* [1918] AC 59, at p 91.} Yet a litigant who has obtained a judgment 'is by law entitled not to be deprived of that judgment without very solid grounds'. {*Brown v Dean* [1910] AC 373, *per* Lord Loreburn LC at p 374.} It is necessary to bear in mind 'the extreme value of the old doctrine *interest reipublicae ut sit finis litium*'. {*Brown v Dean* [1910] AC 373, *per* Lord Loreburn LC at p 374.} This is particularly true where legally-aided appellants are concerned. {*Langdale v Danby* [1982] 3 All ER 129.}

Rights as to legal proceedings are respected by constitutional principles laid down at common law. {As to the implied importation of general rules of constitutional law see s 334 of this Code. For the implied importation of protective rights in criminal proceedings see s 340. As to provisions ousting the jurisdiction of the courts see pp 747–50 below. See also Examples 10.5, 10.11, 143 and 133.1.}

Right not to have legal obligations imposed An important aspect of rights in relation to law is the right not to have legal burdens thrust upon one. It is a detriment to be obliged to carry out statutory duties against one's will, or to incur the risk of being the subject of legal proceedings. This is so even though no economic loss is involved.

Example 2 The power conferred on justices by the Poor Relief Act 1610 to appoint 'four, three or two substantial householders' as unpaid parish overseers was strictly construed. It was held in *R v Loxdale* {(1758) 1 Burr 445.} that an appointment of more than four householders was invalid. Where a parish contained only one householder, it was held in *R v Cousins* {(1864) 33 LJMC 87.} that he could not be appointed as the sole overseer. See also, as to the reluctance of the courts to impose new obligations without clear authority, *Finch v Bannister* {[1908] 2 KB 441.}; *Gaby v Palmer* {(1916) 85 LJKB 1240, at p 1244.}.

European Convention on Human Rights Articles 5 and 6 of the European Convention on Human Rights give alaborate protection for rights in legal proceedings. This covers safeguards in case of arrest, the presumption of innocence, the right to a fair trial, the right of cross-examination, the publicity of proceedings, and other matters. {As to the status of the European Convention on Human Rights in United Kingdom law see pp 322–323 above.}

299. Other interference with rights as a citizen

In addition to the rights referred to in the previous sections of this Part, the principle against doubtful penalization indicates that by the exercise of state power no other right of a person as a citizen should be interfered with except under clear authority of law.

COMMENTARY

Principle against doubtful penalization   The presumption against imposition of a statutory detriment to citizenship rights without clear words is an aspect of the general principle against doubtful penalization. This general principle is explained in s 129 of the Code.

The policy of the law is to protect the rights enjoyed by a person as a citizen. In a notable dissenting judgment, Earl Warren CJ said-

> 'Citizenship *is* man's basic right for it is nothing less than *the right to have rights*. Remove this priceless possession and there remains a stateless person, disgraced and degraded in the eyes of his countrymen.'

{*Perez v Brownell* (1958) 356 US 64. Emphasis in second place added.}

Therefore a residual category is here inserted in this Part of the Code, for it is not possible to list all the rights a citizen has. {The term 'rights as a citizen' is here preferred to 'human rights' because the latter concept is international, and therefore vague and varying; whereas the former inheres in municipal law.} We go on to mention one or two more of them.

Voting rights   The importance attached to voting rights is explained above. {See p 26.} Because of it the courts tend to give a strict construction to any enactment curtailing the franchise. {As to strict and liberal construction see s 154 of this Code.}

Example 1   In *Piercy v Maclean* {(1870) LR 5 CP 252, at p 261.} Willes J said that it was a rule that had been constantly acted on by the courts that words conferring the franchise must be construed 'in their largest ordinary sense'. It was therefore held that a reference to a 'counting-house' for votes must be construed as extending to anything that could reasonably be called a counting-house. {Cf *Randolph v Milman* (1868) LR 4 CP 107 (right of prebendaries to vote at election of proctors).}

Prisoners' rights   A person who is by virtue of any enactment detained in prison or elsewhere retains all his rights as a citizen, except those taken away expressly or by necessary implication. {*Raymond v Honey* [1982] 1 All ER 756, *per* Lord Wilberforce at p 759.} This is an application of the principle that, under English law, rights are removed not conferred. {See pp 291–292 above.} Such rights of citizenship as are not clearly removed by the statute authorising imprisonment therefore continue to be held. {See Example 325.5.}

Rights as a citizen are respected by constitutional principles laid down at common law. {As to the implied importation of general rules of constitutional law see s 334 of this Code.}

European Convention on Human Rights   Protocol 1 to the European Convention on Human Rights requires the holding of free elections at reasonable intervals by secret ballot, under conditions which ensure the free expression of the opinions of the people in the choice of the legislature.

Protocol 4 to the Convention requires that no one shall be expelled, by means either of an individual or of a collective measure, from the territory of the state of which he is a national. It also says that no one shall be deprived of the right to enter the territory of the state of which he is a national. {As to the status of the European Convention on Human Rights in United Kingdom law see pp 322–323 above.}

PART XIV

Legislative Presumptions: the Mischief and its Remedy

Introduction to Part XIV This Part amplifies the presumption set out in s 138 of the Code that Parliament intends the court to apply the remedy provided by the Act for the purpose of remedying a mischief. The meaning of the 'mischief' is discussed (s 300). The resolution in *Heydon's Case* is set out and explained (s 301). We distinguish the social mischief (s 302) from the legal mischief (s 303). Party-political mischiefs are discussed (s 304).

The nature of the mischief is then analysed. We consider its ambit (s 305). Each enactment has its own mischief (s 306). It is important to be sure that Parliament actually legislated for the whole of what seems to be the relevant mischief (s 307). Certain 'mischiefs' arise only in relation to the remedy provided (s 308). Sometimes Parliament phases out a legal mischief rather than abolishing it directly (s 309).

Next we consider the materials used for 'discerning' the mischief (s 310). How is it used in interpretation (s 311)? The remedy provided must be identified and applied (s 312).

300. Meaning of the 'mischief'

Parliament intends that an enactment shall remedy a particular mischief. This may be either a social mischief which is coupled with a legal mischief, or a purely legal mischief.

COMMENTARY

Parliament is taken to do nothing without a reason. Therefore there is a reason for the passing of every Act, and for every enactment within it. Except in the case of purely declaratory provisions, the only reason for passing an Act is to change the existing law. So the reason for an Act's passing must lie in some defect in the existing law. If the existing law were not defective, Parliament would not need or want to change it. That defect is the 'mischief' to which the Act is directed.

On the ground or in the law? If we look more closely, we find however that the term mischief, as used in statutory interpretation, has two different meanings. As well as to a legal defect it may refer to a mischief 'on the ground', that is a factual condition that is causing concern (such as an increase in mugging, or a decline in the birthrate). This the Code calls the 'social mischief'.

While a mischief on the ground may correspond to a defect in the law, this is not necessarily so. An increase in mugging may arise because the law is

631

inadequate. Or it may arise because an adequate law is inadequately enforced. A decline in the birthrate may lie beyond the reach of law altogether.

Furthermore the practice and intention of the law may in rare cases be *not* to remedy what some consider to be a social mischief. Mowbray, a fourteenth-century advocate, argued that law 'ought to be in accordance with reason and to take away mischief *unless the contrary practice has been in use as law*'. {*Tornerghe v Abbot of Furness* YB 15 Edw 3 126. Emphasis added.} Modern lawyers have been known to employ Mowbray's argument.

While in the main lawyers intend, when referring to the 'mischief' of an Act, to point to the defect in the law for which the Act aims to provide a remedy, they sometimes find it convenient to apply the term in the other sense of a mischief 'on the ground', or a social mischief. Often they employ the term ambiguously, since ambiguity has its uses.

Historical   To gain an understanding of the doctrine of the mischief, we need first to look at the early history of statutes. Our law follows a line of organic development; and lawyers are by nature and experience both cautious and conservative. We now trace the distinction between the mischief on the ground (or social mischief) and the legal mischief (or defect in the law corresponding to the social mischief).

In the period following the Norman conquest, statutes expressed the will of the king. Where the nascent common law opposed that will, the king's judges felt themselves to be in difficulty. Within such conflicts were sown the seeds of the idea that the court must presume, in the absence of clear words to the contrary, that an Act is not intended by Parliament to override the common law. {As to this see pp 319–320 above.}

In these early years statutes were of varying types, and few in number. Most dealt with the relations between the king and the barons, or his less powerful subjects. The best-known, Magna Carta, had more the character of a treaty than a law.

Example 1   In 1266 the Statutum de Scaccario {51 Hen 3.} remedied a social mischief graphically described by the eighteenth-century jurist Daines Barrington. It concerned the officers of the Receipt of the Exchequer, who were as inescapable as (and far more deadly than) our own Customs or Inland Revenue officials. Barrington says that every citizen-

> ' . . . had more or less to do with these revenue officers, who were armed with the terrors of the crown process: and it was naturally to be expected, that there should be great abuses and oppressions, *which could only be prevented by the interposition of the legislature.*
>
> What these oppressions were appears by the provisions of the statute. The sheriffs at this time generally farmed the king's revenue, and consequently were guilty of those enormities and exactions which the farmers of the public revenue have in all countries been justly charged with.
>
> One means of oppression was by distraining the farmers (*sic*) cattle used for ploughing (which the statute emphatically says, *gaignent la terre*); and not content with this, he was not permitted to feed his cattle whilst impounded. The poor beasts were either starved, or, if fed by the king's bailiff, the owner was charged at an immoderate price for their sustenance.'

{*Observations upon the Statutes* (2nd edn, 1767) p 42 (emphasis added).}

A little later we find a growth in the number of statutes designed to overcome defects (that is legal mischiefs) in those parts of the common law concerned with the ordinary regulation of society. Usually these statutes are drawn by the judges; and the mischief to which they are directed is plain to see.

Example 2 Edward I deals with a legal mischief consisting in the threat to feudal incidents of wardship and escheat posed by the vesting of lands in monasteries and other ecclesiastical corporations. He procures the passing of the earliest Statutes of Mortmain, 'thereby closing the great gulf, in which all the lands of the kingdom were in danger of being swallowed'. {Kerr Bl (4th edn, 1876) iv 98.}

Example 3 Henry IV tackles a social mischief hindering the enforcement of criminal law. To prevent their giving evidence, malefactors are cutting out the tongues of potential witnesses. {This was checked by 5 Hen 4 c 5 (1403), which was repealed by 9 Geo 4 c 32 (1828) s 1 and 10 Geo 4 c 34 (1829) s 1).}

Example 4 Social mischiefs arising from the greater profitability of pasture over tillage are dealt with by an Act of Henry VII. {4 Hen 7 c 19 (1488).} The preamble recites that-

> 'Great inconveniences daily doth increase by desolation and pulling down and wilfull waste of houses and Towns within [the king's realm], and laying to pasture lands which customarily have been used in tillage, whereby idleness - ground and beginning of all mischiefs - daily doth increase . . . to the subversion of the policy and good rule of this land.'

Example 5 Later we find Edward VI correcting an absurdity of the common law in relation to murder. So refined have the rules of venue become that, where a person is fatally wounded in one county but expires in the next, the offender can be indicted in neither. {This anomaly was put right by 2 & 3 Edw 6 c 24 (1548), which was repealed by the Criminal Law Act 1826, s 32.}

In early times, as always, there are many varieties of social mischief. These expose legal mischiefs, which mar the common law and require correction by Parliament. Arguments begin to arise among common lawyers as to the attitude which the judges administering the common law should adopt towards legislative interventions by Parliament. The judges, having framed 'our lady the common law', are not disposed to acknowledge flaws in their creation. At the instance of the king, the question becomes pressing, and is considered by the Barons of the Exchequer in *Heydon's Case*. {(1584) 3 Co Rep 7a.} What they decided is described in s 301 of this Code. After that we go on to amplify the concept of the mischief.

301. The resolution in *Heydon's Case*

In *Heydon's Case* the Barons of the Exchequer resolved as follows-

> 'That for the sure and true interpretation of all statutes in general (be they penal or beneficial, restrictive or enlarging of

the common law), four things are to be discerned and considered:

(1) what was the common law before the making of the Act;

(2) what was the mischief and defect for which the common law did not provide;

(3) what remedy the Parliament hath resolved and appointed to cure the disease of the commonwealth; and

(4) the true reason of the remedy,

and then the office of all the judges is always to make such construction as shall-

(a) suppress the mischief and advance the remedy, and

(b) suppress subtle inventions and evasions for the continuance of the mischief *pro privato commodo* (for private benefit), and

(c) add force and life to the cure and remedy according to the true intent of the makers of the Act *pro bono publico* (for the public good).

COMMENTARY

This section sets out a slightly modified version of the resolution in *Heydon's Case*. {(1584) 3 Co Rep 7a. See also *Blackwell v England* (1857) 8 El & Bl Rep 541.} It embodies immaterial changes designed to assist reference and improve clarity.

The famous resolution in *Heydon's Case* has been of great importance in the development of statutory interpretation; and continues to be cited today. Like many judicial dicta on the subject, it somewhat rashly attempts to be all-embracing in a few words. Nevertheless it marks the first and indeed only attempt by the judges fully to rationalise the important part of their function which concerns statutory interpretation.

Such brief summaries of a highly complex matter have their uses, but need to be approached with caution. There comes a point when any such compression necessitates the discarding of too many essential distinctions and qualifications for it to be safely relied on as a wholly accurate guide.

The influence of *Heydon's Case* is apparent in many subsequent dicta. Here is one, taken from a case decided more than 250 years later-

'We propose to construe [the Tithe Act 1832] according to the legal rules for the interpretation of statutes, principally by the words of the statute itself, which we are to read in their ordinary sense, and only to modify or alter so far as it may be necessary to avoid some manifest absurdity or incongruity, but no further. It is proper also to consider (1) the state of the law which it proposes or purports to alter; (2) the mischief which existed, and which it was intended to remedy; and (3) the nature of the remedy provided, and then to look at the statutes *in pari materia* as a means of explaining this statute. These are the proper modes of ascertaining the intention of the legislature.'

{*Salkeld v Johnson* (1848) 2 Ex 256, at p 272. As to statutes *in pari materia* see pp 516–517 above. The resolution in *Heydon's Case* was also approved and followed in the following cases, as well as many others down to the present day: *River Wear Comrs v Adamson* (1877) 2 App Cas 743, at p 764; *Re Mayfair Property Co, Bartlett v Mayfair Property Co* [1898] 2 Ch 28, at p 35.}

The final sentence of this confident dictum suggests, as is common, that it contains 'all you need to know about statutory interpretation'. Unhappily the case is otherwise. Such judicial sayings must be treated with the respect due to their origin, but we need to recognise that the way to understanding is not by a quick glance at instant summaries handed down from the bench. It is by careful step-by-step analysis of the enactment under enquiry and the relevant interpretative criteria. {For the enactment as the unit of enquiry see s 72 of this Code. As to the interpretative criteria see Part VI.}

Previous law Paragraph (1) of the resolution in *Heydon's Case* asks what was the common law before the making of the Act. This directs attention to the existing law that in the view of Parliament contained some legal mischief or defect.

Many early statutes were regarded as declaratory of the common law. This should not be taken at face value. The conservative legal profession, already seized of the idea that it provided a shield for the people against royal power, wished to believe that the common law had all the answers.

In a developing society this could not be so. New social mischiefs abounded, and the common law could not keep pace with them. Corresponding legal mischiefs therefore abounded too. Statutes which in reality changed and developed the common law were described as merely declaring it. Lawyers felt it important that legislation should not be openly accepted, in the way it is now, as a tool for change.

This early view conformed to the strange wish lawyers have to be part of an unalterable system. They are too shrewd not to know that every human system must change. Their desire for stability leads them to wish the changes to be unacknowledged. Hence the presumption, faintly regarded now, that an Act does not alter or conflict with common law rules. {See pp 319–320 above.}

As time went on however, it became the main function of legislation to abrogate unsuitable common law rules, or to alter their incidence or effect, or to fill the gaps they left. Because of this the law came over the centuries to be more and more embodied in statute. So the reference to common law in para (1) of the resolution in *Heydon's Case* should nowadays be treated as widened to include statute law, and indeed all forms of law. {See *Ealing LBC v Race Relations Board* [1972] AC 342, *per* Lord Kilbrandon at p 368.} With this modification, the point made by para (1) is of crucial importance; but often gets overlooked.

The existing body of law forms the background to every Act. Unless the contrary intention appears, Parliament is taken to intend this background to control the Act's operation. Where an enactment falls to be construed in relation to a particular factual situation, this means that the enactment is to be treated as embodied in an Act *which is itself part of the whole body of law*. Neither the enactment nor its Act stand in isolation. So far as the Act does not modify existing relevant rules of law, they continue to apply. That is presumed to be Parliament's intention. By implication of law, the express words of the Act are thus greatly enlarged. {See ss 144 and 145 of this Code, and Parts XVIII and XIX.}

Paragraph (2) of the resolution in *Heydon's Case*, dealing with the 'mischief and defect' for which the existing law did not provide, forms the main subject of this and the immediately following sections of the Code. Paragraphs (3) and (4) relate to the nature of the remedy and are discussed in s 312. The duties to suppress the mischief and advance the remedy (para (a)) and 'add force and life' (para (c)) are mainly considered in connection with purposive construction in s 139 and Part XV of the Code. Countering avoidance of the Act's intention (para (b)) is dealt with in s 143 and Part XVII.

Later common law mischiefs   Following *Heydon's Case*, and indeed down to our own time, defects in the common law have continued to engage the attention of Parliament. We now give more examples, so as to illustrate further what is meant by the mischief to which an Act is directed (in the sense considered by the Barons of the Exchequer).

A frequent occasion for legislation is where some anti-social condition arises for which the common law simply does not provide at all.

Example 1   Soon after *Heydon's Case* had been decided, outbreaks of the plague caused alarm. An Act was hastily passed to compel infected sufferers to remain within doors. {1 Ja 1 c 31 (1603), repealed by the Punishment of Offences Act 1837 s 4.}

Example 2   Early in George I's reign the practice became rife of offering rewards for stolen property with no questions asked. The notorious receiver or 'fence' Jonathan Wild, with his confederates, set up a market. Here robbery victims could regain their property on paying the stall-holder half the value. This abuse was checked in 1717 by a provision of 4 Geo 1 c 11. {Repealed by 7 & 8 Geo 4 c 27 (1827), s 1).}

Example 3   Blackstone records how the intervention of Parliament was once called for by-

> ' . . . the insolence of certain weavers and others; who, upon the introduction of some Indian fashions prejudicial to their own manufactures, made it their practice to deface them; either by open outrage, or by privily cutting, or casting *aqua fortis* in the streets upon such as wore them.'

{Kerr Bl (4th edn, 1876) iv 257. The remedial Act was 6 Geo 1 c 23 (1719), repealed by the Criminal Law Act 1826, s 34.}

Example 4   Another social mischief was checked by the famous Waltham Black Act of 1722, passed to counter outrages committed by marauders who blacked their faces for disguise and committed pillage in the countryside around Waltham in Hampshire. {9 Geo 1 c 22 (1722). The Act was repealed by 7 & 8 Geo 4 c 27 (1827) s 1.} J R Spencer notes that this Act 'managed to create 54 new felonies, all of them capital, within the scope of a single section'. {[1981] Crim LR 682, at p 683.}

Common law technicalities   Artificial doctrines of the common law often gave rise to a legal mischief. The law of larceny provides many examples.

Example 5 Deeds of title to land were treated by the common law as being in themselves *realty* (though nothing more substantial than parchment). Because land could not be the subject of larceny, neither therefore could such documents.

Example 6 Different reasoning, to the like effect, applied to bonds, bills or notes evidencing choses in action. The paper composing them had no intrinsic value (being spoilt by having been written on). Therefore, although evidencing assets perhaps of great value, it could not be the subject of larceny. {This anomaly was first corrected by 2 Geo 2 c 25 (1728).} The common law was slow to wake up to the intrinsic value of documents of title.

Example 7 Another defect in the law of larceny related to wrecks. Until seized by or on behalf of the Crown these were the property of no one, and so could be plundered with impunity. {Corrected by 26 Geo 2 c 19 (1753), repealed by the Merchant Shipping Repeal Act 1854 s 4.}

Example 8 Domesticated animals such as dogs, which furnished neither clothing, food nor motive power, were regarded by the common law as having no value. If anything their value was negative, and they were looked on as nothing more than noisy and disease-carrying scavengers. They were therefore incapable of forming the subject of larceny. {This insensitive rule was corrected by an enactment later consolidated as s 18 of the Larceny Act 1861 (repealed by the Theft Act 1968 s 33(3)).}

Example 9 Technicalities of pleading in both civil and criminal cases caused many miscarriages of justice. In indictments for murder the length and depth of the wound had to be stated, so that the court could be satisfied that it was of a mortal nature. {Kerr Bl (4th edn, 1876) iv 323.} Such technicalities in relation to homicide offences caused great scandal. {For an example see *R v Mosley* (1825) 1 Mood CC 97. The matter was put right by s 4 of the Criminal Procedure Act 1851.}

Some technicalities owed their existence to feudal or scholastic origins, and formed notorious blemishes on the common law. Blackstone deals with them in his choicest language-

> 'Both the divinity and the law of those times were therefore frittered into logical distinctions, and drawn out into metaphysical subtilties, with a skill most amazingly artificial; but which serves no other purpose than to show the vast powers of the human intellect, however vainly or preposterously employed. Hence law, in particular, which, being intended for universal reception, ought to be a plain rule of action, became a science of the greatest intricacy, especially when blended with the new refinements engrafted upon feudal property . . . Statute after statute has in latter times been made to pare off these troublesome excrescences, and restore the common law to its pristine simplicity and vigour . . . '

{Kerr Bl (4th edn, 1876) iv 424-5.}

Despite the worship accorded by Blackstone and many other devotees, it had to be admitted that 'our lady the common law' often fell short of the rising standards and requirements of a developing society. Medical advance was held up by the difficulty of obtaining bodies for dissection without robbing graves, which was a misdemeanour. The Anatomy Act 1832 was passed to rectify this. Unfairness in the trial of aliens was remedied by the Juries Act 1825. Section 47 of this Act required that half the members of the jury must be foreigners, if so many were found in the place and the accused alien demanded it. {Section 47 was repealed by the Courts Act 1971 s 56(4).} So it went on, and the upshot was the replacement of many of the old judge-made rules by parliamentary enactments.

302. The social mischief

The social mischief to which an Act is directed is a factual situation, present or shortly expected, which Parliament desires to remedy (if and so far as law can provide a remedy for it). This may range from something obviously wrong (such as an outbreak of a particular type of antisocial behaviour) to the possibility of *improving* an already neutral or even beneficial state of affairs.

COMMENTARY

As explained above {Pp 631–632.}, the social mischief is the factual situation that Parliament considers to be in need of remedying by legislation. It is the mischief on the ground, rather than in the law. {As to the legal mischief see s 303 of this Code.}

Here we come to a fundamental problem of democracy. It is for Parliament (or in practice the majority) to judge whether or not some condition amounts to a social mischief in this sense. On such matters of judgment, opinions may differ. One obvious cause of difference is political ideology, a matter dealt with separately. {See s 304 of this Code.} But there may be differences of opinion not based on party divisions. A former Chief of Police of the Metropolis, Sir Robert Mark, wrote this about two Acts of which he had professional experience, the Police Act 1964 and the Bail Act 1976-

> 'The Bail Act, like the Police Act, is a classic example of doctrinaire reaction to vocal minority pressure pushed through without adequate research, logic or mandate and after a Parliamentary debate remarkable for its irrelevance.'

{*In the Office of Constable* p 295.}

Parliament legislates on many matters as to which it may be said that research is insufficient, or opinions are wrong-headed, or factual situations are misread. The interpreter has to bear this fallibility in mind, and compensate for it as best he properly can.

Objection to the term 'mischief' Because the concept of the social mischief embraces situations of the latter type mentioned in the second sentence of this section of the Code, the term mischief has been objected to. 'It tends' said the Law Commissions 'to suggest that legislation is only designed to deal with an evil and not to further a positive social purpose'. {*The Interpretation of Statutes* (1969) Law Com No 21 p 49 n 177.} This echoes Bentham, who wrote-

'The end of the Law is the suppression of the supposed mischief that gave occasion to it, when it is a mischief; or the procurement or advancement of the benefit, when it is a benefit'.

{*A Comment on the Commentaries* p 107.}

While there is some force in the Law Commissions' criticism, it is nevertheless useful to have a single term to denote the factual state of affairs sought to be remedied or improved by changing the law. Moreover there is conceptually always a legal mischief if the law is not in the desired state, even though on the ground the problem is simply that a beneficent condition is not beneficent enough. Insufficiency of a desired benefit itself constitutes a defect.

The Law Commissions also felt the term mischief to carry an archaic ring, and preferred instead the term 'general legislative purpose'. {*The Interpretation of Statutes* (1969) Law Com No 21 p 19, n 78 and p 49, n 177.} Here it can only be said that modern judges do not appear to find the term mischief archaic, for they very frequently use it in their judgments. Moreover to substitute the term suggested would be a confusion. The purpose of an Act is not the mischief. The purpose is to provide a remedy to cure the mischief.

303. The legal mischief

A legal mischief is a condition which constitutes a defect in the law, or is regarded by Parliament as constituting such a defect. Either the law is defective in not providing, to the fullest extent which is possible for a law, some remedy for a corresponding social mischief (or alleged social mischief), or there is a purely legal defect in the law without a corresponding social mischief.

COMMENTARY

It could be argued that all defects in the law are in themselves social mischiefs. The purpose of the final limb of this section is however to distinguish the case where (disregarding that contention) there is no factual situation which could be characterised as a social mischief.

At first, as we have seen, legal mischiefs were mainly located in the common law. Indeed an early function of statutes was to *declare* a common law rule, but in an improved form. {For examples of common-law legal mischiefs see pp 632ff above.}

Usually the occasion for doing this was a judicial decision exposing the legal defect in question. Obviously such judicial exposure may equally occur in relation to a common-law or a statutory mischief.

Example 1 On one occasion the case in which the judicial decision was given thereafter gave its name to the mischief. *Re Centrebind Ltd* {[1967] 1 WLR 377.} was a decision on a point of company law. As Judge John Finlay QC later remarked, the mischief in question now takes its name from this case: 'in company jargon the mischief is called "centrebinding"'. {*E V Saxton & Sons Ltd v R Miles (Confectioners) Ltd* [1983] 2 All ER 1025, at p 1029.}

The cases reviewed so far in this Part illustrate the kinds of mischief the judges in *Heydon's Case* had in mind when they passed their resolution. The cases reveal clear deficiencies in the public protection afforded the citizen at common law. Not all Acts have been passed for such reasons however. We pass now to enactments designed to remedy defects found not in the common law but in earlier Acts of Parliament.

Statutory mischiefs   As the body of law came more to be inscribed in the statute book than the case reports, it was obvious that legal defects would be found there also. Then arose the type of legal mischief that might be called the statutory mischief. It began early enough. Those who today complain of the deficiencies of statute law will not be surprised to learn that with the first statutes there came the first statutory mischiefs.

Example 2   A statute of 1275 greatly reduced the penalties for rape. {3 Edw 1 (*Stat Westm prim* c 13).} The outcome is thus described by Blackstone-

> 'But this lenity being productive of the most terrible consequences, it was in ten years afterwards, 13 Edw I, found necessary to make the offence of forcible rape felony by statute Westm 2, c 34.'

{Kerr Bl (4th edn, 1876) iv 213.}

Example 3   A few years later an Act was passed to check over-eating. It ordained that no man should be served, at dinner or supper, with more courses than two. An exception was made for specified 'great holidays', when three courses might be served. {10 Edw 3 (1336) St 3.} The Act appears to have been largely ignored, being virtually unenforceable. People eat mainly in their homes, and from earliest times English law has treated a man's house as his castle. {See s 349 of this Code.} The only practical consequence of the Act was to expose householders to blackmail by their own servants. In 1856 it was tardily repealed as obsolete. {19 & 20 Vict c 64.}

Example 4   Legislation of the reign of George II rendered lotteries illegal. This later had the quite unexpected result of curbing the laudable activities of so-called art unions, whose object was to promote a taste for the fine arts on the part of the populace. One way of achieving this was thought to be to appeal to cupidity by offering works of art to be drawn for by lot on penny tickets. This artless scheme was excluded from the anti-lotteries legislation by the passing of a special Act. {Art Unions Act 1846.}

We need not multiply examples of the innumerable cases of statutory mischief. The obvious fact is that law, whether laid down by judges or legislators, will frequently be found defective - either because of initial inadequacy or because of subsequent changes in society. {As to the latter see s 146 of this Code.} Such defects form an important category of 'mischief' requiring remedy by later legislation.

Temporary remedies   On some matters constitutional theory requires that the law be kept in a permanently 'defective' state by insisting that the legislative remedy be merely temporary.

Blackstone pointed out in the eighteenth century that ' ... the [financial] supplies are voted only for one year at a time, and the Mutiny acts are passed for one year only'. {Kerr Bl (4th edn, 1876) i 122.} In our own day supplies continue to be voted for one year at a time, while the practice with regard to the armed forces is to pass an Act every five years that authorises their annual continuance by an Order in Council requiring an affirmative resolution of each House of Parliament. {The current enactment is the Armed Forces Act 1981 s 1.}

There are good constitutional reasons for these special cases, which do not affect the general principle that every enactment is designed to provide a lasting remedy for a legal mischief.

Late revivals The unexpected revival of ancient common law doctrines after a long interval of lapse has occasionally required legislative intervention.

Example 5 In medieval times a lord of Parliament who was to be tried by jury could challenge the array if it did not include at least one knight. In 1749 the Bishop of Worcester asserted his right to claim this ancient privilege. {*R v Bishop of Worcester* (1749) M 23 Geo II BR.} The privilege was thereupon abolished by Act. {24 Geo 2 c 18 (1750), s 4 (repealed by the Statute Law Revision Act 1867).}

Example 6 Another instance of embarrassing revival is furnished by the celebrated early nineteenth-century case of *Ashford v Thornton*. {(1818) 1 B & Ald 405.} Here an appeal of murder was brought, the appellee insisting on his right to wager of battle. Appeals of felony were thereupon abolished by Parliament. {59 Geo 3 c 46 (1819), repealed by the Statute Law Revision Act 1873.}

History shows that it can never be assumed that an ancient doctrine not abolished by statute is incapable of revival. Two more examples may be given.

Example 7 The first relates to the High Court of Chivalry. A nineteenth-century editor of Blackstone's *Commentaries* wrote that the court 'has long been entirely disused'. {Kerr Bl (4th edn, 1876) iv 278.} Yet the High Court of Chivalry sat in full dignity and effectiveness more than a century after this confident statement was uttered. {*Manchester Corpn v Manchester Palace of Varieties* [1955] P 133 (right to use City's coat of arms).}

Example 8 The second example concerns the right of private prosecution in Scotland. Professor Kenny, who for half a century lectured on criminal law in the University of Cambridge, confidently asserted through many editions of his famous textbook that this right was obsolete. {C S Kenny *Outlines of Criminal Law* (15th edn, 1946) p 10.} Yet in 1982 a private prosecution for rape was successfully brought in Scotland. {*R v Sweeney* (1982) *The Times* 29 May.}

304. Party-political mischiefs

A party-political mischief is a so-called mischief considered to be such only by the political party with a majority sufficient to secure the passing of the Act in question. Their opponents may well consider the circumstances against which the Act is directed to be a *benefit* rather than a mischief. They may accordingly determine to restore the status quo if they should later attain power.

COMMENTARY

In modern times there has arisen a new class of legislation. No longer is Parliament largely concerned with repelling the nation's enemies, keeping the Queen's peace, financing the administration and holding the ring between citizens. The legislature becomes an engine of social change. It regulates the national economy. It takes on the management and control of great industries. The subject-matter of its Acts enters the realm of argument and opinion, party-politics, economic theory, religious or sociological controversy, class warfare and other matters as to which there is no consensus.

For example the political left-wing consider the fact that a particular industry is in private ownership to be a mischief, while the right-wing consider it a benefit. The current ownership conditions of that industry are therefore a party-political mischief in the eyes of one or other of the parties. {See further Examples 306.1, 312.2 and 312.3.}

How is the interpreter to regard legislation of this type? The answer is clear. A court of construction is bound to ignore the fact that what to the majority in one Parliament seemed a defect in the existing law may appear the reverse to their successors of a different political persuasion. Until the successors get round to repealing an Act with which they disagree, it stands as the will of the Parliament that made it. {For cases where an incoming government has failed to make commencement orders in relation to its predecessors' legislation see pp 415–416 above. As to the argument that by allowing an Act to remain on the statute book a later Parliament 'legislates' tacitly see p 358.}

The same applies where a decisive change has occurred in the views of a political party since the Act's passing.

Example 1   R v Secretary of State for the Environment, ex p Greater London Council {(1983) *The Times* 2 December.} concerned just such a change. The government currently in power had recently adopted the policy of abolishing the Greater London Council. They therefore did not wish to implement certain provisions of the Town and Country Planning Act 1971 as applied to Greater London. Hodgson J said-

> 'Parliament is supreme, and the Act is an Act of Parliament. Until Parliament amends or repeals it, it remains the will of Parliament. The fact that the executive of the day do not want to do something which it is required by an Act of Parliament to do is nothing to the question: and if that executive because of no other reason than its own political posture exercises its discretion in a way contrary to the intention of Parliament as expressed in the legislation then the courts can and will intervene.'

{The form of such intervention is by judicial review: see s 24 of this Code.}

Judges are not to enter the jungle of politics. If an Act has been passed in a particular Parliament it must be assumed that the majority of legislators in that Parliament considered there to be a defect in the law needing remedy. Moreover the defect must be considered from the viewpoint then prevailing. We considered above what part the original 'mischief' plays in the interpretation brought to bear at a much later time. {See pp 358–360.} It is important not to let confusion creep in by treating the mischief as somehow altered by later events. Later events may indeed require to be taken into account, but not as altering or glossing the historical facts which occasioned the passing of the Act.

305. Ambit of the mischief

In using the mischief for the purposes of interpretation it may be important to determine, so far as necessary for settling the point at issue, the precise scope or ambit of the mischief Parliament intended to remedy.

COMMENTARY

While the general area of the mischief may be easily inferred, more difficulty may be found in deciding whether a particular aspect was within it or not. If it is alleged that a *doubtful* matter was within the mischief aimed at by Parliament, the court will reject the allegation if it can see no good reason for it.

Example 1   In *Hussain v Hussain* {[1982] 3 All ER 369.} it was alleged that s 11(d) of the Matrimonial Causes Act 1973 rendered void a marriage entered into overseas between British-domiciled persons under a foreign law allowing polygamy. The spouse seeking to uphold the marriage admitted polygamy to be contrary to public policy under British law, but showed that in the instant case there was no possibility of a later polygamous marriage. In rejecting the alleged construction, Ormrod LJ said-

'. . . it is difficult to conceive any reason why Parliament, in an increasingly pluralistic society, should have thought it necessary to prohibit persons whose religious or cultural traditions accept polygamy from marrying in their own manner abroad, simply because they are domiciled in England and Wales'. {P 372.}

The wording of the enactment may go wider than the actual mischief for some extraneous reason. It may, for example, assist enforcement of the enactment if it is worded more widely than is legally neccessary to remedy the mischief in question. {For an example related to prostitution see Leng and Sanders 'The CLRC Working Paper on Prostitution' [1983] Crim LR 644 at pp 650-2.}

Common sense may indicate that the ambit of the mischief is narrower than the literal meaning. {For the commonsense construction rule see s 122 of this Code.}

Example 2   In the Australian case of *Ingham v Hie Lie* {(1912) 15 CLR 267.} the court considered a Victorian Act whose purpose was to limit the hours of work of Chinese in factories, laundries etc so as to protect other industries. The defendant, a Chinese laundryman, who had been found *ironing his own shirt*, was charged with an offence under the Act. *Held* No offence had been committed. {Cf Example 289.3.}

See further, as to the ambit of the mischief, Examples, 14.4 to 14.9.

306. The particular mischief of an enactment

The various provisions of an Act may be concerned with several different mischiefs. Where the meaning of a particular enactment is in question, it is important to concentrate attention on the precise mischief that enactment was designed to remedy.

COMMENTARY

Although an Act may have a single main object, its various provisions may nevertheless be concerned with multifarious matters within that object. If one of these is in question the relevant mischief will only indirectly be that involved in the Act's main object. The interpreter will be more closely concerned with the limited mischief at which that particular provision was aimed.

Example 1   The Transport Act 1947, put through by a Labour government, was concerned with one matter only, namely the 'mischief' caused to the national economy by the fact that railways and other forms of transport were in private ownership.

This was a party-political mischief, where no national consensus existed as to whether or not the situation on the ground really constituted a social mischief in need of remedy. {See s 304 of this Code.} Although the Conservative opposition of the day did not agree that rail nationalisation was desirable, that party did not repeal the Act when its turn for office came. The case was different with the nationalisation of steel, which was carried out and then undone several times over.

The Transport Act 1947 had but one object. However it was necessary, in order to carry out this object efficiently, for the Act to make detailed arrangements covering many diferent aspects of the subject. On any of these, doubt might have arisen as to the meaning of a particular enactment. Here it would be necessary to consider the limited mischief of that enactment, though always within the context of the Act's overall purpose.

'Ragbag' Acts   Some Acts are 'ragbag' Acts, covering many areas. The annual Finance Act is an extreme example. It is divided into Parts, dealing respectively with customs and excise duty, value added tax, income tax, capital gains tax, stamp duty, capital transfer tax and so on. Even within a Part of a Finance Act the various provisions have quite different aims. Sections, or groups of sections, are often self-contained.

Example 2   Part III of the Finance Act 1976 deals with so many different matters that it is subdivided into Chapters. Chapter II, consisting of 13 sections, is concerned with the taxing of fringe benefits received by company directors and employees. Chapter II is a 'unit' so far as mischief is concerned. The mischief in question is the unjust avoidance of income tax by the device of the employer paying his employee what is really remuneration in a form which escapes the tax on remuneration. This mischief does not concern any other provision of the Act, and it concerns all the provisions in Chapter II.

Chapter II however contains many different 'enactments'. One of them fell to be construed by the Court of Appeal in *Wicks v Firth (Inspector of Taxes)*. {[1982] 2 All ER 9.} The employer had established an educational trust for the award of scholarships to the children of employees. One of the questions for the court was whether a scholarship so awarded fell within this enactment. Restated using selective comminution {See s 74 of this Code.}, this enactment read-

> 'Where in any year a person is employed, and *by reason of his employment* there is provided for a member of his family any benefit, there is to be treated as emoluments of the employment, and

accordingly chargeable to income tax under Schedule E, an amount
equal to whatever is the cash equivalent of the benefit.'

{Restatement of portions of s 61(1) of the Finance Act 1976 (emphasis added).}

The question here was whether an employee's children received their
scholarships 'by reason of his employment' within the meaning of that phrase as
used in this enactment. For this purpose the 'mischief' of the enactment was the
same as for all the other enactments in Chapter II, namely tax avoidance
through fringe benefits.

We see that whether the Act deals with one matter only, or is a 'ragbag', or is
something in between, the important thing is to identify the particular mischief
with which the enactment under enquiry is concerned.

Even within a single enactment there may be different aspects of the mischief
to which the enactment is directed. A particular point of interpretation may be
concerned with one only of these, and it is then important to determine which.

307. The mischief for which Parliament actually legislated

While the social or legal mischief with which an Act was concerned may
be clearly established, it by no means follows that Parliament intended to
tackle the *whole* of that mischief. This applies even though the Act was
based on the report of a committee of inquiry covering the whole. Nor
does it follow that Parliament took precisely the same view of the nature
or area of the mischief as did other people concerned (for example the
members of a committee of inquiry).

On the other hand Parliament may have decided to legislate for
another mischief *in addition* to the one originally contemplated.

For these reasons it is necessary, so far as relevant to the point of
interpretation at issue, to determine precisely what was the mischief for
which in the end Parliament legislated.

COMMENTARY

Since the enactment is the unit of enquiry in statutory interpretation {See s 72
of this Code.}, what matters in a particular case is not so much the mischief as it
may have been generally regarded but the mischief Parliament actually tackled.
The interpreter needs to make sure that he identifies the correct target.

Here a form of mental dissociation may be required. Initially we must set aside
the requirements the enactment actually lays down, and look only at the defect
(so far as this may be relevant to the factual situation in the instant case).
Moreover we must look not only at the defect as it is in fact, or as it was
originally identified. What we have to seek out and concentrate on is *the defect
for which in the end Parliament actually legislated.*

There is no necessary correlation between a particular defect and a remedial
Act. Society suffers from an excess of defects: Parliament suffers from an
insufficiency of debating time. *Ex hypothesi* there is a mischief for every
enactment; but there cannot be an enactment for every mischief.

It may be helpful to give some examples of this in schematic form.

Example 1 A mischief is identified, which we may call M1. A Bill is introduced into Parliament to remedy M1. It is pointed out in debate that there is also a comparable mischief (M2). The Bill is amended to deal with M2 as well. The fact that M1 alone was identified as the original mischief (perhaps in the report of a committee of inquiry) should not delude the interpreter into supposing that the Act as it finally emerged was not intended by Parliament to cover M2 as well.

Example 2   A mischief with five facets is identified. We may call it A + B + C + D + E. A Bill is introduced to deal with it, but runs into strong opposition. To secure its enactment, the government decides to drop B and D. The fact that B and D in fact formed part of the problem on the ground should not lead the interpreter to conclude that the Act was intended to cover them.

Example 3   A mischief Y is identified. A Bill is introduced to deal with it, but the nature of Y changes radically during the period while the Bill is passing through Parliament. Suitable amendments are made to the Bill. In the end the mischief to which the final Act is directed (Z), though bearing points of resemblance to Y, is broadly different from it. The Act must be construed accordingly.

It very frequently happens that Parliament finds itself unable to tackle a pressing social problem in one operation. It has to be done piecemeal, in stages. It is very important that the interpreter should not confuse the mischief on the ground, or social mischief, with Parliament's intention in relation to it. This whole question was summed up by Lord Wilberforce in relation to legislation to reverse a court decision-

‘ . . . it frequently happens that legislative changes are made in order to reverse decisions of the courts; sometimes, indeed, the courts themselves invite the change. The decision is then the occasion of the enactment. The question may, consequently, arise whether the new enactment is confined to dealing with the particular situation with which the court was concerned or whether it goes further and covers a wider field, and, if so, how much wider. There is no general rule or presumption as to this. Often Parliament, or its expert advisers, may take the opportunity to review the whole matter in principle and make broad changes. (See for example *Central Asbestos Co Ltd v Dodd* {[1973] AC 518.} as to the Limitation Acts.) Legislative time is a precious commodity and it is natural that opportunities, when they arise, will be used . . . On the other hand, there may be cases where Parliament takes a narrow and piecemeal view of the matter; time may not admit of an extensive review which may involve wide policy questions, or necessitate consultation with other interests. All these possibilities must be taken into account by courts in assessing the legislative intention.’

{*Maunsell v Olins* [1975] 1 All ER 16, at p 22.}

It may not be easy to identify the precise mischief with which Parliament intended to deal. This can cause problems where the interpretation turns on it.

Example 4   Section 5(1) of the Misuse of Drugs Act 1971 makes it unlawful for a person ‘to have a controlled drug in his possession’. In *R v Boyesen* {[1982] 2

All ER 161.} the House of Lords had to decide whether, in view of the short title of the Act, it should be treated as concerned only with possession of a *usable* quantity of a controlled drug. Was the mischief the possession of any quantity, however minute, or was it the possession only of an amount sufficient for an addict to use? Lord Scarman said-

> 'If I were disposed, which I am not, to add to the subsection by judicial interpretation words which are not there, I would not accept the words suggested, i e capable of being used in a manner prohibited by the Act. The uncertainty and imprecision of such a criterion of criminal responsibility *would in themselves be mischievous*. But, further, the view that possession is only serious enough, as a matter of legal policy, to rank as an offence if the quantity possessed is itself capable of being misused is a highly dubious one. Small quantities can be accumulated. It is a perfectly sensible view that the possession of any quantity which is visible, tangible, measurable and "capable of manipulation" . . . is a serious matter to be prohibited if the law is to be effective against trafficking in dangerous drugs and their misuse.'

{P 166. Emphasis added. As to counter-mischief see s 326 of this Code.}

308. Mischief which arises only within context of the remedy

The 'mischief' with which a particular enactment is concerned may have only a very indirect connection with the defect the Act is concerned to remedy. It may even be a mischief confined to the context of the remedy itself.

COMMENTARY

Where a remedy is devised to deal with a particular mischief it may have a complex operation. Within that operation there may be room for 'mischiefs' concerned only with the smooth working of the remedy. In appropriate cases, the enactment is to be construed with this in mind.

For example the remedy decided upon to deal with a mischief on the ground, or social mischief, may be the creation of a new criminal offence. Within this context it may be felt that problems will arise if police officers are compelled by the wording of the enactment to obtain a warrant before they are authorised to arrest a person suspected of committing the newly-created offence. So the enactment may give power to arrest without warrant. From this viewpoint the 'mischief' is the likelihood that malefactors will escape justice if the power is not given.

Example 1 In *Wills v Bowley* {[1982] 2 All ER 654. For a full account of the case see Example 162.1.} a question arose as to the nature and extent of the power of arrest conferred by s 28 of the Town Police Clauses Act 1847. The section covers a wide range of offences from the trivial to the grave. Lord Bridge said-

> 'If one next asks what is the mischief which Parliament, by conferring the power of arrest in flagrante delicto, intended to cure, the question admits of an easy answer where the power is applied to a

single offence, as in the case of the drunken driver ... when an offence is apparently being committed of a kind involving a threat to public safety, a power of immediate arrest must be intended to be exercisable on the basis of honest belief on reasonable grounds, *even though the statute has not said so.* But this line of reasoning is not available in those cases where the power applies to a wide range of offences of differing nature and gravity ...'

{P 680. Emphasis added.}

309. Phasing out a legal mischief

Where the mischief is a legal defect consisting of some feature considered obsolete, Parliament may provide for phasing out the mischief rather than abolishing it summarily. This enables the people affected to grow used to the change gradually.

COMMENTARY

The British are a conservative people, and dislike sudden change. They grow accustomed to their institutions and prefer to retain them long after they have ceased to be useful. This particularly applies to an institution which confers honour or dignity on persons connected with it. To ease the transition, and avoid complaint, Parliament may make interim arrangements. The feature of these is usually that the appearance remains when the reality has gone.

Example 1 The Local Government Act 1972 swept away various ancient municipal features such a charters, boroughs, mayors, freemen, and aldermen. Nevertheless ss 245 to 249 of the Act contained elaborate provisions for retaining the appearance of these. A borough became a 'district', but by virtue of s 246 might continue to have the status or style of a borough (while not being allowed to be treated as a borough for the purpose of any existing Act). Though the 1972 Act abolished the office of alderman, s 249 authorised the appointment of 'honorary aldermen', while precluding any councillor so appointed from actually being addressed as alderman or taking part in any ceremony as such. And so on.

This type of provision should not be confused with the ordinary transitional provision, described in s 189 of this Code.

310. Discerning the mischief

The court is instructed by paragraph (2) of the resolution in *Heydon's Case* to 'discern and consider ... the mischief and defect for which the [law] did not provide'. There are various ways in which the mischief may be so 'discerned'.

COMMENTARY

Heydon's Case   For the terms of the resolution in *Heydon's Case* {(1584) 3 Co Rep 7a.} see s 301 of this Code.

The Act may tell us in so many words what the mischief was. Some Acts do this in the long title. For example the long title of 22 & 23 Vict c 17 (1859) was 'An Act to prevent vexatious indictments for certain misdemeanors'. {As to the long title see s 271 of this Code.} Sometimes even the short title is informative. {For the short title see s 275 of this Code.} In *Lonrho Ltd v Shell Petroleum Ltd* {[1982] AC 173, at p 186.} Lord Diplock said of the Dramatic and Musical Performers' Protection Act 1958: 'The Act was passed for the protection of a particular class of individuals, dramatic and musical performers; even the short title said so'.

Or the Act may tell us in a preamble (though in public Acts these are little used nowadays). {As to the preamble see s 272 of this Code.} The preamble to 22 Hen 8 c 10 (1530) explained that the mischief on the ground was the influx into the realm of-

' . . . outlandish people, calling themselves Egyptians, using no craft nor feat of merchandise, who have come into this realm and gone from shire to shire and place to place in great company, and used great, subtil and crafty means to deceive the people . . .'

Another possible source of information about the mischief is a treaty or international agreement to which the Act is intended to give effect. The Recognition of Divorces and Legal Separations Act 1971 was passed to enable the United Kingdom to ratify the Hague Convention on Recognition of Divorces and Legal Separations. {Cmnd 4542; see Law Com No 34.} In *Joyce v Joyce and O'Hare* {[1979] 2 All ER 156.} Lane J said-

'In construing a statute it is proper for the court to look at the mischief at which it is aimed. The mischief at which this statute was aimed is referred to in the hitherto, I think, unreported case of *Quazi v Quazi*. {Since reported in (1978) 8 Fam Law 203.} I have the advantage of having a transcript of the judgment of Wood J in that case. [Wood J said] "the clear mischief at which the convention and indeed the 1971 Act are aimed is that of the 'limping marriage'".' {P 168.}

The term 'limping marriage' neatly combines in one phrase a reference to a legal mischief and a social mischief.

General knowledge   Quite often the mischief is to be gleaned by a combination of general knowledge and inferences drawn from the requirements laid down in the text of the Act. {As to judicial notice of well-known facts see s 21 of this Code. The pre-eminence of the text is explained in s 136 of the Code.} The well-informed judge confidently states the mischief underlying a recent Act.

Example 1   Thus Lord Atkin said in *Coventry Corpn v Surrey CC* {[1935] AC 199, at p 204.}-

'It is well known that [the Poor Law Act 1930] was passed to remedy one of the scandals of the old Poor Law, the breaking up of families by distributing parents and children to different settlements.'

Example 2   Again we find Oliver LJ remarking of the Occupiers' Liability Act 1957-

'Before referring to the Act it is well to remember that its purpose was to eradicate some of the unsatisfactory features of the way in

which the common law had developed as regards the liability of occupiers of premises for injuries sustained by third parties lawfully resorting there . . .'

{*Holden v White* [1982] 2 All ER 328, at p 330.}

Example 3   Lord Denning MR gave two consecutive recapitulations of this kind in *R v Horsham JJ* {[1982] 2 All ER 269, at p 283.}-

'In 1957 there was much concern because when Dr John Bodkin Adams was charged with murder, evidence was given at the committal proceedings of earlier deaths which was not given at his subsequent trial. This concern led to Lord Tucker's Committee in 1958 . . . Their report was implemented by s 3 of the Criminal Justice Act 1967. Then in 1980 there was much concern because, when Mr Jeremy Thorpe and others were charged, one of the accused asked for reporting restrictions to be lifted. The others did not. This concern led to an amendment [made by] the Criminal Justice (Amendment) Act 1981 by which the others could be heard to ask that the reporting restrictions remain.'

Legislative history   As Example 3 shows, a source of knowledge of the mischief is *legislative history*, such as the report of a committee of inquiry on which the Act is based. The discovery of a possible mischief often nowadays leads, not to immediate legislation, but to the institution of an inquiry instructed to investigate the mischief and report on possible remedies. This may be conducted by an ad hoc committee, by a standing committee such as the Criminal Law Revision Committee or the Law Commission, or by a committee set up within the relevant government department.

Referring to a report of the Criminal Law Revision Committee, a commentator remarked of one case that there was no hint in the report 'that a situation in any way approximating to the circumstances of the present case lay within the target area of mischief which the committee intended to hit'. {(1982) 126 Sol Jo 250. For another example see *Dullewe v Dullewe* [1969] 2 AC 313. The rules as to the use of *legislative history* in statutory interpretation are examined in Part X of this Code.}

Unknown mischief   Despite the varied sources of information thus available, it has to be accepted that, particularly with older Acts, it may not be possible for the court to find out what the mischief was. Since the court cannot take into account what it does not know, it must then do the best it can with the Act as it stands.

Example 4   In *Nugent-Head v Jacob (Inspector of Taxes)* {[1948] AC 321.} the House of Lords was asked to construe the second proviso to rule 16 of the All Schedules Rules set out in the Income Tax Act 1918. Lord Uthwatt said-

'That part of [rule 16] which is now embodied in the second proviso made its first appearance in the Income Tax Act 1805, and its present form does not in any material respect differ from its original form. Research inspired by curiosity has failed to reveal the reasons which led to the introduction made in 1805. It may be that the Solicitor-

General is right in his conjecture that the new part, when first introduced, was designed as a collecting provision to deal with the case where the husbands were in India or the plantations and their wives were living in Great Britain. Other conjectures may, however, be made ... But the matter is one of historical interest only. Whatever be the reasons which led to the passing in 1805 of the new provision, those reasons cannot be of any relevance on the question of the construction of the provision as it appears in the Income Tax Act 1918. *That Act must be construed as it stands by reference to its contents.* {P 327. Emphasis added.}

See further s 317 of this Code.

311. Use of the mischief in interpretation

Having identified the correct mischief, the court is to do as required by the resolution in *Heydon's Case*. This states that the office of the judge is always to make such construction as shall suppress the mischief and advance the remedy.

COMMENTARY

Heydon's Case   For the resolution in *Heydon's Case* {(1584) 3 Co Rep 7a.} see s 301 of this Code.

It is presumed that Parliament intended by the enactment to *suppress* the mischief. The law usually does this by ordering those who perpetrate the mischief to desist; and imposing a penalty if they fail. Once the interpeter has correctly marked out the area of the mischief intended to be dealt with by the enactment, he can go on to identify the corresponding penalty or other remedy.

It is further presumed that Parliament did not intend to apply coercive measures going wider than was necessary for the mischief in question. These presumptions as to Parliament's intention may help in construing an enactment whose wording is doubtful. The importance of the mischief goes further than this however. We cannot be sure whether there *is* real doubt or not unless we have the mischief in mind. {As to real doubt see s 4 of this Code.} This is one function of the informed interpretation rule. {See s 119 of this Code.}

In the consideration of opposing constructions of an enactment in relation to a particular factual situation, we may find that bringing the mischief into account helps to decide whether the enactment is intended to be given a wider or narrower construction. {As to opposing constructions see s 84 of this Code.}

Where the mischief favours the wider construction   In some cases consideration of the nature of the mischief which the enactment is intended to remedy may suggest that the enactment is to be given a wider effect.

Example 1   Section 12 of the Criminal Procedure Act 1851 was enacted to remedy the injustice and inconvenience caused in the criminal law by excessive technicalities. In *R v Males* {[1962] 2 QB 500.} Lord Parker CJ held that since the section was directed *against* technicalities it should not to be so construed as to allow the acquittal of a person charged with attempted housebreaking on the technical ground that he had committed the complete offence. 'When one considers', said Lord Parker, 'the mischief aimed at by the Act it seems to this court that that is really the only interpretation that can be put on these words'. {P 505.}

Example 2   Section 1 of the Street Offences Act 1959 was directed to a mischief caused by prostitutes. In increasing numbers, they were standing about in the streets to the annoyance of pedestrians. The section made it an offence to solicit 'in a street'. In *Smith v Hughes* {[1960] 1 WLR 830.} prostitutes who had solicited from balconies or windows looking out on a street were charged with the offence. Lord Parker CJ upheld their conviction by giving the phrase 'in a street' a strained construction. {As to strained construction see ss 92 to 97 of this Code. For strict and liberal construction see s 154.} He said-

> 'For my part, I approach the matter by considering what is the mischief aimed at by this Act. Everybody knows that this was an Act intended to clean up the streets, to enable people to walk along the streets without being molested or solicited by common prostitutes . . . For my part, I am content to base my decision on that ground and that ground alone.'

{P 832. For the argument that judges ought not to widen criminal statutes on this way see Glanville Williams 'Statute Interpretation, Prostitution and the Rule of Law' (comprised in *Crime, Proof and Punishment*, Essays in memory of Sir Rupert Cross). The case is an example of purposive construction (see Part XVIII of this Code). See also *Re Newspaper Proprietors' Agreement* (1962) LR 3 RP 360, at p 375; *Kingsley v Sterling Industrial Securities Ltd* [1967] 2 QB 747, at p 785. As to enactments whose wording goes narrower than the mischief see pp 344–345 above.}

Where the mischief favours the narrower construction   There may on the contrary be cases where consideration of the mischief to which the enactment is directed favours giving it a narrower operation.

Example 3   Section 2(1) of the Matrimonial Causes Act 1963 was passed to remedy the mischief that matrimonial reconciliations were being hindered by the fact that if an attempted reconciliation failed the attempt might be held to amount to condonation of previous matrimonial offences, and so prevent the grant of a divorce decree. In *Brown v Brown* {[1967] P 105.} Simon P held that consideration of the mischief led to the exclusion from the section of cases where the reconciliation was *for a time* succcessful but ultimately failed.

Example 4   An order made under s 75 of the Contagious Diseases (Animals) Act 1869 required pens to be provided for the carriage of animals on board ship. The mischief which the section was intended to remedy was the spread of disease, the risk of which would be lessened by the use of pens. In *Gorris v Scott* {(1874) LR 9 Ex 125.} some sheep were carried in breach of the order without use of pens. In a storm they were washed overboard, which the pens would have prevented. *Held* An action for breach of statutory duty did not lie. {See Example 14.4. As to such actions see s 14 of this Code.}

Example 5   Section 31(1) of the Mines and Quarries Act 1954 required the 'surface entrance' of every mine to be provided with a barrier to prevent persons accidentally falling down the shaft. Section 31(2) required barriers provided 'in pursuance of' s 31(1) to be properly maintained. In *Rodgers v National Coal Board* {[1966] 1 WLR 1559.} the deceased died by a fall from the top deck of a lift cage which was stationary at the head of a shaft. It was alleged that the fall was due to lack of proper maintenance of the barrier round the top deck. Waller J said-

> 'The mischief against which s 31(2) is directed is the mischief of somebody accidentally falling down the shaft from the surface entrance ... This case was an accident which happened when the deceased ... fell down the shaft from inside the shaft ... Therefore there was no breach of statutory duty which caused this accident'.

{P 1563.}

Example 6   Section 2 of the Inheritance (Provision for Family and Dependants) Act 1975 gives the court power to order payments to an applicant out of a deceased person's estate where the deceased did not make reasonable provision for the applicant. Although the Act does not say so, the courts have inferred that the mischief aimed at is limited to the harm arising to persons with a moral claim on the deceased. To the argument that the Act applied wherever it would have been reasonable for the deceased to have made the provision sought, Oliver J replied-

> 'That is not the purpose of this legislation at all ... There must, as it seems to me, be established some sort of moral claim by the applicant ...'

{*Re Coventry (deceased)* [1979] 2 All ER 408. See also *Knapp v The Railway Executive* [1949] 2 All ER 508; *Hartley v Mayoh & Co* [1954] 1 QB 383. As to enactments whose wording goes wider than the mischief see pp 345-346 above.}

Counter-mischief   It may appear to the court that one of the opposing constructions of the enactment, if adopted, would create a mischief of its own. This factor is dealt with below. {See s 326 of the Code. As to opposing constructions see s 84.}

312. Remedy provided for the mischief

The remedy provided by an Act for a mischief takes the form of an amendment of the existing law. It is to be presumed that Parliament, having identified the mischief with which it proposes to deal, intends the remedy to operate in a way which may reasonably be expected to cure the mischief.

COMMENTARY

The 'mischief' may be a social mischief {See s 302 of this Code.} or a legal mischief. {See s 303 of this Code.} Whether or not there is a social mischief, or mischief 'on the ground', there is always a legal mischief. An Act always deals with some actual or supposed defect or inadequacy in the existing law. It follows that the remedy provided must take the form of an amendment of that law.

An Act amends a rule of *common law* by stating that in future the rule shall apply subject to modifications specified by the Act, or shall no longer apply at all. In the latter case the Act may or may not lay down alternative provision.

An Act amends a rule of *statute law* by modifying or else repealing the Act containing it. Again, in the latter case the amending Act may or may not lay down alternative provision.

A third possibility is that the mischief consists in an untoward *judicial decision* on the meaning of an Act. Here the remedy must be to reverse or modify the sub-rule laid down by that decision. {As to sub-rules see s 26 of this Code.}

Example 1   In *Maunsell v Olins* {[1975] 1 All ER 16, at p 18.} Lord Reid said of s 41 of the Housing Repairs and Rents Act 1954: 'There can be no doubt that the primary purpose of the section was to reverse the decision in *Cow v Casey*'. {[1949] 1 KB 474. It concerned the interpretation of s 15(3) of the Increase of Rent and Mortgage Interest (Restrictions) Act 1920.} Lord Dilhorne said of the decision in *Cow v Casey*: 'That was the mischief which s 41 was designed to cure'. {Ibid.}

At its simplest, the remedy for the mischief may consist of removing the obnoxious legal provision and not replacing it by anything. This often happens with a party-political Act when the opposition gets into power. {As to party-political 'mischiefs' see s 304 of this Code.}

Example 2   The Conservative government of 1971 disliked the Land Commission set up by an Act of its Labour predecessors. The very existence of the Commission was conceived to be a mischief, so it was abolished by the Land Commission (Dissolution) Act 1971. That simple procedure, accompanied by a few transitional provisions, constituted the 'remedy'. {Another example from the same year is the Licensing (Abolition of State Management) Act 1971.}

Example 3   A well-known example of a party-political Act tending the other way politically is the Industrial Relations Act 1971. This aroused the fury of the Labour Party. In their manifesto for the next general election, the party pledged themselves to repeal it utterly if returned to power. From their point of view the very existence of the 1971 Act was a 'mischief'.

The Labour Party were returned to power. On examining the 1971 Act more closely they found it contained many useful provisions they wished to retain. Here the 'mischief' became as it were split. From a party-political viewpoint the mischief remained the entirety of the 1971 Act. From the aspect of a *legal* defect, the mischief shrank to a much smaller compass. The draftsman of the reforming Trade Union and Labour Relations Act 1974 solved the problem by saying in s 1(1) of his Act that the 1971 Act 'is hereby repealed' and then adding in s 1(2) that nevertheless Sch 1 to the Act 'shall have effect for re-enacting' specified provisions of the 1971 Act.

In the usual case remedial provisions take a more substantial form than mere abolition of an obnoxious or deficient common-law or statutory rule. They are often both lengthy and far-reaching.

654

Example 4 Towards the end of the nineteenth century the absence of a state system of accident insurance for industrial workers was regarded as a serious social mischief. Parliament remedied it by passing the Workmen's Compensation Act 1897, of which the long title was-

> 'An Act to amend the Law with respect to Compensation to Workmen for accidental Injuries suffered in the course of their Employment.'

Lord Porter later remarked of this long title that the word 'revolutionise' would have given a truer description than 'amend'. {'Case Law in the Interpretation of Statutes' (Presidential address to the Holdsworth Club of the University of Birmingham, 1940) p 7.}

It follows that in the usual case virtually the entire Act constitutes the 'remedy'. Or, where an Act deals with more than one mischief, the relevant provisions of the Act constitute the remedy for each particular mischief. Since the object of the court is to construe the Act, this fact is liable to produce circularity of reasoning. Furthering the remedy is equated to furthering the Act, which does not take the interpreter very far along the road he has to travel.

To supply the answer often requires of the interpreter a feat of constructive imagination. Under our system enactments largely consist of 'cutting edge', or what this Code calls the legal thrust. {See s 79.} They are restricted to the provisions necessary to make the scheme work legalistically; and are short on explanations. The court is required first to fill in the background, and afterwards to do what is needed to implement what it conceives to be the rounded legislative plan.

In order to use the intended remedy as a guide to construction, it is therefore necessary to distil from the wording of the Act the remedy's intended nature and characteristics. The latter part of this section of the Code sketches the basis for doing this, aiming to convey the *attitude* or frame of mind with which the interpreter is expected by Parliament to undertake his task. Parliament intends to provide a remedy which will effectively cure the mischief, so the court must approach the Act in that spirit.

Advancing the remedy Where a difficulty in the working of the Act impairs the effectiveness of the intended remedy, it may be necessary for the court of construction to apply techniques designed to rectify the difficulty. That is no doubt what the Barons of the Exchequer had in mind when they said the court must advance the remedy and 'add force and life' to it. {*Heydon's Case* (1584) 3 Co Rep 7a. For the text of the resolution see s 301 of this Code.}

Certainly the court must endeavour to ensure that the remedy provided by Parliament does not set up some other mischief. {For further examples of the treatment by the courts of a statutory 'remedy' see *Pardo v Bingham* (1869) 4 Ch App 735, at p 740; *Freme v Clement* (1881) 18 Ch D 499, at p 508; *Mersey Steel and Iron Co v Naylor, Benzon & Co* (1882) 9 QBD 648, at p 660; *Lion Mutual Marine Insurance Association Ltd v Tucker* (1883) 12 QBD 176, at p 186; *The Dunelm* (1884) 9 PD 164, at p 171; *Reigate RDC v Sutton District Water Co* (1908) 99 LT 168 and (on appeal) (1909) 78 LJKB 315.}

Counter-mischief Clearly Parliament is unlikely to intend to abolish one mischief at the cost of establishing another which is just as bad, or even worse.

This provides an important guide to construction. It is dealt with in s 326 of this Code.

Purposive construction   The modern name for a reading which advances the remedy provided for a mischief is purposive construction. This is dealt with in detail in Part XV of this Code.

Legislative Presumptions: Purposive Construction

Introduction to Part XV This Part follows on from Part XIV in presenting the modern version of what used to be called the mischief rule, namely purposive construction. Its broad nature is explained (s 313), and then we go on to show that it may either correspond to a literal (s 314) or a strained (s 315) construction.

We consider ways in which the purpose is made known (s 316), and what the interpreter is to do where it is not clear (s 317). The court must loyally accept the purpose (s 318). There is no exclusion from purposive construction in the case of taxing Acts or other special categories (s 319). The British system of purposive construction is less liberal than the continental (s 320).

313. Nature of purposive construction

A construction which promotes the remedy Parliament has provided to cure a particular mischief is known as a purposive construction. Parliament is presumed to intend that in construing an Act the court, by advancing the remedy which is indicated by the words of the Act and the implications arising from those words, should aim to further every aspect of the legislative purpose.

A purposive construction of an enactment is one which gives effect to the legislative purpose by-

(a) following the literal meaning of the enactment where that meaning is in accordance with the legislative purpose (in this Code called a purposive-and-literal construction), or

(b) applying a strained meaning where the literal meaning is not in accordance with the legislative purpose (in the Code called a purposive-and-strained construction).

COMMENTARY

Lord Wilberforce has said that consideration of the purpose of an enactment is always a legitimate part of the process of interpretation. {*Fothergill v Monarch Airlines Ltd* [1980] 2 All ER 696, at p 700.}

As explained in Part XIV of this Code, the purpose or object of Parliament in passing an Act (the legislative purpose) is to provide an appropriate *remedy* to serve as a cure for the *mischief* with which the Act deals. The legislative purpose of a particular enactment contained in the Act is to be arrived at accordingly. In particular, it is deemed to be to remedy the mischief to which *that enactment* is directed. The unit of enquiry is usually a single proposition (an 'enactment'). {For the enactment as the unit of enquiry in statutory interpretation see s 72 of this Code.} As stated above {S 306.}, each enactment has its own limited purpose, to be understood within the larger purpose of the Act containing it.

When judges speak of a purposive construction, they usually mean to refer to what this Code calls a strained-and-purposive construction. {See para (b) of this section.} Thus we find Staughton J referring to 'the power of the courts to disregard the literal meaning of an Act and to give it a purposive construction'. {*A-G of New Zealand v Ortiz* [1982] 3 All ER 432, at p 442.} Lord Diplock speaks of 'competing approaches to the task of statutory construction - the literal and the purposive approach'. {*Kammins Ballrooms Co Ltd v Zenith Investments (Torquay) Ltd* [1971] AC 850, at p 879.}

Nevertheless a purposive construction must obviously be in all cases a construction which gives effect to the legislative intention, whether or not the statutory language needs to be strained to achieve this. Most often a purposive construction, in the true sense, will be a literal construction. {As to the nature of the literal meaning see s 91 of this Code.}

Novelty of the term   The term 'purposive construction' is a new one, but the concept is not. Viscount Dilhorne said that, while it is now fashionable to talk of the purposive construction of a statute, the need for such a construction has been recognised since the seventeenth century. {*Stock v Frank Jones (Tipton) Ltd* [1978] 1 WLR 231.}

In fact the recognition goes considerably further back. Lord Dilhorne was concerned to honour the perspicacity of his own seventeenth-century ancestor, Sir Edward Coke. The difficulties over statutory interpretation belong to the language. There is unlikely to be anything very novel or recent about their solution.

This reasoning explains why, although this Code conforms to modern practice by using the term 'purposive construction', it does not present the underlying meaning in any novel way. On the contrary, the Code sticks closely to old and well-tried concepts. Little has changed over problems of verbal meaning since the Barons of the Exchequer arrived at their famous resolution in *Heydon's Case*. {(1584) 3 Co Rep 7a. See s 301 of this Code.}

Legislation is still about remedying what is thought to be a defect in the law. Even the most 'progressive' legislator, concerned to implement some wholly novel concept of social justice, would be constrained to admit that if the existing law accomodated his ideas there would be no need to change it. No *legal* need that is. Legislation unfortunately possesses a propaganda value also.

Literal construction   Although the term 'purposive construction' is not new, its entry into fashion betokens a swing by the appellate courts away from literal construction. Lord Diplock said in 1975-

> 'If one looks back to the actual decisions of [the House of Lords] on questions of statutory construction over the last 30 years one cannot fail to be struck by the evidence of a trend away from the purely literal towards the purposive construction of statutory provisions.'

{*Carter v Bradbeer* [1975] 3 All ER 158, at p 161.}

The matter was summed up by Lord Diplock in *Jones v Wrotham Park Settled Estates* {[1979] 1 All ER 286, at p 289.}-

'... I am not reluctant to adopt a purposive construction where to apply the literal meaning of the legislative language used would lead to results which would clearly defeat the purposes of the Act. But in doing so the task on which a court of justice is engaged remains one of construction, even where this involves reading into the Act words which are not expressly included in it. *Kammins Ballrooms Co Ltd v Zenith Investments (Torquay) Ltd* {[1971] AC 850.} provides an instance of this; but in that case the three conditions that must be fulfilled in order to justify this course were satisfied. First, it was possible to determine from a consideration of the provisions of the Act read as a whole precisely what the mischief was that it was the purpose of the Act to remedy; secondly, it was apparent that the draftsman and Parliament had by inadvertence overlooked, and so omitted to deal with, an eventuality that required to be dealt with if the purpose of the Act was to be achieved; and thirdly, it was possible to state with certainty what were the additional words that would have been inserted by the draftsman and approved by Parliament had their attention been drawn to the omission before the Bill passed into law. Unless this third condition is fulfilled any attempt by a court of justice to repair the omission in the Act cannot be justified as an exercise of its jurisdiction to determine what is the meaning of a written law which Parliament has passed.'

Lord Diplock's third point is, with respect, overstated. In *R v Schildkamp* {[1971] AC 1.} the House of Lords adopted a purposive-and-strained construction while expressly ruling out any need to formulate the missing words.

Differing 'purposes' The legislative purpose may be stated broadly or narrowly, as needed for the problem of interpretation under examination. At its broadest, the purpose may extend to a number of Acts dealing with the field in question. For example Salmon LJ stated the purpose of the bankruptcy law in these general terms-

'The modern law of bankruptcy has its origins in a number of Victorian statutes which were intended to relieve those in financial difficulties from the burden of debt and the possibilities of loss of liberty in a debtors' prison and to enable them to make a fresh start free from debt. The price they had to pay for these benefits was the surrender to their creditors of all their property save the tools, if any, of their trade and the wearing apparel and bedding of themselves and their families. It was recognised, however, that not all debtors were the victims of misfortune. Some were rogues, some were fools and some were willing to risk other people's money when trying to make their own fortunes. For over a hundred years the law has required the Bankruptcy Court to consider whether the conduct of the bankrupt has been such that the public ought to be protected against his further operations for a period of time or even permanently.'

{*Re Stern (a bankrupt), ex p Keyser Ullmann Ltd v The bankrupt* [1982] 2 All ER 600, at p 605.}

This survey was the prelude to a discussion by Salmon LJ of the specific question whether s 26(7) of the Bankruptcy Act 1914 entitled an opposing creditor at the hearing of an application for the bankrupt's discharge to cross-examine him as of right.

The example illustrates that the concept of legislative purpose is not entirely straightforward. In statutory interpretation the unit of enquiry is usually a single proposition (an 'enactment'). {See s 72 of this Code.} Each enactment has its own limited purpose, to be understood within the larger purpose of the Act containing it - or sometimes within a broader purpose still, when the subject is dealt with by several Acts. Beyond this again is the general purpose of the law as an instrument serving the public welfare. Using the bankruptcy example, we can construct a descending order of purposes as follows-

The purpose of law as an instrument of public welfare

The purpose of the bankruptcy law

The purpose of the Bankruptcy Act 1914

The purpose of s 26 (discharge of bankrupt) of the 1914 Act

The purpose of s 26(7)

Section 26(7) has its own limited purpose, but this partakes to some extent of each of the purposes listed above it.

A further complicating factor is that an Act's purpose can sometimes have quite different aspects. In one sense the purpose of the Bankruptcy Act 1914 is to do the things described in the above dictum of Salmon LJ. In a quite different sense its purpose is simply that indicated by the long title: 'to consolidate the Law relating to Bankruptcy'. Both purposes may be relevant on a point of construction. {As to the significance in relation to interpretation of the fact that the enactment is contained in a consolidation Act see s 232 of this Code.}

Discerning the exact purpose of a particular enactment is often more dificult than discerning the purpose of a whole Act. Moreover exactness may be highly necessary if the point is to be decided correctly.

Example 1   The Treason Act 1695 contained a number of provisions about trials. One said that the prisoner should have a copy of the indictment five days at least 'before the trial'. To determine the precise terminus ad quem of this five-day period it was necessary, as Blackstone perceived, to discern the reasoning behind the enactment: 'that is, upon the true construction of the act, before his arraignment; for then is his time to take any exceptions thereto, by way of plea or demurrer'. {Kerr Bl (4th edn, 1876) iv 362. Cf *Re Daley* [1982] 2 All ER 974 (the moment relevant for determining whether the accused has attained the age entitling him to demand trial by jury is the moment when the court is called on to decide the mode of trial).}

Supervening factor   As always in statutory interpretation, it is necessary, when considering the possibility of applying a purposive construction, to take account of any other applicable criteria as well. The overriding object is to give effect to Parliament's *intention* {See s 98 of this Code.}, and this is unlikely to be to achieve the immediate purpose at no matter what cost. {As to the weighing of interpretative factors see Part VII of this Code.}

It needs to be recognised that contrary purposes of a more general nature may supervene. Parliament is presumed to intend to further the general policy of the law, and to legislate in the knowledge that if it does not expressly provide to the contrary the accepted interpretative criteria will be applied. {For the interpretative criteria see Part VI of this Code.}

Example 2 In *A-G of New Zealand v Ortiz* {[1982] 3 All ER 432.} it was held at first instance that the phrase 'shall be forfeited' in s 12(2) of the New Zealand Historic Articles Act 1962 was ambiguous, and that a purposive construction should be applied to decide whether forfeiture was automatic or depended upon seizure of the historic article in question. The decision was overruled on appeal because, though right as far as it went, it failed to take into account a further (and overriding) criterion. This was the rule of international law which limits the extra-territorial effect of legislation relating to property rights. {As to the implied application of such rules see s 342 of this Code.}

Deeming provisions Acts often deem things to be what they are not. In construing a deeming provision it is necessary to bear in mind the legislative purpose.

Example 3 Section 70(2) of the Rent Act 1977 says that in determining a 'fair rent' for a dwelling-house-

'... it shall be assumed that the number of persons seeking to become tenants of similar dwelling-houses in the locality on the terms (other than those relating to rent) of the regulated tenancy is not substantially greater than the number of such dwelling-houses in the locality which are available for letting on such terms.'

This may be summarised as: in fixing the fair rent assume there is neither a surplus nor a shortage of similar accomodation in the locality.

This apparently simple piece of make-believe is subject to a trap the draftsman did not foresee. Valuers fix hypothetical rents by reference to the actual rents prevailing in the neighbourhood. Section 70(2) could be read as requiring the valuer, in looking at these actual rents for comparison, to assume that they were fixed under the hypothetical conditions, that is with an even balance between available accomodation and would-be tenants.

Such a reading would produce a result exactly opposite to the one intended by Parliament. The scarcity rents would be treated as the norm. In *Western Heritable Investment Co Ltd v Husband* {[1983] 3 All ER 65.}, the House of Lords was called upon to correct this very mistake (made by the Extra Division of the Inner House of the Court of Session in Scotland under the corresponding provision (s 42) of the Rent (Scotland) Act 1971).

314. Purposive-and-literal construction

A purposive-and-literal construction is one which follows the literal meaning of the enactment where that meaning is in accordance with the legislative purpose.

661

COMMENTARY

An interpretation must in the last resort either be literal or strained. {See s 85 of this Code.} The previous section stated that a purposive construction must be either purposive-and-literal or purposive-and-strained. The third type of construction is non-purposive-and-literal. {See below in this commentary.}

The purposive-and-literal is the commonest construction, for usually a literal construction and a purposive construction lead to the same result. For example, Lord Diplock concluded in *Suffolk County Council v Mason* {[1979] 2 All ER 369, at p 372.} that a literal construction of provisions relating to footpaths in the National Parks and Access to the Countryside Act 1949 produced the same answer as a purposive construction.

This correspondence is not surprising; indeed it is what we would expect. Parliament, having a certain purpose, naturally seeks to express this in the words used. If it did otherwise to any great extent, the legislature would be using an inefficient method. {See s 137 of this Code.}

A construction is purposive-and-literal (a) where the literal meaning is clear and reflects the purpose or (b) where the literal meaning is grammatically ambiguous and one of the possible grammatical meanings reflects the purpose.

Ambiguity   The concept of literal construction involves treating both the possible constructions of a grammatically ambiguous enactment as 'literal' meanings. {See s 91 of this Code.} Here the legislative purpose is likely to be decisive in determining which of the ambiguous meanings to adopt, and it seems proper to refer to this also as a 'purposive' construction.

While the classification we have used gives the essence of the matter, its clarity is obscured by the fact that there is likely to be doubt and difference of opinion about (a) whether a particular construction is literal or strained and (b) what the legislative purpose really is.

Example 1   In *R v Cuthbertson* {[1980] 2 All ER 401.} the House of Lords held that it would be a 'strained' construction to say that choses in action came within a statutory power so worded as to enable the court to order *'anything . . . to be forfeited and either destroyed or dealt with in such other manner as the court may order'*. {Emphasis added.} The decision amounted to saying that a chose in action was not 'anything'. A differently-constituted court might well have held that it would be a strained construction to hold that a chose in action did *not* come within the power.

Example 2   It may be thought that the natural meaning of 'side-car' in relation to motor-cycles is an appliance designed to carry a passenger. In *Keen v Parker* {[1976] Crim LR 71.} it was held that, within the meaning of a road traffic regulation requiring the fitting of a side-car where the driver held only a provisional licence, an appliance designed for the carriage of a window cleaner's ladders and tools was a 'side-car'. This was because the purpose of the regulation was to ensure the additional stability provided by a third wheel. Such stability was equally given whether the intended burden was a human being or goods.

It could be argued either that this was a strained interpretation or that the term 'side-car' was ambiguous. Certainly some perspicacity was required to detect the *precise* purpose of the regulation. But in this case it was the precise purpose that mattered. {As to the problems that arise where the purpose is not clear see pp 670–671 below.}

Example 3 Section 76(1) of the Local Government Act 1933 required a councillor to declare his interest and refrain from voting if he had 'any pecuniary interest, direct or indirect, in any contract or proposed contract or other matter' which was under consideration at a meeting at which he was present. In *Rands v Oldroyd* {[1959] 1 QB 204.} the question arose whether the phrase 'or other matter' was to be construed as general or as limited by the *ejusdem generis* canon of construction to matters akin to contracts. {As to this canon see ss 378 to 385 of this Code.} Lord Parker CJ held that, having regard to the fact that the object of the enactment was to prevent conflicts between duty and interest, the phrase should not be narrowly construed. He said-

> 'Whereas, of course, a consideration of the mischief aimed at does not enable the court to construe the words in a wider sense than they appear, it at least means that the court would not be astute to cut down words otherwise wide merely because this was a penal statute.'

{P 212. See also *Quazi v Quazi* [1979] 3 All ER 897, *per* Lord Diplock at p 903.}

Example 4 Section 71 of the Finance Act 1952 provided an exemption from estate duty where the deceased 'died from a wound' if the wound was inflicted when the deceased was on active service against an enemy. In *Barty-King v Ministry of Defence* {[1979] 2 All ER 80.} it was argued by the defendants that dying 'from a wound' meant dying 'from a wound which was the direct cause of death'. Finding, in favour of the plaintiff, that it meant dying 'from a wound which was *a* cause of death', May J said 'if there were any ambiguity . . . the purpose and nature of the legislation seem to me to require a benevolent interpretation in favour of the estate of the deceased. . .' {P 82.}

Example 5 *Post Office v Oxford City Council* {[1980] 2 All ER 439.} concerned the question of whether a disused garage comprising a car showroom, repair shops, petrol filling area etc was subject to a rates surcharge or fell within an exemption for 'factories'. The word 'factory' was ambiguous here because, although a commercial garage is not normally thought of as a factory, this one was registered as such under the Factories Acts (which were not *in pari materia* with the rating legislation). Rejecting the plea for exemption, Stephenson LJ said-

> 'Looking . . . at the real nature of these premises and at the object of the statutory exemption I agree that they are more similar to a shop than to a factory and are constructed mainly for commercial purposes . . .'

{P 443. Shops did not have rating exemption.}

Example 6 This concerns a draftsman's misuse of the definite article (which is properly used only when the substantive to which it is attached has been identified in terms which ensure that it cannot have more than one object). Section 140 of the Law of Property Act 1925 defines 'lessee' as including a person deriving title under a lessee. This produces the result that in relation to any assigned lease where the original lessee is still in existence there must be at least *two* 'lessees'.

Section 146 of the Act provides that forfeiture for breach of covenant cannot be enforced until the lessor serves a notice on 'the' lessee. If the covenant alleged to have been broken is one against assignment without consent there are likely to be two 'lessees'. Upon which of them must the notice be served?

In *Old Grovebury Manor Farm v W Seymour Plant Sales and Hire Ltd (No 2)* {[1979] 3 All ER 504.} the Court of Appeal held that the notice must be served on the 'lessee' who was the assignee of the lease, since the general purpose of s 146 was to afford a cooling-off period during which the person at risk because of the forfeiture could come to terms with the lessor.

Obscure enactments   It could be said that the enactment in the previous example was grammatically defective in using the definite article when there were two or more objects. This would make it a semantically obscure enactment within our terminology. {See s 90 of this Code.} The corrected version would refer to 'one of the lessees' instead of 'the lessee', and would then fall to be treated, in accordance with section 87 of the Code, as ambiguous in its indication of which of the two lessees was to receive the notice. The final step would then be to apply, in the way indicated above, the procedure for using purposive construction to resolve ambiguity.

Non-purposive-and-literal construction   In the sense used in British law, purposive construction is an almost invariable requirement. But a non-purposive construction may be necessary, because unavoidable, where there is insufficient indication of (a) what the legislative purpose is or (b) just how it is to be carried out. Thus in *IRC v Hinchy* {[1960] AC 748.} Lord Keith of Avonholm declined to apply a purposive construction of an income tax enactment because, as he said, the court could not take upon itself the task of working out an assessment in a different way. {P 781.} For a further example see *IRC v Ayrshire Employers Mutual Insurance Association Ltd.* {[1946] 1 All ER 637.}

Non-purposive construction may also be necessary where the court considers a predictable construction is required. {For predictable construction see s 130 of this Code.} Apart from these cases, it is only where the literal (non-purposive) meaning is too strong to be overborne that the court will apply a non-purposive-and-literal construction. {See Example 166.4.}

315. Purposive-and-strained construction

A purposive-and-strained construction is one which applies a strained meaning where the literal meaning is not in accordance with the legislative purpose. The term 'purposive construction' is usually intended by judges to bear this meaning.

COMMENTARY

An interpretation must in the last resort either be literal or strained. {See s 85 of this Code.} Section 313 stated that a purposive construction must be either purposive-and-literal or purposive-and-strained. The third type of construction, as explained in the commentary to the preceding section {P 664 above.}, is non-purposive-and-literal.

This section of the Code describes what is usually meant by judges when they refer to a purposive construction. There are many examples throughout this book of the application of this principle. Here are two more. {See also Example 311.2.}

Example 1 The famous case of *Liversidge v Anderson* {[1942] AC 206.} concerned the interpretation of the wartime power conferred on the Home Secretary to intern certain persons if he had reasonable cause to believe that specified adverse circumstances existed in relation to them. The question for the House of Lords was whether the existence or non-existence of such reasonable cause was a question of fact into which the court could inquire, or whether the words should be construed as meaning in effect 'if he *thinks* he has reasonable cause to believe ...'

By four to one, the House found for the latter meaning. In a celebrated dissenting judgment, Lord Atkin protested that this was 'a strained construction put on words with the effect of giving an uncontrolled power of imprisonment to the minister'. {P 244.} The other law lords found that this strained construction gave effect to the purpose of the regulation, and held that applying it was justified.

Viscount Maugham said the regulation conferring the power should be approached with an intent to 'prefer a construction which will carry into effect the plain intention of those responsible ... rather than one which will defeat that intention'. {P 219.} Lord Macmillan said-

> 'The purpose of the regulation is to ensure public safety, and it is right so to interpret emergency legislation as to promote rather than to defeat its efficacy for the defence of the realm. That is in accordance with a general rule applicable to the interpretation of all statutes or statutory regulations in peace time as well as in war time ...' {P 252.}

Example 2 In *Kammins Ballroom Ltd v Zenith Investments (Torquay) Ltd* {[1971] AC 850.} there was what Lord Diplock called a 'closely balanced division of opinion' {P 879.} in the Court of Appeal and House of Lords as to whether a literal or strained meaning should be given to words in s 29(3) of the Landlord and Tenant Act 1954. These said that no application by a tenant for a new tenancy 'shall be entertained' unless specified time limits had been observed. The question was whether the landlord, for whose benefit the time limits were imposed, could effectively waive the requirement despite its mandatory wording. It was held by a majority of the Lords that he could. Lord Diplock said {P 880.}-

> 'Upon the literal approach, semantics and the rules of syntax alone could never justify the conclusion that the words "*No* application ... *shall be* entertained *unless*" {The emphasis is Lord Diplock's.} meant that some applications should be entertained notwithstanding that neither of the conditions which follow the word 'unless' was fulfilled ... It can be justified only upon the assumption that the draftsman of the Act omitted to state in any words he used in the subsection an exception to the absolute prohibition to which Parliament must have intended it to be subject.'

After analysing the legislative purpose, Lord Diplock reached the conclusion that this assumption concerning an omission by the draftsman should be made; and that a strained construction was therefore necessary.

Courts often strain reality in order to disguise what is really a purposive-and-strained construction as a literal one.

Example 3 In *Kaye v Tyrrell* (1984) *The Times* 9 July the defendant drove through a red light, stopped, and changed seats with his passenger. A few minutes later he was required to take a breath test as being a person who was 'driving or attempting to drive' within the meaning of s 8(1) of the Road Traffic Act 1972.

Held The requirement was properly made since what began when the defendant drove through the red light was a single chain of events.

Here it is obvious that when the requirement was made the defendant, then seated in the passenger seat, was in a literal sense neither driving nor attempting to drive. The court held the contrary by artificially prolonging the period when he was doing so.

Advocates often fail to urge a purposive-and-strained construction when it would help their case to do so. {See for example *Alexander v Tonkin* [1979] 2 All ER 1009.}

316. Statements of purpose

To fulfil its function, a statement of purpose needs to be on the following lines-

> 'The purpose of [*Act or part of Act*] is to remedy the defect in the law consisting of [*description of the mischief*] by amending the law so as to [*description of the remedy*].

A statement of purpose (whether on these lines or not, and whether comprehensive or not) may be found either in the Act itself or in the judgment of a court devising the statement as an aid to construction. When found in the Act, it may be in the long title or preamble, or in a purpose clause or recital.

COMMENTARY

Long title   As to the long title see s 271 of this Code.

Preamble   As to the preamble see s 272 of this Code.

Purpose clause   As to purpose clauses see s 273 of this Code.

Recital   As to recitals see s 274 of this Code.

It is important to distinguish the purpose itself from the various ways in which it is or might be expressed or described. A full statement of the purpose would require a minute setting-out of all aspects of the mischief and the remedy. This would usually be impractical, and the tendency is to devise a brief formula. Wherever it is found, the reader of the statement needs to bear in mind that it *is*

a brief formula and not a full account. Like any summary, it is liable to mislead
by its incompleteness.

Statements of purpose in the Act   Examples of passages by which Acts identify
the mischief with which they deal are given in Part XIV of this Code. Such
passages amount to partial statements of purpose, the rest being derivable from
the provisions of the Act setting out the remedy.

In modern British public Acts, which usually lack a preamble and do not
contain a section designed as a statement of the purpose of the Act, the long title
is often the only guide. This is normally limited to summarising the remedy, but
the mischief and overall purpose may be indicated by implication.

Example 1   The long title of the Obscene Publications Act 1964 is-

'An Act to strengthen the law for preventing the publication for gain
of obscene matter and the publication of things intended for the
production of obscene matter.'

By implication we gather that the mischief consisted in a weakness of the legal
provisions against obscenity. The nature of the remedy is not indicated. We
gather that whatever it is it will strengthen the law, but that is all. To learn more
we must read the Act.

Example 2   The long title of the Corporate Bodies' Contracts Act 1960 is-

'An Act to amend the law governing the making of contracts by or on
behalf of bodies corporate; and for connected purposes.'

This is even less informative. The nature of the mischief is not even hinted at;
nor is the nature of the remedy. This long title is useless as a statement of
purpose.

Such is often the case with long titles. This is not surprising since they are not
designed to be statements of purpose. {For the nature of the long title see s 271
of this Code.} So we are forced to accept that it is seldom possible to find a
satisfactory statement of the purpose of a modern British Act within the Act
itself. {As to the reasons for this, and the use of purpose clauses by some
Commonwealth parliaments, see Bennion *Statute Law* (2nd edn, 1983) pp 98-
100.}

On the other hand Parliament does sometimes explain the purpose of a
particular section.

Example 3   A well-known example of a legislative statement of purpose is found
in s 83 of the Fires Prevention (Metropolis) Act 1774, which is still in force. The
opening recital tells us that the section was enacted-

' . . . in order to deter and hinder ill-minded persons from wilfully
setting their house or houses or other buildings on fire with a view to
gaining to themselves the insurance money, whereby the lives and
fortunes of many families may be lost or endangered . . .'

Example 4   Section 73(1) of the Road Traffic Act 1960 announces that it is
enacted 'with a view to protecting the public against the risks which arise in

cases where the drivers of motor vehicles are suffering from excessive fatigue
. . .' {For a similar provision see Wildlife and Countryside Act 1981 s 39(1).}

Statements of purpose by judges   Whether or not he sets it out in his judgment, a
judge deciding a point of interpretation can scarcely avoid arriving at some
conclusion about the purpose of the enactment under enquiry - and indeed the
purpose of the provisions of which it forms part. Even the literal meaning
cannot safely be arrived at by treating the provision as being in a vacuum. As
Niall MacCormick says-

' . . . the 'obviousness' of an interpretation of enacted words may,
perhaps must, depend on understanding of the principle or principles
which are supposed to inform the enactment.'

{*Legal Reasoning and Legal Theory* (1978) p 205.}
   When attempting to frame a statement of purpose, the judge is likely to
confine it to the enactment under enquiry in the case before him. Sometimes he
frames the statement by reference to an ancillary component such as the long
title or preamble.

Example 5   In a case concerning the National Parks and Access to the
Countryside Act 1949, Lord Diplock said-

'The purposes for which the Act was passed are set out in the long
title. Those that are relevant to the instant appeal are: ". . . to make
further provision for the recording, creation, maintenance and
improvement of public paths and for securing access to open country,
and to amend the law relating to rights of way . . ."'

{*Suffolk County Council v Mason* [1979] 2 All ER 369, at p 372.}
   We see that, like most long titles, this one serves but inadequately as a
statement of purpose. It tells us very little about either the mischief or the nature
of the remedy. A preamble, where used, may provide more help.

Example 6   Lord Diplock had recourse to the preamble in a case under the
Recognition of Divorces and Legal Separations Act 1971. He said-

'The purpose for which the . . . Act was passed is declared by the
preamble to be with a view to the ratification by the United Kingdom
of the Recognition Convention and for other purposes.'

{*Quazi v Quazi* [1979] 3 All ER 897, at p 903. For the juridical nature of a
preamble see s 272 of this Code.}
   This shows that in the case of an Act ratifying an international convention it
may be possible to express the purpose concisely, even though the effect is
merely to transfer the problem of discovering the essential reasons from the Act
to the convention. Sometimes a judge uses the omission of a matter from the
long title or preamble as a ground for concluding that Parliament did not intend
to cover it. This may be unwise.

Example 7   In *Gold Star Publications v Director of Public Prosecutions* {[1981] 2
All ER 257.}, the House of Lords were asked to decide whether the forfeiture
provisions of the Obscene Publications Act 1959 extended to publications

intended for export. In a dissenting judgment, Lord Simon of Glaisdale said of the argument that Parliament intended by the Act to inhibit international trade in pornographic material-

> 'But, if so high-minded an objective had really been one of the purposes of the 1959 Act, it would certainly have been stated in the long title. Its absence is clamant when it comes to a purposive construction of the enacting provsions'. {P 260-1.}

Lord Simon's colleagues appeared not to agree with this inference, which may be thought to put more faith in the drafting of the long title than the practice warrants. {See pp 575–576 above. Having been concerned in the drafting of the 1959 Act, the present author can confirm that Lord Simon's colleagues were right.}

Often a judge will essay his own summary of the purpose, without bringing in the long title or preamble.

Example 8 In a 1930 case on the Landlord and Tenant Act 1927 the first Viscount Hailsham approved one of the opposing constructions advanced because, as he put it-

> 'Any other construction would, it seems to me, defeat the plain purpose of the Act, which obviously was to provide that in the circumstances defined in the Act the tenant should have a right to continue to carry on his trade or business in the premises in the legal sense in which he was carrying them on under the lease for which he seeks . . . renewal.'

{*Whitley v Stumbles* [1930] AC 544, at p 547.}

Example 9 In a 1949 Rent Act case, Lord Evershed MR said-

> ' . . . it appears to me that the general conception (which I of course entirely accept) that the [Rent] Acts are designed to protect occupants of dwelling-houses within the Acts against eviction must be qualified to this extent - against eviction at the suit of persons who may fairly and properly be described as landlords of the occupants [rather than mortgagees].'

{*Dudley and District Building Society v Emerson* [1949] Ch 707, at p 715.}

Example 10 In another Rent Act case Scrutton LJ said-

> ' . . . the fundamental principle of the [1920 Act is] that it . . . is to protect a resident in a dwelling house, not to protect a person who is not a resident in a dwelling house, but is making money by sub-letting it.'

{*Haskins v Lewis* [1931] 2 KB 1, at p 14.}

Note here that (as the previous example illustrates) what Scrutton LJ describes as 'the fundamental principle' is in fact but one of a number of principles underlying the Rent Acts. It was however the only relevant principle in the case before him.

Example 11   In a case concerning s 54 of the Companies Act 1948, Scarman LJ said 'the section must have been enacted to protect company funds and the interests of shareholders as well as creditors'. {*Wallersteiner v Moir* [1974] 1 WLR 991, at p 1032.} He went on: 'I do not agree with the dictum of Harman J in *Essex Aero Ltd v Cross* {[1961] Court of Appeal Transcript 388.} to the effect that the section was enacted not for the company's protection but for that of its creditors'. {Ibid.}

Example 12   In a case on s 7 of the Bankers' Books Evidence Act 1879 Lord Lane CJ said-

> 'The purpose of the provision is unquestionable. It is that to save bankers from the inconvenience of having their books and their staff in courts for the purposes of supplying evidence, it shall be possible for the police officers concerned to obtain an order from the court, and by virtue of that order to be at liberty to inspect the accounts and take notes from them in the bank. Then when the trial comes on the bank will be undisturbed in its business. That is the purpose of the section.'

{*R v Marlborough Street Magistrates' Court Metropolitan Stipendiary Magistrate, ex p Simpson* (1980) 70 Cr App R 291, at p 293.}

The last example is exceptional. Under the British system judges rarely attempt elaborate and comprehensive statements of purpose. They say what seems to them enough to deal with the point at issue, often summarising lengthy and complex provisions in a phrase. Thus we find the purpose of enactments imposing an elaborate system of import duties summed up by a simple reference to 'protection'. {*Newman Manufacturing Co v Marrable* [1931] 2 KB 297. Cf *Powell Lane Manufacturing Co v Putnam* [1931] 2 KB 305.}

317. Where purpose unknown or doubtful

Where the court is unable to find out the purpose of an enactment, or is doubtful as to its purpose, the court is unlikely to depart from the literal meaning.

COMMENTARY

It is apparent from the cases that there is often doubt about the legislative purpose. If the object sought to be achieved by Parliament in passing an Act is uncertain, this is bound to lead to uncertainty in the construction of the Act.

The cause of such uncertainty in modern British Acts usually lies in the absence of any indication of the precise nature and extent of the mischief with which Parliament intended to deal. {See s 306 of this Code.} Our way is to state that the law shall be so, but not why it shall be so.

This is because we legislate piecemeal; and the policy is not thoroughly and consistently thought out and applied. Where it is thought out on one matter, the way it is thought out is unlikely to fit the way it was thought out (perhaps some years earlier) in a neighbouring area. So the law presents a confused appearance.

This is a price which it seems we are forced to pay for the advantages of representative parliamentary democracy. A dictatorship, if it thinks it necessary or worth while, can equip itself with a more logical set of laws. This does not mean that improvement is not possible within our system. {As to the deleterious effects of the British system in the area of industrial injury legislation see P S Atiyah *Accidents, Compensation and the Law* (2nd edn, 1975), pp 146-150.} See also s 310 of this Code.

318. Judicial acceptance of legislator's purpose

It is the duty of the court to accept the purpose decided on by Parliament although disagreeing with it. This applies even where the court considers the result unjust, provided it is satisfied that Parliament really did intend that result.

COMMENTARY

It is fundamental to our modern constitution that the judiciary owe a duty of loyalty to Parliament. Their function is faithfully to carry out what Parliament has decreed. The criteria developed to guide interpretation are designed only to settle doubt as to legislative intention. Where the intention is plain, it must be implemented.

Obviously a particular judge may find the policy of an enactment not to his personal liking. It is axiomatic that he must resolutely thrust aside such considerations when arriving at his decision.

What may not be so obvious is that the judge, once he feels certain of the intention, must also put aside more general considerations. An enactment may strike him as on any view unjust. That cannnot affect his duty. Parliament does sometimes do unjust things.

Example 1 In *Wicks v Firth* {[1982] 2 All ER 9.} the Court of Appeal, against its inclination, felt compelled to hold that s 61(1) of the Finance Act 1976 rendered liable to tax scholarships awarded by a company to children of its employees. Oliver LJ said: 'That is quite clearly the purpose and it is not for this court to question or to evaluate the social justification for the legislation'. {P 14.} Watkins LJ indicated that he concurred, adding 'I derive no pleasure from saying so'. {P 20.}

Example 2 The notorious s 25 of the Matrimonial Causes Act 1973 provided that on a dissolution of marriage the parties were to be placed, so far as practicable, in the financial position they would have been in if the marriage had not broken down. In *Potter v Potter* {[1982] 3 All ER 321.} the Court of Appeal awarded a divorced wife a lump sum. Ormrod LJ said that, but for s 25, 'I would have no doubt that this case was not a case for a lump sum at all'. {P 326.}

It is clear that the court, while loyally applying s 25, felt it produced an unjust result. The section did in fact import the test of injustice as a restriction on its operation, *but only in relation to matrimonial misconduct.* No such misconduct was present in the case, so the court felt compelled by its duty of obedience to Parliament to make what it considered to be an unjust order. Parliament had clearly indicated its opinion that, in the absence of misconduct, it could not be unjust to preserve the pre-divorce financial allocation for however long a period after the divorce. Outside the extreme case, a question of whether injustice arises or not is one of opinion. Parliament had made its opinion clear, and that ended the matter.

This is an example of the application of the principle that where the court has no doubt that Parliament *really intended* an 'adverse' meaning it cannot properly apply a strained construction. If a court were free in such cases to reject Parliament's intention and substitute its own, the law would vary according to which judge happened to try the case. It would be a matter, as Lord Wilberforce has said, of *quot judices tot sententiae*. {*James Buchanan & Co Ltd v Babco Forwarding & Shipping (UK) Ltd* [1977] 3 All ER 1048, at p 1060.}   This phrase is a variant of the saying by Terence: *Quot homines tot sententiae; suus cuique mos* (So many men, so many opinions; his own a law to each). {For a counter argument see Shael Herman, 'Quot judices tot sententiae: A study of the English reaction to continental interpretive techniques' (1981) 1 LS 165. See also the remarks below on the Continental version of purposive construction (s 320 of this Code).} The position was summed up by Lord Scarman in *Duport Steels Ltd v Sirs* {[1980] 1 All ER 529, at p 551.}-

> ' . . . in the field of statute law the judge must be obedient to the will of Parliament as expressed in its enactments. In this field Parliament makes and unmakes the law [and] the judge's duty is to interpret and to apply the law, not to change it to meet the judge's idea of what justice requires. Interpretation does, of course, imply in the interpreter a power of choice where differing constructions are possible. But our law requires the judge to choose the construction which in his judgment best meets the legislative purpose of the enactment. If the result be unjust but inevitable, the judge may say so and invite Parliament to reconsider its provision. But he must not deny the statute. Unpalatable statute law may not be disregarded or rejected, merely because it is unpalatable. Only if a just result can be achieved without violating the legislative purpose of the statute may the judge select the construction which best suits his idea of what justice requires.'

The position is different when the result that seems to the judge unjust was not truly intended by Parliament, or in other words was not truly part of the legislative purpose. {As to such cases see s 128 of this Code.}

319. Purposive construction not excluded for taxing etc Acts

Particular types of Acts (for example taxing Acts) are not excluded from strained-and-purposive construction. The presumption as to purposive construction rule applies to them as to other Acts.

COMMENTARY

Judges have sometimes said that certain types of Act, for example taxing Acts, are excluded from purposive construction. It is submitted that such dicta are contrary to principle and cannot be relied on today. The paramount principle of construction is that the intention of Parliament should be implemented. {See s 98 of this Code.} Lord Russell of Killowen CJ said-

> 'I see no reason why any special canons of construction should be applied to any Act of Parliament, and I know of no authority for

saying that a taxing Act is to be construed differently from any other
Act. The duty of the court is, in my opinion, in all cases the same,
whether the Act to be construed relates to taxation or any other
subject, *viz* to give effect to the intention of the legislature . . .'

{*A-G v Carlton Bank* [1899] 2 QB 158, at p 164. See also *Lord Howard de
Walden v IRC* [1942] 1 KB 389, *per* Lord Greene MR at pp 397-8.}

A modern case where the House of Lords gave a purposive-and-strained
construction to a taxing Act is *Luke v IRC* {[1963] AC 557.}, where Lord Reid
said-

'To apply the words literally is to defeat the obvious purpose of the
legislation and produce a wholly unreasonable result. To achieve the
obvious intention and produce a reasonable result we must do some
violence to the words.' {P 577.}

In a more recent case Lord Wilberforce said in relation to taxing Acts-

'A subject is only to be taxed on clear words, not on 'intendment' or
on the 'equity' of an Act . . . What are 'clear words' is to be
ascertained on normal principles; *these do not confine the courts to
literal interpretation*. There may, indeed should, be considered the
context and scheme of the relevant Act as a whole, and *its purpose
may, indeed should, be regarded* . . .'

{*W T Ramsay Ltd v Inland Revenue Comrs* [1981] 1 All ER 865, at p 871
(emphasis added). See also *IRC v Wesleyan and General Assurance Society* [1946]
2 All ER 749, *per* Lord Greene MR at p 751; *Mangin v IRC* [1971] AC 739, *per*
Lord Donovan at p 746.}

The true principle applying to taxing Acts and other onerous enactments is
that persons should not be subjected to a detriment on the authority of a
doubtful law. {See s 129 and Part XIII of this Code.}

320. British and European versions of purposive construction

The British doctrine of purposive construction is far more literalist than
the European variety, and permits a strained construction only in
comparatively rare cases.

COMMENTARY

It will be seen from the preceding provisions of this Part that the version of
purposive construction applied by British courts does not require or permit a
wholesale jettisoning of the grammatical meaning. Since the purpose is mainly
to be gathered from the langauge used, it must by definition broadly conform to
that language. An animal cannot be different from its skin.

By contrast, the continental version of purposive construction enables the
legislative animal to be skinned alive. This version was thus described by Lord
Denning-

'[European judges] adopt a method which they call in English by
strange words - at any rate they were strange to me - the "schematic
and teleological" method of interpretation. It is not really so alarming

as it sounds. All it means is that the judges do not go by the literal meaning of the words or by the grammatical structure of the sentence. They go by the design or purpose . . . behind it. When they come upon a situation which is *to their minds* within the spirit - but not the letter - of the legislation, they solve the problem by looking at the design and purpose of the legislature - at the effect it was sought to achieve. They then interpret the legislation so as to produce the desired effect. This means they fill in gaps, quite unashamedly, without hesitation. They ask simply: what is the sensible way of dealing with this situation so as to give effect to the presumed purpose of the legislation? *They lay down the law* accordingly.'

{*James Buchanan & Co Ltd v Babco Forwarding & Shipping (UK) Ltd* [1977] 1 All ER 518, at p 522 (emphasis added).}

Lord Denning's reference to the continental way of following the spirit rather than the letter may be contrasted with T S Eliot's sardonic version of the English lawyer's motto: 'The spirit killeth, the letter giveth life'. {Cited by Lord Hailsham LC in *The British Legal System Today* (1983 Hamlyn Lectures) p 49.}

Lord Denning tried hard to persuade the House of Lords to adopt this Continental form of purposive construction, but failed. British lawyers have to reckon with it only where Community law is engrafted on their own.

PART XVI

Legislative Presumptions: Construction against 'Absurdity'

Introduction to Part XVI This Part gives details of the presumption, set out in s 141 of the Code, that Parliament does not intend 'absurd' consequences to flow from the application of its Act. This is one aspect of the presumption favouring a consequential construction, which is described in s 140.

In this context 'absurd' means contrary to sense and reason. The presumption leads to avoidance by the interpreter of six types of undesirable consequence. These are: an unworkable or impracticable result (s 321), an inconvenient result (s 322), an anomalous or illogical result (s 323), a futile or pointless result (s 324), an artificial result (s 325), and a disproportionate counter-mischief (s 326).

321. Avoiding an unworkable or impracticable result

The court seeks to avoid a construction of an enactment that produces an unworkable or impracticable result, since this is unlikely to have been intended by Parliament. Sometimes, however, there are overriding reasons for applying such a construction, for example where it appears that Parliament really intended it or the literal meaning is too strong.

COMMENTARY

Inconvenience For the case where the consequences of a particular construction would be merely inconvenient rather than unworkable or impracticable see s 322 of this Code.

Unworkable or impracticable result Parliament is taken not to intend the carrying out of its enactments to be unworkable or impracticable, so the court will be slow to find in favour of a construction that leads to these consequences. {See Examples 10.10, 114.2 and 323.19.}

Where the enactment is grammatically ambiguous, the court favours a meaning that is workable even where it is grammatically less apt. {As to grammatical ambiguity see ss 87 to 89 of this Code.} As Lord Reid said of the Building (Safety, Health and Welfare) Regulations 1948 {SI 1948/1145.}-

'If the language is capable of more than one interpretation, we ought to discard the more natural meaning if it leads to an unreasonable result, and adopt that interpretation which leads to a reasonably practicable result.'

{*Gill v Donald Humberstone & Co Ltd* [1963] 1 WLR 929, at p 933.}

Lord Reid prefaced this remark by pointing out that here the regulations in question were addressed to practical people and should therefore be construed in the light of practical considerations 'rather than by a meticulous comparison of the language of their various provisions'. {An example of the way judges prefer to minimise the significance of their departures from the most obvious literal meaning.}

Strained construction   We have the authority of Lord Reid for the statement that, to avoid an unworkable result, a strained construction may be justified even where the enactment is not grammatically ambiguous. {As to strained construction see ss 92 to 97 of this Code.} Lord Reid said in *Federal Steam Navigation Co v Department of Trade and Industry* {[1974] 2 All ER 97, at p 100.} that cases where it has properly been held that one word can be struck out of a statute and another substituted include the case where without such substitution the provision would be 'unworkable'.

Clearly this is not the only type of strained construction which is so permissible: to substitute one word for another does not differ in kind from other types of adjustment of the statutory wording.

Example 1   Section 1(2) of the Courts (Emergency Powers) Act 1943 required the court's leave before 'the levying of distress'. In *Watkinson v Hollington* {[1943] 2 All ER 573. See p 577 above.} the question arose of whether this covered the distraining of cattle *damage feasant*. On a literal interpretation it clearly did, but the Court of Appeal rejected that construction on the ground that it would be wholly impractical to obtain the leave of the court before seizing trespassing cattle. {T F T Plucknett observed that in this case the court, in its summary rejection of the plain literal meaning, went back to Edward II and spoke 'with the authentic voice of Bereford': 'Ellesmere on Statutes' (1944) 60 LQR 242 at p 247.}

Example 2   Section 16 of the Factories Act 1937 required the fences guarding dangerous parts of machines to be 'constantly maintained and kept in position while the parts . . . are *in motion* or use'. {Emphasis added.} In *Richard Thomas and Baldwins Ltd v Cummings* {[1955] AC 321.} the House of Lords considered a case where a worker was injured while repairing an unfenced machine. In order to effect the repair it was necessary for the worker to turn the machine by hand, and the repair could not have been done with the fence in position. *Held* The statutory requirement did not apply to repairs in these circumstances.

Lord Reid, dismissing the respondent's contention that since the machine was undoubtedly 'in motion' the requirement applied, said that such a construction would render the repairing of the machine impracticable. Lord Reid went on-

> 'The fact that the interpretation for which the respondent contends would lead to so unreasonable a result is, in my opinion, sufficient to require the more limited meaning of 'in motion' to be adopted unless there is very strong objection to it, and none was suggested. It is true that the Factories Act is a remedial statute and one should therefore lean towards giving a wide interpretation to it, but that does not justify interpreting an *ambiguous* provision in a way which leads to quite unreasonable results.'

{P 334. Emphasis added.}

It will be noticed that Lord Reid refers to the provision as 'ambiguous'. This is not grammatical ambiguity, since there is no doubt about the literal meaning of 'in motion'. The construction adopted by the House of Lords was a strained construction, though in accordance with judicial practice and preference Lord Reid employed the less provocative (if also less accurate) description that suggests a choice between grammatical alternatives.

Logical impossibility An obvious justification for strained construction arises where the literal meaning presents a logical impossibility.

Example 3 Section 54 of the Public Health Act 1875 said that where a local authority 'supply water' within their district they have power to lay mains. Since the authority could not practically satisfy the condition of 'supplying' water unless they first had mains to carry it in, the power was held to operate as soon as the authority had *undertaken* to supply water. {*Jones v Conway Water Supply* [1893] 2 Ch 603. See Example 285.1.}

Unreasonable dilemma A strained construction will also be necessary where the literal meaning places persons who are subject to the Act in a dilemma so unreasonable that Parliament cannot be supposed to have intended it.

Example 4 Section 28 of the Town Police Clauses Act 1847 lists a large number of street offences and imposes on a constable the duty to take into custody 'any person who within his view commits any such offence'. Neglect of this duty was made a criminal offence by s 16 of the Act until that section was repealed by the Police Act 1964. {S 64(3) and Sch 10 Part I.}

In *Wills v Bowley* {[1982] 2 All ER 654. See Example 162.1.} the appellant was arrested under s 28 for an offence of which she was later acquitted. She was however convicted of assaulting the constables who arrested her. On a literal construction of the power of arrest she was not guilty of the assault because the arrest was unlawful in view of the fact that she had not in fact committed the offence in relation to which the duty to arrest was imposed. On her appeal to the House of Lords against the assault conviction: *Held* The conviction would be affirmed since the power of arrest must be taken to include the case where the constable honestly believed, on reasonable grounds based on his own observation, that an offence had been committed. Lord Bridge said-

> 'It would seem to me to be quite ridiculous to construe these provisions in such a way as to force on the constable a choice between the risk of making an unlawful arrrest and the risk of committing a criminal neglect of duty. That would be to impale him on the horns of an impossible dilemma.'

{P 681. See also *Bernard v Gorman* [1941] AC 378 (power to detain 'the offender' included a suspected offender); *Wiltshire v Barrett* [1966] 1 QB 312 (power to arrest 'a person committing an offence' included a person apparently committing an offence); *Trebeck v Croudace* [1918] 1 KB 158 (power to arrest a person who was 'drunk while in charge' of a carriage exonerated an officer with the honest belief that a driver was drunk in charge.}

Administration of Act The courts are ready to impose a strained construction to facilitate the smooth administration of an Act, provided no injustice is caused.

677

Example 5   In *S J Grange Ltd v Customs and Excise Comrs* {[1979] 2 All ER 91. The case is also discussed in Example 114.2.}, Neill J held that it was necessarily implied by s 31 of the Finance Act 1972 that, where a taxpayer had failed to make proper valued-added tax returns, an assessment on him had to be by reference to a specific accounting period and not at large. This ruling was reversed by the Court of Appeal on the ground that it produced an unworkable result. Lord Denning MR said-

> 'I can see the force of it. It is literally correct. But it leads to such impracticable results that it is necessary to do a little adjustment so as to make the section workable.'

{P 101.}

The other judges agreed. Bridge LJ said Neill J's ruling would put 'the greatest practical difficulties in the administration of this tax in the way of the Commissioners of Customs and Excise'. {P 102.} Templeman LJ pointed out that-

> '. . . no one produced any convincing reason as to why the legislature in its wisdom should have devised a scheme in which the trader could in effect play a game of chess with the commissioners . . . in which his eyes were open because he has had the goods and the commissioners' eyes were blindfolded because they could not possibly know what had happened to them.'

{P 104.}

Even to avoid unworkability, the court will not apply a strained construction where this would risk injustice. Thus where an Act puts people under compulsion to undergo some physical activity it will be applied strictly.

Example 6   Section 8 of the Road Traffic Act 1972 requires a motorist 'to supply a specimen of breath for a breath test'. By s 12(1) this must be 'in sufficient *quantity* to enable that test to be carried out'. {Emphasis added.} It was held that where the quantity supplied was sufficient, but the test was vitiated because, contrary to the maker's instructions, the breath was (in good faith) supplied on two intakes of air instead of one, the Act was not contravened. {*Corp v Dalton* (1982) *The Times* 30 July.}

Facilitating legal proceedings   The courts are also anxious to facilitate the smooth working of legal proceedings, again provided that injustice is not caused. Here the judges have a specially close concern. A judge is master of the procedure of his court, subject always to the relevant law and the supervisory powers of higher courts.

Example 7   Section 1(1) of the Poor Prisoners' Defence Act 1930 said-

> 'Any person committed for trial for an indictable offence shall be entitled to free legal aid in the preparation *and conduct* of his defence at the trial and to have solicitor and counsel assigned to him for that purpose . . .'

{Emphasis added.}

The Court of Criminal Appeal held, by a strained construction, that this did not give the accused a right to have a solicitor at the trial. For the accused to possess such a right would mean that-

> '. . . he could repeatedly refuse to have the solicitors assigned when he got advice which he did not like and go to others, and there would be no means whatever to prevent that, with the result that there might be added expense to the country, delays and abuse of the whole procedure.'

{*R v Sowden* [1964] 1 WLR 1454, *per* Lord Parker CJ at p 1458. Cf *Amin v Entry Clearance Officer, Bombay* [1983] 2 All ER 864, *per* Lord Fraser of Tullybelton at p 868 (construction rejected which would give a right of appeal 'unworkable in practice'.}
The courts will not assume the right to enquire into the decisions of an administrative authority where the matter is one where the limited facilities available to a court render any judicial enquiry impracticable or unworkable.

Example 8 In *Liversidge v Anderson* {[1942] AC 206. See Example 97.1.}, the House of Lords gave reg 18B of the Defence (General) Regulations 1939 a strained construction by not enquiring into the sufficiency of the grounds for the detention of the appellant on the order of the Home Secretary. One reason the House gave was that the question was one 'of which the Secretary of State must plainly be a better judge than any court of law can be'. {*Per* Lord Romer at p 281}
As Lord Finlay LC had remarked in an earlier case under reg 18B-

> '. . . no tribunal for investigating the question whether circumstances of suspicion exist warranting some restraint can be imagined less appropriate than a court of law'.

{*R v Halliday* [1917] AC 260, at p 269.}
On the other hand, a supervisory court will not be quick to assume that some form of enquiry is beyond the practicable reach of a lower court.

Example 9 In *Gold Star Publications Ltd v Director of Public Prosecutions* {[1981] 2 All ER 257. See Example 316.7.} the House of Lords was faced with this question in relation to the statutory definition of an obscene article as one likely to 'deprave and corrupt' persons encountering it. {Obscene Publications Act 1959 s 1(1).}
The articles in the case were intended for export, and it was argued that the Act should be treated as confined to articles for home consumption. Magistrates whose duty it was to apply the test could not, it was said, know the attitudes and *mores* of foreigners; and the Act would be unworkable. It was held, Lord Simon of Glaisdale dissenting, that the argument failed. Some articles were obscene by any standard, and for the rest the magistrates would in case of doubt find for the defendants.

Example 10 In another case under the Obscene Publications Act 1959, the court went the other way. *R v Snaresbrook Crown Court, ex p Commissioner of Police of the Metropolis* {(1984) *The Times* 3 April.} concerned the forfeiture provisions of s 3 of the Act. These clearly mean that an article cannot be forfeited as obscene unless the court has inspected it and satisfied itself that such is the case. Yet here the Divisional Court ruled that it was lawful for the court to apply a sampling procedure. Watkins LJ said-

> 'I have no doubt that a judge has considerable power to control proceedings before him and that he must be allowed some latitude to make suitable arrangements to enable proceedings to be fair to the parties. He is entitled to take account of the scale of the problem posed to the courts in hearing such cases as this in view of the vast number of obscene articles seized each year.'

Despite the reference to being fair to the parties, it is clear that fairness to the court was the determining factor here. Where, as often happens, thousands of obscene articles are seized in one raid it is impracticable for courts to inspect and evaluate each one.

Securing convictions   In criminal cases the court will lean against a construction which would render proof of guilt impracticable.

Example 11   A remarkable instance of this occurred in *D (a Minor) v Yates* {(1984) *The Times* 28 March.} The defendant was convicted of using a Superstar 360 FM CB transceiver without a licence, contrary to s 1(1) of the Wireless Telegraphy Act 1949 (which says that no person shall 'use' such apparatus except under a licence). She appealed on the ground that it was not proved that she had used the apparatus during the period of seven days specified in the charge. *Held* The appeal failed, because 'it would be virtually impossible to obtain a conviction if the operator had to be apprehended at the time the set was switched on'. Kerr LJ said: 'The word "use" should be given a broad and sensible interpretation of being available for use'.

Illegality   The unworkable consequences of a particular construction may be relevant indirectly, for example in measuring how far the effects of statutory illegality are to be taken in their application to contractual obligations. Parliament will not be assumed to intend to carry them so far as to make trading impracticable over a wide area.

Example 12   The principle was well described by Lord Devlin when, as Devlin J, he delivered judgment in *St John Shipping Corpn v Joseph Rank Ltd.* {[1957] 1 QB 267, at p 281.} The plaintiffs had transported a cargo of grain on an overloaded ship, thereby committing a criminal breach of statutory duty. The defendants argued that this breach absolved them from paying freight on the cargo.

Lord Devlin pointed out that the argument would mean that no freight would be payable even though the overloading were accidental or trivial. It would lead to 'startling results'. It would logically apply to other types of statutory infringement as well, for example infringement of the duty so to load a cargo as to prevent shifting. The consequences to shipowners would be as serious as if factory owners were unable to recover from their customers the cost of articles manufactured in a factory which did not in all respects comply with the Factories Acts. The argument would even apply to goods carried in a lorry driven at one mile an hour above the permitted speed.

Lord Devlin ended his dismissal of the defendants' case with these words-

'If this is really the law, it is very unenterprising of cargo owners and
consignees to wait until a criminal conviction has been secured before
denying their liabilities. A service of trained observers on all our main
roads would soon pay for itself. An effective patrol of the high seas
would probably be too expensive, but the maintenance of a corps of
vigilantes in all principal ports would be well worth while when one
considers that the smallest infringement of the statute or a regulation
made thereunder would relieve all the cargo owners on the ship from
all liability for freight.

Of course, as [counsel for the defendants] says, one must not be
deterred from enunciating the correct principle of law because it may
have startling or even calamitous results. But I confess that I
approach the investigation of a legal proposition which has results of
this character with a prejudice in favour of the idea that there may be
a flaw in the argument somewhere.'

Establishing a 'contrary intention' Another case in which unworkable
consequences may be relevant indirectly is where a statutory definition or other
provision applies 'unless the contrary intention appears'. {This is the phrase
used in the Interpretation Act 1978 for describing the cases where it does not
apply.}

Example 12 In *Floor v Davis* {[1979] 2 All ER 677.} a question arose as to the
meaning of para 15(2) of Sch 7 to the Finance Act 1965. The question turned on
whether the singular word 'person' was by virtue of s 1(1)(b) of the
Interpretation Act 1889 to be construed as including the plural. {See now
Interpretation Act 1978, s 6(c).} This in turn affected the application of the
definition of 'control' in para 3 of Sch 18 to the Finance Act 1965. Viscount
Dilhorne said {P 684.}-

'If . . . on examination of the application of the Interpretation Act
1889 and construing 'control' in accordance with para 3 led to para
15(2) being unworkable, or, if not unworkable, to a result that
Parliament could not have intended, then it can be concluded that an
intention contrary to the application of the Interpretation Act 1889
appears and that 'control' is not to be so construed.'

Provisions expressly contemplating unworkability Sometimes Parliament
contemplates that an enactment may in some circumstances prove unworkable,
and makes express provision for this.

Example 14 The Coal Mines Act 1911, in laying certain duties on colliery
owners, provided that it should be a defence to an action for contravention of
any of these duties that it was 'not reasonably practicable' to avoid or prevent the
contravention. When this defence was reproduced in s 157 of the Mines and
Quarries Act 1954 the phrase was altered to 'impracticable'.

The cases on these provisions make it clear that impracticability is a question
of fact and degree, and throw light on that concept in its relation to statutory
requirements generally. {See *Watkins v Naval Colliery Co (1897) Ltd* [1912] AC
693; *Butler (or Black) v Fife Coal Co Ltd* [1912] AC 149; *Jayne v National Coal*

Board [1963] 2 All ER 220; *Brown v National Coal Board* [1962] AC 574. As to matters of fact and degree see s 83 of this Code.}

Example 15   Section 43(1) of the Race Relations Act 1976, following s 53(1) of the Sex Discrimination Act 1975, requires the Commission for Racial Equality to draw up and submit to the Secretary of State proposals for amending the Act where they think it necessary. When, in *Commission for Racial Equality v Amari Plastics Ltd* {[1982] 2 All ER 499.}, the commission argued that a construction put forward as to the extent of their power under the Act to issue non-discrimination notices would make the power unworkable, Griffiths LJ unsympathetically retorted that if this was so the remedy lay in the commission's hands. They should make representations to have the Act amended. {P 506.}

322. Avoiding an inconvenient result

The court seeks to avoid a construction that causes unjustifiable inconvenience to persons who are subject to the enactment, since this is unlikely to have been intended by Parliament. Sometimes however there are overriding reasons for applying such a construction, for example where it appears that Parliament really intended it or the literal meaning is too strong.

COMMENTARY

Unworkable or impracticable result   For the case where the consequences of a particular construction would be unworkable or impracticable rather than merely inconvenient rather than see s 321 of this Code.

Inconvenience   The argument from inconvenience is a familiar one to lawyers: *argumentum ab inconvenienti plurimum valet in lege* (an argument based on inconvenience is of great weight in law). {Co Litt 66a, cited by Bowen LJ in *Gard v London Sewers Commrs* (1885) 28 Ch D 486, at p 511.}

After quoting this ancient maxim, Coke adds some remarks which in relation to statutes go much too far: *Non solum quod licet sed quod est conveniens est considerandum. Nihil quod est inconveniens est licitum.* (Not only what is lawful but also what is convenient is to be considered. Nothing that causes inconvenience can be taken as lawful.) {Cf the variant *quod est inconveniens, aut contra rationem, non permissum est in lege* (that which is inconvenient, or against reason, is not permitted in law) - Co Litt 178.} A modern version is given by Lord Shaw-

> 'Where the words of a statute are clear, they must, of course, be followed, but in their Lordships' opinion where alternative constructions are equally open, that alternative is to be chosen which will be consistent with the smooth working of the system which the statute purports to be regulating and that alternative to be rejected which will introduce uncertainty, friction or confusion into the working of the system.'

{*Shannon Realties v Ville de St Michael* [1924] AC 185, at p 192. See also *ITC v Gibbs* [1942] AC 402, at p 414 and *Jones v Director of Public Prosecutions* [1962] AC 635, at p 662.}

Lord Shaw's dictum points a distinction between this section of the Code and the previous one. Whereas the court may find itself compelled to reach a strained construction to avoid unworkable consequences, it is unlikely to reach a strained construction merely to avoid inconvenience.

However it is submitted that Lord Shaw's dictum is inaccurate in stating that the alternative constructions must be 'equally' open. Where the convenient construction is also preferable grammatically, it will obviously be followed (unless some other criterion supervenes). Where the convenient construction is less preferable grammatically, it may still be followed if the court judges this course to be indicated on a weighing of the relevant interpretative factors. {See Part VII of this Code.}

Basis of the principle In the field of statute law, the courts' dislike of inflicting inconvenience mainly arises from the coercive nature of legislation. An Act usually intrudes on the property, time or freedom of the subject. The courts, in their capacity as the subject's protectors, feel that this intrusion, while no doubt necessary in the interests of society generally, should be accomplished without inflicting unneccessary inconvenience. The principle applies generally, but we now present examples of its operation in particular fields.

Uneccessary technicality Modern courts seek to cut down technicalities attendant upon a statutory procedure where these cannot be shown to be necessary to the fulfilment of the purposes of the legislation.

Example 1 Section 1 of the Law of Distress Amendment Act 1908 provides for the service of a statutory declaration on a distraining landlord by a person seeking to protect his goods from seizure. In *Lawrence Chemical Co Ltd v Rubenstein* {[1982] 1 All ER 653.} it was argued that decisions on the section established that where a company made a declaration it must be under seal and signed by an officer of the company. *Held* The declaration need not be under seal, and it was sufficient if it was signed by any duly-authorised agent. Arnold P said-

> 'I can see no reason at all why the method of making the declaration in a case like this should be attended with any such formality . . . To be driven to conclude in the face of every consideration of reasonableness, and certainly in the face of every consideration of convenience, that the seal should be affixed to such a document as this, the proposition must be supported by some special and particular consideration. I can find none.'

{P 658.}

Inconvenience in business Modern regulatory enactments bear heavily on business enterprise. The courts are alert to avoid any inconvenience which is not essential to the operation of the Act, and which may in addition have adverse economic consequences.

Example 2 Section 16(2) of the Betting, Gaming and Lotteries Act 1963 requires the occupier of a licensed horse or dog track, while a totalisator is operating, not to exclude any person from the track by reason only that he proposes to carry on bookmaking, and also (in the case of a dog track only) requires the occupier to take such steps as are necessary to secure that space is available for bookmakers. {It seems that in relation to horse racing, while a person cannot be refused admission on the ground that he proposes to carry on bookmaking, there is no duty to provide space in which he can do so.}

The courts have held that this provision and its predecessor {Betting and Lotteries Act 1934 s 11.} were passed not for the benefit of bookmakers but to ensure for the benefit of the betting public that the totalisator did not enjoy a monopoly. Although not stated by Parliament to be in any way restricted, the right of entry given to bookmakers must be taken as circumscribed by what is convenient. In other words a restriction on the general words is taken to be implied.

> 'It cannot have been intended that the occupier must admit as many bookmakers as may present themselves on any occasion, whether there is room for them or not, and, if an unreasonably large number seek admittance, there is nothing in the Act to indicate who is to be admitted and who may be refused. This omission is not surprising if the obligation on the occupier is only a general obligation to admit an adequate number of bookmakers, but it is, in my view, a clear indication that no further obligation was intended to be imposed.'

{*Cutler v Wandsworth Stadium Ltd* [1949] AC 398, *per* Lord Reid at p 417.}

Two subsequent decisions are of interest.

(1) In *R v Greyhound Racing Association Ltd* {(1955) 39 Cr App R 89, at p 95.} Donovan J said that making the arrangements required by the Act was a matter for the track occupiers 'and if they put the public to inconvenience by what they do in these respects, no doubt they will soon hear about it'.

(2) In *Poole Stadium Ltd v Squires* {[1982] 1 All ER 404, at p 408.}, Phillips J said that the bookmakers' statutory rights were 'subject to what is practical, convenient and proper in the interests of sensible and good management of the licensed track'.

Example 3 Section 8 of the Shops Act 1950 empowers a local authority to make orders fixing the time at which shops, or any specified class of shops, are to be closed for serving customers. By s 74(1) of the Act 'shop' is defined as including any premises where a retail trade or business is carried on. In *Fine Fare Ltd v Aberdare UDC* {[1965] 2 QB 39.} it was held that this did not empower a local authority to make an order by which different 'premises' within one department store had to close at different times, since this would cause the owner of the store unjustified inconvenience.

Example 4 Section 21 of the Weights and Measures Act 1835 provided that a contract made by reference to certain weights and measures abolished by the Act should be void. *Held* To avoid inconvenience to traders, this must be taken not to apply where the weighing or measuring was to be done outside England. 'Otherwise a contract made in China would have to have English weights and measures sent out there'. {*Rosseter v Cahlmann* (1853) 8 Ex 361, *per* Parke B at p 363.}

Example 5 Section 374 of the Merchant Shipping Act 1854 dealt with the licensing of pilots. It provided that a licence issued on any date should not continue in force beyond the following 31st January, but that it might 'be renewed on such 31 day of January' or on any subsequent day. *Held* Renewals could be backdated, since otherwise whole areas would be left for days without qualified pilots being available. This would cause 'the greatest possible inconvenience'. { *The Beta* (1869) 3 Moo PCC NS 23, *per* Turner LJ at p 30.}

Inconvenience to taxpayers The financial demands of the welfare state make modern legislation particularly coercive on the taxpayer. Again the courts are ready to ensure that, even though in the public interest proper taxes must be paid, the taxpayer is not unreasonably harassed by the tax authorities.

Example 6 In *Hallamshire Industrial Finance Trust Ltd v IRC* {[1979] 2 All ER 433.} the Revenue argued that it was sufficient for a tax assessment to specify the amount of the income liable to tax without also stating the actual amount of tax claimed. This was presumably on the basis of the maxim *id certum est quod certum reddi potest* (that is certain which can be rendered certain [by available information]). {9 Co Inst 47. Coke adds: *sed id magis certum est quod de semet ipso est certum* (but that is most certain which is certain on its face).} It does not appear from the report of the case that this maxim was cited however. The maxim would be inappropriate in relation to a financial demand from the state. While the Revenue would have no difficulty in working out the amount of tax due, the taxpayer might well have problems whenever the basis of calculation was in any way complicated. Moreover it would be difficult to know where to draw the line between a reasonable application of the maxim and one which caused the subject unacceptable inconvenience.

Browne-Wilkinson J, rejecting the Revenue's argument that the assessment did not need to specify the amount of tax due, said-

'I do not find this contention attractive. It involves the proposition that the legislature envisaged the possibility of a taxpayer being liable to pay tax in an amount of which he has never been notified prior to a demand for payment under s 60 of the [Taxes Management Act 1970]. The majority of taxpayers on receiving an assessment look only at the amount of tax payable, having neither the time nor the ability (without professional advice) to discover whether that sum is correct. Yet the Crown argues that they would have fully discharged their functions of assessing and giving notice of assessment without specifying any amount of tax payable, merely by stating the facts which would enable someone skilled in tax matters to compute the tax which the Crown is going to demand under s 60, such demand probably not being made until after the time for appealing against the assessment had expired. In my judgment the words of the statute would have to be very clear to force the court to that conclusion.' {P 437.}

Example 7 Under various tax enactments, certain income of a charity was exempted from tax provided it was in fact applied for charitable purposes. The charity paid the income over to another charity which was in law bound to apply it for charitable purposes. The Revenue argued that the exemption could not be claimed unless the first charity proved that the recipient charity had in fact used the money for charitable purposes. *Held* It was sufficient to prove that the recipient charity would be acting unlawfully if it used the money in any other way. Oliver LJ said-

> 'The Crown's proposition is a startling one; it involves this, that the trustees of a charity, although they may discharge themselves as a matter of law by making a grant to another properly constituted charity, are obliged, if they wish to claim exemption under the subsections, to enquire into the application of the funds given and to demonstrate to the Revenue how those funds have been dealt with by other trustees over whom they have no control and for whose actions they are not answerable. Anything more inconvenient would be difficult to imagine, and I find myself quite unable to accept that Parliament, in enacting these sections, can possibly have intended such a result.'

{*IRC v Helen Slater Charitable Trust Ltd* [1981] 3 All ER 98, at p 101.}

Inconvenience in legal proceedings It is stated in the commentary on s 321 of this Code that the courts strive to avoid constructions that render legal proceedings unworkable. For similar reasons, courts seek to avoid uneccessary expense or other inconvenience to litigants or officers of the court.

Example 8 Section 268(2) of the Companies Act 1948 says that in a liquidation the court may examine a person who has relevant knowledge 'and may reduce his answers to writing and require him to sign them'. A witness claimed that requiring him to sign a mere transcript did not comply with this procedure. The gist of each answer should, he asserted, have been first read out to him and then written down. Dismissing this argument, Pennycuik J said that even if that was the literal meaning of the enactment, the procedure would have been 'inconvenient to a degree'. {*Re Milton Hindle Ltd* [1963] 1 WLR 1032, at p 1034.}

Example 9 An enactment empowered the court imposing a sentence of penal servitude also to impose a sentence of preventive detention to follow it. An appeal against a sentence of penal servitude required leave, but an appeal against a sentence of preventive detention did not. By a strained construction, the court announced that to save 'inconvenience and unnecessary expense' it proposed to adopt the policy of treating a person who appealed against a sentence of preventive detention as automatically having leave to appeal against the preliminary sentence of penal servitude. {*R v Smith* [1910] 1 KB 17, at p 21.}

Example 10 In *Marsland v Taggart* {[1928] 2 KB 447.} it was argued that an appeal was vitiated by the fact that one of the three justices who decided a matter had died before the remaining two signed a case stated for consideration by the High Court. Rejecting this, Shearman J said-

> 'Justices come and go, but justice itself should endure. I see no reason to uphold an objection which would result in justice coming to an end owing to the death of a magistrate because s 2 of the Summary Jurisdiction Act 1857 is worded as it is. This sort of objection ought to be as extinct as the thumbscrew.'

{P 450. See also, as to the death of a judge or magistrate during the proceedings, *Newton v Boodle* (1847) 3 CB 795; *Baxendale v McMurray* (1867) 2 Ch App 790; *Wyman v Paterson* [1900] AC 271; *Polurrian Steamship Co Ltd v Young* [1915] 1 KB 922, at p 927; *Norman v Golder* (1944-5) 26 TC 293, at pp 297 and 299.}

Avoiding delay The law's delays are a notorious defect, and the courts regard them as an inconvenience to be avoided. So a construction that tends to draw out proceedings is frowned on.

Example 11 Section 10(5) of the Courts Act 1971 says that the supervisory jurisdiction of the High Court over lower courts does not apply to the Crown Court 'in matters relating to trial on indictment'. Holding that this exclusion covered jury-vetting by a Crown Court judge, the Court of Appeal (Lord Denning MR dissenting) said that to do otherwise would protract proceedings. {*R v Crown Court at Sheffield, ex p Brownlow* [1980] 2 All ER 444.} Shaw LJ explained the ruling in this way-

> 'On the practical side, if decisions made by a judge of the Crown Court as to matters which are related to trial on indictment were subject at any stage to review by the High Court, the trial of a particular cause might be interminably delayed by incidental applications which could then be taken to the High Court by way of case stated or an application for judicial review.' {P 455.}

A particular form of unnecessary inconvenience and expense the courts seek to avoid in modern times is the need to restart proceedings in the same or a different court because of some trivial defect.

Example 12 The proviso to s 2 (5) of the Children Act 1948 says that a juvenile court shall not make an order keeping alive a local authority's resolution vesting in them the parental rights and duties with respect to a child unless, at the time of the juvenile court hearing, there continue to be grounds on which such a resolution could be founded.

In *W v Nottinghamshire County Council* {[1982] 1 All ER 1.} the Court of Appeal had to decide whether the proviso meant that the same grounds as originally existed for the resolution had to continue. *Held* All that the proviso required was that some sufficient grounds existed at the date of the hearing, even if they were not the original grounds. After pointing out that the alternative construction might require the local authority to institute wardship proceedings in the High Court, Ormrod LJ said-

> 'Such an inconvenient, even perverse, result is to be avoided if it is possible to do so. We do not think that our construction puts an undue strain on the language of the proviso; it certainly gives effect to the obvious intention of the legislation.' {P 8.}

Example 13 In *Re Paget's Settlement* {[1965] 1 WLR 1046.} it was argued that the court had no power under the Variation of Trusts Act 1958 to vary a trust made in a foreign country and governed by the law of that country, even though the trust property and all interested persons had for a long period been within the jurisdiction. Instead, it was argued, relief should be sought by bringing proceedings in the foreign country. The argument was supported by the fact that the extent provision (s 2) said that the Act did not extend to Scotland. *Held* The court had unlimited jurisdiction, though it might in a Scottish case feel that the Court of Session was a more appropriate tribunal.

Inconvenience both ways   It sometimes happens that each of the constructions contended for involves some measure of inconvenience. In so far as the court uses inconvenience as a test, it then has to balance the effect of each construction and determine which inconvenience is greater.

Example 14   In *Pascoe v Nicholson* {[1981] 2 All ER 769.} the House of Lords was faced with a question under the breathalyser procedure. Section 9(1) of the Road Traffic Act 1972 says that a person arrested on failing a breath test may, while at a police station, be required to undergo a blood or urine test. The question was whether for this purpose the suspect could be taken to a different police station when no doctor was available at the first one.

On the construction that the suspect could not be taken to another police station, the inconvenience would be to the police. As Lord Roskill said: 'It is not difficult to visualise many parts of the United Kingdom where it might be extremely difficult to obtain the services of a doctor at some isolated police station'. {P 774.} On the opposite construction the inconvenience would be to the suspect. Lord Roskill described it by saying that the suspect might be taken many miles to another police station and then (when he had sobered up) have to return all the way to the first one in order to collect his car. {Ibid.}

The Act contained no express prohibition on the transfer of a suspect to another police station. The House of Lords, settling a conflict of authority between English and Scottish courts, had no difficulty in finding that the balance of convenience lay with the police. In some circumstances it might even go beyond mere inconvenience. Where, as in the Scottish case of *Milne v M'Donald* {(1971) JC 40.}, the police doctor refused to attend at the first police station, the opposite construction would render the provision unworkable.

Inconvenience may operate both ways on questions of the obtaining of evidence. Usually the inconvenience is less for a party having control over the relevant witnesses or documents.

Example 15   In the Jamaican case of *Dillon v The Queen* {[1982] 1 All ER 1017.} the Judicial Committee of the Privy Council had to decide whether, on a charge against a constable of permitting the escape of a prisoner from lawful custody, it was for the prosecution to prove that the custody was in fact lawful. *Held* There could be no presumption of the existence of facts central to an offence, and it was for the prosecution to prove the lawfulness of the custody and not for the defence to disprove it. Lord Fraser of Tulleybelton pointed out that 'there is not likely to be any difficulty for the Crown in proving the lawfulness of the detention, when it exists . . . it should be in the possession of the person in charge of the prison or lock-up'. {P 1020.}

323. Avoiding an anomalous or illogical result

The court seeks to avoid a construction that creates an anomaly or otherwise produces an irrational or illogical result. Sometimes however there are overriding reasons for applying such a construction, for example where Parliament really intended it or the literal meaning is too strong.

COMMENTARY

Common sense   This subsection of the Code deals with an aspect of the principle that Parliament is taken to expect its Acts to be applied with common sense. {For the commonsense construction rule see s 122 of this Code.}

Avoiding anomaly   Every legal system must seek to avoid unjustified differences and inconsistencies in the way it deals with similar matters. As Lord Devlin said, 'no system of law can be workable if it has not got *logic* at the root of it'. {*Hedley Byrne & Co Ltd v Heller and Partners Ltd* [1964] AC 465, at p 516 (emphasis added).}

The logic here referred to is not formal or syllogistic logic. {See s 148 and Part XX of this Code for an explanation of formal logic as applied to statutory interpretation.} It was this formal logic that Lord Halsbury had in mind when he said that 'every lawyer must acknowledge that the law is not always logical'. {*Quinn v Leathem* [1901] AC 495, at p 506.} The American Holmes J is remembered for saying that 'The life of the law has not been logic: it has been experience'. {*The Common Law* p 1.}

While in formal logic the conclusion must inexorably follow from applying the minor premiss (the facts) to the major premiss (the supposed legal rule), in 'informal' logic it is the major premiss itself that is suspect. This is well explained by Professor MacCormick-

'The word "logical" has at least two senses, which are only partially overlapping. In the technical sense of deductive logic ... an argument is logical if it complies with the requirements of [formal] logic, that is to say, if its conclusion follows necessarily from the premisses ... But in everday usage "being logical" has a sense which is wider and in some respects different. Some action, or state of affairs, can be said to be "illogical" in that it "doesn't make sense" ... One of the things which is true of a technically illogical argument is that it does not make sense, in that to utter it is to utter a self-contradiction. To that extent the two usages overlap. But when it is said that a given rule of law "doesn't make sense", what is usually intended is that the law sets a standard of conduct which it is silly or unfair or unreasonable to expect of people. And that introduces a new set of values which are outside the cognizance of "logic" in the technical sense of the term as a name of a specific philosophical discipline. It is in this everyday usage of the term that the major premiss of a legal argument can be stigmatized as "illogical" and therefore also any conclusion which follows from its application.'

{*Legal Reasoning and Legal Theory* p 38.}

Conceptualism   A way by which the law may become illogical in the 'informal' sense is through what has been called conceptualism. This arises where a legal concept is gradually extended by analogies (each of which is impeccable from the point of view of formal logic) until it is taken further than is wise from the viewpoint of legal policy. Conceptualism was condemned by Cardozo J in the American case described in the following Example.

Example 1 Hynes v New York Central Rly Co {(1921) 231 NY 229.} concerned these facts. A boy bathing in a public river was standing on a privately-owned bulkhead preparing to make a dive into the river. At that moment he was struck by falling power lines and fatally injured. From the 'private' viewpoint the boy was a trespasser, towards whom no duty had been broken. From the 'public' viewpoint he was a bather exercising his lawful right to swim in the public river. To decide the case by reference to the 'private' viewpoint would produce an anomalous result. If the boy had happened to dive a moment earlier, and so have been in the water when struck by the power line, there would have been a clear breach of duty. As a trespasser he would be without rights.

It is 'illogical' in the informal sense for a legal duty to go into and out of existence every few moments, according to whether a bather is in the water or on the diving board. Cardozo J held that to apply the law of trespass in what from the viewpoint of pure deduction would be a 'logical' way carried too far the jurisprudence of conceptions. He accordingly found in favour of the dead boy's personal representatives. {The case is examined in a discussion of conceptualism and reasoning by analogy in R Cross *Precedent in English Law* (3rd edn, 1977) pp 188-192. The decision may be condemned by some as an instance of the sacrifice of legal principle to sentiment.}

Our own law nowadays tends to treat logic in the 'informal' way. We go on to discuss various kinds of illogicality or anomaly that may arise in statutory interpretation, beginning with cases where the court decides in favour of a construction which avoids the anomaly. {See also Examples 289.3 and 305.2.}

Remedy not available in like cases Consistency requires that a statutory remedy or benefit should be available, and should operate in the same way, in all cases of the same kind.

Example 2 The literal meaning of the Limitation Act 1623 might well have produced the result that a person under disability had the advantage of two distinct limitation periods. Lord Diplock described the position thus in *Tolley v Morris* {[1979] 2 All ER 561, at p 569.}-

> 'On this construction the two periods might overlap, but there might be an interval between them, during which the infant's right of action would be statute-barred. Such an interregnum during which the plaintiff's rights were temporarily unenforceable would have had no rational justification, and as early as 1670 the Court of King's Bench applied a purposive construction to the statute and held there was but a single limitation period applicable to persons under disability.'

Example 3 Section 1 of the Fatal Accidents Act 1846 (Lord Campbell's Act) gives a claim for damages 'Whensoever the death of a person shall be caused by wrongful act, neglect, or default . . .' In *Davidson v Hill* {[1901] 2 KB 606.} it was held that this entitled the representatives of a foreign seaman killed in a collision with a British ship to recover. Otherwise there would be the anomaly that-

> ' . . . if a foreigner and an Englishman serving on the same ship were both drowned on the high seas by the same collision negligently

caused by an English vessel, the widow of the one could, and the widow of the other could not, obtain by suing the owners of the ship in fault *in personam* that reparation which our legislature ... has declared to be a just reparation'.

{*Per* Kennedy J at p 614. The decision overlooks the necessary limits on the extent and application of a country's law (see s 30 and Part IX of this Code).}

Example 4 In *Gordon v Cradock* {[1964] 1 QB 503.} it was argued that s 31(2) of the Supreme Court of Judicature (Consolidation) Act 1925 should be construed in a way which would mean that a *plaintiff* could cross-appeal only with leave while a *defendant* could appeal without leave. *Held* This would be 'a very strange result', and the suggested construction would accordingly not be followed. {*Per* Willmer LJ at p 506.}

Example 5 In *Dunn v Blackdown Properties Ltd* {[1961] Ch 433.} it was argued that s 162(1)(d)(iv) of the Law of Property Act 1925 produced the result that, on a grant of a right of way over a road coupled with a right to construct and use a drain running under the road, the right of drainage was good but the right of way was not. *Held* Such an anomalous construction could not be accepted. {*Per* Cross J at p 441.}

Example 6 Section 448 of the Companies Act 1948 empowers the court to relieve an officer of a company from liability for 'negligence, default, breach of duty or breach of trust' where he has acted honestly and reasonably and ought fairly to be excused. A director of a betting company which failed to pay general betting duty was sued for the duty under s 2(2) of the Betting and Gaming Duties Act 1972. He applied for relief under s 448. *Held* Although not so limited in words, s 448 was by implication intended to apply only to breach of a duty owed by a person, as an officer of a company, to the company. It would not be fair to give to an officer of a company relief which was not available to other persons caught by s 2(2) of the 1972 Act. {*Customs and Excise Comrs v Hedon Alpha Ltd* [1981] 2 All ER 697.}

Example 7 Section 62 of the Employment Protection (Consolidation) Act 1978 prevents an industrial tribunal from hearing a claim for unfair dismissal following a strike unless there has been victimisation. This is defined as the dismissal of some only of the striking workers. In *McCormick v Horsepower Ltd* {[1981] 2 All ER 746.} the question was at what moment of time this test had to be applied. The appellant argued that it was the date when the claim was made to the tribunal. *Held* The relevant time was the date of the hearing by the tribunal, since otherwise some workers would have a remedy while others might not. O'Connor LJ said-

'The anomalies that would be created by taking the time when a claim is made are quite unacceptable. If all strikers were not dismissed at the same time but at different times during the strike, as happened in this case, then if the first dismissed made a claim at once there would be jurisdiction but not for the last.'

{P 750.}

Example 8   Section 3 of the Law Reform (Miscellaneous Provisions) Act 1934 empowers the court, in any proceedings 'tried in any court of record', to award interest on a judgment debt from the date when the cause of action arose. In *Alex Lawrie Factors Ltd v Modern Injection Moulds Ltd* {[1981] 3 All ER 658.} the question arose of whether such an award could be made where judgment was given in default of appearance.

Held Although the proceedings were not a trial but a mere administrative act, the award could, by a strained construction of s 3, be made. The word 'tried' in that section must be taken to mean 'determined', a construction which accorded with commercial sense. Drake J said-

> 'If a creditor is wrongly kept out of his money he ought in fairness to be able to obtain interest on the sum owing unless there are special circumstances which should disentitle him to interest . . . Why then, in logic, should a debtor who appears but unsuccessfully argues his case be in a worse position as regards having to pay interest than a debtor who does not enter any appearance to the writ?' {P 663.}

Duty not imposed in like cases   The converse of the principle that a statutory remedy should be available in all like cases is that a statutory duty should be imposed in all like cases.

Example 9   Section 42(1) of the National Assistance Act 1948 said that for the purposes of the Act 'a man shall be liable to maintain his wife and his children'. In *Din v National Assistance Board* {[1967] 2 QB 213.} it was argued that this should be construed in accordance with the usual principle of English law that references to marriage mean monogamous marriage and references to children mean legitimate children of such a marriage.

Held The test was whether the marriage was valid under the law governing it, whether monogamous or polygamous. Salmon LJ said-

> 'It would perhaps be as remarkable as it would be unfortunate if a man coming from a country where he is lawfully married to a woman and is lawfully the father of her children may bring them here and leave them destitute with impunity, so that when the National Assistance Board is obliged to come to their assistance, he can avoid all responsibility and thereby throw the burden of maintaining [them] upon the public.'

{P 218.}

Example 10   Section 127 of the Highways Act 1959 rendered it an offence if 'without lawful authority or excuse . . . a hawker or other itinerant trader or a *gipsy* pitches a booth, stall or stand, or encamps, on a highway'. *Held* The word 'gipsy' was not limited to a person of the Romany race, but covered any person leading a nomadic life. It 'is difficult to think that Parliament intended to subject a man to a penalty in the context of causing litter and obstruction on the highway merely by reason of his race'. {*Mills v Cooper* [1967] 2 QB 459, *per* Lord Parker CJ at p 467. See now Highways Act 1980 s 148, which omits the reference to a gipsy.}

Example 11   Section 175 of the Income Tax Act 1952 imposed tax on excess rents. In *T & E Homes Ltd v Robinson (Inspector of Taxes)* {[1979] 2 All ER

522.} it was argued that at common law a payment was not strictly a 'rent' unless the remedy of distraint was available on non-payment, and that this meaning should be applied to the taxing provision. *Held* This reading must be rejected since it would give rise to an anomaly. Templeman LJ said-

> 'The object of s 175 was to tax excess rents, that is to say money received by a landlord in excess of the notional rent which was taxed under Schedule A. Whether or not a rent was excessive depended on the amount and not on the remedy. There would be no sense in taxing excess rents recoverable by distress while allowing excess rents not so recoverable to escape the imposition of tax.' {P 528.}

Example 12 Section 170(2) of the Customs and Excise Management Act 1979 makes it an offence to be concerned in any 'fraudulent' evasion of duty. In *A-G's Reference (No 1 of 1981)* {[1982] 2 All ER 417.} the defendants had attempted to smuggle cannabis by methods that did not involve fraud or other deception. *Held* They were nevertheless guilty, since 'fraudulent' in this connection must be taken to apply to any form of evasion, whether deceitful or not. Lord Lane CJ said-

> 'If deceit is a requirement, then in this sort of case there can never be a conviction under this subsection of the Act. This seems contrary to good sense . . . It seems to us to be a misinterpretation of Parliament's intention, and a path to absurdity, to make guilt depend on whether a customs officer is met and deceived on the one hand, or simply intentionally avoided on the other'. {P 422.}

Example 13 In *R v Denton* {[1982] 1 All ER 65.} the defendant appealed from a conviction of arson under s 1(1) and (3) of the Criminal Damage Act 1971 (which makes it arson to damage property belonging to another by fire without lawful excuse). The defendant had been asked to burn the property by his employer, who owned it, so that the employer could claim the insurance money. *Held* The appeal succeeded. A person did not commit arson if he burned his own property, even where his intent was fraudulent. It would therefore be anomalous if a person whom he asked to do the job for him were held guilty.

The question of whether a case is a 'like' case in relation to a penal enactment may cause difficulty. For instance, enactments frequently refer to the doing of an act in relation to 'any person' without making it clear whether the one who himself does the act is to be treated for this purpose as a 'person'. Is he within the mischief if he does the forbidden act in relation to himself?

Example 14 Section 2 of the Malicious Damage Act 1861, defining an aggravated form of arson, said: 'Whoever shall unlawfully and maliciously set fire to any dwelling house, *any person* being therein, shall be guilty of felony'. In *R v Arthur* {[1968] 1 QB 810.} one Edward David Arthur was arraigned on an indictment charging that he 'on August 31st 1967 maliciously set fire to a dwelling house, one Edward David Arthur being therein, contrary to s 2 of the Malicious Damage Act 1861'. This gave rise to two possibilities of anomaly. It might be anomalous to say that aggravated arson was committed whenever a person was within the house *except* a person who was the one who set fire to it. Or it might be even more anomalous to say that a man could lawfully burn down his own house if he lit it from outside, but not if he lit it from inside and hastily left.

Howard J decided the case by reference to another Act passed in the same year. Section 18 of the Offences Against the Person Act 1861 made it an offence to 'wound or cause grievous bodily harm to *any person*'. After pointing out that no one had heard of anybody being prosecuted under s 18 for causing harm to himself, Howard J ruled that the reference in s 2 to 'any person' must be taken to mean any person other than the setter on fire. {P 813. Cf *Cooper v Motor Insurer's Bureau* (1982) *The Times* 19 July ('any person' in the requirement to insure set out in s 145(3)(a) of the Road Traffic Act 1972 means any person other than than the user of the vehicle himself); *R v Dunbar* [1982] Crim LR 45 (doctor his own patient).}

Decision turning on an immaterial distinction   Even though two cases are not exactly alike, it may still be anomalous to distinguish between them if the difference is immaterial or trivial. Thus the House of Lords held it to be inconceivable that Parliament intended the right to elect to be tried by jury (where the accused attained the age of seventeen between commission of the offence and the full hearing) to depend on whether the accused notified the court of his intention to plead not guilty by post or in person. {*Re Daley* [1982] 2 All ER 974.}

Example 15   Part II of the Landlord and Tenant Act 1954 gives security of tenure to tenants of business premises. It was argued in *Bracey v Read* {[1963] Ch 88.}, where the tenancy related to gallops for training racehorses, that 'premises' did not include open land. *Held* This reading must be rejected as it would lead to the absurd result that a private car park used for business purposes would be outside the Act if it had no building on it, whereas 'if it had a hut in which the attendant sheltered from the rain, or sat when he had no work to do, it would be within the Act'. {*Per* Cross J at p 93.}

Example 16   Section 50 of the Town Police Clauses Act 1847 enables a hackney carriage licence to be revoked 'upon the conviction for the second time . . . for any offence under the provisions of this or the special Act with respect to hackney carriages, or any byelaw made in pursuance thereof'.

In *Bowers v Gloucester Corpn* {[1963] 1 QB 881.} the question was whether the second offence had to be under precisely the same provision as the first, or could be under any other of the named provisions. If two drivers had each been convicted of two offences under the named provisions it would be substantially immaterial that the first had been convicted twice under the same provision while the other had been convicted under two different provisions. *Held* It was irrelevant whether the second conviction was under the same or a different provision. Lord Parker CJ referred to the 'complete absurdity' that would arise if a man could show himself to be utterly unfitted to be a cab driver by committing 30, 40 or 50 offences, and yet not have his licence revoked because he had always committed a different offence. {P 887.}

Example 17   Paragraph 12 of Sch 7 to the Finance Act 1965 provided an exemption from capital gains tax for a gain arising on a disposal of a right to annual payments due under a 'covenant'. In *Rank Xerox Ltd v Lane (Inspector of*

Taxes) {[1979] 3 All ER 657.} the taxpayer company argued that this word covered any contract for annual payments which was made by the company under seal. *Held* The statutory phrase referred to the well-known practice of making unilateral covenants under seal and did not cover ordinary contracts. Lord Wilberforce said that to decide otherwise would be 'paradoxical'. He went on-

> 'If the signature of Xerox to these agreements had not been under seal, the taxpayer company's liability to capital gains tax in respect of the payments could not have been disputed. To make their liability depend on a circumstance so inessential and immaterial as the affixing, or absence, of a seal is arbitrary in the extreme. As a matter of substance it is impossible to detect any reason of fiscal policy why the affixing of a seal to a document should have any relevance to the imposition of the tax.' {P 659.}

Anomaly in legal doctrine   As guardians of the law, courts prefer to avoid coming to a decision which involves creating or accepting an anomalous legal rule or doctrine. Thus Lord Hodson defended the decision of himself and his colleagues in *Director of Public Prosecutions v Schildkamp* {[1971] AC 1.} by arguing {P 12.} that it would be 'highly anomalous' if the criminal remedy for fraudulent trading were held to be wider in scope than the civil.

It would clearly be anomalous for an appeal against sentence to lie where the convict had pleaded *not guilty*, but not to lie where he had pleaded *guilty*. Such was the plain meaning of s 4(3) of the Criminal Appeal Act 1907, but the court applied a strained construction to avoid it. {*R v Ettridge* [1909] 2 KB 24.}

Again, it would, as Widgery LJ put it, be 'perverse' if three murders could be charged in one indictment but two could not. Yet the Indictments Act 1915 allowed joinder of offences only if they formed a 'series'. {Sch, r 3. See now Indictment Rules 1971 (SI 1971/1253) r 9.} Widgery LJ held that, although the word 'series' is not wholly apt to describe only two components, here it was right to give it that strained meaning. {*R v Kray* [1969] 3 WLR 831, at p 836.}

Example 18   Ashworth J said it would be 'odd' if the term *proceedings* in s 1(3) of the Evidence Act 1938 had to be so construed as to let in a statement made when *criminal* proceedings were pending but exclude one made when *civil* proceedings were pending. Accordingly he ruled that the term must be taken to include both criminal and civil proceedings. {*W & M Wood (Haulage) Ltd v Redpath* [1967] 2 QB 520, at p 526.}

Example 19   Eveleigh LJ held that it would be surprising, harsh and ridiculous to hold that a litigant's duty to 'apply to the court' for an order within a stated period was not satisfied because, although his application for a summons was received within the period, the court delayed for a week before actually issuing the summons. The intention of the rule was 'to control the actions of the litigant'. Eveleigh LJ went on-

> 'One has to interpret the rule in a way that makes sense of the whole procedure laid down. It does not make sense to penalize a party who has done everything required of him by the rule, on the basis of something not done in time by the court.'

{*Aly v Aly* (1983) *The Times* 27 December.}

Example 20 The literal meaning of an enactment {2 Geo 3 c 19 s 1, as amended by 39 Geo 3 c 34 s 3.} which laid down close seasons for varieties of game was that it was lawful to kill a game bird at any time up to midnight on the last day of the season but an offence to possess its carcase at the first moment of the following day. *Held* The literal meaning produced an anomaly in the law, and a strained interpretation must be applied. Littledale J said-

> ' . . . if a man may lawfully kill birds on the last moment of the day on the 1st of February, it would be absurd to hold that he would be guilty of an unlawful act by having the same birds in his possession on the 2nd.'

{*Simpson v Unwin* (1832) 3 B & Ad 134, at p 137. Patteson J added (p 138): 'it would be absurd to say that a party who kills the game within the time when he may lawfully do so, must consume it all upon the last day'.}

Example 21 When a construction of s 2(1) of the Agricultural Holdings Act 1948 was put forward which would have meant that in law a farm owner became his own tenant, Harman LJ said: 'When one produces a result as bizarre as that, it is time to pause and consider whether the statute really obliges one to do so'. {*Harrison-Broadley v Smith* [1964] 1 All ER 867, at p 872.}

Example 22 Lord Evershed MR dismissed as 'extravagant' a reading of s 51(2) of the Bankruptcy Act 1914 which would give the trustee in bankruptcy an unfettered right to take the income of property owned outright by the bankrupt but require the leave of the court before he could take the income of property in which the bankrupt had only a life interest. {*Re Cohen (a bankrupt)* [1961] Ch 246, at p 257.}

Example 23 *R v Secretary of State for Home Affairs, ex p Giambi* {[1982] Crim LR 40.} concerned the interpretation of para 2(1) of Sch 3 to the Immigration Act 1971. This excepts from the power to detain persons pending the making of a deportation order against them any person who is 'for the time being released on bail by any court having power so to release him'.

The applicant, a woman who was an Italian national, had been charged with two offences. These were dealt with by different courts. On the first charge the justices committed her for trial, meanwhile granting bail. On the second charge she was convicted and sentenced to 28 days' imprisonment, with a recommendation for subsequent deportation. Having completed the prison term, the applicant now applied for a writ of habeas corpus, claiming that para 2(1) required her to be released pending the making of the deportation order. *Held* Although the literal meaning of para 2(1) required the applicant to be released, it would create an anomaly in the law to apply this meaning. The rule contemplated bail by a court dealing with a connected matter, not one that was irrelevant. Each charge had to be dealt with separately, under the provisions relevant to that charge. Accordingly the application for habeas corpus was refused.

It is clearly anomalous to treat a person as being under a statutory duty where some essential factual pre-requisite that must have been in the contemplation of the legislator is missing.

Example 24 In the Australian case of *Turner v Ciappara* {[1969] VR 851.} the court considered the application of an enactment requiring obedience to automatic traffic signals. On the facts before the court it was shown that through mechanical failure the device was not working properly. *Held* It must be treated as implicit that obedience was required only where the apparatus was in working order.

For examples of other legal anomalies on certain constructions see *Re Lockwood decd* {[1958] Ch 231. See Example 291.2} (distant relatives preferred to nearer on intestacy); *R v Minister of Agriculture and Fisheries, ex p Graham* {[1955] 2 QB 140, at p 168.} (officer of sub-committee could hear representations while officer of main committee could not); *R v Baker* {[1962] 2 QB 530.} (person arrested on suspicion of offence liable to higher penalty than if he had committed the offence).

Anomalous construction nevertheless applied Sometimes, although a particular construction produces an anomalous or illogical result, the court nevertheless feels constrained to apply it. The following are some of the relevant categories.

Where anomaly intended The court may conclude that Parliament actually intended the anomaly. This concludes the matter, for the court's aim is always to arrive at Parliament's true intention and then implement it. Cross J said that the Charitable Trusts (Validation) Act 1954 'is a very odd one'. When it was argued before him that a literal interpretation of the Act would turn a will trust into something the testator could never have envisaged, Cross J retorted that because the Act was so odd 'it is no answer to an argument founded on it that it produces a result which is surprising or even absurd'. {*Re Saxone Shoe Co Ltd's Trust Deed* [1962] 1 WLR 943, at p 956.}

Where a literal construction of s 1 of the Income Tax Act 1853 produced the anomalous result that foreigners were taxed on unremitted income earned abroad, Lord Esher MR, in finding against this construction, acknowledged that-

> 'It is true that if we came to the conclusion that this has been intentionally done we must carry out the law and leave to the government of the country the task of answering objections . . .'

{*Colquhoun v Brooks* (1888) 21 QBD 52, at pp 57–58}

The medieval practice of basing limitation periods on the date of the happening of a specific event, such as the return of King John from Ireland or the coronation of Henry III {Statute of Merton (20 Hen 3 c 8); Stat Westm I (3 Edw 1 c 39).}, inevitably produced anomalies as the cited event grew more and more distant. Yet the inference was irresistible that Parliament intended these anomalies, for otherwise it would instead have appointed (as it later did) a fixed number of years. {This was done by the Limitation of Prescription 1540 (32 Hen 8 c 2), by which time the so-called limitation period extended to more than 300 years!}

An illogical result may have been intended by Parliament because of the difficulty of securing the passage of a fully logical measure. Lord Sumner said of the Married Women's Property Act 1882: 'I fully recognise that the Act of 1882 is illogical, *as reforms often are*'. {*Edwards v Porter* [1925] AC 1, at p 46 (emphasis added).}

Where a complex statutory scheme is first introduced, it is accepted by the courts that Parliament must be taken to have intended the sort of anomalies that are in practice initially inseparable from such schemes. Thus Slade J said of a scheme to provide 'multipliers' for the periodic raising of business rents: 'The introduction of a new "appropriate multiplier" was, I think, bound to produce some anomalies, particularly in the early stages'. {*International Military Services Ltd v Capital and Counties plc* [1982] 2 All ER 20, at p 30.}

Of the provisions in the Finance Act 1975 providing for the institution of capital transfer tax, Lord Russell of Killowen said that anomalies and hard cases 'are, I fear, only to be expected in the introduction of such a radical and complicated experiment in fiscal novelty'. {*Pearson v IRC* [1980] 2 All ER 479, at p 489. See also Lord Keith at p 495.}

Stating the point more broadly, Buckley LJ said in *Alexander v Mercouris* {[1979] 3 All ER 305, at p 308.}-

'Whenever new rights or obligations are created by statute, anomalies will inevitably arise initially. Whatever date is found to be the earliest date at which the new duties, rights or obligations can arise, it will be possible to suggest instances in which one man will escape liability by a day and another, who has followed an exactly similar course of action but 24 hours later, will find himself liable. In such a case an argument by reference to anomalies is, in my opinion, unlikely to be helpful . . .'

Literal meaning too plain Again, the literal meaning may be too plain to be shaken by an anomaly.

Example 25 The result of applying the literal meaning of the statute 4 & 5 Anne c 16 (1705) in the year 1957 was that virtually all European royalty were by statute British subjects. This easily-recognised absurdity did not prevent the House of Lords from applying the literal meaning in *A-G v Prince Ernest Augustus of Hanover*. {[1957] AC 436. See Example 272.2.}

Example 26 The literal meaning of the County Courts Admiralty Jurisdiction Act Amendment Act 1869 gave an action in rem for a claim not exceeding £300 when there was no such remedy for a claim over £300, which was anomalous. Earlier decisions giving a strained construction were reversed because this construction failed to give effect to words which could have no other meaning. {*Gaudet v Brown* (1872) LR 5 PC 134; *Simpson v Blues* (1872) LR 7 CP 290; *Gunnestad v Price* (1875) LR 10 Ex 65; *The Alina* (1880) 5 Ex D 227.}

Example 27 On a literal construction, s 108(1) of the Magistrates' Courts Act 1952 produced the illogical result that, while magistrates could not on the same occasion impose different sentences of imprisonment totalling more than one year, they could do so by adjourning the hearing to another day. Lord Fraser of Tullybelton, delivering the decision of the House of Lords in *Forrest v Brighton JJ* {[1981] 2 All ER 711, at p 717.}, said he regarded the meaning of s 108(1) as 'too plain to be shaken by consequences which may seem to some extent anomalous'.

Example 28 In *Re British Concrete Pipe Association* {[1983] 1 All ER 203.} it was objected that the literal meaning of s 8(1) of the Iron and Steel Act 1969 enabled a nationalised company which retained a shell existence to resume trading free of a previous undertaking to the court. Donaldson MR said {P 206.}-

> 'I agree that that is an odd result, but I do not think that Parliament can be expected to cover every eventuality, and that is one of them. Parliament could of course have provided that the undertaking to the court should be divided into two and become two undertakings, but parliamentary counsel no doubt failed to foresee this interesting possibility and did not provide for it. I am quite unpersuaded by the fact that there is an anomaly to stray away from the natural meaning of the words.'

Other examples of cases where the plain meaning overrode an anomaly are: *Re Duckett* {[1964] Ch 398.} (on a teacher's bankruptcy her allowances and gratuity were available to the creditors, but not her pension contributions); *R v Dooley* {[1964] 1 WLR 648.} (inexplicably different procedures where constable and medical practitioner required taking of blood or urine test); *Macarthys Ltd v Smith* {[1979] 3 All ER 325, at p 335.} (female employee could compare her conditions with those of *previous* male employee on matters not related to pay but not on pay itself).

Anomalies both ways It may happen that each of the opposing constructions produces an anomalous consequence. This will lessen the case for a strained construction. If however it is a matter of choosing between alternative grammatical constructions (that is of grammatical ambiguity), the anomalies incident to each need to be weighed against each other.

Example 29 In a case on RSC Ord 3 r 6 (notice of intention to proceed with action after a year's delay), Nourse J held that the rule was to be construed literally, adding that 'the suggested anomaly caused by this construction of the rule is at the least balanced, if not outweighed, by another anomaly which would flow from the contrary construction'. {*Suedeclub Co Ltd v Occasions Textiles Ltd* [1981] 3 All ER 671, at p 673. See also *International Military Services Ltd v Capital and Counties plc* [1982] 2 All ER 20, *per* Slade J at p 30.}

Example 30 In a case on the meaning of the phrase 'interest in possession' in the capital transfer tax provisions of the Finance Act 1975, the Court of Appeal held that the phrase should be construed in its ordinary sense, although this might conceivably lead to anomalies. Buckley LJ said-

> 'Arguments by reference to anomalies in the construction of a statute of this kind do not seem to me to afford any very valuable assistance. The ingenuity of counsel can almost always produce possible anomalies in either direction, and that has been the case in the present matter.'

{*Pearson v IRC* [1979] 3 All ER 7, at p 12. The dictum was cited approvingly by Lord Dilhorne on appeal: [1980] 2 All ER 479, at p 487.}

Anomaly avoidable by exercise of discretion A possible anomaly carries less weight if there is interposed the discretion of some responsible person, by the sensible exercise of which the risk may be obviated.

Example 31 In *Re a Debtor (No 13 of 1964), ex p Official Receiver* {[1979] 3 All ER 15.} both sides sought to support their arguments by citing anomalies which the opposite view would produce. That of the debtor however depended on the possible making of orders discharging a person from bankruptcy subject to conditions subsequent. Thus it could be avoided by the careful exercise of the power to make such orders, which in practice were rarely made.

Anomaly purely hypothetical The court will pay little attention to a proclaimed anomaly if it is purely hypothetical, and unlikely to arise in practice.

Example 32 In *Home Office v Harman* {[1982] 1 All ER 532.}, a solicitor who was a legal officer of the National Council for Civil Liberties appealed against a finding that she had committed contempt of court by showing to a newspaper reporter documents disclosed on an order for discovery. She argued that it would be anomalous if it was contempt to show the documents themselves but not contempt to show a transcript of the proceedings in which they had been read out.

The House of Lords dismissed this argument. Lord Diplock said {P 538.} that the anomaly was 'hypothetical in the extreme'. He added: 'It does not represent a situation which is even remotely likely to occur in practice . . .'

324. Avoiding a futile or pointless result

The court seeks to avoid a construction that produces a futile or pointless result, since this is unlikely to have been intended by Parliament. Sometimes however there are overriding reasons for applying such a construction, for example where it appears that Parliament really intended it or the literal meaning is too strong.

COMMENTARY

Futile or pointless result Parliament does nothing in vain, a principle also expressed as *lex nil frustra facit* (the law does nothing in vain). {Jenk Cent 17.} It is an old maxim of the law that *quod vanum et inutile est, lex non requirit* (the law does not call for what is vain and useless). {Co Litt 319.} Or as it is put in another form: *lex non praecipit inutilia* (the law does not demand the doing of useless things). {Co Litt 127b.}

Through the inevitable limitations of language, it sometimes nevertheless happens that, in the events that have occurred in the instant case, the literal meaning of the enactment seems to demand the doing of something that is in fact futile or pointless. Here the court will strive to find a more sensible construction. {See Example 9.3.}

Duplicated legal duty Where an enactment appears to impose a legal duty that, by reason of some other enactment or rule of law, already exists *aliunde*, the court strives to avoid pronouncing in favour of such a duplication in the law. The law applies a maxim to this effect in the case of contracts and deeds: *lex rejicit superflua, pugnantia, incongrua* (the law rejects superfluous, contradictory, and incongruous things). {Jenk Cent 133.} It must follow a fortiori that the law should turn against such duplication within its own texts.

Example 1 The Extradition Act 1843 was passed to confer the executive powers needed to give effect to the extradition treaty of 1842 between Britain and the United States of America. The Act provided that each state, on the requisition of the other, should deliver up to justice all persons who, being charged with murder, *piracy*, or other specified crimes committed within the jurisdiction of one of the states, should seek asylum or be found within the territories of the other. {Emphasis added.}

In *Re Ternan* {(1864) 33 LJMC 201.} the question arose of whether the Act operated in relation to piracy not constituting an offence under the municipal law. *Held* The reference to piracy covered only acts (such as slave trading) which were made piracy under the municipal law of the state in question. It did not cover piracy under its more usual meaning, namely piracy *jure gentium*, because under public international law this is within the jurisdiction of all states, and there is no asylum from it anywhere. It could not therefore be within the mischief intended to be remedied by the 1843 Act.

Factual futility Duplication in the law is not the only reason why a purported legal duty may be pointless and therefore ineffective. Unexpected facts may lead to the same result.

Example 2 Section 16(3) of the Gaming Act 1968 requires a gaming licensee who accepts a 'cheque' for gaming to cause it to be delivered within two days to a bank for payment or collection. Failure to comply constitutes an offence. {S 23.} The Act does not define 'cheque', which leaves the free-standing definition of the term in s 3(1) of the Bills of Exchange Act 1882 to apply.

In *Aziz v Knightsbridge Gaming and Catering Services and Supplies Ltd* {(1982) *The Times* 6 July.} it was held that, although the purported cheques in question were drawn on a non-existent bank, it was their appearance that mattered, and judged by that they were 'cheques' within the meaning of s 16(3). However the mischief against which s 16(3) was aimed was the effective grant of credit for gaming. Where the bank was non-existent, and the so-called cheque was a nullity, it was pointless to require the gaming licensee to go through the motions of presenting the 'cheque' to a bank. Accordingly his failure to do so did not constitute an offence.

Disability easily avoidable Where the literal meaning of an enactment appears to impose some legal disability that can be avoided by a trifling rearrangement of affairs, the court will be slow to penalize a person who has inadvertently failed to make this rearrangement or could still easily do so. Thus in *Bishop v Deakin* {[1936] 1 Ch 409.}, Clauson J decided the case by reference to the fact that the effect of an alleged disqualification of a councillor would be that 'he would be eligible at once for re-election to the vacant office'. The learned judge added: 'I cannot think that the legislature intended such a whimsical result'. {P 414. Cf *Holmes v Bradfield RDC* [1949] 2 KB 1, at p 7.}

Example 3   Section 54 of the Public Health Act 1875 provided that 'Where a local authority supply water within their district, they shall have the same powers . . . for carrying water mains . . . as they have . . . for carrying sewers'. In *Jones v Conway and Colwyn Bay Joint Water Supply Board* {[1893] 2 Ch 603.} it was argued that this power to lay mains was conferred only where the local authority were *already* supplying water.

This was clearly the literal meaning of s 54. It would require the local authority to start by supplying water in some other way than by laying mains under the statutory power (for example by contracting for the supply with a private source). Once that supply was effected, even if only to one house for one day, the authority could then say that they did indeed 'supply water within their district'. They could therefore claim the right to exercise the statutory powers. Rejecting this construction, North J said {P 608.}-

> ' . . . it would be very absurd to say that they must in the first place, to some very possibly limited extent, actually supply water, but that as soon as they have turned on water to a single house . . . they come within the words . . . ' {P 608.}

Pointless legal proceedings   The court is always averse to requiring litigants to embark on futile or unnecessary legal proceedings. This includes a stage in proceedings that could without detriment to any party be avoided. Judges are uncomfortably aware of the costs and delays involved in a legal action, and do all in their power to minimize them. Thus Lord Reid ruled against a construction of s 29(3) of the Landlord and Tenant Act 1954 that for no substantial reason would require judges to scrutinize every application for a new business tenancy, and thus incur needless delay and cost. {*Kammins Ballrooms Ltd v Zenith Investments (Torquay) Ltd* [1971] AC 850, at p 860.}

Example 4   In *Marshall v Cottingham* {[1981] 3 All ER 8.} it was alleged that s 109(6) of the Law of Property Act 1925 required a receiver who was appointed by a mortgagee under a debenture by an instrument which did not specify the rate of his commission to obtain a court order to determine this. *Held* It was inappropriate to require the receiver to apply to the court where he did not seek a commission higher than the rate (in this case 5%) that he could originally have demanded. Megarry V-C said {P 11.}-

> ' . . . it is to be borne in mind that the mortgagee is free, without restriction, to fix a rate at 5% (or, of course, less) in the instrument appointing the receiver, and that those who are entitled to the equity in the property have no control over this. I think it improbable that Parliament intended to provide that in every case where the mortgagee had omitted to do this an application to the court must be made, even if the receiver seeks a rate of 5% or less . . . '

It is again pointless to grant a remedy by legal proceedings if it can be instantly nullified by lawful action taken after the proceedings are over. Thus what Blackstone called 'the great and efficacious writ' of habeas corpus *ad subjiciendum* is not issued as of course. As he said-

> ' . . . if it issued of mere course, without showing to the court or judge some reasonable ground for awarding it, a traitor or felon under

sentence of death, a soldier or mariner in the queen's service, a wife, a child, a relation, or a domestic, confined for insanity, or other prudential reasons, might obtain a temporary enlargement by suing out a *habeas corpus*, though sure to be remanded as soon as brought up to the court.'

{Kerr Bl (4th edn, 1875) iii 125.}

Literal meaning too strong Sometimes the court finds the literal meaning too clearly set out to enable it to avoid a futile decision.

Example 5 Section 39(3) of the Powers of Criminal Courts Act 1973 requires the court making a criminal bankruptcy order where there are two or more offences to specify the amount of the loss or damage resulting from each. In *R v Saville* {[1980] 1 All ER 861, at p 862.} Lord Widgery CJ stated the reason for this as being that the figure specified becomes a statement of each petitioning creditor's debt in the bankruptcy proceedings.

In that case Ackner J had fixed a global sum of £35,000 without apportioning it among the different offences. He later remedied this, but on appeal was alleged to have lacked jurisdiction to do so. Holding that Ackner J was merely exercising the inherent jurisdiction of the court to rectify an inchoate order, Lord Widgery remarked that since there was only one creditor, to make the apportionment was 'purely an exercise of futility'. {P 864.} He did not however use this as a ground for dismissing the appeal.

325. Avoiding an artificial result

The court seeks to avoid a construction that leads to an artificial result, since this is unlikely to have been intended by Parliament. Sometimes however there are overriding reasons for applying such a construction, for example where it appears that Parliament really intended it or the literal meaning is too strong.

COMMENTARY

Artificial result The law can deem anything to be the case, however unreal. The law brings itself into disrepute however if it dignifies with legal significance a wholly artificial hypothesis.

Example 1 Thus in the Scottish case of *Maclennan v Maclennan* {(1958) SC 105.} the court declined to rule that a wife's having availed herself, without the husband's knowledge or consent, of AID (artificial insemination by a donor) constituted her adultery within the meaning of that term in the relevant Scottish divorce Act. To do so, the court argued, would lead to wholly artificial results. For example if the donor had happened to die before the date of insemination, the legally-imputed adultery would be with a dead man - involving a kind of constructive necrophilia.

Artificiality need not be so extreme as this to rank as a significant factor in statutory interpretation. One area of importance here concerns corporations. Being entries of purely legal creation, these are imbued with a certain artificiality from the start. Sight must not be lost of the realities behind them.

Example 2 In *Re New Timbiqui Gold Mines Ltd* {[1961] Ch 319.} it was held that a person who purported to have become a member of a company *after it had been dissolved* could not, as a 'member' of the company, petition for its restoration to the register under s 353(6) of the Companies Act 1948. Commenting that s 353(6) already involved 'some degree of make-believe', Buckley J said that this should not be carried further than was absolutely necessary. {P 326.}

Example 3 Section 100 of the Public Health Act 1936 empowers a local authority to bring proceedings for nuisance in the High Court where it is of opinion that summary proceedings would afford an inadequate remedy. In *Warwick RDC v Miller-Mead* {[1962] Ch 441.} it was alleged that where the authority passed a resolution authorising proceedings *after* the writ had been issued in its name this was an insufficient expression of its 'opinion'. *Held* It sufficed if the resolution was passed at any time before the trial of the action. Lord Evershed MR said that because of the fluctuating membership of a local authority the contrary construction would give a result that was 'in a high degree artificial'. {P 454.} Before the action came to trial the authority's composition might have significantly changed, and so might its view of whether the action should proceed.

Fictions Whenever an Act sets up some fiction the courts are astute to limit the scope of its artificial effect. They are particularly concerned to ensure that it does not create harm in ways outside the intended purview of the Act.

Example 4 Section 23 of the Bankruptcy Act 1869 enabled the trustee in bankruptcy to disclaim onerous property. Where the disclaimed property was a lease, s 23 provided that it should be deemed to have been *surrendered* on the date of the adjudication in bankruptcy. The lessor could then prove against the bankrupt's estate for any arrears of rent under the lease.

However in real life a lessor's remedy may not be only against the lessee. If the lessee has sublet, the lessor can enter the sublet land and distrain for rent due to him under the head lease. The right to do this ceases however when the head lease is surrendered. In reality a prudent lessor would not accept a surrender unless his claim for rent were satisfied. What was a lessor's position under the statutory hypothesis?

The answer was supplied in *Re Levy, Ex p Walton* {(1881) 17 Ch D 746.}, where the Court of Appeal held that the lessor did not lose his right to distrain against the sublessee because there had been a fictitious surrender. James LJ said {P 756.}-

> 'Now, when a statute enacts that something shall be deemed to have been done, which in fact and truth is not done, the court is entitled and bound to ascertain for what purposes and between what persons the statutory fiction is to be resorted to . . . when the statute says that a lease which was never surrendered in fact (a true surrender requiring the consent of both parties, the one giving up and the other taking), is deemed to have been surrendered, it must be understood as saying so with the following qualification, which is absolutely necessary to prevent the most grievous injustice, and the most revolting absurdity, "shall as between the lessor on the one hand, and

the bankrupt, his trustee and estate on the other hand, be deemed to have been surrendered".'

This is an example of interstitial articulation by the court. {See s 114 of this Code.} The additional words may be treated as present by implication, as a later court found when approving this decision. {*Hill v East and West India Dock Co* (1884) 9 App Cas 448. As to implication see ss 107 to 110 of this Code.}

Artificial distinctions An area where artificiality may creep into statute law is that of distinctions. Essentially similar cases should be distinguished only on substantial grounds.

Example 5 Rule 47(20) of the Prison Rules 1964 {SI 1964/388.} provides for the punishment of an offence committed by a prisoner against good order and discipline. In *R v Board of Visitors of Highpoint Prison, ex p McConkey* {(1982) *The Times* 23 September.} a prisoner was found guilty of this offence by the board of visitors. He had remained in a cell while other prisoners in the cell were smoking cannabis, though he did not take part or assist. He was awarded 90 days loss of remission, and applied for an order of certiorari.
Held The application would be granted. Such passive conduct would not be an offence under criminal law. While proceedings of this kind had been held not to be 'proceedings in a criminal cause or matter' within the meaning of s 1(1)(a) of the Administration of Justice Act 1960 {See *R v Board of Visitors of Hull Prison, ex p St Germain* [1979] 1 QB 425.}, that was for jurisdictional purposes only. In nature they were very similar to criminal proceedings. Loss of remission for 90 days was virtually equivalent to a sentence of 90 days' imprisonment, which was serious enough to be beyond the jurisdiction of magistrates to impose. McCullough J said-

> 'To found a distinction between a sentence of imprisonment and forfeiture of remission on the basis that remission is a privilege rather than a right is artificial. The reality is that in each case a man who would otherwise be free is in prison.'

He went on to hold that prison rules should be construed no more harshly against a prisoner than would be appropriate were the offences criminal.

326. Avoiding a disproportionate counter-mischief

The court seeks to avoid a construction that cures the mischief the enactment was designed to remedy only at the cost of setting up a disproportionate counter-mischief, since this is unlikely to have been intended by Parliament. Sometimes however there are overriding reasons for applying such a construction, for example where it appears that Parliament really intended it or the literal meaning is too strong.

COMMENTARY

Mischief As to the mischief see s 138 and Part XIV of this Code.

Counter-mischief Clearly it is absurd to suppose that Parliament intended to abolish one mischief only at the cost of establishing another which is just as bad, or even worse. Many legal rules have adverse side-effects, and the policy of the law is to discard possible rules whose disadvantages outweigh their benefits.

Regulatory Acts Some types of remedy necessarily carry in their train corresponding drawbacks. One of the most frequent and inescapable of these is the loss of freedom that accompanies a regulatory measure. Such consequences are manifest, and must be treated as part of Parliament's intention.

Strict construction Where a counter-mischief would arise if the remedy provided by the Act were construed widely, the court may avoid or at least reduce it by limiting the remedy. {As to strict and liberal construction see s 154 of this Code.}

Example 1 Section 1 of the Domestic Violence and Matrimonial Proceedings Act 1976 empowers the county court to make orders excluding a violent husband from the matrimonial home. No limit is specified for the duration of such exclusion orders. The courts have held that, to reduce the counter-mischief of keeping a man out of his own home, exclusion orders should be made only for a brief period.

In *Davis v Johnson* {[1978] 2 WLR 553, at p 569.} Viscount Dilhorne inferred that the purpose of the 1976 Act was 'immediate relief not permanent resolution'. Lord Salmon found it 'difficult to believe that it could ever be fair, save in most exceptional circumstances, to keep a man out of his own flat or house for more than a few months'. {P 576.} In another case Ormrod LJ said the 1976 Act was to be regarded as 'a short term remedy essentially'. {*Hopper v Hopper* [1979] 1 All ER 181, at p 184.}

It may often appear to the court that one of the opposing constructions of the enactment, if adopted, would create a mischief of its own. {As to the opposing constructions see s 84 of this Code.} It is not unusual for a construction contended for by one of the parties to have as one of its consequences the infliction of a serious injustice on the other party. It is unlikely to have been Parliament's intention to remedy one mischief by setting up a counter-mischief of disproportionate severity. The prospect of this would constitute a negative factor in weighing the applicability of the construction in question. {As to positive and negative factors in interpretation see Part VII of this Code.}

The court also has in mind the consequences for the public welfare. {See s 127 of this Code.}

Example 2 Where one possible construction of an enactment intended to remedy the mischief caused by the operations of unskilful river pilots would prevent there being any pilots at all for a period, Dr Lushington looked 'at the mischief which would accrue' from the latter restriction and adopted the other reading of the enactment. {*The Beta* (1865) 3 Moo PCC NS 23, at p 27. See Example 140.2.}

Example 3 Again, where one construction of an enactment meant that the defendant escaped conviction for fraud because in earlier bankruptcy proceedings he had 'disclosed' what was already known, Lord Campbell CJ rejected it as productive of 'great public mischief' outweighing the mischief at which the protective enactment was directed. {*R v Skeen and Freeman* (1859) LJMC 91, at p 95. See Example 363.4.}

A type of mischief which is often the subject of modern legislation is danger to the safety of industrial workers. The court will be reluctant to read an Act as requiring one danger to be obviated at the cost of creating another.

Example 4 Section 157 of the Mines and Quarries Act 1954 said it should be a defence, in any legal proceedings to recover damages for an alleged contravention of the Act, 'to prove that it was impracticable to avoid or prevent the contravention'. In *Jayne v National Coal Board* {[1963] 2 All ER 220.} it was held that the reference to impracticability included the case where, although a protective measure would have been possible in relation to the contravention in question, it might have caused some different danger to arise.

> 'It is, I would have thought, clearly impracticable to take precautions against a danger which could not be known to be in existence, or to take a precaution which has not yet been invented. I think, however, that 'impracticable' means more than this. For instance, if one imagines that as a result of firing a shot in a ripping a dangerous stone is exposed in the roof, it might be immediately possible to remove it by boring and firing another shot; but to do so might well cause greater danger in the surrounding roof than the stone itself.'

{*Per* Veale J at p 224. For an early example where the court held 'there was mischief both ways' see T F T Plucknett *Statutes & their Interpretation in the First Half of the Fourteenth Century* p 157.}

Often it is reasonable to assume that the counter-mischief that has arisen was quite unforeseen by Parliament. Enacted law suffers by comparison with unwritten law in that it involves laying down in advance an untried remedy. This was pointed out by the seventeenth-century Scottish jurist Stair-

> 'Yea, and the nations are more happy whose laws have been entered by long custom, wrung out from their debates on particular cases, until it came to the consistence of a fixed and known custom. For thereby the conveniences and inconveniences thereof through a long tract of time are experimentally seen. So that which is found in some cases convenient, if in other cases afterward it be found inconvenient, it proves abortive in the womb of time, before it attains the maturity of a law. *But in statutes the lawgiver must at once balance the conveniences and inconveniences; wherein he may and often doth fall short . . .'*

{Stair Inst I.1.15. Emphasis added.}

As interpreters of legislation, it is the function of the courts to mitigate this defect of the legislative process so far as they properly can. Where an unforeseen counter-mischief becomes evident it may be reasonable to impute a remedial intention to Parliament. This would be an intention that, if such an untoward event should happen, the court would modify the literal meaning of the enactment so as to remedy the unexpected counter-mischief.

This is one aspect of *consequential construction*, which is explained in s 140 of this Code. Similar considerations may arise where some drafting error has occurred. {As to rectifying construction see s 142 of this Code.} A third possible cause of an unforeseen counter-mischief, or increase in an expected counter-mischief, is social or other change taking place after the passing of the Act. {Updating construction is dealt with in s 146 of this Code.}

PART XVII

Legislative Presumptions: Construction against Evasion

Introduction to Part XVII This Part gives details of the presumption, set out in s 143 of the Code, that Parliament does not intend its Act to be evaded. This is one aspect of the presumption favouring a consequential construction, which is described in s 140.

It is necessary to distinguish legitimate ways of getting round an Act (known as avoidance) from illegitimate ways (known as evasion). This distinction is explained (s 327). Whether or not Parliament includes express anti-evasion provisions does not affect the court's duty to counter evasion (s 328). This includes preventing indirect achievement of what cannot be done directly (s 329). We consider evasion by deferring, rather than cancelling, liability (s 330), and by repetitious acts (s 331).

Finally Part XVII deals with constructions that would hinder legal proceedings under the Act (s 332), or would otherwise defeat the legislative purpose (s 333).

327. Evasion distinguished from avoidance

It is necessary to distinguish, as respects the requirements of an enactment, between lawfully escaping those requirements by so arranging matters that they do not apply (in this Code referred to as avoidance) and unlawfully contravening or failing to comply with the requirements (in the Code referred to as evasion).

COMMENTARY

In ordinary speech the terms avoid and evade are interchangeable. In legal usage, particularly in relation to tax, there has grown up the useful distinction set out in this section of the Code.

Where the meaning of an enactment is doubtful it may not be possible to say with certainty, in advance of a ruling by the court, whether a projected activity amounts to avoidance or evasion. The court is likely to hold it to be the latter if to do otherwise would conflict with Parliament's intention and prejudice the effective operation of the remedy provided. But, as Maxwell says, it is not evading an Act to keep outside it. {*Maxwell on the Interpretation of Statutes* (12th edn, 1969) p 143.} Or, as Grove J expressed it, there can be no objection to 'getting away from the remedial operation of the statute while complying with the words of the statute'. {*Ramsden v Lupton* (1873) LR 9 QB 17, at p 32.}

Substance or sham?   Where a transaction is in a *form* not specified by the Act, the court will consider what its *substance* is.

Example 1   The Malayan Moneylenders Ordinance 1951 defined 'interest' as any amount (by whatsoever name called) in excess of the principal of a loan. When the Judicial Committee of the Privy Council had to consider whether this caught profits made on the exchange of current cheques for post-dated cheques, Lord Devlin said that transactions of this sort could easily be used as a cloak for moneylending. He described the task of the court in this way-

> 'It must first look at the nature of the transaction which the parties have agreed. If in form it is not a loan, it is not to the point to say that its object was to raise money for one of them or that the parties could have produced the same result more conveniently by borrowing and lending money. But if the court comes to the conclusion that the form of the transaction is only a sham and that what the parties really agreed upon was a loan which they disguised, for example, as a discounting operation, then the court will call it by its real name and act accordingly.'

{*Chow Yoong Hong v Choong Fah Rubber Manufactory* [1962] AC 209, at p 216.}

In this case the transaction was held not to be a disguised loan. For an example relating to refinancing of hire-purchase agreements in avoidance of chattel mortgage restrictions in the Bills of Sale Acts see *Snook v London & West Riding Investments Ltd* {[1967] 2 QB 786. Cf *Stoneleigh Finance Ltd v Phillips* [1965] 2 QB 537 and *Kingsley v Sterling Industrial Securities Ltd* [1967] 2 QB 747.}

Tax avoidance   Drawing the line between avoidance and evasion has particularly concerned the courts in tax cases, where very large sums are often at stake. The famous *Westminster* principle that if a transaction is genuine the courts cannot go behind it to some supposed underlying 'substance' was laid down by the House of Lords in 1936, when Lord Tomlin said-

> 'Every man is entitled, if he can, to order his affairs so that tax attaching under appropriate Acts is less than it otherwise would be. If he succeeds in ordering them so as to secure this result, then, however unappreciative the Commissioners of Inland Revenue or his fellow taxpayers may be of his ingenuity, he cannot be compelled to pay an increased tax. The so-called doctrine of 'the substance' seems to me to be nothing more than an attempt to make a man pay notwithstanding that he has so ordered his affairs that the amount of tax sought from him is not legally claimable.'

{*IRC v Westminster (Duke)* [1936] AC 1, at p 19.}

A similar point was made by Lord Greene MR in *Henriksen (Inspector of Taxes) v Grafton Hotel Ltd.* {[1942] 1 All ER 678.} After saying that it frequently happened that the same result in a business sense could be secured by two different legal transactions, one of which would attract tax and the other not, Lord Greene denied that there was any justification for holding that a taxpayer who had adopted the latter method was to be treated as if he had adopted the former. {P 683.}

The position is different where a wholly artificial scheme of tax avoidance has been embarked upon, particularly where nothing of the kind would have had any business point apart from the tax question. The morality of such specially-tailored schemes was attacked by Viscount Simon LC in *Latilla v IRC*. {[1943] AC 377.} After pointing out that those who adopted them often enjoyed the benefits of residence in Britain without accepting their share of the burden of British taxation, he said-

> 'There is, of course no doubt that they are within their legal rights, but that is no reason why their efforts, or those of the professional gentlemen who assist them in the matter, should be regarded as a commendable exercise of ingenuity or as a discharge of the duties of good citizenship. On the contrary, one result of such methods, if they succeed, is of course to increase *pro tanto* the load of tax on the shoulders of the great body of good citizens who do not desire, or do not know how, to adopt these manoeuvres.' {P 381.}

The lack of merit in tailor-made tax avoidance schemes has led the House of Lords to modify the *Westminster* principle by holding that even though each transaction in the scheme is 'genuine' and not a sham, if the sole object is tax avoidance this will not save it where it has no business or commercial purpose.

The new approach was laid down in *W T Ramsay Ltd v IRC* {[1981] 1 All ER 865.}, where Lord Wilberforce said that, while a subject was to be taxed only on clear words, this did not confine the courts to literal construction. He went on-

> 'There may, indeed should, be considered the context and scheme of the relevant Act as a whole, and its purpose may, indeed should, be regarded . . .' {P 871.}

Lord Wilberforce went on to lay down the principle that the court should set its face against purely artificial tax-avoidance devices-

> 'While the techniques of tax avoidance progress and are technically improved, the courts are not obliged to stand still. Such immobility must result either in loss of tax, to the prejudice of other taxpayers, or to Parliamentary congestion or (most likely) to both. To force the courts to adopt, in relation to closely integrated situations, a step by step, dissecting, approach . . . would be a denial rather than an affirmation of the true judicial process.' {P 873.}

What is now known as the *Ramsay* principle was foreshadowed in *Floor v Davis* {[1980] AC 695.} and reinforced by the House of Lords in *IRC v Burmah Oil Co Ltd* {(1982) STC 30.} and *Furniss (Inspector of Taxes) v Dawson*. {[1984] 1 All ER 530. See Example 330.1.}

Tax avoidance schemes often depend on whether an alleged trading element was genuine. The approach of the courts to this is well expressed in the following words of Megarry J-

> 'If on analysis it is found that the greater part of the transaction consists of elements for which there is some trading purpose or explanation . . . then the presence of what I may call 'fiscal elements', inserted solely or mainly for the purpose of producing a fiscal benefit, may not suffice to deprive the transaction of its trading status. The question is whether, viewed as a whole, the transaction is one which

can fairly be regarded as a trading transaction. If it is, then it will not be denatured merely because it was entered into with motives of reaping a fiscal advantage.'

{*Lupton (Inspector of Taxes) v F A & A B Ltd* [1968] 1 WLR 1401, at p 1419. This passage was approved, when the case reached the House of Lords, by Lord Morris of Borth-y-Gest. {*FA & AB v Lupton* [1972] AC 634.}

Another notorious method of tax avoidance is labour-only sub-contracting in the building industry. By this workers (known as 'the lump') who are in essence employees arrange to be treated as self-employed, so both avoiding and evading considerable sums in the way of income tax, national insurance contributions and other imposts. {See *Emerald Construction Co v Lowthian* [1966] 1 WLR 691; *Re C W & A L Hughes* [1966] 1 WLR 1369; *Ready Mixed Concrete (South East) Ltd v Minister of Pensions and National Insurance* [1968] 2 QB 497.} This particular abuse was successfully checked by legislation, though two attempts were needed. {See Finance Act 1971 Part II Chap II, replaced by Finance (No 2) Act 1975 Part III Chap II.}

The way the courts draw the line between avoidance and evasion is further illustrated by the following examples. We first deal with cases held to constitute avoidance.

Example 2   The statute 34 & 35 Vict c 91 (1871) stated that to be appointed as a member of the Judicial Committee of the Privy Council a person must be or have been a judge of one of the superior courts. Sir Robert Collier was then appointed a judge of the Court of Common Pleas. A week later, without ever having sat as a judge, he was appointed to the Judicial Committee. {Cited Craies *Statute Law* (7th edn, 1971) p 79 n 95.} The remedy in such cases is not legal but political. Motions censuring Collier's appointment were narrowly lost in both Houses of Parliament. {Craies, loc cit.}

Example 3   An Act gave a servant the right to a poor law settlement if he was hired for a year. With the intention of avoiding this, an employer hired him for 360 days. *Held* This was outside the Act. {*R v Inhabitants of Little Coggeshall* (1817) 6 M & S 264.}

Example 4   The occupier of a field adjoining a tollgate avoided payment of tolls by using a road he had caused to be specially made which left the turnpike highway just before the tollgate and rejoined it just after. *Held* He was not liable to the payment of tolls. {*Harding v Headington* (1874) LR 9 QB 157. Cf *Wilson v Robertson* (1855) 24 LJQB 185 (goods landed just outside dock limits).}

Example 5   A railway company sought to avoid a statutory borrowing restriction by selling some of its rolling-stock and then leasing it back. *Held* The manoeuvre was successful. {*Yorkshire Railway Wagon Co v Maclure* (1882) 21 Ch D 309. Cf *Maclay v Dixon* [1944] 1 All ER 22 (Rent Act controls on unfurnished tenancies avoided by sale of tenant's furniture to landlord under a contract providing that it would be repurchased at end of tenancy).}

Example 6   A coffee bar was held not to be 'kept open' when, although the doors were locked, food was sold through one of its windows. {*Rogers v Dodd*

[1968] 1 WLR 548. Cf *Deal v Schofield* (1867) LR 3 QB 8 (sale of beer through window to person who immediately drank it).}

Example 7 In order to frustrate the enfranchisement provisions of the Leasehold Reform Act 1967, a company being the freeholder of an estate of 100 houses granted intermediate leases to a connected company. As respects the house concerned in *Jones v Wrotham Park Settled Estates* {[1979] 1 All ER 286.} this meant that, under the statutory formula, instead of paying £300 for enfranchisement the lessee had to pay £4,000. *Held* This was not evasion because the intermediate leases, though highly unusual and potentially disastrous for the intermediate lessee, were genuine transactions and not a sham.

Next we deal with cases where the manoeuvre in question was held to constitute evasion.

Example 8 A shopkeeper was licensed to sell beer for consumption only off the premises. *Held* It was evasion to sell beer to persons who consumed it while sitting on a bench provided by the shopkeeper just outside. {*Cross v Watts* (1862) 32 LJMC 73.}

Example 9 The Theatres Act 1843 prohibited the performance of plays without a licence. *Held* It was evasion for the actors to perform below stage, their actions being reflected by mirrors so that to the audience they appeared to be on stage. {*Day v Simpson* (1865) 34 LJMC 149.}

Example 10 Section 95 of the Companies Act 1948 renders void a charge on 'book debts' which is not registered. A company sought to get round this provision by failing to keep books. *Held* This constituted evasion. The term 'book debts' must be construed as not limited to debts actually entered in a book, but as covering all debts of a kind which in a well-run business normally are so entered. {*Independent Automatic Sales Ltd v Knowles & Foster* [1962] 1 WLR 974, following a dictum by Byles J in *Shipley v Marshall* (1863) 14 CB (NS) 566, at p 573.}

Example 11 The Trade Union and Labour Relations Act 1974 protected employment that was for a 'fixed term'. An employer tried to get round this by entering into contracts for what was in essence a fixed term but which removed the protection by also providing for termination on notice. *Held* This was ineffective. If allowed to succeed it would 'erase in a substantial degree' the intention of the Act and 'give rise to an intolerable absurdity'. {*Dixon v British Broadcasting Corporation* [1979] 2 All ER 112, *per* Shaw LJ at p 117.}

328. Anti-evasion provisions in the Act or other instrument

Sometimes the legislator inserts specific anti-evasion provisions in an Act or other legislative instrument. The presence or absence of these does not however affect the courts' overall duty to counter any attempted evasion of the legislative intention.

COMMENTARY

Sometimes Parliament inserts special provisions in an Act for the purpose of countering evasion of its requirements.

Example 1 An early example was a statute of Edward I against mortmain. {Stat de Viris Mortmain Relig, 7 Edw 1 (1279) St 2, Ruffhead.} An earlier provision of Magna Carta to the like effect having been subject to evasion, this statute said mortmain was not to be effected *quacunque arte vel ingenio* (by whatever art or ingenuity).

Example 2 A modern instance is s 170 of the Customs and Excise Management Act 1979, which provides that a person who does certain acts in relation to goods with intent to evade any prohibition or restriction on the goods, or to evade duty, is guilty of an offence and may be detained.

The presence or absence of such provisions does not affect the general duty of the courts to counter evasion. They are to be regarded as included merely *ex abundanti cautela* (from excess of caution). Provisions apparently unnecessary are often included in Acts for this reason, and are to be treated accordingly.

329. What must not be done directly should not be done indirectly

Where an enactment prohibits the doing of a thing, the prohibition is taken to extend to the doing of it by indirect or roundabout means, even though not expressly referred to.

COMMENTARY

Where Parliament wishes to prohibit the doing of any act, it tends to concentrate in its wording on the obvious and direct ways of doing the act. Yet if the intention is to be achieved, the prohibition must be taken to extend to indirect methods of achieving the same object - even though these are not expressly mentioned. {Cf Example 328.1.}

Example 1 Section 203 of the Army Act 1955 says that any assignment of, or charge on, a payment made in respect of military service shall be void; and that no court shall make an order (1) restraining the beneficiary from receiving such a payment, or (2) directing it to be made to someone else. (Such a direction would be addressed to H M Paymaster General, by whom the payments in question are made.)

In *Walker v Walker* {[1983] 2 ALL ER 909.} the question arose whether s 203 precluded the making of an order under s 37 of the Matrimonial Causes Act 1973 directing H M Paymaster General to make a payment in respect of military service into court, for the ultimate benefit of the divorced wife of the man entitled to it.

Held To make such an order would be to effect indirectly what s 203 said must not be done, and so the order could not be made. Cumming-Bruce LJ said it was clear that the mischief against which s 203 was directed was the loss by service personnel of the right to receive moneys to which it was expedient they should be entitled. He added-

'This was consistent with those provisions of the 1955 Act which have been re-enacted over a period of nearly a century, which provided that there should be a strict control over military pay ... ' {P 912.}

330. Evasion by deferring liability

The court will infer an intention by Parliament to treat as evasion of an Act the deferring of liability under it in ways not envisaged by the Act.

COMMENTARY

If an Act imposes a liability falling at a certain time, it is an evasion of the Act to procure a postponement of the liability by artificial means not contemplated by the Act.

Example 1 In *Furniss (Inspector of Taxes) v Dawson* {[1984] 1 All ER 530.} the House of Lords held a tax deferment scheme ineffective within the *Ramsay* principle {*W T Ramsay Ltd v IRC* [1982] AC 300. See p 711 above.}, even though it was 'a simple and honest scheme which merely seeks to defer payment of tax until the taxpayer has received into his hands the gain which he has made'. {*Per* Lord Brightman at p 536.}

331. Evasion by repetitious acts

The court will infer an intention by Parliament that evasion of an Act should not be countenanced where the method used is constant repetition of acts which taken singly are unexceptionable, but which considered together cumulatively effect an evasion of the purpose of the Act.

COMMENTARY

What substantially amounts to evasion of an enactment can sometimes be effected by constant repetition of acts which in themselves are lawful. An enactment of Edward I countered this device of evasion by repetitious acts in relation to replevin. {Stat Westm II (1285) c 2.} This recited that 'some people bring replevin and after being ordered to return the distress, again replevy it, and keep on repeating this process endlessly'. {T F T Plucknett *Statutes & their Interpretation in the First Half of the Fourteenth Century* p 41.}

Example 1 The Public-Houses Amendment (Scotland) Act 1862 gave magistrates power to order the public houses 'in any particular locality' to close at an earlier hour than the statutory closing time. An attempt was made to use this power to close *all* public houses early by making one order after another until the whole district was covered. *Held* This was unlawful. Lord Cairns said it would be-

' ... adopting a course for the purpose of doing what I must describe as evading an Act of Parliament, and your lordships would not be

715

prepared to sanction, but would discountenance and prevent, the exercise of a power so used.'

{*Macbeth v Ashley* (1874) LR 2 HL(Sc) 352, at p 357. Cf Example 395.4.}

Counter by injunction   Sometimes the penalties for breach laid down by the Act are, or through inflation have become, so inadequate that they no longer deter. Here the court may resort to the use of the injunction procedure to counter the continued repetition of evasive acts. In *A-G v Harris* {[1961] 1 QB 74.} repeated breaches of a byelaw were restrained by injunction, since the statutory penalties were considered by the court insufficient. {See Example 14.12}

Sometimes however the court finds itself helpless to prevent evasion by repetitious acts.

Example 2   The Bills of Sale Act 1854 required a bill of sale to be registered within 21 days. {See now Bills of Sale Act 1878 s 9.} To get round this the parties in *Smale v Burr* {(1872) LR 8 CP 64.} effected a manoeuvre by which, just before the 21 days expired, a new bill was issued in exchange for the first. This was repeated fifteen or sixteen times, but the court did not consider it possible to prevent the practice.

332. Construction which hinders legal proceedings under Act

So that the purpose of an Act may be achieved, it is necessary that any legal proceedings connected with its enforcement and administration should be facilitated and not hindered. Accordingly the courts frown on attempts to construe an enactment in such a way as to frustrate or stultify legal proceedings under the Act.

COMMENTARY

As an aspect of the court's function of enforcing Acts of Parliament {See s 19 of this Code.}, it will not allow legal proceedings under an Act to be stultified or obstructed by inappropriate constructions.

Example 1   Thus in *R v Aubrey-Fletcher, ex p Ross-Munro* {[1968] 1 QB 620, at p 627} Lord Parker CJ rejected a construction of s 19 of the Extradition Act 1870 that would have had-

' . . . another alarming consequence . . . that if, when the person concerned arrives in this country after being surrendered by the foreign state, he is arrested, cautioned and questioned by a police officer, evidence of what he said, whether for him or against him, would be quite inadmissible.'

In a case concerning discovery of documents, Pennycuick J rejected a suggested construction of RSC Ord 6 r 3(1) that he said 'would lead to the most extraordinary results'. He went on-

'It would follow, for example, that if documents came into the possession of persons as executors and they then handed over those documents to themselves in their capacity as trustees of the same will, the moment they have done so they would be exempt from discovery in an action in which they were sued as personal representatives.'

{*Buchanan-Michaelson v Rubinstein* [1965] Ch 258. The order made by Pennycuick J was later discharged on different grounds: [1965] 1 WLR 390.}

A construction that unreasonably hinders the task of the prosecution in enforcing criminal law will be disfavoured.

Example 2   Thus in *R v Holt* {[1981] 2 All ER 854.} the Court of Appeal rejected a construction of s 2(1) of the Theft Act 1978 on which, in the case of an attempt which failed-

'... the prosecution would be in a dilemma since it would either be impossible to charge such an attempt or the prosecution would be obliged to charge attempts in the alternative in which case, since any attempt failed, it would be quite uncertain which of the alternatives it was.'

{*Per* Lawson J at pp 856-7.}

Equally a construction which unreasonably hinders the defence in criminal trials will not be favoured, particularly where the offence is one of absolute or strict liability. {*Rochdale Metropolitan Borough Council v FMC (Meat) Ltd* [1980] 2 All ER 303.}

The principle stated in this section of the Code comes into play whenever a particular construction would allow a legal remedy to be rendered nugatory.

Example 3   A private Act provided that no action should be brought against certain shipowners for damage unless a month's notice of action was given. *Held* This was not intended to apply to Admiralty proceedings *in rem* because if it did the shipowners could easily evade the proceedings by causing the ship to depart before the month was up. {*The Longford* (1889) 14 PD 34.}

An important aspect of the principle concerns cases where an enactment falls to be administered by lay persons, such as jurors, tribunal members, or justices of the peace. Here it is desirable to prefer the simple rather than the abstruse construction of the enactment.

Example 4   In *R v Bloxham* {[1981] 2 All ER 647.} the point at issue concerned the interpretation of the phrase 'for the benefit of another person' in s 22(1) of the Theft Act 1968, which makes it the offence of handling stolen goods where a person 'dishonestly undertakes or assists in their ... realisation by or for the benefit of another person'.

The appellant had bought a car which he later came to believe was stolen property. He then sold it at a low price to another person. The prosecution argued that he had thereby realised it for the benefit of that other person within the meaning of s 22(1). The appellant argued that the words implied that the recipient must be connected with the original theft. Kilner Brown J, after citing the differing views of various text writers including L W Blake, said {P 649.}-

'We have come to the same conclusion as Mr Blake, not so much on academic and metaphysical grounds as on pragmatic grounds. The mischief at which the section is aimed is a dishonest handling. If the words permit of a simple approach capable of being readily understood by a jury this is to be preferred.'

{See also Examples 107.2, 132.5, 142.11, 142.13, 321.7 and 321.10 to 321.12.}

333. Construction which otherwise defeats legislative purpose

The principle requiring a construction against evasion is not limited to cases of deliberate or obvious evasion. It extends to any way by which an Act's integrity of purpose may be undermined, even innocently or unwittingly.

COMMENTARY

An Act has its integrity, which the courts seek to uphold. They turn against a construction which would enable persons to undermine this integrity by using the scheme of the Act in unintended ways.

Example 1 The principle is well illustrated by *Meadows v Clerical, Medical and General Life Assurance Society.* {[1980] 1 All ER 454.} Section 24 of the Landlord and Tenant Act 1954 authorises a person who is the tenant under an expiring business 'tenancy' to apply to the court for a new tenancy. It goes on to state that this shall not prevent a tenancy's termination by forfeiture. The case concerned an application for a new tenancy made while forfeiture proceedings were pending. The leasehold premises were possibly going to be demolished, and by consent the proceedings following issue of the writ claiming forfeiture had been adjourned generally.

Until forfeiture proceedings have been finally resolved it cannot be known whether the tenancy will be held to have come to an end as from the date of the writ claiming forfeiture or will be held to have continued uninterrupted. Meanwhile the tenancy has 'a trance-like existence'. {*Per* Megarry V-C at p 457.} The question here was whether or not, at the time of the application for a new tenancy under s 24, there was in existence a 'tenancy' within the meaning of the section. In other words is a tenancy which (because of possible forfeiture) is in a trance-like state nevertheless to be treated as a 'tenancy'?

Megarry V-C acknowledged that there were difficulties either way. If this were held to be a tenancy within the meaning of the section then other tenants, by dragging out forfeiture proceedings, might in future obtain new tenancies unmeritoriously. But if it were held *not* to be a tenancy, landlords might serve forfeiture notices merely in order to frustrate likely applications for new tenancies. In a passage encapsulating the principle of this section of the Code, Megarry V-C said {P 460.}-

> 'I agree that the Act should, if possible, be construed in such a way as to prevent it being manipulated by either landlords or tenants so as to produce results contrary to its purpose.'

Megarry V-C went on to hold that on the facts of the instant case the trance-like tenancy should indeed be treated as a 'tenancy'. He added however that, in a case where the tenant was found to be unjustly prolonging the forfeiture proceedings, the tenant's claim for relief against forfeiture should be treated as unreal. It would therefore fall to be disregarded, and there would then be no expiring 'tenancy' upon which to found an application for a new tenancy. This would avoid any misuse of the Act.

Example 2 The case of *Stile Hall Properties Ltd v Gooch* {[1979] 3 All ER 848.} concerned a different aspect of the procedure under Part II of the Landlord and Tenant Act 1954. The business tenant applied for a new tenancy by notice to the landlord under s 26 of the Act. By s 26(5), this operated to terminate the existing tenancy on the date specified in the notice as the start of the projected new tenancy. To obtain a court order for the new tenancy, the tenant was required by s 29(3) to make an application to the court within a stated time limit. This she omitted to do. Later she served what purported to be a fresh notice under s 26 for the grant of a new tenancy.
Held The second notice was invalid. It could be effectively served only while the existing tenancy subsisted, but this had previously come to an end by virtue of s 26(5). Edmund Davies LJ said {P 852.}-

> 'The Act vests radical rights in the tenant of business premises. It also recognises that the landlord also has certain rights and must be protected against exploitation and against harassment. If what is suggested here were indeed the position and the tenant could go on indefinitely serving the landlord with fresh requests, it appears to me that a quite impossible situation would result ... The whole scheme [of the Act] would be frustrated were such a request to have any validity.'

To respect the integrity of the Act's purpose does not necessarily mean respecting the literal meaning of what it says. Particularly in a case of *disorganised composition* {See s 76 of this Code.} the literal meaning may be the opposite of what is truly intended.

Example 3 The leading case of *Remon v City of London Real Property Co Ltd* {[1921] 1 KB 49.} also concerned protection for tenants, this time given by the Increase of Rent and Mortgage Interest (Restrictions) Act 1920. Here the protection depended on whether the premises were at the material time 'let as a separate dwelling'. {S 12(2).} In the instant case the premises were not at the material time let at all, the term of the tenancy having expired. *Held* The premises must nevertheless be treated as being let, since otherwise the object of the Act would be frustrated. Scrutton LJ said {P 58.}-

> 'Whom then did [the draftsman] mean to include in the term "tenant"? If a tenant by agreement whose tenancy had expired was not within those terms, the whole purpose of the Act would have been defeated ... I feel I am straining language in speaking of a person whose tenancy has expired ... as a "tenant" ... but such a person appears to be within the clear intention of the legislature ...'

Commenting on this decision in a later case, Brandon LJ said that the Court of Appeal-

> ' ... felt bound to give strained and unnatural meanings to perfectly ordinary words, such as "tenant", "tenancy", "letting" and "let". It did so for one reason, and for one reason only, namely that unless

those words were given strained and unnatural meanings, the manifest purpose of the 1920 Act (to protect from eviction persons whose contractual tenancies had been brought or come to an end) would be defeated.'

{*London Borough of Hammersmith and Fulham v Harrison* [1981] 2 All ER 588, at p 598.}

Perceiving and giving effect to the true purpose of an enactment may often involve giving the words a strained or unexpected meaning.

Example 4 An enactment restricting the supply of controlled drugs allowed a registered medical practitioner to have a drug in his possession 'for the purpose of acting in his capacity as such'. {Misuse of Drugs Regulations 1973 (SI 1973/797), reg 10(1).} Clearly this contemplated the administration of the drug to a patient. In *R v Dunbar* {[1982] 1 All ER 188.} the question was whether a registered medical practitioner who treated *himself* was 'acting in his capacity as such'. The trial judge had withheld this question from the jury on the ground that the answer must in law be no. *Held* The question should have been left to the jury, as it was a question of fact not law, depending on such considerations as the good faith of the practitioner. Lord Lane CJ said {P 191.}-

'It is very much a matter of first impression, as so often in this kind of case. But the way in which it is put on behalf of the Crown is that it is impossible for a person to act in his capacity as a doctor if he is not at the same time treating a patient, other than himself ... That is a proposition which we find ourselves unable to accept. There seem to us to be many occasions on which it can properly be said that a man is acting in his capacity as a doctor which have nothing to do with the existence of any patients.'

{See also Examples 108.1 and 224.5.}

PART XVIII

Legislative Presumptions: Application of Ancillary Rules of Law

Introduction to Part XVIII This Part spells out the effect of the presumption laid down in s 144 of the Code that Parliament is taken to intend general rules of law to apply so far as relevant.

Part XVIII deals in turn with the main areas of general law, as follows: constitutional law (s 334), the decision-making rules required by natural justice and similar factors (s 335), and the rules of equity (s 336), contract (s 337), property (s 338), tort (s 339), crime (s 340), jurisdiction, evidence and procedure (s 341), and private international law (s 342).

334. Rules of constitutional law

Unless the contrary intention appears, an enactment by implication imports any principle or rule of constitutional law (whether statutory or non-statutory) which prevails in the territory to which the enactment extends and is relevant to the operation of the enactment in that territory.

COMMENTARY

General principle As to the general principle under which relevant rules of general law are by implication taken to be imported so far as necessary for the operation of an enactment see s 144 of this Code.

Constitutional law The nature and authority of all legislation is rooted in constitutional law. Even where, as in Britain, the constitution is not formally embodied in a written instrument it must follow that, unless the contrary intention appears, Parliament is presumed to intend to conform to established constitutional patterns.

Since constitutional law is the framework of the state, Acts are taken to operate within its confines. Only where an Act on its face sets out to alter a rule of the constitution will it be taken to intend this. The constitution of a state, even when unwritten, is not to be altered by a sidewind. {Cf s 133 of this Code.}

In practical terms (whatever the statutes may say) the constitution is based on the *current* sense of what is appropriate. The dead do not rule the living.

When the state is settled and mature, the people whose sense of the fitting is relevant in the administration (as opposed to the making) of the law are those who form the establishment, notably the judiciary. Their ideas are based on a knowledge of the history and current stage of development of political institutions. When, as in Britain, these have emerged from slow progress in a uniform direction the essential principles are likely to command almost universal acceptance.

There are many ways in which principles of constitutional law are to be treated as embodied in Acts under interpretation. All we have space for are some examples of the more important aspects. {See also Example 97.1.}

Position of the Crown   Many rules of law touch the position of the Crown. Parliament is presumed to intend that regard shall be had to them in the construction of any enactment.

Thus the Monarch, acting through the Lord Chancellor as head of the Court of Chancery (now the Chancery Division of the High Court), is *parens patriae* (or ex officio guardian) of infants, idiots and lunatics. The courts have held that there is a presumption that the wardship jurisdiction (now largely regulated by statute) which is the modern expression of the *parens patriae* doctrine is not ousted by other provisions for the welfare of children, such as those under which local authorities are granted care orders. {*A v Liverpool City Council* [1982] AC 363, *per* Lord Roskill at p 379.}

This is in line with the presumption that Parliament intends to safeguard the welfare of minors, and others who are not of full legal capacity. Apart from many Acts specifically directed to this end, there are incidental indications of Parliament's concern. Thus the need for leave in order to be able to bring an appeal to the Court of Appeal is dispensed with where the custody, education or welfare of a minor is concerned. {Supreme Court Act 1981 s 18(1)(h)(i).} Where, in any proceedings before any court, the custody or upbringing of a minor, or the application of his property, is in question, the welfare of the minor is the first and paramount consideration. {Guardianship of Minors Act 1971 s 1.} Less concern of this kind is expressly shown for idiots and lunatics.

The role of the Crown as *parens patriae* is but one of many Crown doctrines to be borne in mind in statutory interpretation. Others are dealt with elsewhere in this work. {As to the doctrine of Crown immunity see s 34 of this Code. For instruments made under the royal prerogative see ss 48 and 49.}

Salus populi suprema lex   The rule that the welfare of the people is the supreme law must prevail in any civilised state, and accordingly prevails in the United Kingdom. {13 Co Inst 139; *A-G v De Keyser's Royal Hotel* [1920] AC 508, *per* Lord Moulton at p 552.} Under this rule the law may require of a citizen his time and effort, his property, and even his life. Parliament is presumed to legislate accordingly.

This rule was the basis of impressment, the authority of the state to 'press' or compel the service of the subject for the defence of the realm. An Act of 1555 took away the exemption from impressment of Thames watermen. {2 & 3 Ph & M c 16.} On the other hand many Acts *conferred* such exemptions. {See, e g, 5 Eliz 1 (1562) c 5; 16 Cha 1 (1640) c 5; 2 & 3 Ann (1703) c 13; 14 Geo 2 (1740) c 38; 14 Geo 3 (1774) c 78; 5 & 6 Will 4 (1835) c 24.} In 1799 Parliament ordered a general press of all rogues and vagabonds, for drafting into the regiments.

Necessitas non habet legem   All statutes are subject to the implied rule that in dire emergency their injunctions give way to what necessity demands. It is not so much that 'necessity knows no law' as that the common law in its wisdom provides for such eventualities; and is by implication imported into statute law. As was said in the *Case of the King's Prerogative in Saltpetre* {(1607) 12 Co Rep 12.}-

> 'But when enemies come against the realm to the sea-coast, it is lawful to come upon my land adjoining to the same coast, to make trenches or bulwarks for the defence of the realm, for every subject hath benefit by it. And therefore by the common law, every man may come upon my land for the defence of the realm, as appears from [the statute 8 Edw 4 c 23] ... and for the commonwealth a man shall suffer damage; as, for saving of a city or town, a house shall be plucked down if the next be on fire ... '

One effect of this principle is to require a modified interpretation of legislation where the state is in danger or there is other emergency. Principles such as those in favour of personal liberty {See s 290 of this Code.} may then have to give way. {For examples see *R v Halliday, ex p Zadig* [1917] AC 260 and *Liversidge v Anderson* [1942] AC 206 (Example 97.1).}

As to the necessity principle see further s 352 of this Code.

Electoral provisions   As has been said by distinguished jurists: 'The general structure of government cannot be altered by a side-wind'. {D L Keir and F H Lawson *Cases in Constitutional Law* (4th edn, 1954) p 11.} So an enactment is presumed not to amend basic constitutional provisions unless by explicit provision. This applies for example to provisions as to voting rights in parliamentary elections.

Example 1   In the days before female suffrage and the abolition of university seats, s 27 of the Representation of the People (Scotland) Act 1868 gave voting rights to every 'person' whose name was on the register of the general council of a Scottish university. At that time only males were entitled to be entered on such registers, but by virtue of s 4 of Lord Brougham's Act 1850 {13 & 14 Vict c 21.} all words importing the masculine gender were to be 'deemed and taken to include females ... unless the contrary ... is *expressly* provided'. {Emphasis added.} In s 27 of the 1868 Act the contrary was not expressly provided, and when the University of St Andrews later opened its doors to women they claimed to be within it, and to be therefore entitled to vote.
Held This had not been unequivocally expressed to be Parliament's intention, and the claim could not be admitted. Lord Robertson said-

> ' ... I think that a judgment is wholesome and of good example which puts forward subject-matter and fundamental constitutional law as guides of construction never to be neglected in favour of verbal possibilities.'

{*Nairn v University of St Andrews* [1909] AC 147, at p 161. See also the even stronger decision in *Viscountess Rhondda's Claim* [1922] 2 AC 339. This denied a peeress the right to sit in the House of Lords despite unequivocal words in s 1 of the Sex Disqualification (Removal) Act 1919 (see Bennion 'The Sex

Disqualification (Removal) Act - 60 Inglorious Years' (1979) 129 NLJ 1088; (1980) 130 NLJ 22.}

Taxation only by Parliament   The Bill of Rights (1688) {1 Will & Mar sess 2 c 2.}, after reciting that the late King James II had, by the assistance of 'diverse evill councillors judges and ministers imployed by him', endeavoured to subvert the laws and liberties of the kingdom by levying money otherwise than as granted by Parliament, declared illegal the levying of money for or to the use of the Crown by pretence of prerogative without grant of Parliament.

By a subsequent development culminating in the Parliament Act 1911, it came to be established as a constitutional usage that Parliament here meant the House of Commons alone. {See s 43 of this Code.} This rule is presumed to be incorporated in any relevant enactment, unless the contrary intention appears.

Example 2   By the combined effect of s 4 of the New Ministries and Secretaries Act 1916 and reg 2F of the Defence of the Realm Regulations {Made under s 1(1) of the Defence of the Realm (Consolidation) Act 1914.}, the Food Controller was given wide-ranging powers to make orders for the purpose of encouraging or maintaining the wartime food supply. He made an order prohibiting dealing in milk except under a licence granted only where the licensee agreed to pay the Food Controller twopence a gallon.

In *A-G v Wilts United Dairies Ltd* {(1921) 37 TLR 884.} the power to make this order was challenged. *Held* The order was ultra vires, and therefore void. Atkin LJ said {P 886}-

> 'Though the attention of our ancestors was directed especially to abuses of the prerogative, there can be no doubt that [the Bill of Rights 1688] declares the law that no money shall be levied for or to the use of the Crown except by grant of Parliament. We know how strictly Parliament has maintained this right - and, in particular, how jealously the House of Commons has asserted its predominance in the power of raising money. An elaborate custom of Parliament has prevailed by which money for the service of the Crown is only granted at the request of the Crown made by a responsible Minister and assented to by a resolution of the House in Committee. By constitutional usage no money proposal can be altered by the Second Chamber, whose powers are confined to acceptance or rejection. Similar elaborate checks exist in respect to authority for expenditure of the public revenue . . . '

Atkin LJ went on to say that while Parliament could, whether expressly or by implication, and whether directly or indirectly, have conferred taxing powers on the Food Controller-

> ' . . . the circumstances would be remarkable indeed which would induce the Court to believe that the Legislature had sacrificed all the well-known checks and precautions, and, not in express words, but merely by implication, had entrusted a Minister of the Crown with undefined and unlimited powers of imposing charges upon the subject for purposes connected with his department . . . It makes no

difference that the obligation to pay the money is expressed in the form of an agreement. It was illegal for the Food Controller to require such an agreement as a condition of any licence. It was illegal for him to enter into such an agreement.'

{P 886. The decision was affirmed by the House of Lords: (1922) 38 TLR 781.}

This important decision means that, while charges may be made for the issue of licences, or for any other services provided under statute, the revenue from them must not exceed the cost of administering the service. {*Congreve v Home Office* [1976] QB 629.}

Parliamentary privilege It is to be inferred that, unless the contrary intetion appears, an Act is not intended to operate in a way that infringes established rules of parliamentary privilege.

Example 3 The Licensing (Consolidation) Act 1910 s 65(1) prohibited the sale of intoxicating liquor without a justices' licence. Section 72 contained a list of exemptions, but this did not include sales of liquor within the precincts of the Houses of Parliament. *Held* The sale of intoxicating liquor within the precincts of the House of Commons is a matter falling within the privilege the House possesses of regulating its internal affairs and procedure. It is therefore to be presumed that the Act was not intended to apply to such sales, notwithstanding that they were omitted from the exceptions set out in s 72. {*R v Graham-Campbell, ex p Herbert* [1935] 1 KB 594.}

The presumption does not extend to 'ordinary' criminal acts because parliamentary privilege has never been claimed in respect of them. {See Inskip A-G *arguendo* in *R v Graham-Campbell, ex p Herbert* [1935] 1 KB 594, at p 598.} An 'ordinary' criminal act is one that in itself is generally regarded as reprehensible, irrespective of statute. This involves distinguishing *mala prohibita* from *mala in se*, a distinction which was said to be obsolete by Best J in *Bensley v Bignold*. {(1822) 5 B & Ald 335, at p 341.}

335. Decision-making rules of natural justice etc

Unless the contrary intention appears, the conferring by an enactment of a power or duty to make a decision by implication imports related principles and rules of law. These are the principles and rules (such as the need to observe natural justice) which have been laid down or adopted by the courts to govern the making of such decisions in the territory to which the enactment extends.

COMMENTARY

General principle As to the principle under which relevant rules of general law are by implication taken to be imported so far as necessary for the operation of an enactment see s 144 of this Code.

Decision-making function Many enactments confer on courts, tribunals, public authorities, administrative officials and other functionaries the power or duty to make decisions of one sort or another. The courts have evolved various rules to govern the exercise of this decision-making function, notably the duty to act *fairly*. This duty applies whether or not the decision is made judicially. It is, said Lord Denning MR, the simple precept which now governs the administrative procedure of all public bodies. {*Payne v Lord Harris of Greenwich* [1981] 2 All ER 842, at p 845.} It applies only because Parliament is taken to intend that it shall.

The rules thus imported, though largely within the province of administrative law, also extend to decisions taken (in exercise of the judicial power of the state) by the courts themselves. It follows that the rules apply to every type of functionary upon whom any Act confers a decision-making duty. They are, as Lord Denning put it, 'implicit in the Act'. {*R v Commission for Racial Equality, ex p Hillingdon LBC* (1981) *The Times* 17 July.}

There are many ways in which these rules are to be treated as embodied in Acts under interpretation. All we have space for are some examples of the more important aspects.

Consequences of a decision   We are here concerned only with what is presumed to be the legislative intention giving rise to the legal meaning of the enabling enactment. If a decision taken under the enactment is *affirmative*, action in pursuance of it is likely to follow. This action may be challenged, but if the decision was consonant with the legal meaning of the enactment the challenge will fail. If the decision is *negative* (for example a refusal to issue a licence) no administrative action will follow; and any challenge will lie simply against the decision itself. Again, the challenge will fail if the decision accorded with the enactment under which it was made.

It follows that in either case it is the decision itself that matters from the viewpoint of statutory interpretation. Accordingly we do not here consider the methods by which a decision, or action taken under it, may be challenged (for example by an application for judicial review). {For the principles governing judicial review see s 24 of this Code.} As Lord Brightman said in *Chief Constable of the North Wales Police v Evans* {[1982] 3 All ER 141.}: 'Judicial review is concerned not with the decision, but with the decision-making process'. {P 154.} Lord Brightman added: 'Unless that restriction on the power of the court is observed, the court will in my view, under the guise of preventing the abuse of power, be itself guilty of usurping power'.

The *remedies* for improper decision-making are thus beyond the scope of this section of the Code. It may however be mentioned that it is always presumed, unless the contrary intention appears, that when conferring decision-making powers Parliament intends the normal remedies for abuse to apply.

Requirement of intra vires   One invariable and universal rule is that the decision must be within the power or jurisdiction conferred by the enactment. It must not be ultra vires. This is self-evident, indeed tautologous, because of its nature a statutory power cannot go wider than itself. {For the doctrine of ultra vires see s 58 of this Code.}

Requirement of good faith   A second invariable and universal rule is that every decision under statutory powers must be made in good faith. It is inconceivable the Parliament would show an intention to depart from this.

There are many judicial dicta to the effect that Parliament cannot be taken to intend decisions under its Acts to be arrived at fraudulently, or for private gain or oppression, or for other indirect motive, or otherwise with *mala fides*. {See, e g, *Kruse v Johnson* [1898] 2 QB 91, *per* Lord Russell of Killowen at pp 99-100; *Mayor etc of Westminster v London & North Western Rly Co Ltd* [1905] AC 426, *per* Lord Macnaghten at p 430; *Board of Education v Rice* [1911] AC 179, *per* Lord Loreburn LC at p 182; *Local Government Board v Arlidge* [1915] AC 120, *per* Viscount Haldane LC at pp 132–133; *Nakkuda Ali v M F de S Jayaratne* [1951] AC 66, *per* Lord Radcliffe at p 77. See also Example 4.}

Unless the contrary intention appears The caveat embodied in the phrase 'unless the contrary intention appears' is more than usually apt in this section of the Code. That is because in most cases the wording of the enactment will go some way towards spelling out how the decisions under it are to be taken.

Example 1 A common formula is to empower a functionary to arrive at a specified decision 'if he has reasonable cause to believe' that certain facts exist. {E g the formula in reg 18b of the Defence (General) Regulations 1939, which was the subject of the leading case of *Liversidge v Anderson* [1942] AC 206. The case is discussed above (see Example 97.1).} This formula in itself lays down the main condition regulating the making of the decision, and to that extent displaces implied rules.

It follows that implied ancillary rules will in this area tend to be residual, being modified to a greater or lesser extent by the express words of the enactment.

Apart from this general consideration, there may in rare cases be express statutory provision modifying the common-law rules. This is particularly necessary where all the decision-makers under a particular provision are likely to have a personal interest. Thus s 304 of the Public Health Act 1936 says that a judge or magistrate shall not be disqualified from making decisions under the Act merely because he is a ratepayer. Section 48(5) of the Licensing Act 1953, re-enacted as s 193(6) of the Licensing Act 1964, provides that where a licensing justice is disqualified for interest this shall not invalidate any act done by him. This was relied on in a case where all the licensing justices were members of a co-operative society which was applying for an off-licence.

On the other hand an Act may state expressly that a person with an interest *is* to be treated as disqualified. Thus s 64 of the Justices of the Peace Act 1979 disqualifies members of local authorities from acting as members of the Crown Court or of a magistrates' court in a case where the local authority is a party.

Another type of statutory exception arises where an enactment authorises the making of an application to the court *ex parte*, thus negativing the principle *audi alteram partem*. {*R v Raymond* [1981] 2 All ER 246. As to the *audi alteram partem* principle see s 346 of this Code.}

Natural justice Whenever an enactment confers a *judicial* decision-making function on a person or body, Parliament is prima facie taken to intend that it shall be exercised in accordance with the relevant rules or principles of natural justice.

Thus in *R v Hull Prison Board of Visitors, ex p St Germain (No 2)* {[1979] 3 All ER 545, at p 552.} Geoffrey Lane LJ said-

'For a long time the courts have without objection from Parliament supplemented procedure laid down in legislation where they have found that to be necessary . . .'

This judicial supplementing is not limited to the functions of courts of law, but extends to any body or person with the statutory duty of acting 'judicially'. Lord Morris of Borth-y-Gest explained the principle thus {*Wiseman v Borneman* [1969] 3 All ER 275, at p 278.}-

'My Lords, that the conception of natural justice should at all stages guide those who discharge judicial functions is not merely an acceptable but is an essential part of the philosophy of law . . . Natural justice, it has been said, is only "fair play in action". Nor do we wait for direction from Parliament. The common law has abundant riches; there may we find what Byles J called "the justice of the common law" {*Cooper v Wandsworth Board of Works* (1863) 14 CB(NS) 180, at p 194.}.'

When not exercisable by a judge, these 'judicial functions' have often been termed *quasi-judicial*. An unsatisfactory phrase, it was coined to indicate that some but not all aspects of the statutory function are judicial in nature. Thus the report of the Committee on Ministers' Powers {1932, Cmd 4060.} stated that 'a quasi-judicial decision is only an administrative decision, some stage or element of which possesses judicial characteristics'. But if there is only one decision, and in the course of reaching it the decision-maker necessarily behaves in a judicial way, it is better to say straight out that in his decision making he is acting judicially rather than quasi-judicially. The quality of being judicial is no half-and-half affair.

When is a functionary acting 'judicially'? The cases where a functionary exercising statutory decision-making powers is taken to act judicially fall into two categories. The firts, which is straightforward, comprises the courts which exercise the judicial power of the state. These are described in s 19 of this Code.

The second category is less easy to define, though it is clear that it is limited to executive or administrative functions. As Greene MR said, when reviewing the exercise of the function of licensing cinema performances under the Cinematograph Act 1909 as amended by the Sunday Entertainments Act 1932: 'we are dealing with not a judicial act, but an executive act'. {*Associated Provincial Picture Houses Ltd v Wednesbury Corpn* [1948] 1 KB 223, at p 228.}

So we have the strange concept of a decision-maker performing an executive function who is nevertheless acting 'judicially'. The essential feature is that the functionary is *passing judgment* on the conduct, character, property or other attributes of some person with a view to withholding a benefit or imposing a detriment (though as we shall see the concept does not apply in *all* such cases). Thus Parker J spoke of certiorari lying where an administrative tribunal 'is exercising, after hearing evidence, judicial functions in the sense that it has to decide on evidence between a proposal and an opposition'. {*R v Manchester Legal Aid Committee, ex p R A Brand & Co Ltd* [1952] 2 QB 413, at p 429}. The presumption that the decision is intended to be judicial applies particularly to *appellate* functions. As Viscount Haldane LC said in *Local Government Board v Arlidge* {[1915] AC 120, at p 132}: 'when the duty of deciding an appeal is imposed, those whose duty it is to decide it must act judicially'.

Example 2 By virtue of the Dock Workers (Regulation of Employment) Order 1947, the London Dock Labour Board were required to exercise disciplinary functions in relation to dockers. In *Barnard v National Dock Labour Board* {[1953] 2 QB 18.} the Court of Appeal held that in carrying out this executive function the Board were acting judicially. Denning LJ said {P 40}-

'Under the provisions of the scheme ... the board are put in a judicial position between the men and the employers; they are to receive reports from the employers and investigate them; they have to inquire whether the man has abeen guilty of misconduct, such as failing to comply with a lawful order, or failing to comply with the provisions of the scheme, and if they find against him they can suspend him without pay, or can even dismiss him summarily.'

The next consideration is whether in thus passing judgment the purpose of the enactment requires the functionary to act objectively and impartially or with a bias in favour of some particular *policy*. In the latter case he is not to be treated as acting judicially.

Example 3 Section 1(1) of the New Towns Act 1946 empowered the relevant Minister to designate an area as the site of a new town if satisfied, after consultation with concerned local authorities, that it was expedient to do so in the national interest. Even before the Act was passed it had been decided by the Government that the first new town under it should be at Stevenage. In *Franklin v Minister of Town and Country Planning* {[1948] AC 87.} the order designating land for this purpose was challenged on the ground of bias by the Minister. *Held* The decision was purely administrative, and the Act did not require the Minister to act judicially. Lord Thankerton said {P 102}-

'I am of opinion that no judicial duty is laid on the respondent in discharge of these statutory duties,' and that the only question is whether he has complied with the statutory directions to appoint a person to hold a public inquiry, and to consider that person's report.'

Lord Thankerton went on to point out that a duty to act judicially is imported only where the decision-maker is in the position that 'having to adjudicate as between two or more parties, he must come to his adjudication with an independent mind, without any inclination or bias towards one side or another in the dispute'.

If therefore the decision-maker is a person entrusted by or under the law with wider duties of policy, within the context of which the decision must be made, he is expected to let those considerations influence his decision. He cannot act 'judicially' without failing to carry out what the law requires of him. Thus for example Home Office Ministers as advised by the Parole Board, when deciding whether or not to release or recall a prisoner, act purely administratively within the context of overall penal policy. {*R v Secretary of State for the Home Department, ex p Gunnell* (1983) *The Times* 3 November.}

Even where the decision-making functionary is entrusted with wider policy duties, interpretative criteria may nevertheless indicate that he is intended to act judicially.

Example 4 Two powerful interpretative criteria, namely the presumption against doubtfully-authorised penalization {See Part XIII of this Code.} and the need to preserve public order {See p 289 above.} combined to give this effect in the leading case of *Cooper v Wandsworth Board of Works.* {(1863) 14 CB(NS) 180.} Section 76 of the Metropolis Management Act 1855 required notice to be given to the district board of an intention to build a new house, failing which they could demolish the house. The board exercised this power in relation to the plaintiff's house without giving him an opportunity to be heard. *Held* An action for trespass lay against the board. Erle CJ said {Pp 187–189}-

> 'The conception on the part of the plaintiff has been that, although the words of the statute, taken in their literal sense, without any qualification at all, would create a justification for the act which the district board has done, the powers granted by that statute are subject to a qualification which has been repeatedly recognised, that no man is to be deprived of his property without his having an opportunity of being heard. The evidence here shows that the plaintiff and the district board had not been quite on amicable terms ... the proceedings to demolish, merely because they had ill-will against the party, is a power that the legislature never intended to confer ... I can conceive a great many advantages which might arise in the way of public order, in the way of doing substantial justice, and in the way of fulfilling the purpose of the statute, by the restriction which we put upon them, that they should hear the party before they inflict upon him such a heavy loss.'

{As to the duty to hear both parties see s 346 of this Code.}

Requirements of natural justice If it is decided that a decision-making functionary is intended by Parliament to act judicially, this means that the functionary must observe the requirements of natural justice. The first point to make is that these requirements are not the same in all cases. As Brightman LJ said in *Payne v Lord Harris of Greenwich* {[1981] 1 WLR 754, at p 766}: 'The scope and extent of the principles of natural justice depend on the subject matter to which they are sought to be applied; see *R v Gaming Board for Great Britain, ex p Benaim and Khaide.* {[1970] 2 QB 417, at p 430.}'

One aspect of this is that the functionary is prima facie intended to reach the decision in question by following its normal method of working. Thus in *Local Government Board v Arlidge* {[1915] AC 120, at p 133 (emphasis added).} Viscount Haldane LC said of the Local Government Board-

> 'The result of its inquiry must, as I have said, be taken, in the absence of directions in the statute to the contrary, to be intended to be reached *by its ordinary procedure.*'

The functionary is not therefore required to proceed as if it were a court of justice holding a trial; indeed it may well lack full power to do this (as for example by being unable to administer an oath). {*Board of Education v Rice* [1911] AC 179.}

Another basic point is that, as Lord Diplock said in *Haw Tua Tau v Public Prosecutor* {[1981] 3 All ER 14, at p 21.} 'rules of natural justice change with the times'. He went on-

> 'The procedure for the trial of criminal offences in England at various periods between the abolition of the Court [*sic*] of Star

Chamber and High Commission in the seventeenth century and the passing of the Criminal Evidence Act in 1898 involved practices, particularly in relation to the trial of felonies, that nowadays would unhesitatingly be regarded as flouting fundamental rules of natural justice. Deprivation until 1836 of the right of the accused to legal representation at his trial, and, until 1898, of the right to give evidence on his own behalf are obvious examples.'

The two basic requirements of natural justice Thus both the court and the administrative functionary deciding a question 'judicially' must comply with the rules of natural justice as appropriate to the function and period in question. This brings in two basic requirements, namely to decide without bias and to allow representations to be made before the decision is reached. These are respectively expressed in the maxims *nemo debet esse judex in propria causa* {See s 353 of this Code.} and *audi alteram partem.* {See s 346 of this Code.}

336. Rules of equity

Unless the contrary intention appears, an enactment by implication imports any principle or rule of equity which prevails in the territory to which the enactment extends and is relevant to the operation of the enactment in that territory.

COMMENTARY

General principle As to the principle under which relevant rules of general law are by implication taken to be imported so far as necessary for the operation of an enactment see s 144 of this Code.

Rules of equity Equity acts *in personam* and on the individual conscience. {*Newbury District Council v Secretary of State for the Environment* [1980] 1 All ER 731.} There are many ways by which rules or principles of equity fall to be treated as impliedly embodied in enactments.

One obvious way is where an enactment specifically envisages the application (and perhaps the elaboration by the court) of equitable rules. Thus s 30 of the Law of Property Act 1925, enabling the court to make such orders as it thinks fit where trustees for sale refuse to exercise their powers, contemplates a judicial development of equitable principles similar to that effected under s 7 of the Settled Land Act 1884. {See 27 Halsbury's *Statutes of England* (3rd edn) p 385, and cases there cited. See also *Cousins v Dzosens* (1981) *The Times* 12 December (judicial powers under s 30 used to develop equitable doctrine as to unmarried cohabiters and the dwelling which corresponds to their matrimonial home).}

Again, s 15 of the Trustee Act 1925 empowers trustees under any trust to compromise a 'claim, or thing whatever' relating to the trust. While holding that this did not attract rules of equity restricting the powers of trustees to vary the trust, Buckley LJ nevertheless accepted that an Act might indeed import such restrictions by implication. {*Re Earl of Strafford decd* [1979] 1 All ER 513, at p 522.}

The implied importation of rules of equity must not be confused with the doctrine of equitable construction of statutes (although the two did to some extent share a common origin). {The doctrine of equitable construction is described in s 94 of this Code.} Mellish LJ said in 1876 {*Edwards v Edwards* (1876) 2 Ch D 291, at p 297.}-

> 'The courts of equity have given relief on equitable grounds from provisions in old Acts of Parliament, but this has not been done in the case of modern Acts, which are framed with a view to equitable as well as legal principles.'

{Approved by Cozens-Hardy MR in *Re Monolithic Building Co Ltd* [1915] 1 Ch 643, at p 665. See also *Simpson Motor Sales v Hendon Corpn* [1964] AC 1088, *per* Lord Evershed at p 1126.}

This dictum means that equity will not relieve the supposed harshness of a modern Act in the way it once relieved the harshness of common law or statute. {See, e g, *Leedale (Inspector of Taxes) v Lewis* [1982] 3 All ER 808 (no relief where tax charged on a capital 'gain' which was merely notional).} What the dictum does not do is exclude the importing of equitable doctrines by implication to assist the working of a modern Act. Furthermore, though equity 'subordinates itself to statutes', it will 'never allow a statute to serve as a cloak for fraud; it will never allow an unscrupulous litigant to make an unconscientious use of his rights under a statute'. {H G Hanbury *Modern Equity* (5th edn, 1949) p 24. See *Maddison v Alderson* (1883) 8 App Cas 467, at p 474.}

Example 1   To enable him to evict tenants protected by the Rent Acts, a landlord who was the mortgagor under a bank mortgage of the freehold of the rented property procured his wife to pay off the mortgage. Standing thus in the bank's shoes, she then claimed to evict the tenants on the (true) ground that the lettings had contravened a term of the mortgage deed. {Applying *Dudley and District Benefit Building Society v Emerson* [1949] Ch 707.} *Held* Equity would restrain the wife as mortgagee from obtaining possession. {*Quennell v Maltby* [1979] 1 All ER 568.} Lord Denning MR said {P 571.}-

> 'It seems to me that this is one of those cases where equity steps in . . . If [the landlord] himself had sought to evict the tenants, he would not be allowed to do so. He could not say the tenancies were void. He would be estopped from saying so. They certainly would be protected against him. Are they protected against his wife now that she is the transferee of the charge? In my opinion they are protected, for this simple reason: she is not seeking possession for the purpose of enforcing the loan or the interest or anything of that kind. She is doing it simply for an ulterior purpose of getting possession of the house, contrary to the intention of Parliament as expressed in the Rent Acts.'

The equitable doctrine of undue influence has also been used to counter evasion of the Rent Acts. {See (1981) 131 NLJ 1022.} Other equitable doctrines used in aid of statutory provisions include the equitable doctrine of fraud on a minority {*Estmanco (Kilner House) v Greater London Council* [1982] 1 All ER 437, *per* Megarry V-C at p 445.}, the equitable doctrine of part performance {*Britain v Rossiter* (1882) 11 QBD 123; *Maddison v Alderson* (1883) 8 App Cas 467; *Rawlinson v Ames* [1925] Ch 96; *Stimson v Gray* [1929] 1 Ch 629.}, the equitable doctrine that a person (other than the Crown) who is not bound by a law cannot claim the advantage of it {*The Zollverein* (1856) Swab 96.}, the protection by equity of the bona fide purchaser for value {*Re Brall* [1893] 2 QB 381; *Re Carter and Kenderdine* [1897] 1 Ch 776.} and the doctrine of subrogation borrowed by equity from the common law. {*Lewis v Alleyne* (1888) 4 TLR 560.}

Act effective without recourse to equity Where the scheme of the Act is effective to achieve its object without recourse to equitable doctrines the importation of these will not be inferred.

Example 2 Thus the statutory scheme for professional indemnity insurance set up by the Law Society under s 37(1) of the Solicitors Act 1974 was held by the House of Lords not to import, in relation to commissions received by the Law Society from the insurers, the equitable doctrine of the constructive trust. {*Swain v The Law Society* [1982] 2 All ER 827.} This reversed the decision of the Court of Appeal, who had unanimously held there was a constructive trust. {[1981] 3 All ER 797.} The House of Lords nevertheless left open the possibility of there being a constructive trust in aid of the statutory provisions if the Law Society should be found to have failed in its duty. {See *per* Lord Brightman at p 841.}

Again, subrogation has been held not to apply where this would be contrary to Parliament's express intention.

Example 3 By s 4 of the Bankruptcy (Amendment) Act 1926 relief was given to bankers and others who paid out moneys belonging to a bankrupt 'on or after the date of a receiving order but before notice thereof has been gazetted'. In *Re Byfield (a bankrupt), ex p Hill Samuel & Co Ltd* {[1982] 1 All ER 249.} this was held to exclude application of the equitable doctrine of subrogation where a bank innocently paid out *after* the receiving order had been gazetted. {See further Examples 12.2 and 368.2.}

Equitable remedies The special remedies devised by equity are available to protect rights conferred by statute. {See, e g, *RCA Corpn v Pollard* [1982] 2 All ER 468, *per* Vinelott J at p 478 (injunction to restrain infringement of rights of performers under Performers' Protection Acts 1958 to 1972).}

337. Rules of contract law

Unless the contrary intention appears, an enactment by implication imports any principle or rule of contract law (whether statutory or non-statutory) which prevails in the territory to which the enactment extends and is relevant to the operation of the enactment in that territory.

COMMENTARY

General principle As to the principle under which relevant rules of general law are by implication taken to be imported so far as necessary for the operation of an enactment see s 144 of this Code.

Contract law Where contracts are relevant to the application of an enactment it is presumed, unless the contrary intention appears, that Parliament intended the enactment to operate on the legal incidents of the contracts in accordance with the rules of contract law. {See Examples 345.2 and 368.3.}

Example 1 In *Nokes v Doncaster Amalgamated Collieries Ltd* {[1940] AC 1014.} the House of Lords decided a point under s 154 of the Companies Act 1929. {See now Companies Act 1948 s 208.} This section transferred by operation of law the 'property' of one company to another in a case of reconstruction or amalgamation. The question was whether this operated to transfer rights and obligations under the contracts of service of the transferor company's employees. *Held* The enactment was intended only to effect such transfers as by the law of contract the companies themselves could have agreed should be transferred. This did not include rights and obligations under personal contracts of service. {See also *Denham v Midland Employers' Mutual Assurance Ltd* [1955] 2 QB 437; *Re Skinner* [1958] 3 All ER 273.}

Illegality Where an Act expressly or by implication prohibits the making of a particular kind of contract, any contract made in contravention of the prohibition is void ab initio. {*Archbolds (Freightage) Ltd v Spanglett* [1961] 1 QB 374, *per* Devlin LJ at pp 285-7; *St John Shipping Corpn v Joseph Rank Ltd* [1957] 1 QB 267, at p 285; *Shaw v Groom* [1970] 2 QB 504; *Bedford Insurance Co Ltd v Instituto de Ressaguros do Brasil* (1983) *The Times* 18 November (overruling *Bloxsome v Williams* (1824) 3 B & C 232).}

Where a party needs to rely on his own illegal act in order to recover under a contract, the doctrine of illegality precludes him from doing so. {*Archbolds (Freightage) Ltd v Spanglett* [1961] 1 QB 374, *per* Devlin LJ at pp 285-7. See further s 345 of this Code.}

Effect of Act on existing contracts Where an Act impinges on a contract existing at the date of its commencement the courts look to the terms of the Act to ascertain the effect, rather than assuming that the parties are to be treated as by implication having made advance provision in their contract.

Example 2 In *Frobisher (Second Investments) Ltd v Kiloran Trust Co Ltd* {[1980] 1 All ER 488.}, tenants had covenanted to make maintenance payments in advance. Thereafter s 91A of the Housing Finance Act 1972 rendered these payments irrecoverable. The landlords argued that the doctrine of the law of contract which implies the existence of a term to give business efficacy to an agreement, sometimes known as the doctrine of *The Moorcock* {(1889) 14 PD 64.}, should be applied. *Held* The doctrine of *The Moorcock* did not apply where there had been a disturbance to contractual arrangements as a result of the intervention of a statute. In such a case it was to be assumed that the statute would (expressly or by implication) make consequential provision.

Law merchant The courts assume that Parliament did not intend to interfere with trading practices and the law merchant more than was necessary to achieve the purpose of the enactment.

Example 3 Thus although s 1 of the Gaming Act 1710 says that bills of exchange given for gaming shall be 'utterly void frustrate and of none effect to all intents and purposes whatsoever' the courts have held that this did not affect the rights of an innocent indorsee for value. Abbott CJ said {*Edwards v Dick* (1821) 4 B & Ald 212, at p 214.}-

'I think we must understand the language of the legislature with reference to the object which they had in view, viz, the prevention of gaming, and that will be effectually accomplished by holding the securities to be void for any purpose for enforcing payment of money won at play.'

Private Acts The principles of contract law are particularly relevant to private Acts, since the wording of these is in some respects regarded 'as words of contract to which the legislature has given its sanction [rather] than as words of the legislature itself'. {*Per* Lord Halsbury LC in *Herron v Rathmines & Rathgar Improvement Commrs* [1892] AC 498, at p 501.} This applies only where the private Act is for the benefit of the promoters, and has no relevance to an Act promoted with a public purpose in mind (for example by a local authority). {*Stewart v Thames Conservators* [1908] 1 KB 893.}

Scrutton LJ, speaking of the treatment of private Acts as contracts, said-

'So far as persons not concerned in the Act are concerned, the Act is read strictly against the promoters; so far as the promoters themselves are concerned it is read as a contract between them and is to be construed accordingly.'

{*Harper v Hedges* (1924) 93 LJKB 116, at p 117.}

Thus the doctrine of consideration has been resorted to in construing provisions governing detriment imposed on other parties by a private Act. {*Herron v Rathmines & Rathgar Improvement Commrs* [1892] AC 498.} Again, principles of the interpretation of contracts have been applied to private Acts. {*Townley v Gibson* (1789) 2 TR 701 (intention of parties considered); *Rowbotham v Wilson* (1860) 8 HLC 348, at p 363 (surrounding circumstances at date of Act); *Makin v Watkinson* [1870] LR 6 Ex 25 (unreasonable covenant); *London and South Western Rly Co v Flower* (1875) 1 CPD 77, at p 85 (approving *Makin v Watkinson*); *Savin v Hoylake Rly Co* [1865] LR 1 Ex 9 (Act at variance with earlier agreement between promoters); *Harper v Hedges* (1924) 93 LJKB 116 (construction *contra proferentem*).}

Contrary intention An Act very often spells out its precise effect on the general law of contract. Thus s 40 of the Consumer Credit Act 1974 states that an agreement made in contravention of the Act by an unlicensed trader shall be unenforceable unless a validation order is obtained. Section 170 of the Act makes clear that this is the only civil sanction, thus disapplying the common-law doctrine of illegality discussed above. {Similar provisions are contained in s 62 of the Sex Discrimination Act 1975 (see also s 77) and s 53 of the Race Relations Act 1976 (see also s 72).}

338. Rules of property law

Unless the contrary intention appears, an enactment by implication imports any principle or rule of the law of real or personal property (whether statutory or non-statutory) which prevails in the territory to which the enactment extends and is relevant to the operation of the enactment in that territory.

COMMENTARY

General principle   As to the principle under which relevant rules of general law are by implication taken to be imported so far as necessary for the operation of an enactment see s 144 of this Code.

Rules of property law   There are many ways in which rules of property law are to be treated as embodied in Acts under interpretation. Parliament frequently legislates about property of one sort or another, and does so within the context of the law governing such property. {See Examples 368.1, 368.7 amd 368.8.}

Example 1   Section 23 of the Agricultural Holdings Act 1948 {See now s 1 of the Agricultural Holdings (Notices to Quit) Act 1977.} stated that a notice to quit was invalid if it purported to terminate the tenancy before the expiration of twelve months from the end of the then current year of tenancy. In *Lower v Sorrell* {[1963] 1 QB 959.} the question arose of whether this invalidated a notice to quit given before the commencement of the tenancy, even though there was then no 'current year of tenancy'. *Held* The invalidity of such a notice arose under the common law of landlord and tenant, which was by implication attracted.

Private Acts   Some private Acts, notably estate Acts, are little more than conveyances. The 'little more' amounts to something which the law precluded the parties from doing for themselves, hence the resort to the private Bill procedure. The common lawyer Blackstone said-

> 'Private Acts have often been resorted to as a mode of assurance where, by the ingenuity of some and the blunders of other practitioners, an estate is so grievously entangled by a multitude of resulting trusts, springing uses, executory devises, and the like artificial contrivances - a confusion unknown to the simple conveyances of the common law - that it is out of the power of either the courts of law or equity to relieve the owner . . . A law thus made, though it binds all parties to the Bill, is yet looked upon rather as a private conveyance than as the solemn Act of the legislature.'

{2 Comm 344. Cf *Hornby v Houlditch* (1786), cited 1 TR 93 at p 96.}

It follows that Estate Acts, which are still passed today, are to be construed more as conveyances than statutes. {See *Townley v Gibson* (1789) 2 TR 701, *per* Lord Kenyon at p 705.}

339. Rules of tort law

Unless the contrary intention appears, an enactment by implication imports any principle or rule of the law of tort (whether statutory or non-statutory) which prevails in the territory to which the enactment extends and is relevant to the operation of the enactment in that territory.

COMMENTARY

General principle As to the principle under which relevant rules of general law are by implication taken to be imported so far as necessary for the operation of an enactment see s 144 of this Code.

Law of tort In this section of the Code the term 'tort' is used in its wider sense as including breach of a statutory duty or of the obligations imposed by a bailment. This corresponds to the meaning usually intended by Parliament when it uses the term. {See, e g, s 29(1) of the Post Offce Act 1969 as interpreted in *American Express Co v British Airways Board* [1983] 1 All ER 557). For the tort of breach of statutory duty see s 14 of this Code.}

There are many ways in which rules of tort law, as thus understood, are to be treated as embodied in Acts. One obvious way is where they are expressly attracted. Thus s 1(2) of the Occupiers' Liability Act 1957 says that the persons who are to be treated for the purposes of the Act as the occupier of land and his visitors 'are the same (subject to subsection (4) of this section) as the persons who would at common law be treated as an occupier and his invitees or licensees'.

This method raises a conceptual problem particularly where, as here, the relevant common law doctrine is entirely displaced by the Act. The common law develops from precedent to precedent. How can it develop any further when thus fossilised? The answer is that the development continues, so far as necessary, indirectly. The distinction between invitees and licensees need no longer be refined, but the question of whether a person is one of these or a trespasser will continue to be developed in the guise of statutory interpretation of the term 'visitor' as used in the 1957 Act.

Doctrines such as those relating to vicarious liability and the tort of negligence may by implication be imported where an Act confers a power or imposes a duty.

Example 1 Regulation 4 of the Removal and Disposal of Vehicles Regulations 1968 {SI 1968/43.} empowers a constable to 'arrange for the removal' of an obstructing vehicle. In *Rivers v Cutting* {[1982] 3 All ER 69.} a constable arranged for a garage company to remove a vehicle, in the course of which it suffered damage, presumably by the negligence of one of the garage company's employees. The vehicle owner sued the Chief Constable as being vicariously liable for the presumed negligence. This question of vicarious liability was tried as a preliminary issue. *Held* The regulation by implication authorised the police to employ an independent contractor, thus importing (again by implication) the general rules of law relating to liability for the negligence of such a contractor. Fox LJ said {P 72.}-

> 'I see no reason why there should not be available to the police, if the contractor acts negligently and damages a third party, whatever defences would be available to a private person employing an independent contractor ... I say "whatever defences would be available": the employment of an independent contractor does not necessarily protect the employer from liability in all circumstances ... the constable is not vicariously liable for damage caused by the default of the contractor in carrying out the removal save to such

extent, if any, as liability *is imposed by law for the acts of an independent contractor.*'

{Emphasis added.}

It will be seen that the italicised words import the general rules of the law of vicarious liability for tortious acts.

Trespass Many Acts confer powers of arrest. This imports the common law rules as to arrest. Thus the subject of a wrongful statutory arrest may sue for the torts of assault and false imprisonment. Again, many Acts confer power to search premises. This widens the common-law power of search, which is confined to stolen goods.

Example 2 In *Chic Fashions (West Wales) Ltd v Jones* {[1968] 2 QB 299.} the question arose of whether a statutory power of search imported the ancient common-law doctrine of trespass ab initio. {*Six Carpenters Case* (1610) 8 Co Rep 146a.} Warrants were issued to search the shops owned by the plaintiff company for goods stolen from the factory of Ian Peters Ltd. No such goods were there, but the police found and took away other stolen goods. These they later returned to the plaintiffs, who then sued the police for trespass. The plaintiffs were awarded damages of £500, and the police appealed. *Held* The actions of the police were covered by the warrants, and damages did not lie. The court weighed two conflicting interpretative criteria, as appears in the following extract from the judgment of Lord Denning MR {P 309.}-

> 'At one time the courts held that the constable could seize only those goods which answered the description given in the warrant ... If he seized other goods, not mentioned in the warrant, he was a trespasser in respect of those goods: and not only so, but he was a trespasser on the land itself, a trespasser ab initio, in accordance with the doctrine of the *Six Carpenters Case* {(1610) 8 Co Rep 146a.}, which held that, if a man abuse an authority given by the law, he becomes a trespasser ab initio. If such had remained the law, no constable would be safe in executing a search warrant. The law as it then stood was a boon to receivers of stolen property and an impediment to the forces of law and order. So much so, that the judges gradually altered it ... Now the time has come when we must endeavour to state [the principle]. We have to consider, on the one hand, the freedom of the individual. The security of his home is not to be broken into except for the most compelling reason. On the other hand, we have to consider the interest of society at large in finding out wrongdoers and repressing crime.'

The court came down in favour of repressing crime, and declared that the doctrine of trespass ab initio no longer applied. {Cf *Wiltshire v Barrett* [1966] 1 QB 312 (trespass ab initio not applicable to statutory power of arrest).}

Nuisance The common-law rules relating to nuisance in exercise of a statutory power or duty were thus set out by Webster J {*Department of Transport v North West Water Authority* [1983] 1 All ER 892, at p 895. The rules as thus stated were approved by the House of Lords on appeal: [1983] 3 All ER 273, at p 275.}-

'(1) In the absence of negligence, a body is not liable for a nuisance which is attributable to the exercise by it of a *duty* imposed on it by statute {Emphasis added.}: see *Hammond v St Pancras Corpn* {(1874) LR 9 CP 316.}

(2) It is not liable in those circumstances even if by statute it is expressly made liable, or not exempted from liabilty, for nuisance: see *Stretton's Derby Brewery Co v Derby Corpn* {[1894] 1 Ch 431.} and *Smeaton v Ilford Corpn.* {[1954] Ch 450.}

(3) In the absence of negligence, a body is not liable for a nuisance which is attributable to the exercise by it of a *power* conferred by statute if, by statute, it is not expressly either made liable, or not exempted from liability, for nuisance {Emphasis added.}: see *Midwood & Co Ltd v Manchester Corpn* {[1905] 2 KB 597.}, *Longhurst v Metropolitan Water Board* {[1948] 2 All ER 834.} and *Dunne v North Western Gas Board.* {[1964] 2 QB 806.}

(4) A body is liable for a nuisance by it attributable to the exercise of a *power* conferred by statute, even without negligence, if by statute it is expressly either made liable, or not exempted from liability, for nuisance {Emphasis added.}: see *Charing Cross Electricity Supply Co v Hydraulic Power Co.*' {[1914] 3 KB 772.}

Webster J went on to say that references to nuisance in these four propositions are to be taken as references either to liability in nuisance simpliciter or to liability under the rule in *Rylands v Fletcher* {(1868) LR 3 HL 330.}, while references to negligence are to be construed in the light of the definition given by Lord Wilberforce in *Allen v Gulf Oil Refining Ltd* {[1981] AC 1001, at p 1011.}

Implied application of maxims Maxims of the law of tort will be applied analogously to breaches of statutory duty. Thus in *Holden v White* Stocker J applied to a claim for breach of the duty imposed by the Occupiers' Liability Act 1957 the principle *res ipsa loquitur*. On appeal the judgment was reversed, but the Court of Appeal expressly did not overrule the judge's application of this principle. {See the report of the appellate judgments at [1982] 2 All ER 328.}

As to the implied application of legal maxims see further s 145 and Part XIX of this Code. {For the maxim *volenti non fit injuria* see s 358.}

340. Rules of criminal law

Unless the contrary intention appears, an enactment by implication imports any principle or rule of criminal law (whether statutory or non-statutory) which prevails in the territory to which the enactment extends and is relevant to the operation of the enactment in that territory.

COMMENTARY

General principle As to the principle under which relevant rules of general law are by implication taken to be imported so far as necessary for the operation of an enactment see s 144 of this Code.

739

Rules of criminal law   Since Acts are largely enforced by means of the criminal law it follows that many rules of criminal law are treated as by implication imported, though not set out or referred to in the enactment.

It is a basic principle of legal policy that an act or omission is not criminal unless forbidden by law. {See pp 291–292 above. As to the implied incorporation of this and other principles of legal policy see ss 126 to 134 of this Code.} If the court is of opinion that any matter before it does disclose illegality then, even though the parties do not rely on this, it is the court's duty to take the point of its own motion. {*Malone v Commr of Police of the Metropolis* [1979] 1 All ER, *per* Roskill LJ at p 271.}

Parliament is presumed to legislate within the context of judge-made principles as to the fundamental basis of criminal liability. Lord Wilberforce said in *Director of Public Prosecutions for Northern Ireland v Lynch* {[1975] AC 653, at pp 684-5.}-

'The judges have always assumed responsibility for deciding questions of principle relating to criminal liability and guilt and particularly for setting the standards by which the law expects normal men to act. In all such matters as capacity, sanity, drunkenness, coercion, necessity, provocation [and] self-defence, the common law, through the judges, accepts and sets the standards of right-thinking men of normal firmness and humanity at a level . . . which people can accept and respect.'

Lord Diplock said in *R v Miller* {[1983] 2 AC 161, at p 174.} that criminal enactments-

'. . . fall to be construed in the light of general principles of English law so well established that it is the practice of parliamentary draftsment to leave them unexpressed in criminal statutes, on the confident assumption that a court of law will treat those principles as intended by Parliament to be applicable to the particular offence unless expressley modified or excluded.'

Rules may be thus implied even though the effect of the implication is to prejudice the accused. {As to the principle against penalization under a doubtful enactment see s 129 and Part XIII of this Code.} Thus the definition of every statutory crime not requiring a 'specific intent' must be read as subject to an implied qualification in respect of voluntary self-intoxication-

'When Parliament says "maliciously" . . . the statute must be read as if the word were qualified- "except where the accused was intoxicated through the voluntary taking of drink or drugs".'

{*Director of Public Prosecutions v Majewski* [1976] Crim LR 374, *per* Professor J C Smith at p 376.}

This applies even where, as in s 1(1) of the Criminal Damage Act 1971, Parliament purports to spell out the required mental element in full. {Ibid.}

Criminal law concepts   Where an Act uses a term which has an established meaning at common law, Parliament is taken to intend that meaning to be applied. Thus many criminal enactments use the term 'assault'. This is taken to have its common-law meaning of 'an act by which the defendant intentionally or recklessly causes the complainant to apprehend immediate, or to sustain, unlawful personal violence'. {*Per* Lawton LJ in *R v Kimber* [1983] 3 All ER 316, at p 319. See also *R v Venna* [1976] QB 421, at pp 428-9.}

Mens rea Unless the Act creating the offence indicates to the contrary, proof of a guilty mind is needed to establish the commission of a statutory offence: *actus non facit reum nisi mens sit rea* (the act committed does not establish guilt unless the mind of the actor is guilty). {3 Co Inst 107. See *R v Kimber* [1983] 3 All ER 316, *per* Lawton LJ at p 319.} The House of Lords expressed dislike for the expressions *actus reus* and Mens rea in *R v Miller*. {[1983] 2 AC 161, at p 174.}

Stephen J said in *R v Tolson* {(1889) 23 QBD 168 at p 187}-

> 'The full definition of every crime contains expressly or by implication a proposition as to a state of mind ... The mental element of most crimes is marked by one of the words "maliciously", "fraudulently", "negligently", or "knowingly", but it is the general - I might I think say the invariable - practice of the legislature to leave unexpressed some of the mental elements of crime. In all cases whatever, competent age, sanity, and some degree of freedom from some kinds of coercion are assumed to be essential to criminality, but I do not believe they are ever introduced into any statute by which any particular crime is defined.'

{See also *R v Prince* (1875) LR 2 CCR 154 and *Sweet v Parsley* [1970] AC 132.} In *Sweet v Parsley* {[1970] AC 132, at p 163.} Lord Diplock said-

> '... even where the words used to describe the prohibited conduct would not in any context connote the necessity for any particular [mental] element, they are nevertheless to be read as subject to the implication that a necessary element in the offence is the absence of a belief held honestly and upon reasonable grounds in the existence of facts which if true would make the act innocent.'

Under a judge-made rule, certain crimes are said to be of basic (as opposed to specific) intent. This anomalous rule was created to deal with the special social danger that would arise if by reason of self-induced intoxication the accused could establish that he lacked the necessary mens rea. {*R v Beard* [1920] AC 479; *R v Morgan* [1975] 2 All ER 347; *Director of Public Prosecutions v Majewski* [1976] Crim LR 374; *R v Woods* [1982] Crim LR 42; *R v Bailey (John)* [1983] Crim LR 533. For a list of crimes which respectively do and do not require 'specific intent' see [1976] Crim LR 376.}

Principles of natural justice It is presumed that Parliament intends to import, in an Act creating a criminal offence, the principles of natural justice which the common law recognises as applicable in criminal law. For example it is an 'undoubted fundamental rule of natural justice' that a person charged with a criminal offence is to be presumed innocent until proved guilty according to law. {*Haw Tua Taw v Public Prosecutor* [1981] 3 All ER 14, *per* Lord Diplock at p 21.}

Right to silence Under the adversarial system prevailing at common law, it is treated as fundamental that the accused should have the right of silence. This is the principle against self-incrimination embodied in the maxim *nemo tenetur seipsum accusare*. {Wing Max 486.} The maxim also appears in the form *nemo tenetur prodere seipsum*. {See *Triplex Safety Glass Co v Lancegaye Safety Glass (1934) Ltd* [1939] 2 KB 395; *Rio Tinto Zinc Corpn v Westinghouse Electric Corpn* [1978] AC 547.}

The right to silence means that the accused cannot be compelled to testify, and it may (at the court's discretion) rule out evidence obtained by misleading or tricking him. {*R v Sang* [1979] 3 WLR 263, *per* Lord Scarman at p 290. See also *Haw Tua Taw v Public Prosecutor* [1981] 3 All ER 14.} The right has been seriously weakened by the House of Lords decision in *Holgate-Mohammed v Duke*. {[1984] 1 All ER 1054.} This held that, under s 2(4) of the Criminal Law Act 1967, a constable can arrest without warrant a person whom he reasonably suspects to be guilty of an arrestable offence, even though the sole purpose is to extract a confession.

The right to silence precludes, in the absence of statutory authority, any legal proceeding which might require a person to incriminate himself. {*Rank Film Distributors Ltd v Video Information Centre* [1981] 2 All ER 76 (Anton Piller orders). This decision was reversed by statute: see Supreme Court Act 1981 s 72. For other statutory curtailment of the principle against self-incrimination see Bankruptcy Act 1914 s 15; Civil Evidence Act 1968 s 14(1); Theft Act 1968 s 31.} Even where an enactment expressly confers a right to demand incriminating information, this may be treated as qualified by implied importation of the common-law rule.

Example 1   Paragraph 1(1) of Sch 5 to the Exchange Control Act 1947 empowered the Treasury to direct a person to furnish them with information needed to detect evasion of the Act. *Held* This did not require self-incrimination by a person who had already been cautioned and charged with offences under the Act, since such an interpretation would 'make a mockery of the caution and the concept of the right to silence after a charge has been preferred'. {*A v HM Treasury* [1979] 2 All ER 586, at p 590.}

The right to silence does not operate to defeat a civil claim. {*Green v Weaver* (1827) 1 Sim 404, at p 427; *Robinson v Kitchen* (1856) 8 De G M & G 88; *Jefferson Ltd v Bhetcha* [1979] 2 All ER 1108; *Rank Film Distributors Ltd v Video Information Centre* [1980] 2 All ER 273.} Even in a criminal case, it may be outweighed by other interpretative factors.

Example 2   In the Irish case of *A-G v Conroy* {(1838) Jo Ex Ir 791.} distillers concealed large quantities of spirits so as to avoid paying duty. The court refused to allow them to claim privilege against self-incrimination. The ground for the ruling was that 'so much public inconvenience would result from a contrary decision'. {P 792.}

As to changes in accepted principles of natural justice with the passage of time see the commentary on s 335.

Position of the Crown   Criminal offences were formerly known as pleas of the Crown, in view of the constitutional rule that the sovereign is the person deemed to be injured by every public wrong. Under former practice, an indictment charged an offence as having been committed *contra pacem domini regis, coronam et dignitatem suam* (against the peace of our lord the king, his crown and dignity). This was made unnecessary by the Criminal Procedure Act 1851 s 24, and would now be improper in view of the provisions of the Indictments Act 1916 and the Indictment Rules 1971. {SI 1971/1253.}

Crimes are still prosecuted in the name of the Crown. As successor to the King's Attorney of the thirteenth century, who was charged with the responsibility of maintaining the sovereign's interests before the royal courts, the Attorney-General exercises control over the bringing, conduct and termination of prosecutions. {J Ll J Edwards *The Law Officers of the Crown* (1964) p 3.} The Crown can sue for penalties imposed by Act, where no other beneficiary is indicated. {*Bradlaugh v Clarke* (1883) 8 App Cas 354.}

At common law, time does not run against the Crown. The principle is expressed in the maxim *nullum tempus aut locus occurrit regi* (no time runs against, or place affects, the king). {2 Co Inst 273.} Thus, except where otherwise provided by statute, a crime can be prosecuted at any length of time after its commission.

Blackstone, speaking of rape, says 'the jury will rarely give credit to a stale complaint'. While there has never been a statutory time limit for rape prosecutions, a limit of twelve months is imposed in relation to homosexual offences. {Sexual Offences Act 1967 s 7.} There has long been a time limit of six months for the prosecution of summary offences. {See now Magistrates' Courts Act 1980 s 127.} It is in all cases desirable, as a matter of legal policy, that prosecutions should be brought and heard as soon as possible. Where there is bad faith on the part of the prosecution, an order of prohibition may be granted. {*Director of Public Prosecutions v Humphrys* [1977] AC 1; *R v Grays JJ, ex p Graham* [1982] 3 All ER 653.}

Nemo debet bis vexari Another common-law principle imported by implication is expressed in the maxim *nemo debet bis vexari, si constat curiae quod sit pro una et eadem causa* (no one ought to be twice vexed, if it be proved to the court that it be for one and the same cause). {5 Co Rep 61. The principle is embodied in s 18 of the Interpretation Act 1978, see p 868 below.} This is the basis for the defences of autrefois acquit and autrefois convict. {The latter is expressed in the maxim *nemo debet bis puniri pro uno delicto* (4 Co Rep 43). See s 347 of this Code.}

The principle does not apply as between proceedings before a court of competent jurisdiction and proceedings before some other tribunal. {*R v Statutory Committee of Pharmaceutical Society of Great Britain, ex p Pharmaceutical Society of Great Britain* [1981] 2 All ER 805 (pharmacists convicted of crime of violence later subjected to professional disciplinary proceedings).}

Statement of offence At common law an indictment charging a statutory offence, after describing the act or omission charged, had to conclude with the words 'contra formam statuti' (against the form of the statute(s) in that case made and provided). This is no longer necessary, but the provision creating the offence must be identified. {The Indictment Rules 1971 (SI 1971/1253) r 6.}

The courts construe enactments defining an offence in accordance with general principles of criminal law. Accordingly they strive to avoid a construction which makes it uncertain whether a crime is committed or not, or leaves it to the prosecution to decide. {*Federal Steam Navigation Co Ltd v*

Department of Trade and Industry [1974] 2 All ER 97 ('the owner *or master* of the ship shall be guilty of an offence').} Equally the court will not allow civil procedure to be used so as to prejudice the prosecution of the offence at criminal law. {*Imperial Tobacco Ltd v A-G* [1980] 1 All ER 866 (attempt to obtain civil declaration that act charged as criminal was in fact lawful).} Again, the court will be slow to infer an intention to create vicarious criminal liability, since this not a concept accepted by the common law. {*Wright v Ford Motor Co Ltd* [1967] 1 QB 230.}

Duplicity rule An information, or a count of an indictment, which charges offences in the alternative is void for duplicity. This is because the defendant cannot then know precisely with what he is charged, and may be prevented on a future occasion from pleading autrefois convict or autrefois acquit. {*R v Surrey JJ, ex p Witherick* [1932] 1 KB 450. See Example 74.4.}

The wording of an enactment creating an offence often fits awkwardly when it comes to drafting an information or a count of an indictment so as to avoid the duplicity rule. The problem lies in what constitutes an 'offence'. Where the section constituting the offence is complex, there may be three different conceptions of what constitutes an offence under the section. In reducing scope, these are as follows-

(a) any act or omission that contravenes the section;
(b) an act or omission which is described by alternatives yet, under r 7 of the Indictment Rules 1971 {SI 1971/1253.}, constitutes a single offence for the purpose of the law relating to indictments;
(c) an act or omission which can be separated out from the wording of the section as an act or omission *not* described by alternatives.

Paragraph (a) needs no explanation. To understand para (b) it may be helpful to consider the following comminuted version of r 7 of the Indictment Rules 1971 {SI 1971/1253.} (formerly r 5(1) of Sch 1 to the Indictments Act 1915)-

(1) Where an offence created by or under an enactment
(2) states the offence to be the doing or the omission to do
(3) any one of any different acts in the alternative
OR
(4) any act in any one of any different capacities
OR
(5) any act with any one of any different intentions
(6) or states any part of the offence in the alternative
(7) the acts, omissions, capacities, or intentions, or other matters stated in the alternative in the enactment or subordinate instrument
(8) may be stated in the alternative in an indictment charging the offence.

The former wording of clause 8 was ' . . . in the count charging the offence'. The change, presumably made because an indictment may charge one offence only and so not be divided into counts, is unfortunate. It suggests that the alternatives might need to be stated in separate counts, but this is not the intention. Clauses (1) and (2) are less felicitous than the former version, which ran: 'Where an enactment constituting an offence states . . .' The inelegance of 'Where an offence . . . states the offence' arose because the draftsman wished to include offences made by a subordinate instrument. Matters that by virtue of rule 7 can be stated in the alternative in one count of an indictment constitute a single offence for the purpose of criminal procedure.

Paragraph (c) of the alternatives earlier listed above refers to a factual situation which is covered by the wording of the enactment without reliance on any alternatives. One section or subsection may cover a large number of such separate situations.

Example 3 Section 22(1) of the Theft Act 1968 runs as follows-

> 'A person handles stolen goods if (otherwise than in the course of the stealing) knowing or believing them to be stolen goods he dishonestly receives the goods, or dishonestly undertakes or assists in their retention, removal, disposal, or realisation by or for the benefit of another person, or if he arranges to do so.'

Any one of the actions described would fall within para (a) as 'an offence against section 22(1) of the Theft Act 1968'. So far as paragraph (b) is concerned there are two offences only, namely (1) dishonestly receiving goods and (2) any other offence within s 22(1). {*R v Bloxham* [1982] 1 All ER 582, *per* Lord Bridge at p 584. Professor J C Smith has expressed disagreement, holding it to have been decided that the subsection creates one offence only: [1982] Crim LR 437.} From the second category a very large number of offences can be separated out for the purposes of paragraph (c). Here is just one-

> A person handles stolen goods if (otherwise than in the course of the stealing) knowing them to be stolen he dishonestly assists in their disposal by another person.

{For a graphic depiction of the very large number of paragraph (c) offences in this second category of s 22(1) see V Tunkel 'The Innocent Receiver with Subsequent Mens Rea' (1983) 133 NLJ 844.}

The practical difficulties arise in relation to para (b). Parliamentary draftsmen, when framing a statutory offence, have usually ignored r 7 of the Indictment Rules 1971 {1971/1253.} and its predecessor. They have disregarded this useful suggestion made by Glanville Williams-

> 'Parliamentary counsel can evade the duplicity rule by drafting the offence in single terms and then defining the words of the offence with multiple possibilities. Since the duplicity rule does not operate upon the defining clause, a charge in terms of the verbally single offence will be good.'

{'The Count System and the Duplicity Rule' [1966] Crim LR 255, at p 265.}

It can therefore be very difficult to disentangle the offences which may properly be stated in the alternative in one count of an indictment without contravening the duplicity rule. This creates the risk that persons who should be convicted will escape justice. {See the comments by Professor J C Smith on *British Airways Board v Taylor* [1977] Crim LR 372.}

Example 4 In *R v Molloy* {[1921] 2 KB 364.}, a case under the corresponding provisions of r 5(1) of Sch 1 to the Indictments Act 1915, the defendant was charged with contravening s 8(1) of the Larceny Act 1916, which enacted that 'every person who steals, or, with intent to steal, rips cuts severs or breaks' any fixture should be guilty of felony. Avory J said {P 366.}-

> 'The indictment charges the appellant that he either stole the things or, with intent to steal, that he ripped and severed them. *Those two offences are not necessarily committed by one and the same act*; in other words, the act done may constitute one of the offences but may not constitute the other ... the words of s 8(1) providing that "every person who ... with intent to steal, rips cuts severs or breaks" fixtures ... afford an illustration of the case with which r 5 [of Sch 1 to the Indictments Act 1915] was intended to deal.'

{Emphasis added.}

Example 5 In a case under s 12(1) of the Road Traffic Act 1930, where the statutory words were 'without due care and attention or without reasonable consideration for other persons using the road', Avory J said-

> 'It is not necessary to give illustrations of how a man may be driving with due care and attention ... and yet driving without reasonable consideration for other persons, but, if a person may do one without the other, it follows as a matter of law that an information which charges him in the alternative is bad.'

{*R v Surrey JJ, ex p Witherick* [1932] 1 KB 450, at p 452. The decision was followed in *R v Wilmot* (1934) 24 Crim App R 63, a case under s 11(1) of the Road Traffic Act 1930 where the statutory words were 'recklessly, or at a speed or in a manner which is dangerous to the public'.}

Despite this guidance from Avory J, the principles governing the application of r 7, as worked out by judicial processing, are inconsistent and far from clear. {See Glanvill Williams 'The Count System and the Duplicity Rule' [1966] Crim LR 255.} It remains a problem to determine in particular cases which alternatives stated in a statutory offence may properly be included in a statement of a single offence. Where alternative facts produce a different legal thrust, it is clear there is more than one offence. {See *R v Courtle* [1984] 1 All ER 740 (different penalties for buggery according to age and presence or absence of consent.)}

An indictment need only describe an offence 'shortly'. {Indictment Rules 1971 r 5(1).} In the case of a statutory offence this is done by specifying the relevant enactment by its section number or other description. It is not necessary to specify or negative anything included in the enactment by way of exception, exemption, proviso, excuse or qualification. {Indictment Rules 1971 (SI 1971/1253) r 6(c), following but expanding r 5(2) of Sch 1 to the Indictments Act 1915.}

Standard of proof A criminal enactment by implication requires the question of whether the enactment has been infringed to be determined according to the stricter criteria demanded by the criminal law. Parliament is taken to intend that the enactment shall be applied according to the criminal standard of proof, so that the court or tribunal must ask itself, on the question of guilt, 'am I satisfied so that I am sure?' or 'am I satisfied beyond reasonable doubt?'. {*R v Tottenham Magistrates' Court, ex p Williams* [1982] 2 All ER 705, *per* Donaldson LJ at p

707.} This is in contrast to the civil standard of decision *on a balance of probabilities*.

Onus of proof The onus of discharging the criminal standard rests upon the prosecution. {*Woolmington v Director of Public Prosecutions* [1935] AC 462.} However where an ingredient of the offence relates to a fact peculiarly within the accused's own knowledge, such as whether or not he possessed a licence, the onus is on him to prove the exculpating fact. This, said Professor J C Smith-

' . . . is implicit in an enactment which prohibits the doing of an act save in specified circumstances or by persons of specified classes or with special qualifications or with the licence or permission of specified authorities'.

{*Tynan v Jones* [1975] Crim LR 458, at p 459.}

Sentence The policy of the common law has always been against increasing a sentence once imposed. Accordingly the power, given by s 2(1) of the Courts Act 1971, to 'vary' a sentence by implication was construed not to authorise a variation that would make the original sentence more severe. {*R v Grice* [1978] 66 Cr App R 167.}

341. Rules of jurisdiction, evidence and procedure

Unless the contrary intention appears, an enactment by implication imports any principle or rule relating to jurisdiction, evidence or procedure (whether statutory or non-statutory) which prevails in the territory to which the enactment extends and is relevant to the operation of the enactment in that territory.

COMMENTARY

General principle As to the principle under which relevant rules of general law are by implication taken to be imported so far as necessary for the operation of an enactment see s 144 of this Code.

There are many ways in which rules of jurisdiction, evidence and procedure are to be treated as embodied in Acts under interpretation. All we have space for are some examples of the more important aspects.

Ouster or exclusionary clauses The courts dislike attempts by Parliament to oust or curtail their jurisdiction. {*R v Moreley* (1760) 2 Burr 1040, at p 1042; *Shipman v Henbest* (1790) 4 Term Rep 109; *R v London Corpn* (1829) 9 B & C 1, at p 27; *Balfour v Malcolm* (1842) 8 Cl & Fin 485, at p 500; *Albon v Pyke* (1842) 4 Man & G 421, at p 424; *Smith v Brown* (1871) LR 6 QB 729, at p 733; *Oram v Brearey* (1877) 2 Ex D 346, at p 348; *Seward v The Vera Cruz (Owner), The Vera Cruz* (1884) 10 App Cas 59; *Payne v Hogg* [1900] 2 QB 43, at p 53; *Morris & Bastert Ltd v Loughborough Corpn* [1908] 1 KB 205; *A-G v Boden* [1912] 1 KB 539, at p 561; *Re Vexatious Actions Act 1896* [1915] 1 KB 21, at p 36; *Goldsack v Shore* [1950] 1 KB 708; *Francis v Yiewsley and West Drayton UDC* [1957] 2 QB 136, at p 148; *Pountney v Griffiths* [1976] AC 314, at pp 331,334.}

Lord Campbell CJ attributed the origin of this sentiment to the contests for fees between the early common-law courts. {*Scott v Avery* (1856) 5 HL Cas 811.} A more respectable reason was given by Romer LJ-

> 'The proper tribunals for the determination of legal disputes in this country are the courts and they are the only tribunals which, by training and experience, and assisted by properly-qualified advocates, are fitted for the task.'

{*Lee v Showman's Guild of Great Britain* [1952] 2 QB 329, at p 354.}
While this is no doubt true, a price has to be paid in legal costs and delay. For this reason, and also because advantage may be found in having expert tribunals where, for example, medical or accountancy knowledge is required, a proliferation of statutory tribunals has occurred. The causes which lead to tribunals being set up also militate against rights of appeal or review being given against their decisions.

The courts nevertheless go to great lengths to find implied limitations which water down the literal meaning of ouster clauses. Viscount Simonds said it was a fundamental rule not to be whittled down that the subject's recourse to Her Majesty's courts for the determination of his rights is not to be excluded except by clear words. {*Pyx Granite Co Ltd v Ministry of Housing and Local Government* [1960] AC 260, at p 286.} The cases show that even clear words may not be enough.

Ouster clauses take different forms. One form expressly attempts to oust the type of supervisory jurisdiction now known as judicial review. In the eighteenth and early nineteenth centuries the courts were too inclined to use the prerogative writ of certiorari to quash decisions for technical defects of form. Many Acts therefore said that a decision of a lower court or tribunal 'shall not be taken away by certiorari'. In *R v Cheltenham Commrs* {(1841) 1 QB 467.}, where a tribunal decision was quashed on the ground that some of its members were disqualified, Lord Denman CJ said that these statutory words 'cannot affect our right to see justice executed'. {See also *R v Gillyard* (1848) 12 QB 527 (decision quashed where obtained by fraud). The law on this aspect was summed up by Denning LJ in *R v Medical Appeal Tribunal, ex p Gilmore* [1957] 1 QB 574, at pp 583–585.}

Another form of ouster clause says that the tribunal's decision shall be 'final'. This again has been held not to preclude judicial examination of a ruling not arrived at in accordance with law. Denning LJ said in *R v Medical Appeal Tribunal, ex p Gilmore* {[1957] 1 QB 574, at p 583.}-

> 'The word "final" is not enough. That means only "without recourse to appeal". It does not mean "without recourse to certiorari". It makes the decision final on the facts, but not final on the law.'

{See also *Pyx Granite Co Ltd v Ministry of Housing and Local Government* [1960] AC 260; *Ridge v Baldwin* [1964] AC 40; *R v Crown Court at Knightsbridge, ex p International Sporting Club (London) Ltd* [1981] 3 All ER 417, at p 424.}
A further form of ouster clause states that the tribunal decision 'shall not be called in question in any court of law' {Eg, Foreign Compensation Act 1950 s 4(4).} or 'shall not be questioned in any legal proceedings whatsoever'. {Eg, Housing Act 1957 Sch 4 para 3.} In *Anisminic v Foreign Compensation Commission* {[1969] 2 AC 147.} the House of Lords held that even this wide

formula is not enough to oust the jurisdiction of the courts where the decision in question is a nullity because of error of law. Being a nullity, it is nothing. It therefore cannot be a 'decision' or 'determination' within the meaning of the ouster clause, which accordingly has nothing to bite on. {As to the distinction in this connection between decisions which are 'void' and 'voidable' see *Firman v Ellis* [1978] 3 WLR 1.}

Lord Denning MR went even further than this in *Pearlman v Governors of Harrow School*. {[1978] 3 WLR 736.} The case concerned not one but *two* ouster clauses. The first was the important provision which attempted to avoid the complicating of county court proceedings which necessarily follows where they are subjected to judicial review, namely s 107 of the County Courts Act 1959. The other was embedded in the provision concerned in the case, namely Sch 8 to the Housing Act 1974.

Section 1 of the Leasehold Reform Act 1967 allows a tenant to claim enfranchisement where the rateable value of the premises is below a certain figure. Paragraph 1 of Sch 8 to the 1974 Act permits reduction of the rateable value for this purpose where the tenant has carried out an 'improvement' to the premises made by 'structural alteration, extension or addition'. Any dispute as to whether particular work constitutes an 'improvement' is to be determined by the county court, and the enactment stated that any such determination 'shall be final and conclusive'. {Housing Act 1974 Sch 8 para 2(2).} This was the second ouster clause.

In *Pearlman* the question was whether the installation of central heating fell within the definition of 'improvement'. If it did, the county court judge was required to go on and determine other relevant matters. He held that it did not, and therefore declined to consider the further matters. *Held* This finding was wrong in law. The judge had no jurisdiction to make such an error, and therefore the finding could be quashed despite the two ouster clauses. Lord Denning MR said {P 744.) that the distinction between error of law and want of jurisdiction should be discarded. He went on-

> 'The High Court has, and should have, jurisdiction to control the proceedings of inferior courts and tribunals by way of judicial review. When they go wrong in law, the High Court should have power to put them right. Not only in the instant case to do justice to the complainant. But also so as to secure that all courts and tribunals, when faced with the same point of law, should decide it in the same way ... No court or tribunal has any jurisdiction to make an error of law on which the decision of the case depends.'

Accepting defeat, Parliament repealed s 107 of the County Courts Act 1959 on the quaint ground that it was 'obsolete or unnecessary'. {Courts Act 1981 s 152(4).} The other ouster clause in *Pearlman* has also gone. The Housing Act 1980, without this time vouchsafing any reason, repealed the words stating that determinations under Sch 8 para 2(2) of the Housing Act 1974 'shall be final and conclusive'. {Housing Act 1980 ss 141 and 152(3).}

It is interesting to observe that in other contexts the courts regard such words as meaning what they say. Of the word 'conclusive' as used in s 32(4) of the National Parks and Access to the Countryside Act 1949 (which pronounces a definitive map to be conclusive evidence of the existence of a footpath) Lord Morris of Borth-y-Gest said-

' . . . if Parliament has decreed that in such event the map must be regarded as "conclusive evidence" it follows in my view that Parliament has said that no one must be heard to attack the truth of that which is 'conclusive' . . . To add some further provision would have been superfluous. Finality is reached when something is unreservedly conclusive.'

{*Suffolk County Council v Mason* [1979] 2 All ER 369, at p 377.}

Section 14(1) of the Tribunals and Inquiries Act 1971 states that any provision in an Act passed before 1 August 1958 that any order or determination shall not be called into question in any court, or any provision in such an Act which by similar words excludes any of the powers of the High Court, shall not have effect so as to prevent the removal of the proceedings into the High Court by order of certiorari. Nor is it to prejudice the powers of the High Court to make orders of mandamus. Section 14(3) provides that s 14(1) is not to apply to an order or determination of a court of law, or where an Act makes special provision for application to the High Court within a time limited by the Act. {Eg, Housing Act 1957 Sch 4 para 2.}

Pleading   It is presumed that Parliament intended to import the usual rules of pleading, even though these may have the effect of contradicting the literal meaning of the enactment.

Example 1   Section 1 of the Law Reform (Contributory Negligence) Act 1945 abolishes the common law rule whereby contributory negligence defeats a claim. The opening words read-

'Where any person suffers damage as the result partly of his own fault and partly of the fault of any other person or persons, a claim in respect of that damage shall not be defeated by reason of the fault of the person suffering the damage, *but the damages recoverable in respect thereof shall be reduced to such extent as the court thinks just . . .*' {Emphasis added.}

In *Fookes v Slaytor* {[1979] 1 All ER 137.} the court of first instance was satisfied that the plaintiff was one-third to blame for the damage he had suffered. Although the defendant did not plead contributory negligence, the judge held that the mandatory words of s 1 required him to reduce the damages accordingly. The plaintiff appealed. *Held* The practice whereby contributory negligence is required to be pleaded must be treated as imported. Despite the plain words of the enactment, the plaintiff was therefore entitled to his damages in full.

Evidence   The usual rules relating to evidence are by implication imported whenever it is necessary to establish something referred to in an enactment. {See Example 11.1.}

Example 2   Thus where an enactment enabled a compensation order to be made 'for any . . . loss or damage resulting from an offence' it was held to imply that the liability for, and amount of, the loss or damage must be either proved or agreed. {*R v Vivian* [1979] 1 All ER 48.}

Example 3 Section 5(1) of the Misuse of Drugs Act 1971 says it shall not be lawful for a person to have a controlled drug in his possession. In *R v Boyesen* {[1982] 2 All ER 161, at p 166.} Lord Scarman held that this requires identification of the drug in an acceptable manner. He added-

> 'If it be said that an 'identification' test is itself not expressly stated in the subsection, I would reply that it is implicit. Unless the thing possessed is shown by evidence to be a controlled drug, there is no offence.'

Acts sometimes make provision about one aspect or other of the law of evidence. It follows that they do so against the background of the general rules. Thus a reference in an enactment to 'fresh evidence' imports the usual legal meaning of this phrase as evidence which is not merely additional to that adduced on the former occasion but could not reasonably have been expected to be produced then. {*Re Tarling* [1979] 1 All ER 981, at p 987.}

Example 4 Section 2(1) of the Sexual Offences (Amendment) Act 1976 relates to evidence in a rape trial. It says that without the leave of the judge 'no evidence and no question in cross-examination shall be adduced or asked' about the complainant's sexual experience with other men. In *R v Viola* {[1982] 3 All ER 73.} it was held that the first question the judge must ask himself in deciding whether to give leave is 'are the questions proposed to be put relevant according to the ordinary common law rules of evidence'? {*Per* Lord Lane CJ at p 76.}

Where an enactment allows a departure from the rules of evidence in court proceedings it will be construed strictly. {*R v Ivan Bradley* (1980) 70 Cr App R 200, at p 203.} On the other hand Parliament is taken not to imply that the full rules of evidence must be adhered to in tribunal proceedings. {*R v Greater Birmingham Supplementary Benefit Appeal Tribunal, ex p Khan* [1979] 3 All ER 759, at p 763.}

Estoppel The operation of the rule of evidence known as estoppel in pais (by conduct) may have the effect of altering the normal meaning of an enactment.

Example 5 A lease of a flat was granted for a term of seven years. Since it was not 'for a term of less than seven years', s 32 of the Housing Act 1961 (imposing repairing obligations on the lessor) did not apply. However the rent officer had fixed a higher rent on the basis that s 32 did apply, and for several years the lessors had demanded and received this higher rent. *Held* The lessors were estopped from denying that s 32 applied, even though on the true meaning of the section it did not. {*Brikom Investments Ltd v Seaford* [1981] 2 All ER 783.}

Evidential burden On the trial of statutory offences the doctrine of the evidential burden is taken to be imported unless the contrary intention appears. This means that once the prosecution have made out a prima facie case it is for the defence to adduce such evidence of exculpating facts alleged by them as might, in the judge's opinion, raise a doubt in the minds of a reasonable jury. If the evidential burden is satisfied, the judge must direct the jury to acquit unless they are sure of guilt. {See *R v Powles* [1976] Crim LR 452.}

Standard of proof   Acts frequently determine the incidence of proof of a relevant fact without saying anything about the standard of proof required to be satisfied by the side on whom the burden is thus cast. In such cases the inference is that common law rules as to the standard of proof are to apply. {*R v Ewing* [1983] 2 All ER 645, *per* O'Connor LJ at p 652: 'the standard of proof is governed by common law'. Cf the reference to the common law in Lord Pearce's speech in *Blyth v Blyth* [1966] AC 643, at p 673.}

If the matter is a civil one, proof is therefore to be according to the balance of probabilities. If it is a criminal or quasi-criminal matter the fact must be proved beyond reasonable doubt. Here account must be taken of the rule that some questions in civil proceedings (eg, the existence of fraud) are subject to the criminal standard, while some questions in criminal proceedings (eg, the mental condition of the defendant) are subject to the civil standard.

The position is further complicated by the fact that neither the civil standard nor the criminal standard is necessarily uniform. Thus in *Blyth v Blyth* {[1966] AC 643.} the House of Lords held that while the power to pronounce a decree of divorce conferred by s 4(2) of the Matrimonial Causes Act 1950 was subject to the civil standard, the word 'satisfied' in s 4(2) betokened different degrees of proof for a finding of adultery and a finding of absence of condonation or connivance.

Where the question of proof arises in interlocutory proceedings, the standard may be different again. The court will not wish to determine finally any matter which falls for decision at the trial. Accordingly a statutory reference to 'proof' will be construed as referring merely to a prima facie case, or even an arguable case. {*Sidnell v Wilson* [1966] 2 QB 67; *Land Securities plc v Receiver for the Metropolitan Police District* [1983] 2 All ER 254.}

Public interest immunity   The doctrine of public interest immunity (formerly known as Crown privilege) applies to the disclosure of evidence in proceedings of a civil (as opposed to criminal) nature where ordering this would impede the carrying out of some statutory function. Thus in *Rogers v Secretary of State for the Home Department* {[1972] 2 All ER 1057.} the House of Lords held that disclosure would impede the carrying out by the Gaming Board of its statutory duties. Similarly in *Neilson v Laugharne* {[1981] 1 All ER 829.} it was held that disciplinary inquiries under s 49 of the Police Act 1964 would be prejudiced if witnesses knew their statements might be later disclosed in civil proceedings against accused officers.

Public interest immunity calls for balancing the public interest in the administration of justice, which demands the disclosure of all relevant material, against a competing public interest in withholding that material. {*Neilson v Laugharne* [1981] 1 All ER 829, *per* Oliver LJ at p 838.} The classes of material affected are determined at common law, but the categories are not closed. Lord Salmon said-

> 'The principle is that whenever it is clearly contrary to the public interest for a document or information to be disclosed, then it is in law immune from disclosure. If a new class comes into existence to which this principle applies then that class enjoys the same immunity.'

{*Rogers v Secretary of State for the Home Department* [1972] 2 All ER 1057, at p 1071. See also s 34 of this Code.}

It appears that public interest immunity cannot be waived. {*Hehir v Commr of Police of the Metropolis* [1982] 2 All ER 335.}

Remedies The court is very ready to assume that Parliament intended the usual range of remedies to be available for enforcement of an Act.

Example 6 In *Horner v Horner* {[1982] 2 All ER 495.} the Court of Appeal held that, although the relevant provision of s 1 of the Domestic Violence and Matrimonial Proceedings Act 1976 referred only to 'molestation', s 2 of the Act showed that it gave an implied power to the court to issue the usual form of divorce injunction restraining 'assaulting, molesting or otherwise interfering'. Dunn LJ said: 'By implication s 2 shows that the judge is to have power to make an order restraining the other party to the marriage from using violence'. {P 498.}

342. Rules of private international law (conflict of laws)

Unless the contrary intention appears, an enactment by implication imports any principle or rule of private international law (otherwise known as conflict of laws) which prevails in the territory to which the enactment extends and is relevant to the operation of the enactment in that territory.

COMMENTARY

General principle As to the general principle under which relevant rules of general law are by implication taken to be imported so far as necessary for the operation of an enactment see s 144 of this Code.

Public and private international law There is a distinction between public and private international law, though many judicial dicta do not recognise this. Thus, in a will case turning on a point of private international law Sir James Hannen P said-

> 'Every statute is to be so interpreted and applied, as far as its language admits, as not to be inconsistent with the comity of nations or with established principles of international law.'

{*Bloxam v Favre* (1883) 8 PD 101, at p 104.}

This dictum is more appropriate in relation to public international law. The reason why, in interpreting statutes, a court has regard to the rules of private international law is that they form a necessary part of our municipal law. Public international law is not part of the municipal system, and is not therefore subject to the implied importation of legal rules dealt with in this Part of the Code. {For the presumption that Parliament intends to comply with public international law see s 134 of this Code.}

There are many ways in which rules and principles of private international law are to be treated as embodied in Acts under interpretation. All we have space for are some examples of the more important aspects.

As guides to extent or application of Act   Acts are often drafted in general terms, without express restrictions as to their extent or application. {As to territorial extent see ss 195 to 220 of this Code. As to personal application see ss 221 to 228.} Here the rules of private international law may form a guide to the legislative intention. {See Examples 313.2 and 351.7.}

Where an Act regulates contracts in what might be called worldwide language, that is without exclusionary words, the doctrine of private international law relating to the proper law of the contract will be taken to be applied by implication (of course where not expressly disapplied). Under this doctrine, the proper law of the contract is taken to be that system of law with which the transaction has its closest and most real connection.

Example 1   Section 18(1) of the Trade Union and Labour Relations Act 1974 says that 'any collective agreement' shall be conclusively presumed not to have been intended to be a legally enforceable contract unless it contains an express provision to that effect. This was not intended by Parliament to apply in fact to 'any collective agreement', but only to one where the proper law of the agreement was English law. {See *Monterosso Shipping Co Ltd v International Transport Workers' Federation* [1982] 3 All ER 841.}

Similarly, although an Act may purport to regulate the family or other personal status of persons worldwide, this will be restricted in the light of principles of private international law.

Example 2   Section 2 of the Marriage Act 1949 says: 'A marriage solemnised between persons either of whom is under the age of sixteen shall be void'. {By commonsense implication, this is taken to mean sixteen *years* rather than, say, sixteen months. As to the commonsense construction rule see s 122 of this Code.} On its face this applies to all persons in the world, but in *Pugh v Pugh* {[1951] P 482.} it was held to be limited by the relevant rule of private international law.

This provides that the status of a purported marriage is determined by the domicile of the parties. Here the marriage ceremony had been performed in Austria between a British subject domiciled in England and a fifteen-year old Hungarian girl domiciled in Austria. Although the marriage was valid under the laws of both Hungary and Austria, it was held that s 2 of the 1949 Act invalidated it.

Similarly the width of enactments dealing with succession to property on death will be treated as reduced by the impact of rules of private international law. {*Re Bruce* (1832) 2 Cr & J 436; *Arnold v Arnold* (1837) 6 LJ Ch 218; *Thomson v Advocate-General* (1845) 12 CL & F 1; *A-G v Napier* (1851) 6 Ex 217; *Blackwood v R* (1882) 8 App Cas 81; *Harding v Queensland Commrs of Stamps* [1898] AC 769; *In the Estate of Maldonado decd* [1954] P 223.}

Act frustrated by rule of private international law   Where on a literal construction an enactment would be prevented from achieving its purpose by a rule of private international law, the court presumes that Parliament intended that regard should be had to the rule and a purposive-and-strained construction given accordingly.

Example 3 In *Salmon v Duncombe* {(1886) 11 App Cas 627.} the Judicial Committee of the Privy Council construed a Natal Ordinance of which the long title was-

> 'Ordinance to grant to certain natural-born subjects of Great Britain and Ireland, resident in this district, the right to dispose by last will and testament of their real and personal property according to the law of England'.

The preamble repeated this at greater length, and s 1 said-

> 'Any natural-born subject of Great Britain and Ireland resident within this district may exercise all and singular the rights which such natural-born subject could or might exercise according to the laws and customs of England in regard to the disposal by last will or testament of property, both real and personal, situated in this district, *to all intents and purposes as if such natural-born subject resided in England.*'

{Emphasis added.}

Unfortunately the rules of private international law provide that on death immovables devolve according to the *lex situs* and movables according to the law of the domicile. The country of residence is immaterial, so that the statutory hypothesis called forth by the italicised words made no difference. *Held* The intention was manifest, and the words must be given what this Code calls a purposive-and-strained construction. {See s 315 of the Code.} Lord Hobhouse said {Pp 633-5.}-

> ' ... if the word "resident" be construed in its ordinary sense, and their Lordships see no reason for contruing it otherwise, the Ordinance effects nothing at all ... It is however a very serious matter to hold that when the main object of a statute is clear, it shall be reduced to a nullity by the draftsman's unskilfulness or ignorance of law ... Very likely the draftsman, whose want of skill is shown by other expressions in the Ordinance, attributed to residence a legal effect which it does not possess ... It is very unsatisfactory to be compelled to construe a statute in this way, but it is much more unsatisfactory to deprive it altogether of meaning.'

Refusal to apply foreign law Although under normal rules of private international law a certain foreign law would govern the matter, an English court will refuse to apply that foreign law where to do so would run counter to a fundamental policy of English law. {*Winkworth v Christie, Manson & Woods Ltd* [1980] 1 All ER 1121, at p 1132.}

This rarely-applied exception is but one aspect of the rule that what is by implication imported in the construction of an enactment is not private international law at large, but that law as it exists as part of the *lex fori*.

Unless the contrary intention appears As always, the presumption dealt with in this section of the Code applies only where Parliament does not otherwise provide.

Example 4 Under private international law, devolution of the foreign immovable property of a person adjudged bankrupt under s 18 of the Bankruptcy Act 1914 would be governed by the *lex situs*. However s 167 of the Act states that 'property', where occurring in the Act, includes every description of property whether situate in England or elsewhere. {An example of the bad drafting habit of including as a definition a provision which has substantive effect (see pp 277–278 above).}

Foreign courts   Where it is relevant for an English court to determine what law a foreign court would apply, it will be assumed that the foreign court would conform to the general principles of private international law. {*Breen v Breen* [1964] P 144 (assumed that Irish court would not hold that its constitution impliedly withheld recognition of divorce decree by foreign court of the domicile).}

Legislative Presumptions: Application of Ancillary Legal Maxims

Introduction to Part XIX This Part spells out the effect of the presumption laid down in s 145 of the Code that Parliament is taken to intend general maxims of law to apply so far as relevant in the construction of an enactment. The maxims, all in Latin, are set out in alphabetical order. Sixteen maxims are dealt with here, though various others are discussed elsewhere in the work.

The maxims described in Part XIX cover the following principles: that intentions are deduced from actions (s 343), that acts of God may afford an excuse (s 344), that a person cannot rely on his own illegality (s 345), that both sides should be heard (s 346), that a double detriment should not be inflicted (s 347), the de minimis principle (s 348), that a man's home is his castle (s 349), that impotence excuses (s 350), that law does not expect the impossible (s 351), that necessity knows no law (s 352), that a person should not be judge in his own cause (s 353) or profit from his own wrong (s 354), that things are presumed to be correctly done (s 355), that one who acts through another acts himself (s 356), and that the law requires vigilance if its benefits are to be claimed (s 357). Finally we deal with the volenti principle (s 358).

343. Intentions deduced from actions: *acta exteriora indicant interiora secreta*

Unless the contrary intention appears, an enactment by implication imports the principle of the maxim *acta exteriora indicant interiora secreta* (external actions reveal inner secrets).

COMMENTARY

General principle As to the general principle under which relevant legal maxims are by implication taken to be imported so far as necessary for the operation of an enactment see s 145 of this Code.

The maxim *acta exteriora indicant interiora secreta* (external actions reveal inner secrets) is found in Coke. {8 Co Rep 146, 291.} A person's inner intentions are to be read from his acts and omissions. Whenever in the application of an enactment a person's state of mind is relevant, this maxim comes into play.

Trespass ab initio The principle is the basis of the common law doctrine of trespass ab initio. This applies where authority is given by law to do any act which would otherwise constitute a trespass. If in the course of the act the doer departs from the terms of the authority he is treated as a trespasser from the beginning. {*Six Carpenters' Case* (1610) 8 Co Rep 146a.} The doctrine is disapplied in relation to distress by s 19 of the Distress for Rent Act 1737. {See Example 339.2 and p 738 above.}

344. Act of God: *actus dei nemini facit injuriam*

Unless the contrary intention appears, an enactment by implication imports the principle of the maxim *actus dei nemini facit injuriam* (an Act of God causes legal injury to no one).

COMMENTARY

General principle   As to the general principle under which relevant legal maxims are by implication taken to be imported so far as necessary for the operation of an enactment see s 145 of this Code.

The term Act of God connotes some natural calamity or other event which cannot be avoided and is no one's fault. Equivalent terms are *damnum fatale, vis major*, and inevitable accident.

In principle it is unjust that a person should suffer legal detriment by reason of an Act of God. It therefore falls within the principle that Parliament does not intend injustice. {See s 128 of this Code.}

Unless the contrary intention appears (that is strict liability is intended), a statutory duty does not apply where rendered incapable of fulfilment by Act of God. {*R v Leicestershire JJ* (1850) 15 QB 88 (service of notice on respondent dispensed with by his death). Cf *Campbell v Earl of Dalhousie* (1868) LR 1 Sc & D 259, at p 269; *Harding v Price* [1948] 1 KB 659, at p 701. Strict liability was held to be imposed in *J & J Makin Ltd v London and North Eastern Rly Co* [1943] KB 467, but not in *Brown v National Coal Board* [1962] AC 574 or *Brazier v Skipton Rock Co* [1962] 1 WLR 471.}

Even where the statutory liability is 'strict', it may still not extend to Acts of God.

Example 1   In *The Mostyn* {*Great Western Rly Co v Owners of SS Mostyn* [1928] AC 57.} the House of Lords held that s 74 of the Harbours, Docks and Piers Clauses Act 1847 rendered the owners liable for damage caused by a ship that was still manned, thus distinguishing its earlier decision in *River Wear Comrs v Adamson* {(1877) 2 App Cas 743.} (where the ship causing damage had been abandoned in a storm). *Maxwell* remarks of the distinction thus drawn that it leaves s 74 as an example of an enactment creating a liability which is 'absolute, subject to the defence of Act of God'. {*Maxwell on the Interpretation of Statutes* (12th edn, 1969) p 326.}

Where the statutory duty is intended to have the effect of making the person concerned an insurer, it is likely that it extends to Acts of God. Someone has to bear the financial cost of these, and private Acts often allocate such responsibility to the promoters. {See, e g, *J & J Makin Ltd v London and North Eastern Rly Co* [1943] KB 467 (canal proprietors made liable for damage to lands or buildings 'by the breach of any reservoir . . . or of any of the locks or works . . . or from any other accident'.}

A statutory offence is subject to implied exceptions where, for example, the forbidden act is done 'under duress, to which one might add inevitable accident'. {*Sweet v Parsley* [1970] AC 132, *per* Lord Diplock at p 156. See also Example 350.2.}

345. Reliance on illegality: *allegans suam turpitudinem non est audiendus*

Unless the contrary intention appears, an enactment by implication imports the principle of the maxim *allegans suam turpitudinem non est audiendus* (a person alleging his own wrongdoing is not to be heard).

COMMENTARY

General principle   As to the general principle under which relevant legal maxims are by implication taken to be imported so far as necessary for the operation of an enactment see s 145 of this Code.

The maxim *allegans suam turpitudinem non est audiendus* (a person alleging his own wrongdoing is not to be heard) was put forward by Coke as an important principle of law. {4 Inst 279.} Contravention of a statutory requirement is an unlawful act. This illegality taints the act. It precludes the doer from relying on the unlawful act to found an action or other claim, or establish a defence.

The maxim does *not* mean that a person such as an accomplice will not be heard as a witness merely because his testimony reveals his own wrongdoing. What the policy of the law strikes against is a person seeking a legal benefit where he needs to rely on an illegality. A similar principle is that a person may not benefit from his own wrong. {See s 354 of this Code.} The present principle looks to the case where the illegality is sought to be positively relied on; whereas the principle that a person may not benefit from his own wrong looks to the case where there is an apparently valid cause of action apart from the wrong.

A related maxim is *ex turpi causa non oritur actio* (an action does not arise from a wrongful cause). {Cowp 343.} This is also expressed as *ex dolo malo non oritur actio* (an action does not arise from fraud). {Cowp 343.} *Dolus malus* was defined in Roman law as craft, guile or machination used for the purpose of deception or circumvention. {W W Buckland *A Text-book of Roman Law* (2nd edn, 1950) p 594.} It was contrasted with *dolus bonus*, which signified that degree of allowable dexterity which a person may employ to advance his own interests. {H Broom *Legal Maxims* (1st edn, 1845) p 349.}

The essence of the present principle is that the party needs to establish a wrongful act in order to succeed.

Example 1   In *Goordin v Secretary of State for the Home Department* {(1981) *The Times* 11 August.} the applicant sought the quashing of a deportation order made under s 3(5) of the Immigration Act 1971. In 1972 he had obtained leave of entry for two weeks as a visitor, saying he intended to remain only for that period. This was a lie. He intended to remain as long as he could, and did so.

In 1974 an amnesty was announced for illegal immigrants. If the applicant had been an illegal immigrant, he could have taken advantage of this and, after five years, have obtained leave to remain permanently. In 1976 the deportation order was made under s 3(5) on the ground that he was an overstayer. (Section 3(5) does not apply to persons whose initial entry was illegal.)

The applicant argued that as his statement on entry was a lie this vitiated the entry permit and rendered his initial entry illegal. He could thus claim the benefit of the amnesty and obtain leave to remain permanently. *Held* This was not permissible. The law would not allow the applicant to challenge a procedure he had brought into play by his own deceit.

The present principle is often applicable where the wrongdoing consists in a contravention of the Act under which benefit is sought. This connection is immaterial however. What matters is reliance on a cause of action which depends on something forbidden by law.

An Act may forbid certain conduct either expressly or by implication. This is in accord with the principle that the meaning of an enactment is conveyed by implications as well as express statement. {See s 107 of this Code.}

Example 2 Section 193 of the Public Health Act 1875 prohibited any officer of a local authority from being interested in any contract made by the authority. A penalty was laid down for breach. In *Mellis v Shirley Local Board* {(1885) 16 QBD 446.} the surveyor of a local board was sued under a contract made between him and the board for the execution of certain works under the Act. *Held* The action did not lie, since s 193 by implication rendered the contract illegal. {See also *Elliot v Richardson* (1870) LR 5 CP 744; *Equitable Life Assurance Society of USA v Reed* [1914] AC 587, at p 595; *Farmers' Mart Ltd v Milne* [1915] AC 106; *Re Johns* [1928] Ch 737.}

A provision imposing a penalty for contravention on a certain person may by implication taint the contracts of others with illegality also. {*Musgrove v Chung Teeong Toy* [1891] AC 272 (penalty imposed on shipowner for breach of immigration laws also affected the immigrants).}

The principle of illegality taints a defence as well as a claim: 'no man shall set up his own iniquity as a defence any more than as a cause of action'. {*Montefiori v Montefiori* (1762) 1 W Bla 364, *per* Lord Mansfield CJ (cited by Abbott CJ 2 B & Ald 368).} Elsewhere Lord Mansfield said-

> 'The objection that a contract is immoral or illegal, as between plaintiff and defendant, sounds at all times very ill in the mouth of the defendant. It is not for his sake, however, that the objection is ever allowed, but it is founded in general principles of policy, which the defendant has the advantage of, contrary to the real justice as between him and the plaintiff, by accident, if I may so say.'

{*Holman v Johnson* (1775) 1 Cowp 341.}

This principle makes it possible for tax to be levied on unlawful gains, since the taxpayer cannot resist an assessment by setting up his own wrong. {See *Minister of Finance v Smith* [1927] AC 193, at p 197; *Mann v Nash* [1932] 1 KB 752; *Southern (S.) (Inspector of Taxes v AB* [1933] 1 KB 713; *Collins v Mulvey* [1956] IR 233.}

The defence of illegality can be set up notwithstanding that the defendant has enjoyed performance by the plaintiff of his part of the bargain. {*Young v Mayor etc of Leamington* (1883) 8 App Cas 517 (sanitary authority pleaded want of seal on building contract).}

Contrary intention Not every act or omission in contravention of a statute is tainted with illegality. The question, as always, is what the legislative intention was. While a contravention is presumed to taint the contravener's claim or defence with illegality, the contrary may appear to be Parliament's intention.

A frequent instance is where it seems that Parliament's intention was a limited one (for example protection of the revenue), and that this does not require the broad consequences which would follow from a finding of general illegality. The following Examples show cases on either side of the line.

Example 3 Little v Poole {(1829) 9 B & C 192.} concerned a statute which required a vendor of coals delivered from any ship to give the purchaser a printed ticket stating (1) the number of sacks, (2) the description of the coal, and (3) the name of the vendor. It imposed a penalty of £20 if these requirements were not observed. *Held* The statute was designed for the protection of purchasers. Where a vendor failed to comply with it in the case of a particular contract of sale, there was nothing to displace the usual presumption that he had committed an illegality and so could not enforce the contract.

Example 4 In Learoyd v Bracken {[1894] 1 QB 114.} a stockbroker contravened the Stamp Act 1891 by buying shares for a client without delivering to him a stamped contract note. *Held* the penalty laid down by the Act was regarded by Parliament as a sufficient protection for the revenue, and it was not intended to render unstamped contracts illegal.

An important factor in such cases as the last is one frequently relied on in ascertaining Parliament's intention, namely the disproportionately severe consequences that might ensue if breach of the statute were held to taint transactions affected by it with illegality. {As to consequential construction see s 140 of this Code.}

As always, Parliament may indicate the contrary intention in express words.

Example 5 In Anderson Ltd v Daniel {[1924] 1 KB 138.} it was held that the object of a statutory requirement to give written details on the sale of certain fertilisers and feeding-stuffs was to protect the general public, and that a contract in breach of the requirement could not be enforced by the seller. This decision was reversed by the Fertilisers and Feeding Stuffs Act 1926. Section 1(1) of the Act re-enacted the requirement in question, with modifications. Section 1(2) ran as follows-

> '(2) Failure to give a statutory statement in accordance with the provisions of this section shall not invalidate a contract for sale.'

Severance Where part only of a transaction is tainted by illegality, this does not affect the remainder if it is possible to sever the tainted part from the rest. Severance need not be by textual division, provided it is possible in substance. {*Netherseal Colliery Co Ltd v Bourne* (1889) 14 App Cas 228; *Stanton v Brown* [1900] 1 QB 671. See pp 144–145 above.}

If however the tainted part is inextricably mixed with the rest, the whole transaction will be void. This will happen for example where the stipulations in a contract are based on several distinct considerations, one of which is illegal. In such a case it is not possible to say how far the illegal consideration was the foundation of any promise, so the whole is void. {*Shackell v Rosier* (1836) 2 Bing NC 634; *Egerton v Earl Brownlow* (1853) 4 HLC 1; *Moulis v Owen* [1907] 1KB 746; *Saxby v Fulton* [1909] 2 KB 208; *Carlton Hall Club v Laurence* [1929] 153.}

Judicial initiative   Once the court becomes aware of the fact that a claim or defence is tainted by illegality it must take notice of the fact, even though the party affected does not choose to rely on it. In an action on a contract, Scrutton LJ said-

> 'In my view the Court is bound, once it knows that the contract is illegal, to take the objection and to refuse to enforce the contract, whether its knowledge comes from the statement of the party who was guilty of the illegality, or whether its knowledge comes from outside sources. The Court does not sit to enforce illegal contracts. There is no question of estoppel; it is for the protection of the public that the Court refuses to enforce such a contract.'

{*In re Mahmoud and Ispahani* [1921] 2 KB 716, at p 729. See also *Scott v Brown, Doering & Co* [1892] 2 QB 724; *North Western Salt Co v Electrolytic Alkali Co* [1914] AC 461.}

Construction in bonam partem   As to construction *in bonam partem* see pp 298–300 above.

346. Hearing both sides: *audi alteram partem*

Unless the contrary intention appears, an enactment by implication imports the principle of the maxim *audi alteram partem* (hear the other side).

COMMENTARY

General principle As to the general principle under which relevant legal maxims are by implication taken to be imported so far as necessary for the operation of an enactment see s 145 of this Code.

Unless the contrary intention appears, an enactment by implication imports the maxim *audi alteram partem* (hear the other side). The principle that no man is to be condemned unheard is fundamental to justice. Parliament is presumed not to intend injustice. {See s 128 of this Code.} The principle is a basic precept of natural justice. {As to the requirement to observe natural justice see pp 741–743 above.}

Coke took from Seneca's *Medea* the saying that *qui aliquid statuerit parte inaudita altera, aequum licet dixerit, haud aequum fecerit* (he who decides a thing without the other side having been heard, although he may have said what is right, will not have done what is right). {6 Co Rep 52.}

Erle CJ said that it is 'an indispensable requirement of justice that no man should be condemned unheard or without having had an opportunity of being heard'. {*Re Brook* (1864) 16 CB(NS) 403, at p 416. See the leading case of *Ridge v Baldwin* [1964] AC 40 (holder of a public office removable only for cause could not be dismissed without notice of the reason and an opportunity to be heard).}

The principle has been judicially held to date back to the Garden of Eden. In *R v Chancellor of Cambridge University* {(1723) 1 Stra 557.} Dr Bentley had been deprived of his academic degrees by a decree made without prior notice to him. Fortescue J said-

'The objection for want of notice can never be got over. The laws of God and man both give the party an opportunity to make his defence, if he has any. I remember to have heard it observed by a very learned man, upon such an occasion, that even God himself did not pass sentence upon Adam before he was called on to make his defence. "Adam" (says God), "where art thou? Hast thou not eaten of the tree whereof I commanded thee that thou shouldest not eat?" And the same question was put to Eve also.'

The principle requires not merely an opportunity to be heard, but that all aspects of that hearing are fair. Nevertheless there are no hard and fast rules. Lord Reid said-

'Natural justice requires that the procedure before any tribunal which is acting judicially shall be fair in all the circumstances, and I would be sorry to see this fundamental general principle degenerate into a series of hard and fast rules. For a long time the courts have, without objection from Parliament, supplemented procedure laid down in legislation where they have found that to be necessary for this purpose. But before this unusual kind of power is exercised it must be clear that the statutory procedure is insufficient to achieve justice and that to require additional steps would not frustrate the apparent purpose of the legislation.'

{*Wiseman v Borneman* [1969] 3 All ER 275, at p 277.}

Nor does the principle mean that a party can require to be 'heard' in any manner he chooses. {*Banin* v *MacKinlay (Inspector of Taxes)* [1984] 1 All ER 1116.}

The *audi alteram partem* principle has given rise to many refinements and complexities. The following are a selection of the more important aspects.

Inform the party of the case he has to meet   It is obvious that a party cannot have a reasonable opportunity to be heard unless he is made aware of what it is that he is being heard about. As Lord Fraser of Tullybelton said-

'One of the principles of natural justice is that a person is entitled to
adequate notice and opportunity to be heard before any judicial order
is pronounced against him, so that he, or someone acting on his
behalf, may make such representations, if any, as he sees fit.'

{*Forrest v Brighton JJ* [1981] 2 All ER 711, at p 714 (fact that prisoner not entitled to be present at a hearing did not mean he need not be given notice that it was to be held, and what it was about).}

The terms should not be so widely drawn as to give the decision-making functionary a roving power. {*R v Commission for Racial Equality, ex p Hillingdon LBC* (1981) *The Times* 17 July.} It is sufficient if they convey the substance, though even that is not necessary if the party is already aware of it. {*Payne v Lord Harris of Greenwich* [1981] 2 All ER 842, *per* Lord Denning MR at p 845.}

Allow the party time to prepare his case   A party must be allowed sufficient time, and must not be taken by surprise. Where an adjournment is reasonably needed it must be granted. {*R v Thames Magistrates, ex p Polemis* [1974] 1 WLR 1371.}

Allow reasonable facilities for the making of representations   The party must be afforded appropriate facilities. Unless there is some telling reason to the contrary, this includes the right to be heard *orally* by the decision-making functionary or his representative. {*Local Government Board v Arlidge* [1915] AC 120; *R v Housing Appeal Tribunal* [1920] 3 KB 334; *Brighton Corpn v Parry* (1972) 70 LGR 576.}

At an oral hearing there must be an opportunity to call and cross-examine witnesses. {*Ceylon University v Fernando* [1960] 1 WLR 223; *R v Board of Visitors of Blundeston Prison, ex p Fox-Taylor* (1981) *The Times* 29 October.} Relevant evidence must not be excluded because it is hearsay. {*R v Deputy Industrial Injuries Commr, ex p Moore* [1965] 1 QB 456, *per* Diplock LJ at p 488; *Miller (TA) Ltd v Minister of Housing and Local Government* [1968] 1 .WLR 992.} Legal representation need not be allowed if it is reasonable to deny it. {*Enderby Town FC Ltd v Football Association Ltd* [1971] Ch 591; *Fraser v Mudge* [1975] 1 WLR 1132; *Maynard v Osmond* [1976] 3 WLR 711.}

Do not act on evidence not disclosed to the parties   The principle of the open court requires that the parties should be aware of all that influences the decision-maker. Thus where a rating assessment committee did not disclose an expert report it had commissioned from a valuer the assessment was quashed. {*R v City of Westminster Assessment Committee, ex p Grosvenor House (Park Lane) Ltd* [1941] 1 KB 53. See also *Board of Education v Rice* [1911] AC 179, at p 182.}

This does not mean that *internal* reports, such as that of an inquiry inspector to his Minister, need be disclosed. {*Local Governmant Board v Arlidge* [1915] AC 120.} Nor is disclosure required where it would prejudice national security or breach confidentiality. {*R v Gaming Board, ex p Benaim and Khaida* [1970] 2 QB 417.}

Do not hear one side behind the other's back   In order to conform to natural justice, the decision-maker must not act on representations from one party which the other has not seen and had a chance to comment on. {*R v Manchester Legal Aid Committee, ex p R A Brand & Co Ltd* [1952] 2 QB 413, *per* Parker J at p 429; *Errington v Minister of Health* [1935] 1 KB 249, at p 280.} A party must be given 'a fair opportunity to correct or controvert any relevant statement brought forward to his prejudice'. {*De Verteuil v Knaggs* [1918] AC 557, at p 560.}

If you delegate the hearing of representations consider the delegate's report   Even where it is lawful for the decision-maker to delegate the hearing of objections this does not mean that he can dispense with considering an accurate, if summarised, report of what the objections are. {*R v Chester Borough Council, ex p Quietlynn Ltd* (1984) *The Times* 22 March.}

347. Double detriment: *bona fides non patitur, ut bis idem exigatur*

Unless the contrary intention appears, an enactment by implication imports the principle of the maxim *bona fides non patitur, ut bis idem exigatur* (good faith does not suffer the same thing to be exacted twice).

COMMENTARY

General principle As to the general principle under which relevant legal maxims are by implication taken to be imported so far as necessary for the operation of an enactment see s 145 of this Code.

The maxim *bona fides non patitur, ut bis idem exigatur* (good faith does not suffer the same thing to be exacted twice) is derived from the civil law. {Dig 50, 17, 57.} The principle is also found in the maxim *nemo debet bis vexari* {5 Co Rep 61.}, and in the common law rule repeated in s 18 of the Intepretation Act 1978. {See p 743 above.}

The application of this maxim to statute law is founded in the principle of legal policy that the law, and therefore the legislature, does not intend to inflict injustice. {See s 128 of this Code.} Whenever the literal meaning of an enactment would lead to the infliction of some detriment twice over, the maxim calls for the application of a strained construction to avoid this. {See Example 128.4.}

One aspect of the principle is the rule that two actions cannot be brought in respect of the same cause of action. {See *Buckland v Palmer* (1984) *The Times* 23 June, where the court avoided injustice by allowing the first action to be reopened.}

348. De minimis principle: *de minimis non curat lex*

Unless the contrary intention appears, an enactment by implication imports the principle of the maxim *de minimis non curat lex* (the law does not concern itself with trifling matters).

COMMENTARY

General principle As to the general principle under which relevant legal maxims are by implication taken to be imported so far as necessary for the operation of an enactment see s 145 of this Code.

It is essential to the working of a legal system that it should adopt the principle of the maxim *de minimis non curat lex* (the law does not concern itself with trifling matters). {Cro Eliz 353; Hob 88.} There are a number of reasons for this. Litigious persons and unnecessary litigation must be discouraged: *boni judicis est lites dirimere* (the good judge prevents litigation). {4 Co Inst 15.} Time must not be wasted. Costs must be kept down. The dignity of the law must be preserved.

Parliament is presumed to have regard to all these matters, and by implication to intend that its enactments shall not apply in a *de minimis* case. It is excepted from their operation, as if excluded by an express proviso. Note that in a criminal case this is conceptually different from giving an absolute discharge on the ground of the triviality of the offence. Where *de minimis* applies there is no offence. {For a contrary view, which it is submitted is misconceived, see N L A Barlow 'Possession of Minute Quantities of a Drug' [1977] Crim LR 26. Ursula Ross says, surely rightly, that the application of *de minimis* makes the act in question 'not in itself unlawful' ('Two Cases on Obstructing a Constable' [1977] Crim LR 187, at p 190).}

Substance to be regarded The *de minimis* principle looks to the substance. If a matter at first sight trifling is shown to embody a point of substance, the principle does not apply.

This is shown in relation to fractions of a day, which the law normally disregards. If however a substantial point turns on regard being had to a precise moment of time, the law will abandon its usual view.

Example 1 The bankruptcy statute 6 Geo 4 c 16 (1825) protected the seizure of goods taken in execution where a period of two months had elapsed between the execution and the issuing of a bankruptcy petition. In *Godson v Sanctuary* {(1832) 4 B & Ad 255.} the execution was at 10 a m on 13 August, while the bankruptcy commission was issued at about noon on 13 October. *Held* The court would enquire into the exact time of each event in order to determine whether the two-month period had elapsed. {See also *Thomas v Desanges* (1819) 2 B & Ald 586; *Sadler v Leigh* (1815) 4 Camp 197; *Saunderson v Gregg* (1821) 3 Stark 72; *Clarke v Bradlaugh* (1882) 8 QBD 63.}

Where the subject has substantially complied with a statutory duty, a trivial divergence will be disregarded.

Example 2 In *Customs and Excise Commissioners v J H Corbitt (Numismatists) Ltd* {[1980] 2 All ER 72.} the question arose of whether a trader had kept his accounts in conformity with the requirements of the Commissioners. Lord Simon of Glaisdale said {P 73.}-

> 'The taxpayer can appeal to the value added tax tribunal against an assessment under s 31 [of the Finance Act 1972] on the ground that he has, contrary to the conclusion of the commissioners, in fact complied with the stipulated conditions; and in my view this would extend to a contention that any deviation from those conditions was de minimis.'
>
> See also *Customs and Excise Commrs v Viva Gas Appliances Ltd.* {[1984] 1 All ER 112 ('alteration' of a building).}

The substance is particularly looked at in criminal matters.

Example 3 In *R v Mears* {[1975] Crim LR 155.} the defendant was charged with child stealing, contrary to s 56 of the Offences against the Person Act 1861. He had stopped his car just ahead of a little girl of eight, who was walking along in the same direction. When she reached him, he lifted her up. She screamed, and he at once put her down. *Held* This was sufficient in law to constitute the offence. {Cf *Hawkins v Roots* [1975] Crim LR 521 (triviality of motoring offence not a 'special reason' for not ordering licence to be endorsed); *Delaroy-Hall v Tadman* [1969] 2 WLR 92 (*de minimis* principle does not apply where blood alcohol count only slightly above permitted amount).}

Example 4 In *R v Boyesen* {[1982] 2 All ER 161.} the House of Lords considered whether s 5 of the Misuse of Drugs Act 1971, which renders possession of a controlled drug an offence, applied to a minute quantity which, though measurable, was insufficient for use. *Held* The section did so apply. Lord Scarman said {P 166.}-

> 'Small quantities can be accumulated. It is a perfectly sensible view that the possession of any quantity which is visible, tangible,

measurable and 'capable of manipulation' . . . is a serious matter to be prohibited if the law is to be effective against trafficking in dangerous drugs and their misuse.'

Sometimes the court may hold that, although there is substance in the so-called trivial matter, it is outweighed by contrary factors.

Example 5 In *Squires v Botwright* {[1972] RTR 462.} the appellant had been prevented from entering her house by a police officer in circumstances where no power of arrest had yet arisen. It would have arisen if she had refused his request to produce her licence, but he had not had time to make the request. *Held* The momentary restraint was excusable. The court said {P 468.}-

'I think it would be a very strange situation if in the special and highly peculiar facts of this case the prosecutor was said to have gone beyond the scope of his duty merely because, *for what may have been seconds only,* he sought to prevent the defendant from moving into a particular direction in order to give him time to ask . . .'

{Emphasis added.}
In view of the importance attached by the law to personal liberty (see s 290 of this Code), it is perhaps surprising that the *de minimis* principle was applied here. The court must have regarded the law enforcement factor {See s 127 of this Code.} as of greater weight.

The *de minimis* principle is the basis for the rule that for misdemeanours no distinction is drawn between principals and accessories. {Kerr Bl (4th edn, 1876) iv 28, where Blackstone says 'the law *quae de minimus non curat,* does not descend to distinguish the different shades of guilt in petty misdemeanors'.} By virtue of s 1 of the Criminal Law Act 1967, what were formerly felonies are now on the same footing as misdemeanours. The rule thus applies to all crimes but treason, though the principle underlying it has been lost sight of.

Parliamentary recognition of the principle The principle *de minimis non curat lex* is often recognised by the insertion of express provisions in Acts.

Example 6 Section 44 of the Offences against the Person Act 1861 recognises that it is a ground for the dismissal by magistrates of a complaint of assault or battery preferred by or on behalf of the party aggrieved that the assault or battery was 'so trifling as not to merit any punishment'. {See *Ellis v Burton* [1975] Crim LR 32, which appears to have been decided upon a misreading of the section.}

Procedure The courts take account of the *de minimis* principle in procedural matters. Thus, where magistrates misdirected themselves in making a costs order of small amount, the Divisional Court, while quashing the order, declined to remit the matter to the justices on account of its triviality. {*R v Tottenham JJ, ex p Joshi* [1982] 2 All ER 507.} In *Peake v Automotive Products Ltd* {[1978] QB 233.} the House of Lords refused leave to appeal on the ground of *de minimis*. {See *Ministry of Defence v Jeremiah* [1979] 3 All ER 833, at p 836; (1981) Sol Jo 387; *The Times* (letters) 15 July 1977.} In *R v Gateshead JJ, ex p Usher* {[1981] Crim LR 491.} the Divisional Court held the requirement in s 2(2) of the Bail Act of surrender to custody 'at the time and place' appointed was not infringed by a surrender (with no excuse for the delay) made seven minutes late. {See also *R v Saville* [1980] 1 All ER 861, at p 865 (judge's late alteration to order was one of 'total unimportance').}

349. Domestic sanctuary: *domus sua cuique est tutissimum refugium*

Unless the contrary intention appears, an enactment by implication imports the principle of the maxim *domus sua cuique est tutissimum refugium* (a man's house is his castle).

COMMENTARY

General principle   As to the general principle under which relevant legal maxims are by implication taken to be imported so far as necessary for the operation of an enactment see s 145 of this Code.

The maxim *domus sua cuique est tutissimum refugium*, with its translation 'a man's house is his castle', is found in Coke. {3 Inst c 73.} In *Semayne's Case* {(1604) 5 Co Rep 91b, 92. See H Broom *Legal Maxims* (1st edn, 1845) pp 205-212.} the court arrived at five resolutions on the principle. The first and most important of these began: 'That the house of every one is his castle, as well for his defence against injury and violence, as for his repose', and went on to justify the killing of one caught in the act of arson, burglary or housebreaking.

The law has always paid particular regard to domestic sanctuary, as a vital principle of any civilised community. The legislature has shared in this, with some aberrations. {These began early, when in 1285 the Statute of Wynton required householders to keep arms for the effective pursuit of felons. The statute ordered constables to view houses at stated times to ensure this was done. {C 6. See Daines Barrington *Observations upon the Statutes* (2nd edn, 1767) p 106.}

Example 1   By the statute 14 Cha 2 c 10 (1662) a duty known as hearth-money was imposed on all houses, and granted to the king 'for ever'. However by the statute 1 Will & Mar c 10 (1688) hearth-money was abolished, being declared to be 'not only a great oppression to the poorer sort, but a badge of slavery upon the whole people, exposing every man's house to be entered into and searched at pleasure by persons unknown to him'. {This resounding sentiment was marred by later impositions of house tax and window tax, the latter not being abolished until as late as 1851 (14 & 15 Vict c 36). Some form of taxation on houses has continued to this day.}

The idea that a man is safe in his own house has led to restrictions on entry for arrest or other process of law.

Example 2   Thus arrest upon *mesne process* could be made upon entry into the debtor's home only where his body had been touched outside it: 'For every man's house is looked upon by the law to be his castle of defence and asylum, wherein he should suffer no violence'. {Kerr Bl (4th edn, 1876) iii 293.}

Arrest upon *mesne process* was abolished by s 6 of the Debtor's Act 1869. However the principle remains relevant in the arrest of debtors about to quit England, since s 6 confers a power of arrest in such cases which only operates where the debtor would have been liable to arrest immediately before the commencement of that Act. {An example of archival drafting: see s 286 of this Code. For a recent case under s 6 of the 1869 Act, concerning the writ *ne exeat regno*, see *Felton v Callis* [1969] 1 QB 200.}

The legal protection given to a debtor within doors led to insolvent debtors skulking at home, beyond reach of their creditors. Beginning to 'keep house' is therefore treated as an act of bankruptcy. {Bankruptcy Act 1914 s 1(1)(d); *Dickinson v Foord* (1758) Barnes 160; *Dudley v Vaughan* (1808) 1 Camp 271; *Lloyd v Heathcote* (1820) 2 Brod & Bing 388.}

When Blackstone planned the first university lectures given on English law, he was so impressed with the importance of the principle of domestic sanctuary that he divided crimes against private persons into three categories: against their persons, their habitations, and their property. {Kerr Bl (4th edn, 1876) iv 181.} The crimes against habitations (to which Blackstone devoted a whole chapter of his Commentaries) were stated to consist mainly of arson, burglary and housebreaking. {As to eavesdropping see p 96 above.}

At common law arson was defined as 'maliciously and voluntarily burning the house of another'. {Hawkins 1 PC 137.} It was earlier known as *combustio domororum* or house burning. {Kerr Bl (4th edn, 1876) iv 384.} Arson, said Blackstone, is an offence of very great malignity because it offends 'against that right of habitation, which is acquired by the law of nature as well as by the laws of society'. {Kerr Bl (4th edn, 1876) iv 225.} Unfortunately its domestic connotation has been lost, and the term arson is now applied to the destroying or damaging of any tangible property by fire. {Criminal Damage Act 1971 ss 1(3) and 10(1).}

Burglary consisted in breaking and entering a dwelling-house by night with intent to commit a felony. {Larceny Act 1916 s 25.} Of this crime Blackstone said-

> 'Burglary, or nocturnal housebreaking, *burgi latrocinium*, which by our ancient law was called *ham-socn*, as it is in Scotland to this day, has always been looked upon as a very heinous offence; not only because of the abundant terror that it naturally carries with it, but also as it is a forcible invasion and disturbance of that right of habitation which every individual might acquire even in a state of nature ... And the law of England has so particular and tender a regard to the immunity of a man's house, that it styles it his castle, and will never suffer it to be violated with impunity; agreeing herein with the sentiments of ancient Rome as expressed in the words of Cicero: *quid enim sanctius, quid omni religione munitius, quam domus unius-cujusque civium?* ... the malignity of the offence does not so properly arise from its being done in the dark as *at the dead of night*, when all the creation, except beasts of prey, are at rest; when sleep has disarmed the owner, and rendered his castle defenceless.'

{Kerr Bl (4th edn, 1876) iv 229. For an account of early statutes punishing violation of a dwelling see Daines Barrington *Observations upon the Statutes* (2nd edn, 1767) pp 357-363. See also Larceny Act 1861 ss 51–61 (various offences in relation to dwelling-houses).}

Unfortunately, Parliament has now abandoned the connection between burglary and night-time entry of dwellings. Under s 9 of the Theft Act 1968, burglary may be committed in relation to any type of building at any hour of the day or night.

Modern view The policy of the law continues to uphold the principle of domestic sanctuary. Thus Lord Atkin said in *Balfour v Balfour* {[1919] 2 KB 571, at p 579.} that promises betwen husband and wife are not visited with legal sanctions because the consideration for them 'is that natural love and affection which counts for so little in these cold Courts' and they are made at the domestic hearth. He added: 'each house is a domain into which the King's writ does not seek to run, and to which his officers do not seek to be admitted'.

Although Parliament has often departed from the principle in particular instances, for no doubt compelling reasons, the courts assume prima facie that such is not its intention.

Example 3 In *Morris v Beardmore* {[1980] 2 All ER 753.} the House of Lords considered the application of the principle to the breathalyser legislation. The provisions in question were s 8(2) and (3) of the Road Traffic Act 1972, a selective comminution {As to selective comminution see s 74 of this Code.} of which reads-

'(1) If an accident occurs owing to the presence of a motor vehicle on a road

(2) a constable in uniform may require any person who he has reasonable cause to believe was driving the vehicle at the time of the accident

(3) to provide a specimen of breath for a breath test either at or near the place where the requirement is made.

(4) A person who, without reasonable excuse, fails to provide a specimen of breath for a breath test under [the above] shall be guilty of an offence.'

The car driven by the appellant was involved in an accident at 22.45 hours. At 00.20 three police officers in uniform went to the appellant's home. He was upstairs in a bedroom. The officers were admitted to the house by his son. Despite five messages sent by the son, he refused to come down. He sent a message by his son that the officers were trespassers and should leave. Notwithstanding this, they went to the bedroom and required the appellant to take a breath test. He refused, and was charged under s 8(3). *Held* Because the officers were trespassers, the statutory conditions were not met, and the appellant was therefore not guilty.

Lord Edmund-Davies said {Pp 759-760.}-

' ... I regard it as unthinkable that a policeman may properly be regarded as acting in the execution of his duty when he is acting unlawfully, and this regardless of whether his contravention is of the criminal law or simply of the civil law ... counsel for the prosecutor submitted that such a construction involves writing into the section some such words as 'providing the constable is throughout acting lawfully', and that it is significant that no such qualification was inserted by the legislature. But, to my way of thinking, if any adding to or supplementing of the statutory language is called for, it must be done by those who assert that a constable's powers under s 8 are exercisable regardless of the basic lawlessness of his behaviour.'

Lord Scarman said {Pp 763-4.}-

'When . . . Parliament confers on a constable a power or right which curtails the rights of others, it is to be expected that Parliament intended the curtailment to go no further than its express authorisation . . . it is not the task of judges, exercising their ingenuity in the field of implication, to go further in the invasion of fundamental private rights and liberties than Parliament has expressly authorised .-. .

I have described the right of privacy as "fundamental". I do so for two reasons. First, it is apt to describe the importance attached by the common law to the privacy of the home . . . Second, the right enjoys the protection of the European Convention for the Protection of Human Rights and Fundamental Freedoms {Rome, 4 November 1950, TS 71 (1953); Cmd 8969.}, which the United Kingdom has ratified and under which the United Kingdom permits to those within its jurisdiction the individual right of petition: see arts 8 and 25 . . .

The present appeal is concerned exclusively with the suspect's right to the privacy of his home. The House is not concerned with trespass to land generally, nor with any of the many other difficulties that have arisen in the interpretation and application of this strange and stringent legislation. The appeal turns on the respect which Parliament must be understood, even in its desire to stamp out drunken driving, to pay to the fundamental right of privacy in one's own home, which has for centuries been recognised by the common law.'

{See also *Snook v Mannion* [1982] Crim LR 601; *McLorie v Oxford* [1982] 3 All ER 480, at p 483.}

It has been recently stated by the House of Lords that the principle of domestic sanctuary extends to a person's place of business. {*IRC v Rossminster Ltd* [1980] 1 All ER 80, at pp 82 and 101.} While business premises are no doubt entitled to privacy, they cannot as such possess the peculiar quality investing the home.

It is expected that Parliament will reaffirm its concern for the principle of domestic sanctity by passing the Criminal Trespass Bill 1984, which renders trespass in a dwelling a criminal offence. {At the date of going to press the Bill had not completed its parliamentary stages.}
{See also Examples 303.3 and 326.1.}

350. Impotence: *Impotentia excusat legem*

Unless the contrary intention appears, an enactment by implication imports the principle of the maxim *impotentia excusat legem* (the law does not punish a person for not doing what he lacked power to do, or for being in a situation he was powerless to avoid).

COMMENTARY

General principle   As to the general principle under which relevant legal maxims are by implication taken to be imported so far as necessary for the operation of an enactment see s 145 of this Code.

The maxim *impotentia excusat legem* is mentioned by Coke. {Co Litt 29a.} It is of the very essence of civilised law, for there is something barbaric about punishing the helpless for their very helplessness. The excuse of impotence is a branch of the principle *lex non cogit ad impossibilia*, which is described in s 351 of this Code. Here we are concerned mainly with the physical or mental impotence of a person to do what the law commands.

It is well established in English law that it is a defence even to the grave crime of murder to prove irresistible physical compulsion, as in the use by a man of a woman's arm to 'cudgel' a baby. {Hale *Pleas of the Crown* i 434.} The difficulties arise where some element of blameworthiness is found on the part of the defendant.

Self-induced helplessness   The law does not admit self-induced incapacity, for example by drugs or alcohol, as an excuse. In *R v Beard* {[1920] AC 479, at p 506.} Lord Birkenhead LC referred to the general proposition that 'drunkenness is no excuse for crime'. Various Acts make it an offence to be 'found drunk' in a public place, and the courts show little sympathy for the plea that the accused was incapable of avoiding the offence.

Example 1   Section 12 of the Licensing Act 1872 says that every person found drunk in any highway or other public place shall be liable to a penalty. In *Winzar v Chief Constable of Kent* {(1983) *The Times* 28 March. See 128 SJ 620.} the accused was behaving drunkenly in a hospital waiting room. The police were called. They carried him out, put him in a police car parked outside, and charged him with being found drunk in a highway. *Held* He was properly convicted.

This decision is questionable on several grounds. The police did not 'find' the defendant in the highway but in the hospital. Even if he had been sitting in his car, it is doubtful if he (rather than the car) would have been 'in' the highway within the meaning of s 12. If it is an offence for a person to be in a place, and the police have by force (albeit lawful) put him in that place, it is contrary to principle for him to be held guilty of the offence. Even if it was through his own fault that the police became involved, he is not to be penalized because the police then chose to place him in a position that contravened the Act. {Unless the police had no choice: see *R v Larsonneur* (1933) 24 Cr App R 74 (woman deported from Irish Free State and brought to England in police custody convicted of being 'found' in the United Kingdom). The case is examined by David Lanham in 'Larsonneur Revisited' [1976] Crim LR 276.}

Statutory statement of the principle   As so often with principles of legal policy, the legislator often states the principle expressly. Here too the exception for self-induced incapacity is to be taken as implied.

Example 2   Regulation 9 of the 'Pelican' Pedestrian Crossings Regulations and General Directions 1969 {SI 1969/888.} makes it an offence to park in the approach limits to a pelican crossing, but provides a defence in terms of

772

circumstances beyond the driver's control. In *Oakley-Moore v Robinson* {(1981) *The Times* 17 October.} a driver pleaded that he had run out of petrol at the crucial moment. The car was fitted with a reserve tank, but he was unaware of this. *Held* Although a latent defect unknown to the driver would have been an excuse, a lack of petrol did not fall within that category.

351. Impossibility: *lex non cogit ad impossibilia*

Unless the contrary intention appears, an enactment by implication imports the principle of the maxim *lex non cogit ad impossibilia* (law does not compel the impossible).

COMMENTARY

General principle As to the general principle under which relevant legal maxims are by implication taken to be imported so far as necessary for the operation of an enactment see s 145 of this Code.

All civilised systems of law import the principle that *lex non cogit ad impossibilia*. {Hob 96.} Another version is *nemo tenetur ad impossibilia* (no one is held to the impossible). {Jenk Cent 7. See also 12 Co Rep 89 (*lex non intendit aliquid impossibile*); Dig 50, 17, 185 (*impossibilium nulla obligatio est*).} Broom points out that this should have been the answer to hardships caused by the old doctrine that all Acts dated from the beginning of the session. {H Broom *Legal Maxims* (1st edn, 1845) p 117. As to this doctrine see p 411 above. For an example of its unjust application see *Latless v Holmes* (1792) 4 TR 660.} There have been instances of an Act purporting to require things to be done before it was even passed.

Example 1 Section 9 of the Newspaper Libel and Registration Act 1881 required printers to make certain returns before 31 July 1881. The Act did not receive royal assent until 27 August 1881. A modern court would certainly give this a strained construction, allowing a reasonable time for the making of the returns. To do so would give effect to Parliament's intention, because clearly the error was due to an unexpected delay in the passing of the Act. {Cf *Burns v Nowell* (1880) 5 QBD 444, at p 454.} See also Example 75.2.

Many cases on the impossibility principle concern provisions which require some knowledge by a person that it is impossible for him to have. Here the court varies the literal meaning to allow for the fact that Parliament is taken not to intend anything so unreasonable.

Example 2 Section 15 of the Housing, Town Planning etc Act 1909 imposed on the landlord a condition requiring certain tenanted dwellings to be kept reasonably fit for human habitation, and by implication required the tenant to notify the landlord of defects. In *Fisher v Walters* {[1926] 2 KB 315.} a tenant claimed the benefit of the implied condition without having given the necessary notice. He had been unaware of the defect, and could not have discovered it by reasonable care and vigilance. *Held* The tenant was entitled to the benefit of the condition. {See also *Harding v Price* [1948] 1 KB 695, at p 701 (driver's duty to report accident).}

Legal impossibility   If an enactment requires what is legally impossible it will be presumed that Parliament intended it to be modified so as to remove the impossible element.

Example 3   In *Poulters' Company v Phillips* {(1840) 6 Bing NC 314.} the court construed a byelaw authorising the Poulters' Company to fine any poulterer in the area who refused to be admitted to the Company. By law, a poulterer could not be admitted unless he was a freeman of the City of London. *Held* The byelaw must be treated as limited to poulterers who were freemen. {See also *United Dairies (London) Ltd v Beckenham Corpn* [1963] 1 QB 434, at p 445 (distributor could not comply with duty to ensure full milk bottles were clean without illegally tampering with their seals).} See also Example 75.1.

Supervening impossibility   Where a statutory requirement, while possible to perform when the Act was passed, has become impossible through supervening events, the court will assume that the legislator intended the requirement to be treated as modified accordingly. This is by analogy with the recognition by Parliament that frustrated contracts cannot be performed. {See Law Reform (Frustrated Contracts) Act 1943. As to updating construction see s 146 of this Code.}

Discretionary conditions   Where a court or other functionary has statutory power to impose conditions, these must not be such as are impossible to perform. {*MV Yorke Motors (a firm) v Edwards* [1982] 1 All ER 1024, *per* Lord Diplock at p 1027 (financial condition which was impossible for defendant to fulfil by reason of impecuniosity).} Similarly, a discretionary order such as mandamus should not require the impossible. {*Re Bristol & North Somerset Rly* (1877) 3 QBD 10, at p 13. See also *Hammond v Vestry of St Pancras* (1874) LR 9 CP 316, at p 322 (duty to clean sewers did not extend to things no reasonable care and skill could obviate).}

Drafting error   Where an Act requires what appears to be impossible this may be because of unskilful drafting. If a strained construction is given, the true intention can then be carried out.

Example 4   Section 29(3) of the Landlord and Tenant Act 1954 says that no application under s 24(1) of the Act for a new tenancy 'shall be entertained' unless certain conditiions as to time are satisfied. In *Kammins Ballrooms Co Ltd v Zenith Investments (Torquay) Ltd* {[1971] AC 850, at p 859.} Lord Reid said-

> 'This cannot in my view be read literally. It must mean entertained by the court and the natural meaning of entertained in this connection is taken into consideration. But the court must take the application into consideration before it can discover whether or not it is out of time.'

Impossibility cured by time   An impossibility may be cured by time. Thus where, at the time a statutory duty arose, some necessary item of information was unavailable, the defect may be cured if at or before the hearing it becomes available.

Example 5 Section 3(1) of the Law Reform (Miscellaneous Provisions) Act 1934 empowers the court to add to an award of damages interest for the whole or part of the period since the cause of action arose. In *BP Exploration Co (Libya) Ltd v Hunt (No 2)* {[1982] 1 All ER 925.} it was argued that this could not empower interest to be awarded for a period before the amount of damages was quantified, since the defendant could not have paid over the principal when he did not know its amount. *Held* The difficulty was cured when the court quantified the damages. To disregard this would in some cases work injustice, and it provided an answer to the objection. {See Lord Brandon at p 992.}

Self-induced impossibility An impossibility cannot be pleaded where it was self-induced. {Cf Example 350.2.} It will be treated as self-induced where the subject did not take reasonable steps to avoid or rectify it.

Example 6 Section 9(5) of the Road Traffic Act 1972 requires a motorist to provide two specimens of urine within one hour. In *R v Reynolds* {[1976] Crim LR 385.} the defendant had been injured in an accident and was in bed in hospital. He gave one specimen of urine, but no one came round for the second until the hour had elapsed. He was convicted of failing to supply the second specimen within the hour. He appealed on the ground that it was impossible for him to comply with the statutory procedure since he had not been provided with a container. *Held* The appeal would be dismissed, since the appellant could have asked a nurse for a container but did nothing.

Where impossibility intended The invariable caveat that interpretative criteria apply only unless the contrary intention appears applies even to impossibility. If it is clear that Parliament really did intend to demand the impossible, the court must do the best it can to make the provision work.

Example 7 Section 1(2) of the Domicile and Matrimonial Proceedings Act 1973 says that where, immediately before the commencement of the section, a married woman had her husband's domicile by dependence it is thereafter to be treated as a domicile of choice. In *IRC v Duchess of Portland* {[1982] 1 All ER 784, at p 790.} Nourse J said that the effect of s 1(2) was 'to reimpose the domicile of dependency as a domicile of choice'. He went on-

> 'The concept of an imposed domicile of choice is not one which it is very easy to grasp, but the force of the subsection requires me to do the best I can. It requires me to treat the taxpayer as if she had acquired an English domicile of choice, even though the facts found by the commissioners tell me that that would have been an impossibility in the real world.'

This requirement to do the best one can has not always been observed by judges.

Example 8 The well-known case of *R v Dyott* {(1882) 9 QBD 47.} concerned the common drafting error of applying or extending an enactment without taking proper care to carry through the consequentials. {As to consequential amendments see s 175 of this Code.} Section 1 of the Poor Rate Act 1743, as amended by s 2 of the Parish Notices Act 1837, required publication as a condition of the validity of a poor rate. This was required to be by affixing a notice on or near the door of the church or chapel.

Then s 1 of the Extra-Parochial Places Act 1857 deemed all extra-parochial places to be parishes for poor law purposes. The draftsman should have taken account of the notorious fact that many extra-parochial places possessed neither a church nor a chapel, but he failed to make any consequential provision for this. In *R v Dyott* the court had to deal with the effect of this carelessness in relation to Hopwas Hays in Staffordshire. This possessed one solitary building, a gamekeeper's lodge. *Held* No valid rate could be made for Hopwas Hays, since the condition precedent was impossible of fulfilment. Grove J said {P 49.}-

> 'It would be making legislation, and not interpreting the language of the statutes, were the court to say that the rate could be levied without any prevous publication. It may be that where the language of a statute is merely directory, and it is impossible to follow the direction, the court would give effect to the doctrine of *cy-près*, and say that the direction should be carried out as nearly as possible. The maxim *Nemo tenetur ad impossibilia*, would then apply. But in this case the words of the statute are not directory, but positive and prohibitory. Very likely a provision for publishing a rate in places where there is no church or chapel was omitted from these statutes through a slip, but if so, it is for the legislature to remedy it.'

{As to mandatory and directory provisions see s 10 of this Code. See also *Mayer v Harding* (1867) LR 2 QB 410 (duty to send case stated to superior court during a period throughout which court closed).}

It is submitted that this is an unduly rigid view, which fails to give effect to the obvious intention of Parliament and would not be followed today. {See also *Finney v Godfrey* (1870) LR 9 Eq 356, where James V-C read the requirement of s 2 of the Parish Notices Act 1837 as conditional on the existence of a church or chapel.}

See further the commentary on s 75 of this Code and Examples 75.1 and 75.2.

352. Necessity: *necessitas non habet legem*

Unless the contrary intention appears, an enactment by implication imports the principle of the maxim *necessitas non habet legem* (necessity knows no law). In the Code this is referred to as the necessity principle.

COMMENTARY

General principle As to the general principle under which relevant legal maxims are by implication taken to be imported so far as necessary for the operation of an enactment see s 145 of this Code.

The necessity principle requires careful handling. It appears in various forms: *necessitas non habet legem* (literally, necessity has no law) {Plowd 18. This is proverbial, being attributed to Publilius Cyrus (1st cent BC).}, *necessitas est lex temporis et loci* (necessity is the law when and where it exists) {Hale PC 54.}, *necessitas quod cogit defendit* (necessity excuses what it compels). {Hale PC 54.} There are other versions.

In dire emergency, law gives way to necessity. {See pp 722–723 above.} Any who would deny this are, as Blackstone said-

' . . . forgetting how impossible it is, in any practical system of laws, to point out beforehand those eccentric remedies, which the sudden emergency of national distress may dictate, and which that alone can justify.'

{Kerr Bl (4th edn, 1876) i 221.}

It is presumed that Parliament intends the necessity principle to apply in the case of its enactments. The difficulty is to know what is 'dire' for this purpose. One thing is clear. An enactment will generally give way when the purpose is the saving of human life: *interest reipublicae quod homines conserventur.* {12 Co Rep 62; *Johnson v Phillips* [1975] Crim LR 580.}

The safety of the state is also paramount. {See p 289 above.} The parliament which restored Charles II necessarily met without his summons, and purported to enact many laws. Blackstone said: 'But this was from the necessity of the thing, which supersedes all law; for if they had not so met, it was morally impossible that the kingdom should have been settled in peace'. {Kerr Bl (4th edn, 1876) i 120.}

On the other hand personal hardships such as hunger are not accepted as justifying lawbreaking. {*R v Dudley and Stephens* (1884) 14 QBD 273.} Lord Denning MR said-

'Necessity would open a door which no man could shut . . . So the Courts must, for the sake of law and order, take a firm stand. They must refuse to admit the plea of necessity to the hungry and the homeless; and trust that their distress will be relieved by the charitable and the good.'

{*Southwark London Borough Council v Williams* [1971] Ch 734, at p 744.}

Congruity　The question of when necessity will dispense with obedience to a statutory requirement is essentially a matter of congruity. If the requirement is relatively trifling, a relatively minor degree of necessity will dispense with it. At the other extreme is the rule that necessity can never justify the wilful taking of an innocent life. {*R v Dudley and Stephens* (1884) 14 QBD 273; *Director of Public Prosecutions v Lynch* [1975] AC 653; *Abbot v R* [1977] AC 755. But see *R v Graham* [1982] 1 All ER 801.}

Example 1　In *Johnson v Phillips* {[1975] Crim LR 580.} the police were summoned to an accident in a narrow one-way street. The defendant was ordered by a police officer to reverse up the street in the wrong direction. This was to avoid obstruction to ambulances attending the accident. The defendant refused, saying that to do so would infringe the relevant traffic regulation. He was convicted of obstructing the police officer in the execution of his duty, contrary to s 51(3) of the Police Act 1964. He appealed. *Held* The conviction was justified on the ground of necessity. {Cf *Buckoke v Greater London Council* [1971] 2 All ER 254 (driver of fire engine not justified in passing red light).}

Superior orders　The orders of a superior do not constitute necessity for the purpose of this principle. {*Lewis v Dickson* [1976] Crim LR 442 (factory gateman causing highway obstruction by working to rule).}

Procedure   In procedural matters the court will readily allow a plea of duress. {*R v Inns* [1975] Crim LR 182; *R v Huntingdon Crown Court, ex p Jordan* [1981] Crim LR 641 (guilty plea made under duress).}

353. Judge in own cause: *nemo debet esse judex in propria causa*

Unless the contrary intention appears, an enactment by implication imports the principle of the maxim *nemo debet esse judex in propria causa* (no one should be judge in his own cause).

COMMENTARY

General principle   As to the general principle under which relevant legal maxims are by implication taken to be imported so far as necessary for the operation of an enactment see s 145 of the Code.

This maxim literally means that no one should be judge in his own cause, but it is applied in a wider sense as meaning that no one acting judicially should have, or appear likely to have, a bias in favour of one side or the other.

This has long been treated as a natural law principle. Thus in the seventeenth century, when it was still alleged that an Act contrary to natural law was invalid, it was said that 'Even an Act of Parliament made against natural equity, as, to make a man judge in his own case, is void in itself; for *jura naturae sunt immutabilia*, and they are *leges legum*'. {*Day v Savadge* (1614) Hob 85; cited by Willes J in *Lee v Bude and Torrington Junction Railway Co* (1871) LR 6 CP 576, at p 582.}

By the next century we find Blackstone expressing the principle in a way more fitting to modern ears-

> 'Thus, if an act of parliament gives a man power to try all causes that arise within his manor of Dale; yet if a cause should arise in which he himself is a party, the act is construed not to extend to that, because it is unreasonable that any man should determine his own quarrel.'

{Kerr Bl (4th edn, 1876) i 66.}

As with the maxim *Audi alteram partem* {See s 346 of this Code.},the other basic principle of natural justice, the original application of the present maxim is in relation to courts of law. Thus it was applied to set aside a judgment of Lord Cottenham LC on the ground that he held shares in a company which was a party to the action. {*Dimes v Grand Junction Canal Co* (1852) 3 HLC 759. See also *R v Hertfordshire JJ* (1845) 6 QB 753; *R v Rand* (1866) LR 1 QB 230; *Re Lawson* (1941) 57 TLR 315; *R v Bodmin JJ* [1947] 1 KB 321, at p 325; *R v Caernarvon JJ, ex p Bension* (1948) 113 JP 23; *R v East Kerrier JJ* [1952] 2 All ER 144; *R v Camborne JJ, ex p Pearce* [1955] 1 QB 41.}

The most obvious suspicion of bias arises where the decision-maker has a pecuniary interest in what is at stake. The courts have always taken a strict view of such cases. Blackburn J said in *R v Rand* {(1866) LR 1 QB 230, at p 232}-

> 'There is no doubt that any direct pecuniary interest, however small, in the subject of inquiry, does disqualify a person from acting as a

judge in the matter ... Whenever there is a real likelihood that the judge would, from kindred or any other cause, have a bias in favour of one of the parties, it would be very wrong in him to act.'

The decision is liable to be declared void in the case of a direct pecuniary interest, but is merely voidable in less obvious cases. {*R v Rand* (1866) LR 1 QB 230.} The defect would not operate where full prior disclosure had been made to the parties concerned and they had consented to the functionary's acting.

Whether or not bias actually exists is immaterial where there is reasonable cause for suspecting it. As Lord Hewart CJ said in *R v Sussex JJ, ex p McCarthy* {[1924] 1 KB 256, at p 258.}-

'... it is not merely of some importance but is of fundamental importance that justice should not only be done, but should manifestly and undoubtedly be seen to be done.'

{See also *Metropolitan Properties Co (FGC) Ltd v Lannon* [1969] 1 QB 577 (chairman of rent assessment committee had previously shown opposition to one of the parties). Cf *Hannam v Bradford Corpn* [1970] 1 WLR 937; *R v Altrincham JJ, ex p Pennington* [1975] QB 549.}

It has been suggested that justice is 'seen to be done' where no person with a right to complain of the injustice of the procedure has in fact done so. {*Norwich City Council v Secretary of State for the Environment* [1982] 1 All ER 737, at p 746 (but see p 755).}

The fact that suspicion of bias is directed to only one person out of a large decision-making body will not save the decision. Thus in *R v Hendon RDC, ex p Chorley* {[1933] 2 KB 696.} the unanimous decision of a local authority on an application for a change of use of land was quashed because one of the councillors was an estate agent acting for an interested party.

{See also Example 133.4}

354. Benefit from own wrong: *nullus commodum capere potest de injuria sua propria*

Unless the contrary intention appears, an enactment by implication imports the principle of the maxim *nullus commodum capere potest de injuria sua propria* (no one should be allowed to profit from his own wrong).

COMMENTARY

General principle As to the general principle under which relevant legal maxims are by implication taken to be imported so far as necessary for the operation of an enactment see s 145 of the Code.

The principle against wrongful self-benefit embodied in the maxim of natural law *nullus commodum capere potest de injuria sua propria* is found in Coke. {Co Litt 148.} To similar effect are the following ancient maxims: *nemo ex suo delicto meliorum suam conditionem facere potest* (no one can improve his position by his own wrongdoing) {D 50, 17, 134.}, *nemo ex dolo suo proprio relevetur, aut auxilium capiat* (no one is relieved or assisted by his own fraud), *fraus et dolus nemini patrocinari debent* (fraud and deceit ought not to avail anyone) {3 Co Rep

78b.}, *ex dolo malo non oritur actio* (a cause of action cannot be based on a fraud) {Cowp 343; *Collins v Blantern* (1767) 2 Wils 341.}, *ex turpi causa non oritur actio* (a cause of action cannot be based on wrongdoing), *ex maleficio non oritur contractus* (a contract cannot arise out of an illegal act), *injuria non excusat injuriam* (an injury does not excuse an injury, or two wrongs do not make a right).

The principle against wrongful self-benefit is frequently applied in statutory interpretation, though sometimes without overt acknowledgment. As Widgery LJ said in *Buswell v Goodwin* {[1971] 1 All ER 418 at p 421.}-

> 'The proposition that a man will not be allowed to take advantage of his own wrong is no doubt a very salutary one and one which the court would wish to endorse . . .'

The effect is usually that the literal meaning of the enactment is departed from where it would result in wrongful self-benefit.

Unlawful homicide   The most obvious application of the principle against wrongful self-benefit relates to murder and other unlawful homicide. In this form it is described in s 1 of the Forfeiture Act 1982 as 'the rule of public policy which in certain circumstances precludes a person who has unlawfully killed another from acquiring a benefit in consequence of the killing'. {The term 'rule' here is inappropriate: see p 258 above.}

Example 1   In *R v National Insurance Commr, ex p Connor* {[1981] 1 All ER 769.} the applicant had sought a widow's allowance under s 24(1) of the Social Security Act 1975, but had been refused on the ground of the principle against wrongful self-benefit. She became a widow by stabbing her husband with a knife. Charged with murder, she was convicted of manslaughter in circumstances indicating that the jury found that she used the knife intentionally. *Held* The allowance was rightly refused.

Lord Lane CJ said that there was no doubt the conditions laid down by s 24(1), if taken literally, were satisfied. Nor did the express exclusions contained elsewhere in the Act mention the case where the claimant's own act had caused the loss. Her counsel argued that this was a self-contained modern Act which should be construed literally. That argument must be rejected. Lord Lane said {P 774.}-

> 'The fact that there is no mention in the Act of disentitlement [in such circumstances] is merely an indication, as I see it, that the draftsman realised perfectly well that he was drawing this Act against the background of the law as it stood at the time . . . it is not the label which the law attaches to the crime which has been committed but the nature of the crime itself which in the end will dictate whether public policy demands the court to drive the applicant from the seat of justice.'

{See also *Cleaver v Mutual Reserve Fund Life Assn* [1892] 1 QB 147, at p 156; *In the Estate of Crippen* [1911] P 108, at p 112; *Re Hall's Estate* [1914] P 1; *Tinline v White Cross Insurance Assn Ltd* [1921] 3 KB 327; *James v British General Insurance Co Ltd* [1927] 2 KB 311; *Re Sigsworth* [1935] Ch 89; *Beresford v Royal Insurance Ltd* [1938] AC 586, at pp 596-599; *Re Callaway* [1956] Ch 559; *Re*

Peacock [1957] Ch 310; *St John Shipping Corpn v Joseph Rank Ltd* [1957] 1 QB 267; *Re Giles* [1971] 3 All ER 114; *Gray v Barr* [1971] 2 QB 554.}

The Forfeiture Act 1982 affords relief from the principle against wrongful self-benefit in the case of unlawful killing other than murder. {As to the exclusion of murder see s 5.}

Other applications of principle The principle against wrongful self-benefit is by no means confined to unlawful homicide, but applies generally. It frequently arises as an indirect factor in statutory interpretation.

Example 2 In *R v Exeter City Council, ex p Gliddden* {(1984) *The Times* 15 February.} the applicant had obtained a lease of a dwelling by deception. When the lessor discovered the deception, the applicant did not defend proceedings brought by the lessor for possession. The local authority argued that this failure made the applicant intentionally homeless within s 17 of the Housing (Homeless Persons) Act 1977. *Held* In applying the test of intentional homelessness, the local authority should have disregarded the accomodation obtained by deception and looked at the accomodation previously occupied. The applicant would then not benefit by the deception.

Example 3 Under paras 13 and 15 of Sch 9 to the London Government Act 1963, a local authority were under a duty to owners of land to ensure that drains being installed on the land conformed to a certain standard. The owners, whose agents were installing the drains, were under a different statutory duty to comply with these standards. The agents failed to carry out the latter duty. *Held* Because of the fault of their agents, the owners could not recover compensation from the local authority for breach of the authority's duty. {*Peabody Donation Fund (Governors) v Sir Lindsay Parkinson & Co Ltd* [1983] 3 All ER 417.}

This case is authority for the following proposition-

> Where A is under statutory duty SD1, and B is under another statutory duty (SD2) to ensure that A carries out SD1, A, having failed to carry out SD1, cannot claim against B for breach of SD2.

Contrary intention An intention that the principle against wrongful self-benefit shall not apply is inferred where its application would prevent the operation of a provision designed for the public good generally.

Example 4 Section 17 of the Housing Act 1957 requires a local authority to make a closing order where a house is unfit for occupation. In *Buswell v Goodwin* {[1971] 1 All ER 418.} the tenant argued that the order should not be upheld since the landlord, by whose default the house had been allowed to become unfit, would benefit from it in obtaining possession of the site. *Held* The argument was ineffective since the overriding purpose of the closing order was to safeguard public health. See also *Gardner v Moore*. {[1984] 1 All ER 1100.}

Construction in bonam partem As to construction *in bonam partem* see pp 298–300 above.

355. Presumption of correctness: *omnia praesumuntur rite et solemniter esse acta*

Unless the contrary intention appears, an enactment by implication imports the principle of the maxim *omnia praesumuntur rite et solemniter esse acta* (all things are presumed to be correctly and solemnly done).

COMMENTARY

General principle   As to the general principle under which relevant legal maxims are by implication taken to be imported so far as necessary for the operation of an enactment see s 145 of the Code.

The maxim *omnia praesumuntur rite et solemniter esse acta* is found in Coke. {Co Litt 6. See also Jenk Cent 185.} A fuller version, expressing the obvious fact that the principle applies only until the contrary is proved, is *omnia praesumuntur legitime facta donec probetur in contrarium.* {Co Litt 232.}

The maxim establishes the presumption that an Act is properly passed, or delegated legislation correctly made. {*Akar v A-G of Sierra Leone* [1970] AC 853.} It applies mainly to official or ministerial functions. As Lord Russell of Killowen CJ said of the administration of local government byelaws, 'credit ought to be given to those who have to administer them that they will be reasonably administered'. {*Kruse v Johnson* [1898] 2 QB 91, at p 99. Cf *R v Halliday* [1917] AC 260, at p 268 (it must not be assumed that the powers conferred by an Act on the executive will be abused).} In relation to the issue of a search warrant by a circuit judge, Lord Diplock said in *IRC v Rossminster Ltd* {[1980] 1 All ER 80, at p 91.}-

> 'In the instant case the search warrant did not purport to be issued by the circuit judge under any common law or prerogative power but pursuant to s 20C(1) of the Taxes Management Act 1970 alone. That subsection makes it a condition precedent to the issue of the warrant that the circuit judge should himself be satisfied by information on oath that [certain facts] exist ... It is not, in my view, open to your Lordships to approach the instant case on the assumption that the Common Serjeant did not satisfy himself on both these matters, or to imagine circumstances which might have led him to commit so grave a dereliction of his judicial duties. The presumption is that he acted lawfully and properly ...'

Similarly it will be assumed, in the absence of evidence to the contrary, that justices exercised a statutory discretion as to costs reasonably. {*R v Uxbridge JJ, ex p Commr of Police of the Metropolis* [1981] 3 All ER 129, at p 137.}

The presumption of correctness is applied to any question of whether a person was duly appointed to a public office. {*Berryman v Wise* (1791) 4 Term Rep 366; *R v Borrett* (1833) 6 C & P 124; *Campbell v Wallsend Slipway and Engineering Co Ltd* [1977] Crim LR 351.}

Criminal offences   The maxim *omnia praesumuntur rite et solemniter esse acta* does not raise a strong enough presumption to enable it to be relied on exclusively in proving the existence of a necessary element in the commission of an offence. Referring to the maxim in *Scott v Baker* {[1969] 1 QB 659, at p 672.}, Lord Parker CJ said-

> 'I think for myself that one ought to take very great care in a criminal case as to the length one goes in applying that presumption.'

{See also *Dillon v The Queen* [1982] 1 All ER 1017, at p 1019; *R v Dadson* [1983] Crim LR 540; Example 322.7.}

356. Agency: *qui facit per alium facit per se*

Unless the contrary intention appears, an enactment by implication imports the principle of the maxim *qui facit per alium facit per se* (who acts through another acts himself).

COMMENTARY

General principle As to the general principle under which relevant legal maxims are by implication taken to be imported so far as necessary for the operation of an enactment see s 145 of this Code.

The agency principle is found in Coke. {Co Litt 258.} It mainly applies in the law of contract, but can stand for the general principle that the acts of an agent may be relevant in statutory interpretation. Where an enactment refers to a person, it may be taken as intended to include that person's duly authorised agent. {See Example 8.2.}

Example 1 The Canadian case of *R v Symington* {(1895) 4 BCR 323. Cited E A Driedger *The Construction of Statutes* pp 15-16.} concerned a provision in the Game Protection Act which prohibited the shooting of deer at certain times of year. It exempted 'any resident farmer from killing, at any time, deer that he finds depasturing within his cultivated fields'. The appellant, who was the agent of a resident farmer, was convicted of killing within a prohibited period deer depasturing within the farmer's cultivated fields. He appealed. *Held* The exemption must be taken to extend to a resident farmer's agent.

Example 2 In the Australian case of *McLaughlin v Westgarth* {(1906) 6 SR (NSW) 664. Cited D C Pearce *Statutory Interpretation in Australia* (2nd edn, 1981) p 46.} the Judicial Committee of the Privy Council considered an enactment which protected a person who was the committee of a lunatic from actions brought against him by the lunatic. *Held* The protection must be taken as intended to extend also to persons acting on the instructions of the committee.

Vicarious liability The agency principle is often brought into play where an act forbidden by statute is done by an employee or other agent. {References here to the doing of a forbiddden act include, as usual, failure to do a required act.} Here the question of whether the principal is guilty as well as, or instead of, the agent, depends on the wording of the enactment and the precise facts. All that can be said generally is that a person cannot evade responsibility for a forbidden act by procuring another to do it.

The difficulty comes where the principal was unaware that the prohibited act was to be done by his agent. Here the position was stated in these words by Atkin J-

> 'While prima facie a principal is not to be made criminally responsible for the acts of his servants, yet the Legislature may prohibit an act or enforce a duty in such words as to make the prohibition or the duty absolute; in which case the principal is liable if the act is in fact done by his servants.'

{*Moussell Brothers Ltd v London & North-Western Rly Co* [1917] 2 KB 836, at p 845.}

The agency principle is not displaced by words importing a state of mind. Provided strict liability is intended, the only question is whether the servant who did the act possessed the required frame of mind. {*G Newton Ltd v Smith* [1962] 2 QB 278, at p 284.}

Act done to agent   Where an enactment requires something (such as the serving of a notice) to be done in relation to a person, the question may arise whether this is satisfied if it is done in relation to the agent of that person. Again there is no general rule, and it is matter of gleaning the intention from the words used.

Example 3   CCR Ord 46 r 18(5), relating to applications under s 52 of the Mental Health Act 1959, says-

> 'On the hearing of the application the court may accept as *prima facie* evidence of the facts stated therein any report made by [various functionaries]: Provided that the respondent shall be told the substance of any part of the report bearing on his fitness or conduct which the judge considers to be material . . . '

{This proviso contains two common drafting errors. (1) It states that something shall be done without stating the consequence of failing to do it. (2) It uses the proviso form for a substantive enactment (see p 572 above).}

In *B v B (mental health patient)* {[1979] 3 All ER 494.} the report had been given not to the respondent but to her solicitor, who merely told her the barest outline. It was objected that this did not satisfy the proviso. *Held* the proviso was satisfied. Lawton LJ said {P 498.}-

> 'If a report is handed to the legal adviser of the respondent to an application in circumstances where the legal adviser can give advice and take instructions, that seems to me to be enough to comply with the proviso to para (5).'

If a notice actually reaches the person required to be notified, it is immaterial that it was not served in the specified way. {*Re Poyser and Mills' Arbitration* [1964] 2 QB 467.} As to the case where the notice is actually delivered but is kept from the subject see *Burt v Kirkcaldy* {[1965] 1 WLR 474.} and *Hosier v Goodall.* {[1962] 2 QB 401.}

357. Vigilance: *vigilantibus non dormientibus leges subveniunt*

Unless the contrary intention appears, an enactment by implication imports the principle of the maxim *vigilantibus non dormientibus leges subveniunt* (the vigilant, not the sleeping, are aided by the laws).

COMMENTARY

General principle As to the general principle under which relevant legal maxims are by implication taken to be imported so far as necessary for the operation of an enactment see s 145 of this Code.

The vigilance principle means that coercive statutory powers may be treated as expired or abandoned when not promptly exercised. Where an enactment confers special powers on a person, it is presumed that Parliament intended them to be used expeditiously, particularly where they are at the expense of individuals. This especially applies to powers of compulsory acquisition.

Example 1 In *Grice v Dudley Corp* {[1958] Ch 329.} the defendant local authority had served a notice to treat concerning the plaintiffs' land in 1939. The compensation was then agreed at £6,000. Because of the war, nothing further was done until 1954, when the authority proposed to complete the compulsory purchase at the 1939 price. *Held* The delay was such that the original process must be taken to have been abandoned.

It has been held that the courts should be more indulgent to delay by local authorities than it used to be towards railway companies, 'which were regarded as private undertakers seeking to make profits for themselves'. {*Simpsons Motor Sales (London) Ltd v Hendon Corpn* [1964] AC 1088, *per* Lord Evershed at p 1118.}

358. Volenti principle: *volenti non fit injuria*

Unless the contrary intention appears, an enactment by implication imports the principle of the maxim *volenti non fit injuria* (what one consents to cannot amount to a legal injury).

COMMENTARY

General principle As to the general principle under which relevant legal maxims are by implication taken to be imported so far as necessary for the operation of an enactment see s 145 of the Code.

The maxim *volenti non fit injuria* {Wing 482; Plowd 501.} is mainly applied in tort; though the law generally has tended to be unsympathetic to those who freely agree to undergo a risk and then complain when it is realised. {*Yarmouth v France* (1887) 19 QBD 647, at p 653.} However, mere knowledge of a risk, particularly by an employee, is not taken to establish consent to running it. {*Thomas v Quartermaine* (1887) 18 QBD 685; *Smith v Baker* [1891] AC 325; *Dann v Hamilton* [1939] 1 KB 509.}

Statutory recognition The volenti principle is recognised by Parliament. In laying down the common duty of care owed by occupiers of land, s 2 of the

Occupiers' Liability Act 1957 makes clear that the volenti principle continues to apply. Section 2(5) refers to the principle in the following oblique terms-

'The common duty of care does not impose on an occupier any obligation to a visitor in respect of risks willingly accepted as his by the visitor (the question whether a risk was so accepted to be decided on the same principles as in other cases in which one person owes a duty of care to another).'

A provision corresponding to this, namely s 2(3) of the Occupiers' Liability (Scotland) Act 1960, was applied by the House of Lords in *Titchener v British Railways Board* {[1983] 3 All ER 770.}, where Lord Fraser of Tullybelton said {P 776.}-

'[The volenti principle] is perhaps less often relied on in industrial accident cases at the present time than formerly, but, so far as cases under the 1960 Act are concerned, the principle is expressly stated in s 2(3) and there is no room for an argument that it is out of date or discredited.'

{See also *Simms v Leigh Rugby Football Club* [1969] 2 All ER 923; *White v Blackmore* [1972] 3 All ER 158.}

Breach of statutory duty Where no express mention is made of the volenti principle, does it apply to the tort of breach of statutory duty? {As to this tort see s 14 of the Code.} This must depend on the terms of the enactment imposing the duty, and no general statement is possible.

It is true that Craies makes a general statement that volenti does not apply to breach of statutory duty, citing *Wheeler v New Merton Board Mills Ltd* {[1933] 2 KB 669.} and a dictum by Lord Normand in *Alford v National Coal Board*. {[1952] WN 144. The statement is in *Craies on Statute Law* (7th edn, 1971) at p 246. Halsbury's *Laws of England* (2nd edn) also state (vol 36, para 702) that the defence of volenti is not available in an action founded on breach of statutory duty, citing in addition *Britton v Great Western Cotton Co* (1872) LR 7 Ex 130; *Baddeley v Earl of Granville* (1887) 19 QBD 423; *Davies v Thomas Owen & Co* [1919] 2 KB 39.} If however the statutory duty is framed as a duty of care, equivalent to that imposed by the tort of negligence, then on principle volenti should be available as a defence, though often this is not realised.

Example 1 In *Wallace v Newton* {[1982] 2 All ER 106.} the owner of a horse was held liable under s 2(2) of the Animals Act 1971 without the question of volenti apparently being raised. The plaintiff was a groom injured because of the horse's unpredictable behaviour, which was well known to her.

Criminal breach Consent is an answer to a charge of committing a statutory offence where, as in rape or assault, lack of consent is an ingredient of the offence. {Here the onus is on the prosecution to prove lack of consent: *R v May* [1912] 3 KB 572; *R v Donovan* [1934] 2 KB 498.} This does not however apply where it is contrary to public policy to treat the consent as exculpatory, as where the assault is one causing bodily harm. {*R v Donovan* [1934] 2 KB 498.}

Sometimes an Act spells out the fact that consent is a defence.

Example 2 Section 5(2)(a) of the Criminal Damage Act 1971 states that a person has a lawful excuse for inflicting damage if he believes the owner consented or would have consented to it. The provision refers only to the defendant's *belief* that consent was or would be given. Clearly if this belief was not held, but consent had in fact been given this too would be a defence. {See Glanville Wiliams [1977] Crim LR 207. See also *R v Denton* [1982] 1 All ER 65 (employer asked defendant to burn his mill machinery).}

PART XX

Linguistic Canons of Construction: Use of Deductive Reasoning

Introduction to Part XX This Part contains four sections expanding the remarks in s 148 of the Code on the use of deductive or syllogistic reasoning. The treatment is elementary, but makes the point that it is a universal canon of the construction of verbal expressions that language is to be treated as used in accordance with the rules of formal logic.

The nature of deductive reasoning is briefly explained (s 359). The use of the hypothetical syllogism is discussed (s 360). Then we consider the important part played in statutory ambiguity by the ambiguous middle (s 361). Finally the principle of contradiction, a useful touchstone, is discussed (s 362).

359. Nature of deductive reasoning

The legal meaning of an enactment in its application to a particular factual situation is ascertainable by the process of reasoning known as deductive or syllogistic reasoning. Here the major premiss is the relevant proposition laid down (expressly or not) in the enactment, and the minor premiss is the factual situation. In deciding between opposing constructions of an enactment, deductive reasoning is applied to each construction in turn.

COMMENTARY

Inference is the mental operation which proceeds by so combining two propositions, called premisses, as to cause a consequent conclusion. Deductive or syllogistic inference proceeds from a universal premiss to a particular premiss. Because it is the nature of law to be general, law is applied to facts syllogistically. This is true in science too, where universal principles are called 'laws' and mental acts of assertion are 'judgments'.

Where the legal rule is not 'given', but has to worked out from the judgments of the courts, the logical process is, on the contrary, inductive. So where the law on a topic is uncodified the practitioner reasons inductively, but as soon as it is codified switches to deductive reasoning.

This was neatly expressed by Chalmers, the draftsman of the codifying Sale of Goods Act 1893. {Substantially repealed and re-enacted by the Sale of Goods Act 1979.} The original version of his book on the subject reproduced the clauses of the Sale of Goods Bill, then going through Parliament. The next version reproduced what were by then the sections of the Act. In it Chalmers said the propositions in the original version 'were only law in so far as they were correct and logical *inductions* from the decided cases'. He went on-

'Now the position is reversed. The propositions have become sections of the Act, and the decided cases are only law in so far as they are correct and logical *deductions* from the language of the Act.'

{M D Chalmers *Sale of Goods* (12th edn, 1945) vii. Emphasis added.}

The question of what operation any legal rule (whether statutory or not) has when applied to particular facts is therefore determined by deduction, or syllogistically. Blackstone, while not developing the idea, recognised this when he said that a judgment, though pronounced by the court, is the determination or sentence not of the judges but of the law. 'It is the conclusion that naturally and regularly follows from the premises of law and fact . . .' {Kerr Bl (4th edn, 1876) iii 399.}

This positivist assertion can be criticised as too mechanistic, making no allowance for the legislative function of the court or its discretionary powers. Yet it does recognise an important truth. Blackstone reinforced the statement by drawing attention to the way the standard prefix to a judgment in his day acknowledged this truth: 'not that it is decreed or resolved by the court, for then the judgment might appear to be their own; but "it is considered" . . .' {Ibid.}

A nineteenth-century editor of Blackstone's *Commentaries* pointed out that a recent change had destroyed the subtle constitutional acknowledgment inherent in this prefix: 'The form now is that "*it is this day adjudged*;" or "*the court adjudged*;"'. He added that this was 'a change, and possibly an improvement, though in what respect it is not easy to see'. {Kerr Bl (4th edn, 1876) iii 399.}

Blackstone went on to give the following as an example of the legal syllogism: 'against him who has rode over my corn, I may recover damages by law: but A has rode over my corn; therefore I shall recover damages against A'. {Ibid. This syllogism is examined in Example 361.1.}

The advantage of approaching a problem of statutory interpretation when armed with the implements of syllogistic logic is that we may thereby refine and clarify the question at issue. We equip ourselves with mental tools fashioned at first by Aristotle, and continuously sharpened ever since his time.

These tools are of great value in legal argument. Bentham stressed their practical use when he criticised the teaching of logic in his own day-

'But Logic as studied in the Universities, is an instrument which they pretend to teach how to correct, but never think to teach how to use.
It is not the art of gaining instruction or communicating it: it is the art of disputing as nobody ever disputes.'

{*A Comment on the Commentaries* p 76.}

Admittedly it may well be found impractical for the busy lawyer to go far in this direction. Moreover it is now fashionable in some academic circles to travel beyond Aristotle and engage in symbolic logic. Unfortunately the complications of modern symbolic logic, using algebraic-type symbols to express formal relationships, are scarcely suited to the unscientific products of our parliamentary system, with its untidy debates, unsystematic concessions to lobbying by outside interests, and piecemeal amendments to Bills. This is generally true notwithstanding that precision in drafting has improved in recent years. {See s 76 of this Code.}

Some modern enactments *are* precise and mechanistic enough to lend themselves to treatment by the processes of symbolic logic, as is shown by the fact that flow charts can be constructed from them. See for example the flow chart by Steven Wilton on the penalty points system under the Transport Act 1981 {(1982) 132 NLJ 412.} and the flow charts by the present author on the complex requirements as to the service of copies of agreements under the Consumer Credit Act 1974. {Bennion *Consumer Credit Control* (Oyez Longman, 1976 updated) Vol I, Introduction pp 14 and 16.} The topic is discussed generally in Lewis, Horabin and Gane *Flow Charts, Logical Trees and Algorithms for Rules and Regulations.* {HMSO 1967.}

These instances are proportionately few in number however. Not until a specially-devised language such as Legol can be brought into general use will we gain much practical help from symbolic logic. {As to Legol, a specially-invented language or 'legal formulism', see Bennion 'Legol and the Electronic Home Lawyer' (1981) *The Law Society's Gazette* 1334. For the use of symbolic logic see Layman Allen 'Symbolic Logic: A Razor Edged Tool for Drafting and Interpreting Legal Documents' (1957) 66 Yale LJ 833.}

Modern symbolic logic bears the usual defect of highly-developed systems in any field. Its complexities, while in some ways making it more useful, place it beyond the reach of all but the specialist. The ordinary lawyer must content himself with formal or classical logic, which may have some help to offer in refining the issues that face an interpreter. As Mellone said-

> 'The exercise of paraphrasing . . . assertions so as to express them in one or other of the four standard forms, is a valuable exercise in accuracy of thought and clearness of expression, and strengthens the habit of exact interpretation.'

Mellone went on to add that use of the general rules of the syllogism 'is a valuable exercise in clearness and distinctness of thought and expression, and throws light on many confusions which occur in ordinary reasonings'. {S H Mellone *Elements of Modern Logic* pp 65, 124. As to the four standard forms see Example 361.1.}

360. The hypothetical syllogism

The effect of an enactment can be expressed in the form of the hypothetical syllogism 'If F then L', where F is the factual outline and L is the legal thrust of the enactment.

COMMENTARY

As explained in s 78 of this Code, the factual outline (F) is the framework of fact that triggers the operation of an enactment, while the legal thrust (L) is the effect in law produced by the enactment when the facts of the instant case fall within the outline. The position can be rendered in the form of the hypothetical syllogism 'If F then L'. This is called by logicians an implicative proposition, because the antecedent F implies the consequent F.

It may also be called a conditional proposition. L applies (that is the legal thrust operates in the instant case) upon the condition that F is satisfied. The proposition is logically universal: wherever and whenever F is satisfied, L comes into play.

To view a problem of statutory interpretation in this light may help in concentrating attention on the key questions. What precisely is the factual outline that triggers this enactment? Just what is the legal thrust of the enactment? Do the facts of the instant case really fall within the outline, and thus bring the enactment into play?

For the assistance that can be given by the logical concept of the undistributed middle see s 361 of this Code.

361. The ambiguous middle term

Deductive logic is of value in dealing with the ambiguous middle term, a frequent problem in statutory interpretation.

COMMENTARY

In formal logic the common factor in both the major and the minor premiss is known as the middle term. In Blackstone's example given above {P 790.}, the middle term is 'riding over another person's corn'. For the major premiss (the enactment) to apply to the facts, the middle term must be contained in the minor premiss in the same form as it is in the major. {This lies behind the concept of the 'factual outline' discussed in s 78 of this Code.} The 'ambiguous middle' is a common breach of the rules of the syllogism.

A well-known example of an ambiguous middle is found in the syllogism 'all metals are elements: brass is a metal: therefore brass is an element'. We know by the definition of an element that brass is not one; so the conclusion is false. The middle term 'metal' is used with one meaning in the major premiss and a different meaning in the minor. This is the logical fallacy of *equivocation*, an error in reasoning due to the use of a term in different senses during the course of the same argument.

We now return to Blackstone's syllogism and use it to illustrate briefly the main logical problem in this field, the ambiguous middle.

Example 1   First, on the assumption that the law in question is laid down by statute, let us frame Blackstone's syllogism in conformity with logical principle, using C and D for claimant and defendant-

> *Major premiss (the enactment)*
> Every person who has ridden over the corn of another person is a person who must pay that other person damages.
>
> *Minor premiss (the factual situation)*
> D is a person who has ridden over the corn of another person (named C).
>
> *Conclusion (the judgment)*
> D is a person who must pay C damages.

This is in the first of the four standard forms, which may be expressed as 'all S is P' (where S is the subject, 'is' is the copula, and P is the predicate). This is known as the universal affirmative proposition. The other three standard forms are 'no S is P' (the universal negative proposition), 'some S is P' (the particular affirmative proposition), and 'some S is not P' (the particular negative proposition).

Now we consider Blackstone's middle term, namely 'riding over another person's corn'. If his syllogism were the subject of a genuine problem of statutory interpretation arising in the course of litigation, a likely ground of dispute would be whether or not the middle term is the same in both the major and minor premiss. In other words, did D's act amount to riding over C's corn within the meaning of the enactment?

Let us say that D is proved to have ridden on horseback across C's field of ripe wheat awaiting harvest. D might argue that wheat is not 'corn', or that there is an implication that damage must be proved, or that his horse bolted because of an act of God such as a lightning flash. D might even be bold enough to argue that the enactment referred not to a man's corn growing in his field but to a man's corn growing on his foot. All these problems, and many more that can easily be imagined, would raise the problem of the ambiguous middle.

The ambiguous middle is the main logical problem in statutory interpretation because of an inherent difficulty of language. With many (though not all) propositions it is a practical impossibility to state the middle term comprehensively. The draftsman may (though this is unlikely) *think* all the judgments of which his inference consists, but he can seldom as a practical matter *state* all the propositions inherent in its expression.

Indeed this is a universal limitation of language. The ultimate ellipsis is the cry of 'Fire!', wherein an infinity of imagined but unexpressed propositions are frantically concealed.

It can be seen that another way of looking at the typical case calling for statutory interpretation is that it turns on the question *which of the opposing constructions put forward correctly expresses the midddle term?* {As to opposing constructions see s 84 of this Code.} The middle term is unlikly to be clearly stated in the enactment itself, for if it were there would be little difficulty in interpretation.

The usual difficulty is to identify a middle term which is inherent in what the enactment says and also fits the facts. Cross recognises this when he says-

> '... the crucial decision is made before the reasoning can be cast into syllogistic form. Not only is the syllogism constructed after the facts have been found, but it is also constructed after any legal problems concerning the scope of the rule have been solved.'

{R Cross *Precedent in English Law* (3rd edn, 1977) p 179.}

Cross cites Hart's statement that-

> 'A division of the judicial process into two independent types of inquiry viz (a) what is the relevant rule (question of law)? and (b) did the party in fact do what the rule requires (question of fact)? may mislead; it conceals the fact that until the meaning of the legal rule is settled it is impossible to refer to the facts of the case *in its terms*.'

{H L A Hart *Proceedings of the Aristotelian Society* Supp Vol xxix p 260 (emphasis added).}

While Cross's statement is true, it does not deprive syllogistic reasoning of value. The syllogism can be formed by the court in the course of working out its judgment, so as to test its tentative conclusion. If it reinforces that conclusion, so that it forms the basis of the judgment, the syllogism can be used afterwards to state the law declared by that judgment. This is the basis of what this Code calls interstitial articulation. {See ss 112 to 114.} Unless the court expressed the syllogism in its judgment (which would be unusual) the conclusion would need to be *reconstructed* in terms of formal logic. {See Twining and Miers *How To Do Things With Rules* (1st edn, 1976) p 141.}

362. The principle of contradiction

A logical principle of importance in statutory interpretation is the *principium contradictionis* or principle of contradiction, namely that contradictory statements cannot both at the same time be true.

COMMENTARY

The *principium contradictionis*, or principle of contradiction, was stated by Aristotle in the form that contradictory statements cannot both at the same time be true. Thus one cannot without defect of reasoning advance both a universal affirmative proposition ('all S is P') and a particular negative proposition ('some S is not P'). Equally one cannot legitiimately advance both a universal negative proposition ('no S is P') and a particular affirmative proposition ('some S is P').

Inconsistent enactments   A common application of this principle is in relation to contradictory enactments within the same Act. Enactment A may in itself be clear and unambiguous. So may enactment B, located elsewhere in the Act. But if they contradict each other they cannot both be applied literally. A undoes B, and B undoes A. The court must do the best it can to reconcile them, but this can be achieved only be giving one or both a strained construction. {For strained construction see ss 92 to 97 of this Code. Conflicting enactments are dealt with in s 149.}

Inconsistent dicta   Mention of strained construction leads us to another important application of the principle of contradiction. Many distinguished judges have maintained, and some still do, that a clear enactment may not lawfully be given a strained construction. No doubt they would except the case just mentioned, where strained construction is logically impelled by contradiction within the Act (though frequently the dicta contemplate no exceptions). Otherwise these literalist judges are adamant. If the grammatical meaning is clear and unambiguous it must be applied, whatever the consequences.

This matter is examined in detail elsewhere. {See s 93 of this Code.} Here we may find it instructive to apply the logical principle of contradiction to a combination of the so-called literal rule of construction and the undoubted fact that many courts, from the House of Lords down, in fact depart from it.

The so-called literal rule of interpretation can be stated in this form-

> Except when logically impelled by contradiction, a strained construction can never lawfully be applied to an enactment.

The position as demonstrated by what courts actually do can be stated in this form-

Some judges apply a strained construction to an enactment when not logically impelled by contradiction.

The logical contradiction which vitiates the 'rule' of literal construction can be exposed in this way.

It is a reasonable *universal affirmative proposition* to say that all judges carry out their duties as the law requires. While there might be (very rare) exceptions, these would not invalidate the proposition as a statement of what is generally, and for practical purposes, true. A judge who did not carry out his duties in the way required by law would evidently be a bad and extraordinary judge who, if he did not mend his ways, would soon be dismissed.

Neil MacCormick said that the 'must' in the proposition that the judge 'must' give judgment in favour of the party who has won in law is not the 'must' of causal or logical necessity but the 'must' of obligation. He went on-

'. . . it would be so strange as to be barely imaginable that a judge having established the justifiability of one decision by logical argument from sound legal premisses and findings of fact should then issue some diametrically different order.'

{*Legal Reasoning and Legal Theory* pp 33-4.}

The *particular negative proposition*, as we have seen, can be stated as *some judges apply a strained construction when not logically impelled*. Now we have our contradictory syllogisms.

First syllogism

Major premiss
A judge is a person who carries out his duties as the law requires.

Minor premiss
J is a person who is a judge.

Conclusion
J carries out his duties as the law requires.

Second syllogism

Major premiss
The law requires a judge not to apply a strained construction unless logically impelled.

Minor premiss
J is a judge who applies a strained construction when not logically impelled.

Conclusion
J does not carry out his duties as the law requires.

There is only one way to resolve the plain contradiction between the two conclusions. The major premiss of the second syllogism must be altered to something on these lines: *The law allows a judge, where he thinks fit in accordance with legal principle to do so, to apply a strained construction when not logically impelled*. This means the rejection of the so-called literal rule of interpretation.

This inevitable conclusion is one our judges have been reluctant to recognise, yet it is of great importance. It means that instead of arguing about whether or not it is lawful to depart from the 'literal rule' we should accept that there is no such rule. Instead we should concentrate on working out the principles governing the choice between a literal and a strained construction. That is what the present work seeks to do.

PART XXI

Linguistic Canons of Construction: Interpretation of Individual Words and Phrases

Introduction to Part XXI   This Part amplifies s 151 of the Code, dealing with the linguistic canons which govern the straightforward interpretation of individual words and phrases.

The concept of the 'ordinary' meaning of a word or phrase is discussed (s 363). We consider composite expressions (s 364), and then go on to four sections dealing with technical terms. The nature of a technical term is examined (s 365), and then we look at legal terms (s 366) and non-legal terms (s 367). Lastly we consider terms that have both a technical and an ordinary meaning (s 368).

Various special cases are then dealt with, namely neologisms and slang (s 369), archaisms (s 370), terms in a foreign context (s 371), abbreviations (s 372), homonyms (s 373), and terms that are strictly meaningless (s 374).

Part XXI ends with two sections dealing with the ways meaning is established, namely under the doctrine of judicial notice (s 375) or by adducing evidence (s 376).

363. Ordinary meaning

The starting point in statutory interpretation is to consider the ordinary meaning of the word or phrase in question, that is its proper and most known signification. If there is more than one ordinary meaning, the most common and well-established is preferred (other things being equal).

COMMENTARY

This section of the Code is concerned with the first task of the interpreter, namely to arrive at the ordinary meaning of the word or phrase in question. Whether or not that is to be regarded as its legal meaning within the relevant enactment is a separate matter. {As to the legal meaning see s 2 and Part IV of this Code.}

The phrase 'proper and most known signification' appears in a famous passage from Pufendorf which has been adopted by our judges. {And also (without attribution) by Blackstone: Kerr Bl (4th edn, 1876) i 39.} This runs-

> 'As for words, the rule is, unless there be reasonable objections against it, they are to be understood in their proper and most known signification; not so much according to grammar, as to the general use of them.'

{Pufendorf *Of the Law of Nature and Nations* (4th edn, 1729) p 535.}

There are many judicial variants expressing the same idea. Dr Lushington spoke of '*Uti loquitur vulgus*'. {*The Fusilier* (1864) 34 LJPM & A 25, at p 27.} Lord Tenterden said words are to be applied 'as they are understood in common language'. {*A-G v Winstanley* (1831) 2 D & Cl 302, at p 310.} Parke B spoke of adhering to 'the grammatical and ordinary sense of the words used' {*Grey v Pearson* (1857) 6 HL Cas 61, at p 106. See also *Becke v Smith* (1836) 2 M & W 191, at p 195.}; Viscount Dilhorne LC required words to be given 'their ordinary natural meaning'. {*Selvey v Director of Public Prosecutions* [1970] AC 304, at p 330.}; Graham J said 'the words must be treated as having their ordinary English meaning as applied to the subject matter with which they are dealing'. {*Exxon Corpn v Exxon Insurance Consultants International Ltd* [1981] 2 All ER 495, at p 502.}

Educated or uneducated usage?   The dicta suggest that there is a uniform usage throughout the country, but this is clearly not so. There are regional and class variations. In *Brock v Wollams* {[1949] 2 KB 388, at p 395.} Cohen LJ formulated what has since been called 'the Cohen question'. {So described by Lord Diplock in *Carega Properties SA (formerly Joram Developments Ltd) v Sharratt* [1979] 2 All ER 1084, at p 1086.} The point concerned who is a 'member of the family' within the meaning of the Rent Acts. Cohen LJ said that the question the county court judge should have asked himself was: 'Would an ordinary man, addressing his mind to the question whether Mrs Wollams was a member of the family or not, have answered "Yes" or "No"?'
In *Langdon v Horton* {[1951] 1 KB 666, at p 669.}, Lord Evershed MR borrowed from *Henry V* to amplify the description 'an ordinary man' in the Cohen question as a man 'base, common, and popular'. {*Henry V* iv i 37.} This appears misconceived, having regard to Shakespeare's use of the latter phrase. Pistol challenges the disguised King Henry, who replies that he is a friend. Pistol goes on-

> 'Discuss unto me; art thou officer? Or art thou base, common, and popular?

The standard can hardly be that of the ordinary man in this sense; and it seems that the Cohen question needs reframing. The words to be construed are put together by draftsmen, and draftsmen are not ordinary men. Like learned judges, they are highly educated men. The standard must be at least that of the ordinary person of good education. When choosing their words, draftsmen do not consciously don the mental equipment of a Pistol (even supposing they were able to). Perhaps the right balance is struck by Buckley LJ with his reference to 'a man who speaks English and understands English accurately but not pedantically'. {*Benson (Inspector of Taxes) v Yard Arm Club Ltd* [1979] 1 WLR 347, at p 351.}

This is a vexed question, allied to that of whether the layman should be expected to understand statutes. {The latter is discussed above, p 311.} Certainly when ordinary words are to be put to a jury there is a strong case for leaving them free of judicial explanation. Dunn LJ said of the word *necessary* as used in s 2(2)(c) of the Health and Safety at Work etc Act 1974-

> ' . . . the judge did not analyse the meaning of the word 'necessary'.
> No complaint is made about that, and indeed we think that the judge

was right to take that course. The word 'necessary' is an ordinary English word and it would have only confused the jury to embark on some philosophical analysis of what the word means.'

{*R v Swan Hunter Shipbuilders Ltd* [1982] 1 All ER 264, at p 272.}

The same might be said of many words which juries are called upon to understand, though judicial exegesis is all too frequent. {For a protest against this in relation to the word *recklessly* see Bennion 'Leave My Word Alone' (1981) 131 NLJ 596. As to *dishonestly* see *R v McIvor* [1982] 1 All ER 491. For the case where an ordinary word has acquired a peculiar legal meaning see s 365 of this Code.}

Confused words Particular care needs to be taken with words that are often confused with each other.

Example 1 Sir Ernest Gowers said that there is no excuse for confusing the adjectives *economical* and *economic*. {E Gowers *The Complete Plain Words* (2nd ed rev, 1977) p 61.} Yet the draftsman of the Transport (London) Act 1969 did appear to confuse them when in s 1 he placed on the Greater London Council a duty to promote 'integrated, efficient and *economic* transport facilities'. {Emphasis added.}

In the 'Fair Fares' case this led to much judicial head-scratching, going right up to the House of Lords. {*Bromley London Borough Council v Greater London Council* [1982] 1 All ER 129.} As inevitably happens with such drafting, the various courts were compelled to give the enactment a minutely particularising examination, endeavouring to extract help as to the intended meaning from every possible quarter.

Unexpected word Sometimes the draftsman uses an unexpected word, when a more common term might have seemed more obvious. Here the court may be assisted in its task of construction if it can spot the reason for this.

Example 2 In *Newbury District Council v Secretary of State for the Environment* {[1980] 1 All ER 731.} the House of Lords considered the meaning of the word 'repository' in Class X of the Town and Country Planning (Use Classes) Order 1950. {SI 1950/1131.} Lord Fraser of Tullybelton said that the word was seldom used, and that 'store' would have been more natural. He went on: 'The reason why the draftsman preferred the word repository to the commoner word "store" may be that "store" is sometimes used to include a retail shop such as a "department store"'. {P 743.}

Several ordinary meanings Many terms have more than one ordinary meaning. Here the starting point is the most common and well-established meaning. {*R v Income Tax Commrs* (1888) 22 QBD 296, *per* Fry LJ ('The words of a statute are to be taken in their primary, and not in their secondary, signification'). See also *A-G of Ontario v Mercer* (1883) 8 AC 767, at p 778.} However the context may quickly drive the interpreter to one of the others. This may be a quite different meaning, or a subdivision of the common meaning.

Example 3 The ordinary meaning of the noun *drink* extends to anything potable. Section 15 of the Road Traffic Act 1930 made it an offence to drive a car while under the influence of 'drink or a drug'. In *Armstrong v Clark* {[1957] 2 QB 391.} it was suggested that this covered a non-alcoholic drink. Lord Goddard CJ said {P 394.}-

> 'If that were so, I should be inclined to apply the dictum of Martin B where the bailiff was sworn to keep the jury without meat or drink, or any light but candlelight, and a juryman asked if he might have a glass of water. Martin B said: "Well it is certainly not meat and I should not call it drink. He can have it." I think 'drink' means alcoholic drink.'

Bowen LJ said that-

> ' ... if a word in its popular sense and read in an ordinary way is capable of two constructions, it is wise to adopt such a construction as is based on the assumption that Parliament merely intended to give so much power as was necessary for carrying out the objects of the Act and not to give any unnecessary powers.'

{*Wandsworth Board of Works v United Telephone Co* (1884) 13 QBD 904, at p 920. Cf *Lord Colchester v Kewney* (1867) LR 1 Ex 368 ('hospital' given wide meaning in tax exemption provision).}

This is simply to say that the court should give a purposive construction. {As to purposive construction see s 139 and Part XVI of this Code.} It is not limited to cases where the Act gives coercive powers.

Example 4 In *R v Skeen and Freeman* {(1859) 28 LJMC 91.} the Court for Crown Cases Reserved sat with 14 judges to consider a problem on the meaning of *disclose* in s 6 of the statute 5 & 6 Vict c 39 (1842). This stated that an agent could not be convicted of committing a fraudulent act if, at any time before indictment, he had 'disclosed' it on examination in bankruptcy. The question was whether this was equivalent to 'stated', or was restricted to disclosure of facts not previously known. *Held* The latter was the intended meaning. The judges divided 9 against 5. Delivering the majority opinion, Lord Campbell CJ said that ether the wider or the narrower meaning was grammatically possible. He went on {P 94.}-

> 'But, if the language employed admit of two constructions, and according to one of them the enactment would be absurd and mischievous, and according to the other it would be reasonable and wholesome, we surely ought to put the latter construction upon it as that which the legislature intended.'

Pollock CB added {P 101.} that 'if we have to construe the word "disclose" as merely to "state", we should entirely repeal the statute'.

Parts of speech Different parts of speech may present their own problems. The draftsman's choice of a preposition can be decisive. {See, e g, *Medical Defence Union Ltd v Department of Trade* [1979] 2 All ER 421, at pp 431-2 (Megarry V-C, saying that prepositions 'may be important', distinguished between contracts of insurance and contracts for insurance).} Again, what Lord Diplock called 'a bold and ingenious argument' was founded on the fact that the draftsman had selected the definite rather than the indefinite article. {*Tolley v Morris* [1979] 2 All ER 561, at pp 570, 572.}

Order of words The precise order in which words are placed in the sentence may be important. Bayley J said that it was very desirable to give words 'that sense which is their natural import in the order in which they are placed'. {*R v Ramsgate (Inhabitants)* (1827) 6 B & C 712, at p 715. See also Example 166.4.}

Tense The tense used may be decisive.

Example 5 A provision empowered the Minister to make a certain order if satisfied that a school 'is being administered' in contravention of the Act. Counsel for the Minister argued that it was permissible to take account of the past running of the school. *Held* Only the current method of administration at the time of the order could be considered. {*Maradana Mosque (Board of Trustees) v Mahmud* [1967] AC 13.}

Example 6 Section 1(3) of the Children Act 1948 removes the right of a local authority to keep a child in care under the section 'if any parent or guardian desires to take over the care of the child'. *Held* This applies only where the parent or guardian expresses a wish to take on the immediate care of the child. {*Re S (an infant)* [1965] 1 WLR 94 (reversed on other grounds at p 483).}

Words presumed to be used correctly It is presumed that a draftsman uses words with correct meaning and grammar. Lord Macmillan said-

'. . . words are used in an Act of Parliament correctly and exactly and not loosely or inexactly. Upon those who assert that the rule has been broken the burden of establishing their proposition lies heavily . . .'

{*Mayor etc of the Borough of New Plymouth v Taranaki Electric Power Board* [1933] AC 680, at p 682. See s 77 of this Code.}

364. Composite expressions

A composite expression must be construed as a whole, but it is incorrect to assume that the whole is necessarily the sum of its parts. Because a certain meaning can be collected by taking each word in turn and then combining their several meanings, it does not follow that this is the true meaning of the whole phrase. Each word in the phrase may modify the meaning of the others, giving the whole its own meaning.

COMMENTARY

Lord Halsbury LC said in *Mersey Docks and Harbour Board v Henderson* {(1883) 13 App Cas 595, at p 599.}-

'It certainly is not a satisfactory method of arriving at the meaning of a compound phrase to sever it into several parts, and to construe it by the separate meaning of each of such parts when severed.'

In considering what he called the 'triad' in the phrase 'efficiency, economy and safety of operation' in s 5 of the Transport (London) Act 1969, Lord Wilberforce said 'the triad must be taken as a whole'. {*Bromley London Borough Council v Greater London Council* [1982] 1 All ER 129, at p 155. See also Example 122.10.}

Example 1 In *Exxon Corpn v Exxon Insurance Consultants International Ltd* {[1981] 3 All ER 241.} the Court of Appeal considered whether the made-up trade name *Exxon* was an 'original literary work' within the meaning of s 2(1) of the Copyright Act 1956. They accepted that it was original, that it was literary in the sense of being composed of letters and having a written form, and that it was a work, in that much time and effort had been spent in inventing it. *Held* It was nevertheless not an 'original literary work'. Oliver LJ said {P 249.}-

> 'But "original literary work" as used in the 1956 Act is a composite expression, and for my part I do not think that the right way to apply a composite expression is, or at any rate is necessarily, to ascertain whether a particular subject matter falls within the meaning of each of the constituent parts, and then to say that the whole expression is merely the sum total of the constituent parts. In my judgment it is not necessary, in construing a statutory expression, to take leave of one's common sense . . .'

{Cf *Lee v Showmen's Guild of Great Britain* [1952] 2 QB 329, at p 338 (meaning of 'unfair competition'). As to the commonsense construction rule see s 122 of this Code.}

Example 2 In *ACT Construction Ltd v Commrs of Customs and Excise* {[1982] 1 All ER 84.} the House of Lords considered the composite expression 'repair or maintenance' in Sch 4 to the Finance Act 1972. Section 12 of the Act, dealing with zero-rating for VAT, relieves from tax supplies of a description specified in Sch 4. Section 12(4) empowers the Treasury to vary Sch 4 by order. Section 46(2) says that Sch 4 shall be interpreted in accordance with the notes contained therein, and that the power to vary Sch 4 extends to these notes.

As varied by para 3 of the Value Added Tax (Consolidation) Order 1976 {SI 1976/128.}, Sch 4 exempts supplies of services in the course of building or engineering work. An appended note says that this does not include 'any work of repair or maintenance'. In *ACT Construction Ltd* the question was whether the latter phrase included the underpinning of foundations. *Held* It did not. Lord Roskill said {P 88.}-

> ' . . . the argument in the court below appears to have proceeded on the basis that the words 'repair or maintenance' are used in antithesis to one another . . . The two words are not used in antithesis to one another. The phrase is a single composite phrase "repair or maintenance" and in many cases *there may well be an overlap between them* . . . '

{Emphasis added.}

Hendiadys The figure of speech known as hendiadys, from a Greek phrase meaning 'one by means of two', may be employed by the draftsman. An old example of its use in law is the term *law and heraldry*, meaning heraldic law.

If an Act made it an offence 'to take and drive away' a motor vehicle, this would be a hendiadys. It would not be an offence merely to take a vehicle, nor merely to drive one away. Both elements would be required to be proved.

Example 3 Professor Pearce gives as an example of hendiadys the enactment dealt with in the Australian case of *Traders Prudent Insurance Co Ltd v Registrar of Workers' Compensation Commission* {[1971] 2 NSWLR 513. See D C Pearce *Statutory Interpretation in Australia* (2nd edn, 1981) p 48.} This read: 'Every insurer shall promptly co-operate with the Committee and assist to carry out its duties under this section'. *Held* One obligation only was imposed by this, and it was insufficient merely to charge failure to co-operate.

365. Technical terms: general

If a word or phrase has a technical meaning in relation to a particular expertise, and is used in a context dealing with that expertise, it is to be given its technical meaning, unless the contrary intention appears.

COMMENTARY

Technical terms are not terms in ordinary use, but require knowledge of the expertise with which they are connected in order to be correctly understood. As Blackstone said, they must be taken according to the acceptation of the learned in each art, trade and science. {Kerr Bl (4th edn, 1876) i 39.}

The position is different according to whether the expertise is the law of the court's jurisdiction, or some other expertise (whether foreign law, or a different field of knowledge than law). In the former case the court takes judicial notice of the meaning of the technical term; in the latter case evidence may be required. {For judicial notice of the meaning of words see s 375 of this Code. As to evidence of meaning see s 376.}

Where it is possible to identify a particular expertise with which the Act is dealing, then at once it is assumed that the words are used in the sense understood by those who practise the expertise. As Lord Esher MR said, where used in connection with a particular business, words are presumed to be used in the sense in which they are understood in regard to that business. {*Unwin v Hanson* [1891] 2 QB 115, at p 119.} Or as Farwell LJ put it: 'If it is a word which is of a technical or scientific meaning then it must be construed according to that which is its primary meaning, namely its technical or scientific meaning'. {*Holt & Co v Collyer* (1881) 16 Ch D 718, at p 720. As to words with both a technical and an ordinary meaning see s 368 of this Code.} If it is a legal term, then what matters is the branch of law with which the Act is dealing. {For legal terms see s 366 of this Code. As to non-legal technical terms see s 367.}

Technical term with different meaning Where a technical expression incorporates an ordinary word and gives it a special meaning, it does not then conform to the word as used in an enactment with its ordinary meaning. An obvious example is Bombay duck, which is not duck at all but fish. It would not be covered by an enactment regulating 'duck'.

Example 1 The Excise Acts place a tax on 'spirits', without elaborating the meaning. In *A-G v Bailey* {(1847) 1 Ex 281.} it was held that this, being a word of known import, is used in the sense in which it is ordinarily understood. It therefore does not cover sweet spirits of nitre, which is a known article of commerce not ordinarily described as 'spirits'.

Term with more than one meaning The interpreter needs to recognise that a technical term may have different meanings, or a wider and narrower meaning. Lord Macmillan once said that the term *assessment* was used in the Income Tax Acts with no less than eight different meanings. {*Commrs for the General Purposes of the Income Tax Acts for the City of London v Gibbs* [1942] AC 402, at p 424.} The court's choice of the intended meaning will depend on the context, and on other relevant interpretative criteria. {As to the interpretative criteria see Part VI of this Code.}

Example 2 Section 2(1) of the Inheritance (Family Provision) Act 1938 said that an order under the Act could be made only 'within six months from the date on which representation in regard to the testator's estate for general purposes is first taken out'. In *Re Bidie* {[1949] Ch 121.} the deceased appeared to be intestate, and a grant of administration was made. Later a will was discovered. The grant of administration was revoked, and a grant of probate made. By that time more than six months had elapsed since the grant of administration.

On an application by the widow under the 1938 Act the judge held that the application was out of time. The widow appealed. *Held* The term 'administration' had a wide and a narrow meaning. Here it must be given the narrow meaning as referring only to probate. The court had no jurisdiction under the Act in cases of intestacy, and the purpose of the Act anyway so required. Hence the widow's application was not out of time.

366. Technical legal terms

If a word or phrase has a technical meaning in a certain branch of law, and is used in a context dealing with that branch, it is to be given its technical legal meaning, unless the contrary intention appears.

COMMENTARY

Each branch of law has its own jargon. If an enactment is dealing with a particular branch, and uses one of these technical expressions, the inference is almost irresistible that it has its usual meaning. This will not be displaced by showing that some popular misconcepton accords it a different meaning.

Example 1 In *R v Slator* {(1881) 8 QBD 267.} it was argued that the term *indictment* as used in s 7 of the Corrupt Practices Prevention Act 1863 applied to any form of criminal proceeding. *Held* The contention would be rejected. Denman J said {P 272.}: 'It always requires the strong compulsion of other words in an Act to induce the court to alter the well-known meaning of a legal term'. Bowen J said {P 274.}-

'The whole of the argument fails if it is not shown that there is a popular use of the term 'indictment' as including 'information'.

There is certainly no such popular use of the term among lawyers, and if there is among persons ignorant of the law, it is an incorrect use of the term.'

Example 2 In *Jenkins v IRC* {[1944] 2 All ER 491.} the Court of Appeal were faced with an argument that 'irrevocable' in s 38 of the Finance Act 1938 was intended to bear an enlarged meaning. Lord Greene MR said {P 495.}-

'It seems to me quite illegitimate to take a word which has a technical and precise meaning in conveyancing and then to argue that it has some extended meaning. If the legislature wished to give the word 'irrevocable' some unusual and extended meaning of this sort, I ask myself why in the world it did not do so.'

Free-standing terms These legal technical terms stand on their own feet, without definition. {As to statutory definitions see s 125 of this Code.} They are free-standing terms, and have a meaning in law which exists for all purposes, not just for those of a particular enactment.

This general meaning may be given by statute or at common law. Thus *highway* is defined at common law whereas *highway maintainable at the public expense* is defined generally by s 36(2) of the Highways Act 1980. A common law meaning may be more or less precisely worked out by the decided cases. For example Ormrod LJ said of *contempt of court*: 'As is well known, this phrase, though very widely used, has always been a source of confusion'. {*Whitter v Peters* [1982] 2 All ER 369, at p 371.}

A term is called a free-standing term because it has a legal meaning when used by itself, without accompanying definition. Unless the contrary intention appears, Parliament is taken, when so using it, to intend that its meaning in the enactment shall correspond to the legal meaning assigned to it generally.

Any system of law contains terms which can be used without definition because they stand for well-understood concepts within that system. By contrast, an Act often defines terms for the purposes of that Act only. These definitions may be applied to other Acts in *pari materia* {*R v Titterton* [1895] 2 QB 61, at p 67; *Lennon v Gibson & Howes Ltd* [1919] AC 709, at p 714; *Bickerdike v Lucy* [1920] 1 KB 707.}, but not in any wider way. {*Macbeth v Chislett* [1910] AC 220, at p 223; *Powell v Cleland* [1949] 1 KB 262, at p 273. See s 125 of this Code.}

While the Interpretation Act 1978 assigns general meanings, it does not make the terms it defines free-standing terms. Its definitions apply in strictly limited contexts, whereas a free-standing term can be used without explanation in any legal frame of reference, whether statutory, contractual or otherwise. {As to the Interpretation Act 1978 see pp 283ff above, and Appendix D.} Except where the term has been given a general meaning by statute, one is driven, as Ackner LJ put it in relation to the term *brothel* as used in s 33 of the Sexual Offences Act 1956, to the meaning at common law. {*Kelly v Purvis* [1983] 1 All ER 525, at p 527.}

In earlier times the law tended to allot persons or things a status, either generally or in a specific connection. It then legislated for them by reference to the term denoting that status, without adding a definition.

Many such terms bore the prefix 'common'. Thus a place might be in law a common bawdy-house. {See *Kelly v Purvis* [1983] 1 All ER 525, at p 527.} A person might be a common barrator {The offence of being a common barrator was abolished by the Criminal Law Act 1967 s 13(1)(a).}, a common informer {See the enactments listed in the Schedule to the Common Informers Act 1951, which abolished the common informer procedure.}, a common scold {The offence of being a common scold was abolished by the Criminal Law Act 1967 s 13(1)(a).}, or a common night walker. {The offence of being a common night walker was also abolished by the Criminal Law Act 1967 s 13(1)(a).}

The status of being a common prostitute still has legal significance. {*R v De Munck* [1918] 1 KB 635; *R v Webb* [1963] 3 All ER 177.} Use of this term in legislation without definition goes back at least to the Vagrancy Act 1824. Abandonment of the term was recommended by the Street Offences Committee of 1928 {Cmd 3231.} as it 'tends to prejudge the merits of the case'. {Para 48.} Nevertheless it is still in use. {See Sexual Offences Act 1956 s 22(1)(a).}

Other 'status' terms which have now disappeared from the criminal law include 'suspected person' {See Example 179.1.} and 'habitual criminal' {Prevention of Crime Act 1908. See *R v Norman* [1924] 2 KB 315 (status of being an habitual criminal might be lost with time).}

Meaning uncertain   Occasionally it may happen that the legal meaning of a technical term used in an Act is uncertain. Since the court is obliged to take judicial notice of the term, it must, where the decision of the case requires it, determine the meaning.

Example 3   Section 127(1) of the Magistrates' Courts Act 1980 says that in general a court shall not try an information or hear a complaint unless the information was laid or the complaint made within six months. In relation to the predecessor of this subsection, namely s 104 of the Magistrates' Courts Act 1952, the question arose in *R v Leeds JJ, ex p Hanson* {[1981] 3 All ER 72. Affd *sub nom Hill v Anderton* [1982] 2 All ER 963.} of exactly what constitutes the *laying* of an information.

Held   The essence of the matter is the doing by the prosecutor of all that lies in his power to initiate the proceedings. Accordingly an information is *laid* when its contents are brought to the attention of a magistrate or the clerk to the justices as a part of the prosecution process, whether or not they are taken into account by him. The same applies to the making of a complaint.

Multi-jurisdictional enactments   Where an enactment extends to territories with different legal systems (for example England and Scotland), the draftsman may select a word which is not a term of art in any one system but is suitable for all. The interpreter should be alert to this possible explanation when dealing with what might appear an unexpected term.

Example 4   Section 2 of the Succession Duty Act 1853 used the term 'devolution by law'. In *Earl of Zetland v Lord Advocate* {(1878) 3 App Cas 505, at p 522.} Lord Blackburn said-

> '"Devolving an estate or devolution by law" is not a technical set of words either in England or in Scotland; it is used in this Act which is meant to apply equally to English and Irish estates and to Scottish

estates; probably it was purposely chosen as being a phrase which the law had neither appropriated nor to which it had given any particular meaning, and we have to arrive at its meaning by taking the whole context and looking to the subject-matter, and thus seeing what the words do mean.'

Alternatively, a technical term may be selected which belongs to one only of the legal systems in question. This does not indicate that the term is to be used in a sense other than its usual one, but that the usual meaning is to be applied throughout. {*Commrs of Income Tax v Pemsel* [1891] AC 531 ('charitable purposes' in s 61 of Income Tax Act 1842 to be given its technical English meaning in Scotland, not its popular meaning). Cf *Edinburgh Water Co v Hay* (1854) 1 Macq HL (Sc) 682; *Rank Xerox Ltd v Lane (Inspector of Taxes)* [1979] 3 All ER 657, *per* Lord Keith of Kinkel at pp 665-6. See s 197 of this Code.}
   {See further Examples 125.3 and 323.17.}

367. Technical non-legal terms

If a word or phrase has a technical meaning in relation to a certain area of trade, business, technology, or other non-legal expertise, and is used in a context dealing with that expertise, it is to be given its technical meaning, unless the contrary intention appears.

COMMENTARY

Pufendorf, quoting Cicero, said that terms of art which are above the reach of the common people must be taken according to the definition of the learned in each art. {As to evidence of the meaning of technical terms see s 376 of this Code.} 'The logicians, says Cicero, use not the same words as other men; they have terms of their own, as indeed all other arts have'. {*Of the Law of Nature and Nations* (4th edn, 1729) p 536.}
   Modern legislation aims to regulate a great many areas where technical activities of one sort or another take place. It follows that the legislature must occasionally employ appropriate technical terms, expecting them to be understood in their technical sense. Its doing so is assisted by the fact that Members of Parliament are drawn from many walks of life, and often have technical knowledge in the area concerned. They are assisted by the expertise of civil servants and others.
   A technical term may have no other meaning but its technical one, or may have an ordinary meaning too. {As to the latter case see s 368 of this Code.} It may be English or foreign; in a living or dead language. Botanical terms, for instance, used to appear in English but are now usually in Latin. The statute 4 & 5 Will & Mary c 23 (1692) made it an offence punishable with whipping or confinement in the house of correction to burn on any waste, between Candlemas and Midsummer, any grig, ling, heath, furze, goss, or fern. The Weeds Act 1959 states the names of weeds in both English and Latin. {See s 1(2).} The Dangerous Drugs Act 1965 uses English in the body of the Act {See, e g, s 1 (raw opium, coca leaves, poppy-straw, cannabis etc).} and Latin (or pseudo-Latin) in the Schedule.
   A term may be technical notwithstanding that it is made up of ordinary words.

Thus 'historic cost' is a technical term of accountancy, though its components are ordinary words. {In normal use *historical* would be preferred for the meaning here, since *historic* has acquired the sense of 'epoch-making'.}

Legislation may contain a definition of a technical term in ordinary language. This should dispense with any argument as to its meaning.

Example 1   A definition of the insurance term *zillmerising* is contained in reg 4(1)(l) of the Insurance Companies (Accounts and Statements) (Amendment) Regulations 1982. {SI 1982/305.}

Technical terms may have to be understood by the interpreter, even though not used in the enactment itself. This is because the working of the enactment cannot be followed otherwise. Thus a judge deciding a case relative to the television business may need to learn what a *facility company* is. {See *Hadmor Productions Ltd v Hamilton* [1982] 1 All ER 1042, at p 1046.} If a case concerns the oil industry, the judge may have to grapple with terms like *farm-in agreement, farm-in payment, farm-in oil, came on stream* and so on. {See *BP Exploration Co (Libya) Ltd v Hunt (No 2)* {[1982] 1 All ER 925, at p 987.}

Brett MR said in *The Dunelm* {(1884) 9 PD 164, at p 171.}-

> 'My view of an Act of Parliament which is made applicable to a large trade or business is that it should be construed, if possible, not according to the strictest and nicest interpretation of language, but according to a reasonable and business interpretation of it with regard to the trade or business with which it is dealing.'

Brett MR (who had by then become Lord Esher) said in *R v Comrs of Income Tax* {(1888) 22 QBD 296, at p 306.} that this 'reasonable and business interpretation' did not extend to technical terms that had not gained acceptance with 'as large a body as that to which the statute applies'. {Cf *London and North Eastern Rly Co v Berriman* [1946] AC 278, at p 305-6.}

Example 2   The Metage on Grain (Port of London) Act 1872 applied to 'grain brought into the port of London for sale'. Grain could be brought in for sale as grain, or for manufacture into other products which would then be sold. In *Cotton v Vogan & Co* {[1895] 2 QB 652.} it was held that only the former was covered, because this was the business meaning of the words.

Example 3   Regulation 31(3)(a) of the Building (Safety, Health and Welfare) Regulations 1948 {SI 1948/1145.} required 'crawling boards' to be used in certain operations. In *Jenner v Allen West & Co Ltd* {[1959] 1 WLR 554.} it was argued that this should be given the literal meaning of plain boards over which workmen could crawl. Evidence showed however that the term had a technical meaning in the trades concerned. This required cross battens to be fitted to the boards, so as to prevent men from slipping. *Held* The technical meaning should be applied.

A term may be shown to be used as a technical term of a particular type of business where it is mentioned along with other technical terms of that type of business, even though if standing alone it might have been taken as an ordinary term.

Example 4   A public health enactment required a licence for the establishment of 'the business of blood-boiler, bone-boiler, fellmonger, slaughterer of cattle, horses, or animals of any description, soap-boiler, tallow-melter, tripe-boiler, *or other noxious or offensive business, trade or manufacture*. {Emphasis added.} The italicised words are very wide, yet the specific terms are all connected with trades dealing with animals, and must therefore be treated as limited to such trades. Accordingly it was held in *Wanstead Local Board of Health v Hill* {(1863) 32 LJMC 135.} that the italicised words did not cover a brickworks. {See also *Withington Local Board of Health v Manchester Corpn* [1893] 2 Ch 19 (smallpox hospital not covered). See further s 378 of this Code.}

Although the meaning of a technical term may not be entirely clear, what matters is whether it is clear enough to decide the instant case.

Example 5 The case of *Phillips v Prosser* {[1976] Crim LR 262} concerned a local traffic order, under which a sign had been erected reading 'No access except for buses and service vehicles'. The defendant had driven his private hire car past the sign. *Held* While the precise meaning of 'service vehicle' might be uncertain, it was clear that a private hire car was not one.

The distinction between an ordinary and a technical term may become virtually non-existent where almost everyone knows the technical meaning.

Example 6 Section 65 of the Highway Act 1835 conferred on justices power to order trees near the highway to be 'pruned or lopped'. In *Unwin v Hanson* {[1891] 2 QB 115.} the question was whether this enabled an order to be made requiring the *tops* of trees to be cut off. *Held* It did not. There is a clear distinction between the technical terms *lop* and *top*, as evidence called in the case showed. However every countryman is familiar with the distinction, so there is no need to treat the words as technical terms.

A word may be a technical term of two or more different fields of expertise. It is then necessary to determine which field is intended.

Example 7 In *Chesterfield Tube Co Ltd v Thomas (Valuation Officer)* {[1970] 1 WLR 1483.} the Court of Appeal held that the meaning of the technical phrase 'generation . . . of power' in the General Rate Act 1967 Sch 3 para 1(a) was what the phrase meant to rating valuers not physicists.

368. Terms with both ordinary and technical meaning

Where an enactment uses a term which has both an ordinary and a technical meaning, the question of which meaning the term is intended to have is determined by the context. If the context is technical, the presumption is that the technical meaning of the term is intended. Otherwise the ordinary meaning is taken as meant.

COMMENTARY

Many words and phrases have both an ordinary and a technical meaning. In deciding which is intended, it is necessary to consider the surrounding words. If these are technical, it is a reasonable assumption that the term is intended to bear its technical meaning. If however the term is used in a non-technical context it is presumed to have its ordinary meaning.

Example 1 The term *interest* has a technical meaning in real property law. In ordinary speech however, a person may be said to be 'interested' in some question concerning land even though he is not the owner of an interest in the land. *R v Dudley Crown Court, ex p Pask* {(1983) *The Times* 18 June.} concerned the meaning of 'interested' in s 6(1) of the Licensing Act 1964. This empowers justices to grant a provisional on-licence on the application of 'a person interested in any premises'. An application was made in relation to school premises by the headmaster and deputy headmaster. They were merely employees of the owner of the school premises, and had no legal interest in them.

Held The applicants were 'persons interested' in the school premises within the meaning of s 6(1). Taylor J said-

> 'There is no reason here to import into the word "interest" a requirement that such interest be a legal or equitable one in the special property sense. In the ordinary sense of the word the headmaster and his deputy are persons interested in the premises.'

{See also *Pennine Raceway Ltd v Kirklees Metropolitan Council* [1983] QB 382 ('person interested in the land' in s 164(1) of the Town and Country Planning Act 1971 includes a person granted a right to use the land).}

It may be difficult to determine whether the context is or is not 'technical'.

Example 2 In the New Zealand case of *In the Estate of Rangi Kerehoma (deceased)* {[1924] NZLR 1007.} the court considered an enactment which empowered the Native Land Court to determine what provision ought 'in equity' to be made for the support of a person. *Held* Although a matter of law was involved, this was not intended to be a reference to the technical doctrines of equity, but to the everyday concept of fairness.

Example 3 Section 1(1) of the Restriction of Offensive Weapons Act 1959 said that any person 'who manufactures, sells or *offers for sale* or hire, or lends or hires, to any other person' any flick-knife is guilty of an offence. {Emphasis added.} In *Fisher v Bell* {[1961] 1 QB 394.} a shopkeeper was accused of offering a flick-knife for sale by putting it in his shop-window. The question was whether 'offer' was used in its popular or technical sense. *Held* It was used in its technical sense in the law of contract, under which placing goods in a shop window does not constitute an 'offer'.

This decision can be criticised as giving insufficient weight to the mischief. {As to the mischief see s 138 and Part XV of this Code. For purposive construction see s 139 and Part XVI.} Yet the difficulty over context is a real one. While in one sense the context is the legal one of sale of goods, in another it is the commercial one of any dealing in flick-knives.

On scientific matters, judges sometimes get impatient with expert evidence and come down in favour of the popular meaning.

Example 4 In *R v Commrs under Boiler Explosions Act 1882* {[1891] 1 QB 703, at p 716.} Lord Esher MR, when considering in the light of scientific evidence the meaning of the word 'boiler' said-

> 'I apprehend that in this Act it was not meant to draw these scientific distinctions but to deal with the thing in which there is steam under pressure which is likely to explode.'

Case law may give an ordinary word a technical meaning. As Lord Wilberforce said in connection with 'office' as used in the Income Tax Acts, many words of ordinary meaning acquire a signification coloured over the years by legal construction in a technical context such that return to the pure source of common parlance is no longer possible. {*Edwards (Inspector of Taxes) v Clinch* [1981] 3 All ER 543, at p 545.}

Example 5 This happened with *fraudulently*, which once meant much the same as *dishonestly*. The contrast between the two was thus stated by Lawton LJ-

'We do not agree that the judges should define what "dishonestly" means. This word is in common use whereas the word "fraudulently" which was used in s 1(1) of the Larceny Act 1916, had acquired as a result of case law a special meaning.'

{*R v Feely* [1973] 1 All ER 341, at pp 344-5.}

Here it may be noted that *fraudulently* acquired its technical meaning only because the courts did not do what they are now saying should be done with *dishonestly*. In *A-G's Reference (No 1 of 1981)* {[1982] 2 All ER 417.} the Court of Appeal gave *fraudulently*, as used in s 170(2) of the Customs and Excise Management Act 1979, a meaning equivalent to *dishonestly*.

Example 6 In relation to the term *plant* in its industrial sense, Oliver LJ said of its appearance in s 41(1)(a) of the Finance Act 1971 that it is used 'in an artificial and largely judge-made sense'. {*Cole Bros Ltd v Phillips (Inspector of Taxes)* [1981] STC 671, at p 675.}

On the other hand a word may travel in the opposite direction; that is a technical term may acquire a popular meaning.

Example 7 The term *premises* was (and still is) a technical legal term. The position regarding it was thus described by Lord Wilberforce in *Maunsell v Olins* {[1975] 1 All ER 16, at p 21.}-

' . . . this is a word of conveyancing jargon, meaning, strictly (and pace Viscount Hailsham in *Whitley v Stumbles* {[1930] AC 544, at p 546.}) everything in a deed which precedes the habendum. From this it has passed into the vernacular, at least a quasi-legal vernacular, as referring to some sort of property, but not with any precise connotation . . . a number of meanings have been acquired of which the most central appears to be buildings or some kinds of buildings, but it would be far too much to say that there is any prima facie, still less any grammatical meaning from which one should start.'

{Cf, as to 'premises', *Bracey v Read* [1963] Ch 88.}

Conveyancing terms are often taken to be used in a popular sense in taxing Acts, where the object is to secure uniformity by reference to the substance rather than the form of transactions. {See, e g, *T & E Homes Ltd v Robinson (Inspector of Taxes)* [1979] 2 All ER 522 (meaning of 'rent'). Cf *Rank Xerox Ltd v Lane* [1979] 3 All ER 657 ('covenant').} Similar considerations apply to social legislation.

Example 8 In *Centrax Trustees Ltd v Ross* {[1979] 2 All ER 952, at p 955.} Goulding J said of s 8 of the Administration of Justice Act 1973 (mortgages of dwelling-houses): 'it is unlikely that in what may be called social legislation of this sort Parliament intended an occupier's situation to depend on distinctions in conveyancing'. {Cf *Lee-Verhulst (Investments) Ltd v Harwood Trust* [1973] 1 QB 204, *per* Sachs LJ at p 214 ('It is ... the tendency in recent statutes to use "occupied" with the express intention of avoiding technical distinctions between leases and licences'). See also *Land Reclamation Co Ltd v Basildon District Council* [1979] 2 All ER 993, at p 1005 ('enjoyment' and 'occupation' of land); *Methuen-Campbell v Walters* [1979] 1 All ER 608 ('appurtenances').}

369. Neologisms and slang

Occasionally the legislator may use a term which appears to be a newly-coined or slang word. Here the interpreter must not be put off by its unorthodox nature, but must give it what appears to be the intended meaning.

COMMENTARY

The sovereign power of Parliament means that it can make use of whatever expressions it chooses. {As to parliamentary sovereignty see s 31 of this Code.} Though the court may disapprove of Parliament's choice of a word, it is not entitled to reject it. In this respect at least, Parliament is in the position of a Roman emperor; and the judge cannot play Marcellus-

> 'When Tiberius had used a word which was not Latin, Capito said, that in honour of the Emperor, it ought to pass current for the future, although nobody before him had made use of it. But one Marcellus replied, that Caesar might, if he pleased, naturalize men, but words he could not.'

{Pufendorf *Of the Law of Nature and Nations* (4th edn, 1729) p 535.}
   Parliament (or rather the draftsman) invents words not infrequently.

Example 1 This was done in s 2(6) of the Immigration Act 1971, as Lord Denning MR remarked-

> 'In 1971 the Parliament of the United Kingdom invented a new word. It made a new man. It called him "patrial". Not a patriot, but a patrial. Parliament made him one of us: and made us one of them. We are all now patrials. We are no longer, in the eye of the law, Englishmen, Scotsmen or Welshmen. We are just patrials.'

{*R v Home Secretary, ex p Phansopkar* [1976] QB 606, at p 615.}
   The way s 2(6) was worded provides another variant of the definition form. {As to statutory definitions see s 125 of this Code.} The earlier provisions of s 2 spelt out who was to have the right of abode in the United Kingdom. Section 2(6) then said: 'In the following provisions of this Act the word "patrial" is used of persons having the right of abode in the United Kingdom'.
   It may be noted that Lord Denning was therefore wrong to say 'We are now all patrials'. This was not made a free-standing term. It was a term that could not be used elsewhere without definition. {After a ten-year life, the term 'patrial' has now disappeared from our law: British Nationality Act 1981 s 39(2).} In a later

case Lord Denning referred to 'patriating' the Canadian constitution, 'to use a coined word'. {*R v Secretary of State for Foreign and Commonwealth Affairs, ex p Indian Assn of Alberta* [1982] 2 All ER 118, at p 129.}

Another example of a word coined by Parliament is 'custodianship'. {Children Act 1975 Pt II.} Coinages are often made for the purposes of a particular statutory system. Thus the Consumer Credit Act 1974 coins many terms, including 'consumer credit business', 'credit-token agreement', 'debtor-creditor-supplier agreement', 'fixed-sum credit' and 'pawn-receipt'. {See Consumer Credit Act 1974 s 189(1).}

Neologisms or slang terms used in legislation include 'hijacking' {Hijacking Act 1971.}, 'house to house collection' {House to House Collections Act 1939.}, 'know-how' {Income and Corporation Taxes Act 1970 Pt XIV chap I.}, and 'Quaker' {Quakers and Moravians Act 1833. At that time the word Quaker was scarcely established; indeed it has never been formally adopted by the Society of Friends.}

The courts recognise a particular usage by draftsmen. {As to 'Humpty-Dumptyism' by draftsmen see Bennion *Statute Law* (2nd edn, 1983) pp 174, 177.}

Example 2 In *Bromley London Borough Council v Greater London Council* {[1982] 1 All ER 129, at p 160.}, Lord Diplock said of the word *transport* that it is 'an expression which it has become the practice of parliamentary draftsmen to confine to the carriage of passengers and goods by road, rail, water or air'.

The law discourages trade appropriation of common words. Fry LJ said that there is a perpetual struggle going on 'to enclose and appropriate as private property certain little strips of the great open common of the English language'. He added that this is a kind of trespass against which the courts ought to set their faces. {Re Dunn's Trade-Marks (1889) 41 Ch D 439, at p 455.} On the other hand the law protects coined words. Section 64 of the Patents, Designs, and Trade Marks Act 1883 gave protection to 'a fancy word or words not in common use'. A commision of enquiry on the Act objected to the term 'fancy word'. It is certainly not, they said, a happy one 'and has naturally given rise to considerable differences of opinion as to its meaning'. {See *Eastman Photographic Materials Co Ltd v Comptroller-General of Patents, Designs, and Trade-Marks* [1898] AC 571, at p 574.}

A peculiar usage in legislation may be dictated by prudery.

Example 3 Section 4 of the Vagrancy Act 1824 sets out a list of persons who are to be deemed rogues and vagabonds and liable to imrisonment. This includes 'every *person* wilfully, openly, lewdly, and obscenely exposing his *person* . . . with intent to insult any female'. {Emphasis added.} This is obviously in breach of the principle that a word should not be used with different meanings in the same enactment; but the difficulties do not stop there. What exactly does *person* mean in the second place where it occurs?

In *R v Holmes* {As reported in (1853) 1 WR 416.} Maule J said: '"The person," in Old Bailey language, means "private parts"', while Lord Campbell CJ added: 'The word is modern slang'. In *Evans v Ewels* {[1972] 1 WLR 671.} it was held that the word meant 'penis' and nothing else. Even this did not lay the problems to rest, for by virtue of s 6(a) of, and Sch 2 para 1 to, the

Interpretation Act 1978 words in this provision importing the masculine gender include the feminine! Cf *Woodling v Secretary of State for Social Services* {[1984] 1 All ER 593 ('bodily functions').}

Judges sometimes use terms that can only be called colloquial, but still have a clear legal meaning. A colloquial term may by usage become a new technical term.

Example 4 RSC Ord 14 r 3(1) precludes the making of an order for summary judgment where there is 'an issue or question in dispute which ought to be tried'. In *MV Yorke Motors (a firm) v Edwards* {[1982] 1 All ER 1024, at p 1027.} Lord Diplock said that the expression 'triable issue' is commonly used as a paraphrase of this. The term 'triable issue' may thus be said to have become by practice a technical legal term in its own right.

Example 5 A person's case is often said to have 'no merits' where 'on the merits' the decision should go to his opponent. Referring to the *Report of the Foreign Judgments (Reciprocal Enforcement) Committee* {(1932) Cmd 4213.} (on which the Foreign Judgments (Reciprocal Enforcements) Act 1933 was based), and its reference to a judgment of the District Court of Munich, Viscount Dilhorne said-

> 'It was not a judgment "on the merits", an expression used not infrequently by lawyers, and used by the committee in para 1 of their report and one to which I must confess I have no difficulty in attaching a meaning.'

{*Black-Clawson International Ltd v Papierwerke Waldhof-Aschaffenberg AG* [1975] 1 All ER 810, at p 825. See also Lord Wilberforce at p 830. And see on this phrase: *Ricardo v Garcias* (1845) 12 Cl & Fin 368, at pp 377, 389, 390; *Godard v Gray* (1870) LR 6 QB 139, at p 150; American Law Institute (Restatement-Second) Conflict of Laws s 110 (1971) i 324-5.}

Example 6 In *Robinson v Torbay Borough Council* {[1982] 1 All ER 726, at p 730.} Judge Goodall said of subs-s (1) and (2) of s 17 of the Housing (Homeless Persons) Act 1977-

> 'I have come to the conclusion that perhaps the sense of the two subsections can best be expressed by a colloquialism, as is so often the case in English. [The test is] if the fair-minded bystander could say to himself, "He asked for it," and say that in either sense of those words.'

In a later passage {P 733.}, the learned judge said: 'Applying the test I formulated earlier, I think the ordinary man in the street would say of the plaintiffs, "Well, they asked for it." I am afraid, in the colloquial sense, they *did* ask for it'.

Other examples of colloquial judicial usage or acceptance include 'bootleg record' {*Warner Bros Records Inc v Parr* [1982] 2 All ER 455, at p 458.}, 'a disregard' {*O'May v City of London Real Property Co Ltd* [1982] 1 All ER 660, at pp 665, 670.}, 'hassle' {*Walker v Boyle* [1982] 1 All ER 634, at p 641.}, 'lost years' {*Benson v Biggs Wall & Co Ltd* [1982] 3 All ER 300, at pp 33-4.}, 'minicab' {*Armitage v Walton* [1976] Crim LR 70.}, and 'one-off'. {*BVS SA v Kerman Shipping Co* [1982] 1 All ER 616, at p 619; *International Sea Tankers Inc v Hemisphere Shipping Co Ltd* [1982] 2 All ER 437, at p 440. See also Example 303.1.}

370. Archaisms

Rarely the legislator may use a term which is archaic or obsolete. Here the interpreter must give the term what appears to be its intended meaning, having regard to changes since it was current.

COMMENTARY

Sometimes (though very seldom) a term is inserted in an Act even though it is known to be archaic. This may be a technical or non-technical term. It is presumed that the term is intended to have its archaic meaning, though that does not prevent its meaning in the Act from being developed by the courts in the ordinary way.

Example 1 Section 28(6) of the Trade Marks Act 1938 says that the registrar must refuse an application under the section 'if it appears to him that the grant thereof would tend to facilitate *trafficking* in a trade mark'. In *Re American Greetings Corp's Application* {[1983] 2 All ER 609.} Dillon LJ said-

> 'Trafficking in a trade mark has from the outset been one of the cardinal sins of trade mark law. But there is no statutory definition of trafficking, and one may suspect that, as with usury in the Middle Ages, though it is known to be a deadly sin, it has become less and less clear, as economic circumstances have developed, what the sin actually comprehends.' {P 619. Cf Example 375.1.}

Updating construction As to the presumption that an updating construction is to be applied see s 146 of this Code.

371. Terms applied in a foreign context

Where a term in an enactment is applied in a context outside the territory to which the enactment extends, the term is presumed to be intended to have a like meaning as it has to matters within that territory.

COMMENTARY

Difficulty may arise where the court is asked to construe an enactment which uses English words, but applies in a foreign context where the words have a different meaning. {Eg, the industrial term 'plant' has a meaning in Australia different from that in England: *Cole Bros Ltd v Phillips (Inspector of Taxes)* [1982] 2 All ER 247, at p 252.} The presumption is that the words should be given 'their ordinary meaning in the English language as applied to such a subject-matter'. {*Per* Lord Esher MR in *Clerical, Medical & General Life Assurance Society v Carter* (1889) 22 QBD 444, at p 448.} Here the reference to the English language means that language as understood in the territory to which the enactment extends. {As to the 'extent' of an enactment see s 195 of this Code. For enactments extending to more than one legal system (eg, England and Scotland) see s 197.}

Example 1   The word *marry* has varying meanings. In particular it may refer either to monogamous or polygamous marriage. In *Hyde v Hyde* {(1866) LR 1 P & D 130.} the validity of a Mormon marriage was in question. Lord Penzance said {P 133.} that there is 'no magic in a name', and that if the relationship in Utah between man and wife is not what we recognise as marriage but another and altogether different relationship 'the use of a common term to express these two relations will not make them one and the same'. Accordingly the term *marriage* in a British Act is taken to mean monogamous marriage. {See *Bethell's Case* (1887) 38 Ch D 220; *Brinkley v A-G* (1890) 15 PD 76.}

Example 2   Section 1 of the Education Act 1962 {As substituted by the Education Act 1980 s 19 and Sch 5.}, taken with reg 7 of the Education (Mandatory Awards) Regulations 1980 {SI 1980/974.}, required a local education authority to make awards for full-time courses which were either for a first degree of a United Kingdom university or a comparable first degree course. In *R v Leeds City Council, ex p Datta* {1982) *The Times* 27 April.} the applicant had two degrees from the University of Calcutta, and had been admitted to a degree course at Leeds University. The question was whether, in the light of evidence that Calcutta degrees were not of United Kingdom standard, the Leeds course was in the applicant's case 'for a first degree'. *Held* Here the term *degree* meant a degree as conferred in the United Kingdom, so the Calcutta 'degrees' were to be disregarded.

{See also Examples 197.1 to 197.3, 199.6, 323.9 and 323.10.}

372. Abbreviations

If an abbreviation is used in an enactment it is to be construed as if the term were set out in full.

COMMENTARY

Abbreviation, also known as abridging or contraction, was very frequent in old statutes. Thus *rationabilem* was written as *ronabilem* in the Statute *De Prerogativa Regis* (1323). The word *every* was often written as 'evy'. {See, e g, 22 Hen 8 c 5 (1530) s 4.}

The statute 4 Geo 2 c 26 (1730) required that all law proceedings should be in words at length, and not abbreviated. This was alleviated by 6 Geo 2 c 14 (1732), which permitted numbers to be expressed in figures rather than words. {See also practice note at [1923] WN 288.} Nevertheless Acts continued to use words instead of figures until 1963.

Abbreviations have been known to give rise to legal terms.

Example 1   The term *culprit* is said by Blackstone to originate in this way. When the prisoner pleaded not guilty, the clerk of arraigns was supposed to answer on behalf of the Crown that he was indeed guilty (*culpabilis*), and that he (the clerk) was ready to prove this (*prit praesto sum*). This was taken down by the abbreviation *cul. prit.*. {Kerr Bl (4th edn, 1876) iv 352-3.}

373. Homonyms

A homonym is a word or phrase with more than one meaning. It is presumed that where the legislator uses a homonym in an Act or other instrument it is intended to have the same meaning in each place. The same applies to cognate expressions.

COMMENTARY

Many words of the same spelling are capable of different meanings. The same applies to phrases. Philologists call these terms *homonyms*. A draftsman needs to take especial care not to use homonyms with different meanings in the same Act without making his intentions clear. {For a detailed example of where this care was not taken see Bennion *Statute Law* (2nd edn, 1983) pp 175-6.} Since drafting is presumed to be competent {See s 77 of this Code.}, it is presumed that a word or phrase has the same meaning throughout unless the contrary intention is shown. This is an aspect of the principle that an Act should be drafted and construed as a whole. {As to this see s 149 of the Code.}

Thus Cleasby B said: 'It is a sound rule of construction to give the same meaning to the same words occurring in different parts of an Act of Parliament'. {*Courtauld v Legh* (1869) LR 4 Ex 126, at p 130.} Where through unskilful drafting there is doubt as to whether this was indeed Parliament's intention, much difficulty may be caused.

Example 1 The court said in *Doe d Angell v Angell* (1846) 9 QB 328, at p 355.}-

> 'Considerable difficulty arises in the construction of the Real Property Limitation Act 1833 by reason of the word "rent" being used in two different senses throughout - *viz* in the sense of a rent charged upon land, and of a rent reserved under a lease.'

Sometimes the drafting is so grossly deficient that the intention to use different meanings is beyond doubt.

Example 2 The law of bigamy is still contained in s 57 of the Offences against the Person Act 1861. This begins 'Whosoever, being *married*, shall *marry* any other person during the life of the *former* husband or wife . . . ' {Emphasis added.} The word *former* is hopelessly wrong, because the whole point of bigamy is that there is a *present* spouse when the second ceremony takes place. The cognate expressions *married* and *marry* here must have a different meaning by logical necessity.

In our monogamous system it is impossible for a person 'being married' to marry in the same sense; the second ceremony is necessarily void. Therefore the interpreter is compelled to give a different meaning to 'marry' here. As the court said in *R v Allen* {(1872) LR 1 CCR 367, at p 374.}: 'it is at once self-evident that the proposition that the same effect must be given to the term 'marry' in both parts of the sentence cannot possibly hold good'.

This is a case where a strained construction is unavoidable. {As to strained construction see ss 92 to 97 of this Code.} The opening of s 57 must be treated as rewritten along the following lines: 'Whosoever, being married, shall purport to marry any other person during the life of the former's husband or wife . . .'

{It seems likely that 'former's' was intended all along, and that 'former' was a misprint.} See also Example 369.3.

Where an artificial meaning is given to a term for a particular purpose, it will not apply to use of the term where that purpose does not operate.

Example 3   By s 27(2) of the Metropolitan Building Act 1855, each set of chambers in a large building was to be treated as a separate 'building' for the purpose of fireproofing etc. A Schedule to the Act empowered the district surveyor to charge a fee of a specified amount in respect of each 'building' surveyed by him. In *Moir v Williams* {[1892] 1 QB 264.} the question was whether the surveyor could charge a fee for each set of chambers. *Held* The treatment of a set of chambers as a 'building' did not extend to the fee-charging provision.
See also Example 93.3.

374. Meaningless terms

Where the legislator makes use of a meaningless term, the court must do its best to arrive at the meaning most likely to have been intended.

COMMENTARY

It is not unknown for Parliament to employ terms which strictly speaking are meaningless. Apart from sheer error, this may be because they possess an appearance of meaning which deceives the legislator, or are party shibboleths {As to these see Bennion *Statute Law* (2nd edn, 1983) p 159.}, or have a vogue use. {As to vogue words see E Gowers *The Complete Plain Words* (2nd edn rev, 1977) pp 283-5.}

Example 1   The long title of the Leasehold Reform Act 1967 describes it as being (in addition to other things) an Act 'to enable tenants of *houses* held on long leases at low rents to acquire the freehold'. {Emphasis added.} It is notoriously difficult to say what is and is not a 'house', particularly since it and similar terms (such as 'dwelling') have often been artificially extended by statute. So s 2(1) sets out to throw light on the meaning. The term 'house', it says, includes 'any building designed and adapted for living in *and reasonably so called*'. {Emphasis added.} It goes on to say that, where the building is divided horizontally, the flats or other units into which it is divided are not 'houses', though the building as a whole may be.

In *Tandon v Trustees of Spurgeon's Homes* {[1982] 1 All ER 1086.} the House of Lords was asked to say whether a building forming part of a purpose-built parade of shops with living accomodation over was 'reasonably called a house'. This is a meaningless question, though their Lordships were too polite to say so. It is incapable of any satisfactory answer, though of course the House had to do its best. The Court of Appeal, divided two to one, had reversed the decision of the judge. By three to two the House of Lords reversed the decision of the Court of Appeal, and held that the building could be 'reasonably called a house'. Such divisions of judicial opinion are inevitable when meaningless terms are used in legislation; and the law is thereby brought into disrepute.

Example 2 Section 1 of the Guardianship of Infants Act 1925 requires the court, in determining questions of custody, to regard the welfare of the child as 'the first and paramount consideration'. The word 'first' here is meaningless. It can add nothing to 'paramount', which is stronger. In *J v C* {[1970] AC 668, at p 710.} Lord MacDermott made a valiant effort to find a meaning for it, and spoke of the child's welfare as being 'the top item in a list of items' and 'of first importance'.

Even worse was to follow. During the passage of the Bill that became the Children Act 1975 the House of Lords insisted, against the advice of the Lord Chancellor, on an amendment to what became s 3. As enacted, this requires a court or adoption agency to 'have regard to all the circumstances, first consideration being given to the need to safeguard and promote the welfare of the child . . .'

The unamended version had 'full account being taken of' instead of 'first consideration being given to'. Since the latter phrase is meaningless, it has naturally given rise to great difficulty. {See *Re B (Adoption: Parental Consent)* [1976] 2 WLR 755, at p 760; *Re P (Adoption: Parental Consent)* [1977] 1 All ER 182; *Re D (an infant) (parent's consent)* [1977] AC 602; *Re H (A Minor)* [1982] 3 WLR 501; (1976) 126 NLJ 671; (1982) 132 NLJ 591; (1984) 134 NLJ 135. For a full account see Bennion '"First Consideration": A Cautionary Tale' (1976) 126 NLJ 1237.} Lord Simon of Glaisdale, who had supported the amendment, gave his articulation as follows-

> 'In adoption proceedings, the welfare of the child is not the paramount consideration (i e outweighing all others) as with custody and guardianship; but it is the first consideration (i e outweighing any other).'

{*Re D (an infant) (parent's consent)* [1977] AC 602, at p 638.}

This is another valiant attempt to give meaning to a meaningless expression, but it attributes to the metaphorical weighing of factors an arithmetical precision that is beyond it. {Once a pernicious expression takes root it is difficult to remove. Section 3 of the Matrimonial and Family Proceedings Act 1984 requires 'first consideration' to be given to a child's welfare.}
See also Examples 75.1, and 75.2, 90.2 and 367.5.

375. Judicial notice of meaning

Judicial notice is taken of the meaning of words in Acts and delegated legislation. This does not apply to technical terms (other than those of the law prevailing within the court's jurisdiction).

COMMENTARY

Judicial notice For the general principles relating to the doctrine of judicial notice see s 21 of this Code.

Judges are presumed to be learned. This learning is taken to extend to the law prevailing within their jurisdiction and the language in which that law is expressed. As Martin B said: 'Is not the Judge bound to know the meaning of all words in the English language?' {*Hills v London Gaslight Co* (1857) 27 LJ Ex 60, at p 63.} Pollock CB remarked that 'Judges are philologists of the highest order'. {*Ex p Davis* (1857) 5 WR 522, 523.}

Law or fact?   The question of what a word means in its context within the Act is a question of legal interpretation, and therefore of law. The court is required to arrive at the *legal* meaning of the term. {See s 2 of this Code.} This does not mean that a jury cannot be left to apply an ordinary word without judicial exegesis. Nor does it mean that an interpretation put on an ordinary word by lay magistrates or any other lay tribunal is to be disturbed on appeal unless it is within the *Wednesbury* principle. {*Brutus v Cozens* [1973] AC 854 (meaning of 'insulting behaviour'). As to the *Wednesbury* principle see p 69 above. For the function of juries see pp 798–799 above.}

Buckley LJ said of the meaning of 'plant' in the Income Tax Acts-

> 'The statutes have not at any time contained a definition of the meaning of "plant". Consequently the question is: what does that word mean and how does it apply to the particular circumstances of this case? That is a question of law, being one of interpretation, but nevertheless it is a jury question in the sense that the word "plant" is not a term of art: it must be interpreted according to its ordinary meaning as a word in the English language in the context in which it has to be construed; that is to say, the court of construction must interpret it as a man who speaks English and understands English correctly but not pedantically would interpret it . . .'

{*Benson (Inspector of Taxes) v Yard Arm Club Ltd* [1979] 2 All ER 336, at pp 338-9. See also *Carega Properties SA v Sharratt* [1979] 2 All ER 1084, at p 1087; *ACT Construction Ltd v Commrs of Customs and Excise* [1979] 2 All ER 691 (affd [1982] 1 All ER 84). See p 802 above}

Dictionaries   Most judges allow their putative memories to be refreshed by the citation of dictionaries and other works of reference. {Exceptionally, Lord Wilberforce informed the present author that he never used dictionaries and shut his ears if they were referred to in court.} Lord Coleridge said of dictionaries 'it is a well-known rule of courts of law that words should be taken to be used in their ordinary sense, and we are therefore sent for instruction to these books'. {*R v Peters* (1886) 16 QBD 636, at p 641.} A dictionary cited should be 'well-known and authoritative'. {*Per* Cozens-Hardy MR in *Camden (Marquess) v IRC* [1914] 1 KB 641, at p 647.}

If the court is concerned with the contemporary meaning of a word at the time the Act was passed, it may be important to consult a dictionary of around that time. {See *Hardwick Game Farm v Suffolk Agricultural and Poultry Producers Assn Ltd* [1966] 1 All ER 309, at p 323; *R v Bouch* [1982] 3 All ER 918, at pp 921-2. As to updating construction see s 146 of this Code.} An English dictionary published in another country may be an unreliable guide. {See *Hardwick Game Farm v Suffolk Agricultural and Poultry Producers Assn Ltd* [1966] 1 All ER 309, at p 323 (citation of dictionary published in USA on the meaning of 'poultry').}

Dictionaries can be used to arrive at the etymology of the word, which may guide the court.

Example 1   Thus Donovan J, in deciding on the meaning of 'reckless' in s 12(1) of the Prevention of Fraud (Investments) Act 1939, said that it literally meant 'without reck'. He added: '"Reck" is simply an old English word, now, perhaps, obsolete, meaning "heed", "concern" or "care"'. {*R v Bates* [1952] 2 All ER 842, at p 845-6.}

If the term has been judicially defined in a relevant context, this will be treated by the court as a more reliable guide to its meaning than a dictionary is likely to provide. In *Midland Rly v Robinson* {(1889) 15 App Cas 19, at p 34.}, Lord Macnaghten said that on a point such as whether 'mine' in s 77 of the Railways Clauses Consolidation Act 1845 included surface workings 'the opinions of such judges as Kindersley V-C, Turner LJ and Sir George Jessel are probably a safer guide than any definitions or illustrations to be found in dictionaries'. {See also *Kerr v Kennedy* [1942] 1 KB 409, at p 413.}

As to the citing of legal textbooks see s 6 of this Code.

Technical terms If there is doubt as to the meaning of a technical term, other than a term of the law prevailing within the jurisdiction, this may be resolved by evidence. The matter is discussed in s 376 of this Code.

376. Evidence of meaning

Evidence may not be adduced of the meaning of terms of which the court takes judicial notice; but is admissible as respects the meaning of other terms.

COMMENTARY

Ordinary words Evidence may not be adduced of the meaning of words as to which the court takes judicial notice. {For these see s 375 of this Code.}

Example 1 In *Camden (Marquess) v IRC* {[1914] 1 KB 641.} the evidence of a valuer as to the meaning of 'nominal rent' in s 13 of the Finance Act 1910 was held inadmissible. Phillimore LJ said {P 650.}-

' . . . in construing a modern statute, not dealing with the particular customs of a particular trade, but of general application, evidence such as is sought to be adduced in this case is inadmissible.'

{See also *R v Calder and Boyars Ltd* [1969] 1 QB 151; *R v Anderson* [1972] 1 QB 304; *R v Stamford* [1972] 2 QB 391.}
This decision must be near the borderline. If it had been the fact that 'nominal rent' was indeed a valuer's technical term, then it would have been arguable that Parliament's intention was to use it in the technical sense.

It seems that evidence should be admitted to establish whether or not a term *is* a technical term. {See *London and North Eastern Rly Co v Berriman* [1946] AC 278, at p 305.} If the evidence shows it is, then the court determines whether it was intended in the technical sense. If the court finds it was, then evidence of what the technical meaning is becomes admissible.

Technical non-legal terms Evidence may be given of the meaning of words used in a technical sense (other than legal terms of which the court takes judicial notice). {See, e g, *Prophet v Platt Bros & Co Ltd* [1961] 1 WLR 1130 (fettling of metal castings); *Blankley v Godley* [1952] 1 All ER 436n (aircraft 'taking off');

London and North Eastern Rly Co v Berriman [1946] AC 278 (repairing of permanent way).

Reference books   Reference books may be consulted in lieu of evidence. Thus books by Mill and Stephen were cited in *Re Castioni* {[1891] 1 QB 149.} on the question of what offences are 'of a political character' within the meaning of s 3(1) of the Extradition Act 1870. Cf *Bank of Toronto v Lambe* (1887) 12 App Cas 575, at p 581 (works on political economy cited as to meaning of 'direct taxation' in British North America Act 1867; *R v Bouch* [1982] 3 All ER 918, at pp 921-2 (*Encyclopedia Britannica* cited as to definition of 'explosive substance' in s 3(1) of the Explosive Substances Act 1883).}

Linguistic Canons of Construction: Elaboration of Meaning of Words and Phrases

Introduction to Part XXII This Part amplifies s 152 of the Code, dealing with the linguistic canons which govern the elaboration of meaning of individual words and phrases by the drawing of certain inferences. In several cases, the principles are embedded in well-known Latin maxims.

We begin with the *noscitur a sociis* principle (s 377). The next eight sections explain the *ejusdem generis* principle derived from it (ss 378 to 385). Then comes the principle, also derived from it, that draws inferences from the respective ranks of items mentioned (s 386).

Part XXII continues with the maxims *reddendo singula singulis* (s 387) and *expressum facit cessare tacitum* (s 388). The most important aspect of the latter maxim, namely the principle *expressio unius est exclusio alterius*, is described in the next six sections (ss 389 to 394).

Finally Part XXII shows how an implication may fall to be drawn from an oblique statement or other reference (s 395), and explains the implication that arises where a statutory condition or other description is only partly met (s 396).

377. *Noscitur a sociis* principle

A statutory term is recognised by its associated words. The Latin maxim *noscitur a sociis* states this contextual principle, whereby a word or phrase is not to be construed as if it stood alone but in the light of its surroundings. While of general application and validity, the maxim has given rise to particular precepts such as the *ejusdem generis* principle and the rank principle.

COMMENTARY

A word or phrase in an enactment must always be construed in the light of the surrounding words. As Viscount Simonds said in *A-G v Prince Ernest Augustus of Hanover* {[1957] AC 436, at p 461.}-

' ... words, and particularly general words, cannot be read in isolation; their colour and their content are derived from their context.'

This section of the Code deals with the manifestations of that principle traditionally subsumed under the rubric *noscitur a sociis* (it is recognised by its associates). {3 TR 87.}

A like principle states that *noscitur ex socio, qui non cognoscitur ex se* (what cannot be known in itself may be known from its associate). {Moore 817.} A related maxim is: *quae non valeant singula, juncta juvant* (what has no meaning by itself is effective when combined). {3 Buls 132.}

Bacon tells us that *copulatio verborum indicat acceptationem in eodem sensu* (the linking of words suggests treatment of them in the same sense). {Bac iv 26.} Two detailed applications of the principle are dealt with separately in subsequent provisions of this Code. These are the *ejusdem generis* principle {See ss 378 to 385.} and the rank principle. {See s 386.}

The general contextual principle was well stated by Stamp J-

> 'English words derive colour from those which surround them. Sentences are not mere collections of words to be taken out of the sentence, defined separately by reference to the dictionary or decided cases, and then put back into the sentence with the meaning which you have assigned to them as separate words . . . '

{*Bourne v Norwich Crematorium Ltd* [1967] 2 All ER 576, at p 578.}

Example 1   Thus in considering whether a county court is an inferior court for the purposes of the Contempt of Court Act 1981, the House of Lords in *Peart v Stewart* {[1983] 1 All ER 859.} was influenced by the way, in the definition of 'court' in s 19, certain general words were 'sandwiched' between descriptions of superior courts, as Lord Diplock put it. {P 862.} He went on to say that these were words 'to which the principle of construction noscitur a sociis applies'. {Ibid.}

As always with an interpretative criterion, other considerations may displace the principle. For example the draftsman may have specified certain terms not so as to give colour to a general phrase but to prevent any doubt as to whether they are included. Viscount Dilhorne said that where an Act defines a thing as including specified matters it is not always right to 'interpret the general words in the light of the particular instances given'. He added-

> 'It is a familiar device of a draftsman to state expressly that certain matters are to be treated as coming within a definition to avoid argument on whether they did or not.'

{*IRC v Parker* [1966] AC 141, at p 161. For another case where the principle was displaced see note *Words in diminishing order* at p 827 below.}

Words used in same sense   The basic operation of the principle is to require related words to be treated as used in the same sense. Section 6 of the Trade Descriptions Act 1968 says that a person exposing goods for supply or having goods in his possession for supply shall be deemed to offer to supply them. Section 11 makes it an offence for the offeror to indicate that the goods are being offered at a price less than that at which they are in fact being offered. In *Miller v F A Sadd & Son Ltd* {[1981] 3 All ER 265.} it was alleged that a person fell within this provision where, following a completed sale of apples, he for the time being retained possession of them. He had the apples 'in his possession for supply' and was therefore, it was said, to be treated as offering them. Accepting that this was literally so, McNeill J rejected the argument. He said {P 269.}-

' ... the words "in his possession for supply" must be read sui generis with "exposing ... for supply" and in the context of a definition of "offering to supply". Moreover ... the word "indication" [in s 11] makes no sense in the context of a concluded contract.'

Determining the meaning of a neutral word Where an enactment includes a word which in itself is neutral or colourless, the context provides the colouring agent. Walton J said that the word *payment* 'has no one settled meaning but ... takes its colour very much from the context in which it is found'. {*Garforth (Inspector of Taxes) v Newsmith Stainless Ltd* [1979] 2 All ER 73, at p 76.} In another case Stamp LJ said-

' ... the words "occupation" and "occupier" are not words of art having an ascertained legal meaning applicable, or prima facie applicable, wherever you find them in a statute, but take their colour from the context of the statute in which they are found ... '

{*Lee-Verhulst (Investments) Ltd v Harwood Trust* [1973] 1 QB 204, at p 217.}
  A word of very vague and wide meaning, when taken by itself, is 'facilities'. As used in s 14(1) of the Trade Descriptions Act 1968, which penalizes the making of a false statement as to the nature of 'any services, accomodation or facilities provided', it is cut down by the context and does not include shopping facilities. {*Westminster CC v Ray Alan (Manshops) Ltd* [1982] 1 All ER 771 (false statement that shop was holding a 'closing down sale').} As used in s 29(1) of the Sex Discrimination Act 1975, which makes it unlawful to discriminate in the provision of 'goods, facilities or services to the public', it 'is not to be given a wholly unrestricted meaning but must be limited or confined to facilities that are akin to goods or services'. {*Kassam v Immigration Appeal Tribunal* [1980] 2 All ER 330, *per* Ackner LJ at p 335.}
  The neutral word *case* was held to mean a solid case, and not such a container as a linen bag, because of its context in the phrase 'case or canister' as the required container for gunpowder when taken into a mine. {*Foster v Diphwys Casson Slate Co* (1887) 18 QBD 429.}

Example 2 Section 1(1) of the Transport (London) Act 1969 required the Greater London Council to 'develop policies ... which will promote the provision of integrated, efficient and *economic* transport facilities and services for Greater London'. {Emphasis added.} In *Bromley LBC v Greater London Council* {[1982] 1 All ER 129. See Example 363.1.} the question was whether the word 'economic' here imported financial economy or referred to the science of economics. Lord Scarman said {P 174.}-

'As a matter of English usage, the term "economic" ... has several meanings. They include both that for which the appellants contend and that for which Bromley contend. It is a very useful word: chameleon-like, taking its colour from its surroundings."

Adopting a restricted meaning The context may restrict the literal or usual meaning.

Example 3 Thus s 11(4) of the Supreme Court Act 1980, following the Act of Settlement (1700), says that a judge of the Supreme Court 'shall hold that office

825

during good behaviour, subject to a power of removal by Her Majesty on an address presented to Her by both Houses of Parliament'. Though the point is undecided, it is arguable that the first limb restricts the second, so that an address can be presented only on bad behaviour. {W Anson *Law and Custom of the Constitution* (4th edn) ii 234-5; W P M Kennedy 6 U of Toronto LJ 464-5.}

Example 4   In *London County Council v Tann* {[1954] 1 WLR 371.} it was held that the word 'ordinance' must be given a limited meaning because of its association with the word 'Act'.

Example 5   In *Kearns v Cordwainers' Company* {(1859) 28 LJCP 285.} the word 'right' was given a restricted meaning because of its associates in a saving for 'any right, claim, privilege, franchise, exemption, or immunity' in s 179 of the Thames Conservancy Act 1857. It thus did not include a right of navigation enjoyed by the public at large.

Example 6   The case of *London & North Eastern Rly Co v Berriman* {[1946] AC 278.} concerned the interpretation of the words 'for the purpose of relaying or repairing the permanent way' in safety regulations requiring a look-out to be posted where men were working for the stated purpose. The question was whether the routine oiling of signalling apparatus fell within the word 'repairing'. The House of Lords held by three to two that it did not. Lord Porter, one of the majority, said {P 307.}-

> ' . . . the combining of "repairing" with "relaying", if it has any effect at all, seems to me to narrow, not to widen the meaning of the former word. The one word suggests renewal, the other the putting of something into proper order, not the prevention of some future fault. The combined words suggest the putting of the track into proper order, either by renewing or mending.'

Adopting a less usual meaning   The context may indicate that the less usual meaning of a word is to be adopted.

Example 7   The word *whisky* has a well-understood meaning. This is obviously displaced when the word is found in a provision such as the local Act which was the subject of enquiry in *Simpson v Teignmouth Bridge Co.* {(1903) 72 LJKB 204.} This authorised the levying of a toll on any 'coach, chariot, hearse, chaise, berlin, landau and phaeton, gig, whisky, chair or coburg and every other carriage hung on springs'. {A whisky was a light two-wheeled one-horse carriage. The case actually concerned the question whether toll could be levied on a bicycle. It was held it could not.}

Example 8   Section 2 of the Ecclesiastical Courts Jurisdiction Act 1860 penalizes 'riotous, violent, or *indecent* behaviour' in churches and churchyards. {Emphasis added.} *Abrahams v Cavey* {[1968] 1 QB 479.} concerned a prosecution under s 2 where the defendant had shouted out in a Methodist church service (held in connection with the Labour Party conference): 'Oh you hypocrites, how can you use the word of God to justify your policies?'. *Held* In s 2 the word 'indecent' did not have its usual sexual connotation but, because of the surrounding words, must be taken to refer to the indecency of creating some disturbance within a sacred place.

Determining extent of qualifying term Where a string of words is followed by a general expression which is as much applicable to the first and other words as to the last, that expression is not limited to the last, but applies to all. So in the phrase 'horses, oxen, pigs, and sheep, *from whatever country they may come*' the italicised words would apply to horses as much as sheep. {*Great Western Rly Co v Swindon etc Railway Co* (1884) 9 App Cas 787, *per* Lord Bramwell at p 808. See also *Rye v Rye* [1962] AC 496, *per* Lord MacDermott at p 508.}

Applying a special meaning The context may show that language is being treated in a special way, or from a particular viewpoint. The ambience may be that of a particular industry or profession, or of some overseas country (as where an English court construes a Commonwealth enactment). As Glanville Williams put it, 'the document may be its own dictionary, showing an intention to use words in some special shade of meaning'. {*Learning the Law* (11th edn, 1982), p 98.} A common example is the interpretation of an old statute, where the whole language is that of a different age.

Words in diminishing order A string of near-synonyms may not be intended to have equivalent meanings, but to operate in diminishing order. Several sections of the Offences against the Person Act 1861 contain the phrase 'poison or other destructive or noxious thing'. Tudor Evans J said in relation to the meaning of the phrase in s 24-

> 'It was submitted that the meaning of the word 'noxious' must take colour from the preceding words. We do not accept that construction. It seems to us, looking at the relevant sections, that the statute is dealing with offences in a declining order of gravity and that by "noxious" is meant something different in quality from and of less importance than poison or other destructive things.'

{*R v Marcus* [1981] 2 All ER 833, at p 837 (insertion of sleeping tablets in neighbour's bottle of milk held administration of a noxious thing within the meaning of s 24 of the 1861 Act).}

Other examples The *noscitur a sociis* principle has also been applied in the following cases. *Muir v Keay* {(1875) LR 10 QB 594.} (in the phrase 'for public refreshment, resort and entertainment' in s 6 of the Refreshment Houses Act 1860, 'entertainment' means reception of the public rather than entertaining them by a theatrical etc performance). *Pengelly v Bell Punch Co Ltd* {[1964] 2 All ER 945.} (in the phrase 'floors, steps, stairs, passages and gangways' in s 28(1) (obstruction) of the Factories Act 1961, 'floors' meant *parts* of floors over which workman were likely to pass and repass). *Mills v Cooper* {[1967] 2 QB 459.} (in laying down an offence committed when 'a gypsy encamps on a highway', s 127(c) of the Highways Act 1959 was taken to use the term 'gypsy' in a loose rather than an ethnic sense, since this fitted the scheme of the Act in dealing with various types of highway obstruction). {See now s 148(d) of the Highways Act 1980, where the reference to a gypsy has been omitted.} *R v Patterson* {[1962] 2 QB 429.} (s 28(2) of the Larceny Act 1916, in penalizing the possession by night of 'any key, picklock, crow, jack, bit, *or other implement of housebreaking*', intended the italicised phrase to be applied objectively as covering all implements *capable* of use in housebreaking). {The point is put beyond doubt by the wording of the replacing provision, s 25 of the Theft Act 1968 (see sub-s (3)).}

{See also Examples 125.2 and 395.13.}

378. *Ejusdem generis* principle: description of

The Latin words *ejusdem generis* (meaning 'of the same kind or nature'), have been attached to a principle of construction whereby wide words associated in the text with more limited words are taken to be restricted by implication to matters of the same limited character. The principle may apply whatever the form of the association, but the most usual form is a list or string of genus-describing terms followed by wider residuary or sweeping-up words.

COMMENTARY

The *ejusdem generis* principle arises from the linguistic implication by which words having literally a wide meaning (when taken in isolation) are treated as reduced in scope by the verbal context. It may be regarded as an instance of ellipsis, or reliance on implication. {See Glanville Williams 'The Origins and Logical Implications of the *Ejusdem Generis* Rule' 7 Conv (NS) 119.}

As Rupert Cross put it: 'the draftsman must be taken to have inserted the general words in case something which ought to have been included among the specifically enumerated items had been omitted . . .' {*Statutory Interpretation* p 116.} Or, as Odgers says, it is assumed 'that the general words were only intended to guard against some accidental omission in the objects of the kind mentioned and were not intended to extend to objects of a wholly different kind'. {*Construction of Deeds and Statutes* (5th edn, 1967) p 184.} It follows that the principle is presumed to apply unless there is some contrary indication. {*Tillmans & Co v Knutsford (SS) Ltd* [1908] 2 KB 385.}

Romer LJ expressed the rationale of the *ejusdem generis* principle when he said that it is an aspect of the wider principle that 'where reasonably possible, some significance and meaning should be attributed to each and every word and phrase in a written instrument'. {*Brownsea Haven Properties Ltd v Poole Corpn* [1958] Ch 574, at p 610.} The validity of this depends on the presumed competence of the draftsman. Lord Devlin said of commercial contracts, which are known to be frequently ill-drawn: 'The presumption against surplusage is of little value in ascertaining the intention of the parties to commercial documents as many great commercial judges have recognised'. {*Chandris v Isbrandtsen-Moller Co Inc* [1951] 1 KB 240, at p 244. Cf s 76 of this Code.}

Thus the phrase 'having in possession', if taken alone, embraces the concept of legal as well as physical possession. When used in an enactment which reads 'having in possession or conveying in any manner' (where 'conveying' is clearly limited to physical removal) the phrase has by implication a more limited meaning. As Blackburn J said in *Hadley v Perks* {(1866) LR 1 QB 444, at p 457.}, it must be limited: 'making the one co-extensive with the other, and confining it to "having" *ejusdem generis* with "conveying"'.

In the same way Lord Cairns LC said in *Ashbury Railway Carriage & Iron Co v Riche* {(1875) LR 7 HL 653.} that, where a company was empowered by its memorandum and articles to carry on the business of 'mechanical engineers and general contractors', the latter phrase was by implication limited in scope because of its juxtaposition with the reference to mechanical engineers. It therefore applied only to the making of contracts connected with general engineering.

The principle is not tied to any particular formula. It does not, as has been suggested, apply only where there is a string of genus-describing terms followed by wide residuary or sweeping-up words (though this is a common example of its application). Thus for example the wider words may merely follow on from the generic words.

Example 1   The case of *Brownsea Haven Properties Ltd v Poole Corpn* {[1958] Ch 574.} concerned the first part of s 21 of the Town Police Clauses Act 1847, which reads-

> 'The commissioners may from time to time make orders for the route to be observed by all carts, carriages, horses, and persons, and for preventing obstruction of the streets ... in all times of public processions, rejoicings, or illuminations, *and in any case where the streets are thronged or liable to be obstructed* . . .'

{Emphasis added.}

The Court of Appeal held that the italicised words were by implication restricted to causes of congestion *ejusdem generis* with public processions, rejoicings or illuminations, since otherwise there was no point in mentioning these things. {P 610. Cf *Papworth v Coventry* [1967] 2 All ER 41, where *Brownsea Haven Properties Ltd v Poole Corpn* was distinguished.}

Example 2   An even clearer example of how the principle is not tied to the formula usually associated with it is furnished by *East London Rly Co v Whitchurch*. {(1874) LR 7 HL 81.} An Act authorising the construction of a railway line by a company said that while the company was possessed of any land assessed to a parochial or church rate the company, until the railway line was completed and *assessed, or liable to be assessed,* must make good 'the deficiency in the assessment for such rates'. {Emphasis added.}

The question was whether the whole line had to be completed before this liability to make good the deficiency ceased, or only the part running through the parish. It was decided by applying the *ejusdem generis* principle to the word 'assessed' in the italicised phrase. The earlier reference to a parochial or church rate showed that the genus was rates of a parochial nature *levied only within the parish in question.*

Since it is independent of form, the *ejusdem generis* principle does not necessitate use of the word *other* in the residuary phrase (e g 'offal, garbage, or other refuse'). {*Brownsea Haven Properties Ltd v Poole Corpn* [1958] Ch 574, at p 598.} Nor need a word like 'similar' be used; indeed the point of the principle is to treat the presence of such a word as *implied.*

The *ejusdem generis* principle is captured by E A Driedger in these words-

> 'The result of the decisions appears to be as follows: if no class can be found, the rule cannot apply and a broad construction may be

favoured; if a class can be found but the specific words exhaust the class, then rejection of the rule may be favoured because its adoption would make the general words unnecessary; if, however, the specific words do not exhaust the class, then adoption of the rule may be favoured because its rejection would make the specific words unnecessary.'

{ *The Construction of Statutes* p 95. As to exhaustion of the genus see *R v Payne* (1866) LR 1 CCR 27; *Fenwick v Schmalz* (1868) LR 3 CP 313, at p 315.}

Long title   As to the application of the *ejusdem generis* principle to the long title of an Act see *R v Noble*. {[1974] 2 All ER 811. The long title is dealt with in s 271 of this Code.}

Noscitur a sociis   The *ejusdem generis* principle is a branch of the principle *noscitur a sociis*, which is dealt with in s 377 of this Code. {So too is the rank principle, described in s 386. below.} There are of course other reasons for giving a wide phrase a narrow construction. {See *Director of Public Prosecutions v Jordan* [1977] AC 699, at p 719.}

Drafting error   The *ejusdem generis* principle is unnecessary where enactments are properly drafted. If residuary or other words are to be limited by reference to a genus, this limitation should be expressly imposed. There is then no need for conjecture. The modern precision draftsman accepts this obvious principle, and aims to word his productions accordingly. As Reed Dickerson says: 'Instead of relying on the curative rules of 'construction', he tries to avoid the situations that give rise to them in the first place'. {*Materials on Legal Drafting* (West Publishng Co, 1981) p 129.}

Where the principle does apply there is sometimes a drafting error in the depiction of the genus. {For an example see *Allen v Emmerson* [1944] 1 KB 362, *per* Asquith J at p 367.}

379. *Ejusdem generis* principle: nature of a 'genus'

For the *ejusdem generis* principle to apply there must be a sufficient indication of a category that can properly be described as a class or genus, even though not specified as such in the enactment. Furthermore the genus must be narrower than the words it is said to regulate. The nature of the genus is gathered by implication from the express words which suggest it (in this Code referred to as the genus-describing terms). Usually these consist of a list or string of substantives or adjectives (in the Code referred to as the generic string).

COMMENTARY

The genus-describing terms are the words from which the nature of the intended genus is inferred. Usually these take the form of a simple list or 'string'. This most frequently consists of substantives.

Example 1 Section 43 of the Customs Consolidation Act 1876 reads: 'The importation of arms, ammunition, gunpowder, *or any other goods* may be prohibited by proclamation or Order in Council'. {Emphasis added.} Although the italicised words are completely general, it is obvious that some limitation is intended. Otherwise why did not the draftsman simply say 'The importation of any goods may be prohibited . . .'?

In *A-G v Brown* {[1920] 1 KB 773.} it was held that the *ejusdem generis* principle applied. Sankey J, who relied on the history of the royal prerogative among other factors, refrained from describing what the genus was. He was content to hold that the substance in question, pyrogallic acid, was outside it.

The *ejusdem generis* principle has been applied to strings of adjectives.

Example 2 Thus in *Re Stockport Ragged, Industrial & Reformatory Schools* {[1898] 2 Ch 687.} the Court of Appeal held that in the phrase 'cathedral, collegiate, chapter or other schools', used in s 62 of the Charitable Trusts Act 1853, the residuary words 'or other schools' needed to be given a restricted meaning. Lindley MR said {P 696.}-

> 'I cannot conceive why the legislature should have taken the trouble to specify in this section such special schools as cathedral, collegiate and chapter, except to show the type of school which they were referring to, and in my opinion other schools must be taken to mean other schools of that type.'

The tendency of the courts is to restrict the imputed genus to an area that goes no wider than is necessary to encompass the entire generic string.

Example 3 Thus a string specified as 'boots, shoes, stockings and other articles' would import the genus *footwear* rather than the wider category of wearing apparel. {*Magnhild (SS) v McIntyre Bros & Co* [1920] 2 KB 321, *per* McCardie J at p 331.}

Example 4 The string 'wherries or lighters' imports a narrower genus with which to restrict the residuary words 'or other craft' than does a string specified as 'boats and vessels'. Wherries and lighters carry persons or things. Hence a tug, which carries neither goods nor passengers, would not be a 'craft' within the residuary words 'or other craft'. Where the string is 'boats and vessels' the residuary words 'or other craft' would however include a tug. {Compare *Reed v Ingham* (1854) 32 LJMC 156 with *Tisdell v Combe* (1838) 7 A & E 788.}

Example 5 The string 'a railway, road, pipeline or other facility' imports a facility for conveying goods, and so excludes storage facilities. {See the Australian case of *Canwan Coals Pty Ltd v FCT* (1974) 4 ALR 223.}

It is necessary to be able to formulate the genus; for if it cannot be formulated it does not exist. 'Unless you can find a category', said Farwell LJ, 'there is no room for the application of the *ejusdem generis* doctrine'. {*Tillmans & Co v SS Knutsford* [1908] 2 KB 385, at p 403. See also *Russell v Scott* [1948] AC 422.}

As McCardie J remarked, it is necessary to ask first, what common quality the specified things possess which constitutes them a genus and second, whether the (unspecified) thing at issue in the instant case possesses that quality. He went on-

'So far as I can see the only test seems to be whether the specified things which precede the general words can be placed under some common category. By this I understand that the specified things must possess some common and dominant feature.'

{*SS Magnild (Owners) v Macintyre Bros & Co* [1920] 3 KB 321.}
So with the string 'wherries and lighters' {*Reed v Ingham* (1854) 23 LJMC 156. See Example 4.} one might formulate the genus as 'craft carrying goods or passengers'.

Example 6   Where an enactment restricted the conduct of an offensive business, the string identifying the type of business was-

' . . . a blood-boiler, bone-boiler, fellmonger, slaughterer of cattle, horses, or animals of any description, soap-boiler, tallow-melter, tripe-boiler . . . '

The residuary words were very wide: ' . . . or other noxious or offensive business, trade or manufacture'. Nevertheless the genus was held to be businesses concerned with animal matter only. {See, e g, *Wanstead Local Board of Health v Hill* (1863) 32 LJMC 135 (brickworks not included); *Withington Local Board of Health v Manchester Corpn* [1893] 2 Ch 19 (smallpox hospital not included).} Why specify just those animal products if you meant to cover every type of commercial activity? Yet it has to be remembered that this was nineteenth-century drafting, a product of the age of disorganised composition. {See s 76 of this Code.}
   In addition to the generic string, other parts of the context may give assistance in finding the genus.

Example 7   Section 8(4) of the Finance Act 1894 contained the string 'every trustee, guardian, committee, or other person'. It was held in *Re Latham, IRC v Barclays Bank Ltd* {[1962] Ch 616.} that the genus was persons holding property in a fiduciary capacity, but this was helped by previous mention in the subsection of persons holding beneficially.
   If a genus cannot be found, the principle does not apply.

Example 8   In *NALGO v Bolton Corpn* {[1943] AC 166.} the House of Lords considered a definition of 'workman' describing him as any person who has entered into a works under a contract with an employer, whether the contract be by way of manual labour, clerical work 'or otherwise'. They held there was no genus indicated. The terms 'manual labour' and 'clerical work' do not belong to a single genus, said Viscount Simon. {P 176.} Lord Wright pointed out that the *ejusdem generis* principle is merely a principle of construction, not a rule of law. 'It presupposes a "genus" but here the only "genus" is "a contract with an employer"'. {P 185.}
   If the genus is as wide as the residuary words there is no room for the principle to operate in.

Example 9   In s 3 of the Game Act 1831 the string was 'any dog, gun, net or other engine or instrument'. It was held in *Allen v Thompson* {(1870) LR 5 QB 336.}, which concerned the use of a snare, that 'dog, gun, net' did not connote any narrower genus than 'other engine or instrument', and that the genus certainly included a snare. {Cf *R v Munks* [1964] 1 QB 304, discussed at p 367 above.}

Judges do not always trouble to formulate the genus fully. It is enough to indicate how it might be framed.

Example 10 Where the generic string was 'building, engineering, mining', Widgery J said-

' . . . without attempting to define the genus in detail, it seems clear to me that it is restricted to operations of the scale, complexity and difficulty which require a builder or an engineer or some mining expert.'

{*Coleshill and District Investment Co Ltd v Minister of Housing and Local Government* [1968] 1 All ER 62, at p 65.}

380. *Ejusdem generis* principle: single genus-describing term

The *ejusdem generis* principle may apply where one term only establishes the genus, though in such cases the presumption favouring the principle is weakened.

COMMENTARY

Judges sometimes say that it requires the mention of several terms to establish a genus. {Said by Asquith J in *Allen v Emerson* [1944] 1 KB 362, at p 367 ('theatres and other places'). See also *Cork & Bandon Rly Co Ltd v Goode* (1853) 22 LJCP 198 ('bond or other specialty' held to include specialty by Act); *Roe v Hemmings* [1951] 1 KB 676. The point is usefully discussed in a note 'No Genus' in 70 LQR 172.}

In *United Towns Electric Co Ltd v A-G for Newfoundland* {[1939] 1 All ER 423.} the House of Lords refused to restrict to local taxation the meaning of 'taxation' in an enactment saying that a company was liable to water rates but was otherwise exempt from taxation. Australian courts have ruled that in the phrase 'building or other place' the word 'place' is not restricted to places akin to buildings. {*Lake Macquarie Shire Council v Ades* [1977] 1 NSWLR 126; *Plummer v Needham* (1954) 56 WALR 1.}

However a rule that two or more genus-describing words are *always* required would be too rigid. The question is always one of the intention conveyed by the entirety of the passage, and there can be no absolute rule. The better view appears to be that usually the *ejusdem generis* principle should be applied in the one-word case in recognition of the fact that the draftsman must have specified the word for some purpose.

Example 1 Thus in *A-G v Seccombe* {[1911] 2 KB 688.} it was held that the words 'or otherwise' in the phrase 'any benefit to him by contract or otherwise' in s 11(1) of the Customs and Inland Revenue Act 1889 must be construed *ejusdem generis* with 'contract'. {Cf Example 385.1.}

Example 2 In *Lewisham BC v Maloney* {[1948] 1 KB 51.} it was held that in the phrase 'easement, right or other privilege' in the definition of a Class D land charge contained in s 10(1) of the Land Charges Act 1925, the word 'right' must be construed *ejusdem generis* with 'easement'.

Example 3   In *Parkes v Secretary of State for the Environment* {[1979] 1 All ER 211.} the Court of Appeal held that in the phrase 'building or other operations' in s 290 of the Town and Country Planning Act 1971 the other operations must be read as akin to building. {For other examples of a single genus-decribing term see two cases described above: *Hadley v Perks* (1866) LR 1 QB 444 and *Ashbury Railway Carriage & Iron Co v Riche* (1875) LR 7 HL 653. Further examples of a single generic term arise in *Watson v Martin* (1865) 34 LJMC 50 ('table or instrument of gaming'); *Williams v Golding* (1865) LR 1 CP 69 (district surveyor 'or other person'); *Humber Conservancy Board v Federated Coal & Shipping Co Ltd* [1928] 1 KB 492 ('"port" includes "place"').}

It is true that the mention of one genus-describing term only may make it difficult to arrive at the nature of the genus. {As to the need for arriving at this see s 379 of this Code.}

Example 4   Section 47 of the Coal Mines Act 1911 required haulage roads to be 'kept clear as far as possible of pieces of coal and other obstructions'. In *Alexander v Tredegar Iron & Coal Co Ltd* {[1944] KB 390, at p 396. See Example 385.2.} Scott LJ said of the application of the *ejusdem generis* principle to these words-

> 'If one tries to apply it, one is at once met with the difficulty that, there being only one species, viz pieces of coal, there is no basis for formulating a genus.'

Example 5   A famous early example of this difficulty was given by Best CJ in *Fletcher v Lord Sondes* {(1827) 3 Bing (HL) 501, at p 580.}-

> 'By 14 Geo 2 c 6, persons who should steal sheep or *any other cattle* were deprived of the benefit of clergy, but until the legislature distinctly provided what cattle were meant to be included, the judges felt that they could not apply the statute to any other cattle but sheep.'

{Emphasis added. Cited Craies *Statute Law* (7th edn, 1971) p 179, where the New Zealand case of *Cooney v Covell* (1901) 21 NZLR 106 is also cited as an instance of applying the *ejusdem generis* principle to a single genus-describing term ('advertisements or other publications'). See also p 385 above.}

Example 6   In *Quazi v Quazi* {[1979] 3 All ER 897.} the House of Lords held that s 2 of the Recognition of Divorces and Legal Separations Act 1971, in referring to a foreign divorce obtained by 'judicial or other proceedings', did not import the *ejusdem generis* principle. As Viscount Dilhorne put it, there was no genus and the 'other proceedings' must simply be proceedings which were not judicial. {P 904.} Counsel's argument that they must be *quasi-judicial* was rejected.

In an obiter dictum, Lord Diplock went so far as to lay down a rule that there can be never be an application of the *ejusdem generis* principle without at least two preceding terms. {P 902.} This would be too rigid, and is contrary to authority. The question must always be What did Parliament intend by including the specific term? Here it is difficult to see why the word 'judicial' was mentioned if the intention was not in some way to limit the meaning of 'proceedings'.

{See also Example 314.3.}

381. *Ejusdem generis* principle: genus-describing terms followed by wider residuary words

The most common case for the application of the *ejusdem generis* principle is where a phrase beginning with genus-describing terms is concluded by wider residuary words. The effect of the principle is then to curtail the literal meaning of the residuary words so as to confine it to the genus described.

COMMENTARY

This form of the principle was stated by Cockburn CJ in these words-

> 'According to well-established rules in the construction of statutes, general terms following particular ones apply only to such persons or things as are *ejusdem generis* with those comprehended in the language of the legislature.'

{*R v Cleworth* (1864) 4 B & S 927, at p 932.}

To like effect Lord Campbell said that 'where there are general words following particular and specific words, the general words must be confined to things of the same kind as those specified'. {*R v Edmundson* (1859) 28 LJMC 213, at p 215.}

To avoid confusion it may be necessary to state that, though in such dicta the residuary words are described as *general* terms, the whole point is that whatever their genus may be when used alone they are now to be confined to some other, narrower, meaning. Equally the introductory words are perhaps confusingly referred to as particular or specific words when the point is that they are used to establish a generic category.

This application of the principle is undoubtedly the most common, and is indeed stated by some authorities as its only application. Thus Daines Barrington, writing in 1766, says-

> '[It is] a rule in the construction of statutes, *"that, if particular words are followed by those which are more general, the more general words shall receive a confined construction:"* as what is first mentioned, must be supposed to have been chiefly in the contemplation of the legislature.'

{*Observations upon the Statutes* (2nd edn, 1767) p 114.}

The following are examples of this application of the *ejusdem generis* principle. 'Trustee, guardian, committee' (residuary words 'or other person in whom the property is vested' did not include beneficiaries, but were limited to the genus of those holding in a fiduciary capacity) {*Re Latham decd* [1962] Ch 616.}; 'tenure, custom, prescription' (residuary words 'or otherwise' did not include purely contractual obligations since the genus is obligations imposed by law on land)

{*Eton RDC v River Thames Conservators* [1950] Ch 540.}; 'tradesman, artificer, workman, labourer' (residuary words 'or other person whatsoever' did not include persons above the level of artisans, such as a coach proprietor, barber or yeoman farmer) {*Sandiman v Breach* (1827) 5 LJ(OS) KB 298; *Palmer v Snow* [1900] 1 QB 725; *R v Cleworth* (1864) 4 B & S 927.}; 'corn and grass, hops, roots, fruits, pulse' (residuary words 'or other product whatsoever' did not include more substantial crops such as trees and shrubs) {*Clark v Gaskarth* (1818) 8 Taunt 431; cf *R v Hodges* (1829) Moo & M 341.}; 'house, office, or room' (residuary words 'or other place' did not apply to an outdoor betting enclosure) {*Powell v Kempton Park Racecourse Co* [1899] AC 143.}; 'arms, ammunition, gunpowder' (residuary words 'or any other goods' did not include pyrogallic acid, even though it is used (for photographic purposes) in war) {*A-G v Brown* [1920] 1 KB 773.}; 'signals, warning sign posts, direction posts, signs' (residuary words 'or other devices' in this definition of 'traffic sign' did not include a white line painted on the road) {*Evans v Cross* [1938] 1 KB 694.}; 'spring gun, mantrap' (residuary words 'or other engine' confined to contrivances of a mechanical nature). {*R v Munks* [1964] 1 QB 304.}

382. *Ejusdem generis* principle: genus-describing terms surrounding wider word

Where a word of wider meaning is included in a string of genus-describing terms of narrower meaning, the *ejusdem generis* principle may operate to restrict the meaning of the wider word so as to keep it within the genus.

COMMENTARY

This section applies where, within a string of terms each of which is qualified in some way, there appears an unqualified word.

Example 1   Section 25 of the Dublin Carriages Act 1853 required a licence to be held before any person could lawfully 'use or let to hire any hackney carriage, job carriage, stage carriage, *cart*, or job horse'. {Emphasis addded.} In *Shaw v Ruddin* {(1859) 9 Ir CLR 214.} it was held that hackney carriage, job carriage, stage carriage and job horse were genus-describing words, the genus being conveyances used for hire. Accordingly the unrestricted word *cart*, when found in their company, must be construed as limited to carts used for hire.

Example 2   In *Scales v Pickering* {(1828) 4 Bing 448.} the court considered a local Act empowering a water company to 'break up the soil and pavement of roads, highways, footways, commons, streets, lanes, alleys, passages and public places'. There was thought to be an urban flavour about this string. Accordingly the word 'footways' was held not to apply to a path across a field.

383. *Ejusdem generis* principle: general words followed by narrower genus-describing terms

The *ejusdem generis* principle is presumed not to apply where apparently general words are followed by narrower words suggesting a genus more limited than the initial general words, if taken by themselves, would indicate. The question is however, as always, one of the legislator's intention.

COMMENTARY

Where apparently wide words are followed by terms indicating a narrower genus, this may suggest an intention to curtail the width of the initial words. Nevertheless the courts have been reluctant to treat this as an instance of the *ejusdem generis* principle. Craies goes so far as to state that 'There cannot be an inverse application of the rule'. {*Statute Law* (7th edn, 1971) p 182 n 64.} He cites as authority a dictum of Cohen LJ-

'I have never heard before of an inverse application of the *ejusdem generis* rule and I think it would be very dangerous here to attempt to cut down by the application of any such principle the wide words which precede . . .'

{*Re Wellsted's Will Trusts* [1949] Ch 296, at p 318.}

Maxwell agrees with Craies. The *ejusdem generis* principle, he says, 'applies only to general words *following* words which are less general'. {*The Interpretation of Statutes* (12th edn, 1969) p 298.} He cites as authority a statement by Lord Cave LC-

'I know of no authority for applying that rule to . . . a case where, to begin with, the whole clause is governed by the initial general words.'

{*Ambatielos v Anton Jurgens Margarine Works* [1923] AC 175, at p 183. See also, to the like effect, *Canadian National Railways v Canadian Steamship Lines Ltd* [1945] AC 204, at p 211; *Re Wellsted's Will Trusts* [1949] Ch 296, at p 305.}

384. *Ejusdem generis* principle: express exclusion of

An intention to exclude the *ejusdem generis* principle may be indicated by the use of express words making clear that the residuary words are not to be treated as reduced in scope by the genus-describing terms.

COMMENTARY

If he desires to indicate that the *ejusdem generis* principle is not to apply, the draftsman qualifies the residuary or sweeping-up words by a suitable generalisation such as 'or things *of whatever description*'. {*A-G v Leicester Corpn* [1910] 2 Ch 359, *per* Neville J at p 369. Cf *Skinner & Co v Shew & Co* [1893] 1 Ch 413 and *Larsen v Sylvester & Co* [1908] AC 295.}

However the word 'whatsoever' in the phrase 'or other person whatsoever' in the Sunday Observance Act 1677 was held *not* to disapply the principle. {See the cases, described above (p 836) of *Sandiman v Breach* (1827) 5 LJ(OS) KB 298; *Palmer v Snow* [1900] 1 QB 725; and *R v Cleworth* (1864) 4 B & S 927.} Again, the *ejusdem generis* principle was applied to the phrase 'corn and grass, hops, roots, fruits, pulse' notwithstanding that the residuary words were 'or other product *whatsoever*'. {*Clark v Gaskarth* (1818) 8 Taunt 431.}

These examples show that the only safe drafting method is to use in relation to the residuary words explicit disapplying words such as 'whether or not of the same kind as those mentioned'. This was done in s 61(2) of the Finance Act 1976, which speaks of benefits 'whether or not similar to any of those mentioned above in this subsection'. {See Example 104.1.} Another method is to include a *definition* of the residuary words. This will be construed on its own, without reference to the *ejusdem generis* principle. {*Beswick v Beswick* [1968] AC 58, *per* Lord Guest at p 87.}

Widening by amending Act   Very strong words may be needed if an amending Act is to succeed in disapplying the *ejusdem principle*.

Example 1   The Public Bodies Corrupt Practices Act 1889 was intended to deal with corruption in local government only, and accordingly in s 7 laid down the following definition of 'public body'-

> 'The expression "public body" means any council of a county or county of a city or town, any council of a municipal borough, also any board, commissioners, select vestry, or other body which has power to act under and for the purposes of any Act relating to local government.'

The Prevention of Corruption Act 1916 intended to widen the scope of the 1889 Act. Accordingly s 4(2) provided that in that Act the expression 'public body' should include, in addition to the bodies mentioned in it, 'local and public authorities *of all descriptions*'. {Emphasis added.} It might be thought the the italicised words were sufficient to disapply the *ejusdem principle*, yet in *R v Newbould* {[1962] 1 All ER 693.} the principle was applied so as to exclude the National Coal Board. Winn J said of the italicised words-

> 'A rational and sufficient connotation can be given to the words if they are taken to comprise no more than local authorities and public authorities of the general kind, character, and genus referred to in the earlier phrase contained in s 7.'

385. *Ejusdem generis* principle: implied exclusion of

An intention to exclude the *ejusdem generis* principle may be treated as implied where the application of the principle would produce a result contrary to the legal meaning taken to be intended by Parliament.

COMMENTARY

Like all other linguistic canons of construction, the *ejusdem generis* principle applies only where the contrary intention does not appear. It is moreover but one of the interpretative criteria that may be applicable in a particular case. Accordingly it may be overridden by indications that the result it produces would not conform to Parliament's intended meaning of the enactment. In *Quazi v Quazi* {[1979] 3 All ER 897, at p 916.} Lord Scarman said-

> 'If the legislative purpose of a statute is such that a statutory series should be read ejusdem generis, so be it; the rule is helpful. But, if it is not, the rule is more likely to defeat than to fulfil the purpose of the

statute. The rule, like many other rules of statutory interpretation, is a useful servant but a bad master.'

Example 1   By s 76(1) of the Local Government Act 1933, a member of a local authority was required to disclose his interest and refrain from voting where he had 'any pecuniary interest, direct or indirect, in any contract or proposed contract *or other matter.* {Emphasis added.} In *Rands v Oldroyd* {[1959] 1 QB 204.} Lord Parker CJ held that the mischief at which the enactment was directed required the italicised phrase to be given its unrestricted meaning. {Cf Example 380.1. He said {P 212.}-

'Whereas, of course, a consideration of the mischief aimed at does not enable the court to construe the words in a wider sense than they appear, it at least means that the court would not be acute to cut down words otherwise wide merely because this was a penal statute.'

The first half of this dictum, which was unnecessary to the decision, must be treated, like many such judicial utterances, with caution. Lord Parker, in company with many other judges, not infrequently came to a decision which contradicts it. {See, e g, *Fisher v Bell* [1961] 1 QB 394 and *Adler v George* [1964] 2 QB 7.}

Example 2   When the coal mine obstruction case of *Alexander v Tredegar Iron & Coal Co Ltd* {Cited above, see Example 380.4.} went to the House of Lords they decided the *ejusdem generis* principle did not apply. This was not because of the difficulty of applying it to a single genus-describing term but because the enactment in question, namely s 47 of the Coal Mines Act 1911, was not intended to cover an obstruction consisting of a moving vehicle. {For another example see *Skinner & Co v Shew & Co* [1893] 1 Ch 413 (threats made 'by circulars, advertisements or otherwise').}

Example 3   In *R v Edmundson* {(1859) 28 LJMC 213.} Lord Campbell CJ, while stating that he was applying the *ejusdem generis* principle, in fact rejected it in favour of a construction based on the mischief. Section 10 of the Frauds by Workmen Act 1777 authorised the issue of search warrants for stolen goods suspected of being in 'any dwelling-house, outhouse, yard, garden or other place'. The genus here is clearly places being or associated with dwelling-houses, yet the court treated a warehouse over a mile from the dwelling-house in question as a 'place' within the meaning of the section. Lord Campbell said {P 215.}-

' ... warehouses are *ejusdem generis* with the dwelling-houses, outhouses and yards ... the mischief provided against ... was that of persons who were the receivers of stolen property ... I have no doubt that warehouses ... come within the mischief contemplated by the Act.'

This justifies the comment by Bowen LJ that 'there are many classes of cases in which it is obvious the [*ejusdem generis* principle] would have to bend'. {*Earl of Jersey v Guardians of Neath Poor Law Union* (1899) 22 QBD 555, at p 561. For another example see *R v Spratley* (1856) 6 E & B 363 (voting paper required to state 'street, lane, or other place' in which property situated; name of parish held sufficient).}

Use of residuary term elsewhere An implication against the application of the *ejusdem generis* principle to narrow a term arises where the term has been used elsewhere in the Act in a wide sense.

Example 4 An Act empowered an inspector of nuisances to inspect foodstuffs located in 'any place'. Elsewhere the Act imposed a penalty on persons who prevented an inspector from entering any 'slaughter-house, shop, building, market, *or other place*' where carcases were stored. {Emphasis added.} *Held* The unrestricted use of 'place' in the provision conferring the power of inspection indicated that it was intended to have the same wide meaning in the second provision. {*Young v Grattridge* (1868) LR 4 QB 166.}

386. Rank principle

Where a string of items of a certain level is followed by residuary words, it is presumed that the residuary words are not intended to include items of a higher rank.

COMMENTARY

From a sense of what is fitting, it is assumed that the draftsman did not intend to include in residuary words items of higher rank than is possessed by those specifically mentioned in the preceding words. This is a particular application of the *noscitur a sociis* principle. {See s 377 of this Code.} By specifying only items of lower rank the impression is created that higher ranks are not intended to be covered. If they were, then their mention would be expected *a fortiori*.

Example 1 Coke gives as an example the statute of Henry VIII which suppressed monasteries and other religious houses. {31 Hen 8 c 13 (1539).} This discharged from payment of tithes all lands which had passed to the Crown by dissolution, renouncing, relinquishing, forfeiture, giving up, 'or by any other means'. These residuary words did not include conveyance by Act of Parliament 'which is the highest manner of conveyance that can be'. {*Archbishop of Canterbury's Case* (1596) 2 Co Rep 46a.}

Example 2 An earlier Act relating to religious houses dealt with alienation of land. {13 Edw 1 c 41 (1285).} The string began with land in the possession of abbeys, and ended with other religious houses. Coke concluded that it did not include episcopal lands: 'bishops are not comprehended within this Act, for they are superior to abbots and these words [other religious houses] shall extend to houses inferior to them that were mentioned before'. {2 Inst 457.}
Blackstone said of this-

> 'A statute, which treats of things or persons of an inferior rank, cannot by any general words be extended to those of a superior. So a

statute, treating of deans, prebendaries, parsons, vicars, and others having spiritual promotion, is held not to extend to bishops, though they have spiritual promotion; deans being the highest persons named, and bishops being of a still higher order.'

{*Commentaries* (1813 edn), i 104.}

Example 3 Where an Act prohibited salmon fishing in 'the waters of the Humber, Ouse, Trent ... and all other waters wherein salmons be taken' this was held not to include the great River Thames in the days (soon perhaps to be revived) when salmon lived in its waters. {2 Inst 478.}

Other examples of the application of the rank principle include the following. In s 1 of the Sunday Observance Act 1677, the string 'tradesman, artificer, workman, labourer, or other person whatsoever' was held not to include persons above the artisan class. {*Gregory v Fearn* [1953] 1 WLR 974.} The string 'copper, brass, pewter, and tin, and all other metals' in a local Act of 1825 {6 Geo 4 c clxx.} was held not to include precious metals such as gold and silver. {*Casher v Holmes* (1831) 2 B & Ad 592.} A power given to the Barons of the Exchequer by s 26 of the Queen's Remembrancer Act 1859 to make procedural rules for their court did not extend to giving rights of appeal to higher courts. {*A-G v Sillem* (1864) 10 HLC 704. Cf *Hotel and Catering Industry Training Board v Automobile Proprietary Ltd* [1968] 1 WLR 1526.} Megarry V-C suggests that the principle may apply to exclude a judge from the provision that in Welsh legal proceedings the Welsh language may be spoken 'by any party, witness or other person who desires to use it'. {Welsh Language Act 1967 s 1(1). See R E Megarry *A Second Miscellany-at-Law* p 169.} Another modern example is the phrase 'an officer or examiner of the court or some other person' in RSC Ord 39 r 4(a). The concluding words have been held not to include judges. {*Re Brickman's Settlement* [1982] 1 All ER 336.}

Tapering strings The rank principle has been held to apply where the string was regarded as tapering down, and the item in question, though not superior to items at the beginning, was superior to those listed towards the end. Thus where the string was 'horse, mare, gelding, mule, ass, ox, cow, heifer, steer, sheep or other cattle' bulls were held to be excluded. Although not superior to horses, they were regarded as superior to oxen, cows etc. {*Ex p Hill* (1827) 3 C & P 225.}

Necessary disapplication The rank principle does not apply if no items are left for the residuary words to cover but those of higher rank, or as Blackstone puts it, where 'the general words would otherwise be entirely void'. {Kerr Bl (4th edn, 1876) i 63.} He gives as an example the provision in the Statute of Marlborough {52 Hen 3 (1267).} which lists essoigns 'in counties, hundreds, or in courts baron, or in other courts'. Since there were no other courts of lower or equal jurisdiction, the latter words were held to include the king's courts of record at Westminster. {2 Inst 137.}

Inverse application   The rank principle may have an opposite application in excluding persons of *lower* rank from the ambit of residuary words. Thus the Dean of St Pauls was held not to be within the exemption from tithes conferred by the Tithes in London Act 1545 on 'great men and noblemen and noblewomen'. He was not a nobleman, and the words 'great men' applied only 'to persons superior, in certain respects, to noblemen and noblewomen, of which description there are certainly persons in this country'. {*Warden of St Paul's v Bishop of Lincoln* (1817) 4 Price 65, *per* Richards CB at p 79.}

387. *Reddendo singula singulis* principle

Where a complex sentence has more than one subject, and more than one object, it may be the right construction to *render each to each*, by reading the provision distributively and applying each object to its appropriate subject. A similar principle applies to verbs and their subjects, and to other parts of speech.

COMMENTARY

The *reddendo singula singulis* principle concerns the use of words distributively.

Example 1   The typical application of this principle is where a testator says 'I *devise and bequeath* all my *real and personal* property to B'. The term *devise* is appropriate only to real property. The term *bequeath* is appropriate only to personal property. Accordingly, by the application of the principle *reddendo singula singulis*, the testamentary disposition is read as if it were worded 'I devise all my real property, and bequeath all my personal property, to B'.

Example 2   If an enactment spoke of what was to happen when 'anyone shall draw or load a sword or gun . . . ' this would similarly be read as 'anyone shall draw a sword or load a gun . . . '.

Example 3   Section 1 of the Immigration Act 1971 lays down general principles. It begins-

> 'All those who are in this Act expressed to have the right of abode in
> the United Kingdom shall be free to live in , and to come and go into
> and from, the United Kingdom without let or hundrance . . . '

The phrase 'to come and go into and from' the United Kingdom appears clumsy. Applied *reddendo singula singulis*, it is to be read as if it said 'to come into the United Kingdom and go from it'. Why did not the draftsman put in this way? Because he wished to keep the evocative phrase 'come and go'.

These are obvious examples. The principle is of real utility in more complex cases.

Example 4 Overseers of Wigton v Overseers of Snaith {(1851) 16 QB 496.} concerned the interpretation of s 5 of the Poor Law Amendment Act 1849. This provided for the transfer of a lunatic pauper from one poor law union to another, and gave the receiving union a right to compensation from the other. The right was to receive the expenses incurred 'in and about the obtaining any order of justices for the removal *and maintenance* of a lunatic pauper'. {Emphasis added.} The question was whether the receiving union could claim for the ongoing maintenance of the pauper. An order of the justices was required only for removal, and not for maintenance.

Held The intention was to give a right to compensation (a) for the cost of obtaining the removal order, and (b) for the maintenance of the pauper. The phrase 'in and about' should be treated as repeated before 'maintenance', so that the true articulation of the provision read-

(1) The receiving union shall be entitled to the expenses incurred
(2) in and about the obtaining any order of justices for the removal of a lunatic pauper
and
(3) in and about the maintenance of a lunatic pauper so removed.

Enactments often need to be read *reddendo singula singulis*. An important modern example is s 2(1) of the European Communities Act 1972. {See the extensive explanation of how this is to be read in Bennion *Statute Law* (2nd edn, 1983) pp 65-6.} For an instructive example founded on s 59(1) of the Local Government Act 1933 see *Bishop v Deakin*. {[1936] Ch 409. The case is fully analysed in Bennion *Statute Law* (2nd edn, 1983) pp 171-2. See also *Stracey v Nelson* (1844) 12 M & W 535; *Badger v South Yorkshire Rly* (1858) 1 E & E 359, at p 364; *Phillips v Highland Rly* (1883) 8 App Cas 329, at p 336.}

Disorganised composition Need to apply the *reddendo singula singulis* principle is usually a symptom of what in this work is called disorganised composition. {See s 76 of this Code.}

Punctuation The way an enactment is punctuated may assist in determining whether it is to be read distributively, though this cannot be relied on. {As to the punctuation of Acts see s 284 of this Code.}

388. *Expressum facit cessare tacitum*

To state a thing expressly ends the possibility that something inconsistent with it is implied.

COMMENTARY

As explained above {See ss 107 to 110.}, many statutory propositions are implied rather than being directly expressed. This calls for accurate inference by the statute reader. The maxim *expressum facit cessare tacitum* {Co Litt 183b, 210a.} embodies the important principle that no inference is proper if it goes against the express words Parliament has used. 'Express enactment shuts the door to further implication'. {*Per* Lord Dunedin in *Whiteman v Sadler* [1910] AC 514, at p 527. See Example 12.3.}

Codifying enactments   Where an enactment codifies a rule of common law, equity, custom or prerogative it is presumed to displace that rule altogether. This applies even where the term codification is not used. Accordingly the statutory formulation of the rule, whether or not it is to the like effect as the previous rule, by implication disapplies any aspect of that rule not embodied in the new formulation. As Broom says of statutory exemptions from a former common-law rule-

> ' . . . where a general Act of Parliament confers immunities which expressly exempt certain persons from the effect and operation of its provisions, it excludes all exemptions to which the subject might have been before entitled at common law; for the introduction of the exemption is necessarily exclusive of all other independent extrinsic exceptions.'

{*Legal Maxims* (1st edn, 1845) p 286, citing *Dwarris on Statutes* (1st edn) ii 712-3; *R v Cunningham* (1804) 5 East 478, 3 TR 442. See also *R v Eastern Archipelago Co* (1853) 1 E & B 310, at p 343. As to codifying Acts see s 233 of this Code.}
Note that this principle raises a purely linguistic assumption. It does not affect the possibility that a *strained* construction may be called for. {See s 93 of this Code.}

Expressio unius principle   The chief application of the principle *expressum facit cessare tacitum* lies in the so-called *expressio unius* principle. This is dealt with in the next six sections of the Code.

389. *Expressio unius* principle: description of

The maxim *expressio unius est exclusio alterius* (to express one thing is to exclude another) is an aspect of the principle *expressum facit cessare tacitum*. Known for short as the *expressio unius* principle, it is applied where a statutory proposition might have covered a number of matters but in fact mentions only some of them. Unless these are mentioned merely as examples, or *ex abundanti cautela*, or for some other sufficient reason, the rest are taken to be excluded from the proposition.

The *expressio unius* principle is also applied where a formula which in itself may or may not include a certain class is accompanied by words of *extension* naming only some members of that class. The remaining members of the class are then taken to be excluded.

Again, the principle may apply where an item is mentioned in relation to one matter but not in relation to another matter equally eligible.

COMMENTARY

Expressum facit cessare tacitum   The principle *expressum facit cessare tacitum* is described in s 388 of this Code.

Like all canons of construction the *expressio unius* principle, which Coke gives in the form *designatio unius est exclusio alterius* {Co Litt 210a, where the form *expressio unius personae vel rei est exclusio alterius* also occurs.}, operates only where not outweighed by other interpretative factors. {As to the weighing of factors see Part VII of this Code.} Subject to this, it is of common application, being based on the argument that (unless some other reason appears) there was no reason for the draftsman to mention some only of the possible items unless the intention was that they were intended to be the only ones dealt with, so that the rest are excluded. Cross says-

> ' . . . it is doubtful whether the maxim does any more than draw attention to a fairly obvious linguistic point, viz that in many contexts the mention of some matters warrants an inference that other cognate matters were intentionally excluded.'

{*Statutory Interpretation* p 120. See Examples 104.2 and 125.6.}

Disorganised composition Need to apply the *expressio unius* principle is usually a symptom of what in this work is called disorganised composition. {See s 76 of this Code.} Such sloppy drafting calls for special care in applying the principle, since it cannot be assumed that logically-impelled implications were truly intended. Chitty LJ said of a Thames Conservancy Act, 'To an Act drawn as this is, I think it would be dangerous to apply the rule of *expressum facit cessare tacitum*'. {*River Thames Conservators v Smeed, Dean & Co* [1897] 2 QB 334.}

Example 1 Section 16 of the Licensing Act 1872, an imperfectly-drafted Act, laid down three separate offences against public order. In the statement of the first offence the word 'knowingly' was included, but it was omitted in the case of the other two. This gave rise to the logical implication that these could be committed with or without knowledge, and it was so held in *Mullins v Collins* {(1874) LR 9 QB 292, *per* Archibald J at p 295.} However in *Somerset v Wade* {[1894] 1 QB 574.}, which concerned the contrast between 'permitting' in s 13 of the Act and 'knowingly permitting' in s 14, the decision went against the application of the *expressio unius* principle.

In *Colquhoun v Brooks* {(1887) 19 QBD 400, at p 406.} Wills J said 'The failure to make the *expressio* complete very often arises from accident . . . ' On appeal this was supported by Lopes LJ-

> 'The *exclusio* is often the result of inadvertence or accident and the maxim ought not to be applied where its application, having regard to the subject-matter to which it is to be applied, leads to inconsistency or injustice.'

{*Colquhoun v Brooks* {(1888) 21 QBD 52, at p 65. These dicta were applied, so as to reject the *expressio unius* principle, in *Dean v Wiesengrund* [1955] 2 QB 120 (see Example 394.2).}

390. *Expressio unius* principle: words of designation

The principle *expressio unius est exclusio alterius* applies where some only out of a possible series of substantives or other items are expressly designated.

COMMENTARY

In line with Coke's version of the principle in the form *designatio unius est exclusio alterius* {Co Litt 210a.}, probably its main application is where words of designation are used.

Example 1 In *R v Caledonian Rly* {(1850) 16 QB 19.} an Act authorised the company to build bridges 'of the heights and spans' shown on the deposited plan. The plan also showed inclinations. While conforming to the specified heights and spans, the company departed from the inclinations.
Held The company had not infringed the Act. Lord Campbell CJ said {P 30.}-

> ' . . . we are clearly of opinion that there is no obligation beyond the heights and spans of the bridges as delineated on the plans. These are mentioned in the enactment; and nothing is said as to the rates of inclination of the road. *Expressio unius est exclusio alterius.*'

Example 2 The Diplomatic Privileges Act 1964 gave the force of law to certain provisions of the Vienna Convention on Diplomatic Relations 1961. These protected, in relation to a foreign mission, what were defined as the 'premises of the mission'. {See art 1 of the Convention, set out in Sch 1 to the Diplomatic Privileges Act 1964.} In *Intpro Properties (UK) Ltd v Sauvel* {[1983] 2 All ER 495.} it was alleged that a private dwelling occupied by a financial counsellor at the French embassy in London was the subject of diplomatic immunity as being 'premises of the mission'. The definition of this phrase in art 1 of the Convention is-

> ' . . . the buildings or parts of buildings and the land ancillary thereto, irrespective of ownership, used for the purposes of the mission including *the residence of the head of the mission*'. {Emphasis added.}

Held The specific mention of the residence of the *head* of the mission made it clear that the residences of other members of the mission could not form part of the premises of the mission.

391. *Expressio unius* principle: words of extension

Where it is doubtful whether a stated term does or does not include a certain class, and words of extension are added which cover some only of the members of the class, it is implied that the remaining members of the class are excluded.

COMMENTARY

The most common technique of extending the indisputable meaning of a term is by the use of an enlarging definition, that is one in the form 'A includes B'. {See p 282 above.} Where the stated B does not exhaust the class of which it is a member, the remaining class members are taken to be excluded from the ambit of the enactment.

Example 1 Section 2 (3) of the Immigration Act 1971 states that for the purposes of s 2(1) of the Act the word 'parent' includes the *mother* of an illegitimate child. The class to which this extension relates is the *parents* of an illegitimate child. In *R v Immigration Appeals Adjudicator, ex p Crew* {(1982) *The Times* 26 November.} Lord Lane CJ said: 'Under the rule *expressio unius exclusio alterius*, that express mention of the mother implies that the father is excluded'.

392. *Expressio unius* principle: words of exception

The principle *expressio unius est exclusio alterius* is often applied to words of exception. An excepting provision may except certain categories either from the Act in which the provision is contained, or from the law generally.

COMMENTARY

Where an Act contains specific exceptions, it is presumed that these are the only exceptions of the kind intended. Particular caution is needed in the application of the *expressio unius* principle here however.

Example 1 The statute 37 Hen 8 c 12 contained exceptions from its own operation. It imposed annual tithes on 'the citizens and inhabitants of London', but specified certain exempt citizens. The Dean of St Paul's, who was not so specified, claimed the benefit of the principle that relevant legal maxims are taken to be attracted. {See s 145 and Part XIX of this Code.} He relied on the common-law maxim *ecclesia ecclesiae decimas solvere non debet* (one church is not obliged to pay tithes to another church). {Cro Eliz 479.}
Held The *expressio unius* principle here carried the greater weight, and the Dean could not be treated as exempted. {*Warden of St Paul's v Dean of St Paul's* (1817) 4 Price 65.}

Example 2 Section 79 of the Road Traffic Regulation Act 1967 contains an exception from the law generally. It states-

> 'No statutory provision imposing a speed limit on motor vehicles shall apply to any vehicle on an occasion when it is being used for fire brigade, ambulance or police purposes, if the observance of those provisions (*sic*) would be likely to hinder the use of the vehicle for the purpose for which it is being used on that occasion.'

Speed limits are not the only statutory restrictions which might hinder official vehicles in an emergency. What about those relating to traffic lights for example? Lord Denning MR said of traffic light restrictions-

> 'Those provisions, *taken in all their strictness*, apply to fire engines, ambulances and police cars, as much as to anyone else. None of them is exempt from obeying the red lights. But by special permission they are exempt from obeying the speed limit.'

{*Buckoke v Greater London Council* [1971] 2 All ER 254, at p 258 The italics, which are added, highlight a phrase perhaps indicating Lord Denning's uneasiness at the consequences of applying the *expressio unius* principle here.}
This dictum suggests that the *expressio unius* principle indeed applies to s 79

of the Road Traffic Regulation Act 1967. Why should Parliament single out speed limits if it intends traffic lights and other restrictions (for example one-way streets) also to be suspended in an emergency? This is a typical case for the application of the principle.

Yet such a reading may attribute too much rationality to Parliament, taken in its practical rather than its ideal aspect. {See s 101 of this Code.} In a case of pressing emergency it is unlikely that the courts would hold that any of these statutory restrictions were intended to apply - even to a private citizen, if acting as rescuer. {See *Johnson v Phillips* [1975] Crim LR 580. As to implied exceptions for emergency see pp 722–723 above.} As Farwell LJ said: 'It is not enough that the express and the tacit are merely incongruous; it must be clear that they cannot reasonably be intended to co-exist'. {*Lowe v Dorling & Son* [1906] 2 KB 772, at p 784.}

Similarly it was said by Megarry V-C in *Malone v Commr of Police of the Metropolis (No 2)* {[1979] 2 All ER 620, at p 642.} that the limited power conferred by reg 55(2) of the Telephone Regulations 1971 {SI 1971/2075.} to tap telephones for the purpose of terminating indecent calls cannot 'negate any general power to tap telephones for police purposes in relation to crime'.

393. *Expressio unius* principle: words providing remedies etc

Where an Act sets out specific remedies, penalties or procedures it is presumed that other remedies, penalties or procedures that might have been applicable are by implication excluded.

COMMENTARY

It is commonly said by judges that where an Act lays down specific remedies, penalties, procedures etc these are intended to be the only ones available.

Example 1 Section 103 of the County Courts Act 1959 applies the general principles of High Court practice to the county court, while s 20 of the Act specifically empowers the making of county court rules enabling the court to order a party to make an interim payment. In *Felix v Shiva* {[1982] 3 All ER 263.} it was argued that because no such county court rule had been made a corresponding High Court rule for interim payment could be relied on by virtue of s 103.
Held Rules under s 20 were the only available method, and in their absence s 103 could not be relied on. Eveleigh LJ said {P 266.}-

> 'If a power is given by statute, and the statute lays down the way in which that power is to be brought into existence, it must be brought into existence by that method and none other.'

Example 2 Section 51 of the Parliamentary Voters Registration Act 1843 specified a particular penalty where the overseer wilfully inserted the names of unqualified persons in the voters' list. It was held that this meant no indictment would lie against him for statutory misdemeanor. {*R v Hall* [1891] 1 QB 747; cf *R v Buchanan* (1846) 8 QB 883 and *R v Gregory* (1853) 5 B & Ad 555.}

Example 3 An Act provided that in certain circumstances Crown land could be forfeited and was then liable to be sold at auction. It was held that the latter words precluded any other mode of dealing with forfeited land by the Crown. {*Blackburn v Flavelle* (1881) 6 App Cas 628, at p 634.}

The same principle applies to other forms of statutory remedy, apart from those arising from illegality.

Example 4 Section 62(3) of the Criminal Justice Act 1967 states that where a prisoner released on licence is recalled to prison he must be given reasons for his recall. No such requirement is imposed where a request for release on licence is refused. In *Payne v Lord Harris of Greenwich* {[1981] 2 All ER 842, at p 853.} Brightman LJ said-

> 'As the duty to give reasons is expressly imposed where recall to prison is in issue, but not where release on licence is in issue, it seems fairly obvious that the duty was not intended to be imposed in the latter case.'

Similarly it was held that where an Act contained numerous provisions imposing an express obligation on the Secretary of State for the Environment to give notice of planning determinations 'it is impossible to imply a statutory obligation (as opposed to a duty in the course of good administration) to give notice, where no express obligation is imposed'. {*Griffiths v Secretary of State for the Environment* [1983] 1 All ER 439, *per* Lord Bridge at p 446.}

394. *Expressio unius* principle: where other cause for the expressio

The principle *expressio unius est exclusio alterius* does not apply where it appears that there is a reason for singling out the named terms other than an intention to exclude other terms.

COMMENTARY

There is no room for the application of the *expressio unius* principle where some reason other than the intention to exclude certain items exists for the express mention of the items in question. Thus they may be used merely as examples, or be included *ex abundanti cautela*, or for some other purpose.

Examples If it appears that particular items were singled out for mention merely as examples, there is no room for the *expressio unius* principle to apply.

Example 1 By s 1 of the Poor Relief Act 1601 a poor-rate was imposed on occupiers of 'lands, houses, tithes and coal mines'. This wording indicated, by the application of the *expressio unius* principle, that 'lands' was used in a restricted sense as not including buildings and minerals. {For similarly restricted references to land see *R v Midland Rly* (1855) 4 E & B 958; *Crayford Overseers v D & C Rutter* [1897] 1 QB 650; *Gilmore (Valuation Officer) v Baker-Carr* [1962] 1 WLR 1165, at p 1172. At the opposite extreme, for a widening of 'buildings and hereditaments' to include land of every description see *R v Shrewsbury Gas Co* (1832) 1 LJMC 18.}

The application of the principle also suggested that buildings other than houses, and mines other than coal mines, were not rated. In *R v Inhabitants of Sedgley* {(1831) 2 B & Ad 65.} the argument that other mines were also intended to be rated, and that coal mines were mentioned merely as an example, was rejected. {See also, as to the mention of items merely as examples, *C Maurice & Co Ltd v Minister of Labour* [1968] 1 WLR 1337, *per* Diplock LJ at p 1345; *Prestcold (Central) Ltd v Minister of Labour* [1969] 1 WLR 89; *Lead Smelting Co v Richardson* (1762) 3 Burr 1341.}

Mention ex abundanti cautela   An item may have been singled out for mention by the draftsman *ex abundanti cautela* (from abundance of caution), perhaps under pressure from persons with a vested interest. Its mention then has little significance in relation to items not mentioned. {See *McLaughlin v Westgarth* (1906) 75 LJPC 117, *per* Lord Halsbury at p 118 (savings in private Acts); *Duke of Newcastle v Morris* (1870) LR 4 HL 661, *per* Lord Hatherley at p 671 (peers' privilege of freedom from arrest).} Here the ruling maxim is *abundans cautela non nocet* (abundance of caution does no harm). {11 Co Rep 6. See the Canadian case of *Docksteader v Clark* (1903) 11 BCR 37, cited E A Driedger *The Construction of Statutes* p 99.}

Expressio otherwise explained   There is no room for the application of the *expressio unius* principle where there was some other reason for singling out the item in question for express mention.

Example 2   Section 14(1) of the Increase of Rent and Mortgage Interest (Restrictions) Act 1920 said that in case of overpayment by the tenant 'the sum so paid shall be recoverable from the landlord . . . who received the payment *or his legal personal representative* by the tenant'. {Emphasis added.} There was no mention of the legal personal representative of the *tenant*. In *Dean v Wiesengrund* {[1955] 2 QB 120.} it was argued that the mention only of the landlord's legal personal representative meant that where the tenant had died before claiming a repayment his personal representative could not claim it on behalf of his estate.

Held   The landlord's personal representative was mentioned for a transitional reason. It might otherwise have been argued that where the landlord had died before the Act came into force his personal representative would not be liable. Jenkins LJ said {P 130-1.} that the *expressio unius* principle is-

> ' . . . after all, no more than an aid to construction, and has little, if any, weight where it is possible, as I think it is in the present case, to account for the *inclusio unius* on grounds other than an intention to effect the *exclusio alterius*.'

Excluded item new   If an item which on the application of the *expressio unius* principle would be excluded is of a class which came into existence only after the passing of the enactment, it is probably right to disregard the principle as an aid to construction. {*A-G for Northern Ireland's Reference (No 1 of 1975)* [1977] AC 105, *per* Lord Diplock at p 132.}

395. Implication by oblique reference

Uncertainty in one part of a proposition may be resolved by implication from what is said in another part, even though that other part is ñot directly referring to the first part. Accordingly account is to be taken of a meaning of one provision in an Act that logically if obliquely arises from what is said elsewhere in the Act. Equally an express statement in an enactment may carry oblique implications respecting the legal meaning of other Acts, or of unenacted rules of law.

COMMENTARY

It must often happen that what is expressed in one place throws light on the meaning intended elsewhere. Thus doubt as to whether treason was a felony was settled by a passage in the Treason Act 1351 which, speaking of some dubious crimes, directed a reference to Parliament that it may there be adjudged 'whether they be treason, or *other* felony'. {Emphasis added. See Kerr Bl (4th edn, 1874) iv 82.} Doubt as to whether 'interest' was confined to annual interest in the phrase 'interest, annuities or other annual payments' occurring in the Income Tax Act 1952 was set at rest by the necessary implication arising from the reference to *other* annual payments. {*IRC v Frere* [1965] AC 402. The same result is produced by applying the *noscitur a sociis* principle (see s 377 of this Code.} Here are some further examples.

Example 1 An Act requiring Members of Parliament to swear 'on the true faith of a Christian' was held by necessary implication to exclude Jews from Parliament. {*Miller v Salomons* (1853) 7 Ex 475; *Salomons v Miller* (1853) 8 Ex 778.}

Example 2 When it was expressly enacted that an offence triable by magistrates might be committed within territorial waters, an implied jurisdiction to *try* that offence was held to be created. {*R v Kent JJ, ex p Lye* [1967] 2 QB 153, at p 178.}

Example 3 The requirement in s 26 of the Firearms Act 1968 that an application for a firearm certificate must be made to the chief constable for the area in which the applicant resides implies that a person who is not resident in an area which has a chief constable is not entitled to a certificate. {*Burditt v Joslin* [1981] 3 All ER 203 (applicant a British army officer resident in Germany).}

Example 4 The power conferred on a minister by para 4(3) of Sch 3 to the Housing Act 1957 to exclude any part of the affected land from a compulsory purchase order made by a local authority in connection with their clearance area resolution (thereby excluding that part also from the clearance area) necessarily implies a power, not expressly given, for the minister in effect to cancel the clearance area resolution by excluding *all* the land. {*R v Secretary of State for the Environment, ex p Wellingborough BC* (1981) *The Times* 3 November. Cf Example 331.1.}

Example 5   The power conferred on the Treasury by s 18(2) of the Exchange Control Act 1947 to *validate* an issue or transfer which purported to be made in contravention of the Act implied that such an issue or transfer was otherwise a nullity. {*Re Transatlantic Life Assurance Co Ltd* [1979] 3 All ER 352.}

Example 6   The statement in para 6 of Sch 6 to the Agricultural Holdings Act 1948 that the parties to an arbitration must within 28 days from the arbitrator's appointment deliver to him statements of their cases, and that no amendment or addition shall be allowed after the expiration of the 28 days 'except with the consent of the arbitrator', implies that a statement is not void because it is initially defective. {*E D & A D Cooke Bourne (Farms) Ltd v Mellows* [1982] 2 All ER 208.} 'Otherwise there would be no point in seeking leave to add necessary particulars'. {*Per* Cumming-Bruce LJ at p 220.}

Example 7   The reference in s 54(4)(b) of the Taxes Management Act 1970 to 30 days having elapsed since notification of a taxpayer's intention to withdraw an appeal without the inspector having notified his objection to the withdrawal implies that the inspector possesses a right of objection amounting to a veto. {*Beach v Willesden General Commrs of Income Tax* (1981) *The Times* 2 November.}

Example 8   The statement in s 2(1) of the Limitation Act 1963 that an application by the prospective plaintiff for the leave of the court under s 1 (extension of time-limits) of the Act must be made *ex parte* by implication prevents the defendant in the subsequent action from applying to discharge the order which gave the plaintiff leave. {*Cozens v North Devon Hospital Management Committee* [1966] 2 QB 330.}
Here are some more detailed examples.

Example 9   Section 1(2) of the Leasehold Property (Repairs) Act 1938 says that a lessor cannot recover damages for breach of a repairing covenant from the lessee unless he has first served on him a notice such as is specified in s 146(1) of the Law of Property Act 1925 and allowed one month for it to be complied with. The wording of s 146(1) indicates that the notice can only be served *before* the breach is remedied. *Held* This implies that the lessor is not entitled to recover damages where he has carried out urgent repairs himself before serving the s 146(1) notice, even though the lease provides for this. {*SEDAC Investments Ltd v Tanner* [1982] 3 All ER 646.}

Example 10   In *Re Duke of St Albans's Will Trusts* {[1963] Ch 365.} the question arose of whether the term 'actual tenant in tail' in the Fines and Recoveries Act 1833 covered a contingent remainderman. The wording of the definition in s 1 of the Act made it unlikely that it did so. The court decided that it did because of the implication arising from s 15 of the Act, which spoke of 'every actual tenant in tail, whether in possession, remainder, *contingency* or otherwise'. {Emphasis added.}

Example 11   In *Whitney v IRC* {[1926] AC 37.} it was argued by a taxpayer that the provisions relating to an 'individual' in s 4 of the Income Tax Act 1918 meant that non-residents were not intended to be taxed. This was refuted on the ground that s 7(2) of the Act provided for tax returns to be made by the representatives or agents of non-residents, which would not have been necessary if all non-residents had been tax-exempt. {See the speech of Viscount Cave LC (dissenting, but not on this point) at p 43.}

Example 12 Section 102(1) of the Mental Health Act 1959 {See now s 96(1) of the Mental Health Act 1983.} dealt with the powers of the judge in relation the property of a mentally-disordered patient. Paragraph (b) referred to the maintenance or other benefit of the patient's 'family', without defining that word. Paragraph (c) referred to making provision for other persons for whom the patient might be expected to provide if sane. In *Re DML* {[1965] Ch 1133.} the question was whether the word 'relative' in para (b) included mere collateral relatives. *Held* It did not. The implication from para (c) was that para (b) covered only persons for whom the patient might be expected to provide if sane, and this was confined to near relatives.

Ruling out other interpretative criterion An oblique implication may determine whether or not some other interpretative criterion applies.

Example 13 In *Letang v Cooper* {[1965] 1 QB 232.} it was argued that the *noscitur a sociis* principle governed the construction of the term 'breach of duty' as occurring in the phrase 'any action for damages for negligence, nuisance or breach of duty' in s 1(2) of the Limitation Act 1963. Since damages for negligence or nuisance lie only on proof of actual damage, it was argued that a similar limitation applied to breach of duty as here mentioned. The argument was refuted by the fact that the words 'breach of duty' were followed by the words '(whether the duty exists by virtue of a contract . . . or independently of any contract . . .)'. Since damages lie for breach of contract irrespective of actual damage the oblique implication was that no such restriction was intended.

See also Examples 10.2, 10.3, 146.6 and 290.1.

396. Implication where statutory description only partly met

Where the facts of the instant case substantially though not entirely correspond to a description in the relevant enactment, it is presumed that the enactment is intended to apply in the same way as it would if they did entirely correspond. Where on the other hand the statutory description is partly but not substantially met, it is presumed that the enactment is intended to apply in the same way as it would if the description were not met at all.

COMMENTARY

Where a statutory description is only partly met on the facts of the instant case, the question whether the enactment nevertheless applies is usually one of fact and degree. {See s 83 of this Code.} Necessary compression of statutory language makes it difficult for the draftsman to use all the words needed to supply adequate connotation. This principle assists by providing guidance in the frequent cases where the statutory description is only partially complied with.

Cases of substantial correspondence   An Act prohibiting the making of 'wooden buttons' was held to be infringed by making buttons of wood with a shank of wire. {*R v Roberts* (1701) 1 Ld Raym 712.} Section 15(1) of the Vehicles (Excise) Act 1949 penalized a person who kept on a road an unlicensed 'mechanically propelled vehicle'. A car minus its engine was held still to be within this description. {*Newberry v Simmonds* [1961] 2 QB 345.} Section 8(1) of the Road Traffic Act 1972 says that a 'constable in uniform' may require the taking of a breath test. For this purpose a uniformed officer not wearing his official helmet or cap is treated as nevertheless 'in uniform'. {*Wallwork v Giles* [1970] RTR 117; *Taylor v Baldwin* [1976] Crim LR 137.}

Sometimes the purpose of the enactment indicates a more precise test than merely that of substantial correspondence.

Example 1   Section 3(1) of the Insurance Brokers (Registration) Act 1977 provides that a person is entitled to be registered under the Act if he has 'carried on business as an insurance broker' for a period of not less than five years. In *Pickles v Insurance Brokers' Registration Council* {[1984] 1 All ER 1073.} the applicant had a mixed business and the question arose of whether the enactment required the business in fact carried on by an applicant for the requisite period to consist entirely of insurance broking. *Held* The legal meaning of s 3 was that the applicant's business need not consist entirely of insurance broking, but he had to have engaged in insurance broking to an extent which provided him with *adequate practical experience* of that activity.

Cases falling short of correspondence   Where the facts do not substantially answer to the required description, the enactment does not apply.

Example 2   Under reg 7(1)(d) of the Social Security (Unemployment, Sickness and Invalidity Benefit) Regulations 1975 {SI 1975/564.} a person is not entitled to unemployment benefit if he has received a capital payment 'in lieu . . . of the remuneration he would have received'. An officer in the RAF made redundant received a payment of compensation for curtailment of his service career. This contained an element of payment in lieu of remuneration, but the proportion was speculative and unquantifiable. It was held that reg 7(1)(d) did not apply. {*R v National Insurance Comrs, ex p Stratton* [1979] 1 All ER 1.}

Example 3   Section 15(1) of the Vehicles (Excise) Act 1949 penalized a person who kept on a road an unlicensed 'mechanically propelled vehicle'. A car bought for scrap, of which the engine was rusted up, the tyres were flat, and the gearbox and electrical apparatus were missing was held not to be a mechanically propelled vehicle. Lord Parker CJ said-

> 'It seems to me as a matter of common sense that some limit must be put, and some stage must be reached, when one can say: "This is so immobile that it has ceased to be a mechanically propelled vehicle".

{*Smart v Allan* [1963] 1 QB 291, at p 298. Cf *Newberry v Simmons* above. As to the commonsense construction rule see s 122 of this Code.}

Substantial correspondence is lacking where a device (such as a traffic signal) upon whose functioning the legal thrust of an enactment depends is in fact malfunctioning. {See Example 323.24.}

APPENDIX A

Court Technique

As explained in s 3 of this Code, the interpreter's duty is to arrive at the *legal meaning* of the enactment under enquiry. The following account details the steps to be gone through. It is presented from the advocate's viewpoint, but largely reflects the judicial function also. Further assistance may be gained from the checklist in Appendix B.

The following assumes, which will not always be the case, that the advocate chooses to make use of the optional techniques of selective comminution {See s 74 of this Code.} and interstitial articulation. {See s 113.} Where this is not done, the account needs to be read with appropriate adaptations.

Before going into court

1. Determine, by reference to the facts of your case, the date, territory and application of the law to be applied. {As to the temporal, territorial and personal operation of Acts see s 30 of this Code.}

2. Obtain the relevant statutory text or texts, including the texts containing any amending, repealing, commencement or transitional provisions. {The statutory texts are described in Part II of this Code. As to amendments, repeals etc see Part VIII.}

3. Identify the enactment which is the *unit of enquiry* in relation to the problem of statutory interpretation. {For the enactment as the unit of enquiry see s 72 of this Code.}

4. Ascertain the relevant juridical factual outline, that is the factual outline laid down by the enactment which is the unit of enquiry or (where that has been the subject of judicial processing) the narrower factual outline laid down by the court. {As to this see s 78 of this Code.}

5. Ascertain the relevant legal thrust of the enactment. {See s 79 of this Code.}

6. Relate the juridical factual outline to the actual factual outline, based on the relevant facts of the instant case.

7. Frame the crucial question of law.

8. Determine the *opposing constructions* of the enactment under enquiry. {As to the opposing constructions see s 84 of this Code.}

9. Decide whether there is a *real doubt* as to which of the opposing constructions embodies Parliament's intention. {For the concept of 'real doubt' see s 3 of this Code.} If there is no real doubt that a particular construction of the enactment embodies the legislator's intention, that construction is to be followed. Otherwise it is necessary to proceed further.

10. Diagnose the cause of the doubt. {Causes of doubt are dealt with in s 85 of this Code.}

11. If necessary, work out a *selective comminution* of the enactment under enquiry. {For selective comminution see s 74 of this Code.}

12. Check the comminution against the relevant facts of the instant case.

13. Work out an *interstitial articulation* for each of the opposing constructions. {Interstitial articulation is described in ss 112 to 114 of this Code.}

14. Identify the relevant *interpretative criteria*. {The concept of the interpretative criterion is explained in s 115 of this Code. The various criteria are set out in Part VI.}

15. Assemble from the relevant interpretative criteria, by applying the criteria to the text of the enactment and the relevant facts of the instant case, the *interpretative factors*

855

that bear on the point of interpretation in question. {Interpretative factors are explained in Part VII of this Code.}

16. Devise the arguments that support the factors in your favour and undermine those of your opponent.

In court

17. Hand copies of the comminution to the court and your opponent, making clear that it consists only of the actual wording of the enactment (subject to any necessary 'carpentry'). {As to briefs to the court see s 263 of this Code.}

18. Explain the point of interpretation to the court by reference to the numbered clauses of the comminution.

19. Hand copies of the two articulations to the court and your opponent, making clear that they consist of the actual wording of the enactment elaborated as might have been done by the draftsman if he had desired to determine the point at issue by express words.

20. Present the arguments to the court, which, after hearing your opponent, will determine which of the opposing constructions (as articulated) is supported by the heavier weight of interpretative factors.

{For a worked example see Example 162.1.}

APPENDIX B

Checklist of interpretative criteria

The following is offered as a checklist for use when resolving a problem of statutory interpretation. To locate the description of a particular item consult the index.

Preliminary questions

What is the relevant enactment?

Is the enactment in a consolidation Act?

Is the enactment in a codifying Act?

Does the enactment extend to the territory in question?

Does the enactment apply to the person or matter in question?

Does the doctrine of Crown immunity apply?

Has the enactment come into force?

Has the enactment been expressly or impliedly repealed?

Has the enactment expired?

Has the enactment ceased to be enforced?

Has the enactment been expressly or impliedly amended?

Is the enactment the subject of an extra-statutory concession?

Is the enactment subject to transitional provisions?

Is the enactment retrospective?

Is there any doubt as to the validity of the enactment?

Is the drafting precise or disorganised?

Have sub-rules been produced by judicial or other processing?

What is the statutory or judicial factual outline?

What are the material facts of the instant case?

What is the legal thrust of the enactment?

Does the doubt concern the factual outline, or the legal thrust, or both?

Is the doubt 'real'?

What was the legislator's purpose or object?

What was the legislator's motive?

What was the legislator's intention?

Is the enactment ambiguous in relation to the facts?

Is there semantic obscurity, and if so what is the 'corrected version'?

Appendix B: *Checklist of interpretative criteria*

Does the enactment require a strained construction?

What are the opposing constructions of the enactment?

Possible guides to legal meaning of the enactment

The juridical nature of the enactment.

Surrounding information required for an *informed* interpretation (subject to need to minimize unpredictability and lengthening of proceedings), including: pre-enacting history, enacting history, post-enacting history.

Implications arising from the express words of the enactment.

The 'plain' meaning of the enactment (if it has one).

The rule that, where there is no 'plain' meaning, the legal meaning is to be ascertained by weighing and balancing the relevant interpretative factors as they apply to the opposing constructions of the enactment.

Common sense.

A descriptive component (such as a sidenote or heading) of the Act or instrument containing the enactment.

A rule or definition laid down by the Interpretation Act 1978 or some other statutory provision.

Legal (or public) policy.

The principle against doubtful penalization.

Rules as to standard of proof (whether civil or criminal).

The principle that law should serve the public interest.

The principle that law should be just.

The principle that law should not operate retrospectively.

The principle that law should be certain and predictable.

The principle that law should be coherent and self-consistent.

The principle that law should not be subject to casual change.

The principle that the common law is said to be in a favoured position in relation to statute law.

The principle that municipal law should conform to public international law.

The presumption that the text is intended to be the primary indication of intention.

The presumption that an Act is normally intended to be given its literal meaning.

The presumption that the court is intended to have regard to the respective consequences of the opposing constructions.

The presumption that the court is intended to apply the remedy provided for the 'mischief'.

The presumption that the court is intended to apply a purposive construction.

The presumption that the court is intended to rectify drafting errors where this is required to carry out the overall legislative intention.

The presumption that the court is intended to avoid an unworkable or impractical result.

The presumption that the court is intended to avoid an inconvenient result.

The presumption that the court is intended to avoid an anomalous or illogical result.

The presumption that the court is intended to avoid a futile or pointless result.

The presumption that the court is intended to avoid an artificial result.

The presumption that the court is intended to avoid creating a disproportionate counter-mischief.

The presumption that the court is intended to adopt a construction which will not permit evasion of the enactment.

The presumption that the court is intended to apply ancillary rules and maxims of law, and have regard to implications arising from them.

The presumption that the court is intended to apply an updating construction where this is required to carry out the legislative intention.

The maxim *cessante ratione legis, cessat ipsa lex.*

The maxim *communis error facit jus.*

The canon that an enactment is to be construed by use of deductive reasoning.

The canon that an Act or other instrument is to be read as a whole.

The canon that each word is to be given a meaning (subject to the possiblity that it is inserted *ex abundanti cautela*).

The canon that the same words are to be given the same meaning.

The canon that different words are to be given different meanings.

The maxim *generalibus specialia derogant.*

The maxim *generalia specialibus non derogant.*

The *noscitur a sociis* principle.

The *ejusdem generis* principle.

The rank principle.

The *reddendo singula singulis* principle.

The maxim *expressum facit cessare tacitum.*

The *expressio unius* principle.

Other linguistic canons, such as those relating to technical terms.

APPENDIX C

List of Terms

Note The following are defined or explained in the Code or Commentary, or in the Interpretation Act 1978 (set out in Appendix D). The numbers indicate the pages on which the terms are referred to. In many cases more extensive references will be found in the Index.

Appendix C: List of Terms

Updated text of Interpretation Act 1978 (c 30)

An Act to consolidate the Interpretation Act 1889 and certain other enactments relating to the construction and operation of Acts of Parliament and other instruments, with amendments to give effect to recommendations of the Law Commission and the Scottish Law Commission.

[20 July 1978]

General provisions as to enactment and operation

1 Words of enactment Every section of an Act takes effect as a substantive enactment without introductory words.

Annotations
This section derived from the Interpretation Act 1889 s 8.

2 Amendment or repeal in same Session Any Act may be amended or repealed in the Session of Parliament in which it is passed.

Annotations
This section derived from the Interpretation Act 1889 s 10.

3 Judicial notice Every Act is a public Act to be judicially noticed as such, unless the contrary is expressly provided by the Act.

Annotations
This section derived from the Interpretation Act 1889 s 9.

4 Time of commencement An Act or provision of an Act comes into force—
  (a) where provision is made for it to come into force on a particular day, at the beginning of that day;
  (b) where no provision is made for its coming into force, at the beginning of the day on which the Act receives the Royal Assent.

Annotations
This section derived from the Acts of Parliament (Commencement) Act 1793 and the Interpretation Act 1889 s 36(2).

Interpretation and construction

5 Definitions In any Act, unless the contrary intention appears, words and expressions listed in Schedule 1 to this Act are to be construed according to that Schedule.

6 Gender and number In any Act, unless the contrary intention appears,—
  (a) words importing the masculine gender include the feminine;
  (b) words importing the feminine gender include the masculine;

865

(c) words in the singular include the plural and words in the plural include the singular.

Annotations
This section derived from the Interpretation Act 1889 s 1(1).

7 References to service by post   Where an Act authorises or requires any document to be served by post (whether the expression 'serve' or the expression 'give' or 'send' or any other expression is used) then, unless the contrary intention appears, the service is deemed to be effected by properly addressing, pre-paying and posting a letter containing the document and, unless the contrary is proved, to have been effected at the time at which the letter would be delivered in the ordinary course of post.

Annotations
This section derived from the Interpretation Act 1889 s 26.

8 References to distance   In the measurement of any distance for the purposes of an Act, that distance shall, unless the contrary intention appears, be measured in a straight line on a horizontal plane.

Annotations
This section derived from the Interpretation Act 1889 s 34.

9 References to time of day   Subject to section 3 of the Summer Time Act 1972 (construction of references to points of time during the period of summer time), whenever an expression of time occurs in an Act, the time referred to shall, unless it is otherwise specifically stated, be held to be Greenwich mean time.

Annotations
This section derived from the Statutes (Definition of Time) Act 1880 s 1.

10 References to the Sovereign   In any Act a reference to the Sovereign reigning at the time of the passing of the Act is to be construed, unless the contrary intention appears, as a reference to the Sovereign for the time being.

Annotations
This section derived from the Interpretation Act 1889 s 30.

11 Construction of subordinate legislation   Where an Act confers power to make subordinate legislation, expressions used in that legislation have, unless the contrary intention appears, the meaning which they bear in the Act.

Annotations
This section derived from the Interpretation Act 1889 s 31.

Statutory powers and duties

12 Continuity of powers and duties   (1) Where an Act confers a power or imposes a duty it is implied, unless the contrary intention appears, that the power may be exercised, or the duty is to be performed, from time to time as occasion requires.

(2) Where an Act confers a power or imposes a duty on the holder of an office as such, it is implied, unless the contrary intention appears, that the power may be exercised, or the duty is to be performed, by the holder for the time being of the office.

Annotations
This section derived from the Interpretation Act 1889 s 32(1), (2).

13 Anticipatory exercise of powers   Where an Act which (or any provision of which) does not come into force immediately on its passing confers power to make subordinate legislation, or to make appointments, give notices, prescribe forms or do any other thing for the purposes of the Act, then, unless the contrary intention appears, the power may be exercised, and any instrument made thereunder may be made so as to come into force, at any time after the passing of the Act so far as may be necessary or expedient for the purpose—
  (a) of bringing the Act or any provision of the Act into force; or
  (b) of giving full effect to the Act or any such provision at or after the time when it comes into force.

Annotations
This section derived from the Interpretation Act 1889 s 37.

14 Implied power to amend   Where an Act confers power to make—
  (a) rules, regulations or byelaws; or
  (b) Orders in Council, orders or other subordinate legislation to be made by statutory instrument,
it implies, unless the contrary intention appears, a power, exercisable in the same manner and subject to the same conditions or limitations, to revoke, amend or re-enact any instrument made under the power.

Annotations
This section derived from the Interpretation Act 1889 s 32(3).

Repealing enactments

15 Repeal of repeal   Where an Act repeals a repealing enactment, the repeal does not revive any enactment previously repealed unless words are added reviving it.

Annotations
This section derived from the Interpretation Act 1889 s11(1).

16 General savings   (1) Without prejudice to section 15, where an Act repeals an enactment, the repeal does not, unless the contrary intention appears,—
  (a) revive anything not in force or existing at the time at which the repeal takes effect;
  (b) affect the previous operation of the enactment repealed or anything duly done or suffered under that enactment;
  (c) affect any right, privilege, obligation or liability acquired, accrued or incurred under that enactment;
  (d) affect any penalty, forfeiture or punishment incurred in respect of any offence committed against that enactment;
  (e) affect any investigation, legal proceeding or remedy in respect of any such right, privilege, obligation, liability, penalty, forfeiture or punishment;
and any such investigation, legal proceeding or remedy may be instituted, continued or enforced, and any such penalty, forfeiture or punishment may be imposed, as if the repealing Act had not been passed.
  (2) This section applies to the expiry of a temporary enactment as if it were repealed by an Act.

Annotations
Sub-s (1) derived from the Interpretation Act 1889 s 38(2).

17 Repeal and re-enactment (1) Where an Act repeals a previous enactment and substitutes provisions for the enactment repealed, the repealed enactment remains in force until the substituted provisions come into force.

(2) Where an Act repeals and re-enacts, with or without modification, a previous enactment then, unless the contrary intention appears,—

(a) any reference in any other enactment to the enactment so repealed shall be construed as a reference to the provision re-enacted;

(b) in so far as any subordinate legislation made or other thing done under the enactment so repealed, or having effect as if so made or done, could have been made or done under the provision re-enacted, it shall have effect as if made or done under that provision.

Annotations
This section derived from the Interpretation Act 1889 ss 11(2), 38(1).

Miscellaneous

18 Duplicated offences Where an act or omission constitutes an offence under two or more Acts, or both under an Act and at common law, the offender shall, unless the contrary intention appears, be liable to be prosecuted and punished under either or any of those Acts or at common law, but shall not be liable to be punished more than once for the same offence.

Annotations
This section derived from the Interpretation Act 1889 s 33.

19 Citation of other Acts (1) Where an Act cites another Act by year, statute, session or chapter, or a section or other portion of another Act by number or letter, the reference shall, unless the contrary intention appears, be read as referring—

(a) in the case of Acts included in any revised edition of the statutes printed by authority, to that edition;

(b) in the case of Acts not so included but included in the edition prepared under the direction of the Record Commission, to that edition;

(c) in any other case, to the Acts printed by the Queen's Printer, or under the superintendence or authority of Her Majesty's Stationery Office.

(2) An Act may continue to be cited by the short title authorised by any enactment notwithstanding the repeal of that enactment.

Annotations
Sub-s (1) derived from the Interpretation Act 1889 s 35(2); sub-s (2) derived from the Short Titles Act 1896 s 3.

20 References to other enactments (1) Where an Act describes or cites a portion of an enactment by referring to words, sections or other parts from or to which (or from and to which) the portion extends, the portion described or cited includes the words, sections or other parts referred to unless the contrary intention appears.

(2) Where an Act refers to an enactment, the reference, unless the contrary intention appears, is a reference to that enactment as amended, and includes a reference thereto as extended or applied, by or under any other enactment, including any other provision of that Act.

Annotations
Sub-s (1) derived from the Interpretation Act 1889 ss 31, 37, 39.

Supplementary

21 Interpretation etc (1) In this Act 'Act' includes a local and personal or private Act; and 'subordinate legislation' means Orders in Council, orders, rules, regulations, schemes, warrants, byelaws and other instruments made or to be made under any Act.

(2) This Act binds the Crown.

Annotations
This section derived from the Interpretation Act 1889 ss 30, 31, 37, 39.

22 Application to Acts and Measures (1) This Act applies to itself, to any Act passed after the commencement of this Act and, to the extent specified in Part I of Schedule 1, to Acts passed before the commencement of this Act.

(2) In any of the foregoing provisions of this Act a reference to an Act is a reference to an Act to which that provision applies; but this does not affect the generality of references to enactments or of the references in section 19 (1) to other Acts.

(3) This Act applies to Measures of the General Synod of the Church of England (and, so far as it relates to Acts passed before the commencement of this Act, to Measures of the Church Assembly passed after 28th May 1925) as it applies to Acts.

Annotations
Sub-s (3) derived from the Interpretation Measure 1925 s 1.

23 Application to other instruments (1) The provisions of this Act, except sections 1 to 3 and 4 (b), apply, so far as applicable and unless the contrary intention appears, to subordinate legislation made after the commencement of this Act and, to the extent specified in Part II of Schedule 2, to subordinate legislation made before the commencement of this Act, as they apply to Acts.

(2) In the application of this Act to Acts passed or subordinate legislation made after the commencement of this Act, all references to an enactment include an enactment comprised in subordinate legislation whenever made, and references to the passing or repeal of an enactment are to be construed accordingly.

(3) Sections 9 and 19(1) also apply to deeds and other instruments and documents as they apply to Acts and subordinate legislation; and in the application of section 17(2)(a) to Acts passed or subordinate legislation made after the commencement of this Act, the reference to any other enactment includes any deed or other instrument or document.

(4) Subsections (1) and (2) of this section do not apply to Orders in Council made under section 5 of the Statutory Instruments Act 1946, section 1 (3) of the Northern Ireland (Temporary Provisions) Act 1972 or Schedule 1 to the Northern Ireland Act 1974.

24 Application to Northern Ireland (1) This Act extends to Northern Ireland so far as it applies to Acts or subordinate legislation which so extend.

(2) In the application of this Act to Acts passed or subordinate legislation made after the commencement of this Act, all references to an enactment include an enactment comprised in Northern Ireland legislation whenever passed or made; and in relation to such legislation references to the passing or repeal of an enactment include the making or revocation of an Order in Council.

(3) In the application of section 14 to Acts passed after the commencement of this Act which extend to Northern Ireland, 'statutory instrument' includes statutory rule for the purposes of the {Statutory Rules Northern Ireland Order 1979}.

(4) The following definitions contained in Schedule 1, namely those of—
. . .;
The Communities and related expressions;
The Corporation Tax Acts;
The Income Tax Acts;
The Tax Acts,

apply unless the contrary intention appears, to Northern Ireland legislation as they apply to Acts.

(5) In this section 'Northern Ireland legislation' means—

(a) Acts of the Parliament of Ireland;

(b) Acts of the Parliament of Northern Ireland;

(c) Orders in Council under section 1(3) of the Northern Ireland (Temporary Provisions) Act 1972;

(d) Measures of the Northern Ireland Assembly; and

(e) Orders in Council under Schedule 1 to the Northern Ireland Act 1974.

Annotations

Sub-s (3): amended by the Statutory Rules (Northern Ireland) Order 1979 (SI 1979/1573) art 11(1), Sch 4 para 25.

Sub-s (4): words omitted repealed by the British Nationality Act 1981 s 52(8), Sch 9.

25 Repeals and savings (1) The enactments described in Schedule 3 are repealed to the extent specified in the third column of that Schedule.

(2) Without prejudice to section 17(2)(a), a reference to the Interpretation Act 1889, to any provision of that Act or to any other enactment repealed by this Act, whether occurring in another Act, in subordinate legislation, in Northern Ireland legislation or in any deed or other instrument or document, shall be construed as referring to this Act, or to the corresponding provision of this Act, as it applies to Acts passed at the time of the reference.

(3) The provisions of this Act relating to Acts passed after any particular time do not affect the construction of Acts passed before that time, though continued or amended by Acts passed thereafter.

Annotations

Sub-s (3) derived from the Interpretation Act 1889 s 40.

26 Commencement This Act shall come into force on 1st January 1979.

27 Short title This Act may be cited as the Interpretation Act 1978.

SCHEDULE 1: WORDS AND EXPRESSIONS DEFINED (s 5)

Note: The years or dates which follow certain entries in this Schedule are relevant for the purposes of paragraph 4 of Schedule 2 (application to existing enactments).

Definitions

'Associated state' means a territory maintaining a status of association with the United Kingdom in accordance with the West Indies Act 1967. (16th February 1967)

'Bank of England' means, as the context requires, the Governor and Company of the Bank of England or the bank of the Governor and Company of the Bank of England.

'Bank of Ireland' means, as the context requires, the Governor and Company of the Bank of Ireland or the bank of the Governor and Company of the Bank of Ireland.

'British Islands' means the United Kingdom, the Channel Islands and the Isle of Man. (1889)

'British possession' means any part of Her Majesty's dominions outside the United Kingdom; and where parts of such dominions are under both a central and a local legislature, all parts under the central legislature are deemed, for the purposes of this definition, to be one British possession. (1889)

. . .

'Building regulations', in relation to England and Wales, means regulations made under section 61(1) of the Public Health Act 1936.

'Central funds', in an enactment providing in relation to England and Wales for the payment of costs out of central funds, means money provided by Parliament.

'Charity Commissioners' means the Charity Commissioners for England and Wales referred to in section 1 of the Charities Act 1960.

'Church Commissioners' means the Commissioners constituted by the Church Commissioners Measure 1947.

'Colonial legislature', and 'legislature' in relation to a British possession, mean the authority, other than the Parliament of the United Kingdom or Her Majesty in Council, competent to make laws for the possession. (1889)

'Colony' means any part of Her Majesty's dominions outside the British Islands except—

(a) countries having fully responsible status within the Commonwealth;

(b) territories for whose external relations a country other than the United Kingdom is responsible;

(c) associated states;

and where parts of such dominions are under both a central and a local legislature, all parts under the central legislature are deemed for the purposes of this definition to be one colony. (1889)

'Commencement', in relation to an Act or enactment, means the time when the Act or enactment comes into force.

'Committed for trial' means—

(a) in relation to England and Wales, committed in custody or on bail by a magistrates' court pursuant to {section 6 of the Magistrates' Courts Act 1980} or by any judge or other authority having power to do so, with a view to trial before a judge and jury; (1889)

(b) in relation to Northern Ireland, committed in custody or on bail by a magistrates' court pursuant to {Article 37 of the Magistrates' Courts (Northern Ireland) Order 1981}, or by a court, judge, resident magistrate, justice of the peace or other authority having power to do so, with a view to trial on indictment. (1st January 1979)

'The Communities', 'the Treaties' or 'the Community Treaties' and other expressions defined by section 1 of and Schedule 1 to the European Communities Act 1972 have the meanings prescribed by that Act.

'Comptroller and Auditor General' means the Comptroller-General of the receipt and issue of Her Majesty's Exchequer and Auditor-General of Public Accounts appointed in pursuance of the Exchequer and Audit Departments Act 1866.

'Consular officer' has the meaning assigned by Article 1 of the Vienna Convention set out in Schedule 1 to the Consular Relations Act 1968.

'The Corporation Tax Acts' means—

(a) Parts X and XI of the Income and Corporation Taxes Act 1970;

(b) all other provisions of that or any other Act relating to corporation tax or to any other matter dealt with in Part X or Part XI of that Act;

(c) all the provisions of Part IV of the Finance Act 1965 and of any other enactment which, at the passing of the said Act of 1970, formed part of or was to be construed with the Corporation Tax Acts.

'County court' means—

(a) in relation to England and Wales, a court held for a district under the {County Courts Act 1984}; (1846)

(b) in relation to Northern Ireland, a court held for a division under the County Courts {(Northern Ireland) Order 1980}. (1889)

'Court of Appeal' means—

(a) in relation to England and Wales, Her Majesty's Court of Apeal in England;

(b) in relation to Northern Ireland, Her Majesty's Court of Appeal in Northern Ireland.

'Court of summary jurisdiction', 'summary conviction' and 'Summary Jurisdiction

Acts', in relation to Northern Ireland, have the same meanings as in Measures of the Northern Ireland Assembly and Acts of the Parliament of Northern Ireland.

'Crown Court' means—

(a) in relation to England and Wales, the Crown Court constituted by section 4 of the Courts Act 1971;

(b) in relation to Northern Ireland, the Crown Court constituted by section 4 of the Judicature (Northern Ireland) Act 1978.

'Crown Estate Commissioners' means the Commissioners referred to in section 1 of the Crown Estate Act 1961.

'England' means, subject to any alteration of boundaries under Part IV of the Local Government Act 1972, the area consisting of the counties established by section 1 of that Act, Greater London and the Isles of Scilly. (1st April 1974)

'Financial year' means, in relation to matters relating to the Consolidated Fund, the National Loans Fund, or moneys provided by Parliament, or to the Exchequer or to central taxes or finance, the twelve months ending with 31st March. (1889)

'Governor-General' includes any person who for the time being has the powers of the Governor-General, and 'Governor', in relation to any British possession, includes the officer for the time being administering the government of that possession. (1889)

'High Court' means—

(a) in relation to England and Wales, Her Majesty's High Court of Justice in England;

(b) in relation to Northern Ireland, Her Majesty's High Court of Justice in Northern Ireland.

'The Income Tax Acts' means all enactments relating to income tax, including any provisions of the Corporation Tax Acts which relate to income tax.

'Land' includes buildings and other structures, land covered with water, and any estate, interest, easement, servitude or right in or over land. (1st January 1979)

'Lands Clauses Acts' means—

(a) in relation to England and Wales, the Lands Clauses Consolidation Act 1845 and the Lands Clauses Consolidation Acts Amendment Act 1860, and any Acts for the time being in force amending those Acts; (1889)

(b) (applies to Scotland);

(c) in relation to Northern Ireland, the enactments defined as such by section 46(1) of the Interpretation Act (Northern Ireland) 1954. (1889)

'Local land charges register', in relation to England and Wales, means a register kept pursuant to section 3 of the Local Land Charges Act 1975, and 'the appropriate local land charges register' has the meaning assigned by section 4 of that Act.

'London borough' means a borough described in Schedule 1 to the London Government Act 1963, 'inner London borough' means one of the boroughs so described and numbered from 1 to 12 and 'outer London borough' means one of the boroughs so described and numbered from 13 to 32, subject (in each case) to any alterations made under Part IV of the Local Government Act 1972.

'Lord Chancellor' means the Lord High Chancellor of Great Britain.

'Magistrates' court' has the meaning assigned to it—

(a) in relation to England and Wales, by {section 148 of the Magistrates' Courts Act 1980};

(b) in relation to Northern Ireland, by {Article 2(2) of the Magistrates' Courts (Northern Ireland) Order 1981}.

'Month' means calendar month. (1850)

'National Debt Commissioners' means the Commissioners for the Reduction of the National Debt.

'Northern Ireland legislation' has the meaning assigned by section 24(5) of this Act. (1st January 1979)

'Oath' and 'affidavit' include affirmation and declaration, and 'swear' includes affirm and declare.

'Ordnance Map' means a map made under powers conferred by the Ordnance Survey Act 1841 or the Boundary Survey (Ireland) Act 1854.

'Parliamentary Election' means the election of a Member to serve in Parliament for a constituency. (1889)

'Person' includes a body of persons corporate or unincorporate. (1889)

'Police area', 'police authority' and other expressions relating to the police have the meaning or effect described—

(a) in relation to England and Wales, by section 62 of the Police Act 1964;

(b) . . .

'The Privy Council' means the Lords and others of Her Majesty's Most Honourable Privy Council.

{'Registered' in relation to nurses, midwives and health visitors, means registered in the register maintained by the United Kingdom Central Council for Nursing, Midwifery and Health Visiting by virtue of qualifications in nursing, midwifery or health visiting, as the case may be.}

'Registered medical practitioner' means a fully registered person within the meaning of {the Medical Act 1983}. (1st January 1979)

'Rules of Court' in relation to any court means rules made by the authority having power to make rules or orders regulating the practice and procedure of that court, and in Scotland includes Acts of Adjournal and Acts of Sederunt; and the power of the authority to make rules of court (as above defined includes power to make such rules for the purpose of any Act which directs or authorises anything to be done by rules of court. (1889)

'Secretary of State' means one of Her Majesty's Principal Secretaries of State.

. . .

'Statutory declaration' means a declaration made by virtue of the Statutory Declarations Act 1835.

'Supreme Court' means—

(a) in relation to England and Wales, the Court of Appeal and the High Court together with the Crown Court;

(b) in relation to Northern Ireland, the Supreme Court of Judicature of Northern Ireland.

'The Tax Acts' means the Income and Corporation Taxes Act 1970 and all other provisions of the Income Tax Acts and the Corporation Tax Acts. (12th March 1970)

'The Treasury' means the Commissioners of Her Majesty's Treasury.

'United Kingdom' means Great Britain and Northern Ireland. (12th April 1927)

'Wales' means, subject to any alteration of boundaries made under Part IV of the Local Government Act 1972, the area consisting of the counties established by section 20 of that Act. (1st April 1974)

'Water authority', in relation to England and Wales, means an authority established in accordance with section 2 of the Water Act 1973; and 'water authority area', in relation to any functions of such an authority, means the area in respect of which the water authority are for the time being to exercise those functions.

'Writing' includes typing, printing, lithography, photography and other modes of representing or reproducing words in a visible form, and expressions referring to writing are construed accordingly.

Construction of certain expressions relating to children.

In relation to England and Wales the following expressions and references, namely—

(a) the expression 'the parental rights and duties';

(b) the expression 'legal custody' in relation to a child (as defined in the Children Act 1975); and

(c) any reference to the person with whom a child (as so defined) has his home,

are to be construed in accordance with Part IV of that Act. (12th November 1975)

Construction of certain expressions relating to offences.

In relation to England and Wales—

    (a) 'indictable offence' means an offence which, if committed by an adult, is triable on indictment, whether it is exclusively so triable or triable either way;

    (b) 'summary offence' means an offence which, if committed by an adult, is triable only summarily;

    (c) 'offence triable either way' means an offence which, if committed by an adult, is triable either on indictment or summarily;

and the terms 'indictable', 'summary' and 'triable either way', in their application to offences, are to be construed accordingly.

In the above definitions references to the way or ways in which an offence is triable are to be construed without regard to the effect, if any, of {section 22 of the Magistrates' Courts Act 1980} on the mode of trial in a particular case.

Annotations

This Schedule derived from the British Nationality Act 1948 s 1(1), (2); the Costs in Criminal Cases Act 1973 s 13(1); the Courts Act 1971 s 1(1); the Criminal Law Act 1977 s 64; the European Communities Act 1972 s 1(2); the Income and Corporation Taxes Act 1970 s 526(1)(a), (b), (2); the Interpretation Act 1889 ss 2(1), 3, 6, 12(1), (3), (5), (12), (14)–(20), 13(1)–(3), (11), 14, 15(4), 17(1), 18(1)–(3), (6), (7), 19–23, 25, 27, 36(1); the Interpretation Act (Northern Ireland) 1954 s 46(1); the Judicature (Northern Ireland) Act 1978 s 41; the Local Government Act 1972 s 269; the Local Land Charges Act 1975 s 4; the London Government Act 1963 s1(1), (6); the Magistrates' Courts Act 1952 s 124; the Magistrates' Courts (Northern Ireland) Act 1964 s 1; the Medical Act 1978 s 31(1), Sch 6 para 48(b); the Northern Ireland Act 1962 s 27; the Police Act 1964 s 62; the Public Health Act 1936 s 61(1); the Revenue Act 1884 s 14; the Royal and Parliamentary Titles Act 1927 s 2(2); the Water Act 1973 s 2(3); the West Indies Act 1967 s 1(3).

Words omitted apply to Scotland only; definition 'British subject' and 'Commonwealth citizen' repealed by the British Nationality Act 1981 s 52(8), Sch 9; definitions 'committed for trial' and 'Magistrates' court' amended by the Magistrates' Courts Act 1980 s 154, Sch 7 para 169 and the Magistrates' Courts (Northern Ireland) Order 1981 (SI 1981/1675) art 170(2), Sch 6 Part I, para 56; definition 'County Court' amended by the County Courts Act 1984 s 148(1) and Sch 2 and the County Courts (Northern Ireland) Order 1980 (SI 1980/397) art 68(2), Sch 1, Part II; definition 'Registered' added by the Nurses, Midwives and Health Visitors Act 1979 s 23(4), Sch 7, para 30; final amendment made by the Magistrates' Courts Act 1980 s 154, Sch 7; definition 'Registered medical practitioner' amended by the Medical Act 1983 Sch 5, para 18.

SCHEDULE 2: APPLICATION OF ACT TO EXISTING ENACTMENTS
(ss 22, 23)

Part I Acts

1. The following provisions of this Act apply to Acts whenever passed:—

Section 6(a) and (c) so far as applicable to enactments relating to offences punishable on indictment or on summary conviction

    Section 9

    Section 10

    Section 11 so far as it relates to subordinate legislation made after the year 1889

    Section 18

    Section 19(2).

2. The following apply to Acts passed after the year 1850:—

    Section 1

    Section 2

    Section 3

    Section 6(a) and (c) so far as not applicable to such Acts by virtue of paragraph 1

    Section 15

    Section 17(1).

3. The following apply to Acts passed after the year 1980:—

    Section 4

    Section 7

Section 8
Section 12
Section 13
Section 14 so far as it relates to rules, regulations or byelaws
Section 16(1)
Section 17(2)(a)
Section 19(1)
Section 20(1).

4. (1) Subject to the following provisions of this paragraph—
  (a) paragraphs of Schedule 1 at the end of which a year or date earlier than the commencement of this Act is specified apply, so far as appllicable, to Acts passed on or after the date, or after the year, so specified; and
  (b) paragraphs of that Schedule at the end of which no year or date is specified apply, so far as applicable, to Acts passed at any time.

(2) The definition of 'British Islands', in its application to Acts passed after the establishment of the Irish Free State but before the commencement of this Act, includes the Republic of Ireland.

(3) The definition of 'colony', in its application to an Act passed at any time before the commencement of this Act, includes—
  (a) any colony within the meaning of section 18(3) of the Interpretation Act 1889 which was excluded, but in relation only to Acts passed at a later time, by any enactment repealed by this Act;
  (b) any country or territory which ceased after that time to be part of Her Majesty's dominions but subject to a provision for the continuation of existing law as if it had not so ceased;
and paragraph (b) of the definition does not apply.

(4) The definition of 'Lord Chancellor' does not apply to Acts passed before 1st October 1921 in which that expression was used in relation to Ireland only.

(5) The definition of 'person', so far as it includes bodies corporate, applies to any provision of an Act whenever passed relating to an offence punishable on indictment or on summary conviction.

(6) This paragraph applies to the National Health Service Reorganisation Act 1973 and the Water Act 1973 as if they were passed after 1st April 1974.

5. The following definitions shall be treated as included in Schedule 1 for the purposes specified in this paragraph—
  (a) in any Act passed before 1st April 1974, a reference to England includes Berwick upon Tweed and Monmouthshire and, in the case of an Act passed before the Welsh Language Act 1967, Wales;
  (b) in any Act passed before the commencement of this Act and after the year 1850, 'land' includes messuages, tenements and hereditaments, houses and buildings of any tenure;
  (c) . . .

Annotations
This Schedule derived from the Wales and Berwick Act 1746 s 3; the Interpretation Act 1889 ss 1(2), 2(1), 3, 12(1), 18(3); the Irish Free State (Consequential Adaptation of Enactments) Order 1923 (SR & O 1923/405) art 2, Schedule; the National Health Service Reorganisation Act 1973 s 55(2) and the Water Act 1973 s 38(2).
Words omitted apply to Scotland only.

Part II Subordinate Legislation
6. Sections 4(a), 9 and 19(1), and so much of Schedule 1 as defines the following expressions, namely—
British subject and Commonwealth citizen;
England;

Local land charges register and appropriate local land charges register;
. . .
United Kingdom;
Wales,

apply to subordinate legislation made at any time before the commencement of this Act as they apply to Acts passed at that time.

7. The definition in Schedule 1 of 'county court', in relation to England and Wales, applies to Orders in Council made after the year 1846.

Annotations
Para 7 derived from the Interpretation Act 1889 s 6.
  Words omitted apply to Scotland only.

White Paper on Interpretation Act 1978

1. Under section 36(2) of the Interpretation Act 1889 an Act which is expressed to come into operation on a particular day is to be construed as coming into operation 'immediately on the expiration of the previous day'. Under the Acts of Parliament (Commencement) Act 1793 an Act which makes no provision for its commencement comes into force 'on' the date endorsed as the date of Royal Assent. In that case, the Act has effect from the first moment of the day of Royal Assent (*Tomlinson v Bullock* (1879) 4 QBD 230).

A. There is no practical distinction for purposes of commencement between the beginning of one day and the end of the previous day, and we recommend that in reproducing the above enactments the moment of commencement should be expressed as the beginning of the relevant day, whether appointed by the Act or depending on the date of Royal Assent.

B. Subsection (2) of section 36 has also become technically defective in the light of two modern developments in the field of commencement. It is common practice for different provisions of the same Act to be brought into force on different dates and for the date (or dates) of commencement to be fixed by order made under the Act, rather than by the Act itself. There is no room for a different rule as to the moment of commencement in such cases, and we recommend that in reproducing section 36 (2) they should be treated in the same way as the case where a whole Act is expressed to come into operation on a day specified in the Act.

Effect is given to the above recommendations in clause 4 of the draft Bill.

2. Section 1(1) of the Interpretation Act 1889 directs that unless the contrary intention appears in an Act passed after 1850—

(a) words importing the masculine gender shall include females; and
(b) words in the singular shall include the plural, and words in the plural shall include the singular.

This provision was derived from the first sentence of section 4 of Lord Brougham's Act of 1850 (13 Vict c 21) which was to the same effect, and has probably contributed more than any other single enactment to the declared objective of Lord Brougham's Act ('An Act for shortening the language of Acts of Parliament'). The contribution would have been little if any greater if the gender rule had been drawn so as to operate both ways, as in section 61 of the Law of Property Act 1925 (c 20) (construction of deeds, contracts, wills, orders and other instruments). It has however been represented to us that there are legislative contexts (such as nursing and consent to adoption) where the feminine pronoun might with advantage be used to include the masculine, instead of vice versa. It is occasionally so used without the benefit of section 1(1) of the Interpretation Act 1889, as in the following passage in section 36(1) of the Finance Act 1977 (c 36)—

'living accommodation is job-related for a person if it is provided for him by reason of his employment, or for his spouse by reason of hers'.

Appendix E: *White Paper on Interpretation Act 1978*

In this passage 'him' and 'his' include 'her' and 'hers' by virtue of section 1(1): but common sense alone requires the final 'hers' to be read as 'his' where the person whose accommodation is in question is a married woman.

We recommend that in reproducing 1889 section 1(1) the rule should be made to operate both ways. Effect is given to this recommendation in clause 6 of the draft Bill.

3. The text of section 37 of the Interpretation Act 1889 is as follows—

'37. Where an Act passed after the commencement of this Act is not to come into operation immediately on the passing thereof, and confers power to make any appointment, to make, grant, or issue any instrument, that is to say, any Order in Council, order, warrant, scheme, letters patent, rules, regulations, or byelaws, to give notices, to prescribe forms, or to do any other thing for the purposes of the Act, that power may, unless the contrary intention appears, be exercised at any time after the passing of the Act, so far as may be necessary or expedient for the purpose of bringing the Act into operation at the date of the commencement thereof, subject to this restriction, that any instrument made under the power shall not, unless the contrary intention appears in the Act, or the contrary is necessary for bringing the Act into operation, come into operation until the Act comes into operation.'

The section has been expounded in *R v Minister of Town and Country Planning* [1951] 1 KB 1 and *Usher v Barlow* [1952] Ch. 255, which established that the word 'operation' is used in two senses, namely (1) commencement, and (2) effective working. The distinction is expressly drawn in clause 13 of the Bill. We recommend that the following additional amendments should be made in reproducing section 37.

A. As already mentioned, it is common practice for different provisions of an Act to be brought into force at different times. That situation is not expressly contemplated by section 37, but the principle of that section should apply whether it is a whole Act or a particular provision which is to be brought into 'operation'.

B. It has been represented to us that there are cases in which statutory powers have to be exercised before an Act or provision comes into force in order to secure the effective working of the Act or provision, not at the time when the Act or provision comes into force but at a subsequent but relatively early date. This is not warranted by section 37, which requires that the purpose must be to bring the Act into operation 'at the date of commencement thereof', but it is within the spirit of the section, and should be covered expressly.

C. Section 37 confers a limited power to do things in advance for the specified purpose of bringing the Act into operation, but subject to the 'restriction' that an instrument made under the power must not come into operation until the Act comes into operation unless that is necessary for the same purpose. We consider that the restriction is little more than a repetition in negative form of the limitation contained in the power itself, and could be omitted without detriment; and we recommend accordingly.

Effect is given to the above recommendations in clause 13 of the draft Bill.

4. Section 32(3) of the Interpretation Act 1889 provides that where an Act confers power to make 'rules, regulations or by-laws', the power (in the absence of a contrary intention) is to be construed as including power to rescind, revoke, amend or vary the rules, regulations or by-laws.

A. A power to amend or revoke is usually required for other kinds of subordinate legislation to be made under an Act, and the restriction of section 32(3) to rules, regulations and by-laws has led to a proliferation of *ad hoc* provisions authorising amendment and revocation of Orders in Council, Ministerial orders and other instruments. To take only one volume of recent statutes, such provisions are to be found in 1975 c 68 s 38(2) and (3); c 69 s 26 (2); c 70 s 28 (2); c 71 s 123(4); c 72 s 106(3); c 76 s 18(3); c 77 s 55(4) and c 78 s 13(6) and s 14(4). We consider that when section 32(3) is reproduced, it should be extended so as to dispense with the need for such *ad hoc* provisions in the future. On the other hand there are certain instruments made under

878

statutory powers for which a power to revoke or amend is unnecessary, and others for which such a power would be inappropriate. Two of the enactments mentioned above (1975 c 71 s 123(4) and c 77 s 53(4)) exclude particular orders from the power to revoke or amend. There are other instances, for example compulsory purchase orders, where power to revoke or amend is never conferred. Some selectivity is therefore required if section 32(3) is extended as we propose. The line is not easy to draw but we believe that it will be sufficient for practical purposes to exclude from the extended provision any subordinate legislation which is not made by statutory instrument.

Accordingly we recommend that the existing provision should be extended so as to cover, in addition to rules, regulations and by-laws, Orders in Council, orders and other types of subordinate legislation made by statutory instrument. With this limitation there should seldom be need for an express provision excluding the implied power to revoke or vary. Effect is given to this recommendation in clause 14 of the draft Bill, coupled with the definition of 'subordinate legislation' in clause 21(1) and clause 24(3).

B. In connection with section 32(3), it has been represented to us that there are certain cases in which it would be desirable to bring together in a single instrument the effects of a series of previous instruments without revoking the latter. This situation is no doubt rare, but we recommend that the opportunity should be taken to make it clear that collation as well as amendment and revocation is covered by the implied power. Effect is also given to this recommendation in clause 14.

5. Section 38(2) of the Interpretation Act 1889 contains a number of important saving provisions which are implied (subject to the contrary intention) where an Act repeals any other enactment. The common law rule was that when an Act is repealed it is treated as if it had never been enacted except as to matters and transactions past and closed; and the effect of section 38(2) is to modify that rule by preserving the previous operation of the repealed Act and rights and liabilities acquired or incurred under it. It is settled that the benefit of these savings is not confined to express repeals but extends to any enactment which abrogates or limits the effect of a previous enactment (*Moakes v Blackwell Colliery Co* [1925] 2 KB 64 at p 70).

The common law rule applies, and section 38(2) does not, where a temporary Act expires by effluxion of time. Accordingly *ad hoc* savings have been necessary in such Acts. The usual saving, e.g. section 17(3) of the Prevention of Terrorism (Temporary Provisions) Act 1976 (c 8), is to the effect that section 38(2) of the Interpretation Act is to apply on the expiration of the temporary Act as if it was then repealed by another Act. Temporary Acts are not a major feature of modern legislation, but we recommend that such savings should be generalised by extending section 38(2) to expirations. Effect is given to this recommendation in subsection (2) of clause 16 of the draft Bill.

6. Section 38(1) of the Interpretation Act 1889 provides that where an Act repeals any provisions of a former Act and re-enacts them with or without modification, references in 'any other Act' to the provisions so repealed are to be construed (unless the contrary intention appears) as references to the provisions so re-enacted.

A. The words 'any other Act' are ambiguous, and it is unsettled whether the translation operates upon internal references to the provisions repealed which occur in the Act containing those provisions. We recommend that this ambiguity should be resolved so as to include internal, as well as external, references to the repealed provisions. Effect is given to this recommendation in clause 17(2)(a) of the draft Bill.

Under clause 22(1) and paragraph 3 of Schedule 2, this restatement of section 38(1) will operate in relation to repeals and re-enactments effected by Acts passed after 1889. The change, if it is one, can safely be made retrospective to this extent. In so far as section 38(1) has been relied upon for the translation of 'internal' references, the restatement will give effect to the intention. In so far as the section has not been so relied upon, the restatement will (harmlessly) duplicate express translations effected by former Acts. What is inconceivable is that any former Act which intended *not* to translate internal (as opposed to external) references to provisions repealed and re-enacted would have relied for that purpose on the doubt whether section 38(1) applied to them. In such a case (if there ever was one) an express provision would have been necessary, and this would establish the contrary intention for the purposes of clause 17(2).

B. Section 38(1) is also defective in so far as the translation of references to the repealed enactment is confined to references which appear in other Acts. In practice the translation is equally required for references which appear in subordinate legislation or in documents which are not legislative in character. Accordingly section 38(1) is seldom if ever relied upon in Consolidation Acts. The normal practice is to include an express saving (without prejudice to the operation of section 38) to the following effect:

> 'Where any enactment or document refers . . . to any of the repealed enactments, the reference shall, except where the context otherwise requires, be construed as a reference to this Act or to the corresponding provision of this Act'.

We recommend that section 38(1) be extended so as to cover references to enactments repealed and re-enacted, whether those references occur in Acts of Parliament or any other enactment or document. Effect to this recommendation is given in clause 17(2)(a), clause 23(2) and (3) and clause 24(2) of the draft Bill.

C. Another standard saving, which appears regularly in Consolidation Acts, provides that subordinate legislation made, and other things done, under the enactments repealed are to be treated as made or done under the corresponding provision of the Consolidation Act. Frequently this, and the extended version of section 38(1) referred to above, are the only savings needed in a Consolidation Act—see for example Costs in Criminal Cases Act 1973 (c 14) s 21(3) and (4); Independent Broadcasting Authority Act 1973 (c 19) s 39(2) to (4); Legal Aid Act 1974 (c 4) s 42(2) and (3). We recommend that this additional saving be introduced alongside the original saving in section 38(1). Effect to this recommendation is given in subsection (2)(b) of clause 17 of the draft Bill.

7. Subsections (1) and (2) of section 35 of the Interpretation Act 1889 read as follows—

> '(1) In any Act, instrument or document, an Act may be cited by reference to the short title, if any, either with or without a reference to the chapter, or by reference to the regnal year in which the Act was passed, and where there are more statutes or sessions than one in the same regnal year, by reference to the statute or session, as the case may require, and where there are more chapters than one, by reference to the chapter, and any enactment may be cited by reference to the section or subsection of the Act in which the enactment is contained.
>
> (2) Where any Act passed after the commencement of this Act contains such reference as aforesaid, the reference shall, unless a contrary intention appears, be read as referring, in the case of statutes included in any revised edition of the statutes purporting to be printed by authority, to that edition, and in the case of statutes not so included, and passed before the reign of King George the First, to the edition prepared under the direction of the Record Commission; and in other cases to the copies of the statutes purporting to be printed by the Queen's Printer, or under the superintendence or authority of Her Majesty's Stationery Office.'

A. Subsection (1) was derived from section 3 of Lord Brougham's Act which was to the same effect but with certain differences of detail—

> (1) The earlier section did not authorise citation by short title. Short titles were by no means unknown in 1850 (see e.g. Towns Improvement Clauses Act 1847, s 4; House of Commons Costs Taxation Act 1847, s 11), but were not the general rule. By 1889 the practice was firmly established. Only a handful of Acts of the previous decade, and none later than 1893, received short titles under the Short Titles Act 1896.
>
> (2) In prescribing the details of citation by regnal year and chapter, Lord Brougham's Act distinguished between Acts made before 7 Henry 7 and those made after 4 Henry 7 (the apparent overlap was illusory). In the former case provision was

made for citation by statute if more than one in the same regnal year; in the latter for citation by statute or session if more than one in the same regnal year (see e.g. I Mary, Sessions 1 to 3, 13 Chas 2 Stats 1 and 2. The Act of 1889 omitted this distinction, and referred to 'statutes or sessions' regardless of the date of the Act to be recited.

(3) Lord Brougham's Act directed that the citation by regnal year, statute or session and chapter should be sufficient 'without reciting the title of such Act [or the provision of such section] so referred to'. This was omitted in 1889, no doubt as having already done its work.

To return to the text of section 35(1) as it stands, we observe in the first place that it is otiose in so far as it purports to authorise the citation of an Act by a short title by which it is otherwise authorised to be cited. This applies to all the 2,000 odd enactments scheduled to the Short Titles Act 1896 and to every other Act which includes a short title clause. Secondly the provision for citation by regnal year, statute/session and chapter cannot be taken literally as authority for the subsidiary citations which are used in the Chronological Table of the Statutes and in Schedules of amendments or repeals, such as Schedule 3 to the draft Bill. Only two of the references in the first column of that Schedule identify 'the regnal year in which the Act was passed' (these being comparatively rare cases in which the relevant Session of Parliament was begun and ended in the same regnal year). Thirdly section 35(1) is and always has been inappropriate to the Acts of the Parliament of Scotland, which were numbered by calendar year and chapter and not by reference to regnal years (This defect was not inherent in the Bill for the Interpretation Act as introduced, which referred to regnal or calendar years; but for reasons which do not appear on the record the calendar year was dropped in the course of the parliamentary proceedings).

These problems, as well as the change in the citation of Acts of 1963 onwards introduced by the Acts of Parliament (Numbering and Citation) Act 1962. could be looked after by suitable redrafting of subsection (1) of section 35 in the Consolidation Bill. But the question is whether that is worth doing. The methods used for identifying previous statutes would be exactly as they are if subsection (1) of section 35 were not in force. There is no comparable provision for the identification in U.K. Acts of Acts of the Parliament of Northern Ireland either by their short titles or by regnal year (or calendar year since 1944) and chapter; and there is no provision authorising the identification in such Acts of subordinate legislation by SR & O or SI year and number. Both are regularly so identified in U.K. statutes without specific statutory authority. The choice therefore lies between expanding section 35 (1) so as to authorise these citations, and repealing it as unnecessary. We recommend the latter option, to which effect is given by Schedule 3 to the draft Bill.

B. Subsection (2) of section 35 was and is still required in order to govern the selection between the chapters or sections attributed to the same Act in different editions of the earliest statutes. A once well-known instance of the problem was 6 Ann c 41 sections 24 and 25 (Statutes of the Realm) *alias* 6 Ann c 7 sections 25 and 26 (Statutes at Large). A similar problem, not dealt with by subsection (2) as it stands, arises in relation to some of the Acts of the Parliament of Scotland. We recommend that in these cases also preference should be given to the edition published by authority. Effect is given to this recommendation by subsection (1) of clause 19 of the draft Bill.

8. The great majority of Acts of Parliament contain references of some kind to other existing enactments which, or some of which, have been amended by intervening legislation. This raises the theoretical question whether the reference is intended to denote the enactment in the form in which it was originally passed or in the form in which it stands at the time of the reference. The intention is almost invariably the latter. Where it is not, words are added to make that clear—see for example paragraph 7(1) of Schedule 2 to the Acquisition of Land (Authorisation Procedure) Act 1946, which refers to sections 78 to 85 of the Railways Clauses Consolidation Act 1845 'as originally enacted

and not as amended . . . by section 15 of the Mines (Working Facilities and Support) Act 1923.'

Nevertheless the practice has grown up, no doubt to be on the safe side, of including in Acts which contain such references a clause to the effect that they are to be construed as referring to the enactments in question as amended by subsequent Acts. On an approximate estimate such a clause now appears in two out of every three Acts. Although the general purpose is the same, these clauses differ from each other in detail, ranging from the simplest form—'Any reference in this Act to any enactment is a reference that enactment as amended by any subsequent enactment'. to the full treatment—'Unless the context otherwise requires, any reference in this Act to any other enactment is a reference thereto as amended, and includes a reference thereto as extended or applied, by or under any other enactment, including this Act'.

Apart from the expenditure of paper and ink upon clauses the need for which is at best doubtful, these provisions are disturbing because it is seldom self-evident why the clause appears in different forms in different Acts, and does not appear at all in the others.

We recommend accordingly that the consolidation should include a clause designed to eliminate these recurrent *ad hoc* clauses. Effect to this recommendation is given in clause 20(2) of the draft Bill.

9. The application of the Interpretation Act 1889 to subordinate legislation is selective, not to say capricious. Section 6 (meaning of 'county court' in England and Wales) applies to Orders in Council as well as Acts. Contrast section 29 ('county court' in Northern Ireland) which applies only to Acts. Subsection (1) of section 35 authorises the citation of Acts by short title, or by regnal year and chapter, where the citation is made in 'any Act, instrument or document'. But subsection (2), which governs the references to regnal year and chapter in the case of the early statutes for which there were variations in different editions, applies only to references occurring in Acts of Parliament; and subsection (3), under which a quotation of words from a previous Act is treated as inclusive, applies only where the quotation is made in an Act. Similarly in section 36 subsection (1) defines 'commencement' when used in and in relation to Acts only; while subsection (2) regulates the time of day at which an Act or subordinate legislation comes into operation when expressed to come into operation on a particular day. The effects of sections 11 and 38 (repeals) depend upon the meaning of the word 'enactment' as used in those sections. It is clear that subsection (1) of section 38, which translates references to provisions repealed and re-enacted, applies only to the repeal of Acts by Acts and is confined to references in other Acts. On the other hand the savings contained in section 11(1) and section 38(2) may and probably do apply where (as occasionally happens) subordinate legislation is repealed by Act of Parliament, though not by subsequent subordinate legislation. The general definitions contained in the Act of 1889 (sections 12 to 30) apply only to Acts of Parliament. Under section 31 expressions used in subordinate legislation have the same meaning as in the parent Act, but this provision imports the general definitions only where the expression defined occurs both in the parent Act and in the subordinate legislation, not where it occurs in the latter only.

Naturally the draftsmen of subordinate legislation have not left it there. Most instruments of any elaboration contain a clause applying the Interpretation Act as it applies to an Act of Parliament; and instruments which revoke previous subordinate legislation usually go on to provide expressly that section 38 is to apply as if the revocation were a repeal of an Act by an Act. The practice (as of 1971) is described in Halsbury's Statutes, Vol. 32 'Statutes' at p 407. A great deal of space in the Statutory Instruments series is occupied by such provisions, which would not be needed if the Interpretation Act were directly applied to subordinate legislation without the curious distinctions described above.

Accordingly we recommend that (subject to certain minor exceptions referred to below) the following amendments should be made in the application of the Act of 1889 to subordinate legislation—

(1) All definitions, and all other provisions except those capable only of application to Acts of Parliament (sections 8, 9 and 10) should apply, so far as applicable and unless the contrary intention appears, to subordinate legislation made after the consolidation comes into force.

(2) The provisions relating to repeals (sections 11(1) and (2) and section 38(1) and (2)) should also apply where subordinate legislation is repealed either by Act or by subordinate legislation.

The exceptions referred to above relate to Orders in Council under section 5 of the Statutory Instruments Act 1946, which are *sui generis*, and Orders in Council under two Acts relating to Northern Ireland, which are dealt with by another Recommendation.

Effect is given to this recommendation in subsections (1), (2) and (4) of clause 23 of the draft Bill.

10. The Interpretation Act does not apply to Acts of the Parliament of Northern Ireland. It was originally extended to such Acts by the Interpretation Act 1921 (12 Geo 5 [NI] c 4): but that Act, and the Act of 1889 as applied by it, were repealed by the Interpretation Act (Northern Ireland) 1954 section 48(1) and (2). In general therefore the two codes are separate, the one applying to Acts of the Parliament of the United Kingdom and the other to Acts of the Parliament of Northern Ireland, to Measures of the Northern Ireland Assembly, and (by specific application) to Orders in Council under modern legislation which have the effect of such Acts.

The question does arise however whether how far the provisions of the Interpretation Act 1889 relating to the effects of repeals (sections 11 and 38) operate in cases where Acts of the Parliament of Northern Ireland are repealed by Acts of the Parliament of the United Kingdom, or contain references to enactments of either Parliament which are so repealed. If an Act of Northern Ireland which repealed a previous Act of Northern Ireland is itself repealed by U.K. legislation, is the original repeal preserved by section 11(1) or section 38(2)(a) of the Act of 1889? If an enactment referred to in an Act of Northern Ireland is repealed and re-enacted by U.K. legislation, is the reference translated into a reference to the new enactment by section 38(1) of the Act of 1889?

It is on account of such doubts that *ad hoc* applications of section 38 are often included in Acts which repeal Northern Ireland legislation. A recent example of such an Act is the Social Security (Consequential Provisions) Act 1975 (c 18), section 2(4)(b) of which provides as follows:

'(4) Section 38 of the Interpretation Act 1889 (effect of repeals)—

. . .

(b) has the same operation in relation to any repeal by this Act of an enactment of the Parliament of Northern Ireland or of the Northern Ireland Assembly (or of any provision of an Order made under, or having the same effect as, such an enactment) as it has in relation to the repeal of an Act of the Parliament of the United Kingdom (references in section 38 of the 1889 Act to Acts and enactments being construed accordingly).'

Such provisions would be unnecessary if it were made clear that while the Interpretation Act 1889 continues to apply only to the provisions made by Acts of the Parliament of the United Kingdom, the impact of those provisions upon other 'enactments' extends to enactments of the Parliament of Northern Ireland and other Northern Ireland legislation; and we recommend accordingly. Effect is given to this recommendation in clause 24(2) of the draft Bill.

11. Section 27 of the Interpretation Act 1889 did not define 'committed for trial' as respects Ireland. The reason for this omission is not clear, but it may have been that Irish lawyers were content to rely on some dicta of Palles CB in *R (Feely) v Fitzgibbon* (delivered in Nov. 1888 and reported in Judgments of the Superior Courts in Ireland (1890) ref 191 at page 195) regarding the meaning of the expression 'return for trial'

which was then more commonly used in Ireland. The learned Chief Baron appeared to regard 'trial' as referring exclusively to trial by a jury, summary offences being 'heard' or 'heard and determined' as opposed to 'tried'. Unfortunately, the work in which this Judgment appears has not been available to the public for a very long time and, as most enactments now in force in Northern Ireland refer to 'committed for trial' rather than 'returned for trial', the absence of a definition of the former corresponding to that in force in England, suggests inconsistency in the interpretation of the law of two parts of the United Kingdom. Any such inconsistency has already been removed, as respects Northern Ireland enactments, by the inclusion in section 42(4) of the Interpretation Act (Northern Ireland) 1954 (c 33) of a Northern Irish version of the definition in section 27 of the Act of 1889. We recommend that a similar version should be made applicable to Westminster Acts extending to Northern Ireland, but with one change, namely, the substitution of the words 'on indictment' for the words 'before a judge and jury'. This change is necessary because, for a temporary period, section 2 of the Northern Ireland (Emergency Provisions) Act 1973 c 53 (as amended by section 18 of the Northern Ireland (Emergency Provisions) (Amendment) Act 1975 c 62) authorises certain indictable offences to be tried without a jury. It is, however, desirable that the expression 'committed for trial' should cover committals for trial of these offences and the form of the definition we recommend for Northern Ireland provides accordingly.

Effect is given to this recommendation in paragraph (b) of the definition in Schedule 1 to the draft Bill.

12. Section 3 of the Interpretation Act 1889 defines 'land' as including messuages, tenements, and hereditaments, houses, and buildings of any tenure. The definition was derived from section 4 of Lord Brougham's Act. It has never been appropriate for Scotland, where messuages and hereditaments are unknown to the law. Most modern Acts in which the meaning of 'land' is significant contain their own definition (see for example the Town and Country Planning Act 1971 (c 78) section 290(1), the Town and Country Planning (Scotland) Act 1972 (c 52) section 275(1) and the Community Land Act 1975 (c 77) section 6(1)). The points looked after by such definitions are the inclusion of (1) buildings and structures, (2) lakes, rivers and foreshore (land covered with water), (3) particular estates or interests in land and (4) easements (in Scotland servitudes) and other rights over and in land. We recommend that for the purposes of future Acts the definition in section 3 should be re-written so as to cover these points. Effect is given to this recommendation in Schedule 1 to the draft Bill. It is very improbable that any damage would be done by applying this definition retrospectively to Acts passed since 1850 which do not contain their own: but in order to be on the safe side the draft Bill retains the present definition for such Acts (Schedule 2 paragraph 5).

INDEX

Note The names of persons are in general included in this Index only where their actual words are quoted in the work.

All references are to page numbers

Box principle 366–367, 457
Bramwell B 332, 504
Brandeis brief 562
Brandon, Lord 450, 719–720
Bridge, Lord 13, 178, 258, 267, 403–404, 552, 647–648, 677, 678, 849
Brightman, Lord 160, 307, 445, 622, 715, 726, 730, 849
British Islands 469
British possession 469–470
Broad terms 61, 184–185, 188, 192, 204, 234, 310–311, 318–319, 379–381, 613–614
Brook, R 610
Broom, H 32, 174–175, 219, 326, 346
Brougham, Lord 179, 498, 499
Brown, Stephen J 175
Browne LJ 301, 429
Browne-Wilkinson LJ 685
Brutum fulmen 33
Buckland, W W 7, 9, 218
Buckley LJ 620, 698, 699, 798, 820
Burn, R 51, 95
Burrow, James 599–600
Byelaws—
  nature of 152–153
  ultra vires doctrine 144
  when void for uncertainty 204
Byles J 728,

Cairns, Lord 13, 379, 715–716, 829
Campbell, Lord 214, 457, 748, 800, 813, 835, 839, 846
Canada 351, 368–369, 464–465, 477
Cantley J 377
Canons of construction—
  broad terms — *see* Broad terms
  construction as a whole — *see* Construction as a whole
  deductive reasoning, use of 373
  distinguished from rules, principles and presumptions 256–259
  literal meaning, use in ascertaining 372–373
  nature of 372–373
Cardozo J 334–335, 622, 690
Casus omissus — *see* Rectifying construction
Carus, Sjt 308
Castle, man's home is — *see* Domestic sanctuary, principle of
Cave, Viscount 5, 267
Certiorari — *see* Judicial review
Cessante ratione legis cessat ipsa lex 212, 345–346
Chalmers, MD 265, 789–790
Chancery Roll — *see* Roll
Channel Islands 470–471
Chapter number (of Act) 374, 567, 586–588
Chitty LJ 845
Cicero 769, 807
Citizen, the — *see* Doubtful penalization, principle against; Subject, the

Clauses Act 88–89
Clauson J 701
Clausula derogatoria 171
Cleasby B 817
Clerk of the Crown 111, 113
Clerk of the Parliaments—
  appointment of 119
  Crown, agent of 110, 113, 119
  date of passing of Act, insertion by 588–589
  settling of text of Act by 119–120
Cockburn CJ 278, 348, 594, 835
Codifying Act—
  interpretation of 519–520
  interstitial articulation and 253
  nature of 87, 97–98
  sub-rules, and 79
Cohen LJ 798, 837
Cohen question, the 798
Coke, Sir E 5, 10, 19, 29, 33, 38, 54, 82, 161, 195, 218, 225, 242, 308, 312–313, 319, 355, 371, 375, 457, 474, 483, 497, 610, 658, 682–683, 685, 762, 840
Coleridge, Lord 38, 241, 348, 510, 820
Collective title 516, 604–607
Collier, R 712
Colony 471–473
Commencement provisions—
  form of 93, 274–275, 410
  interpretation of 275, 302
  meaning of 'commencement' 409–410, 589, 773
  preparatory orders etc 417
  substituted provisions 438–439
  suspension of commencement 414–416
  types of 410–417
  — *and see* Retrospectivity; Transitional provisions
Comminution—
  meaning 168, 389, 399, 598, 744
  selective 168–170, 184–185, 203, 290, 342, 396, 399, 401–404, 432, 493, 550, 644–645, 770
Common law—
  Act presumed not to change? 319–320, 558, 620–621, 632, 635
  advantage over statute 707
  basis of 295
  declared by Act — *see* Declaratory Act
  developed by reference to Act 247–249, 320, 360, 502
  evasion of 347–348
  inadequacies of 636–640, 649–650
  interpretative criteria as part of 257–258
  justice and 51
  modified by Act 41, 95–98, 248, 304, 317–320, 352–354, 433–434, 437, 633, 635–638, 654
  natural justice and 728
  nature of 8, 358
  relation to statute law 286, 386, 620–621, 737, 740–741, 844

All references are to page numbers

All references are to page numbers

Index

Dias, R W M 4
Dicey, A V 173, 617
Dickerson, Reed 196, 202, 227, 830
Dictionaries, use of 820–822, 824, 827
Different words—
  construed in different ways 376–377
  construed in same way 376–377
Differential readings 393, 662
Dilhorne, Viscount 225, 279, 315, 548, 549,
    566, 654, 658, 681, 706, 798, 814,
    824
Dillon J 189
Diplock, Lord 6, 11, 14, 100, 153, 160, 170–
    171, 182, 184, 197, 216, 238, 243, 307–
    310, 312, 313, 321, 322, 357, 362, 370–
    371, 405, 423–424, 497, 514, 515, 525–
    526, 528, 531, 535, 543, 550, 658–659,
    665, 668, 690, 700, 730–731, 740, 741,
    758–759, 782, 800–801, 813, 814, 824,
    834
Director of Public Prosecutions 48
Directory requirements 21–26, 34, 215, 443,
    776
  — and see Mandatory requirements
Discretion, statutory 27, 60, 69, 140–141,
    267, 362, 388, 400, 622–623, 625, 642,
    700, 774
  — and see Decision-making, rules
    governing; Judicial review
Disobedience of law—
  civil sanctions for 35–43
  criminal sanctions for 33–35, 848
  persistent 42
  — and see Evasion of Act; Judicial review
Dispensing power 428–429
Distance 284, 866
Domestic sanctuary, principle of 640, 706,
    738, 768–771
  — and see Doubtful penalization,
    principle against
*Domus sua cuique est tutissimum
    refugium* — see Domestic sanctuary,
    principle of
Donaldson MR 53, 168, 170, 189, 224, 280,
    328, 331, 423, 699, 746–747
Donovan, Lord 684, 820–821
Double detriment — see *Bona fides non
    patitur, ut bis idem exigatur*
Doubt—
  causes of 383–384
  consequential construction and 332
  must be real 5–6, 329
  when real 5–6, 197–198, 261, 560–561
Doubtful penalization, principle against—
  family rights, interference with 614–616
  free association, interference with 617–618
  free speech, interference with 618
  legal rights, impairment of 145, 625–627
  life, health or safety, detriment to 246, 491,
    609–612, 777

Doubtful penalization, principle against—
    continued
  nature of 292, 296, 302–306, 312, 334, 389,
    392, 445, 609–629
  physical restraint of the person 25, 221–222,
    397, 403, 611–614, 678, 705, 747, 767
  privacy, infringement of 611, 624–625 — *and
    see* Domestic sanctuary, principle of
  property, interference with 25, 31, 304, 386,
    618–623
  religious freedom, interference with 616–617
  reputation or status, detriment to 623–624
  rights as citizen, interference with 142, 145,
    291–292, 625–629
  voting rights, interference with 26, 38, 628,
    723–724, 840
  — *and see* Retrospectivity; Strict and
    liberal construction; Updating
    construction
Drafting—
  Acts *in pari materia* 517
  amendments to Bills, of 16
  breach of duty, intended result of 21–22, 36
  common sense and 267
  competence presumed 180–181, 801
  compression of language 207–208, 398–400,
    853–854
  criticism of 423–424
  disorganized composition 28, 30, 33, 177–
    180, 209, 278–279, 327–328, 336–338,
    344, 375, 403, 455–456, 536, 568, 572,
    593, 620, 719–720, 828, 832, 845
  general principle approach 240, 374
  implication, use of 240, 242
  Magna Carta, of 178
  precision drafting 31, 33, 37, 61, 101, 177–
    180, 240, 251, 327–328, 375, 379, 423–
    424, 433–434, 572, 595
  procedure 229–232
  — *and see* Definitions; Delegated
    legislation; Drafting error;
    Draftsman; Incorporation by
    reference
Drafting error—
  ejusdem generis principle and 830
  foreign aspects 492, 500
  foresight, lack of 699, 776
  frequency of 337–338
  ignorance, caused by 661
  impossibility, causing 774
  legal doctrine flouted 318, 337, 344, 352–353,
    754–755
  legislative history, and 549
  long title 577
  missed consequentials 426
  punctuation 597–600
  repeals 436–437
  royal assent procedure 110, 118
  tautology — *see* Tautology
  transitional provisions — *see* Transitional
    provisions

All references are to page numbers

All references are to page numbers

All references are to page numbers

All references are to page numbers

Index

Moorcock, The, doctrine of 734
Morality, preservation of — *see* **Legal policy**
More, Sir T 14
Morris, Lord 290
Morris of Borth-y-Gest, Lord 229, 247, 283, 334, 450, 728
Morton, Lord 282
Mowbray 632
Murphy, WT 11, 202
Mustill J 331

Natural justice—
    judicial powers and 727–728
    mandatory and directory requirements 24
    negligence and 40–41
    requirements of 730–731, 741–743
    — *and see* **Audi alteram partem**; *Nemo debet esse judex in propria causa*
Natural law 174
Necessitas non habet legem 722–723, 776–778
Necessity — *see* Necessitas non habet legem
Negligence 40, 41, 405, 738–739
Nemo debet bis vexari 743, 765
Nemo debet esse judex in propria causa, 175, 318, 731, 778–779
Neologisms 812–815
New Zealand 464–466, 477
Newman, Cardinal 5
Nicholl MR 566
Non liquet, principle of 4, 204, 208, 234
    — *and see* **Meaningless terms**
Non obstante, device of 129
Normand, Lord 193, 559
North J 702
Northern Ireland—
    meaning 481–482
    Privy Council of 139
    — *and see* **Ireland**
Noscitur a sociis 823–828, 853
    — *and see* **Ejusdem generis** principle; **Rank principle**
Notice, statutory requirement to give 25, 26, 29, 438, 719–720, 775–776, 784, 849
— *and see* **Audi alteram partem**
Nourse J 275, 620, 699, 775
Nuisance 738–739
Nullus commodum capere potest de injuria sua propria 285–286, 294, 298, 779–781
Number 284, 865–866
Numbering 109

Obedience to law—
    duty *sub modo* 16–17, 28, 29, 31
    legal duty of 15–18
    mandatory and directory requirements 21–27
    moral duty of 15–16, 174–175
    over-performance 17–18
    whether compliance need be exact 17, 21–27

Obscurity, semantic 207–210, 214–215, 232–233, 339–346, 398–400, 597–600, 664, 817–818
    — *and see* **Plain meaning rule**; **Rectifying construction**
Offence—
    alternative verdicts 398–400
    composite acts 509–510
    duplicated 284, 315–316, 744–746
    extra-territorial 499, 502–510
    meaning 744–746
    prosecution policy 47–50, 281
    sentencing policy 310–311
Oliver LJ 6, 17, 31, 297, 649–650, 671, 686, 802, 811
Omissions 509–510
Omne majus continet in se minus 17, 268–269, 651–652, 702
Omnia praesumuntur rite et solemniter esse acta 126, 272–273, 782–783
Opposing constructions—
    adjudicating authority and 53
    ambiguity and 204–206
    consequential construction and 332, 706
    interstitial articulation and 253, 396–400
    significance of 192–197, 432, 793–794
    weighing 206
    — *and see* **Interpretative factors**
Order in Council 130–131, 138
Order of Council 139
Ordinary meaning—
    nature of 797–798
    prima facie to be given 331, 797–798
    term with both ordinary and technical meaning 809–812
Ormrod LJ 145, 316, 364, 441–442, 671, 706, 805

Pacta privata juri publico derogare non possunt 30–33
Pardon, Bill for 106
Parke B — *see* **Lord Wensleydale**
Parker CJ 170, 214, 327, 367, 483, 566, 651–652, 663, 679, 694, 716, 728, 773, 839, 854
Parliament—
    can legislate only by Act 98–100
    duration of, altering 118–119, 173
    infallibility of 230–233
    jurisdiction of 454–455
    powers of, curbs on 170–177
    privilege 530–532, 725
    procedure of 83–84, 418
    prorogation of 114–115
    slowness of 217
    sovereignty of 94–100, 125, 176
    taxing powers 724–725
    — *and see* **Bill, parliamentary**; **Clerk of the Parliaments**; **Commons, House**

All references are to page numbers